Statistical Forecasts of the United States

Statistical Forecasts of the United States

Edited by
Sean R. Pollock

Gale Research Inc.
An International Thomson Publishing Company

ITP
Changing the Way the World Learns

NEW YORK • LONDON • BONN • BOSTON • DETROIT • MADRID
MELBOURNE • MEXICO CITY • PARIS • SINGAPORE • TOKYO
TORONTO • WASHINGTON • ALBANY NY • BELMONT CA • CINCINNATI OH

STAFF

Edited by Sean R. Pollock

Keith Jones, *Managing Editor*

Linda Irvin, Donna Wood, *Senior Editors*
Jacqueline K. Barrett, Kim Ellen Forster, Leslie A. Norback, *Editors*
Deborah A. Tracy, Kristin G. Hart, *Associate Editors*
James J. Makowski, Suzanne E. Safran, *Editorial Associates*

Marlene Lasky, *Permissions Supervisor*
Tyra Y. Phillips, *Permissions Assistant*

Victoria B. Cariappa, *Research Manager*
Maureen Richards, *Research Specialist*
Eva M. Felts, *Research Associate*
Laurel Sprague, Amy Beth Wieczorak, *Research Assistants*

Mary Beth Trimper, *Production Director*
Deborah Milliken, *Production Assistant*
Cynthia Baldwin, *Product Design Manager*
Terrence Glenn, *Cover Design*

Editorial Code and Data, Inc. Staff

Gary Alampi, *Programmer/Analyst*
Sherae R. Carroll, *Data Entry Associate*

Library of Congress Catalog Card Number HC106.8.S7357 1995
ISBN 0-8103-8935-5
CIP data may be found on page xxxiii

Printed in the United States of America

10 9 8 7 6 5 4 3 2 1

ITP™ Gale Research Inc., an International Thomson Publishing Company.
ITP logo is a trademark under license.

TABLE OF CONTENTS

CHAPTER 1 - AGRICULTURE

CHAPTER 1 - AGRICULTURE (continued)

CHAPTER 2 - BUSINESS, BANKING, AND FINANCE

CHAPTER 2 - BUSINESS, BANKING, AND FINANCE (continued)

CHAPTER 2 - BUSINESS, BANKING, AND FINANCE (continued)

CHAPTER 3 - CONSTRUCTION AND HOUSING

CHAPTER 4 - CRIME, LAW ENFORCEMENT, AND PRISONS

CHAPTER 4 - CRIME, LAW ENFORCEMENT, AND PRISONS (continued)

CHAPTER 5 - DEFENSE AND THE SPACE PROGRAM

CHAPTER 5 - DEFENSE AND THE SPACE PROGRAM (continued)

CHAPTER 6 - ECONOMICS

CHAPTER 6 - ECONOMICS (continued)

CHAPTER 7 - EDUCATION

CHAPTER 7 - EDUCATION (continued)

CHAPTER 7 - EDUCATION (continued)

CHAPTER 7 - EDUCATION (continued)

CHAPTER 8 - ENERGY

CHAPTER 8 - ENERGY (continued)

CHAPTER 8 - ENERGY (continued)

CHAPTER 9 - ENVIRONMENTAL ISSUES AND NATURAL RESOURCES

CHAPTER 9 - ENVIRONMENTAL ISSUES AND NATURAL RESOURCES (continued)

CHAPTER 9 - ENVIRONMENTAL ISSUES AND NATURAL RESOURCES (continued)

CHAPTER 10 - HEALTH, MEDICAL CARE, AND HUMAN SERVICES

CHAPTER 10 - HEALTH, MEDICAL CARE, AND HUMAN SERVICES (continued)

CHAPTER 10 - HEALTH, MEDICAL CARE, AND HUMAN SERVICES (continued)

CHAPTER 11 - INCOME, TAXES, PRICES, AND SPENDING

CHAPTER 11 - INCOME, TAXES, PRICES AND SPENDING (continued)

CHAPTER 11 - INCOME, TAXES, PRICES AND SPENDING (continued)

CHAPTER 12 - LABOR, EMPLOYMENT, OCCUPATIONS, AND EARNINGS

CHAPTER 12 - LABOR, EMPLOYMENT, OCCUPATIONS, AND EARNINGS (continued)

CHAPTER 12 - LABOR, EMPLOYMENT, OCCUPATIONS, AND EARNINGS (continued)

CHAPTER 13 - POPULATION AND VITAL STATISTICS

CHAPTER 13 - POPULATION AND VITAL STATISTICS (continued)

CHAPTER 13 - POPULATION AND VITAL STATISTICS (continued)

CHAPTER 14 - SCIENCE AND TECHNOLOGY

CHAPTER 14 - SCIENCE AND TECHNOLOGY (continued)

CHAPTER 15 - TRANSPORTATION

CHAPTER 15 - TRANSPORTATION (continued)

CHAPTER 15 - TRANSPORTATION (continued)

INTRODUCTION

STATISTICAL FORECASTS OF THE UNITED STATES (SFUS) is a compilation of published information forecasting all aspects of American life through the year 2000 and beyond.

The need for *SFUS* was prompted by the lack of a single reference source from which a broad spectrum of statistical projections might be extracted. Of equal importance, the approach of the twenty-first century—termed "The Information Century" by many—emphasized the need for a resource that would provide statistical forecasts relevant to a wide range of information seekers. *SFUS* is not a guide indicating how best to prepare for the twenty-first century; rather, it is a comprehensive source book from which the reader is free to draw for the purpose of assembling reports, compiling studies, or simply satisfying personal curiosity.

The statistical material presented is drawn from governmental, corporate, and private sources. *SFUS* provides the reader with:

- Over 800 discrete tables, charts, graphs, and narratives.
- Broad coverage of subject areas pertinent to life in the United States.
- Easy-to-access chapters organized by topic and subtopic.
- A key to pertinent acronyms.
- An index of projections by year.
- A detailed subject index.

SCOPE

SFUS provides statistical coverage of a wide range of subjects concerning future life and living conditions in the United States. And since the data which follows is largely drawn from current reports, books, and periodicals, *SFUS* reflects contemporary concerns and emphases. For example, the chapters on Economics and Health address President Clinton's battle to tame the federal deficit and the rising cost of health care, while Defense deals with the decline of military spending in the Cold War era. The majority of tables offer data for the late 1990s and the early twenty-first century. For certain topics, retrospective data is used to track trends across past decades and to forecast these trends into the future.

Care has been taken to present as balanced a view as possible of all topics. The editors have not injected their own philosophical preconceptions into the selection, presentation, or interpretation of the data. In response to reviewer suggestions , a greater proportion of prose has been included in the second edition of *SFUS* to further clarify and expand on the data supplied. Readers seeking a broader understanding of the methodological assumptions behind the individual forecasts are encouraged to revisit the original sources cited beneath each table.

SOURCES

Data published in *SFUS* was culled from federal and state governmental publications, corporate sources, private organizations, and other non-governmental material published in books and periodicals. Much of this material, before appearing in this volume, was not otherwise indexed in a manner useful to the reader interested in statistical forecasts. Several thousand articles and reports were examined during the preparation of *SFUS 2*, and of these some 725 discrete items are edited for inclusion here.

ORGANIZATION

Statistical Forecasts of the United States is divided into fourteen chapters, each of which focus upon specific topics. Within each topic there appear individual tables and other statistical media, organized by subtopic.

Each table title, or headline, is preceded by a table number. (All tables, which are numbered and bordered by stars—e.g., ★ 24 ★—may be accessed by headline or number from the Table of Contents. Statistical data may also be accessed via the Index of Forecasts by Year.) Immediately beneath the headline, statistical data is displayed as a table, a graph, a chart, a prose statement, or a combination of the above.

At the bottom of each table, the **source** of the data is identified. If the source cited has identified another source from which data was derived, that preceding source is also identified under the rubric **primary source**. Footnotes or other explanatory **notes** are placed after the source information. Where possible, abbreviations and acronyms are defined; most definitions also appear in the section titled List of Abbreviations, while others appear within the footnotes.

INDEXES

SFUS features a detailed **Index of Forecasts by Year** (see p. 777) and **Subject Index**. Entries listed in the **Index of Forecasts by Year** are arranged by individual year (or a range of years where statisticians provide a percentage change over a specific time period). This index is arranged by primary topic, followed by table and page numbers. The **Subject Index** (see p. 792) similarly provides fast and easy access to data on specific topics.

SUGGESTIONS ARE WELCOME

Readers who wish to suggest new features or subject areas to appear in future editions of *SFUS* are cordially invited to write to the editor.

Library of Congress Cataloging-in-Publication Data

Statistical Forecasts of the United States / edited by Sean R. Pollock.
813 p.
Includes bibliographical references and index.
ISBN 0-8103-8935-5 (acid-free paper) : $89.50
1. Economic forecasting—United States—Statistics. 2. Social prediction—United States—Statistics. 3. United States—Economic condi-tions—forecasting—Statistics. 4. United States—Social conditions—Forecasting—Statistical methods. 5. United States—Economic conditions—Statistics. 6. United States—Social conditions—Statistics. Pollock, Sean R., 1961- . HC106.8.S7357 1995
330.973'001'12—dc20 93-7565
CIP

LIST OF ABBREVIATIONS

AC	Alternating Current
ACE	Advanced Computing Environment
ACEEE	American Council for an Energy Efficient Economy
ACI	Airports Council International
ADA	Average Daily Attendance
ADL	Activities of Daily Living
AEO	Annual Energy Outlook
AFR	Away-From-Reactor
AFUE	Annual Fuel Utilization Efficiency
AFV	Alternative Fuel Vehicle
AIDS	Acquired Immune Deficiency Syndrome
AIDS	Acquired Immunodeficiency Disease
AMA	American Medical Association
AMSA	Association of Metropolitan Sewerage Agencies
ANL	Argonne National Laboratory
API	American Petroleum Institute
APL	Applied Physics Laboratory
APR	Annual Percentage Rate
ARP	Acreage Reduction Program
ARTCC	Air Route Traffic Control Center
ASIC	Application-Specific Integrated Circuits
AT&T	American Telephone and Telegraph Co.
ATM	Asynchronous Transmission Mode
Avg.	Average
BA	Budget Authority
BIF	Bank Insurance Fund
BLS	Bureau of Labor Statistics
BOP	Bureau of Prisons
bST	Bovine Somatotropin
BTS	Boeing Test Support
Btu	British thermal unit
bu	bushel
c.j.	criminal justice
CA	California
CAA	Clean Air Act
CAAA	Clean Air Act Amendment
CAD/CAM	Computer Aided Design/Computer Aided Manufacturing
CAGR	Compound Annual Growth Rate
CBO	Congressional Budget Office
CCC	Commodity Credit Corporation
CD-ROM	Compact Disc Read-Only Memory
CDPD	Cellular Digital Packet Data
CEO	Chief Executive Officer
CFC	Chlorofluorocarbon

cmty . . . . community
CO . . . . Carbon Monoxide
CO_2 . . . . Carbon Dioxide
COGME . . . . (medical association)
Constr. . . . . Construction
COP . . . . Coefficient of Performance
CPI . . . . Consumer Price Index
CPS . . . . *Current Population Survey*
CRP . . . . Conservation Reserve Program
CRS . . . . Congressional Research Service
CSO . . . . Combined Sewer Overflow
CSU . . . . Channel Service Unit
cwt . . . . hundredweight (100 pounds)
(D) . . . . Democrat
DC . . . . Direct Current
DDT . . . . Dichlorodiphenyltrichloroethane
Det. . . . . Detention
DFP . . . . Designated Force Potential
DI . . . . Federal Disability Insurance
DOD . . . . U.S. Department of Defense
DOE . . . . Department of Energy
doll . . . . dollar
DOS (PC-DOS) . . . . Disk Operating System (IBM)
DOT . . . . *Dictionary of Occupational Titles*
DOT . . . . Department of Transportation
doz . . . . dozen
DRAM . . . . Dynamic Random Access Memory
DRI . . . . Data Resources Inc.
DSP . . . . Digital Sign Processing
DSU . . . . Data Service Unit
E . . . . Estimated
ECAR . . . . East Central Area Reliability Coordination Agreement
EDA . . . . Department of Commerce Community Diversification EDP
EEG . . . . Electroencephalogram
EEI . . . . Edison Electric Institute
EER . . . . Energy Efficiency Ratio
EF . . . . Efficiency Factor
EIA . . . . Energy Information Administration
EITC . . . . Earned Income Tax Credit
EKG . . . . Electrocardiogram; Electrocardiograph
Elec. . . . . Electronic
EOR . . . . Enhanced Oil Recovery
EPA . . . . Environmental Protection Agency
EPACT . . . . Energy Policy Act of 1992
EPRI . . . . Environmental Protection Research Institute
Equipt. . . . . Equipment
ERCOT . . . . Electric Reliability Council of Texas
Est. . . . . Estimated
Excl. . . . . Excludes
Exist. . . . . Existing
F.S.U. . . . . Former Soviet Union
FAA . . . . Federal Aviation Administration
Fac. . . . . Facility

FACTA-90 . . . . Food, Agriculture, Conservation, and Trade Act of 1990
FAPRI . . . . Food and Agricultural Policy Research Institute
FBI . . . . Federal Bureau of Investigation
FCC . . . . Federal Communications Commission
FDIC . . . . Federal Deposit Insurance Corporation
FFB . . . . Federal Financing Bank
FHA . . . . Federal Housing Administration
FHA . . . . Federal Highway Administration
FTE . . . . Full-Time Equivalent
FY . . . . Fiscal Year
GATT . . . . General Agreement on Tariffs and Trade
GDP . . . . Gross Domestic Product
GE . . . . General Electric
GED . . . . General Education Development
GHG . . . . Greenhouse Gas
GNP . . . . Gross National Product
GPO . . . . Government Printing Office
GRI . . . . Gas Research Institute
GVW . . . . Gross Vehicle Weight
hab . . . . Horizontal Assembly Building
HC . . . . Hydrocarbon
HDTV . . . . High-definition television
HFC . . . . Hydrofluorocarbon
HI . . . . Federal Hospital Insurance
HIV . . . . Human Immunodeficiency Virus
HL . . . . Hyperlearning
HMO . . . . Health Maintenance Organization
HOPE . . . . Home Ownership and Opportunity for People Everywhere
hp . . . . horsepower
HSPF . . . . Heating Seasonal Performance Factor
HUD . . . . Department of Housing and Urban Development
Hydro . . . . Hydroelectric Power
IATA . . . . International Air Transport Association
IBM . . . . International Business Machines
IC . . . . Integrated Circuit (microprocessor)
ICE . . . . Internal Combustion Engine
ICE . . . . Integrated Circuit Engineering Corp.
IEA . . . . International Energy Agency
IFR . . . . Instrument Flight Rules
III . . . . Interstate Identification Index
IMF . . . . International Monetary Fund
Inc. . . . . Incorporated
Incl. . . . . Includes
IPAA . . . . Independent Petroleum Association of America
IPCC . . . . Intergovernmental Panel on Climate Change
IPEDS . . . . Integrated Postsecondary Education Data System
IVHS . . . . Intelligent Vehicle-Highway Systems
JEM . . . . Japanese Experiment Module
Juv. . . . . Juvenile
kbps . . . . Kilobytes per second
KEDI . . . . Kent Economic and Development Institute
kV . . . . kilovolts
kW . . . . Kilowatt
kWh . . . . Kilowatt-Hours

LAN . . . . Local Area Network
lb . . . . pound
LDV . . . . Light-Duty Vehicle
LEP . . . . Limited English-Proficiency
LNG . . . . Liquefied Natural Gas
Lower 48 . . . . United States excluding Alaska and Hawaii
LTC . . . . Long-term Care
MA . . . . Master of Arts
MAAC . . . . Mid-Atlantic Area Council
Mac . . . . Macintosh
MAIN . . . . Mid-America Interconnected Network
MAPP . . . . Mid-Continent Area Power Pool
Max. . . . . Maximum
Mbps . . . . Megabytes per second
Med. . . . . Medium
MESUR . . . . Mars Environment Survey
Min. . . . . Minimum
MIPS . . . . Millions of Instructions Per Second
MIS . . . . Management Information System
MMT . . . . Million Metric Tons
MMTCE . . . . Million Metric Tons of Carbon Equivalent
MPG . . . . Miles Per Gallon
MPLM . . . . Lunar Module
MPU . . . . Microprocessor Unit
MS-DOS . . . . Microsoft Disk Operating System
MSW . . . . Municipal Solid Waste
MTBE . . . . methyl tertiary butyle ether
MTU . . . . Metric Tons of Uranium
n.e.c. . . . . not elsewhere classified
NA . . . . Not Available
NAFTA . . . . North American Free Trade Agreement
NAHB . . . . National Association of Home Builders of the United States
NAR . . . . National Association of Realtors
NASA . . . . National Aeronautics & Space Administration
NATA . . . . North American Telecommunications Association
NBC . . . . National Broadcasting Corporation
NCES . . . . National Center for Education Statistics
NEMS . . . . National Energy Modeling System
NEPOOL . . . . New England Power Pool
NERA . . . . National Economic Research Association
NERC . . . . North Eastern Reliability Council
NFF . . . . National Fingerprint File
NHS . . . . National Highway System
NHTSA . . . . National Highway Traffic and Safety Administration
NIA/USC . . . . National Institute on Aging
NIE . . . . Newly Industrialized Economies
NIH . . . . National Institutes of Health
NIST . . . . National Institute of Standards and Technology
NO . . . . Northern
non-c.j. . . . . non-criminal justice
NOOA . . . . National Oceanic and Atmospheric Administration
NO_x . . . . Nitrous Oxide
NPC . . . . National Petroleum Council
NPCC . . . . Northeastern Power Coordinating Council

NPR . . . National Park Renewal

NR . . . Northern Rocky

NSF . . . National Science Foundation

NSTC . . . National Science and Technology Council

N_2O . . . Nitrous Oxide

NUGs . . . Non Utility Generators

NW . . . Northwest

NY . . . New York

O&M . . . Operation and Maintenance

OASI . . . Federal Old-Age and Survivors Insurance

OBRA-90 . . . Omnibus Budget Reconciliation Act of 1990

OBRA-93 . . . Omnibus Budget Reconciliation Act of 1993

OECD . . . Organization for Economic Cooperation and Development

OEM . . . Original Equipment Manufacturer

OL . . . Outlays

OMB . . . Office of Management and Budget

OPEC . . . Organization of Petroeum Exporting Countries

OS . . . Operating System

OTA . . . Office of Technology Assessment

P . . . Projected

PA-RISC . . . (see RISC)

PAYGO . . . Pay as You Go

PC . . . Personal Computer

PC-DOS . . . Personal Computer Disk Operating System (IBM)

PCB . . . Polychlorinated Biphenyl

PCB . . . Printed Circuit Board

PCMCIA . . . Personal Computer Memory Card International Association

PDA . . . Personal Digital Assistant

PFC . . . Perfluorocarbon

Ph.D . . . Doctor of Philosophy

PHD . . . Piled Higher and Deeper

PN . . . Pacific North

PRB . . . Population Reference Bureau

PV . . . Planetary Vehicle

PW . . . *Publishers Weekly*

R&D . . . Research and Development

RAM . . . Random Access Memory

RbST . . . See bST

RCRA . . . Resource Conservation and Recovery Act

RECS . . . *Residential Energy Consumption Survey*

RISC . . . Reduced Instruction Set Computer

ROMPER . . . Robotic Melon Picker

RPK . . . Revenue Passenger Kilometers

RPM . . . Revenue Passenger Miles

RPM . . . Revolutions Per Minute

RSPA . . . Research and Special Programs Administration

S&L . . . Savings and Loan

S&P . . . Standard and Poore

SDI . . . Strategic Defence Initiative

SDWA . . . Safe Drinking Water Act

Sec. . . . Security

SEER . . . Seasonal Energy Efficiency Ratio

SERC . . . Southeastern Electric Reliability Council

SERP . . . Super-Efficient Refrigerator Program
SIC . . . Standard Industrial Classification
SMI . . . Federal Supplementary Medical Insurance
SMR . . . Specialized Mobile Radio services
SNF . . . Spent Nuclear Fuel
SO . . . Southern
SONET . . . Synchronous Optical Network
SO_2 . . . Sulfur Oxide
SPP . . . Southwest Power Pool
SRAM . . . Static Random Access Memory
SST . . . Supersonic Transport
SST . . . Super Sonic Transport
START, START II . . . Strategic Arms Reduction Treaties
STD . . . Sexually Transmitted Disease
STP . . . Surface Transportation Program
SW . . . Southwest
TAV . . . Trans-Atmospheric Vehicle
TFR . . . Total Fertility Rate
TMT . . . Ton-Mile Traveled
TMT . . . Thousand Metric Tons
TRP . . . Technology Reinvestment Project
U.N. . . . United Nations
U.S.S.R. . . . United Soviet Socialist Republic
U_3O_8 . . . Uranium ore concentrate
UK . . . United Kingdom
UNESCO . . . United Nations Educational, Scientific, and Cultural Organization
USAAA . . . United States Clean Air Act
USDA . . . United States Department of Agriculture
USN&WR . . . U.S. News & World Report
VA . . . Department of Veterans Affairs
VAT . . . Value-Added Tax
VMT . . . Vehicle Miles Traveled
VOC . . . Volatile Organic Compound
VOD . . . Video-on-demand
WEC . . . World Energy Conference
WEFA . . . Wharton Econometric Forecasting Associates
WIC . . . Women, Children, and Infant food program
WICHE . . . Western Interstate Commission for Higher Education
WNP . . . Washington Nuclear Plant
WSCC . . . Western Systems Coordinating Council
Yr. . . . Year
ZPG . . . Zero Population Growth

Statistical Forecasts
of the United States

Second Edition

Chapter 1
AGRICULTURE

Scientific Advances and Biotechnology

★1★

Trends in Agriculture, 1991-2000

Among the many trends forecasters Cetron and Davies identify as impacting future U.S. agriculture are the following:

"In the United States, the family farm is quickly disappearing. Yet, giant agribusinesses reap vast profits, while small, part-time 'hobby' farms also survive. This trend will begin to affect other developed nations during the 1990s and will eventually spread to the rest of the world...

"According to the U.S. Office of Technology Assessment, biotechnology and other yield-increasing developments will account for five-sixths of the growth in world harvests by 2000; the rest will come from newly cultivated croplands...

"We already know how to cut water use and waste-water flows by up to 90%. In the next decade, the industrialized countries will finally adopt many of these water-saving techniques. Developing countries reuse little of their waste water, because they lack the sewage systems required to collect it. By 2000, building this needed infrastructure will become a high priority in many parched lands."

Source: Marvin J. Cetron and Owen Davies, "Trends Shaping the World," in *The Futurist*, September-October 1992, pp. 13-14. *Primary source:* Adapted from Cetron and Davies, *Crystal Globe*: *The Haves and HaveeNots of the New World Order*, St. Martin's Press, 1991.

★2★

Scientific Advances and Biotechnology

Agriculture and Robotics, 2000

"A robotic harvester that can identify whether melons and other crops are ripe enough to pick may revolutionize farming. By the year 2000, a farmer will be able to purchase such a robot for the price of a new pickup truck, according to Purdue University agricultural engineer Gaines Miles.

"Current harvesting machines not only are unable to tell if what they have picked is ripe, but they also often destroy new crops. That's where the Robotic Melon Picker (ROMPER) will be able to transplant, cultivate, and harvest round, or 'head' crops such as melons, lettuce, cabbage, and pumpkins...

"The electronic components for an agricultural robot could cost less than $2,000 in the next decade, Miles believes. As the costs of technology drop, more farmers will be able to afford such devices."

Source: "Robot Farming," *The Futurist*, July-August 1993, p. 54. *Primary source:* Rebecca J. Goetz, "But Do They Do Windows?" *Forefront*, Winter 1992, Agricultural Experiment Station, Agricultural Administration Building, Purdue University, West Lafayette, Indiana 47907.

★3★

Scientific Advances and Biotechnology

Trends in Biotechnology, 1990-2000

"In the 1990s in many parts of the developing world, farmers will need to learn more about the principles of intensive yet sustainable farming practices. Farmers with such kinds of knowledge can make maximum profit from advanced varieties, and furthermore, they themselves will be able to add to the knowledge about making the new varieties fully profitable and productive...

"Other new technologies will begin to have impact in the 1990s, but the major effects—the most important results—will come from those already in place: plant breedings, the present bundle of knowledge-intensive farming practices, and the interactions now present between the farming and research communities. Nothing can be more important in the near term than to expand, fine-tune, and produce products—both material and intellectual—with these three technologies...

"Despite the importance of present technologies for progress in the next decade, the future of the developing world beyond the 1990s depends on sound development—during the 1990s—of the new wave of molecular and cell biology technologies, many of which are subsumed under the title of biotechnology. To properly utilize biotechnology will require a new pattern of behavior, expectations, and responsibilities for most developing countries."

Source: Donald Duvick, "Technology for the 1990s: Rate and Potential Limitation of Technology Generation," in *Agricultural Issues in the 1990s: Proceedings of the Eleventh Agriculture Sector Symposium*, edited by Lisa Garbus, Anthony Pritchard, and Odin Knudsen (Washington D.C.: The International Bank for Reconstruction and Development/The World Bank), 1991, pp. 50-1, 53. *R *I.

★4★

Scientific Advances and Biotechnology

Adoption of Bovine Somatotropin (bST) Dairy Technology by U.S. Farmers, 1991-2000

"OTA's analysis indicates that during the first year that bST is commercially available, no more than 17 percent of farmers will use it. After 5 years, bST adoption is forecast to range from 25 percent in the Corn Belt to 46 percent in the Pacific region. After 10 years, bST adoption is forecast to range from 31 percent in the Corn Belt to 67 percent in the Pacific region."

[Percent of farmers adopting]

Region	1991	1995	2000
Pacific	17%	46%	67%
Lakes States	15	35	46
Northeast	15	31	43
Appalachia	15	32	46
Southeast	15	29	39

[Continued]

★4★

Adoption of Bovine Somatotropin (bST) Dairy Technology by U.S. Farmers, 1991-2000

[Continued]

Region	1991	1995	2000
Southern Plains	13	34	42
Corn Belt	13	25	31

Source: U.S. Congress, Office of Technology Assessment, *U.S. Dairy Industry at a Crossroad: Biotechnology and Policy Choices—Special Report*, (Washington, DC: U.S. Government Printing Office, May 1991), p. 74. *Primary source:* Office of Technology Assessment, 1991. *Note:* 1. bST is assumed to be commercially available in 1991.

Government Programs and Impacts

★5★

Impact of bST Adoption on Other Agricultural Sectors, 1995-1998

"The adoption of bST appears to have relatively minor impacts on agricultural sectors outside of dairy..."

"The adoption of bST does create a marginal increase in demand for feed in the dairy industry. However, the net effect, when all markets adjust, is extremely small. Among all crops, impacts on the all hay price are largest with bST adoption; average hay prices increase by $1.25 to $2.50/ton depending on the policy scenario."

[Number of units]

Commodity (units)	Policy scenarios					
	Fixed price support		Trigger price		Quota	
	No bST	bST	No bST	bST	No bST	bST
Corn ($bu)	2.85	2.86	2.85	2.86	2.85	2.86
Grain sorghum ($bu)	2.54	2.54	2.54	2.54	2.54	2.54
Barley ($bu)	2.60	2.61	2.60	2.61	2.60	2.61
Oats ($bu)	1.39	1.40	1.39	1.40	1.39	1.39
Wheat ($bu)	3.09	3.09	3.09	3.09	3.09	3.09
Soybeans ($bu)	6.46	6.47	6.46	6.46	6.46	6.46
Cotton ($lb)	0.86	0.86	0.86	0.86	0.86	0.86
All hay ($/ton)	103.06	105.55	102.95	104.64	102.77	104.03
Yearling cattle ($/cwt)	74.87	74.94	74.92	74.79	75.08	74.97
Calf ($/cwt)	81.84	82.01	81.93	81.84	82.16	82.06
Cows ($/cwt)	56.97	57.11	57.05	56.84	57.33	57.14
Hogs ($cwt)	51.08	51.09	51.06	51.11	51.01	51.04
Broilers (/lb)	61.38	61.45	61.43	61.43	61.46	61.47
Turkeys (/lb)	69.32	69.38	69.41	69.29	69.55	59.49
Eggs (/dozen)	81.15	81.20	81.14	81.18	81.14	81.16
Lamb ($/cwt)	91.46	91.63	91.45	91.62	91.41	91.51

Source: U.S. Congress, Office of Technology Assessment, *U.S. Dairy Industry at a Crossroad: Biotechnology and Policy Choices—Special Report*, (Washington, DC: U.S. Government Printing Office, May 1991), p. 101. *Primary source:* Office of Technology Assessment, 1991. *Note:* bu=bushel; cwt=hundredweight (100 pounds); lb=pound.

★6★

Government Programs and Impacts

Summary of U.S. Department of Agriculture Budget Projections, 1994-1999

[Millions of dollars]

		1993 Actual	1994	1995	1996	1997	1998	1999
Discretionary Spending	BA	15,600	16,400	15,400	15,500	15,700	15,700	15,800
	OL	14,600	16,200	15,700	15,500	15,600	15,700	15,900
Discretionary Budget Authority (excluding International Programs)		14,052	15,018	14,170	14,241	14,402	14,436	14,595
Discretionary Outlays (excluding International Programs)		13,095	14,572	14,398	14,195	14,371	14,483	14,671
Mandatory and Receipts Paygo (deficit impact)								
Comprehensive reform of Federal Crop Insurance program:								
Increase insurance program		NA	-	168	701	877	977	1,159
Eliminate ad-hoc disaster payments		NA	-	-500	-1,000	-1,000	-1,000	-1,000
Deficit impact, comprehensive crop reform		NA	-	-332	-299	-123	-23	159

Source: Executive Office of the President of the United States, Office of Management and Budget, *Budget of the United States Government: Fiscal Year 1995* (Washington, D.C.: U.S. Government Printing Office, 1994), pp. 237-38, 240, 243, 248, 250-53. *Primary source:* Tables 7-3, 7-4, 7-6, 7-9, 7-11, 7-12, 7-13, and 7-14 of 1995 budget.

★7★

Government Programs and Impacts

Proposed U.S. Agricultural Investments, 1993-1999

[Millions of dollars]

		1993 Enacted	Estimate		Change: 1994 to 1995	Estimate			
			1994	1995		1996	1997	1998	1999
Rural development initiative:									
Grant levels	BA	878	1,039	1,148	109	1,300	1,285	1,262	1,148
	OL	621	787	895	108	1,009	1,170	1,248	1,229
Loan levels	(Loans)	(3,119)	(4,046)	(5,728)	(1,682)	(5,728)	(5,728)	(5,728)	(5,728)
WIC (Special supplemental food program for women, infants & children)	BA	2,860	3,210	3,564	354	3,914	4,166	4,245	4,394
	OL	2,846	3,222	3,538	316	3,896	4,147	4,239	4,383
USDA-National Science and Technology Council (NSTC)	BA	161	171	189	18	200	208	215	214
	OL	90	119	130	11	194	197	192	207
Food safety	BA	494	517	534	17	535	537	541	541
	OL	494	511	533	22	535	537	541	541
Food safety research	BA	16	16	41	25	41	41	41	41
	OL	15	16	40	24	41	41	41	41
Natural resource protection and environmental infrastructure	BA	749	735	782	47	865	874	874	874

[Continued]

★7★

Proposed U.S. Agricultural Investments, 1993-1999

[Continued]

		1993 Enacted	Estimate		Change: 1994 to 1995	Estimate			
			1994	1995		1996	1997	1998	1999
	OL	757	750	768	18	839	876	871	874
National research initiative	BA	98	112	130	18	130	130	130	130
	OL	60	75	106	31	116	126	130	130
Climate change action plan	BA	...	2	12	10	17	24	30	30
	OL	...	2	11	9	15	23	27	30
Pacific Northwest Forest Plan implementation	BA	...	60	97	37	97	97	97	97
	OL	...	48	77	29	97	97	97	97

Source: Executive Office of the President of the United States, Office of Management and Budget, *Budget of the United States Government: Fiscal Year 1995* (Washington, D.C.: U.S. Government Printing Office, 1994), pp. 233-34.

★8★

Government Programs and Impacts

U.S. Program Provisions, 1994-2003

"FAPRI projections incorporate provisions of the **Food, Agriculture, Conservation, and Trade Act of 1990** (FACTA-90) and the **Omnibus Budget Reconciliation Acts of 1990 and 1993** (OBRA-90, OBRA-93). Provisions of the three acts are assumed to be extended indefinitely. The projections incorporate the North American Free Trade Agreement (NAFTA), but they do not incorporate a General Agreement on Tariffs and Trade (GATT)."

	94/95	95/96	96/97	97/98	98/99	99/00	00/01	01/02	02/03
	(Dollars per Bushel)								
Target Prices									
Corn	2.75	2.75	2.75	2.75	2.75	2.75	2.75	2.75	2.75
Sorghum	2.61	2.61	2.61	2.61	2.61	2.61	2.61	2.61	2.61
Barley	2.36	2.36	2.36	2.36	2.36	2.36	2.36	2.36	2.36
Oats	1.45	1.45	1.45	1.45	1.45	1.45	1.45	1.45	1.45
Wheat	4.00	4.00	4.00	4.00	4.00	4.00	4.00	4.00	4.00
Rice (Dollars/cwt)	10.71	10.71	10.71	10.71	10.71	10.71	10.71	10.71	10.71
Cotton (Dollars/lb)	0.73	0.73	0.73	0.73	0.73	0.73	0.73	0.73	0.73
Loan Rates									
Corn	1.89	1.80	1.75	1.73	1.73	1.72	1.72	1.73	1.73
Sorghum	1.80	1.71	1.67	1.64	1.64	1.63	1.63	1.64	1.65
Barley	1.54	1.46	1.43	1.41	1.41	1.40	1.40	1.41	1.41
Oats	0.97	0.92	0.90	0.89	0.89	0.88	0.88	0.89	0.89
Soybeans	4.92	4.92	4.92	4.92	4.92	4.92	4.92	4.92	4.92
Wheat	2.58	2.45	2.33	2.21	2.14	2.13	2.25	2.31	2.37
Rice (Dollars/cwt)	6.50	6.50	6.50	6.50	6.50	6.50	6.50	6.50	6.50
Cotton (Dollars/lb)	0.52	0.50	0.50	0.50	0.50	0.50	0.50	0.50	0.50
Sugarcane (Cents/lb)	18.00	18.00	18.00	18.00	18.00	18.00	18.00	18.00	18.00

[Continued]

★8★

U.S. Program Provisions, 1994-2003

[Continued]

	94/95	95/96	96/97	97/98	98/99	99/00	00/01	01/02	02/03
	(Percent)								
Acreage Reduction Program (ARP) Rate									
Corn	0.0	7.5	7.5	7.5	7.5	7.5	7.5	7.5	7.5
Sorghum	0.0	5.0	5.0	5.0	5.0	5.0	5.0	5.0	5.0
Barley	0.0	5.0	5.0	5.0	5.0	5.0	5.0	5.0	5.0
Oats	0.0	0.0	0.0	0.0	0.0	0.0	0.0	0.0	0.0
Wheat	0.0	5.0	5.0	5.0	5.0	5.0	5.0	5.0	5.0
Rice	0.0	0.0	0.0	0.0	0.0	0.0	0.0	0.0	0.0
Cotton	11.0	10.0	12.5	12.5	12.5	12.5	12.5	12.5	12.5
	(Percent)								
Normal Flexed Area Rate	15.0	15.0	15.0	15.0	15.0	15.0	15.0	15.0	15.0
	(Million Acres)								
Other Idled Area									
Conservation Reserve	36.42	38.00	35.96	22.29	13.53	8.18	4.08	3.60	2.60
0-92/85, 50-92/85	13.2	13.2	13.6	15.1	16.7	17.0	17.2	17.2	16.7

Source: Food and Agricultural Policy Research Institute, *FAPRI 1994 U.S. Agricultural Outlook*, #1-94 (Iowa State University/University of Missouri-Columbia, April 1994), p. 21. "This material is based upon work supported by the Cooperative State Research Service, U.S. Department of Agriculture. Any opinions, findings, conclusions, or recommendations are those of the authors and do not necessarily reflect the view of the USDA." *Notes:* Source also includes information for 1992/1993 and 1993/1994, as well as data for export program expenditures, milk support price, and producer milk assessment.

★9★

Government Programs and Impacts

Proposed Changes to Mandatory Programs, 1994-1997

"Making government work for the next century means reforming programs that don't work and updating policies and programs that were designed to meet the needs of an earlier era."

[Outlays in millions of dollars]

	1994	1995	1996	1997	1998	1994-1997 Total
Eliminate subsidies to honey producers	-12	-10	-6	-4	-3	-32
Target CCC subsidies to farmers with off-farm incomes below $100,000	-75	-115	-140	-140	-140	-470
Increase non-eligible payment acres (triple base) staring in 1996	...	...	-310	-720	-720	-1,030
Eliminate 0/92 and 50/92 (PAY/92) programs starting in 1996	...	...	-273	-664	-640	-937
Increase assessments on "non-program" crops starting in 1996	...	...	-450	-450	-450	-900

[Continued]

★9★

Proposed Changes to Mandatory Programs, 1994-1997

[Continued]

	1994	1995	1996	1997	1998	1994-1997 Total
Limit payments on wool and mohair to $50 thousand per person	-10	-68	-68	-66	-66	-212
Permanently extend market promotion program at 1993 level	-52	-52	-52	-52	-52	-208

Source: Executive Office of the President of the United States, Office of Management and Budget, *A Vision of Change for America* (Washington, D.C.: U.S. Government Printing Office, May 1991), p. 126. *Note:* Source also includes data for other government departments.

Land Use and Management

★10★

Planted and Idled Area, 1994-2003

"Summing across planted and idled area, the **total area** devoted to 15 principal crops is projected to increase through 1995/96 as increases in idled area more than offset declines in planted area. Beginning in 1996/97 with the expiration of CRP contracts, total area decreases as some of the CRP acres do not return to production or annual idled programs."

[Millions of acres]

	94/95	95/95	96/97	97/98	98/99	99/00	00/01	01/02	02/03
15-Crop Total Area	317.4	319.6	319.2	314.6	311.6	310.0	309.2	309.2	308.5
Planted	266.3	258.0	258.8	266.1	270.1	273.5	276.7	277.2	278.4
Payment	122.7	116.1	117.4	118.3	120.5	120.1	119.1	118.8	116.2
Non-Payment	143.6	141.9	141.4	147.8	149.6	153.4	157.6	158.4	162.2
Idled	51.1	61.5	60.4	48.4	41.5	36.5	32.5	32.0	30.2
ARP, PLD, 0-92/85	14.7	23.5	24.5	26.2	28.0	28.3	28.4	28.4	27.6
CRP	36.4	38.0	36.0	22.3	13.5	8.2	4.1	3.6	2.6
Wheat Total Area	87.8	89.2	89.5	89.4	90.1	89.8	90.8	90.6	90.4
Planted	71.5	69.4	70.0	72.6	75.7	76.8	79.2	79.2	79.3
Payment	49.5	46.7	47.0	48.2	48.8	49.3	48.8	48.9	48.6
Non-Payment	22.0	22.7	23.0	24.4	26.9	27.5	30.3	30.3	30.7
ARP, PLD, 0-92/85	5.4	8.6	8.8	9.7	10.3	10.7	10.7	10.6	10.5
CRP	10.8	11.2	10.6	7.0	4.1	2.4	0.9	0.8	0.5
Corn Total Area	87.0	87.7	88.2	88.2	87.9	88.1	88.1	87.8	87.9
Planted	79.5	75.6	75.9	77.9	77.7	78.6	79.0	78.8	79.6
Payment	48.6	46.0	47.0	46.3	47.4	46.4	45.7	45.4	43.2
Non-Payment	30.9	29.6	28.9	31.6	30.3	32.3	33.2	33.4	36.4
ARP, PLD, 0-92/85	3.1	7.5	7.7	7.9	8.4	8.2	8.2	8.2	7.8

[Continued]

★ 10 ★

Planted and Idled Area, 1994-2003

[Continued]

	94/95	95/95	96/97	97/98	98/99	99/00	00/01	01/02	02/03
CRP	4.1	4.7	4.5	2.4	1.8	1.3	0.9	0.8	0.6
Sorghum Total Area	16.1	15.7	15.6	15.3	14.9	14.8	14.6	14.6	14.5
Planted	12.5	11.0	11.0	11.5	11.4	11.7	11.6	11.6	11.8
Payment	6.7	6.0	6.0	6.2	6.5	6.5	6.5	6.5	6.4
Non-Payment	5.7	5.0	5.0	5.3	5.0	5.2	5.1	5.1	5.4
ARP, PLD, 0-92/85	1.2	2.2	2.3	2.5	2.8	2.8	2.8	2.8	2.7
CRP	2.5	2.5	2.3	1.3	0.7	0.4	0.2	0.1	0.1
Barley Total Area	12.8	12.9	12.8	12.6	12.3	12.2	12.0	11.9	11.9
Planted	7.9	7.5	7.5	8.2	8.4	8.6	8.8	8.8	8.9
Payment	4.7	4.3	4.3	4.6	4.6	4.7	4.9	4.9	5.0
Non-Payment	3.1	3.2	3.2	3.6	3.7	3.9	3.9	3.9	3.9
ARP, PLD, 0-92/85	2.1	2.5	2.5	2.6	2.9	3.0	3.0	3.1	2.9
CRP	2.8	2.9	2.7	1.8	1.0	0.5	0.1	0.1	0.1
Oats Total Area	9.7	10.0	9.8	9.5	9.3	9.2	9.1	9.1	9.0
Planted	7.8	8.1	7.8	7.9	8.0	8.1	8.1	8.1	8.1
Payment	1.2	1.2	1.3	1.3	1.3	1.3	1.3	1.3	1.3
Non-Payment	6.6	6.9	6.5	6.6	6.7	6.8	6.8	6.8	6.8
ARP, PLD, 0-92/85	0.5	0.5	0.6	0.6	0.7	0.8	0.8	0.8	0.8
CRP	1.4	1.5	1.4	0.9	0.6	0.4	0.2	0.2	0.1
Soybean Total Area	65.6	65.5	65.3	65.1	64.8	65.1	65.0	65.6	65.6
Planted	61.4	61.0	61.1	62.5	63.0	63.9	64.2	64.9	65.1
CRP	4.2	4.5	4.2	2.6	1.8	1.2	0.8	0.7	0.5
Cotton Total Area	14.8	14.6	14.8	15.0	15.4	15.3	15.3	15.2	15.1
Planted	12.9	12.9	12.7	12.7	12.8	12.8	12.8	12.8	12.6
Payment	9.1	9.2	8.8	9.0	9.1	9.1	9.1	9.1	9.0
Non-Payment	3.8	3.7	3.9	3.7	3.9	3.7	3.7	3.7	3.6
ARP, PLD, 50-92/85	1.9	1.8	2.1	2.3	2.4	2.4	2.5	2.5	2.5
CRP	1.4	1.5	1.5	0.8	0.5	0.3	0.2	0.2	0.2
Rice Total Area	3.7	3.6	3.6	3.6	3.7	3.6	3.6	3.6	3.6
Planted	3.2	3.2	3.1	3.2	3.2	3.2	3.2	3.2	3.2
Payment	2.8	2.8	2.9	2.8	2.8	2.8	2.8	2.8	2.7
Non-Payment	0.4	0.3	0.3	0.3	0.4	0.4	0.4	0.5	0.5
ARP, PLD, 50-92/85	0.4	0.4	0.4	0.4	0.4	0.4	0.4	0.4	0.4
CRP	0.0	0.0	0.0	0.0	0.0	0.0	0.0	0.0	0.0
Sugar									
Harvested	2.3	2.3	2.3	2.4	2.4	2.4	2.4	2.4	2.4
6 Other Crops[1]									
Planted[2]	7.3	7.2	7.2	7.3	7.3	7.3	7.4	7.4	7.4

[Continued]

★ 10 ★

Planted and Idled Area, 1994-2003

[Continued]

	94/95	95/95	96/97	97/98	98/99	99/00	00/01	01/02	02/03
Other CRP Area	10.4	10.8	10.2	6.3	3.6	2.1	1.0	0.9	0.7
Hay									
Harvested	61.2	61.3	61.4	62.1	62.7	62.9	63.0	62.9	62.9
15 Crops + Hay	378.6	380.8	380.6	376.6	374.3	372.9	372.2	372.1	371.4
Planted	327.5	319.3	320.2	328.2	332.8	336.4	339.7	340.1	341.2
Payment	122.7	116.1	117.4	118.3	120.5	120.1	119.1	118.8	116.2
Non-Payment	204.8	203.2	202.8	209.9	212.3	216.3	220.6	221.3	225.0
Idled	51.1	61.5	60.4	48.4	41.5	36.5	32.5	32.0	30.2
ARP, PLD, 0-92/85	14.7	23.5	24.5	26.2	28.0	28.3	28.4	28.4	27.6
CRP	36.4	38.0	36.0	22.3	13.5	8.2	4.1	3.6	2.6

Source: Food and Agricultural Policy Research Institute, *FAPRI 1994 U.S. Agricultural Outlook*, #1-94 (Iowa State University/ University of Missouri-Columbia, April 1994), pp. 96, 98. "This material is based upon work supported by the Cooperative State Research Service, U.S. Department of Agriculture. Any opinions, findings, conclusions, or recommendations are those of the authors and do not necessarily reflect the view of the USDA." *Notes:* Source also includes data for 1992/1993 and 1993/1994. 1. Sunflowers, peanuts, edible beans, tobacco, rye, and flaxseed. 2. Harvested area for tobacco and rye.

★ 11 ★

Land Use and Management

Conservation Reserve, Total Acreage, and Flexibility Shifts for Major Crops, 1991-2001

"The Environmental Conservation Acreage Reserve Program moves 40 million acres to conserving uses by the mid-1990s. Land enrolled in this program includes CRP acreage and 1 million acres in the Wetlands Reserve Program. This land becomes available for production consideration when contracts expire, most after 10 years, with market price incentives determining how much actually is used for production."

[Millions of acres]

	Selected history		1995/96	1996/97	1997/98	1998/99	1999/2000	2000/01
	1991/92	1992/93						
Conservation Reserve Program acreage, 8 major crops								
Corn	3.9	4.1	4.6	4.8	2.6	2.1	1.6	1.2
Sorghum	2.4	2.4	2.5	2.3	1.3	0.7	0.3	0.1
Barley	2.8	2.8	3.0	3.0	2.1	1.3	0.7	0.4
Oats	1.3	1.4	1.5	1.4	1.0	0.6	0.4	0.2
Wheat	10.4	10.6	11.2	10.6	7.0	4.1	2.4	0.9
Rice	---	---	---	---	---	---	---	---
Upland cotton	1.3	1.4	1.5	1.5	0.9	0.6	0.3	0.2
Soybeans	3.8	4.0	4.3	4.3	2.6	1.5	1.2	0.8
Total	25.9	26.7	28.6	27.9	17.5	10.9	6.9	3.8
Total acreage, with CRP, 8 major crops								
Corn	87.3	88.7	86.6	87.1	87.0	86.7	86.6	86.9
Sorghum	16.0	17.7	15.6	15.5	15.4	15.3	15.2	15.2
Barley	13.9	12.7	12.7	12.7	12.6	12.4	12.4	12.4
Oats	10.6	10.1	7.7	7.4	7.4	7.3	7.2	7.2
Wheat	96.2	90.2	88.2	88.4	87.9	87.4	87.1	86.7
Rice	3.6	3.6	3.6	3.6	3.6	3.6	3.6	3.6

[Continued]

★ 11 ★

Conservation Reserve, Total Acreage, and Flexibility Shifts for Major Crops, 1991-2001

[Continued]

	Selected history		1995/96	1996/97	1997/98	1998/99	1999/2000	2000/01
	1991/92	1992/93						
Upland cotton	16.3	16.1	16.3	16.3	15.7	15.3	15.4	15.3
Soybeans	63.0	63.3	66.3	66.6	65.1	64.0	64.2	63.8
Total	306.9	302.3	297.0	297.6	294.7	292.1	291.7	291.1
Total acreage, without CRP, 8 major crops								
Corn	83.4	84.6	82.0	82.3	84.4	84.6	85.0	85.7
Sorghum	13.6	15.3	13.1	13.2	14.1	14.6	14.9	15.1
Barley	11.1	9.9	9.7	9.7	10.5	11.1	11.7	12.0
Oats	9.3	8.7	6.2	6.0	6.4	6.7	6.8	7.0
Wheat	85.8	79.6	77.0	77.8	80.9	83.3	84.7	85.8
Rice	3.6	3.6	3.6	3.6	3.6	3.6	3.6	3.6
Upland cotton	15.0	14.7	14.8	14.8	14.8	14.7	15.1	15.1
Soybeans	59.2	59.3	62.0	62.3	62.5	62.5	63.0	63.0
Total	281.0	275.7	268.4	269.7	277.2	281.1	284.8	287.3

Source: United States Department of Agriculture, World Agricultural Outlook Board, *Long-Term Agricultural Baseline Projections,* WAOB-93-1 (Washington, D.C.: U.S. Government Printing Office, October 1993), p. 19. *Notes:* 1. Historical data as of June 1993. —Less than 50,000 acres. Baseline projections present one plausible scenario, representative of the long-term direction for the agricultural sector. The projections are a conditional, current law (as of June 1993) scenario with no shocks, based on a special set of assumptions regarding the macroeconomy, the weather, and international developments. The projections were prepared in June 1993, based on policy decisions and other information known at that time. The short-term outlook would now differ from that used in these baseline projections, although it is expected that by 1995 agricultural sector will have adjusted to the near-term disruptions in supply and use.

★ 12 ★

Land Use and Management

Base Reductions Attributable to the Conservation Reserve Program (CRP), 1994-2003

"Under the 1993 Budget Reconciliation Package, **CPR enrollment** is capped at 38 million acres. Through 12 signups, enrollment for 1994/95 stands at 36.4 million acres with 23.3 million acres coming from base reductions of program commodities. Wheat base acreage represents the largest single commodity contribution with 11.2 million acres of projected enrollment by 1995/96.

"As **CRP contracts** begin to expire in 1996/97, it is assumed that none of the contracts are extended. However, it is not assumed that all of the land returns to production. Across feed grains, wheat, cotton, rice, and soybeans, it is assumed that between 50 and 60 percent of CRP acres return to production. A portion of the land is assumed to be enrolled in the 0-85 and 50-85 programs, while some will go to hay and pasture."

[Millions of acres]

	94/95	95/96	96/97	97/98	98/99	99/00	00/01	01/02	02/03
Wheat	10.83	11.16	10.61	6.99	4.06	2.35	0.89	0.79	0.54
Corn	4.29	4.66	4.51	2.35	1.83	1.29	0.88	0.79	0.60
Sorghum	2.47	2.53	2.30	1.30	0.68	0.38	0.17	0.15	0.11
Barley	2.83	2.88	2.74	1.79	1.01	0.53	0.15	0.12	0.07
Oats	1.40	1.46	1.39	0.95	0.60	0.36	0.17	0.15	0.11
Cotton	1.43	1.53	1.48	0.84	0.50	0.31	0.22	0.20	0.15
Rice	0.01	0.02	0.01	0.01	0.01	0.01	0.00	0.00	0.00
Total Base Reductions	23.27	24.23	23.03	14.24	8.69	5.23	2.48	2.20	1.59

[Continued]

★ 12 ★

Base Reductions Attributable to the Conservation Reserve Program (CRP), 1994-2003

[Continued]

	94/95	95/96	96/97	97/98	98/99	99/00	00/01	01/02	02/03
Reduced Soybean Area	4.16	4.47	4.22	2.57	1.77	1.17	0.78	0.70	0.51
Other	9.62	10.26	7.50	-3.31	-2.48	-1.69	-1.93	0.43	-0.11
Total CRP Area	36.42	38.00	35.96	22.29	13.53	8.18	4.08	3.60	2.60

Source: Food and Agricultural Policy Research Institute, *FAPRI 1994 U.S. Agricultural Outlook*, #1-94 (Iowa State University/University of Missouri-Columbia, April 1994), pp. 96-7. "This material is based upon work supported by the Cooperative State Research Service, U.S. Department of Agriculture. Any opinions, findings, conclusions, or recommendations are those of the authors and do not necessarily reflect the view of the USDA." *Note:* Source also includes data for 1992/1993 and 1993/1994.

★ 13 ★

Land Use and Management

Net Flexed Area, 1994-2003

"Given the price paths of program crops, **flexible acreage** is projected to continue shifting into soybeans and minor oilseeds and out of feed grains and food grains. Flexible acreage is projected to continue shifting into cotton throughout the projection period."

[Millions of acres]

	94/95	95/96	96/97	97/98	98/99	99/00	00/01	01/02	02/03
Wheat	-2.17	-2.20	-2.24	-2.36	-2.31	-2.36	-2.25	-2.27	-2.30
Corn	-2.60	-2.54	-2.58	-2.51	-2.59	-2.47	-2.41	-2.38	-2.19
Sorghum	-0.25	-0.33	-0.34	-0.36	-0.42	-0.41	-0.42	-0.42	-0.40
Barley	-0.72	-0.69	-0.69	-0.70	-0.73	-0.74	-0.76	-0.76	-0.76
Oats	-0.26	-0.27	-0.29	-0.30	-0.30	-0.31	-0.32	-0.33	-0.34
Rice	-0.17	-0.26	-0.30	-0.27	-0.23	-0.25	-0.23	-0.23	-0.22
Cotton	0.05	0.09	0.11	0.07	0.08	0.06	0.05	0.05	0.03
Soybeans	4.96	5.02	5.11	5.18	5.23	5.21	5.12	5.12	4.99
Minor Oilseeds	0.38	0.39	0.40	0.41	0.42	0.42	0.41	0.41	0.41
Other Crops	0.77	0.79	0.82	0.84	0.85	0.85	0.82	0.82	0.79

Source: Food and Agricultural Policy Research Institute, *FAPRI 1994 U.S. Agricultural Outlook*, #1-94 (Iowa State University/University of Missouri-Columbia, April 1994), pp. 96-7. "This material is based upon work supported by the Cooperative State Research Service, U.S. Department of Agriculture. Any opinions, findings, conclusions, or recommendations are those of the authors and do not necessarily reflect the view of the USDA." *Note:* Source also includes data for 1992/1993 and 1993/1994.

Farm Income and Trade

★ 14 ★

Farm Income Statistics, 1994-2002

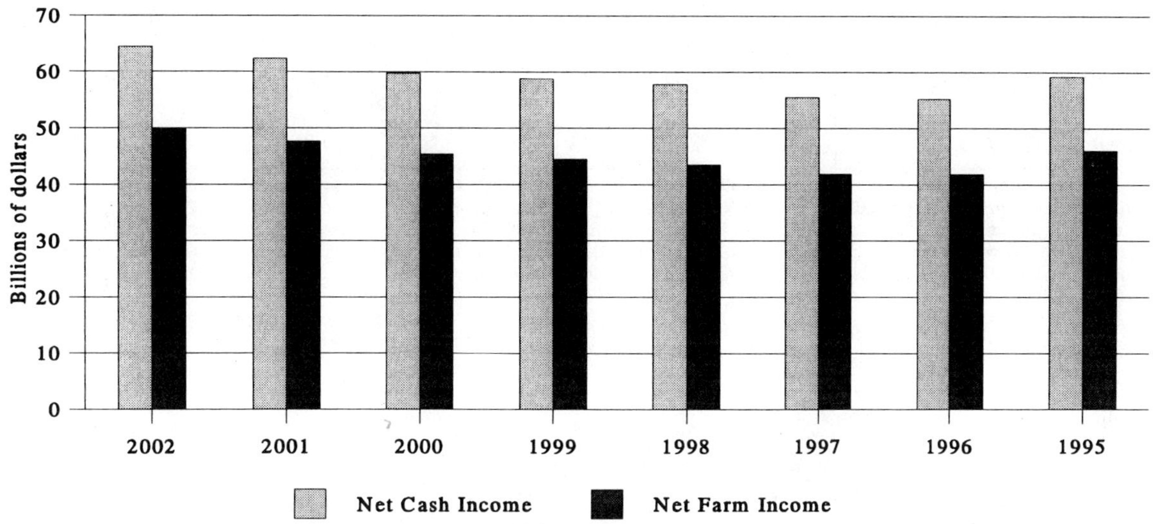

"On a cash basis, net income is actually expected to have reached levels in 1993 despite the effects of the Midwest flooding. **Net cash income** in 1993 is estimated to have grown by $4.53 billion as the result of higher livestock receipts and government payments, and only a modest increase in expenses. However, net cash income is expected to drop by $4.15 billion in 1994 with a $3.00 billion dollar decline in government payments and a $2.79 billion increase in cash production expenses. Higher crop cash receipts and lower expenses are expected to generate a $1.09 billion dollar increase in net cash income in 1995. Net cash income drops by $4.03 billion in 1996 with the cattle cycle, but grows steadily after 1997 when the livestock sector recovers."

[Billions of dollars]

	1994	1995	1996	1997	1998	1999	2000	2001	2002
Farm Receipts	183.60	184.56	182.45	188.16	192.92	196.69	200.37	206.19	211.88
Crops	86.20	87.94	88.15	90.14	91.69	93.80	95.58	97.63	100.24
Livestock	89.71	88.84	86.36	89.85	92.83	94.28	95.95	99.51	102.35
Farm-Related[1]	7.69	7.78	7.94	8.17	8.40	8.61	8.85	9.06	9.29
Government Payments	8.76	8.26	8.48	7.14	6.75	5.94	5.63	5.01	4.25
Gross Cash Income (1+2)	192.36	192.82	190.94	195.29	199.67	202.64	206.00	211.21	216.13
Nonmoney Income	6.05	6.03	6.00	6.28	6.52	6.60	6.63	6.82	7.00
Value of Inventory Change	4.71	0.17	0.47	0.64	0.19	0.46	0.75	0.48	0.76
Gross Farm Income (3+4+5)	203.11	199.02	197.40	202.21	206.39	209.70	213.37	218.50	223.89

[Continued]

★ 14 ★

Farm Income Statistics, 1994-2002

[Continued]

	1994	1995	1996	1997	1998	1999	2000	2001	2002
Cash Expenses[2]	134.25	133.63	135.78	139.84	141.89	143.89	146.25	148.81	151.62
Total Expenses	154.25	152.98	155.56	160.32	162.87	165.23	168.00	170.81	173.97
Net Cash Income (3-7)	58.10	59.19	55.16	55.46	57.71	58.75	59.75	62.39	64.51
Net Farm Income (6-8)	48.86	46.04	41.84	41.89	43.52	44.47	45.37	47.69	49.91
Deflated (1987 $)[3]	38.32	35.06	30.86	29.91	30.15	29.86	29.53	30.10	30.53

Source: Food and Agricultural Policy Research Institute, *FAPRI 1994 U.S. Agricultural Outlook*, #1-94 (Iowa State University/University of Missouri-Columbia, April 1994), pp. 110-11. "This material is based upon work supported by the Cooperative State Research Service, U.S. Department of Agriculture. Any opinions, findings, conclusions, or recommendations are those of the authors and do not necessarily reflect the view of the USDA." *Notes:* Source also includes data for 1992 and 1993. 1. Income from machine hire, custom work, sales of forest products, and other miscellaneous cash sources. 2. Excludes capital consumption, perquisites to hired labor, and farm household expenses. 3. Deflated by the GNP price deflator, 1987=1.

★ 15 ★

Farm Income and Trade

Farm Receipts, Expenses, and Incomes, 1991-2000

"In the baseline scenario, net farm income is relatively constant in nominal terms at about $4 billion below the 1992 record of $48.7 billion. Real net farm income declines. Much of the decline in real net farm income is due to lower Government payments as market prices rise and target prices are assumed to remain at current levels. With Government payments falling, the agriculture sector increasingly relies on the marketplace for its income. Both crop and livestock receipts are up in nominal terms, due to larger production and higher prices. Crop receipts fall in real terms while real livestock receipts are nearly constant. Production expenses also increase in nominal terms, but are nearly flat in real terms."

	Selected history[1]		1995	1996	1997	1998	1999	2000
	1991	1992						
	Billons of dollars							
Cash receipts:								
Crops	81.9	84.8	86.3	88.9	91.1	93.0	94.9	97.2
Livestock and products	86.8	86.4	88.2	90.3	93.5	96.9	100.0	103.5
All commodities	168.7	171.2	174.6	179.2	184.6	189.9	194.9	200.7
Government payments	8.2	9.2	10.4	9.2	8.3	7.9	7.5	7.0
Value of inventory change	-0.3	3.9	1.4	0.5	0.5	0.3	0.7	1.1
Gross cash income	184.7	187.6	193.1	196.8	201.4	206.6	211.4	217.0
Gross farm income	190.3	197.8	200.4	203.4	208.4	213.7	219.3	225.6
Cash expenses	131.3	130.1	133.9	136.1	140.8	145.1	149.9	155.0
Total production expenses	150.3	149.1	155.6	158.4	163.9	169.0	174.6	180.4

[Continued]

★ 15 ★

Farm Receipts, Expenses, and Incomes, 1991-2000

[Continued]

	Selected history[1] 1991	1992	1995	1996	1997	1998	1999	2000
Net cash income	53.4	57.5	59.2	60.7	60.6	61.4	61.5	62.0
Net farm income	40.0	48.7	44.8	45.0	44.5	44.7	44.8	45.2
Total farm assets	843.9	861.2	926.5	958.5	993.7	1,027.2	1,058.6	1,087.4
Total farm debt	138.8	138.3	143.1	146.1	150.3	155.0	159.8	164.7
	Percent							
Debt/equity ratio	19.7	19.1	18.3	18.0	17.8	17.8	17.8	17.8
Debt/assets ratio	16.4	16.1	15.4	15.2	15.1	15.1	15.1	15.1

Source: United States Department of Agriculture, World Agricultural Outlook Board, *Long-term Agricultural Baseline Projections*, WAOB-93-1 (Washington, D.C.: U.S. Government Printing Office, October 1993), p. 44. *Note:* 1. Historical data as of June 1993.

★ 16 ★

Farm Income and Trade

Average Nominal and Real Income to Farm Operating Households, 1991-2000

"In the baseline scenario, net farm income is relatively constant in nominal terms at about $4 billion below the 1992 record of $48.7 billion. Real net farm income declines. Much of the decline in real net farm income is due to lower Government payments as market prices rise and target prices are assumed to remain at current levels. With Government payments falling, the agriculture sector increasingly relies on the marketplace for its income. Both crop and livestock receipts are up in nominal terms, due to larger production and higher prices. Crop receipts fall in real terms while real livestock receipts are nearly constant. Production expenses also increase in nominal terms, but are nearly flat in real terms."

	Selected history[1] 1991	1992	1995	1996	1997	1998	1999	2000
	Dollars per operator household							
Farm income to household	4,397	4,337	4,823	5,000	4,921	4,978	4,925	4,932
Off-farm income	31,638	35,731	38,061	39,812	41,723	43,684	45,737	47,887
Farm operator household income	36,035	40,068	42,884	44,812	46,644	48,662	50,662	52,819
	1987 dollars per operator household[2]							
Farm income to household	3,733	3,587	3,665	3,684	3,510	3,438	3,294	3,194

[Continued]

★ 16 ★

Average Nominal and Real Income to Farm Operating Households, 1991-2000

[Continued]

	Selected history[1]		1995	1996	1997	1998	1999	2000
	1991	1992						
Off-farm income	26,857	29,554	28,922	29,338	29,760	30,169	30,593	31,015
Farm operator household income	30,590	33,141	32,587	33,022	33,270	33,607	33,888	34,209

Source: United States Department of Agriculture, World Agricultural Outlook Board, *Long-term Agricultural Baseline Projections*, WAOB-93-1 (Washington, D.C.: U.S. Government Printing Office, October 1993), p. 45. *Notes:* 1. Historical data as of June 1993. 2. Nominal dollar values divided by the GDP deflator.

★ 17 ★

Farm Income and Trade

Net Returns for Eight Crops, 1994-2003

"Despite higher prices, lower yields result in lower **program participant per-acre net returns** for feed grains and cotton in 1993/94. With the exceptions of wheat and rice, participant returns should rebound as higher yields and lower ARP rates more than offset lower prices. With frozen target prices and program yields, participant net returns decline throughout the projection period.

"**Nonparticipant per-acre net returns** follow movements in market prices throughout the projection period. Nonparticipant returns for grain sorghum, barley, oats, and cotton decline throughout the period as cost increases more than offset yield increases. Stronger prices for wheat, corn, soybeans, and rice provide some support for returns in the final years of the projection period.

"**Aggregate net returns**, including disaster payments, fell by $3 billion in 1993/94 with lower yields and acreage. Corn returns suffered the largest drop. The declinc was somewhat mitigated by the inclusion of $2.3 billion in disaster payments.

"**Total returns** should increase in 1994/95 with higher yields and planted area. Higher ARP rates reduce total returns in 1995/96, but returns increase as acreage with the expiration of CRP contracts."

	94/95	95/96	96/97	97/98	98/99	99/00	00/01	01/02	02/03
Net Returns									
	(Dollars per Acre)								
Wheat									
Participant	94.36	88.08	86.04	84.77	83.24	83.87	81.79	81.52	81.15
Nonparticipant	64.62	61.40	57.80	57.94	56.76	63.85	62.00	64.58	67.67
Corn									
Participant	186.67	170.32	170.74	164.33	165.00	163.77	161.07	163.80	162.69
Nonparticipant	137.80	130.78	135.79	121.29	127.76	128.57	124.54	137.66	140.21
Sorghum									
Participant	91.36	84.95	84.09	80.25	79.14	77.46	75.74	75.55	73.83
Nonparticipant	62.05	60.02	60.90	50.92	52.19	50.72	49.71	55.01	54.63
Barley									
Participant	77.43	72.70	71.91	68.48	66.83	65.48	63.41	62.97	61.40
Nonparticipant	62.20	62.15	62.45	56.75	55.53	55.46	53.28	55.71	55.74

[Continued]

★ 17 ★

Net Returns for Eight Crops, 1994-2003

[Continued]

	94/95	95/96	96/97	97/98	98/99	99/00	00/01	01/02	02/03
Oats									
Participant	51.26	48.73	48.03	45.84	43.44	40.92	38.46	36.69	34.33
Nonparticipant	45.23	39.84	39.74	37.46	35.29	32.49	29.28	28.16	26.12
Soybeans	128.97	121.06	128.18	124.07	123.93	124.10	128.91	132.41	138.18
Cotton									
Participant	195.68	195.69	189.58	186.36	175.80	172.50	168.19	163.38	162.38
Nonparticipant	143.08	142.30	135.49	133.72	117.44	114.23	110.52	106.15	110.03
Rice									
Participant	204.16	198.90	199.58	196.34	187.78	183.05	176.65	170.57	165.89
Nonparticipant	42.88	25.89	42.14	51.05	43.18	47.42	49.34	53.84	63.87
	(Billion Dollars)								
Total Net Returns	34.52	32.42	32.97	32.51	32.86	33.24	33.14	33.98	34.38
Wheat	6.61	6.27	6.14	6.33	6.45	6.79	6.75	6.81	6.87
Corn	13.92	12.98	13.28	12.74	13.07	13.09	12.83	13.38	13.39
Sorghum	1.60	1.42	1.42	1.39	1.39	1.38	1.35	1.37	1.36
Barley	0.73	0.69	0.69	0.70	0.71	0.72	0.71	0.72	0.70
Oats	0.39	0.36	0.35	0.34	0.32	0.30	0.28	0.27	0.25
Soybeans	7.92	7.39	7.83	7.76	7.81	7.93	8.28	8.59	9.00
Cotton	2.69	2.67	2.60	2.60	2.47	2.42	2.36	2.28	2.26
Rice	0.67	0.66	0.67	0.66	0.62	0.61	0.59	0.57	0.55
Disaster Payments	0.00	0.00	0.00	0.00	0.00	0.00	0.00	0.00	0.00

Source: Food and Agricultural Policy Research Institute, *FAPRI 1994 U.S. Agricultural Outlook*, #1-94 (Iowa State University/ University of Missouri-Columbia, April 1994), pp. 100-01. "This material is based upon work supported by the Cooperative State Research Service, U.S. Department of Agriculture. Any opinions, findings, research, conclusions, or recommendations are those of the authors and do not necessarily reflect the view of the USDA." *Note:* Source also includes data for 1992/1993 and 1993/1994.

★ 18 ★

Farm Income and Trade

Quantity of U.S. Exports, 1994-2002

"The volume of agricultural exports falls by nearly 14 percent in fiscal year 1994 primarily because of high U.S. grain and oilseed prices and a sluggish world economy. Total exports are not projected to reach fiscal year 1993 and levels until 1998, reflecting a poor short-term outlook for world economic recovery.

"The volume of animal and animal product exports shows steady growth throughout the projection period, increasing by 42 percent from 3.7 mmt in fiscal year 1992 to 4.9 mmt in fiscal year 2002. The grains and feeds sector show less dramatic growth of 16 percent over the same period, while oilseeds and products stagnate at about 8 percent growth."

[1,000 metric tons, fiscal year]

	1994	1995	1996	1997	1998	1999	2000	2001	2002
Total	124,222	132,373	134,891	139,267	145,376	151,726	156,082	159,691	163,228
Animals and Animal Products	3,798	3,846	4,016	4,130	4,298	4,527	4,782	4,906	4,929
Grains and Feeds	89,422	94,910	96,034	99,002	103,708	108,677	111,687	114,226	116,872
Wheat (Unmilled and Flour)	32,286	30,492	29,132	30,273	32,499	35,147	37,308	38,513	39,175
Rice (Paddy Milled)	2,714	2,532	2,582	2,605	2,639	2,682	2,672	2,679	2,666
Feed Grains and Products	39,796	46,274	47,695	48,336	49,941	51,488	51,655	52,482	53,917
Other Grains and Feeds	14,625	15,613	16,625	17,788	18,629	19,360	20,051	20,553	21,114
Oilseeds and Products	23,530	25,490	26,471	27,435	28,226	28,931	29,716	30,401	31,020
Cotton (excl. Linters)	1,364	1,453	1,453	1,446	1,455	1,455	1,432	1,404	1,371
Other Products	6,108	6,673	6,918	7,254	7,690	8,136	8,466	8,754	9,036

Source: Food and Agricultural Policy Research Institute, *FAPRI 1994 U.S. Agricultural Outlook*, #1-94 (Iowa State University/University of Missouri-Columbia, April 1994), p. 102-03. "This material is based upon work supported by the Cooperative State Research Service, U.S. Department of Agriculture. Any opinions, findings, conclusions, or recommendations are those of the authors and do not necessarily reflect the view of the USDA." *Note:* Source also includes data for 1992 and 1993.

★ 19 ★

Farm Income and Trade

Value of U.S. Exports, 1994-2002

"Total value of agricultural exports is shifting from dependence on exports of grains, feeds, and oilseeds to animals and animal products. The value of poultry products has grown dramatically in the past decade and is projected to more than double over the projection period. The value of meat and meat product exports also shows impressive growth of approximately 80 percent from fiscal year 1992 to 2002.

"Despite strong growth in the value of meat and poultry exports, the historical high of $43.8 billion in 1981 is not projected to be surpassed until fiscal year 1998."

[Million dollars, fiscal year]

	1994	1995	1996	1997	1998	1999	2000	2001	2002
Total	40,028	40,231	40,845	42,470	44,414	46,777	48,940	50,556	52,060
Animal and Animal Products	8,952	9,007	9,206	9,530	10,341	11,216	11,931	12,350	12,467
Meat and Meat Products	3,651	3,766	3,818	3,996	4,594	5,199	5,588	5,798	5,768

[Continued]

★ 19 ★

Value of U.S. Exports, 1994-2002

[Continued]

	1994	1995	1996	1997	1998	1999	2000	2001	2002
Poultry and Poultry Products	1,820	1,822	1,984	1,988	2,036	2,178	2,384	2,483	2,587
Dairy Products	653	608	596	598	599	603	606	609	612
Hides and Skins	1,412	1,449	1,445	1,528	1,616	1,668	1,717	1,764	1,782
Other Animal Products	1,415	1,361	1,363	1,419	1,496	1,567	1,637	1,697	1,718
Grains and Feeds	12,403	11,973	11,919	12,276	12,692	13,438	14,170	14,567	15,315
Wheat (Unmilled and Flour)	4,356	3,858	3,627	3,709	4,047	4,390	4,989	5,181	5,411
Rice (Paddy Milled)	847	777	828	863	881	902	923	949	974
Feed Grains and Products	4,968	5,144	5,200	5,383	5,372	5,686	5,748	5,839	6,250
Corn	4,162	4,306	4,382	4,548	4,521	4,782	4,821	4,885	5,251
Other Feed Grains	806	838	818	835	851	905	927	953	999
Other Grains and Feeds	2,232	2,195	2,264	2,320	2,392	2,459	2,511	2,599	2,681
Oilseeds and Products	6,562	6,565	6,605	7,080	7,222	7,447	7,703	8,064	8,380
Soybeans	4,395	4,386	4,400	4,689	4,715	4,816	4,949	5,167	5,353
Other Oilseeds and Products	2,167	2,178	2,205	2,391	2,507	2,631	2,754	2,897	3,028
Cotton (excl. Linters)	1,914	1,991	2,002	1,958	1,981	1,956	1,928	1,899	1,858
Other Products	10,197	10,696	11,114	11,627	12,178	12,720	13,208	13,675	14,040

Source: Food and Agricultural Policy Research Institute, *FAPRI 1994 U.S. Agricultural Outlook*, #1-94 (Iowa State University/University of Missouri-Columbia, April 1994), pp. 102-03. "This material is based upon work supported by the Cooperative State Research Service, U.S. Department of Agriculture. Any opinions, findings, conclusions, or recommendations are those of the authors and do not necessarily reflect the view of the USDA." *Note:* Source also includes data for 1992 and 1993.

★ 20 ★

Meat Trade, 1994-2002

"World **beef trade** increases 17 percent in 1994, primarily due to an 8 percent production increase in the European Union resulting from the herd build-up in the recent past that took advantage of headage payments.

"World **beef trade** after 1994 is projected to decline at an average rate of 1.1 percent, reversing the 2.8 percent annual growth of the 1985-92 period. The projections show reductions in exports from the European Union and imports by the United States, Mexico, and Canada. Strong import growth is likely in Japan and Korea. Slow but steady growth in production and exports are likely in New Zealand, Brazil, and Argentina.

"**Pork trade**, after declining during the past five years, is projected to rebound over the projection period with an annual growth rate of about 3 percent. The growth in trade comes from favorable prices, relative to beef, that increase import demands in Japan and Mexico, as well as from a delayed economic upturn in the former Soviet Union and Eastern Europe.

"Continued growth in **poultry trade** is projected through 2002, but at a reduced annual rate of 3.3 percent compared to 6 percent during the 1985-92 period. While health concerns and relative prices favor the share of poultry in total meat consumption, import demand growth is subdued by production increases resulting from low feed prices."

[1,000 metric tons]

	1994	1995	1996	1997	1998	1999	2000	2001	2002
Beef and Veal									
Net Exporters									
Argentina	258	273	272	274	284	297	288	285	278
Australia	1,080	1,157	1,295	1,286	1,170	1,101	1,055	1,021	1,040
Brazil	311	315	314	325	331	339	346	352	357
Eastern Europe	26	31	25	32	42	52	64	74	82
European Union	1,160	717	542	418	346	229	209	194	200
New Zealand	453	470	483	489	496	504	513	523	533
Total Net Exports	3,288	2,963	2,931	2,824	2,669	2,522	2,475	2,449	2,490
Net Importers									
Canada	65	64	65	69	71	71	65	51	30
Japan	699	784	873	915	947	977	988	998	1,009
Mexico	113	124	140	163	161	125	77	55	11
United States	422	397	380	276	126	69	73	68	143
Former Soviet Union	521	217	183	159	142	99	92	84	73
Other Importers/Residual	1,469	1,378	1,291	1,241	1,221	1,181	1,180	1,193	1,224
Total Net Imports	3,288	2,963	2,931	2,824	2,669	2,522	2,475	2,449	2,490
Pork									
Net Exporters									
Canada	283	295	304	310	319	314	292	274	271
China	130	135	141	146	152	158	165	172	178
Eastern Europe	126	126	92	97	55	32	3	42	46
European Union	453	489	531	566	613	662	691	702	714
Other Western Europe	8	0	0	0	0	0	0	0	0
Taiwan	308	324	324	330	344	351	351	357	369
Total Net Exports	1,308	1,369	1,392	1,449	1,483	1,517	1,502	1,547	1,578

[Continued]

★ 20 ★

Meat Trade, 1994-2002

[Continued]

	1994	1995	1996	1997	1998	1999	2000	2001	2002
Net Importers									
Hong Kong	225	236	242	240	236	239	242	239	236
Japan	689	712	724	756	790	824	854	878	899
Mexico	45	54	68	69	71	81	98	101	109
United States	136	125	107	163	175	107	-9	-19	-22
Former Soviet Union	100	111	111	77	80	130	175	199	216
Other Importers/Residual	112	132	141	144	132	137	141	148	140
Total Net Imports	1,308	1,369	1,392	1,449	1,483	1,517	1,502	1,547	1,578
Broiler Meat									
Net Exporters									
Brazil	319	314	302	300	299	295	286	298	309
Eastern Europe	1	0	-14	-5	4	14	22	37	48
European Union	380	442	471	526	539	524	514	485	438
Thailand	200	203	204	215	226	236	246	257	268
United States	907	903	1,008	982	1,008	1,086	1,195	1,229	1,265
Total Net Exports	1,807	1,862	1,971	2,018	2,076	2,155	2,263	2,306	2,328
Net Importers									
Canada	62	65	92	101	101	113	143	145	132
Hong Kong	194	198	206	212	219	226	233	239	245
Japan	482	505	573	611	648	689	730	748	753
Mexico	74	105	111	115	118	123	128	133	138
Saudi Arabia	252	256	262	266	270	275	281	284	289
Former Soviet Union	50	51	63	75	95	122	151	182	216
Other Importers/Residual	694	683	663	637	625	609	596	576	555
Total Net Imports	1,807	1,862	1,971	2,018	2,076	2,155	2,263	2,306	2,328
	(Dollars per Metric Ton)								
U.S. Market Prices									
Nebraska Direct Steers	1,644	1,595	1,502	1,537	1,603	1,679	1,769	1,842	1,905
Iowa-Southern Minnesota Barrows and Gilts	1,070	1,010	928	1,009	1,099	1,038	971	1,032	1,107
12-City Broilers	1,203	1,217	1,191	1,216	1,234	1,242	1,225	1,267	1,275
Eastern Region Wholesale Turkey	1,398	1,425	1,374	1,419	1,505	1,523	1,500	1,548	1,571

Source: Food and Agricultural Policy Research Institute, *FAPRI 1994 U.S. Agricultural Outlook*, #1-94 (Iowa State University/University of Missouri-Columbia, April 1994), pp. 44-5. "This material is based upon work supported by the Cooperative State Research Service, U.S. Department of Agriculture. Any opinions, findings, conclusions, or recommendations are those of the authors and do not necessarily reflect the view of the USDA." *Note:* Source also includes data for 1992 and 1993.

Dairy Projections

★21★

Dairy Projections

Dairy Supply and Utilization, 1991-2001

"In the crops sector, productive capacity is projected to rise due to increases in resource and input use and in productivity. For most crops, yields are projected to rise at or near their long-term trends. Reflecting, in part, the assumption that the Conservation Reserve Program (CRP) is not extended when contracts expire, land used for crop production increases as some CRP land returns to production. Also, generally lower annual Acreage Reduction Program (ARP) levels contribute to increased land being used for crops. Domestic demand for crops is projected to grow slowly, largely reflecting gains in population."

	Units	Selected history[1]		1995/96	1996/97	1997/98	1998/99	1999/2000	2000/01
		1991/92	1992/93						
Milk production	Bil. lbs.	150.9	151.2	158.4	158.5	159.0	160.5	162.4	163.5
Commercial use	Bil. lbs.	141.3	143.7	151.9	153.5	155.0	156.5	158.4	159.5
Net removals:									
Milkfat basis	Bil. lbs.	10.3	8.3	7.2	5.7	4.7	4.7	4.7	4.7
Total solids	Bil. lbs.	5.3	5.7	7.2	5.7	4.7	4.7	4.7	4.7
Production data:									
Number of cows	Thousand	9,868	9,755	9,445	9,320	9,200	9,120	9,040	8,965
Milk per cow	Pounds	15,296	15,495	16,770	17,005	17,275	17,595	17,960	18,235
bST use	% of cows	0	0	30	33	35	40	45	50
Prices:									
Support	Doll. per cwt	10.10	10.10	10.10	10.10	10.35	10.35	10.60	10.60
All milk	Doll. per cwt	13.25	12.80	12.00	12.40	12.70	12.80	12.95	13.05
Assessments	Doll. per cwt	0.097	0.113	0.117	0.113	0.113	0.113	0.113	0.113
Effective price	Doll. per cwt	13.15	12.69	11.88	12.29	12.59	12.69	12.84	12.94
Costs and returns:									
Concentrate costs	Doll. per cwt milk	4.09	4.03	4.22	4.30	4.35	4.38	4.43	4.54
Other cash costs	Doll. per cwt milk	7.20	7.35	7.45	7.55	7.65	7.70	7.75	7.80
Returns above cash costs	Doll. per cwt milk	1.86	1.31	0.21	0.44	0.59	0.61	0.66	0.60

Source: United States Department of Agriculture, World Agricultural Outlook Board, *Long-term Agricultural Baseline Projections*, WAOB-93-1 (Washington, D.C.: U.S. Government Printing Office, October 1993), p. 20. *Notes:* 1. Historical data as of June 1993. Baseline projections present one plausible scenario, representative of the long-term direction for the agricultural sector. The projections are a conditional, current law (as of June 1993) scenario with no shocks, based on a special set of assumptions regarding the macroeconomy, the weather, and international developments. The projections were prepared in June 1993, based on policy decisions and other information known at that time. The short-term outlook would not differ from that used in these baseline projections, although it is expected that by 1995 the agricultural sector will have adjusted to the near-term disruptions in supply and use.

★ 22 ★

Dairy Projections

Regional Dairy Supply, 1994-2002

"**Milk production** is expected to expand by more than 1.5 billion pounds in 1994 as production per cow increases by nearly 500 pounds. Largely because of rBST use, milk production increases on average 0.93 percent per year during the period of 1995 to 1998; production grows at an average rate of only 0.68 percent per year for the remainder of the projection period.

"**Dairy cow numbers** decline to 9.5 million head in 1994. Dairy cow numbers continue to contract over the entire projection period, reaching 8.5 million head in 2002. Contraction is greater in the mid-1990s in an effort to adjust for increases in production per cow. Nearly half of the projected decline in dairy cow numbers between 1994 and 2002 occurs in the Upper Midwest region."

	1994	1995	1996	1997	1998	1999	2000	2001	2002
	(Thousand Head)								
Average Cows on Farms:									
Appalachian	561	535	512	491	472	456	442	429	416
Corn Belt	836	817	800	784	770	759	748	737	725
Upper Midwest	2,610	2,511	2,436	2,369	2,310	2,259	2,215	2,176	2,139
Northeast	1,956	1,925	1,899	1,875	1,854	1,838	1,823	1,809	1,794
Pacific	1,614	1,631	1,635	1,638	1,641	1,646	1,652	1,658	1,662
Southeast	275	270	266	263	265	273	285	298	313
Southern Plains	369	363	357	353	352	356	362	372	384
Other States	1,303	1,267	1,229	1,197	1,172	1,154	1,138	1,124	1,117
United States	9,522	9,319	9,135	8,969	8,836	8,741	8,664	8,602	8,549
United States, Jan. 1	9,656	9,445	9,249	9,076	8,917	8,810	8,726	8,656	8,601
	(Pounds)								
Milk Production per Cow									
Appalachian	13,437	14,071	14,664	15,090	15,571	15,869	16,169	16,462	16,744
Corn Belt	14,717	15,351	15,946	16,378	16,849	17,139	17,440	17,739	18,035
Upper Midwest	15,393	16,030	16,631	17,075	17,552	17,862	18,182	18,502	18,828
Northeast	16,027	16,706	17,340	17,798	18,310	18,638	18,975	19,306	19,630
Pacific	19,684	20,413	21,110	21,653	22,215	22,622	23,040	23,463	23,893
Southeast	14,986	15,661	16,277	16,273	17,215	17,509	17,814	18,122	18,413
Southern Plains	15,467	16,132	16,765	17,241	17,739	18,071	18,410	18,749	19,089
Other States	15,437	16,113	16,747	17,221	17,728	18,064	18,408	18,753	19,092
United States	16,073	16,769	17,420	17,908	18,430	18,778	19,135	19,400	19,843
	(Million Pounds)								
Milk Production									
Appalachian	7,534	7,527	7,506	7,406	7,354	7,243	7,149	7,062	6,970
Corn Belt	12,299	12,543	12,763	12,847	12,981	13,003	13,036	13,067	13,072
Upper Midwest	40,169	40,257	40,521	40,447	40,539	40,357	40,281	40,261	40,275
Northeast	31,344	32,153	32,923	33,368	33,952	34,248	34,584	34,917	35,215
Pacific	31,767	33,299	34,518	35,460	36,447	37,227	38,052	38,892	39,701
Southeast	4,120	4,226	4,332	4,396	4,561	4,787	5,075	5,407	5,758
Southern Plains	5,707	5,850	5,991	6,081	6,238	6,428	6,673	6,970	7,323

[Continued]

★ 22 ★

Regional Dairy Supply, 1994-2002

[Continued]

	1994	1995	1996	1997	1998	1999	2000	2001	2002
Other States	20,107	20,419	20,581	20,614	20,783	20,851	20,942	21,083	21,325
United States	153,047	156,274	159,133	160,619	162,855	164,145	165,792	167,659	169,638

Source: Food and Agricultural Policy Research Institute, *FAPRI 1994 U.S. Agricultural Outlook*, #1-94 (Iowa State University/University of Missouri-Columbia, April 1994), p. 90. "This material is based upon work supported by the Cooperative State Research Service, U.S. Department of Agriculture. Any opinions, findings, conclusions, or recommendations are those of the authors and do not necessarily reflect the view of the USDA." *Note:* Source also includes data for 1992 and 1993.

★ 23 ★

Dairy Projections

Milk Production with Permanently Reduced Milk Demand, 1990-1998

"This table shows the impact of reduced demand on milk production (given medium bST adoption) with alternative policies-fixed support price, trigger-adjusted support price, production quota, and a dairy termination program. Differences in the time path of milk production under the quota and the other polices are readily apparent. The quota results in a quick downward adjustment in dairy herd size necessary to avoid large government expenditures while maintaining milk price at the $10.60 support level. The dairy termination program (buyout occurs in 1992) adjusts herd size in a manner similar to the quota in 1992, but herd size and total milk production climb rapidly before declining again in 1998. The trigger policy results in an eventual but much delayed decline in milk production. The fixed support price policy, as expected, maintains the highest level of milk production of the alternative policies."

[Billions of lbs]

Year	Fixed	Trigger	Quota	Daily termination program
1990	144	144	144	144
1991	146	146	146	146
1992	146	146	131	0
1993	153	153	132	146
1994	153	152	136	146
1995	156	155	137	152
1996	157	154	140	152
1997	160	156	142	156
1998	161	155	144	154

Source: U.S. Congress, Office of Technology Assessment, *U.S. Dairy Industry at a Crossroad: Biotechnology and Policy Choices-Special Report*, OTA-F-470 (Washington, DC: U.S. Government Printing Office, May 1991), p. 100. *Primary source:* Office of Technology Assessment, 1991. *Note:* Magnitudes estimated from published chart.

★ 24 ★

Dairy Projections

Butter Supply and Utilization, 1994-2002

"The **wholesale butter price** at about 67 cents per pound is expected to remain near the CCC purchase price for butter in 1994. Over the projection period, wholesale butter prices remain within 3 cents per pound of the CCC purchase price since CCC removals of butter continue.

"Annual **per capita butter consumption** is expected to remain relatively constant throughout the projection period, increasing to 4.46 pounds by 2002 from the 1993 level of 4.39 pounds. The last tilt in butter/powder prices that lowered the butter purchase price to 65 cents per pound has and will continue to result in some additional commercial disappearance of butter."

	1994	1995	1996	1997	1998	1999	2000	2001	2002
	(Million Pounds)								
Supply	1,680	1,664	1,691	1,687	1,705	1,688	1,681	1,652	1,640
Beginning Stocks	276	233	237	244	241	236	222	207	178
Production	1,399	1,427	1,450	1,439	1,460	1,448	1,455	1,440	1,458
Imports	4	4	4	4	4	4	4	4	4
Utilization	1,447	1,427	1,448	1,446	1,469	1,466	1,473	1,473	1,492
Total Foreign Use	301	241	241	241	241	241	241	241	241
Exports	300	240	240	240	240	240	240	240	240
Shipments	1	1	1	1	1	1	1	1	1
Domestic Use	1,146	1,186	1,207	1,205	1,228	1,225	1,232	1,232	1,251
Commercial	1,026	1,066	1,087	1,085	1,108	1,105	1,112	1,112	1,131
Government Donations	120	120	120	120	120	120	120	120	120
Ending Stocks	233	237	244	241	236	222	207	178	148
Commercial	23	25	27	27	29	30	32	32	34
Government	210	212	217	214	207	192	176	146	114
Carry-in	260	210	212	217	214	207	192	176	146
Removals	345	397	400	392	388	380	379	365	363
DEIP	45	45	45	45	45	45	45	45	45
Domestic Donations	120	120	120	120	120	120	120	120	120
Other Disappearance	275	275	275	275	275	275	275	275	275
	(Pounds)								
Per Capita Consumption	4.39	4.50	4.54	4.49	4.53	4.48	4.47	4.43	4.46
	(Cents per Pound)								
Prices									
Wholesale	66.60	66.52	66.45	67.13	67.29	67.62	67.95	68.30	68.35
CCC Price	65.00	65.00	65.00	65.00	65.00	65.00	65.00	65.00	65.00
Retail	1.54	1.54	1.54	1.55	1.56	1.57	1.57	1.57	1.57

Source: Food and Agricultural Policy Research Institute, *FAPRI 1994 U.S. Agricultural Outlook*, #1-94 (Iowa State University/ University of Missouri-Columbia, April 1994), pp. 91, 94. "This material is based upon work supported by the Cooperative State Research Service, U.S. Department of Agriculture. Any opinions, findings, conclusions, or recommendations are those of the authors and do not necessarily reflect the view of the USDA." *Note:* Source also includes data for 1992 and 1993.

★ 25 ★

Dairy Projections

Cheese Supply and Utilization, 1994-2002

"The **wholesale cheese price** is expected to increase by nearly 4 cents per pound in 1994. Throughout the projection period, the wholesale price continues to run well above the CCC purchase price for cheese, which remains at $1.12 per pound. The increase in wholesale cheese prices tends to lend support to the all-milk price over the projection period.

"Annual **per capita cheese consumption** is projected to continue increasing throughout the projection period, exceeding 31 pounds by 2002. Any weakness in cheese demand would likely result in lower cheese prices and, thus, lower milk prices."

	1994	1995	1996	1997	1998	1999	2000	2001	2002
	(Million Pounds)								
Supply	7,407	7,744	8,024	8,205	8,412	8,660	8,886	9,186	9,357
Beginning Stocks	502	501	509	514	520	529	539	548	560
Production	6,609	6,947	7,218	7,395	7,595	7,835	8,052	8,342	8,501
Imports	296	296	296	296	296	296	296	296	296
Utilization	6,907	7,234	7,510	7,685	7,883	8,121	8,338	8,626	8,788
Foreign Use	71	71	71	71	71	71	71	71	71
Exports	25	25	25	25	25	25	25	25	25
Shipments	46	46	46	46	46	46	46	46	46
Domestic Use	6,836	7,163	7,439	7,614	7,812	8,050	8,267	8,555	8,717
Commercial	6,814	7,141	7,417	7,592	7,790	8,028	8,245	8,533	8,695
Government Donations	22	22	22	22	22	22	22	22	22
Ending Stocks	501	509	514	520	529	539	548	560	569
Commercial	498	506	511	517	526	536	545	557	566
Government	3	3	3	3	3	3	3	3	3
Carry-in	3	3	3	3	3	3	3	3	3
Removals	0	0	0	0	0	0	0	0	0
Non-Support Removals	45	45	45	45	45	45	45	45	45
DEIP	7	7	7	7	7	7	7	7	7
Domestic Donations	22	22	22	22	22	22	22	22	22
Other Disappearance	23	23	23	23	23	23	23	23	23
	(Pounds)								
Per Capita Consumption	26.2	27.2	28.0	28.3	28.8	29.4	30.0	30.7	31.1
	(Cents per Pound)								
Prices									
Wholesale 40lb Block	132.26	132.15	135.24	136.73	138.05	139.04	140.15	140.68	141.85
CCC Price	112.03	112.03	112.03	112.03	112.03	112.03	112.03	112.03	112.03
Retail	3.41	3.45	3.54	3.61	3.67	3.73	3.79	3.85	3.91

Source: Food and Agricultural Policy Research Institute, *FAPRI 1994 U.S. Agricultural Outlook*, #1-94 (Iowa State University/University of Missouri-Columbia, April 1994), pp. 91-2. "This material is based upon work supported by the Cooperative State Research Service, U.S. Department of Agriculture. Any opinions, findings, conclusions, or recommendations are those of the authors and do not necessarily reflect the view of the USDA." *Note:* Source also includes data for 1992 and 1993.

Livestock Projections

★ 26 ★

Livestock Production and Prices, 1994-2002

"**Production** of beef, pork, broilers, and turkeys increases more than 1.5 billion pounds in 1994 as only pork production fails to exceed the 1993 level. Annual increases are projected for the remainder of the period, and total production of these four products exceeds 77 billion pounds by 2002.

"**Livestock prices** are mixed in 1994, with beef and broiler prices decreasing while pork and turkey prices increase. By the end of the projection period, all of the livestock prices are higher than 1994 levels."

	1994	1995	1996	1997	1998	1999	2000	2001	2002
	(Billion Pounds)								
Production									
Beef	23.99	24.33	24.92	25.17	24.86	24.23	23.65	23.48	23.26
Pork	16.54	17.13	17.65	17.53	17.11	17.51	18.01	17.63	17.49
Broiler	23.17	23.84	24.56	25.40	26.36	27.41	28.44	29.51	30.59
Turkey	4.90	4.99	5.09	5.16	5.28	5.44	5.61	5.78	5.96
Total	68.60	70.29	72.23	73.24	73.61	74.59	75.71	76.40	77.31
Change	2.3%	2.5%	2.8%	1.4%	0.5%	1.3%	1.5%	0.9%	1.2%
	(Dollars per Hundredweight)								
Prices									
1100-1300lb Nebraska Direct Steers	74.58	72.35	68.14	69.72	72.72	76.18	80.22	83.57	86.40
230-250lb Iowa-Southern Minnesota Barrows and Gifts	48.53	45.83	42.11	45.79	49.83	47.06	44.05	46.82	50.19
12-City Wholesale Broiler	54.58	55.21	54.02	55.17	55.95	56.33	55.56	57.47	57.83
Eastern Region Wholesale Turkey	63.43	64.63	62.32	64.37	68.27	69.08	68.04	70.22	71.25

Source: Food and Agricultural Policy Research Institute, *FAPRI 1994 U.S. Agricultural Outlook*, #1-94 (Iowa State University/ University of Missouri-Columbia, April 1994), pp. 86-7. "This material is based upon work supported by the Cooperative State Research Service, U.S. Department of Agriculture. Any opinions, findings, conclusions, or recommendations are those of the authors and do not necessarily reflect the view of the USDA." *Note:* Source also includes data for 1992 and 1993.

★ 27 ★

Livestock Projections

Per Capita Meat Consumption and Expenditures, 1994-2002

"Annual **per capita meat consumption** generally varies with total domestic production over the projection period. In 1994, annual per capita consumption increases almost 2 pounds from the 1993 level as rising consumption of beef, broiler, and turkey more than overpowers a decline in pork consumption. After 1994, per capita consumption is projected to increase modestly, gaining about 5 pounds over the remainder of the period as increases in poultry per capita consumption more than offset the declines in beef and pork per capita consumption.

"Annual **per capita expenditures** are projected to increase by $31 during the projection period as consumers continue to substitute less expensive poultry products for more expensive red meat products. This substitution continues to allow consumers to receive a bargain at the meat counter.

"The **implied meat bundle price** increases by only 9 cents over the projection period as the mix of meat products continues to shift towards the less expensive poultry products."

	1994	1995	1996	1997	1998	1999	2000	2001	2002
					(Pounds)				
Consumption									
Beef	66.8	66.9	67.7	67.2	64.9	62.4	60.4	59.4	58.8
Pork	50.1	51.2	52.1	51.7	50.1	50.3	50.5	49.1	48.2
Broiler	71.0	72.2	72.7	74.6	76.4	78.1	79.4	81.4	83.3
Turkey	18.0	18.2	18.4	18.5	18.8	19.1	19.6	20.1	20.5
Total	205.9	208.5	210.9	211.9	210.2	209.9	210.0	210.0	210.8
Change	0.9%	1.2%	1.2%	0.5%	-0.8%	-0.1%	0.0%	-0.0%	0.4%
					(Dollars)				
Expenditures									
Beef	192.68	190.62	187.48	189.55	190.79	189.67	190.32	192.38	195.55
Pork	100.16	100.52	98.47	101.04	101.25	99.90	97.83	99.98	102.71
Broiler	62.92	65.35	65.10	68.67	72.39	74.83	75.32	80.17	83.27
Turkey	18.32	18.91	18.95	19.50	20.66	21.41	21.52	22.77	23.64
Total	374.08	375.41	370.00	378.75	385.09	385.81	384.99	395.29	405.18
Change	0.1%	0.4%	-1.4%	2.4%	1.7%	0.2%	-0.2%	2.7%	2.5%
					(Dollars per Pound)				
Implied Meat Bundle Price	1.82	1.80	1.75	1.79	1.83	1.84	1.83	1.88	1.92
Change	-0.9%	-0.9%	-2.6%	1.9%	2.5%	0.3%	-0.3%	2.7%	2.1%

Source: Food and Agricultural Policy Research Institute, *FAPRI 1994 U.S. Agricultural Outlook,* #1-94 (Iowa State University/University of Missouri-Columbia, April 1994), pp. 86-7. "This material is based upon work supported by the Cooperative State Research Service, U.S. Department of Agriculture. Any opinions, findings, conclusions, or recommendations are those of the authors and do not necessarily reflect the view of the USDA." *Note:* Source also includes data for 1992 and 1993.

★28★

Livestock Projections

Beef Supply and Utilization, 1994-2002

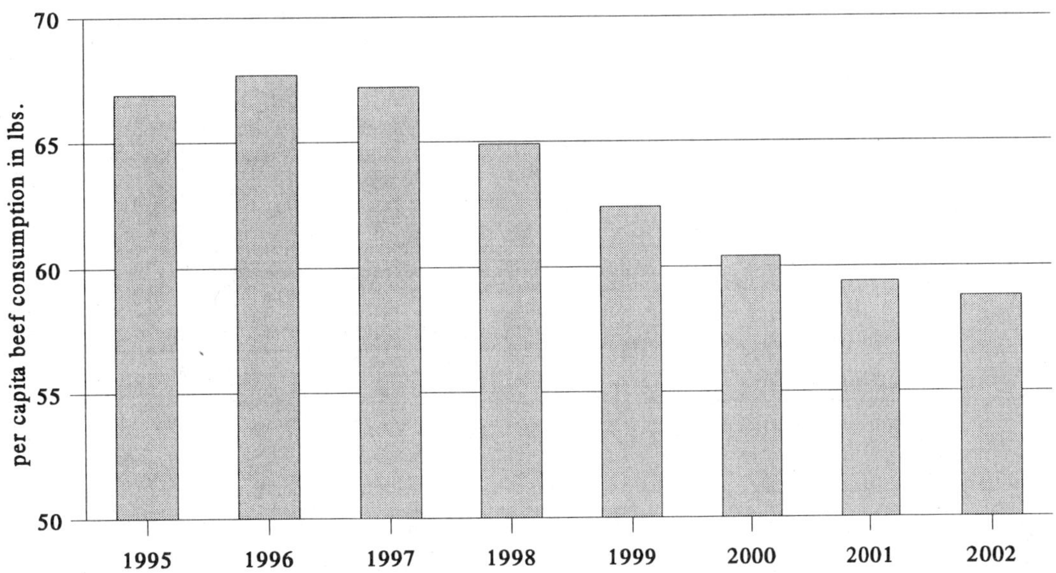

"Improved **cow-calf returns** over the last few years have caused cow-calf producers to expand the beef cow herd. Expansion is expected to be much slower and smaller than has been experienced in previous cycles. The beef cow herd is expected to fall just short of 35 million head in 1996 before contracting to 30.4 million head in 2002 as cow-calf returns weaken substantially during the latter part of the projection period.

"Although lessened by a decline in net imports, beef **consumption** parallels the production cycle with a peak of 25.8 billion pounds in 1997. On a per capita basis, beef consumption reaches its highest level, 67.7 pounds, in 1996 and falls during the next six years of the projection period to 58.8 pounds.

"**Retail beef prices** generally move with fed-steer prices, but the percent changes are usually smaller. From 1994 to 2002, beef retail prices rise at less than half the projection inflation rate. Further weakening of beef demand is evident as both real beef prices per capita beef consumption decline over the projection period relative to 1993 levels."

	1994	1995	1996	1997	1998	1999	2000	2001	2002
					(Million Head)				
Cattle and Calves (Jan. 1)	102.4	103.2	104.3	103.8	102.5	100.8	99.4	98.8	98.2
Beef Cows (Jan. 1)	34.5	34.7	34.9	34.3	33.4	32.1	31.1	30.6	30.4
Total Cattle Slaughter	34.5	35.0	36.0	36.0	35.2	34.2	33.1	32.5	32.0
					(Million Pounds)				
Supply	26,781	27,147	27,751	28,016	27,709	27,067	26,470	26,280	26,064
Beginning Stocks	450	482	490	508	508	497	481	465	462
Imports	2,340	2,340	2,340	2,340	2,340	2,340	2,340	2,340	2,340
Production	23,991	24,326	24,921	25,168	24,861	24,230	23,649	23,475	23,262
Disappearance	26,300	26,657	27,243	27,507	27,212	26,586	26,005	25,819	25,608
Domestic Use	24,890	25,193	25,740	25,775	25,150	23,397	23,826	23,630	23,584
Exports	1,410	1,464	1,503	1,732	2,062	2,189	2,179	2,189	2,024

[Continued]

★ 28 ★

Beef Supply and Utilization, 1994-2002

[Continued]

	1994	1995	1996	1997	1998	1999	2000	2001	2002
Ending Stocks	482	490	508	508	497	481	465	462	456
	(Dollars per Hundredweight)								
Prices									
1100-1300 lb									
Nebraska Direct Steers	74.58	72.35	68.14	69.72	72.72	76.18	80.22	83.57	86.40
Change	-2.2%	-3.0%	-5.8%	2.3%	4.3%	4.7%	5.3%	4.2%	3.4%
600-700lb									
Oklahoma City Feeder Steers	88.25	83.18	75.59	79.64	82.67	85.43	90.70	96.10	98.30
Change	-3.0%	-5.8%	-9.1%	5.4%	3.7%	3.3%	6.2%	6.0%	2.3%
Utility Cows, Sioux Falls	46.01	44.06	4.125	42.43	44.42	45.92	47.82	49.90	50.57
Change	-3.4%	-4.2%	-6.4%	2.9%	4.7%	3.4%	4.1%	3.3%	2.4%
	(Dollars per Pound)								
Beef Retail	2.89	2.85	2.77	2.82	2.94	3.04	3.15	3.24	3.32
Change	-1.7%	-1.3%	-2.8%	1.9%	4.1%	3.4%	3.7%	2.8%	2.7%
	(Dollars per Cow)								
Net Returns									
Cow-Calf	69.15	42.36	0.35	13.26	24.14	35.17	56.85	75.87	77.90
	(Dollars per Hundredweight)								
Feedlot	-2.25	-0.46	-0.12	-1.32	-0.30	1.16	1.89	1.58	2.48

Source: Food and Agricultural Policy Research Institute, *FAPRI 1994 U.S. Agricultural Outlook*, #1-94 (Iowa State University/University of Missouri-Columbia, April 1994), pp. 78-9. "This material is based upon work supported by the Cooperative State Research Service, U.S. Department of Agriculture. Any opinions, findings, conclusions, or recommendations are those of the authors and do not necessarily reflect the view of the USDA." *Notes:* Source also includes data for 1992 and 1993, as well as projections on per capita consumption (see graphic below).

★ 29 ★

Livestock Projections

Pork Supply and Utilization, 1994-2002

"Pork **production** is expected to fall to 16.5 billion pounds in 1994, which is 500 million pounds less than the 1993 level. Pork production increases in 1995 as hog producers respond to favorable returns. Since grain stocks are at relatively low levels, the pork cycle could change markedly if adverse weather conditions occur.

"The pork **breeding herd** fell 100 thousand head from December 1992 to December 1993. By December 1994, the breeding herd remains virtually unchanged as producers remain cautious about grain production in 1994. Continued increases in technological efficiencies allow increases in pork production from a smaller breeding herd. Increases in pigs per litter and farrowings per sow, as well as heavier carcass weights, are the main reasons this continues to occur.

"**Foreign trade** will strengthen total demand as the United States becomes a net exporter of pork by 2000.

"**Retail pork prices** mirror barrow and gilt prices, but the changes are proportionately smaller. Facing a lower supply, retail pork prices rise to $2.00 in 1994 and tend to increase over the projection period, reaching $2.13 by 2002."

	1994	1995	1996	1997	1998	1999	2000	2001	2002
	(Million Head)								
Hogs on Farms									
Market (Dec. 1)	50.4	50.7	51.5	51.0	49.9	50.2	51.9	51.8	51.4
Breeding (Dec. 1)	7.07	7.26	7.33	6.87	6.63	6.98	7.04	6.81	6.60
Total Hog Slaughter	91.2	93.9	96.6	95.5	93.1	95.2	97.6	95.6	95.0
	(Million Pounds)								
Supply	17,613	18,173	18,697	18,655	18,234	18,545	18,945	18,571	18,401
Beginning Stocks	375	354	380	400	380	367	391	408	381
Imports	700	687	668	730	743	668	541	529	526
Production	16,538	17,131	17,649	17,525	17,111	17,509	18,014	17,634	17,495
Disappearance	17,259	17,793	18,297	18,275	17,867	18,154	18,537	18,191	18,024
Domestic Use	16,859	17,381	17,865	17,905	17,510	17,722	17,978	17,620	17,450
Exports	400	412	432	370	357	432	559	571	574
Ending Stocks	354	380	400	380	367	391	408	381	377
	(Pounds)								
Per Capita Consumption									
Carcass Weight	64.6	66.0	67.1	66.7	64.6	64.8	65.2	63.3	62.2
Retail Weight	50.1	51.2	52.1	51.7	50.1	50.3	50.5	49.1	48.2
Change	-4.2%	2.1%	1.8%	-0.7%	-3.1%	0.3%	0.6%	-2.8%	-1.8%
	(Dollars per Hundredweight)								
Prices									
230-250lb									
Iowa-Southern Minnesota									
Barrows and Gifts	48.53	45.83	42.11	45.79	49.83	47.06	44.05	46.82	50.19
Change	5.3%	-5.6%	-8.1%	8.8%	8.8%	-5.6%	-6.4%	6.3%	7.2%
6 Market Sows	37.26	35.46	32.55	33.85	35.55	34.17	31.77	33.21	34.76

[Continued]

★ 29 ★

Pork Supply and Utilization, 1994-2002

[Continued]

	1994	1995	1996	1997	1998	1999	2000	2001	2002
Change	0.5%	-4.8%	-8.2%	4.0%	5.0%	-3.9%	-7.0%	4.5%	4.7%
	(Dollars per Pound)								
Pork Retail	2.00	1.96	1.89	1.95	2.02	1.99	1.94	2.04	2.13
Change	1.2%	-1.7%	-3.8%	3.3%	3.4%	-1.6%	-2.6%	5.2%	4.6%
	(Dollars per Hundredweight)								
Net Returns Farrow-Finish	4.48	3.36	-0.62	2.33	6.15	2.42	-1.21	0.68	2.70

Source: Food and Agricultural Policy Research Institute, *FAPRI 1994 U.S. Agricultural Outlook*, #1-94 (Iowa State University/University of Missouri-Columbia, April 1994), pp. 80-1. "This material is based upon work supported by the Cooperative State Research Service, U.S. Department of Agriculture. Any opinions, findings, conclusions, or recommendations are those of the authors and do not necessarily reflect the view of the USDA." *Note:* Source also includes data for 1992 and 1993.

★ 30 ★

Livestock Projections

January Beef Cow and Breeding Ewe Supply, 1973-2030

[Million head]

Year	Beef cows and heifers	Breeding ewes
1977	41.4	8.8
1978	38.7	8.6
1979	37.1	8.4
1980	37.1	8.5
1981	38.7	8.8
1982	39.3	8.3
1983	38.1	8.3
1984	37.5	7.9
1985	35.4	7.2
1986	33.6	6.8
1987	33.9	6.8
1988	34.0	7.1
1990[1]	25.6	6.9
2000[1]	39.5	9.1
2030[1]	51.2	15.0

Source: USDA Forest Service, *Factors Affecting the Demand for Grazed Forage in the United States,* RM-210 (Washington, D.C.: U.S. Government Printing Office, January 1992), p. 14. *Primary source:* For historical data, USDA, 1974, 1987. *Notes:* 1. Baseline scenario. Source also includes data for 1965-1977 and high and low projections for 1990-2030.

★31★

Livestock Projections

Regional Distribution of Breeding Ewes, 1974-2030

[Percent]

Year	Region					
	PN	CA	SW	NR	NO	SO
1974	3.51	7.59	6.93	42.04	18.73	21.20
1975	3.49	7.73	7.23	41.89	18.09	21.57
1976	3.50	8.70	7.94	39.90	16.99	22.97
1977	3.35	8.70	8.02	38.24	18.02	23.67
1978	3.66	9.08	9.45	39.08	14.98	23.75
1979	3.99	10.01	8.39	39.52	15.44	22.65
1980	3.69	10.00	8.65	43.86	11.22	22.58
1981	4.16	9.69	8.07	40.28	15.81	21.99
1982	4.60	9.71	7.99	40.32	16.44	20.94
1983	4.22	9.67	7.89	39.46	16.93	21.83
1984	4.27	10.10	7.78	41.54	15.97	20.34
1985	4.29	10.64	7.45	40.07	16.36	21.19
1986	4.68	10.63	7.57	41.04	14.84	21.24
1987	4.37	10.01	7.10	39.22	17.32	21.98
Average	3.97	9.40	7.89	40.46	16.37	21.99
STD[1]	0.4447	0.9863	0.6571	1.4787	2.136	1.0197
CV[2]	0.11	0.10	0.08	0.04	0.13	0.05
			Projections			
1990	4.88	11.37	7.69	40.45	14.62	20.99
2000	5.82	13.46	7.47	40.55	12.77	19.93
2030	8.87	20.26	7.01	39.24	7.42	17.20

Source: USDA Forest Service, *Factors Affecting the Demand for Grazed Forage in the United States*, RM-210 (Washington, D.C.: U.S. Government Printing Office, January 1992), p. 17. *Notes:* PN=Pacific North; CA=California; SW=Southwest; NR=Northern Rocky; NO=Northern; SO=Southern. 1. Standard deviation. 2. Coefficient of variation.

★ 32 ★

Livestock Projections

Young Chicken Supply and Utilization, 1991-2000

"Record meat supplies are projected to continue for the rest of the decade, reflecting moderate feed prices, small increases in other production costs, and ample forage supplies. Consumers purchase more meat, but a larger proportion is poultry. The long-term decline in the real price of meats continues. Declining real prices along with increases in real disposable income allow consumers to buy more meat with a smaller proportion of disposable income."

	Unit	Selected history[1]		1995	1996	1997	1998	1999	2000
		1991	1992						
Beginning stocks	Mil. lbs.	26	36	30	30	30	30	30	30
F.I. slaughter	Mil. lbs.	19,728	21,052	23,656	24,285	24,950	25,616	26,310	27,025
Production	Mil. lbs.	19,591	20,907	23,492	24,117	24,777	25,438	26,127	26,837
Total supply	Mil. lbs.	19,617	20,943	23,522	24,147	24,807	25,468	26,157	26,867
Exports	Mil. lbs.	1,261	1,489	1,850	1,900	1,950	2,000	2,040	2,080
Ending stocks	Mil. lbs.	36	33	30	30	30	30	30	25
Consumption	Mil. lbs.	18,320	19,421	21,642	22,217	22,827	23,438	24,087	24,762
Per capita, carcass wgt	Pounds	72.5	76.0	82.3	83.8	85.4	87.0	88.7	90.5
Per capita, retail wgt	Pounds	63.9	66.8	72.3	73.7	75.1	76.5	78.0	79.5
Prices:									
Broilers, farm	Cents per lb.	30.90	31.90	32.90	33.20	33.70	34.50	35.50	36.50
12-city market price	Cents per lb.	52.00	52.60	54.82	55.36	56.19	57.54	59.23	60.77
Costs and returns:									
Total costs	Cents per lb.	47.00	49.60	48.68	49.60	50.86	51.91	53.03	54.27
Net returns	Cents per lb.	5.00	3.00	6.14	5.77	5.33	5.65	6.20	6.50

Source: United States Department of Agriculture, World Agricultural Outlook Board, *Long-term Agriculture Baseline Projections*, WAOB-93-1 (Washington, D.C.: U.S. Government Printing Office, October 1993), p. 38. *Notes:* Baseline projections present one plausible scenario, representative of the long-term direction for the agricultural sector. The projections are a conditional, current law (as of June 1993) scenario with no shocks, based on a special set of assumptions regarding the macroeconomy, the weather, and international developments. The projections were prepared in June 1993, based on policy decisions and other information known at that time. The short-term outlook would not differ from that used in these baseline projections, although it is expected that by 1995 the agricultural sector will have adjusted to the near-term disruptions in supply and use. 1. Historical data as of June 1993.

★ 33 ★

Livestock Projections

Turkey Supply and Utilization, 1991-2000

"Record meat supplies are projected to continue for the rest of the decade, reflecting moderate feed prices, small increases in other production costs, and ample forage supplies. Consumers purchase more meat, but a larger proportion is poultry. The long-term decline in the real price of meats continues. Declining real prices along with increases in real disposable income allow consumers to buy more meat with a smaller proportion of disposable income."

	Unit	Selected history[1]		1995	1996	1997	1998	1999	2000
		1991	1992						
Beginning stocks	Mil. lbs.	306	264	260	260	260	260	260	260
F.I. slaughter	Mil. lbs.	4,652	4,829	5,300	5,900	6,286	6,722	7,090	7,410
Production	Mil. lbs.	4,603	4,778	5,247	5,847	6,233	6,669	7,037	7,357
Total supply	Mil. lbs.	4,909	5,042	5,507	6,107	6,493	6,929	7,297	7,617
Exports	Mil. lbs.	103	171	212	224	236	248	250	262
Ending stocks	Mil. lbs.	264	272	260	260	260	260	260	260
Consumption	Mil. lbs.	4,542	4,599	5,035	5,623	5,997	6,421	6,787	7,095
Per capita	Pounds	18.0	18.0	19.1	21.2	22.4	23.8	25.0	25.9
Prices:									
Turkey, farm	Cents per lb.	37.70	37.70	35.80	34.00	32.60	32.00	31.90	32.00
Hen turkey (whsle) East	Cents per lb.	61.30	60.20	59.70	56.62	54.28	53.37	53.20	53.33
Costs and returns:									
Total costs	Cents per lb.	60.30	57.39	55.08	45.91	47.88	48.73	49.22	49.67
Net returns	Cents per lb.	1.00	2.81	4.61	10.71	6.40	4.64	3.98	3.66

Source: United States Department of Agriculture, World Agricultural Outlook Board, *Long-term Agriculture Baseline Projections*, WAOB-93-1 (Washington, D.C.: U.S. Government Printing Office, October 1993), p. 39. *Notes:* Baseline projections present one plausible scenario, representative of the long-term direction for the agricultural sector. The projections are a conditional, current law (as of June 1993) scenario with no shocks, based on a special set of assumptions regarding the macroeconomy, the weather, and international developments. The projections were prepared in June 1993, based on policy decisions and other information known at that time. The short-term outlook would not differ from that used in these baseline projections, although it is expected that by 1995 the agricultural sector will have adjusted to the near-term disruptions in supply and use. 1. Historical data as of June 1993.

★ 34 ★

Livestock Projections

Egg Supply and Utilization, 1991-2000

	Unit	Selected history[1]		1995	1996	1997	1998	1999	2000
		1991	1992						
Beginning stocks	Mil. doz.	12	13	12	13	14	13	14	13
Production	Mil. doz.	5,758	5,883	5,962	5,974	5,986	5,998	6,010	6,022
Imports	Mil. doz.	2	4	5	10	3	10	5	10
Total supply	Mil. doz.	5,772	5,900	5,978	5,997	6,003	6,021	6,029	6,045

[Continued]

★ 34 ★

Egg Supply and Utilization, 1991-2000

[Continued]

	Unit	Selected history[1]		1995	1996	1997	1998	1999	2000
		1991	1992						
Hatching use	Mil. doz.	708	728	850	875	900	925	950	975
Exports	Mil. doz.	154	157	157	154	155	150	155	150
Ending stocks	Mil. doz.	13	14	13	14	13	14	13	14
Consumption	Mil. doz.	4,896	5,001	4,958	4,954	4,935	4,932	4,911	4,906
Per capita	Number	232.5	235.0	226.2	224.2	221.5	219.7	217.0	215.1
Prices:									
Eggs, farm	Cents per doz.	66.3	56.4	62.3	67.5	63.1	68.3	64.9	67.5
New York, Grade A large	Cents per doz.	77.5	65.4	72.0	78.0	73.0	79.0	75.0	78.0
Costs and returns:									
Total costs	Cents per doz.	66.10	55.60	74.96	75.73	76.78	77.98	79.51	81.07
Net returns	Cents per doz.	11.40	9.80	-2.96	2.27	-3.78	1.02	-4.51	-3.07

Source: United States Department of Agriculture, World Agricultural Outlook Board, *Long-term Agriculture Baseline Projections*, WAOB-93-1 (Washington, D.C.: U.S. Government Printing Office, October 1993), p. 40. *Notes:* Baseline projections present one plausible scenario, representative of the long-term direction for the agricultural sector. The projections are a conditional, current law (as of June 1993) scenario with no shocks, based on a special set of assumptions regarding the macroeconomy, the weather, and international developments. The projections were prepared in June 1993, based on policy decisions and other information known at that time. The short-term outlook would not differ from that used in these baseline projections, although it is expected that by 1995 the agricultural sector will have adjusted to the near-term disruptions in supply and use. 1. Historical data as of June 1993.

Crop Supply and Utilization

★ 35 ★

Corn Supply and Utilization, 1991-2001

"In the crops sector, productive capacity is projected to rise due to increases in resource and input use and in productivity. For most crops, yields are projected to rise at or near their long-term trends. Reflecting, in part, the assumption that the Conservation Reserve Program (CRP) is not extended when contracts expire, land used for crop production increases as some CRP land returns to production. Also, generally lower annual Acreage Reduction Program (ARP) levels contribute to increased land being used for crops. Domestic demand for crops is projected to grow slowly, largely reflecting gains in population."

	Selected history[1]		1995/96	1996/97	1997/98	1998/99	1999/2000	2000/01
	1991/92	1992/93						
Supply and use (million bushels):								
Beginning stocks	1,521	1,100	1,798	1,803	1,728	1,808	1,848	1,823
Imports	20	4	5	5	5	5	5	5
Production	7,475	9,479	9,075	9,245	9,550	9,660	9,770	9,950
Supply	9,016	10,583	10,878	11,053	11,283	11,473	11,623	11,778
Feed and residual	4,878	5,250	5,625	5,750	5,775	5,800	5,850	5,900
Food, seed, & industrial	1,454	1,495	1,800	1,875	1,925	1,975	2,025	2,075

[Continued]

★ 35 ★

Corn Supply and Utilization, 1991-2001

[Continued]

	Selected history[1] 1991/92	1992/93	1995/96	1996/97	1997/98	1998/99	1999/2000	2000/01
Domestic	6,332	6,745	7,425	7,625	7,700	7,775	7,875	7,975
Exports	1,584	1,725	1,650	1,700	1,775	1,850	1,925	2,000
Total use	7,916	8,470	9,075	9,325	9,475	9,625	9,800	9,975
Ending stocks	1,100	2,113	1,803	1,728	1,808	1,848	1,823	1,803
Prices (dollars per bushel):								
Target price	2.75	2.75	2.75	2.75	2.75	2.75	2.75	2.75
Loan rate	1.62	1.72	1.58	1.57	1.57	1.62	1.62	1.63
Farm price	2.37	2.05	2.20	2.25	2.25	2.25	2.25	2.30
Deficiency payments (million dollars)	0.41	0.73	0.55	0.50	0.50	0.50	0.5	0.45
Deficiency payments (million dollars)	2,080	3,622	3,056	2,771	2,806	2,858	2,913	2,635
Variable costs of production (dollars)								
Per acre	135.17	135.25	142.60	146.92	151.96	156.90	161.74	166.56
Per bushel	1.24	1.03	1.14	1.16	1.18	1.21	1.23	1.25
Returns over variable costs (dollars per acre)								
Participant	144.78	187.97	182.59	183.46	181.79	180.22	178.76	179.50
Nonparticipant	122.21	134.12	133.50	138.83	138.83	135.60	134.14	139.34
Normal flex acres	122.21	134.12	133.50	138.83	137.17	135.60	134.14	139.34
Optional flex acres	165.10	211.06	191.25	191.33	189.67	188.10	186.64	186.59

Source: United States Department of Agriculture, World Agricultural Outlook Board, *Long-term Agriculture Baseline Projections*, WAOB-93-1 (Washington, D.C.: U.S. Government Printing Office, October 1993), p. 20. *Notes:* Baseline projections present one plausible scenario, representative of the long-term direction for the agricultural sector. The projections are a conditional, current law (as of June 1993) scenario with no shocks, based on a special set of assumptions regarding the macroeconomy, the weather, and international developments. The projections were prepared in June 1993, based on policy decisions and other information known at that time. The short-term outlook would not differ from that used in these baseline projections, although it is expected that by 1995 the agricultural sector will have adjusted to the near-term disruptions in supply and use. Source also includes data from program variables, acreage, and yields per acre. 1. Historical data as of June 1993.

★ 36 ★

Crop Supply and Utilization

Sorghum Supply and Utilization, 1991-2001

"In the crops sector, productive capacity is projected to rise due to increases in resource and input use and in productivity. For most crops, yields are projected to rise at or near their long-term trends. Reflecting, in part, the assumption that the Conservation Reserve Program (CRP) is not extended when contracts expire, land used for crop production increases as some CRP land returns to production. Also, generally lower annual Acreage Reduction Program (ARP) levels contribute to increased land being used for crops. Domestic demand for crops is projected to grow slowly, largely reflecting gains in population."

	Selected history[1] 1991/92	1992/93	1995/96	1996/97	1997/98	1998/99	1999/2000	2000/01
Supply and use (million bushels):								
Beginning stocks	143	53	104	96	93	105	117	119
Imports	0	0	0	0	0	0	0	0
Production	585	884	695	710	740	760	765	780
Supply	727	937	799	806	833	865	882	899

[Continued]

★ 36 ★

Sorghum Supply and Utilization, 1991-2001

[Continued]

	Selected history[1] 1991/92	1992/93	1995/96	1996/97	1997/98	1998/99	1999/2000	2000/01
Feed and residual	374	475	395	390	395	400	410	420
Food, seed, & industrial	9	8	8	8	8	8	8	8
Domestic	383	483	403	398	403	408	418	428
Exports	292	275	300	315	325	340	345	345
Total use	674	758	703	713	728	748	763	773
Ending stocks	53	180	96	93	105	117	119	126
Prices (dollars per bushel):								
Target price	2.61	2.61	2.61	2.61	2.61	2.61	2.61	2.61
Loan rate	1.54	1.63	1.50	1.49	1.49	1.54	1.55	1.55
Farm price	2.25	1.85	2.05	2.10	2.10	2.10	2.10	2.15
Deficiency payments (million dollars)	0.37	0.76	0.56	0.51	0.51	0.51	0.51	0.46
Deficiency payments (million dollars)	175	345	264	247	262	270	272	249
Variable costs of production (dollars)								
Per acre	74.67	74.99	79.34	81.63	84.20	86.73	89.21	91.70
Per bushel	1.26	1.03	1.18	1.21	1.24	1.27	1.29	1.32
Returns over variable costs (dollars per acre)								
Participant	69.58	91.70	86.09	85.70	84.17	82.70	81.26	80.80
Nonparticipant	58.75	59.69	58.01	60.12	58.60	57.12	55.69	57.73
Normal flex acres	58.75	59.69	58.01	60.12	58.60	57.12	55.69	57.73
Optional flex acres	80.21	104.61	91.05	90.21	88.69	87.21	85.78	84.87

Source: United States Department of Agriculture, World Agricultural Outlook Board, *Long-term Agriculture Baseline Projections*, WAOB-93-1 (Washington, D.C.: U.S. Government Printing Office, October 1993), p. 21. *Notes:* Baseline projections present one plausible scenario, representative of the long-term direction for the agricultural sector. The projections are a conditional, current law (as of June 1993) scenario with no shocks, based on a special set of assumptions regarding the macroeconomy, the weather, and international developments. The projections were prepared in June 1993, based on policy decisions and other information known at that time. The short-term outlook would not differ from that used in these baseline projections, although it is expected that by 1995 the agricultural sector will have adjusted to the near-term disruptions in supply and use. Source also includes data from program variables, acreage, and yields per acre. 1. Historical data as of June 1993.

★ 37 ★

Crop Supply and Utilization

Barley Supply and Utilization, 1991-2001

"In the crops sector, productive capacity is projected to rise due to increases in resource and input use and in productivity. For most crops, yields are projected to rise at or near their long-term trends. Reflecting, in part, the assumption that the Conservation Reserve Program (CRP) is not extended when contracts expire, land used for crop production increases as some CRP land returns to production. Also, generally lower annual Acreage Reduction Program (ARP) levels contribute to increased land being used for crops. Domestic demand for crops is projected to grow slowly, largely reflecting gains in population."

	Selected history[1] 1991/92	1992/93	1995/96	1996/97	1997/98	1998/99	1999/2000	2000/01
Supply and use (million bushels):								
Beginning stocks	135	129	152	152	151	165	179	174
Imports	25	12	30	30	35	35	35	35
Production	464	456	410	415	445	465	480	490

[Continued]

★ 37 ★

Barley Supply and Utilization, 1991-2001

[Continued]

	Selected history[1] 1991/92	1992/93	1995/96	1996/97	1997/98	1998/99	1999/2000	2000/01
Supply	624	597	592	597	631	665	694	699
Feed and residual	230	195	190	190	205	220	235	250
Food, seed, & industrial	171	165	165	166	166	166	175	175
Domestic	401	360	355	356	371	386	410	425
Exports	94	80	85	90	95	100	110	110
Total use	495	440	440	446	466	486	520	535
Ending stocks	129	157	152	151	165	179	174	164
Prices (dollars per bushel):								
Target price	2.36	2.36	2.36	2.36	2.36	2.36	2.36	2.36
Loan rate	1.32	1.40	1.29	1.28	1.28	1.32	1.33	1.33
Farm price	2.10	2.03	2.10	2.10	2.05	2.05	2.05	2.08
Deficiency payments (million dollars)	0.62	0.56	0.49	0.49	0.52	0.49	0.50	0.45
Deficiency payments (million dollars)	173	153	141	142	161	165	180	155
Variable costs of production (dollars)								
Per acre	59.54	59.78	63.13	64.97	67.06	69.12	71.15	73.16
Per bushel	1.08	0.96	1.09	1.11	1.14	1.16	1.19	1.21
Returns over variable costs (dollars per acre)								
Participant	73.01	83.44	78.28	77.50	74.71	72.47	71.87	70.69
Nonparticipant	56.38	66.89	58.67	57.88	53.89	62.85	51.85	52.68
Normal flex acres	56.38	66.89	58.67	57.88	53.86	52.85	51.85	52.68
Optional flex acres	85.02	92.87	81.74	80.96	78.38	75.93	75.40	73.87

Source: United States Department of Agriculture, World Agricultural Outlook Board, *Long-term Agriculture Baseline Projections*, WAOB-93-1 (Washington, D.C.: U.S. Government Printing Office, October 1993), p. 22. *Notes:* Baseline projections present one plausible scenario, representative of the long-term direction for the agricultural sector. The projections are a conditional, current law (as of June 1993) scenario with no shocks, based on a special set of assumptions regarding the macroeconomy, the weather, and international developments. The projections were prepared in June 1993, based on policy decisions and other information known at that time. The short-term outlook would not differ from that used in these baseline projections, although it is expected that by 1995 the agricultural sector will have adjusted to the near-term disruptions in supply and use. Source also includes data from program variables, acreage, and yields per acre. 1. Historical data as of June 1993.

★38★

Crop Supply and Utilization

Oats Supply and Utilization, 1991-2001

"In the crops sector, productive capacity is projected to rise due to increases in resource and input use and in productivity. For most crops, yields are projected to rise at or near their long-term trends. Reflecting, in part, the assumption that the Conservation Reserve Program (CRP) is not extended when contracts expire, land used for crop production increases as some CRP land returns to production. Also, generally lower annual Acreage Reduction Program (ARP) levels contribute to increased land being used for crops. Domestic demand for crops is projected to grow slowly, largely reflecting gains in population."

	Selected history[1]		1995/96	1996/97	1997/98	1998/99	1999/2000	2000/01
	1991/92	1992/93						
Supply and use (million bushels):								
Beginning stocks	171	128	101	96	91	95	108	118
Imports	75	50	65	65	65	65	65	65
Production	243	295	235	225	240	250	260	265
Supply	489	472	401	386	396	410	433	448
Feed and residual	235	230	175	165	170	185	195	205
Food, seed, & industrial	125	125	125	125	126	112	115	116
Domestic	360	355	300	290	296	297	310	321
Exports	2	6	5	5	5	5	5	5
Total use	362	361	305	295	301	302	315	326
Ending stocks	128	111	96	91	95	108	118	122
Prices (dollars per bushel):								
Target price	1.45	1.45	1.45	1.45	1.45	1.45	1.45	1.45
Loan rate	0.83	0.88	0.81	0.81	0.81	0.83	0.84	0.84
Farm price	1.20	1.33	1.35	1.40	1.35	1.30	1.30	1.30
Deficiency payments (million dollars)	0.35	0.17	0.10	0.05	0.10	0.15	0.15	0.15
Deficiency payments (million dollars)	30	15	10	5	10	17	12	12
Variable costs of production (dollars)								
Per acre	47.43	47.38	49.97	51.50	53.30	55.07	56.81	58.53
Per bushel	0.94	0.72	0.89	0.91	0.94	0.97	0.99	1.02
Returns over variable costs (dollars per acre)								
Participant	27.90	46.89	29.89	29.52	27.37	25.21	23.86	22.53
Nonparticipant	13.41	39.87	25.77	27.46	23.25	19.03	17.68	16.35
Normal flex acres	13.41	39.87	25.77	27.46	23.25	19.03	17.68	16.35
Optional flex acres	30.46	48.13	30.62	29.88	28.10	26.30	24.95	23.63

Source: United States Department of Agriculture, World Agricultural Outlook Board, *Long-term Agriculture Baseline Projections*, WAOB-93-1 (Washington, D.C.: U.S. Government Printing Office, October 1993), p. 23. *Notes:* Baseline projections present one plausible scenario, representative of the long-term direction for the agricultural sector. The projections are a conditional, current law (as of June 1993) scenario with no shocks, based on a special set of assumptions regarding the macroeconomy, the weather, and international developments. The projections were prepared in June 1993, based on policy decisions and other information known at that time. The short-term outlook would not differ from that used in these baseline projections, although it is expected that by 1995 the agricultural sector will have adjusted to the near-term disruptions in supply and use. Source also includes data from program variables, acreage, and yields per acre. 1. Historical data as of June 1993.

★ 39 ★

Crop Supply and Utilization

Wheat Supply and Utilization, 1991-2001

"In the crops sector, productive capacity is projected to rise due to increases in resource and input use and in productivity. For most crops, yields are projected to rise at or near their long-term trends. Reflecting, in part, the assumption that the Conservation Reserve Program (CRP) is not extended when contracts expire, land used for crop production increases as some CRP land returns to production. Also, generally lower annual Acreage Reduction Program (ARP) levels contribute to increased land being used for crops. Domestic demand for crops is projected to grow slowly, largely reflecting gains in population."

	Selected history[1]		1995/96	1996/97	1997/98	1998/99	1999/2000	2000/01
	1991/92	1992/93						
Supply and use (million bushels):								
Beginning stocks	866	472	675	644	624	614	619	612
Imports	1,981	2,459	2,404	2,436	2,503	2,555	2,605	2,635
Production	41	72	85	90	95	100	105	110
Supply	2,888	3,003	3,164	3,170	3,222	3,269	3,329	3,357
Food	789	830	875	890	905	920	935	945
Seed & industrial	94	93	95	96	98	100	102	104
Feed and residual	254	225	300	285	280	280	280	280
Domestic	1,136	1,148	1,270	1,271	1,238	1,300	1,317	1,329
Exports	1,280	1,355	1,250	1,275	1,325	1,350	1,400	1,425
Total use	2,416	2,503	2,520	2,546	2,608	2,650	2,717	2,754
Ending stocks	472	500	644	624	614	619	612	603
Prices (dollars per bushel):								
Target price	4.00	4.00	4.00	4.00	4.00	4.00	4.00	4.00
Loan rate	2.04	2.21	2.21	2.10	2.06	2.06	2.11	2.13
Farm price	3.00	3.25	2.85	2.90	2.95	2.95	3.00	3.05
Deficiency payment rate	1.35	0.81	1.15	1.10	1.05	1.05	1.00	0.95
Deficiency payments (million dollars)	2,247	1,370	2,144	2,037	2,026	2,065	2,003	1,933
Variable costs of production (dollars)								
Per acre	52.33	52.42	55.33	56.98	58.87	60.73	62.56	64.38
Per bushel	1.53	1.33	1.44	1.48	1.52	1.56	1.60	1.63
Returns over variable costs (dollars per acre)								
Participant	73.53	93.49	87.83	87.22	86.38	85.11	84.37	83.65
Nonparticipant	50.57	75.63	54.11	54.96	55.59	54.32	55.04	55.79
Normal flex acres	50.57	75.63	54.11	54.96	55.59	54.32	55.04	55.79
Optional flex acres	97.01	103.50	93.78	92.91	91.81	90.54	89.54	88.57

Source: United States Department of Agriculture, World Agricultural Outlook Board, *Long-term Agriculture Baseline Projections*, WAOB-93-1 (Washington, D.C.: U.S. Government Printing Office, October 1993), p. 24. *Notes:* Baseline projections present one plausible scenario, representative of the long-term direction for the agricultural sector. The projections are a conditional, current law (as of June 1993) scenario with no shocks, based on a special set of assumptions regarding the macroeconomy, the weather, and international developments. The projections were prepared in June 1993, based on policy decisions and other information known at that time. The short-term outlook would not differ from that used in these baseline projections, although it is expected that by 1995 the agricultural sector will have adjusted to the near-term disruptions in supply and use. Source also includes data from program variables, acreage, and yields per acre. 1. Historical data as of June 1993.

★ 40 ★

Crop Supply and Utilization

Rice Supply and Utilization, 1991-2001

"In the crops sector, productive capacity is projected to rise due to increases in resource and input use and in productivity. For most crops, yields are projected to rise at or near their long-term trends. Reflecting, in part, the assumption that the Conservation Reserve Program (CRP) is not extended when contracts expire, land used for crop production increases as some CRP land returns to production. Also, generally lower annual Acreage Reduction Program (ARP) levels contribute to increased land being used for crops. Domestic demand for crops is projected to grow slowly, largely reflecting gains in population."

	Selected history[1]		1995/96	1996/97	1997/98	1998/99	1999/2000	2000/01
	1991/92	1992/93						
Supply (million cwt.):								
Beginning stocks	24.6	27.3	32.7	29.7	29.0	28.4	29.1	30.7
Production	157.5	179.1	173.2	172.6	171.9	171.3	172.3	173.2
Imports	5.3	6.0	7.9	8.7	9.5	10.5	11.4	12.3
Total supply	187.4	212.4	213.8	211.0	210.4	210.2	212.8	216.2
Utilization (million cwt.):								
Domestic	84.7	88.5	97.1	100.0	103.0	106.1	109.1	112.3
Exports	66.4	76.0	78.0	73.0	70.0	66.0	64.0	63.0
Residual	9.0	9.0	9.0	9.0	9.0	9.0	9.0	9.0
Total use	160.1	173.5	184.1	182.0	182.0	181.1	182.1	184.3
Ending stocks (million cwt.)	27.3	38.9	29.7	29.0	28.4	29.1	30.7	31.9
Prices (dollars per cwt.):								
Target price	10.71	10.71	10.71	10.71	10.71	10.71	10.71	10.71
Loan rate	6.50	6.50	6.50	6.50	6.50	6.50	6.50	6.50
Average market price	7.58	5.90	5.84	6.07	6.31	6.44	6.51	6.64
Deficiency payment rate	3.07	4.21	4.21	4.21	4.21	4.21	4.21	4.13
World price	5.90	5.37	4.50	4.65	4.80	4.95	5.10	5.25
Deficiency payments (million dollars)	458	615	653	666	678	677	678	667
Variable costs of production (dollars)								
Per acre	330.31	332.83	351.85	361.87	373.11	384.34	395.63	407.04
Per cwt.	5.82	5.82	6.23	6.40	6.59	6.78	6.95	7.12
Returns over variable costs (dollars per acre)								
Participant	248.67	281.07	261.99	259.92	254.38	242.49	228.42	214.51
Nonparticipant	99.78	4.77	-21.92	-18.46	-15.62	-19.12	-25.02	-27.59
Normal flex acres	136.66	107.77	88.25	86.18	80.64	68.76	54.69	43.89
Optional flex acres	285.52	311.66	292.65	290.58	285.04	273.15	259.08	244.62

Source: United States Department of Agriculture, World Agricultural Outlook Board, *Long-term Agriculture Baseline Projections*, WAOB-93-1 (Washington, D.C.: U.S. Government Printing Office, October 1993), p. 25. *Notes:* Baseline projections present one plausible scenario, representative of the long-term direction for the agricultural sector. The projections are a conditional, current law (as of June 1993) scenario with no shocks, based on a special set of assumptions regarding the macroeconomy, the weather, and international developments. The projections were prepared in June 1993, based on policy decisions and other information known at that time. The short-term outlook would not differ from that used in these baseline projections, although it is expected that by 1995 the agricultural sector will have adjusted to the near-term disruptions in supply and use. Source also includes data from program variables, acreage, and yields per acre. 1. Historical data as of June 1993.

★ 41 ★

Crop Supply and Utilization

Hay Supply and Utilization, 1994-2002

"Hay **area harvested** in 1993/94 rebounded from the low levels of 1992/93. The increase can be attributed in part to relaxed restrictions of harvesting on conservation acres and relatively low levels of hay stocks at the beginning of the year. In response to higher prices, harvested area is projected to increase in 1994/95 and then remain relatively stable through 1996/97. As CRP contracts expire, it is assumed that a portion of that land will go into hay production. As this occurs, hay area harvested begins to increase in 1998/99...

"U.S. average **all-hay price** increases almost $9.00 per ton in 1993/94 as total hay supplies fall with lower beginning stocks. After a decline in 1994/95, hay prices strengthen through 1997/98, but then decline as CRP land returns to hay production."

	94/95	95/96	96/97	97/98	98/99	99/00	00/01	01/02	02/03
	(Million Acres)								
Area	61.2	61.3	61.4	62.1	62.7	62.9	63.0	62.9	62.9
	(Tons per Acre)								
Yield	2.51	2.52	2.53	2.52	2.52	2.52	2.53	2.55	2.56
	(Million Tons)								
Supply	174.0	177.5	179.7	181.3	183.6	186.0	187.9	188.9	189.2
Production	153.7	154.5	155.3	156.7	157.9	158.9	159.6	160.1	160.7
Beginning Stocks	20.4	23.1	24.5	24.6	25.6	27.1	28.3	28.7	28.5
Disappearance	151.0	153.1	155.1	155.6	156.5	157.7	159.1	160.4	160.9
Ending Stocks	23.1	24.5	24.6	25.6	27.1	28.3	28.7	28.5	28.3
	(Dollars)								
Prices									
All-Hay (crop year)	73.66	72.21	74.37	78.07	75.56	70.19	66.47	67.02	68.88
Alfalfa (calendar year)	82.69	78.78	79.98	83.59	82.87	77.84	73.13	72.32	73.95

Source: Food and Agricultural Policy Research Institute, *FAPRI 1994 U.S. Agricultural Outlook*, #1-94 (Iowa State University/University of Missouri-Columbia, April 1994), pp. 60-1. "This material is based upon work supported by the Cooperative State Research Service, U.S. Department of Agriculture. Any opinions, findings, conclusions, or recommendations are those of the authors and do not necessarily reflect the view of the USDA." *Note:* Source also includes data for 1992/1993 and 1993/1994.

★ 42 ★

Crop Supply and Utilization

Cotton Supply and Utilization, 1991-2001

"In the crops sector, productive capacity is projected to rise due to increases in resource and input use and in productivity. For most crops, yields are projected to rise at or near their long-term trends. Reflecting, in part, the assumption that the Conservation Reserve Program (CRP) is not extended when contracts expire, land used for crop production increases as some CRP land returns to production. Also, generally lower annual Acreage Reduction Program (ARP) levels contribute to increased land being used for crops. Domestic demand for crops is projected to grow slowly, largely reflecting gains in population."

	Selected history[1]		1995/96	1996/97	1997/98	1998/99	1999/2000	2000/01
	1991/92	1992/93						
Supply and use (thousand bales)								
Beginning stocks	2,262	3,583	5,000	4,900	5,100	5,300	5,400	5,500
Imports	13	2	2	2	2	2	2	2
Production	17,216	15,710	16,700	17,300	17,600	17,800	18,100	18,300
Supply	19,491	19,295	21,702	22,202	22,702	23,102	23,502	23,802
Domestic use	9,548	9,835	10,600	10,800	11,000	11,200	11,400	11,600
Exports	6,348	5,025	6,300	6,400	6,500	6,600	6,700	6,800
Total use	15,896	14,860	16,900	17,200	17,500	17,800	18,180	18,400
Ending stocks	3,583	4,471	4,900	5,100	5,300	5,400	5,500	5,500
Prices (dollars per pound):								
Target price	0.729	0.729	0.729	0.729	0.729	0.729	0.729	0.729
Loan rate	0.5077	0.5235	0.5005	0.5000	0.5000	0.5000	0.5020	0.5160
Deficiency payments (million dollars)	552	1,019	860	791	724	680	626	593
Variable costs of production (dollars)								
Per acre	282.5	288.97	303.81	312.71	322.81	333.13	343.32	353.66
Per pound	0.43	0.42	0.44	0.44	0.45	0.46	0.47	0.47
Returns over variable cost (dollars per acre)								
Participant	164.35	210.87	183.77	188.48	184.75	182.81	176.61	174.37
Nonparticipant	124.31	137.70	134.10	143.31	145.65	148.56	153.55	154.31
Normal flex acres	124.31	137.70	134.10	143.31	145.65	148.56	153.55	154.31
Optional flex acres	183.90	257.47	240.30	235.71	230.25	227.16	226.75	223.61

Source: United States Department of Agriculture, World Agricultural Outlook Board, *Long-term Agriculture Baseline Projections*, WAOB-93-1 (Washington, D.C.: U.S. Government Printing Office, October 1993), p. 26. *Notes:* Baseline projections present one plausible scenario, representative of the long-term direction for the agricultural sector. The projections are a conditional, current law (as of June 1993) scenario with no shocks, based on a special set of assumptions regarding the macroeconomy, the weather, and international developments. The projections were prepared in June 1993, based on policy decisions and other information known at that time. The short-term outlook would not differ from that used in these baseline projections, although it is expected that by 1995 the agricultural sector will have adjusted to the near-term disruptions in supply and use. Source also includes data from program variables, acreage, and yields per acre. 1. Historical data as of June 1993.

★ 43 ★

Crop Supply and Utilization

Soybean Supply and Utilization, 1991-2001

"In the crops sector, productive capacity is projected to rise due to increases in resource and input use and in productivity. For most crops, yields are projected to rise at or near their long-term trends. Reflecting, in part, the assumption that the Conservation Reserve Program (CRP) is not extended when contracts expire, land used for crop production increases as some CRP land returns to production. Also, generally lower annual Acreage Reduction Program (ARP) levels contribute to increased land being used for crops. Domestic demand for crops is projected to grow slowly, largely reflecting gains in population."

	Selected history[1]		1995/96	1996/97	1997/98	1998/99	1999/2000	2000/01
	1991/92	1992/93						
Supply (million bushels)								
Beginning stocks, Sept. 1	329	278	260	280	300	315	305	305
Production	1,987	2,197	2,185	2,215	2,245	2,265	2,305	2,325
Imports	3	2	3	3	4	5	5	5
Total supply	2,319	2,477	2,448	2,498	2,549	2,585	2,615	2,635
Disposition (million bushels)								
Crush	1,254	1,280	1,320	1,335	1,350	1,370	1,380	1,390
Seed, feed, & residual	102	112	98	98	99	100	100	100
Exports	685	775	750	765	785	810	830	850
Total disposition	2,041	2,167	2,168	2,198	2,234	2,280	2,310	2,340
Carryover stocks, Aug. 31								
Total ending stocks	278	310	280	300	315	305	305	295
Prices (dollars per bushel):								
Loan rate	5.02	5.02	5.02	5.02	5.02	5.02	5.02	5.02
Effective marketing loan	4.92	4.92	4.92	4.92	4.92	4.92	4.92	4.92
Soybean price, farm	5.58	5.50	5.90	5.85	5.80	5.85	5.85	5.95
Variable costs of production								
Per acre	72.76	73.44	77.80	79.94	82.39	84.77	87.10	89.47
Per bushel	2.13	1.95	2.17	2.21	2.25	2.30	2.34	2.38
Returns over variable costs								
Net returns (dollars per acre)	118.08	133.36	134.01	131.83	129.89	131.10	131.11	134.25

Source: United States Department of Agriculture, World Agricultural Outlook Board, *Long-term Agriculture Baseline Projections*, WAOB-93-1 (Washington, D.C.: U.S. Government Printing Office, October 1993), p. 27. *Notes:* Baseline projections present one plausible scenario, representative of the long-term direction for the agricultural sector. The projections are a conditional, current law (as of June 1993) scenario with no shocks, based on a special set of assumptions regarding the macroeconomy, the weather, and international developments. The projections were prepared in June 1993, based on policy decisions and other information known at that time. The short-term outlook would not differ from that used in these baseline projections, although it is expected that by 1995 the agricultural sector will have adjusted to the near-term disruptions in supply and use. Source also includes data from program variables, acreage, soybean oil, and soybean meal. 1. Historical data as of June 1993.

★ 44 ★

Crop Supply and Utilization

Sugar Supply and Utilization, 1994-2002

"Total **imports** of raw sugar fell to 2.0 million tons in fiscal year 1993 with marketing quotas coming into place. Marketing quotas are in place for portions of fiscal years 1993 and 1994 with quota imports for the two years coming in at 2.5 million tons. In fiscal year 1995 and beyond, given stock levels and domestic demand growth, quota imports range between 1.4 million and 1.6 million tons. Thus, marketing quotas are not in effect after fiscal year 1994.

"Sugar **consumption** is projected to increase throughout the projection period as population increases and per capita consumption remains relatively flat.

"**Ending stocks** of sugar are projected to fall below 1.3 million tons in fiscal year 1994. With increases in production, ending stocks should increase throughout the projection period."

	1994	1995	1996	1997	1998	1999	2000	2001	2002
	(1,000 Short Tons, Raw Value, Fiscal Year)								
Supply	11,111	11,237	11,346	11,459	11,575	11,698	11,810	11,913	12,025
Beginning Stocks	1,756	1,294	1,389	1,441	1,474	1,498	1,518	1,562	1,615
Production	7,540	7,725	7,826	7,925	7,992	8,066	8,137	8,210	8,280
Imports	1,815	2,218	2,131	2,093	2,109	2,134	2,155	2,141	2,129
Quota	1,165	1,568	1,481	1,443	1,459	1,484	1,505	1,491	1,479
Non-Quota	650	650	650	650	650	650	650	650	650
Utilization	9,817	9,848	9,905	9,985	10,077	10,180	10,249	10,298	10,352
Disappearance	9,237	9,298	9,355	9,435	9,527	9,630	9,699	9,748	9,802
Exports	580	550	550	550	550	550	550	550	550
Error Adjustment	0	0	0	0	0	0	0	0	0
Ending Stocks	1,294	1,389	1,441	1,474	1,498	1,518	1,562	1,615	1,673
	(Cents per Pound, Fiscal Year)								
Prices									
N.Y. Spot Raw Sugar	21.67	21.37	21.37	21.37	21.37	21.37	21.37	21.37	21.37
Cane Loan Rate	18.00	18.00	18.00	18.00	18.00	18.00	18.00	18.00	18.00

Source: Food and Agricultural Policy Research Institute, *FAPRI 1994 U.S. Agricultural Outlook*, #1-94, (Iowa State University/University of Missouri-Columbia, April 1994), p. 75. "This material is based upon work supported by the Cooperative State Research Service, U.S. Department of Agriculture. Any opinions, findings, conclusions, or recommendations are those of the authors and do not necessarily reflect the view of the USDA." *Note:* Source also includes data for 1992 and 1993.

★ 45 ★

Crop Supply and Utilization

Fruit Supply and Utilization, 1991-2000[1]

"In the crops sector, productive capacity is projected to rise due to increases in resource and input use and in productivity. For most crops, yields are projected to rise at or near their long-term trends. Reflecting, in part, the assumption that the Conservation Reserve Program (CRP) is not extended when contracts expire, land used for crop production increases as some CRP land returns to production. Also, generally lower annual Acreage Reduction Program (ARP) levels contribute to increased land being used for crops. Domestic demand for crops is projected to grow slowly, largely reflecting gains in population."

	Unit	Selected history[2]		1995	1996	1997	1998	1999	2000
		1991	1992						
Utilized production:									
All fruits	Million short tons	26.8	31.3	32.9	33.8	34.6	35.2	35.8	36.3
Apples	Million pounds	9,834	10,296	10,574	10,685	10,786	10,878	10,963	11,044
Oranges	Thousand short tons	8,907	11,165	12,149	12,814	13,402	13,894	14,283	14,609
Imports:[3]									
All fruit	Million short tons	8.5	7.7	7.8	7.8	7.8	7.8	7.8	7.9
Apples	Million pounds	2,858	2,462	2,514	2,500	2,493	2,495	2,506	2,522
Oranges	Thousand short tons	2,344	1,683	1,537	1,427	1,342	1,280	1,239	1,208
Exports:[3]									
All fruit	Million short tons	3.8	4.1	4.3	4.5	4.6	4.7	4.8	4.9
Apples	Million pounds	1,459	1,477	1,569	1,625	1,676	1,719	1,755	1,787
Oranges	Thousand short tons	1,245	1,483	1,562	1,612	1,656	1,693	1,722	1,747
Grower prices:									
All fruits	1977=100	262	183	161	161	162	164	167	171
Apples	Cents per pound	18.1	15.0	16.1	16.2	16.5	16.8	17.2	17.7
Oranges	Dollars per ton	180	150	155	153	152	152	154	156

Source: United States Department of Agriculture, World Agricultural Outlook Board, *Long-term Agriculture Baseline Projections*, WAOB-93-1 (Washington, D.C.: U.S. Government Printing Office, October 1993), p. 28. *Notes:* Price indexes are for calendar years; other estimates are for crop years. 1. Excludes tree nuts. 2. Historical data as of June 1993. 3. Includes farm weight equivalent of fresh and processed products.

★ 46 ★

Crop Supply and Utilization

Vegetables Supply and Utilization, 1991-2000[1]

"In the crops sector, productive capacity is projected to rise due to increases in resource and input use and in productivity. For most crops, yields are projected to rise at or near their long-term trends. Reflecting, in part, the assumption that the Conservation Reserve Program (CRP) is not extended when contracts expire, land used for crop production increases as some CRP land returns to production. Also, generally lower annual Acreage Reduction Program (ARP) levels contribute to increased land being used for crops. Domestic demand for crops is projected to grow slowly, largely reflecting gains in population."

	Unit	Selected history[2]		1995	1996	1997	1998	1999	2000
		1991	1992						
Production:									
All vegetables	Million cwt	686	700	728	737	746	755	764	773
Potatoes	Million cwt	418	412	417	425	429	435	440	445
Sweet potatoes	Million cwt	11.2	12.0	12.2	12.3	12.4	12.4	12.5	12.6
Dry beans	Million cwt	33.8	22.0	25.5	26.0	26.5	27.0	27.5	28.0
Imports:[3]									
All vegetables	Million cwt	73.12	90.57	98.07	99.29	100.48	101.67	102.87	104.04
Potatoes	Million cwt	17.27	15.74	17.70	18.00	18.35	18.67	19.01	19.35
Sweet potatoes	Million cwt	0.51	0.62	0.58	0.59	0.60	0.61	0.61	0.62
Dry beans	Million cwt	0.73	0.68	0.72	0.73	0.74	0.75	0.76	0.77
Exports:[3]									
All vegetables	Million cwt	46.76	52.32	43.75	44.30	44.84	45.38	45.93	46.46
Potatoes	Million cwt	19.76	24.87	23.66	24.73	25.21	26.02	26.71	27.58
Sweet potatoes	Million cwt	0.16	0.19	0.18	0.19	0.20	0.20	0.21	0.22
Dry beans	Million cwt	9.96	6.50	8.32	8.70	9.08	9.46	9.85	10.24
Grower prices:									
All vegetables	1977=100	135	151	158	160	162	165	168	170
Potatoes	Dollars per cwt	4.96	5.28	5.50	5.48	5.68	5.78	5.93	6.06
Sweet potatoes	Dollars per cwt	13.30	13.30	13.81	13.98	14.15	14.33	14.51	14.69
Dry beans	Dollars per cwt	15.60	20.70	24.22	24.58	24.95	25.33	25.71	26.09

Source: United States Department of Agriculture, World Agricultural Outlook Board, *Long-term Agriculture Baseline Projections*, WAOB-93-1 (Washington, D.C.: U.S. Government Printing Office, October 1993), p. 28. *Notes:* 1. Price indexes are for calendar years; other estimates are for crop years. 2. Historical data as of June 1993. 3. Includes farm weight equivalent of processed products.

★ 47 ★

Crop Supply and Utilization

Flue-cured Tobacco Supply and Utilization, 1991-2001

"In the crops sector, productive capacity is projected to rise due to increases in resource and input use and in productivity. For most crops, yields are projected to rise at or near their long-term trends. Reflecting, in part, the assumption that the Conservation Reserve Program (CRP) is not extended when contracts expire, land used for crop production increases as some CRP land returns to production. Also, generally lower annual Acreage Reduction Program (ARP) levels contribute to increased land being used for crops. Domestic demand for crops is projected to grow slowly, largely reflecting gains in population."

	Unit	Selected history[1]		1995/96	1996/97	1997/98	1998/99	1999/2000	2000/01
		1991/92	1992/93						
Acreage Yield, and production:									
Planted area	1,000 acres	403	402	360	352	341	332	324	316
Harvested area	1,000 acres	403	402	360	352	341	332	324	316
Yield	lbs./ac.	2,265	2,257	2,250	2,250	2,250	2,250	2,250	2,250
Production	Mil. lbs.	912	906	810	793	768	747	729	711
Supply:									
Beg. stocks	Mil. lbs.	1,216	1,223	1,109	1,064	1,027	990	937	896
Marketings	MIl. lbs.	882	901	810	793	768	747	729	711
Total[2]	Mil. lbs.	2,098	2,124	1,919	1,857	1,795	1,737	1,666	1,607
Use:									
Domestic	Mil. lbs.	471	525	460	440	420	420	400	380
Export	Mil. lbs.	404	425	395	390	385	380	370	370
Total[2]	Mil. lbs.	875	950	855	830	805	800	770	750
Ending stocks:									
Total	Mil. lbs.	1,223	1,174	1,064	1,027	990	937	896	857
Price:									
Avg. to growers	$/Cwt	172.3	172.6	183	186	189	192	195	198
Support	$/Cwt	152.8	156.0	164	167	170	173	176	179

Source: United States Department of Agriculture, World Agricultural Outlook Board, *Long-term Agriculture Baseline Projections*, WAOB-93-1 (Washington, D.C.: U.S. Government Printing Office, October 1993), p. 28. *Notes:* 1. Historical data as of June 1993. 2. Domestic tobacco only.

★ 48 ★

Crop Supply and Utilization

Burley Tobacco Supply and Utilization, 1991-2001

"In the crops sector, productive capacity is projected to rise due to increases in resource and input use and in productivity. For most crops, yields are projected to rise at or near their long-term trends. Reflecting, in part, the assumption that the Conservation Reserve Program (CRP) is not extended when contracts expire, land used for crop production increases as some CRP land returns to production. Also, generally lower annual Acreage Reduction Program (ARP) levels contribute to increased land being used for crops. Domestic demand for crops is projected to grow slowly, largely reflecting gains in population."

	Unit	Selected history 1991/92	Selected history 1992/93	1995/96	1996/97	1997/98	1998/99	1999/2000	2000/01
Acreage Yield, and production:									
Planted area	1,000 acres	312	332	248	250	262	265	265	265
Harvested area	1,000 acres	312	248	250	262	265	265	265	265
Yield	lbs./ac.	2,110	2,163	2,100	2,100	2,100	2,100	2,100	2,100
Production	Mil. lbs.	658	719	520	525	550	557	557	557
Supply:									
Beg. stocks	Mil. lbs.	765	778	793	718	658	628	610	597
Marketings	Mil. lbs.	657	700	520	525	550	557	557	557
Total[2]	Mil. lbs.	1,422	1,478	1,313	1,243	1,208	1,185	1,167	1,154
Use:									
Domestic	Mil. lbs.	436	410	370	360	350	340	330	320
Export	Mil. lbs.	208	215	225	225	230	235	240	245
Total[2]	Mil. lbs.	644	625	595	585	580	575	570	565
Ending stocks:									
Total	Mil. lbs.	778	853	718	658	628	610	597	589
Price:									
Avg. to growers	$/Cwt	179.0	181.0	187	191	195	198	201	203
Support	$/Cwt	158.0	165.0	177	181	185	188	190	193

Source: United States Department of Agriculture, World Agricultural Outlook Board, *Long-term Agriculture Baseline Projections*, WAOB-93-1 (Washington, D.C.: U.S. Government Printing Office, October 1993), p. 28. *Notes:* 1. Historical data as of June 1993. 2. Domestic tobacco only.

Chapter 2
BUSINESS, BANKING, AND FINANCE

Business: Various Projections

★ 49 ★

Effect of Lower Interest Rates on Business Investment, 1997

"The bondmarket remains a mystery to many Americans. But the impact of falling interest rates is as tangible as a cheap mortgage or a surge in auto sales. To gauge the impact, *U.S. News* asked the WEFA Group, a prominent forecasting firm, to simulate the effects of lower interest rates on its econometric model of the American economy...

"[According to the WEFA Group, with]:

6% long-term interest rates, business investment soars from $560 billion to $780.6 billion by 1997.

6.5% long term interest rates, business investment reaches $766.2 billion by 1997.

7.5% long term interest rates, business investment totals just $740.5 billion by 1997."

Source: David Hage, "Tonic for a Sick Economy," in *U.S. News & World Report,* 23 August 1993, pp. 44-5.

★ 50 ★

Business: Various Projections

Decrease in Business Costs Due to Federal Expense Deduction, 1993-1999

"As Congress struggles to fill in the remaining blanks in President Clinton's budget bill, small-businesses owners can smile with the knowledge that they have apparently bagged one lucrative tax goodie.

"This is a sweetening of the provision that lets companies deduct equipment expenditures for tax purposes in the year of purchase, rather than depreciate the assets over several years. Experts say companies should start planning now on how to get most out of the break...

"The increase will make it all the more worthwhile for small-business owners to get the most our of the provision-which already contains more advantageous wrinkles than many realize...

"For instance, Richard Herring, general manager of Gloucester Co., a Franklin, Mass., manufacturer of sealing compounds, says his firm is spending about $20,000 to upgrade its controller that regulates colors and other ingredients in batches of sealant. 'I'm not sure if the controller qualifies' for the expensing deduction, Mr. Herring says. Good news. As long as Gloucester Co. spends less on equipment that $200,000, it can use the full deduction. If a company spends more than that on equipment—as most large firms do—the amount of the deduction is reduced one dollar for every dollar spent beyond $200,000."

[Thousands of dollars]

Year	Annual amount of depreciation
1993	5
1994	1.3
1995	1
1996	.6
1997	.6
1998	.4
1999	0

Source: Eugene Carlson, "Small Business Gaze Hungrily at Sweeter Tax Provision," in *The Wall Street Journal*, 29 July 1993, p. B2. *Primary source:* Grant Thornton. *Note:* Magnitudes estimated from published chart.

★51★

Business: Various Projections

Generic Pharmaceutical Drug Market, 1985-2000

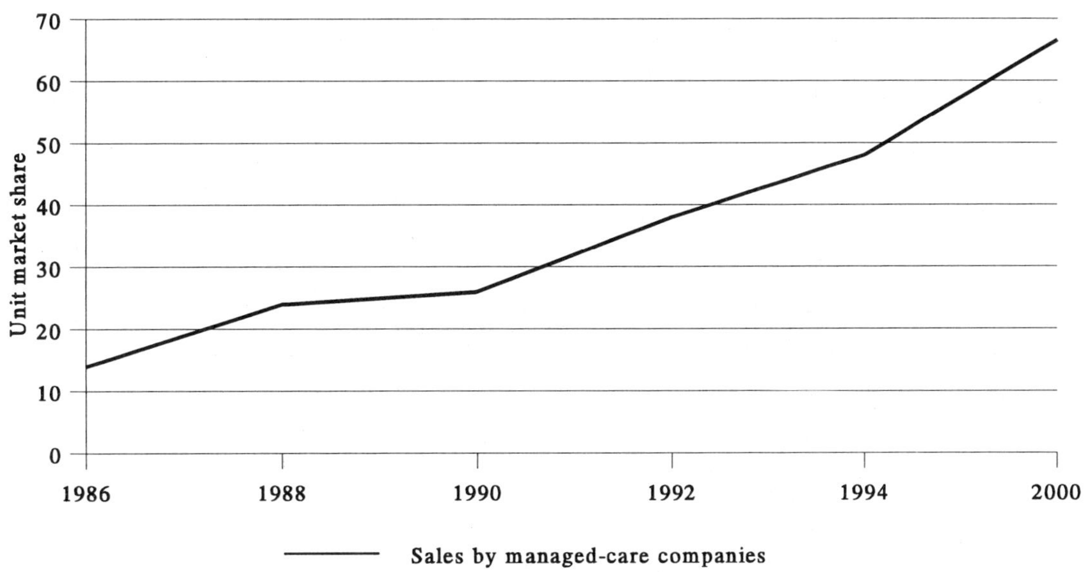

"The downward pressure on prices from generic brand pharmaceutical drugs seems certain to build. 'If the government mandates prescribing generics, a big part of the drug industry will look like computer clones,' says John Klein, president of the generic manufacturer Zenith Laboratories. Additional pressure is coming as the main pharmaceutical market changes from thousands of doctors who ignore prices to HMOs, mail-order companies, and other providers that make price a top priority. Steven Gerber, a security analyst with Oppenheimer & Co., predicts that managed-care companies will account for two-thirds of the drug industry's sales by the year 2000, vs. one-third [in 1993]."

[Unit market share]

1985	14
1986	17
1987	21
1988	24
1989	27
1990	26
1991	29
1992	38
1993	43
1994	48
1995	52
2000	66.6

Source: Shawn Tully, "Why Drug Prices Will Go Lower," in *Fortune*, 3 May 1993, pp. 60, 62. *Primary source:* Hemant K. Shah, pharmaceutical analyst, HKS & Co. *Note:* Magnitudes estimated from published chart.

★52★

Business: Various Projections

Plastics Healthcare Packaging Market, 1989-1997

"A study projects a 4.5% growth in plastic sales for use in healthcare packaging. The sale of plastics for blister cards is projected to increase by 8.9%."

[Application sales in millions of dollars]

	Application sales
1989	163
1992	191
1997	238

Source: Michael Bordenaro, "Pharmaceuticals Focus on Labeling and Automation," in *Packaging*, January 1994, p. 45. *Primary source:* TPC Business Research Group.

★53★

Business: Various Projections

Shipments of Business Forms and Related Products by U.S. Forms Manufacturers, 1992-1996

"Two basic assumptions are behind this forecast: (1) The U.S. economy will continue to experience slow economic growth for the foreseeable future, with real GDP growth in the 2.0 to 3.0 percent range at best; (2) There will be an acceleration in the impact of forms-displacing technologies on the forms industry's core product lines over the next three to four years, as more end-users seek to eliminate paper from their business processes."

[Year-to-year percent change in shipment values]

Product	1992-93	1993-94	1995-95	1995-96	Average 1992-1996
Business Forms					
Custom Continuous	-2.9%	-2.7%	-2.5%	-2.4%	-2.6%
Stock Continuous	-9.5	-4.7	-4.3	-4.1	-5.7
Unit Sets	-4.0	-3.5	-3.2	-3.1	-3.5
Salesbooks/Pegboard	-2.7	-2.0	-1.7	-1.9	-2.1
Total	-4.7	-3.3	-3.0	-3.0	-3.5
Related Products					
Pre-printed Cutsheets	9.5	7.5	6.0	4.5	6.9
Pressure Sensitive Labels	12.5	10.5	9.0	8.5	10.1

[Continued]

★ 53 ★

Shipments of Business Forms and Related Products by U.S. Forms Manufacturers, 1992-1996

[Continued]

Product	1992-93	1993-94	1995-95	1995-96	Average 1992-1996
Total Business Forms and Related Products:	-2.2	-1.1	-0.9	-0.9	-1.3

Source: Douglas C. Taylor, in *Perspective '93: The Present and the Future of the North American Forms Industry* (International Business Forms Industries, Inc.), 1993, pp. 27-8. *Primary source:* International Business Forms Industries Inc.

★ 54 ★

Business: Various Projections

Supercenter Discount Store Growth, 1997

"Competition among discount stores remains high, in part because selling space has doubled in the past ten years. 'Good management is crucial in this kind of economic environment,' says Edward F. Johnson of the Johnson Redbook Services research firm. 'Category killer' stores such as Home Depot, Staples, and Petsmart remain strong. And Dean Witter analyst Patrick McCormick says membership warehouse club revenues should rise 21%, to $40 billion, by the end of this year and another 20% next. New investment is going into 'supercenters' that combine grocery and discount stores. McCormick says that total is projected to grow from 50 today to 1,000 by 1997. If that happens, he adds, their sales will total $55 billion to $60 billion."

Source: Therese Eiben and John Wyatt, "How the Industries Stack Up," in *Fortune*, 12 July 1993, p. 88.

The Automobile Industry

★ 55 ★

Truck and Auto Sales, 1994-2000

"This year automakers expect to sell 15.2 million cars and trucks at an average of about $19,000 each. Says Chrysler economist Donald Hilty: 'The bad times are over, and the good times are beginning.' He points to growing household income and a shrinking burden of consumer debt, along with pent-up demand of more than seven million units. Hilty thinks the boom could continue until 1997 and peak at a record 17.8 million units in annual sales."

[Millions of units]

1994	15.2
1995	16.7
1996	17.3
1997	17.8
1998	17.6
1999	17.0
2000	16.7

Source: Alex Taylor III, "U.S. Automakers Go Flat Out," in *Fortune,* 21 February 1994, p. 10. *Notes:* U.S. truck and auto sales include medium and heavy trucks. Magnitudes estimated from published chart. Source also includes data for 1990-1993.

★ 56 ★

The Automobile Industry

Autofutures Vehicle Sales Forecast, 1992-1997

"Until recently, forecasters had been predicting booming vehicle sales in the latter part of the decade, mostly as a result of pent-up demand. Car and truck sales usually average about 15 million units a year, but they have been running almost two million units below that for the past four years as hard-pressed consumers postponed big-ticket purchases. The need to replace aging vehicles, combined with growth of the car-buying population, had been expected to push sales from this year's estimated 14.1 million units to a record 17 million by 1996.

"Now Autofutures of Ann Arbor, Michigan, one of the best known auto industry research firms, is stepping on the brakes. It says sales will peak at just 14.8 million in 1995 and decline slowly from there until they reach 13.4 million in 1998. Reasons: slow economic growth, declining real incomes, and the high price of new cars. Says Autofutures analyst Alan L. Baum: 'The economy determines the sales trend, not the other way around. The average cost of a new car is $18,000 now, or 26 weeks of the median family income, up from 22.8 weeks in 1990. It just doesn't add up'."

[Sales in millions of vehicles]

Year	Bullish forecasters	Autofutures' forecast
1992	11.9	11.9
1993	14.4	14.2
1994	15.3	14.6
1995	16.2	14.9
1996	17.0	14.8
1997	17.0	14.1
1998	17.0	13.4

Source: Alex Taylor III, "Will Car Sales Soon Sputter?" in *Fortune*, 1 November 1993, p. 26. *Primary source:* Autofutures of Ann Arbor, MI. *Note:* Magnitudes estimated from published chart.

★ 57 ★

The Automobile Industry

Japanese Automobile Manufacturing in the U.S., 1992-1998

"Japan's favored strategy will be to continue moving production to the U.S. to take advantage of the lower costs that the weak dollar assures. In 1992, Japanese manufacturers sold 1.4 million cars and trucks made at American transplants—up from 60,000 a decade ago—45% of their total U.S. sales. Some analysts expect the transplant share to grow to 60% by 1998."

Source: Justin Martin, "Jolt for Japan," in *Fortune*, 20 September 1993, p. 13.

★ 58 ★

The Automobile Industry

Vehicle Production by Japanese Automakers, 1985-2000

"Rather than beginning a period of decline, Japanese carmakers are in transition from a growth industry to a cyclical one. For three decades after the end of World War II, auto production in Japan rose almost without interruption. The growth path steepened in the 1980s, when a relatively weak yen combined with low interest rates to create Japan's short-lived 'bubble economy,' which finally burst."

[Millions of units]

1985	12.40
1986	12.30
1987	12.35
1988	12.80
1989	12.90
1990	13.60
1991	13.20
1992	12.35
1993	11.40
1994	11.50
1995	11.70
1997	11.95
1998	11.70
1999	11.35
2000	11.10

Source: Alex Taylor III, "Here Come Japan's Carmakers—Again," in *Fortune*, 13 December 1993, p. 130. *Note:* Magnitudes estimated from published chart.

★ 59 ★

The Automobile Industry

Vehicles Exported from North America by Detroit's Big Three Automakers, 1988-1999

"Detroit, once renowned for its provincialism, is finally becoming expert-minded. For foreign sales of Big Three cars and trucks have grown fourfold since 1986 and, as the [table] shows, could more than double by the end of the decade."

[Thousands of vehicles]

Year	GM	Ford	Chrysler
1988	80	40	50
1989	90	30	70
1990	100	65	30
1991	125	45	68
1992	130	50	80

[Continued]

★ 59 ★

Vehicles Exported from North America by Detroit's Big Three Automakers, 1988-1999

[Continued]

Year	GM	Ford	Chrysler
1993	140	70	100
1999	250	225	180

Source: Alex Taylor III, "Detroit's Exports Take Off," in *Fortune*, 1 November 1993, p. 12. *Note:* Magnitudes estimated from published chart.

The Communications Industry

★ 60 ★

Consumer Telecommunications Market, 1991-1996

"The market for all types of corded telephones increased from $523 million in 1985 to $652 in 1991. It is expected to increase to slightly over $1 billion by 1996."

	1991	1992	1993	1994	1995	1996	CAGR
Corded Telephone Instruments							
Standard							
Value: $ millions	267	266	261	249	236	243	-3.0
Quantity: million units	12	12	12	12	11	10	-0.7
One Piece							
Value: $ millions	25	18	12	7	3	1	-41.1
Quantity: million units	3	2	1	1	1	1	-17.6
Decorator							
Value: $ millions	71	68	68	66	64	63	-2.6
Quantity: million units	2	1	1	1	1	1	-5.4
Full-featured							
Value: $ millions	289	342	403	475	641	782	22.0
Quantity: million units	2	3	3	4	5	6	21.0
Total							
Value: $ millions	652	693	743	797	945	1,036	9.7
Quantity: million units	18	18	18	18	18	18	*
Cordless Telephones							
Value: $ millions	710	707	800	980	950	1,022	7.6
Quantity: million units	9	9	10	11	11	12	5.1
Telephone Answering Machines							
Value: $ millions	758	770	790	780	775	765	0.2
Quantity: million units	11	11	12	12	13	14	4.3

[Continued]

★ 60 ★

Consumer Telecommunications Market, 1991-1996

[Continued]

	1991	1992	1993	1994	1995	1996	CAGR
Total							
Value: $ millions	2,120	2,170	2,333	2,557	2,670	2,823	5.9

Source: Mitchell B. Wander, ed., et al, in *Telecommunications Market Review and Forecast*, pp. 194, 196. *Primary source:* NATA Market Research Department. *Notes:* Less than 0.5 percent. Totals may not equal sum of categories due to rounding. CAGR = Compound Annual Growth Rate (percent). Source also includes data for 1985-1990.

★ 61 ★

The Communications Industry

Total Set-top and Server Market as a Percentage of TV Households, 1994- 2000

"As it becomes increasingly apparent that video-on-demand will likely give the initial stimulus to revenue to growth it's not surprising that a growing number of research reports are looking at this potential new revenue stream...

"The first, published by the Multimedia Research Group of Sunnyvale, California, reflects the findings of an eight-month effort by three analysts...

"Essentially, the study predicts that the VOD market (including an $8 billion hardware segment for set-top boxes and video servers) will approximate $23 billion in gross revenues by the end of this decade. At that time, about 41 million homes, or 42 percent of all TV households, will have the enabling technology for VOD. Under this scenario, new movies will rent for about $4 (1994 dollars)."

"On average, each household will spend about $31 monthly for the following services: movies and replays of TV programs ($20); games and game-related services ($10); and on-line connections ($1). In addition, the average interactive customer will spend about $37/month to purchase an array of products."

Summary VOD market	1994	1995	1996	1997	1998	1999	2000	TOTAL
Total TV Households (millions)[1]	93.66	94.22	94.79	95.36	95.93	96.50	97.08	
Cable households (percent)[1]	59	60	61	61	62	62	63	
Cable Households (million)[1]	55	57	58	58	59	60	61	
GR. TOTAL: SET-TOPS								
Units (000)	28	549	1,995	3,756	6,746	9,249	18,594	40,917
% of U.S. TV households	0.03	0.58	2.10	3.94	7.03	9.58	19.15	42
Dollars (million)	$8	$165	$598	$1,127	$2,024	$2,775	$5,578	
GR. TOTAL: SERVERS								
Units	9	67	161	320	609	899	1,788	3,852
Dollars (million)	$22	$141	$321	$646	$1,000	$1,281	$2,492	
GRAND TOTAL: (million)	$30	$305	$920	$1,773	$3,024	$4,056	$8,071	

Source: "VOD: Yes, No or Maybe," in *Cablevision*, 19 September 1994, p. 24. *Primary source:* 1994 Multimedia Research Group. *Notes:* Includes all distribution media, including cable, telco and wireless. VOD=Video on Demand. 1. Nielsen Media Research ('91-93).

★ 62 ★

The Communications Industry

Subscriptions to Wireless Communications Market, 1993-1998

"Brace yourself for a new world. It's a world in which invisible communications networks grid every major metropolitan area, link workers inside office builders and warehouses, and surround the Earth via flotillas of satellites. It's a world in which wireless devices combine the functions of telephones and computers, sending and receiving voice, text and graphics, and sifting through reams of information on behalf of their human masters. It's a world in which we are all reachable—anytime, anyplace. And it's a world about which the main question isn't if, but when. 'It's amazing,' says Ira Brodsky, president of Datacomm Research Co., a Wilmette, Ill., telecommunications consulting firm. 'You get this sense that it's a volcano about to erupt'."

[Thousands of U.S. subscribers]

	1993	1994	1995	1996	1997	1998	Growth[1]
Voices services							
Cellular	14,163	17,350	20,965	25,182	29,917	35,500	20.2%
SMR[2]	1,620	1,750	1,890	2,040	2,200	2,380	8.0
Data services							
Cellular	600	1,150	1,535	1,818	2,083	2,500	33.0%
Paging	17,655	21,250	25,500	30,600	36,720	44,064	20.2
Mobile data networks	300	500	800	1,000	1,200	1,400	38.0
Satellite phone services	50	60	72	86	120	160	26.2
Total	34,388	42,060	50,762	60,726	72,240	86,004	20.1%

Source: G. Christian Hill, "Look No Wires! The Cord Has Been Cut, and Communications May Never Be the Same," in *The Wall Street Journal*, 11 February 1994, pp. R1, R5. *Primary source:* Link Resources Corp. *Notes:* 1. Compound annual growth rate. 2. Specialized mobile radio services, such as fleet dispatches.

★63★

The Communications Industry

Market Developments for Hand-held Wireless Data Services, 1993-1998

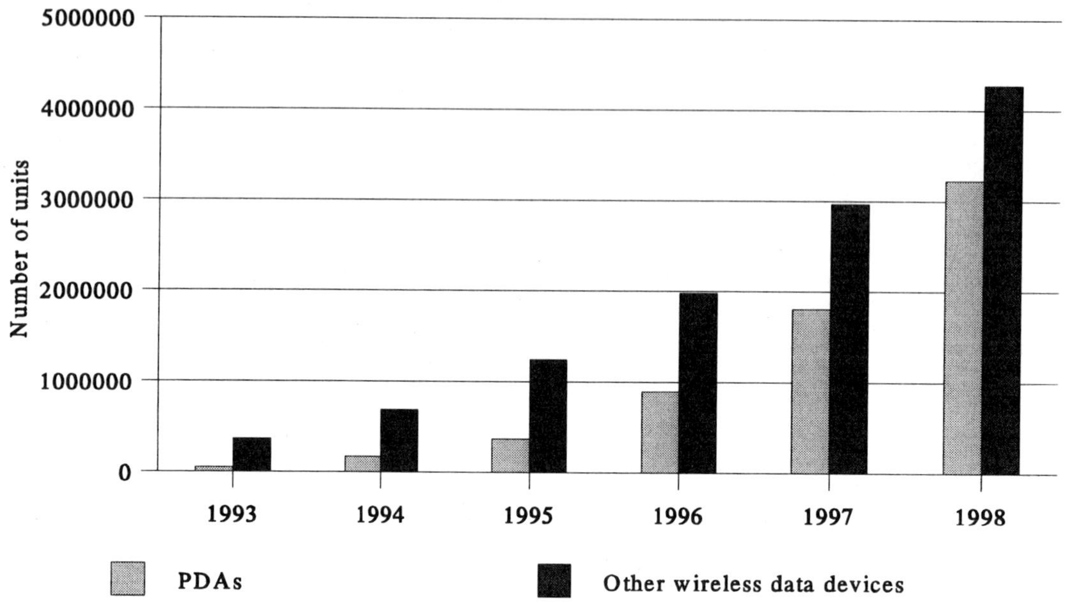

"Most market researchers—and most people in general—haven't spent a lot of time thinking about all the other possibilities of powerful networks and powerful devices. But the uses are limitless. To cite a couple of examples: **Qualcomm** Corp. of San Diego tracks 40,000 trucks via satellite, constantly monitoring their locations and even engine conditions. And **Cincinnati Microwave** Inc., Cincinnati, has developed a wireless system for vending machines to talk to a computer at headquarters, ordering more goods or reporting vandalism. Motorola, in fact, says anything that has a switch, including car engines, can be turned on or off by a wireless network, and it plans to try to sell the idea to the masses."

[Timeline of expected developments]

Year	Installed Base		Expected events
	PDAs[1]	Other wireless data devices[2]	
1993	52,000	364,000	Data-only networks, Ardis and Ram, start to upgrade service; first PDAs--Newton, Simon, Zoomer--are introduced.
1994	170,000	685,000	Radio modems and cellular phones on small slip-in cards are introduced for PDAs and portable computers; Motorola, Compaq, Sony ship more-advanced PDAs; two new data networks--specialized mobile radio, or SMR, and cellular digital packet data, or CDPD--are introduced; FCC awards licenses for personal communications services; AT&T launches first intelligent network service, PersonaLink.
1995	368,000	1,245,000	Regional personal communications systems for data and voice are established; companies complete national massaging network and national SMR network; Phillips, Matsushita, others introduce PDAs, as devices and applications proliferate.

[Continued]

★63★

Market Developments for Hand-held Wireless Data Services, 1993-1998

[Continued]

Year	Installed Base		Expected events
	PDAs[1]	Other wireless data devices[2]	
1996	895,000	1,980,000	CDPD becomes a seamless national network, promoting transmission of voice and data on single devices; hundreds of services become available on intelligent networks through easy-to-use software applications; demand for data devices soars.
1997	1,808,000	2,967,000	Hand-held wireless data devices become a mass market.
1998	3,224,000	4,278,000	

Source: G. Christian Hill, "Look! No Wires! The Cord Has Been Cut, and Communications May Never Be the Same," in *The Wall Street Journal*, 11 February 1994,p. R5. *Primary source:* BIS Strategic Decisions for estimates of installed base. *Notes:* 1. Personal digital assistants; excludes palmtop computers. 2. Computers such as subnotebooks, laptops and desktops equipped for wireless use.

★64★

The Communications Industry

Data Communications Equipment Market, 1991-1996

"**Data service units** (DSUs) are devices used to send digital data over transmission lines from a data terminal without a modem. DSUs may require use of a channel service unit (CSU), an apparatus which connects certain digital equipment to digital phone lines, in cases when the terminal lacks digital line interface capability.

"**Front-end processors** are auxiliary computers attached to a network to perform control operations, freeing up the host computer for data processing...

"**Concentrators** are devices that perform a function similar to both multiplexers and packet switches in the sense that both types of equipment are designed to maximize the capacity of a given telecommunications transmission circuit...

"**LANs** are dedicated data communications facilities providing high-speed switched connections, generally over a distance of less than a few miles, typically within an office building or campus environment...

"The data communications market has increased rapidly over the last several years from almost $2.9 billion in 1985 to $7.2 billion in 1991 and is expected to approach $9.6 billion by 1996. Part of the increase in sales of data communications equipment can be attributed to increasing sales by interconnect companies."

[Millions of dollars]

	1991	1992	1993	1994	1995	1996	CAGR
Front-end processors	483	532	557	583	616	644	5.9
Local area networks (LANs)	2,210	2,390	2,590	2,800	3,030	3,275	8.2
Modems	1,532	1,568	1,581	1,568	1,444	1,422	-1.5
Packet switching equipment	634	661	690	719	750	783	4.3
Multiplexers	1,159	1,265	1,311	1,346	1,426	1,501	5.1
T-1 multiplexers	580	635	760	880	1,000	1,125	12.3

[Continued]

★ 64 ★

Data Communications Equipment Market, 1991-1996

[Continued]

	1991	1992	1993	1994	1995	1996	CAGR
Concentrators	245	255	250	240	235	230	-1.3
DSUs/CSUs	325	382	450	530	625	735	17.7
Other	620	710	785	840	910	1,005	10.1
Total	7,208	7,763	8,214	8,625	9,036	9,595	5.9

Source: Mitchell B. Wander, ed., et al, in *Telecommunications Market Review and Forecast*, pp. 150-51, 153. Primary source: NATA Market Research Department. *Notes:* CAGR = Compound Annual Growth Rate (percent). Source also includes data for 1985-1990.

★ 65 ★

The Communications Industry

Mobile Communications Market, 1991-1996

	1991	1992	1993	1994	1995	1996	CAGR
Radio Pagers							
Annual sales value: $ millions	598	620	642	665	689	714	3.6
Annual sales volume: millions	3.8	4.2	4.6	5.1	5.6	6.2	10.3
Pagers in use: millions	13.4	14.7	16.0	17.5	19.2	21.0	9.4
Cellular Telephones							
Annual sales value: $ millions	1,955	2,094	2,242	2,402	2,572	2,755	7.1
Annual sales volumes: millions	2,265	3,024	4,037	5,389	7,194	9,604	33.5
Total							
Annual sales value: $ millions	2,553	2,713	2,884	3,067	3,261	3,468	21.5

Source: Mitchell B. Wander, ed., et al, in *Telecommunications Market Review and Forecast*, pp. 199, 208. *Primary source:* NATA Market Research Department. *Notes:* CAGR = Compound Annual Growth Rate (percent). Source also includes data for 1985-1990.

★ 66 ★

The Communications Industry

Annual Shipments of Electronic Personal Communicators, 1993-1998

"Cellular telephone with fax, paging and data functions."

[Thousands of units]

1993	0
1994	100
1995	300
1996	750
1997	1450
1998	2500

Source: G. Christian Hill and Jim Carlton, "Getting Personal," in *The Wall Street Journal*, 11 February 1994, p. R6. *Primary source:* Link Resources Corp. *Note:* Magnitudes estimated from published chart.

★ 67 ★

The Communications Industry

Connector Consumption, 1993-1998

"Connector makers are popping the champagne corks over the surge of orders related to the estimated $100 billion information superhighway. By 1998 annual connector sales of almost $4 billion are predicted by Bishop & Associates, Inc. in West Chicago, IL. It forecasts 8-percent rate of computer related parts. Computer OEMs [Original Equipment Manufacturers], systems integrators, and other electronic-data-processing applications will continue to be the largest connector buyers, though, consuming more than $6.5 billion by 1998."

	Annual growth rate (percent)		Worldwide market (billions of dollars)	
	1993	1998	1993	1998
Computers	8.0	7.0	4.7	6.5
Communications	7.7	8.0	2.5	3.7
All sectors	5.0	5.8	14.6	19.4

Source: Jodi V. Buonanno, "Communications Boom Spurs Connector Spurt," in *Electronic Business Buyer*, March 1994, p. 30. *Primary source:* Bishop & Associates.

★ 68 ★

The Communications Industry

Worldwide and North American Optic Fiber Consumption, 1993-1998

"[While General Instrument's product manager John Chamberlain claims that the market for fiber optics] 'is going bananas internationally,' U.S. exports of cable components may be limited. Countries that lack the infrastructure also lack the cash to buy it. And those countries with cash are building their own fiber plants, some with government subsidies that would undercut U.S. firms. Among the few bright spots for U.S. exports, according to Corning's manager and market analyst John Lively, are the U.K. due to deregulation and China."

[Billions of dollars]

Year	Worldwide	North American
1993	0	0
1994	4.3	1.6
1995	4.9	1.8
1996	5.5	2.1
1997	6.6	2.4
1998	7.6	2.9

Source: Vanessa Craft, in *Electronic Business Buyer,* April 1994, p. 36. *Primary source:* ElectroniCast, KMI. *Note:* Magnitudes estimated from published chart.

★ 69 ★

The Communications Industry

Worldwide Demand for Networking Chips, 1993-1997

"**TransSwitch Corp.** is on the threshold of the '90s dream. As the United States begins building the information superhighway, the company has become a leading supplier of advanced data-communications chip sets. Corporate users' exploding demand for the high-speed and wide bandwidth services known as synchronous optical network (SONET) and asynchronous transmission mode (ATM) will create a $1.1 billion chip market by 1997, according to In-Stat Inc., in Scottsdale, AZ., up from 1993 sales of almost $34 million."

[Millions of dollars]

Year	
1993	0
1994	125
1995	450
1996	650
1997	1,100

Source: Carol Rosen, "Datacom Chip Maker is at Right Place, Right Time," in *Electronic Business Buyer*, April 1994, p. 70. *Primary source:* In-Stat. *Note:* Magnitudes estimated from published chart.

The Computer Industry

★ 70 ★

U.S. Shipments of Portable Computers, 1993-1997

"As a group, corporate PC buyers are opting with a vengeance for notebook computers. Notebooks are the fastest growing segment of the PC market, according to Gerald Purdy, industry analyst with Dataquest Inc. in San Jose. Docking stations that link notebooks to corporate local area networks give users the opportunity to compute on the same machine in the office and on the road. Improved displays, larger disk drives, and fast and powerful microprocessors offer notebook users desktop capabilities without taking up the space. Notebook sales are expected to rise by 20 percent this year, reaching 3.1 million units by 1996."

[Millions of units sold in the U.S.]

	1993	1995	1997
Desktop PC	10.70	11.80	14.40
Notebook	21.8	2.93	3.15
Subnotebook[1]	0.33	1.29	2.83

Source: Lamont Wood, "Stalking the Best PCs," in *Electronic Business Buyer,* November 1993, p. 115. *Primary source:* Dataquest. *Note:* 1. Includes Personal Digital Assistants (PDAs).

★ 71 ★

The Computer Industry

Worldwide Shipments of Portable Computers, 1981-1997

"Since Univac's introduction in 1952, info tech has had little discernible impact on productivity. But experts see the technology as set to drive growth dramatically."

[Millions shipped worldwide]

Year	MIPS
1981	400
1985	450
1989	500
1993	700
1997	5,400

Source: John Huey, "Waking Up to the New Economy," in *Fortune,* 27 June 1994, pp. 38, 81. *Primary source:* Dataquest. *Notes:* Magnitudes estimated from published chart. MIPS - millions of instructions per second. (A measure of computing power).

★ 72 ★

The Computer Industry

Shipments of Multimedia-ready PCs and Multimedia PC Upgrade Kits, 1991- 1996

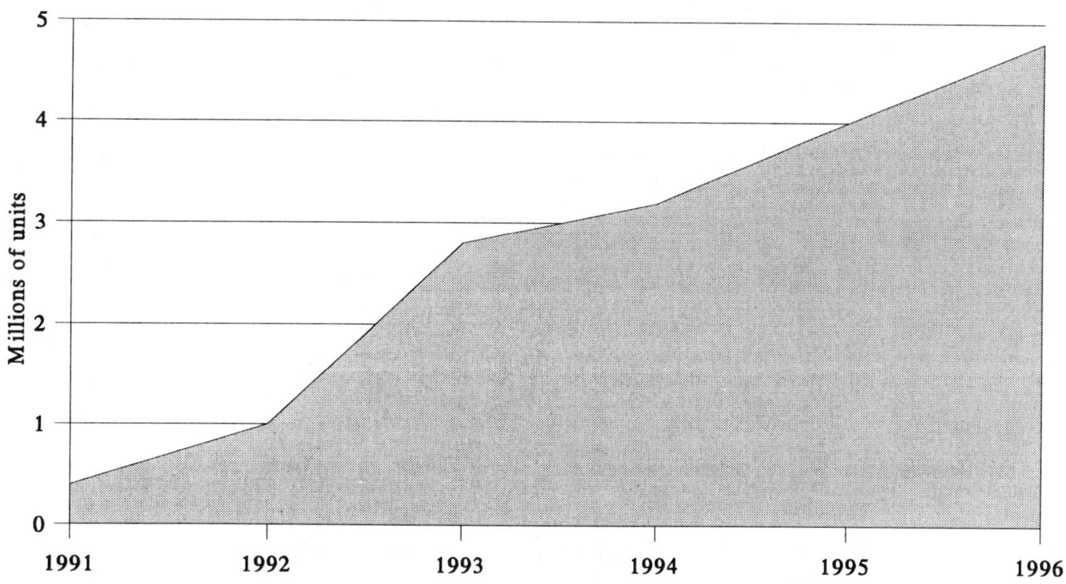

"Multimedia, an elusive term usually defined as the combination of computer data, sound, animation and video, has become more than a toy technology...

"A typical multimedia setup for a personal computer includes a CD-ROM compact disk player, audio gear and special hardware allowing the display of sophisticated graphics.

"Even using a narrow definition of multimedia, [Gregory Sheppard principal analyst with Dataquest, Inc. of San Jose, CA] estimated that delivery of multimedia equipped personal computers rose from about 200,000 in 1991 to about one million last year. By 1996, he predicted, the number would reach 4.5 million."

[Millions of units]

Year	
1991	.4
1992	1.0
1993	2.8
1994	3.2
1995	4.0
1996	4.8

Source: Jerry Schwartz, "Corporate Paperwork Gets Sound and Action," in *The New York Times*, 7 July 1993, p. D6. *Primary source:* Dataquest. *Note:* Magnitudes estimated from published chart.

★ 73 ★

The Computer Industry

Home versus Business and Government PC Sales, 1992-1996

"Personal computer sales are expected to more than double from 1992-1996, to 46 million units sold."

[In percent]

	1992	1996
Business and government	73	58
Home	27	42

Source: Deirdre Schwiesow and Sam Ward, in *USA* Today, 12 May, 1994, p. 1A. *Primary source:* Channel Marketing Corp.

★ 74 ★

The Computer Industry

Worldwide 3.3 Volt Dynamic Random Access Memory (DRAM) Chip Market, 1992-1997

[Worldwide DRAM market in millions of dollars; 3.3 V-units' share in percent]

Year	3.3 Volt units' share
1992	2
1993	10
1994	14
1995	50
1996	70
1997	78

Source: J. Robert Lineback, in *Electronic Business Buyer*, December 1993, p. 36. *Primary source:* Mitsubishi Electric and ICE. *Note:* Magnitudes estimated from published chart.

★75★

The Computer Industry

Worldwide Sales of Digital Sign Processing (DSP) Chip Market, 1991-1996

"What's the magic of DSP? It enables software engineers to translate familiar continuously varying analog signals—voice and image signals, for instance—into the discrete digital language of computing by using DSP chips. Once transformed into the 1's and 0's of computer code, the signals can be manipulated in a variety of ways impossible when they are in analog form. Example: Digitized audio signals can be greatly compressed so they take less space in the airwaves, opening up new channels for cellular telephones in big cities where capacity is already strained. With analog technology, only a single phone conversation can be transmitted over a radio bandwidth; digital systems can squeeze three or more conversations into the same space."

[Worldwide sales growth; index: 1983 = 100]

Year	General purpose DSP chips	All chips
1991	1,750	300
1992	2,500	325
1993	3,375	500
1994	4,500	650
1995	6,250	675
1996	7,800	700

Source: Gene Bylinsky, "A U.S. Comeback in Electronics," in *Fortune*, 20 April 1992, pp. 78, 82. *Notes:* Magnitudes estimated from published chart. Source also includes data for 1983-1990.

★76★

The Computer Industry

Worldwide Merchant Microprocessor Market, 1991-1997

[Thousands of units]

	1991	1992	1993	1994	1995	1996	1997
PowerPC	0.0	0.0	100.0	896.0	1,758.2	3,255.5	4,486.0
Sparc	194.6	392.7	844.9	1,134.1	1,365.2	1,540.3	1,658.4
MIPS	140.4	283.6	392.4	502.5	603.1	719.7	797.2
ARM	30.0	40.9	184.3	375.0	484.0	583.0	715.0
Hobbit	0.0	0.0	75.0	225.0	303.8	486.0	646.4
Transputer	26.0	38.6	35.0	36.0	37.3	44.5	46.7
Alpha	0.0	0.0	0.0	9.6	32.8	30.8	33.4
88K	24.7	42.3	90.0	75.0	57.8	25.0	15.8
PA-RISC	0.0	0.0	4.5	9.3	11.1	12.0	12.0
Total RISC	415.7	798.0	1,726.1	3,262.6	4,653.2	6,696.8	8,410.9

Source: Robert Ristelhueber, "The Microprocessor Free-For-all," in *Electronic Business Buyer*, November 1993, pp. 55, 60. *Primary source:* In-Stat. *Note:* Sales of 32-bit or greater MPUs for the PC and workstation market.

★ 77 ★

The Computer Industry

Cost Increase in High-performance Semiconductor Production, 1992-2000

"Is the semiconductor industry spending itself into oblivion?

"The impending arrival of the $1 billion wafer fab is an unwelcome landmark for semiconductor makers. The cost of building new plants will have risen roughly 500 percent in the past decade. The depreciation costs of these immense factories alone now represent nearly half the total cost of producing a wafer.

"The biggest culprit of this upward spiral has been the expense of production equipment, now 70 to 75 percent of fab costs. Semiconductor makers have long grumbled about the rising costs of their capital equipment, but have been willing to pay the price to keep innovating. The scramble to break the half-micron barrier, however, is driving up costs so sharply that even in the largest chip suppliers wonder whether they can stay in the race. Equipment costs increase geometrically as line widths shrink below 0.8 microns, according to an analysis by **Intel Corp**. in Santa Clara."

[Capital cost per wafer per week, in thousands of dollars]

Year	
1990	100
1991	120
1992	150
1993	190
1994	250
1995	300
1996	370
1997	430
1998	500
1999	550
2000	600

Source: Robert Ristelhueber, "New Fabs Don't Have the Cost $1 Billion," in *Electronic Business Buyer*, December 1993, pp. 63-4. *Primary source:* Intel. *Note:* Source also includes data for 1970-1991.

★78★

The Computer Industry

Cost Increase in High-performance Semiconductor Manufacturing Sectors, 1991-2000

"Intel's Michael Splinter [general manager of component manufacturing] contends that the productivity of equipment is inadequate considering its cost. 'The cost of equipment has grown faster than the productivity of equipment,' he says. 'For chip makers to stay profitable, equipment productivity must increase at a rate equal to or faster than the cost of that equipment.'

"Splinter estimated that seminconductor production equipment adds value to the wafer only 10 to 30 percent of the time; the rest of the time it's cooling and moving wafers. 'There's all kinds of overhead designed into these systems that we haven't figured out how to get rid of,' he concedes."

[Percent increase]

Capital equipment	3.2
Chip area	2.4
Raw materials	2.0
Process steps	1.8
Test	1.5

Source: Robert Ristelhueber, "New Fabs Don't Have to Cost $1 Billion," in *Electronic Business Buyer*, December 1993, pp. 64-5. *Primary source:* Texas instruments. *Note:* Magnitudes estimated from published chart.

★79★

The Computer Industry

Personal Digital Assistant (PDA) Market, 1992-1996

"Standard, plain-vanilla word processing, spreadsheets, and electronic mail are driving the soaring demand for portable computers, not the special sales-tracking applications commonly considered the ideal use of notebooks, laptops, pen-based tablets, and other mobile personal computers, according to a new report by Forrester Research, Inc. in Cambridge, MA. MIS managers at 50 large companies estimated that laptop and notebook computer use will jump by more than 100 percent by 1996. Purchases of personal digital assistants like Cupertino, CA based **Apple Computer Inc.'s** Newton and other PC 'mutants' will outpace traditional laptops and notebooks, though—up 600 percent, according to analysts Neal Hill and William Bluestein."

[Average number of units in each company]

	1992	1996
Laptop/notebook PCs	566	1,123
Tablets, PDAs and other mutants	75	345

Source: "PDA Demand Scenarios May Be for Real," in *Electronic Business Buyer*, November 1993, p. 36. *Primary source:* Forrester Research. *Note:* PDA = Personal Digital Assistant.

★ 80 ★

The Computer Industry

Decrease in Prices of PDAs, 1993-2000

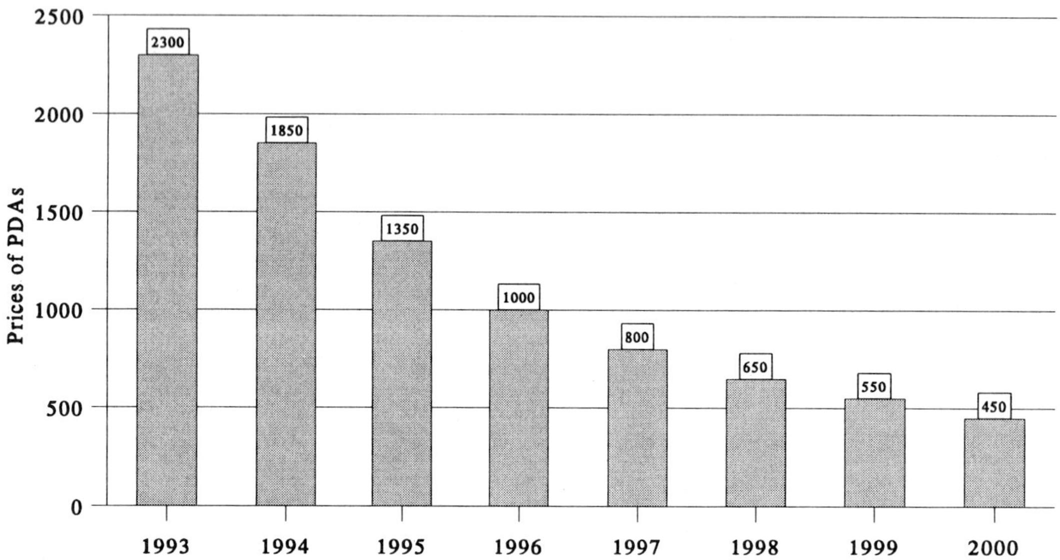

[Prices of PDAs with both voice and data capability]

Year	
1993	2,300
1994	1,850
1995	1,350
1996	1,000
1997	800
1998	650
1999	550
2000	450

Source: G. Christian Hill and Jim Carlton, "Getting Personal," in *The Wall Street Journal*, 11 February 1994, p. R6. *Primary source:* BIS Strategic Decisions. *Note:* Magnitudes estimated from published chart.

★ 81 ★

The Computer Industry

Annual Shipments of Electronic Information Organizers, 1993-1998

"Small keyboards, programmable for tasks like data collection and accounting."

[Thousands of units]

Year	Information organizer
1993	710
1994	760
1995	740
1996	675
1997	620
1998	600

Source: G. Christian Hill and Jim Carlton, "Getting Personal," in *The Wall Street Journal*, 11 February 1994, p. R6. *Primary source:* Link Resources Corp. *Note:* Magnitudes estimated from published chart.

★ 82 ★

The Computer Industry

Annual Shipments of Electronic Personal Agents, 1993-1998

"Pen-based input, smart software to assist user and improve time management."

[Thousands of units]

Year	Electronic personal agent
1993	50
1994	90
1995	130
1996	230
1997	400
1998	758

Source: G. Christian Hill and Jim Carlton, "Getting Personal," in *The Wall Street Journal*, 11 February 1994, p. R6. *Primary source:* Link Resources Corp. *Note:* Magnitudes estimated from published chart.

★ 83 ★

The Computer Industry

Annual Shipments of Intelligent Electronic Books, 1993-1998

"Reads multimedia material on CD-ROM disks or slip-in cards."

[Thousands of units]

Year	Intelligent electronic book
1993	20
1994	40
1995	70
1996	130
1997	260
1998	550

Source: G. Christian Hill and Jim Carlton, "Getting Personal," in *The Wall Street Journal*, 11 February 1994, p. R6. *Primary source:* Link Resources Corp. *Note:* Magnitudes estimated from published chart.

★ 84 ★

The Computer Industry

Annual Shipments of Electronic Tablets or Notebooks, 1993-1998

"Pen-based notepad for data and image capture, suited to mobile data collection."

[Thousands of units]

Year	Electronic tablet or notebook
1993	15
1994	40
1995	95
1996	160
1997	280
1998	375

Source: G. Christian Hill and Jim Carlton, "Getting Personal," in *The Wall Street Journal*, 11 February 1994, p. R6. *Primary source:* Link Resources Corp. *Note:* Magnitudes estimated from published chart.

★ 85 ★

The Computer Industry

Annual Shipments of Entertainment Personal Agents, 1993-1998

"Combines game capability with personal organizing tools."

[Thousands of units]

Year	Entertainment personal agent
1993	0
1994	0
1995	30
1996	80
1997	175
1998	340

Source: G. Christian Hill and Jim Carlton, "Getting Personal," in *The Wall Street Journal*, 11 February 1994, p. R6. *Primary source:* Link Resources Corp. *Note:* Magnitudes estimated from published chart.

★ 86 ★

The Computer Industry

Sales of Client-server Development Tools, 1992-1997

"Overall, the U.S. market for software licenses and maintenance fees will grow 12.8 percent this year to $36.2 billion, according to market research firm International Data Corp. (IDC), up from $32.1 billion in 1993. IDC predicts that the U.S. market will continue to grow at better than 12 percent per year, reaching $51.7 billion by 1997.

"Among the industry's many trends, the movement away from hierarchical mainframe installations to client/server computing represents one of the most critical, says Jennifer Scholze, an IDC software analyst. The growing power to desktop PCs and workstations is permitting the distribution of application code that once resided on large central computers. Growth in software targeted at those machines, consequently, is slowing. Meanwhile, software tools that assist in the production of client/server applications are growing rapidly due to this shift in the data-processing paradigm."

[Billions of dollars]

Year	
1992	4.5
1994	10.4
1997	22.4

Source: Dwight B. Davis, "Solid Growth Hides Weak Spots," in *Electronic Business Buyer*, January 1994, p. 73. *Primary source:* International Data Corporation (IDC).

★ 87 ★

The Computer Industry

Worldwide Market for Automated Client-server Software Testing, 1993-1997

"If a product can automate a job that no one wants, it can make money. If that job is the drudgery of software testing, the product could make a fortune. That is the idea fueling the growth of **Auto Tester Inc.**, a three-year-old start-up owned by privately held **Software Recording Co.** in Dallas.

"The company offers testing tools and systems that automatically enter data to exercise and validate a wide range of software, from business programs to embedded-control applications. The tests are performed at the functional level of the software. As a result, the tests can provide a realistic view of how software-based applications will hold up in the hands of users or in real-world situations, says Linda G. Hayes, company president."

[Millions of dollars]

Year	
1993	50
1994	90
1995	140
1996	200
1997	300

Source: J. Robert Lineback, "Software Testing—A Job Nobody Wants," in *Electronic Business Buyer*, April 1994, p. 68. *Primary source:* Hambrecht & Quist. *Note:* Magnitudes estimated from published chart.

★ 88 ★

The Computer Industry

European Operating Software Market, 1992-1997

"September 1993 will see the release of Novell DOS 7, a new version of an alternative disk operating system for IBM-compatible PCs by Desktop Systems Division of **Novell Inc.** of Provo, Utah. Novell's European Development Center at Hungerford, England, developed the software, which challenges **Microsoft Corp.** of Redmond, Washington, and **IBM Corp.** of Armonk, N.Y. Both recently launched the 6th version of their respective MS-DOS and PC-DOS.

"Microsoft's UK-based personal products manager, Mark Edwards, isn't concerned. He claims 8 million copies of his MS-DOS 6 software has shipped in two months. **"Novell has clearly missed the boat with this one,"** he says. **Ovum Ltd.** of London agrees: The market research firm projects that by 1997, Windows will dominate Europe's OS market."

[Percent]

	1992	1997
Windows	43	76
DOS	41	9
OS/2	4	3
Mac	9	10
Unix	3	2

Source: Peter Flectcher, "Novel DOS 7 Coming in September," in *Electronics*, 26 July 1993, p. 3.

★ 89 ★

The Computer Industry

North American Printed Circuit Board Consumption, 1994-1997

"Multilayer printed-circuit boards, the backbone of most computer and telecommunications equipment, will enjoy faster growth in the next three years than other board types, according to market research BPA (Technology & Management) Inc., Cold Spring Harbor, NV. Multilayer boards, which have the highest average selling price, account for one half of the North American market, which will total $8.5 billion by 1997."

[Percent growth in consumption, in percent]

Flexible	14.3
Glass epoxy	18.1
Multilayer	23.3
Paper & composite	11.0
Total	20.1

Source: "Multilayer Boards Make Further Inroads in PCB Market," in *Electronic Business Buyer*, April 1994, p. 34. *Primary source:* BPA.

★ 90 ★

The Computer Industry

Worldwide Video Decoder Shipments, 1994-2000

"Interactive multimedia, video on demand, and video teleconferencing have more in common than excessive hype—they depend on compression and decompression algorithms and chips. **C-Cube Microsystems Corp.** of Milpitas, CA is the reigning king of the video compression market and its already riding the growth rocket...

"This year, global demand will be 1-million decoder units and 10,000 encoder systems, predicts Gerry Kaulfhold, vice president of multimedia for In-Stat Inc., a market research firm in Scottsdale, AZ. C-Cube has about half of the decoder market, he estimates. By 1996 worldwide decoder box demand will increase to more than 10-million units, rising to more than 27-million units by the year 2000. C-Cube is likely to hold onto a lot of that huge market—more than industry observers would expect of a small company that has attracted major competitors such as **SGS-Thomson,** Phillips, **AT&T, Motorola,** and TI."

[Millions of shipments]

Year	
1994	1.0
1996	8.0
1998	17.5
2000	27.0

Source: Carol Rosen, "C-Cube Becomes the King of Compression," in *Electronic Business Buyer,* April 1994, p. 66. *Primary source:* In-Stat. *Note:* Magnitudes estimated from published chart.

★ 91 ★

The Computer Industry

Flat-panel Video Screen Sales, 1992-2000

"No one doubts that flat-panel displays are a crucial technology for the Information Age. Sales were $3.2 billion last year and are expected to hit $9.4 billion by 2000. And since Japanese companies own more than 95% of the market, the U.S. faces a daunting challenge in getting back into the race. 'It's going to take all the best resources that the U.S. government and industry can muster,' says Peter Mills, chief executive of the U.S. Display Consortium, a 10-company, ARPA-funded effort to develop the basic materials and manufacturing processes needed for fabricating displays."

[Billions of dollars]

Year	
1992	3.2
1996	6
2000	9.4

Source: John Carey, "Industrial Policy, or Industrial Folly?" in *Business Week,* 17 May 1993, p. 38. *Primary source:* Stanford Resources Inc. *Note:* Magnitudes estimated from published chart.

★ 92 ★

The Computer Industry

North American Shipments of Subminiature Switches, 1994-1997

"For years switch makers have responded to the demand for tiny toggles and puny pushbuttons, but meeting that requirement is pushing switch-makers into entirely new dimensions. Manufacturing have shrunk switches to as small as 0.244x0.106x0.332 inches...

"Miniaturization is sweeping into all type of switches, says David Wyman, project analyst of Venture Development Corp. in Natick, MA. Manufacturers are looking for space savings in terms of thinness. That means growth for miniature and subminiature switches.

"Wyman predicts that while the entire North American switch market will grow only about 4.5 percent annually over the next five years, demand growth for subminiature and ultraminiature switches will be 6 to 7 percent. Soaring sales of portable computers and peripherals, cellular telephones, video games, and other electronic equipment are accelerating the switch market, says Wyman. This increase will offset the declining demand for the defense and aerospace industries."

[Millions of dollars]

	1994	1997
All switches	1,100	1,248
Subminiature switches*	157	226

Source: James Carbone, "Small is Beautiful to Switch Users," in *Electronic Business Buyer,* April 1994, p. 131. *Primary source:* Venture Development. *Note:* *Includes DIP switches, most of which are subminiature.

★93★

The Computer Industry

Local Area Network (LAN) Hub Cost, 1993-1997

"The boom times are ending for the legion of suppliers in the $1.5 billion local-area network (LAN) hub market. Most corporate PCs are already networked, while competition and improved technology are squeezing prices...

"Prices for certain types of Ethernet connections for PCs fell from 50 to 67 percent over a few years, notes David Fowler, the vice president of marketing at **Chipcom Corp.**, a Southborough, Mass., wiring-hub supplier. The Boston-based Yankee Group estimates that hub-connection prices will drop 50 percent by 1997."

[Cost per hub on a per connection basis]

Year	Ethernet	Token ring
1993	800	325
1994	625	275
1995	500	225
1996	400	175
1997	325	150

Source: "The LAN Meteors are Crashing," in *Electronic Business Buyer*, November 1993, p. 32. *Primary source:* Yankee Group. *Note:* Magnitudes estimated from published chart.

Company Projections

★94★

Wal-Mart Supercenters in Operation and Supercenter Food Sales, 1992-1997

"Counting sales in its regular discount stores, Sam's Clubs warehouse units, and wholesaler McLane Co., Wal-Mart is likely to grow from a $13.8 billion grocer to the nation's largest by 1997, eclipsing the current leader, $22 billion Kroger Co., according to Burt P. Flickinger III, a principal at Booz Allen & Hamilton Inc. who has studied the Supercenters."

[Billions of dollars]

Year	Supercenters in operation	Supercenter food sales[1]
1992	40	.6
1993	80	1.4
1994	150	2.6
1995	190	4.0

[Continued]

★ 94 ★

Wal-Mart Supercenters in Operation and Supercenter Food Sales, 1992-1997

[Continued]

Year	Supercenters in operation	Supercenter food sales[1]
1996	350	6.6
1997	450	9

Source: Wendy Zellner, "When Wal-Mart Starts a Food Fight, It's a Doozy," in *Business Week*, 14 June 1993, p. 92. *Primary source:* Oppenheimer & Co. *Notes:* 1. Includes some nonfood items typically found in supermarkets. Magnitudes estimated from published chart. Source also includes data for 1991.

★ 95 ★

Company Projections

Revenues for *USA Today*, 1983-1997

"Critics called it McPaper. Fast-food journalism. And worse." "But *USA Today*, pretty weather map and all, has survived. And now, the newspaper that an analyst once labeled "the most unprofitable newspaper in the history of the world" is making money. It just completed its first profitable year."

[Millions of dollars]

Year	
1983	50
1984	120
1985	170
1986	220
1987	260
1988	290
1989	325
1990	330
1991	320
1992	340
1993	370
1994	395
1995	440
1996	475
1997	505

Source: William Glaberson, "After Decade of Losses, USA Today has First Profit," in *The New York Times*, 10 January 1994, pp. D1, D6. *Primary source:* Sanford C. Bernstein & Company estimates. *Notes:* Figures after 1993 are projections. Magnitudes estimated from published chart. Source also includes data for estimated operating profits and losses, 1983-1997.

★ 96 ★

Company Projections

IBM Merchant Sales, 1994-1996

"IBM has lots to sell. Its product portfolio includes a broad line of semiconductors that encompasses microprocessors, high-density dynamic RAMs (DRAMs) and static RAMs (SRAMs), mixed-signal ICs, and application-specific ICs (ASICs). It has started selling its formidable packaging capabilities, peripherals, and single-board computers. It's also ramping up a big PCMCIA card business, which includes direct sales and private labeling.

"Behind this move is an effort to bolster its finances. Gross margins have slumped from 57 percent in 1988 to 45 percent in 1992 and are now in the high 30s. Revenue estimates for 1993 vary, but analyst John Jones of Salomon Brothers, San Francisco, CA, estimates a continued revenue slide to $61.7 billion with an $8-billion loss, most of that from huge restructuring costs incurred in the second quarter of 1993. Next year, according to Jones, the hemorrhaging will stop."

[Millions of dollars]

Year	
1994	1,200
1995	1,800
1996	2,400

Source: "IBM Wants to Sell EVERYTHING!" in *Electronic Business Buyer*, April 1994, p. 114. *Primary source:* Salomon Brothers' estimates. *Notes:* Excludes disk drives. Magnitudes estimated from published chart. Source also includes data for 1990-1993.

★ 97 ★

Company Projections

General Electric Service Revenues as a Percent of Total Revenues, 1988- 1996

"The service economy, already representing over three-quarters of the GDP, is growing much faster than smokestack industries. At GE, revenues for the company's main service businesses—NBC and GE Capital—have bulged from $14.3 billion in 1988 to $25.2 billion last year, an annual growth rate of 12%...

"At this rate, nonmanufacturing operations will account for more than half the company's revenues by 1996, and GE will be, in effect, a service company."

Year	
1988	31
1990	34
1992	40
1994	47
1996	51

Source: Terence P. Pare, "GE as a Service Company," in *Fortune*, 18 April 1994, p. 16. *Primary source:* Year-end figures, 1988-1993. *Note:* Magnitudes estimated from published chart.

Banking and Finance

★98★

Financial Projections for the Bank Insurance Fund (BIF), 1991-1997

[By fiscal year, in billions of dollars]

	Actual 1991	1992	1993	1994	1995	1996	1997
	Outlays						
Gross Spending[A]	18.5	27.4	35.1	31.2	26.5	18.8	15.9
Collections	11.1	12.9	17.8	22.3	24.7	25.8	25.6
Net Budget Outlays[B]	7.4	14.5	17.3	8.9	1.7	-7.0	-9.7
	Accrued Income or Losses						
Gross Losses[C]	07.9	-10.0	-13.0	-11.0	-9.0	-6.0	-5.0
Net Income or Losses[D]	-8.1	-7.1	-5.9	-3.8	-1.1	1.3	2.6
	End-of-Year Balances						
Cumulative Borrowings from FFB and Treasury	8.5	19.0	36.3	45.1	46.9	39.9	30.2
Accrued Fund Balance[E]	2.4	-4.7	-10.6	-14.4	-15.5	-14.2	-11.6

Source: U.S. Congress, Congressional Budget Office, *CBO Projections of the Banking Industry and the BIF*, (Washington, D.C.: U.S. Government Printing Office), 1 April 1992, p. 52. *Primary source:* Congressional Budget Office. *Notes:* FFB=Federal Financing Bank. A. Includes cash disbursed for bank failures, plus other cash expenditures. B. Gross spending less collections. C. Losses accrued in resolving failed banks. D. Assessment income less gross losses, additional reserves for future losses, and other expenses. E. Includes reserve for a portion of the subsequent year's losses.

★99★

Banking and Finance

Comparison of Baseline Projections about the Bank Insurance Fund, 1991- 1997

[By fiscal year, in billions of dollars]

	Actual 1991	1992	1993	1994	1995	1996	1997
Net Outlays							
OMB[A]	7.4	33.0	38.0	13.7	7.5	-4.5	-19.3
CBO[B]	7.4	14.5	17.3	8.9	1.7	-7.0	-9.7
FDIC[C]	7.4	19.0	13.6	N.A	N.A.	N.A.	N.A.

[Continued]

★ 99 ★

Comparison of Baseline Projections about the Bank Insurance Fund, 1991- 1997

[Continued]

	Actual 1991	1992	1993	1994	1995	1996	1997
Losses on Failed Banks							
OMB	7.9	16.9	23.3	16.8	14.6	11.0	6.5
CBO	7.9	10.0	13.0	11.0	9.0	6.0	5.0
FDIC	7.9	13.2	12.6	N.A.	N.A.	N.A.	N.A.
Assets of Failed Banks							
OMB	57.0	80.0	110.5	85.6	82.7	70.5	43.2
CBO	57.0	58.0	76.0	64.0	52.0	35.0	29.0
FDIC	57.0	86.0	82.3	N.A.	N.A.	N.A.	N.A.
Fund Net Worth							
OMB[D]	2.4	-2.2	-18.3	-28.1	-35.4	-38.9	-37.5
CBO	2.4	-4.7	-10.6	-14.4	-15.5	-14.2	-44.6
FDIC	2.4	-9.6	-18.3	N.A.	N.A.	N.A.	N.A.
Cumulative Borrowing							
OMB	8.3	33.0	71.0	84.7	92.2	87.7	68.4
CBO	8.3	19.0	36.3	45.1	46.9	39.9	30.2
FDIC	8.3	33.8	47.4	N.A.	N.A.	N.A.	N.A.
Deposit Base Growth[E]							
OMB	N.A.	1.1	3.3	3.4	3.4	3.3	3.4
CBO	N.A.	4.5	4.5	5.5	5.5	5.5	5.5
FDIC	N.A.	4.5	4.5	N.A.	N.A.	N.A.	N.A.

Source: U.S. Congress, Congressional Budget Office, *CBO Projections of the Banking Industry and the BIF*, (Washington, D.C.: U.S. Government Printing Office), 1 April 1992, p. 60. *Primary source:* Congressional Budget Office (CBO), using data from the Office of Management and Budget (OMB) and the Federal Deposit Insurance Corporation (FDIC). *Notes:* N.A. = Not available. A. OMB projections have been converted to a cash basis; assumes premiums rise to $0.30 per $100 of assessable deposits by 1994; also includes special premium assessments beginning in 1992 as required in certain circumstances by the FDIC Improvement Act of 1991. B. Assumes premiums increase to $0.30 per $100 of assessable deposits by 1994. C. FDIC projections released October 1991; calendar year basis; D. Except for 1991, does not include a reserve for future losses. E. Annual growth rate in percent.

★ 100 ★

Banking and Finance

Bank Insurance Fund Financial Projections, 1987-2006

[Millions of dollars]

Year	Total income	Total expense	BIF net income (loss)	Total D-- Bank Dep. Self-insured deposits	Insured deposits as a percent of total deposits			Est. yield on BIF's treasury securities	Total domestic bank at end of the	
					All banks	Savings bank	Commercial bank		Commercial banks	Savings banks
2006	6,316.7	2,037.2	4,279.5	4,592,406	74.9%	96.0%	74.0%	5.50%	4,611,410	186,506
2005	3,938.1	1,960.6	3,977.5	4,415,775	74.9%	96.0%	74.0%	5.50%	4,412,833	182,849
2004	3,581.3	1,886.9	3,694.3	4,245,937	74.9%	96.0%	74.0%	5.50%	4,222,807	179,264
2003	3,245.1	1,815.9	3,429.2	4,082,632	74.9%	96.8%	74.0%	5.50%	4,040,963	175,749
2002	4,928.4	1,747.7	3,180.7	3,925,608	75.8%	96.8%	74.0%	5.50%	3,866,950	172,303
2001	4,630.0	1,682.1	2,947.9	3,774,623	75.8%	96.8%	74.0%	5.50%	3,700,431	168,924
2000	4,348.8	1,418.9	2,729.9	3,629.445	75.8%	96.8%	74.0%	5.50%	3,341,082	165,612
1999	4,084.0	1,588.2	2,525.8	3,489,851	75.8%	96.8%	74.0%	5.50%	3,388,596	162,365
1998	3,034.6	1,499.8	2,334.9	3,333,626	75.8%	96.8%	74.0%	5.50%	3,242,675	159,181
1997	3,399.8	1,443.4	2,136.3	3,226,363	75.1%	96.8%	74.0%	5.50%	3,103,038	156,060
1996	3,379.0	1,405.2	1,973.8	3,102,465	75.1%	96.0%	74.0%	5.50%	2,969,415	153,000
1995	4,868.4	1,792.5	3,075.9	2,963,139	75.1%	96.0%	74.0%	5.50%	2,841,545	150,000
1994	6,377.0	3,155.0	3,222.0	2,868,403	75.2%	96.0%	74.0%	5.50%	2,719,182	160,000
1993	6,102.8	7,875.0	1,772.2	2,758,080	75.4%	96.0%	74.0%	5.50%	2,602,088	170,000
1992	6,074.1	12,302.5	6,228.4	2,682,000	75.5%	96.0%	74.0%	5.50%	2,490,036	185,000
1991	5,750.0	8,520.0	2,770.0	2,550,000	76.8%	96.2%	74.3%	5.00%	2,382,810	200,566
1990	3,838.3	4,586.4	748.1	2,540,930	75.9%	94.8%	76.2%	8.30%	2,336,551	212,630
1989	3,494.6	4,799.0	3,304.4	2,465,922	76.8%	93.5%	74.2%	9.16%	2,236,737	223,934
1988	3,347.7	6,628.1	3,200.2	2,330,768	75.1%	95.4%	73.0%	8.64%	2,116,380	220,934
1987	3,319.4	2,488.2	831.2	2,201,549	75.3%	95.0%	73.3%	9.39%	1,993,383	204,800

Source: U.S. Congress, Congressional Budget Office, *CBO Projections of the Banking Industry and the BIF*, (Washington, D.C.: U.S. Government Printing Office), 1 April 1992, p. 66. *Primary source:* Ely & Company, Inc., Alexandria, Virginia. *Notes:* Also includes BIF history from 1961-1986, as well as BIF income, expense, and end-of-year figures according to individual categories. Explanatory notes and assumptions supplied separately.

★ 101 ★

Banking and Finance

Savings and Commercial Bank Reserve Ratios, 1985-2005

[Reserve ratio at year end]

Year	Commercial bank reserve ratio at year end	BIF reserve ratio at year end	Savings Bank reserve ratio at year end
1985	1.15	1.15	-.37
1987	1.15	1.15	-.15
1989	.75	.75	0
1991	.50	.50	2.1
1993	.05	.05	
1995	1.30	.37	
1997	1.4	.37	

[Continued]

★ 101 ★

Savings and Commercial Bank Reserve Ratios, 1985-2005

[Continued]

Year	Commercial bank reserve ratio at year end	BIF reserve ratio at year end	Savings Bank reserve ratio at year end
1999	1.67	.55	
2001	1.80	.87	
2003	1.95	1.05	
2005	2.12	1.15	

Source: U.S. Congress, Congressional Budget Office, *CBO Projections of the Banking Industry and the BIF*, (Washington, D.C.: U.S. Government Printing Office), 1 April 1992, p. 101. *Primary source:* C 1992 Ely & Company, Inc., Alexandria, Virginia. *Notes:* Magnitudes estimated from published chart. Data for 1991 is estimated and data for 1992-2005 is projected. Magnitude of negative savings bank reserve ratio becomes irrelevant after 1991.

★ 102 ★

Banking and Finance

Yield on One-year Treasury Bills, 1993-2004

[Percent]

Year	As of January 14
1993	.4
1995	5.60
1996	6.60
1997	7.00
1998	7.50
1998	7.80
2001	8.00
2002	8.20
2003	8.25
2004	8.30

Source: Thomas T. Vogel, Jr., "Rates Appear to Shed the 'Inflation Premium,' in *The Wall Street Journal*, 23 August 1993, pp. C1, C19. *Notes:* Inflationary expectations were calculated by studying the relationship between prices for different bond futures contracts, as of January 14, 1993. Source also includes projections as of August 10, 1993. Magnitudes estimated from published chart.

★ 103 ★

Banking and Finance

Decline in Number of Bank Branches, 1989-2000

"The decline in branches is pronounced. Some 4,000 bank and thrift branches closed from 1990 to 1992. Seamus P. McMahon, a vice-president at Booz, Allen & Hamilton Inc., predicts that there will be as many as 15,000 fewer branches by the end of the decade."

[Thousand of banks and thrift branches]

Year	Banks and thrift branches
1989	83
1990	85
1991	81
1992	79
2000	65

Source: Kelley Holland, et al, "Next Bank, 100 Miles," in *Business Week*, 10 May 1993, p. 55. *Primary source:* Office of Thrift Supervision, Booz Allen & Hamilton Inc. *Note:* Magnitudes estimated from published chart.

★ 104 ★

Banking and Finance

High, Low, and Average Annual Rates of Return for S&P Stocks, 1950-1999

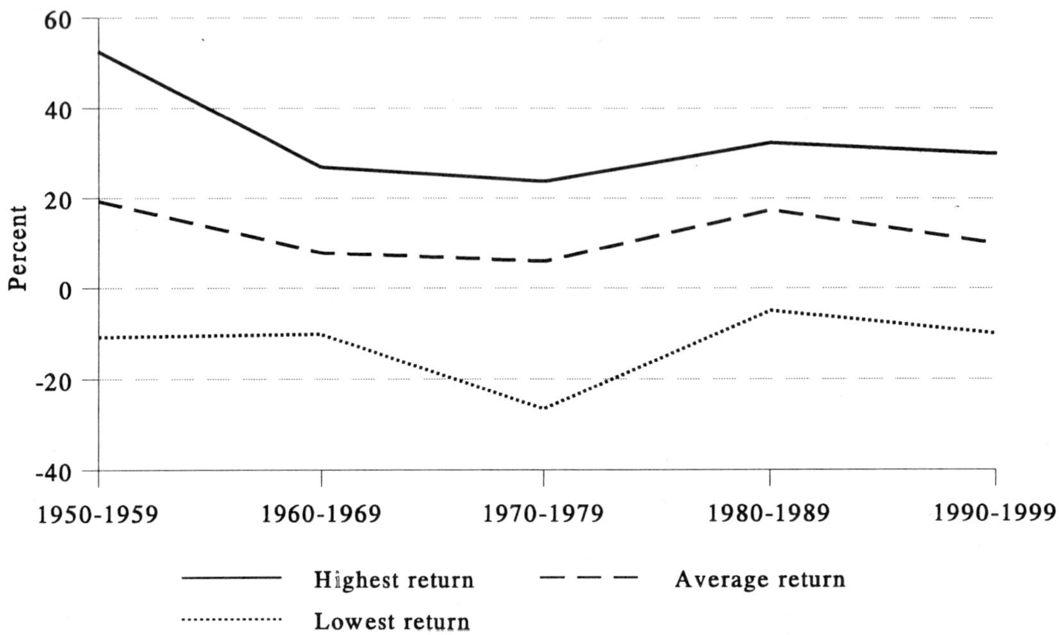

"When average returns on the market are high, the prospect of making 20 percentage points more or less than the norm is either joyful or blah—but not terrible. In the 1980s, stocks returned an annual average of 17.5%, so the *expected* deviations would have ranged from a high of 37.5% (17.5 plus 20) to a low of minus 2.5% (17.5 minus 20). The *actual* high was a 32.4% gain in 1980, while the low was a 4.9% loss in 1981.

"But the expected 10% average annual return in the 1990s, which is the average stocks have posted since 1926, subjects investors to far greater risks. Normal swings could produce annual highs of 30% or losses of 10%. And who's to say that the market will stay within its range? In the Seventies, stocks swung well wide of the expected band and investors lost a bundle. Such prospects are sobering. Says Roger Hertog, president of Sanford C. Bernstein: 'We are in a period of tremendous caution'."

[Percent]

Year	Highest return	Average return	Lowest return
1950-1959	52.6	19.4	-10.8
1960-1969	26.9	7.8	-10.1
1970-1979	23.8	5.9	-26.5
1980-1989	32.4	17.5	-4.9
1990-1999	30	10	-10

Source: Susan E. Kuhn, "The New Perilous Stock Market," in *Fortune*, 27 December 1993, p. 54. *Primary source:* Sanford C. Bernstein, Ibbotson Associates. *Notes:* Based on historical volatility, annual returns in the 1990s could swing as much as 20 percentage points above or below the expected annual return.

Chapter 3
CONSTRUCTION AND HOUSING

Government Programs and Impacts

★ 105 ★

Budget Summary of U.S. Department of Housing and Urban Development, 1993-1999

[Millions of dollars]

	1993 (actual)	1994	1995	1996	1997	1998	1999
Discretionary Spending							
BA	25,500	25,100	26,100	33,500	35,200	37,500	38,800
OL	25,000	27,500	29,500	30,500	31,200	31,200	31,900
Discretionary Budget Authority	25,524	25,105	26,064	33,537	35,152	37,544	38,785
Discretionary Outlays	24,965	27,498	29,477	30,514	31,183	31,163	31,892
Mandatory and Receipts PAYGO Proposals to Reform Disposition of Multifamily Housing Properties (deficit impact)	NA	-520	-	-	-	-	-
Nondiscretionary Budget Authority	26,500	25,600	27,500	34,800	36,300	38,500	39,700
Nondiscretionary Outlays	25,200	25,500	27,700	28,400	28,100	27,900	28,500

Source: Executive Office of the President of the United States, Office of Management and Budget, *Budget of the United States Government* (Washington, D.C.: U.S. Government Printing Office, 1994), pp. 28, 237-8, 240, 250, 252. *Notes:* Combines data from tables I-3, 7-3, 7-4, 7-6, 7-11, and 7-13. BA = Budget Authority; OL = Outlays.

★ 106 ★

Government Programs and Impacts

Proposed Housing and Urban Development Investments, 1993-1999

[Millions of dollars]

		1993 Enacted	Estimate		Change: 1994 to 1995	Estimate			
			1994	1995		1996	1997	1998	1999
Housing and Urban Development (totals)	BA	1,972	2,782	5,140	2,358	4,993	5,162	5,999	6,751
	OL	7,142	7,732	8,511	779	9,484	10,527	11,486	12,525
Detail:									
Multifamily property disposition	BA	93	555	733	178	763	858	511	779
	OL	93	102	119	17	142	170	200	333
Community partnership against crime	BA	...	...	265	265	265	265	265	265
	OL	...	...	19	19	152	265	265	265
Incremental housing vouchers	BA	1,307	1,404	2,743	1,339	2,812	2,882	4,062	4,542
	OL	6,877	7,407	7,863	456	8,410	9,040	9,708	10,471
Homeless programs: homeless assistance grants and innovative homeless initiative programs	BA	572	823	1,250	427	1,000	1,000	1,000	1,000
	OL	172	223	509	286	631	899	1,156	1,295
Moving to independence	BA	...	...	149	149	153	157	161	165
	OL	...	...	1	1	149	153	157	161

Source: Executive Office of the President of the United States, Office of Management and Budget, *Budget of the United States Government*, (Washington, D.C.: U.S. Government Printing Office, 1994), pp. 243, 245. *Note:* BA = Budget Authority; OL = Outlays.

★ 107 ★

Government Programs and Impacts

Housing Investment Proposals, 1994-1998

[Millions of dollars]

	1994	1995	1996	1997	1998	1994-1997 Total
Housing:						
100% vouchers (100,000 units)	7	65	222	422	654	716
Preservation and restoration of assisted housing	37	155	282	384	519	858
Supportive housing program	...	22	81	138	183	241
Mortgage revenue bonds (tax incentive)	104	145	160	172	174	581
Extend low-income housing tax credit (tax incentive)	214	478	791	1,114	1,442	2,597
Real estate investment (tax incentive)	254	387	164	17	-158	822
Urban Partnership Against Crime	6	52	116	138	133	312
Severely distressed public housing	...	17	68	121	167	206

[Continued]

★ 107 ★

Housing Investment Proposals, 1994-1998

[Continued]

	1994	1995	1996	1997	1998	1994-1997 Total
HOPE youthbuild	...	5	19	34	48	58
Subtotal, Housing	622	1,326	1,903	2,540	3,162	6,391

Source: Executive Office of the President of the United States, Office of Management and Budget, *A Vision of Change for America*, (Washington, D.C.: U.S. Government Printing Office, February 1993), p. 136. *Note:* HOPE = Home Ownership and Opportunity for People Everywhere.

★ 108 ★

Government Programs and Impacts

Expiring Section 8 Contracts, 1993-1996

"The Section 8 program is the largest single federal housing assistance program, providing housing subsidies to more than two million households. Under Section 8, the government pays a housing owner the difference between a negotiated 'contract rent' and 30 percent of a resident's adjusted income...

"The Section 8 program was first authorized in 1974 and began full-scale operations in 1976. During the 1990s, millions of contracts with public housing authorities and private owners will expire, requiring Congressional action to prevent low income residents from losing their housing assistance."

[Billions of dollars]

Fiscal year	Units with expiring contracts	Funds needed to renew the contracts
1993	197,416	$5.8
1994	173,401	5.3
1995	222,023	7.0
1996	367,840	11.7
Total	960,680	$29.8

Source: Edward B. Lazere, et al., *A Place to Call Home: The Low Income Housing Crisis Continues* (Washington, D.C.: Center on Budget and Policy Priorities/Low Income Housing Information Service, December 1991), p. 58.

★ 109 ★

Government Programs and Impacts

Outlays and Budget Authority: Commerce and Housing Credit, 1993-1999

[Billions of dollars]

Function	1993 Actual	Estimate					
		1994	1995	1996	1997	1998	1999
Outlays							
Commerce and housing credit	-22.7	0.5	-5.5	-9.0	-5.7	-5.4	-3.9
On-budget	(-24.2)	(-1.2)	(-8.7)	(-9.2)	(-5.2)	(-4.3)	(-2.4)
Off-budget	(1.4)	(1.7)	(3.3)	(0.2)	(-0.5)	(-1.1)	(-1.5)
Budget Authority							
Commerce and housing credit	9.9	28.2	11.3	8.1	5.4	5.9	5.0
On-budget	(7.7)	(23.9)	(5.9)	(6.0)	(5.1)	(4.4)	(5.0)
Off-budget	(2.2)	(4.3)	(5.3)	(2.1)	(0.3)	(1.6)	1

Source: Executive Office of the President of the United States, Office of Management and Budget, *Budget of the United States Government*, (Washington, D.C.: U.S. Government Printing Office, 1994), pp. 251, 253. *Note:* 1. $50 million or less.

Housing: Prices, Values, and Starts

★ 110 ★

Housing Values, 2000

"What is likely to happen in the next several years to the value of owner-occupied housing? Some analysts have argued that home values will decline substantially during the 1990s. Economists Gregory Mankiw and David Weil have been especially pessimistic, estimating that the inflation-adjusted price of housing may decline by as much as 47% between now and 2010. In their widely-cited 1989 *Regional Science and Urban Economics* article 'The Baby Boom, the Baby Bust, and the Housing Market,' the twosome argues that the recent past's increase in the demand for owner-occupied housing, seen especially in the late 1970s, came about largely through changes in the age distribution of the population. Mankiw and Weil suggest that a larger population of people in their peak home-buying years may have increased the average per-household demand and, in turn, the asset price for owner-occupied residences.

"Because demographic forecasts for the 1990s and the early part of the 21st century indicate substantial declines in the population segments responsible for the home-buying boom of the 1970s and 1980s, Mankiw and Weil predict that demand will diminish and that inflation-adjusted housing prices will fall substantially. If this dire forecast proves even remotely true, then there are dark days ahead for the individuals, businesses, and governments that are affected by the value of the nation's housing.

[Continued]

★ 110 ★

Housing Values, 2000

[Continued]

"Such a pervasive decline in home values across the U.S. is seen as quite unlikely, however, by many economists. The [following projections] offer the more optimistic estimate that the aggregate stock of owner-occupied housing will rise in value by almost 25%, in inflation-adjusted terms, during the 1990s. An increase of such magnitude would make this decade a better period for home ownership than were the 1980s, though the gain would fall short of the 30% rise in inflation-adjusted values experienced during the 1970s.

"U.S. population is expected to rise by approximately 18 million people during the next ten years. If the average household size and the aggregate home ownership rate remain constant during the 1990s, then the number of owner-occupant households will increase in proportion to population growth. Of course, changes in the rate of home ownership, and in the proportion of each group represented by heads of households, are likely to be observed.

"One factor that surely will affect future trends in the home owernship rate is the expected change in the age distribution of the population. We will become an older society during the 1990s. In particular, growth is expected among the 45-64 age group relative to the 25-34 age group. Because the ownership rate traditionally has been higher for older age groups, the number of owner households will likely increase in the coming decade, in contrast to the Mankiw-Weil finding, even if the ownership rate within each group stays constant. A precise estimate of this aging's effect on the number of owners is, however, difficult to achieve.

"The home ownership rates traditionally observed among age groups may also change during the 1990s, especially if there are changes in average household incomes and in the price of owning relative to that of renting. In fact, the responsiveness of these ownership rates to changes in income and to the relative price of owning versus renting is an important adjustment mechanism incorporated into the analysis underlying this article. If no other factors change, then a higher average income increases both the demand for housing per household and the number of owner-occupant households in the country. These increases, in turn, place upward pressure on the asset price of housing, and this upward price pressure forces the amount of housing per household and the number of owner-occupant households back downward.

"A statistical model of the housing market based on these considerations has been used in generating forecasts of housing market conditions in the year 2000. Three sets of forecasts are provided: the base case, the best case, and the worst case. The key assumptions of each case pertain to changes expected in the economic and demographic factors that work together to determine the value of housing. Some assumptions are common to the three cases: for example, population in the year 2000 is expected to have increased by 7.2% to 268.75 million people, and the proportion of the population between 45 and 64 years of age is expected to rise from 29% to 31.8% by the end of this decade.

"The base case provides for no change in the relative price of owning versus renting and for a 5% increase in the inflation-adjusted replacement cost, an outcome consistent with the idea that the housing supply will be more hindered in the 1990s by zoning issues, environmental concerns, and limited availability of land than it has been in the past. The forecast for this scenario is further based on the assumption that each percentage increase in the population of 45-64 year-olds is accompanied by a .33% increase in the number of home owners. This factor and others that determine ownership rates show the population increase, in this base case, to be accompanied by a projected 17.3% increase in the number of owner-occupant households.

[Continued]

★ 110 ★

Housing Values, 2000

[Continued]

"Income, adjusted for inflation, is expected to grow by 14% during the decade, down from growth rates of 18% during the 1980s and 16% during the 1970s. Housing per owner household is projected to rise by 6.7%. This increase is less than the projected 14% rise in income, since a predicted 7.3% upward movement in the inflation-adjusted price of a constant quality housing unit reduces the response of housing consumption to higher income. Most of the rise in the asset price is generated by the 5% increase in replacement cost, while the remainder results from a 24% (6.7% + 17.3%) increase in housing demand, i.e., the sum of the percentage changes in housing services and the number of owning households. The key result of this base case forecast is an increase in the inflation-adjusted value of the owner-occupied housing stock to $7.38 trillion, a 31.2% increase over the 1990 level, by the year 2000. The base case forecast is considerably more optimistic than is that presented by Mankiw and Weil, even though it incorporates an assumed slowdown in economic growth relative to the two previous decades...

"An ongoing study of our nation's urban housing, which this author has conducted with Donald Leavens and Orawin Velz of the National Association of Realtors (NAR), may be a promising source of information about housing in America's metropolitan areas. Preliminary results suggest that NAR's Existing Home Sales Survey Data, in combination with other information, might provide for better forecasting at the regional and local levels. The NAR data may be even more valuable if ways can be found to improve the reliability of reporting and especially, if more information can be provided about the size and quality of each house sold. With such information, market observers could develop better indicators of movements in the constant quality price of housing. Academic researchers should be encouraged to work with real estate boards and other industry representatives to develop even better data sources. Such cooperative efforts can greatly enhance our understanding of the country's housing markets."

Source: James R. Follain, "Housing Values in the Year 2000," in *Illinois Real Estate Letter*, Winter/Spring 1993, pp. 2-3, 5-7.

★ 111 ★

Housing: Prices, Values, and Starts

Home Prices, 1992-1997

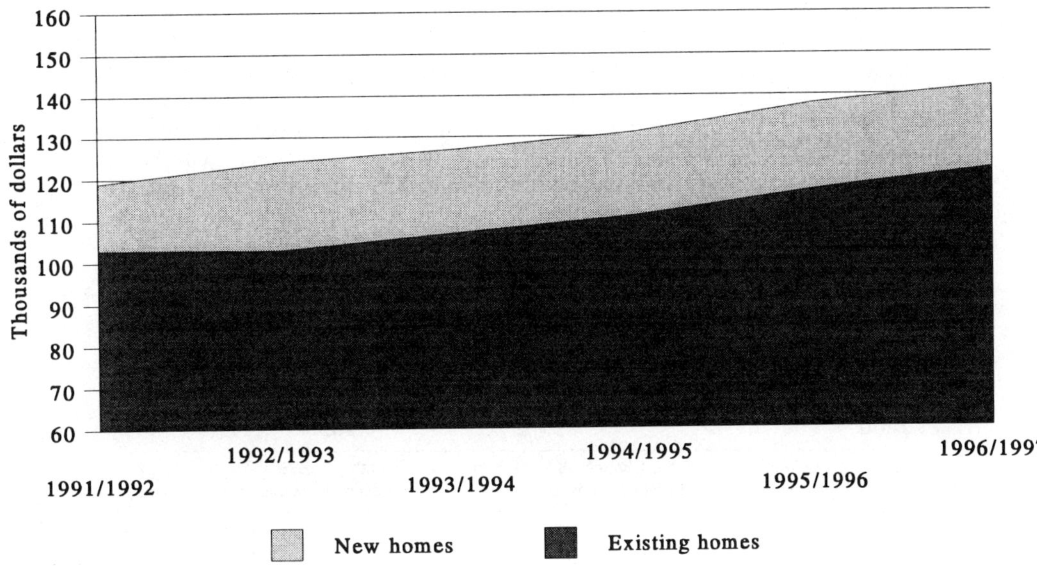

"Prices of both new and existing homes grew faster than inflation in 1993. The median price of new homes rose 4.1%, while the price of resales increased 3.0%; consumer prices climbed a mere 2.9% in 1993. However, the increase in home prices was not seen everywhere in the country. Prices of existing homes fell 0.9% in the West and dropped 0.4% in the Northeast.

"According to the NAR forecast, home prices will continue to climb at a faster pace than inflation. By 1995, prices of both existing and new homes will rise at an annual rate of over 4%."

[Thousands of dollars]

	New homes	Existing homes
1991/1992	119	103
1992/1993	124	103
1993/1994	127	107
1994/1995	131	111
1995/1996	138	117
1996/1997	142	122

Source: Eileen A. Neely, "Home Prices: Healthy Increases Continue," in *Real Estate Outlook: Market Trends & Insights*, February 1994, p. 4. *Primary source:* National Association of Realtors (NAR). *Note:* Magnitudes estimated from published chart.

★ 112 ★

Housing: Prices, Values, and Starts

Demographic Trends in Realty Purchases, 1990-2000

"With the aging of the baby boomers come trends in demographics and household formation that will create niche marketing opportunities for savvy realtors. Increasing levels of immigration will help offset the so called 'baby bust' and may increase home ownership rates as well as sales volume in the late '90s. The Harvard Joint Center for Housing Studies now predicts that the population will grow faster than was thought previously, primarily due to these higher levels of immigration. Higher household formation generally means more housing sales. In particular, niche markets will exist in the first-time, trade-down and recreation/second homebuyer segments."

[Millions of households]

1990	92.3
1995	98.9
2000	105.4

Source: Lisa Cole, "Planning for Change: A Look into the 21st Century," in *Real Estate Outlook: Market Trends & Insights*, February 1994, p. 10. *Primary source:* Harvard Joint Center for Housing Studies.

★ 113 ★

Housing: Prices, Values, and Starts

Home Sales and Starts, 1992-1996

[Thousands]

	1992	1993	1994	1995	1996
Total Single-Family Sales	4,519	4,889	5,197	4,953	4,854
Existing Single-Family Sales	3,520	3,799	3,980	3,792	3,744
New Single-Family Sales	610	669	752	708	684
Housing Starts	1,200	1,285	1,446	1,393	1,362
Single-Family Units	1,030	1,123	1,255	1,197	1,145
Multifamily Units	170	162	191	196	217
2-4 Family Units	31	31	36	38	44
5+ Family Units	139	131	155	158	173
Mobile Homes Shipped	211	254	270	250	243
Percent change - Year Ago					
Total Single-Family Sales	12.0	8.2	6.3	-4.7	-2.0
Existing Single-Family Sales	9.3	7.9	4.8	-4.7	-1.3
New Single-Family Sales	19.8	9.7	12.4	-5.8	-3.4
Housing Starts	18.3	7.1	12.5	-3.6	-2.2
Single-Family Units	22.6	9.1	11.7	-4.6	-4.3
Multifamily Units	-2.3	-4.7	17.9	2.8	10.5

[Continued]

★ 113 ★

Home Sales and Starts, 1992-1996

[Continued]

	1992	1993	1994	1995	1996
2-4 Family Units	-14.7	-0.7	16.6	7.2	14.3
5+ Family Units	0.7	-5.6	18.5	1.8	9.6

Source: "U.S. Economic Outlook: February 1994," in *Real Estate Outlook: Market Trends & Insights*, February 1994, p. 18. *Primary source:* Forecast produced using Lawrence H. Meyer & Associates' model of the U.S. economy. Assumptions and simulations by Dr. John Tuccilo and Eileen A. Neely. *Notes:* Total single-family sales equals single-family resales plus 97% of single-family housing starts. Quarterly figures are seasonally adjusted annual rates. Source also includes more detailed quarterly data for 1993-1995.

★ 114 ★

Housing: Prices, Values, and Starts

Lease Aging Profile, 1992-2001

"This snapshot of the square feet, cost, and number of leases committed in existing agreements can help managers identify how and when to restructure occupancy costs."

[Rentable square feet in thousands; total lease commitment in millions; number of leases coming due in thousands]

Year	Leases coming due	Rentable square feet	Total lease commitment
1992	83	660	13.4
1993	86	780	15.2
1994	77	670	13.5
1995	42	450	7.2
1996	43	580	11.2
1997	17	270	4.9
1998	0	0	0.0
1999	3	70	1.6
2000	1	20	0.0
2001	4	90	1.8

Source: "Lease Aging Profile," in *Harvard Business Review*, May-June 1993, p. 130. *Note:* Some magnitudes estimated from published chart.

★ 115 ★

Housing: Prices, Values, and Starts

Homeownership Rates, 1940-2000

"According to Fannie Mae chief economist David Berson, the national homeownership rate will set a new record by the turn of the century, when, Berson says, an estimated 68.1 percent of the nation's households will own their own homes. That would mean some 9 million households shift from renting to owning over the next six years...

"Homeownership rates could go even higher if certain public policy proposals, like higher FHA loan limits and lender outreach efforts to minorities, go through. Bersons's best-case scenario has ownership topping 69 percent by 2000—which would mean some 12 million new buyers between now and then."

[Percent]

Year	Rate
1940	43.6
1950	55.0
1960	61.9
1970	62.9
1980	64.4
1990	63.9
2000[1]	66.3
2000[2]	68.1
2000[3]	69.2

Source: Brad German, "Homeownership Rates: Ready for Lift-Off?" in *Builder*, February 1994, p. 36. *Primary source:* National Association of Home Builders of the United States (NAHB), Fannie Mae. *Notes:* FHA = Federal Housing Administration. 1. Based on current rate of improvement. 2. Based on Fannie Mae prediction. 3. Based on best case scenario.

★ 116 ★

Housing: Prices, Values, and Starts

Low-Cost Housing, 1993-2003

"Designers can now build prototypes almost instantly using computer images of a proposed part, then guiding a laser beam over a vat of light-sensitive resin and building up the prototype layer by layer.

"On a larger scale, the technique could be used to build low-cost housing one layer at a time, says Joseph Pegna, an assistant professor of mechanical engineering at Rensselaer Polytechnic Institute in Troy, New York. He envisions a huge robot that could deposit thin layers of various materials, following a script included in the computer design. Wiring and plumbing would be built in, and appliances could be set into place as the house rose.

"Pegna believes that such building techniques could be a reality within 10 years."

Source: "Houses Built Layer by Layer," in *The Futurist*, 1993, p. 8. *Primary source:* Rensselaer Polytechnic Institute, News and Communications, Troy, New York 12180.

★ 117 ★

Housing: Prices, Values, and Starts

Alternate Projections in Housing Prices, 1994-2010

"For the past few years, the real estate and construction industries, already staggering under the burden of a depressed market, have been further dispirited by a forecast predicting that real housing prices will fall dramatically by 2010. The forecast, produced by two economists, N. Gregory Mankiw of Harvard University and David N. Weil of Brown University, predicts that by 2010 real housing prices in the United States will have declined by 47 percent. Such a scenario, of course, would be devastating to homeowners, bankers, builders and investors.

"In their 1989 article in *Regional Science and Urban Economics*, Mankiw and Weil linked future housing prices to America's changing age structure. During the 1970s and 1980s, a larger-than-usual portion of the U.S. population were in their home-buying years. In the 1990s, the aging of the population would reduce housing demand, Mankiw and Weil reasoned, causing real (inflation-adjusted) prices to slide downward...

[Continued]

★ 117 ★

Alternate Projections in Housing Prices, 1994-2010

[Continued]

"Now comes a study by Patric H. Hendershott of Ohio State University, published by the National Bureau of Economic Research, which challenges the validity of the Mankiw-Weil forecast. In its place, Hendershott offers a model that predicts a much brighter future for housing prices. To the non-housing-industry business leader, the real significance of Hendershott's work is that it exposes some of the pitfalls of using demographic data to make business and economic decisions.

"To make their forecast, Mankiw and Weil used a simple supply-and-demand model. According to the model, the supply of housing responds positively to changes in real prices. The demand for housing, on the other hand, responds negatively to changes in real prices and positively to a 'demand shifter.' Because both supply and demand vary with the real price of housing, the influence of real price change on supply and demand is pretty much eliminated. That makes the demand shifter the variable that moves things around. In other words, to forecast real housing prices all you need to do is look at changes in the demand shifter. And Mankiw and Weil, of course, decided that the demand shifter was a demographic variable—the changing age distribution of the U.S. population...

"To link the age distribution of Americans to U.S. housing prices, Mankiw and Weil calculated 99 coefficients—which they called 'propensities to consume housing space'—assigning one to every possible age year. Once they did this, they could forecast the real housing prices for any future year merely by looking at the forecast for the age distribution of the U.S. population in that year. As the Census Bureau adjusted its forecasts, the housing price predictions would similarly change.

"And so the gloomy forecast was generated. According to Mankiw and Weil's coefficients, as individuals pass into their 40s their propensity to consume housing space decreases steadily. Thus when the proportion of Americans over 40 rises past a critical point, housing demand will become so soft that real housing prices will drop...

"But compelling as the Mankiw-Weil model may be, it doesn't, as Patric Hendershott points out in his study, hold up to scrutiny. Although the model worked well when it was used to 'hindcast' the 1950s and '60s, its forecasts were increasingly inaccurate when they were compared with the actual numbers for the '70s and '80s. If the Mankiw-Weil model cannot properly forecast the preceding two decades, Hendershott concludes, there is little reason to place much credence in its predictions for the 1990s and beyond...

"The Hendershott revision produced a somewhat better fit for the 1970s and 1980s than did the original model, casting Mankiw and Weil's gloomy forecast in doubt.

[Continued]

★ 117 ★

Alternate Projections in Housing Prices, 1994-2010

[Continued]

"Using the revised model, Hendershott predicts that if there is any decline in real housing prices during the next 20 years, it will be mild. This would be the best of all possible worlds. Housing would become more affordable, but the value of housing assets in the portfolios of investors and homeowners would rise almost as fast as any inflation that should occur.

"A 1993 multiple-variable housing-price model produced by James R. Follain, chairman of the economics department at Syracuse University, similarly debunks the Mankiw-Weil projections. The median estimate calculated by Follain's model promises a 5 percent increase in real housing prices by the year 2000" [See entry 110].

Source: Norman Weinberg, "The Art of Forecasting: How Housing-Price Projections Were Led Astray," in *Forecast*, July/August 1994, pp. 17-18, 20.

Construction

★ 118 ★

Homebuilding and Housing Prices, 1991-2000

"It is projected that an average of 1.3 to 1.5 million new housing units (including mobile homes) will be built annually in the 1990s, compared to about 1.75 million in the 1980s and nearly 2 million in the 1970s. This will be a negative influence on residential construction industries and the demand for household furnishings. Because new units will tend to be larger and more expensive, on average, the value of home construction may not decline.

"This study disputes forecasts of severe declines in housing prices. The demand for higher-priced housing will increase as the baby boomers age, although the trend will be moderated by the fact that the baby boomers will be less successful in their quest for higher incomes than earlier generations. At the same time, prices will sag for small and lower-quality dwellings, occupied mainly by young people and others with low incomes.

"The future strength of housing and the prices of other assets will be closely related to future interest rates. Prospective home buyers are greatly influenced by mortgage finance costs. If inflation is moderate and interest rates are allowed to subside, housing prices could rise faster than other prices."

Source: Library of Congress, Congressional Research Service, *Demographic Change and the Economy of the Nineties*, (Washington, D.C.: U.S. Government Printing Office, 1991), p. IX.

★ 119 ★

Construction

Nonresidential Construction, 1991-2000

"Office and commercial construction soared in the 1980s, when the nation's supply of office and shopping space nearly doubled. The construction boom occurred largely because of the generous depreciation allowances provided in the tax reduction act of 1981. Deregulation of the thrift institutions also encouraged lenders to make loans on nonresidential projects despite rising vacancy rates.

"Commercial real estate now faces a prolonged depression while the present high vacancy rates come down. It is likely to take several years for vacancy rates to come down to healthy levels. Because of demographic trends, the need for new structures will grow more slowly than in the past. Hence, office and commercial construction may never regain the levels reached in the 1980s.

"Building for manufacturing and utilities, which slumped in the 1980s, could increase over the next several years. After the year 2000, the demographic slowdown is likely to reduce the need for most types of construction."

Source: Library of Congress, Congressional Research Service, *Demographic Change and the Economy of the Nineties* (Washington, D.C.: U.S. Government Printing Office, 1991), p. IX.

★ 120 ★

Construction

State Wastewater Facility Needs, 2008

[Millions of dollars]

State	Year 2008 needs
1 New York	$12,721
2 CALIFORNIA	6,539
3 FLORIDA	6,186
4 Massachusetts	5,836
5 TEXAS	4,975
6 NEW JERSEY	3,754
7 [Ohio]	3,579
8 [Michigan]	3,321
9 [Illinois]	2,958
10 WASHINGTON	2,685
11 NORTH CAROLINA	1,799
12 [Indiana]	1,721
13 [Pennsylvania]	1,644
14 Puerto Rico	1,592
15 Tennessee	1,467
16 [Kentucky]	1,457

[Continued]

★ 120 ★

State Wastewater Facility Needs, 2008

[Continued]

State	Year 2008 needs
17 [Wisconsin]	1,399
18 Connecticut	1,392
19 Oregon	1,273
20 Missouri	1,222
21 Louisiana	1,189
22 Minnesota	1,106
23 GEORGIA	1,007
24 ARIZONA	979
25 [West Virginia]	976
26 Virginia	957
27 MARYLAND[1]	919
28 NEW HAMPSHIRE	854
29 Alabama	781
30 Kansas	720
31 SOUTH CAROLINA	684
32 [Iowa]	646
33 UTAH	583
34 Mississippi	548
35 Oklahoma	476
36 HAWAII	413
37 Rhode Island	408
38 Arkansas	370
39 Maine	341
40 [District of Columbia]	278
41 ALASKA	221
42 Vermont	209
43 COLORADO	196
44 NEVADA	165
45 NEW MEXICO	130
46 DELAWARE	127
47 Idaho	124
48 [Nebraska]	114
49 South Dakota	87
50 [Montana]	69
51 [North Dakota]	34
52 [Wyoming]	18
Total	$83,249

Source: Library of Congress, Congressional Research Service, *Demographic Change and the Economy of the Nineties* (Washington, D.C.: U.S. Government Printing Office, 1991), p. 153. *Notes:* States shown in all capital letters are projected to experience above-average population gains over the next 20 years. States shown in brackets are those projected to experience population decreases, according to Census Bureau reports. Table excludes Guam, American Samoa, Pacific Trust Territories and Virgin Islands. 1. Median.

★ 121 ★

Construction

Growth in State Wastewater Facility Needs, 1991-2010

[Millions of dollars]

State	Growth needs
1 FLORIDA	$2,202
2 TEXAS	1,669
3 CALIFORNIA	1,282
4 New York	1,038
5 NORTH CAROLINA	587
6 Tennessee	569
7 WASHINGTON	542
8 [Ohio]	438
9 ARIZONA	437
10 NEW JERSEY	403
11 GEORGIA	392
12 Massachusetts	391
13 [Kentucky]	349
14 Louisiana	335
15 Oregon	291
16 UTAH	291
17 Missouri	267
18 SOUTH CAROLINA	243
19 Kansas	235
20 Alabama	234
21 [Pennsylvania]	205
22 Minnesota	204
23 VIRGINIA	202
24 [Michigan]	196
25 [Wisconsin]	195
26 [Illinois]	194
27 Oklahoma[1]	191
28 HAWAII	177
29 NEW HAMPSHIRE	145
30 [Indiana]	139
31 Mississippi	138
32 [Iowa]	135
33 Connecticut	125
34 [West Virginia]	124
35 ALASKA	114
36 Arkansas	113
37 NEVADA	64
38 Idaho	59
39 Maine	53
40 MARYLAND	53
41 DELAWARE	45
42 Rhode Island	44
43 NEW MEXICO	38
44 COLORADO	33
45 Puerto Rico	23
46 [Nebraska]	15

[Continued]

★ 121 ★

Growth in State Wastewater Facility Needs, 1991-2010

[Continued]

State	Growth needs
47 [Montana]	12
48 Vermont	7
49 South Dakota	6
50 [District of Columbia]	4
51 [North Dakota]	3
52 [Wyoming]	1
Total	$15,252

Source: Library of Congress, Congressional Research Service, *Demographic Change and the Economy of the Nineties* (Washington, D.C.: U.S. Government Printing Office, 1991), p. 154. *Notes:* States shown in all capital letters are projected to experience above-average population gains over the next 20 years. States shown in brackets are those projected to experience population decreases, according to Census Bureau reports. Table excludes Guam, American Samoa, Pacific Trust Territories and Virgin Islands. 1. Median.

★ 122 ★

Construction

Supercities, 1993-1998

"With the world population constantly growing and putting ever more pressures on urban areas, the creativity of city planners will become extremely important during the next several decades.

"Many city design and renewal efforts around the world can be classified as super projects—macroengineering efforts seeking new, multidisciplinary approaches for transportation, commercial, residential, and industrial site planning and development. Some cities have already begun such efforts, and many of the ideas on the drawing boards for the city of the future may put past feats of construction and planning to shame...

"The U.S.- based World City Corporation has a project called the Phoenix World City under development. A cruise ship capable of carrying more than 5,000 passengers, it would truly be a floating city, with several medium-rise apartment units, marina, conference center, and many other amenities. Construction is scheduled to begin in early 1994 and completed by either 1997 or 1998."

Source: McKinley Conway, "Tomorrow's Supercities for Land, Sea, and Air," in *The Futurist*, May-June 1993, pp. 27-9.

Chapter 4
CRIME, LAW ENFORCEMENT, AND PRISONS

Federal Expenditures

★ 123 ★

Summary of U.S. Department of Justice Budget Projections, 1993-1999

"The 1995 budget marks a new beginning in America's fight against crime, illegal immigration, and drugs. It holds the line on the growth of our Federal crime control bureaucracy, invests in the communities and the people most affected by crime and drugs, and commits the resources required to ensure that violent criminals and serious drug traffickers serve stiff sentences behind bars. It proposes initiatives to put more police on our streets, provides innovative programs to prevent non-violent first-time offenders from becoming hardened criminals, and attacks hard-core drug use directly and with substantial new spending for treatment programs. The 1995 budget, together with the provisions and funding offered by the pending Violent Crime Control and Law Enforcement Act, will begin the shift in emphasis from a wholly Federal response to a response which empowers States and communities to fight crime and drug abuse locally. Finally, the budget will significantly improve border security and will upgrade efforts to restrain illegal immigration."

[Millions of dollars]

	1993 Actual	1994	1995	1996	1997	1998	1999
Discretionary Budget Authority	9,315	9,376	12,144	14,343	15,240	16,000	17,255
Discretionary Outlays	9,153	9,705	10,614	12,943	14,332	15,521	17,068
Mandatory and Receipts PAYGO Proposal:							
Deficit Reduction Resulting from Creation of a 15% surcharge against debtors	--	-39	-39	-39	-39	-39	-39
Proposed investments: Budget Authority (total)[1]	150	25	2,491	4,358	5,074	5,578	6,581
Proposed investments: Outlays (total)[1]	8	83	819	2,407	4,008	5,065	6,487
Federal Employment (full-time equivalent in thousands)	95.4	97.2	101.9	--	--	--	--

Source: Executive Office of the President of the United States, Office of Management and Budget, *Budget of the United States Government: Fiscal Year 1995* (Washington, D.C.: U.S. Government Printing Office, 1994), pp. 237-38, 240, 243, 248. *Notes:* 1. See entry 124 for detail. Table combines data from tables 7-3, 7-4, 7-6, 7-8, and 7-9.

★ 124 ★

Federal Expenditures

Proposed Investments in U.S. Department of Justice, 1993-1999

[Millions of dollars]

		1993 Enacted	Estimate		Change: 1994 to 1995	Estimate			
			1994	1995		1996	1997	1998	1999
Community policing	BA	150	25	1,720	1,695	2,070	2,270	1,900	...
	OL	8	83	444	361	1,074	1,879	2,085	1,631
Brady Bill/Criminal records upgrade	BA	...	...	100	100	100	...	...	...
	OL	...	...	22	22	57	73	43	5
Border security and illegal immigration	BA	...	...	300	300	350	350	350	350
	OL	...	...	255	255	328	348	350	350
Other crime bill (miscellaneous bureaus)	BA	...	...	303	303	1,767	2,380	3,250	6,150
	OL	...	...	44	44	883	1,637	2,510	4,421
Employer sanctions and naturalization initiatives	BA	...	...	68	68	71	74	78	81
	OL	...	...	54	54	65	71	77	80

Source: Executive Office of the President of the United States, Office of Management and Budget, *Budget of the United States Government: Fiscal Year 1995* (Washington, D.C.: U.S. Government Printing Office, 1994), p. 245.

Government Expenditures

★ 125 ★

Federal and State, and Local Law Enforcement Expenditures, 1990-1998

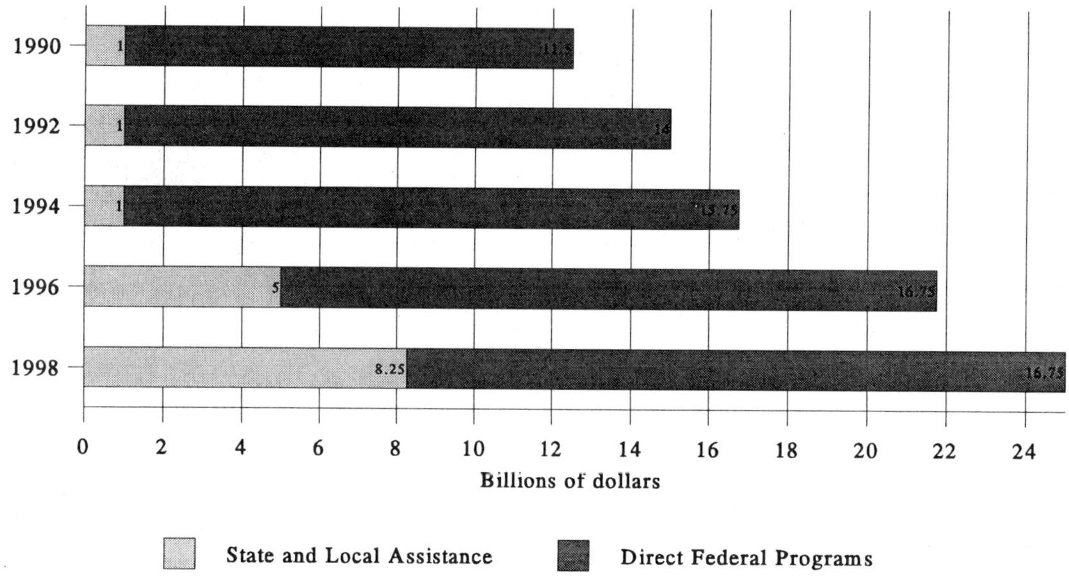

[Billions of dollars]

	1990	1992	1994	1996	1998
State and Local Assistance	1.00	1.00	1.00	5.00	8.25
Direct Federal Programs	11.50	14.00	15.75	16.75	16.75
Total	12.50	15.00	16.75	21.75	25.00

Source: Executive Office of the President of the United States, Office of Management and Budget, *Budget of the United States Government: Fiscal Year 1995* (Washington, D.C.: U.S. Government Printing Office, 1994), p. 200. *Notes:* Includes both mandatory and discretionary funding. Fiscal Year 1995 total budget is $18.9 billion.

★ 126 ★

Government Expenditures

Major Crime Control Initiatives, 1994-1998

"One of the cornerstones of the President's program to combat crime, particularly violent crime in our urban communities, is increasing the number of police officers on our streets. For 1995, $1.7 billion in new funding is requested to provide State and local grants to begin hiring these officers. These grants will assist States and localities in establishing community policing programs across the Nation. A total of $6 billion more will be provided for 1996-1999 to ensure that as many as 100,000 new police officers are added to the State and local police rolls. This program will ultimately increase the number of police officers by over 15 percent.

"The 1995 budget proposes to eliminate the formula portion of the Byrne drug law enforcement grant program. While saving over $300 million, this funding will be replaced in large part by the President's new community policing initiative and various other new grant programs supporting State and local law enforcement authorized by the pending House- and Senate-passed crime bills. Also, the budget proposes an increase of $50 million for the discretionary portion of the Byrne grant program, effectively doubling those projects that target specific needs."

[Increased budget authority in millions of dollars]

New police officers	1,720
Criminal records upgrade (Brady Bill)	100
Juvenile Crime Prevention	69
Total	1,889

Source: Executive Office of the President of the United States, Office of Management and Budget, *Budget of the United States Government: Fiscal Year 1995* (Washington, D.C.: U.S. Government Printing Office, 1994), pp. 199-200.

Adult and Federal Corrections

★ 127 ★

Anticipated Capacity of Adult Correctional Institutions, 1994

"A total of 959,388 [prison system] beds are anticipated in 52 agencies based on 86,117 that are currently under construction and 115,062 that are in the planning stages."

State	Current capacity	Under construction	Beds planned	Anticipated capacity
Alabama	16,475		900	17,375
Alaska[1]	2,466	50		2,516
Arizona	16,091	1,450	2,218	19,759
Arkansas	8,014	69	4,463	12,546
California	69,013	8,814		77,827
Colorado[2]	7,880	378	2,689	10,947
Connecticut	12,133	1,838	600	14,571
Delaware	3,025			3,025
District of Columbia	8,752			8,752
Florida	54,043	6,951	26,699	87,693
Georgia[3]	27,740	4,172	1,000	32,912
Hawaii	1,672	218	3,024	4,914
Idaho	2,115	128	56	2,299
Illinois[4]	25,417	189	1,372	26,978
Indiana	12,255	1,264		13,519
Iowa	4,625		950	5,575
Kansas	6,448		85	6,533
Kentucky	9,383	58	912	10,353
Louisiana	16,487		200	16,687
Maine	1,358			1,358
Maryland	12,297	911	1,296	14,504
Massachusetts	6,528		2,600	9,128
Michigan	28,985	1,200		30,185
Minnesota	3,845	440	1,705	5,990
Mississippi	8,571			8,571
Missouri	15,911	400		16,311
Montana[5]	1,180		388	1,568
Nebraska	2,013		90	2,103
Nevada	6,440	617	152	7,209
New Hampshire	1,716		300	2,016
New Jersey	18,520	296	3,232	22,048
New Mexico	3,571		500	4,071
New York[6]	61,761		300	62,061
North Carolina	18,925	1,700		20,625
North Dakota	600		15	615
Ohio	22,521	5,220	2,010	29,751
Oklahoma	12,466			12,466
Oregon	6,397		108	6,505

[Continued]

★ 127 ★

Anticipated Capacity of Adult Correctional Institutions, 1994

[Continued]

State	Current capacity	Under construction	Beds planned	Anticipated capacity
Pennsylvania	18,844	2,288		21,132
Rhode Island	2,902			2,902
South Carolina	16,214	3,390		19,604
South Dakota	1,496			1,496
Tennessee[7]	11,957		1,000	12,957
Texas	72,854	24,294	36,119	133,267
Utah	3,183	40	1,194	4,417
Vermont	785		100	885
Virginia	15,359	1,200	3,389	19,948
Washington	7,996		2,241	10,237
West Virginia	1,875	1,006		2,881
Wisconsin	6,190	1,400	1,100	8,690
Wyoming	1,003	30	55	1,088
Federal[8]	59,912	16,106	12,000	88,018
Total	758,209	86,117	115,062	959,388

Source: Camille Graham Camp and George M. Camp, *The Corrections Yearbook, 1994: Adult Corrections* (South Salem, N.Y.: Criminal Justice Institute, Inc.), 1994, pp. 43-4. *Notes:* 1. Current Capacity as of 1/1/93. Beds under-construction are double-bunking. 2. Beds planned include 1,211 future contract beds. 3. Total beds under construction from six new and one existing institution. 4. Beds planned exclude increase of 208 Elec. Det. and 1 Federal bed. 5. Beds planned include 225 medium and 163 minimum. 6. Beds planned are medical beds. 7. Beds planned are proposed by Governor. 8. Data for main facilities and exclude contract facilities.

★ 128 ★

Adult and Federal Corrections

Adult Correctional Institutions under Construction, Adding Beds, and Number of Beds Being Added, 1994

"As of 1/1/94, 78 new facilities are under construction in 24 jurisdictions and 78 facilities are being added to in 22 jurisdictions. 86,117 beds are being added, of which 21,984 are maximum, 41,887 are medium, and 20,262 are minimum. 24 agencies will spend $1.9 billion to add facilities and beds."

State	Institutions		Beds				Cost ($)
	New	Existing	Total	Maximum	Medium	Minimum	
Alaska[1]		1	50	50			213,000
Arizona	3		1,450		1,450		43,952,061
Arkansas		2	69		69		1,860,000
California[2]	4		8,814	5,922	100	808	
Colorado[3]	1	1	378		250	128	2,100,000
Connecticut	3	2	1,838	96	1,742		179,289,370
Florida[4]	4	13	6,951	5,248	1,703		119,022,067
Georgia[4,5]	6	1	4,172	676	3,048	448	100,000,000
Hawaii		2	218	6	156	56	21,300,000
Idaho	1		128	32	36	60	

[Continued]

★ 128 ★

Adult Correctional Institutions under Construction, Adding Beds, and Number of Beds Being Added, 1994

[Continued]

State	Institutions		Beds				Cost ($)
	New	Existing	Total	Maximum	Medium	Minimum	
Illinois[6]	1		189		29	160	2,500,000
Indiana	1	1	1,264		1,144	120	2,500,000
Kentucky	1	1	58		58		2,709,000
Maryland	1	6	911	811		100	54,520,000
Michigan	1		1,200	300	900		
Minnesota		1	440		440		20,500,000
Missouri	1	2	400		220	180	949,000
Nevada	1	1	617		539	78	41,500,000
New Jersey		2	296		264	32	11,900,000
North Carolina	6	20	1,700		650	1,050	
Ohio	4	5	5,220		3,988	1,232	140,500,000
Pennsylvania	2		2,288	120	2,020	148	
Rhode Island[7]		1					7,000,000
South Carolina	3		3,390			3,390	117,000,000
Texas[8]	16		24,294	6,696	16,598	1,000	
Utah		1	40			40	100,000
Vermont	1						
Virginia	1	1	1,200		1,200		35,328,859
West Virginia	2		1,006	206	600	200	
Wisconsin	1	2	1,400	500	900		125,000,000
Wyoming		1	30			30	734,891
Fed[9]	13	11	16,106	1,321	3,783	11,002	820,000,000
Total	78	78	86,117	21,984	41,887	20,262	1,850,478,248

Source: Camille Graham Camp and George M. Camp, *The Corrections Yearbook, 1994: Adult Corrections* (South Salem, N.Y.: Criminal Justice Institute, Inc.), 1994, p. 42. *Notes:* 1. Total is double-bunking. 2. Total including 1,984 unspecified female beds. Medium beds are reception. 3. Existing excluding 4 fac. renovations that do not impact beds. 250 is mixed levels. 4. Close, not maximum, security. 5. New is 4 prisons, 1 inmate boot camp unit, 1 pre-transitional center. Medium including minimum. Minimum is boot camp unit and pre-transitional center. 6. Minimum including 55 cmty. beds. Cost estimate to be at least figure shown. 7. Cost estimated. 8. Medium includes 550 psychiatric facility beds. 9. Figures are for main facilities and excluding contract facilities. High, not maximum, security. Minimum includes 1,833 minimum, 5,644 low, and 3,505 administrative.

★ 129 ★

Adult and Federal Corrections

Number and Cost of Adult Correctional Institution Beds under Construction for Different Security Levels, 1994

"115,062 beds were planned in 36 agencies. Among 35 agencies, the average construction cost per bed for maximum security was $80,004. In 41 agencies, the average cost per bed for medium security was $58,509, and 36 agencies reported an average cost of $28,194 for minimum security beds."

State	Planned beds	Maximum	Medium	Minimum
Alabama	900		$22,222	
Arizona	2,218	$41,000	$35,311	$30,000
Arkansas	4,463	$52,000	$27,000	$27,000
California[1]		$113,187	$91,247	$59,186
Colorado[2]	2,689	$105,000	$75,000	$48,000
Connecticut	600	$147,000	$82,787	
District of Columbia		$190,000	$108,000	$70,000
Florida	26,699	$23,445	$19,865	$9,542
Georgia	1,000	$35,000	$27,000	$22,000
Hawaii	3,024	$155,000	$220,000	$70,00
Idaho[3]	56	$87,500	$40,000	$15,000
Illinois[4]	1,372	$98,000	$64,000	$48,000
Indiana		$62,891	$58,928	$18,000
Iowa	950		$29,333	
Kansas	85	$78,125	$38,000	$10,500
Kentucky	912	$62,025	$50,000	$12,500
Louisiana	200		$10,415	
Maryland	1,296	$66,091		$16,250
Massachusetts	2,600	$100,000	$80,000	$75,000
Michigan		$71,780	$50,286	$24,500
Minnesota	1,705	$100,000	$75,000	
Mississippi		$35,000	$30,000	$25,000
Missouri		$75,000	$50,000	$25,000
Montana[5]	388		$40,000	
Nebraska	90	$102,102	$63,815	$38,288
Nevada	152	$76,000	$160,000	$9,000
New Hampshire	300			
New Jersey	3,232	$90,000	$40,000	$30,000
New Mexico	500	$71,000	$64,000	$19,000
New York[6]	300	$110,000	$90,000	$20,000
North Carolina		$48,000	$20,000	$6,000
North Dakota	15			
Ohio[7]	2,010		$24,093	$27,124
Oklahoma		$60,000	$40,000	$20,000
Oregon	108		$91,000	
Pennsylvania		$75,000	$55,000	$25,000
South Carolina		$48,000	$40,000	$10,500
South Dakota[8]			$69,445	
Tennessee[9]	1,000	$55,000	$38,000	$22,000
Texas	36,119	$32,000	$24,000	$20,000
Utah	1,194			

[Continued]

★ 129 ★

Number and Cost of Adult Correctional Institution Beds under Construction for Different Security Levels, 1994

[Continued]

State	Planned beds	Maximum	Medium	Minimum
Vermont	100			$20,000
Virginia	3,389			
Washington	2,241	$110,000	$94,130	$36,088
West Virginia		$50,000	$40,000	$35,000
Wisconsin[10]	1,100	$90,000	$65,000	$42,000
Wyoming	55			$11,503
Federal[11]	12,000	$85,000	$56,000	$18,000
Total/Average	115,062	$80,004	$58,509	$28,194

Source: Camille Graham Camp and George M. Camp, *The Corrections Yearbook, 1994: Adult Corrections* (South Salem, N.Y.: Criminal Justice Institute, Inc.), 1994, pp. 45-6. *Notes:* 1. Medium and Minimum costs averages. 2. Includes 1,211 future contract beds. 3. Bed costs averaged. 4. Excludes increase of 208 Elec. Det. and 1 Federal bed. 5. 225 medium, 163 minimum. 6. Medical beds. 7. Average cost per ADM/ Medical bed is $112,500. 8. Average cost for maximum, medium, and minimum beds. 9. Governor proposed beds. 10. Costs FY'93. Source: Annual Fiscal Year Report, June 1993. 11. High, not maximum. Excludes contract facilities.

★ 130 ★

Adult and Federal Corrections

Actual and Projected BOP (Bureau of Prisons) Population and Capacity, 1992-2002

"[The Bureau of Prisons'] inmate population continues to grow at a rate faster than BOP's ability to increase prison capacity. BOP's expansion program is closing the gap between population and capacity as shown in the table below. However, population projections beyond 1997 indicate that, if no changes are made to sentencing laws and if prison construction is not funded in the budgets for fiscal years 1994 and beyond, the gap between population and capacity could increase to levels that could renew BOP's concerns about overcrowded prisons."

[In thousands]

Year	Year-end population	Year-end capacity
1992	70,000	47,000
1993	80,000	57,000
1994	87,000	61,000
1995	95,000	80,000
1996	100,000	91,000
1997	102,000	97,000
1998	108,000	108,000
1999	112,000	112,000
2000	115,000	115,000

[Continued]

★ 130 ★

Actual and Projected BOP (Bureau of Prisons) Population and Capacity, 1992-2002

[Continued]

Year	Year-end population	Year-end capacity
2001	120,000	120,000
2002	122,000	122,000

Source: United States General Accounting Office, General Government Division, *Federal Prison Expansion Overcrowding Reduced But Inmate Population Growth May Raise Issue Again* (Washington, D.C.: U.S. Government Printing Office, December 1993), p. 4. *Primary source:* BOP. *Notes:* Data are as of the end of the year for 1980, which are as of January 1, 1981. Also, the actual population is shown from 1980 through 1992 and the projected population is for 1993 through 2002. The actual capacity is shown for 1980 through 1992 and the projected capacity is from 1993 through 1997. Magnitudes estimated from published chart. Source also includes data for 1980 through 1991.

★ 131 ★

Adult and Federal Corrections

Rated Capacity for BOP Facilities through 1996 and Amount Attributed to Policy Changes, 1993-1996

"[As] of March 1993, BOP increased its existing rated capacity by 8,927, or about 17 percent, and its rated capacity for facilities planned through 1996 by 16,857, or about 37 percent, as a result of its policy revisions... In addition to the policy change for double-bunking, BOP revised the standard cell size for new construction from 90 square feet to a nominal 75 square feet. The calculated increase in rated capacity due to policy changes includes all policy changes; however, according to BOP officials, most of the increase is attributable to double-bunking."

Sources of increased rated capacity	Rated capacity as of March 1993	Amount of rated capacity attributable to revised policy
Existing facilities as of March 1993	52,013	8,927
New construction	38,283	13,952
Acquired facilities	4,576	2,045
Expansion projects planned at existing facilities	2,454	860
Total	97,326	25,784

Source: United States General Accounting Office, General Government Division, *Federal Prison Expansion Overcrowding Reduced But Inmate Population Growth May Raise Issue Again* (Washington, D.C.: U.S. Government Printing Office, December 1993), pp. 26-7. *Primary source:* BOP.

★ 132 ★

Adult and Federal Corrections

Projected Prison Population Compared to Planned Rated Capacity for Minimum to Low Security Level Prisons, 1993-1997

"An analysis of future capacity plans for each of BOP's security levels indicates that the current and projected capacity for medium-security-level institutions is greater than the projected populations. The projected capacity for high-security-level institutions is expected to exceed populations in fiscal years 1994 through 1997. However, population projections for inmates classified at low- and medium-security levels will exceed rated capacity for those security levels for fiscal years 1993 through 1997."

Classification and fiscal year	Population projections as of January 1993	Rated capacity planned as of June 1993	Percent of population projections to rated capacity
Minimum security			
1993	20,307	15,137	134
1994	21,754	15,893	137
1995	23,107	17,557	132
1996	24,414	20,373	120
1997	25,656	20,885	123
Low security			
1993	24,646	10,860	227
1994	26,322	12,460	211
1995	27,888	13,452	207
1996	30,867	19,846	156
1997	32,318	26,246	123

Source: United States General Accounting Office, General Government Division, *Federal Prison Expansion Overcrowding Reduced But Inmate Population Growth May Raise Issue Again* (Washington, D.C.: U.S. Government Printing Office, December 1993), p. 14.

Juvenile Corrections

★ 133 ★

Potential Rise in Juvenile Crime, 1994-2005

"The federal government recently launched massive research that will try to determine how violent behavior can be short-circuited. The results will come none too soon. By the year 2005, the number of 15-to-19-year-olds—the most violent-prone age group—will increase by 23 percent."

Source: Scott Minerbrook, "A Generation of Stone Killers," in *U.S. News & World Report*, 17 January 1994, p. 37.

★ 134 ★

Juvenile Corrections

Number and Cost of Planned Beds in Juvenile Institutions, 1994

"5,997 beds were in the planning stages in 19 agencies. The anticipated average cost per bed was $97,321, as estimated by 19 agencies."

State	Beds	Average cost
Arkansas[1]	50	
California	1,550	$91,000
Colorado[2,3]	298	$110,000
Delaware[4]	60	$200,000
District of Columbia[5]	68	
Hawaii		$301,672
Illinois[3,6]	100	$60,000
Indiana		50,000
Kentucky		$41,666
Maryland[7]	339	$105,000
Massachusetts	300	$75,000
Michigan		$135,000
Mississippi	510	$44,333
Missouri	180	$109,000
New Mexico	32	$7,800
New York[8]	105	$167,000
North Carolina	24	$43,134
Ohio	144	$100,000
Pennsylvania	114	$88,500
Rhode Island	12	
Texas[9]	2,000	$55,000
Utah	66	$65,000

[Continued]

★ 134 ★

Number and Cost of Planned Beds in Juvenile Institutions, 1994

[Continued]

State	Beds	Average cost
Wisconsin	45	
Total/Average	5,997	$97,321

Source: Camille Graham Camp and George M. Camp, *The Corrections Yearbook, 1994: Juvenile Corrections*. (South Salem, NY: Criminal Justice Institute, Inc.), 1994. *Notes:* 1. Non-institutional beds. 2. Detention beds. 3. Cost estimated. 4. Planned is replacement facility, no new capacity. 5. Planned contracted beds. 6. Juvenile Boot Camp. 7. Beds per ten-year plan. Cost includes design, construction, inspection and equipment. 8. Cost per bed includes fees, landscaping and equipment. 9. Net cost.

Jail Systems

★ 135 ★

Number and Cost of State Jail Beds Planned, But Not Under Construction, 1994-2006

"28,900 beds were planned in 51 systems. 43 systems reported projected costs of $1.2 billion."

	Beds	Cost
Maricopa County, AZ	402	$3,100,000
Mohave County, AZ	600	
Pinal County, AZ	420	$11,300,000
Yuma County, AZ	60	$870,000
San Bernadino County, CA	232	$9,100,000
Denver County, CO	800	$50,000,000
Alachua County, FL	70	
Brevard County, FL[1]	575	
Broward County, FL	1,200	
Collier County, FL	256	$8,000,000
Hillsborough County, FL	512	$16,800,000
Orange County, FL[2]	3,080	$182,000,000
Osceola County, FL[3]	120	$2,155,000
Pinellas County, FL	800	$30,000,000
Cobb County, GA	1,086	$39,000,000
Gwinnett County, GA	576	
Richmond County, GA	244	$200,000
Marion County, IN	200	$8,000,000
Sedgwick County, KS[4]	450	$12,000,000
Iberia Parish, LA	32	$350,000
Jefferson Parish, LA	700	$18,000,000
Anne Arudel County, MD	384	$26,000,000

[Continued]

★ 135 ★

Number and Cost of State Jail Beds Planned, But Not Under Construction, 1994-2006

[Continued]

	Beds	Cost
Frederick County, MD	112	$5,800,000
Harford County, MD	172	$10,000,000
Montgomery County, MD[4]	800	$44,000,000
Prince George's County, MD	192	$18,000,000
Oakland County, MI	40	$500,000
St. Louis County, MO[5]	1,200	$100,000,000
Ocean County, NJ	18	$18,000
Niagara County, NY	160	$24,557,627
Oneida County, NY	571	$30,000,000
Onondaga County, NY[6]	224	$50,000,000
Mecklenburg County, NC	1,800	$22,000,000
Hamilton County, OH	300	$20,000,000
Dauphin County, PA	128	$5,000,000
Delaware County, PA	1,000	$60,000,000
Greenville County, SC	192	$2,110,445
Richland County, SC[7]	192	$7,000,000
Dallas County, TX[8]	1,920	$8,600,000
El Paso County, TX	1,100	$35,000,000
Limestone County, TX	1,000	
Montgomery County, TX	96	$380,000
Tarrant County, TX	672	$3,700,000
Salt Lake County, UT	1,200	$100,000,000
Fairfax County, VA	750	$53,000,000
Prince William-Manassas, VA	200	$20,000,000
Roanoke City, VA	300	$7,900,000
King County, WA[9]	896	$150,000,000
Pierce County, WA	670	
Yakima County, WA[10]	196	$5,300,000
Total	28,900	$1,199,741,072

Source: Camille Graham Camp and George M. Camp, *The Corrections Yearbook, 1994: Jail Systems* (South Salem, NY: Criminal Justice Institute, Inc.), 1994, pp. 40-1. *Notes:* 1. Average beds. 2. Beds and cost estimate planned through year 2006. 3. Beds estimated. 4. Cost estimated. 5. Site preparation began April 94. 6. Cost estimated. 7. Beds planned for juvenile, medium security, and maximum security facilities. 8. Beds planned to be completed 6/94. 9. Includes 344 beds planned for year 2000, for cost unknown. Cost includes 23 courtrooms and offices. 10. Adding beds to existing cells.

★ 136 ★

Jail Systems

Jail Beds Under Construction, 1994

"21,348 beds are under construction in 28 jail systems."

	Beds
Pima, AZ	412
Butte, CA	416
Los Angeles, CA	5,800
Sonoma, CA	239
Stanislaus, CA	156
Ventura, CA	758
Alachua, FL	560
Manatee, FL	976
DeKalb, GA	3,543
Richmond, GA	422
Cook, IL	1,532
St. Louis City, MO	224
Passaic, NJ[1]	150
Broome, NY	400
Onondaga, NY	616
Sullivan, NY	1
Mecklenburg, NC	600
Stark, OH	104
Tulsa, OK	96
Berks, PA[2]	223
Erie, PA	204
Philadelphia, PA	2,016
Greenville, SC	288
Richaland, SC	336
Spartanburg, SC	396
Denton, TX	384
Dane, WI	487
Manitowoc, WI	9
Total	21,348

Source: Camille Graham Camp and George M. Camp, *The Corrections Yearbook, 1994: Jail Systems* (South Salem, NY: Criminal Justice Institute, Inc.), 1994, p. 40. *Notes:* 1. Estimate. 2. Renovations of existing units.

Further Developments in Law Enforcement

★ 137 ★

Non-lethal Law Enforcement Weapons Development, 2000-2100

"Guns are one of the most effective methods available today for self-defense against violence. A gun puts people on equal footing—men and women, young, and old. With proper training, anyone can use a gun effectively.

"However, guns can be extremely deadly—not only in the hands of criminals, but also in the hands of law-abiding users. Accidents with firearms claim some 1,500 lives a year in the United States.

"Today's guns could easily be converted into less-lethal weapons. For instance, how about guns with a safety catch locked by a combination? The user would have to program the right numbers in order to operate this weapon. Most firearms now have some type of safety catch; we could simply improve on this concept by making it harder for an unauthorized person to operate.

"Yet another option is to develop firearms with computerized handles that can read the user's fingerprints. The gun would only function when used by the owner. This concept would go a long way in reducing gun violence precipitated by stolen weapons.

"But non-lethal weapon technologies are also available today that could give people the protection they need without the deadly force of traditional guns. These technologies could be further refined to create an ideal non-lethal weapon...

"[In] the future, firearms as we now know them will disappear. Guns in the twenty-first century will take the same place that crossbows and swords do today. People own crossbows and swords for sport and collection but not for self-defense. The same thing will occur with firearms. In the future, people will collect firearms and use them for sport or hunting, but not to defend themselves. The 'gun' of the future will be much more effective for paralyzing its target, but much less deadly."

Source: Abraham N. Tennenbaum and Angela M. Moore, "Non-lethal Weapons: Alternatives to Deadly Force," in *The Futurist*, September-October 1993, pp. 20, 23.

★ 138 ★

Further Developments in Law Enforcement

Electronic Crime Control Technologies, 1993-2001

"Alternatives to imprisonment are increasingly being offered, but humanitarianism alone is not enough to justify releasing prisoners for good behavior, conferring leniency on first-time offenders, or offering work-release or other such programs where the offender is supervised in the community.

"One revolutionary alternative for controlling criminals is a system known as the Electronic Supervision Program. It may prove a precursor of felon-supervision systems in the new millennium. The Electronic Supervision Program is now a popular system for managing offenders by means of electronic monitors. The system enables law-enforcement agents to keep better track of inmates released from prison.

"The Electronic Supervision Program's home-detention system is based on current technology available from a variety of national and international corporations. This first-generation system consists of an anklet transponder electronically linked to a telephone modem. Its purpose is to alert a central monitoring station when the offender moves outside of a 100-foot radius around the modem. The system also periodically checks the offender's location. Attempts to leave the specified location or to tamper with the transponder are relayed back to the monitoring station automatically...

"A second-generation monitoring system consisting of computer-controlled radio receivers will likely be in place between 1995 and 2000. This system will instantly record every place the offender goes—not just when he or she is out of the range of the home-detention modem.

"An anklet (or bracelet) transponder would send out a blip signal every five to 10 seconds that would be picked up by the two separate receivers. The arrival times of the blips would determine the offender's approximate location on a city or regional grid map. The signal would also include a unique frequency code to identify whose transponder was 'blipping.' (This system could also be adapted to use cellular phone transmitters, providing even greater accuracy in determining an offender's location.)...

"The end of the 1990s will likely see a hugely improved system of parolee and probationer supervision at a greatly reduced cost. If the system succeeds, the public may support the release of nonviolent, low-risk offenders from costly correctional facilities, leaving only the violent, high-risk criminals behind bars.

"The third generation of electronic supervision incorporating radio monitors, fuzzy logic, and medical implants will likely be in place sometime after 2001. Custom-programmed microprocessor chips would monitor the offender's physiological patterns and reactions and would recognize the advent of a violent or severely aberrant phase. The microprocessor could then send out an alarm to the nearest receiver, which would relay it to the central monitoring station."

Source: Max Winkler, "Walking Prisons: The Developing Technology of Electronic Controls," in *The Futurist*, July-August 1993, pp. 34-6.

★ 139 ★

Further Developments in Law Enforcement

Private Security and Law Enforcement Spending, 1980-2000

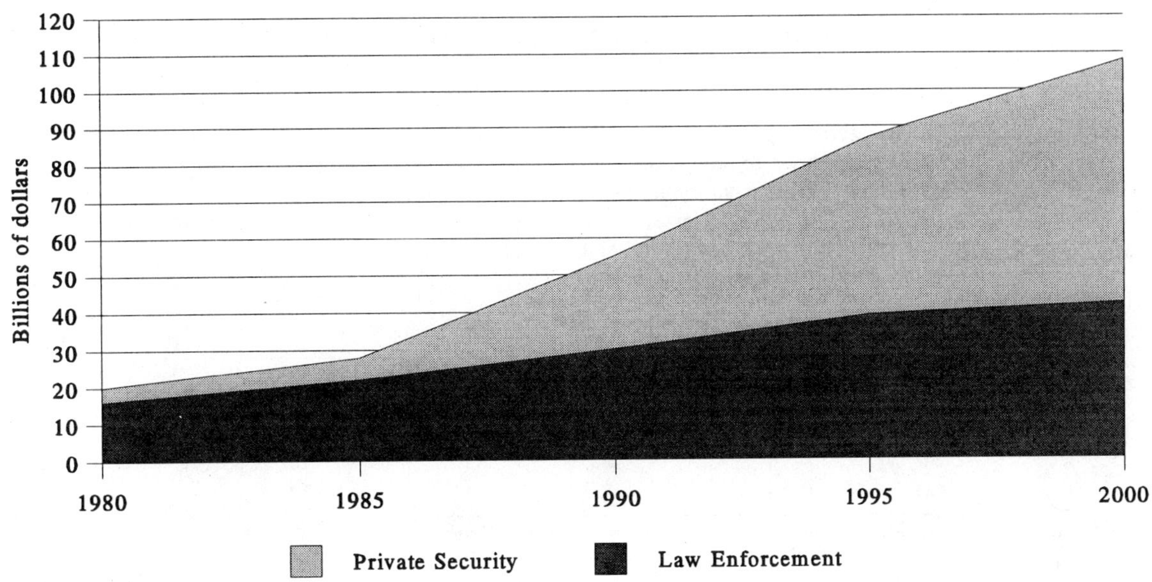

"During the last decade, the private security industry has mushroomed, winning jobs patrolling malls, neighborhoods, even prisons. This week, Sussex, N.J., will become a charity—a U.S. town that is hiring a private firm as its police force. The money-strapped community disbanded its four-man police force a year ago and later decided to rely on a private firm instead of the state police. Executive Security Inc. will charge $48,000 for a six-month trial, compared with an annual police budget of over $200,000. Many law-enforcement officials express concern about the arrangement, urging that consolidating with a nearby town is a better solution than hiring out the work."

[Billions of dollars]

	1980	1985	1990	1995	2000
PS	20	28	55	87	108
LE	16	22	30	39	42

Source: Rod Little, "On the Rent-a-Cop Beat," in *U.S. News & World Report*, 7 June 1994, p. 10. *Primary source:* Hallcrest Systems Inc. *Notes:* Magnitudes estimated from published chart. PS=Private Security, LE=Law Enforcement.

★ 140 ★

Further Developments in Law Enforcement

Private Security and Law Enforcement Employment, 1980-2000

"[The] privatization of public safety... has been growing for a decade. Increasingly in city business districts, private residential communities and public housing complexes, hired security is being used to augment, and sometimes replace, services once provided by police.

"Private security guards—1.5 million in 1990—outnumbered public law enforcement three to one, according to the Hallcrest Report II, a study commissioned by the National Institute of Justice, the research arm of the Justice Department. Businesses, communities and individuals spent $52 billion on private security in 1990, almost twice the amount raised by taxes for public law enforcement."

[Millions]

Year	Public	Private
1980	.6	1.0
1990	.6	1.5
2000	.7	1.9

Source: Milo Geyelin, "Hired Guards Assume More Police Duties as Privatization of Public Safety Spreads," in *The Wall Street Journal*, 1 June 1993, p. B1. *Primary source:* Hallcrest Systems Inc. *Note:* Magnitudes estimated from published chart.

★ 141 ★

Further Developments in Law Enforcement

Volume of Fingerprint Cards Submitted to Identify by Source, 2000

[Thousands of cards per day]

State/local c.j. contingency	12.0
State/local non-c.j. new applications	6.0
Federal non-c.j. new applications	7.3
Federal non-c.j. base	11.2
State/local non-c.j. base	11.7
State/local c.j. new applications	2.6
Federal c.j. new applications	0.8
Federal c.j. base	1.1
State/local c.j. base	8.4

Source: Congress of the United States, Office of Technology Assessment, *The FBI Fingerprint Identification Automation Program: Issues and Options—Background Paper* (Washington, D.C.: U.S. Government Printing Office, November 1991), p. 25. *Primary source:* Office of Technology Assessment, 1991. *Note:* c.j. = criminal justice; non-c.j. = non-criminal justice.

★ 142 ★

Further Developments in Law Enforcement

Range of Daily FBI Fingerprint Card Submissions, 2000

"[The Office of Technology Assessment National Fingerprint File/Interstate Identification Index] has identified six scenarios for fingerprint card submissions... The OTA-1, OTA-2, and OTA-3 scenarios assume full National Fingerprint File/Interstate Identification Index implementation; the OTA-4 scenario assumes half NFF/III implementation. The OTA-5 and OTA-6 scenario assume no NFF/III implementations. The OTA-1 scenario assumes no major new fingerprint check applications beyond what can be accommodated in the baseline growth. The OTA-2 scenario provides a margin for some new applications. The OTA-3, OTA-4, and OTA-5 scenarios provide margins for substantial additional baseline growth and new fingerprint check applications, assuming full, half, and no NFF/III implementation, respectively. The OTA-6 scenario assumes a much greater than expected growth in fingerprint checks with no NFF/III implementation, and reflects the unverified results of the FBI's user survey."

	OTA-1	OTA-2	OTA-3	OTA-4	OTA-5	OTA-6
Criminal justice	11,000	13,000	13,000	25,000	34,000	50,000
Noncriminal justice	23,000	30,000	36,000	36,000	36,000	50,000
Total	34,000	43,000	49,000	61,000	70,000	100,000

Source: Congress of the United States, Office of Technology Assessment, *The FBI Fingerprint Identification Automation Program: Issues and Options—Background Paper* (Washington, D.C.: U.S. Government Printing Office, November 1991), pp. 25-6. *Primary source:* Office of Technology Assessment, 1991. *Notes:* The FBI subsequently adjusted its estimate from about 100,000 fingerprint cards per day, based on the unverified survey results, to 78,000 cards per day with no NFF/III, after verifying the survey results and correcting for double counting, purely speculative projections, and other anomalies.

Chapter 5
DEFENSE AND THE SPACE PROGRAM

Defense: Budget Impacts

★ 143 ★

Department of Defense Budget, 1990-1997

[Billions of dollars]

1990	294
1991	291
1992	281
1993	256
1994	252
1995	248
1996	238
1997	233

Source: Eugene Carlson, "Thinking Small Pays Off for These Federal Contractors," in the *Wall Street Journal*, 12 October 1993, p. B2. *Primary source:* White House Budget Office. *Notes:* Figures for fiscal years 1990-1992 are actual. Fiscal year 1993 is estimated and later years are President Clinton's requests. Figures aren't adjusted for inflation. Magnitudes estimated from published chart.

★ 144 ★

Defense: Budget Impacts

Funding Summary for National Defense, 1993-1999

"The 1995 defense budget request and the 1995-1999 projected defense plan continue the reduction of defense resources since the end of the Cold War."

[Billions of dollars]

	1993 Actual	1994 Estimate	Proposed 1995	1996	1997	1998	1999
Department of Defense-Military:							
Budget Authority	262.4	250.0	252.8	244.2	241.0	247.5	253.8
Outlays	280.1	268.3	259.8	249.9	245.4	245.5	246.3
Atomic Energy Defense Activities:							
Budget Authority	12.1	10.9	10.6	11.0	10.9	11.0	11.2
Outlays	11.0	11.2	10.5	10.8	10.	11.0	11.1
Other Defense Related Activities:							
Budget Authority	1.7	0.9	0.7	0.7	0.7	0.7	0.7
Outlays	1.3	1.1	0.8	0.9	0.7	0.7	0.7
Total National Defense:							
Budget Authority	276.1	261.7	264.2	255.9	252.6	259.2	265.7
Outlays	292.4	280.6	271.1	261.6	257.0	257.1	258.1

Source: Executive Office of the President of the United States, Office of Management and Budget, *Budget of the United States Government* (Washington, D.C.: Government Printing Office, 1994), p. 224.

★ 145 ★

Defense: Budget Impacts

Defense Budget Authority Trend, 1950-1999

"In real (inflation-adjusted) dollars, the budget levels projected for DOD by the end of the five-year planning period are 35 percent below the last Cold War (1989) budget level, and 42 percent below the 1985 peacetime defense spending peak... As a share of the GDP, DOD spending will fall from 3.7 percent in 1995 to 2.8 percent in 1999. This compares to an average DOD share of 8.5 percent of GDP during the mid 1950's to mid 1960's."

[Billions of dollars]

1950	120
1952	430
1955	227
1965	264
1968	352
1975	235
1977	250

[Continued]

★ 145 ★

Defense Budget Authority Trend, 1950-1999

[Continued]

1985	390
1990	347
1995	252
1999	227

Source: Executive Office of the President of the United States, Office of Management and Budget, *Budget of the United States Government* (Washington, D.C.: Government Printing Office, 1994), p. 224-5. *Note:* DOD=U.S. Department of Defense.

★ 146 ★

Defense: Budget Impacts

Defense Reinvestment and Conversion, 1993-1997

"[The] conversion program brings together activities from across the Federal Government. In almost all cases, increased funding has been requested for 1995. These increases, when combined with additional 1993 and 1994 spending in key conversion programs, bring the defense conversion program to about $22 billion over five years—$2 billion over the $20 billion level announced in March 1993."

[Budget Authority in millions of dollars]

	1993 Actual	1994 Estimate	Proposed 1995	Proposed 1996	Proposed 1997	Total 1993-97
Department of Defense Personnel Assistance and Community Support	1,020	1,265	1,192	1,192[2]	1,192[2]	5,861
Department of Energy Worker and Community Transition Program	92	200	125	100	100	617
Department of Labor Workforce Security Program	[3]	125[4]	195[4]	195[4]	195[4]	710
Department of Commerce Community Diversification Assistance (EDA)	[5]	80	140	140	140	500
Total: Worker and Community Assistance Programs	1,112	1,670	1,652	1,627	1,627	7,688
Department of Defense Dual-Use Technology	882	1,441	1,429	1,454	1,479	6,685
Technology Reinvestment Project (TRP)	465[6]	554	625	650	675	2,969
Other Dual-use Initiatives	417	887	804	804[2]	804[2]	3,716

[Continued]

★ 146 ★

Defense Reinvestment and Conversion, 1993-1997

[Continued]

	1993 Actual	1994 Estimate	Proposed 1995	1996	1997	Total 1993-97
New Federal High Technology Investments (Conversion Opportunities)[7]	...	907	1,734	2,054	2,444	7,139
Other Industry Assistance Programs	...	50[8]	50[8]	...	...	100
Grand total: Programs that will assist defense workers, communities and firms	1,994	4,068	4,865	5,135	5,550	21,612

Source: Executive Office of the President of the United States, Office of Management and Budget, *Budget of the United States Government* (Washington, D.C.: Government Printing Office, 1994), p. 123. *Notes:* 1. This program reflects funding above 1993 levels plus that portion of existing programs re-directed to conversion efforts. 2. This is the 1995 level. Specific estimates for 1996 and 1997 are not yet available. 3. 475 million was transferred in 1993 from the Department of Defense to the Department of Labor. 4. This is the portion of the overall investment increase that could be expected to be used to assist displaced defense workers. 5. In addition, $80 million was transferred in 1993 from the Department of Defense. 6. In addition to $465 million of TRP funding, the 1993 TRP solicitation included $7 million in separately budgeted Small Business Innovative Research funds for a total of $472 million. 7. This includes investment programs that provide direct conversion opportunities (e.g. NASA's aeronautics initiative) and 50 percent of programs that provide some conversion opportunities (e.g. Department of Commerce program for Information Highways). 8. This reflects the National Shipbuilding Initiative which the Congress funded in 1994 in the defense budget. Funding for 1995 loan subsidies is provided in the Department of Transportation budget.

★ 147 ★

Defense: Budget Impacts

Summary of National Defense Budget Adjustments, 1997

"Planned funding for national defense over the next four years fulfills the promise of an additional $60 billion in program savings. Combined with government-wide pay and benefit changes and additional reductions to offset projected underfunding, this program will yield $37 billion in outlay savings in 1997. We will implement those reductions carefully as part of our effort to redesign the force. As we undertake a major strategic review over the coming months, we will identify new changes, savings and additions that will fit our new strategy."

[Billions of dollars]

	1997 Outlays
Bush adjusted baseline	287
Adjustments to baseline:	
Program reductions[1]	-26
Pay and benefit changes	-6
Additional reductions to offset projected underfunding	-5

[Continued]

★ 147 ★

Summary of National Defense Budget Adjustments, 1997

[Continued]

	1997 Outlays
Total adjustments	-37
Revised budget level[2]	249

Source: Executive Office of the President of the United States, Office of Management and Budget, *A Vision of Change for America* (Washington, D.C.: Government Printing Office, 17 February 1993), p. 70-1. *Notes:* Details may not add due to rounding. 1. These outlay savings reflect 1994-1997 budget authority reductions of about $60 billion from national defense programs. 2. These estimates do not include the investment package initiatives for defense conversion and for energy efficiency in Federal buildings.

★ 148 ★

Defense: Budget Impacts

Military and Military-Related Employment, 1993-2000

"The job shortfall in the lagging U.S. economy [was, as of March, 1993] some 8 to 10 million; cuts in the military services will contribute an additional half million job seekers a year to the year 2000, substantially increasing the need for job creation. But that burden will be lightened by the immediate federal budget savings and the lower cost of investment required for civilian jobs compared to those in the defense industry."

[Millions of people]

	1993	Proposed 2000
Active military	1.8	0.6
Military reserves	1.1	0.5
Defense Department employees	1.1	0.4
Defense industry workers	3	0.8

Source: "The Men and Women of the Armed Forces," in *Bulletin of the Atomic Scientists*, March 1993, p. 23.

★ 149 ★

Defense: Budget Impacts

Defense Spending by Service and Function, 2000

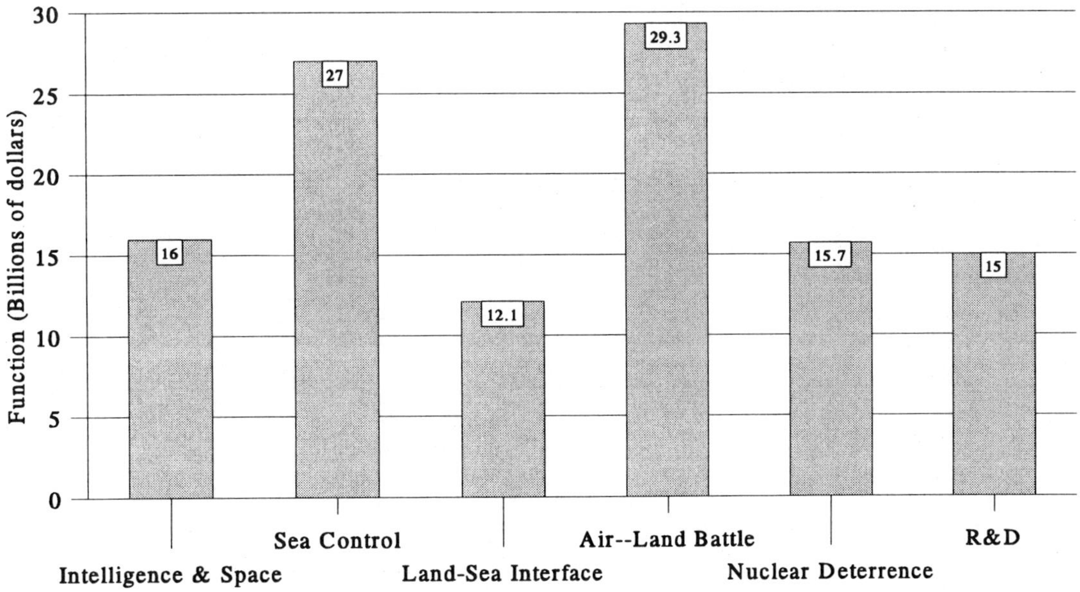

[Billions of dollars]

By service	
Army	19.5
Marines	7.1
Intelligence	11.9
R&D	15.0
Navy	33.0
Air Force	28.7
By function	
Sea Control	27.0
Intelligence & Space	16.0
R&D	15.0
Nuclear Deterrence	15.7
Air-Land Battle	29.3
Land-Sea Interface	12.1

Source: "The Defense Dollar in the Year 2000," in *Bulletin of the Atomic Scientists*, March 1993, p. 17. *Notes:* This distribution assumes a total military budget of $115 billion dollars (in constant 1990 dollars) by the year 2000.

★ 150 ★

Defense: Budget Impacts

Defense Spending as a Percent of GDP, 1990-1998

"The budget contains $440 [million] for a combination of counter-proliferation measures and continued efforts at nuclear-arms reduction. Perhaps the biggest surprise is that the Strategic Defense Initiative (SDI) survives virtually untouched. The only change: a bigger share of its $3.8 billion budget will go towards short-range tactical defense."

[Percent]

1990	5.3
1991	4.9
1992	4.8
1993	4.7
1994	4
1995	3.7
1996	3.5
1997	3.1
1998	3.0

Source: "Fading Firepower," in *The Economist*, 3 April 1993, p. 31. *Primary source:* United States Defense Department. *Notes:* Magnitudes estimated from published chart. Figures from 1950-1989 are excluded.

★ 151 ★

Defense: Budget Impacts

Defense Spending Projections: Bush vs. Clinton Administration, 1993-1998

"CLINTON'S CUTS: Reduction of active forces by 9% (1994 savings: $6 billion), scrapping part of the Star Wars program ($2.5 billion), early retirement of Navy ships ($1.2 billion), reduction in Army divisions from 14 to 12 and tactical air wings from 28 to 25 ($800 million). ADDITIONS: $914 million for more F-16 aircraft, $300 million for peacekeeping activities, $40 million to curb the proliferation of nuclear and biological weapons, $400 million to boost U.S. efforts to rid former Soviet republics of nuclear weapons."

[Billions of dollars]

	1993	1994	1995	1996	1997	1998
Bush	273	276	277	278	285	291
Clinton	273	262	260	253	250	253

Source: Bruce Van Voorst; "Man in a Minefield," in *Time*, 5 April 1993, p. 31. *Primary source:* Defense Budget Project. *Note:* Magnitudes estimated from published chart.

★ 152 ★

Defense: Budget Impacts

Defense Spending Projections: Aspin vs. Kaufmann Plan, 1997

"[The] five-year budget plan favored by Les Aspin, Bill Clinton's choice for Defense Secretary, would pare America's arsenal and active-duty troops well below current levels... But George Bush envisioned cuts that were only slightly less deep. Bush would have kept 1.6 million uniformed personnel by 1997, vs. Aspin's 1.4 million. Over the next five years, Aspin proposes spending just 6% less on the military than the departing Administration...

"William Kaufmann, a respected military analyst at the Brookings Institution, believes the military budget by 1997 could drop as low as $182 billion in today's dollars. His plan is the 'more radical' one on the table.

"Kaufmann would save by spending *more* on some things. To ensure a flexible force he would retain more Marine divisions (18,000 troops each) than Aspin, since they can be rapidly deployed. But he would trim more ruthlessly the number of heavily equipped Army divisions (12,000 troops each), which can't be so easily moved. To strengthen America's capacity to engage an enemy quickly, he and Aspin both propose to build more military transport planes and ships."

	At present	Aspin plan	Kaufmann plan
1997 Budget (billions of 1993 dollars)	$276	$234	$182
Uniformed personnel (millions)	1.9	1.4	1.1
Air Force			
Tactical aircraft	3,638	1,400	2,135
Strategic nuclear bombers[1]	229	140	0
Army/Marines			
Army divisions	16	9	7
Marine divisions	3	2	3
Navy			
Aircraft carriers	15	12	7
Missile submarines	25	18	18
Other ships	488	310	259
Sealift ships	33	61	53

Source: Suneel Ratan; "Staying Strong Without Breaking the Bank," in *Fortune*, 8 February 1993, pp. 92-3. *Note:* 1. *Fortune* estimate.

★ 153 ★

Defense: Budget Impacts

Pentagon Procurement, 1960-2000

"The American defence industry grew fat during the cold war, especially during the Reagan years. But after continuous steady growth since the early 1960s, the Pentagon's spending on research, development and new equipment has fallen in real terms by nearly 50% since 1986—down from $150 billion (in 1993 dollars) to little more than $80 billion today. Overall American defence spending is expected to fall from a peak of 6.5% of GDP in 1986 to no more than 3.2% of GDP by 1997—the biggest slide since the decline of the 1920s and 1930s that followed the first world war."

[1993 prices in billions of dollars]

Year	
1960	87
1962	100
1965	87
1967	117
1975	62
1986	148
1990	115
1995	88
2000	76

Source: "Victims of Their Own Success," in *The Economist*, 3 September 1994, p. 3. *Primary source:* Booz Allen & Hamilton.

★ 154 ★

Defense: Budget Impacts

Shifts in Defense Priorities, 1994-1997

"The Clinton administration proposed the first defense budget shaped specifically for the post-Cold War world...

"The proposed budget would buy no fighter jets for the Air Force, no tanks for the Army, and only six ships for the Navy. It would spend as much on environmental cleanup jobs as on the Army's entire acquisition plan, and more on peackeeping than the Marines spend on weapons and ammunition. And while spending $725.9 million to bolster the U.S. ballistic-missile arsenal, it would spend about half that amount on dismantling the old Soviet nuclear stockpile.

"It is a stand-down budget, but not a plan for wholesale demobilization. It would trim the size of the military and spend enough on operations, maintenance and training to keep that smaller force ready.

"But it is really designed for the future, cutting weapons procurement to invest billions in defense research and subsidize key parts of the defense industry.

" 'There are no Cold-War relics in this budget', Defense Secretary William Perry told reporters at the Pentagon yesterday...

"The budget is designed to produce a ready, technologically superior force, but not a military that will be the world's policeman.

" 'The United States cannot and should not shoulder a disproportionate share of the human and economic costs of maintaining international peace and security,' the budget states."

"Most notably, the budget would spend at least $3.46 billion in implementing the Pentagon's new defense industrial policy to ensure that U.S. industry will be capable of outfitting the forces of the future. This new policy, aimed at keeping alive 'defense-unique' sectors, such as nuclear-submarine yards, while helping the rest of the defense industry shrink, is probably the Clinton administration's biggest departure from the past at the Pentagon."

"The single biggest item in the new industrial policy is CVN-76, the Navy's next aircraft carrier, which is expected to cost about $4.48 billion, half of that coming out of 1995 spending. Aides to then-Defense Secretary Les Aspin late last year considered delaying the start of its construction, but ultimately decided that doing so could diminish the capability of **Tenneco** Inc.'s Newport News Shipbuilding & Dry Dock Co., which will build the carrier, to construct nuclear-repelled vessels."

"In addition, the budget calls for spending $335 million to upgrade FMC Corp.'s Bradley Fighting Vehicles and General Dynamics Corp.'s M-1 Abrams battle tanks in order to sustain a production capability for tracked combat vehicles."

[Billions of dollars of outlays]

	1994	1995	1996	1997
Defense	$279.8	$270.7	$261.0	$256.4

Source: Thomas E. Ricks, "A Post-Cold War Defense Plan Maps a Smaller But Ready Force," in the *Wall Street Journal*, 8 February 1994, p. A12.

★ 155 ★

Defense: Budget Impacts

Defense Industry Restructuring, 1985-2000

"Few businesses have seen their engines fail so dramatically as the U.S. defense industry. Since 1985, its major customer—the Pentagon—has seen its procurement spending authority fall in real terms from $127 billion to $54 billion. Now President Clinton promises to cut even deeper. To stay aloft, major defense contractors like Grumman have been frantically laying off workers, cutting capital expenditures, paring debt, and boosting foreign sales.

"The surprising result: Industry balance sheets have never been stronger. 'Everyone talks about the bad news,' says Judith Bollinger, vice president of investment research at Goldman Sachs. 'But defense companies are all generating phenomenal excess cash. The next five years will be incredible for cash flow.' Reacting to that welcome news, the share prices of some of the most actively traded defense stocks easily outpaced the 4.5% growth turned in by Standard & Poor's 500 in 1992. General Dynamics led the way with a 93% gain, followed by Lockheed (26%), Raytheon (23%), and Martin Marietta (17%).

"Still, despite their heroic efforts, many defense companies—possibly one or two of the largest—will fall to earth in the next few years. Since 1985, 259 defense contractors have sold out to stronger or better-positioned rivals, according to JSA International, a consulting firm in Cambridge, Massachusetts. Analysts at Booz Allen & Hamilton estimate that 75% to 80% of the top 100 defense companies or divisions that remain could be gone by 2000."

Source: Nancy J. Perry, "What's Next for the Defense Industry," in *Fortune,* 22 February 1993, p. 94.

Defense: Technological and Political Impacts

★ 156 ★

Trends in Warfare

"[According to forecasters Cetron and Davies, trends in future warfare will include the following:]

—The United States and the Soviet Union will sign a long procession of arms treaties in the next decade. The two countries will make a virtue of necessity, but both will act primarily to cut expensive military programs from their budgets...

[Continued]

★ 156 ★

Trends in Warfare

[Continued]

—Terrorist states will continue to harbor chemical and biological weapons until the international community finally takes a firm stand.

—Brushfire wars will grow more frequent and bloody. Among the most likely are:

Israel vs. the Arab countries. We foresee one last conflict in this region before the peace that now seems near actuality becomes a reality. Israel will win this one, too.

India vs. Pakistan. The two have feuded with each other since the British left in 1947; religious differences, separatism in Kashmir, and small stocks of nuclear weapons make this a hot spot to watch carefully.

Northern Ireland vs. itself. This perpetually troubled land will remain its own worst enemy. In trying to keep Ireland under control, the British face an increasingly unpleasant task.

Tactical alliances formed by the common interests to meet immediate needs will replace long-term commitments among nations.

—In the Middle East, 'the enemy of your enemy is your friend.' Iran and Iraq will tolerate each other in their stronger hatred for the West. The United States and Syria will never be friends, but both dislike Iraq."

Source: Marvin Cetron and Owen Davies, "50 Trends Shaping the World," in *The Futurist*, September-October 1991, p. 20. *Primary source:* Marvin J. Cetron and Owen Davies, *Crystal Globe: The Haves and Have-Nots of the New World Order* (St. Martin's Press), 1991.

★ 157 ★

Defense: Technological and Political Impacts

High-tech Weapons Development

"Rail guns, hypercannons, coaxial launchers, and ram accelerators may soon become part of the battlespeak of the future. These experimental, aircraft-based systems may solve some of the problems posed by conventional weapons during the next century, according to studies at Lockheed Aircraft Service Company.

"Today's gunship aircraft are too large and vulnerable to enemy fire to be completely effective, says engineer Craig H. Smyser, principal investigator of advanced weapons system integration at Lockheed. Also, the chemical reactions of gunpowder-based propellants are inherently inefficient: Projectiles don't travel as fast as they could. This causes pilots to fly at lower altitudes while in enemy airspace in order to compensate for the accuracy lost traveling at higher altitudes...

[Continued]

★ 157 ★

High-tech Weapons Development
[Continued]

"The new systems use a variety of ways to propel projectiles. The rail gun and the coaxial launcher, or coilgun, employ the basic magnetic principles of attraction and repulsion for propulsion. Ignitable media such as gases or liquids would be used in electrothermal chemical guns and liquid propellant systems. High pressure and compression would be used in systems such as light-gas guns, thermal hypervelocity launchers ('hypercannons'), and ram accelerators ('ram cannons').

"Of these, the rail gun is currently the leading candidate for development, according to Smyser. More sophisticated systems using directed energy, such as lasers and particle beams, are ' not mature enough for tactical applications. ' However, the use of high-powered microwave devices is already being investigated by Lockheed.

"Smyser speculates that the 'thousand-year reign of gunpowder in the annals of warfare may be toppled by these futuristic weapons.'"

Source: "Hyperweapons: Goodbye, Gunpowder?" in *The Futurist*, July-August 1993, pp. 55-6. *Primary source:* Craig H. Smyser, "The Future of Firepower," in *Lockheed Horizons*, January 1993.

★ 158 ★

Defense: Technological and Political Impacts

START (Strategic Arms Reduction Treaty) Limitations on Nuclear Warheads, 1993-2003

"Arms control cannot offer quick solutions. Implementation of the landmark START (Strategic Arms Reduction Treaty) and START II accords, which would cut strategic nuclear arsenals in the United States and former Soviet Union by about two thirds over the next decade, is on hold because of disputes between Russia and Ukraine over Soviet nuclear weapons stationed in Ukraine. Even if implemented now, the START cuts could take a decade to complete—an eternity given the instability in the former Soviet Union...

"The mounting animosity is turning the strategic-arms-control process into a deadlock. Conservatives in the Russian parliament cite Ukrainian intransigence on START as reason not to ratify START II. The situation 'is quickly moving to the point of no return,' says Konovalov. The tension could also slow efforts now underway to disarm, even without the START accords. 'We want to get as much fissile material out of weapons, and out of Russia, as possible,' says Thomas Graham Jr., acting director of the Arms Control and Disarmament Agency. Starting last year under the Bush administration, the United States sent Moscow a list of the systems it planned to retire under START and began unilaterally dismantling Minuteman II strategic missiles and retiring aging Poseidon nuclear-missile submarines. The Russians also began retiring missile submarines and some of their older strategic missiles, partly on the expectation of American financial help...

"The Clinton administration will also only go so far in reducing its arsenal without formal implementation of START. Officials say they would continue to retire older submarines no matter what, but would rethink further cuts. Not implementing START would hurt at home. According to Steven Kosiak, of the Defense Budget Project, the United States would save as much as $60 billion over the next 15 years if the full START and START II cuts are made."

	1993 (current)	1996	1998	2000	2003
U.S.	10,563	9,150	7,950	6,000	
C.I.S.	10,301	9,150	7,950	6,000	
START II					
U.S.				3,800-4,250	3,000-3,500
C.I.S.				3,800-4,250	3,000-3,500

Source: Tim Zimmermann and Bruce B. Auster with Kenneth T. Walsh and Douglas Stanglin and Peter Vassiliev, "Are Nukes on the Loose?" in *U.S. News & World Report*, 19 April 1993, pp. 40-2.

★ 159 ★

Defense: Technological and Political Impacts

Military Challenges to World Peace, 1993-2025

"The end of the Cold War did not end all wars—it merely changed the paradigm in which conflicts arise and escalate, says military scholar Russell Ramsey, a distinguished visiting professor at the U.S. Army School of the Americas, Fort Benning, Georgia...

"Ramsey identifies four major challenges to world peace through the year 2025, in order of likelihood:

1. **Regional Ethnic Conflict**. The world will comprise some 200 nation-states by the early 2000s, whose sovereignty and authority will increasingly be challenged by 4,000 ethnic minorities. 'Non-acceptance of the nation-state fuels perhaps 20 armed conflicts in 1993 and is the greatest threat to world peace until 2025,' says Ramsey.

2. **Arms and Engineers for Hire**. This scenario appears very likely due to the 'flood' of arms and experts in the former Soviet Union, together with 'contract-hungry' arms producers in the West and ongoing regional conflicts around the world. Ramsey believes that the new North-South Economic World paradigm will tend to fuel this trafficking in arms and engineers for hire.

3. **Regional Pariah Regimes.** Panama's Manuel Noriega, Iraq's Saddam Hussein, North Korea's Kim II Sung, and Serbia's Slobodan Milosevic are present examples of pariahs who are able to gain support and to initiate and sustain armed conflict.

4. **Focused Economic Grievance Syndrome**. A single economic issue such as famine, control of a natural resource, or tariffs and government subsidies could become both a catalyst and a sustaining force behind a major conflict, says Ramsey."

Source: "World War: Four Scenarios," in *The Futurist*, September-October 1993, p. 55. *Primary source:* Russell W. Ramsey, "World Systems, Challenges: 1993-2025," in *The Officer*, April 1993.

★ 160 ★

Defense: Technological and Political Impacts

Designated Force Potential of Iraq and Iran, 1991-2000

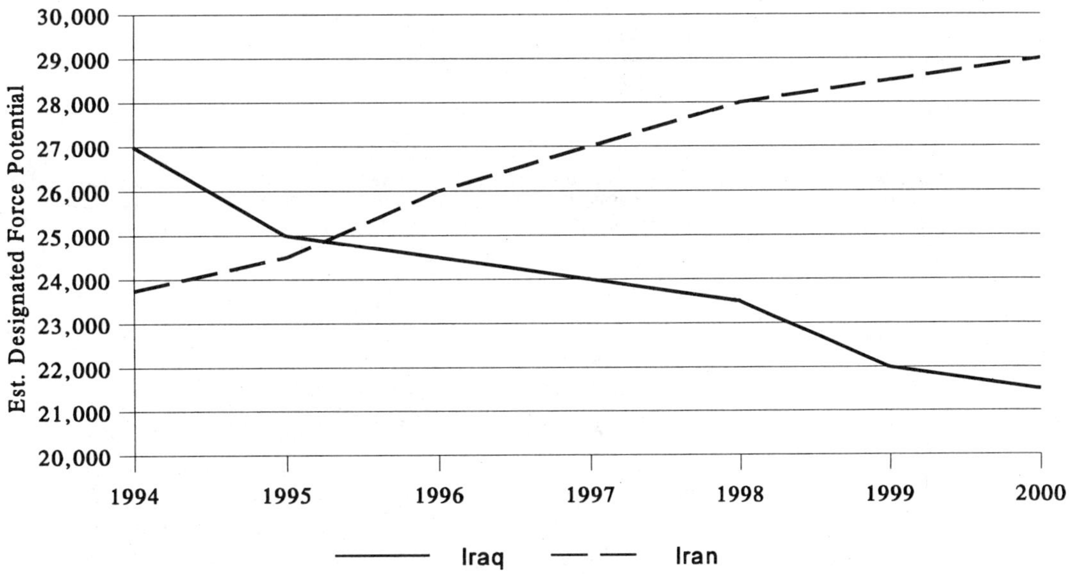

"[The table below and graphic above plots] the current and likely future range of DFP [Designated Force Potential] indices for both Iraq and Iran to the end of the decade.

"The [opposing] lines reflect the changes in air-ground combat power noted since the close of the Gulf War. The negative slope of the Iraqi line reflects the contraction of that country's forces after the Gulf war.

"The Iranian line is extended to the end of the decade to indicate the probable DFP index that Tehran might realize if it did no more than build its forces at the rate established over the last two years.

"The [high and low projections] reflect an annual degradation of Iraqi equipment of 2 to 3 percent over coming years and likely upper and lower ranges of Iranian improvements to be obtained from fulfillment of known procurement plans."

[Likely range of designated force potential]

	Iraq		Iran		
	Low	High	Low	Middle	High
1991	-	31,000[1]	-	22,000[1]	-
1992	-	29,000[1]	-	23,000[1]	-
1993	-	27,000[1]	-	24,000[1]	-
1994	27,000	-	23,750	24,000	24,500
1995	25,000	-	24,500	25,000	27,000
1996	24,500	25,000	26,000	27,000	29,000
1997	24,000	24,500	27,000	28,000	31,000
1998	23,500	24,000	28,000	29,000	32,500

[Continued]

★ 160 ★

Designated Force Potential of Iraq and Iran, 1991-2000

[Continued]

	Iraq		Iran		
	Low	High	Low	Middle	High
1999	22,000	23,000	28,500	30,000	34,000
2000	21,500	22,500	29,000	31,000	36,000

Source: Maj. Gen. Edward B. Atkeson, "The Gulf's Shifting Balance: Will Iran Be Our Next Foe?" in *Army*, July 1994, p. 12. *Notes:* Equipment on order is assumed to be delivered between 1996 and 1998. Iraqi force structure contracted between 1991 and 1993. Thereafter its material is assumed to degrade between 2 and 3 percent per year. 1. Actual. Magnitudes estimated from published chart.

★ 161 ★

Defense: Technological and Political Impacts

"The Obsolescence of War," 1993-2025

"I imagine a future where the propensity to use force is very low and the frequency of conflict is reduced to the greatest extent in history. I do not imagine this occurring or even coming into view within the next three to five years, but certainly by the end of the first quarter of the twenty-first century.

"Little explanation is required to rationalize the years of residual conflict that lie ahead. Saddam Hussein is not the last of the autocrats who possess significant armies; the end of the cold war has not meant that the global trade in arms will end in the near future; and the processes of self-determination and democratization now occurring appear to be neither trouble-free nor irreversible. If we do indeed reach a total of two hundred members of the United Nations by the year 2000, some new countries will only be created by turmoil. Many will be created from the chaos associated with the breakup of empires (especially the Soviet-Communist hegemony and satellite system), and others will emerge from the divisions caused by long-repressed ethnic and religious strife. On the sidelines, extremists and terrorists will probably resort increasingly to terroristic weapons in order to obtain resolution of terms they judge to be favorable. They will undoubtedly apply pressure and perhaps resort to private armies in order to gain a legitimate political role.

"Fortunately, this period is likely to be relatively short. Some isolated, lingering conflicts, such as those in Northern Ireland or among Palestinian Liberation Organization factions in the Middle East, may continue beyond this point, but their impact will be of declining regional and global consequence, and they will eventually solicit membership in the international system as the benefits of cooperation and integration into that system appear more appealing than the gains of vengeance."

Source: Allan E. Goodman, *A Brief History of the Future* (Boulder, CO: Westview Press), 1993, pp. 82-3.

★ 162 ★

Defense: Technological and Political Impacts

Technological Developments in Warfare, 2000-2100

"The battlefield of 2020 will use millions of computer systems and components. These systems, ranging from tiny microprocessors embedded in weapons to mobile command-and-control centers, will be ubiquitous, critical, and essential. They will be interlinked by a wide range of communications media.

"The effectiveness of individual *soldiers* in the future will be enhanced by computational tools that give them constant access to command-and-control centers, help them navigate, monitor their physical condition, and provide an instant source of up-to-date knowledge in the form of 'smart manuals.'

"Data bases, nearly instantaneous communications and analysis, intelligent decision aids, and multisensory information displays will provide *commanders* with an unprecedented awareness of the battlefield. While the potential for a good commander to affect the outcome will be multiplied, so will the potential for command errors to prove disastrous."

"For *logisticians*, the most significant changes will be in the planning and control of logistics operations.

"For *strategic planning*, warfare fought with computers and unmanned systems may become at once more common and more threatening. The publics of advanced nations may find war more acceptable if the number of casualties can be kept low. The rewards of aggression may be higher because of the aggressor's ability to exploit a temporary advantage in system sophistication.

"Computers, data bases, and software will themselves become targets in warfare. Our computational resources must be protected while exploiting any vulnerability in the opponent's systems. This *computer warfare* will involve at least four components: information security; injection of, and protection against, electronic viruses; sabotage; and exploiting the computational predictability of the opponent's systems...

"[Software] design will remain a difficult problem in 2020, but very-high-level languages will have shifted most software development out of the hands of programmers and into those of subject-area experts. [By] 2020 the Army will have the infrastructure, design tools, languages, and silicon foundry engineering to deploy to forward maintenance depots a silicon compiler for automated design and production of VLSI chips...

"In the area of *design simulation* and visualization tools, by 2020 high-resolution simulations will be calculable from first-principle non-linear equations and physical relationships. Real-time, interactive simulations of complex systems and operational environments will be achievable by networking thousands of individual simulators.

[Continued]

★ 162 ★

Technological Developments in Warfare, 2000-2100

[Continued]

"*Optimization* programs will be available to vary the parameters of a simulated design to seek the best set of design parameters. However, this optimization approach will still depend on having an initial design to simulate; the form in which a design problem is represented can control its solutions...

"Advances in knowledge representation will increase the reliability of software by providing formal structures and mathematicians to describe key information about the battlefield, such as terrain, the degree of certainty about the enemy's forces and intentions, and sets of potential outcomes...

"[Envisioned] is a *battle control language* that will give commanders controls of computational power analogous to the control that the current spreadsheet packages give users to 'program' their own calculations and tables. The high-level language will use statements that look like operations, orders, unit TOEs (Tables of Organization and Equipment), and map graphics. The language will let commanders control, interrogate, and understand a nearly instantaneous information flow about unit status and logistics. Incoming intelligence will be correlated and displayed in seconds. Continuous simulations, which will run in the background, will be used to test alternatives. Broad mission orders from the commander will automatically generate implementing instructions to units.

"The networks of 2020 will carry voice and data at high data rates. Connection into the network will be available anywhere in the field. However, some of the unsolved problems of network management today are likely to continue. These problems include delay, redundancy, and priorities...

"Today, the level of distributed processing has advanced to the point that a new application process needs to interact only with operating system or network protocol, one step above interaction at the hardware level... [This] level of required interaction will advance by 2020 so that applications will interact at a level of abstraction (meaning) that is far above the hardware level. This level of interaction will enable more powerful application programs for sensor fusion, situation assessment, operations planning, and sophisticated modeling.

"The technology to support this future level of distributed processing will include massively distributed worldwide networks; dynamic, real-time protocols for distributed operating systems; and distributed object data base management systems...

"In the area of *human factors*, technological advances will occur in visual display techniques, force-feedback controls, information presentation optimized for low data transmission rate, and workload optimization for control of multiple systems by a single operator."

"*Heads-up displays*, which project an image from a lipstick-size tube onto eyeglasses, are just appearing as commercial products. By 2020 stereo heads-up displays will be standard...

[Continued]

★ 162 ★

Technological Developments in Warfare, 2000-2100

[Continued]

"[By] 2020 interface media and modes will be customized to the user's job, expertise, and personal preferences. One operator will be able to control multiple systems simultaneously and efficiently. Controls will switch between pure program control, operator monitoring, and operator control, according to circumstances. Structured voice will be the standard mode of entering responses to option menus. Other input modes may include analysis of facial and body gestures from TV images or direct monitoring of physiological responses (although the semantic content of such input will be far less sophisticated than linguistic expression).

"In the *hypermedia* area, users will be able to navigate consistently, through many different kinds of information, including drawings, photographs, video, synthesized voice, and diverse textual formats. The technology and human factors expertise for hypermedia is just beginning to emerge...

"[Users] of map information in 2020 will be able to switch freely between, or superimpose, symbolic data and simulated or real scenes. Synthesized speech will supplement visual displays. Computer-aided drawing will convey nonverbal information...

"[By] 2020, unmanned systems will probably still be less capable than manned systems. They will be useful because, if properly designed, they can be far more numerous than manned systems. The highest payoffs from battlefield robots will come from putting large numbers of sensors in places where soldiers should not go and from integrating the information from the sensors into a coherent picture...

"[A] more relevant model for conceiving of battlefield robots is the land mine rather than the human soldier. That is military robots will evolve as 'smart mines' with increasingly sophisticated sensors, weapons, and modes of propulsion, rather than as 'mechanical foot soldiers.' The sensors weapons, and propulsion methods used by these robot mines will differ greatly from those used by soldiers...

"For robot weapons, the most practical concept may be explosively propelled projectiles that achieve armor-piercing velocity with low weight and cost. By 2020 single-missile robot tubes, hidden in ground cover, are likely to be more secure than missile batteries mounted on vehicles."

Source: National Research Council, Commission on Engineering and Technical Systems, Board on Army Science and Technology, *Star 21-Strategic Technologies for the Army of the Twenty—First Century* (Washington, D.C.: National Academy Press), 1992, pp. 113-23.

The Space Program

★ 163 ★

Summary of Space Program Budget Proposals, 1994-1998

[Millions of dollars]

	1994	1995	1996	1997	1998	1994-1997 Total
NASA civil aviation	36	121	171	222	267	550
NASA short-haul aircraft research	3	10	17	20	20	50

Source: Executive Office of the President of the United States, Office of Management and Budget, *A Vision of Change for America* (Washington, D.C.: U.S. Government Printing Office, 17 February 1993), p. 136.

★ 164 ★

The Space Program

Proposed Investments in NASA, 1993-1999

[Millions of dollars]

		1993 Enacted	Estimate		Change: 1994 to 1995	Estimate			
			1994	1995		1996	1997	1998	1999
National Aeronautics and Space Administration	BA	1,091	1,438	1,726	288	1,836	1,894	2,022	1,906
	OL	885	1,236	1,542	306	1,772	1,858	1,958	1,939

Source: Executive Office of the President of the United States, Office of Management and Budget, *Budget of the United States Government* (Washington, D.C.: U.S. Government Printing Office, 1994), p. 243. *Note:* BA = Budget Authority. OL = Outlays.

★ 165 ★

The Space Program

Future Military Space Operations, 2020

"A comprehensive joint-service study conducted by 350 participants under auspices of the Air Force's Air University recently produced a candidate blueprint for future space operations. Called 'SPACECAST 2020,' the full study report is still in the review process, but an unclassified executive summary states: 'The United States must not only be able to be in space, it must be able to act from space and to protect space-based assets.' The summary outlines a number of concepts aimed at assuring 'global presence, global reach and global power' using space...

"Although put forth in the SPACECAST 2020 executive summary without supporting details, several highlighted options include:

—A composite aerospace wing with a squadron of rocket-powered TAVs capable of either orbiting 5,000-lb. payloads or delivering them via suborbital trajectory to any point on the globe within hours of launch. Modified KC-135Q tankers carrying noncryogenic propellants could transfer fuel to the TAVs after takeoff and before they accelerate to orbital velocities.

—An information architecture that can 'collect, analyze, assess, synthesize and disseminate' fused data from hyperspectral and other imaging sensors, as well as laser, radar and acoustic systems.

—A 'Super Global Positioning System' that provides three-dimensional navigation capabilities. It would be integrated into real-time battle management plans, and all information made available to users at all levels.

—A means to track and control myriad transatmospheric and space vehicles—a 'space traffic control' system. These would consist of "space-based sensors to provide continuous, in-flight deconfliction of orbital space systems without operator intervention.' Users would alter a flight plan and automatically be cleared for use of a 'spaceway,' according to the summary.

—Space 'weather' information disseminated directly to military and civil centers via data superhighways. Forecasting may depend on deep-space satellites that monitor and report solar plasma emissions or solar wind, with warnings of radiation threats to operations. Enhanced atmospheric sensing also could warn of potential communications, radar and navigation systems disruption or blackout. Sensors might be deployed on future GPS and commercial satellite constellations to enable daily, world-wide ionosphere mapping.

[Continued]

★ 165 ★

Future Military Space Operations, 2020

[Continued]

—Far-future unconventional spacelift concepts such as Earth-orbiting and geostationary tethers, nuclear propulsion and anti-matter-based fuels. When he commanded the then-Air-Force Astronautics Laboratory, Nunn predicted that anti-matter-enriched rocket fuels would definitely become feasible. Recently, however, the demise of the U.S. superconducting supercollider program "put the anti-matter option back to zero" for the U.S., simply because the necessary quantities of anti-particles cannot be obtained from overseas. Although it may not happen in the U.S., anti-matter-augmented propulsion "will be in Boeing someday, though. It offers true SSTO capability and substantial in-orbit maneuvering and evasive [potential]. It's definitely a long-term effort though," he said.

—Information warfare capability. This broad category encompasses psychological operations such as use of holographic images projected from space to 'achieve information superiority'."

Source: William B. Scott, "Cutbacks Foster Novel Military Space Concepts," in *Aviation Week & Space Technology*, 5 September 1994, pp. 101, 103, 105.

★ 166 ★

The Space Program

World Missions to Mars, 1994-1996

"From the beginning, Mars has exerted an uncommonly powerful tug on the human psyche. The ancients associated the red planet with destruction, and the Romans later named it for their god of war. What appeared to be canals on Mars's surface once fueled widespread speculation that an advanced civilization had inhabited the cold and rugged planet, and fancifully imagined Martians have long been a staple of science fiction tales. Indeed, earthlings are so enchanted by the possibility of Martian life that in 1938 Orson Welles was able to panic the entire nation with his dramatic radio 'newscast' of an invasion from our neighboring planet.

"But Welles and many others had the invasion backward. While no Martian, benign or terrifying, has set down here, scientists have spent a generation investigating the red planet's secrets. That exploration will soon accelerate. Nearly two decades since the last successful mission to Mars, space agencies from the United States, Russia, Japan and Europe all are aiming scientific probes in its direction...

[Continued]

★ 166 ★

World Missions to Mars, 1994-1996

[Continued]

"Russia plans to launch spacecraft in 1994 and 1996 that will land small stations on the surface. Planet B, a Japanese orbiter, will be sent in 1996 to study the upper atmosphere. In the same year, the National Aeronautics and Space Administration expects to deploy a lander carrying a six-wheeled rover whose mission will be to examine the chemistry of nearby rocks. Ten or more seismic and weather stations and rovers could be deployed late in the decade to provide a global network of monitors called Mars Environment Survey (MESUR, pronounced 'measure'). The European Space Agency will decide this fall whether to mount a complementary effort...

"The many images of the Martian surface that Observer will soon send home may help explain our neighboring planet's form and evolution. But after looking at satellite photographs of Mars and trying to decipher what they see, planetary scientists will want to study the terrain at close range. Since they cannot visit the planet themselves and turn the soil with their own hands, the plan is to send robotic observers to verify what remote sensing satellites have reported and to uncover details that are impossible to detect from orbit.

"NASA's MESUR project, planned for the end of the decade, would place a network of 10 or more small landers at strategic locations across the planet's surface. The principal tasks of the heavily instrumented landers would be to document shifts in the local weather and to keep a continuous record of seismic activity for at least a year. Each lander would carry and dispatch a small rover that could drive up to nearby rocks and determine their chemical composition."

"The network of seismometers would record 'marsquakes' from several points to explore what the mysterious interior of the planet is really like. Much of what scientists know about Earth's internal structure and dynamics has been learned by studying earthquakes, since the waves that are generated by such cataclysmic rumblings change as they pass through various layers of the Earth's interior. 'That's a whole class of science we just can't get from orbital imaging,' says Golombek.

"Deploying a swarm of landers is a huge technical challenge, however, and since money is tight, NASA will test a new, low-cost exploratory scheme with a single lander called 'pathfinder.' Initial funds for that mission, to be launched in late 1996, are expected to be included in the 1994 budget now before Congress. By using rough landing techniques pioneered years ago by the Russians, safety ideas from the American auto industry and powerful off-the-shelf electronics, NASA expects to build the initial lander for $150 million and its microrover for an additional $25 million—bargain basement prices for space exploration. Both are to be hoisted into space on a medium-class Delta rocket like the ones now used to launch communications satellites. The full fleet of landers envisioned for the MESUR project is expected to cost about half a billion dollars. By contrast, the complex Viking mission of the 1970s, with its two orbiters and two landers, would cost $3.2 billion in today's dollars."

Source: William J. Cook, "The Invasion of Mars," in *U.S. News & World Report*, 23 August 1993, pp. 51-53.

★ 167 ★

The Space Program

Historical Decline in NASA's Five-year Budget Requests, 1996-1999

"A quarter of a century after man first landed there, the moon is again a focus of space-going attention. But whereas the world held its breath for Apollo 11, few have heard of *Clementine*, the little craft following in its orbits...

"When planetary scientists and engineers met recently to discuss small missions at the Applied Physics Laboratory (APL) of Johns Hopkins University, in Maryland, they were acutely aware of *Clementine* looking down on them from the waxing moon; many wanted to use its technologies. They are not merely entranced by the possibilities. They are moved by necessity. Once *Cassini*, a big mission to Saturn, is off the books, NASA plans only small planetary probes for the foreseeable future...

"As well as Mars..., NASA's plans include the 'Discovery programme', a series of missions each costing under $150m. The APL meeting was full of potential Discoveries: spacecraft to orbit Mercury (which has the sort of polar ice *Clementine* is looking for on the moon), to look at Venus in the infra-red, to puncture comets and to study the volcanoes of Jupiter's moons...

"At the heart of the NASA programme is the space station it plans to build with Russia, Europe and Japan, a programme that would buy 100 Discovery missions. Last year the House of Representatives voted by a majority of one to keep the project alive. This year critics will attack it again. Some will say that it saves too many jobs in Russia and not enough in California; others that Russian co-operation is not cutting costs as much as promised. If, as expected, the House appropriations committee gives NASA less than the president has asked for, then even George Brown, chair of the science committee and a long-standing station supporter, says he will vote to kill it rather than see NASA's other projects gutted."

[Billions of dollars]

	1996	1997	1998	1999
1993	17.70	20.30	-	-
1994	16.25	16.60	16.90	-
1995	14.50	14.60	14.70	14.80

Source: "Beyond This Horizon," in *The Economist*, 30 April 1994, pp. 94-95. *Primary source:* Congressional Budget Office; NASA. *Notes:* Magnitudes estimated from published chart. Source also includes data for 1990-1995.

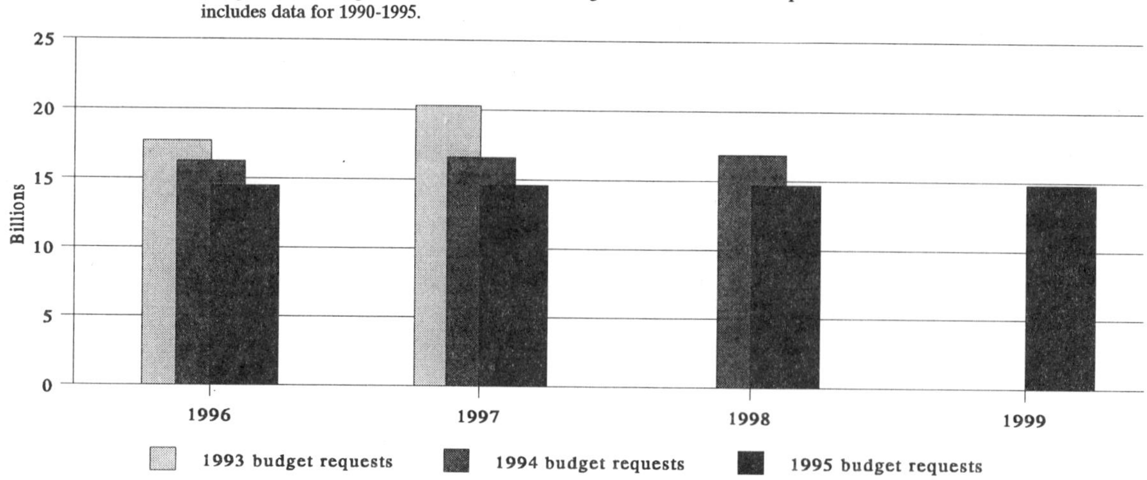

★ 168 ★

The Space Program

Space Station Freedom Program, 1987-2000

"Space Station Freedom's mission is three-fold. First, it will provide a permanent outpost where we will learn to live and work productively in space. Freedom will be an orbiting research base with essential resources of volume, power, data handling, and communications to accommodate experiments for long-duration studies of human physiology and well-being in space, research that is required before the nation can embark on achievable, long-range human exploration goals. Second, Freedom will provide an advanced research laboratory to explore space and employ its resource for the benefit of humanity. Space Station Freedom will be a permanent, multi-purpose research laboratory and outpost in space unsurpassed in equipment and capabilities with the constant presence of a hands-on crew for learning how to use the unique microgravity environment of space, enabling the study of new materials, new medicines and new technologies. And finally, Freedom will provide the opportunity to learn to build, operate and maintain systems in space. Space Station Freedom will be an engineering testbed, located in low Earth orbit where we will perfect our ability to live and function, to allow development of the systems, the logistics, the knowledge and the talents required for the full-scale utilization, and exploration of space."

Source: NASA, Office of Space Systems Development, *Space Station Freedom Media Handbook* (Washington, D.C.: March 1991), pp. III, 21.

★ 169 ★

The Space Program

Space Station Freedom Configuration Capabilities, 1997-2000

	Man tended capability 1997	Permanently manned capability 2000
Power	18.75 kW-1PV module	56.25 kW-3 PV modules
Module length	27ft. -1 microgravity lab	27ft. -1 lab. 1 hab
U.S. lab user racks (ISPRs)	12	12
User research power	11 kW	30 kW
Logistic module capacity	MPLM - 8 racks	PLM - 20 racks
Command uplink	70 kbps	70 kbps
Data downlink	43 Mbps	43 Mbps
Gravity level	1 ug	1 ug
Attached payload accommodations	2 ports	4 ports
U.S. assembly and logistics flights	6	17
Permanent crew size	0	4 expandable to 8
Dedicated crew for research	4 (while on station)	2 (continuous)
Utilization flights (MTC to PMC)	8	N/A
Truss	4 segments built and checked out on ground	7 segments built and checked out on ground
Length (total)	158 ft.	353

[Continued]

★ 169 ★

Space Station Freedom Configuration Capabilities, 1997-2000

[Continued]

	Man tended capability 1997	Permanently manned capability 2000
Pressurized resource nodes	1	2
International hardware:		
Canada	Mobile Servicing System (simplified)	Mobile Servicing System
Japan	none	JEM - 10 ISPRs
Europe	none	APM - 20 ISPRs
Life Support	Shuttle supported	regenerative water loop
Propulsion	2 downsized modules	4 modules
Pressurized docking adapter	1	2
Airlock	0	1
Assured Crew Return Vehicle	0 - use Shuttle	1

Source: NASA, Office of Space Systems Development, *Space Station Freedom Media Handbook* (Washington, D.C.: March 1991), p. 23.

Chapter 6
ECONOMICS

The American Economy: General Projections

★ 170 ★

Economic Trends

"[Forecasters Cetron and Davies predict that in the future] Washington, D.C. will supplant New York as the world financial capital. The stock exchanges and other financial institutions, especially those involved with international transactions, will move south to be near Congress, the World Bank, and key regulatory bodies.

"Among the key economic players already in Washington: the Federal Reserve Board, the embassies and commercial/cultural attaches of nearly every country in the world, and the headquarters of many multi-national and international corporations.

"In addition, several agencies cooperating with the United Nations, including the International Monetary Fund and the General Agreement on Tariffs and Trade, have their headquarters or routinely conduct much of their business in Washington."

Source: Marvin J. Cetron and Owen Davies, "Trends Shaping the World," in *The Futurist*, September-October 1991, pp. 18-19. *Primary source:* Marvin J. Cetron and Owen Davies, *Crystal Globe: The Haves and HaveeNots of the New World Order* (St. Martin's Press, 1991).

★ 171 ★

The American Economy: General Projections

KEDI Economic Survey Highlights of the U.S. Economy, 1994-1996 and Later

"The Kent Economic Development Inc. (KEDI) long-term outlook for the economy is as follows: Growth of the economy will accelerate in 1994. The upward trend will continue throughout 1994 and 1995. It will slow down in 1996. Forecast data for 1994 and afterward do not point to recession or major downturn. In 1994, and years that follow, short-and long-term interest rates will be increasing. Federal budget deficits will keep declining in 1994 and the following years. In 1994, the export-import gap is expected to be increasingly negative. It will be declining in 1996 and afterward."

Source: Kent Economic and Development Institute Inc., *KEDI Economic Survey*, March 1994, p.2.

★ 172 ★

The American Economy: General Projections

The Future U.S. Economic Crisis

"All catastrophe theorists agree that we are heading for a precipice. There is disagreement as to the severity of the crash. Paul Erdman [in *What's Next? How to Prepare Yourself for the Crash of '89* (1988)] foresees a severe but short recession, with relativity good times a couple of years later. Howard Ruff [*How to Prosper During the Coming Bad Years* (1979)] prophesies total chaos and advocates "survivalism"—store enough food for one year, gun and bullets, etc. The others predict something in between. Almost all predict:

1. A crash in the stock market, with stocks and bonds losing at least 50% of their value.

2. Inflation, perhaps even hyperinflation.

3. Very extensive bank failures.

4. Collapse of real estate values.

5. A sharp decline in the value of the dollar and a sharp increase in the price of gold.

[Continued]

★ 172 ★

The Future U.S. Economic Crisis

[Continued]

6. A general loss of confidence in the government of the United States and in its institutions.

"Some of these things have already happened to some extent; but they are predicted to become much more serious. It should be recognized that while the segment of the economic field discussed in this chapter has been crying wolf for the past decades, others have been consistently optimistic. For example, Herman Kahn's *The Coming Boom*, published in 1982, foresaw only good times ahead. Any many other furturologists have published similar analyses since then.

"A substantial portion of each of the popular books that predict an economic catastrophe is devoted to suggestions and tips. These are designed to help the reader to weather the coming storm and to emerge in good shape economically. People with money to invest are advised to reduce their stocks and bonds portfolio and to avoid real estate altogether. U.S. government debt instruments such as T-bills, Swiss francs, and gold are favored by many advisers.

"Many of the investment programs are frankly recommended as disaster strategies. They are designed to play it safe, even if that means losing out on some good investment opportunities. But that can also be expensive in the long run. Had you followed the advice of the catastrophe crowd in the late 1970s, for example, and converted most of your nest egg into gold, you would have been deliriously happy for a few years in the early 1980s when the price of gold shot up to over $800 an ounce. But it promptly dropped back to below $400. In the meantime, you have been renting instead of owning your own home—when, in some parts of the country, the value of your house may well have increased four-or-fivefold in the past ten years. So, what price insurance?...

"In this discussion we are not concerned with economic models in general, but only with the use of these models to predict an out-and-out castastrophe. All that I know about models and all that I have observed leads me to conclude that catastrophe predictions based on economic models are almost completely devoid of credibility. Sooner or later a genuine economic catastrophe will descend upon us, and some fortunate author will have predicted it more or less correctly and will therefore be lauded as a true prophet and a genius. But in my view, his success will have nothing to do with his skill or his foresight. It will be strictly a matter of luck."

Source: Walter J. Karplus, "Economic Collapse: Another 'Great Depression'," in his *The Heavens Are Falling: The Scientific Prediction of Catastrophes in Out Time* (New York: Plenum Press), 1992, pp. 239-41.

★ 173 ★

The American Economy: General Projections

U.S. Economic Outlook, 1994-1996

	1994 III	1994 IV	1995 I	1995 II	1992	1993	1994	1995	1996
U.S. Economy									
Annual Growth Rate									
Real GDP	2.9	2.8	2.7	2.9	2.6	3.0	3.9	2.9	2.8
Civilian Employment	1.8	1.9	2.1	1.6	0.6	1.5	2.3	1.9	1.6
Consumer Prices	2.9	3.0	3.1	2.7	3.0	3.0	2.6	2.9	2.9
Percent									
Civilian Unemployment	6.3	6.2	6.3	6.2	7.4	6.8	6.4	6.2	6.2
Interest Rates, Percent									
Federal Funds Rate	3.8	3.9	4.0	4.0	3.5	3.0	3.6	4.0	4.0
3-Month T-Bill Rate	3.7	3.9	4.0	4.0	3.4	3.0	3.6	4.0	4.0
Prime Rate	6.3	6.3	6.3	6.3	6.3	6.3	6.3	6.3	6.3
Discount Rate	3.3	3.3	3.3	3.5	3.3	3.0	3.2	3.4	3.5
Corporate AAA Bond Yield	7.3	7.2	7.2	7.0	8.1	7.2	7.3	7.0	6.7
30-Year Government Bond	6.7	6.6	6.6	6.4	7.7	6.6	6.7	6.4	6.1
Mortgage Rates, Percent									
30-Year Fixed Rate	7.5	7.4	7.4	7.3	8.4	7.3	7.5	7.3	7.1
1-Year Adjustable	5.1	5.4	5.5	5.5	5.6	4.6	4.9	5.6	5.6

Source: "U.S. Economic Outlook: April 1994," in *Real Estate Outlook*, April 1994, p. 18. *Primary source:* Forecast produced using Laurence H. Meyer & Associates' model of the U.S. economy. Assumptions and simulations by Dr. John Tuccillo and Eileen A. Neely. *Notes:* Quarterly rates are seasonally adjusted rates. Source also includes data for 1993 and the first half of 1994, as well as information on Home Sales & Starts and Median Home Prices (see table 113).

★ 174 ★

The American Economy: General Projections

KEDI Economic Survey, 1993-1999

"KEDI's long-term outlook for the economy calls for continuing expansion of output this year and in 1995...Forecast of State and Local budgets is optimistic with constantly increasing surpluses for the entire forecast period."

Indicator	Unit	1993	1997	1998	1999
Gross domestic	bil. 87$	5137.6	5766.5	5945.3	6129.6
product	% change	3.0	2.6	3.1	3.1
Index of indust.	1987=100	111.5	130.1	134.1	138.5
prod.	% change	4.6	2.2	3.1	3.3
Capacity	%	80.8	84.6	84.3	84.2
utiliz.	% change	3.9	.1	-.3	-.1
Unemployment	%	7.0	5.9	5.9	5.9
rate	% change	-8.5	-.4	.2	.1

[Continued]

★ 174 ★

KEDI Economic Survey, 1993-1999

[Continued]

Indicator	Unit	1993	1997	1998	1999
Private housing	mil. units	1.3	1.3	1.3	1.3
starts	% change	4.8	23.8	-.6	.1
Car sales	mil. units	9.2	10.0	10.2	10.5
	% change	9.4	2.0	2.2	3.1
Implicit GDP	1987=100	124.0	146.4	151.3	156.3
price def.	% change	2.3	3.9	3.4	3.3
Consumer Price	82-84=100	144.1	168.3	174.4	180.3
Index	% change	3.0	3.8	3.6	3.4
Prod. Price Index	1982=100	124.9	158.0	164.3	170.7
(fin. goods)	% change	1.4	4.7	4.0	3.9
Federal Deficit	bil. $	-270.4	-176.0	-159.8	-149.6
	% change	-1.6	-8.0	-9.2	-6.4
Personal Income	bil. $	5281.9	7642.9	8338.4	9105.6
	% change	2.5	8.8	9.1	9.2
Prime Rate	%	6.0	7.3	7.7	8.2
	% change	-4.0	2.0	5.4	6.7
Mortgage Rate	%	8.2	9.4	9.6	9.4
	% change	-3.2	5.7	1.6	-1.9
Currency+demand	bil. $	1062.4	1415.5	1494.8	1572.5
deposits	% change	10.4	7.1	5.6	5.2
Commercial+ind.	bil. $	617.7	634.4	652.8	669.1
loans	% change	5.3	2.7	2.9	2.5
Raw steel	mil. sh. tons	90.1	92.0	91.6	91.5
production	% change	2.4	2.1	-.4	-.1
Electric power	mil. kw-hr	3248	3316.0	3422.1	3435.8
production	% change	2.0	2.1	3.2	.4
Bituminous coal	mil. sh. tons	981	1000.6	1019.6	1043.1
production	% change	.8	2.0	1.9	2.3
Crude oil	avg. daily bbl.	2891	2885.2	2853.5	2847.8
output	% change	-.3	-.2	-1.1	-.2
Retail sales	bil. $	2112.5	2838.2	3065.2	3319.6
	%change	7.2	7.4	8.0	8.3

Source: Kent Economic and Development Institute, *KEDI Economic Survey*, prepared by the staff of Kent Economic and Development Institute, Inc., Vol. 18, No. 4, March 1994, pp. 1, 3. *Primary source:* U.S. Department of Commerce fourth quarter 1993 second estimates of Income and Product data; Board of Governors of the Federal Reserve System release of the Index of Industrial Production, February 1994; and latest available data on prices, employment, industrial and financial developments. *Note:* Numbers in "% change" rows show percent changes over the previous year.

★ 175 ★

The American Economy: General Projections

Gross Domestic Product by Major Demand Category, 1979-2005-I

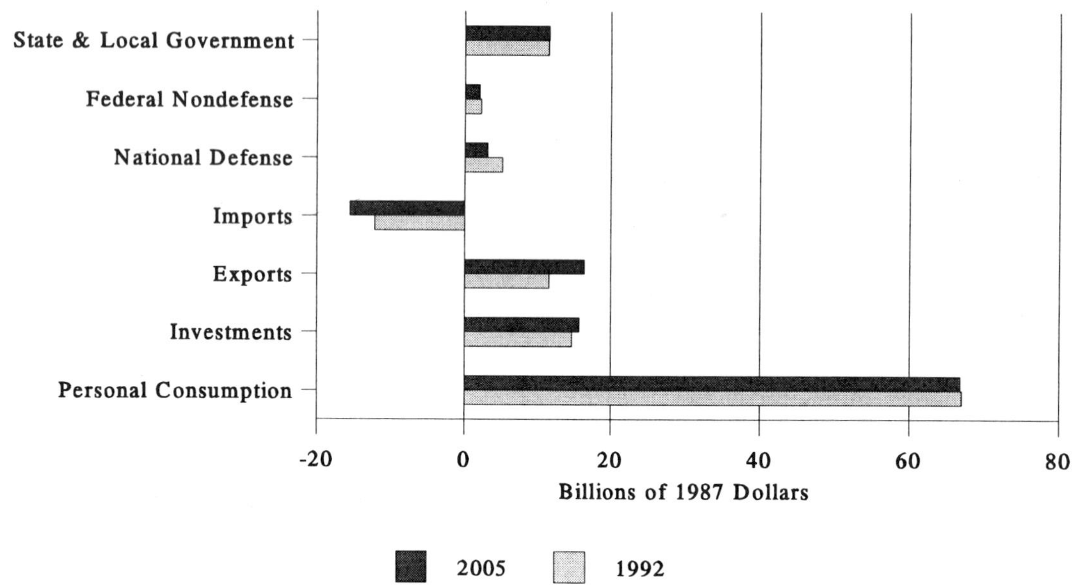

"[Real] GDP is expected to grow at an average annual rate of 2.2 percent between 1992 and 2005 in the moderate-growth scenario. This compares favorably with the rate of growth of 2.1 percent annually during the 1979-92 period, but is slower than the 1979-89 rate of growth of 2.5 percent. To understand why the GDP is expected to slow somewhat in the future, one must examine the behavior of the major factors of production—labor and capital. The growth of the supply of labor, as represented by the civilian labor force, will slow to a 1.3-percent rate over the 1992-2005 period, down 0.2 percentage point from the 1979-92 growth rate of 1.5 percent. As population growth slows, so too, will labor force growth, in spite of assumptions of higher immigration. Offsetting this decline in labor force growth to some extent is a higher utilization rate for labor. Real GDP per employee, estimated to increase at an annual rate of 0.8 percent between 1992 and 2005, will be unchanged from the growth experienced during the 1979-92 period."

[Billions of 1987 dollars]

Category	1979	1989	1992	2005 Low	2005 Moderate	2005 High
Gross domestic product	$3,796.8	$4,838.0	$4,986.3	$6,028.2	$6,629.1	$7,331.2
Personal consumption	2,448.3	3,223.3	3,341.8	4,104.6	4,426.5	4,699.0
Investment	669.8	784.1	732.9	929.0	1,043.2	1,376.2
Exports	293.6	471.8	578.0	940.7	1,088.4	1,264.7
Imports	-304.1	-545.4	-611.6	-955.6	-1,037.4	-1,182.6
National defense	185.1	281.4	261.2	197.9	203.4	208.8
Federal nondefense	86.6	94.8	111.8	122.2	133.6	141.7
State and local government	417.6	528.3	572.2	689.2	771.4	823.4
Percent distribution						
Gross domestic product	100.0	100.0	100.0	100.0	100.0	100.0
Personal consumption	64.5	66.6	67.0	68.1	66.8	64.1
Investment	17.6	13.7	14.7	15.4	15.7	18.8

[Continued]

★ 175 ★

Gross Domestic Product by Major Demand Category, 1979-2005-I

[Continued]

Category	1979	1989	1992	2005		
				Low	Moderate	High
Exports	7.7	11.2	11.6	15.6	16.4	17.3
Imports	-8.0	-11.6	-12.3	-15.9	-15.6	-16.1
National defense	4.9	5.9	5.2	3.3	3.1	2.8
Federal nondefense	2.3	2.2	2.2	2.0	2.0	1.9
State and local government	11.0	11.5	11.5	11.4	11.6	11.2

Source: U.S. Department of Labor, Bureau of Labor Statistics, *The American Work Force: 1992-2005* (Washington, D.C.: U.S. Government Printing Office, April 1994), pp. 12-13. *Primary source:* Historical data, Bureau of Economic Analysis; projected data, Bureau of Labor Statistics.

★ 176 ★

The American Economy: General Projections

Gross Domestic Product by Major Demand Category, 1979-2005-II

"[Real] GDP is expected to grow at an average annual rate of 2.2 percent between 1992 and 2005 in the moderate-growth scenario. This compares favorably with the rate of growth of 2.1 percent annually during the 1979-92 period, but is slower than the 1979-89 rate of growth of 2.5 percent. To understand why the GDP is expected to slow somewhat in the future, one must examine the behavior of the major factors of production—labor and capital. The growth of the supply of labor, as represented by the civilian labor force, will slow to a 1.3-percent rate over the 1992-2005 period, down 0.2 percentage point from the 1979-92 growth rate of 1.5 percent. As population growth slows, so too, will labor force growth, in spite of assumptions of higher immigration. Offsetting this decline in labor force growth to some extent is a higher utilization rate for labor. Real GDP per employee, estimated to increase at an annual rate of 0.8 percent between 1992 and 2005, will be unchanged from the growth experienced during the 1979-92 period."

[Billions of 1987 dollars]

Category	Average annual rates of change					
	1979-89	1989-92	1979-92	1992-2005		
				Low	Moderate	High
Gross domestic product	2.5	1.0	2.1	1.5	2.2	3.0
Personal consumption	2.8	1.2	2.4	1.6	2.2	2.7
Investment	1.6	-2.2	.7	1.8	2.8	5.0
Exports	4.9	7.0	5.3	3.8	5.0	6.2
Imports	6.0	3.9	5.5	3.5	4.1	5.2
National defense	4.3	-2.5	2.7	-2.1	-1.9	-1.7
Federal nondefense	.9	5.7	2.0	.7	1.4	1.8
State and local government	2.4	2.7	2.5	1.4	2.3	2.8

Source: U.S. Department of Labor, Bureau of Labor Statistics, *The American Work Force: 1992-2005* (Washington, D.C.: U.S. Government Printing Office, April 1994), pp. 12-13. *Primary source:* Historical data, Bureau of Economic Analysis; projected data, Bureau of Labor Statistics.

★ 177 ★

The American Economy: General Projections

Gross Private Domestic Investment, 1979-2005-I

"This component of GDP, hereinafter referred to as private investment, is comprised of business fixed investment, that is, purchases of nonresidential structures and purchases of producers' durable equipment; construction of residential buildings; and changes inventories. Over the historical period, private investment has accounted for a remarkably stable share of GDP—16.5 percent during the 1970's and 16.3. percent during the 1980's. This seeming stability in the averages can be deceptive, however.

"Business investment in the form of purchases of plant and equipment has traditionally been the most volatile component of GDP, responding sharply and even widely at times to swings in the business cycle. Equipment purchases, for example, ranged from a low 4.7 percent of real GDP in 1961 to a high of 7.6 percent in 1988. Even more noteworthy is the spectacular range of annual changes over the post-World War II period, from a low of an 11.3-percent decline in 1975 to a high of 18-percent growth in 1984. Over the projection period, the Bureau expects producers' durable equipment purchases to continue to grow more rapidly than overall GDP by 2005. What is notable, however, about producers' durable equipment growth in the 1980's and that growth projection to 2005 is the growing proportion accounted for by computers. Because of the enormous increases in the quality of business computing over the past 10 years, constant-dollar estimates of this commodity grew at a phenomenal pace during the 1980's. Many analysts of the computer industry expect this growth to continue almost unabated throughout the projection period."

[Billions of 1987 dollars]

Category	1979	1989	1992	2005		
				Low	Moderate	High
Gross private investment	$669.7	$784.00	$732.9	$929.0	$1,043.5	$1,376.2
Business fixed investment	448.8	540.1	529.2	699.0	808.4	1,042.7
Producers' durable equipment	285.5	362.5	378.6	538.3	637.4	807.1
Nonresidential construction	163.3	177.6	150.6	160.7	171.0	235.6
Residential construction	207.4	214.2	197.1	217.2	220.1	307.9
Change in business inventories	13.6	29.8	6.5	12.8	14.7	25.6
			Percent distribution			
Gross private investment	100.0	100.0	100.0	100.0	100.0	100.0
Business fixed investment	67.0	68.9	72.2	75.2	77.5	75.8
Producers' durable equipment	42.6	46.2	51.7	57.9	61.1	58.6
Nonresidential construction	24.4	22.7	20.5	17.3	16.4	17.1
Residential construction	31.0	27.3	26.9	23.4	21.1	22.4
Change in business inventories	2.0	3.8	.9	1.4	1.4	1.9

Source: U.S. Department of Labor, Bureau of Labor Statistics, *The American Work Force: 1992-2005*, (Washington, D.C.: U.S. Government Printing Office, April 1994), p. 16. *Primary source:* Historical data, Bureau of Economic Analysis; projected data, Bureau of Labor Statistics.

★ 178 ★

The American Economy: General Projections

Gross Private Domestic Investment, 1979-2005-II

"This component of GDP, hereinafter referred to as private investment, is comprised of business fixed investment, that is, purchases of nonresidential structures and purchases of producers' durable equipment; construction of residential buildings; and changes in business inventories. Over the historical period, private investment has accounted for a remarkably stable share of GDP—16.5 percent during the 1970's and 16.3. percent during the 1980's. This seeming stability in the averages can be deceptive, however.

"Business investment in the form of purchases of plant and equipment has traditionally been the most volatile component of GDP, responding sharply and even widely at times to swings in the business cycle. Equipment purchases, for example, ranged from a low 4.7 percent of real GDP in 1961 to a high of 7.6 percent in 1988. Even more noteworthy is the spectacular range of annual changes over the post-World War II period, from a low of an 11.3-percent decline in 1975 to a high of 18-percent growth in 1984. Over the projection period, the Bureau expects producers' durable equipment purchases to continue to grow more rapidly than overall GDP by 2005. What is notable, however, about producers' durable equipment growth in the 1980's and that growth projection to 2005 is the growing proportion accounted for by computers. Because of the enormous increases in the quality of business computing over the past 10 years, constant-dollar estimates of this commodity grew at a phenomenal pace during the 1980's. Many analysts of the computer industry expect this growth to continue almost unabated throughout the projection period."

[Billions of 1987 dollars]

Category	Average annual rates of change					
	1979-89	1989-92	1979-92	1992-2005		
				Low	Moderate	High
Gross private investment	1.6	-2.2	.7	1.8	2.8	5.0
Business fixed investment	1.9	-.7	1.3	2.2	3.3	5.4
Producers' durable equipment	2.4	1.5	2.2	2.7	4.1	6.0
Nonresidential construction	.8	-5.3	-.6	.5	1.0	3.5
Residential construction	.3	-2.7	-.4	.7	.9	3.5

Source: U.S. Department of Labor, Bureau of Labor Statistics, *The American Work Force: 1992-2005,* (Washington, D.C.: U.S. Government Printing Office, April 1994), p. 16. *Primary source:* Historical data, Bureau of Economic Analysis; projected data, Bureau of Labor Statistics.

★ 179 ★

The American Economy: General Projections

Exports and Imports of Goods and Services, 1979-2005

"It is safe to say that U.S. exports and imports of goods and services are the two components of GDP that have gained the most in importance over the past 30 years. In 1960, real gross exports accounted for 4.4 percent of GDP, while real gross imports tallied a 4.7-percent share. By 1992, the shares had risen to 11.6 percent for real gross exports and 12.3 percent for real gross imports. Until the early 1980's, growth in both categories of U.S. foreign trade had proceeded apace, with some years showing small real trade deficits and others small surpluses. In nominal terms, the U.S. economy had not experienced a trade deficit since 1945...

"During the latter half of the 1980's, all categories of real exports grew at dramatic rates. Capital goods exports, which had declined 3.5 percent a year between 1980 and 1985, grew more than 14 percent each year, in real terms, between 1985 and 1990. This category was followed by real consumer goods exports, which grew 20.2 percent each year, on average, the second half of the 1980's...

"The result of all this growth, including the slower growth from 1985 to 1990, has been a major improvement in both the exchange rate and U.S. trade balances. U.S. direct investment abroad grew from $215 billion in 1980 to $421 billion in 1990, an average annual rate of growth of almost 7 percent. Problems still exist, however. During the 1980's, the U.S. economy saw huge increases in foreign ownership of domestic industries: from 1980 to 1990, foreign direct investment in the United States grew from $83 billion to $404 billion, an average growth rate of more than 17 percent per year. The flow of income out of the country due to these investments will continue to be an important factor in U.S. foreign trade for the foreseeable future...

"Nonetheless, BLS projections for foreign trade are not bleak. The largest drops in the value of the dollar appear to be behind the Nation, but the exchange rate is expected to continue to decline at a moderate pace, reaching a level of 65.3 by 2005, down from 83.5 in 1992 and representing an average annual decline of 1.9 percent. The exchange rate in the macroeconomic model is affected primarily by the real nonoil trade balance relative to overall exports and secondarily by relative wholesale prices and relative bond rates. As exports grow the trade balances improve as a result of, among other things, declining exchange rates, the exchange rate declines will moderate."

[Billions of 1987 dollars]

Category	1979	1989	1992	2005		
				Low	Moderate	High
Exports of goods and services	$293.6	$471.8	$578.0	$940.7	$1,088.4	$1,264.7
Foods, feeds, and beverages	25.7	30.0	35.7	53.5	58.3	62.1
Industrial supplies and materials	61.8	85.8	97.5	149.6	165.5	194.4
Capital goods	82.1	136.6	178.4	333.0	396.1	496.4
Computers	1.7	28.1	51.0	120.6	147.2	208.7
Other capital goods	80.4	108.5	127.4	212.4	248.9	287.7
Automobile and parts	28.7	33.4	41.9	59.0	60.5	66.9
Consumer and other goods	27.5	58.1	69.1	111.6	115.4	129.9
Services	67.8	128.0	155.4	234.0	292.6	315.0
Imports of goods and services	304.1	545.4	611.6	955.6	1,037.4	1,182.6
Foods, feeds, and beverages	20.2	24.6	26.0	28.4	37.5	40.2
Industrial supplies and materials	105.9	116.7	123.2	175.1	180.3	204.2
Petroleum	55.7	51.3	51.2	81.1	82.1	78.9
Other supplies and materials	50.2	65.4	72.0	94.0	98.2	125.3
Capital goods	30.5	109.4	148.8	293.2	324.2	395.7
Computers	.4	25.4	59.7	116.2	137.5	195.4
Other capital goods	30.1	84.0	88.7	177.0	186.7	200.3
Automobiles and parts	42.7	80.7	79.7	99.8	112.1	115.1

[Continued]

★ 179 ★

Exports and Imports of Goods and Services, 1979-2005

[Continued]

Category	1979	1989	1992	2005 Low	2005 Moderate	2005 High
Consumer and other goods	49.5	119.1	134.7	202.4	215.8	251.0
Services	55.3	95.1	99.7	156.7	167.5	176.4
Net foreign trade	-10.6	-73.6	-33.6	-14.9	51.0	82.1
			Percent distribution			
Exports of goods and services	100.0	100.0	100.0	100.0	100.0	100.0
Foods, feeds, and beverages	8.8	6.4	6.2	5.6	5.4	4.9
Industrial supplies and materials	21.0	18.2	16.9	15.8	15.2	15.3
Capital goods	28.0	28.9	30.9	35.6	36.4	39.5
Computers	.6	6.0	8.8	12.8	13.5	16.5
Other capital goods	27.4	23.0	22.0	22.8	22.9	23.0
Automobiles and parts	9.8	7.1	7.2	6.3	5.6	5.3
Consumer and other goods	9.4	12.3	11.9	11.9	10.6	10.3
Services	23.1	27.1	26.9	24.7	26.9	24.7
Imports of goods and services	100.0	100.0	100.0	100.0	100.0	100.0
Foods, feeds, and beverages	6.6	4.5	4.3	3.0	3.6	3.4
Industrial supplies and materials	34.8	21.4	20.1	18.3	17.4	17.3
Petroleum	18.3	9.4	8.4	8.5	7.9	6.7
Other supplies and materials	16.5	12.0	11.8	9.8	9.5	10.6
Capital goods	10.0	20.1	24.3	30.6	31.3	33.1
Computers	.1	4.7	9.8	12.1	13.3	16.4
Other capital goods	9.9	15.4	14.5	18.5	18.0	17.0
Automobiles and parts	14.0	14.8	13.0	10.4	10.8	9.7
Consumer and other goods	16.3	21.8	22.0	21.2	20.8	21.6
Services	18.2	17.4	16.3	16.5	16.1	14.9

Source: U.S. Department of Labor, Bureau of Labor Statistics, *The American Work Force: 1992-2005*, (Washington, D.C.: U.S. Government Printing Office, April 1994), pp. 17-19. *Primary source:* Historical data, Bureau of Economic Analysis; projected data, Bureau of Labor Statistics. *Note:* Source also contains data on average rates of change.

Effects of Government Entitlements on the U.S. Economy

★ 180 ★

Federal Entitlement Spending without Budget Controls, 1980-1998

"The President has long clung to the notion that the silver bullet for controlling entitlements lies in health care reform. He has a point. Since 1980, Medicare and Medicaid spending has more than *quadrupled*. Says Stanley Collender, Price Waterhouse's chief budget watcher: 'When you look at entitlements, controlling Medicare and Medicaid are the top five priorities, period'."

[Billions of dollars]

	1980	1994	1998
Federal retirement	30	67	85
Veterans' benefits	13	20	21
Social Security	100	320	400
Unemployment	17	25	28
Welfare	7	17	20
Medicare	30	120	240
Food stamps	9	25	28
Farm subsidies	3	10	9
Medicaid	10	90	140
Supplemental Security Income	6	25	31
Earned-income tax credit	1	11	22

Source: Suneel Ratan, "How to Really Cut the Budget Deficit," in *Fortune*, 4 October 1993, p. 102. *Note:* Magnitudes estimated from published chart.

★ 181 ★

Effects of Government Entitlements on the U.S. Economy

Cost of Government Entitlements as a Percentage of GDP, 1995-2030

"A presidential commission is struggling to devise a plan to control the federal deficit and rein in the fastest-growing part of the budget, 'entitlements' ranging from Social Security and Medicare to welfare and farm subsidies.

"There are no recommendations yet, but a draft of the 75 options that Friday will go to the Bipartisan Commission on Entitlements and Tax Reform is already setting off shock waves. Among the big ones:

Raising the retirement age for Social Security to 70.

Raising the eligibility age for Medicare to 70.

Increasing Medicare premiums that the elderly pay for health care by $60 a month, raising deductibles and making recipients pay other costs.

Restricting or eliminating some middle-class tax breaks, such as deductions for interest paid on home mortgages and for state and local taxes.

Taxing the value of employer-paid health insurance and Medicare benefits.

Increasing Social Security payroll taxes.

Denying Social Security and Medicare benefits for the most affluent Americans."

Year	Percentage
1995	10.9
2000	12
2010	14.9
2020	18
2030	20.4

Source: William W. Welch, "Elderly Could Lose in Budget Numbers Game," in *USA Today*, 7 December 1994, p. 4A. *Primary source:* Bipartisan Commission on Entitlements and Tax Reform; GDP projections based on Social Security Estimates. *Notes:* Magnitudes for 2000-2020 estimated from published chart. 1995 figure based on a GDP of $7.1 trillion; 2030, $11.5 trillion.

★ 182 ★

Effects of Government Entitlements on the U.S. Economy

Rising Cost of Health versus Nonhealth Entitlements, 1993-1998

"A key concession President Clinton made to get his budget through the House of Representatives was agreeing to new speed limits on fast-growing entitlements. That was a first; never before has Washington set targets to rein in these programs, from Social Security to farm price supports. But as barriers to burgeoning spending go, these constitute 'a hurdle about 6 inches high,' notes economist Rudolph Penner of the accounting firm KPMG Peat Marwick...

"The new speed limits, which Clinton agreed to at the behest of conservative Democrats, wouldn't change the upward drift of entitlements. In effect, they would only set overall targets, allowing these programs to grow as fast as they are projected to do anyway. Thus, Medicaid could still expand by about 15 percent a year, adding a whopping $12 billion in 1994 alone. The only catch would come if entitlements and mandatory spending exceeded the targets by more than 0.5 percent a year, or about $4 billion at present. In that case, the President could recommend raising taxes, cutting other spending or doing nothing; Congress could either follow his advice or ignore it."

[Percentage of GDP]

	1993	1994	1995	1996	1997	1998
Medicaid/Medicare	4.0	4.2	4.5	4.9	5.1	5.3
Social Security	9.0	8.9	8.7	8.5	8.5	8.5

Source: Susan Dentzer, "The Easy Way Out on Entitlements," 7 June 1993, p. 61. *Primary source:* Congressional Budget Office. *Note:* Source also includes data for 1960-1992.

The 1995 U.S. Budget

★ 183 ★

Economic Assumptions of the 1995 Budget, 1992-1999[1]

"The Administration's economic assumptions through 1999 project a continuation of the trends evident in 1993: real economic growth sufficiently strong to lower unemployment gradually without reigniting inflation."

[Calendar years]

	1992 Actual	Projections						
		1993	1994	1995	1996	1997	1998	1999
Gross Domestic Product (GDP):								
Percent change, fourth quarter over fourth quarter:								
Current dollars	6.7	5.0	5.8	5.6	5.7	5.7	5.7	5.6
Constant (1987) dollars	3.9	2.3	3.0	2.7	2.7	2.6	2.6	2.5
Implicit price deflator (1987=100)	2.8	2.6	2.7	2.8	2.9	3.0	3.0	3.0

[Continued]

★ 183 ★

Economic Assumptions of the 1995 Budget, 1992-1999

[Continued]

	1992 Actual	Projections 1993	1994	1995	1996	1997	1998	1999
Consumer Price Index (all urban):[2]								
Percent change, fourth quarter over fourth quarter	3.1	2.8	3.0	3.2	3.3	3.4	3.4	3.4
Unemployment rate, civilian, percent:[3]								
Fourth quarter level	7.3	6.7	6.4	6.0	5.8	5.6	5.5	5.5
Interest rates, percent:								
91-day Treasury bills[4]	3.5	3.0	3.4	3.8	4.1	4.4	4.4	4.4
10-year Treasury notes	7.0	5.9	5.8	5.8	5.8	5.8	5.8	5.8

Source: Executive Office of the President of the United States, Office of Management and Budget, *Budget of the United States Government: Fiscal Year 1995* (Washington, D.C.: U.S. Government Printing Office, 1994), p. 15. *Notes:* 1. Based on information available as of December 1993. 2. CPI for all urban customers. 3. Pre-1994 basis. A February 1994 change in survey methodology is expected to add about 0.5 percentage points to the measured unemployment rate. 4. Average rate (bank discount basis) on new issues within period.

★ 184 ★

The 1995 U.S. Budget

Federal Government Financing and Debt, 1993-1999[1]

[Billions of dollars]

	1993 Actual	Estimate 1994	1995	1996	1997	1998	1999
FINANCING							
Surplus or deficit (-)	-254.7	-234.8	-165.1	-169.6	-186.4	-190.5	-181.1
(On-budget)	-300.0	-290.1	-225.0	-236.3	-265.5	-279.2	-278.6
(Off-budget)	45.3	55.3	59.9	66.7	79.2	88.7	97.6
Means of financing other than borrowing from the public:							
Change in:[2]							
Treasury operating cash balance	6.3	12.5	-	-	-	-	-
Checks outstanding, etc.[3]	0.4	-0.9	-0.4	-	-	-	-
Deposit funds balances	-0.4	-0.5	-1.7	-	-	-	-
Seigniorage on coins	0.4	0.6	0.6	0.6	0.6	0.6	0.6
Less: Net financing disbursements:							
Direct loan financing accounts	-3.8	-6.4	-10.1	-15.9	-17.9	-18.9	-19.0
Guaranteed loan financing accounts	4.6	4.2	3.0	2.5	2.3	1.4	0.4
Total, requirement for borrowing from the public	-247.3	-225.2	-173.7	-182.4	-201.4	-207.3	-199.1
Reclassification of debt[4]	-1.3	-	-	-	-	-	-
Change in debt held by the public	248.5	225.2	173.7	182.4	201.4	207.3	199.1
DEBT, END OF YEAR[1]							
Gross Federal debt:							
Debt issued by Treasury	4,326.5	4,652.1	4,936.0	5,243.0	5,577.2	5,929.4	6,281.4
Debt issued by other agencies	24.8	23.9	24.2	24.1	24.1	24.1	24.1
Total, gross Federal debt	4,351.2	4,676.0	4,960.1	5,267.1	5,601.3	5,953.5	6,305.4

[Continued]

★ 184 ★

Federal Government Financing and Debt, 1993-1999

[Continued]

	1993 Actual	Estimate 1994	1995	1996	1997	1998	1999
Held by:							
Government accounts	1,104.0	1,203.6	1,314.0	1,438.5	1,571.3	1,716.3	1,869.1
The public	3,247.2	3,472.4	3,646.1	3,828.5	4,029.9	4,237.2	4,463.3
(Federal Reserve Banks)	325.7						
(Other)	2,921.5						
DEBT SUBJECT TO STATUTORY LIMITATION, END OF YEAR							
Debt issued by Treasury	4,326.5	4,652.1	4,936.0	5,243.0	5,577.2	5,929.4	6,281.4
Less: Treasury debt not subject to limitation[5]	-15.6	-15.6	-15.6	-15.6	-15.6	-15.6	-15.6
Agency debt subject to limitation	0.2	0.1	0.1	0.1	0.1	0.1	0.1
Adjustment for discount and premium[6]	4.5	4.5	4.5	4.5	4.5	4.5	4.5
Total, debt subject to statutory limitation[7]	4,315.6	4,641.1	4,925.0	5,232.0	5,566.2	5,918.4	6,270.3

Source: Executive Office of the President of the United States, Office of Management and Budget, *Budget of the United States Government: Fiscal Year 1995* (Washington, D.C.: U.S. Government Printing Office, 1994), p. 249. *Notes:* 1. Treasury securities held by the public and zero-coupon bonds held by Government accounts are almost entirely measured at sales price plus amortized discount or less amortized premium. Agency debt is almost entirely measure at face value. Treasury securities in the Government account series are measured at face value less unrealized discount (if any). 2. A decrease in the Treasury operating cash balance (which is an asset) is a means of financing the deficit. It therefore has a positive sign, which is opposite to the sign of the deficit. An increase in checks outstanding or deposit fund balances (which are liabilities) is also a means of financing the deficit and therefore also has a positive sign. 3. Besides checks outstanding, includes accrued interest payable on Treasury debt, miscellaneous liability accounts, allocations of special drawing rights, and as an offset, cash and monetary assets other than the Treasury operating cash balance, miscellaneous asset accounts, and profits on sale of gold. 4. The Farm Credit System Financial Assistance Corporation was reclassified from a Government-sponsored enterprise to a Federal Agency as of October 1, 1992, and its debt was accordingly reclassified as Federal Agency debt. This reclassification does not constitute borrowing. 5. Consists primarily of Federal Financing Bank debt. 6. Consists of unamortized discount (less premium) on public issues of Treasury notes and bonds (other than zero-coupon bonds) and unrealized discounts on Government account series securities. 7. The statutory debt limit is $4,900 billion.

★ 185 ★

The 1995 U.S. Budget

Budget Summary of Receipts, Outlays, and Surpluses or Deficits, 1980- 1999

[Millions of dollars]

Year	Total Receipts	Total Outlays	Total Surplus or Deficit (-)	On-Budget Receipts	On-Budget Outlays	On-Budget Surplus or Deficit (-)	Off-Budget Receipts	Off-Budget Outlays	Off-Budget Surplus or Deficit (-)
1980	517,112	590,947	-73,835	403,903	476,618	-72,715	113,209	114,329	-1,120
1981	599,272	678,249	-78,976	469,097	543,053	-73,956	130,176	135,196	-5,020
1982	617,766	745,755	-127,989	474,299	594,351	-120,052	143,467	151,404	-7,937
1983	600,562	808,380	-207,818	453,242	661,272	-208,030	147,320	147,108	212
1984	666,457	851,846	-185,388	500,382	686,032	-185,650	166,075	165,813	262
1985	734,057	946,391	-212,334	547,886	769,584	-221,698	186,171	176,807	9,363
1986	769,091	990,336	-221,245	568,862	806,838	-237,976	200,228	183,498	16,731
1987	854,143	1,003,911	-149,769	640,741	810,079	-169,339	213,402	193,832	19,570
1988	908,954	1,064,140	-155,187	667,463	861,449	-193,986	241,491	202,691	38,800
1989	990,691	1,143,172	-152,481	727,026	932,261	-205,235	263,666	210,911	52,754
1990	1,031,321	1,252,705	-221,384	749,666	1,027,640	-277,974	281,656	225,065	56,590
1991	1,054,272	1,323,793	-269,521	760,388	1,082,106	-321,719	293,885	241,687	52,198
1992	1,090,453	1,380,856	-290,403	788,027	1,128,518	-340,490	302,426	252,339	50,087

[Continued]

★ 185 ★

Budget Summary of Receipts, Outlays, and Surpluses or Deficits, 1980- 1999

[Continued]

Year	Total			On-Budget			Off-Budget		
	Receipts	Outlays	Surplus or Deficit (-)	Receipts	Outlays	Surplus or Deficit (-)	Receipts	Outlays	Surplus or Deficit (-)
1993	1,153,535	1,408,205	-254,670	841,601	1,141,618	-300,017	311,934	266,587	45,347
1994 estimate	1,249,071	1,483,829	-234,758	912,892	1,202,953	-290,061	336,179	280,876	55,303
1995 estimate	1,353,815	1,518,945	-165,130	998,594	1,223,582	-224,987	355,221	295,364	59,857
1996 estimate	1,427,312	1,596,877	-169,564	1,052,606	1,288,898	-236,292	374,706	307,979	66,727
1997 estimate	1,505,072	1,691,443	-186,371	1,107,581	1,373,129	-265,548	397,491	318,314	79,177
1998 estimate	1,586,925	1,777,416	-190,491	1,165,532	1,444,760	-279,228	421,393	332,656	88,737
1999 estimate	1,672,946	1,854,023	-181,077	1,227,811	1,506,455	-278,644	445,135	347,568	97,567

Source: Executive Office of the President of the United States, Office of Management and Budget, *Budget of the United States Government: Fiscal Year 1995* (Washington, D.C.: U.S. Government Printing Office, 1994), p. 255. *Note:* *$500 thousand or less. Source also includes data for 1798-1979.

★ 186 ★

The 1995 U.S. Budget

Clinton Administration Private-sector Investment Proposals, 1994-1998

[Millions of dollars]

	1994	1995	1996	1997	1998	1994-1997 Total
Investment Tax Incentives:						
Targeted capital gains exclusion (tax incentive)	12	93	155	207	247	467
Earned income tax credit (EITC) (tax incentive)	(525)	(6,228)	(6,445)	(6,662)	(6,927)	(19,860)
Mortgage revenue bonds (tax incentive)	(104)	(145)	(160)	(172)	(174)	(581)
High-speed rail bonds (tax incentive)	...	(1)	(4)	(11)	(20)	(16)
Extend R&E tax credit (tax incentive)	(1,207)	(1,503)	(1,750)	(1,977)	(2,200)	(6,437)
Extend low-income housing tax credit (tax incentive)	(214)	(478)	(791)	(1,114)	(1,442)	(2,597)
Small business investment tax credit (tax incentive)	2,795	3,133	3,027	3,309	3,501	12,264
Alternative minimum tax depreciation preference (tax incentive)	188	307	396	404	273	1,295
Temporary incremental investment tax credit (tax incentive)	6,399	3,584	107	-961	-572	9,129
Small issue manufacturing bonds (tax incentive)	14	28	35	37	37	114
Alternative minimum tax exception for gifts of appreciated property (tax incentive)	70	73	75	77	79	295
Small business credit availability	60	131	153	157	160	501
SUBTOTAL, TAX INCENTIVES	9,478	7,218	3,795	3,073	3,565	23,564
SUBTOTAL, SPENDING INCENTIVES	60	131	153	157	160	501

[Continued]

★ 186 ★

Clinton Administration Private-sector Investment Proposals, 1994-1998

[Continued]

	1994	1995	1996	1997	1998	1994-1997 Total
TOTAL, PRIVATE-SECTOR INCENTIVES	9,538	7,349	3,948	3,230	3,725	24,065
TAX INCENTIVES, ALL CATEGORIES	12,763	17,092	14,779	15,278	17,039	59,912
SPENDING INCENTIVES, ALL CATEGORIES	8,817	19,877	31,586	39,422	44,592	99,702
TOTAL, ALL CATEGORIES	21,580	36,969	46,365	54,700	61,631	159,614

Source: Executive Office of the President of the United States, Office of Management and Budget, *A Vision of Change for America* (Washington, D.C.: U.S. Government Printing Office, 17 February 1993), p. 138.

★ 187 ★

The 1995 U.S. Budget

Government Growth by Administration, 1961-1997

[Real average annual percent change]

	FYs	Total Spending	Domestic Spending	Defense Spending	Net Interest
Kennedy	1961-64	4.0	8.5	0.4	5.1
Johnson	1964-69	5.4	6.1	4.8	5.5
Nixon	1969-75	2.7	9.3	-6.9	4.0
Ford	1975-77	3.0	5.1	-2.0	5.1
Carter	1977-81	4.0	3.3	2.9	13.1
Reagan	1981-89	2.5	0.7	4.7	7.4
Bush	1989-93	1.5	4.2	-4.7	0.5
Clinton	1993-97	1.6	3.8	-5.9	1.3

Source: Ed Rubenstein, "How Quickly We Forget," in *National Review*, 1 August 1994, p. 17.

★ 188 ★

The 1995 U.S. Budget

Council of Economic Advisers' Projections for Annual Economic Growth under the Clinton Plan, 1993-1997

"If everything works according to plan, President Clinton's economic package will give the recovery an extra push this year through a big jobs program, and will help sustain growth later by reducing the country's huge budget deficit and encouraging investment.

"But analysts say the plan may not play out that way. By slapping nearly $245 billion in net new taxes onto individuals and businesses over the next six years, the plan risks slowing down the economy once it begins showing healthy growth.

"Some analysts worry about even more dire prospects.

" 'Clinton is heightening the risk of renewed recession by raising personal income tax rates,' warns Morgan Stanley Co. chief economist Stephen Roach. 'It could unnerve consumer confidence and make Americans throw in the towel'."

[Percent]

Year	Percentage
1993	3.1
1994	3.3
1995	2.7
1996	2.5
1997	2.5

Source: Rick Wartzman, "Proposed Tax Increases Hit the Rich Hardest," *The Wall Street Journal*, 18 February 1993, p. A10. *Primary source:* Council of Economic Advisers. *Notes:* For purposes of calculating the deficit under the economic plan, the White House uses more conservative economic assumptions provided by the Congressional Budget Office. Magnitudes estimate from published chart.

★ 189 ★

The 1995 U.S. Budget

Impact of Clinton's Proposals on GDP, CPI, and Unemployment: CBO versus Clinton Administration Projections, 1993-1998

"Mr. Clinton's package, the toughest budget-cutting program proposed by a President since World War II, would raise taxes and lower Government spending so that the annual deficit, now more than $300 billion, would be reduced by $140 billion by the 1997 fiscal year, the last of Mr. Clinton's term.

"Over five years, the deficit reduction would come almost equally from spending cuts and tax increases.

"The main elements would be higher income taxes on families with incomes above about $180,000, new taxes on energy that would cost most families $100 to $150 a year, reduced military spending, a freeze in the pay of Government workers, limits in Medicare and Medicaid payments to doctors and hospitals and relatively small spending cuts in many other Government programs."

[Percent]

	Congressional Budget Office projections	Clinton Administration projections
Gross domestic product		
1993	2.80	3.00
1994	3.00	3.30
1995	2.75	2.70
1996	2.50	2.50
1997	2.20	2.50
1998	1.80	2.50
Consumer price index		
1993	2.8	3.0
1994	2.7	3.1
1995	2.7	3.3
1996	2.7	3.3
1997	2.7	3.4
1998	2.7	3.4
Unemployment		
1993	7.2	7.0
1994	6.6	6.4
1995	6.2	6.1
1996	6.0	5.9
1997	5.8	5.7
1998	5.7	5.5

Source: David E. Rosenbaum, "Battle Lines Begin to Form on Clinton Economic Plan," in *The New York Times*, 19 February 1993, p. A1. *Primary source:* Office of Management and Budget. *Notes:* GDP and CPI track percent change fourth quarter to fourth quarter of calendar years. Unemployment figures track annual average. Magnitudes estimated from published chart.

Impacts of the Budget on Government Spending, Taxes, and Programs

★ 190 ★

Federal Domestic Spending, 1975-1999

"The 1993 Budget Act supposedly 'capped' discretionary spending in nominal dollars, forcing real spending reductions. The defense budget, however, will bear the brunt of this restraint. The Clinton budget pours money saved at the Pentagon into job training, Head Start, infrastructure, data highway entitlements, and other 'investment' programs. As a result, discretionary spending will rise by $9 billion (1993 dollars) in 1994, and another $5 billion in FY1995, a 6 percent real rise in just two years. Fiscal discipline, such as it is, is evident only after the 1996 election..."

[Billions of 1993 dollars]

	Discretionary	Mandatory entitlements	Total	As percentage of GDP
1975	$180.0	$443.7	$623.7	15.3%
1980	227.5	513.7	741.2	15.9
1988	185.5	578.7	764.2	13.6
1993	229.4	760.9	990.3	15.7
1994E	237.6	781.9	1,019.5	15.8
1999E	244.2	919.2	1,163.4	16.2

Source: Ed Rubenstein, "The Wrong Numbers," in *National Review*, 7 March 1994, p. 20. *Primary source:* CBO. Calculations by Ed Rubenstein.

★ 191 ★

Impacts of the Budget on Government Spending, Taxes, and Programs

Clinton Administration Spending Plan Compared to That of Bush Administration, 1993-1997

"The success of President Clinton's budget plan rests on his ability to persuade Congress not only to cut the deficit but to redirect billions toward public investments he believes are important to the nation's economy.

"After long resisting Republican presidents, Democrats now face one of their own in the White House, and he demands choices that challenge old alliances governing spending priorities. Compromises will be required before the budget clears Congress. But if Mr. Clinton moves too far from his mark, he risks undermining his credibility and the voters' willingness to accept the large tax increases so important to his plan."

[Change from Bush Administration Policy, in billions of dollars]

Fiscal year	Defense	Entitle-ments[1]	Domestic[2]
1993	-	-	-9
1994	-7	-9	+11
1995	-12	-18	+12
1996	-20	-30	+17
1997	-37	-41	+19
1993-97	-76	-98	+68

Source: David Rogers and David Wessel, "Clinton Faces Task of Altering Spending Habits," in *The Wall Street Journal*, 22 February 1993, p. A12. *Primary source: A Vision for Change in America. Notes:* 1. Includes Medicare cuts, increased taxation of Social security benefits, savings from shift in borrowing to shorter maturities. 2. Includes all "investment" spendings.

★ 192 ★

Impacts of the Budget on Government Spending, Taxes, and Programs

Composition of Federal Spending on Programs by Administration, 1970-1997

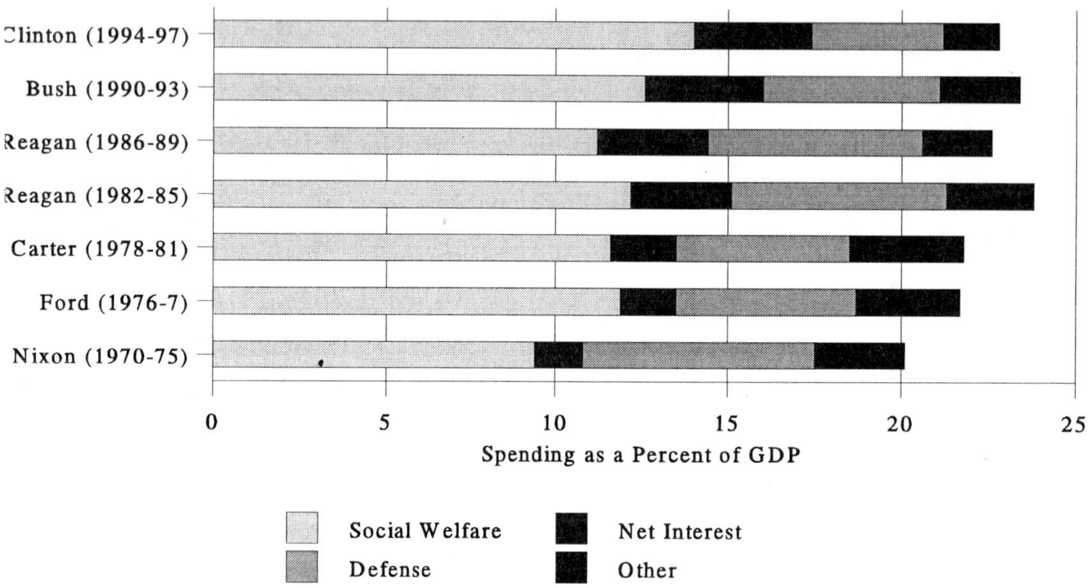

"Since 1960 each 1.0 percentage point rise in taxes as a percentage of GDP has been followed, after a one-year lag, by a 1.8 percentage-point reduction in economic growth. This consistent tradeoff is uncovered in an economic model developed by William C. Dunkelberg, dean of the School of Business and Management at Temple University. When applied to the Joint Tax Committee's projection of a 0.5 percentage point rise in the federal tax burden in 1994, the Denkelberg model indicates a 0.9 percentage-point drop in the rate of economic growth from the Clinton program.

"So instead of growing at a rate of 3.0 percent, we'll grow by 2.1 percent. By 1998, according to the National Center for Policy Analysis, the new budget will destroy at least 1.34 million jobs that would have existed under current policies. A family of of four will receive $4,000 less income that year because of this plan.

"In analyzing this legislation, moreover, economists have focused exclusively on taxes. They have largely overlooked negatives on the spending side of the ledger."

[Spending as a percent of GDP]

President (FYs)	Social welfare	Net interest	Defense	Other	Total
Nixon (1970-75)	9.4	1.4	6.7	2.6	20.1
Ford (1976-7)	11.9	1.6	5.2	3.0	21.7
Carter (1978-81)	11.6	1.9	5.0	3.3	21.8
Reagan (1982-85)	12.2	2.9	6.2	2.5	23.8
Reagan (1986-89)	11.2	3.2	6.2	2.0	22.6

[Continued]

★ 192 ★

Composition of Federal Spending on Programs by Administration, 1970-1997

[Continued]

President (FYs)	Social welfare	Net interest	Defense	Other	Total
Bush (1990-93)	12.6	3.4	5.1	2.3	23.4
Clinton (1994-97)	14.0	3.4	3.8	1.6	22.8

Source: Ed Rubenstein, "Things to Come," in *National Review*, 6 September 1993, p. 16. *Primary source:* Congressional Research Service (calculations by Ed Rubenstein).

★ 193 ★

Impacts of the Budget on Government Spending, Taxes, and Programs

Effect of Clinton Budget on Domestic, Defense, and Entitlements Spending, 1990-1999

"Over the next five years, Mr. Clinton proposes to increase what's known as budget authority (the money that goes into agency checkbooks) for domestic programs by $33 billion or 15%. But outlays the (checks that agencies write from budget authority granted in the past) would rise by $22.5 billion or 8.7%...

"Adjusted for inflation, Mr. Clinton's budget looks tough... Over the next five years-provided the caps hold—outlays for defense are to fall a steep 21% and outlays for domestic program by 6%.

"For 1995 Mr. Clinton projects that outlays for domestic and defense discretionary spending will come in just under the cap and actually fall by $7.7 billion (without making an adjustment for inflation). That hasn't happened since 1969. Domestic outlays are to rise by $2.8 billion, defense and foreign aid to fall by $10.5 billion.

"Over the next five years, even assuming that Mr. Clinton's health plan passes and works as he predicts, spending on federal budget programs will climb by $325 billion, or 29%—to $1.1 trillion in fiscal 1999, a 29% increase. Outlays for Medicare alone are projected to rise by $74 billion, or 53%."

[Billions of dollars]

Year	Budget Authority Increase[1]		Unadjusted Outlays[2]		Adjusted Outlays[3]		Dom, Defense, and Benefits Spending[4]	
	Domestic	Defense	Domestic	Defense	Domestic	Defense	Dom/Def	Benefits
1990	170	300	180	300	160	275	500	550
1991	190	330	195	320	165	280	540	565
1992	210	300	220	305	180	255	540	685
1993	215	275	248	295	188	237	545	725
1994	220	260	250	280	195	222	550	785
1995	230	262	265	270	195	205	545	810
1996	245	262	263	265	195	200	545	890
1997	250	255	265	255	190	190	545	950
1998	250	253	265	255	185	185	545	1030
1999	250	260	265	255	180	180	545	1100

Source: David Wessel, "Clinton Retains Desire for Spending, But Budget Reveals the Restraints of Deficit Cutting Laws," in *The Wall Street Journal*, 11 February 1994, p. A14. *Primary source:* Office of Management and Budget. *Notes:* 1. Amount of money that goes into agency checkbooks, not adjusted for inflation. 2. Outlays, not adjusted for inflation. 3. Outlays, in 1987 dollars. 4. Outlays if Clinton's health plan passes, not adjusted for inflation. Magnitudes estimated from published chart.

★ 194 ★

Impacts of the Budget on Government Spending, Taxes, and Programs

Effects of Clinton Budget on Spending and Taxes, 1993-1998

"Some may say that with the population and economy growing, government spending may be expected to increase. But a Congressional Budget Office analysis shows outlays as a percentage of GDP rising from 23.4 percent in 1993 to 24.1 percent in the year 2000. So it's not being reduced by that measure, either. Incidentally, 2000 is the first year in which outlays ($2,055 billion) are expected to exceed the number of the year. The fact is, spending is not being reined in."

[Billions of dollars]

	1993	1994	1995	1996	1997	1998
Spending:	1468	1515	1574	1625	1690	1781
Receipts:	1146	1251	1328	1413	1476	1531
Deficit:	322	264	246	212	214	250
Defense Outlays:	277	264	258	252	234	239

Source: Tom Bethell, "The Poisoned Chalice Revisited," in *The American Spectator*, September 1993, p. 16. *Primary source:* Above figures, purporting to show "equal parts spending and tax increases," were published by the Office of Management and Budget on 8 April 1993.

★ 195 ★

Impacts of the Budget on Government Spending, Taxes, and Programs

Effect of Decreased Government Spending on Taxes as a Share of GDP, 1990-1998

[Percent of GDP]

Year	Federal Spending		Taxes		Deficit	
	Budget as is	Clinton Plan	Budget as is	Clinton Plan	Budget as is	Clinton Plan
1990	22.75	NA	18.70	NA	4.00	NA
1991	23.30	NA	18.60	NA	4.70	NA
1992	23.10	23.10	18.30	NA	4.90	NA
1993	23.30	23.40	18.10	18.10	5.00	5.20
1994	22.50	22.45	18.10	18.60	4.25	3.95
1995	22.30	22.00	18.10	18.60	4.20	3.30
1996	22.00	21.50	18.10	18.75	4.00	2.70
1997	22.10	21.20	17.75	18.60	4.50	2.65
1998	22.20	21.20	17.50	18.25	4.70	2.80

Source: Ann Reilly Dowd, "Clintonomics," *Fortune*, 22 March 1993, p. 31. *Primary source:* Office of Management and Budget. *Note:* Magnitudes estimated from published chart.

★ 196 ★

Impacts of the Budget on Government Spending, Taxes, and Programs

Effect of Omnibus Budget Reconciliation Act of 1993 on Taxes, 1993-1998

"The central elements of the Omnibus Budget Reconciliation Act would raise the tax rates on upper-income taxpayers, increase the Federal tax on gasoline by 4.3 cents a gallon, reduce military spending and limit the explosive growth in Medicare spending.

"The latest calculations by Congressional statisticians of how much additional taxes various income groups would bear show that taxpayers with incomes over $200,000 would have an average tax increase of 5.4 percent. In no other category would the tax increase be more than 1 percent, and taxpayers with incomes below $20,000 would, on average, get a tax cut.

"The tax cut at the low end of the income range would result from a large increase in the earned-income tax credit, a program that gives a tax break and in some instances rebates to workers who are poor or have incomes just above the poverty line. Democrats called this provision the most important antipoverty measure since the 1970's."

[Percent]

Income	Average tax change
Less than $10,000	-1.28%
10,000 to 20,000	-0.30
20,000 to 30,000	+0.02
30,000 to 40,000	+0.21
40,000 to 50,000	+0.29
50,000 to 75,000	+0.39
75,000 to 100,000	+0.54
100,000 to 200,000	+0.86
200,000 and over	+5.39
Total all Taxpayers	+0.97

Source: David E. Rosenbaum, "House Debates Budget, Feeling the Heat," in *The New York Times*, 6 August 1993, pp. A1, A14. *Primary source:* Joint Committee on Taxation estimates. *Notes:* For this chart, income includes adjusted gross income plus: tax-exempt interest, employer contributions for health plans and life insurance, employer share of FICA tax, workers' compensation, nontaxable Social Security benefits, insurance value of Medicare benefits, corporate income tax liability attributed to stockholders, alternative minimum tax preference items and excluded income of U.S. citizens living abroad.

★ 197 ★

Impacts of the Budget on Government Spending, Taxes, and Programs

Proposed Federal Program Cutbacks, 1994-1998

"This January we produced a budget proposal that would reduce baseline federal expenditures in 1998 by about $250 billion below what the president's budget yields. Our plan would reduce the deficit to below 1% of gross domestic product (it is now 5%) by allowing federal outlays to climb only from $1.46 trillion this year to $1.52 trillion in 1998. We do not believe that there are a large number of Americans who think that the federal government cannot do the things it is supposed to do for $1.52 trillion."

[Billions of dollars]

Program to kill	Savings 1994-98
Department of Energy	$24.0
IMF and World Bank	5.5
Aid to Egypt and Israel	6.5
Super Collider	7.5
Space Station	9.0
Farm Programs	18.0
Rural Electrification Admin.	6.5
Urban Mass Transit	8.5
Arts Subsidies	3.5
David-Bacon Act	8.0
Low Income Energy Assist.	6.0
Public Housing Construction	12.0
TOTAL	$115.0

Source: William Niskanen and Stephen Moore, "The Budget Cuts Clinton Missed," in *The Wall Street Journal*, 16 August 1993, p. A14. *Primary source:* Authors.

★ 198 ★

Impacts of the Budget on Government Spending, Taxes, and Programs

Authority for Discretionary Domestic Programs, 1977-1999

"The Clinton years are continuing the Bush pattern of talking tough but silently spending away. The chart shows healthy gains in domestic spending through 1996; the fiscal discipline, such as it is, occurs only in the 'out years,' as people in Washington like to say, which means in Bill Clinton's second term, which means it will never happen.

"Even by Mr. Clinton's own budget table, domestic spending will climb by $11 billion in fiscal 1995 to $227.2 billion, or a healthy 5%. Tim Muris, a budget expert from the Reagan era now at George Mason University, has inspected the fine print and says we should include another $4.9 billion in FY 1995 for user fees and health spending. That puts the 1995 increase alone at 7.3%; or two-and-a-half times the rate of inflation."

[Billions of dollars]

Year	
1977	122
1981	138
1985	130
1989	143
1993	212
1997	248
1999	251

Source: "Leon Darman," in *The Wall Street Journal*, 9 February 1994, p. A14. *Primary source:* Fiscal 1995 Budget, historical tables. *Note:* Magnitudes estimated from published chart.

The U.S. Annual Federal Deficit

★ 199 ★

U.S. Budget Deficit, 1993-1998

"When the Social Security 'surplus' is netted out, the deficit outlook is less than impressive: In the long run the relationship between federal debt and the size of the economy is crucial. Debt cannot grow faster than GDP without cheating financial instability. Eventually investors demand exorbitantly high interest rates, or cease buying federal debt entirely, reflecting doubts about the government's ability to raise sufficient revenues to pay interest. The government's own numbers show the national debt increasing by more than $1.5 trillion over the next five years. With GDP growth lagging debt growth, the nation is in a dangerous debt trap."

[Billions of dollars]

	Official deficit	ex Social Security	Gross Federal Debt	
			Total	As percentage of GDP
1993	$-254.7	$-300.0	$4,351.2	69.2%
1994	-234.8	-290.0	4,676.0	70.4
1995	-176.1	-236.0	4,960.1	70.7
1995	-173.1	-239.8	5,267.1	70.9
1997	-180.8	-259.9	5,601.3	71.5
1998	-187.4	-276.1	5,953.5	72.0

Source: Ed Rubenstein, "The Wrong Numbers," in *National Review*, 7 March 1994, p. 20. *Primary source:* OMB, FY1995 Budget.

★ 200 ★

The U.S. Annual Federal Deficit

Senator Hank Brown's Alternative to Clinton's Deficit Reduction Plan, 1994-1998

"President Clinton challenged critics of his tax increases to come forward with their own specific proposals to reduce the deficit. Last week, I presented the president with a plan that would cut the deficit by $679 billion over the next five years. The plan proposes to do this by cutting spending and *not* raising taxes.

"There are many in Congress who believe that improving the economy and American competitiveness in world markets will come from eliminating wasteful programs—not from increasing the tax burden on working Americans.

"Ironically, none of the plan's $679 billion in cuts are draconian. While special interest groups will oppose them, the general public will wonder why Congress spent money on the programs to begin with.

"The plan cuts $94 billion in defense spending and eliminates $338 billion in mandatory spending increases and $147 billion in discretionary spending during the next five years. Social Security would not be affected."

[Billions of dollars]

	Brown's	Clinton's	CBO uncapped
1994	255	270	300
1995	230	260	315
1996	200	225	320
1997	170	210	345
1998	160	235	380

Source: Hank Brown, "My Deficit-reduction Plan," in *The Wall Street Journal*, 9 March 1993, p. A18. *Primary source:* Clinton's deficit as estimated by CBO. *Note:* Magnitudes estimated from published chart.

★ 201 ★

The U.S. Annual Federal Deficit

Deficit Outlook under Alternative Scenarios, 1993-2003

"The Congressional Budget Office says the White House plan falls $18 billion short of its claim that it will cut the deficit by $140 billion by 1997. The Joint Congressional Committee on Taxation says Clinton's proposed taxes on the nation's top income earners will fall $6.6 billion short of his estimated revenues.

"In his own party, Clinton has heard from House Budget Committee Chairman Martin Sabo (D) of Minnesota, who pledges to come up with $3 billion in additional spending cuts over the next year. Some House Democrats are pushing for a plan to devote all of the spending reductions and tax revenues to chipping away at the federal deficit."

[Billions of dollars]

	A	B	C	D
1994	305	275	260	250
1995	300	230	225	220
1996	300	200	180	140
1997	330	210	170	125
1998	375	230	195	125
1999	425	260	200	105
2000	460	285	210	95
2001	510	320	225	85
2002	560	350	250	75
2003	625	380	275	50

Source: Amy Kaslow, "High Hopes Fill 1993 Budget Arena," in *The Christian Science Monitor*, 16 March 1993, p. 9. *Primary source: A Vision of Change for America*, Office of Management and Budget. *Notes:* Magnitudes estimated from published chart. A= If spending and revenues do not change. B= If Clinton's program is enacted. C= If Clinton's program is enacted and it fosters a stronger economy. D= If the program is enacted, the economy gets stronger, and healthcare costs are controlled.

★ 202 ★

The U.S. Annual Federal Deficit

Deficit Outlook with Stabilized Health Care Costs, 1994-2004

"Making economic predictions beyond 2004 is generally foolish, but one sure fact is that the baby boomers, the oldest of whom turn 48 this year, will be closer to retirement at that time. And the closer the baby boomers are to retiring, the harder it will be for politicians to make the changes in Social Security and Medicare that most economists think are needed to prevent enormous deficits or huge tax increases in the future.

"The baby boomers will get whatever retirement benefits have been promised. 'We will be politically powerful enough to ensure that,' says Deborah Steelman, a Republican baby boomer who headed a commission that examined all this in 1991. 'We will hurt the generations behind us.'

"The law already provides that the Social Security retirement age is to climb gradually from 65 to 66 in 2009 and 67 in 2027. With people living longer and longer, Mr. Bentsen has said it is time to think about accelerating that timetable or raising the age further. Others suggest making the elderly pay more of the Medicare tab or trimming or taxing benefits paid to the relatively well-off or imposing new broad-based taxes now."

[Percentage of GDP]

Year	If health costs were stable[1]	Current policy
1994	3.4	3.4
1995	2.2	2.4
1996	1.8	2.2
1997	1.8	2.3
1998	1.4	2.2
1999	1.2	2.4
2000	1.1	2.5
2001	1.0	2.7
2002	.9	2.9
2003	.8	3.1
2004	.7	3.3

Source: David Wessel, "Prepare for a New Dose of Deficit Medicine," in *The Wall Street Journal*, 9 February 1994, p. A1. *Primary source:* Congressional Budget Office. *Note:* 1. If Medicare and Medicaid spending grows only as fast as the economy.

★ 203 ★

The U.S. Annual Federal Deficit

Clinton Budget Deficit Reduction with Health Cost Controls, 1993-2003

"[Advocates] of managed competition like Stanford University economist Alain Enthoven maintain that Clinton's new health care system will squeeze out billions of dollars' worth of unneeded care.

"Whatever the short-term costs inherent in gearing up for Clinton's plan—for example, in extending coverage to the uninsured—it is these long-term savings that will matter the most. Current projections show that health spending will rise from 14 percent of gross domestic product to 19 percent by the end of the century. Over that same period, Medicare and Medicaid will more than double in size; by 1995 alone, federal health spending will exceed any other type of government spending, including defense or Social Security. A health reform plan that managed to keep national health spending to around 16 percent of GDP could save as much as $4 trillion by the year 2000 and tens of trillions of dollars in the next century."

[Billions of dollars]

	1994	1995	1996	1997	1998	1999	2000	2001	2002	2003
Current	280	280	290	320	350	400	450	500	570	640
With cuts	250	230	200	190	200	215	230	260	300	230
With controls	230	190	130	120	110	100	85	70	55	50

Source: Susan Dentzer, "Grim Fairy Tales about Health Costs," in *U.S. News & World Report*, 10 May 1993, p. 61. *Note:* Magnitudes estimated from published chart.

★ 204 ★

The U.S. Annual Federal Deficit

Decrease in Federal Deficit Due to Decrease in Costs of S&L Bailout and Persian Gulf War, 1989-1996

"The deficit's size is distorted by the effects of the Gulf war and the S&L bailout. The war actually reduced the fiscal 1991 deficit by $24 billion, since the U.S. collected more in contributions from its allies than it paid out. In 1992, however, war finances will add an estimated $16.8 billion to the deficit as spending to replace used-up weapons continues while contributions fall.

"Far larger is the impact of the money spent to shut or sell failed savings and loans. Government bean counters record the expense of making depositors whole only when S&Ls are sold or closed. Because the government has been slow to shed moribund thrifts, those costs in 1991 turned out lower than estimated, which improved the deficit in 1991 and will worsen it in 1992. If all goes well, most big payments to depositors should be finished by the end of 1993. Once that's over, proceeds from additional sales of S&L assets are expected to cut the deficit by tens of billions per year."

[Billions of current dollars]

	Federal Deficit	Deficit net of costs of S&L Bailout and Gulf War
1989	170	140
1990	230	165
1991	300	230
1992	365	220
1993	270	190
1994	160	130
1995	90	75
1996	65	60

Source: Rob Norton, "Should You Worry about the Deficit?" in *Fortune*, 7 October 1991, p. 103. *Primary source:* Council of Economic Advisers; Office of Management and Budget. *Notes:* Magnitudes estimated from published chart. Source also includes data for 1981-1988. Federal deficit amounts to 6.5% of GNP in 1983; 5.8% of GNP in 1992; and 0.7% of GNP in 1996.

U.S. and World Trade Projections

★ 205 ★

The World Economy, 2000

"A recent report by the Organization for Economic Cooperation and Development (OECD), entitled *Long-Term Prospects for the World Economy,* offers a hopeful view [of the world economy]. 'Projections for the global economy in the 1990s and beyond are by and large optimistic,' the report states. Industrialized countries are predicted to fare as well as a result of restructuring that has occurred in recent years, provided that the international financial markets remain relatively stable.

"Average economic output in North America and Europe is predicted to grow between 2.5% and 3% annually; in Japan, between 3% and 4%; in the Asia-Pacific region as a whole, over 5.5%; and in Latin America 3%, according to the report.

"The OECD believes that North America should benefit from NAFTA, which would foster substantial economic growth. The trade agreement would help reduce consumer prices within the North American marketplace and speed up the introduction of new technologies."

Source: "The World Economy in the 21st Century," in *The Futurist,* March-April 1993, p. 51. *Primary source:* Organization for Economic Cooperation and Development (OECD), *Long-term Prospects for the World Economy* (Washington, D.C.: OECD Publications and Information Center), 1992.

★ 206 ★

U.S. and World Trade Projections

The World's Largest Economies, 2020

"Big economies are not necessarily rich economies: compare India and Italy today. Nonetheless, it is striking that, if [the forecasts below] are right, within a generation China will overtake America as the world's biggest economy; and that by 2020 as many as nine of the top 15 economies will be from today's third world."

[United States = 100]

	2020
China	140
U.S.	100
Japan	46
Indian	36
Indonesia	32
Germany	26
South Korea	21

[Continued]

★ 206 ★

The World's Largest Economies, 2020

[Continued]

	2020
Thailand	20
France	18
Taiwan	17
Brazil	16
Italy	16
Russia	15
Britain	15
Mexico	14

Source: "War of the Worlds," in *The Economist*, 1 October 1994, p. 4. *Primary source:* World Bank. *Note:* Forecasts in the World Bank's *Global Economic Prospects.*

★ 207 ★

U.S. and World Trade Projections

Distribution of GDP and Growth Rates among Industrialized Nations, 1967- 2013

"According to the traditional measure published by The International Monetary Fund (IMF) in 1992 the developing economies accounted only for 17 percent of the total world economy.

"We now find however that our taken-for-granted belief about where the action is doesn't wash. Yes, it's true that most people in the developing world live in what, by our standards, are poverty conditions. But they're not as poor as we used to think. The IMF recently revised its calculations of the world economic output in a way that created dramatically higher totals for the developing countries."

[Percent]

	Distribution of GDP: Old View*	Distribution of GDP: New View*	Distribution of GDP: 2013	Growth Rates: 1967-1992	Growth Rate: 1993-2013
U.S.	25	22	14	2.4	2.4
Developed economies	70	54	40	2.9	2.6
F.S.U. plus	13	8	6	2.0	3.0
Developing economies	17	38	54	4.9	6.0
China	2	7	16	7.5	9.0

Source: Edgar R. Fiedler, "The Third World—Where the Action Is," in *Economic Times*, January 1994, p. 4. *Primary source:* International Monetary Fund, Capital Group, Lombard Street Research. *Notes:* "Old View" based on market exchange rates, "New View" on PPP exchange rates. "F.S.U. plus"=former Soviet Union, Vietnam, North Korea and Cuba. U.S. is included in "Developed Economies," China is included in "Developing Economies."

★ 208 ★

U.S. and World Trade Projections

U.S. GDP Compared to That of Other Industrialized Countries, 1960-2020

"Industrializing not only fosters economic growth, but rapid economic growth. As Brian Reading has observed, 'fast growth comes from starting behind the world leaders and catching up.' The United Kingdom led the world into the Industrial Revolution about 1780. The United States, Germany and Japan, as the table below shows, all started later and achieved growth in per-capita income that overtook Britain. The chart also shows the strides made by Korea, which started industrializing in the early 1950s and is projected to catch the advanced nations not too far into the next century, and some less dramatic but still impressive progress achieved more recently by China, where industrialization started in the 1960s...

"[Based] on Reading's country-by-country projections of future growth (which don't seem unreasonable) by 2013 the developing economics will have far outstripped the industrialized world in terms of total global output. What we now call the Third World will account for 54 percent of global GDP, while the developed counties will then produce only 40 percent. Measured in terms of the incremental output over the two decades, the developing nations will record two-thirds of the growth, the industrial world only a little more than one fourth.

"Among individual countries, the most dramatic story ahead will be the displacement of the United States as the world's largest economy. Reading is projecting that China, which has been growing at a rate of 7.5 percent per year for the past 25 years, will advance at an average pace of 9 percent over the next two decades, and that the United States will continue to expand at the 2.4 percent of the past quarter century. Under those assumptions, by 2013 China will produce 16 percent of world GDP, while the output of the United States will have declined to 14 percent of the world total.

"In terms of the standard of living (per capita income), the United States in 2013 will remain far ahead of China, by a factor of four or five. But with a total population that will be almost five times that of the United States,' China's aggregate economic output will have surpassed the U.S. total."

[GDP per capita; United Kingdom = 100]

	1960	1980	2000	2013	2020
U.S.	142	150	143	142	138
United Kingdom	100	100	100	100	100
Germany	197	125	102	105	115
Japan	47	100	130	140	148
Korea	12	25	50	68	145
China	2	5	8	13	35

Source: Edgar R. Fiedler, "The Third World—Where the Action Is," in *Economic Times*, January 1994, p. 5. *Primary source:* International Monetary Fund, Capital Group, Lombard Street Research. *Notes:* Magnitudes estimated from published chart. Source also includes data for 1780-1959.

★ 209 ★

U.S. and World Trade Projections

Real GDP Growth: Industrial Versus Developing Countries, 1974-2003

"Over the next 25 years, the world will see the biggest shift in economic strength for more than a century. Today the so-called industrial economies dominate the globe, as they have for the past 150 years or so. Yet within a generation several are likely to be dwarfed by newly emerging economic giants. History suggests, alas, that such shifts in economic power are rarely smooth. A growing number of people in the rich industrial world are already urging their governments to prepare for battle against the upstarts. The upstarts are heartwarmingly many. Scores of counties in the third world and the former Soviet block have embraced market-friendly economic reforms and opened their borders to trade and investment. These policies promise rapid growth in more economies than ever before. The four Asian tigers (Hong Kong, Singapore, South Korea and Taiwan) that have pushed aggressively into western markets in the past three decades have a combined population of only 73m; even adding in Japan, the original Asian tiger, the total is less than 200m. Now, however, more than 3 billion people in Asia, Latin America and Eastern Europe are joining the rich world's 1 billion or so in the market-economy club."

[Real GDP growth, annual average percent]

	1974-1993	1994-2003
Rich industrial countries	2.9	2.7
Developing countries	3.0	4.8
of which:		
East Asia	7.5	7.6
South Asia	4.8	5.3
Latin America	2.6	3.4
Eastern Europe and former Soviet Union	1.0	2.7
Sub-Saharan Africa	2.0	3.9
Middle East and North Africa	1.2	3.8

Source: "War of the Worlds," in *The Economist*, 1 October 1994, p. 3. *Primary source:* World Bank.

★ 210 ★

U.S. and World Trade Projections

Increase in Pacific Rim Exports, 1975-1998

"Bill Clinton and his chief trade negotiator, Mickey Kantor, have been playing a game of bad cop/bad cop with Tokyo lately in an effort to open Japan's huge market to more American products. But a new analysis of world trade shows that the Pacific Rim harbors an even bigger challenge to U.S. exports—and to U.S. jobs and wages...

"While this trade battle is fought largely in the ports and factories of the Pacific Rim, it is inflicting casualties here in the United States. One reason for stagnant wages and sluggish hiring in the current U.S. recovery, which has seen job growth at about one eighth the typical post-recession pace, is that American employers are scrambling to slash labor costs to compete with NIEs. Labor costs in the Asian developing nations, for example, average $4.23 per hour, compared with $15.45 in the United States. The WEFA Group predicts that the unemployment rate will remain above 6 percent in America and above 8 percent in Western Europe through the mid-'90s as industrialized nations struggle to stay ahead of their new competitors."

[Percent share]

Year	Percentage
1975	7
1980	10
1985	12
1990	14
1993	19
1998	23

Source: David Hage, "Caught in the Undertow," in *U.S. News & World Report*, 17 May 1993, p. 61. *Primary source:* The WEFA Group. *Note:* NIE = Not otherwise classified.

★ 211 ★

U.S. and World Trade Projections

Effect of Increased Japanese Economic Growth on American Growth, 1990- 2020

"[Most forecasters] expect Japan's GDP growth to continue to outpace America's by one to two percentage points a year, on average. Assume Japanese growth at the upper end of that range and a modest 1% annual decline in the dollar's value against the yen, and by 2010 a country the size of Montana, with half the U.S. population, will have a bigger economy than America's."

[GDP in billions of 1992 dollars]

Year	Japan	U.S.
1990	3,000	6,000
2000	5,200	7,000
2010	8,500	8,500
2020	15,000	10,500

Source: Richard I. Kirkland, Jr., "What If Japan Triumphs?" in *Fortune*, 18 May 1992, pp. 60-1.
Note: Assumes Japan's real growth averages 4% a year and America's only 2%.

Chapter 7
EDUCATION

General Trends in Education

★212★

World Universities, 2000

"[By circa 2000], Universities—especially those in the United States—will belong to the world. There will be more universities and more seats in them throughout the world, but there will also be larger numbers of foreign students in schools in North America and Europe than at present. The great centers of learning that exist on these continents will have made the transformation from state and class institutions to world learning environments. In the future, our present concern with the large and growing numbers of advanced degrees and patents given to foreign students compared to Americans will be replaced by a concern that we ensure that our centers of advanced learning fully reflect the global nature of our links and trade as well as the diversity of the planet's population...

"Sometime during this decade or the next, we will shift substantially to computer-delivered tutorial courses to provide such basic information and theories and to allow students to learn at individual rates. When this technology becomes widely available, we will hold the means to transmit such learning around the globe and allow professors to develop much more specialized or advanced courses for smaller groups of students. Some businesses like IBM, which every working day instruct more than twenty thousand employees in a classroom or other learning environment, are already using such advanced educational techniques, with a record of great pedagogical success."

Source: Allan E. Goodman, *A Brief History of the Future: The United States in a Changing World Order* (Boulder, CO: Westview Press), 1993, p. 98.

★ 213 ★

General Trends in Education

The Hyperlearning Revolution, 2001-2100

"[If] we really want to prepare ourselves and our children for 'the future,' we need to be thinking about the world of 2030, 2050, and beyond. Does that sound farfetched? You think that's too 'futuristic' to have any meaning to you today?

"Ponder this. In America today, there are babies alive now, babies bouncing on fathers' knees, babies nestling in mothers' arms, who will be alive in the year 2100. That's not a typo—I mean 2100, not just 2001. And we're not talking about just a handful of babies but thousands. There are several hundred 108-year-olds in the United States today, and with our larger population and further advances in medical science, it's virtually certain that several thousand of today's children will live right on through the next century.

"So if you've touched a baby lately, you may well have touched a resident of the twenty-second century. That future is alive now, and it's worth thinking about today...

"The reality is that a new generation of technology has blown the social role of learning completely inside out:

—Learning used to be a distinctly human process. Now learning is a transhuman process people share with increasingly powerful artificial networks and brains. Even today, expert systems and neural networks are being 'trained' by human knowledge engineers; the machines' automated expertise in turn is providing 'just-in-time learning' for car mechanics, power plant operators, and a growing legion of other workers.

—Learning was an activity thought to be confined to the box of a school classroom. Now learning permeates every form of social activity—work, entertainment, home life—outside of school. For what piano lessons would cost, you now can buy an electronic piano that will teach you to play it. Only a quarter of American adults know how to program a VCR; a new model will teach you how in any of six languages. The fastest growing cable TV networks—The Discovery Channel and The Learning Channel—are devoted to learning. Of the more than sixty million Americans who learned how to use personal computers since 1980, most learned from vendors, books, other users, and the computers themselves, not in schools.

—Learning was presented as the result of instruction: a linear hierarchical process in which an 'expert' teacher would pour knowledge into the empty head of an obedient student. With knowledge doubling every year or so, 'expertise' now has a shelf life measured in days; everyone must be both learner and teacher; and the sheer challenge of learning can be managed only through a globe-girdling network that links all minds and all knowledge.

[Continued]

★213★

The Hyperlearning Revolution, 2001-2100

[Continued]

—Learning or education was a task of childhood in preparation for entering adult life and work. Now learning is literally the work of the majority of U.S. jobs and will be what virtually all adults—whether employed, unemployed, or 'on welfare' - will do for a living by the early years of the twenty-first century.

"I call this new wave of technology *hyperlearning*, or just HL for short. It is not a single device or process, but a universe of new technologies that both possess and enhance intelligence. The *hyper* in hyperlearning refers not merely to an unprecedented degree of connectedness of knowledge, experience, media, and brains—both human and nonhuman. The *learning* in HL refers most literally to the transformation of knowledge and behavior through experience—what learning means in this context goes as far beyond mere education or training as the space shuttle goes beyond the dugout canoe."

Source: Lewis J. Perelman, *School's Out: Hyperlearning, the New Technology, and the End of Education* (New York: William Morrow and Company, Inc.), 1992, pp. 21-3.

★214★

General Trends in Education

The Plug-in School, 2000

"In the future, technologies will allow learning to take place virtually everywhere. School buildings as they now exist could even be eliminated, replaced with a ubiquitous array of stimulating, interactive, and flexible learning technologies embedded in all human habitats...

"New, integrated technologies enrich the learning experience by giving students access to encyclopedic amounts of information and data in any of their subject areas, integrated with rich images and animation. Curriculums enhanced by these exciting technologies could help teachers expose students to history and its meanings: Names and dates of historical events and actors come alive in full costumes of the times, embellished by period music.

"The advanced physical learning environment would also teach students about life in the twenty-first century—at work, at home, and in places yet to be imagined.

[Continued]

★ 214 ★

The Plug-in School, 2000

[Continued]

"The school, the workplace, and the home are clearly integrating. Responsibilities, functions, activities, and tasks that once occurred exclusively within each domain are crossing over into the other environments. Corporate workers have home offices, students and older learners take cable-access university courses, and parents bring their toddlers to day-care learning centers at work sites. It may no longer be sensible to think about the school, the office, and the home as separate from one another. These three once-distinct entities are breaking apart, combining, and overlapping in new and unexpected ways. The next-generation school can lead this process of blending aspects of learning, living, and working...

"The 'Plug-In School' is a possible first step toward the flexible learning environments of the twenty-first century. As now envisioned, this facility serves as a hub for receiving learning modules 'injected' into its classrooms. The school has a physical structure that opens its walls to become part of the library, museum, science center, planetarium, laboratory, and corporation that is plugged into it. Yet, the school never loses its own identity as the students' and teachers' environment.

"The Plug-In School is conceived as a facility that, in addition to its traditional roles, functions at the center of a delivery and distribution system for education 'packages'. A key goal is to strengthen the school's relationships with informal learning centers and with employers to create both academic and career-oriented instructional programs."

Source: David Pesanelli, "The Plug-in School: A Learning Environment for the 21st Century," in *The Futurist*, September-October 1993, pp. 29-31.

★ 215 ★

General Trends in Education

World-Class Learning Communities, 2000

"By 2020, the top fifth of American earners will earn more than 60 percent of American income, with the bottom fifth dropping to 2 percent. The high-tech elite will withdraw further into their secure enclaves, living a life with excellent health care, challenging work, effective schools, and global travel and linkages. They can tolerate the disorder beyond the pale of walling themselves off, both physically and psychologically, from those who have been left out. Moreover, one might expect more moves toward a security state with investment in electronically equipped security forces, more high-security prisons, and a stepping up of executions for those who have truly 'stepped over the line'. There will be less contact between these enclaves and the rest of society. The urban and rural poor will live largely out of sight in their own decaying sectors. The despair and hopelessness of their children will be a fact of life—as will be the human warehousing of thousands of minority youth in prisons.

[Continued]

★ 215 ★

World-Class Learning Communities, 2000

[Continued]

"We may choose that way. It is not a vision of America as 'a light on the hill' to the rest of the world's burgeoning and impoverished population. But it is not our only choice. We could be guided by another vision—one that Lynn White in *Dynamo and Virgin Reconsidered* refers to as a 'high democratic culture—one in which human values and excellence of aristocratic traditions would be combined with the democratic concern for the dignity of each and the desire to include all in meaningful participation.

"Such a culture would require a recognition by America's leaders that a dangerously divided society, in the long run, is an intolerable threat to the country's moral and material well-being and survival. It would require a decision to take the power of new technology and combine it with the values of our democratic tradition. It would require recognition that the best bet for America's social well-being is a population equipped across the board with symbolic-analytic skills tempered by ecological awareness and deep appreciation for the values and traditions of democracy. Where work is concerned, it would require a commitment to seize the advantage of having thoroughly educated workers to create environments that would combine high tech with high worker involvement—the informating style...

"To create a society of world-class schools for a world-class economy would demand a dramatic change in priorities. It would demand an investment in education, at all levels, of the order employed in building a high-tech military machine during the Cold War. Just the sheet cost of razing the decayed shells of inner-city school buildings and replacing them with modern centers to support symbolic-analytic learning would itself be enormous. A decision would be needed to create exciting learning centers with physical accoutrements comparable to those of American corporations—with readily available computer facilities for all students and teachers, fine laboratories for the sciences, the arts, and language instruction, and, difficult to imagine, air conditioning. Such schools, led by leaders committed to the new vision, would attract to teaching some of our most able and imaginative young adults. The real test of progress will be to count how many inner-city schools have been turned into such world-class learning communities by the year 2000."

Source: Arthur G. Wirth, *Education and Work for the Year 2000: Choices We Face* (San Francisco: Jossey-Bass Publishers) 1992, pp. 199-201.

★ 216 ★

General Trends in Education

Technological Trends Affecting Education, 1988-2020

"Some of the possible short-term future trends in technology are quite easy to see—at least in nonspecific ways—and seem to be probable. Among those that would appear to be highly relevant to education are the following:

[Continued]

★ 216 ★

Technological Trends Affecting Education, 1988-2020

[Continued]

—The speed of the devices used for computing and for storing information will continue to increase, while their size, power requirements and cost will continue to decrease. These trends have characterized computer technology for several decades and will probably continue to do so for the foreseeable future.

—Computer systems that realize orders of magnitude increases in computing power by exploiting parallel multi-processor architectures will become increasingly common.

—Remote wireless terminals will provide access to computer networks and thereby to central repositories of information of nearly every conceivable type.

—Microprocessor-based computing power will be everywhere—in household appliances, in hand tools, in games and toys, in clothing.

—Software will be available for an increasingly extensive array of applications and much of it will have potential for serving educational purposes.

—Software also will be developed that will permit the supplementation of conventional text with dynamic graphics, including process simulations, that should enhance the effectiveness of expository material.

—Multimedia communication facilities, allowing the mixing of text, images, and speech will become widely available.

—User-oriented languages and 'front ends' to applications software will become increasingly easy for people without technical training to use. How soon truly natural-language capabilities will be available is difficult to say; however, systems with useful aspects of natural language and limited speech input and output capabilities will proliferate.

—Computer-based information services addressed to a diversity of objectives—job posting, want ads, selective news, information searchers—will also proliferate.

—Increasingly powerful tools to facilitate interacting with very large data bases—both for directed searching and for browsing—will be developed."

Source: Raymond S. Nickerson, "Technology in Education in 2020: Thinking about the Not-Distant Future," in *Technology in Education: Looking toward 2020*, edited by Raymond S. Nickerson and Philip P. Zodhiates (Hillsdale, NJ: Lawrence Erlbaum Associates, Publishers), 1988, p. 2.

Literacy, Attendance, and Retention Rates

★ 217 ★

Rise in Global Literacy Rates, 1970-2000

"The worldwide rate of literacy will continue to increase during the 1990s, predicts the United Nations Educational, Scientific, and Cultural Organization (UNESCO).

"Between 1970 and 1990, the world literacy rate for adults jumped from 61.5% to 73.5%. If present trends continue, the rate will rise to 78.2% by the year 2000.

"But despite the rising literacy rate, population growth caused the total number of illiterate persons to increase from 890 million in 1970 to 948 million in 1990. That figure is expected to fall slightly to 935 million by the turn of the century."

Source: "World Literacy Rate Rises," in *The Futurist*, September-October 1991, p. 47. *Primary source: UNESCO Sources* (Paris, France), February 1991.

★ 218 ★

Literacy, Attendance, and Retention Rates

Relative Illiteracy Rates, 1985-2000

"The proportion of illiterates among the world's adult population has steadily decreased, although the absolute number has grown. In developing countries, the proportion of illiterates will drop from 39% in 1985 to 28% by 2000, while the number of illiterate adults will have climbed by 10 million."

Source: Marvin Cetron and Owen Davies, 50 Trends Shaping the World, in *The Futurist*, September-October 1991, p. 17. *Primary source:* Marvin Cetron and Owen Davies, *The Have and Have-Nots of the New World Order* (St. Martin's Press), 1991.

★ 219 ★

Literacy, Attendance, and Retention Rates

Limited English-proficiency (LEP) Student Growth Rates, 1978-2000

"America is characterized by diversity. Within its borders, one can move from tropics to tundra, from desert to rainforest. In terms of population, one can find peoples from all over the world who speak many different languages. We find such diversity in our schools as well, the children of recent immigrants and the children of native peoples, children of plenty and children of want. They come, each to be educated, to be given the tools that will let them achieve their own version of the American dream.

"For millions of Americans the dream continues to be deferred. It is likely that in the year 2020 schools will be populated by a student group that has an even larger percentage of poor and disadvantaged children than today, more children who are members of minority groups, more children from single-parent families, and more children with special needs. The budget deficits at the federal level, a conservative turn in attitudes regarding federal investment in education, and a rearrangement in spending priorities make it less and less likely that the federal government will mount any major national initiative to address the problems of this segment of the society, even as its proportion increases...

"Limited English-proficiency (LEP) students have been described as the 'fastest growing segment of school age population in the United States.' Although the overall population of students aged 5 to 14 declined by 6.2% from 1978 to 1982, the LEP population grew by 10.3%. Projections developed in 1981 show the total number of LEP children ages 5 to 14 increasing 16.7% between 1980 and 1990 and increasing 41.7% between 1980 and 2000."

Source: Shirley M. Malcolm, Technology in 2020: Educating a Diverse Population," in *Technology in Education: Looking toward 2020*, edited by Raymond S. Nickerson and Philip P. Zodhiates (Hillsdale, NJ: Lawrence Erlbaum Associates, Publishers), 1988, pp. 215-216.

★ 220 ★

Literacy, Attendance, and Retention Rates

Average Daily Attendance (ADA) in Public Elementary and Secondary Schools, Change in ADA, the Population, and ADA as a Proportion of the Population, 1979-2004

Year ending	ADA (in thousands)	Change in ADA	Population (in millions)	ADA as a proportion of the population
1979	39,076	-1,003,590	223.8	0.175
1980	38,289	-787,089	226.4	0.169
1981	37,704	-585,167	228.8	0.165
1982	37,095	-609,092	231.1	0.161
1983	36,636	-458,784	233.2	0.157
1984	36,363	-272,890	235.3	0.155
1985	36,404	41,283	237.4	0.153
1986	36,523	118,842	239.6	0.152
1987	36,864	340,764	241.7	0.153
1988	37,051	186,840	243.9	0.152
1989	37,268	217,365	246.2	0.151
1990	37,799	531,224	248.6	0.152
1991	38,427	627,247	251.3	0.153
1992[2]	38,972	545,677	254.1	0.153
1993	39,594	621,376	256.9	0.154
1994	40,321	727,476	259.7	0.155
1995	41,063	742,322	262.5	0.156
1996	41,801	737,682	265.1	0.158
1997	42,672	871,300	267.8	0.159
1998	43,458	785,933	270.4	0.161
1999	44,010	552,102	272.9	0.161
2000	44,472	461,168	275.4	0.161
2001	44,859	387,863	277.8	0.161
2002	45,193	334,045	280.3	0.161
2003	45,480	286,722	282.7	0.161
2004	45,727	246,822	285.1	0.160

Source: Debra E. Gerald and William J. Hussar, U.S. Department of Education, National Center for Education Statistics, *Projections of Education Statistics to 2004* (Washington, D.C.: U.S. Government Printing Office), October 1993, p. 149. *Primary source:* U.S. Department of Commerce, Bureau of the Census, "U.S. Population Estimates, by Age, Sex, Race, and Hispanic Origin: 1980 to 1991," Series P-25, No. 1095, February 1993 and unpublished tabulations: U.S. Department of Education, National Center for Education Statistics, *Statistics of State School Systems;* Common Core of Data survey; and the Early Estimates survey: DRI/McGraw-Hill, 'U.S. Quarterly Model.' This table was prepared October 1993. *Notes:* 1. Projections for average daily attendance were made by multiplying the forecasts for enrollment by the average value of the ratio average daily attendance to the enrollment from 1982 to 1991; approximately 0.93 percent. 2. Average daily attendance is estimated on the basis of past data.

★ 221 ★

Literacy, Attendance, and Retention Rates

Public School Grade Retention Rates, 1991-2004

Grade	1991	Projected	
		1999	2004
1 to 2	96.0	95.4	95.4
2 to 3	100.2	100.1	100.1
3 to 4	100.5	100.4	100.4
4 to 5	100.6	100.5	100.5
5 to 6	101.3	101.3	101.3
6 to 7	102.3	102.8	102.8
7 to 8	98.5	98.3	98.3
8 to 9	111.1	110.5	110.5
9 to 10	92.0	92.3	92.3
10 to 11	91.3	91.1	91.1
11 to 12	91.5	90.9	90.9

Source: Debra E. Gerald and William J. Hussar, U.S. Department of Education, National Center for Education Statistics, *Projections of Education Statistics to 2004* (Washington, D.C.: U.S. Government Printing Office), October 1993, p. 111.

Elementary and Secondary School Enrollment

★ 222 ★

Preprimary School-Age Populations, 1979-2004

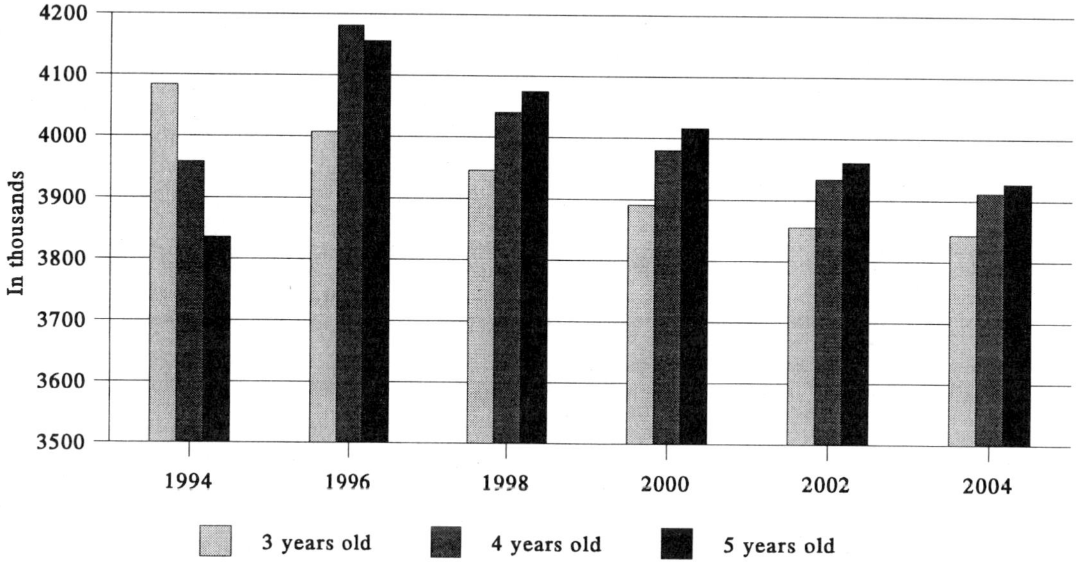

[In thousands]

Year (July 1)	3 years old	4 years old	5 years old	3-5 years old
1979	3,077	3,175	3,092	9,344
1980	3,238	3,128	3,180	9,546
1981	3,261	3,274	3,129	9,664
1982	3,361	3,297	3,274	9,932
1983	3,479	3,398	3,296	10,173
1984	3,527	3,518	3,397	10,442
1985	3,566	3,568	3,518	10,652
1986	3,578	3,609	3,568	10,755
1987	3,509	3,623	3,610	10,742
1988	3,620	3,556	3,627	10,803
1989	3,646	3,669	3,559	11,036
1990	3,659	3,698	3,679	11,036
1991	3,718	3,717	3,702	11,437
1992	3,813	3,778	3,722	11,313
1993	3,894	3,829	3,781	11,504
1994	4,084	3,958	3,836	11,878
1995	4,114	4,150	3,963	12,227
1996	4,007	4,181	4,156	12,344
1997	3,976	4,076	4,185	12,231
1998	3,946	4,040	4,075	12,061
1999	3,917	4,010	4,046	11,974

[Continued]

★ 222 ★

Preprimary School-Age Populations, 1979-2004

[Continued]

Year (July 1)	3 years old	4 years old	5 years old	3-5 years old
2000	3,891	3,980	4,016	11,887
2001	3,871	3,954	3,986	11,811
2002	3,856	3,934	3,961	11,751
2003	3,848	3,920	3,941	11,709
2004	3,844	3,912	3,927	11,683

Source: Debra E. Gerald and William J. Hussar, U.S. Department of Education, National Center for Education Statistics, *Projections of Education Statistics to 2004* (Washington, D.C.: U.S. Government Printing Office), October 1993, p. 146. *Primary source:* U.S. Department of Commerce, Bureau of the Census, "U.S. Population Estimates, by Age, Sex, Race, and Hispanic Origin: 1980 to 1991," in *Current Population Reports*, Series P-25, No. 1095, February 1993 and unpublished tabulations. This table was prepared May 1993.

★ 223 ★

Elementary and Secondary School Enrollment

School-Age Populations, 1979-2004

[In thousands]

Year (July 1)	5 years old	6 years old	5-13 years old	14-17 years old
1979	3,092	3,164	31,431	16,611
1980	3,180	3,111	31,091	16,144
1981	3,129	3,186	30,711	15,610
1982	3,274	3,133	30,528	15,057
1983	3,296	3,276	30,279	14,741
1984	3,397	3,297	30,061	14,726
1985	3,518	3,398	29,892	14,888
1986	3,568	3,518	30,078	14,824
1987	3,610	3,568	30,503	14,502
1988	3,627	3,611	31,029	14,023
1989	3,559	3,625	31,413	13,536
1990	3,679	3,561	31,999	13,312
1991	3,702	3,681	32,500	13,424
1992	3,722	3,705	33,006	13,649
1993	3,781	3,747	33,424	13,802
1994	3,836	3,785	33,870	14,088
1995	3,963	3,838	34,263	14,591
1996	4,156	3,966	34,868	14,933
1997	4,185	4,156	35,387	15,333
1998	4,075	4,186	35,808	15,600
1999	4,046	4,077	36,253	15,639
2000	4,016	4,047	36,547	15,811
2001	3,986	4,017	36,805	15,900
2002	3,961	3,987	36,991	16,034

[Continued]

★ 223 ★

School-Age Populations, 1979-2004

[Continued]

Year (July 1)	5 years old	6 years old	5-13 years old	14-17 years old
2003	3,941	3,962	37,107	16,277
2004	3,927	3,943	37,080	16,522

Source: Debra E. Gerald and William J. Hussar, U.S. Department of Education, National Center for Education Statistics, *Projections of Education Statistics to 2004* (Washington, D.C.: U.S. Government Printing Office), October 1993, p. 147. *Primary source:* U.S. Department of Commerce, Bureau of the Census, "U.S. Population Estimates, by Age, Sex, Race, and Hispanic Origin: 1980 to 1991," in *Current Population Reports*, Series P-25, No. 1095, February 1993 and unpublished tabulations. This table was prepared May 1993.

★ 224 ★

Elementary and Secondary School Enrollment

Elementary Enrollment Rates, by Age and Sex, 1991-2004

Age	Boys		Girls	
	1991	1993-2004	1991	1993-2004
5	5.1	5.0	6.3	6.1
6	83.9	83.9	87.7	88.7
7	104.1	103.8	106.5	104.2
8	105.5	105.0	105.9	105.2
9	100.3	100.6	98.7	100.1
10	101.4	100.9	104.1	102.5
11	104.5	104.3	101.3	102.8
12	106.0	103.5	103.7	102.5
13	96.9	96.7	97.6	96.2
14	35.4	36.8	26.2	26.0
15	5.9	6.8	3.3	3.6
16	0.2	0.5	0.1	0.2
17	0.0	0.1	0.0	0.0
18	0.0	0.0	0.3	0.1

Source: Debra E. Gerald and William J. Hussar, U.S. Department of Education, National Center for Education Statistics, *Projections of Education Statistics to 2004* (Washington, D.C.: U.S. Government Printing Office), October 1993, p. 107.

★ 225 ★

Elementary and Secondary School Enrollment

Secondary Enrollment Rates, by Age and Sex, 1991-2004

Age	Boys		Girls	
	1991	1993-2004	1991	1993-2004
12	0.1	0.2	0.1	0.3
13	5.0	5.1	6.5	7.0
14	62.5	63.2	70.4	72.2
15	90.4	89.1	91.1	91.1
16	91.0	91.3	93.0	92.9
17	81.8	80.2	79.1	78.5
18	27.0	25.8	17.5	17.5
19	7.9	6.5	4.4	3.9
20	1.9	1.4	1.6	1.3
21	0.8	0.8	0.5	0.7
22	0.6	0.5	0.4	0.4
23	0.3	0.3	1.1	0.6
24	0.4	0.5	0.4	0.3
25-29	0.2	0.2	0.3	0.4
30-34	0.2	0.2	0.4	0.3

Source: Debra E. Gerald and William J. Hussar, U.S. Department of Education, National Center for Education Statistics, *Projections of Education Statistics to 2004* (Washington, D.C.: U.S. Government Printing Office), October 1993, p. 107.

★ 226 ★

Elementary and Secondary School Enrollment

Enrollment in Grades K-8 and 9-12 of Elementary and Secondary Schools, by Control of Institution, 1979-2004

[In thousands]

Year	Total			Public			Private		
	K-12[1]	K-8[1]	9-12	K-12[1]	K-8[1]	9-12	K-12[1]	K-8[1]	9-12
1979	46,651	31,734	14,916	41,651	28,084	13,616	5,000	3,700	1,300
1980	46,208	31,639	14,570	40,877	27,647	13,231	5,331	3,992	1,339
1981	45,544	31,380	14,164	40,044	27,280	12,764	5,500	4,100	1,400
1982	45,166	31,361	13,805	39,566	27,161	12,405	5,600	4,200	1,400
1983	44,967	31,296	13,671	39,252	26,981	12,271	5,715	4,315	1,400
1984	44,908	31,205	13,704	39,208	26,905	12,304	5,700	4,300	1,400
1985	44,979	31,229	13,750	39,422	27,034	12,388	5,557	4,195	1,362
1986	45,205	31,536	13,669	39,753	27,420	12,333	5,452	4,116	1,336
1987	45,488	32,165	13,323	40,008	27,933	12,076	5,479	4,232	1,247
1988	45,430	32,537	12,893	40,189	28,501	11,687	5,241	4,036	1,206
1989	45,898	33,314	12,583	40,543	29,152	11,390	5,355	4,162	1,193
1990	46,448	33,973	12,475	41,217	29,878	11,338	5,232	4,095	1,137
1991	47,199	34,544	12,655	42,000	30,470	11,530	5,199	4,074	1,125
1992	48,045	35,157	12,888	42,670	30,945	11,725	5,375	4,212	1,163

[Continued]

★ 226 ★

Enrollment in Grades K-8 and 9-12 of Elementary and Secondary Schools, by Control of Institution, 1979-2004

[Continued]

Year	Total			Public			Private		
	K-12[1]	K-8[1]	9-12	K-12[1]	K-8[1]	9-12	K-12[1]	K-8[1]	9-12
1993	48,925	35,727	13,198	43,454	31,447	12,007	5,471	4,280	1,191
1994	49,819	36,170	13,649	44,254	31,837	12,417	5,565	4,333	1,232
1995	50,709	36,668	14,041	45,049	32,275	12,774	5,660	4,393	1,267
1996	51,762	37,311	14,451	45,988	32,841	13,147	5,774	4,470	1,304
1997	52,714	37,940	14,773	46,835	33,395	13,440	5,879	4,545	1,333
1998	53,382	38,398	14,984	47,430	33,798	13,632	5,952	4,600	1,352
1999	53,942	38,793	15,149	47,927	34,145	13,782	6,015	4,648	1,367
2000	54,412	39,129	15,283	48,345	34,441	13,904	6,067	4,688	1,379
2001	54,816	39,389	15,427	48,705	34,670	14,035	6,111	4,719	1,392
2002	55,162	39,589	15,573	19,914	34,846	14,168	6,148	4,743	1,405
2003	55,159	39,713	15,746	49,280	34,955	14,325	6,179	4,758	1,421
2004	55,706	39,676	16,029	49,506	34,923	14,583	6,200	4,753	1,446

Source: Debra E. Gerald and William J. Hussar, U.S. Department of Education, National Center for Education Statistics, *Projections of Education Statistics to 2004* (Washington, D.C.: U.S. Government Printing Office), October 1993, p. 8. *Primary source:* U.S. Department of Education, National Center for Education Statistics, *Statistics of Public Elementary and Secondary Schools;* Common Core of Data surveys, "Selected Public and Private Elementary and Secondary Education Statistics," *NCES Bulletin*, October 23, 1979; "Private Elementary and Secondary Education, 1983; Enrollment, Teachers, and Schools," *NCES Bulletin*, December 1984; 1985 Private School Survey: "Key Statistics for Private Elementary and Secondary Education: School Year 1988-89," *Early Estimates*: "Key Statistics for Private Elementary and Secondary Education: School Year 1990-91," *Early Estimates*: "Public and Private Elementary and Secondary Education Statistics School Year 1991-92," *Early Estimates*: and "Public and Private Elementary and Secondary Education Statistics: School Year 1992-93," *Early Estimates*. This table was prepared May 1993. *Notes:* 1. Includes most Kindergarten and some nursery school enrollment. Some data have been revised from previously published figures. Projections are based on data through 1991. Because of rounding, details may not add to totals.

★ 227 ★

Elementary and Secondary School Enrollment

Enrollment Rates in Public Schools, by Grade Level, 1991-2004

[Percent of total enrollment]

Grade level	Population base age	1991	Projected	
			1999	2004
Kindergarten	5	99.0	97.3	97.3
Grade 1	6	96.6	96.7	96.7
Elementary upgraded and special	5-13	1.7	1.7	1.7
Secondary upgraded and special	14-17	1.9	2.0	2.0
Postgraduate	18	0.4	0.4	0.3

Source: Debra E. Gerald and William J. Hussar, U.S. Department of Education, National Center for Education Statistics, *Projections of Education Statistics to 2004* (Washington, D.C.: U.S. Government Printing Office), October 1993, p. 111.

★ 228 ★

Elementary and Secondary School Enrollment

Total High School Enrollments by Region, 1978-1998

Year	West*		South Southcentral*		Northcentral		Northeast*	
	Public	Nonpublic**	Public	Nonpublic**	Public	Nonpublic**	Public	Nonpublic**
1978-79	7,289,829		12,567,810		10,337,129		9,003,831	
1979-80	7,189,792		12,433,091		9,980,346		8,616,121	
1980-81	7,135,773		12,322,815		9,637,258		8,308,308	
1981-82	7,145,350		12,193,447		9,330,445		7,980,390	
1982-83	7,114,426		12,576,753		9,060,214		7,700,652	
1983-84	7,153,515		12,057,727		8,962,987		7,502,856	
1984-85	7,249,298		12,066,256		8,835,956		7,343,029	
1985-86	7,374,760		12,096,361		8,782,483		7,249,166	
1986-87	7,539,170		12,199,947		8,784,635		7,187,913	
1987-88	7,752,249		12,334,869		8,939,871		7,225,153	
1988-89	7,949,103		12,413,338		8,907,004		7,171,880	
1989-90	8,164,669	693,150	12,495,609	994,610	8,900,613	1,243,370	7,156,158	1,382,530
1990-91	8,426,277	707,030	12,602,132	999,880	8,963,932	1,223,880	7,223,254	1,341,500
1991-92	8,706,172	722,320	12,798,547	1,002,020	9,081,857	1,213,670	7,350,379	1,306,120
1992-93	8,910,444	737,580	12,985,959	1,019,700	9,198,481	1,206,660	7,472,946	1,296,820
1993-94	9,174,410	755,380	13,178,150	1,029,680	9,289,590	1,196,720	7,609,940	1,284,720
1994-95	9,470,300	775,590	13,400,460	1,040,880	9,402,710	1,190,010	7,768,380	1,280,860
1995-96	9,789,740	798,060	13,622,980	1,053,530	9,509,660	1,186,220	7,930,550	1,282,880
1996-97	10,147,720	823,660	13,861,740	1,066,290	9,629,320	1,187,160	8,091,110	1,288,220
1997-98	10,446,070	845,400	14,065,720	1,077,540	9,680,440	1,184,530	8,232,220	1,290,780

Source: Western Interstate Commission for Higher Education (WICHE), *High School Graduates: Projections by State, 1992-2009* (Boulder, CO: WICHE Publications), October 1993, p. 12. *Notes:* *West: includes public school enrollment projections for 1992-93 for Arizona, which could not supply enrollment projections for that year. South Central: includes public school enrollment projections for 1992-93 for Louisiana which could not supply enrollments for that year. Northeast: nonpublic enrollments for the District of Columbia are for Catholic schools only. **Historical data are incomplete prior to 1989-90.

High School Graduates and Earned Degrees Conferred

★ 229 ★

Total U.S. High School Enrollments and Graduates, 1989-2009

Year	Total Enrollments 1978-79 through 1992-93 (actual) 1993-94 through 1997-98 (projected)		High School Graduates 1978-79 through 1991-92 (actual) 1992-93 through 2008-09 (projected)	
	Public[1]	Nonpublic[2]	Public[3]	Nonpublic[2]
1989-90	36,717,049	4,313,660	2,320,597	257,930
1990-91	37,215,595	4,272,290	2,231,054	243,490
1991-92	37,936,955	4,244,130	2,233,768	241,230
1992-93	38,567,830	4,260,760	2,266,900	239,650
1993-94	39,252,090	4,266,490	2,254,150	236,870
1994-95	40,041,860	4,287,330	2,341,250	240,790
1995-96	40,852,920	4,320,690	2,376,790	241,370
1996-97	41,729,380	4,365,330	2,453,170	242,300
1997-98	42,424,450	4,398,250	2,539,060	245,740
1998-99			2,598,190	244,480
1999-00			2,658,040	242,660
2000-01			2,679,940	238,100
2001-02			2,708,120	237,270
2002-03			2,765,370	238,300
2003-04			2,740,980	235,850
2004-05			2,795,970	243,740
2005-06			2,874,190	250,660
2006-07			2,971,050	259,340
2007-08			3,056,830	266,470
2008-09			3,003,030	261,540

Source: Western Interstate Commission for Higher Education (WICHE), *High School Graduates: Projections by State, 1992-2009* (Boulder, CO: WICHE Publications), October 1993, p. 9. *Notes:* 1. Includes public school enrollment projections for 1992-93 for Arizona and Louisiana, which could not supply grade level enrollments for that year. 2. Historical data are incomplete prior to 1989-90. Nonpublic enrollments and graduates for the District of Columbia are for Catholic Schools only. 3. 1989-90 includes a graduate projection for Indiana, which could not supply graduate data for that year; 1991-92 includes graduate projections for Ohio and Vermont which could not supply graduate data for that year; 1990-91 includes graduate projections for Vermont which could not supply graduate data for that year. Source also includes data for 1978-1989.

★ 230 ★

High School Graduates and Earned Degrees Conferred

High School Graduates, by Control of Institution, 1979-2004

[In thousands]

Year ending	Total	Public	Private
1979	3,101	2,801	300
1980	3,043	2,748	295
1981	3,020	2,725	295
1982	2,995	2,705	290
1983	2,888	2,598	290
1984	2,767	2,495	272
1985	2,677	2,414	263
1986	2,643	2,383	260
1987	2,694	2,429	265
1988	2,773	2,500	273
1989	2,727	2,459	268
1990	2,586	2,320	266
1991	2,506	2,238	268
1992	2,502	2,246	256
		Projected	
1993	2,514	2,257	257
1994	2,526	2,267	258
1995	2,648	2,377	271
1996	2,669	2,396	273
1997	2,763	2,480	283
1998	2,890	2,595	296
1999	2,955	2,653	302
2000	3,009	2,701	308
2001	3,039	2,728	311
2002	3,066	2,753	314
2003	3,096	2,779	317
2004	3,116	2,797	319

Source: Debra E. Gerald and William J. Hussar, U.S. Department of Education, National Center for Education Statistics, *Projections of Education Statistics to 2004* (Washington, D.C.: U.S. Government Printing Office), October 1993, p. 52. *Primary source:* U.S. Department of Education, National Center for Education Statistics, *Statistics of Public Elementary and Secondary Schools*; Common Core of Data surveys, "Selected Public and Private Elementary and Secondary Education Statistics," *NCES Bulletin*, October 23, 1979; "Private Elementary and Secondary Education, 1983; Enrollment, Teachers, and Schools," *NCES Bulletin*, December 1984; 1985 Private School Survey: "Key Statistics for Private Elementary and Secondary Education: School Year 1988-89," *Early Estimates*: "Key Statistics for Private Elementary and Secondary Education: School Year 1991-92," *Early Estimates*: and "Public and Private Elementary and Secondary Education Statistics: School Year 1992-93," *Early Estimates*. This table was prepared May 1993. *Notes:* Prior to 1980-90, numbers for private high school graduates were estimated by the National Center for Education Statistics (NCES). Because of rounding, details may not add to totals.

★ 231 ★

High School Graduates and Earned Degrees Conferred

Total High School Graduates by Region, 1988-2009

Year	West		South Southcentral		Northcentral		Northeast	
	Public	Nonpublic**	Public	Nonpublic**	Public*	Nonpublic**	Public*	Nonpublic**
1988-89	480,865		785,875		664,372		533,207	
1989-90	461,122	36,040	750,099	58,430	617,808	67,310	491,568	96,160
1990-91	454,915	35,010	724,878	55,500	585,110	62,500	466,151	90,480
1991-92	468,682	36,860	719,538	55,570	577,589	61,140	467,959	87,670
1992-93	486,350	36,580	724,420	55,850	590,780	61,340	465,360	85,890
1993-94	490,790	37,160	718,210	56,770	583,490	60,250	461,670	82,680
1994-95	508,570	38,980	745,350	58,610	608,740	61,640	478,590	81,560
1995-96	520,250	40,750	755,480	59,950	613,500	60,400	487,570	80,270
1996-97	546,800	41,810	775,690	60,160	633,910	61,410	496,770	78,930
1997-98	576,080	43,620	802,190	61,750	657,610	62,050	503,180	78,320
1998-99	600,680	44,630	821,410	61,870	661,100	60,840	515,010	77,150
1999-00	623,880	45,210	837,530	62,510	663,940	59,540	532,700	75,400
2000-01	636,100	45,130	841,940	62,390	663,190	57,840	538,710	72,730
2001-02	646,640	45,910	850,080	62,210	665,610	57,460	545,780	71,690
2002-03	661,150	46,500	866,020	63,240	680,730	57,460	557,460	71,100
2003-04	666,320	46,910	850,380	62,310	667,980	56,020	556,300	70,610
2004-05	686,980	48,860	870,670	63,360	663,030	56,370	575,300	75,160
2005-06	715,500	51,060	892,020	64,970	674,550	57,110	592,120	77,530
2006-07	748,050	53,760	919,190	66,870	694,140	58,540	609,670	80,170
2007-08	788,880	57,110	940,320	68,280	711,140	59,730	616,490	81,340
2008-09	776,900	56,450	934,240	67,700	678,550	58,280	613,350	79,110

Source: Western Interstate Commission for Higher Education (WICHE), *High School Graduates: Projections by State, 1992-2009* (Boulder, CO: WICHE Publications), October 1993, p. 13. *Notes:* *Northcentral: historical data include graduate projections for states that could not supply data for some years—1989-90 for Indiana and 1991-92 for Ohio. Northeast: historical data include graduate projections for 1991-92 for Vermont which could not supply data for those years. **Historical data are incomplete prior to 1989-90. Nonpublic graduates for the District of Columbia are for Catholic schools only. Source also includes data for 1978-1987.

★ 232 ★

High School Graduates and Earned Degrees Conferred

Public and Nonpublic High School Graduates by State, 2000-2009

State	2000 2001	2001 2002	2002 2003	2003 2004	2004 2005	2005 2006	2006 2007	2007 2008	2008 2009
Alabama									
Public	41,577	41,027	40,469	39,750	40,788	41,584	42,834	43,463	41,427
Nonpublic[alt]	3,702	3,588	3,316	3,423	3,474	3,545	3,651	3,704	3,529
Alaska									
Public	7,548	7,880	8,202	8,069	7,963	7,873	8,398	8,794	7,145
Nonpublic[1]	120	134	138	128	135	129	135	138	130
Arizona									
Public	46,216	46,489	46,589	50,488	52,559	54,429	55,733	57,225	56,114

[Continued]

★ 232 ★

Public and Nonpublic High School Graduates by State, 2000-2009

[Continued]

State	2000 2001	2001 2002	2002 2003	2003 2004	2004 2005	2005 2006	2006 2007	2007 2008	2008 2009
Nonpublic[alt]	2,087	2,050	2,080	2,092	2,269	2,350	2,407	2,472	2,423
Arkansas									
Public	28,909	28,613	28,014	27,109	27,456	27,828	28,524	28,957	27,473
Nonpublic[2,alt]	963	982	952	901	933	946	969	985	934
California									
Public	326,526	334,631	345,568	346,519	371,122	393,042	420,203	451,637	446,525
Nonpublic	28,676	29,343	29,775	30,169	32,101	33,997	36,347	39,067	38,626
Colorado									
Public	42,334	42,466	43,829	45,848	44,843	45,362	43,749	41,714	42,060
Nonpublic[alt]	1,864	1,875	2,010	1,983	1,894	1,876	1,853	1,882	1,897
Connecticut									
Public	31,644	32,478	33,151	32,654	33,784	34,579	35,219	35,326	36,603
Nonpublic[2,alt]	3,817	3,814	3,789	3,665	4,039	4,135	4,256	4,312	4,154
Delaware									
Public	6,621	6,623	6,893	7,067	7,468	8,240	8,622	8,207	8,254
Nonpublic	1,641	1,669	1,649	1,730	1,738	1,828	1,886	1,952	1,963
District of Columbia									
Public	2,997	2,962	2,922	2,931	3,163	3,267	3,654	3,674	3,090
Nonpublic	1,705	1,703	1,700	1,686	1,756	1,812	2,029	2,039	1,714
Florida									
Public	125,455	129,717	135,722	133,121	144,758	152,174	159,622	164,753	160,718
Nonpublic[2,alt]	11,606	11,833	11,978	11,939	12,876	13,536	14,199	14,656	14,296
Georgia									
Public	73,509	72,518	74,513	74,805	80,389	83,068	86,478	88,355	86,283
Nonpublic	4,778	4,719	4,814	4,606	5,067	5,234	5,452	5,568	5,438
Hawaii									
Public	11,472	11,398	11,086	11,199	11,261	11,529	11,724	12,404	12,116
Nonpublic	2,368	2,311	2,247	2,184	2,342	2,398	2,435	2,577	2,518
Idaho									
Public	17,287	17,709	17,900	16,811	15,288	14,606	13,986	14,473	15,177
Nonpublic[2,alt]	811	795	702	716	671	662	668	689	725
Illinois									
Public	112,211	117,426	120,425	119,471	124,489	129,746	136,048	142,500	125,452
Nonpublic[2,alt]	11,185	11,303	11,234	10,915	11,222	11,481	11,820	12,160	12,049
Indiana									
Public	63,046	62,307	61,596	59,930	60,191	62,549	63,947	66,052	64,897
Nonpublic	3,344	3,278	3,251	3,229	3,197	3,324	3,398	3,511	3,449
Iowa									
Public	35,394	34,416	34,933	33,588	31,187	31,366	32,108	32,430	29,633
Nonpublic[2,alt]	3,358	3,281	3,281	3,146	3,010	3,029	3,100	3,131	2,860
Kansas									
Public	30,835	30,355	30,786	30,080	29,701	30,122	30,280	30,704	28,320
Nonpublic[2,alt]	1,585	1,799	1,642	1,546	1,557	1,570	1,567	1,579	1,508
Kentucky									
Public	39,667	39,503	39,837	36,994	37,113	36,881	38,592	39,268	39,667
Nonpublic[2,alt]	2,701	2,535	2,642	2,489	2,501	2,486	2,600	2,645	2,673

[Continued]

★ 232 ★

Public and Nonpublic High School Graduates by State, 2000-2009

[Continued]

State	2000 2001	2001 2002	2002 2003	2003 2004	2004 2005	2005 2006	2006 2007	2007 2008	2008 2009
Louisiana									
Public	30,033	32,252	31,713	31,114	29,522	29,496	29,037	28,814	29,759
Nonpublic[2,alt]	7,825	7,712	7,802	7,372	7,007	7,000	6,893	6,837	7,063
Maine									
Public	13,638	13,837	14,076	13,391	13,713	13,979	14,219	14,129	13,496
Nonpublic	1,533	1,568	1,526	1,484	1,505	1,533	1,560	1,551	1,478
Maryland									
Public	50,629	51,554	52,310	51,788	56,088	588,581	60,513	62,043	65,298
Nonpublic[2,alt]	5,588	5,539	5,633	5,581	6,023	6,289	6,497	6,662	7,012
Massachusetts									
Public	55,372	57,207	58,880	57,906	60,893	63,590	65,991	66,806	62,239
Nonpublic[2,alt]	6,730	6,755	6,911	6,730	7,106	7,421	7,699	7,798	7,263
Michigan									
Public	93,952	95,184	98,435	96,187	97,540	96,941	103,052	106,645	106,410
Nonpublic[2,alt]	7,303	7,068	7,222	6,846	7,274	7,230	7,685	7,953	7,935
Minnesota									
Public	62,608	63,320	65,048	64,151	61,669	63,160	63,887	64,354	63,417
Nonpublic[2,alt]	3,523	3,493	3,470	3,348	3,370	3,451	3,491	3,517	3,465
Mississippi									
Public	24,964	24,610	24,260	23,726	23,283	23,724	24,274	24,564	24,542
Nonpublic[alt]	3,062	2,960	2,801	2,669	2,683	2,736	2,798	2,830	2,828
Missouri									
Public	55,108	54,439	55,974	55,555	54,032	55,000	55,992	56,990	56,078
Nonpublic[2,alt]	6,834	6,653	6,546	6,435	6,540	6,655	6,776	6,897	6,787
Montana									
Public	12,548	12,881	12,973	12,886	12,079	11,532	11,521	11,457	11,389
Nonpublic[2,alt]	497	519	536	497	467	446	445	442	440
Nebraska									
Public	20,688	20,856	20,796	20,290	19,410	19,480	19,731	19,865	19,502
Nonpublic[2,alt]	1,869	1,890	1,904	1,872	1,768	1,773	1,795	1,806	1,775
Nevada									
Public	16,617	17,511	18,378	19,132	19,394	20,953	22,814	25,134	26,732
Nonpublic[2,alt]	314	297	299	289	327	354	386	424	452
New Hampshire									
Public	13,805	13,851	14,474	14,169	15,874	16,185	16,600	16,376	14,969
Nonpublic[2,alt]	1,493	1,471	1,354	1,327	1,571	1,603	1,648	1,622	1,483
New Jersey									
Public	73,621	75,114	77,047	78,298	82,966	86,184	89,168	89,497	86,202
Nonpublic[2,alt]	13,816	13,217	13,341	13,673	14,674	15,243	15,770	15,830	15,247
New Mexico									
Public	18,834	18,621	18,823	18,537	18,461	18,268	18,498	18,531	19,044
Nonpublic[2,alt]	1,719	1,715	1,715	1,710	1,677	1,660	1,680	1,682	1,729
New York									
Public	154,941	156,505	159,258	158,442	162,068	165,882	170,948	173,199	179,423
Nonpublic[2,alt]	19,736	19,078	18,799	18,566	19,988	20,615	21,408	21,857	21,477

[Continued]

★ 232 ★

Public and Nonpublic High School Graduates by State, 2000-2009

[Continued]

State	2000 2001	2001 2002	2002 2003	2003 2004	2004 2005	2005 2006	2006 2007	2007 2008	2008 2009
North Carolina									
Public	64,995	67,025	68,059	67,892	71,328	74,440	77,893	79,739	78,150
Nonpublic[2,alt]	2,560	2,618	2,633	2,721	2,819	2,943	3,079	3,151	3,090
North Dakota									
Public	8,512	8,152	8,048	7,620	7,114	6,978	6,610	6,389	6,263
Nonpublic[2,alt]	464	446	467	434	401	392	372	359	351
Ohio									
Public	108,787	107,329	110,979	108,571	108,269	110,113	112,460	114,493	108,815
Nonpublic[2,alt]	12,443	12,335	12,524	12,381	12,361	12,573	12,841	13,072	12,424
Oklahoma									
Public	39,360	38,966	38,594	38,277	34,841	34,498	34,480	34,673	34,427
Nonpublic[2,alt]	1,528	1,458	1,519	1,531	1,366	1,353	1,352	1,360	1,350
Oregon									
Public	33,766	33,935	34,403	34,069	33,386	34,556	35,616	37,005	36,933
Nonpublic[2,alt]	2,134	2,136	2,150	2,206	2,154	2,231	2,299	2,389	2,384
Pennsylvania									
Public	119,163	118,788	121,875	123,563	122,104	124,347	126,723	129,092	126,558
Nonpublic[2,alt]	14,926	15,200	14,730	14,540	15,007	15,283	15,575	15,866	15,556
Rhode Island									
Public	9,243	9,713	9,622	9,374	10,245	10,374	10,770	11,083	10,641
Nonpublic[2,alt]	1,113	1,045	1,037	1,003	1,113	1,128	1,171	1,203	1,157
South Carolina									
Public	35,407	35,038	35,321	34,055	34,282	36,577	37,769	38,330	39,968
Nonpublic[2,alt]	3,809	3,633	4,108	4,022	4,065	4,244	4,414	4,513	4,445
South Dakota									
Public	9,487	9,387	9,354	9,064	8,759	8,530	8,447	8,382	8,414
Nonpublic[2,alt]	1,081	1,151	1,177	1,204	1,060	1,032	1,022	1,013	1,018
Tennessee									
Public	45,233	45,237	46,223	45,052	46,773	48,681	50,378	51,607	50,328
Nonpublic[2,alt]	5,384	5,421	5,598	5,530	5,629	5,858	6,062	6,211	6,057
Texas									
Public	205,065	207,223	212,412	209,550	207,911	208,914	211,837	217,868	224,160
Nonpublic[2,alt]	10,046	10,141	10,321	10,501	10,211	10,260	10,403	10,700	11,008
Utah									
Public	31,473	30,864	30,220	29,914	29,251	30,086	29,908	30,737	28,046
Nonpublic[2,alt]	717	749	764	820	750	763	753	768	744
Vermont									
Public	7,039	7,152	6,956	6,716	6,931	6,915	7,242	7,053	6,574
Nonpublic[2,alt]	636	633	631	624	637	636	668	650	608
Virginia									
Public	68,853	70,544	73,338	71,681	75,962	78,312	81,400	83,547	81,241
Nonpublic[2,alt]	3,496	3,654	3,771	3,750	3,902	4,023	4,182	4,291	4,174
Washington									
Public	64,871	65,668	66,711	66,814	65,938	67,943	70,620	74,269	70,971
Nonpublic[2,alt]	3,821	3,977	4,078	4,115	4,065	4,190	4,353	4,579	4,377

[Continued]

★ 232 ★

Public and Nonpublic High School Graduates by State, 2000-2009

[Continued]

State	2000 2001	2001 2002	2002 2003	2003 2004	2004 2005	2005 2006	2006 2007	2007 2008	2008 2009
West Virginia									
Public	18,912	17,811	17,543	17,254	16,262	15,842	16,071	16,378	16,095
Nonpublic[2,alt]	926	957	986	855	826	802	814	832	816
Wisconsin									
Public	62,564	62,438	64,359	63,474	60,667	60,562	61,576	62,339	61,349
Nonpublic[2,alt]	4,855	4,767	4,742	4,664	4,605	4,598	4,674	4,733	4,658
Wyoming									
Public	6,606	6,585	6,474	6,032	5,434	5,324	5,284	5,504	4,645
Nonpublic[2,alt]	4	4	4	4	3	3	3	3	3
U.S. Total									
Public	2,679,942	2,708,115	2,765,366	2,740,975	2,795,972	2,874,192	2,971,050	3,056,828	3,003,032
Nonpublic	238,096	237,272	238,299	235,851	243,736	250,659	259,340	266,468	261,540

Source: Western Interstate Commission for Higher Education (WICHE), *High School Graduates: Projections by State, 1992-2009* (Boulder, CO: WICHE Publications), October 1993, pp. 22-30. *Notes:* alt designates states for which the alternate method was used to generate nonpublic estimates. 1. Designates states for which nonpublic enrollments by grade are available, but data on nonpublic graduates are not. 2. Designates states for which nonpublic enrollments and in most cases, graduates are available from the state department of education but did not meet criteria for generating nonpublic estimates. All projections and nonpublic estimates are rounded to the nearest tenth. Detail may not add to total due to rounding. Source also includes data for 1982-1999.

Teachers and Student/Teacher Ratios

★ 233 ★

Supply and Demand for Teachers, 1990-2000

[Number of teachers in millions]

Year	Demand	Supply
1990	2.775	2.760
1991	2.850	2.775
1992	2.875	2.800
1993	2.960	2.850
1994	2.975	2.860
1995	3.250	2.875
1996	3.750	2.900
1997	3.100	2.910
1998	3.150	2.920
1999	3.175	2.930
2000	3.250	2.930
2001	3.270	2.940

Source: "The Teacher Gap," in *Fortune*, 8 March 1993, p. 11. *Primary source:* American Federation of Teachers. *Note:* Magnitudes estimated from published chart.

★ 234 ★

Teachers and Student/Teacher Ratios

Classroom Teachers in Elementary and Secondary Schools, by Control of Institution and Organizational Level, with Alternative Projections, 1992-2004

[In thousands]

Year	Total			Public			Private		
	K-12	Elementary	Secondary	K-12	Elementary	Secondary	K-12	Elementary	Secondary
1992	2,814	1,738	1,076	2,541	1,478	973	363	260	103
				Middle alternative projections					
1993	2,841	1,753	1,088	2,475	1,491	984	366	262	104
1994	2,890	1,736	1,155	2,520	1,476	1,044	370	260	111
1995	2,950	1,768	1,181	2,572	1,504	1,068	378	265	113
1996	3,017	1,810	1,207	2,630	1,539	1,091	386	271	116
1997	3,070	1,843	1,227	2,677	1,568	1,109	393	276	117
1998	3,109	1,866	1,243	2,711	1,587	1,124	398	279	119
1999	3,145	1,885	1,260	2,742	1,603	1,140	403	282	121
2000	3,179	1,903	1,276	2,772	1,618	1,154	407	285	122
2001	3,211	1,920	1,291	2,800	1,633	1,167	411	287	124
2002	3,241	1,935	1,306	2,827	1,645	1,181	414	289	125
2003	3,268	1,943	1,325	2,851	1,653	1,198	418	291	127
2004	3,296	1,949	1,347	2,875	1,658	1,218	420	292	129
				Low alternative projections					
1993	2,828	1,746	1,082	2,463	1,485	978	365	261	104
1994	2,856	1,717	1,139	2,490	1,460	1,030	366	257	109
1995	2,904	1,741	1,163	2,532	1,481	1,052	372	260	111
1996	2,963	1,775	1,188	2,584	1,510	1,074	379	266	114
1997	3,012	1,804	1,208	2,626	1,534	1,093	385	270	116
1998	3,048	1,826	1,223	2,658	1,553	1,106	390	273	117
1999	3,078	1,842	1,236	2,684	1,566	1,118	394	275	118
2000	3,109	1,859	1,250	2,711	1,581	1,131	398	278	120
2001	3,140	1,874	1,266	2,738	1,594	1,145	402	280	121
2002	3,170	1,889	1,281	2,765	1,606	1,159	405	283	123
2003	3,196	1,896	1,299	2,788	1,613	1,175	408	284	124
2004	3,220	1,900	1,319	2,809	1,616	1,193	411	284	126
				High alternative projections					
1993	2,856	1,763	1,094	2,488	1,499	989	368	264	105
1994	2,933	1,761	1,171	2,557	1,498	1,059	376	263	112
1995	3,002	1,801	1,201	2,618	1,532	1,086	384	269	115
1996	3,078	1,850	1,228	2,684	1,573	1,111	394	277	118
1997	3,137	1,888	1,250	2,735	1,605	1,130	402	282	120
1998	3,183	1,915	1,268	2,775	1,629	1,146	408	287	121
1999	3,228	1,941	1,288	2,185	1,650	1,165	414	290	123
2000	3,270	1,964	1,306	2,851	1,671	1,181	419	294	125
2001	3,309	,987	1,322	2,885	1,690	1,195	424	297	127
2002	3,346	2,007	1,340	2,918	1,706	1,211	428	300	128

[Continued]

★ 234 ★

Classroom Teachers in Elementary and Secondary Schools, by Control of Institution and Organizational Level, with Alternative Projections, 1992-2004

[Continued]

Year	Total			Public			Private		
	K-12	Elementary	Secondary	K-12	Elementary	Secondary	K-12	Elementary	Secondary
2003	3,383	2,022	1,361	2,950	1,719	1,231	433	302	130
2004	3,422	2,036	1,386	2,985	1,731	1,253	427	305	133

Source: Debra E. Gerald and William J. Hussar, U.S. Department of Education, National Center for Education Statistics, *Projections of Education Statistics to 2004* (Washington, D.C.: U.S. Government Printing Office), October 1993, p. 72. *Primary source:* U.S. Department of Education, National Center for Education Statistics, *Statistics of Public Elementary and Secondary Schools*; Common Core of Data surveys, "Selected Public and Private Elementary and Secondary Education Statistics," *NCES Bulletin*, October 23, 1979; "Private Elementary and Secondary Education, 1983; Enrollment, Teachers, and Schools," *NCES Bulletin*, December 1984; 1985 Private School Survey: "Key Statistics for Private Elementary and Secondary Education: School Year 1988-89," *Early Estimates:* "Key Statistics for Private Elementary and Secondary Education: School Year 1990-91," *Early Estimates*: "Public and Private Elementary and Secondary Education Statistics School Year 1991-92," *Early Estimates*: and "Public and Private Elementary and Secondary Education Statistics: School Year 1992-93," *Early Estimates*. This table was prepared May 1993. *Notes:* The numbers of elementary and secondary teachers reported separately by National Education Association were prorated to the National Center for Education Statistics (NCES) totals for each year. Projections are based on data through 1992. Because of rounding, details may not add to totals. Source also includes data for 1979-1991.

★ 235 ★

Teachers and Student/Teacher Ratios

Pupil-Teacher Ratios in Elementary and Secondary Schools, by Control of Institution and Organizational Level, with Alternative Projections, 1992-2004

Year	Total		Public		Private	
	Elementary	Secondary	Elementary	Secondary	Elementary	Secondary
1992	18.5	14.8	18.9	15.2	16.2	11.3
			Middle alternative projections			
1993	18.6	15.0	19.0	15.4	16.3	11.5
1994	19.0	14.6	19.4	15.0	16.7	11.4
1995	18.9	14.6	19.3	15.0	16.6	11.2
1996	18.8	14.7	19.2	15.1	16.5	11.3
1997	18.8	14.7	19.2	15.1	16.5	11.4
1998	18.8	14.7	19.2	15.1	16.5	11.4
1999	18.8	14.7	19.2	15.1	16.5	11.3
2000	18.8	14.7	19.2	15.0	16.5	11.3
2001	18.7	14.6	19.1	15.0	16.4	11.3
2002	18.6	14.6	19.0	15.0	16.4	11.2
2003	18.5	14.7	18.9	15.0	16.4	11.2
2004	18.4	14.7	18.8	15.1	16.3	11.2
			Low alternative projections (Based on high alternative projections of teachers)			
1993	18.5	14.9	18.9	15.3	16.2	11.3
1994	18.7	14.4	19.1	14.8	16.4	11.0
1995	18.6	14.4	18.9	14.8	16.3	11.0
1996	18.4	14.4	18.8	14.8	16.2	11.1
1997	18.3	14.5	18.7	14.8	16.1	11.1

[Continued]

★ 235 ★

Pupil-Teacher Ratios in Elementary and Secondary Schools, by Control of Institution and Organizational Level, with Alternative Projections, 1992-2004

[Continued]

Year	Total		Public		Private	
	Elementary	Secondary	Elementary	Secondary	Elementary	Secondary
1998	18.3	14.5	18.7	14.8	16.1	11.1
1999	18.3	14.4	18.6	14.7	16.0	11.1
2000	18.2	14.3	18.6	14.7	16.0	11.0
2001	18.1	14.3	18.5	14.6	15.9	11.0
2002	18.0	14.3	18.3	14.6	15.8	11.0
2003	17.8	14.3	18.2	14.6	15.7	10.9
2004	17.6	14.3	18.0	14.7	15.6	10.9
	High alternative projections (Based on low alternative projections of teachers)					
1993	18.7	15.1	19.1	15.5	16.4	11.5
1994	19.2	14.8	19.6	15.2	16.9	11.3
1995	19.2	14.9	19.6	15.2	16.9	11.4
1996	19.2	14.9	19.6	15.3	16.8	11.5
1997	19.2	15.0	19.6	15.3	16.8	11.5
1998	19.2	15.0	19.6	15.4	16.8	11.6
1999	19.2	15.0	19.6	15.3	16.9	11.5
2000	19.2	15.0	19.6	15.3	16.9	11.5
2001	19.2	14.9	19.6	15.3	16.8	11.5
2002	19.1	14.9	19.5	15.3	16.8	11.5
2003	19.0	15.0	19.4	15.3	16.8	11.4
2004	18.9	15.0	19.3	15.4	16.7	11.5

Source: Debra E. Gerald and William J. Hussar, U.S. Department of Education, National Center for Education Statistics, *Projections of Education Statistics to 2004* (Washington, D.C.: U.S. Government Printing Office), October 1993, p. 73. *Primary source:* U.S. Department of Education, National Center for Education Statistics, *Statistics of Public Elementary and Secondary Schools*: Common Core of Data surveys, "Selected Public and Private Elementary and Secondary Education Statistics," *NCES Bulletin*, October 23, 1979; "Private Elementary and Secondary Education, 1983; Enrollment, Teachers and Schools,: *NCES Bulletin*, December 1984; 1985 Private School Survey: "Key Statistics for Private Elementary and Secondary Education: School Year 1988-89," *Early Estimates*: "Key Statistics for Private Elementary and Secondary Education: School Year 1989-90," *Early Estimates*: "Key Statistics for Public and Private Elementary and Secondary Education: School Year 1990-91," *Early Estimates*: "Public and Private Elementary and Secondary Education Statistics: School Year 1991-92," *Early Estimates*: and "Public and Private Elementary and Secondary Education Statistics: School Year 1992-93," *Early Estimates*. This table was prepared June 1993. *Notes:* Projections are based on data through 1992. Because of rounding, details may not add to totals. Source also includes data for 1979-1991.

★ 236 ★

Teachers and Student/Teacher Ratios

Average Annual Salaries of Classroom Teachers in Public Elementary and Secondary Schools, with Alternative Projections, 1992-2004

Year	Constant 1991-92 dollars[1]	Current dollars[2]
1992	34,098	34,098
1993	34,316	35,334
	Middle alternative projections	
1994	34,632	36,711
1995	35,388	38,729
1996	36,330	41,081
1997	37,055	43,289
1998	37,589	45,459
1999	37,774	-
2000	37,819	-
2001	37,995	-
2002	38,205	-
2003	38,397	-
2004	38,572	-
	Low alternative projections	
1994	34,520	36,997
1995	34,985	39,301
1996	35,572	41,993
1997	36,066	44,665
1998	36,592	47,560
1999	36,657	-
2000	36,647	-
2001	36,705	-
2002	36,879	-
2003	37,015	-
2004	37,121	-
	High alternative projections	
1994	35,084	37,016
1995	36,251	39,236
1996	37,398	41,509
1997	38,146	43,487
1998	38,737	45,515
1999	38,995	-
2000	39,090	-
2001	39,280	-
2002	39,494	-

[Continued]

★ 236 ★

Average Annual Salaries of Classroom Teachers in Public Elementary and Secondary Schools, with Alternative Projections, 1992-2004

[Continued]

Year	Constant 1991-92 dollars[1]	Current dollars[2]
2003	39,708	-
2004	39,939	-

Source: Debra E. Gerald and William J. Hussar, U.S. Department of Education, National Center for Education Statistics, *Projections of Education Statistics to 2004* (Washington, D.C.: U.S. Government Printing Office), October 1993, p. 85. *Primary source:* National Education Association, *Estimates of State School Statistics*, 1993. *Notes:* 1. Based on the Consumer Price Index for all urban consumers, Bureau of Labor Statistics, U.S. Department of Labor. 2. Projections in current dollars are not shown after 1998 due to the uncertain behavior of inflation over the long term.

Higher Education Enrollment

★ 237 ★

College-Age Populations, 1979-2004

[In thousands]

Year (July 1)	18 years old	18-24 years old	25-29 years old	30-34 years old	35-44 years old
1979	4,316	30,048	19,178	17,025	25,176
1980	4,245	30,360	19,792	17,810	25,868
1981	4,186	30,505	20,275	18,798	26,454
1982	4,136	30,433	20,816	18,781	28,095
1983	3,978	30,174	21,259	19,137	29,336
1984	3,774	29,706	21,584	19,576	30,575
1985	3,686	29,151	21,804	20,102	31,767
1986	3,623	28,467	22,018	20,552	33,081
1987	3,703	27,928	21,982	21,058	34,299
1988	3,803	27,585	21,868	21,470	35,258
1989	3,889	27,379	21,690	21,758	36,494
1990	3,603	27,038	21,356	21,990	37,845
1991	3,391	26,599	20,844	22,242	39,352
1992	3,307	26,063	20,278	22,343	39,973
1993	3,349	26,278	20,402	22,579	40,440
1994	3,422	25,990	19,830	22,552	41,333
1995	3,385	25,609	19,382	22,446	42,219
1996	3,540	25,261	19,216	22,119	43,087
1997	3,574	24,590	19,262	21,604	43,879
1998	3,703	25,029	19,138	20,981	44,499
1999	3,883	25,524	18,852	20,399	44,946

[Continued]

★ 237 ★

College-Age Populations, 1979-2004

[Continued]

Year (July 1)	18 years old	18-24 years old	25-29 years old	30-34 years old	35-44 years old
2000	3,873	26,055	18,459	19,937	45,192
2001	3,971	26,607	18,012	19,761	45,164
2002	3,964	27,186	17,524	19,805	44,891
2003	3,918	27,563	17,431	19,684	44,336
2004	4,044	28,026	17,594	19,405	43,714

Source: Debra E. Gerald and William J. Hussar, U.S. Department of Education, National Center for Education Statistics, *Projections of Education Statistics to 2004* (Washington, D.C.: U.S. Government Printing Office), October 1993, p. 148. *Primary source:* U.S. Department of Commerce, Bureau of the Census, "U.S. Population Estimates, by Age, Sex, Race, and Hispanic Origin: 1980 to 1991," *Current Population Reports*, Series P-25, No. 1095, February 1993 and unpublished tabulations. This table was prepared May 1993.

★ 238 ★

Higher Education Enrollment

College Enrollment, Degrees, and High-School Graduates, 1995-2003

	1995	1996	1997	1998	1999	2000	2001	2002	2003
College enrollment									
Total	14,591,000	14,739,000	14,922,000	15,167,000	15,431,000	15,634,000	15,814,000	15,993,000	16,124,000
Men	6,471,000	6,551,000	6,658,000	6,794,000	6,956,000	7,071,000	7,194,000	7,300,000	7,386,000
Women	8,120,000	8,188,000	8,264,000	8,373,000	8,475,000	8,563,000	8,620,000	8,693,000	8,738,000
Full-time	8,131,000	8,224,000	8,355,000	8,542,000	8,755,000	8,916,000	9,087,000	9,218,000	9,327,000
Part-time	6,460,000	6,515,000	6,567,000	6,625,000	6,676,000	6,718,000	6,727,000	6775,000	6,797,000
Full-time equivalent*	10,465,000	10,578,000	10,727,000	10,934,000	11,165,000	11,342,000	11,515,000	11,664,000	11,780,000
Four-year institutions									
Total	9,117,000	9,203,000	9,320,000	9,481,000	9,662,000	9,800,000	9,935,000	10,058,000	10,155,000
Public	6,177,000	6,235,000	6,317,000	6,428,000	6,552,000	6,649,000	6,742,000	6,825,000	6,891,000
Private	2,940,000	2,968,000	3,003,000	3,053,000	3,110,000	3,151,000	3,193,000	3,233,000	3,264,000
Two-year institutions									
Total	5,474,000	5,536,000	5,602,000	5,686,000	5,769,000	5,834,000	5,879,000	5,935,000	5,969,000
Public	5,199,000	5,259,000	5,320,000	5,398,000	5,477,000	5,537,000	5,578,000	5,632,000	5,664,000
Private	275,000	277,000	282,000	288,000	292,000	297,000	301,000	303,000	305,000
Undergraduate									
Total	12,443,000	12,582,000	12,755,000	12,992,000	13,245,000	13,447,000	13,623,000	13,787,000	13,909,000
Public	10,065,000	10,178,000	10,315,000	10,499,000	10,696,000	10,852,000	10,984,000	11,113,000	11,206,000
Private	2,378,000	2,404,000	2,440,000	2,493,000	2,549,000	2,595,000	2,639,000	2,674,000	2,703,000
Graduate									
Total	1,822,000	1,831,000	1,839,000	1,847,000	1,856,000	1,857,000	1,859,000	1,871,000	1,877,000
Public	1,177,000	1,181,000	1,187,000	1,192,000	1,197,000	1,198,000	1,199,000	1,206,000	1,211,000
Private	645,000	650,000	652,000	655,000	659,000	659,000	660,000	650,000	666,000
First-professional									
Total	326,000	326,000	328,000	328,000	330,000	330,000	332,000	335,000	338,000

[Continued]

★ 238 ★

College Enrollment, Degrees, and High-School Graduates, 1995-2003

[Continued]

	1995	1996	1997	1998	1999	2000	2001	2002	2003
Public	134,000	135,000	135,000	135,000	136,000	136,000	137,000	138,000	138,000
Private	192,000	191,000	193,000	193,000	194,000	194,000	195,000	197,000	200,000
Degrees									
Associate									
Total	497,000	489,000	502,000	510,000	517,000	528,000	540,000	548,000	557,000
Men	200,000	197,000	202,000	206,000	209,000	214,000	220,000	224,000	228,000
Women	297,000	292,000	300,000	304,000	308,000	314,000	320,000	324,000	329,000
Bachelor's									
Total	1,166,000	1,170,000	1,146,000	1,173,000	1,186,000	1,208,000	1,239,000	1,275,000	1,303,000
Men	535,000	532,000	524,000	538,000	547,000	559,000	574,000	594,000	607,000
Women	631,000	638,000	622,000	635,000	639,000	649,000	665,000	681,000	696,000
Master's									
Total	354,000	354,000	350,000	350,000	351,000	353,000	358,000	361,000	365,000
Men	166,000	166,000	163,000	163,000	165,000	167,000	173,000	175,000	179,000
Women	188,000	188,000	187,000	187,000	186,000	186,000	185,000	186,000	186,000
Doctorate									
Total	40,900	41,100	41,300	41,400	41,900	41,600	41,600	41,700	41,800
Men	24,200	23,900	23,700	23,400	23,400	22,700	22,300	22,00	21,700
Women	16,700	17,200	17,600	18,000	18,500	18,900	19,300	19,700	20,100
First-professional									
Total	85,700	85,200	85,700	85,400	86,200	86,600	87,300	87,300	88,000
Men	49,100	49,100	49,800	49,800	50,400	50,800	51,500	51,500	52,200
Women	36,600	36,100	35,900	35,600	35,800	35,800	35,800	35,800	35,800
High-school graduates									
Total	2,601,000	2,631,000	2,748,000	2,863,000	2,921,000	2,978,000	3,009,000	3,010,000	3,011,000
Public	2,345,000	2,372,000	2,478,000	2,581,000	2,634,000	2,685,00	2,713,000	2,714,000	2,715,000
Private	256,000	259,000	270,000	282,000	287,000	293,000	296,000	296,000	296,000

Source: The Chronicle of Higher Education, 6 January, 1993, p. A40. *Primary source:* U.S. Department of Education. *Notes:* *Estimate based on full-time employment plus the full-time equivalent of part-time enrollment as reported by institutions. The table shows the "middle alternative forecast," which represents the most likely outcome. Details may not add to totals because of rounding. Source also includes data for 1992-1994.

★ 239 ★

Higher Education Enrollment

College Enrollment Rates, by Age, Sex, and Attendance Status, with Alternative Projections, 1991-2004

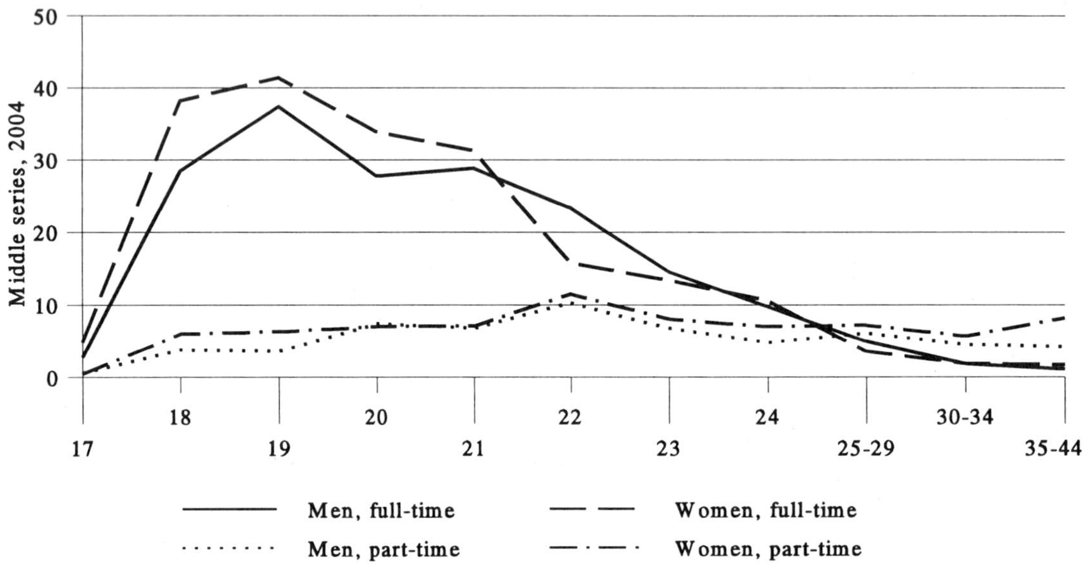

Age, sex, and attendance status	1991	Low alternative 1999	Low alternative 2004	Middle alternative 1999	Middle alternative 2004	High alternative 1999	High alternative 2004
Men							
Full-time:							
16	0.1	0.1	0.1	0.1	0.1	0.1	0.1
17	2.0	2.5	2.5	2.8	2.8	2.8	2.8
18	27.6	26.8	26.8	28.6	28.5	28.8	28.8
19	31.2	31.9	31.9	35.2	37.4	35.2	37.4
20	25.7	24.6	24.6	27.3	27.8	28.4	28.9
21	25.8	27.1	27.1	28.9	28.9	31.9	31.9
22	19.9	22.3	22.3	23.4	23.4	23.9	23.9
23	14.0	14.1	14.1	14.6	14.6	16.3	16.3
24	9.8	9.6	9.6	9.8	9.8	10.1	10.2
25-29	4.7	4.8	4.8	5.0	5.0	5.6	5.6
30-34	1.7	1.9	1.9	1.9	1.9	2.0	2.0
35-44	1.0	1.1	1.1	1.1	1.1	1.2	1.2
Part-time:							
16	0.0	0.0	0.0	0.0	0.0	0.0	0.0
17	0.4	0.5	0.5	0.6	0.6	0.6	0.6
18	3.1	3.8	3.8	3.8	3.8	3.8	3.8
19	3.4	3.4	3.4	3.6	3.6	4.1	4.3
20	5.5	5.7	5.7	6.8	7.4	6.8	7.4
21	5.5	5.8	5.8	6.3	6.8	6.9	7.7
22	9.0	9.4	9.4	10.3	10.3	11.4	11.4
23	6.4	6.8	6.8	6.8	6.8	7.0	7.0

[Continued]

★ 239 ★

College Enrollment Rates, by Age, Sex, and Attendance Status, with Alternative Projections, 1991-2004

[Continued]

Age, sex, and attendance status	1991	Low alternative		Middle alternative		High alternative	
		1999	2004	1999	2004	1999	2004
24	4.4	4.6	4.6	4.7	4.8	4.7	4.8
25-29	5.6	5.9	5.9	6.1	6.1	6.5	6.5
30-34	4.3	4.4	4.4	4.5	4.5	5.1	5.1
35-44	4.0	4.1	4.1	4.2	4.2	4.3	4.3
Women							
Full-time:							
16	0.2	0.2	0.2	0.2	0.2	0.3	0.3
17	4.4	4.9	4.9	4.9	4.9	5.2	5.2
18	36.3	38.2	38.2	38.2	38.2	39.3	39.3
19	38.3	40.2	40.2	41.4	41.4	43.0	43.0
20	30.7	31.0	31.0	33.9	33.9	35.1	35.1
21	31.4	30.7	30.7	31.3	31.3	33.7	33.7
22	15.3	15.5	15.5	15.8	15.8	16.4	16.4
23	10.9	11.0	11.0	12.5	13.4	14.1	14.1
24	9.8	10.6	10.6	10.6	10.6	11.9	11.9
25-29	3.6	3.6	3.6	3.6	3.6	3.9	3.9
30-34	1.9	1.9	1.9	1.9	1.9	2.0	2.0
35-44	1.7	1.6	1.6	1.7	1.7	1.7	1.7
Part-time:							
16	0.0	0.0	0.0	0.0	0.0	0.0	0.0
17	0.0	0.5	0.5	0.5	0.5	0.5	0.5
18	5.1	5.1	5.1	6.0	6.0	6.5	6.5
19	5.4	5.7	5.7	6.3	6.3	6.8	6.8
20	6.1	6.1	6.1	6.8	7.0	7.0	7.2
21	6.1	6.4	6.4	7.1	7.1	7.2	7.2
22	9.5	9.7	9.7	11.1	11.5	11.7	11.7
23	6.8	6.5	6.5	8.1	8.1	8.2	8.2
24	6.1	6.4	6.4	7.0	7.0	7.3	7.3
25-29	6.6	6.6	6.6	7.2	7.2	7.3	7.8
30-34	5.3	5.5	5.5	5.7	5.7	6.0	6.0
35-44	7.9	8.2	8.2	8.2	8.2	8.4	8.4

Source: Debra E. Gerald and William J. Hussar, U.S. Department of Education, National Center for Education Statistics, *Projections of Education Statistics to 2004* (Washington, D.C.: U.S. Government Printing Office), October 1993, p. 108.

★ 240 ★

Higher Education Enrollment

Public College Enrollment as a Percent of Total Enrollment, by Attendance Status, Sex, Level Enrolled, and by Type of Institution, 1991-2004

Enrollment category	Men			Women		
	1991	1999	2004	1991	1999	2004
Full-time, undergraduate, 4-year institutions	69.9	69.7	69.7	69.1	69.1	69.1
Part-time, undergraduate, 4-year institutions	73.0	73.1	73.1	69.9	70.1	70.1
Full-time, undergraduate, 2-year institutions	91.7	91.5	91.5	90.2	89.8	89.8
Part-time, undergraduate, 2-year institutions	98.1	97.5	97.5	98.5	98.2	98.2
Full-time, postbaccalaureate, 4-year institutions	56.2	56.3	56.3	59.0	59.6	59.6
Part-time, postbaccalaureate, 4-year institutions	59.0	58.9	58.9	66.2	66.8	66.8

Source: Debra E. Gerald and William J. Hussar, U.S. Department of Education, National Center for Education Statistics, *Projections of Education Statistics to 2004* (Washington, D.C.: U.S. Government Printing Office), October 1993, p. 114.

★ 241 ★

Higher Education Enrollment

Total Enrollment in All Institutions of Higher Education, by Sex, Attendance Status, and Control of Institution, with Alternative Projections, 1992-2004

[In thousands]

Year	Total	Sex		Attendance status		Control	
		Men	Women	Full-time	Part-time	Public	Private
1992	14,558	6,654	7,904	8,139	6,419	11,377	3,181
				Middle alternative projections			
1993	14,994	6,842	8,152	8,355	6,639	11,722	3,272
1994	15,005	6,831	8,174	8,312	6,693	11,736	3,269
1995	14,946	6,781	8,165	8,242	6,704	11,695	3,251
1996	14,938	6,752	8,186	8,220	6,718	11,696	3,242
1997	14,999	6,765	8,234	8,257	6,742	11,746	3,253
1998	15,111	6,811	8,300	8,346	6,765	11,836	3,275
1999	15,304	6,892	8,412	8,511	6,793	11,986	3,318
2000	15,462	6,970	8,492	8,657	6,805	12,108	3,354
2001	15,607	7,041	8,566	8,795	6,812	12,220	3,387
2002	15,738	7,116	8,622	8,923	6,815	12,318	3,420
2003	15,802	7,161	8,641	8,992	6,810	12,365	3,437
2004	15,892	7,216	8,676	9,087	6,805	12,431	3,461
				Low alternative projections			
1993	14,589	6,608	7,981	8,104	6,485	11,408	3,181

[Continued]

★ 241 ★

Total Enrollment in All Institutions of Higher Education, by Sex, Attendance Status, and Control of Institution, with Alternative Projections, 1992-2004

[Continued]

Year	Total	Sex		Attendance status		Control	
		Men	Women	Full-time	Part-time	Public	Private
1994	14,549	6,602	7,947	8,029	6,520	11,379	3,170
1995	14,448	6,533	7,915	7,938	6,510	11,303	3,145
1996	14,396	6,480	7,916	7,893	6,503	11,268	3,128
1997	14,424	6,479	7,945	7,917	6,507	11,292	3,132
1998	14,500	6,504	7,996	7,987	6,513	11,352	3,148
1999	14,649	6,564	8,085	8,131	6,518	11,468	3,181
2000	14,776	6,620	8,156	8,255	6,521	11,565	3,211
2001	14,887	6,670	8,217	8,370	6,517	11,648	3,239
2002	14,985	6,720	8,265	8,475	6,510	11,722	3,263
2003	15,017	6,745	8,272	8,523	6,494	11,744	3,273
2004	15,083	6,784	8,299	8,604	6,479	11,791	3,292
				High alternative projections			
1993	15,493	7,107	8,386	8,673	6,820	12,103	3,390
1994	15,619	7,142	8,477	8,683	6,936	12,206	3,413
1995	15,599	7,124	8,475	8,617	6,982	12,200	3,399
1996	15,634	7,116	8,518	8,625	7,009	12,231	3,403
1997	15,718	7,145	8,573	8,680	7,038	12,301	3,417
1998	15,858	7,207	8,651	8,792	7,066	12,411	3,447
1999	16,054	7,291	8,763	8,963	7,091	12,564	3,490
2000	16,225	7,371	8,854	9,112	7,113	12,696	3,529
2001	16,382	7,449	8,933	9,254	7,128	12,817	3,565
2002	16,525	7,528	8,997	9,383	7,142	12,926	3,599
2003	16,597	7,578	9,019	9,452	7,145	12,980	3,617
2004	16,699	7,638	9,061	9,551	7,148	13,058	3,641

Source: Debra E. Gerald and William J. Hussar, U.S. Department of Education, National Center for Education Statistics, *Projections of Education Statistics to 2004* (Washington, D.C.: U.S. Government Printing Office), October 1993, p. 26. *Primary source:* U.S. Department of Education, National Center for Education Statistics, Fall Enrollment in Colleges and Universities Surveys and Integrated Postsecondary Education Data System (IPEDS) Survey. This table was prepared June 1993. *Notes:* Projections are based on data through 1991. Because of rounding, details may not add to totals. Source also includes data for 1979-1991.

★ 242 ★

Higher Education Enrollment

Total Enrollment in All Institutions of Higher Education, by Sex and Attendance Status, with Alternative Projections, 1992-2004

[In thousands]

Year	Total	Men		Women	
		Full-time	Part-time	Full-time	Part-time
1992	14,558	3,992	2,662	4,147	3,757
		Middle alternative projections			
1993	14,994	4,104	2,738	4,251	3,901
1994	15,005	4,071	2,760	4,241	3,933
1995	14,946	4,031	2,750	4,211	3,954
1996	14,938	4,010	2,742	4,210	3,976
1997	14,999	4,024	2,741	4,233	4,001
1998	15,111	4,067	2,744	4,279	4,021
1999	15,304	4,145	2,747	4,366	4,046
2000	15,462	4,218	2,752	4,439	4,053
2001	15,607	4,285	2,756	4,510	4,056
2002	15,738	4,354	2,762	4,569	4,053
2003	15,802	4,396	2,765	4,596	4,045
2004	15,892	4,446	2,770	4,641	4,035
		Low alternative projections			
1993	14,589	3,938	2,670	4,166	3,815
1994	14,549	3,904	2,698	4,125	3,822
1995	14,448	3,847	2,686	4,091	3,824
1996	14,396	3,806	2,674	4,087	3,829
1997	14,424	3,810	2,669	4,107	3,838
1998	14,500	3,837	2,667	4,150	3,846
1999	14,649	3,899	2,665	4,232	3,853
2000	14,776	3,956	2,664	4,299	3,857
2001	14,887	4,008	2,662	4,362	3,855
2002	14,985	4,059	2,661	4,416	3,849
2003	15,017	4,087	2,658	4,436	3,836
2004	15,083	4,128	2,656	4,476	3,823
		High alternative projections			
1993	15,493	4,263	2,844	4,410	3,976
1994	15,619	4,247	2,895	4,436	4,041
1995	15,599	4,207	2,917	4,410	4,065
1996	15,634	4,199	2,917	4,426	4,092
1997	15,718	4,229	2,916	4,451	4,122
1998	15,858	4,288	2,919	4,504	4,147
1999	16,054	4,367	2,924	4,596	4,167
2000	16,225	4,441	2,930	4,671	4,183
2001	16,382	4,513	2,936	4,741	4,192
2002	16,525	4,584	2,944	4,799	4,198

[Continued]

★ 242 ★

Total Enrollment in All Institutions of Higher Education, by Sex and Attendance Status, with Alternative Projections, 1992-2004

[Continued]

Year	Total	Men		Women	
		Full-time	Part-time	Full-time	Part-time
2003	16,597	4,627	2,951	4,825	4,194
2004	16,699	4,682	2,956	4,869	4,192

Source: Debra E. Gerald and William J. Hussar, U.S. Department of Education, National Center for Education Statistics, *Projections of Education Statistics to 2004* (Washington, D.C.: U.S. Government Printing Office), October 1993, p. 32. *Primary source:* U.S. Department of Education, National Center for Education Statistics, Fall Enrollment in Colleges and Universities Surveys and Integrated Postsecondary Education Data System (IPEDS) Survey. This table was prepared June 1993. *Notes:* Projections are based on data through 1991. Because of rounding, details may not add to totals. Source also includes data for 1979-1991.

★ 243 ★

Higher Education Enrollment

Part-time Enrollment in Higher Education, by Level Enrolled and Type of Institution, as a Percent of Total Enrollment, for Each Age and Sex Classification, 1991-2004

Age	Men			Women		
	1991	1999	2004	1991	1999	2004
	Undergraduate, 4-year institutions					
16-17 years old	0.0	11.5	11.5	0.0	8.9	8.9
18-19 years old	10.9	16.1	16.1	13.3	15.3	15.3
20-21 years old	18.2	20.7	20.7	23.5	24.9	24.9
22-24 years old	31.9	33.1	33.1	26.8	29.4	29.4
25-29 years old	26.9	29.6	29.6	24.4	28.3	28.3
30-34 years old	26.8	27.6	27.6	27.4	26.9	26.9
35 years and over	32.5	29.3	29.3	28.1	26.5	26.5
	Undergraduate, 2-year institutions					
16-17 years old	94.6	82.8	82.8	0.0	48.3	48.3
18-19 years old	83.4	77.7	77.7	81.7	79.7	79.7
20-21 years old	74.9	73.1	73.1	71.2	69.5	69.5
22-24 years old	57.5	54.9	54.9	59.4	56.9	56.9
25-29 years old	55.7	51.9	51.9	57.1	52.9	52.9
30-34 years old	51.0	50.5	50.5	57.1	56.6	56.6
35 years and over	42.4	45.0	45.0	51.8	53.0	53.0
	Postbaccalaureate, 4-year institutions					
16-17 years old	5.4	5.7	5.7	0.0	2.8	2.8
18-19 years old	5.7	6.2	6.2	5.0	5.0	5.0
20-21 years old	6.9	6.2	6.2	5.4	5.6	5.6

[Continued]

★ 243 ★

Part-time Enrollment in Higher Education, by Level Enrolled and Type of Institution, as a Percent of Total Enrollment, for Each Age and Sex Classification, 1991-2004

[Continued]

Age	Men			Women		
	1991	1999	2004	1991	1999	2004
22-24 years old	10.6	12.0	12.0	13.8	13.7	13.7
25-29 years old	17.4	18.5	18.5	18.4	18.9	18.9
30-34 years old	22.2	22.0	22.0	15.5	16.5	16.5
35 years and over	25.1	25.7	25.7	20.1	20.5	20.5

Source: Debra E. Gerald and William J. Hussar, U.S. Department of Education, National Center for Education Statistics, *Projections of Education Statistics to 2004* (Washington, D.C.: U.S. Government Printing Office), June 1993, p. 113. *Note:* Projections shown for 1999 and 2004 were adjusted to add to 100 percent.

★ 244 ★

Higher Education Enrollment

Full-time Enrollment in Higher Education, by Level Enrolled and Type of Institution, as a Percent of Total Enrollment, for Each Age and Sex Classification, 1991-2004

Age	Men			Women		
	1991	1999	2004	1991	1999	2004
	Undergraduate, 4-year institutions					
16-17 years old	71.9	70.8	70.8	59.7	64.6	64.6
18-19 years old	65.9	66.3	66.3	67.8	69.1	69.1
20-21 years old	79.0	79.9	79.9	82.2	82.3	82.3
22-24 years old	66.4	66.6	66.6	56.1	60.0	60.0
25-29 years old	41.0	40.5	40.5	38.7	40.2	40.2
30-34 years old	28.3	29.0	29.0	35.4	37.1	37.1
35 years and over	29.0	29.5	29.5	41.6	41.6	41.6
	Undergraduate, 2-year institutions					
16-17 years old	28.1	29.0	29.0	40.4	35.4	35.4
18-19 years old	34.1	33.7	33.7	32.2	30.9	30.9
20-21 years old	21.0	20.1	20.1	17.8	17.7	17.7
22-24 years old	17.5	15.7	15.7	18.0	17.3	17.3
25-29 years old	19.8	17.3	17.3	29.1	27.4	27.4
30-34 years old	19.7	18.9	18.9	46.0	39.1	39.1
35 years and over	31.9	27.0	27.0	35.9	34.2	34.2
	Postbaccalaureate, 4-year institutions					
16-17 years old	-	-	-	-	-	-
18-19 years old	-	-	-	-	-	-
20-21 years old	-	-	-	-	-	-

[Continued]

★ 244 ★

Full-time Enrollment in Higher Education, by Level Enrolled and Type of Institution, as a Percent of Total Enrollment, for Each Age and Sex Classification, 1991-2004

[Continued]

Age	Men			Women		
	1991	1999	2004	1991	1999	2004
22-24 years old	16.1	17.7	17.7	25.9	22.7	22.7
25-29 years old	39.3	42.3	42.3	32.2	32.4	32.4
30-34 years old	52.0	52.1	52.1	18.6	23.7	23.7
35 years and over	39.2	43.5	43.5	22.5	24.3	24.3

Source: Debra E. Gerald and William J. Hussar, U.S. Department of Education, National Center for Education Statistics, *Projections of Education Statistics to 2004* (Washington, D.C.: U.S. Government Printing Office), October 1993, p. 112. *Notes:* -= Not applicable. Projections shown for 1999 and 2004 were adjusted to add to 100 percent.

★ 245 ★

Higher Education Enrollment

Full-time Equivalent Enrollment in All Institutions of Higher Education, by Level of Student and Type of Institution, with Alternative Projections, 1992-2004

[In thousands]

Year	Total	Undergraduate		Graduate 4-year	First-professional 4-year
		4-year	2-year		
1992	10,454	5,903	3,154	1,093	304
Middle alternative projections					
1993	10,751	6,068	3,246	1,124	313
1994	10,727	6,026	3,253	1,133	315
1995	10,662	5,976	3,247	1,127	312
1996	10,644	5,966	3,254	1,117	307
1997	10,689	5,995	3,280	1,110	304
1998	10,787	6,067	3,312	1,107	301
1999	10,962	6,194	3,365	1,103	300
2000	11,112	6,306	3,406	1,102	298
2001	11,252	6,419	3,439	1,096	298
2002	11,382	6,515	3,472	1,096	299
2003	11,448	6,569	3,481	1,099	299
2004	11,540	6,636	3,501	1,303	300
Low alternative projections					
1993	10,444	5,884	3,160	1,096	304
1994	10,382	5,814	3,153	1,408	307
1995	10,287	5,747	3,135	1,101	304
1996	10,240	5,719	3,134	1,088	299

[Continued]

★ 245 ★

Full-time Equivalent Enrollment in All Institutions of Higher Education, by Level of Student and Type of Institution, with Alternative Projections, 1992-2004

[Continued]

Year	Total	Undergraduate 4-year	Undergraduate 2-year	Graduate 4-year	First-professional 4-year
1997	10,265	5,737	3,149	1,083	295
1998	10,337	5,793	3,173	1,077	293
1999	10,483	5,904	3,217	1,071	291
2000	10,608	5,999	3,250	1,070	289
2001	10,721	6,094	3,274	1,065	288
2002	10,823	6,176	3,297	1,061	289
2003	10,865	6,214	3,299	1,063	290
2004	10,941	6,271	3,314	1,066	290
		High alternative projections			
1993	11,133	6,276	3,347	1,478	333
1994	11,186	6,266	3,380	1,201	339
1995	11,136	6,221	3,380	1,199	336
1996	11,154	6,239	3,396	1,189	331
1997	11,219	6,282	3,427	1,183	327
1998	11,341	6,372	3,465	1,179	325
1999	11,521	6,504	3,519	1,174	323
2000	11,678	6,617	3,565	1,173	322
2001	11,825	6,737	3,599	1,168	321
2002	11,959	6,838	3,631	1,168	321
2003	12,028	6,892	3,644	1,170	322
2004	12,128	6,964	3,667	1,173	324

Source: Debra E. Gerald and William J. Hussar, U.S. Department of Education, National Center for Education Statistics, *Projections of Education Statistics to 2004* (Washington, D.C.: U.S. Government Printing Office), October 1993, p. 46. *Primary source:* U.S. Department of Education, National Center for Education Statistics, Fall Enrollment in Colleges and Universities Surveys and Integrated Postsecondary Education Data System (IPEDS) Survey. This table was prepared June 1993. *Notes:* Projections are based on data through 1991. Because of rounding, details may not add to totals. Source also includes data for 1979-1991.

★ 246 ★

Higher Education Enrollment

Full-time Equivalent Enrollment in Private Institutions of Higher Education, by Level of Student and Type of Institution, with Alternative Projections, 1992-2004

[In thousands]

Year	Total	Undergraduate		Graduate 4-year	First-professional 4-year
		4-year	2-year		
1992	2,583	1,792	215	397	179
		Middle alternative projections			
1993	2,653	1,842	220	408	183
1994	2,644	1,828	220	411	185
1995	2,625	1,814	219	409	183
1996	2,615	1,810	220	405	180
1997	2,624	1,820	223	402	179
1998	2,644	1,841	225	401	177
1999	2,686	1,881	229	400	176
2000	2,723	1,915	233	400	175
2001	2,757	1,949	235	398	175
2002	2,790	1,978	239	397	176
2003	2,808	1,995	239	399	175
2004	2,832	2,015	241	400	176
		Low alternative projections			
1993	2,576	1,786	215	397	178
1994	2,560	1,764	214	402	180
1995	2,534	1,744	213	399	178
1996	2,518	1,735	213	395	175
1997	2,521	1,741	214	393	173
1998	2,537	1,758	216	391	172
1999	2,571	1,792	220	389	170
2000	2,602	1,821	223	388	169
2001	2,631	1,851	225	387	169
2002	2,657	1,876	227	385	169
2003	2,669	1,887	227	385	170
2004	2,690	1,905	229	386	170
		High alternative projections			
1993	2,755	1,905	227	428	195
1994	2,766	1,902	229	436	198
1995	2,747	1,887	228	435	196
1996	2,748	1,893	230	432	193
1997	2,760	1,906	232	430	191
1998	2,789	1,934	236	428	190
1999	2,830	1,975	240	427	189
2000	2,868	2,009	245	426	188
2001	2,904	2,045	247	424	188

[Continued]

★ 246 ★

Full-time Equivalent Enrollment in Private Institutions of Higher Education, by Level of Student and Type of Institution, with Alternative Projections, 1992-2004

[Continued]

Year	Total	Undergraduate		Graduate 4-year	First-professional 4-year
		4-year	2-year		
2002	2,938	2,077	249	424	188
2003	2,957	2,093	251	425	188
2004	2,982	2,115	252	426	189

Source: Debra E. Gerald and William J. Hussar, U.S. Department of Education, National Center for Education Statistics, *Projections of Education Statistics to 2004* (Washington, D.C.: U.S. Government Printing Office), October 1993, p. 48. *Primary source:* U.S. Department of Education, National Center for Education Statistics, Fall Enrollment in Colleges and Universities Surveys and Integrated Postsecondary Education Data System (IPEDS) Survey. This table was prepared June 1993. *Notes:* Projections are based on data through 1991. Because of rounding, details may not add to totals. Source also includes data for 1979-1991.

★ 247 ★

Higher Education Enrollment

Full-time Equivalent Enrollment in Public Institutions of Higher Education, by Level of Student and Type of Institution, with Alternative Projections, 1992-2004

[In thousands]

Year	Total	Undergraduate		Graduate 4-year	First-professional 4-year
		4-year	2-year		
1992	7,872	4,111	2,939	696	126
		Middle alternative projections			
1993	8,098	4,226	3,026	716	130
1994	8,082	4,198	3,032	722	130
1995	8,036	4,162	3,027	718	129
1996	8,029	4,156	3,034	712	127
1997	8,067	4,176	3,058	708	125
1998	8,143	4,226	3,087	706	124
1999	8,275	4,313	3,136	702	124
2000	8,389	4,391	3,173	702	123
2001	8,496	4,470	3,204	699	123
2002	8,592	4,537	3,233	699	123
2003	8,641	4,574	3,242	701	124
2004	8,707	4,621	3,260	702	124
		Low alternative projections			
1993	7,868	4,098	2,946	699	126
1994	7,822	4,050	2,939	706	127

[Continued]

★ 247 ★

Full-time Equivalent Enrollment in Public Institutions of Higher Education, by Level of Student and Type of Institution, with Alternative Projections, 1992-2004

[Continued]

Year	Total	Undergraduate		Graduate 4-year	First-professional 4-year
		4-year	2-year		
1995	7,753	4,003	2,923	702	126
1996	7,722	3,983	2,921	693	124
1997	7,744	3,996	2,936	690	122
1998	7,800	4,035	2,958	686	121
1999	7,912	4,112	2,997	682	121
2000	8,006	4,178	3,027	681	120
2001	8,090	4,243	3,049	678	119
2002	8,167	4,300	3,070	676	120
2003	8,196	4,327	3,072	678	120
2004	8,251	4,366	3,086	679	120
			High alternative projections		
1993	8,379	4,371	3,120	750	138
1994	8,420	4,364	3,150	765	140
1995	8,389	4,334	3,152	763	140
1996	8,406	4,346	3,166	757	138
1997	8,460	4,376	3,195	753	136
1998	8,553	4,437	3,230	751	135
1999	8,691	4,530	3,279	748	134
2000	8,809	4,608	3,320	747	134
2001	8,921	4,691	3,352	744	133
2002	9,021	4,762	3,383	744	133
2003	9,072	4,799	3,394	745	134
2004	9,146	4,849	3,415	747	135

Source: Debra E. Gerald and William J. Hussar, U.S. Department of Education, National Center for Education Statistics, *Projections of Education Statistics to 2004* (Washington, D.C.: U.S. Government Printing Office), June 1993, p. 47. *Primary source:* U.S. Department of Education, National Center for Education Statistics, Fall Enrollment in Colleges and Universities Surveys and Integrated Postsecondary Education Data System (IPEDS) Survey. This table was prepared June 1993. *Notes:* Projections are based on data through 1991. Because of rounding, details may not add to totals. Source also includes data for 1979-1991.

★ 248 ★

Higher Education Enrollment

Total Enrollment in Four-year Institutions of Higher Education, by Sex, Attendance Status, and Control of Institution, with Alternative Projections, 1992-2004

[In thousands]

Year	Total	Sex		Attendance status		Control	
		Men	Women	Full-time	Part-time	Public	Private
1992	9,060	4,328	4,732	6,177	2,883	6,139	2,921
			Middle alternative projections				
1993	9,323	4,452	4,871	6,343	2,980	6,318	3,005
1994	9,340	4,439	4,871	6,302	3,008	6,308	3,002
1995	9,255	4,399	4,856	6,239	3,016	6,270	2,985
1996	9,234	4,374	4,860	6,212	3,022	6,259	2,975
1997	9,259	4,375	4,884	6,228	3,031	6,276	2,983
1998	9,329	4,404	4,925	6,291	3,038	6,326	3,003
1999	9,455	4,456	4,999	6,410	3,045	6,413	3,042
2000	9,563	4,508	5,055	6,519	3,044	6,489	3,074
2001	9,668	4,557	5,111	6,628	3,040	6,563	3,105
2002	9,761	4,608	5,153	6,726	3,035	6,628	3,133
2003	9,816	4,642	5,174	6,786	3,030	6,666	3,150
2004	9,884	4,680	5,204	6,861	3,023	6,712	3,172
			Low alternative projections				
1993	9,063	4,293	4,770	6,147	2,916	6,142	2,921
1994	9,023	4,283	4,740	6,084	2,939	6,112	2,911
1995	8,946	4,233	4,713	6,007	2,939	6,059	2,887
1996	8,898	4,190	4,708	5,962	2,936	6,028	2,870
1997	8,909	4,186	4,723	5,971	2,938	6,036	2,873
1998	8,958	4,201	4,757	6,019	2,939	6,071	2,887
1999	9,058	4,240	4,818	6,122	2,936	6,142	2,916
2000	9,149	4,280	4,869	6,215	2,934	6,206	2,943
2001	9,234	4,317	4,917	6,307	2,927	6,265	2,969
2002	9,308	4,353	4,955	6,389	2,919	6,317	2,991
2003	9,342	4,375	4,967	6,433	2,909	6,341	3,001
2004	9,396	4,404	4,992	6,497	2,899	6,378	3,018
			High alternative projections				
1993	9,654	4,633	5,021	6,594	3,060	6,538	3,116
1994	9,708	4,645	5,063	6,591	3,117	6,573	3,135
1995	9,678	4,622	5,051	6,532	3,141	6,551	3,122
1996	9,682	4,609	5,073	6,530	3,152	6,558	3,124
1997	9,723	4,623	5,100	6,560	3,163	6,587	3,136
1998	9,811	4,663	5,148	6,640	3,171	6,649	3,162
1999	9,940	4,717	5,223	6,764	3,176	6,739	3,201
2000	10,052	4,768	5,284	6,874	3,178	6,818	3,234
2001	10,166	4,823	5,343	6,987	3.179	6,898	3,268
2002	10,267	4,877	5,390	7,088	3,179	6,967	3,300

[Continued]

★ 248 ★

Total Enrollment in Four-year Institutions of Higher Education, by Sex, Attendance Status, and Control of Institution, with Alternative Projections, 1992-2004

[Continued]

Year	Total	Sex		Attendance status		Control	
		Men	Women	Full-time	Part-time	Public	Private
2003	10,322	4,912	5,410	7,146	3,176	7,006	3,316
2004	10,397	4,953	5,444	7,225	3,172	7,058	3,339

Source: Debra E. Gerald and William J. Hussar, U.S. Department of Education, National Center for Education Statistics, *Projections of Education Statistics to 2004* (Washington, D.C.: U.S. Government Printing Office), October 1993, p. 27. *Primary source:* U.S. Department of Education, National Center for Education Statistics, Fall Enrollment in Colleges and Universities Surveys and Integrated Postsecondary Education Data System (IPEDS) Survey. This table was prepared June 1993. *Notes:* Projections are based on data through 1991. Because of rounding, details may not add to totals. Source also includes data for 1979-1991.

★ 249 ★

Higher Education Enrollment

Total Enrollment in Two-year Institutions of Higher Education, by Sex, Attendance Status, and Control of Institution, with Alternative Projections, 1992-2004

[In thousands]

Year	Total	Sex		Attendance status		Control	
		Men	Women	Full-time	Part-time	Public	Private
1992	5,498	2,326	3,172	1,962	3,536	5,238	260
Middle alternative projections							
1993	5,671	2,390	3,281	2,012	3,659	5,404	267
1994	5,695	2,392	3,303	2,010	3,685	5,428	267
1995	5,691	2,382	3,309	2,003	3,688	5,425	266
1996	5,704	2,378	3,326	2,008	3,696	5,437	267
1997	5,740	2,390	3,350	2,029	3,711	5,470	270
1998	5,782	2,407	3,375	2,055	3,727	5,510	272
1999	5,849	2,436	3,413	2,101	3,748	5,573	276
2000	5,899	2,462	3,437	2,138	3,761	5,619	280
2001	5,939	2,484	3,455	2,167	3,772	5,657	282
2002	5,977	2,508	3,469	2,197	3,780	5,690	287
2003	5,986	2,519	3,467	2,206	3,780	5,699	287
2004	6,008	2,536	3,472	2,226	3,782	5,719	289
Low alternative projections							
1993	5,526	2,315	3,211	1,957	3,569	5,266	260
1994	5,526	2,319	3,207	1,945	3,581	5,267	259
1995	5,502	2,300	3,202	1,931	3,571	5,244	258
1996	5,498	2,290	3,208	1,931	3,567	5,240	258
1997	5,515	2,293	3,222	1,946	3,569	5,256	259

[Continued]

★ 249 ★

Total Enrollment in Two-year Institutions of Higher Education, by Sex, Attendance Status, and Control of Institution, with Alternative Projections, 1992-2004

[Continued]

Year	Total	Sex		Attendance status		Control	
		Men	Women	Full-time	Part-time	Public	Private
1998	5,542	2,303	3,239	1,968	3,574	5,281	261
1999	5,591	2,324	3,267	2,090	3,582	5,326	265
2000	5,627	2,340	3,287	2,040	3,587	5,359	268
2001	5,653	2,353	3,300	2,063	3,590	5,383	270
2002	5,677	2,367	3,310	2,086	3,591	5,405	272
2003	5,675	2,370	3,305	2,090	3,585	5,403	272
2004	5,687	2,380	3,307	2,107	3,580	5,413	274
			High alternative projections				
1993	5,839	2,474	3,365	2,079	3,760	5,565	274
1994	5,911	2,497	3,414	2,092	3,819	5,633	278
1995	5,926	2,502	3,424	2,085	3,841	5,649	277
1996	5,952	2,507	3,445	2,095	3,857	5,673	279
1997	5,995	2,522	3,473	2,120	3,875	5,714	281
1998	6,047	2,544	3,503	2,152	3,895	5,762	285
1999	6,114	2,574	3,540	2,199	3,914	5,825	289
2000	6,173	2,603	3,570	2,238	3,935	5,878	295
2001	6,216	2,626	3,590	2,267	3,949	5,919	297
2002	6,258	2,651	3,607	2,295	3,963	5,959	299
2003	6,275	2,666	3,609	2,306	3,969	5,974	301
2004	6,302	2,685	3,617	2,326	3,976	6,000	302

Source: Debra E. Gerald and William J. Hussar, U.S. Department of Education, National Center for Education Statistics, *Projections of Education Statistics to 2004* (Washington, D.C.: U.S. Government Printing Office), October 1993, p. 28. *Primary source:* U.S. Department of Education, National Center for Education Statistics, Fall Enrollment in Colleges and Universities Surveys and Integrated Postsecondary Education Data System (IPEDS) Survey. This table was prepared June 1993. *Notes:* Projections are based on data through 1991. Because of rounding, details may not add to totals. Source also includes data for 1979-1991.

★ 250 ★

Higher Education Enrollment

Undergraduate Enrollment in All Institutions of Higher Education, by Sex and Attendance Status, with Alternative Projections, 1992-2004

[In thousands]

Year	Total	Men		Women	
		Full-time	Part-time	Full-time	Part-time
1992	12,450	3,427	2,165	3,740	3,118
		Middle alternative projections			
1993	12,823	3,520	2,227	3,838	3,238
1994	12,815	3,483	2,243	3,825	3,264
1995	12,761	3,452	2,232	3,798	3,279
1996	12,765	3,440	2,224	3,804	3,297
1997	12,833	3,461	2,223	3,832	3,317
1998	12,949	3,508	2,226	3,881	3,334
1999	13,147	3,591	2,231	3,969	3,356
2000	13,309	3,667	2,237	4,041	3,364
2001	13,462	3,738	2,243	4,112	3,369
2002	13,596	3,807	2,251	4,169	3,369
2003	13,659	3,847	2,256	4,192	3,364
2004	13,747	3,895	2,262	4,233	3,357
		Low alternative projections			
1993	12,469	3,377	2,171	3,758	3,163
1994	12,406	3,332	2,190	3,717	3,167
1995	12,313	3,281	2,178	3,688	3,166
1996	12,278	3,252	2,166	3,691	3,169
1997	12,313	3,261	2,161	3,716	3,175
1998	12,396	3,293	2,159	3,762	3,182
1999	12,555	3,361	2,159	3,846	3,189
2000	12,687	3,420	2,160	3,913	3,194
2001	12,806	3,475	2,160	3,977	3,194
2002	12,910	3,528	2,161	4,030	3,191
2003	12,944	3,554	2,161	4,047	3,182
2004	13,011	3,592	2,162	4,085	3,172
		High alternative projections			
1993	13,227	3,634	2,312	3,980	3,301
1994	13,309	3,608	2,351	3,996	3,354
1995	13,287	3,575	2,367	3,972	3,373
1996	13,334	3,578	2,367	3,994	3,395
1997	13,423	3,615	2,365	4,024	3,419
1998	13,568	3,679	2,369	4,079	3,441
1999	13,700	3,763	2,375	4,173	3,459
2000	13,944	3,841	2,383	4,246	3,474
2001	14,108	3,916	2,391	4,318	3,483
2002	14,253	3,989	2,400	4,374	3,490

[Continued]

★ 250 ★

Undergraduate Enrollment in All Institutions of Higher Education, by Sex and Attendance Status, with Alternative Projections, 1992-2004

[Continued]

Year	Total	Men		Women	
		Full-time	Part-time	Full-time	Part-time
2003	14,325	4,030	2,409	4,397	3,489
2004	14,424	4,082	2,416	4,437	3,489

Source: Debra E. Gerald and William J. Hussar, U.S. Department of Education, National Center for Education Statistics, *Projections of Education Statistics to 2004* (Washington, D.C.: U.S. Government Printing Office), October 1993, p. 37. *Primary source:* U.S. Department of Education, National Center for Education Statistics, Fall Enrollment in Colleges and Universities Surveys and Integrated Postsecondary Education Data System (IPEDS) Survey. This table was prepared June 1993. *Notes:* Projections are based on data through 1991. Because of rounding, details may not add to totals. Source also includes data for 1979-1991.

★ 251 ★

Higher Education Enrollment

Graduate Enrollment in All Institutions of Higher Education, by Sex and Attendance Status, with Alternative Projections, 1992-2004

[In thousands]

Year	Total	Men		Women	
		Full-time	Part-time	Full-time	Part-time
1992	1,790	383	477	302	628
		Middle alternative projections			
1993	1,844	396	490	307	651
1994	1,861	399	496	309	657
1995	1,859	392	497	307	663
1996	1,852	386	497	302	667
1997	1,848	381	497	298	672
1998	1,847	379	497	296	675
1999	1,843	375	495	295	678
2000	1,841	374	494	296	677
2001	1,833	370	492	296	675
2002	1,829	370	490	297	672
2003	1,830	372	489	300	669
2004	1,831	374	488	303	666
		Low alternative projections			
1993	1,802	380	479	303	640
1994	1,822	388	488	303	643
1995	1,817	384	488	299	646
1996	1,805	375	488	294	648
1997	1,802	372	488	291	651

[Continued]

★ 251 ★

Graduate Enrollment in All Institutions of Higher Education, by Sex and Attendance Status, with Alternative Projections, 1992-2004

[Continued]

Year	Total	Men		Women	
		Full-time	Part-time	Full-time	Part-time
1998	1,797	369	488	288	652
1999	1,789	364	486	287	652
2000	1,786	364	484	287	651
2001	1,779	361	482	287	649
2002	1,772	359	480	287	646
2003	1,769	361	477	289	642
2004	1,768	364	474	291	639
		High alternative projections			
1993	1,919	426	511	319	663
1994	1,956	433	521	327	675
1995	1,960	429	527	325	679
1996	1,953	421	527	321	684
1997	1,952	416	528	318	690
1998	1,949	413	527	316	693
1999	1,945	410	526	314	695
2000	1,943	407	524	316	696
2001	1,937	405	522	314	696
2002	1,935	403	521	316	695
2003	1,934	405	519	318	692
2004	1,935	407	517	321	690

Source: Debra E. Gerald and William J. Hussar, U.S. Department of Education, National Center for Education Statistics, *Projections of Education Statistics to 2004* (Washington, D.C.: U.S. Government Printing Office), October 1993, p. 40. *Primary source:* U.S. Department of Education, National Center for Education Statistics, Fall Enrollment in Colleges and Universities Surveys and Integrated Postsecondary Education Data System (IPEDS) Survey. This table was prepared June 1993. *Notes:* Projections are based on data through 1991. Because of rounding, details may not add to totals. Source also includes data for 1979-1991.

★ 252 ★

Higher Education Enrollment

Graduate Enrollment as a Percent of Total Postbaccalaureate Enrollment, by Sex and Attendance Status, and by Type and Control of Institution, 1991-2004

Enrollment category	Men			Women		
	1991	1999	2004	1991	1999	2004
Full-time, 4-year public	77.6	71.1	76.1	81.4	80.6	80.6
Part-time, 4-year public	98.8	98.9	98.9	99.5	99.5	99.5
Full-time, 4-year private	58.3	57.1	57.1	66.5	65.1	65.1
Part-time, 4-year private	91.6	91.7	91.7	95.5	95.6	95.6

Source: Debra E. Gerald and William J. Hussar, U.S. Department of Education, National Center for Education Statistics, *Projections of Education Statistics to 2004* (Washington, D.C.: U.S. Government Printing Office), October 1993, p. 114.

★ 253 ★

Higher Education Enrollment

First-Professional Enrollment in All Institutions of Higher Education, by Sex and Attendance Status, with Alternative Projections, 1992-2004

[In thousands]

Year	Total	Men		Women	
		Full-time	Part-time	Full-time	Part-time
1992	318	182	20	105	11
Middle alternative projections					
1993	327	188	21	106	12
1994	329	189	21	107	12
1995	326	187	21	106	12
1996	321	184	21	104	12
1997	318	182	21	103	12
1998	315	180	21	102	12
1999	314	179	21	102	12
2000	312	177	21	102	12
2001	312	177	21	102	12
2002	313	177	21	103	12
2003	313	177	20	104	12
2004	314	177	20	105	12
Low alternative projections					
1993	318	181	20	105	12
1994	321	184	20	105	12
1995	318	182	20	104	12

[Continued]

★ 253 ★

First-Professional Enrollment in All Institutions of Higher Education, by Sex and Attendance Status, with Alternative Projections, 1992-2004

[Continued]

Year	Total	Men		Women	
		Full-time	Part-time	Full-time	Part-time
1996	313	179	20	102	12
1997	309	177	20	100	12
1998	307	175	20	100	12
1999	305	174	20	99	12
2000	303	172	20	99	12
2001	362	172	20	98	12
2002	303	172	20	99	12
2003	304	172	20	100	12
2004	304	172	20	100	12
		High alternative projections			
1993	347	203	21	111	12
1994	354	206	23	113	12
1995	352	203	23	113	13
1996	347	200	23	111	13
1997	343	198	23	109	13
1998	341	196	23	109	13
1999	339	194	23	109	13
2000	338	193	23	109	13
2001	337	192	23	109	13
2002	337	192	23	109	13
2003	338	192	23	110	13
2004	340	193	23	111	13

Source: Debra E. Gerald and William J. Hussar, U.S. Department of Education, National Center for Education Statistics, *Projections of Education Statistics to 2004* (Washington, D.C.: U.S. Government Printing Office), October 1993, p. 43. *Primary source:* U.S. Department of Education, National Center for Education Statistics, Fall Enrollment in Colleges and Universities Surveys and Integrated Postsecondary Education Data System (IPEDS) Survey. This table was prepared June 1993. *Notes:* Projections are based on data through 1991. Because of rounding, details may not add to totals. Source includes data for 1979-1991.

Degrees Conferred in Institutions of Higher Education

★ 254 ★

Associate Degrees Conferred, by Sex of Recipient, with Alternative Projections, 1992-2004

Year ending	Total	Men	Women
1992	485,000	204,000	281,000
	Middle alternative projections		
1993	497,000	207,000	290,000
1994	504,000	210,000	294,000
1995	518,000	216,000	302,000
1996	518,000	215,000	303,000
1997	516,000	214,000	302,000
1998	517,000	214,000	303,000
1999	522,000	216,000	306,000
2000	528,000	219,000	309,000
2001	538,000	223,000	315,000
2002	547,000	227,000	320,000
2003	554,000	236,000	324,000
2004	560,000	233,000	327,000
	Low alternative projections		
1993	497,000	207,000	290,000
1994	504,000	210,000	294,000
1995	505,000	208,000	297,000
1996	502,000	207,000	295,000
1997	499,000	205,000	294,000
1998	499,000	204,000	295,000
1999	503,000	205,000	298,000
2000	508,000	207,000	301,000
2001	518,000	211,000	307,000
2002	525,000	214,000	311,000
2003	531,000	216,000	315,000
2004	536,000	218,000	318,000
	High alternative projections		
1993	497,000	207,000	290,000
1994	504,000	210,000	294,000
1995	535,000	222,000	313,000
1996	538,000	222,000	316,000
1997	538,000	222,000	316,000
1998	540,000	223,000	317,000
1999	545,000	225,000	320,000
2000	552,000	228,000	324,000

[Continued]

★ 254 ★

Associate Degrees Conferred, by Sex of Recipient, with Alternative Projections, 1992-2004

[Continued]

Year ending	Total	Men	Women
2001	564,000	233,000	331,000
2002	573,000	237,000	336,000
2003	580,000	240,000	340,000
2004	586,000	243,000	343,000

Source: Debra E. Gerald and William J. Hussar, U.S. Department of Education, National Center for Education Statistics, *Projections of Education Statistics to 2004* (Washington, D.C.: U.S. Government Printing Office), October 1993, p. 60. *Primary source:* U.S. Department of Education, National Center for Education Statistics, Fall Enrollment in Colleges and Universities Surveys and Integrated Postsecondary Education Data System (IPEDS) Survey. This table was prepared June 1993. *Notes:* Projections are based on data through 1990-91. Because of rounding, details may not add to totals. Source includes data for 1979-1991.

★ 255 ★

Degrees Conferred in Institutions of Higher Education

Bachelor's Degrees Conferred, by Sex of Recipient, with Alternative Projections, 1992-2004

Year ending	Total	Men	Women
1992	1,120,000	518,000	602,000
	Middle alternative projections		
1993	1,145,000	529,000	616,000
1994	1,165,000	537,000	628,000
1995	1,178,000	548000	630,000
1996	1,214,000	565,000	649,000
1997	1,206,000	560,000	646,000
1998	1,194,000	556,000	638,000
1999	1,487,000	553,000	634,000
2000	1,190,000	556,000	634,000
2001	1,203,000	563,000	640,000
2002	1,229,000	575,000	654,000
2003	1,254,000	587,000	667,000
2004	1,278,000	598,000	680,000
	Low alternative projections		
1993	1,143,000	527,000	616,000
1994	1,163,000	535,000	628,000
1995	1,176,000	546,000	630,000
1996	1,173,000	539,000	634,000
1997	1,159,000	533,000	626,000
1998	1,143,000	525,000	618,000
1999	1,134,000	520,000	614,000
2000	1,135,000	521,000	614,000

[Continued]

★ 255 ★

Bachelor's Degrees Conferred, by Sex of Recipient, with Alternative Projections, 1992-2004

[Continued]

Year ending	Total	Men	Women
2001	1,144,000	525,000	619,000
2002	1,167,000	534,000	633,000
2003	1,187,000	543,000	644,000
2004	1,208,000	552,000	656,000
	High alternative projections		
1993	1,150,000	534,000	616,000
1994	1,171,000	543,000	628,000
1995	1,186,000	556,000	630,000
1996	1,269,000	592,000	677,000
1997	1,267,000	588,000	679,000
1998	1,254,000	583,000	671,000
1999	1,254,000	583,000	671,000
2000	1,261,000	589,000	672,000
2001	1,277,000	599,000	678,000
2002	1,305,000	611,000	694,000
2003	1,329,000	623,000	706,000
2004	1,354,000	635,000	719,000

Source: Debra E. Gerald and William J. Hussar, U.S. Department of Education, National Center for Education Statistics, *Projections of Education Statistics to 2004* (Washington, D.C.: U.S. Government Printing Office), October 1993, p. 61. *Primary source:* U.S. Department of Education, National Center for Education Statistics, Fall Enrollment in Colleges and Universities Surveys and Integrated Postsecondary Education Data System (IPEDS) Survey. This table was prepared June 1993. *Notes:* Projections are based on data through 1990-91. Because of rounding, details may not add to totals. Source includes data for 1979-1991.

★ 256 ★

Degrees Conferred in Institutions of Higher Education

Master's Degrees Conferred, by Sex of Recipient, with Alternative Projections, 1992-2004

Year ending	Total	Men	Women
1992	349,000	163,000	186,000
	Middle alternative projections		
1993	364,000	170,000	194,000
1994	370,000	176,000	194,000
1995	377,000	182,000	195,000
1996	383,000	188,000	195,000
1997	389,000	194,000	195,000
1998	383,000	188,000	195,000
1999	378,000	182,000	196,000
2000	371,000	176,000	195,000

[Continued]

★ 256 ★

Master's Degrees Conferred, by Sex of Recipient, with Alternative Projections, 1992-2004

[Continued]

Year ending	Total	Men	Women
2001	364,000	170,000	194,000
2002	364,000	170,000	194,000
2003	363,000	170,000	193,000
2004	363,000	170,000	193,000
		Low alternative projections	
1993	356,000	166,000	190,000
1994	358,000	169,000	189,000
1995	361,000	172,000	189,000
1996	363,000	175,000	188,000
1997	366,000	178,000	188,000
1998	362,000	175,000	187,000
1999	358,000	172,000	186,000
2000	354,000	169,000	185,000
2001	354,000	166,000	185,000
2002	347,000	163,000	184,000
2003	347,000	163,000	184,000
2004	347,000	163,000	184,000
		High alternative projections	
1993	372,000	174,000	198,000
1994	384,000	183,000	201,000
1995	393,000	192,000	201,000
1996	402,000	201,000	201,000
1997	412,000	210,000	202,000
1998	403,000	201,000	202,000
1999	394,000	192,000	202,000
2000	385,000	183,000	202,000
2001	376,000	174,000	202,000
2002	379,000	177,000	202,000
2003	379,000	177,000	202,000
2004	379,000	177,000	202,000

Source: Debra E. Gerald and William J. Hussar, U.S. Department of Education, National Center for Education Statistics, *Projections of Education Statistics to 2004* (Washington, D.C.: U.S. Government Printing Office), October 1993, p. 62. *Primary source:* U.S. Department of Education, National Center for Education Statistics, Fall Enrollment in Colleges and Universities Surveys and Integrated Postsecondary Education Data System (IPEDS) Survey. This table was prepared June 1993. *Notes:* Projections are based on data through 1990-91. Because of rounding, details may not add to totals. Source includes data for 1979-1991.

★ 257 ★

Degrees Conferred in Institutions of Higher Education

Doctoral Degrees Conferred, by Sex of Recipient, with Alternative Projections, 1992-2004

Year ending	Total	Men	Women
1992	40,100	25,200	14,900
		Middle alternative projections	
1993	41,200	25,600	15,600
1994	41,300	25,200	16,100
1995	41,300	24,800	16,500
1996	41,300	24,400	16,900
1997	41,400	24,000	17,400
1998	41,400	23,600	17,800
1999	41,400	23,200	18,200
2000	41,400	22,800	18,600
2001	41,400	22,400	19,000
2002	41,400	22,000	19,400
2003	41,400	21,600	19,800
2004	41,400	21,200	20,200
		Low alternative projections	
1993	39,800	24,200	15,600
1994	39,800	23,800	16,000
1995	39,800	23,400	16,400
1996	39,900	23,000	16,900
1997	39,900	22,600	17,300
1998	39,900	22,200	17,700
1999	39,900	21,800	18,100
2000	39,900	21,400	18,500
2001	39,900	21,000	18,900
2002	39,900	20,600	19,300
2003	39,900	20,200	19,700
2004	39,900	19,800	20,100
		High alternative projections	
1993	42,600	27,000	15,600
1994	43,100	27,000	16,000
1995	43,600	27,000	16,600
1996	44,000	27,000	17,000
1997	44,500	27,000	17,500
1998	44,900	27,000	17,900
1999	45,300	27,000	18,300
2000	45,700	27,000	18,700
2001	46,100	27,000	19,100
2002	46,500	27,000	19,500

[Continued]

★ 257 ★

Doctoral Degrees Conferred, by Sex of Recipient, with Alternative Projections, 1992-2004

[Continued]

Year ending	Total	Men	Women
2003	46,900	27,000	19,900
2004	47,300	27,000	20,300

Source: Debra E. Gerald and William J. Hussar, U.S. Department of Education, National Center for Education Statistics, *Projections of Education Statistics to 2004* (Washington, D.C.: U.S. Government Printing Office), October 1993, p. 63. *Primary source:* U.S. Department of Education, National Center for Education Statistics, Fall Enrollment in Colleges and Universities Surveys and Integrated Postsecondary Education Data System (IPEDS) Survey. This table was prepared June 1993. *Notes:* Projections are based on data through 1990-91. Because of rounding, details may not add to totals. Source includes data for 1979-1991.

★ 258 ★

Degrees Conferred in Institutions of Higher Education

First-Professional Degrees Conferred, by Sex of Recipient, with Alternative Projections, 1992-2004

Year ending	Total	Men	Women
1992	71,600	43,200	28,400
	Middle alternative projections		
1993	73,900	43,900	30,000
1994	74,700	44,000	30,700
1995	75,100	44,100	31,000
1996	75,300	44,200	31,100
1997	74,700	44,100	30,600
1998	74,300	44,000	30,300
1999	74,000	43,900	30,100
2000	73,900	43,800	30,100
2001	73,800	43,700	30,100
2002	73,700	43,600	30,100
2003	73,800	43,500	30,300
2004	74,000	43,400	30,600
	Low alternative projections		
1993	73,100	43,100	30,000
1994	73,400	43,000	30,400
1995	73,300	42,900	30,400
1996	73,400	42,800	30,600
1997	72,800	42,700	30,100
1998	72,100	42,600	29,500
1999	72,000	42,500	29,500
2000	71,700	42,500	29,200
2001	71,700	42,500	29,200
2002	71,500	42,500	29,000

[Continued]

★ 258 ★

First-Professional Degrees Conferred, by Sex of Recipient, with Alternative Projections, 1992-2004

[Continued]

Year ending	Total	Men	Women
2003	71,700	42,500	29,200
2004	72,000	42,500	29,500
		High alternative projections	
1993	74,700	44,700	30,000
1994	77,100	45,000	32,100
1995	77,900	45,300	32,600
1996	78,600	45,600	33,000
1997	78,000	45,500	32,500
1998	77,800	45,400	32,400
1999	77,700	45,300	32,400
2000	77,500	45,100	32,400
2001	77,300	44,900	32,400
2002	77,100	44,700	32,400
2003	76,900	44,500	32,400
2004	77,000	44,300	32,700

Source: Debra E. Gerald and William J. Hussar, U.S. Department of Education, National Center for Education Statistics, *Projections of Education Statistics to 2004* (Washington, D.C.: U.S. Government Printing Office), October 1993, p. 64. *Primary source:* U.S. Department of Education, National Center for Education Statistics, Fall Enrollment in Colleges and Universities Surveys and Integrated Postsecondary Education Data System (IPEDS) Survey. This table was prepared June 1993. *Notes:* Projections are based on data through 1990-91. Because of rounding, details may not add to totals. Source includes data for 1979-1991.

Expenditures and Financial Aspects of Education

★ 259 ★

Education Revenue Receipts from State Source per Capita in Constant 1991-92 Dollars, with Alternative Projections, 1994-2004

Year ending	Middle alternative projections	Low alternative projections	High alternative projections
1994	438	$444	$442
1995	450	448	464
1996	470	458	489
1997	485	466	504
1998	492	473	513
1999	495	474	518

[Continued]

★ 259 ★

Education Revenue Receipts from State Source per Capita in Constant 1991-92 Dollars, with Alternative Projections, 1994-2004

[Continued]

Year ending	Middle alternative projections	Low alternative projections	High alternative projections
2000	499	476	522
2001	503	476	527
2002	508	480	532
2003	513	483	537
2004	517	486	542

Source: Debra E. Gerald and William J. Hussar, U.S. Department of Education, National Center for Education Statistics, *Projections of Education Statistics to 2004* (Washington, D.C.: U.S. Government Printing Office), October 1993, p. 151. *Primary source:* U.S. Department of Education, National Center for Education Statistics, *Statistics of State School Systems*, Common Core of Data survey and Early Estimates survey: and National Education Association, annual *Estimates of State School Statistics*. Latest edition 1992-93. Copyright by the National Education Association 1993. This table was prepared June 1993. *Notes:* Based on the Consumer Price Index for all urban consumers, Bureau of Labor Statistics, U.S. Department of Labor.

★ 260 ★

Expenditures and Financial Aspects of Education

Current Expenditures and Current Expenditures per Pupil in Average Daily Attendance (ADA) in Public Elementary and Secondary Schools, with Alternative Projections, 1992-2004

Year ending	ADA (in thousands)	Current expenditures			
		Constant 1991-92 dollars[1]		Current dollars[2]	
		Total (in billions)	Per pupil in ADA	Total (in billions)	Per pupil in ADA
1992[3]	38,972	209.2	5,368	209.2	5,368
1993[3]	39,594	211.9	5,352	218.2	5,511
Middle alternative projections					
1994	40,321	217.7	5,400	230.8	5,724
1995	41,063	226.5	5,515	247.9	6,036
1996	41,801	238.0	5,694	269.1	6,439
1997	42,672	247.9	5,810	289.6	6,788
1998	43,458	254.9	5,865	308.2	7,093
1999	44,010	260.0	5,907	-	-
2000	44,472	264.8	5,955	-	-
2001	44,859	269.8	6,015	-	-
2002	45,193	275.0	6,085	-	-
2003	45,480	279.8	6,152	-	-

[Continued]

★ 260 ★

Current Expenditures and Current Expenditures per Pupil in Average Daily Attendance (ADA) in Public Elementary and Secondary Schools, with Alternative Projections, 1992-2004

[Continued]

Year ending	ADA (in thousands)	Current expenditures: Constant 1991-92 dollars[1]: Total (in billions)	Current expenditures: Constant 1991-92 dollars[1]: Per pupil in ADA	Current expenditures: Current dollars[2]: Total (in billions)	Current expenditures: Current dollars[2]: Per pupil in ADA
2004	45,727	284.4	6,218	-	-
Low alternative projections					
1994	40,321	216.7	5,373	232.2	5,759
1995	41,063	222.5	5,420	250.0	6,088
1996	41,801	230.5	5,514	272.1	6,510
1997	42,672	237.9	5,576	294.7	6,905
1998	43,458	244.6	5,628	317.9	7,315
1999	44,010	248.3	5,642	-	-
2000	44,472	252.5	5,678	-	-
2001	44,859	256.1	5,709	-	-
2002	45,193	260.8	5,771	-	-
2003	45,480	264.9	5,825	-	-
2004	45,727	268.6	5,874	-	-
High alternative projections					
1994	40,321	222.0	5,507	234,3	5,810
1995	41,063	234.9	5,720	254.2	5,191
1996	41,801	248.6	5,947	275.9	6,601
1997	42,672	259.0	6,069	295.2	6,919
1998	43,458	266.7	6,137	313.4	7,211
1999	44,010	272.7	6,197	-	-
2000	44,472	278.2	6,257	-	-
2001	44,859	283.5	6,320	-	-
2002	45,193	288.8	6,391	-	-
2003	45,480	294.0	6,463	-	-
2004	45,727	299.2	6,543	-	-

Source: Debra E. Gerald and William J. Hussar, U.S. Department of Education, National Center for Education Statistics, *Projections of Education Statistics to 2004* (Washington, D.C.: U.S. Government Printing Office), October 1993, p. 83. *Primary source:* U.S. Department of Education, National Center for Education Statistics, *Statistics of State School Systems*: Common Core of Data survey, and the Early Estimates survey; and National Education Association, annual *Estimates of State School Statistics*. (Latest edition 1992-93, copyright 1993 by the National Education Association. All rights reserved). This table was prepared June 1993. *Notes:* 1. Based on the Consumer Price Index for all urban consumers, Bureau of Labor Statistics, U.S. Department of Labor. 2. Projections in current dollars are not shown after 1998 due to the uncertain behavior of inflation over the long term. 3. Current expenditures and average daily attendance are estimated on the basis of past data. Projections in current dollars are not shown after 1998 due to the uncertain behavior of inflation over the long term. Current expenditures and average daily attendance are estimated on the basis of past data. Source also includes data for 1979-1991.

★ 261 ★

Expenditures and Financial Aspects of Education

Current Expenditures and Current Expenditures per Pupil in Fall Enrollment in Public Elementary and Secondary Schools, with Alternative Projections, 1992-2004

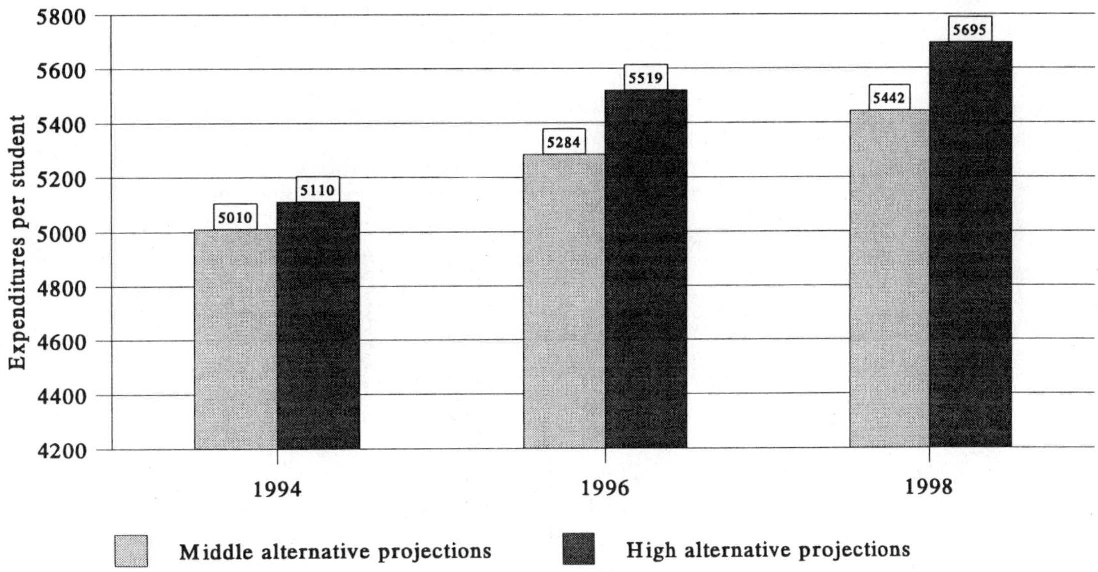

Year ending	Fall enrollment[1] (in thousands)	Current expenditures: Constant 1991-92 dollars[2]		Current expenditures: Current dollars[3]	
		Total (in billions)	Per pupil in fall enrollment	Total (in billions)	Per pupil in fall enrollment
1992	42,000	209.2	4,981	209.2	4,981
1993	42,670	211.9	4,967	218.2	5,114
Middle alternative projections					
1994	43,454	217.7	5,010	230.8	5,311
1995	44,254	226.5	5,118	247.9	5,601
1996	45,049	238.0	5,284	269.1	5,975
1997	45,988	247.9	5,391	289.6	6,298
1998	46,835	254.9	5,442	308.2	6,581
1999	47,430	260.0	5,481	-	-
2000	47,927	264.8	5,526	-	-
2001	48,345	269.8	5,581	-	-
2002	48,705	275.0	5,647	-	-
2003	49,014	279.8	5,709	-	-
2004	49,280	284.4	5,770	-	-
Low alternative projections					
1994	43,454	216.7	4,986	232.2	5,344

[Continued]

★ 261 ★

Current Expenditures and Current Expenditures per Pupil in Fall Enrollment in Public Elementary and Secondary Schools, with Alternative Projections, 1992-2004

[Continued]

Year ending	Fall enrollment[1] (in thousands)	Current expenditures: Constant 1991-92 dollars[2]: Total (in billions)	Current expenditures: Constant 1991-92 dollars[2]: Per pupil in fall enrollment	Current expenditures: Current dollars[3]: Total (in billions)	Current expenditures: Current dollars[3]: Per pupil in fall enrollment
1995	44,254	222.5	5,029	250.0	5,649
1996	45,049	230.5	5,117	272.1	6,040
1997	45,988	237.9	5,174	294.7	6,407
1998	46,835	244.6	5,223	317.9	6,788
1999	47,430	248.3	5,235	-	-
2000	47,927	252.5	5,268	-	-
2001	48,345	256.1	5,298	-	-
2002	48,705	260.8	5,355	-	-
2003	49,014	264.9	5,405	-	-
2004	49,280	268.6	5,451	-	-
		High alternative projections			
1994	43,454	222.0	5,110	234.3	5,391
1995	44,254	234.9	5,308	254.2	5,744
1996	45,049	248.6	5,519	275.9	6,125
1997	45,988	259.0	5,631	295.2	6,420
1998	46,835	266.7	5,695	313.4	6,691
1999	47,430	272.7	5,750	-	-
2000	47,927	278.2	5,806	-	-
2001	48,345	283.5	5,864	-	-
2002	48,705	288.8	5,930	-	-
2003	49,014	294.0	5,997	-	-
2004	49,280	299.2	6,071	-	-

Source: Debra E. Gerald and William J. Hussar, U.S. Department of Education, National Center for Education Statistics, *Projections of Education Statistics to 2004* (Washington, D.C.: U.S. Government Printing Office), October 1993, p. 84. *Primary source:* U.S. Department of Education, National Center for Education Statistics, *Statistics of State School Systems: Statistics of Public Elementary and Secondary Schools*: "Selected Public and Private Elementary and Secondary Education Statistics," NCES Bulletin, October 23, 1979; Common Core of Data Survey; and the *Early Estimates* survey; and National Education Association, annual *Estimates of State School Statistics*, (Latest edition 1992-93. Copyright 1993 by the National Education Association.) This table was prepared June 1993. *Notes:* 1. Each enrollment number is for the fall of the school year ending in the school year shown in column 1. Hence, the enrollment number listed for 1979 is for fall 1978. 2. Based on the Consumer Price Index for all urban consumers, Bureau of Labor Statistics, U.S. Department of Labor. 3. Projections in current dollars are not shown after 1998 due to the uncertain behavior of inflation over the long term. Source also includes data for 1979-1991.

★ 262 ★

Expenditures and Financial Aspects of Education

Total Higher Education Expenditures, 1980-2003

[Billions of constant 1990-91 dollars]

Characteristic	1980-81	1991-92 (estimate)	2002-2003 (projected)	Percent change 1980-81 to 1991-92	Percent change 1991-92 to 2002-2003
Current-fund expenditures	$99.1	$150.6	$208.1	52	38
Public	65.4	95.7	133.3	46	39
Private	33.7	54.9	74.8	63	36

Source: William J. Hussar, U.S. Department of Education, National Center for Education Statistics, *Pocket Projections: Projections of Education Statistics to 2003* (Washington, D.C.: U.S. Government Printing Office), January 1993, p. 5. *Note:* Includes public and private institution expenditures.

★ 263 ★

Expenditures and Financial Aspects of Education

Current-Fund Expenditures of Public and Private Institutions of Higher Education, with Alternative Projections, 1992-2004

Year ending	Constant 1991-92 dollars[1] (in billions)			Current dollars (in billions)		
	Total	Public	Private	Total	Public	Private
1992	155.6	98.8	57.3	155.6	98.3	57.3
1993	159.8	100.7	59.1	164.6	103.7	60.9
Middle alternative projections						
1994	164.8	103.8	60.9	174.7	110.0	64.6
1995	169.8	106.9	63.0	185.8	116.9	68.9
1996	175.2	110.1	65.0	198.1	124.5	73.5
1997	180.2	113.2	67.0	210.5	132.3	78.3
1998	184.8	116.0	68.8	223.5	140.3	83.2
1999	189.3	118.7	70.5	-	-	-
2000	194.1	121.8	72.4	-	-	-
2001	199.1	124.8	74.2	-	-	-
2002	204.1	128.0	76.1	-	-	-
2003	209.1	131.2	78.0	-	-	-
2004	214.0	134.1	79.9	-	-	-
Low alternative projections						
1994	163.9	103.7	60.2	175.6	111.1	64.5
1995	168.0	106.0	62.0	188.7	119.1	69.6
1996	172.9	109.0	64.0	204.2	128.6	75.5
1997	178.0	112.0	66.0	220.4	138.7	81.7

[Continued]

★ 263 ★

Current-Fund Expenditures of Public and Private Institutions of Higher Education, with Alternative Projections, 1992-2004

[Continued]

Year ending	Constant 1991-92 dollars[1] (in billions)			Current dollars (in billions)		
	Total	Public	Private	Total	Public	Private
1998	182.6	114.7	67.8	237.3	149.1	88.2
1999	187.0	117.4	69.6	-	-	-
2000	191.8	120.4	71.4	-	-	-
2001	196.8	123.4	73.3	-	-	-
2002	201.9	126.7	75.2	-	-	-
2003	207.0	129.9	77.1	-	-	-
2004	211.9	132.9	79.0	-	-	-
			High alternative projections			
1994	165.4	104.0	61.5	174.5	109.7	64.8
1995	171.5	107.8	63.7	185.6	116.7	68.9
1996	177.4	111.5	65.8	196.9	123.8	73.1
1997	182.4	114.7	67.7	207.9	130.7	77.2
1998	187.0	117.6	69.4	219.7	138.2	81.6
1999	191.6	120.4	71.2	-	-	-
2000	196.6	123.5	73.0	-	-	-
2001	201.5	126.7	74.9	-	-	-
2002	206.6	129.8	76.8	-	-	-
2003	211.7	133.0	78.7	-	-	-
2004	216.6	136.0	80.6	-	-	-

Source: Debra E. Gerald and William J. Hussar, U.S. Department of Education, National Center for Education Statistics, *Projections of Education Statistics to 2004* (Washington, D.C.: U.S. Government Printing Office), October 1993, p. 91. *Primary source:* U.S. Department of Education, National Center for Education Statistics, "Financial Statistics of Institutions of Higher Education" and "Fall Enrollment in Colleges and Universities," surveys. This table was prepared June 1993. *Notes:* 1. Based on the Consumer Price Index for all urban consumers, Bureau of Labor Statistics, U.S. Department of Labor. 2. Projections in current dollars are not shown after 1998 due to the uncertain behavior of inflation over the long term. Source also includes data for 1979-1991.

★ 264 ★

Expenditures and Financial Aspects of Education

Educational and General Expenditures of Public and Private Institutions of Higher Education, with Alternative Projections, 1992-2004

Year ending	Constant 1991-92 dollars[1] (in billions)			Current dollars (in billions)		
	Total	Public	Private	Total	Public	Private
1992	121.8	78.7	43.1	121.8	78.7	43.1
1993	124.9	80.2	44.7	128.6	82.5	46.1
	Middle alternative projections					
1994	128.4	82.3	46.1	136.1	87.3	48.9
1995	132.1	85.1	47.0	144.6	93.2	51.4
1996	136.1	88.3	47.8	153.8	99.8	54.0
1997	139.6	91.1	48.6	163.1	106.4	56.7
1998	142.8	93.5	49.3	172.7	113.1	59.6
1999	145.9	95.7	50.2	-	-	-
2000	149.2	98.0	51.2	-	-	-
2001	152.6	100.4	52.2	-	-	-
2002	156.1	102.8	53.3	-	-	-
2003	159.6	105.3	54.3	-	-	-
2004	162.9	107.7	55.2	-	-	-
	Low alternative projections					
1994	127.6	82.2	45.4	136.7	88.1	48.6
1995	130.3	84.4	46.0	146.4	94.8	51.7
1996	134.0	87.2	46.7	158.1	102.9	55.2
1997	137.5	90.0	47.6	170.3	111.4	58.9
1998	140.7	92.4	48.4	182.9	120.1	62.9
1999	143.7	94.5	49.2	-	-	-
2000	147.0	96.8	50.2	-	-	-
2001	150.4	99.1	51.3	-	-	-
2002	154.0	101.6	52.4	-	-	-
2003	157.6	104.2	53.4	-	-	-
2004	160.9	106.6	54.3	-	-	-
	High alternative projections					
1994	129.1	82.5	46.6	136.2	87.0	49.2
1995	133.7	86.0	47.7	144.7	93.1	51.6
1996	138.1	89.5	48.6	153.3	99.3	54.0
1997	141.7	92.4	49.4	161.6	105.3	56.3
1998	144.9	94.9	50.0	170.3	111.5	58.8
1999	148.1	97.2	50.9	-	-	-
2000	151.6	99.6	52.0	-	-	-
2001	155.0	102.0	53.0	-	-	-
2002	158.5	104.5	54.0	-	-	-

[Continued]

★ 264 ★

Educational and General Expenditures of Public and Private Institutions of Higher Education, with Alternative Projections, 1992-2004

[Continued]

Year ending	Constant 1991-92 dollars[1] (in billions)			Current dollars (in billions)		
	Total	Public	Private	Total	Public	Private
2003	162.0	107.0	55.1	-	-	-
2004	165.5	109.4	56.1	-	-	-

Source: Debra E. Gerald and William J. Hussar, U.S. Department of Education, National Center for Education Statistics, *Projections of Education Statistics to 2004* (Washington, D.C.: U.S. Government Printing Office), October 1993, p. 92. *Primary source:* U.S. Department of Education, National Center for Education Statistics, "Financial Statistics of Institutions of Higher Education," and "Fall Enrollment in Colleges and Universities," surveys. This table was prepared June 1993. *Notes:* Projections in current dollars are not shown after 1998 due to the uncertain behavior of inflation over the long term. Source also includes data for 1979-1991. 1. Based on the Consumer Price Index for all urban consumers, Bureau of Labor Statistics, U.S. Department of Labor.

★ 265 ★

Expenditures and Financial Aspects of Education

Educational and General Expenditures and Educational and General Expenditures per Full-Time Equivalent (FTE) Student of Private Four-Year Institutions, with Alternative Projections, 1992-2004

Year ending	FTE (in thousands)	Current-fund expenditures			
		Constant 1991-92 dollars[1]		Current dollars	
		Total (in billions)	Per student in FTE	Total (in billions)	Per student in FTE
1992[2]	2,286	41.8	18,292	41.8	18,292
1993[2]	2,368	43.4	18,343	44.7	18,888
Middle alternative projections					
1994	2,433	44.8	18,408	47.5	19,514
1995	2,424	45.6	18,829	50.0	20,607
1996	2,406	46.5	19,321	52.6	21,848
1997	2,395	47.3	19,729	55.2	23,049
1998	2,401	48.0	19,986	58.0	24,170
1999	2,419	48.8	20,180	-	-
2000	2,457	49.8	20,282	-	-
2001	2,490	50.8	20,417	-	-
2002	2,522	51.9	20,564	-	-
2003	2,551	52.8	20,716	-	-
2004	2,569	53.8	20,935	-	-

[Continued]

★ 265 ★

Educational and General Expenditures and Educational and General Expenditures per Full-Time Equivalent (FTE) Student of Private Four-Year Institutions, with Alternative Projections, 1992-2004

[Continued]

Year ending	FTE (in thousands)	Current-fund expenditures: Constant 1991-92 dollars[1] Total (in billions)	Constant 1991-92 dollars[1] Per student in FTE	Current dollars Total (in billions)	Current dollars Per student in FTE
		Low alternative projections			
1994	2,433	44.1	18,110	47.2	19,409
1995	2,424	44.7	18,425	50.2	20,699
1996	2,406	45.4	18,884	53.6	22,293
1997	2,395	46.2	19,304	57.3	23,907
1998	2,401	47.0	19,585	61.1	25,456
1999	2,419	47.9	19,783	-	-
2000	2,457	48.9	19,890	-	-
2001	2,490	49.9	20,041	-	-
2002	2,522	51.0	20,204	-	-
2003	2,551	51.9	20,362	-	-
2004	2,569	52.9	20,579	-	-
		High alternative projections			
1994	2,433	45.3	18,630	47.8	19,656
1995	2,424	46.4	19,142	50.2	20,718
1996	2,406	47.3	19,673	52.5	21,835
1997	2,395	48.0	20,058	54.8	22,866
1998	2,401	48.7	20,284	57.2	23,833
1999	2,419	49.5	20,480	-	-
2000	2,457	50.6	20,589	-	-
2001	2,490	51.6	20,721	-	-
2002	2,522	52.6	20,868	-	-
2003	2,551	53.6	21,028	-	-
2004	2,569	54.6	21,262	-	-

Source: Debra E. Gerald and William J. Hussar, U.S. Department of Education, National Center for Education Statistics, *Projections of Education Statistics to 2004* (Washington, D.C.: U.S. Government Printing Office), October 1993, p. 98. *Primary source:* U.S. Department of Education, National Center for Education Statistics, "Financial Statistics of Institutions of Higher Education" and "Fall Enrollment in Colleges and Universities," surveys. This table was prepared June 1993. *Notes:* 1. Based on the Consumer Price Index for all urban consumers, Bureau of Labor Statistics, U.S. Department of Labor. 2. Estimated on the basis of past data. Projections in current dollars are not shown after 1998 due to the uncertain behavior of inflation over the long term. Source also includes data for 1979-1991.

★ 266 ★

Expenditures and Financial Aspects of Education

Educational and General Expenditures and Educational and General Expenditures per Full-Time Equivalent (FTE) Student of Public Four-Year Institutions, with Alternative Projections, 1992-2004

Year ending	FTE (in thousands)	Current-fund expenditures			
		Constant 1991-92 dollars[1]		Current dollars	
		Total (in billions)	Per student in FTE	Total (in billions)	Per student in FTE
1992[2]	4,796	62.6	13,063	62.6	13,063
1993[2]	4,933	64.3	13,036	66.2	13,423
		Middle alternative projections			
1994	5,072	66.0	13,015	70.0	13,797
1995	5,050	68.3	13,528	74.8	14,805
1996	5,009	70.8	14,127	80.0	15,974
1997	4,995	73.0	14,618	85.3	17,077
1998	5,009	75.1	14,988	90.8	18,127
1999	5,056	77.0	15,239	-	-
2000	5,139	79.0	15,378	-	-
2001	5,216	81.1	15,543	-	-
2002	5,292	83.2	15,717	-	-
2003	5,359	85.3	15,918	-	-
2004	5,399	87.5	16,198	-	-
		Low alternative projections			
1994	5,072	66.0	13,004	70.7	13,937
1995	5,050	68.0	13,460	76.4	15,121
1996	5,000	70.3	14,035	83.0	16,569
1997	4,995	72.6	14,525	89.8	17,988
1998	5,009	74.6	14,891	96.9	19,355
1999	5,056	76.5	15,136	-	-
2000	5,139	78.5	15,273	-	-
2001	5,216	80.5	15,440	-	-
2002	5,292	82.7	15,620	-	-
2003	5,359	84.8	15,877	-	-
2004	5,399	87.0	16,110	-	-
		High alternative projections			
1994	5,072	66.1	13,027	69.7	13,745
1995	5,050	68.7	13,601	74.3	14,720
1996	5,009	71.3	14,233	79.1	15,798
1997	4,995	73.6	14,733	83.9	16,795
1998	5,009	75.7	15,112	88.9	17,756
1999	5,056	77.7	15,367	-	-
2000	5,139	79.7	15,512	-	-

[Continued]

★ 266 ★

Educational and General Expenditures and Educational and General Expenditures per Full-Time Equivalent (FTE) Student of Public Four-Year Institutions, with Alternative Projections, 1992-2004

[Continued]

Year ending	FTE (in thousands)	Current-fund expenditures			
		Constant 1991-92 dollars[1]		Current dollars	
		Total (in billions)	Per student in FTE	Total (in billions)	Per student in FTE
2001	5,216	81.8	15,678	-	-
2002	5,292	83.9	15,851	-	-
2003	5,359	86.0	16,053	-	-
2004	5,399	88.2	16,338	-	-

Source: Debra E. Gerald and William J. Hussar, U.S. Department of Education, National Center for Education Statistics, *Projections of Education Statistics to 2004* (Washington, D.C.: U.S. Government Printing Office), October 1993, p. 94. *Primary source:* U.S. Department of Education, National Center for Education Statistics, "Financial Statistics of Institutions of Higher Education" and "Fall Enrollment in Colleges and Universities," surveys. This table was prepared October 1993. *Notes:* 1. Based on the Consumer Price Index for all urban consumers, Bureau of Labor Statistics, U.S. Department of Labor. 2. Estimated on the basis of past data. Projections in current dollars are not shown after 1998 due to the uncertain behavior of inflation over the long term. Source also includes data for 1979-1991.

★ 267 ★

Expenditures and Financial Aspects of Education

Educational and General Expenditures and Educational and General Expenditures per Full-Time Equivalent (FTE) Student of Public Two-Year Institutions, with Alternative Projections, 1992-2004

Year ending	FTE (in thousands)	Current-fund expenditures			
		Constant 1991-92 dollars[1]		Current dollars	
		Total (in billions)	Per student in FTE	Total (in billions)	Per student in FTE
1992[2]	3,067	16.1	5,241	16.1	5,241
1993[2]	2,939	15.8	5,391	16.2	5,551
Middle alternative projections					
1994	3,026	16.3	5,386	17.3	5,709
1995	3,032	16.8	5,546	18.4	6,070
1996	3,027	17.5	5,779	19.8	6,535
1997	3,034	18.0	5,945	21.1	6,945
1998	3,058	18.4	6,021	22.3	7,281
1999	3,087	18.7	6,048	-	-
2000	3,136	19.0	6,054	-	-
2001	3,173	19.3	6,086	-	-

[Continued]

★ 267 ★

Educational and General Expenditures and Educational and General Expenditures per Full-Time Equivalent (FTE) Student of Public Two-Year Institutions, with Alternative Projections, 1992-2004

[Continued]

Year ending	FTE (in thousands)	Current-fund expenditures: Constant 1991-92 dollars[1] Total (in billions)	Constant 1991-92 dollars[1] Per student in FTE	Current dollars Total (in billions)	Current dollars Per student in FTE
2002	3,204	19.7	6,134	-	-
2003	3,233	20.0	6,187	-	-
2004	3,242	20.3	6,249	-	-
		Low alternative projections			
1994	3,026	16.2	5,362	17.4	5,747
1995	3,032	16.4	5,402	18.4	6,068
1996	3,027	16.9	5,583	20.0	6,591
1997	3,034	17.4	5,745	21.6	7,115
1998	3,058	17.8	5,812	23.1	7,554
1999	3,087	18.0	5,827	-	-
2000	3,136	18.3	5,828	-	-
2001	3,173	18.6	5,865	-	-
2002	3,204	19.0	5,926	-	-
2003	3,233	19.4	5,991	-	-
2004	3,242	19.6	6,060	-	-
		High alternative projections			
1994	3,026	16.4	5,412	17.3	5,710
1995	3,032	17.3	5,703	18.7	6,173
1996	3,027	18.2	6,007	20.2	6,668
1997	3,034	18.8	6,191	21.4	7,058
1998	3,058	19.2	6,285	22.6	7,384
1999	3,087	19.5	6,323	-	-
2000	3,136	19.9	6,340	-	-
2001	3,173	20.2	6,376	-	-
2002	3,204	20.6	6,424	-	-
2003	3,233	20.9	6,477	-	-
2004	3,242	21.2	6,548	-	-

Source: Debra E. Gerald and William J. Hussar, U.S. Department of Education, National Center for Education Statistics, *Projections of Education Statistics to 2004* (Washington, D.C.: U.S. Government Printing Office), October 1993, p. 96. *Primary source:* U.S. Department of Education, National Center for Education Statistics, "Financial Statistics of Institutions of Higher Education" and "Fall Enrollment in Colleges and Universities," surveys. This table was prepared June 1993. *Notes:* 1. Based on the Consumer Price Index for all urban consumers, Bureau of Labor Statistics, U.S. Department of Labor. 2. Estimated on the basis of past data. Projections in current dollars are not shown after 1998 due to the uncertain behavior of inflation over the long term. Source also includes data for 1979-1991.

★ 268 ★

Expenditures and Financial Aspects of Education

Current-Fund Expenditures and Current-Fund Expenditures per Full-Time Equivalent (FTE) Student of Public Two-Year Institutions, with Alternative Projections, 1992-2004

Year ending	FTE (in thousands)	Current-fund expenditures: Constant 1991-92 dollars[1] Total (in billions)	Constant 1991-92 dollars[1] Per student in FTE	Current dollars Total (in billions)	Current dollars Per student in FTE
1992[2]	3,067	17.2	5,613	17.2	5,613
1993[2]	2,939	17.1	5,804	17.6	5,976
		Middle alternative projections			
1994	3,026	17.5	5,791	18.6	6,139
1995	3,032	18.1	5,958	19.8	6,521
1996	3,027	18.8	6,198	21.2	7,008
1997	3,034	19.3	6,370	22.6	7,442
1998	3,058	19.7	6,451	23.9	7,802
1999	3,087	20.0	6,485	-	-
2000	3,136	20.4	6,493	-	-
2001	3,173	20.7	6,529	-	-
2002	3,204	21.1	6,582	-	-
2003	3,233	21.5	6,639	-	-
2004	3,242	21.8	6,711	-	-
		Low alternative projections			
1994	3,026	17.5	5,768	18.7	6,181
1995	3,032	17.6	5,819	19.8	6,537
1996	3,027	18.2	6,009	21.5	7,094
1997	3,034	18.7	6,178	23.2	7,651
1998	3,058	19.1	6,251	24.8	8,124
1999	3,087	19.4	6,272	-	-
2000	3,136	19.7	6,275	-	-
2001	3,173	20.0	6,316	-	-
2002	3,264	20.4	6,381	-	-
2003	3,233	20.9	6,451	-	-
2004	3,242	21.2	6,529	-	-
		High alternative projections			
1994	3,026	17.6	5,816	18.6	6,136
1995	3,032	18.5	6,109	20.0	6,612
1996	3,027	19.4	6,418	21.6	7,124
1997	3,034	20.0	6,608	22.9	7,533
1998	3,058	20.5	6,706	24.1	7,880
1999	3,087	20.8	6,750	-	-
2000	3,136	21.2	6,769	-	-
2001	3,173	21.6	6,808	-	-

[Continued]

★ 268 ★

Current-Fund Expenditures and Current-Fund Expenditures per Full-Time Equivalent (FTE) Student of Public Two-Year Institutions, with Alternative Projections, 1992-2004

[Continued]

Year ending	FTE (in thousands)	Current-fund expenditures: Constant 1991-92 dollars[1] Total (in billions)	Constant 1991-92 dollars[1] Per student in FTE	Current dollars Total (in billions)	Current dollars Per student in FTE
2002	3,204	22.0	6,861	-	-
2003	3,233	22.4	6,919	-	-
2004	3,242	22.7	7,000	-	-

Source: Debra E. Gerald and William J. Hussar, U.S. Department of Education, National Center for Education Statistics, *Projections of Education Statistics to 2004* (Washington, D.C.: U.S. Government Printing Office), October 1993, p. 95. *Primary source:* U.S. Department of Education, National Center for Education Statistics, "Financial Statistics of Institutions of Higher Education" and "Fall Enrollment in Colleges and Universities," surveys. This table was prepared June 1993. *Notes:* 1. Based on the Consumer Price Index for all urban consumers, Bureau of Labor Statistics, U.S. Department of Labor. 2. Estimated on the basis of past data. Projections in current dollars are not shown after 1998 due to the uncertain behavior of inflation over the long term. Source also includes data for 1979-1991.

★ 269 ★

Expenditures and Financial Aspects of Education

Current-fund Expenditures and Current-fund Expenditures per Full-Time Equivalent (FTE) Student of Private Four-year Institutions, with Alternative Projections, 1992-2004

Year ending	FTE (in thousands)	Current-fund expenditures: Constant 1991-92 dollars[1] Total (in billions)	Constant 1991-92 dollars[1] Per student in FTE	Current dollars Total (in billions)	Current dollars Per student in FTE
1992[2]	2,286	55.9	24,458	55.9	24,458
1993[2]	2,368	57.7	24,384	59.5	25,108
Middle alternative projections					
1994	2,433	59.5	24,459	63.1	25,928
1995	2,424	61.5	25,380	67.3	27,776
1996	2,406	63.6	26,438	71.9	29,895
1997	2,395	65.6	27,373	76.6	31,979
1998	2,401	67.3	28,037	81.4	33,907
1999	2,419	69.1	28,555	-	-
2000	2,457	70.9	28,845	-	-
2001	2,490	72.7	29,195	-	-
2002	2,522	74.6	29,565	-	-
2003	2,551	76.4	29,958	-	-
2004	2,569	78.3	30,489	-	-

[Continued]

★ 269 ★

Current-fund Expenditures and Current-fund Expenditures per Full-Time Equivalent (FTE) Student of Private Four-year Institutions, with Alternative Projections, 1992-2004

[Continued]

Year ending	FTE (in thousands)	Current-fund expenditures			
		Constant 1991-92 dollars[1]		Current dollars	
		Total (in billions)	Per student in FTE	Total (in billions)	Per student in FTE
		Low alternative projections			
1994	2,433	58.8	24,161	63.0	25,894
1995	2,424	60.5	24,974	68.0	28,055
1996	2,406	62.6	26,000	73.8	30,693
1997	2,395	64.5	26,950	79.9	33,376
1998	2,401	66.4	27,643	86.3	35,929
1999	2,419	68.1	28,168	-	-
2000	2,457	69.9	28,465	-	-
2001	2,490	71.8	28,832	-	-
2002	2,522	73.7	29,216	-	-
2003	2,551	75.6	29,617	-	-
2004	2,569	77.5	30,149	-	-
		High alternative projections			
1994	2,433	60.0	24,666	63.3	26,025
1995	2,424	62.2	25,676	67.4	27,789
1996	2,406	64.4	26,773	71.5	29,716
1997	2,395	66.3	27,678	75.6	31,553
1998	2,401	68.0	28,305	79.9	33,258
1999	2,419	69.7	28,821	-	-
2000	2,457	71.5	29,115	-	-
2001	2,490	73.4	29,463	-	-
2002	2,522	75.2	29,831	-	-
2003	2,551	77.1	30,229	-	-
2004	2,569	79.1	30,772	-	-

Source: Debra E. Gerald and William J. Hussar, U.S. Department of Education, National Center for Education Statistics, *Projections of Education Statistics to 2004* (Washington, D.C.: U.S. Government Printing Office), October 1993, p. 97. *Primary source:* U.S. Department of Education, National Center for Education Statistics, "Financial Statistics of Institutions of Higher Education" and "Fall Enrollment in Colleges and Universities," surveys. This table was prepared June 1993. *Notes:* 1. Based on the Consumer Price Index for all urban consumers, Bureau of Labor Statistics, U.S. Department of Labor. 2. Estimated on the basis of past data. Projections in current dollars are not shown after 1998 due to the uncertain behavior of inflation over the long term. Source also includes data for 1979-1991.

★ 270 ★

Expenditures and Financial Aspects of Education

Current-fund Expenditures and Current-fund Expenditures per Full-Time Equivalent (FTE) Student of Public Four-year Institutions, with Alternative Projections, 1999-2004

Year ending	FTE (in thousands)	Current-fund expenditures			
		Constant 1991-92 dollars[1]		Current dollars	
		Total (in billions)	Per student in FTE	Total (in billions)	Per student in FTE
1992	4,766	81.0	16,899	81.0	16,899
1993	4,933	83.6	16,951	86.1	17,454
		Middle alternative projections			
1994	5,072	86.3	17,013	91.5	18,035
1995	5,050	88.8	17,582	97.2	19,242
1996	5,009	91.4	18,242	103.3	20,628
1997	4,995	93.9	18,793	109.7	21,955
1998	5,009	96.3	19,218	116.4	23,242
1999	5,056	98.7	19,526	-	-
2000	5,139	101.4	19,731	-	-
2001	5,216	104.1	19,962	-	-
2002	5,292	106.9	20,203	-	-
2003	5,359	109.7	20,470	-	-
2004	5,390	112.3	20,808	-	-
		Low alternative projections			
1994	5,072	86.2	16,999	92.4	18,218
1995	5,050	88.3	17,493	90.2	19,651
1996	5,009	90.8	18,121	107.2	21,392
1997	4,995	93.3	18,669	115.5	23,120
1998	5,009	95.6	19,090	124.3	24,812
1999	5,056	98.0	19,389	-	-
2000	5,139	100.7	19,591	-	-
2001	5,216	103.4	19,825	-	-
2002	5,292	106.2	20,074	-	-
2003	5,359	109.1	20,349	-	-
2004	5,399	111.7	20,691	-	-
		High alternative projections			
1994	5,072	86.4	17,030	91.1	17,967
1995	5,050	89.3	17,679	96.6	19,134
1996	5,009	92.1	18,383	102.2	20,404
1997	4,995	94.6	18,945	107.9	21,597
1998	5,009	97.1	19,382	114.1	22,773
1999	5,056	99.6	19,696	-	-
2000	5,139	102.3	19,907	-	-
2001	5,216	105.1	20,140	-	-

[Continued]

★ 270 ★

Current-fund Expenditures and Current-fund Expenditures per Full-Time Equivalent (FTE) Student of Public Four-year Institutions, with Alternative Projections, 1999-2004

[Continued]

Year ending	FTE (in thousands)	Current-fund expenditures			
		Constant 1991-92 dollars[1]		Current dollars	
		Total (in billions)	Per student in FTE	Total (in billions)	Per student in FTE
2002	5,292	107.9	20,381	-	-
2003	5,359	110.7	20,649	-	-
2004	5,399	113.3	20,992	-	-

Source: Debra E. Gerald and William J. Hussar, U.S. Department of Education, National Center for Education Statistics, *Projections of Education Statistics to 2004* (Washington, D.C.: U.S. Government Printing Office), October 1993, p. 93. *Primary source:* U.S. Department of Education, National Center for Education Statistics, "Financial Statistics of Institutions of Higher Education" and "Fall Enrollment in Colleges and Universities," surveys. This table was prepared June 1993. *Notes:* Source also contains data for 1979-1998. Projections in current dollars are not shown after 1998 due to the uncertain behavior of inflation over the long term. 1. Based on the Consumer Price Index for all urban consumers, Bureau of Labor Statistics, U.S. Department of Labor.

Education and Employment Statistics

★ 271 ★

Effect of Employment Growth on College-Graduate Job Market, 1990-2005

"Overall economic growth between 1990 and 2005 will be slower than in past decades, according to [economist Kristina J. Shelley, writing in *Occupational Outlook Quarterly*]. This is largely due to the aging of the baby-boom generation. 'In the 1990s and early part of the twenty-first century, employment growth will be slow because the number of young people entering the labor force will change little and the labor force participation of women will grow less rapidly,' she says...

"On the other hand, the need to, replace workers leaving the work force for such reasons as retirement, death, disability, relocation, or family needs may benefit college graduates. While the annual rate of replacement for 1984-1990 was 1.06%, it should reach 1.34% between 1990 and 2005."

Source: "Too Many Graduates, Too Few Jobs," in *The Futurist*, March-April 1993, p. 58. *Primary source:* Kristina J. Shelley, U.S. Department of Labor, Bureau of Labor Statistics, "More College Graduates May Be Chasing Fewer Jobs," in *Occupational Outlook Quarterly*, Summer, 1992.

★ 272 ★

Education and Employment Statistics

Distribution of Employment in Major Occupational Groups by Educational Attainment, 1992-20

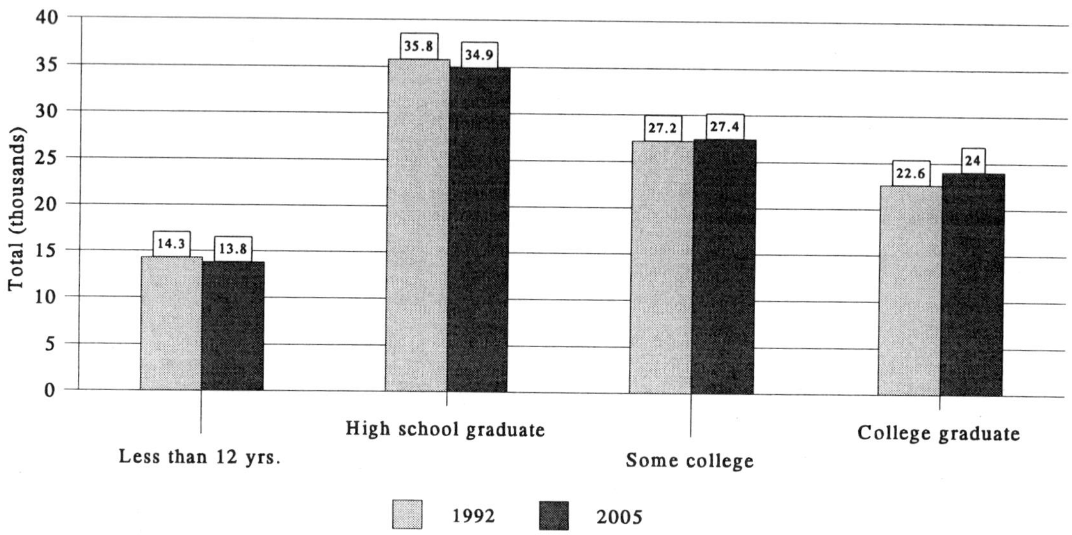

[Employment in thousands]

Occupation	Total employment		Educational attainment											
			Total, all workers		College graduate		Some college		High school graduate		Less than 12 years	
	1992	2005	1992	2005	1992	2005	1992	2005	1992	2005	1992	2005
Total, all occupations	121,099	147,482	100.0	100.0	22.6	24.0	27.2	27.4	35.8	34.9	14.3	13.8
Executive, administrative, and managerial occupations	12,066	15,195	100.0	100.0	47.2	47.7	27.2	27.2	21.7	21.7	3.2	3.2
Professional specialty occupations	16,592	22,801	100.0	100.0	71.5	71.2	19.6	19.8	7.7	7.7	1.3	1.3
Technicians and related support occupations	4,282	5,664	100.0	100.0	28.9	29.3	45.3	45.9	23.2	23.4	2.5	2.5
Marketing and sales occupations	12,993	15,664	100.0	100.0	22.0	22.4	32.0	32.4	33.1	33.5	12.3	12.5
Administrative support occupations, including clerical	22,349	25,406	100.0	100.0	13.1	13.4	37.5	37.7	43.6	43.8	6.0	6.1
Service occupations	19,358	25,820	100.0	100.0	6.4	6.5	35.4	35.8	40.8	40.8	27.0	25.9
Agriculture, forestry, fishing, and related occupations	3,530	3,650	100.0	100.0	7.7	7.3	17.2	17.8	38.2	37.6	36.7	37.5
Precision production, craft, and repair occupations	13,580	15,380	100.0	100.0	6.3	6.3	26.2	26.1	49.1	48.7	18.7	18.7
Operators, fabricators, and laborers	16,349	17,902	100.0	100.0	3.4	3.5	17.7	18.1	52.1	52.0	28.1	27.8

Source: U.S. Department of Labor, Bureau of Labor Statistics, *The American Work Force: 1992-2005* (Washington, D.C.: U.S. Government Printing Office), April 1994, p. 83.
Notes: Projected 2005 is the change due to occupational employment shifts, 1992-2005. Source also includes data on median weekly earnings.

Chapter 8
ENERGY

General Trends in National Energy Supply and Use

★ 273 ★

General Trends in the Energy Supply, 2000

[Forecasters Cetron and Davies forecast the following trends for energy in the 21st century]:

"Despite all the calls to develop alternative sources of energy, oil will provide more of the world's power in 2000 than it did in 1990.

"OPEC will supply most of the oil used in the 1990s. Demand for OPEC oil grew from 15 million barrels a day in 1986 to over 20 million just three years later. By 2000, it will easily top 25 million barrels daily.

"Oil prices are not likely to rise; instead, by 2000 they will plummet to between $7 and $9 a barrel. A number of factors will undermine oil prices within the next 10 years:

—Oil is inherently cheap. It costs only $1.38 per barrel to lift Saudi oil out of the ground. Even Prudhoe Bay and North Sea oil cost only $5 per barrel.

—The 20 most-industrialized countries will have three-month supplies of oil in tankers and storage tanks. Most have another three months' worth in "strategic reserves." If OPEC raises its prices too high, their customers can afford to stop buying until the costs come down. This was not the case during the 1970s oil shocks.

—OPEC just is not very good at throttling back production to keep prices up when their market is glutted. They will not get any better at doing so in the 1990s.

"Growing competition from other energy sources will also help to hold down the price of oil:

—Natural gas burns cleanly, and there is enough of it available to supply the world's entire energy need for the next 200 years.

[Continued]

★ 273 ★

General Trends in the Energy Supply, 2000

[Continued]

—Solar, geothermal, wind-generated, and wave-generated energy sources will contribute where geographically and economically feasible, but their total contribution will be small.

—Nuclear plants will supply 12% of the energy in Eastern Europe and the Soviet Union by the end of the century."

Source: Marvin Cetron and Owen Davies, "Trends Shaping the World," in *The Futurist*, September-October 1991, p. 14. *Primary source:* Cetron and Davies, *Crystal Globe: The Haves and Have-Nots of the New World Order* (St. Martin's Press, 1991).

★ 274 ★

General Trends in National Energy Supply and Use

Total Energy Supply and Disposition Summary, 1990-2010

[Quadrillion Btu per year, unless otherwise noted]

Supply, Disposition, and Prices	Reference Case					Annual Growth 1990-2010 (percent)	Annual Growth 1992-2010 (percent)
	1990	1992	2000	2005	2010		
Production							
Crude oil and lease condensate	15.57	15.22	11.01	10.25	10.80	-1.8%	-1.9%
Natural gas plant liquids	2.17	2.36	2.54	2.70	2.70	1.1%	0.8%
Dry natural gas[1]	18.49	18.51	19.63	20.87	20.89	0.6%	0.7%
Coal	22.46	21.62	23.38	24.28	26.47	0.8%	1.1%
Nuclear power	6.20	6.64	7.21	7.30	6.57	0.3%	-0.1%
Renewable energy/other[2]	6.20	6.28	7.29	7.82	8.69	1.7%	1.8%
Total	71.08	70.64	71.06	73.23	76.12	0.3%	0.4%
Imports							
Crude oil[3]	12.80	13.24	18.73	19.78	19.62	2.2%	2.2%
Petroleum products[4]	3.40	2.71	6.90	8.55	9.81	5.4%	7.4%
Natural gas	1.54	2.15	3.19	3.59	4.16	5.1%	3.7%
Other imports[5]	0.73	0.96	1.49	1.47	1.61	4.1%	2.9%
Total	18.46	19.07	30.31	33.39	35.21	3.3%	3.5%
Exports							
Petroleum	1.82	2.02	2.12	2.12	2.12	0.7%	0.2%
Natural gas	0.09	0.22	0.24	0.27	0.30	6.4%	1.7%
Coal	2.70	2.68	3.31	3.54	3.75	1.7%	1.9%
Total	4.61	4.92	5.68	5.92	6.17	1.5%	1.3%
Discrepancy[6]	-0.65	1.01	0.05	0.10	0.07	NA	-13.9%
Consumption							
Petroleum products[7]	33.55	33.65	38.23	40.29	42.00	1.1%	1.2%
Natural gas	19.30	20.15	22.67	24.31	24.89	1.3%	1.2%
Coal	19.01	18.99	20.29	20.95	22.88	0.9%	1.0%

[Continued]

★ 274 ★

Total Energy Supply and Disposition Summary, 1990-2010

[Continued]

Supply, Disposition, and Prices	Reference Case					Annual Growth 1990-2010 (percent)	Annual Growth 1992-2010 (percent)
	1990	1992	2000	2005	2010		
Nuclear power	6.20	6.64	7.21	7.30	6.57	0.3%	-0.1%
Renewable energy/other[8]	6.23	6.37	7.34	7.94	8.89	1.8%	1.9%
Total	84.28	85.80	95.73	100.79	105.23	1.1%	1.1%
Net Imports - Petroleum	14.37	13.93	23.51	26.22	27.32	3.3%	3.8%
Prices (1992 dollars per unit)							
World oil price (dollars per barrel)[9]	23.22	18.20	20.72	24.90	28.16	1.0%	2.5%
Gas wellhead price (dollars per Mcf)[10]	1.83	1.75	2.42	2.89	3.47	3.3%	3.9%
Coal minemouth price (dollars per ton)	23.22	21.03	25.29	27.00	30.87	1.1%	2.2%

Source: Department of Energy, Energy Information Administration, Office of Integrated Analysis and Forecasting, *Annual Energy Outlook 1994: With Projections to 2010,* (Washington, D.C.: U.S. Government Printing Office, January 1994), p. 55. *Primary sources:* 1990: Energy Information Administration (EIA), *Annual Energy Review 1992* 1990 and 1992 natural gas values: EIA, *Natural Gas Annual 1992 Volume 1* (Washington, D.C., November 1993). *Notes:* Btu = British Thermal Unit. Mcf = Thousand cubic feet. NA = Not applicable. Totals may not equal sum of components due to independent rounding. Figures for 1990 may differ from published data due to internal conversion factors within the Annual Energy Outlook (AEO) 1994 National Energy Modeling System. Projections: EIA, AEO 1994 National Energy Modeling System run AEO94B. D1221934. 1. Includes synthetic gas. 2. Includes utility and nonutility electricity from hydroelectric, geothermal, wood and wood waste, municipal solid waste, other biomass, wind, photovoltaic and solar thermal sources; nonelectric energy from renewable resources, such as active and passive solar system, ground-water heat pumps, and wood, alcohol fuels from renewable resources; and, in addition to renewables, electricity from waste heat, liquid hydrogen, and methanol. 3. Includes imports of crude oil for the Strategic Petroleum Reserve. 4. Imports of finished petroleum products. Does not include imports of unfinished oils or blending components. 5. Includes coal, coal coke (net), and electricity (net), methanol, methyl tertiary butyle ether (MTBE), and imports of unfinished oils. 6. Balancing item. Includes unaccounted for supply, losses, and gains. 7. Includes natural gas plant liquids, crude oil consumed as fuel, and nonpetroleum based liquids for blending, such as ethanol. 8. Includes utility and non-utility electricity from hydroelectric, geothermal, wood and wood waste, municipal solid waste, other biomass, wind, photovoltaic and solar thermal sources; nonelectric energy from renewable resources, such as active and passive solar system, ground-water heat pumps, and wood, alcohol fuels from renewable resources; and, in addition to renewables, electricity from waste heat, plus coal coke imports, net electricity imports, methanol, and liquid hydrogen. 9. Average refiner acquisition cost for imported crude oil. 10. Represents Lower-48 onshore and offshore supplies.

★ 275 ★

General Trends in National Energy Supply and Use

Energy Consumption by End-Use Consumption and Energy Source, 2010

"The distinction between primary (including electricity generation and transmission losses) and delivered end-use energy consumption is illustrated in the table below, which contrasts percentage shares based solely on delivered energy to shares that include electricity generation and transmission losses in the electricity totals.

"Overall, electric utilities consume about 3.2 Btu for every Btu of electricity delivered to customers. In terms of end-use energy consumption, electricity accounts for only 15 percent of energy consumed by final customers in 2010. In terms of total energy requirements, however, 36 percent of the Nation's energy is used to generate and distribute electricity. This distinction is particularly important in estimating the energy requirements and conservation potential of the residential and commercial sectors, because these sectors depend most heavily on electricity."

End-user sector and energy source	End-use consumption		With electricity losses	
	Percent	Quads	Percent	Quads
Residential		10.6		18.5
Electricity	34	3.6	62	11.6
Natural gas	47	5.0	27	5.0
Petroleum	12	1.3	7	1.3
Other	7	0.7	4	0.7
Commercial		7.6		15.2
Electricity	46	3.5	73	11.2
Natural gas	40	3.0	20	3.0
Petroleum	11	0.8	5	0.8
Other	2	0.2	1	0.2
Industrial		31.7		41.5
Electricity	14	4.5	35	14.3
Natural gas	34	10.7	26	10.7
Petroleum	34	10.8	26	10.8
Other	18	5.7	13	5.7
Transportation		29.5		29.9
Electricity	1	0.2	2	0.6
Natural gas	4	1.1	4	1.1
Petroleum	95	28.1	94	28.1
Other	-	0.1	-	0.1
Total (all sectors)		79.3		105.2
Electricity	15	11.8	36	37.7
Natural gas	25	19.8	19	19.8
Petroleum	52	41.1	39	41.1
Other	8	6.7	6	6.7

Source: Department of Energy, Energy Information Administration, Office of Integrated Analysis and Forecasting, *Annual Energy Outlook 1994: With Projections to 2010*, (Washington, D.C.: U.S. Government Printing Office, January 1994), p. 10.

★ 276 ★

General Trends in National Energy Supply and Use

Energy Consumption by End-use Sector and Source, 1990-2010

[Quadrillion Btu per year]

Sector and Source	Reference Case					Annual Growth 1990-2010	Annual Growth 1992-2010
	1990	1992	2000	2005	2010	(percent)	(percent)
Residential							
Distillate fuel	0.84	0.85	0.90	0.89	0.87	0.2%	0.1%
Kerosene	0.06	0.06	0.06	0.06	0.06	-0.5%	-0.3%
Liquefied petroleum gas	0.36	0.41	0.36	0.34	0.33	-0.5%	-1.2%
Natural gas	4.52	4.83	5.00	4.97	4.99	0.5%	0.2%
Coal	0.06	0.06	0.05	0.05	0.05	-1.3%	-1.2%
Renewable energy[1]	0.61	0.63	0.65	0.66	0.66	0.4%	0.3%
Electricity	3.15	3.19	3.39	3.49	3.63	0.7%	0.7%
Total	9.61	10.04	10.41	10.46	10.60	0.5%	0.3%
Commercial							
Distillate fuel	0.49	0.49	0.52	0.51	0.49	0.1%	0.1%
Kerosene	0.01	0.01	0.01	0.01	0.01	-0.5%	-0.5%
Motor gasoline[2]	0.11	0.09	0.11	0.11	0.11	0.2%	1.3%
Residential fuel	0.23	0.23	0.22	0.22	0.22	-0.4%	-0.4%
Natural gas	2.70	2.89	2.88	2.94	3.01	0.6%	0.2%
Other[3]	0.16	0.16	0.15	0.15	0.15	-0.2%	-0.2%
Renewable energy[4]	0.01	0.01	0.03	0.03	0.03	5.2%	4.9%
Electricity	2.86	2.91	3.30	3.44	3.51	1.0%	1.1%
Total	6.57	6.78	7.22	7.41	7.55	0.7%	0.6%
Industrial[5]							
Distillate fuel	1.18	1.19	1.37	1.47	1.56	1.4%	1.5%
Liquefied petroleum gas	1.61	1.83	1.99	2.20	2.40	2.0%	1.5%
Motor gasoline[2]	0.18	1.20	0.23	0.25	0.26	1.8%	1.6%
Petrochemical feedstocks	1.10	1.23	1.32	1.46	1.59	1.9%	1.5%
Residential fuel	0.42	0.34	0.46	0.44	0.45	0.4%	1.5%
Other petroleum[6]	3.82	3.83	4.38	4.43	4.55	0.9%	1.0%
Natural gas[7]	8.50	8.96	9.61	10.20	10.69	1.2%	1.0%
Metallurgical coal	1.04	0.87	0.74	0.65	0.57	-2.9%	-2.3%
Steam coal	1.71	1.65	1.91	2.11	2.24	1.4%	1.7%
Net coal coke imports	0.00	0.03	0.01	0.02	0.02	NA	-2.6%
Renewable energy	1.96	1.99	2.40	2.62	2.84	1.9%	2.0%
Electricity	3.23	3.29	3.84	4.18	4.50	1.7%	1.8%
Total	24.78	25.42	28.27	30.02	31.68	1.2%	1.2%
Transportation							
Distillate fuel	3.83	3.76	4.87	5.32	5.82	2.1%	2.5%
Jet fuel[8]	3.13	3.00	3.72	4.08	4.44	1.8%	2.2%
Motor gasoline[2]	13.58	13.69	15.03	15.50	15.76	0.7%	0.8%
Residential fuel	1.03	1.09	1.32	1.49	1.65	2.3%	2.3%
Liquefied petroleum gas	0.02	0.02	0.08	0.13	0.20	12.3%	13.8%
Other petroleum[9]	0.22	0.20	0.21	0.22	0.24	0.3%	0.9%

[Continued]

★ 276 ★

Energy Consumption by End-use Sector and Source, 1990-2010

[Continued]

Sector and Source	Reference Case					Annual Growth 1990-2010 (percent)	Annual Growth 1992-2010 (percent)
	1990	1992	2000	2005	2010		
Pipeline fuel natural gas	0.68	0.61	0.69	0.782	0.73	0.3%	1.0%
Compressed natural gas	0.00	0.00	0.13	0.24	0.37	NA	NA
Renewables (ethanol)[10]	0.00	0.00	0.01	0.03	0.06	33.4%	33.4%
Liquid hydrogen	0.00	0.00	0.00	0.00	0.00	94.9%	74.4%
Methanol[11]	0.00	0.00	0.01	0.03	0.06	38.7%	29.2%
Electricity	0.01	0.01	0.08	0.13	0.19	15.9%	17.8%
Total	22.50	22.38	26.16	27.91	29.50	1.4%	1.5%
Electric Utilities[12]							
Distillate fuel	0.02	0.03	0.08	0.13	0.11	7.7%	8.4%
Residential fuel	1.23	0.90	0.93	0.97	0.81	-2.1%	-0.6%
Natural gas	2.88	2.86	4.36	5.24	5.10	2.9%	3.3%
Steam coal	16.10	16.30	17.49	18.05	19.93	1.1%	1.1%
Nuclear power	6.20	6.40	7.21	7.30	6.57	0.3%	0.1%
Renewable energy/other[13]	3.64	3.20	4.23	4.55	5.21	1.8%	2.7%
Total	30.07	29.69	34.30	36.24	37.74	1.1%	1.3%
Primary Energy Consumption							
Distillate fuel	6.36	6.31	7.72	8.34	8.86	1.7%	1.9%
Kerosene	0.08	0.07	0.07	0.07	0.07	-0.5%	-0.3%
Jet fuel[3]	3.13	3.00	3.72	4.08	4.44	1.8%	2.2%
Liquefied petroleum gas	2.06	2.32	2.49	2.74	3.00	1.9%	1.4%
Motor gasoline[2]	13.87	13.98	15.37	15.86	16.14	0.8%	0.8%
Petrochemical feedstocks	1.10	1.23	1.32	1.46	1.59	1.9%	1.5%
Residential fuel	2.91	2.56	2.94	3.12	3.11	0.3%	1.1%
Other petroleum[14]	4.04	4.03	4.59	4.65	4.79	0.8%	1.0%
Natural gas	19.30	20.15	22.67	24.31	24.89	1.3%	1.2%
Metallurgical coal	1.04	0.87	0.74	0.65	0.57	-2.9%	-2.3%
Steam coal	17.96	18.05	19.54	20.29	22.31	1.1%	1.2%
Net coal coke imports	0.0	0.03	0.01	0.02	0.02	NA	-2.6%
Nuclear power	6.20	6.40	7.21	7.30	6.57	0.3%	0.1%
Renewable energy/other[15]	6.22	5.83	7.32	7.92	8.87	1.8%	2.4%

[Continued]

★ 276 ★

Energy Consumption by End-use Sector and Source, 1990-2010

[Continued]

Sector and Source	Reference Case					Annual Growth 1990-2010 (percent)	Annual Growth 1992-2010 (percent)
	1990	1992	2000	2005	2010		
Total	84.29	84.86	95.73	100.79	105.23	1.1%	1.2%
Electricity Consumption (all sectors)	9.25	9.45	10.62	11.25	11.84	1.2%	1.3%

Source: Department of Energy, Energy Information Administration, Office of Integrated Analysis and Forecasting, *Annual Energy Outlook 1994: With Projections to 2010* (Washington, D.C.: U.S. Government Printing Office, January 1994), pp. 56-7. *Primary source:* 1990 Coal Consumption: Energy Information Administration (EIA), *Quarterly Coal Report* (Washington, D.C., May 1991), and EIA, *State Energy Data Report* (Washington, D.C., May 1993). 1990 and 1992 natural gas consumption: EIA, *Natural Gas Annual 1992 Volume 1* (Washington, D.C., November 1993). 1990 and 1992 consumption other than coal and natural gas: EIA, *Monthly Energy Review* (Washington, D.C., July 1993) and Office of Coal, Nuclear, Electric, and Alternative Fuels estimates. Figures for 1990 may differ from published data due to internal conversion factors within the AEO 1994 National Energy Modeling System. Projections: EIA, AEO 1994 National Energy Modeling System run AEO94B.D1221934. *Notes:* Btu = British thermal unit. NA = Not applicable. Totals may not equal to sum of components due to independent rounding. Reference case projections. 1. Includes electricity generated by the sector for self-use from hydroelectric, geothermal, wood and wood waste, municipal solid waste, other biomass, wind, photovoltaic and solar thermal sources, and non-electric energy from renewable sources such as solar and solar thermal sources, and non-electric energy from renewable sources such as solar thermal water heaters, ground water heat pumps, and wood. 2. Includes ethanol (blends of 10 percent or less) and ethers blended into gasoline. 3. Includes liquefied petroleum gas and coal. 4. Includes commercial sector electricity co-generated using wood and wood waste, municipal solid waste, and other biomass; non-electric energy from renewable sources, such as active and passive solar systems, geothermal heat pumps, and solar water heating systems. 5. Fuel consumption includes consumption for cogeneration. 6. Includes petroleum coke, asphalt, road oil, lubricants, still gas, and miscellaneous petroleum products. 7. Includes lease and plant fuel. 8. Includes naphtha and kerosene type. 9. Includes aviation gas and lubricants. 10. Only E85 (85 percent ethanol). 11. Only M85 (85 percent methanol). 12. Includes consumption of energy by electric utilities, independent power producers, and small power producers that sell power to the grid. 13. Includes electricity sold to utilities by nonutilities, including cogenerators, from hydroelectric, geothermal, wood and wood waste, municipal solid waste, other biomass, wind, photovoltaic and solar thermal sources, plus waste heat and net electricity imports. Does not include own use. 14. Includes unfinished oils, natural gasoline, motor gasoline blending compounds, aviation gasoline, lubricants, still gas, asphalt, road oil, and miscellaneous petroleum products. 15. Includes electricity generated for sale to electric utilities and for self-use from renewable resources, non-electric energy from renewable sources, electricity generated from waste heat, net electricity imports, liquid hydrogen, and methanol.

Residential, Commercial, and Industrial Energy Use

★277★

Building Energy Use, 1990-2010

"A modeling effort by the Energy Information Administration, conducted as part of the National Energy Strategy, estimated the business-as-usual and cost-effective levels of energy use in buildings in 2010. This study estimated that, relative to the predicted business-as-usual 2010 consumption, 13 percent of energy used in buildings could be saved with cost-effective technologies, and that 26 percent of energy could be saved with technically feasible, but not necessarily cost-effective technologies. These estimates are at the low end of the range of cost-effective savings found in other studies, probably due in part to conservative assumptions concerning building shell retrofits."

[Quads per year]

Sector	Energy Use			
	Business-as-usual		Cost-effective	Technical potential
	1990	2010	2010	2010
Residential	10.7	11.7	10.2	8.3
Commercial	6.8	8.7	7.5	6.8
Total	17.5	20.4	17.7	15.1

Source: U.S. Congress, Office of Technology Assessment, *Building Energy Efficiency* (Washington, D.C.: U.S. Government Printing Office, May 1992), pp. 26, 28-9. *Primary source:* U.S. Department of Energy, Energy Information Administration, *Energy Consumption and Conservation Potential: Supporting Analysis for the National Energy Strategy* (Washington, D.C.: December 1990). *Notes:* Business-as-usual forecast assumes "current government policies and programs remain in effect" (p. 56). Cost-effective forecast is the "high conservation excursion," and assumes "full penetration of cost-effective, energy efficient technologies and other conservation measures" where "cost-effectiveness is defined as an energy-savings investment that generates a positive net present value" (p. 59). A 10 percent discount rate is assumed. Technical potential is the "very high conservation excursion," and assumes that the most efficient technologies are installed when in-place units fail. There is no premature scrapping of capital equipment in either case.

★278★

Residential, Commercial, and Industrial Energy Use

Residential Sector Key Indicators and End-Use Consumption, 1990-2010

[Quadrillion Btu per year, unless otherwise noted]

Key Indicators and Consumption	Reference Case					Annual Growth 1990-2010 (percent)	Annual Growth 1992-2010 (percent)
	1990	1992	2000	2005	2010		
Household Characteristics							
Households (millions)							
Single-family	64.36	65.60	71.64	75.09	78.70	1.0%	1.0%

[Continued]

★ 278 ★

Residential Sector Key Indicators and End-Use Consumption, 1990-2010

[Continued]

Key Indicators and Consumption	Reference Case					Annual Growth 1990-2010	Annual Growth 1992-2010
	1990	1992	2000	2005	2010	(percent)	(percent)
Multifamily	24.42	24.27	24.72	25.43	26.37	0.4%	0.5%
Mobile homes	5.21	5.19	5.31	5.38	5.39	0.2%	0.2%
Total	93.99	95.06	101.67	105.90	110.46	0.8%	0.8%
Housing Starts (millions)							
Single-family	0.90	1.04	1.05	1.08	1.04	0.7%	0.0%
Multifamily	0.30	0.17	0.38	0.39	0.46	2.0%	5.6%
Mobile homes	0.19	0.21	0.22	0.22	0.21	0.5%	-0.1%
Total	1.39	1.42	1.66	1.69	1.71	1.0%	1.0%
Energy Intensity							
(million Btu per year per household)							
Heating	54.59	58.45	56.55	53.91	51.19	-0.3%	-0.7%
Total	102.23	105.60	102.40	98.82	95.93	-0.3%	-0.5%
Fuel Consumption							
Distillate							
Space heating	0.75	0.77	0.82	0.82	0.80	0.3%	0.2%
Water heating	0.08	0.08	0.07	0.07	0.07	-0.7%	-0.6%
Other uses[1]	0.00	0.00	0.00	0.00	0.00	1.0%	1.0%
Total	0.84	0.85	0.90	0.89	0.87	0.2%	0.1%
Liquefied Petroleum Gas							
Space heating	0.23	0.27	0.24	0.23	0.22	-0.3%	-1.2%
Water heating	0.08	0.09	0.07	0.07	0.07	-1.0%	-1.6%
Cooking[2]	0.05	0.04	0.04	0.04	0.04	-1.0%	-0.4%
Other uses[1]	0.01	0.01	0.01	0.01	0.01	0.9%	0.9%
Total	0.36	0.41	0.36	0.34	0.33	-0.5%	-1.2%
Natural Gas							
Space heating	3.12	3.42	3.56	3.52	3.49	0.6%	0.1%
Space cooling	0.00	0.00	0.00	0.00	0.01	NA	NA
Water heating	1.09	1.10	1.11	1.12	1.16	0.3%	0.3%
Cooking[2]	0.18	0.18	0.19	0.20	0.21	0.8%	0.9%
Clothes dryers	0.08	0.08	0.07	0.06	0.6	-1.3%	-1.4%
Other uses[3]	0.06	0.06	0.06	0.07	0.07	1.0%	1.0%
Total	4.52	4.83	5.00	4.97	4.99	0.5%	0.2%
Electricity							
Space heating	0.30	0.33	0.38	0.40	0.41	1.5%	1.1%
Space cooling	0.52	0.51	0.52	0.53	0.54	0.2%	0.3%
Water heating	0.34	0.34	0.35	0.35	0.35	0.2%	0.1%
Refrigeration	0.53	0.52	0.45	0.39	0.33	-2.3%	-2.5%
Cooking	0.15	0.15	0.16	0.17	0.18	1.0%	1.0%

[Continued]

★ 278 ★

Residential Sector Key Indicators and End-Use Consumption, 1990-2010

[Continued]

Key Indicators and Consumption	Reference Case					Annual Growth 1990-2010 (percent)	Annual Growth 1992-2010 (percent)
	1990	1992	2000	2005	2010		
Clothes dryers	0.17	0.18	0.18	0.18	0.18	0.3%	0.2%
Freezers	0.15	0.14	0.11	0.09	0.07	-3.6%	-3.7%
Lighting	0.30	0.30	0.32	0.33	0.34	0.5%	0.7%
Other uses[4]	0.69	0.72	0.92	1.07	1.23	2.9%	3.0%
Total	3.15	3.19	3.39	3.49	3.63	0.7%	0.7%
Renewables							
Wood[5]	0.59	0.61	0.63	0.63	0.63	0.3%	0.1%
Geothermal[6]	0.01	0.01	0.01	0.02	0.02	7.9%	7.3%
Solar[7]	0.01	0.01	001	0.01	0.01	1.1%	1.1%
Total	0.61	0.63	0.65	0.66	0.66	0.4%	0.3%
Other Fuels[8]	0.13	0.12	0.11	0.11	0.11	-0.9%	-0.8%
Total Fuels							
Space heating	5.13	5.53	5.75	5.71	5.66	0.5%	0.1%
Space cooling	0.52	0.51	0.53	0.54	0.56	0.4%	0.5%
Water heating	1.60	1.67	1.62	1.62	1.67	0.2%	0.0%
Cooking	0.37	0.37	0.39	0.41	0.42	0.7%	0.7%
Clothes dryers	0.25	0.26	0.25	0.24	0.24	-0.2%	-0.4%
Other uscs	1.73	1.75	1.87	1.95	2.05	0.8%	0.9%
Total	9.61	10.04	10.41	10.46	10.60	0.5%	0.3%

Source: Department of Energy, Energy Information Administration, Office of Integrated Analysis and Forecasting, *Annual Energy Outlook 1994: With Projections to 2010* (Washington, D.C.: U.S. Government Printing Office, January 1994), pp. 60-1. *Primary source:* 1990: Energy Information Administration (EIA), *State Energy Data Report* (Washington, D.C., May 1993). 1990 and 1992 natural gas values: EIA, *Natural Gas Annual 1992 Volume 1* (Washington, D.C., November 1993). Projections: EIA, AEO 1994 National Energy Modeling System run AEO94B.D1221934. *Notes:* Reference-case projections. Btu = British Thermal Unit. NA= Not applicable. Totals may not equal sum of components due to independent rounding. 1. Includes such appliances as swimming-pool and hot-tub heaters. 2. Does not include outdoor grills. 3. Includes such appliances as swimming-pool heaters, outdoor grills, and outdoor lighting. 4. Includes such appliances as microwave ovens, television sets, and dishwashers. 5. Includes wood used for primary and secondary heating in wood stoves and fireplaces as reported by the *Residential Energy Consumption Survey: 1990 (RECS)*. 6. Includes primary energy displaced by ground-source (geothermal) heat pumps in space heating and cooling applications. 7. Includes primary energy displaced by solar thermal water heaters. 8. Includes kerosene and coal.

★ 279 ★

Residential, Commercial, and Industrial Energy Use

Residential Sector Energy Use by Type of Equipment, 1990-2010

Equipment Stock Data	Reference Case				Annual Growth 1990-2010 (percent)
	1990	2000	2005	2010	
Equipment Stock (million units)					
Main Space Heaters					
Electric heat pumps	6.44	8.67	9.84	11.12	2.8%
Electric other	15.09	15.83	16.31	16.82	0.5%
Natural gas heat pumps	0.00	0.11	0.18	0.25	NA
Natural gas other	51.73	57.32	59.99	62.80	1.0%
Distillate	10.41	10.05	10.10	10.14	-0.1%
Liquid petroleum gas	4.39	3.91	3.75	3.61	-1.0%
Kerosene	1.09	0.91	0.84	0.78	-1.6%
Wood stoves	3.89	3.79	3.75	3.71	-0.2%
Geothermal heat pumps	0.15	0.36	0.48	0.61	7.3%
Total	93.19	100.96	105.23	109.84	0.8%
Space Cooling (million units)					
Electric heat pumps	6.44	8.67	9.84	11.12	2.8%
Natural gas heat pumps	0.00	0.11	0.18	0.25	N/A
Geothermal heat pumps	0.15	0.36	0.48	0.61	7.3%
Central air conditioners	30.68	37.47	40.93	44.49	1.9%
Room air conditioners	40.20	40.23	40.33	40.49	0.0%
Total	77.47	86.84	91.76	96.95	1.1%
Water Heaters (million units)					
Electric	35.28	37.71	39.15	40.77	0.7%
Natural gas	50.37	55.81	58.61	61.55	1.0%
Distillate	5.14	5.15	5.20	5.26	0.1%
Liquid petroleum gas	3.20	3.00	2.93	2.88	-0.5%
Solar thermal	0.55	0.62	0.66	0.69	1.1%
Total	94.55	102.29	106.55	111.16	0.8%
Cooling Equipment (million units)[1]					
Electric	54.85	60.11	62.96	66.00	0.9%
Natural gas	33.78	36.76	38.35	40.05	0.9%
Liquid petroleum gas	5.36	4.80	4.59	4.42	-1.0%
Total	93.99	101.66	105.89	110.46	0.8%
Clothes Dryers (million units)					
Electric	49.46	54.55	57.02	59.56	0.9%
Natural gas	15.22	14.38	13.95	13.54	-0.6%
Total	64.66	68.93	70.97	73.10	0.6%
Other Appliances (million units)					
refrigerators	101.83	110.14	114.67	119.55	0.8%
freezers	32.41	31.40	31.05	30.89	-0.2%

[Continued]

★ 279 ★

Residential Sector Energy Use by Type of Equipment, 1990-2010

[Continued]

Equipment Stock Data	Reference Case				Annual Growth 1990-2010 (percent)
	1990	2000	2005	2010	
Stock Average Equipment Efficiency					
Main space heaters					
Electric heat pumps (HSPF)	6.76	7.32	7.49	7.60	0.6%
Natural gas heat pumps (COP)	1.04	1.25	1.25	1.25	0.9%
Geothermal heat pumps (HSPF)	9.35	11.60	11.96	12.17	1.3%
Natural gas furnace (AFUE)	0.67	0.73	0.76	0.78	0.7%
Distillate furnace (AFUE)	0.76	0.79	0.80	0.81	0.3%
Space Cooling Systems					
Electric heat pumps (SEER)	8.56	9.76	10.12	10.35	0.9%
Natural gas heat pumps (COP)	0.93	1.07	1.07	1.07	0.7%
Geothermal heat pumps (SEER)	9.62	11.96	12.34	12.56	1.3%
Central air conditioners (SEER)	8.60	9.52	9.87	10.11	0.8%
Room air conditioners (EER)	7.47	8.80	10.03	10.26	1.6%
Water Heaters					
Electric (EF)	0.83	0.87	0.89	0.91	0.4%
Natural gas (EF)	0.51	0.54	0.56	0.56	0.5%
Distillate (EF)	0.48	0.54	0.57	0.57	0.8%
Liquid petroleum gas (EF)	0.51	0.54	0.56	0.56	0.5%
Other Appliances (kilowatt-hour per year)					
Refrigerators	1,188.00	923.66	762.69	614.02	-3.2%
Freezers	984.00	737.50	614.87	496.04	-3.4%

Source: Department of Energy, Energy Information Administration, *Supplement to the Annual Energy Outlook* (Washington, D.C.: U.S. Government Printing Office, March, 1994), pp. 120-21. *Primary source:* 1990: Energy Information Administration (EIA), *Household Energy Consumption and Expenditures 1990* (Washington, D.C., February 1993), and EIA, *State Energy Data Report* (Washington, D.C., May 1993). Projections: EIA, AEO 1994 National Energy Modeling System run AEO94B.D1221934. *Notes:* HSPF = Heating Seasonal Performance Factor: The total heating output of a heat pump during its normal annual usage period for heating divided by total electric input in watt-hours during the same period. COP = Coefficient of Performance: Energy efficient rating measure determined, under specific testing conditions, by dividing the energy output by the energy input. AFUE = Annual Fuel Utilization Efficiency: Efficiency rating based on average usage, including on and off cycling, as set out in the standardized Department of Energy test procedures. SEER = Seasonal Energy Efficiency Ratio: The total cooling of a central unitary air conditioner or a unitary heat pump in Btu during its normal annual usage period for cooling divided by the total electric energy input in watt-hours during the same period. EER = Energy Efficiency Ratio: A ratio calculated by dividing the cooling capacity in Btu per hour by the power input in watts at any given set of rating conditions, expressed in Btu per hour per watt. EF = Efficiency Factor: Efficiency (measured in Btu out/Btu in) of water heaters under certain test conditions specified by the Department of Energy. Btu = British Thermal Unit. NA = Not applicable. Totals may not equal to sum of components due to independent rounding. 1. Does not include microwave ovens or outdoor grills.

★ 280 ★

Residential, Commercial, and Industrial Energy Use

Commercial Sector Key Indicators and End-use Consumption, 1990-2010

[Quadrillion Btu per year, unless otherwise noted]

Key Indicators and Consumption	Reference Case					Annual Growth 1990-2010 (percent)	Annual Growth 1992-2010 (percent)
	1990	1992	2000	2005	2010		
Key Indicators							
Total Employment (millions)	109.8	108.4	124.5	132.8	139.6	1.2%	1.4%
Total Floorspace (billion square feet)							
Surviving	62.7	64.7	71.0	74.0	77.0	1.0%	1.0%
New additions	1.5	1.4	1.4	1.5	1.6	0.3%	0.9%
Total	64.3	66.1	72.4	75.4	78.6	1.0%	1.0%
Energy Consumption Intensity (Thousand Btu per square feet)	102.3	102.6	99.7	98.3	96.0	-0.3%	-0.4%
End-Use Consumption							
Electricity							
Space heating	0.06	0.06	0.05	0.04	0.04	-2.0%	-2.0%
Space cooling	0.26	0.26	0.26	0.26	0.26	0.0%	-0.1%
Lighting	1.20	1.20	1.21	1.20	1.19	0.0%	-0.1%
Water heating	0.03	0.03	0.04	0.05	0.06	4.1%	4.4%
Office equipment	0.39	0.41	0.78	0.94	1.01	4.8%	5.1%
Other uses[1]	0.93	0.95	0.96	0.96	0.96	0.2%	0.1%
Total electricity	2.86	2.91	3.30	3.44	3.51	1.0%	1.1%
Natural Gas							
Space heating	1.36	1.38	1.33	1.30	1.28	-0.3%	-0.4%
Space cooling	0.01	0.01	0.02	0.02	0.02	3.3%	2.5%
Water heating	0.37	0.39	0.38	0.38	0.37	0.0%	-0.2%
Other uses[2]	0.96	1.11	1.14	1.24	1.34	1.7%	1.1%
Total natural gas	2.70	2.89	2.88	2.94	3.01	0.6%	0.2%
Distillate							
Space heating	0.31	0.31	0.34	0.33	0.32	0.2%	0.2%
Water heating	0.03	0.03	0.03	0.03	0.02	-1.1%	-1.2%
Other uses[2]	0.15	0.15	0.15	0.15	0.15	0.0%	0.0%

[Continued]

★ 280 ★

Commercial Sector Key Indicators and End-use Consumption, 1990-2010

[Continued]

Key Indicators and Consumption	Reference Case					Annual Growth 1990-2010 (percent)	Annual Growth 1992-2010 (percent)
	1990	1992	2000	2005	2010		
Total distillate	0.49	0.49	0.52	0.51	0.49	0.1%	0.1%
Other Fuels[3]	0.51	0.49	0.50	0.49	0.49	-0.2%	0.0%
Renewables[4]	0.01	0.01	0.03	0.03	0.03	5.2%	4.9%
Total Consumption	6.57	6.78	7.22	7.41	7.55	0.7%	0.6%

Source: Department of Energy, Energy Information Administration, Office of Integrated Analysis and Forecasting, *Annual Energy Outlook 1994: With Projections to 2010* (Washington, D.C.: U.S. Government Printing Office, January 1994), p. 62. *Primary source:* 1990 and 1992 natural gas values: Energy Information Administration (EIA), *Natural Gas Annual 1992 Volume 1* (Washington, D.C., November 1993). Projections: EIA, AEO 1994 National Energy Modeling System run AEO94B.D1221934. *Notes:* Reference-case projections. Btu=British Thermal Unit. N/A=Not applicable. Totals may not equal sum of components due to independent rounding. 1. Includes ventilation, cooking, refrigeration, and other miscellaneous commercial uses. 2. Includes cooking and other miscellaneous commercial uses. 3. Includes residual fuel oil, liquefied petroleum, gas, coal, motor gasoline, and kerosene. 4. Includes solar, geothermal, and biomass energy.

★ 281 ★

Residential, Commercial, and Industrial Energy Use

Commercial Sector Energy Use by Function, 1990-2010

[1992 dollars per million Btu]

Indicators	Reference Case				Annual Growth 1990-2010 (percent)
	1990	2000	2005	2010	
Building Energy Consumption[1] (quadrillion Btu)					
Assembly	0.45	0.42	0.39	0.37	-0.9%
Education	0.68	0.62	0.58	0.53	-1.2%
Food Sales	0.19 0	.20 0	.20 0	.21 0	.5%
Food Service	0.31	0.31	0.32	0.32	0.3%
Health Care	0.43	0.49	0.49	0.50	0.7%
Lodging	0.42	0.42	0.41	0.40	-0.2%
Office-Large	0.71	0.84	0.88	0.90	1.2%
Office-Small	0.56	0.65	0.69	0.70	1.1%
Merchantile/Service	1.09	1.29	1.39	1.48	1.5%
Warehouse	0.56	0.63	0.65	0.65	0.8%
Other	0.49	0.44	0.41	0.38	-1.3%

[Continued]

★ 281 ★

Commercial Sector Energy Use by Function, 1990-2010

[Continued]

Indicators	Reference Case				Annual Growth 1990-2010 (percent)
	1990	2000	2005	2010	
Total	5.89	6.33	6.42	6.45	0.5%
Efficiency Indicators					
Space Heating (coefficient of performance)[2]					
Electricity	1.19	1.33	1.38	1.42	0.9%
Natural Gas	0.71	0.76	0.78	0.80	0.6%
Distillate	0.72	0.87	0.80	0.81	0.6%
Space Cooling (coefficient of performance)[2]					
Electricity	2.83	3.32	3.54	3.75	1.4%
Natural Gas	1.04	1.20	1.23	1.26	1.0%
Water Heating (coefficient of performance)[2]					
Electricity	0.76	0.83	0.84	0.85	0.5%
Natural Gas	0.67	0.71	0.73	0.74	0.5%
Distillate	0.67	0.71	0.73	0.74	0.5%
Lighting Efficacy$_2$ (lumens per watt)					
Electricity	41.55	47.04	49.60	51.93	1.1%

Source: Department of Energy, Energy Information Administration, *Supplement to the Annual Energy Outlook* (Washington, D.C.: U.S. Government Printing Office, March, 1994), p. 122. *Primary source:* 1990 and Projections: EIA, AEO 1994 National Energy Modeling System run AEO94B.D1221934. *Notes:* Btu=British Thermal Unit. Totals may not equal sum of components due to independent rounding. 1. Excludes commercial sectors energy consumption (from uses such as street lights) that is not attributable to buildings. 2. Energy efficiency rating measure determined, under specific testing conditions, by dividing the energy output by the energy input. 3. A ratio of the measure of light produced by a light source to the electrical power used to produce that quality of light, expressed in lumens per watt.

★ 282 ★

Residential, Commercial, and Industrial Energy Use

Industrial Sector Key Indicators and Consumption, 1990-2010

[Quadrillion Btu per year, unless otherwise noted]

Key Indicators and Consumption	Reference Case					Annual Growth 1990-2010 (percent)	Annual Growth 1992-2010 (percent)
	1990	1992	2000	2005	2010		
Key Indicators							
Value of Gross Output (billion 1987 dollars)							
Manufacturing	2536	2552	3186	3616	4076	2.4%	2.6%
Nonmanufacturing	883	875	1061	1158	1246	1.7%	2.0%
Total	3419	3427	4247	4774	5322	2.2%	2.5%
Energy Prices (1992 dollars per million Btu)							
Electricity	15.22	14.87	15.03	15.32	16.11	0.3%	0.4%
Natural gas	3.46	3.07	3.85	4.37	4.93	1.8%	2.7%
Steam coal	1.64	1.56	1.70	1.80	1.91	0.8%	1.1%
Residual oil	3.30	2.54	3.54	4.28	4.80	1.9%	3.6%
Distillate oil	6.02	4.88	5.20	6.00	6.65	0.5%	1.7%
Liquefied petroleum gas	5.84	4.95	6.41	7.61	8.67	2.0%	3.2%
Motor gasoline	10.01	9.07	10.30	11.18	11.80	0.8%	1.5%
Metallurgical coal	1.87	1.80	2.08	2.25	2.20	0.8%	1.1%
Energy Consumption							
Consumption[1] (quadrillion Btu per year)							
Purchased electricity	3.23	3.29	3.84	4.18	4.50	1.7%	1.8%
Natural gas[2]	8.50	8.96	9.61	10.20	10.69	1.2%	1.0%
Steam coal	1.71	1.65	1.91	2.11	2.24	1.4%	1.7%
Metallurgical coal and coke[3]	1.05	0.90	0.76	0.67	0.59	-2.8%	-2.3%
Residual fuel	0.42	0.34	0.46	0.44	0.45	0.4%	1.5%
Distillate	1.18	1.19	1.37	1.47	1.56	1.4%	1.5%
Liquefied petroleum gas	1.61	1.83	1.99	2.20	2.40	2.0%	1.5%
Petrochemical feedstocks	1.10	1.23	1.32	1.46	1.59	1.9%	1.5%
Other Petroleum[4]	4.00	4.03	4.61	4.68	4.81	0.9%	1.0%
Renewables	1.96	1.99	2.40	2.62	2.84	1.9%	2.0%
Total	24.78	25.42	28.27	30.02	31.68	1.2%	1.2%
Consumption per Unit of Output[1] (thousand Btu per 1987 dollars)							
Purchased electricity	0.94	0.96	0.90	0.88	0.85	-0.5%	-0.7%
Natural gas[2]	2.49	2.61	2.26	2.14	2.01	-1.1%	-1.4%
Steam coal	0.50	0.48	0.45	0.44	0.42	-0.9%	-0.7%
Metallurgical coal and coke[3]	0.31	0.26	0.18	0.14	0.11	-4.9%	-4.6%
Residual fuel	0.12	0.10	0.11	0.09	0.08	-1.8%	-1.0%
Distillate	0.35	0.35	0.32	0.31	0.29	-0.8%	-0.9%
Liquefied petroleum gas	0.47	0.53	0.47	0.46	0.45	-0.2%	-0.9%
Petrochemical feedstocks	0.32	0.36	0.31	0.31	0.30	-0.4%	-1.0%
Other petroleum[4]	1.17	1.18	1.08	0.98	0.90	-1.3%	-1.5%

[Continued]

★ 282 ★

Industrial Sector Key Indicators and Consumption, 1990-2010

[Continued]

Key Indicators and Consumption	Reference Case					Annual Growth 1990-2010 (percent)	Annual Growth 1992-2010 (percent)
	1990	1992	2000	2005	2010		
Renewables	0.57	0.58	0.56	0.55	0.53	-0.4%	-0.5%
Total	7.25	7.41	6.66	6.29	5.95	-1.0%	-1.2%

Source: Department of Energy, Energy Information Administration, Office of Integrated Analysis and Forecasting, *Annual Energy Outlook 1994: With Projections to 2010* (Washington, D.C.: U.S. Government Printing Office, January 1994), p. 63. *Primary source:* 1990: Energy Information Administration (EIA), *State Energy Data Report* (Washington, D.C.: May 1993). 1990 and 1992 natural gas values: EIA, *Natural Gas Annual 1992 Volume 1* (Washington, D.C., November 1993). Projections: EIA, AEO 1994 National Energy Modeling System run AEO94B.D1221934. *Notes:* Reference-case projections. Btu=British Thermal Unit. Totals may not equal sum of components due to independent rounding. 1. Fuel consumption includes consumption for cogeneration. 2. Includes lease and plant fuel. 3. Includes net imports of coal coke 4. Includes petroleum coke, asphalt, road oil, lubricants, motor gasoline, still gas, and miscellaneous petroleum products.

Transportation Energy Supply and Use

★ 283 ★

Transportation Sector Key Indicators and End-use Consumption, 1990-2010

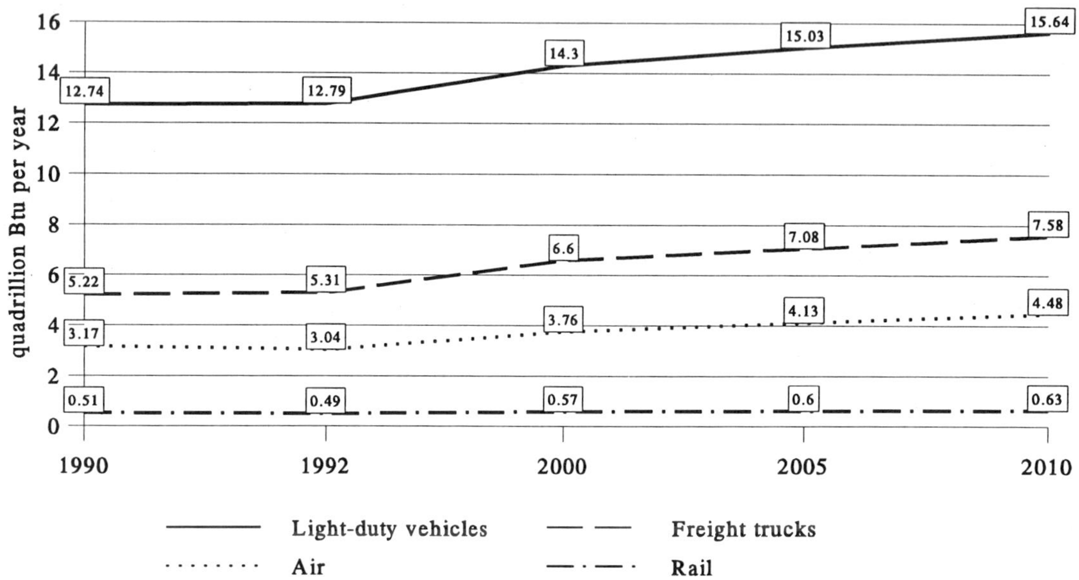

Key Indicators and Consumption	Reference Case					Annual Growth 1990-2010 (percent)	Annual Growth 1992-2010 (percent)
	1990	1992	2000	2005	2010		
Key Indicators							
Level of travel index (1990=1.0)							
Light-duty vehicles	1.00	1.01	1.18	1.29	1.38	1.6%	1.7%
Freight trucks	1.00	1.09	1.34	1.47	1.61	2.4%	2.2%
Air	1.00	1.07	1.45	1.67	1.89	3.2%	3.2%
Rail	1.00	1.04	1.16	1.25	1.34	1.5%	1.4%
Marine	1.00	0.99	1.07	1.13	1.20	0.9%	1.1%
Energy Efficiency Indicators							
New car MPG[1]	28.20	28.05	29.50	30.60	31.41	0.5%	0.6%
New light truck MPG[1]	20.91	20.98	22.41	23.38	24.16	0.7%	0.8%
Light duty fleet MPG[2]	18.90	19.26	20.21	20.90	21.63	0.7%	0.6%
Aircraft efficiency index	1.00	1.01	1.07	1.11	1.14	0.7%	0.7%
Freight truck efficiency index	1.00	1.01	1.09	1.13	1.18	0.8%	0.8%
Rail efficiency index	1.00	1.00	1.04	1.06	1.07	0.3%	0.4%
Domestic shipping efficiency index	1.00	1.00	1.01	1.01	1.02	0.1%	0.1%
Energy Use by Mode (quadrillion Btu per year)							
Light-duty vehicles[1]	12.74	12.79	14.30	15.03	15.64	1.0%	1.1%
Freight trucks[3]	5.22	5.31	6.60	7.08	7.58	1.9%	2.0%

[Continued]

★ 283 ★

Transportation Sector Key Indicators and End-use Consumption, 1990-2010

[Continued]

Key Indicators and Consumption	Reference Case					Annual Growth 1990-2010	Annual Growth 1992-2010
	1990	1992	2000	2005	2010	(percent)	(percent)
Air	3.17	3.04	3.76	4.13	4.48	1.7%	2.2%
Rail	0.51	0.49	0.57	0.60	0.63	1.0%	1.4%
Marine	1.53	1.59	1.88	2.08	2.26	2.0%	2.0%
Pipeline fuel	0.68	0.61	0.69	0.72	0.73	0.3%	1.0%
Other[4]	0.15	0.15	0.17	0.18	0.19	1.3%	1.5%
Total[5]	22.50	22.38	26.16	27.91	29.50	1.4%	1.5%

Source: Department of Energy, Energy Information Administration, Office of Integrated Analysis and Forecasting, *Annual Energy Outlook 1994: With Projections to 2010* (Washington, D.C.: U.S. Government Printing Office, January 1994), p. 64. *Primary source:* 1990: Federal Highway Administration (FHA), *Highway Statistics 1991*; Oak Ridge National Laboratory, *Transportation Energy Data Book: 12 and 13* (March 1993); Federal Aviation Administration (FAA), *Faa Aviation Forecasts Fiscal years 1993-2004*; National Highway Traffic and Safety Administration (NHTSA), *Summary of Fuel Economy Performance*, February 1993; Energy Information Administration (EIA), *Residential Transportation Energy Consumption Survey 1991*; Argonne National Laboratory, FRATE Model 1990. 1990 and 1992 natural gas values: EIA *Natural Gas Annual 1992 Volume 1* (Washington, D.C., November 1993). Projections: EIA, AEO 1994 National Energy Modeling System run AEO94B.D1221934. *Notes:* Reference-case projections. Totals of table may not equal sum of components due to independent rounding. 1. Environmental Protection Agency rated miles per gallon. 2. Combined car and light truck "on-the-road" estimate. 3. Includes light-duty trucks used for freight. 4. Includes lubricants. 5. Total will not equal sum of components due to independent rounding.

★ 284 ★

Transportation Energy Supply and Use

Transportation Sector Energy Use by Mode and Type, 1990-2010

[Trillion Btu per year]

Mode and Type	Reference Case				Annual Growth 1990-2010
	1990	2000	2005	2010	(percent)
Energy Use by Mode					
Highway					
Light-duty vehicles	12,738.1	14,295.3	15,031.6	15,640.0	1.0%
Automobiles	11,318.4	11,788.6	12,090.5	12,418.2	0.5%
Light trucks[1]	1,387.2	2,472.8	2,906.5	3,186.2	4.2%
Motorcycles	32.5	33.8	34.7	35.6	0.5%
Buses	93.7	102.2	106.9	110.4	0.8%
Freight trucks[2]	5,039.0	6,422.9	6,902.0	7,391.8	1.9%
Small(<10,000 pounds)	1,550.4	1,906.3	2,011.1	2,114.1	1.6%
Medium (10,000-19,500 pounds)	989.6	1,280.8	1,387.1	1,497.2	2.1%
Large (<19,500 pounds)	2,499.0	3,235.7	3,503.8	3,780.5	2.1%
Non-Highway					
Air[3]	2,379.9	3,190.1	3,551.8	3,898.4	2.5%
General aviation	156.5	192.4	209.4	225.3	1.8%
Domestic air carriers	1,678.0	2,062.0	2,225.7	2,392.2	1.8%
International air carriers	259.6	427.2	473.8	522.9	3.6%
Freight carriers	285.7	508.4	642.9	757.6	5.0%

[Continued]

★ 284 ★

Transportation Sector Energy Use by Mode and Type, 1990-2010

[Continued]

Mode and Type	Reference Case				Annual Growth 1990-2010
	1990	2000	2005	2010	(percent)
Water[4]	1,535.0	1,883.7	2,078.5	2,263.9	2.0%
Freight	1,291.0	1,624.6	1,812.3	1,990.2	2.2%
Domestic shipping	308.6	333.2	354.9	378.8	1.0%
International shipping	982.4	1,291.4	1,457.4	1,611.4	2.5%
Recreational boats	244.0	259.1	266.2	273.8	0.6%
Rail	512.9	566.7	596.2	626.6	1.0%
Lubricants	176.0	170.3	178.6	193.7	0.5%
Pipeline fuel natural gas	680.3	691.0	722.6	726.6	0.3%
Military Use	902.1	656.2	660.3	670.5	-1.5%
Aviation[5]	795.0	570.1	573.7	582.5	-1.5%
Residual fuel use	15.6	12.7	12.7	12.9	-0.9%
Distillate fuel use	91.5	73.4	73.9	75.0	-1.0%
Total[4]	22,506.5	26,156.9	27,905.5	29,496.6	1.4%
Energy Use by Type					
Oil	21,783.2	24,228.4	26,746.3	28,097.7	1.3%
Motor gasoline	13,577.1	15,030.2	15,497.1	15,760.7	0.7%
Distillate (diesel)	3,830.5	4,865.3	5,324.4	5,819.4	2.1%
Jet fuel (kerosene & naphtha)	3,129.5	3,717.6	4,083.2	4,438.8	1.8%
Residual oil	1,030.2	1,324.3	1,486.4	1,638.1	2.3%
Aviation gasoline	45.0	42.6	42.3	42.1	-0.3%
Liquid petroleum gas	21.8	78.2	134.4	204.7	11.9%
Lubricants	176.0	170.3	178.6	193.7	0.5%
Methanol	0.1	7.9	29.7	62.7	38.7%
Ethanol	0.2	10.6	31.6	55.2	33.4%
Electricity	14.1	84.7	132.6	191.2	13.9%
Compressed natural gas	2.1	134.3	242.8	365.2	29.4%
Liquid hydrogen	0.0	0.0	0.0	0.0	94.9%
Pipeline fuel natural gas	680.3	691.0	722.6	726.6	0.3%
Total Consumption[6]	22,506.5	26,156.9	27,905.5	29,498.6	1.4%

Source: Department of Energy, Energy Information Administration, Office of Integrated Analysis and Forecasting, *Supplement to the Annual Energy Outlook 1994* (Washington, D.C.: U.S. Government Printing Office, March 1994), p. 124. *Primary source:* 1990: Energy Information Administration (EIA), *State Energy Data Report* (Washington, D.C., May 1993); EIA, *Fuel Oil and Kerosene Sales 1991* (Washington, D.C., November 1992); Oak Ridge National Laboratory, *Transportation Energy Book: 12 and 13* (March 1993); and Department of Defense, Defense Fuel Supply Center. Projections: EIA, AEO 1994 National Energy Modeling System run AEO94B.D1221934. *Notes:* Reference-case projections. Btu=British thermal unit. Totals may not equal sum of components due to independent rounding. 1. Includes personal vehicles, fleet vehicles, and freight light trucks. 2. Does not include commercial bus and military use. 3. Does not include military jet fuel use. 4. Does not include military residual oil. 5. Includes jet fuel and naphtha use. 6. Total may not equal sum of components due to double counting of freight light truck consumption.

★ 285 ★

Transportation Energy Supply and Use

Transportation Sector Energy Use by Fuel Type within a Mode, 1990-2010

[Trillion Btu per year]

Mode and Type	Reference Case				Annual Growth 1990-2010 (percent)
	1990	2000	2005	2010	
Light-Duty Vehicles[1]					
Motor gasoline	12,516.62	13,912.13	14,388.58	14,666.35	0.8%
Methanol	0.09	7.87	29.67	62.72	38.7%
Ethanol	0.17	10.64	31.56	55.25	33.4%
Compressed natural gas	2.10	135.95	244.53	367.01	29.5%
Liquid petroleum gas	8.75	61.48	116.32	185.25	16.5%
Electricity	0.30	24.83	71.73	129.90	35.4%
Liquid Hydrogen	0.00	0.00	0.00	0.00	94.9%
Distillate (diesel)	175.19	142.51	149.34	173.66	0.0%
Total	12,738.18	14,295.40	15,031.72	15,640.14	1.0%
Freight Trucks[2]					
Motor gasoline	2,303.09	2,659.01	2,716.85	2,758.21	0.9%
Distillate (diesel)	2,722.88	3,747.08	4,169.99	4,614.15	2.7%
Methanol	0.00	0.00	0.00	0.00	N/A
Compressed natural gas	0.00	0.00	0.00	0.00	N/A
Liquid petroleum gas	13.05	16.77	18.11	19.49	2.0%
Total	5,039.02	6,422.85	6,901.95	7,391.84	1.9%
Freight Rail[3]					
Distillate (diesel)	456.87	510.01	538.64	568.61	1.1%
Total	456.87	510.01	538.64	568.61	1.1%
Domestic Shipping					
Distillate (diesel)	214.19	231.25	246.36	262.96	1.0%
Residual oil	94.37	101.92	108.55	115.82	1.0%
Motor gasoline	0.00	0.00	0.00	0.00	N/A
Total	368.56	333.17	354.91	378.77	1.0%
International Shipping					
Distillate (diesel)	62.20	81.74	92.27	102.06	2.5%
Residual oil	920.24	1,209.70	1,365.11	1,509.33	2.5%
Total	982.44	1,291.44	1,457.38	1,611.38	2.5%
Air Transportation					
Jet fuel	2,334.55	3,147.50	3,509.52	3,856.30	2.5%
Aviation gasoline	45.36	42.56	42.26	42.14	-0.4%
Total	2,379.90	3,190.06	3,551.06	3,898.44	2.5%
Miscellaneous Transportation Military Use					
Jet fuel (kerosene)	451.55	334.13	336.23	341.44	-1.4%
Jet fuel (naphtha)	343.40	235.95	237.43	241.11	-1.8%
Residual fuel	15.58	12.66	12.74	12.94	-0.9%
Distillate	91.52	73.41	73.87	75.02	-1.0%

[Continued]

★ 285 ★

Transportation Sector Energy Use by Fuel Type within a Mode, 1990-2010

[Continued]

Mode and Type	Reference Case				Annual Growth 1990-2010 (percent)
	1990	2000	2005	2010	
Total	902.06	656.16	660.28	670.51	-1.5%
Bus Transportation					
Total	93.73	102.21	106.86	110.45	0.8%
Rail Transportation					
Total	56.07	56.66	57.55	57.96	0.2%
Recreation Boats	243.99	259.07	266.20	273.77	0.6%
Lubricants	176.00	170.32	178.61	193.71	0.5%
Pipeline Fuel Natural Gas	680.27	690.97	722.57	726.64	0.3%
Total Miscellaneous	2,195.42	1,935.40	1,992.06	2,033.05	-0.4%
Total Consumption	22,506.50	26,156.91	27,905.48	29,498.64	1.4%

Source: Department of Energy, Energy Information Administration, Office of Integrated Analysis and Forecasting, *Supplement to the Annual Energy Outlook 1994* (Washington, D.C.: U.S. Government Printing Office, March 1994), p. 125-2. *Primary source:* 1990: Energy Information Administration (EIA), *State Energy Data Report* (Washington, D.C., May 1993); EIA, *Fuel Oil and Kerosene Sales 1991* (Washington, D.C., November 1992); Oak Ridge National Laboratory, *Transportation Energy Book: 12 and 13* (March 1993); and Department of Defense, Defense Fuel Supply Center. Projections: EIA, AEO 1994 National Energy Modeling System run AEO94B.D1221934. *Notes:* Reference-case projections. N/A=Not applicable. Totals may not equal sum of components due to independent rounding. 1. Includes personal vehicles, fleet vehicles, and freight light trucks. 2. Freight light trucks are included in both light duty vehicles and freight trucks. Does not include military distillate. Does not include commercial buses. 3. Does not include passenger rail.

★ 286 ★

Transportation Energy Supply and Use

Light-duty Vehicle Energy Consumption by Technology and Fuel Type, 1990-2010

[Trillion Btu per year]

Technology Type	Reference Case				Annual Growth 1990-2010 (percent)
	1990	2000	2005	2010	
Light-Duty Consum. by Tech. Type					
Conventional Vehicles[1]					
Gasoline ICE vehicles	12.516.55	13,903.49	14,349.06	14,567.02	0.8%
Distillate (diesel) ICE	175.19	142.51	149.34	173.66	0.0%
Alternative-Fuel Vehicles					
Alcohol Fuel Technology					
Methanol-flex fuel ICE	0.12	9.84	35.18	74.60	37.9%
Methanol-neat ICE	0.00	0.10	0.91	3.57	51.0%
Ethanol-flex fuel ICE	0.20	13.04	39.59	67.62	33.7%

[Continued]

★ 286 ★

Light-duty Vehicle Energy Consumption by Technology and Fuel Type, 1990-2010

[Continued]

Technology Type	Reference Case				Annual Growth 1990-2010 (percent)
	1990	2000	2005	2010	
Ethanol-neat ICE	0.00	0.08	0.84	3.31	55.3%
Total Alcohol	0.32	23.06	76.52	149.10	35.9%
Natural Gas Technology					
Compressed natural gas ICE	2.10	134.30	242.79	365.26	29.4%
Liquid petroleum gas ICE	8.75	63.13	118.06	187.12	16.5%
Total Natural Gas	45.82	197.43	360.85	552.38	13.3%
Electric Technology					
Electric vehicle	0.30	20.75	47.52	82.00	32.4%
Electric hybrid	0.00	8.06	45.95	77.94	93.7%
Electric hybrid 2 stroke	0.00	0.09	2.43	16.82	99.2%
Electric hybrid turbine	0.00	0.00	0.05	1.12	N/A
Total Electricity	0.30	28.90	95.94	177.87	37.6%
Turbine Technology					
Gas turbine gasoline	0.00	0.00	0.00	0.00	N/A
Gas turbine compressed natural gas	0.00	0.00	0.00	0.01	N/A
Total turbine	0.00	0.00	0.00	0.07	N/A
Fuel Cell Technology					
Fuel cell methanol	0.00	0.00	0.00	0.00	95.0%
Fuel cell hydrogen	0.00	0.00	0.00	0.00	94.9%
Total fuel cell	0.00	0.00	0.00	0.00	94.9%
Light-Duty Consumption by Fuel Type[1]					
Motor gasoline	12,516.62	13,912.13	14,388.58	14,668.35	0.8%
Distillate (diesel)	175.19	142.51	149.34	173.66	0.0%
Methanol	0.09	7.87	29.67	62.72	38.7%
Ethanol	0.17	10.64	31.56	55.25	33.4%
Compressed natural gas	2.10	135.95	244.53	367.01	29.5%
Liquid petroleum gas	8.75	61.48	116.32	185.25	16.5%
Electricity	0.30	24.83	71.73	129.90	35.4%
Liquid hydrogen	0.00	0.00	0.00	0.00	94.9%

Source: Department of Energy, Energy Information Administration, Office of Integrated Analysis and Forecasting, *Supplement to the Annual Energy Outlook 1994* (Washington, D.C.: U.S. Government Printing Office, March 1994), p. 127. *Primary source:* 1990 and Projections: EIA, AEO 1994 National Energy Modeling System run AEO94B.D1221934. *Notes:* N/A=Not applicable. ICE=Internal Combustion Engine. 1. Includes personal vehicles, fleet vehicles, and freight line trucks. Includes both cars and trucks.

★ 287 ★

Transportation Energy Supply and Use

Light-duty Vehicle MPG by Technology Type, 1990-2010

[MPG gasoline equivalents]

Technology Type	Reference Case				Annual Growth 1990-2010 (percent)
	1990	2000	2005	2010	
Automobiles[1]					
Conventional Vehicles					
Gasoline ICE vehicles	28.16	29.44	30.45	31.13	0.5%
Distillate (diesel) ICE	30.26	31.63	32.67	33.37	0.5%
Alternate-Fuel Vehicles					
Alcohol Fuel Technology					
Methanol-flex fuel ICE	28.75	31.80	34.38	35.31	1.0%
Methanol-neat ICE	30.83	32.22	33.28	34.00	0.5%
Ethanol-flex fuel ICE	29.71	31.42	32.16	33.05	0.5%
Ethanol-neat ICE	32.83	34.31	35.44	36.20	0.5%
Natural Gas Technology					
Compressed natural gas ICE	27.02	28.44	28.99	29.62	0.5%
Liquid Petroleum gas ICE	36.73	38.67	39.40	40.26	0.5%
Electric Technology					
Electric vehicle	43.40	45.30	46.28	47.44	0.4%
Electric hybrid	39.96	40.62	42.02	42.91	0.4%
Electric hybrid 2 stroke	39.96	41.77	42.15	43.07	0.4%
Electric hybrid turbine	39.96	41.77	43.14	42.69	0.3%
Turbine Technology					
Gas turbine gasoline	37.11	38.79	40.06	40.93	0.5%
Gas turbine compressed natural gas	37.11	38.79	40.06	40.93	0.5%
Fuel Cell Technology					
Fuel cell methanol	45.67	47.74	49.31	50.37	0.5%
Fuel cell hydrogen	45.67	47.74	49.31	50.37	0.5%
Average New Car MPG	28.20	29.50	30.60	31.41	0.5%
Light-Duty Trucks[2]					
Conventional Vehicles					
Gasoline ICE vehicles	20.72	22.19	23.00	23.59	0.6%
Distillate (diesel) ICE	28.76	29.98	30.97	31.64	0.5%
Alternative-Fuel Vehicles					
Alcohol Fuel Technology					
Methanol-flex fuel ICE	27.32	31.66	33.07	33.90	1.1%
Methanol-neat ICE	29.30	30.55	31.56	32.24	0.5%
Ethanol-flex fuel ICE	29.26	29.96	30.72	31.45	0.4%
Ethanol-neat ICE	31.20	32.53	33.60	34.33	0.5%

[Continued]

★ 287 ★

Light-duty Vehicle MPG by Technology Type, 1990-2010

[Continued]

Technology Type	Reference Case				Annual Growth 1990-2010
	1990	2000	2005	2010	(percent)
Natural Gas Technology					
Compressed natural gas ICE	25.92	26.97	27.89	28.49	0.5%
Liquid petroleum gas ICE	35.48	36.92	38.18	39.01	0.5%
Electric Technology					
Electric vehicle	40.80	42.58	44.39	45.29	0.5%
Electric hybrid	37.98	40.39	42.02	42.95	0.6%
Electric hybrid 2 stroke	37.98	39.60	42.03	42.95	0.6%
Electric hybrid turbine	37.98	39.60	40.91	42.95	0.6%
Turbine Technology					
Gas turbine gasoline	35.27	36.77	37.99	38.80	0.5%
Gas turbine compressed natural gas	35.27	36.77	37.99	38.80	0.5%
Fuel Cell Technology					
Fuel cell methanol	43.41	45.26	46.75	47.76	0.5%
Fuel cell hydrogen	43.41	45.26	46.75	47.76	0.5%
Average New Truck MPG	20.91	22.41	23.38	24.16	0.7%
Fleet Average Stock Car MPG[3]	20.28	22.02	22.91	23.78	0.8%
Fleet Average Stock Truck MPG[3]	15.04	16.65	17.37	18.04	0.9%
Fleet Average Stock Vehicle MPG[3]	18.90	20.21	20.90	21.63	0.7%

Source: Department of Energy, Energy Information Administration, Office of Integrated Analysis and Forecasting, *Supplement to the Annual Energy Outlook 1994* (Washington, D.C.: U.S. Government Printing Office, March 1994), pp. 132-33. *Primary source:* 1990: Decision Analysis Corporation of Virginia and Science Applications U\International Corporation, "Alternative-fuel Vehicle Model Database," Draft Report, Subtask 4. Prepared for EIA, 15 September 1992; Department of Energy, IDEAS Model, Prepared by Energy and Environmental Analysis Inc. for the Office of Domestic and International Energy Policy; National Highway Traffic and Safety Administration, "Summary of Fuel Economy Performance" (February 1993). Projections: EIA, AEO 1994 National Energy Modeling System run AEO94B.D1221934. *Notes:* MPG=Miles Per Gallon. ICE=Internal Combustion Engine. 1. Fuel efficiencies are EPA rated. Includes personal and fleet vehicles. 2. Fuel efficiencies are EPA rated. Includes personal vehicles, fleet vehicles, and freight light trucks. 3. Stock values are on-road efficiencies. Includes personal vehicles, fleet vehicles and freight light trucks.

★ 288 ★

Transportation Energy Supply and Use

Air Travel Energy Use, 1990-2010

Indicators	Reference Case				Annual Growth 1990-2010 (percent)
	1990	2000	2005	2010	
Travel Demand (billion of miles)					
Revenue passenger miles domestic	362.7	478.0	532.9	590.6	2.5%
RPM personal	195.2	258.2	284.1	314.6	2.4%
RPM business	166.9	219.2	248.2	275.4	2.5%
Load factor domestic[1]	0.6	0.6	0.6	0.6	N/A
Revenue passenger miles international	126.7	223.8	256.3	291.8	4.3%
Load factor international[1]	0.7	0.7	0.7	0.7	N/A
Revenue ton miles freight (billion)	10.1	19.3	25.2	30.6	5.7%
GDP (billion 1986 dollars)	4,877.4	6,040.7	6,736.3	7,396.7	2.1%
Exports (billion 1987 dollars)	509.9	922.2	1,233.6	1,529.6	5.6%
Ticket price (yield, 1987 cents per passenger mile)	14.1	13.6	14.2	14.8	0.2%
Operating cost (1987 dollars per available seat-mile)					
Fuel cost (1991 dollars per thousand Btu)	5.0	4.5	5.1	5.7	0.6%
Seat miles demanded (billion)	786.6	1.137.7	1,310.3	1,484.9	3.2%
Aircraft Sales					
Narrow body aircraft	279	244	206	225	-1.1%
Wide body aircraft	55	76	80	90	2.5%
Aircraft Stock					
Narrow body aircraft	3,675	4,806	5,265	5,675	2.2%
Wide body aircraft	721	1,170	1,415	1,676	4.3%
Aircraft New Efficiency (seat miles per gallon)					
Narrow body aircraft	44.1	49.4	51.0	52.6	0.9%
Wide body aircraft	55.1	60.3	61.7	63.8	0.7%
Average aircraft efficiency	45.6	51.6	53.6	55.4	1.0%
Aircraft Stock Efficiency (seat miles per gallon)					
Narrow body aircraft	44.0	47.1	48.6	50.2	0.7%
Wide body aircraft	55.0	57.6	58.9	60.2	0.5%
Average aircraft stock efficiency	48.2	51.8	53.5	55.1	0.7%
Seat Miles Demanded (billion)					
Narrow body aircraft	440.5	576.2	631.1	680.1	2.2%
Wide body aircraft	346.1	561.5	679.2	804.8	4.3%
Fuel Consumption (trillion Btu) Commercial					
Jet fuel	2,334.5	3,147.5	3,509.5	3,856.3	2.5%
Aviation Gasoline	45.4	42.6	42.3	42.1	-0.4%

[Continued]

★ 288 ★

Air Travel Energy Use, 1990-2010

[Continued]

Indicators	Reference Case				Annual Growth 1990-2010 (percent)
	1990	2000	2005	2010	
Military					
Jet fuel	795.0	570.1	573.7	582.5	-1.5%

Source: Department of Energy, Energy Information Administration, Office of Integrated Analysis and Forecasting, *Supplement to the Annual Energy Outlook 1994* (Washington, D.C.: U.S. Government Printing Office, March 1994), p. 139. *Primary source:* Federal Aviation Administration (FAA), *FAA Aviation Forecasts, Fiscal Years 1991-2002*, and previous editions; United States Department of Transportation (DOT), Research and Special Programs Administration (RSPA), *Fuel Cost and Consumption Tables*, annual summaries, 1979-1990; DOT, RSPA, *Air Carrier Financial Statistics Quarterly*, December 1990/1989, and prior issues; DOT, RSPA, *Air Carrier Traffic Statistics Monthly*, December 1990/1989, and prior issues; Greene, D.L., "Energy Efficiency Improvement Potential of Commercial Aircraft to 2010," ORNL-6622, 6/1990; and Rathi, A., B. Peterson, and D. Greene, *Air Transport Energy Use Model*, Oak Ridge National Laboratory, April 1991, Draft. Projections: EIA, AEO 1994 National Energy Modeling System run AEO94B.D1221934. *Notes:* 1. Fraction of seats filled. RPM=Revenue Passenger Miles. GDP=Gross Domestic Product. Btu=British thermal unit. N/A=Not Applicable.

★ 289 ★

Transportation Energy Supply and Use

Freight Transportation Energy Use, 1990-2010

Technology and Fuel	Reference Case				Annual Growth 1990-2010 (percent)
	1990	2000	2005	2010	
Trucks					
Fuel Efficiency (miles per gallon of fuel)					
Small (10,000 pounds)					
Gasoline	14.18	15.44	16.09	16.67	0.8%
Diesel	17.14	18.66	19.44	20.15	0.8%
Alcohol	15.81	17.21	17.94	18.59	0.8%
Liquid petroleum gas	15.81	17.21	17.94	18.59	0.8%
Medium (10,000-19,500 pounds)					
Gasoline	6.83	7.08	7.20	7.27	0.3%
Diesel	7.49	7.76	7.88	7.97	0.3%
Alcohol	5.04	5.22	5.30	5.36	0.3%
Liquid petroleum gas	5.04	5.22	5.30	5.36	0.3%
Heavy (>19,500 pounds)					
Gasoline	5.43	5.62	5.71	5.78	0.3%
Diesel	5.33	5.52	5.61	5.67	0.3%
Alcohol	5.02	5.20	5.29	5.35	0.3%
Liquid petroleum gas	5.02	5.20	5.29	5.35	0.3%
Vehicle Miles Traveled (billion)					
Small (<10,000 pounds)	170.34	227.81	250.66	273.40	2.4%
Gasoline	166.02	217.89	236.40	253.14	2.1%
Diesel	4.17	9.72	14.04	20.02	8.2%

[Continued]

★ 289 ★

Freight Transportation Energy Use, 1990-2010

[Continued]

Technology and Fuel	Reference Case				Annual Growth 1990-2010 (percent)
	1990	2000	2005	2010	
Alcohol	0.00	0.00	0.00	0.00	N/A
Liquid petroleum gas	0.15	0.21	0.23	0.25	2.4%
Medium (10,000-19,500 pounds)	51.96	69.49	76.46	83.40	2.4%
Gasoline	36.57	42.69	43.28	43.05	0.8%
Diesel	15.03	26.30	32.64	39.76	5.0%
Alcohol	0.00	0.00	0.00	0.00	N/A
Liquid petroleum gas	0.37	0.49	0.54	0.59	2.4%
Heavy (<19,500 pounds)	93.38	124.88	137.41	149.88	2.4%
Gasoline	4.07	2.04	1.36	0.90	-7.3%
Diesel	89.25	122.77	135.97	148.89	2.6%
Alcohol	0.00	0.00	0.00	0.00	N/A
Liquid petroleum gas	0.06	0.07	0.08	0.09	2.4%
Total Vehicle Miles Traveled Trucks	315.68	422.18	464.53	506.68	2.4%
Trucks					
Fuel Consumption (trillion Btu)					
Diesel	2,722.88	3,747.08	4,166.99	4,614.15	2.7%
Motor gasoline	2,303.09	2,659.01	2,716.85	2,758.21	0.9%
Alcohol	0.00	0.00	0.00	0.00	N/A
Liquid petroleum gas	13.05	16.77	18.11	19.49	2.0%
Railroads					
Tons miles by rail (billion ton miles)	898.99	1,046.40	1,119.74	1,200.59	1.5%
Fuel efficiency (ton miles per 1,000 Btu)	2.03	2.12	2.15	2.18	0.3%
Fuel consumption (trillion Btu)					
Diesel (distillate)	456.87	510.01	538.64	568.61	1.1%
Residual oil	0.00	0.00	0.00	0.00	N/A
Electricity	0.00	0.00	0.00	0.00	N/A
Domestic Shipping					
Ton miles shipping (billion ton miles)	771.11	825.87	874.96	928.72	0.9%
Fuel efficiency (ton miles per 1,000 Btu)	0.37	0.37	0.38	0.38	0.1%
Fuel consumption (trillion Btu)					
Diesel (distillate)	214.19	231.25	246.36	262.96	1.0%
Residual oil	94.37	101.92	108.55	115.82	1.0%
Motor gasoline	0.00	0.00	0.00	0.00	N/A
International Shipping					
Gross trade (billion 1987 dollars)	1,071.73	1,836.96	2,333.07	2,847.05	5.0%
Exports (billion 1987 dollars)	509.93	922.21	1,233.55	1,529.59	5.6%
Imports (billion 1987 dollars)	561.80	914.75	1,099.52	1,317.46	4.4%

[Continued]

★ 289 ★

Freight Transportation Energy Use, 1990-2010

[Continued]

Technology and Fuel	Reference Case				Annual Growth 1990-2010 (percent)
	1990	2000	2005	2010	
Fuel consumption (million Btu)					
Diesel (distillate)	62.20	81.74	92.27	102.06	2.5%
Residual oil	920.24	1,209.70	1,365.11	1,509.33	2.5%

Source: Department of Energy, Energy Information Administration, Office of Integrated Analysis and Forecasting, *Supplement to the Annual Energy Outlook 1994* (Washington, D.C.: U.S. Government Printing Office, March 1994), pp. 140-41. *Primary source:* Oak Ridge National Laboratory, *Transportation Energy Book: 12 and 13* (March 1993); Argonne National Laboratory, *FRATE Model*, 1990; United States Department of Transportation, *1989 Carload Waybill Statistics Traffic and Revenue by Commodity Classes*, September 1991 and prior issues; Reebie Associates, *TRANSEARCH Database* (Greenwich, CN, 1989); and Army Corps of Engineers, *Waterborne Commerce of the United States* (New Orleans), 1991 and prior issues. Projections: EIA, AEO 1994 National Energy Modeling System run AEO94B.D1221934. *Note:* Btu=British thermal unit. N/A=Not applicable.

Coal

★ 290 ★

Coal Supply, Disposition, and Prices, 1990-2010

[Million short tons per year, unless otherwise noted]

Supply Disposition and Prices	Reference Case					Annual Growth 1990-2010 (percent)	Annual Growth 1992-2010 (percent)
	1990	1992	2000	2005	2010		
Production[1]							
East of the Mississippi	630	589	630	630	650	0.2%	0.5%
West of the Mississippi	399	409	451	491	573	1.8%	1.9%
Total[2]	1029	998	1081	1121	1223	0.9%	1.1%
Net Imports							
Imports	3	4	10	10	11	7.1%	5.9%
Exports	106	103	133	144	152	1.8%	2.2%
Total	-103	-99	-123	-134	-142	1.6%	2.0%
Total Supply	926	899	358	987	1081	0.8%	1.0%
Consumption by Sector							
Residential and commercial	7	6	6	6	5	-1.0%	-0.8%
Industrial	76	74	87	94	101	1.5%	1.8%
Coke plants	39	32	28	24	21	-2.9%	-2.2%
Electricity[3]	774	780	837	862	950	1.0%	1.1%
Total	895	892	958	987	1079	0.9%	1.1%

[Continued]

★ 290 ★

Coal Supply, Disposition, and Prices, 1990-2010

[Continued]

Supply Disposition and Prices	Reference Case					Annual Growth 1990-2010 (percent)	Annual Growth 1992-2010 (percent)
	1990	1992	2000	2005	2010		
Discrepancy and Stock Change[4]	31	-6	0	0	3	-11.3%	N/A
Average Minemouth Price							
(1992 dollars per short ton)	23.22	21.03	25.29	27.00	30.87	1.4%	2.2%
Delivered Prices (1992 dollar per short ton)							
Industrial	35.85	32.78	37.43	40.37	42.30	0.8%	1.4%
Coke plants	50.93	47.92	55.81	60.38	58.91	0.7%	1.2%
Electricity	32.49	29.36	34.11	35.52	40.32	1.1%	1.8%
Average[5]	33.59	30.32	35.05	36.60	40.88	1.0%	1.7%
Average price to all users							
(1992 dollars per million Btu)	1.58	1.42	1.64	1.71	1.92	1.0%	1.7%
Exports[6]	45.49	41.34	50.96	54.71	55.95	1.0%	1.7%

Source: Department of Energy, Energy Information Administration, Office of Integrated Analysis and Forecasting, *Annual Energy Outlook 1994: With Projections to 2010* (Washington, D.C.: U.S. Government Printing Office, January 1994), p. 72. *Primary source:* 1990: Energy Information Administration (EIA), *Quarterly Coal Report* (Washington, D.C., May 1991), and EIA, *Coal Production* (Washington, D.C., September 1991). 1992: EIA, *Quarterly Coal Report* (Washington, D.C., November 1993), and EIA, *Coal Production* (Washington, D.C., October 1993). Projections: EIA, AEO 1994 National Energy Modeling System run AEO94B.D1221934. *Notes:* Reference case projections. Btu=British thermal unit. N/A=Not Applicable. Totals may not equal sum of components due to independent rounding. 1. Includes anthracite, bituminous coal, and lignite. 2. Production plus net imports. 3. Includes consumption by cogenerators. 4. Includes consumption by independent power producers. 5. Balancing item: the sum of production and net imports, minus total consumption. 6. Free alongside ship price at U.S. port of exit.

★ 291 ★

Coal

U.S. Domestic Coal Supply, Disposition, and Prices, 1990-2010

Supply Disposition and Prices	Reference Case				Annual Growth 1990-2010 (percent)
	1990	2000	2005	2010	
Sources of Supply (million short tons)					
Distribution From					
Northern Appalachia	148.6	175.4	187.8	216.4	1.9%
Southern Appalachia	232.9	245.3	255.0	266.9	0.7%
Interior	204.0	173.8	156.0	154.3	-1.4%
Northern Great Plains	250.2	284.4	296.8	339.9	1.5%
Other west	77.5	68.7	81.2	92.8	0.9%
Non-contiguous	0.8	0.4	0.4	0.4	-3.2%

[Continued]

★ 291 ★

U.S. Domestic Coal Supply, Disposition, and Prices, 1990-2010

[Continued]

Supply Disposition and Prices	Reference Case				Annual Growth 1990-2010
	1990	2000	2005	2010	(percent)
Total Distribution (excludes exports)[1]	914.0	947.9	977.1	1,070.8	0.8%
Imports	2.7	9.7	10.0	10.6	71.%
Total Supply	916.6	967.6	987.1	1,061.4	0.8%
Consumption (million short tons)					
Residential/commercial	6.7	6.1	5.9	5.5	-1.0%
Industrial	76.3	86.9	94.1	101.4	1.4%
Coke plants	38.9	27.8	24.3	21.4	-3.0%
Electricity	773.5	836.9	862.4	950.4	1.0%
Total Consumption	895.5	957.7	966.8	1,078.6	0.9%
Discrepancy[2]	21.2	-0.2	0.3	2.8	-9.7%
Delivered Prices (1992 dollars per short ton)					
Industrial	35.85	37.43	40.37	42.30	0.8%
Coke plants	50.93	55.81	60.38	58.91	0.7%
Electricity	32.49	34.11	35.52	40.32	1.1%
Average Price[3]	33.16	35.05	36.60	40.88	1.1%

Source: Department of Energy, Energy Information Administration, Office of Integrated Analysis and Forecasting, *Supplement to the Annual Energy Outlook 1994* (Washington, D.C.: U.S. Government Printing Office, March 1994), p. 206. *Primary source:* 1990: Energy Information Administration (EIA), *Coal Distribution January-December 1990* (Washington, D.C., April 1991). 1990 imports: U.S. Bureau of the Census, Form IM-145. 1990 consumer stock withdrawals: EIA, *Quarterly Coal Report, October-December 1991* (Washington, D.C., May 1992), and EIA, *Quarterly Coal Report, October-December 1990* (Washington, D.C., May 1991). 1990 consumption: residential/ commercial, electricity, total industrial, and total consumption: EIA *State Energy Consumption Report, Consumption Estimates 1960-1990* (Washington, D.C., May 1992). Other 1990 industrial and coke plant consumption estimated from sectorial coal distribution: *Quarterly Coal Report, October-December 1990* (Washington, D.C., May 1991). 1990 delivered prices: *Quarterly Coal Report, October-December 1990* (Washington, D.C., May 1991). Projections: EIA, AEO 1994 National Energy Modeling System run AEO94B.D1221934. *Notes:* N/A=Not Applicable. Totals may not equal sum of components due to independent rounding. 1. Excludes distribution to unknown destinations to unknown origins. 2. Includes stock changes. 3. Weighted average.

★ 292 ★

Coal

Coal Production by Region and Type, 1990-2010

[Million short tons per year]

Supply Regions and Coal Types	Reference Case 1990	2000	2005	2010	Annual Growth 1990-2010 (percent)
Appalachia	488.99	523.63	546.76	582.48	0.9%
Bituminous	488.99	523.63	546.76	582.48	0.9%
Low sulfur	60.85	131.39	156.60	188.70	5.8%
Medium sulfur	339.04	309.15	297.22	296.51	-0.7%
High sulfur	89.11	83.09	92.97	97.26	0.4%
Lignite (medium sulfur)	0.00	0.00	0.00	0.00	N/A
Interior	205.65	179.34	162.93	168.99	-1.0%
Bituminous	147.07	117.58	97.15	93.16	-2.3%
Low sulfur	0.77	0.88	2.12	2.27	5.6%
Medium sulfur	18.94	35.56	44.17	50.99	5.1%
High sulfur	127.36	81.14	50.86	39.90	-5.6%
Lignite	58.59	61.76	65.79	75.82	1.3%
Medium sulfur	43.18	48.74	50.07	63.48	1.9%
High sulfur	15.40	13.02	15.72	12.35	-1.1%
West	334.43	377.78	411.41	471.43	1.7%
Bituminous	60.65	62.25	83.01	108.70	3.0%
Low sulfur	54.82	56.82	75.18	95.34	2.8%
Medium sulfur	5.83	5.43	7.81	13.35	4.2%
High sulfur	0.00	0.00	0.02	0.01	N/A
Sub-Bituminous	244.27	287.11	298.86	329.54	1.5%
Low sulfur	189.61	233.17	241.81	248.48	1.4%
Medium sulfur	53.60	52.72	55.63	79.46	2.0%
High sulfur	1.07	1.22	1.42	1.59	2.0%
Lignite	29.50	28.43	29.55	33.20	0.6%
Low sulfur	0.10	0.08	0.09	0.10	-0.1%
Medium sulfur	26.55	25.64	26.67	29.84	0.6%
High sulfur	2.86	2.71	2.78	3.27	0.7%
Subtotals: All Regions					
Bituminous	696.71	703.46	726.94	784.34	0.6%
Sub-bituminous	244.27	287.11	298.86	329.54	1.5%
Lignite	88.09	90.18	95.33	109.02	1.1%
Low sulfur	306.15	422.34	475.80	534.89	2.8%
Medium sulfur	487.14	477.24	481.57	533.63	0.5%

[Continued]

★ 292 ★

Coal Production by Region and Type, 1990-2010

[Continued]

Supply Regions and Coal Types	Reference Case				Annual Growth 1990-2010 (percent)
	1990	2000	2005	2010	
High sulfur	235.79	181.17	163.76	154.37	-2.1%
U.S. Total	1,029.06	1,060.75	1,121.13	1,222.89	0.9%

Source: Department of Energy, Energy Information Administration, Office of Integrated Analysis and Forecasting, *Supplement to the Annual Energy Outlook 1994* (Washington, D.C.: U.S. Government Printing Office, March 1994), p. 208. *Primary source:* 1990: Energy Information Administration (EIA), *Coal Production 1990* (Washington, D.C., September 1991), Tables 1 and 5. Projections: EIA, AEO 1994 National Energy Modeling System run AEO94B.D1221934. *Notes:* Appalachia: PA, OH, MD, WV, VA, TN, AL, GA, EAST KY. Interior: MI, IL, IN, IA, MO, KS, AR, OK, LA, TX, WEST KY. West: ND, SD, MT, WY, CO, UT, AZ, NM, WA, OR, AK, CA. Sulfur definitions: Low Sulfur=0-0.60 pounds of sulfur per million Btu; Medium Sulfur=0.61-1.67 pounds of sulfur per million Btu; High Sulfur=Over 1.67 pounds of sulfur per million Btu. Btu=British thermal unit. N/A=Not Applicable. Totals may not equal sum of components due to independent rounding.

★ 293 ★

Coal

Comparative Coal Forecasts, 2000-2010

[Million short tons, except where noted]

Projection	EIA AEO94			Other Forecasts		
	Reference	High Economic Growth	Low Economic Growth	DRI	GRI	WEFA
2000						
Production	1,081	1,094	1,065	1,090	1,091	1,060
Consumption by Sector						
Electricity	837	847	822	844	863	847
Coking plants	28	28	28	32	26	32
Industrial/other	93	95	90	105	78	79
Total	958	971	939	981	973	958
Net Coal Exports	123	123	123	109	117	102
Minemouth Price (1992 dollars per short ton)	25.29	26.86	25.13	NA	NA	24.99
Average Delivered Price: Electricity (1992 dollars per short ton)	34.11	35.60	33.72	29.66	26.66	34.28

[Continued]

★ 293 ★

Comparative Coal Forecasts, 2000-2010

[Continued]

Projection	EIA AEO94 Reference	EIA AEO94 High Economic Growth	EIA AEO94 Low Economic Growth	Other Forecasts DRI	Other Forecasts GRI	Other Forecasts WEFA
2010						
Production	1,223	1,287	1,165	1,379	1,333	1,278
Consumption by Sector						
Electricity	950	1,006	901	1,004	1,077	1,053
Coking plants	21	22	21	29	22	28
Industrial/other	107	114	101	204	82	84
Total	1,079	1,142	1,023	1,237	1,182	1,165
Net Coal Exports	142	142	142	136	146	112
Minemouth Price (1992 dollars per short ton)	30.87	32.95	29.97	NA	NA	27.08
Average Delivered Price: Electricity (1992 dollars per short ton)	40.32	43.17	38.91	33.03	24.98	41.13

Source: Department of Energy, Energy Information Administration, Office of Integrated Analysis and Forecasting, *Annual Energy Outlook 1994: With Projections to 2010* (Washington, D.C.: U.S. Government Printing Office, January 1994), p. 168. *Primary source:* EIA, AEO94 Forecasting System, runs AEO94B.D1221934 (Reference Case), HMAC94.D1221932 (High Economic Growth Case), and LMAC94.D1221932 (Low Economic Growth Case). DRI: DRI/McGraw-Hill, *Energy Review* (Second Quarter 1993). GRI: Gas Research Institute, *GRI Baseline Projection of U.S. Energy Supply and Demand*, 1994 edition (August 1993). WEFA: The Wharton Econometric Forecasting Associates (WEFA) Group, *Coal and Electricity Report* (Summer 1993). *Note:* NA=Not Applicable.

★ 294 ★

Coal

Coal Production and Minemouth Prices by Region, 1990-2010

Supply Regions	Reference Case 1990	Reference Case 2000	Reference Case 2005	Reference Case 2010	Annual Growth 1990-2010 (percent)
Production (million short tons per year)					
Northern Appalachia	165.90	181.86	198.20	229.80	1.6%
Southern Appalachia	323.10	341.77	348.59	352.68	0.4%
Interior	205.70	179.34	162.93	168.99	-1.0%
North Great Plains	251.10	294.19	308.06	349.47	1.7%
Other West	81.60	81.87	101.65	119.77	1.9%
Non-contiguous	1.70	1.72	1.71	2.19	1.3%
Appalachian	489.00	523.63	546.79	582.48	0.9%
Interior	205.70	179.34	162.93	168.99	-1.0%
West	334.40	377.78	411.41	471.43	1.7%

[Continued]

★ 294 ★

Coal Production and Minemouth Prices by Region, 1990-2010

[Continued]

Supply Regions	Reference Case				Annual Growth 1990-2010 (percent)
	1990	2000	2005	2010	
East of Mississippi River	630.20	629.89	629.68	649.85	0.2%
West of Mississippi River	398.90	450.87	491.44	573.05	1.8%
U.S. Total	1,029.10	1,080.75	1,121.13	1,222.90	0.9%
Minemouth Prices (1992 dollars per short ton)					
Northern Appalachia	W	32.39	34.76	35.05	N/A
Southern Appalachia	W	36.20	40.13	39.76	N/A
Interior	22.89	21.81	22.12	23.33	0.1%
North Great Plains	9.06	10.14	10.75	24.06	5.0%
Other West	W	26.13	24.06	27.35	N/A
Non-contiguous	W	21.87	20.90	22.04	N/A
Appalachia	30.83	34.88	38.18	37.90	1.0%
Interior	22.89	21.81	22.12	23.33	0.1%
West	12.38	13.66	14.08	24.89	3.6%
East of Mississippi River	29.98	33.43	37.02	37.34	1.1%
West of Mississippi River	12.60	13.92	14.17	23.53	3.2%
U.S. Total	23.22	25.29	27.00	30.87	1.4%

Source: Department of Energy, Energy Information Administration, Office of Integrated Analysis and Forecasting, *Supplement to the Annual Energy Outlook 1994* (Washington, D.C.: U.S. Government Printing Office, March 1994), p. 207. *Primary source:* 1990 distribution: Energy Information Administration (EIA), *Coal Production 1990* (Washington, D.C., September 1991), Tables 1, 17, and 19. Projections: EIA, AEO 1994 National Energy Modeling System run AEO94B.D1221934. *Notes:* Appalachia: PA, OH, MD, WV, VA, TN, AL, GA, EAST KY. Interior: MI, IL, IN, IA, MO, KS, AR, OK, LA, TX, WEST KY. West: ND, SD, MT, WY, CO, UT, AZ, NM, WA, OR, AK, CA. W=Withheld to prevent disclosure of proprietary data. N/A=Not Applicable. Totals may not equal sum of components due to independent rounding.

★ 295 ★

Coal

World Steam Coal Import Demand by Import Region, 1995-2010

[Million metric tons of coal equivalent]

Import Regions[1]	1995	2000	2005	2010
The Americas	17.9	24.5	26.3	30.0
United States	6.0	8.2	8.6	9.5
Canada	7.8	7.5	7.0	6.0
Mexico	1.3	2.8	3.7	6.2
South America	2.8	6.0	7.0	8.3

[Continued]

★ 295 ★

World Steam Coal Import Demand by Import Region, 1995-2010

[Continued]

Import Regions[1]	1995	2000	2005	2010
Europe	102.3	126.8	151.5	169.1
Scandinavia	16.0	15.1	14.6	13.7
U.K./Ireland	8.7	15.4	22.6	27.3
Germany	9.8	14.0	16.6	24.1
Other NW Europe	28.9	32.6	36.8	37.3
Iberia	15.0	17.3	19.9	20.0
Italy	10.6	14.2	17.8	18.6
Med/E Europe	13.3	18.2	23.2	28.1
Asia	114.4	160.8	214.6	242.2
Japan	60.9	86.5	107.9	118.0
East Asia	35.2	45.5	60.0	68.5
China/Hong Kong	9.5	13.3	18.8	22.3
ASEAN	4.5	6.3	11.7	16.2
Indian Sub	4.3	9.2	16.2	17.2
Total	234.6	312.1	392.4	441.3

Source: Department of Energy, Energy Information Administration, Office of Integrated Analysis and Forecasting, *Supplement to the Annual Energy Outlook 1994* (Washington, D.C.: U.S. Government Printing Office, March 1994), p. 69. *Primary source:* Energy Information Administration, Office of Integrated Analysis and Forecasting. *Notes:* 1. Import regions: **United States:** United States; **Canada:** Canada; **Scandinavia:** Denmark, Finland, Norway, Sweden; **U.K./ Ireland:** Ireland, United Kingdom; **Germany:** Austria, Germany; **Other NW Europe:** Belgium, France, Luxembourg, Netherlands; **Iberia:** Portugal, Spain; **Italy:** Italy; **Med/E Europe:** Algeria, Bulgaria, Croatia, Egypt, Greece, Israel, Malta, Morocco, Romania, Tunisia, Turkey; **Mexico:** Mexico; **South America:** Argentina, Brazil, Chile; **Japan:** Japan; **East Asia:** North Korea, South Korea, Taiwan; **China/Hong Kong:** China, Hong Kong; **ASEAN:** Malaysia, Philippines, Thailand; **Indian Sub:** Bangladesh, India, Iran, Pakistan, Sri Lanka. One "metric ton of coal equivalent" contains 27.78 million Btu. Totals may not equal sum of components due to independent rounding.

★ 296 ★

Coal

World Steam Coal Flows by Importing Regions and Exporting Countries, 1990-2010

[Million short tons]

Import and Export Regions	Reference Case				Annual Growth 1990-2010
	1990	2000	2005	2010	(percent)
Steam Coal Exports to Europe					
Australia	11.0	0.0	15.9	20.5	3.2%
United States	24.0	50.7	58.8	62.0	4.9%
South Africa	31.0	65.7	63.8	64.6	3.7%
Former U.S.S.R.	14.0	8.2	8.7	8.6	-2.4%
Poland	23.0	7.9	6.3	6.5	-6.1%
Canada	1.0	4.6	1.8	0.0	N/A

[Continued]

★ 296 ★

World Steam Coal Flows by Importing Regions and Exporting Countries, 1990-2010

[Continued]

Import and Export Regions	Reference Case 1990	2000	2005	2010	Annual Growth 1990-2010 (percent)
China	3.0	3.3	3.3	5.0	2.5%
South America	11.0	4.2	9.9	18.7	2.7%
Other	11.0	11.9	18.7	22.0	3.5%
Total	130.0	156.5	187.1	207.9	2.4%
Steam Coal Exports to Asia					
Australia	41.0	93.6	113.0	123.7	5.7%
United States	6.0	11.4	18.9	26.6	7.7%
South Africa	18.0	0.0	14.9	22.1	1.0%
Former U.S.S.R.	3.0	4.4	4.1	3.8	1.2%
Poland	0.0	0.0	0.0	0.0	N/A
Canada	3.0	4.0	7.0	8.9	5.6%
China	8.0	18.2	20.9	21.8	5.1%
South America	1.0	39.7	55.9	60.3	22.7%
Other	5.0	24.4	26.3	27.2	8.8%
Total	84.0	195.7	261.0	294.5	6.5%
Steam Coal Exports to Others					
Australia	0.0	0.2	0.2	0.2	N/A
United States	11.0	9.2	7.7	8.8	-1.1%
South Africa	1.0	2.3	1.6	2.0	3.4%
Former U.S.S.R.	0.0	2.4	2.9	4.0	N/A
Poland	0.0	0.6	2.6	2.4	N/A
Canada	1.0	1.1	1.1	1.1	0.5%
China	0.0	1.4	1.7	2.0	N/A
South America	2.0	8.3	9.2	10.3	8.6%
Other	0.0	3.7	4.5	5.0	N/A
Total	15.0	29.1	31.4	35.8	4.4%
Total Steam Coal Exports					
Australia	54.0	93.8	129.1	144.4	5.0%
United States	42.0	71.2	85.4	97.4	4.3%
South Africa	50.0	68.0	80.3	88.8	2.9%
Former U.S.S.R.	18.0	14.9	15.7	16.4	-0.4%
Poland	19.0	8.4	8.9	8.9	-3.7%
Canada	5.0	9.7	9.9	10.0	3.5%
China	17.0	23.0	25.9	28.7	2.7%
South America	16.0	52.2	74.9	89.4	9.0%

[Continued]

★ 296 ★

World Steam Coal Flows by Importing Regions and Exporting Countries, 1990-2010

[Continued]

Import and Export Regions	Reference Case				Annual Growth 1990-2010
	1990	2000	2005	2010	(percent)
Other	14.0	40.0	49.5	54.2	7.0%
Total	236.0	381.3	479.5	538.2	4.2%

Source: Department of Energy, Energy Information Administration, Office of Integrated Analysis and Forecasting, *Supplement to the Annual Energy Outlook 1994* (Washington, D.C.: U.S. Government Printing Office, March 1994), p. 209. *Primary source:* Energy Information Administration, *Supplement to the Annual Energy Outlook 1993* (Washington, D.C., February 1993). Projections: EIA, AEO 1994 National Energy Modeling System run AEO94B.D1221934. *Notes:* Totals may not equal sum of components due to independent rounding. N/A = Not Applicable.

★ 297 ★

Coal

World Metallurgical Coal Import Demand by Import Region, 1995-2010

[Million metric tons of coal equivalent]

Import Regions[1]	1995	2000	2005	2010
The Americas	18.4	18.0	17.6	16.7
United States	0.0	0.0	0.0	0.0
Canada	4.0	4.0	3.5	3.0
Mexico	1.6	1.5	1.7	1.4
South America	12.8	12.5	12.4	12.3
Europe	50.2	47.2	47.9	46.8
Scandinavia	2.4	2.0	1.8	1.7
U.K./Ireland	8.1	7.4	7.1	6.7
Germany	3.8	3.9	6.0	7.5
Other NW Europe	12.5	10.7	10.1	9.3
Iberia	1.5	1.7	1.6	1.5
Italy	4.4	3.9	3.7	3.5
Med/E Europe	17.5	17.6	17.6	16.6
Asia	87.9	84.0	81.5	76.9
Japan	59.1	52.7	49.1	45.5
East Asia	17.1	19.2	19.1	18.2
China/Hong Kong	2.2	2.2	2.7	3.2
ASEAN	0.0	0.0	0.0	0.0

[Continued]

★ 297 ★

World Metallurgical Coal Import Demand by Import Region, 1995-2010

[Continued]

Import Regions[1]	1995	2000	2005	2010
Indian Sub	9.5	9.9	10.6	10.0
Total	156.5	149.2	147.0	140.4

Source: Department of Energy, Energy Information Administration, Office of Integrated Analysis and Forecasting, *Supplement to the Annual Energy Outlook 1994* (Washington, D.C.: U.S. Government Printing Office, March 1994), p. 70. *Primary source:* Energy Information Administration, Office of Integrated Analysis and Forecasting. *Notes:* 1. Import regions: **United States**: United States; **Canada**: Canada; **Scandinavia**: Denmark, Finland, Norway, Sweden; **U.K./ Ireland**: Ireland, United Kingdom; **Germany**: Austria, Germany; **Other NW Europe**: Belgium, France, Luxembourg, Netherlands; **Iberia**: Portugal, Spain; **Italy**: Italy; **Med/E Europe**: Algeria, Bulgaria, Croatia, Egypt, Greece, Israel, Malta, Morocco, Romania, Tunisia, Turkey; **Mexico**: Mexico; **South America**: Argentina, Brazil, Chile; **Japan**: Japan; **East Asia**: North Korea, South Korea, Taiwan; **China/Hong Kong**: China, Hong Kong; **ASEAN**: Malaysia, Philippines, Thailand; **Indian Sub**: Bangladesh, India, Iran, Pakistan, Sri Lanka. One "metric ton of coal equivalent" contains 27.78 million Btu. Totals may not equal sum of components due to independent rounding.

★ 298 ★

Coal

World Metallurgical Coal Flows by Importing Regions and Exporting Countries Regions, 1990-2010

[Million short tons]

Import and Export Regions	Reference Case				Annual Growth 1990-2010
	1990	2000	2005	2010	(percent)
Metallurgical Coal Exports to Europe					
Australia	14.0	11.4	10.7	10.1	-1.6%
United States	35.0	25.6	25.9	25.3	-1.6%
South Africa	0.0	0.0	0.0	0.0	N/A
Former U.S.S.R.	13.0	3.4	3.1	3.2	-6.8%
Poland	4.0	8.4	11.4	11.5	5.6%
Canada	3.0	5.5	3.8	3.5	0.8%
China	0.0	0.0	0.0	0.0	N/A
South America	0.0	0.0	0.0	0.0	N/A
Other	5.0	0.0	0.0	0.0	N/A
Total	74.0	54.1	55.0	53.8	-1.6%
Metallurgical Coal Exports to Asia					
Australia	48.0	51.3	52.7	50.5	0.3%
United States	14.0	23.2	19.8	17.7	1.2%
South Africa	4.0	5.0	5.0	5.0	1.2%
Former U.S.S.R.	6.0	1.1	1.3	1.1	-8.0%
Poland	0.0	0.0	0.0	0.0	N/A
Canada	26.0	15.9	15.0	14.1	-3.0%
China	1.0	1.9	1.9	1.9	3.2%
South America	0.0	0.0	0.0	0.0	N/A

[Continued]

★ 298 ★

World Metallurgical Coal Flows by Importing Regions and Exporting Countries Regions, 1990-2010

[Continued]

Import and Export Regions	Reference Case				Annual Growth 1990-2010
	1990	2000	2005	2010	(percent)
Other	0.0	0.0	0.0	0.0	N/A
Total	100.0	96.4	95.7	90.4	-0.5%
Metallurgical Coal Exports to Others					
Australia	2.0	0.0	0.0	0.0	N/A
United States	12.0	13.2	13.2	12.0	0.0%
South Africa	0.0	0.0	0.0	0.0	N/A
Former U.S.S.R.	0.0	2.5	2.7	2.6	N/A
Poland	3.0	0.4	0.3	0.2	-13.4%
Canada	2.0	0.7	0.6	0.6	-5.8%
China	0.0	2.2	2.2	2.2	N/A
South America	0.0	0.0	0.0	0.0	N/A
Other	0.0	0.0	0.0	0.0	N/A
Total	18.0	19.0	19.0	17.6	-0.1%
Total Metallurgical Coal Exports					
Australia	63.0	62.6	63.4	60.6	-0.2%
United States	63.0	62.0	59.0	55.0	-0.7%
South Africa	4.0	5.0	5.0	5.0	1.2%
Former U.S.S.R.	25.0	6.9	7.1	6.9	-6.2%
Poland	12.0	8.8	11.7	11.7	-0.1%
Canada	30.0	22.0	19.4	18.3	-2.5%
China	2.0	4.1	4.1	4.1	3.7%
South America	1.0	0.0	0.0	0.0	N/A
Other	6.0	0.0	0.0	0.0	N/A
Total	205.0	171.4	169.7	161.6	-1.2%

Source: Department of Energy, Energy Information Administration, Office of Integrated Analysis and Forecasting, *Supplement to the Annual Energy Outlook 1994* (Washington, D.C.: U.S. Government Printing Office, March 1994), p. 210. *Primary source:* Energy Information Administration, *Supplement to the Annual Energy Outlook 1993* (Washington, D.C., February 1993). Projections: EIA, AEO 1994 National Energy Modeling System run AEO94B.D1221934. *Notes:* N/A=Not Applicable. Totals may not equal sum of components due to independent rounding.

★ 299 ★

Coal

World Total Coal Flows by Importing Regions and Exporting Countries Regions, 1990-2010

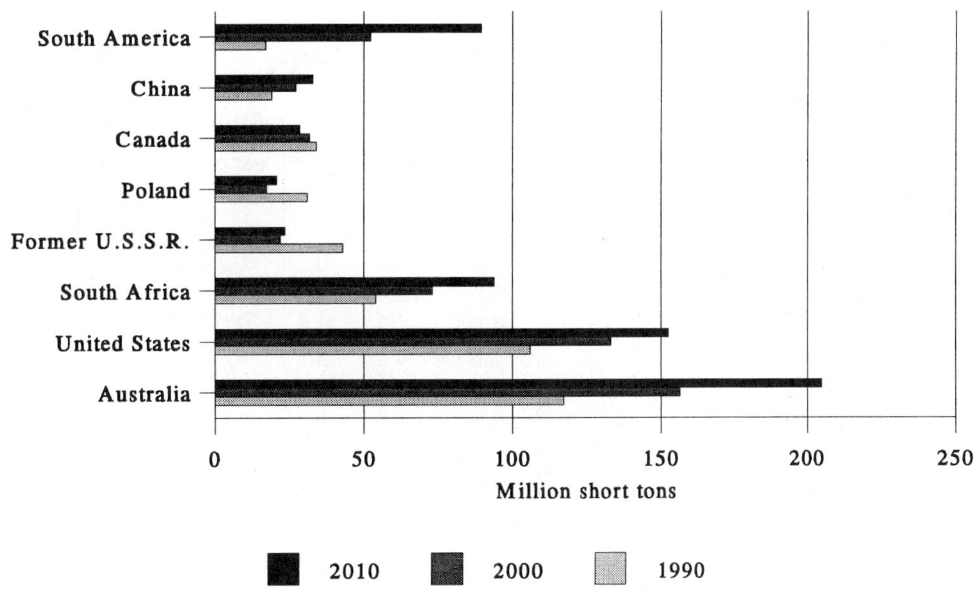

[Million short tons]

Import and Export Regions	Reference Case				Annual Growth 1990-2010 (percent)
	1990	2000	2005	2010	
Total Coal Exports to Europe					
Australia	24.0	11.4	26.5	30.6	1.2%
United States	59.0	76.2	84.8	87.3	2.0%
South Africa	32.0	65.7	63.8	64.6	3.6%
Former U.S.S.R.	27.0	11.6	11.8	11.8	-4.0%
Poland	27.0	16.2	17.7	18.0	-2.0%
Canada	4.0	10.1	5.5	3.5	-0.6%
China	3.0	3.3	3.3	5.0	2.5%
South America	11.0	4.2	9.9	18.7	2.7%
Other	16.0	11.9	18.7	22.0	1.6%
Total	204.0	210.6	242.0	261.6	1.3%
Total Coal Exports to Asia					
Australia	89.0	144.9	165.7	174.3	3.4%
United States	21.0	34.6	38.6	44.3	3.8%
South Africa	22.0	5.0	19.9	27.2	1.1%
Former U.S.S.R.	9.0	5.5	5.5	5.0	-2.9%
Poland	0.0	0.0	0.0	0.0	N/A
Canada	28.0	19.9	22.0	23.0	-1.0%
China	9.0	20.1	22.8	23.7	5.0%
South America	1.0	39.7	55.9	60.3	22.7%
Other	5.0	24.4	26.3	27.2	8.3%

[Continued]

★ 299 ★

World Total Coal Flows by Importing Regions and Exporting Countries Regions, 1990-2010

[Continued]

Import and Export Regions	Reference Case				Annual Growth 1990-2010 (percent)
	1990	2000	2005	2010	
Total	184.0	294.0	356.7	384.9	3.8%
Total Coal Exports to Others					
Australia	2.0	0.2	0.2	0.2	-11.3%
United States	23.0	22.4	21.0	20.8	-0.5%
South Africa	1.0	2.3	1.6	2.0	3.4%
Former U.S.S.R.	0.0	4.8	5.5	6.6	N/A
Poland	3.0	1.0	2.9	2.6	-0.7%
Canada	3.0	1.8	1.8	1.7	-2.7%
China	0.0	3.7	3.9	4.2	N/A
South America	2.0	8.3	9.2	10.3	8.6%
Other	0.0	3.7	4.5	5.0	N/A
Total	33.0	48.1	50.5	53.4	2.4%
Total Coal Exports					
Australia	117.0	156.44	192.4	205.0	2.8%
United States	106.0	133.2	144.4	152.4	1.8%
South Africa	54.0	73.1	85.3	93.8	2.8%
Former U.S.S.R.	43.0	21.9	22.8	23.4	-3.0%
Poland	31.0	17.2	20.6	20.6	-2.0%
Canada	34.0	31.7	29.3	28.3	-0.9%
China	19.0	27.1	30.0	32.8	2.8%
South America	17.0	52.2	74.9	89.4	8.7%
Other	20.0	40.0	49.5	54.2	5.1%
Total	441.0	552.7	649.2	699.9	2.3%

Source: Department of Energy, Energy Information Administration, Office of Integrated Analysis and Forecasting, *Supplement to the Annual Energy Outlook 1994* (Washington, D.C.: U.S. Government Printing Office, March 1994), p. 211. *Primary source:* Energy Information Administration, *Supplement to the Annual Energy Outlook 1993* (Washington, D.C., February 1993). Projections: EIA, AEO 1994 National Energy Modeling System run AEO94B.D1221934. *Notes:* Totals may not equal sum of components due to independent rounding. N/A=Not Applicable.

Electricity

★ 300 ★

Electric Power Supply and Demand, 1990-2010

Electricity Supply and Demand	Reference Case				Annual Growth 1990-2010 (percent)
	1990	2000	2005	2010	
Electricity Generating Capacity[1] (gigawatts)					
Utilities					
Capacity					
Coal steam	299.53	297.24	299.18	317.07	0.3%
Other fossil steam[2]	143.85	129.73	123.49	120.38	-0.9%
Combined cycle	7.17	17.63	28.45	34.98	8.2%
Combustion turbine/diesel	45.62	64.40	70.35	73.89	2.4%
Nuclear power	99.59	102.58	103.79	90.73	-0.5%
Pumped storage/other[3]	17.64	20.20	20.20	20.20	0.7%
Renewable[4]	76.00	77.48	78.06	88.43	0.5%
Total utilities capability	669.38	709.23	723.23	740.65	0.4%
Cumulative Planned Additions[5]					
Coal steam	0.00	8.30	13.35	16.25	N/A
Other fossil steam[2]	0.00	1.54	1.64	1.64	N/A
Combined cycle	0.00	9.14	14.30	14.99	N/A
Combustion turbine/diesel	0.00	18.84	24.18	24.55	N/A
Nuclear power	0.00	4.70	5.91	5.91	N/A
Pumped storage/other[3]	0.00	2.56	2.56	2.56	N/A
Renewable[4]	0.00	1.13	1.14	1.14	N/A
Total (planned)	0.00	46.20	63.06	67.03	N/A
Cumulative Unplanned Additions[6]					
Coal steam	0.00	0.00	0.00	17.79	N/A
Other fossil steam[2]	0.00	0.00	0.00	0.00	N/A
Combined cycle	0.00	1.45	7.09	12.94	N/A
Combustion turbine/diesel	0.00	0.50	2.68	5.93	N/A
Nuclear power	0.00	0.00	0.00	0.00	N/A
Pumped storage/other[3]	0.00	0.00	0.00	0.00	N/A
Renewable[4]	0.00	0.37	0.88	6.22	N/A
Total (planned)	0.00	2.31	10.65	42.87	N/A
Cumulative Total Utility Additions	0.00	48.52	73.72	109.91	N/A
Cumulative Utility Retirements	0.00	30.34	41.38	60.43	N/A
Nonutilities (excludes cogenerators)[6]					
Capacity[7]					
Coal steam	0.09	1.51	1.53	8.55	25.5%

[Continued]

★ 300 ★

Electric Power Supply and Demand, 1990-2010

[Continued]

Electricity Supply and Demand	Reference Case				Annual Growth 1990-2010 (percent)
	1990	2000	2005	2010	
Other fossil steam[2]	0.23	0.83	0.83	0.83	6.6%
Combined cycle	1.27	9.47	15.93	23.19	15.6%
Combustion turbine/diesel	0.90	5.50	9.34	12.85	14.2%
Nuclear power	0.00	0.00	0.00	0.00	N/A
Pumped storage/other[3]	0.00	0.00	0.00	0.00	N/A
Renewable[4]	6.64	13.52	17.49	26.19	7.1%
Total Utilities Capability	9.13	30.82	45.11	71.59	10.8%
Cogenerators[9]	33.74	43.49	43.99	44.47	1.4%
Electricity Demand (billion kilowatthours)					
Residential	919.21	989.52	1,018.47	1,059.51	0.7%
Commercial/Other	833.70	960.36	1,002.09	1,022.34	1.0%
Industrial	940.62	1,119.90	1,220.03	1,311.86	1.7%
Transportation	17.39	24.72	38.65	55.71	6.0%
Total Sales	2,710.92	3,094.49	3,279.24	3,449.43	1.2%
Net Energy for Load (billion kilowatthours)[10]					
Net international electricity imports	2.00	26.43	28.16	29.94	14.5%
Net international electricity imports	-1.78	-1.72	-1.71	-2.01	0.6%
Purchase from nonutilities (including cogenerators)[11]	116.04	236.95	313.47	429.39	6.8%
Generation by utilities	2,808.14	3,072.39	3,201.41	3,260.46	0.7%
Total Net Energy for Load	2,924.41	3,334.06	3,541.32	3,717.78	1.2%
Generation by Fuel Type (billion kilowatthours)					
Utility Generation					
Coal	1,559.60	1,687.17	1,741.48	1,886.17	1.0%
Petroleum	117.02	84.55	90.33	73.91	-2.3%
Natural gas	264.09	335.00	392.20	373.39	1.7%
Nuclear	576.86	671.26	679.88	612.06	0.3%
Pumped storage/other[12]	-1.92	-11.05	-11.06	-11.05	9.1%
Renewable[13]	292.50	305.46	808.57	325.98	0.5%
Total Utility Generation	2,808.14	3,072.39	3,201.41	3,260.46	0.7%
Cogenerators (billion kilowatthours)[14]	177.87	210.39	222.78	235.04	1.4%
Nonutility Generation Including Cogeneration (billion kilowatthours)					
Coal	0.63	9.31	9.43	54.21	25.%
Petroleum/Other[15]	1.04	0.66	0.84	0.41	-4.6%
Natural gas	8.91	72.07	119.19	144.41	14.9%
Renewable	28.82	68.81	94.77	138.53	8.2%

[Continued]

★ 300 ★

Electric Power Supply and Demand, 1990-2010

[Continued]

Electricity Supply and Demand	Reference Case				Annual Growth 1990-2010 (percent)
	1990	2000	2005	2010	
Total Nonutility Generation	39.40	150.85	224.23	337.55	11.3%
End-Use Prices[16]					
(1992 cents per kilowatthour)					
Residential	8.5	8.7	9.1	9.8	0.7%
Commercial	7.7	7.6	7.8	8.1	0.3%
Industrial	5.2	5.1	5.2	5.5	0.3%
Transportation	5.1	5.2	5.3	5.4	0.2%
All sectors average	7.1	7.0	7.2	7.6	0.3%
Price Components[16]					
(1992 cents per kilowatthour)					
Capital component	3.0	2.7	2.6	2.7	-0.5%
Fuel component	1.4	1.4	1.6	1.7	1.0%
O&M component	2.6	2.6	2.6	2.6	0.1%
Wholesale power cost	0.1	0.3	0.4	0.6	7.2%
Total	7.1	7.0	7.2	7.6	0.3%
Fuel Consumption (trillion Btu)	1.32	1.66	2.15	2.60	3.4%
Utilities[17]					
Coal	16.10	17.39	17.94	19.39	0.9%
Natural gas	2.88	3.66	4.13	3.79	1.4%
Oil	1.26	0.90	0.98	0.80	-2.2%
Nonutilities[18]					
Coal	0.01	0.10	0.10	0.54	25.3%
Natural gas	0.06	0.66	1.06	1.26	16.4%
Oil	0.00	0.01	0.01	0.00	7.3%
Emissions (million short tons)[19]					
Total carbon	472.35	525.39	553.63	595.85	1.2%

[Continued]

★ 300 ★

Electric Power Supply and Demand, 1990-2010

[Continued]

Electricity Supply and Demand	Reference Case 1990	2000	2005	2010	Annual Growth 1990-2010 (percent)
Carbon dioxide	1,735.35	1,933.06	2,037.94	2,195.36	1.2%
Sulfur dioxide	14.53	9.66	8.35	8.28	-2.8%

Source: Department of Energy, Energy Information Administration, Office of Integrated Analysis and Forecasting, *Supplement to the Annual Energy Outlook 1994* (Washington, D.C.: U.S. Government Printing Office, March 1994), pp. 183-85. *Primary source:* 1990 (except for nonutility generation and prices): Energy Information Administration (EIA), *Electric Power Annual 1991* (Washington, D.C.: February 1993). 1990 Nonutility generation: Form EIA-861, "Annual Electric Utility Report" and Form EIA-867, "Annual Nonutility Power Producer Report." The Form EIA-867 is filed by nonutilities reporting the energy delivered, while the EIA-861 is filed by electric utilities reporting the energy received. Because the Form EIA-861 collects data from the universe of utilities, these data are used for electricity sold to utilities. Own use data is from Form EIA-867. Prices and all projections: EIA, AEO 1994 National Energy Modeling System run AEO94B.D1221934. *Notes:* 1. Net summer capability is the steady hourly output that generating equipment is expected to supply to system load (exclusive of auxiliary power), as demonstrated by tests during summer peak demand. 2. Incudes oil-, gas-, and dual-fired capability. 3. Other includes methane and propane and blast furnace gas. 4. Includes conventional hydroelectric, geothermal, wood, wood waste, municipal solid waste, other biomass, solar, and wind power. 5. Cumulative additions after December 31, 1990. 6. Includes small power producers, independent power producers, exempt wholesale generators, which produce electricity for sales to utilities. 7. Nameplate capacity is reported for nonutilities. Nameplate capacity is designated by the manufacturer. 8. Other includes hydrogen, sulfur, batteries, chemicals, fish oil, and spent sulfite liquor. 9. Includes cogenerators at industrial, commercial and other facilities whose primary function is not electricity production. Nameplate capacity is reported for nonutilities. Nameplate capacity is designated by the manufacturer. 10. Generation to meet system load by source. 11. Includes small power producers, independent power producers, and exempt wholesale generators, which produce electricity for sales to utilities. 12. Other includes methane, propane, and blast furnace gas. 13. Includes conventional hydroelectric, geothermal, wood, wood waste, municipal solid waste, other biomass, solar, and wind power. 14. Includes cogenerators at industrial, commercial and other facilities whose primary function is not electricity production. 15. Other includes hydrogen, sulfur, batteries, chemicals, fish oil, and spent sulfite liquor. 16. Prices represent average revenue per kilowatthour. 17. In the end-use energy consumptions tables, projected fuel consumption in the utility sector includes fuel used by independent power producers. In this table, power used by independent power producers is included in the nonutility category. 18. Includes fuel consumption by independent power producers and exempt wholesale generators, which produce electricity for sales to utilities. 19. Estimated emissions from utilities and independent power producers. O&M=Operation and Maintenance. N/A=Not Applicable. Totals may not equal sum of components due to independent rounding.

★ 301 ★

Electricity

Electricity Supply, Disposition, and Prices, 1990-2010

[Billion kilowatthours, unless otherwise noted]

Supply, Disposition and Prices	Reference Case 1990	1992	2000	2005	2010	Annual Growth 1990-2010 (percent)	Annual Growth 1992-2010 (percent)
Electric Utilities							
Generation by Fuel Type							
Coal	1560	1576	1687	1741	1886	1.0%	1.0%
Petroleum	117	89	85	90	74	-2.3%	-1.0%
Natural gas	264	264	335	392	373	1.7%	1.9%
Nuclear power	577	619	671	680	612	0.3%	-0.1%
Pumped storage/other[1]	-2	-4	-11	-11	-11	9.1%	5.8%
Renewable sources[2]	293	254	305	309	326	0.5%	1.4%
Total	2809	2798	3072	3201	3260	0.7%	0.9%
Nonutilities (excluding cogenerators)[3]							
Generation by Fuel Type							
Coal	1	2	9	9	54	25.0%	22.0%

[Continued]

★ 301 ★

Electricity Supply, Disposition, and Prices, 1990-2010

[Continued]

Supply, Disposition and Prices	Reference Case					Annual Growth 1990-2010 (percent)	Annual Growth 1992-2010 (percent)
	1990	1992	2000	2005	2010		
Petroleum/other[4]	1	1	1	1	0	-4.6%	-4.9%
Natural gas	9	16	72	119	144	14.9%	13.0%
Renewable sources[2]	29	40	69	95	139	8.2%	7.1%
Total	39	60	151	224	338	11.3%	10.1%
Cogeneration[5]	178	192	210	223	235	1.4%	1.1%
Net Imports	2	28	26	28	30	14.5%	0.4%
Electricity Sales by Sector							
Residential	924	936	995	1024	1065	0.7%	0.7%
Commercial	839	850	967	1009	1030	1.0%	1.1%
Industrial	946	973	1126	1226	1318	1.7%	1.7%
Transportation	4	4	25	39	56	14.1%	15.8%
Total	2713	2763	3112	3298	3469	1.2%	1.3%
End-Use Prices (1992 cents per kilowatthour)[6]							
Residential	8.5	8.1	8.7	9.1	9.8	0.7%	1.0%
Commercial	7.7	7.5	7.6	7.8	8.1	0.3%	0.5%
Industrial	5.2	5.1	5.1	5.2	5.5	0.3%	0.4%
Transportation	5.1	5.1	5.2	5.3	5.4	0.2%	0.3%
All Sectors Average	7.1	6.8	7.0	7.2	7.6	0.3%	0.6%
Price Components (1992 cents per kilowatthour)[6]							
Capital component	3.0	2.9	2.7	2.6	2.7	-0.5%	-0.4%
Fuel component	1.4	1.3	1.4	1.6	1.7	1.0%	1.8%
O&M component	2.6	2.6	2.6	2.6	2.6	0.1%	0.1%
Net Wholesale Power Component	0.1	0.1	0.3	0.4	0.6	7.2%	8.0%
Total	7.1	6.8	7.0	7.2	7.6	0.3%	0.6%

Source: Department of Energy, Energy Information Administration, Office of Integrated Analysis and Forecasting, *Annual Energy Outlook 1994: With Projections to 2010* (Washington, D.C.: U.S. Government Printing office, January 1994), p. 65. *Primary source:* 1990 (except for nonutility generation and prices): Energy Information Administration (EIA), *Electric Power Annual 1991* (Washington, D.C.: February 1993). 1992 (except for nonutility generation and prices): Energy Information Administration (EIA), *Electric Power Annual 1992* (Washington, D.C.: February 1994). 1990 Nonutility generation: Form EIA-861, "Annual Electric Utility Report" and Form EIA-867, "Annual Nonutility Power Producer Report." The Form EIA-867 is filed by nonutilities reporting the energy delivered, while the EIA-861 is filed by electric utilities reporting the energy received. Because the Form EIA-861 collects data from the universe of utilities, these data are used for electricity sold to utilities. Own use data if from Form EIA-867. Prices, 1992 cogeneration, 1992 cogeneration, and all projections: EIA, AEO 1994 National Energy Modeling System run AEO94B.D1221934. *Notes:* O&M=Operation and Maintenance. Totals may not equal sum of components due to independent rounding. 1. Other includes methane and propane and blast furnace gas. 2. Includes conventional hydroelectric, geothermal, wood, wood waste, municipal solid waste, other biomass, solar and wind power. 3. Includes small power producers, independent power producers, and exempt wholesale generators, which produce electricity for sales to the grid. 4. Other includes hydrogen, sulfur, batteries, chemicals, fish oil, and spent sulfite liquor. 5. Includes cogeneration at industrial, commercial and other facilities whose primary function is not electricity production. Includes both sales to utilities and generation for own use. 6. Prices represent average revenue per kilowatthour.

★ 302 ★

Electricity

Electricity Generating Capability, 1990-2010

[Thousand megawatts]

Net Summer Capability[1]	Reference Case 1990	1992	2000	2005	2010	Annual Growth 1990-2010 (percent)	Annual Growth 1992-2010 (percent)
Electric Utilities							
Capability							
Coal steam	299.5	298.7	297.2	299.2	317.1	0.3%	0.3%
Other fossil steam[2]	143.9	142.5	129.7	123.5	120.4	-0.9%	-0.9%
Combined cycle	7.2	7.8	17.6	28.4	35.0	8.2%	8.7%
Combustion turbine/diesel	45.6	47.9	64.4	70.4	73.9	2.4%	2.4%
Nuclear power	99.6	99.0	102.6	103.8	90.7	-0.5%	-0.5%
Pumped storage/other[3]	17.6	19.1	20.2	20.2	20.2	0.7%	0.3%
Renewable sources[4]	76.0	76.2	77.5	78.1	83.4	0.5%	0.5%
Total	689.4	691.2	709.2	723.5	740.7	0.4%	0.4%
Cumulative Planned Additions[5]							
Coal steam	0.00	1.29	8.30	13.35	16.25	N/A	N/A
Other fossil steam[2]	0.00	0.95	1.54	1.64	1.64	N/A	N/A
Combined cycle	0.00	0.67	9.14	14.30	14.99	N/A	N/A
Combustion turbine /diesel	0.00	2.50	18.84	24.18	24.55	N/A	N/A
Nuclear power	0.00	0.00	4.70	5.91	5.91	N/A	N/A
Pumped storage/other[3]	0.00	1.41	2.56	2.56	2.56	N/A	N/A
Renewable sources[4]	0.00	0.28	1.13	1.14	1.14	N/A	N/A
Total	0.00	7.10	46.20	63.08	67.03	N/A	N/A
Cumulative Unplanned Additions[5]							
Coal steam	0.00	0.00	0.00	0.00	17.79	N/A	N/A
Other fossil steam[2]	0.00	0.00	0.00	0.00	0.00	N/A	N/A
Combined cycle	0.00	0.00	1.45	7.09	12.94	N/A	N/A
Combustion turbine/diesel	0.00	0.00	0.50	2.68	5.93	N/A	N/A
Nuclear power	0.00	0.00	0.00	0.00	0.00	N/A	N/A
Pumped storage/other[3]	0.00	0.00	0.00	0.00	0.00	N/A	N/A
Renewable sources[4]	0.00	0.00	0.37	0.88	6.22	N/A	N/A
Total	0.00	0.00	2.31	10.69	42.87	N/A	N/A
Cumulative Total Utility Additions[5]	0.00	7.10	48.52	73.72	109.91	N/A	N/A
Cumulative Utility Retirements	1.20	6.46	30.34	41.38	60.43	N/A	N/A
Nonutilities (excludes cogenerators)[5]							
Installed Capability[7]							
Coal steam	0.09	0.35	1.51	1.53	8.55	25.5%	19.5%
Other fossil steam[2]	0.23	0.40	0.83	0.83	0.83	6.6%	4.1%
Combined cycle	1.27	2.88	9.47	15.93	23.19	15.6%	12.3%
Combustion turbine/diesel	0.90	1.48	5.50	9.34	12.85	14.2%	12.7%
Nuclear power	0.00	0.00	0.00	0.00	0.00	N/A	N/A
Pumped storage/other[8]	0.00	0.00	0.00	0.00	0.00	N/A	N/A
Renewable sources[4]	6.64	7.42	13.52	17.49	26.19	7.1%	7.3%

[Continued]

★ 302 ★

Electricity Generating Capability, 1990-2010

[Continued]

Net Summer Capability[1]	Reference Case					Annual Growth 1990-2010 (percent)	Annual Growth 1992-2010 (percent)
	1990	1992	2000	2005	2010		
Total	9.13	12.53	30.82	45.11	71.59	10.8%	10.2%
Cogenerators[7,9]	33.74	37.78	43.49	43.47	44.47	1.4%	0.9%
Cumulative Nonutility Additions[5,7]	0.00	7.44	31.45	46.24	73.20	N/A	13.5%

Source: Department of Energy, Energy Information Administration, Office of Integrated Analysis and Forecasting, *Annual Energy Outlook 1994: With Projections to 2010* (Washington, D.C.: U.S. Government Printing Office, January 1994), p. 66. *Primary source:* 1990: Energy Information Administration (EIA), *Electric Power Annual 1991* (Washington, D.C.: February 1993). 1992: Energy Information Administration (EIA), *Electric Power Annual 1992* (Washington, D.C.: February 1994). Projections: EIA, AEO 1994 National Energy Modeling System run AEO94B.D1221934. *Notes:* N/A=Not Applicable. Totals may not equal sum of components due to independent rounding. 1. Net summer capability is the steady hourly output that generating equipment is expected to supply to system load (exclusive of auxiliary power), as demonstrated by tests during summer peak demand. 2. Includes oil-, gas-, and dual-fired capability. 3. Other includes methane and propane and blast furnace gas. 4. Includes conventional hydroelectric, geothermal, wood, wood waste, municipal solid waste, other biomass, solar, and wind power. 5. Cumulative additions after December 31, 1990. 6. Includes small power producers, independent power producer, and exempt wholesale generators, which produce electricity for sales to the grid. 7. Nameplate capacity is reported for nonutilities. Nameplate capacity is designated by the manufacturer. 8. Other includes hydrogen, sulfur, batteries, chemicals, fish oil, and spent sulfite liquor. 9. Includes cogenerators at industrial, commercial and other facilities whose primary function is not electricity production.

★ 303 ★

Electricity

Electric Generating Capacity by Type of Fuel, 1993-2002

[Percent total]

	1993						2002					
	Coal	Nuclear	Hydro	Oil/ gas	Other (Util)	NUGs	Coal	Nuclear	Oil/ Hydro	Other gas	(Util)	NUGs
United States-Summer												
ECAR	80.2	7.5	0.6	6.5	3.6	1.5	73.6	6.8	0.6	11.8	4.4	2.8
ERCOT	26.6	8.7	0.8	59.0	0.0	4.9	26.5	7.8	0.7	61.4	0.0	3.7
MAAC	21.5	23.0	2.0	45.0	3.3	5.2	19.9	21.2	1.7	45.7	2.2	9.2
MAIN	54.7	29.9	1.1	13.6	0.7	0.1	49.5	26.4	0.9	21.9	1.1	0.1
MAPP	63.4	11.8	9.3	13.9	0.5	1.2	62.3	11.4	8.3	15.7	1.1	1.2
NPCC	12.6	19.0	9.3	44.6	4.7	10.0	12.0	18.1	8.8	42.6	4.5	14.1
SERC	46.8	19.4	7.6	19.5	3.6	3.0	40.3	18.2	6.3	26.9	3.8	4.5
SPP	38.1	8.3	3.7	48.1	0.5	1.2	36.5	8.0	3.7	50.1	0.5	1.2
WSCC	23.9	7.3	32.5	24.6	4.3	7.3	21.7	6.6	29.8	26.5	6.3	9.1
Total U.S.	41.5	14.2	9.4	27.9	2.8	4.0	38.0	13.3	8.5	31.5	3.4	5.4
Canada-Winter												
MAPP	24.5	0.0	71.1	4.4	0.0	0.0	23.3	0.0	72.2	4.5	0.0	0.0
NPCC	17.5	22.3	48.8	10.3	0.0	1.1	15.2	19.9	51.2	91	0.4	4.2

[Continued]

★ 303 ★

Electric Generating Capacity by Type of Fuel, 1993-2002

[Continued]

	1993						2002					
	Coal	Nuclear	Hydro	Oil/ gas	Other (Util)	NUGs	Coal	Nuclear	Oil/ Hydro	Other gas	(Util)	NUGs
WSCC	29.1	0.0	57.1	11.9	0.0	1.9	28.2	0.0	54.8	9.3	2.4	5.3
Total Canada	20.4	16.1	52.3	10.1	0.0	1.2	18.3	14.5	53.4	8.8	0.7	4.1

Source: North American Electric Reliability Council, *Electricity Supply & Demand, 1993-2002: Summary of Electric Utility Supply and Demand Projections*, June 1993, p. 13. *Notes:* ECAR=East Central Area Reliability Coordination Agreement; ERCOT=Electric Reliability Council of Texas; MAAC=Mid-Atlantic Area Council; MAIN=Mid-America Interconnected Network; MAPP=Mid-Continent Area Power Pool; NPC=Northeastern Power Coordinating Council; NUGS=Nonutility Generators; SERC=Southeastern Electric Reliability Council; SPP=Southwest Power Pool; WSCC=Western Systems Coordinating Council. Percentages may not add due to rounding.

★ 304 ★

Electricity

Comparison of Alternate Electricity Forecasts, 2000-2010

[Billion kilowatthours, except where noted]

Projection	EIA AEO94			Other Forecasts					
	Reference	High Economic Growth	Low Economic Growth	WEFA	GRI	DRI	NERC	EEI	NERA
2000									
Average End-Use Price									
(1992 cents per kilowatthour)	7.00	7.10	6.90	7.33	6.35	6.50	NA	7.10	NA
Residential	8.70	8.80	8.50	8.80	7.48	7.60	NA	8.38	NA
Commercial	7.60	7.80	7.50	7.98	6.73	7.00	NA	7.73	NA
Industrial	5.10	5.20	5.00	5.20	4.81	5.00	NA	5.32	NA
Net Energy for Load	3,335	3,411	3,273	3,485	3,472	3,537	3,479	3,693	3,810
Coal	1,687	1,714	1,654	1,727	1,795	1,720	1,764	1,859	1,760
Petroleum	85	94	76	128	114	116	61	121	180
Natural gas	335	354	335	403	342	349	354	671	500
Nuclear	671	671	671	601	664	696	678	677	640
Hydroelectric/other[1]	294	295	295	354	287	336	277	301	380
Nonutility sales of grid	237	258	215	214	233	286	280	NA	270
Net imports	26	26	26	59	37	34	65	64	80
Electricity Sales	3,112	3,178	3,046	3,227	3,153	3,228	NA	3,427	3,570
Residential	995	1,012	976	1,113	1,063	1,129	NA	1,121	1,130
Commercial/other[2]	992	1,004	980	1,004	1,000	1,011	NA	1,066	1,150
Industrial	1,126	1,162	1,090	1,110	1,090	1,088	NA	1,240	1,290
Capability (gigawatts)[3,4,5]	740.0	745.2	737.6	747.0	787.7	791.5	718.5	813.4	789.0
Coal steam	298.7	298.7	298.7	306.5	339.2	335.8	294.6	318.6	335.0
Oil and gas	227.5	232.3	225.1	235.0	243.3	247.2	229.8	296.1	242.0
Nuclear	102.6	102.6	102.6	101.4	109.9	113.0	103.1	101.8	112.0
Hydroelectric/other[1]	111.2	111.6	111.0	104.1	95.4	95.6	91.0	96.9	100.0

[Continued]

★ 304 ★

Comparison of Alternate Electricity Forecasts, 2000-2010

[Continued]

Projection	EIA AEO94 Reference	EIA AEO94 High Economic Growth	EIA AEO94 Low Economic Growth	Other Forecasts WEFA	GRI	DRI	NERC	EEI	NERA
2010									
Average End-Use Price									
(1992 cents per kilowatthour)	7.60	7.90	7.20	8.01	618	6.50	NA	7.18	NA
Residential	9.80	10.30	9.20	9.74	7.37	7.40	NA	8.48	NA
Commercial	8.10	8.40	7.70	8.64	6.56	7.00	NA	7.82	NA
Industrial	5.50	5.70	5.20	5.65	4.72	5.30	NA	5.38	NA
Net Energy for Load	3,720	3,894	3,556	4,121	4,118	4,390	NA	4,672	NA
Coal	1,886	1,990	1,794	2,136	2,183	2,048	NA	2,355	NA
Petroleum	74	68	81	204	124	138	NA	150	NA
Natural gas	373	371	345	498	374	405	NA	1,017	NA
Nuclear	612	612	612	566	648	713	NA	689	NA
Hydroelectric/other[1]	315	313	321	362	292	336	NA	393	NA
Nonutility sales to grid	430	510	373	285	446	702	NA	NA	NA
Net imports	30	30	30	71	53	48	NA	67	NA
Electricity Sales	3,469	3,621	3,307	3,816	3,707	3,982	NA	4,343	NA
Residential	1,065	1,108	1,019	1,308	1,201	1,402	NA	1,319	NA
Commercial/other[2]	1,086	1,128	1,045	1,210	1,153	1,208	NA	1,394	NA
Industrial	1,318	1,396	1,243	1,298	1,353	1,372	NA	1,630	NA
Capability (gigawatts)[3,4,5]	812.3	850.1	780.8	877.8	860.5	879.2	NA	924.8	NA
Coal steam	325.7	347.2	311.3	365.4	391.1	384.7	NA	340.6	NA
Oil and gas	266.2	276.6	249.5	304.4	266.1	285.9	NA	360.8	NA
Nuclear	90.7	90.7	90.7	101.0	107.8	113.0	NA	103.8	NA
Hydroelectric/other[1]	129.8	135.8	129.4	107.0	95.5	95.6	NA	119.7	NA

Source: Department of Energy, Energy Information Administration, Office of Integrated Analysis and Forecasting, *Annual Energy Outlook 1994: With Projections to 2010* (Washington, D.C.: U.S. Government Printing Office, January 1994), p. 165. *Primary source:* Energy Information Administration (EIA), AEO94 Forecasting System, run AEO94B.D1221934 (Reference Case), HMAC94.D1221932 (High Economic Growth Case), and LMAC94.D1221932 (Low Economic Growth Case). WEFA: The Wharton Econometric Forecasts (WEFA) Group, *Coal and Electricity Report* (Summer 1993). Gas Research Institute (GRI): *GRI Baseline Projection of U.S. Energy Supply and Demand*, 1994 edition (August 1993). North American Electric Reliability Council (NERC), *Electricity Supply and Demand 1993-2002* (June 1993). Edison Electric Institute (EEI), *Electricity Futures Project* (draft report). National Economic Research Association (NERA), *NERA Energy Outlook* (December 1992). *Notes:* 1. Other includes conventional hydroelectric, geothermal, wood, wood waste, municipal solid waste, other biomass, solar, and wind power, plus a small quantity of petroleum coke. For nonutility generators, other also includes waste heat, blast furnace gas, and coke oven gas. 2. Other includes sale of electricity to government, railways, and street lighting authorities. 3. For GRI, capability represents nameplate capacity; for the others, capability represents net summer capability. 4. WEFA's DRI's, and EEI's capability projections include cogeneration. 5. GRI, DRI and NERC do not provide nonutility capacity but plant type. The total nonutility capacity in 2000 is 27.1, 86.8, and 41.2 gigawatts for GRI, DRI, and NERC, respectively. In 2010, the projections are 65.3 and 164.8 gigawatts for GRI and DRI, respectively. NA = Not available.

★ 305 ★

Electricity

Existing and Planned Electric Transmission Lines, 2002

[Circuit miles]

	AC VOLTAGE (kV)					DC VOLTAGE (+kV)					AC & DC
	230	345	500	765	Total	250-300	400	450	500	Total	Total
ECAR	1180	11970	1059	2137	16346	0	0	0	0	0	16346
ERCOT	0	7604	0	0	7604	0	0	0	0	0	7604
MAAC	5206	172	1989	0	7367	0	0	0	0	0	7367
MAIN	241	5495	0	90	5826	0	0	0	0	0	5826
Cmnwlth Edison	0	2814	0	90	2904	0	0	0	0	0	2904
East Missouri	90	863	0	0	953	0	0	0	0	0	953
S. Cent. Illinois	48	830	0	0	878	0	0	0	0	0	878
Wis.-Upper Mich.	103	988	0	0	1091	0	0	0	0	0	1091
MAPP U.S.	7501	5728	342	0	13571	465	436	0	0	901	14472
NPCC U.S.	1575	4495	5	314	6389	0	0	192	0	192	6581
New York	1090	2623	5	314	4032	0	0	0	0	0	4032
NEPOOL	485	1872	0	0	2357	0	0	192	0	192	2549
SERC	22077	2	8813	0	30892	0	0	0	0	0	30892
Florida	5359	0	1799	0	7158	0	0	0	0	0	7158
Southern	6808	0	2262	0	9070	0	0	0	0	0	9070
TVA	30	2	2557	0	2589	0	0	0	0	0	2589
VACAR	9880	0	2195	0	12075	0	0	0	0	0	12075
SPP	5032	5021	2043	0	12096	0	0	0	0	0	12096
Southeast	2722	97	1950	0	4769	0	0	0	0	0	4769
West Central	1798	2586	47	0	4431	0	0	0	0	0	4431
Northern	512	2338	46	0	2896	0	0	0	0	0	2896
WSCC U.S.	33193	10733	14338	0	58264	0	0	0	1333	1333	59597
NW Power Pool	13867	4275	6985	0	25127	0	0	0	264	264	25391
Rocky Mtn.	4160	1428	0	0	5588	0	0	0	0	0	5588
Ariz.-N. Mex.	2816	4464	2332	0	9612	0	0	0	0	0	9612
Calif.-So. Nev.	12350	566	5021	0	17937	0	0	0	1069	1069	19006
TOTAL U.S.	76005	51220	28589	2541	158355	465	436	192	1333	2426	160781

Source: North American Electric Reliability Council, *Electricity Supply & Demand, 1993-2002: Summary of Electric Utility Supply and Demand Projections*, June 1993, p. 93. *Notes:* AC=Alternating Current; DC=Direct Current. ASCC=Alaska Systems Coordinating Council; ECAR=East Central Area Reliability Coordination Agreement; MAAC=Mid-Atlantic Area Council; MAIN=Mid-America Interconnected Network; MAPP=Mid-Continent Area Power Pool; NEPOOL=New England Power Pool; NPCC=Northeast Power Coordinating Council; SERC=Southeastern Electric Reliability Council; SPP=Southwest Power Pool; TVA=Tennessee Valley Authority; VACAR=Virginia Central Area Reliability Coordination Agreement; WSCC=Western Systems Coordinating Council. Includes transmission lines 230 kV and above. For WSCC, some 287 kV and 360 kV lines are included in the 345 kV category. Source also includes data for Canada and Mexico.

★ 306 ★

Electricity

Construction Status of Electric Generating Unit Additions, 1993-2002

[Thousands of megawatts]

	United States	Canada
Coal	6.7	1.0
Not Yet Under Construction[1]	3.4	0.0
Under Construction	3.3	1.0
Nuclear[2]	5.9	1.8
Not Yet Under Construction[1]	0.0	0.0
Under Construction	5.9	1.8
Hydro	0.6	4.3
Not Yet Under Construction[1]	0.4	1.7
Under Construction	0.2	2.6
Oil/Gas	47.3	0.6
Not Yet Under Construction[1]	41.8	0.2
Under Construction	5.5	0.4
Pumped Storage	1.3	0.0
Not Yet Under Construction[1]	0.1	0.0
Under Construction	1.2	0.0
Other (Utility)	5.3	0.5
Not Yet Under Construction[1]	5.1	0.5
Under Construction	0.2	0.0
Total (Utility)	67.1	8.2
Not Yet Under Construction[1]	50.8	2.4
Under Construction	16.3	5.8
Non-Utility Generators	15.2	3.9
Total (All Additions)	82.3	12.1

Source: North American Electric Reliability Council, *Electricity Supply & Demand, 1993-2002: Summary of Electric Utility Supply and Demand Projections*, June 1993, p. 93. *Notes:* 1. Includes units planned but not utility authorized, units with regulatory approval pending, and units with regulatory approval received but not yet under construction. 2. Units WNP 1 and WNP 3, located in WSCC's Northwest Power Pool Area, are in some stage of construction but are not included. WNP=Washington Nuclear Plant; WSCC=Western Systems Coordinating Council. Includes generators from the United States and Canada for the period January 1, 1993 to December 31, 2002.

Nuclear Energy and Uranium

★ 307 ★

Historical Forecasts of Nuclear Energy Use, 2000

"In the 1960s, nuclear energy was at its peak of public visibility. Not only was nuclear energy perceived as the possible destroyer of mankind, it was simultaneously seen as a provider of future wonders. But the most wondrous outcome of nuclear technology was that nearly every forecast for it proved wrong.

"It started with expectations of skyrocketing demand for electric power, driven by demographic and life-style trends. Planners thought the baby boom represented a permanent shift in birth rates and thus projected that the U.S. population would increase rapidly for many years. Moreover, per capita electricity consumption was forecasted to grow wildly as electric gadgets proliferated. Electric heating elements imbedded in suburban driveways, for example, were expected to eliminate the need for snow shoveling and enable wintertime barbecuers to grill to their heart's delight. By the year 2000, reported *The Wall Street Journal*, per capita consumption levels would be three times their 1960s level.

"Surging demand for electric power meant that huge generation plants would be needed. Utilities were advised by industry planners to build big, build often and build nuclear. By the year 2000, it was predicted, all large power plants would be nuclear and the last of the old oil-fired plants would shut down...

"In the end, none of these applications was realized. Nuclear energy turned out to be one of the biggest strategic traps of the 20th century. The fortune spent on nuclear generating plants was for naught because forecasted consumption levels were vastly overstated: The baby boom turned into the baby bust, and the '70s energy crisis caused the country to reduce its per capita electricity consumption. Other nuclear energy applications, such as the Nucleon, provided technologically unfeasible. But the most important reason forecasters erred in their predictions was that they didn't anticipate the safety issues—be they real or imaged—that framed public discussion of the technology and that effectively vaporized nuclear expansion plans in America."

Source: Steven P. Schnaars, "If They'd Only Known: Why Nuclear Energy Self-Destructed," in *Forecast: The Magazine of Demographics and Business Statistics*, July-August 1994, p. 64.

★ 308 ★

Nuclear Energy and Uranium

Cumulative Quantities of Spent Nuclear Fuel, 1985-2010

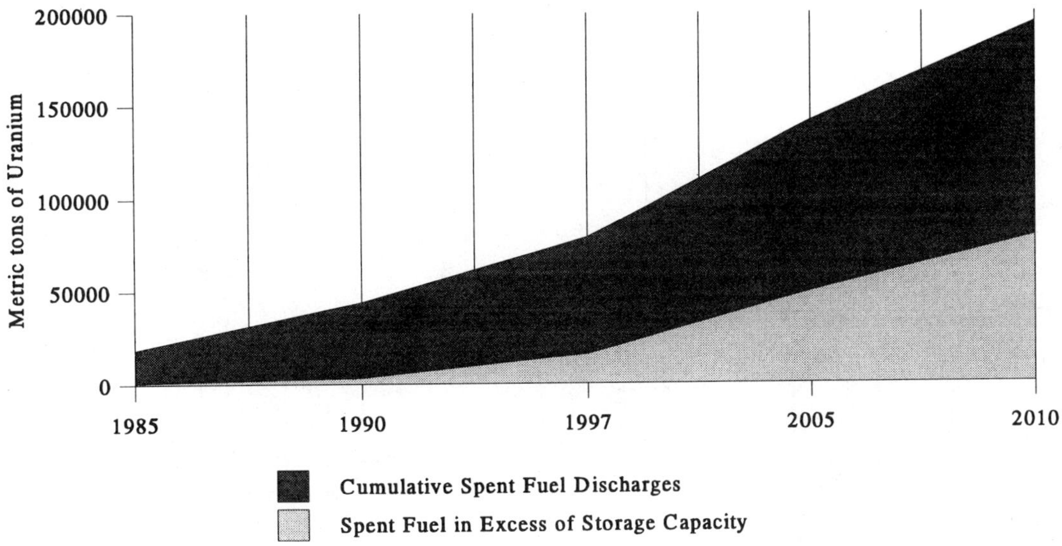

"An estimate of the cumulative quantity of spent fuels that will result from nuclear power plant operation in the U.S. through 2010 is given [below]. Also shown is the prediction of the cumulative quantity of spent fuel in excess of storage capacity at the reactors which would have to be transported to an away-from-reactor storage facility (AFR). This prediction assumes that utilities will expand their reactor storage pools to the maximum capacity and that no transshipment between reactors will occur. If a repository became operational in 1997, the away-from-reactor storage requirements would peak at about 20,000 MTU during 2001... Transporting the spent fuel from reactor to AFRs and then to a repository would require an additional 87 rail casks during 2005 if a repository is operating in 1997."

[Metric Tons of Uranium]

Year	Cumulative Spent Fuel Discharges	Cumulative Spent Fuel in Excess of Reactor Storage Capacity
1985	18,700	800
1990	44,100	3,300
1997	78,800	16,100
2005	141,400	49,500
2010	194,400	79,000

Source: U.S. Department of Energy, National Waste Terminal Storage Program, *National Site Characterization and Selection Plan and Environmental Assessment*, NWTS-4 (Washington, D.C.: U.S. Government Printing Office, January 1981), pp. 13-14.

★ 309 ★

Nuclear Energy and Uranium

Apparent Uranium Market Requirements of Utilities, 1993-2001

[Million pounds U_3O_8 equivalent]

Year of Delivery	Quantity of Natural Uranium Under Contract	Unfilled Requirements	Apparent Market Requirements	Reported Enrichment Feed Deliveries
1993	30.7	1.2	32.0	38.0
1994	31.5	6.2	37.7	43.4
1995	30.8	8.8	39.6	42.0
1996	22.5	15.4	37.9	48.3
1997	18.3	22.2	40.5	46.9
1998	12.5	29.8	42.3	48.5
1999	8.0	32.4	40.4	45.8
2000	5.8	38.1	43.8	49.5
2001	2.7	40.8	43.5	46.0

Source: U.S. Department of Energy, Energy Information Administration, *Uranium Industry Annual 1992* (Washington, D.C.: U.S. Government Printing Office, October 1993), p. 65. *Primary source:* EIA, form EIA-858, "Uranium Industry Annual Survey" (1992). *Notes:* As of December 31, 1992. Totals may not equal to sum of components due to independent rounding.

★ 310 ★

Nuclear Energy and Uranium

Commitments for Delivery of Uranium from Foreign Suppliers to Domestic Utilities and Suppl under Purchase-Contract Imports, 1992-2000 and Later

"[The data below] reveal that utilities accounted for roughly 51 percent of 1992 purchase-contract imports. For years beyond 1992, utility commitments account for 92 percent of the total quantity under purchase contracts from foreign suppliers as of December 31, 1992."

[Million pounds U_3O_8 equivalent]

Year of delivery	Imports by Utilities[1]				Imports by Suppliers[1]				Combined Imports[1]			
	Firm	Optional	Total	Cumulative	Firm	Optional	Total	Cumulative	Firm	Optional	Total	Cumulative
1992	11.8	0	11.8	11.8	11.5	0	11.5	11.5	23.3	0	23.3	23.3
1993	12.0	0.8	12.8	24.6	4.9	0	4.9	16.4	16.9	0.8	17.7	41.0
1994	12.3	2.8	15.1	39.8	0.5	0.3	0.8	17.2	12.8	3.1	15.9	56.9
1995	11.1	3.3	14.4	54.2	0.4	0.3	0.7	17.9	11.5	3.6	15.1	72.1
1996	10.1	2.9	13.0	67.2	0.4	0	0.4	18.3	10.6	2.9	13.4	85.5
1997	8.7	3.5	12.2	79.4	0.4	0	0.4	18.7	9.1	3.5	12.5	98.0
1998	4.9	3.2	8.1	87.4	0	0.2	0.2	18.9	4.9	3.4	8.3	106.3
1999	3.1	2.6	5.7	93.1	0	0.1	0.1	19.0	3.1	2.7	5.8	112.1

[Continued]

★ 310 ★

Commitments for Delivery of Uranium from Foreign Suppliers to Domestic Utilities and Suppliers under Purchase-Contract Imports, 1992-2000 and Later

[Continued]

Year of delivery	Imports by Utilities[1]				Imports by Suppliers[1]				Combined Imports[1]			
	Firm	Optional	Total	Cumulative	Firm	Optional	Total	Cumulative	Firm	Optional	Total	Cumulative
2000 and Later	4.2	5.0	9.2	102.3	0	0.1	0.1	19.1	4.2	5.1	9.3	121.4
Total	78.2	24.1	102.3	-	18.1	1.0	19.1	-	96.2	25.1	121.4	-

Source: U.S. Department of Energy, Energy Information Administration, *Uranium Industry Annual 1992* (Washington, D.C.: U.S. Government Printing Office, October 1993), p. 56. *Primary source:* Energy Information Administration, Form EIA-858, "Uranium Industry Annual Survey" (1992). *Notes:* Totals may not equal sum of components because of independent rounding. N/A=Not Applicable. 1. For 1992, includes domestic utility, supplier, and trader/broker purchases reported as imports of foreign-origin uranium materials into the United States. Uranium materials reported as imports under loan and exchange transactions are excluded. For 1993-2000 and later, the figure shown equals the amount of import commitments in each year under purchase contracts by utilities, suppliers, and traders/brokers. U_3O_8=Uranium ore concentrate.

★ 311 ★

Nuclear Energy and Uranium

Commitments for Delivery of Uranium from Domestic Suppliers to U.S. Utilities, 1992-2000 and Later

"The annual delivery commitments to domestic utilities from domestic uranium suppliers are listed in [the table below]. Actual deliveries in 1992 were 23.4 million pounds U_3O_8, 12.3 million pounds more than the expected deliveries for contracts in place at the beginning of 1992. Low spot-market prices for uranium during 1992 appear to be a contributing factor for this increase. Projected cumulative deliveries reported from current contracts for the years beyond 1992 are 77.5 million pounds, up from the 64.9 million pounds reported for 1991. For the period 1993 and beyond, firm delivery commitments were increased by 19.1 million pounds and optional deliveries were increased by 4.6 million pounds, bringing the total increase in delivery commitments to 23.7 million pounds U_3O_8 for the period 1993 and later."

[Million pounds U_3O_8 equivalent]

Year of Delivery	As of December 31, 1991				As of December 31, 1992				Change in Total from December 31, 1991 to December 31, 1992	
	Firm	Optional	Total	Cumulative	Firm	Optional	Total	Cumulative	Total	Cumulative
1992	10.4	0.7	11.1	11.1	23.4	0	23.4	23.4	12.3	12.3
1993	11.0	1.3	12.3	23.3	17.1	0.8	17.9	41.3	5.6	18.0
1994	8.3	1.2	9.6	32.9	13.3	3.1	16.4	57.7	6.8	24.8
1995	8.2	2.1	10.3	43.2	13.0	3.4	16.4	74.1	6.1	30.9
1996	5.8	1.7	7.5	50.7	6.2	3.3	9.5	83.6	2.0	32.9
1997	5.2	1.1	6.2	56.9	4.5	1.6	6.1	89.7	-0.1	32.8
1998	2.3	1.3	3.6	60.5	3.0	1.4	4.4	94.2	0.9	33.7
1999	1.3	0.7	2.0	62.5	1.7	0.6	2.3	96.4	0.3	33.9
2000 and Later	1.9	0.5	2.4	64.9	4.1	0.3	4.4	100.8	2.0	36.0
Total	54.3	10.6	64.9	-	86.3	14.5	100.8	-	-	-

Source: U.S. Department of Energy, Energy Information Administration, *Uranium Industry Annual 1992* (Washington, D.C.: U.S. Government Printing Office, October 1993), p. 48. *Primary source:* Energy Information Administration, Form EIA-858, "Uranium Industry Annual Survey" (1992). *Notes:* N/A=Not applicable. U_3O_8=Uranium ore concentrate. Totals may not equal sum of components because of independent rounding.

★ 312 ★

Nuclear Energy and Uranium

Uncommitted Uranium Available for Sale, 1993-2002

[Million pounds U_3O_8 equivalent]

Year of Sale	Price Category[1]					
	$10 Per Pound or Less	$20 Per Pound or Less	$30 Per Pound or Less	$40 Per Pound or Less	$50 Per Pound or Less	Unlimited Price
1993	0.5	5.6	5.6	5.6	5.6	5.6
1994	0	4.2	4.2	4.2	4.2	4.2
1995	0	3.9	4.9	4.9	4.9	4.9
1996	0	4.9	5.9	5.9	5.9	5.9
1997	0	5.9	6.9	6.9	6.9	6.9
1998	0	6.8	7.8	7.8	7.8	7.8
1999	0	7.9	8.9	8.9	8.9	8.9
2000	0	7.9	8.9	8.9	8.9	8.9
2001	0	7.9	8.9	8.9	8.9	8.9
2002	0	6.6	7.6	7.6	7.6	7.6
Total	0.5	61.6	69.7	69.7	69.7	69.7

Source: U.S. Department of Energy, Energy Information Administration, *Uranium Industry Annual 1992* (Washington, D.C.: U.S. Government Printing Office, October 1993), p. 67. *Primary source:* Energy Information Administration, Form EIA-858, "Uranium Industry Annual Survey" (1992). *Notes:* Totals may not equal sum of components because of independent rounding. Quantities of U_3O_8 in price categories are cumulative within each year, that is, for each year the quantities of higher price categories include all quantities in the lower price categories. U_3O_8 = Uranium ore concentrate. 1. Prices are in constant 1993 dollars. These data are based on estimates made by domestic suppliers as of December 31, 1992.

Oil and Natural Gas

★ 313 ★

Comparative Forecasts of U.S. Oil Production and Imports, 2010

"Projections of domestic [oil] production reflect differing forecasts of the size of resources, the costs of development, and the application of new technology. In the AEO94 reference case, for example, production is projected to decline in the 1990s but increase slightly between 2006 and 2010 because of rising prices and technology improvements. The GRI forecast shows a similar pattern for petroleum production, but the WEFA and DRI forecasts project a decline in production throughout the forecast period."

Forecast	AEO94	DRI	GRI	WEFA
World oil price (1992 dollars per barrel)	28.16	30.03	27.27	26.84
Crude oil and natural gas liquids production (millions barrels per day)	7.1	7.0	8.5	6.8
Total net imports (million barrels per day)	12.8	13.1	9.9	10.4

Source: Department of Energy, Energy Information Administration, Office of integrated Analysis and Forecasting, *Annual Energy Outlook 1994: With Projections to 2010* (Washington, D.C.: U.S. Government Printing Office, January 1994), p. 37. *Notes:* AEO94=Annual Energy Outlook 1994; DRI=Data Resources, Inc.; GRI=Gas Research Institute; WEFA=Wharton Econometric Forecasting Associates.

★ 314 ★

Oil and Natural Gas

Comparative Forecasts of World Oil Prices, 2000-2010

"Variation in OPEC's production rate is a key assumption in establishing the low and high world oil price paths. For the low price case, assumptions about OPEC production rates are optimistic, consistent with market conditions in the past several years. For the high price case, OPEC production assumptions are more pessimistic. OPEC production for 2010 is about 11 percent higher in the low price case than in the reference case-and about 8 percent lower in the high price case...

"Three out of four other forecasts have world oil prices in the $27-30 range in 2010, with the AEO94 reference case in the middle. The range between the low and high cases encompasses the spread of these other forecasts."

[1992 dollars per barrel]

Forecast	1992 dollars per barrel		
	2000	2005	2010
AEO94 reference case	20.72	24.90	28.16
AEO94 low price case	15.44	17.49	20.15
AEO94 high price case	24.16	29.90	34.11
DRI	22.66	26.66	29.95
WEFA	20.34	22.79	24.94
IEA	26.70	29.30	29.30
GRI	21.01	23.82	27.02

Source: Department of Energy, Energy Information Administration, Office of Integrated Analysis and Forecasting, *Annual Energy Outlook 1994: With Projections to 2010* (Washington, D.C.: U.S. Government Printing Office, January 1994), p. 37. *Notes:* AEO94=Annual Energy Outlook 1994; DRI=Data Resources, Inc.; WEFA=Wharton Econometric Forecasting Associates; IEA=International Energy Agency; GRI=Gas Research Institute.

★ 315 ★

Oil and Natural Gas

Increase in Iraqi Daily Production of Crude Oil and Liquid Natural Gas Compared to OPEC, 1990-1998

"Expressing confidence that the United Nations embargo on Iraqi oil exports will be lifted by early next year, Iraq's Oil Minister is preparing to triple oil production over the next few years from an initial two million barrels a day.

"Revenues from the increasing oil production could offset the cost of the reparations that Iraq must pay for its 1990 invasion of Kuwait. But it could also put pressure on world oil prices, unless demand keeps growing and production declines elsewhere...

"If Iraq succeeds in pushing up its oil production sharply, and if oil prices do not plunge because of increased supply, Iraq may by the end of the century be offsetting the painful economic consequences of invading Kuwait. It would be pumping enough new oil to compensate itself for the 30 percent slice of oil revenues that it must pay in reparations under the United Nations Security Council's terms for the gulf war cease-fire."

[Millions of barrels]

Year	Iraq*	Saudi Arabia	Kuwait	OPEC as a whole
1990	2.0	6.0	1.0	24.5
1991	.3	8.0	0.0	25.0
1992	.5	7.5	1.0	24.0
1993	.5	7.5	2.0	25.0
1994	1.0	NA	NA	28.0
1995	3.0	NA	NA	30.0
1996	4.0	NA	NA	31.0
1997	4.5	NA	NA	32.0
1998	5.5	NA	NA	34.0

Source: Paul Lewis, "Ambitious Plans for Iraqi Oil," in *The New York Times*, July 30, 1994, p. 35. *Primary source:* *Oil & Gas Journal*. *Notes:* NA=Not available. OPEC=Organizational for Petroleum Exporting Countries. Figures for individual countries are not available. Magnitudes estimated from published chart. Source also includes data for 1982-1989. 1. Projections assume U.N. sanctions are lifted early in 1995.

★316★

Oil and Natural Gas

Crude Oil Recoverable Resources, 1990-2010

"Expected recoverable resource estimates reflect static technology and economic conditions. Within the projection period of the model, the state of technology development and penetration proceeds, thus expanding the volume of economically recoverable resources. The initial recoverable resource estimates reflect the 1990 level of technological development and penetration. The 2010 estimates are based on the assumed rate of technological progress."

[Billion barrels]

Crude Oil Resource Category	Technology		Technology Improvement Rate (percent)
	1990 Level	2010 Level	
Undiscovered	43.21	64.22	--
Onshore	33.53	49.83	2.0
Offshore	9.68	14.39	2.0
Inferred Reserves	26.34	39.45	--
EOR	6.17	9.47	2.2
Other Onshore	17.70	26.30	2.0
Offshore	2.47	3.68	2.0
Total Lower 48 States Unproved	69.55	103.67	--
Alaska	10.53	15.65	2.0
Total U.S. Unproved	80.08	119.32	--
Proved Reserves	26.25	26.25	--
Total Crude Oil	106.33	145.57	--

Source: Department of Energy, Energy Information Administration, Office of Integrated Analysis and Forecasting, *Supplement to the Annual Energy Outlook 1994* (Washington, D.C.: U.S. Government Printing Office, March 1994), p. 47. *Primary source:* Energy Information Administration (EIA), Office of Integrated Analysis and Forecasting. *Note:* EOR = Enhanced oil recovery.

★ 317 ★

Oil and Natural Gas

Oil and Gas Supply, 1990-2010

Production and Supply	Reference Case					Annual Growth 1990-2010 (percent)	Annual Growth 1992-2010 (percent)
	1990	1992	2000	2005	2010		
Crude Oil							
Lower 48 Average Wellhead Price[1] (1992 dollars per barrel)	23.02	17.38	20.19	23.99	26.98	0.8%	2.5%
Production (million barrels per day)[2]							
U.S. Total	7.36	7.17	5.17	4.84	5.10	-1.8%	-1.9%
Lower 48 Onshore	4.63	4.38	3.62	3.59	3.63	-1.2%	-1.0%
Conventional	3.97	3.68	3.05	2.88	2.80	-1.7%	-1.5%
Enhanced Oil Recovery	0.66	0.71	0.57	0.71	0.84	1.2%	1.0%
Lower 48 Offshore	0.95	1.07	0.68	0.65	0.72	-1.4%	-2.1%
Alaska	1.77	1.71	0.87	0.00	0.74	-4.2%	-4.5%
U.S. End of Year Reserves (billion barrels)	27.56	24.97	18.84	17.46	18.31	-2.0%	-1.7%
Natural Gas							
Lower 48 Average Wellhead Price[1] (1992 dollars per thousand cubic feet)	1.83	1.75	2.42	2.89	3.47	3.3%	3.9%
Production (trillion cubic feet)[3]							
U.S. Total	17.81	17.84	18.93	20.13	20.19	0.6%	0.7%
Lower 48 Onshore	12.15	12.50	14.87	14.82	14.55	0.9%	0.8%
Associated-Dissolved[4]	2.07	2.11	1.64	1.64	1.67	-1.1%	-1.3%
Non-Associated	10.08	10.39	13.22	13.18	12.88	1.2%	1.2%
Conventional	8.63	8.53	9.95	9.78	9.51	0.5%	0.6%
Unconventional	1.45	1.86	3.27	3.40	3.38	4.3%	3.4%
Tight Sands	1.13	1.19	1.99	2.11	2.15	3.3%	3.3%
Coal Bed Methane	0.19	0.51	0.92	0.93	0.89	8.1%	3.2%
Devonian Shale	0.12	0.16	0.35	0.36	0.33	5.1%	4.2%
Lower 48 Offshore	5.28	4.93	3.57	4.83	5.16	-0.1%	0.3%
Associated-Dissolved[4]	0.63	0.68	0.58	0.57	0.59	-0.3%	-0.8%
Non-Associated	4.65	4.25	2.99	4.26	4.57	-0.1%	0.4%
Alaska	0.38	0.41	0.50	0.49	0.47	1.1%	0.8%

[Continued]

★ 317 ★

Oil and Gas Supply, 1990-2010

[Continued]

Production and Supply	Reference Case					Annual Growth 1990-2010 (percent)	Annual Growth 1992-2010 (percent)
	1990	1992	2000	2005	2010		
U.S. End of Year Reserves (trillion cubic feet)	169.35	165.02	164.83	156.73	152.38	-0.5%	-0.4%
Supplemental Gas Supplies[5]	0.12	0.12	0.11	0.12	0.07	-2.4%	-2.6%
Total Wells Completed	31.17	23.01	37.551	54.27	76.50	4.6%	6.9%

Source: Department of Energy, Energy Information Administration, Office of Integrated Analysis and Forecasting, *Annual Energy Outlook 1994: With Projections to 2010* (Washington, D.C.: U.S. Government Printing Office, January 1994), p. 71. *Primary source:* 1990: Lower 48 Onshore, Lower 48 Offshore, Alaska Crude Oil Production—Energy Information Administration (EIA), *Petroleum Supply Annual 1990* (Washington, D.C.: May 1991); U.S. Crude Oil Reserves, U.S. Natural Gas Reserves, Lower 48 Offshore Natural Gas Production—EIA, *U.S. Crude Oil, Natural Gas, and Natural Gas Liquids Reserves* (Washington, D.C., September 1991). 1992: Lower 48 Onshore, Lower 48 Offshore, Alaska Crude Oil Reserves Production—Energy Information Administration (EIA), *Petroleum Supply Annual 1992* (Washington, D.C., May 1993); U.S. Crude Oil Reserves, U.S. Natural Gas Reserves, Lower 48 Offshore Natural Gas Production—EIA, *U.S. Crude Oil, Natural Gas, and Natural Gas Liquids Reserves* Washington, D.C., September 1993). 1990 and 1992: Crude Oil Lower 48 Average Wellhead Prices—EIA, *Annual Energy Review 1992* (Washington, D.C.: June 1993); Natural Gas Lower 48 Average Wellhead Prices, Alaska and Total Natural Gas Production, Supplemental Gas Supplies—EIA, *Natural Gas Annual 1992* (Washington, D.C., November 1993); Total Wells Completed—*Monthly Energy Review* (Washington, D.C., November 1993); Other 1990 and 1992 values: EIA, Office of Integrated Analysis and Forecasting. Figures for 1990 and 1992 may differ from published data due to internal conversion factors within the AEO 1994 National Energy Modeling System. Projections: EIA, AEO 1994 National Energy Modeling System run ARO94B.D1221934. *Notes:* Reference case projections. Btu=British thermal units. Totals may not equal sum of components because of independent rounding. 1. Represents Lower 48 onshore and offshore supplies. 2. Includes lease condensate. 3. Dry marketed production minus nonhyrdrocarbon gases removed. 4. Gas which occurs in crude oil reserves either as free gas (associated) or as gas in solution with free oil (dissolved). 5. Synthetic natural gas, propane air, coke oven gas, refinery gas, biomass gas, air injected for Btu stabilization, and manufactured gas comingled and distributed with natural gas.

★ 318 ★

Oil and Natural Gas

Oil and Gas Reserves, 1990-2010

Categories	Reference Case				Annual Growth 1990-2010 (percent)
	1990	2000	2005	2010	
Crude Oil[1]					
Reserves (billion barrels)					
U.S. Total	27.56	18.84	17.46	18.31	-2.0%
Lower 48 onshore	17.33	11.75	11.46	11.50	-2.0%
Conventional	14.24	9.22	8.32	7.80	-3.0%
Enhanced oil recovery	3.08	2.53	3.14	3.70	0.9%
Lower 48 offshore	3.70	2.28	2.09	2.11	-2.8%
Alaska	6.52	4.80	3.91	4.71	-1.6%
Dry Natural Gas					
Reserves (trillion cubic feet)					
U.S. Total	169.3	164.8	156.7	152.4	-0.5%
Lower 48 onshore	127.0	122.8	115.9	113.8	-0.5%
Associated-dissolved[2]	17.3	13.3	13.2	13.5	-1.3%
Non-associated	109.7	109.5	102.7	100.3	-0.4%
Conventional	89.0	76.4	70.6	68.8	-1.3%

[Continued]

★ 318 ★

Oil and Gas Reserves, 1990-2010

[Continued]

Categories	Reference Case				Annual Growth 1990-2010
	1990	2000	2005	2010	(percent)
Unconventional	20.6	33.2	32.1	31.5	2.1%
Tight sands	13.5	19.1	19.0	19.2	1.8%
Coal bed methane	5.1	10.8	10.1	9.4	3.1%
Devonian shale	2.0	3.2	3.0	2.8	1.6%
Lower 48 offshore	33.1	31.8	30.2	27.3	-0.9%
Associated-dissolved[2]	7.1	5.6	5.5	5.7	-1.1%
Non-associated	26.0	26.2	24.7	21.6	-0.9%
Alaska	9.3	10.3	10.6	11.3	1.0%

Source: Department of Energy, Energy Information Administration, Office of Integrated Analysis and Forecasting, *Annual Energy Outlook 1994: With Projections to 2010* (Washington, D.C.: U.S. Government Printing Office, January 1994), p. 195. *Primary source:* 1990 conventional, enhanced oil recovery crude oil, unconventional, tight sands, coal bed methane, devonian shale natural gas reserves: Energy Information Administration (EIA), Office of Integrated Analysis and Forecasting. Other 1990: EIA, *U.S. Crude Oil, Natural Gas, and Natural Gas Liquids Reserves* (Washington, D.C., September 1991). Figures for 1990 may differ from published data due to internal conversion factors within the AEO 1994 National Energy Modeling System. Projections: EIA, AEO 1994 National Energy Modeling System run AEO94B.D1221934. *Notes:* Totals may not equal sum of components because of independent rounding. 1. Includes lease condensate. 2. Gas which occurs in crude oil reservoirs either as free gas (associated) or as gas in solution with crude oil (dissolved).

★ 319 ★

Oil and Natural Gas

Comparative Forecasts for Natural Gas, 2010

"The complexities of gas market analysis do not allow easy conclusions regarding the factors that determine specific gas prices. Nevertheless, tentative conclusions can be drawn from some comparisons. The highest gas prices generally correspond to projects that include the highest oil prices (DRI and NPC). Oil is a substitute fuel that competes with gas for market share. Higher oil prices reduce competitive pressure, allowing for higher gas prices. Aggregate production levels are a rough measure of the degree of exploitation of increasingly costly supplies. DRI shows relatively high production volumes and the highest prices. AGA's projections shows the maximum production level, but its price is the lowest, reflecting a more optimistic outlook on the potential recoverable resource base, the use of new technology to maintain recent levels of productivity, and a relatively low oil price."

Forecast	AEO94	DRI	GRI	AGA	NPC
World oil price (1992 dollars per barrel)	28.16	30.03	27.27	24.47	29.72
Average wellhead price, lower 48 states (1992 dollars per thousand cubic feet)	3.47	3.88	3.22	2.89	3.77

[Continued]

★ 319 ★

Comparative Forecasts for Natural Gas, 2010

[Continued]

Forecast	AEO94	DRI	GRI	AGA	NPC
U.S. natural gas production (trillion cubic feet)	20.2	21.8	21.6	21.9	20.5
U.S. natural gas consumption (trillion cubic feet)	24.1	24.8	25.3	25.4	24.0

Source: Department of Energy, Energy Information Administration, Office of Integrated Analysis and Forecasting, *Annual Energy Outlook 1994: With Projections to 2010* (Washington, D.C.: U.S. Government Printing Office, January 1994), p. 37. *Notes:* AEO94=Annual Energy Outlook 1994; DRI=Data Resources, Inc.; GRI=Gas Research Institute; AGA=American Gas Association; NPC=National Petroleum Council.

★ 320 ★

Oil and Natural Gas

Natural Gas Recoverable Resources, 1990-2010

[Trillion cubic feet]

Natural Gas Resource Category	Technology		Technology Improvement Rate (percent)
	1990 Level	2010 Level	
Undiscovered	356.63	529.93	--
Onshore	234.53	348.49	2.0
Offshore	122.10	181.44	2.0
Inferred Reserves	145.30	215.91	--
Other Onshore	114.42	170.02	2.0
Offshore	30.89	45.90	2.0
Unconventional Gas Recovery	316.63	470.50	--
Tight Gas	232.40	345.33	2.0
Devonian	21.23	31.55	2.0
Coalbed	63.00	93.61	2.0
Total Lower 48 States Unproved	818.56	1,216.34	--
Alaska	33.31	49.50	2.0
Total U.S. Unproved	851.87	1,265.84	--
Proved Reserves	169.35	169.35	--
Total Natural Gas	1,021.22	1,435.19	--

Source: Department of Energy, Energy Information Administration, Office of Integrated Analysis and Forecasting, *Supplement to the Annual Energy Outlook 1994* (Washington, D.C.: U.S. Government Printing Office, March 1994), p. 48. *Primary source:* Energy Information Administration (EIA), Office of Integrated Analysis and Forecasting.

★ 321 ★

Oil and Natural Gas

Natural Gas Supply, Disposition, and Prices, 1990-2010

[Trillion cubic feet per year, unless otherwise noted]

Supply, Disposition, and Prices	Reference Case					Annual Growth 1990-2010	Annual Growth 1992-2010
	1990	1992	2000	2005	2010	(percent)	(percent)
Production							
Dry Gas Production[1]	17.81	17.84	18.93	20.13	20.19	0.6%	0.7%
Supplemental Natural Gas[2]	0.12	0.12	0.11	0.12	0.07	-2.4%	-2.6%
Net Imports	1.45	1.92	2.93	3.31	3.85	5.0%	3.9%
Canada	1.43	2.03	2.67	2.76	2.92	3.6%	2.0%
Mexico	-0.02	-0.10	-0.05	0.00	0.17	N/A	N/A
LNG	0.03	-0.01	0.31	0.55	0.75	17.2%	N/A
Total Supply	19.38	19.88	21.97	23.56	24.11	1.1%	1.1%
Consumption by Sector							
Residential	4.39	4.69	4.85	4.83	4.85	0.5%	0.2%
Commercial	2.62	2.80	2.80	2.85	2.93	0.6%	0.2%
Industrial[3]	7.02	7.53	8.01	8.52	9.00	1.2%	1.0%
Electric utilities[4]	2.79	2.77	4.22	5.06	4.93	2.9%	3.3%
Lease and plant fuel[5]	1.24	1.17	1.32	1.38	1.38	0.5%	0.9%
Pipeline fuel	0.66	0.59	0.67	0.70	0.70	0.3%	1.0%
Transportation[6]	0.00	0.00	0.13	0.24	0.35	N/A	N/A
Total	18.72	19.54	21.99	23.58	24.14	1.3%	1.2%
Discrepancy[7]	0.66	0.33	-0.02	-0.03	-0.03	N/A	N/A
Average Wellhead Price[8] **(1992 dollars per thousand cubic feet)**	1.83	1.75	2.42	2.89	3.47	3.3%	3.9%
Delivered Prices (1992 dollars per thousand cubic feet)							
Residential	6.19	5.89	7.26	7.85	8.55	1.6%	2.1%
Commercial	5.15	4.88	6.22	6.80	7.49	1.9%	2.4%
Industrial[9]	3.57	3.17	3.96	4.50	5.08	1.8%	2.7%
Electric utilities	2.54	2.36	3.02	3.63	4.22	2.6%	3.3%
Transportation	3.62	4.05	9.90	10.76	11.41	5.9%	5.9%
Average[10]	4.33	4.03	4.92	5.42	6.07	1.7%	2.3%

Source: Department of Energy, Energy Information Administration, Office of Integrated Analysis and Forecasting, *Annual Energy Outlook 1994: With Projections to 2010* (Washington, D.C.: U.S. Government Printing Office, January 1994), p. 70. *Primary source:* 1990 and 1992 industrial and transportation delivered prices: Energy Information Administration (EIA), AEO 1994 National Energy Modeling System run AEO94B.D1221934. Other 1990 and 1992: EIA, *Natural Gas Annual 1992 Volume 1* (Washington, D.C., November 1993). Projections: EIA, AEO 1994 National Energy Modeling System run AEO94B.D1221934. *Notes:* LNG=Liquefied natural gas. N/A=Not applicable. Totals may not equal sum of components because of independent rounding. 1. Dry marketed production minus nonhydrocarbon gases removed. 2. Synthetic natural gas, propane air, coke oven gas, refinery gas, biomass gas, air injected for Btu stabilization, and manufactured gas comingled and distributed with natural gas. 3. Includes consumption by cogenerators. 4. Includes consumption by independent power producers. 5. Represents natural gas used in the field gathering and processing plant machinery. 6. Compressed natural gas used as a vehicle fuel. 7. Balancing item. Reflects natural gas lost, the net result of converting flow data measured at varying temperatures and pressures to a standard temperature and pressure, and the merger of different data reporting systems which vary in scope, format, definition, and respondent type. 8. Represents Lower-48 onshore and offshore supplies. 9. Excludes uses for lease and plant fuel. 10. Weighted average price. Weights used are the sectoral consumption values excluding lease, plant, and pipeline fuel.

★ 322 ★

Oil and Natural Gas

Detailed Comparative Forecasts for Natural Gas Production, 2000-2010

Projection	EIA AEO94 Reference	EIA AEO94 High Economic Growth	EIA AEO94 Low Economic Growth	Other Forecasts WEFA	GRI	DRI	AGA	NPC
2000								
Wellhead Price (1992 dollars per thousand cubic feet)	2.42	2.56	2.31	2.39	2.58[1]	2.56	2.26[1]	3.23
Dry Gas Production	18.9	19.6	18.4	19.2	19.3	19.9	19.8	18.3
Net Imports	2.9	2.9	2.9	2.6	2.7	2.7	NA	NA
Consumption	22.0	22.7	21.5	21.8	22.4	22.3	22.9	20.8
Residential	4.9	4.9	4.8	4.7	4.8	4.8	5.0	20.8
Commercial	2.8	2.8	2.8	3.0	3.0	3.0	3.4	2.9
Industrial	8.0	8.2	7.8	8.0	9.8	9.0	10.1	7.6
Electric utility	4.2	4.6	4.0	3.9	3.8	3.5	3.6	3.7
Other	2.1	2.2	2.1	2.2	1.1	1.9	0.8	1.8
2010								
Wellhead Price (1992 dollars per thousand cubic feet)	3.47	3.88	2.93	3.13	3.22[1]	3.88	2.89[1]	3.77
Dry Gas Production	20.2	21.3	19.2	20.3	21.6	21.8	21.9	20.5
Net Imports	3.9	3.9	3.9	3.1	3.3	3.4	NA	NA
Consumption	24.1	25.3	23.1	23.3	25.3	24.8	25.4	24.0
Residential	4.9	5.0	4.7	4.8	4.9	4.7	5.1	4.8
Commercial	2.9	3.0	2.9	3.3	3.5	3.1	4.0	3.4
Industrial	9.0	9.4	8.7	7.8	11.3	10.9	10.7	8.6
Electric utility	4.9	5.2	4.5	4.8	4.2	3.9	4.1	5.2
Other	2.4	2.7	2.3	2.7	1.4	2.1	1.6	2.0

Source: Department of Energy, Energy Information Administration, Office of Integrated Analysis and Forecasting, *Annual Energy Outlook 1994: With Projections to 2010* (Washington, D.C.: U.S. Government Printing Office, January 1994), p. 167. *Primary source:* Energy Information Administration (EIA), AEO94 Forecasting System, runs AEO94B.D1221934 (Reference Case), HMAC94.D1221932 (High Economic Growth Case), and LMAC94.D1221932 (Low Economic Growth Case). WEFA: The Wharton Econometric Forecasts (WEFA) Group, *Energy Analysis Quarterly* (Winter 1993). Gas Research Institute (GRI): *GRI Baseline Projection of U.S. Energy Supply and Demand*, 1994 edition (August 1993). DRI: DRI/McGraw-Hill, *Energy Review* (Spring-Summer 1993). AGA: American Gas Association, *1993 AGA-TERA Base Case* (March 1993). NPC: National Petroleum Council, *The Potential for Natural Gas in the United State, Vol. VI* (December 1992). *Notes:* NA = Not available. 1. Average acquisition price.

★ 323 ★

Oil and Natural Gas

Natural Gas Imports and Exports, 1990-2010

"Pipeline import and export flows from Mexico, Canadian import (from the United States) and export (to the United States) capacities, and liquefied natural gas (LNG) imports and exports are projected exogenously to the National Energy Modeling System (NEMS). Exogenously specified projections of pipeline import and export values from Canada and Mexico are shown below.

"Mexican import and export volumes for natural gas were drawn heavily from the analysis work supporting the recent National Petroleum Council study, *The Potential for Natural Gas in the United States* (Washington, DC, 1993).

"Canadian production and exports to the United States are determined endogenously within the model. Assumed Canadian gas consumption levels (with an associated price) also affect the wellhead price by limiting the gas supply available for export to the United States. The consumption of gas in Canada was assumed to grow at 1.2 percent per year throughout the projection and in each scenario from its historical level of 2.47 trillion cubic feet in 1990 (taken from the *International Energy Annual*). Natural gas exports to Canada from the United States are expected to grow annually by 14 billion cubic feet from the 1990 level of approximately 17.4 billion cubic feet, reaching 238 billion cubic feet by 2010. The Canadian resource base estimate used in the model for the beginning of year 1990 is 304 trillion cubic feet for gas, derived from figures published by the National Energy Board. This quantity was assumed to increase at a rate of 2 percent each projection year to reflect improvements in and penetration of technology."

[Billion cubic feet per year]

Year	Canada		Mexico		Liquefied Natural Gas	
	Imports	Exports	Imports	Exports	Imports	Exports
1990	1,778	17	0	16	84	50
1995	3,000	62	0	82	193	50
2000	3,167	144	0	50	359	50
2005	3,323	204	10	10	602	50
2010	3,556	250	183	10	803	50

Source: Department of Energy, Energy Information Administration, Office of Integrated Analysis and Forecasting, *Supplement to the Annual Energy Outlook 1994* (Washington, D.C.: U.S. Government Printing Office, March 1994), p. 50. *Primary source:* Energy Information Administration (EIA), Office of Integrated Analysis and Forecasting. *Notes:* Canadian "import" figures represent design capacity, not actual flow projections, because flows are not an assumption. Canadian import flows are determined endogenously within the model.

Petroleum

★ 324 ★

International Petroleum Supply and Disposition Summary, 1990-2010

[Million barrels per day, unless otherwise noted]

Supply and Disposition	Reference Case					Annual Growth 1990-2010 (percent)	Annual Growth 1992-2010 (percent)
	1990	1992	2000	2005	2010		
World Oil Price (1992 dollars per barrel)[1]	23.22	18.20	20.72	24.90	28.16	1.0%	2.5%
Production[2]							
U.S. (50 states)	9.59	9.77	8.01	7.81	8.13	-0.8%	-1.0%
Canada	2.03	2.12	2.22	2.52	2.45	1.0%	0.8%
OECD Europe[3]	4.58	5.08	6.42	5.28	4.75	0.2%	-0.4%
OPEC	25.04	26.38	35.54	40.92	44.02	2.9%	2.9%
Rest of the World[4]	11.06	11.00	12.95	12.27	12.07	0.4%	0.5%
Total Production	52.30	54.35	65.13	68.80	71.42	1.6%	1.5%
Net Eurasian Exports	1.88	1.58	1.24	1.42	1.60	-0.8%	0.1%
Total Supply	53.60	55.93	66.37	70.22	73.02	1.6%	1.5%
Consumption							
U.S. (50 states)	16.99	17.03	19.34	20.40	21.30	1.1%	1.2%
U.S. Territories	0.21	0.21	0.25	0.27	0.27	1.4%	1.4%
Canada	1.69	1.64	1.87	1.89	1.89	0.6%	0.8%
Japan	5.14	5.45	6.78	7.14	7.23	1.7%	1.6%
Australia & New Zealand	0.82	13.61	15.49	1.01	15.95	1.1%	0.9%
OECD Europe	12.90	13.61	15.49	15.88	15.95	1.1%	0.9%
Rest of the World[4]	15.78	17.56	21.99	23.93	25.60	2.4%	2.1%
Total Consumption	53.53	56.33	66.67	70.52	73.32	1.6%	1.5%
Discrepancy	-0.07	0.40	0.30	0.30	0.30	N/A	-1.6%
Consumption Aggregations							
OECD	37.75	38.77	44.68	46.60	47.71	1.2%	1.2%
OPEC	4.61	4.95	5.89	6.51	7.18	2.2%	2.1%
Rest of the World[4]	11.18	12.61	16.10	17.42	18.42	2.5%	2.1%
Non-OPEC Production[4]	27.26	27.97	29.59	27.88	27.40	0.0%	-0.1%
OPEC Summary							
Market Share	0.47	0.47	0.53	0.58	0.60	1.3%	1.4%

[Continued]

★ 324 ★

International Petroleum Supply and Disposition Summary, 1990-2010

[Continued]

Supply and Disposition	Reference Case 1990	1992	2000	2005	2010	Annual Growth 1990-2010 (percent)	Annual Growth 1992-2010 (percent)
Production capacity[5]	29.80	28.90	38.40	44.10	47.75	2.4%	2.8%
Capacity utilization	0.84	0.91	0.93	0.93	0.92	0.5%	0.1%

Source: Department of Energy, Energy Information Administration, Office of Integrated Analysis and Forecasting, *Annual Energy Outlook 1994: With Projections to 2010* (Washington, D.C.: U.S. Government Printing Office, January 1994), p. 76. *Primary source:* 1990: Energy Information Administration (EIA), *International Energy Annual 1991*, and EIA, International Petroleum Statistics Report. 1992: (EIA), *International Energy Annual 1992*, and EIA, *Monthly Energy Review*. Projections: EIA, AEO 1994 National Energy Modeling System run AEO94B.D1221934. *Notes:* N/A=Not applicable. Totals may not equal sum of components because of independent rounding. 1. The average cost to domestic refiners of imported crude oil. 2. Includes production of crude oil (including lease condensates), natural gas plant liquids, other hydrogen and hydrocarbons for refinery feedstocks, alcohol, liquids produced from coal and other sources, and refinery gains. 3. Organization for Economic Cooperation and Development (OECD) Europe includes unified Germany. 4. Does not include Eurasia. 5. Maximum sustainable production capacity. OECD includes Australia, Austria, Belgium, Canada, Denmark, Finland, France, Germany, Greece, Ireland, Italy, Japan, Luxembourg, the Netherlands, New Zealand, Norway, Portugal, Spain, Sweden, Switzerland, Turkey, the United Kingdom, and the United States (including territories). OPEC=Organization for Petroleum Exporting Countries=Algeria, Gabon, Indonesia, Iran, Iraq, Kuwait, Libya, Nigeria, Qatar, Saudi Arabia, the United Arab Emirates, and Venezuela. Eurasia=Albania, Bulgaria, China, Czech Republic, Hungary, Poland, Romania, Slovak Republic, the former Soviet Union, and the former Yugoslavia.

★ 325 ★

Petroleum

Comparative Forecasts for Petroleum, 2000-2010

[Million barrels per day, except where noted]

Projection	EIA AEO94 Reference	EIA AEO94 High World Oil Price	EIA AEO94 Low World Oil Price	Other Forecasts WEFA	GRI	DRI	AGA	IPAA
2000								
World Oil Price (1992 dollars per barrel)	20.72	24.16	15.44	20.62[1]	21.21[1]	22.74[1]	21.54[1]	NA
Crude Oil and NGL Production	7.0	7.3	6.6	7.9	7.9	8.1	NA	7.7
Crude Oil	5.2	5.5	4.8	6.2	6.1	6.4	NA	6.0
Natural Gas Liquids	1.8	1.8	1.8	1.8	1.8	1.8	NA	1.7
Total Net Imports	10.9	10.5	12.0	8.7	9.2	9.7	NA	9.2
Petroleum Demand	19.3	19.0	20.0	18.3	15.2	18.7	NA	18.5
Motor Gasoline	8.0	7.9	8.3	7.6	7.1	7.7	NA	7.6
Jet Fuel	1.8	1.8	1.8	1.6	1.7	1.7	NA	1.8
Distillate Fuel	3.6	3.6	3.7	3.2	3.5	3.4	NA	3.4
Residual Fuel	1.3	12.	1.5	1.3	1.3	1.2	NA	1.2
Other	4.6	4.6	4.7	4.6	4.9	4.6	NA	4.5
2010								
World Oil Price (1992 dollars per barrel)	28.16	34.11	20.15	26.84[1]	27.27[1]	30.03[1]	24.47[1]	NA

[Continued]

★ 325 ★

Comparative Forecasts for Petroleum, 2000-2010

[Continued]

Projection	EIA AEO94 Reference	EIA AEO94 High World Oil Price	EIA AEO94 Low World Oil Price	Other Forecasts WEFA	GRI	DRI	AGA	IPAA
Crude Oil and NGL Production	7.1	7.9	5.6	6.8	8.5	7.0	NA	NA
Crude Oil	5.1	5.9	3.7	4.8	6.8	5.2	NA	NA
Natural Gas Liquids	2.0	1.9	1.9	2.0	1.8	1.7	NA	NA
Total Net Imports	12.8	11.3	15.3	10.4	9.9	13.1	NA	NA
Petroleum Demand	21.3	20.6	22.4	18.9	19.4	20.9	NA	NA
Motor Gasoline	8.4	8.0	8.9	7.7	6.9	8.2	NA	NA
Jet Fuel	2.1	2.1	2.2	1.6	1.9	2.0	NA	NA
Distillate Fuel	4.2	4.1	4.3	3.3	4.0	4.2	NA	NA
Residual Fuel	1.4	1.3	1.7	1.7	1.3	1.3	NA	NA
Other	5.2	5.1	5.4	4.5	5.5	5.2	NA	NA

Source: Department of Energy, Energy Information Administration, Office of Integrated Analysis and Forecasting, *Annual Energy Outlook 1994: With Projections to 2010* (Washington, D.C.: U.S. Government Printing Office, January 1994), p. 166. *Primary source:* Energy Information Administration (EIA), AEO94 Forecasting System, runs AEO94B.D1221934 (Reference Case), HWOP94.D1221932 (High World Oil Price Case), and LWOP94.D1221932 (Low World Oil Price Case). WEFA: The Wharton Economic Forecasts Group, *Energy Analysis Quarterly* (Winter 1993). Gas Research Institute (GRI): *Draft of the GRI Baseline Projection of U.S. Energy Supply and Demand*, 1994 edition (August 1993). DRI: DRI/McGraw-Hill, *Energy Review* (Spring-Summary 1993). AGA: American Gas Association, An Overview of the *1993 AGA-TERA Base Case* (June 1993). IPAA: Independent Petroleum Association of America, *IPAA Supply and Demand Committee Long-Run Forecast 1993-2000* (March 1993). *Notes:* N/A=Not available. 1. Refiner's acquisition cost.

★ 326 ★

Petroleum

Imported Petroleum by Source, 1990-2010

[Million barrels per day]

Sources	Reference Case 1990	2000	2005	2010	Annual Growth 1990-2010 (percent)
Crude Oil					
Canada	0.30	0.00	0.00	1.29	7.5%
Mexico	0.05	0.00	0.00	0.34	10.0%
North Sea	0.01	0.00	0.00	0.13	11.7%
OPEC	0.36	0.00	0.00	2.76	10.7%
Latin America	0.11	0.00	0.00	0.95	11.4%
North Africa	0.00	0.00	0.00	0.02	9.8%
West Africa	0.06	0.00	0.00	0.43	10.7%
Indonesia	0.03	0.00	0.00	0.09	5.3%
Persian Gulf	0.16	0.00	0.00	1.27	11.0%
Other Middle East	0.00	0.00	0.00	0.02	7.3%
Other Latin America	0.01	0.00	0.00	0.06	8.6%
Other Africa	0.03	0.00	0.00	0.20	11.0%
Other Asia	0.06	0.00	0.00	0.21	6.7%

[Continued]

★ 326 ★

Imported Petroleum by Source, 1990-2010

[Continued]

Sources	Reference Case				Annual Growth 1990-2010 (percent)
	1990	2000	2005	2010	
Light Refined Products[1]					
Canada	0.19	0.56	0.69	0.91	8.2%
Northern Europe	0.03	0.06	0.08	0.09	5.0%
Southern Europe	0.04	0.05	0.06	0.07	2.4%
OPEC	0.06	0.00	0.00	0.43	10.7%
Latin America	0.09	0.16	0.23	0.29	5.9%
North Africa	0.01	0.02	0.04	0.05	6.9%
West Africa	0.00	0.00	0.00	0.00	-1.5%
Indonesia	0.00	0.00	0.00	0.00	N/A
Persian Gulf	0.09	0.05	0.07	0.09	0.1%
Caribbean Basin	0.08	0.21	0.36	0.45	9.2%
Asian Exporters	0.02	0.01	0.02	0.02	2.1%
Other	0.04	0.03	0.04	0.04	-0.1%
Heavy Refined Products[2]					
Canada	0.10	0.09	0.11	0.16	2.3%
Northern Europe	0.02	0.02	0.03	0.03	3.7%
Southern Europe	0.02	0.01	0.01	0.01	-1.8%
OPEC	0.10	0.13	0.19	0.22	3.9%
Latin America	0.04	0.04	0.05	0.06	1.9%
North Africa	0.03	0.05	0.09	0.09	6.6%
West Africa	0.01	0.00	0.00	0.01	-0.9%
Indonesia	0.01	0.03	0.04	0.05	8.4%
Persian Gulf	0.02	0.01	0.01	0.01	-2.5%
Caribbean Basin	0.07	0.06	0.06	0.07	-0.4%
Asian Exporters	0.03	0.04	0.05	0.07	5.1%
Other	0.05	0.04	0.05	0.06	1.4%

Source: Department of Energy, Energy Information Administration, Office of Integrated Analysis and Forecasting, *Supplement to the Annual Energy Outlook 1994* (Washington, D.C.: U.S. Government Printing Office, March 1994), p. 50. *Primary source:* Energy Information Administration, AEO 1994 National Energy Modeling System run AEO94B.D1221934. *Notes:* N/A= Not applicable. 1. Includes gasoline, distillate, jet fuel, and liquefied petroleum gases. 2. Includes residual fuel oil and other refined products. OPEC=Organization for Petroleum Exporting Countries—Algeria, Gabon, Indonesia, Iran, Iraq, Kuwait, Libya, Nigeria, Qatar, Saudi Arabia, the United Arab Emirates, and Venezuela. Caribbean basin=Colombia, Ecuador, Guatemala, Jamaica, Mexico, Netherlands Antilles, Panama, Puerto Rico, Trinidad and Tobago, Venezuela, and the Virgin Islands.

★ 327 ★

Petroleum

Market Share for Gasoline Types by Census Division, 1990-1997 and Later

[Percent]

Gasoline Type/Year	Census Division								
	1	2	3	4	5	6	7	8	9
Traditional Gasoline									
1990-1991	100.00	100.00	100.00	100.00	100.00	100.00	100.00	100.00	100.00
1992	96.47	89.10	100.00	100.00	100.00	100.00	100.00	95.63	87.20
1993	89.31	66.97	100.00	100.00	100.00	100.00	100.00	86.77	61.20
1994	89.31	66.97	100.00	100.00	100.00	100.00	100.00	88.77	61.20
1995	9.05	7.69	75.82	83.93	79.00	100.00	70.15	86.77	36.53
1996	9.05	7.69	35.00	72.90	57.02	67.43	66.39	66.62	17.81
1997 forward	9.05	7.69	35.00	62.97	50.18	67.43	63.65	66.62	17.81
Oxygenated Gasoline (2.7% oxygen)									
1990-1991	0.00	0.00	0.00	0.00	0.00	0.00	0.00	0.00	0.00
1992	3.53	10.90	0.00	0.00	0.00	0.00	0.00	4.37	12.80
1993	10.69	33.03	0.00	0.00	0.00	0.00	0.00	13.23	38.80
1994	10.69	33.03	0.00	0.00	0.00	0.00	0.00	13.23	38.80
1995	0.00	0.00	0.00	16.07	0.00	0.00	0.00	13.23	17.77
1996	0.00	0.00	0.00	16.07	0.00	0.00	0.00	8.82	6.13
1997 forward	0.00	0.00	0.00	26.00	0.00	0.00	0.00	8.82	6.13
Reformulated - Oxygenated Gasoline (2.7% oxygen)									
1990-1991	0.00	0.00	0.00	0.00	0.00	0.00	0.00	0.00	0.00
1992	0.00	0.00	0.00	0.00	0.00	0.00	0.00	0.00	0.00
1993	0.00	0.00	0.00	0.00	0.00	0.00	0.00	0.00	0.00
1994	0.00	0.00	0.00	0.00	0.00	0.00	0.00	0.00	0.00
1995	10.69	32.15	0.00	0.00	0.00	0.00	0.00	0.00	0.00
1996	10.69	32.15	0.00	0.00	0.00	0.00	0.00	0.00	0.00
1997 forward	10.69	32.15	0.00	0.00	0.00	0.00	0.00	0.00	0.00
Reformulated Gasoline (2.0% oxygen)									
1990-1991	0.00	0.00	0.00	0.00	0.00	0.00	0.00	0.00	0.00
1992	0.00	0.00	0.00	0.00	0.00	0.00	0.00	0.00	0.00
1993	0.00	0.00	0.00	0.00	0.00	0.00	0.00	0.00	0.00
1994	0.00	0.00	0.00	0.00	0.00	0.00	0.00	0.00	0.00
1995	80.26	60.16	24.18	0.00	21.00	0.00	29.87	0.00	45.70
1996	80.26	60.16	65.00	11.03	42.98	32.57	33.61	24.55	76.06
1997 forward	80.26	60.16	65.00	11.03	49.82	32.57	36.35	24.55	76.06

Source: Department of Energy, Energy Information Administration, Office of Integrated Analysis and Forecasting, *Supplement to the Annual Energy Outlook 1994* (Washington, D.C.: U.S. Government Printing Office, March 1994), p. 65. *Primary source:* Energy Information Administration, Office of Integrated Analysis and Forecasting.

★ 328 ★

Petroleum

Petroleum Product Prices, 1990-2010

[1992 cents per gallon unless otherwise noted]

Sector and Fuel	Reference Case					Annual Growth 1990-2010	Annual Growth 1992-2010
	1990	1992	2000	2005	2010	(percent)	(percent)
World Oil Price (dollars per barrel)	23.32	18.20	20.72	24.90	28.16	1.0%	2.5%
Delivered Sector Product Prices							
Residential							
Distillate Fuel	118.5	92.7	104.2	115.7	124.0	0.2%	1.6%
Liquefied Petroleum Gas	106.6	86.7	96.0	106.1	116.4	0.4%	1.6%
Commercial							
Distillate Fuel	90.3	66.0	72.5	83.5	92.0	0.1%	1.9%
Residual Fuel	54.8	39.3	53.3	63.3	70.7	1.3%	3.3%
Residual Fuel (dollars per barrel)	23.02	16.50	22.37	26.58	29.69	1.3%	3.3%
Industrial							
Distillate Fuel	84.1	67.6	72.2	83.3	92.2	0.5%	1.7%
Liquefied Petroleum Gas	52.6	42.7	55.4	65.7	74.8	1.8%	3.2%
Petrochemical Feedstocks	83.7	64.1	50.6	60.7	70.4	-0.9%	0.5%
Residual Fuel	49.5	38.0	53.0	64.1	71.8	1.9%	3.6%
Residual Fuel (dollars per barrel)	20.80	15.95	22.26	26.92	30.17	1.9%	3.6%
Transportation							
Distillate Fuel[1]	125.2	111.2	128.7	141.3	150.7	0.9%	1.7%
Jet Fuel[2]	81.8	61.0	72.6	83.7	98.3	0.7%	2.4%
Motor Gasoline[3]	121.7	113.7	128.8	139.7	147.5	1.0%	1.5%
Residual Fuel	47.6	32.1	48.3	58.4	67.7	1.8%	4.2%
Residual Fuel (dollars per barrel)	19.99	13.47	20.28	24.52	28.43	1.8%	4.2%
Electric Utilities							
Distillate Fuel	83.2	62.6	67.2	78.6	87.5	0.3%	1.9%
Residual Fuel	52.7	37.5	52.0	63.2	71.1	1.5%	3.6%
Residual Fuel (dollars per barrel)	22.14	15.77	21.86	26.55	29.88	1.5%	3.6%
Refined Petroleum Product Prices[4]							
Distillate Fuel	113.9	97.6	111.5	123.8	133.7	0.8%	1.8%
Jet Fuel	81.8	61.0	72.6	83.7	93.3	0.7%	2.4%
Liquefied Petroleum Gas	58.9	51.9	63.6	73.9	83.6	1.8%	2.7%
Motor Gasoline	121.7	113.7	128.8	139.7	147.5	1.0%	1.5%
Petrochemical Feedstocks	83.7	64.1	50.6	60.7	70.4	-0.9%	0.5%
Residual Fuel	50.6	35.5	50.6	61.0	69.4	1.6%	3.8%

[Continued]

★ 328 ★

Petroleum Product Prices, 1990-2010

[Continued]

Sector and Fuel	Reference Case					Annual Growth 1990-2010	Annual Growth 1992-2010
	1990	1992	2000	2005	2010	(percent)	(percent)
Residual Fuel (dollars per barrel)	21.26	14.90	21.25	25.64	29.14	1.6%	3.8%
Average	102.2	90.8	103.4	113.9	122.2	0.9%	1.7%

Source: Department of Energy, Energy Information Administration, Office of Integrated Analysis and Forecasting, *Annual Energy Outlook 1994: With Projections to 2010* (Washington, D.C.: U.S. Government Printing Office, January 1994), p. 69. *Primary source:* 1990 prices: Energy Information Administration (EIA), *State Energy Price and Expenditures Report* (Washington, D.C., September 1993). 1992 prices for gasoline, distillate, and jet fuel are based on prices in the EIA, *Petroleum Marketing Annual 1992* (Washington, D.C., July 1993). 1992 prices for all other petroleum prices are derived from the EIA, *State Energy Price and Expenditures Report* (Washington, D.C., September 1993). Projections: EIA, AEO 1994 National Energy Modeling System run AEO93B.D1221934. *Notes:* Reference case projections. 1. Includes Federal and State taxes and excludes county and local taxes. 2. Kerosene-type jet fuel. 3. Average price for all grades. Incudes Federal and State taxes and excludes county and local taxes. 4. Weighted averages of end-use fuel prices are derived from the prices in each sector and the corresponding sectoral consumption.

Renewable Resources and Alternative Fuels

★ 329 ★

Renewable Energy, 1990-2010

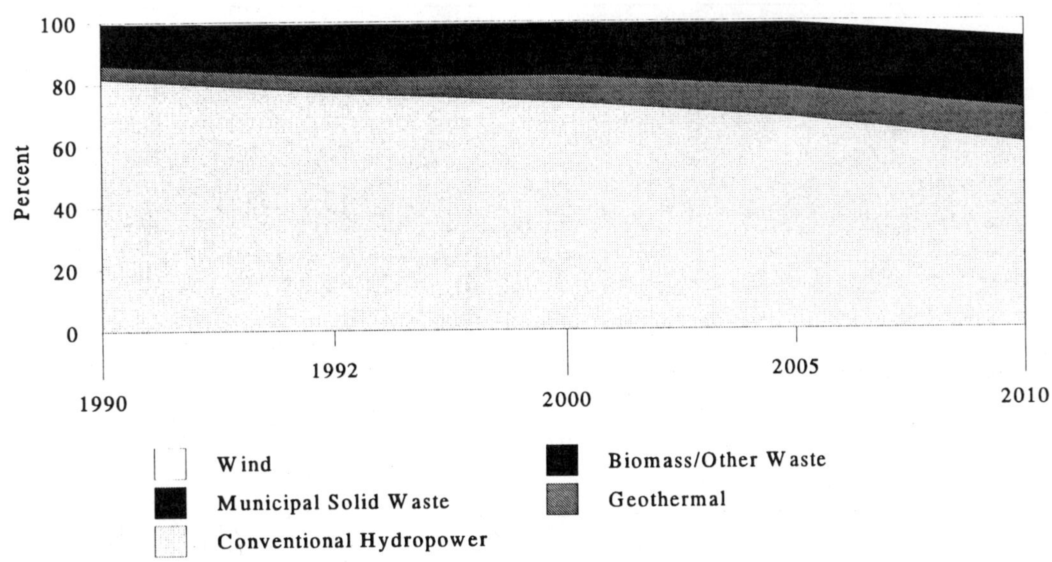

Quadrillion Btu per year, unless otherwise noted]

Electric and Nonelectric	Reference Case					Annual Growth 1990-2010 (percent)	Annual Growth 1992-2010 (percent)
	1990	1992	2000	2005	2010		
Electricity							
Capability (gigawatts)							
Conventional Hydropower	75.30	75.54	78.29	78.43	78.53	0.2%	0.2%
Geothermal[1]	2.91	2.89	5.54	6.56	8.54	5.5%	6.2%
Municipal Solid Waste	2.13	2.66	3.64	4.43	5.24	4.6%	3.8%
Biomass/Other Waste[2]	6.86	7.29	9.23	12.20	15.17	4.0%	4.2%
Solar[3]	0.36	0.36	0.73	0.98	1.33	6.7%	7.5%
Wind[4]	1.55	1.65	1.76	1.98	10.65	10.1%	10.9%
Total	89.11	90.40	99.20	104.56	119.45	1.5%	1.6%
Generation (billion kilowatthours)							
Conventional Hydropower	288.04	247.88	305.07	305.89	306.58	0.4%	1.3%
Geothermal[1]	15.86	16.68	36.01	43.19	57.15	6.6%	7.1%
Municipal Solid Waste	12.32	17.24	20.17	26.04	32.04	5.5%	4.0%
Biomass/Other Waste[2]	34.14	41.73	48.42	65.94	83.63	13.6%	13.8%
Solar[3]	0.70	1.75	2.35	3.36	4.81	10.1%	5.8%
Wind[4]	2.38	2.91	2.91	3.55	29.09	13.3%	13.6%

[Continued]

★ 329 ★

Renewable Energy, 1990-2010

[Continued]

Electric and Nonelectric	Reference Case					Annual Growth 1990-2010 (percent)	Annual Growth 1992-2010 (percent)
	1990	1992	2000	2005	2010		
Total	353.44	328.19	414.93	447.97	513.30	1.9%	2.5%
Consumption Equivalent							
Conventional Hydropower	2.98	2.57	3.16	3.17	3.17	0.4%	1.3%
Geothermal[1]	0.16	0.17	0.37	0.45	0.59	6.6%	7.2%
Municipal Solid Waste	0.13	0.18	0.21	0.27	0.33	5.5%	4.1%
Biomass/Other Waste[2]	0.35	0.43	0.50	0.68	0.87	13.6%	17.2%
Solar[3]	0.01	0.01	0.02	0.03	0.05	10.1%	9.3%
Wind[4]	0.02	0.03	0.03	0.04	0.30	13.3%	13.9%
Total	3.66	3.40	4.30	4.64	5.32	1.9%	2.5%
Nonelectric Renewable Energy							
Residential, Commercial, and Industrial							
Geothermal	0.01	0.01	0.01	0.02	0.02	7.9%	7.3%
Biofuels	2.53	2.57	3.00	3.22	3.44	1.6%	1.6%
Solar Thermal	0.02	0.02	0.04	0.04	0.04	3.8%	4.0%
Transportation							
Ethanol	0.06	0.09	0.11	0.12	0.13	3.9%	2.0%
Total	2.62	2.69	3.16	3.39	3.63	1.8%	1.9%
Total Renewable Energy	6.28	6.07	7.45	8.02	8.94	1.8%	1.9%

Source: Department of Energy, Energy Information Administration, Office of Integrated Analysis and Forecasting, *Annual Energy Outlook 1994: With Projections to 2010* (Washington, D.C.: U.S. Government Printing Office, January 1994), p. 73. *Primary source:* 1990 and 1992 ethanol: Energy Information Administration (EIA), *Weekly Petroleum Status Report* (Washington, D.C., January 1993). Other 1990 and 1992: EIA, sum of EIA-860 "Annual Electric Generator Report" and EIA-867 "Annual Nonutility Power Producer Report." Projections: EIA, AEO 1994 National Energy Modeling System run AEO94B.D1221934. *Notes:* Btu=British thermal unit. Includes renewables used in industrial power generation and cogeneration. Totals may not equal sum of components because of independent rounding. 1. Includes hydrothermal resources only (hot water and steam). 2. Does not include projections for energy crops. 3. Utility-grid connected generation only. 4. Includes horizontal-axis wind turbines only.

★ 330 ★

Renewable Resources and Alternative Fuels

U.S. Electricity Net Generation Using Renewable Resources, 1990-2010

"If renewable resources are to provide a greater share of the Nation's electricity supply, the cost of using them will need to decline relative to alternatives. In some cases, such as wind and solar thermal generation, small improvements in generating costs may significantly increase their market penetration. In other cases, such as photovoltaic and most forms of geothermal power, large cost reductions are needed to spur greater market penetration. Of course, other events may also work to accelerate the use of renewable resources. Increases in fossil-fuel costs and additional environmental regulations on fossil-fueled plants could make the use of renewable resources economically more attractive. In addition, social policies, including favorable tax treatments or other forms of assistance, could promote interest in renewable resource use."

[Billion kilowatthours]

	1990	Reference Case 2010	Annual Percentage Rate of Growth 1990-2010[1]
Conventional Hydroelectric	288	306	0.3
Geothermal	15	62	7.2
Municipal Solid Waste	10	54	8.5
Biomass	31	59	3.2
Solar[2]	1	4	9.2
Wind	2	16	10.4
Total, Renewable Resources	348	501	1.8
Fossil/Storage/Other	2,098	2,975	1.8
Nuclear	577	636	0.5
Total Generation	3,023	4,112	1.5

Source: Department of Energy, Energy Information Administration, *Renewable Resources in the U.S. Electricity Supply* (Washington, D.C.: U.S. Government Printing Office, February 1993), p. viii. Primary source: Energy Information Administration. 1990: For utilities, EIA-861 "Annual Electric Utility Report;" for nonutilities, EIA-867, "Annual Nonutility Power Producer Report." 2010 projections: *Annual Energy Outlook 1993,* AEO 1993 Forecasting System run AEO93B.D0918921 (Washington, D.C., January 1993). *Notes:* 1. Annual percentage rates of growth are calculated using unrounded values. 2. Includes solar thermal and less than 0.02 billion kilowatthours grid-connected photovoltaic operation. Totals may not equal sum of components because of independent rounding. Electric utility generation data exclude internal generating station use (net); nonutility data include internal use (gross).

★ 331 ★

Renewable Resources and Alternative Fuels

U.S. Electric Generating Capacity and Net Generation Using Renewable Resources, 2010

Technology	1990[1]	2010 Reference	2010 High Economic Growth	2010 Low Economic Growth	2010 High World Oil Price	2010 Low World Oil Price
Net Summer Capability (Gigawatts)						
Conventional Hydropower	72.9	76.9	76.9	76.9	76.9	76.9
Geothermal	2.6	8.5	8.5	8.5	9.7	7.3
Municipal Solid Waste	2.0	11.4	13.9	10.9	11.4	11.4
Biomass/Other Waste[2]	6.0	8.1	8.3	7.2	8.1	8.1
Solar[3]	0.4	1.9	1.9	1.9	2.2	1.7
Wind	1.4	6.3	6.3	6.3	7.3	5.3
Total Capacity, Renewable	85.2	113.1	115.9	111.7	115.5	110.7
Fossil/Nuclear/Other[4]	647.8	767.0	814.2	722.1	759.4	780.6
Total Generating Capacity	733.0	880.1	930.1	833.8	874.9	891.3
Percent Renewable	11.6	12.9	12.5	13.4	13.2	12.4
Net Generation (Billion Kilowatthours)						
Conventional Hydropower	288	306	306	306	306	306
Geothermal	15	62	62	62	72	53
Municipal Solid Waste	10	54	70	50	54	54
Biomasss/Other Waste[2]	31	59	60	54	59	59
Solar[3,5]	1	4	4	4	4	3
Wind	2	16	16	16	19	14
Total Renewable	348	501	519	492	513	488
Fossil/Nuclear/Other[4]	2,675	3,611	3,816	3,393	3,576	3,679
Total Net Generation	3,023	4,112	4,335	3,885	4,089	4,167
Percent Renewable	11.5	12.2	12.0	12.7	12.5	11.7

Source: Department of Energy, Energy Information Administration, *Renewable Resources in the U.S. Electricity Supply* (Washington, D.C.: U.S. Government Printing Office, February 1993), p. 16. *Primary source:* Energy Information Administration. 1990: For utilities, EIA-861 "Annual Electric Utility Report"; for nonutilities, EIA-867, "Annual Nonutility Power Producer Report." Projections for 2000 and 2010: *Annual Energy Outlook 1993*, DOE/EIA-0383 (93). *Notes:* Totals may not equal sum of components due to independent rounding. 1. The 1990 data shown in the table are actual EIA published values (preliminary data), while the 1990 values published in the *Annual Energy Outlook 1993* are estimates. 2. Includes wood, wood waste, and other biomass. 3. Includes both solar thermal and grid-connected photovoltaic capacity. 4. Includes pumped-storage hydroelectric. 5. Includes solar thermal and less than 0.02 billion kilowatthours grid-connected photovoltaic generation. Forecasts of renewable electric generating capacity for the High and Low Oil and Gas Recovery Cases are the same as for the Reference Case.

★ 332 ★

Renewable Resources and Alternative Fuels

Comparison of Forecasts for Renewable Resources, 2010

	EIA Reference Case	WEFA	DRI[1]	GRI[1]	UCS Reference Case	UCS Climate Stabilization Case
Generating Capability (Net Summer Capability) (Gigawatts)						
Conventional Hydroelectric	76.9	97.9[2]	71.6	71.5	99	NA
Geothermal	8.5				7	NA
Biomass/Waste (MSW)	19.5	9.1[3]	9.9[3]	4.1	15	NA
Solar	1.9				6	NA
Wind	6.3				8	NA
Total Renewables (Utilities and Nonutilities)	113.1	107.0	NA	NA	135	NA
Total Capability	860.1	879.8	NA	NA	953	NA
Percent Renewables	12.9	12.2	NA	NA	14.2	NA
Total Renewables (Utilities Only)	81.0	NA	81.5	75.6	NA	NA
Total Capacity	766.3	NA	920.4	827.9	NA	NA
Percent Renewables	10.6	NA	8.9	9.1	NA	NA
Net Generation (Billion Kilowatthours)						
Conventional Hydroelectric	306.5	331.2	335.8	283.3[2]	326	343
Geothermal	62.1				53	60
Biomass/Waste (MSW)	112.4	30.5[3]	17.7[3]	9.9	113	136
Solar	3.8				13	39
Wind	16.2				17	117
Total Renewables (Utilities and Nonutilities)	500.9	361.7	NA	NA	522	695
Total Generation	4,112.0	3,867.6	NA	NA	4,430	2,576
Percent Renewables	12.2	9.4	NA	NA	11.8	27.0
Total Renewables (Utilities Only)	335.2	NA	353.5	293.2	NA	NA
Total Generation	3,522.4	NA	3,867.1	3,394.8	NA	NA
Percent Renewables	9.5	NA	9.1	8.6	NA	NA

Source: U.S. Department of Energy, Energy Information Administration, *Renewable Resources in the U.S. Electricity Supply* (Washington, D.C.: U.S. Government Printing Office, February 1993), p. 19. *Primary source:* Energy Information Administration, AEO 1993 Forecasting System run AEO93B.D0918921 (reference case). WEFA: The Wharton Econometric Forecasts Group, *Energy Analysis Quarterly* (Summer 1992). DRI: DRI/McGraw-Hill, *Energy Review* (Second Quarter 1992). Gas Research Institute (GRI): *Implications of the GRI Baseline Projection of U.S. Energy Supply and Demand*, 1993 edition (August 1992) and *Draft of GRI93 Baseline Projections* (August 1992). UCS: The Union of Concerned Scientists, *America's Energy Choices, Investing in a Strong Economy and a Clean Environment* (Cambridge, MA 1991). *Notes:* NA=Not available. MSW=Municipal Solid Waste. 1. Electric utilities only (excluding nonutilities), nameplate capacity. 2. Includes pumped storage hydroelectric. 3. Includes small amounts of "other" such as waste heat and petroleum coke.

★ 333 ★

Renewable Resources and Alternative Fuels

Utility and Nonutility Electric Capability for Renewable Technologies, 2000-2010

[Gigawatts]

Renewables	2000		2010	
	Utility	Nonutility	Utility	Nonutility
Conventional Hydroelectric	75.0	1.9	75.0	1.9
Wind	0.0	3.6	0.0	6.3
Solar Thermal	0.1	1.2	0.3	1.7
Geothermal	2.8	2.4	4.3	4.3
Photovoltaic	0.0	0.0	0.0	0.0
Wood	0.4	7.3	0.5	7.6
Municipal Solid Waste	0.5	6.2	1.0	10.4
Total	78.7	22.5	81.0	32.1

Source: U.S. Department of Energy, Energy Information Administration, *Renewable Resources in the U.S. Electricity Supply* (Washington, D.C.: U.S. Government Printing Office, February 1993), p. 30. *Primary source:* Energy Information Administration, Office of Integrated Analysis and Forecasting. *Note:* Totals may not equal sum of components due to independent rounding.

★ 334 ★

Renewable Resources and Alternative Fuels

Maximum Hydroelectric Capacity, 1990-2000

[Megawatts]

Year	Maximum capacity	Year	Maximum capacity
1990	74,640	2000	77,530
1991	74,640	2001	77,540
1992	74,930	2002	77,550
1993	75,030	2003	77,560
1994	75,340	2004	77,580
1995	75,470	2005	77,590
1996	75,670	2006	77,600
1997	75,800	2007	77,620
1998	76,690	2008	77,620
1999	77,500	2009	77,620
		2010	77,620

Source: Department of Energy, Energy Information Administration, Office of Integrated Analysis and Forecasting, *Supplement to the Annual Energy Outlook 1994* (Washington, D.C.: U.S. Government Printing Office, March 1994), p. 73. *Primary source:* Energy Information Administration, Office of Integrated Analysis and Forecasting. Data for hydroelectric capacity are derived from capacity changes report on Forms EIA-860 and EIA-867 and are outputs from the Hydroelectric Power Submodule.

★ 335 ★

Renewable Resources and Alternative Fuels

U.S. Coalbed Methane Production, 1980-2010

"With current coalbed methane technology, it is feasible to produce large amounts of coalbed methane in Appalachia: An estimated 70 to 110 billion cubic feet (Bcf) of coalbed methane could be cost-effectively produced in 2000, and 518 to 583 Bcf in 2010. These estimates are based on analyses conducted by the Gas Research Institute (GRI) and the U.S. Environmental Protection Agency (EPA) and include both coalbed methane production in conjunction with coal mining and from non-mining areas. At these production levels, coalbed methane would represent a significant fraction of Appalachian natural gas production. In 2000, for example, coalbed methane would account for an estimated 7 to 10 percent of regional natural gas production. By 2010, its share could grow to 15 to 20 percent. Annual production would still represent only a small percentage of total coalbed methane resources, which are large in Appalachia. The basin's total coalbed methane resources are estimated by GRI to be 66 trillion cubic feet (Tcf), which represents 10 percent of U.S. coalbed methane resources."

[In Bcf (Billion cubic feet)]

Year	San Juan Basin	Black Warrior Basin	Other Basins[1]	Total
1980	<1	<1	0	<1
1985	2	9	0	11
1990	154	37	0	190
1995	440	145	30	615
2000	1,101	308	111	1,520
2010	816	392	715	1,923

Source: Environmental Protection Agency, Office of Air and Radiation, Global Change Division, *The Environmental and Economic Benefits of Coalbed Methane Development in Appalachia* (Washington, D.C.: U.S. Government Printing Office, November 1992), pp. 1,7. *Primary source:* 1980-1990 data from Advanced Resources International, Inc.; projections are from *Baseline Projection Data Book*, Gas Research Institute, 1992. *Notes:* "Other Basins" includes the Appalachian and Peceance basins, as well as other western coal basins.

★ 336 ★

Renewable Resources and Alternative Fuels

Reduction in Methane Emissions from Coal Mining by Coal Basin, 1988-2010

"If all of Appalachia's profitable reductions are made in 2000, the region's methane emissions from coal mining could be reduced by 3 to 25 percent, and U.S. methane emissions from coal mining by 2 to 15 percent. These reductions would be equivalent to 2 to 17 million tons of carbon dioxide. For comparison, these reductions represent the amount of CO_2 emitted by 0.5 to 3.9 million cars. Similarly, in 2010, the emission reductions would represent 10 to 30 percent of the regions, emissions and 5 to 20 percent of U.S. emissions from coal mining. Achieving comparable greenhouse gas emissions through transportation changes would require displacing 1.9 to 6.3 million cars."

[In Bcf (Billion cubic feet)]

Basin	1988	2000	2010
Appalachia	120-200	120-225	145-280
Black Warrior	35-40	40-45	55-75
Illinois	15-20	20-25	30-40
Western	15-25	30-55	45-75
Total	180-285	205-350	270-470

Source: U.S. Environmental Protection Agency, Office of Air and Radiation, Global Change Division, *The Environmental and Economic Benefits of Coalbed Methane Development in Appalachia* (Washington, D.C.: U.S. Government Printing Office, November 1992), pp. 1,7. *Primary source: Anthropogenic Methane Emissions in the United States: Report to Congress*, final draft, August 1992.

Chapter 9
ENVIRONMENTAL ISSUES AND NATURAL RESOURCES

Effects and Costs of Federal Mandates

★ 337 ★

Trends in Environmental Issues, 1985-2050

"Air pollution and other atmospheric issues will dominate eco-policy discussions for years to come.

—Soot and other particulates will be more carefully scrutinized in the near future. Recent evidence shows that they are far more dangerous than sulfur dioxide and other gaseous pollutants formerly believed to present major health risks. In the United States alone, medical researchers estimate that as many as 60,000 people may die each year as a direct result of breathing particulates. Most are elderly and already suffering from respiratory illness.

—By 1985, the concentration of carbon dioxide in the atmosphere had increased 25 times since pre-industrial days. By 2050, the concentration is likely to increase 40% over today's levels if energy use continues to grow at its current pace. Burning fossil fuel will spew about 7 billion tons of carbon into the air each year by 2000, 10-14 billion in 2030, and 13-23 billion in 2050.

—Blame global warming for at least some of the spread of Africa's deserts. Before the process runs its course, two-fifths of Africa's remaining fertile land could become arid wasteland. Up to one-third of Asia's non-desert land and one-fifth of Latin America's may follow. Global warming will not only hurt agriculture, but will also raise sea levels, with consequent impacts on habitation patterns and industries.

—Brazil and other nations will soon halt the irrevocable destruction of the earth's rain forests for very temporary economic gain. Those countries will need economic help to make the transition. The World Bank and the International Monetary Fund (IMF) will help underwrite alternatives to rain-forest destruction.

—Acid rain such as that afflicting the United States and Canada will appear whenever designers of new power plants and factories neglect emission-control equipment. Watch for it in most developing countries.

"Disposal of mankind's trash is a growing problem, especially in developed nations. Within the next decade, most of the industrialized world will all but run out of convenient space in its landfills.

[Continued]

★ 337 ★

Trends in Environmental Issues, 1985-2050

[Continued]

—The U.S. Environmental Protection Agency estimates that existing technologies could reduce the total amount of hazardous waste generated in the United States by 15%—30% by 2000.

—For now, recycling is a necessary nuisance. By 2000, recyclables will become valuable resources, as research finds profitable new uses for materials currently being discarded. Recycling will save energy as well: Remanufacturing requires less energy than does the full iron-ore-to-Cadillac production process."

Source: Martin Cetron and Owen Davies, "Trends Shaping the World," in *The Futurist*, September-October 1991, pp. 14-15. *Primary source:* Marvin J. Cetron and Owen Davies, *Crystal Globe: The Haves and Haveenots of the New World Order* (St. Martin's Press, 1991).

★ 338 ★

Effects and Costs of Federal Mandates

U.S. Pollution Control Expenditures, 1972-2000

[Millions of 1991 dollars]

Year	
1972	52
1976	70
1980	82
1984	80
1988	97
1992	130
1996	143
2000	162

Source: U.S. Actions for a Better Environment (Washington, D.C.: U.S. Government Printing Office, 1991, p. 1. *Primary source:* Environmental Investments: The Cost of a Clean Environment, 1991. *Note:* Magnitudes estimated from published chart.

★ 339 ★

Effects and Costs of Federal Mandates

Regulatory Costs of Government Mandates, 1977-2000

"The next President will have to contend with major new laws—such as the Americans With Disabilities Act and the 1990 Clean Air Act, which have yet to be fully translated into rules for business and local governments to meet. Paul R. Portney, a senior fellow at Resources for the Future, a non-partisan environmental economics research group in Washington, says the act is one reason Americans will be spending 2.8% of Gross Domestic Product (GDP) to comply with federal environmental mandates by the end of the decade. Germans are no less green and face a monumental challenge in cleaning up the former East. Yet, Portney estimates, Germany will be spending 1.6% to 1.8% of Gross National Product (GNP). None of these estimates include the unknown potential cost of legislation being considered that would impose tough recycling standards on the packaging industry, or whatever actions are taken to tackle global warming."

[Billions of 1991 dollars]

	1977	1992	2000
Paperwork	120	200	215
Other economic and social	430	250	285
Environmental	25	130	160
TOTAL	575	580	660

Source: Louis S. Richman, "Bringing Reason to Regulation," in *Fortune*, 19 October 1992, p. 95. *Primary source:* Thomas Hopkins, Rochester Institute of Technology. *Notes:* Costs are annualized in billions of 1991 dollars. Magnitudes estimated from published chart.

★ 340 ★

Effects and Costs of Federal Mandates

Cost to Local Governments of Compliance with EPA Regulations, 1987-2000

"The Environmental Protection Agency (EPA) conservatively estimates that the cost (in real, uninflated, dollars) to local governments of complying with its regulations will be as much as 85 percent higher in the year 2000 as in 1987. The costs to local taxpayers by 2000, according to the EPA, will exceed $32 billion (in 1986 dollars). This does not include the costs imposed on businesses and consumers. These estimates are especially alarming in the light of the fact that, in the past, the EPA's cost projections have been underestimated by as much as a multiple of 30...

"To be conservative, let us assume the EPA's cost estimates are off by only a multiple of two, not twenty or thirty, as too often has been the case. Then by its own estimates, the cost to local taxpayers of complying with environmental mandates could be approximately $64 billion by the end of this decade.

[Continued]

★ 340 ★

Cost to Local Governments of Compliance with EPA Regulations, 1987-2000

[Continued]

"Most of these costs are borne ostensibly to improve public health by cleaning up the air, water, and land. To put the $64 billion into perspective, it is five to six times what is currently spent on medical research in the United States each year...

"Between 1991 and 2000, according to the city of Columbus' study of *major* environmental regulations, city taxpayers would pay over $1.6 billion (in constant 1991 dollars) just for the environmental mandates in existence in 1991. At the time the report was published, some 600 additional regulatory rules were being developed. Furthermore, the study only reported the direct costs. (Indirect or hidden costs were not considered)...

"Soon after the study was released, economic journalist Warren Brookes estimated that, if other American cities must bear the same costs as Columbus does, then local taxpayers will pay about $400 billion for environmental mandates during the decade of the 1990s. The Columbus study and Brookes' cost estimate came before the Clean Air Act Amendments of 1990 went into effect. Waiting in the wings of Congress are reauthorization proposals for the Resource Conservation and Recovery Act (RCRA), and the Comprehensive Environmental Response Compensation and Liability Act (or Superfund).

"As the Boston-based National Consumer Law Center concluded in a study of how regulatory costs affect the poor, the costs of clean water laws 'hit low-income people especially hard' because 'water bills represent a relatively large portion of their income, and the poor often live in apartments with leaky plumbing over which they have no control.' In Boston, the Center estimates, average water bills will increase from $500 annually to over $1600 by 2000, which will force many of the poor to 'cut back on food, clothing and material care'."

Source: Thomas J. DiLorenzo, Center for the Study of American Business, *Unfunded Federal Mandates: Environmentalism's Achilles Heel?* (St. Louis: Washington University), 1993, pp. 4-6, 10.

★ 341 ★

Effects and Costs of Federal Mandates

EPA Increases in Local User Fees and Taxes Due to Environmental Mandates, 1987-2000

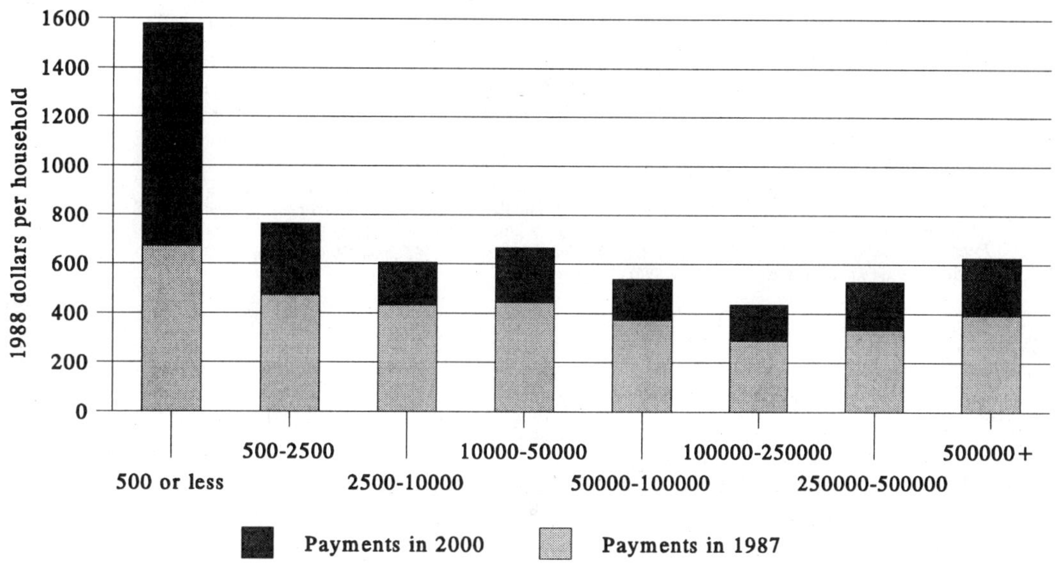

"As shown [in the table below], the EPA acknowledges the special burden its regulations place on smaller communities. Unfortunately, there is little reason to believe that these estimates are any more accurate than the estimates mentioned earlier that were off by multiples of 20 and 30. Regardless, [the table] does show significant 'diseconomies of scale' for environmental mandates placed on local governments.

"Taxpayers will be paying these increased costs through escalating state and local taxes and fees of various kinds. Currently, states charge for water and sewer services through myriad means, including water usage fees, connection fees, population-based operating fees, and water delivery taxes, to mention a few. The National Governors Association states: 'The public undoubtedly will pay a growing share of SDWA [Safe Drinking Water Act] costs through [increased] fees and state taxes'."

[Constant 1988 dollars per household]

City population	Payments in 1987	Payments in 2000	Percent change (1987 to 2000)
500 or less	$670	$1,580	136%
500-2,500	473	763	61%
2,500-10,000	433	605	40%
10,000-50,000	444	665	50%
50,000-100,000	373	539	45%
100,000-250,000	291	436	50%
250,000-500,000	335	529	58%

[Continued]

★ 341 ★

EPA Increases in Local User Fees and Taxes Due to Environmental Mandates, 1987-2000

[Continued]

City population	Payments in 1987	Payments in 2000	Percent change (1987 to 2000)
500,000 or more	393	626	59%
Population weighted average	419	647	54%

Source: Thomas J. DiLorenzo, Center for the Study of American Business, *Unfunded Federal Mandates: Environmentalism's Achilles Heel?* (St. Louis: Washington University), 1993, pp. 6, 9. *Primary source: A Preliminary Analysis of the Public Costs of Environmental Protection: 1981-2000* (Washington, D.C.: U.S. Environmental Protection Agency, May 1990).

★ 342 ★

Effects and Costs of Federal Mandates

Revenues Required to Maintain Water Quality Programs, 1990-2010

[Billions of dollars]

Year	O&M	Debt service[1]	Total
1990	4.84	1.74	6.58
1995	7.86	4.20	12.06
2000	12.78	6.36	19.14
2005	20.77	6.59	27.36
2010	33.75	5.47	39.22

Source: U.S. House of Representatives, Committee on Merchant Marine and Fisheries, *Clean Water Funding: A Proposal for a National Clean Water Investment Corporation* (Washington, D.C.: U.S. Government Printing Office, August 1992), p. 118. *Notes:* AMSA=Association of Metropolitan Sewerage Agencies. 1. The Debt Service is based on a 20-year bond at 7% annual interest rate. Projections of debt service and operation and maintenance needs for the 1990-2010 period indicate that high costs will not diminish in the future. AMSA's Needs Survey results focus only on costs associated with compliance with existing requirements. As communities face new environmental mandates, the cost burden will continue to escalate.

★ 343 ★

Effects and Costs of Federal Mandates

Cost of Maintaining Municipal Wastewater Needs, 2000-2010

[Millions of dollars]

State	Secondary treatment	Advanced treatment	Infil/ inflow	Replacement/Rehabilitation			Collection system	CSOs	Separate stormwater	Air toxics/ Air quality	Total
				Sewers	Treatment plant	Pumping stations					
Alaska 001	20.0		5.0	30.0	10.0	1.5	5.0				71.5
Alaska 001				30.0							30.0
Alaska 002			3.0	7.0		3.0					13.0
Arizona 001	20.0	10.0				5.0	15.0				50.0
Arizona 002	17.0	49.9		2.0	41.5	4.0	2.8			7.2	124.4
California 001											
California 002	200.0	100.0		50.0	150.0	20.0					520.0
California 003	2.0	5.0		25.0	5.0	5.0	16.0			2.0	60.0
California 004											
California 005	17.9		2.9	97.7	25.0	12.3					155.8
California 006		459.0						487.0			946.0
California 008	187.0	613.0	5.0				35.0				840.0
California 009	109.8	201.0									310.8
California 010											
California 011											
California 013		120.0									120.0
Colorado 001											
Colorado 002		3.0		10.0	4.5	0.2	10.5				30.2
Connecticut 001								80.0			80.0
District of Columbia 001											
Florida 001											
Florida 002		40.0		4.0		15.0					59.0
Florida 003				10.0							10.0
Florida 005			1.4	0.9		10.3	3.3				15.9
Florida 006			5.0	6.0	1.0	3.5	13.5		20.0		46.0
Florida 008											
Florida 009		15.0	10.0								25.0
Florida 010											
Georgia 001					30.0	5.0					35.0
Georgia 002											
Georgia 003											
Hawaii 001	402.5		100.0	25.0	10.0	20.0	61.0				618.5
Iowa 001											
Idaho 001											
Illinois 001	10.0	10.0	180.0	49.0	31.0	50.0	90.0	160.0	100.0		680.0
Illinois 003			1.0	6.0	6.0						13.0
Illinois 004			2.0								2.0
Illinois 006					60.0			50.0			110.0
Indiana 001		10.0	46.4		81.5	50.8	87.8	30.0	150.0		456.7
Kansas 001		30.0			6.5		0.6				37.1
Kansas 002											
Kentucky 001								15.0	2.0		17.0
Louisiana 001											
Massachusetts 001			10.0								10.0
Massachusetts 002	3.0		10.0	1.6		0.3		10.0		2.0	28.9
Massachusetts 004											
Massachusetts 005				33.0		3.5		1.0			39.5
Maryland 001											
Maryland 003		214.7		60.0	100.0	20.0	138.4				333.3
Michigan 002											
Michigan 003								127.2			127.2
Minnesota 001											
Minnesota 002		59.6		99.4	212.7	22.9	20.0				414.6
Missouri 001				25.0	7.0	2.0	4.0	10.0	7.0	1.0	56.0
Missouri 002								500.0			500.0
Missouri 003	5.0						1.0				6.0

[Continued]

★ 343 ★

Cost of Maintaining Municipal Wastewater Needs, 2000-2010

[Continued]

State	Secondary treatment	Advanced treatment	Infil/ inflow	Replacement/Rehabilitation			Collection system	CSOs	Separate stormwater	Air toxics/ Air quality	Total
				Sewers	Treatment plant	Pumping stations					
Nebraska 001											
New Jersey 001											
New Jersey 004											
New Jersey 005											
New Jersey 006											
New Jersey 007											
New Mexico 001											
Nevada 001											
New York 001											
New York 002				1,600.0							1,600.0
New York 003											
New York 005											
Ohio 003	20.0	40.0		40.0	3.0	1.0	80.0	226.0		20.0	430.0
Ohio 004									33.0		33.0
Ohio 005											
Ohio 006									1.0		1.0
Oregon 001		37.1	10.0		54.5	2.0	10.0				113.6
Oregon 002	138.0		2.0	300.0	70.0	50.0	20.0	500.0	100.0		1,180.0
Oregon 003											
Oregon 004	20.0		3.0	20.0	25.0	3.0	9.5		12.0		92.5
Oregon 005	10.4		0.6				3.0				14.0
Oregon 007											
Pennsylvania 002	150.0		464.0	104.0	104.0	204.0	148.0	52.0	630.0		1,856.0
Pennsylvania 003											
Rhode Island 001											
Tennessee 001			2.5	5.0	10.0	1.0	1.0				18.5
Tennessee 002					10.0	2.0					12.0
Tennessee 003	12.0			30.0					60.0		102.0
Tennessee 004								1.5			1.5
Texas 001	27.0	13.0	0.5	10.0	10.0	0.6	20.0				81.1
Texas 002		100.0	20.0	50.0	20.0	10.0	60.0			6.0	266.0
Texas 003											
Texas 004	200.9	32.3									233.2
Texas 005			2.0	16.0		4.0				0.5	22.5
Texas 006			20.0				30.2				50.2
Texas 007											
Texas 009											
Utah 001	40.0		3.0	3.0	10.0	1.0	15.0		15.0		87.0
Utah 002	44.0	10.0			1.5						55.5
Virginia 001											
Virginia 003	35.0			43.8	200.0	5.0	15.0				298.8
Virginia 004											
Virginia 005											
Virginia 006											
Virginia 007		11.0			127.5						138.5
Virginia 008	1.3				0.1		0.8	94.0	0.3		96.5
Washington 001	210.0		0.7		12.0	25.0	85.0				332.7
Washington 002			25.0				25.0				50.0
Wisconsin 001		53.1									53.1
Wisconsin 002				4.0	3.0	4.0	5.0				16.0
Wisconsin 003											
Wisconsin 004											
Total	1,904.8	2,238.7	935.2	2,797.4	1,442.3	565.9	1,030.6	2,343.7	1,130.3	38.7	14,427.6

[Continued]

★ 343 ★

Cost of Maintaining Municipal Wastewater Needs, 2000-2010

[Continued]

State	Secondary treatment	Advanced treatment	Infil/ inflow	Replacement/Rehabilitation			Collection system	CSOs	Separate stormwater	Air toxics/ Air quality	Total
				Sewers	Treatment plant	Pumping stations					
Average	17.6	20.7	8.7	25.9	13.4	5.2	9.5	21.7	10.5	0.4	133.6
Maximum	402.5	613.0	464.0	1,600.0	212.7	204.0	148.0	500.0	630.0	20.0	1,856.0

Source: U.S. House of Representatives, Committee on Merchant Marine and Fisheries, *Clean Water Funding: A Proposal for a National Clean Water Investment Corporation* (Washington, D.C.: U.S. Government Printing Office, August 1992), pp. 128-9. *Primary source:* The Cost of Clean: A National Survey of Municipal Wastewater Management Needs. *Note:* CSO = Combined Sewer Overflow.

★ 344 ★

Effects and Costs of Federal Mandates

Air Quality Expenditures by the Petroleum Industry, 1980-2000

[Millions of dollars]

Year	Number
1980	5,000
1981	4,100
1982	4,300
1983	3,000
1984	2,500
1990	2,800
1991	3,800
2000 (L)	11,500
2000 (H)	15,000

Source: Jody Perkins, *Costs to the Petroleum Industry of Major New and Future Federal Government Environmental Requirements* (American Petroleum Institute: Washington, D.C.), 1993, p. 43. *Primary source: 1980 to 1984 estimates*: API, "Environmental Expenditures of the United States Petroleum Industry: 1972-1981," Publication No. 4351, [1981], pp. 2 and 5. API, "Environmental Expenditures of the United States Petroleum Industry: 1975-1984," Publication No. 4404, [1985], pp. 2 and 6. *1990 and 1991 estimates:* API, "Petroleum Industry Environmental Performance 1992," [1992], pp. 34-40, and API, "Environmental Expenditures of the U.S. Petroleum Industry: 1991," May 1993 draft report, forthcoming. *Of GNP Deflator:* EPA, *Environmental Investments: The Cost of A Clean Environment*, Report to Congress, (Washington, DC: November 1990), p. 1-14, and "National Income and Product Accounts Table," *Survey of Current Business*, 72 no. 7, July 1992, Table 7.3 (See Appendix B). *Notes:* Estimates are in 1991 dollars. Estimates are not available for years 1985-1989 and 1992-1999. Estimates for 1980 to 1984 were extrapolated to 100 percent of refining capacity based on estimated shares of refining capacity reflected in survey responses. Estimates for 2000 based on 1991 estimate and simulation results described in this paper. Distribution by medium was based on percentage shares of simulated mean of total costs. Magnitudes estimated from published chart. Chart also includes data for 1972 to 1979, as well as for water, and land and other. API = American Petroleum Institute; EPA = Environmental Protection Agency; GNP = Gross National Product; L = Low; H = High.

★ 345 ★

Effects and Costs of Federal Mandates

Environmental Expenditures by the Petroleum Industry as a Share of Nationwide Environmental Expenditures, 1980-2000

[Percent]

Year	Number
1980	12.20
1981	11.50
1982	11.00
1983	8.75
1984	7.25
1990	6.75
1991	6.75
2000 (L)	13.5
2000 (H)	17.5

Source: Jody Perkins, *Costs to the Petroleum Industry of Major New and Future Federal Government Environmental Requirements* (American Petroleum Institute: Washington, D.C.), 1993, p. 44. *Primary source: For petroleum industry expenditures*: Estimates presented in entry 342 (above); *For U.S. total environmental expenditures*: EPA, *Environmental Investments: The Cost of A Clean Environment*, Report to Congress, November 1990, Tables 8-17 and 8-17A and p. 1-14. *Of GNP deflator*: EPA, *Environmental Investments: The Cost of A Clean Environment*, Report to Congress, November 1990, p. 1-14, and "National Income and Product Accounts Tables," *Survey of Current Business*, 72 no. 7, July 1992, Table 7.3 (See Appendix B). *Notes:* Estimates are not available for years 1985-1989 and 1992-1999. U.S. total expenditures adjusted to 1991 dollars using a GNP deflator. Magnitudes estimated from published chart. Chart also contains data for 1972-1979. EPA=Environmental Protection Agency; GNP=Gross National Product; L=Low; H=High.

World Climate and Trends in Air Pollutant Emissions

★ 346 ★

Impacts of Global Warming, 1992-2050

"Most forecasts of global warming and the accompanying side effects are followed by sets of prescriptions of things that should be done to avoid the most catastrophic consequences. The predictions, therefore, tend to deal with what may happen if we fail to mend our ways and with what is to be expected if we take some preventative actions—many best-, medium-, and worst-case scenarios. These scenarios require at least three distinct steps.

[Continued]

★ 346 ★

Impacts of Global Warming, 1992-2050

[Continued]

"Having fairly well established that certain greenhouse gases, particularly Carbon Dioxide (CO_2), are responsible for the greenhouse effect, we must predict how the levels of these atmospheric gases will change in coming years. Then we must predict how this will affect worldwide, and possibly local, temperatures. Finally, it is necessary to predict the nature and magnitude of the unpleasant consequences of these temperature changes.

"There is tremendous uncertainty as to the amount of the build-up of CO_2, let alone all the other greenhouse gases, to be expected in the coming decades. It depends strongly on the predicted growth in the developed as well as the developing world, the extent to which energy can be economized, and the extent to which fossil fuels can be replaced by alternative sources of energy. Certainly, how we treat or mistreat our forests will also have a significant effect. Other sources of greenhouse gases include 'natural' phenomena such as the decomposition of dead organic matter and the release of CO_2 from carbonate sediments in the oceans. Hence, all reputable prognosticators hedge their predictions. However, there is general agreement that unless we take very drastic actions at once, sometime in the first half of the twenty-first century the level of atmospheric greenhouse gases will be twice what it is now. The only question is how soon.

"In order to predict the effect on the temperature of the build-up of greenhouse gases, one has to specify or guess the significance of various negative and positive feedback processes and make a host of other assumptions. These are too complex to include their discussion at this point. The bottom line, however, is that most authoritative scientists venturing predictions place temperature increases between now and the year 2050 at about 0.3C (or about 0.2F) every ten years, if there is no concerted effort to reduce the emission of greenhouse gases. Others put this figure above 0.5C per decade. If strong mitigating actions are taken, it may be possible to hold this increase to 0.1C per decade. This would mean an increase in the world average temperature anywhere from 0.6C to 3.0C. These are global averages. The prediction of regional or local temperature change is much tougher still.

"Stephen Schneider *[in Global Warming (1989)]* lists the following consequences of global warming over the next several decades:

Increased rainfall in the tropics,

Wetter springtimes in high and middle latitudes,

Drier midsummer conditions (droughts) in the United States,

Increased probability of extreme heat waves, increased likelihood of forest and brush fires,

Increase in sea level by as much as a meter over the next hundred years.

[Continued]

★ 346 ★

Impacts of Global Warming, 1992-2050

[Continued]

Others would add a sharply increasing number of blizzards, hurricanes, dust-bowl conditions (in the United States), and many other disasters.

"Every environmentalist has his own list of remedies, but by and large they all contain the following major items:

Sharply increased funding for research; systematic large-scale programs to develop a better understanding of climatology, as well as the many problems related to the reduction of emissions of greenhouse gases.

Reduced energy consumption by all segments of society.

More efficient use of energy.

Shifting from coal to less harmful fossil fuels, such as natural gas.

Phasing out harmful chemicals—first chlorofluorocarbons (CFCs) and gradually fossil fuels, at least to some extent, by developing and introducing alternative sources of energy.

Planting a large number of trees and preventing the decimation of the tropical rain forests.

"All this will cost lots of money. Schneider proposes an annual expenditure equal to '5% of the defense budget each year to the year 2000 A.D.' to finance the development and implementation of installations in line with the above list.

"While environments strongly favor the curtailing of fossil-fuel power generators, they are also nearly unanimous in condemning one obvious source of energy that does not emit greenhouse gases—nuclear power. No doubt, fear of pollution as a result of disposal is the basis for their opposition to fission reactors. High development costs are usually cited as the principal objection to yet-to-be-invented reactors that operate by nuclear fusion."

Source: Walter J. Karplus, *The Heavens Are Falling: The Scientific Prediction of Catastrophes in Our Time* (New York: Plenum Press), 1992, pp. 152-4.

★ 347 ★

World Climate and Trends in Air Pollutant Emissions

Greenhouse Gas Emissions, 1990-2000

"The major greenhouse gases are carbon dioxide (CO_2), methane, nitrous oxides, and hydrofluorocarbons (HFCs). As shown [in the table below], net emissions of these gases in the U.S. are projected to grow by about 7 percent between 1990 and 2000 without the Action Plan, from 1,462 million metric tons of carbon equivalent (MMTCE) to 1,568 MMTCE. [All gases are converted to MMTCE by conversion factors based on radiative forcing, called 'global warming potential.' The emission estimates for 1990 are taken from *Emissions of Greenhouse Gases in the United States, 1985-1990* (EIA, 1993) and *Anthropogenic Methane Emissions in the United States, Estimates for 1990* (EPA, 1993). The nitrous oxide emissions from agriculture were provided by USDA. Projections are based on analysis conducted by DOE, EPA, and USDA for the Climate Change Action Plan. Baseline estimates of emissions may change as internationally recognized methodologies evolve]...

"Net carbon emissions alone are projected to grow to 1,337 by the year 2000—over 8 percent above 1990 levels—without the policies in outlined in the Action Plan. [Although projections of greenhouse gases are given as point estimates, considerable uncertainty surrounds any projection that depends on future economic activities. A broad range of outcomes are plausible]. Methane and nitrous oxide emissions are expected to decline slightly, but HFCs are expected to increase to 45 MMTCE. These projections already account for some policies recently enacted and programs implemented by the Administration that reduce CO_2, methane, and nitrous oxide emissions. Without these programs, U.S. greenhouse gas emissions would rise to 1,674 MMTCE by 2000, according to Administration estimates. Thus, while significant progress has been made, more is needed to meet the President's goal. In order to return U.S. greenhouse gas emission to 1990 levels by the year 2000, the Action Plan must reduce the projected emission level by about 106 million metric tons below the year 2000 forecasted level."

[Carbon-equivalent in million metric tons]

Year	GHG emissions	HFC	N20	Methane	Carbon
1990	1462	20	39	166	1,237
2000 Baseline	1568	45	36	150	1,337
2000 Action plan	1459	33	31	134	1,261

Source: The Climate Change Action Plan (Washington, D.C.: U.S. Government Printing Office, October 1993), pp. 5-6, 9. *Notes:* Carbon reported as sources less sinks. Forest sinks are 130 MMT in 1990 and 137 MMT in 2000 in baseline; 147 MMT in Action Plan. GHG=Greenhouse Gas; HFC=Hydrofluorocarbon; MMT=Million Metric Tons; N_2O=Nitrous Oxide.

★ 348 ★

World Climate and Trends in Air Pollutant Emissions

International Climate Variations, 1650-2000

"[A] reconstruction of the Northern Hemisphere's climate from 1400 to 1970 by Dr. Raymond S. Bradley and Dr. Philip D. Jones of the University of East Anglia in England showed not a single, long-term pattern of any kind but rather a wide range of variations in different parts of the world, with oscillations between warmer and cooler regional climates taking place on scales of a decade or two...

"This record can be read in two ways, says Dr. Bradley. If one considers the period from the mid-16th century to the late 20th century, a steady warming trend appears to underlie the decade-to-decade temperature fluctuations. This perspective, says Dr. Bradley, seems to favor those who see the recent warming of the 20th century as part of a natural phenomenon. But if one considers the period from 1400 to 1900, the decade-to-decade fluctuations oscillate around an unchanging average somewhat below the 1860-to-1970 benchmark. Then it jumps sharply upward in the 20th century. This perspective, said Dr. Bradley, seems to favor those who see the 20th century as an aberration and attribute it to emissions of industrial gases that trap heat in the atmosphere."

[Degrees centigrade]

Year	North America	Europe	China	Northern Hemisphere
1650	-0.8	-0.5	-4.0	-0.7
1700	-1.0	-0.5	-0.8	-0.6
1750	-.09	0.0	-0.9	-0.2
1800	-1.5	0.5	-0.6	-0.3
1850	-0.5	-0.2	-1.2	-0.2
1900	-0.2	-0.5	-.06	0.0
1950	0.3	0.3	-1.2	0.8
2000	1.0	1.0	-1.2	0.3

Source: William K. Stevens, "In New Data on Climate Changes, Decades, Not Centuries, Count," in *The New York Times*, 7 December 1993, p. C4. *Primary source:* Dr. Raymond S. Bradley and Dr. Philip D. Jones. *Notes:* A study of climate patterns from A.D. 1400 to the present, combining many kinds of historical, tree-ring and ice-core data, indicates that different climatic conditions prevailed in different parts of the world at any given time. The zero line approximates the mean temperature for 1860 to 1959 in degrees centigrade. One unit of variation is 0.12 degrees centigrade. Magnitudes estimated from published chart. Source also includes data for 1400-1600.

★ 349 ★

World Climate and Trends in Air Pollutant Emissions

Summary of Greenhouse Gas Emission Reductions and Economic Impacts, 1994-2010

"As shown [in the table below], the [Climate Change] Action Plan will return net U.S. greenhouse gas emission to 1990 levels by the year 2000. The combined impact of all actions reduces emissions from projected levels by 108 MMTCE. Net carbon emissions are likely to be slightly higher—about 2 percent above their 1990 levels. The rate of increase in HFC emissions is cut in half. Offsetting these gains in emissions are further reductions in methane and nitrous oxide emissions..

"Many of the programs outlined here will encourage individuals and firms to invest in energy savings equipment or other technologies that yield significant cost savings over the long term. Comparing the magnitude of these investments with the value of energy savings indicates the overall cost-effectiveness of the Action Plan. While investing over $60 billion in greenhouse gas emission reductions between 1994 and 2000, individuals and firms realize over $60 billion in energy savings between 1994 and 2000, and realize continued returns in the form of an additional $207 billion in energy savings between 2001 and 2010."

[Outlays, investment, and energy savings in millions of dollars]

Sector	Greenhouse gas reduction (MMTCE) 2000	Federal outlay (millions) 1994-2000	Private capital investment (millions) 2000	Cumulative value of energy savings (millions)	
				1990-2000	2001-2010
Energy demand					
Commercial	10.6	$445	$20,500	$8,600	$36,700
Residential	16.3	$397	$31,200	$14,800	$62,300
Industrial	19.0	$247	$4,900	$14,200	$65,900
Transportation	8.1	-$2,132	$2,200	$18,600	$31,200
Energy supply	10.8	$57	$1,200	$4,400	$9,000
Methane reduction and recovery	16.3	$93	$860	$650	$2,000
HFC, PFC and Nitrous Oxides reductions	16.3	$26	N/A	N/A	N/A
Forestry actions	10.0	$75	$40	N/A	N/A
TOTAL	108.6	-$793	$60,900	$61,250	$207,100

Source: The Climate Change Action Plan (Washington, D.C.: U.S. Government Printing Office, October, 1993), pp. 7-8. *Notes:* Dollar figures for private investment and the value of energy savings are in undiscounted 1991$. Federal outlay is in current year dollars. HFC=Hydrofluorocarbon; MMTCE=Million Metric Tons of Carbon Equivalent; PFC=Perfluorocarbon.

★ 350 ★

World Climate and Trends in Air Pollutant Emissions

Effect of Doubling Greenhouse Gases on the U.S. Economy, 2025

"The rising atmospheric concentration of greenhouse gases is potentially the most economically disruptive and costly change that has been set in motion by our modern industrial society. William Cline, an economist with the Washington-based Institute for International Economics, has looked at the long term economic effects of global warming. As part of this study, he analyzed the effect of a doubling of greenhouse gases on the U.S. economy, which could come as early as 2025. He estimates that heat stress and drought would cost U.S. farmers $18 billion in output, that the increased electricity for air conditioning would require an additional $11 billion, and that dealing with sea level rise would cost about $7 billion per year. In total, Cline estimates the cost at nearly $60 billion, roughly 1% of the 1990 U.S. Gross National Product (GNP)."

Source: Lester R. Brown, "The World Transformed: Envisioning an Environmentally Safe Planet," in *The Futurist*, May-June 1993, pp. 17-18.

★ 351 ★

World Climate and Trends in Air Pollutant Emissions

Effects of Pollution on European and North American Forests

"Many scientists predict the demise of most forests in those areas of Europe and North America that are already hard-hit by the effects of acid rain—this unless heroic measures are taken at once to abate the emission of the major pollutants. They further foresee a spread of the consequences of acid rain, until all regions of the globe are substantially affected.

"The Community exhorts us to stop emitting oxides of sulfur and nitrogen! We must repair the damage already done. Unfortunately, this is much easier said than done.

"Approximately one-half of the pollutants that cause acid rain are emitted by power stations that burn coal or oil. There are a number of ways to reduce this amount.

1. Conserve energy so as to consume less fuel. A number of successful moves in this direction have already been undertaken in the developed countries. However, the energy requirements of Third World nations are expected to increase in the coming decades.

2. Switch to low-sulfur fuels. Some fossil fuels are much richer in sulfur than others. There are low-sulfur coals and low-sulfur oils on the market, but usually at a higher price than the garden variety.

[Continued]

★351★

Effects of Pollution on European and North American Forests

[Continued]

3. Switch to alternative fuels. These include natural gas, wood, and kerosene as well as a number of so-called renewable energy sources, such as the sun, tidal forces, hydroelectricity, and winds. Nuclear power would also help mitigate the acid rain problem, but perhaps this would eventually inflict even greater damage to the environment in the form of low-level radiation.

4. Clean coal before burning. There are methods of 'washing' coal to remove about 10 to 15% of its sulfur.

5. Remove sulfur during or after burning. This can be done by mixing limestone with the coal. Alternatively, the gaseous combustion products can be 'scrubbed' by passing them over or through limestone.

"There are also a number of practical ways of limiting the emission of oxides of nitrogen by power stations and by internal combustion engines. These involve the addition of special exhaust scrubbers and the introduction of improved automobile engines and gasoline.

"All of the above remedial measures entail considerable expense, both in installation and in operation. For example, the U.S. Office of Technology Assessment estimated that to reduce the level of atmospheric sulfur dioxide in the eastern United States by 35% by 1995 would cost anywhere from three to six billion dollars. For that reason, the adoption of draconian remedial measures has often been opposed, not only by the energy industries but also by a number of governmental agencies.

"There is evidence that some irreversible damage has already been done to the environment. That is, even if the emission of all man-made acid rain pollutants were to cease at once, the environment would not return to its pre-acid rain state. Too much acid in the soil and the water already exists in many places. To counteract the presence of the acids that were deposited during the acid rain episodes, it is necessary to 'sweeten' the soil and water by introducing large quantities of lime. This method has been used with some success in Sweden, but at very considerable cost. To employ this approach on a worldwide basis would entail enormous expenditures for the mining, the conditioning, the distribution, and the application of the powdered limestone."

Source: Walter J. Karplus, *The Heavens Are Falling: The Scientific Prediction of Catastrophes in Our Time* (New York: Plenum Press), 1992, pp. 185-6.

★ 352 ★

World Climate and Trends in Air Pollutant Emissions

World Carbon Dioxide Emissions by Fuel Type, 1980-2010

"All hydrocarbon fuels, by definition, contain carbon, which is emitted into the atmosphere when the fuel is burned (i.e. combined with oxygen), mainly as carbon dioxide (CO_2). Concerns have been raised in recent years regarding the long-term effects of CO_2 and other gaseous emissions on the environment, particularly as they might help trap heat near the Earth's surface and thus contribute to what has become popularly known as the 'greenhouse effect.' These concerns center primarily on the possibility that large-scale anthropogenic emissions of so-called 'greenhouse gases' (mainly CO_2, methane, nitrous oxide, tropospheric ozone, and chlorofluorocarbons, or CFCs) will result in an excessive level of global warming in coming years."

[Billion metric tons (cumulative)]

Year	Oil	Gas	Coal	Total
1980	2.7	.8	1.9	5.4
1985	2.5	1.9	2.1	5.6
1990	2.8	1.1	2.4	6.1
1995	2.9	1.2	2.6	6.4
2000	3.0	1.3	2.7	7.1
2005	3.2	1.4	2.9	7.4
2010	3.3	1.5	3.0	7.8

Source: U.S. Department of Energy, Energy Information Administration, *International Energy Outlook 1991: A Post-War Review of Energy Markets*, (Washington, D.C.: U.S. Government Printing Office, June 1991), pp. 25-6. *Primary source:* History: Consumption of oil, gas, and coal derived from *International Energy Annual*, and *The Energy Journal*, Volume 4, No. 3. Projections: Derived from *The Energy Journal*, Volume 4, No. 3, and Table 6. Individual figures may not sum to total due to rounding. *Note:* Magnitudes estimated from published chart.

★ 353 ★

World Climate and Trends in Air Pollutant Emissions

Annual National Carbon Monoxide (CO) Emissions, 1980-2010

[Million short tons]

	1980	1990	2000	2010
Highway vehicles	88.0	59.8	43.8	46.0
All other sources	41.0	32.6	28.4	28.2
Total	129.0	92.4	72.2	74.2

Source: United States Environmental Protection Agency, Office of Air Quality Planning and Standards, *National Air Pollutant Emission Trends, 1900-1992* (Library Services Office (MD-35), U.S. Environmental Protection Agency, Research Triangle Park, NC 27711, October 1993), p. 6-10. *Notes:* Historical emissions were updated from the previous version of this report. The projected 'All Other' source emissions are based on a September 1991 analysis.

★354★

World Climate and Trends in Air Pollutant Emissions

Global Carbon Dioxide (CO_2) Concentrations, 2000-2100

"The International Energy Agency (IEA) predicts that [developing countries] will produce just under 45% of the world's carbon dioxide (CO_2) emissions by 2010, compared with 16% in 1970. The World Energy Conference (WEC) foresees even more use of renewable energy in the rich world; it reckons the developing countries will produce more than half of world emissions of CO_2 by 2010."

[Parts per million]

Year	Reference scenario	Ecologically-driven scenario
2000	360	360
2010	400	395
2020	425	405
2030	460	430
2040	490	445
2050	510	450
2060	550	470
2070	580	480
2080	610	485
2090	670	485
2100	710	480

Source: "The New Price," in *The Economist*, 18 June 1994, p. 15. *Primary source:* Grossman & Krueger, Princeton University; World Energy Council. *Note:* Magnitudes estimated from published chart.

★355★

World Climate and Trends in Air Pollutant Emissions

Annual National Sulfur Oxide (SO_2) Emissions, 1980-2010

[Million short tons]

	1980	1990	2000	2010
Electric utilities	17.5	15.9	9.7	9.0
Nonutility, point services	6.7	5.3	5.4	5.6
All other sources	2.0	1.6	1.5	1.2
Total	26.2	22.8	16.6	15.8

Source: United States Environmental Protection Agency, Office of Air Quality Planning and Standards, *National Air Pollutant Emission Trends, 1900-1992* (Library Services Office (MD-35), U.S. Environmental Protection Agency, Research Triangle Park, NC 27711, October 1993), p. 6-13. *Notes:* Historical emissions were updated from the previous version of this report. The projected "All Other" source emissions are based on a September 1991 analysis. SO_2=Sulfur oxide.

★ 356 ★

World Climate and Trends in Air Pollutant Emissions

Decline in Global Emissions of Carbon Monoxide (CO), Sulfur Oxide (SO_2) and Volatile Organic Compound (VOC) Concentrations, 1970-2000

"Chlorofluorocarbons (CFCs) were discovered by General Motors in 1928; the fact that they destroy ozone in the stratosphere become apparent when a large ozone hole was discovered over Antarctica in 1985. Widely used as solvents, refrigerants, and fire retardants, CFCs are gradually eating away the shield that protects us against the sun's ultraviolet rays. A 1987 agreement called the Montreal Protocol mandated a 50% reduction in CFCs by 1999. But environmentalists, including Democratic vice presidential candidate Al Gore—who considers stratospheric ozone a public health emergency—wanted quicker action.

"It turns out they got it from a most unlikely source. Last winter the National Aeronautics and Space Administration forecast a possible ozone hole over New England, near President Bush's vacation home in Kennebunkport, Maine. Coincidentally or not, Bush, who until then had opposed a Senate Proposal to quickly phase out the production of CFCs, did an about-face. He directed CFC manufacturers, including big companies like Du Pont and Allied-Signal, to cease all production by 1995. The CFC manufacturers at first balked at the phase-out. But now, says Eileen Clausen of the Environmental Protection Agency (EPA), they are diligently working to find substitutes."

[Million of metric tons per year]

	1970	1990	2000
CO	100	60	40
SO_2	25	20	12
VOC	25	20	12

Source: Faye Rice, "Next Steps for the Environment," in *Fortune* 19 October 1992, pp. 99-100. *Primary source:* Environmental Protection Agency.

★ 357 ★

World Climate and Trends in Air Pollutant Emissions

Annual National Nitrous Oxide (NO_x) Emissions, 1980-2010

[Million short tons]

	1980	1990	2000	2010
Electric utilities	7.0	7.5	6.7	8.2
Industrial sources	4.1	4.4	3.9	4.5
Highway vehicles	8.7	7.8	6.3	6.1
All other sources	3.9	3.9	3.3	3.5
Total	23.7	23.6	20.2	22.3

Source: United States Environmental Protection Agency, Office of Air Quality Planning and Standards, *National Air Pollutant Emission Trends, 1900-1992* (Library Services Office (MD-35), U.S. Environmental Protection Agency, Research Triangle Park, NC 27711, October 1993), p. 6-11. *Notes:* Industrial sources include industrial fuel combustion and processes. Historical emissions were updated from previous report. NO_x = Nitrous oxide.

★ 358 ★

World Climate and Trends in Air Pollutant Emissions

Comparison of Peak Ozone Season and Annual Average NO_x Emissions, 1987-2010

[Thousand short tons per day]

	Peak ozone season			Annual average		
	1987	2000	2010	1987	2000	2010
Highway vehicles	16.4	17.0	16.6	21.6	17.4	16.8
All other sources	40.3	38.0	44.4	38.6	38.0	44.4
Total	56.7	55.0	61.0	60.2	55.4	61.2

Source: United States Environmental Protection Agency, Office of Air Quality Planning and Standards, *National Air Pollutant Emission Trends, 1900-1992* (Library Services Office (MD-35), U.S. Environmental Protection Agency, Research Triangle Park, NC 27711, October 1993), p. 6-14. *Notes:* The projection year nitrous oxide (NO_x) emissions are from a September 1992 analysis of the 1990 Clean Air Act Amendment (CAAA). Emission estimates for the years 2000 and 2010 reflect additional reductions needed for areas to meet estimated 3% reductions or attainment targets. More reductions may be needed. Some may come from NO_x after 1996.

★ 359 ★

World Climate and Trends in Air Pollutant Emissions

Annual National Volatile Organic Compound (VOC) Emissions, 1980-2010

[Million short tons]

	1980	1990	2000	2010
Highway vehicle	11.0	7.0	4.9	4.7
All other sources	17.4	16.7	12.8	12.8
Total	28.4	23.7	17.7	17.5

Source: United States Environmental Protection Agency, Office of Air Quality Planning and Standards, *National Air Pollutant Emission Trends, 1900-1992* (Library Services Office (MD-35), U.S. Environmental Protection Agency, Research Triangle Park, NC 27711, October 1993), p. 6-12. *Notes:* Historical emissions were updated from the previous version of this report. The projected "All Other" source emissions are based on a September 1991 analysis.

★ 360 ★

World Climate and Trends in Air Pollutant Emissions

Comparison of Peak Ozone Season and Annual Average Volatile Organic Compound (VOC) Emissions, 1987-2010

[Thousand short tons per day]

	Peak ozone season			Annual average		
	1987	2000	2010	1987	2000	2010
Highway vehicle	27.0	12.0	11.5	22.6	13.3	13.0
All other sources	39.0	32.4	32.7	40.2	35.1	35.1
Total	66.0	44.4	44.2	62.8	48.4	48.1

Source: United States Environmental Protection Agency, Office of Air Quality Planning and Standards, *National Air Pollutant Emission Trends, 1900-1992* (Library Services Office (MD-35), U.S. Environmental Protection Agency, Research Triangle Park, NC 27711, October 1993), p. 6-14. *Notes:* The projection year Volatile Organic Compound (VOC) emissions are from the ERCAM-VOC model results, based on a September 1992 analysis of the 1990 Clean Air Amendment (CAAA). Emission estimates for the years 2000 and 2010 reflect additional reductions needed to meet estimated 3 percent reductions or attainment targets. More reductions may be needed.

★ 361 ★

World Climate and Trends in Air Pollutant Emissions

Global Shares of Net Methane Emissions, 1990-2025

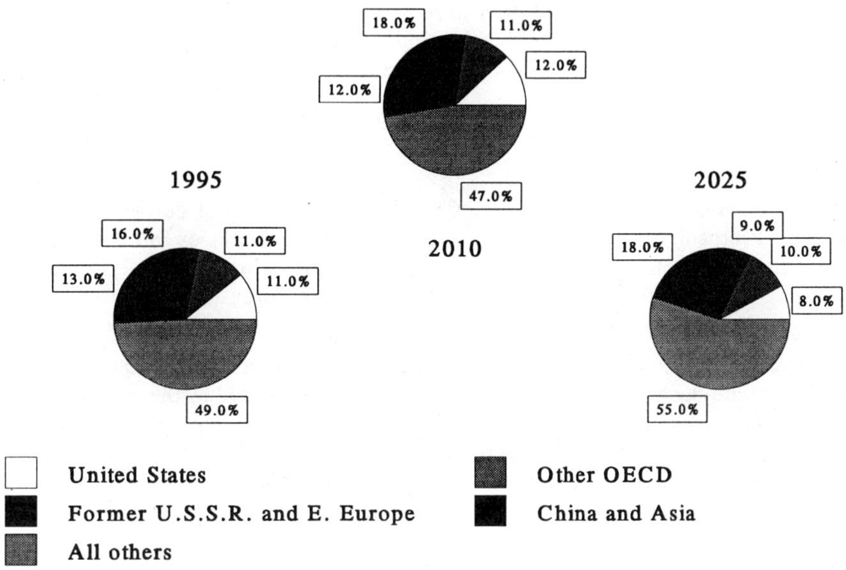

[Percent of regional shares]

Year	United States	Other OECD	Former USSR and E. Europe	China and Asia	All other
1990	12	11	19	12	46
1995	12	11	18	12	47
2000	12	11	17	13	47
2005	11	11	16	13	49
2010	11	11	14	14	50
2015	10	10	11	16	53
2020	9	10	9	18	54
2025	8	10	9	18	55

Source: U.S. Actions for a Better Environment (Washington, D.C.: U.S. Government Printing Office), 1991, p. 5. *Primary source:* Emissions Scenarios for the Intergovernmental Panel on Climate Change (IPCC), An Update: Assumptions, Methodology and Results, May 1992. *Notes:* OECD=Organization for Economic Cooperation and Development. USSR=United Soviet Socialist Republic. Magnitudes estimated from published chart.

★ 362 ★

World Climate and Trends in Air Pollutant Emissions

U.S. Commitment to Chloroflurocarbon Phase-out, 1990-2000

"The U.S. has been the world's leader in responding to the depletion by various chlorine (CFCs) and bromine (halons) compounds of the stratospheric ozone layer which protects the earth's surface from ultraviolet radiation.

—*Ban on CFC use as spray can propellants*. In 1978, the U.S. banned CFC spray can propellants in non-essential uses. Only a few countries followed in this action.

—*Montreal Protocol CFC Phase-Out*. At the London Meeting of Parties to the Montreal Protocol, the U.S. supported, and achieved agreement on, a complete world-wide phase-out of CFCs, halons, and certain other ozone-depleting substances such as carbon tetrachloride and methyl chloroform.

—*Accelerated U.S. CFC Phase-out*. The U.S., under the Clean Air Act, adopted legislative provisions which will phase out U.S. production and consumption of specified ozone-depleting substances more quickly than required by the amended Montreal Protocol. The U.S. law also includes a schedule for phase-out of HCFCs which is not required under the provision of the Protocol. The U.S. enacted a tax on ozone-depleting chemicals during the phase-out to accelerate the reductions. President Bush in February of [1991] announced that the U.S. would seek: A production phase-out of CFCs halons, carbon tetrachloride, and methyl chloroform by December 31, 1995, with limited exceptions; a voluntary cut to 50 percent below baseline levels by the end of the year; agreement by all nations to join the U.S. in accelerating the phase-out.

"[The table below] shows the U.S. commitments to phase out ozone-depleting compounds more quickly than required by the Montreal Protocol and the London amendments."

[Percent of Base Year]

Year	Annual/ projected	USCAA	Protocol
1990	64	100	100
1992	50	80	100
1994	25	65	100
1996	0	40	50
1998	0	15	15
2000	0	0	0

Source: U.S. Actions for a Better Environment (Washington, D.C.: U.S. Government Printing Office), 1991, p. 7. *Primary source:* Environmental Protection Agency (EPA) Stratospheric Ozone Protection Branch. *Notes:* USCAA = United States Clean Air Act. Magnitudes estimated from published chart.

★ 363 ★

World Climate and Trends in Air Pollutant Emissions

Decline in Chlorofluorocarbon - 11 Emissions, 1978-2000

"Under an agreement signed by 87 countries last November in Copenhagen, the manufacture of Chlorofluorocarbons (CFC's) is to be phased out by the end of 1995, while halon manufacture is to stop by the end of this year. Controls were first placed on CFC production by the Montreal Protocol of 1987.

"The deadlines were moved up in 1990 and again last November after scientists found that ozone depletion was more extensive than had been believed. In October 1991, for instance, scientists working under United Nations auspices reported for the first time that the ozone layer in the latitudes of the United States had depleted in the previous summer."

[Parts per trillion]

Year	Observed	Industry estimate
1978	10.0	12.0
1979	9.0	10.5
1980	8.5	8.5
1985	12.5	10.0
1990	6.0	9.0
1995	0.0	2.5
2000	0.0	0.0

Source: William K. Stevens, "Scientists Startled by a Drop in Ozone-Killing Chemicals," in *The New York Times*, 26 August 1993, p. A18. *Primary source:* National Oceanic and Atmospheric Administration (NOAA). *Notes:* Magnitudes estimated from published chart. Source also includes data for 1981-1984, 1986-1989, 1991-1994, and 1996-1999.

Environmental Impacts of Overpopulation

★ 364 ★

Effect of Population Growth on Wetlands, 1790-2050

"The continental United States lost more than half of its original wetlands in a 200-year period, according to data from the U.S. Fish and Wildlife Service. During the same period, U.S. population doubled more than six times, growing from about 4 million in 1790 to 255 million in 1993...

"U.S. population is now projected to grow by 50% to 383 million people in 2050, according to the U.S. Census Bureau. [At the historical rate of wetlands loss to population growth, the U.S. will lose approximately 8.3% of its remaining wetlands by this date.] Unless the trend is halted, preserving the remaining wetlands may become impossible, Population-Environment- Balance warns."

Source: "Wetlands Versus Population Growth," in *The Futurist*, September-October 1993, pp. 55-6. *Primary source:* Population-Environment Balance, 1325 G St., N.W., Suite 1003, Washington, D.C. 20005; Bureau of the Census, Public Information Office, Economics and Statistics Administration, U.S. Department of Commerce, Washington, D.C. 20230.

Environmental Impacts of Hazardous Waste

★ 365 ★

Impacts of Radioactive Contamination

"Over the past thirty-five years, enormous quantities of radioactive materials, some with very long half-lives, have been released into the atmosphere, the oceans, lakes, streams, and underground water reservoirs. The atmospheric nuclear bomb testing that ended in 1963 was just the beginning. In addition to the known nuclear reactor accidents, there may have been a number of incidents that were hushed up, at least according to some observers. Then there are the radioactive wastes, many improperly stored. The environment has been terribly mistreated for a long time, and there is little that can be done about it now...

"Many of the results of our past sins involving low-level radiation are irreversible. All that we can hope to do is refrain from making things even worse. The Community says we must convince our governments to phase out and eventually close all nuclear facilities throughout the world.

[Continued]

★ 365 ★

Impacts of Radioactive Contamination

[Continued]

"The U.S. government has estimated the cost of getting rid of its military nuclear plants: $175 billion. The cost for doing this for all civilian nuclear facilities may well exceed several thousand billion dollars. And that's for the United States alone. Remember that many countries are counting on nuclear energy to help them to develop their economies and pull their standard of living closer to that of the developed countries. Also, major research and development efforts are required to devise means for the relatively safe disposal of the radioactive wastes that have accumulated and that will continue to increase in volume until all reactors are turned off."

Source: Walter J. Karplus, *The Heavens Are Falling: The Scientific Prediction of Catastrophes in Our Time* (New York: Plenum Press), 1992, pp. 175-7.

★ 366 ★

Environmental Impacts of Hazardous Waste

High-level Radioactive Nuclear-plant Waste in the U.S., 1991-2030

"Nuclear waste, now about 30,000 metric tons, is projected to rise to nearly 88,000 tons by 2030. Almost all the spent fuel sits in water-filled pools designed to cool the radioactive waste. These pools, which were supposed to be temporary storage, are running out of room."

[Metric tons]

Year	
1991	23,000
2000	43,000
2010	60,000
2020	77,000
2030	88,000

Source: Mary Beth Regan, "Nuclear Fuel Rods Along the Sand Dunes?" 10 May 1993, p. 27. *Primary source:* Energy Information Administration. *Note:* Magnitudes estimated from published chart.

★ 367 ★

Environmental Impacts of Hazardous Waste

Waste Acceptance Rates for Spent Nuclear Fuel, 1998-2007

[Metric tons of uranium]

Year	SNF
1998	400
1999	600
2000	900
2001	900
2002	900
2003	900
2004	900
2005	900
2006	900
2007	900
Total	8,200

Source: U.S. Department of Energy, Office of Civilian Radioactive Waste Management, *Annual Capacity Report* (Washington, D.C.: U.S. Government Printing Office, December 1991), p. 5. *Note:* SNF = Spent Nuclear Fuel.

Recycling, Reclamation, and Alternative Energy Sources

★ 368 ★

Paper and Paperboard Manufacture Consumption of Primary and Reclaimed Materials, 1992-1996

"In 1993, recovered paper consumption for paper and paperboard manufacture is expected to reach 29.2 million tons, increasing to 34.4 million tons in 1996, assuming full utilization of productive capacity. At this level, recovered paper would comprise better than one-third of total fiber consumed by the industry. The four-year increase, 1992-1996, is projected at 7.9 million tons. This translates to an average annual rate of increase of 6.8%, twice the rate of growth in consumption for all fiber, and more than three times the rate of growth in papermaking capacity."

[Thousands short tons]

Grades	1992		1993	1994	1995	1996		
	Annual tons	Percent	Annual tons	Annual tons	Annual tons	Annual tons	Percent	Average annual growth 1993-1996*
Total consumption	87,915	100.0	90,585	95,106	97,194	98,905	100.0	3.0
Primary materials								
Wood pulp from Primary fibers	40,120	45.6	40,512	41,507	41,769	41,922	42.2	1.1

[Continued]

★ 368 ★

Paper and Paperboard Manufacture Consumption of Primary and Reclaimed Materials, 1992-1996

[Continued]

Grades	1992 Annual tons	1992 Percent	1993 Annual tons	1994 Annual tons	1995 Annual tons	1996 Annual tons	Percent	Average annual growth 1993-1996*
Reclaimed materials	47,795	54.4	50,073	53,599	55,425	56,983	57.6	4.5
Wood pulp from								
Reclaimed fibers	21,142	24.1	20,717	22,189	22,281	22,364	22.6	1.4
Recovered paper**	26,476	30.1	29,169	31,199	32,931	34,405	34.8	6.8
Other	177	0.2	187	211	213	214	0.2	4.9

Source: American Forest & Paper Association, *Paper Paperboard Pulp Capacity and Fiber Consumption* (Washington, D.C.: American Forest & Paper Association), 1993, p. 6. *Notes:* Consumption for 1994-1996 assumes capacity levels of production. *Four-year increase. **Includes tonnage consumed in the manufacture of molded pulp products ranging from 295,000 tons in 1992 to 313,000 tons in 1996.

★ 369 ★

Recycling, Reclamation, and Alternative Energy Sources

Earth 21 Strategies, 1990-2030

"New Earth 21 [proposed by Japan's Ministry of International Trade and Industry] is a framework for a program of actions over the next 100 years [addressed] to the recovery of this planet from 200 years of damage done by the accumulation of carbon dioxide and other greenhouse gases.

"The first 50 years will be devoted to five decade-long tasks: The first decade focuses on improving and implementing energy efficiently [see projection in Chapter 14, "Science and Technology," under "Environmental Technologies"]. This will be accomplished through increased use of available technologies while promoting intensified scientific and economic research in new, efficient technologies. Research and development of clean energy resources will be spurred. And carbon-dioxide absorption sinks will be enhanced through increased reforestation and improved forestry management.

"The second decade will aim at the promotion of clean energies such as inherently safe nuclear energy and renewable energies. The third decade will see the spread of non-greenhouse-gas substitutes for chlorofluorocarbons (CFCs), carbon dioxide reutilization technologies, and low-energy production processes.

"In the fourth decade, carbon dioxide absorption will advance dramatically through reforestation and the afforestation of deserts using biotechnology. The technology to enhance oceanic sinks, where phytoplankton absorb carbon dioxide, will also be available by this time. The fifth decade will be the dawn of a new generation of technologies such as fusion, orbiting solar-power plants, magma electricity generation, as well as superconductors and other new energy-related technologies.

"All of these programs... will be implemented in a global partnership with all countries, including developed and developing countries alike.

"In the second 50 years, the results of the first five decades will be integrated to complete the work of regreening the planet."

	1990	2000	2010	2020	2030
Intensified scientific research to reduce uncertainties	X				
Accelerated energy conservation	X				
CFCs phase out	X				
Safer nuclear power plants	X				
New and renewable energy sources		X			
Third generation CFC substitutes		X			
CO_2 fixation and reulitization technology		X			
Environment-friendly production process			X		
Reforestation	X				
Reversing desertification through bio-tech (salt-and-drought-resistant plants)			X		
Enhancing oceanic sinks				X	
Nuclear fusion					X
Space solar power generation					X

Source: Yasuhiko Ishida, "Regreening the Earth: Japan's 100-Year Plan," in *The Futurist*, July-August 1993, pp. 20-2. *Note:* CFC=Chlorofluorocarbon; CO_2=Carbon Dioxide.

★ 370 ★

Recycling, Reclamation, and Alternative Energy Sources

Annual Production Growth Assumptions for Geothermal Heat Pump Systems, 1988-1995

	1988	1989	1990	1991	1992	1993	1994	1995
Growth	25.0%	25.0%	25.0%	25.0%	25.0%	25.0%	25.0%	25.0%
Production	12,000	15,000	18,750	23,438	29,297	36,621	45,776	57,220
Number of Units	45,000	60,000	78,750	102,188	131,484	168,105	213,882	271,102
Northeast-Residential	6,750	9,000	11,813	15,328	19,723	25,216	32,082	40,665
Northeast-Commercial	2,250	3,000	3,938	5,109	6,574	8,405	10,694	13,555
Midwest-Residential	20,250	27,000	35,438	45,984	59,168	75,647	96,247	121,996
Midwest-Commercial	6,750	9,000	11,813	15,328	19,723	25,216	32,082	40,665
South-Residential	5,738	7,650	10,041	13,029	16,764	21,433	27,270	34,566
South-Commercial	1,913	2,550	3,347	4,343	5,588	7,144	9,090	11,522
West-Residential	1,013	1,350	1,772	2,299	2,958	3,782	4,812	6,100
West-Commercial	338	450	591	766	986	1,261	1,604	2,033
Site (million Btu saved/unit)								
Northeast	24.6	24.6	24.6	24.7	24.8	24.7	24.8	24.8
Midwest	32.6	32.6	32.6	32.5	32.4	32.2	32.1	32.1
South	23.8	23.8	23.8	22.8	21.9	20.9	20.0	20.0
West	23.2	23.2	23.2	22.2	21.4	20.6	19.6	19.6

Source: U.S. Department of Energy, Energy Information Administration, *Assumptions for the Annual Energy Outlook 1993* (Washington, D.C.: U.S. Government Printing Office, 1993), p. 14. *Primary source:* Energy Information Administration, Office of Integrated Analysis and Forecasting. *Notes:* Calculations are used to estimated the energy contribution of geothermal heat pumps from 1988 to 1995. After 1995, the market penetration model is used.

★ 371 ★

Recycling, Reclamation, and Alternative Energy Sources

Alternative-fuel Vehicle Sales, 2010

[Thousands]

Vehicle type	Oil price case		
	Low oil price ($18)	Mid-level price ($29)	High oil price ($38)
Light-duty vehicles	1025	1025	1279
Medium-duty trucks	7	11	15
Heavy-duty trucks	0	3	7

Source: U.S. Department of Energy, Energy Information Administration, *Assumptions for the Annual Energy Outlook 1993* (Washington, D.C.: U.S. Government Printing Office, 1993), p. 28. *Primary source:* Energy Information Administration, Office of Integrated Analysis and Forecasting.

★ 372 ★

Recycling, Reclamation, and Alternative Energy Sources

Alternative-fuel Vehicle Sales and Stock, 2010

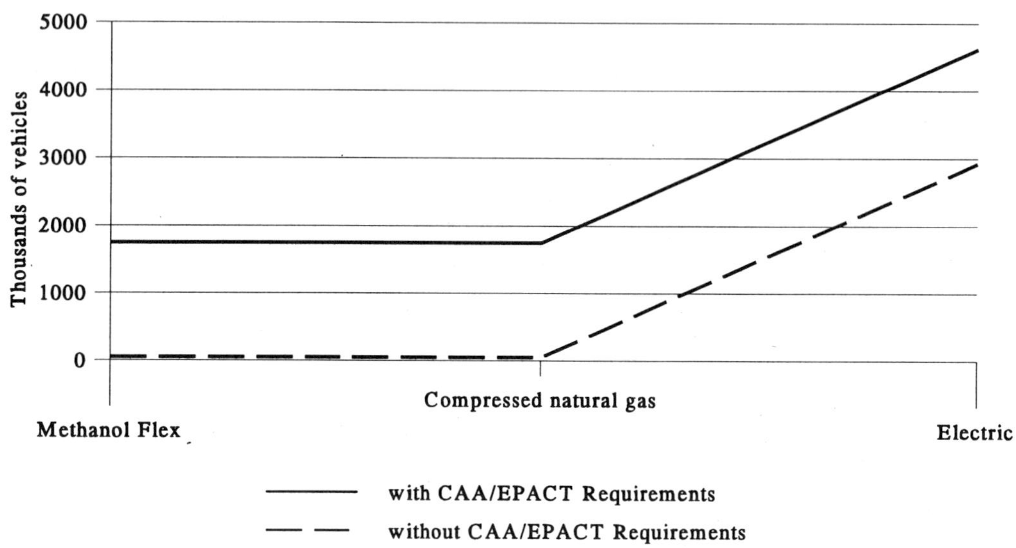

[Thousands]

Vehicle type	AEO92	AEO93 W/O HR776	AEO93 W/HR776
Sales			
Light-duty vehicles	17,960	18,012	18,012
Alternative-fuel vehicles	234	346	1,025
Stock			
Light-duty vehicles	235,188	238,787	238,792
Methanol Flex		52	1,743
Compressed natural gas		52	1,743
Electric	1,946	2,930	4,621
Conventional	233,242	235,753	230,685

Source: U.S. Department of Energy, Energy Information Administration, *Assumptions for the Annual Energy Outlook 1993* (Washington, D.C.: U.S. Government Printing Office, 1993), p. 29. *Primary source:* Energy Information Administration, Office of Integrated Analysis and Forecasting. *Notes:* AEO=Annual Energy Outlook. HR776=House of Representatives version of Energy Policy Act.

★373★

Recycling, Reclamation, and Alternative Energy Sources

New Fleet Vehicle Purchases Required by EPACT/CAA, 1993-2006

"In passing the CAA and EPACT legislation, Congress recognized fleets as being uniquely suited for introducing new fuel and vehicle technologies. Fleet vehicles typically accumulate higher annual mileage than private vehicles and are replaced sooner. By using alternative-fuel vehicles, fleets can shorten the amount of time it takes to improve our air quality and pave the country's route to energy independence."

[Percent]

Year	Clean Air Act		Energy Policy Act			
	GVW less than 8,500 lb. (% of CFVs)	GVW less than 26,000 lb. (% of CFVs)	Federal[2] (% or number of AFVs)	State (% of AFVs)	Fuel provider (% of AFVs)	Municipal/ private[3] (% of AFVs)
1993			7,500[1]			
1994			11,250[1]			
1995			15,000[1]			
1996			25%	10%	30%	
1997			33%	15%	50%	
1998	30%	50%	50%	25%	70&	
1999	50%	50%	75%	50%	90%	20%
2000	70%	50%	75%	75%	90%	20%
2001	70%	50%	75%	75%	90%	20%
2002	70%	50%	75%	75%	90%	30%
2003	70%	50%	75%	75%	90%	40%
2004	70%	50%	75%	75%	90%	50%
2005	70%	50%	75%	75%	90%	60%
2006	70%	50%	75%	75%	90%	70%

Source: U.S. Department of Energy, Argonne National Laboratory, *Taking an Alternative Route* (Washington, D.C.: U.S. Government Printing Office, 1994), p. 8. *Notes:* AFV=Alternative Fuel Vehicle; CAA=Clean Air Act; CFV=Conventionally Fueled Vehicle; EPACT=Energy Policy Act of 1992; GVW=Gross Vehicle Weight. 1. As required by Executive Order No. 12844. 2. Fiscal year for Federal Fleet Acquisition Requirements; Model Year for all others. 3. May be required by regulations if DOE finds these *voluntary* acquisitions unlikely to be met.

★ 374 ★

Recycling, Reclamation, and Alternative Energy Sources

Clean Coal Technology Commercial Readiness, 1985-2004

"[If] the nation's $5 billion plus investment in clean coal technologies is successful, just over the horizon may lie a new coal era for the U.S. and the world."

[Year readiness]

Year	Pre-combustion		Combustion				Post-combustion		Conversion
	Advanced physical cleaning	Chemical/ biological cleaning	Atmospheric fluidized bed	Pressurized fluidized bed	Advanced combustors	Gas reburning	Duct injection	Advanced scrubbers	Gasification combined cycle
1985									D
1986			D						
1987							D		
1988					D				
1989				D		D			
1990	D						D	D	
1991		D					F		
1993	F				F	F			
1995							W	F	
1996		F	F		W	W			
1997									
1998	W			F					F
1999								W	
2000		W							
2001			W	W					
2004								W	

Source: U.S. Department of Energy, Assistant Secretary for Fossil Energy, *Clean Coal Technology: The New Coal Era* (Washington, D.C.: U.S. Government Printing Office, March 1992), p. 38. *Note:* D = Demonstrations; F = First Commercial Plants; W = Widespread use.

★375★

Recycling, Reclamation, and Alternative Energy Sources

Retirement or Repowering of Coal-fired Power Plants Thirty Years Old or Older, 1985-2010

"By the mid-1990s, more than half of all existing coal-fired boilers in the U.S. will be 30 years old and older, and the percentage of aging plants will rise even more sharply around the year 2000. At the same time, demand for electricity is continuing to increase. As much as 100,000 to 150,000 megawatts of additional new capacity beyond what is currently planned—the equivalent of 200 to 300 moderately sized (500-megawatt) power plants—could be required by the end of the century.

"These two trends—aging power plants and growing electricity demand—could pose serious problems for utilities wishing to use coal unless new technology is available. Today's baseload coal-fired power plant takes 10 to 12 years to design, permit, and build. It is probably too late to count on major new baseload construction to meet much of the new power demand by the year 2000.

"Many clean coal technologies, however, offer the option of repowering older power plants..., not only reducing their emissions but extending their lifetime by 20 to 30 years. Because of their higher efficiencies, the new technologies can boost an older plant's electrical output by 40% to 200%. For some installations, the effect could be the equivalent of two or more power plants at the original plant site, with sulfur emissions as much as 99% lower and NO_x emissions 40% lower than the older plant. Repowering concepts may also become the technologies of choice for future, new plant construction."

[Coal-fired plants Thirty Years or Older, by percentage of megawatts]

Year	Percent of megawatts
1985	12
1990	18
1995	27
2000	43
2005	65
2010	83

Source: U.S. Department of Energy, Assistant Secretary for Fossil Energy, *Clean Coal Technology: The New Coal Era* (Washington, D.C.: U.S. Government Printing Office, March 1992), pp. 34-36. *Note:* Magnitudes estimated from published chart.

★ 376 ★

Recycling, Reclamation, and Alternative Energy Sources

Carbon Removal by "America the Beautiful" Program, 2000-2010

"As part of his 'America the Beautiful' program, President Bush... proposed one of the most ambitious reforestation programs in the world: a program to plant a billion trees per year across America above and beyond the number of trees that are normally planted. This reforestation initiative will contribute to cleaner air and water and energy conservation, and will reduce net carbon dioxide emissions. Urban tree planting under the program has increased 25 percent over the last year. Funding at the President's requested level would have significant impacts on net carbon dioxide emissions."

[Million metric tons of carbon]

Year	Carbon dioxide removed from atmosphere
2000	6
2010	33

Source: U.S. Actions for a Better Environment (Washington, D.C.: U.S. Government Printing Office), 1991, p. 5, 9. *Primary source:* Environmental Protection Agency (EPA), Climate Change Division.

★ 377 ★

Recycling, Reclamation, and Alternative Energy Sources

Environmental Effects of Energy-saving Computer Technologies, 2000

"The widespread penetration of energy-saving computer technologies offers significant benefits to consumers, the economy, and the environment. The cost of operating a typical 150-watt personal computer 24 hours per day year round can be $105/year (assuming electricity costs at $0.08/kWh) and uses 1,314 kWh/yr. Turning the machine off at night reduces the operating cost to $35/year and cuts energy consumption to 433 kWh/year. Using technology that conserves power when the machine is not active during the day could cut costs to $17/year for 216 kWh/year. Environmental Protection Agency (EPA) estimates that green computers could save a total of $1.5 to $2 billion in annual electricity bills and avoid emissions of 20 million tons of carbon dioxide, 140,000 tons of sulfur dioxide, and 75,000 tons of nitrogen dioxide by 2000."

Source: U.S. Congress, Office of Technology Assessment, *Energy Efficiency: Challenges and Opportunities for Electric Utilities* (Washington, D.C.: U.S. Government Printing Office, September 1993), p. 87. *Primary source:* U.S. Environmental Protection Agency, *Office of Atmospheric Programs, 1992 Accomplishments and Prospects for 1993*, vol. 1: Global Change Division, Environmental Protection Agency (EPA) 430-K-92-031, November 1992, pp. 9-10. Brian J. Johnson and Catherine R. Zoi, "EPA Energy Star Computers: The Next Generation of Office Equipment," in American Council for an Energy-Efficient Economy, *ACEEE 1992 Summer Study of Energy Efficiency in Buildings*, vol. 6 (Washington, D.C.: American Council for an Energy-Efficient Economy, 1992), pp. 6.107-6.114. kWh/yr. = Kilowatt hours per year.

★ 378 ★

Recycling, Reclamation, and Alternative Energy Sources

Emissions Savings from Telecommuting, 1992-2002

"The pollution created by highway vehicles in 1990 was 5.085 million tons of nitrogen oxides, 4.63 million tons of hydrocarbons, and 27.48 million tons of carbon monoxide (U.S. Environmental Protection Agency (EPA), National Air Pollution Emission Estimates 1940-1990, Nov. 1991). The estimated amount of reduction of these pollutants due to telecommuting is shown... below.

"[The table below] shows a relatively limited impact of telecommuting on air quality. However, these results could be very misleading when applied to a specific locality. The degree to which telecommuting is adopted depends in part on the overall transportation environment. In areas suffering serious congestion and air quality problems, in which stringent transportation demand and control measures are in force, firms and employees will have much greater incentive to explore and implement telecommuting. The result could be a substantially higher rate of adoption than used in this analysis, particularly for individuals who face the more lengthy or congested commuting trips. Under those circumstances, it is also less likely that latent demand will appear as telecommuters disappear from the highways. The resulting reduction in congestion will result in emission reductions for all traffic—an effect that could be as great in magnitude as that from removal of the telecommuters. With a higher number of telecommuters and reduced congestion for all vehicles, the total reduction in emissions could conceivably be several times that suggested [below]."

	Emissions	1992		1997--5 year		2002--10 year	
		Tons saved	% of total[1]	Tons saved	% of total[1]	Tons saved	% of total[1]
Upper bound	NO_x	11,852	0.23%	41,061	0.81%	111,479	2.19%
	HC	14,571	0.31%	50,468	1.09%	137,047	2.70%
	CO	98,753	0.36%	342,118	1.25%	928,836	3.38%
Lower bound	NO_x	11,852	0.23%	31,593	0.62%	55,739	1.10%
	HC	14,571	0.31%	38,839	0.84%	68,524	1.35%
	CO	98,753	0.36%	263,229	0.95%	464,418	1.69%

Source: U.S. Department of Transportation, *Transportation Implications of Telecommuting* (Washington, D.C.: U.S. Government Printing Office, April 1993), p. 78. *Notes:* CO=Carbon monoxide; HC=Hydrocarbon; NO_x=Nitrogen oxide. 1. Percentages based on 1990 levels.

Natural Resources

★ 379 ★

Increase in Wolf Population in Idaho and Yellowstone National Park, 1995-2003

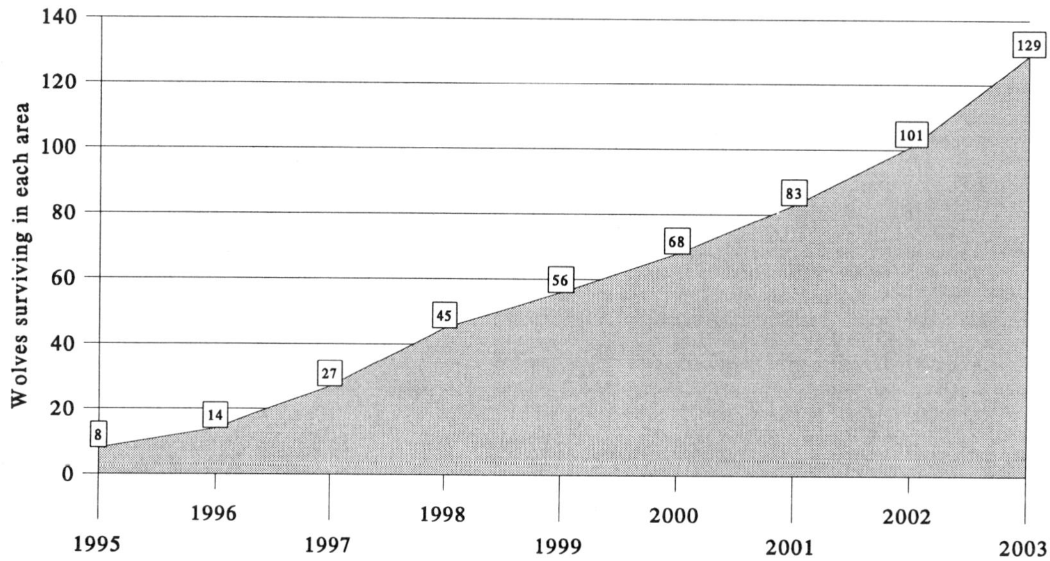

"Biologists are poised to set free four gray wolves into Idaho and eight into Yellowstone National Park in an effort to build breeding populations of the endangered species. Eighteen more should follow by the end of the year.

"Thirty wolves, 15 going to each area, are to be released each year for the next 3-5 years. Biologists hope the population will reach about 100 in each area by 2002."

[Wolves surviving in each area]

Year	
1995	8
1996	14
1997	27
1998	45
1999	56
2000	68
2001	83
2002	101
2003	129

Source: Marty Baumann, "Endangered Gray Wolves to be Released Into the Wild," in *USA TODAY*, 13 January 1995, p. 5D. *Primary source:* Department of the Interior, *USA TODAY* research.

★ 380 ★

Natural Resources

Refuges 2003 Alternatives, 1993-2003

"**Refuges 2003** identifies, defines and evaluates seven different approaches to the management of the National Wildlife Refuge System over the next decade. They represent a wide spectrum of policies and programs, and reflect diverse management orientations towards natural resource and public use management. They would all be technically feasible within the constraints of statutory authorities governing management of the Refuge System, as well as associated compatibility determinations.

"[The table below] summarizes the relative management emphasis for all Alternatives and enables the reader to identify the primary differences in Management Actions at a glance."

Management actions	Balanced (Proposed action)	Sanctuary	Wildlife observation	Ecosystem management	Hunting, trapping, fishing	Maximum multiple use
Develop individual refuge plans	MME	MLE	LE	LE	ME	MLE
Develop refuge system infrastructure	SE	ME	ME	ME	ME	ME
Collect and manage data	ME	SE	ME	ME	ME	SE
Regulate and manage uses	MME	MME	ME	ME	ME	LE
Acquire land	SE	MLE	LE	ME	ME	LE
Designate and manage special management areas	ME	LE	ME	MME	ME	LE
Conserve and restore biological diversity	ME	MLE	ME	MME	SE	MLE
Protect air quality	ME	MME	ME	MME	ME	SE
Investigate and clean up refuge contaminants	ME	MME	ME	ME	SE	ME
Graze and hay refuge lands	LE	MLE	LE	LE	LE	MME
Farm refuge lands	LE	MLE	LE	LE	ME	MME
Manage forests on refuge lands	SE	MLE	SE	LE	ME	MME
Explore and extract oil, gas and minerals	SE	MLE	SE	SE	SE	MME
Manage fire	ME	MLE	ME	MME	ME	LE
Manage or restore water rights	ME	MME	SE	MME	ME	SE
Manage fishery resources	ME	MLE	ME	ME	MME	MME
Manage game species	ME	MLE	ME	SE	MME	ME
Manage nongame species	ME	MLE	MME	MME	LE	SE
Manage and recover threatened and endangered species	ME	MLE	ME	ME	LE	LE
Control predation	SE	MLE	LE	LE	MME	ME
Manage pests	LE	MLE	MLE	LE	SE	ME
Provide hunting opportunities	SE	MLE	MLE	LE	MME	ME
Provide trapping opportunities	ME	MLE	MLE	LE	ME	ME
Provide fishing opportunities	ME	MLE	LE	LE	MME	MME
Provide other wildlife-oriented recreation and education	ME	MLE	MME	LE	LE	ME
Provide nonwildlife-oriented recreation	MLE	MLE	MLE	MLE	MLE	MME
Inventory and protect cultural resources	ME	LE	MME	ME	ME	MME

Source: U.S. Department of the Interior, U.S. Fish and Wildlife Service, *Refuges 2003* (Washington, D.C.: U.S. Government Printing Office, January 1993), pp. 2-1, 2-9.
Notes: MME=Much More Emphasis; ME=More Emphasis; LE=Less Emphasis; MLE=Much Less Emphasis.

★ 381 ★

Natural Resources

Environmental Effects of Refuges 2003 Alternatives, 1993-2003

Environmental impact topics	Projected current (No action)[1]	Balanced (proposed action)[2]	Sanctuary[2]	Wildlife observation[2]	Ecosystem management[2]	Hunting, trapping, fishing[2]	Maximum multiple use[2]
Air quality	-	+ +	+ +	+ +	+ +	+ +	- -
Water quality	+	+	+ +	+	+	+	- -
Biological diversity	+	+ +	-	+	+ + +	-	- -
Game mammals	+	+ +	-	+	+	+ + +	+
Game birds	+	+	- -	+	-	+ + +	+ +
Nongame species	+	+ +	-	+ +	+ + +	- -	- -
Aquatic species	-	+	+ +	+	+ + +	-	- -
Threatened and endangered species	+	+ +	-	+	+ + +	- -	-
Wetland habitat	+	+	- -	+ +	+ + +	+	- - -
Terrestrial habitat	+	+ +	+	+	+ + +	+	- -
Local economies	+ +	+ +	- - -	+ + +	-	-	+ + +
Social values	+	+ +	-	+	+	-	- -
Wildlife-oriented recreation	+	+ +	- - -	+ + +	-	+	+
Nonwildlife-oriented recreation	- -	- - -	- - -	- - -	- - -	- - -	+ + +
Wilderness and other management areas	+	+	- - -	+ +	+ + +	+	- - -
Cultural resources	- -	+	+	+ +	+	+	- -

Source: U.S. Department of the Interior, U.S. Fish and Wildlife Service, *Refuges 2003* (Washington, D.C.: U.S. Government Printing Office, January 1993), p. 4-2. *Notes:* + + + = Large Positive Effects; + + = Moderate Positive Effects; + = Slightly Positive Effects; - = Slightly Negative Effects; - - = Moderate Negative Effects; - - - = Large Negative Effects. 1. Effects of No Action Alternative as compared to Current Situation. 2. Effects of other Alternative as compared to the No Action Alternative.

Recreational Resources

★ 382 ★

Federal Mandatory and Receipts PAYGO Proposals for the Department of the Interior, 1994-1999

[Deficit impact in millions of dollars]

Year	1994	1995	1996	1997	1998	1999
Implement NPR recommendation to increase park fees to enhance park facilities and make 15 percent of estimated receipts available for fee collection costs. Create a new National Park Renewal Fund to expend 50 percent of net new receipts and return them to the collection park	-	-1	-4	-4	-3	-2
Impose 8% royalty on hardrock minerals removed from Federal lands	-	-	-16	-112	-110	-108

[Continued]

★ 382 ★

Federal Mandatory and Receipts PAYGO Proposals for the Department of the Interior, 1994-1999

[Continued]

Year	1994	1995	1996	1997	1998	1999
Establish hardrock reclamation fund to reclaim abandoned mine sites on federal lands	-	-	-	1	29	49

Source: Executive Office of the President of the United States, Office of Management and Budget, *Budget of the United States Government* (Washington, D.C.: U.S. Government Printing Office, 1994), p. 240. *Note:* NPR=National Park Renewal. PAYGO=Pay as you go.

★ 383 ★

Recreational Resources

Federal Investment Proposals in the Department of the Interior, 1993-1999

[Millions of dollars]

		1993 Enacted	Estimate		Change: 1994 to 1995	Estimate			
			1994[1]	1995		1996	1997	1998	1999
Natural resource protection and environmental infrastructure (includes NAFTA environmental activities)	BA	1,783	1,813	1,964	151	2,013	2,028	2,048	2,056
	OL	1,732	1,757	1,942	185	2,003	2,025	2,045	2,053
Pacific Northwest Forest Plan	BA	...	27	71	44	85	85	85	86
	OL	...	19	58	39	81	85	85	85
South Florida ecosystem restoration	BA	26	17	45	28	45	45	45	45
	OL	10	15	31	16	47	45	45	45
National Biological Survey	BA	...	167	177	10	187	192	200	210
	OL	...	82	156	74	179	188	196	205
National spatial data infrastructure initiative	BA	...	1	7	6	7	7	7	7
	OL	...	1	7	6	7	7	7	7
BuRec wastewater reclamation & reuse pilot program (So. Cal.)	BA	...	10	10	...	37	34	21	1
	OL	...	9	10	1	32	34	23	4
Climate change action plan	BA	...	[1]	[1]	[1]	...	...	...	...
	OL	...	[1]	[1]	[1]	...	...	...	...

Source: Executive Office of the President of the United States, Office of Management and Budget, *Budget of the United States Government* (Washington, D.C.: U.S. Government Printing Office, 1994), p. 245. *Notes:* 1. Less than 1 percent. BA=Budget Authority; NAFTA=North American Free Trade Agreement; OL=Outlays.

★ 384 ★

Recreational Resources

Projected Decrease in Land, Water, and Snow and Ice Resources Available for Outdoor Recreation, 2000-2040

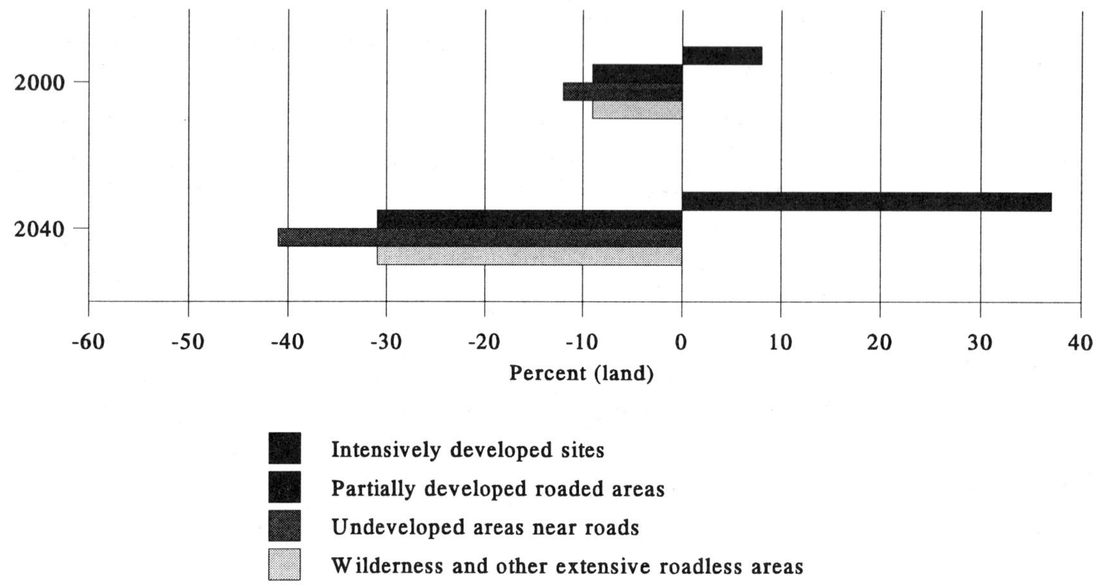

[Percent]

Resources and environments	Projected percentage change from 1987				
	2000	2010	2020	2030	2040
Land					
Wilderness and other extensive roadless areas	-9	-15	-21	-26	-31
Undeveloped areas near roads	-12	-20	-28	-35	-41
Partially developed roaded areas	-9	-15	-21	-26	-31
Intensively developed sites	8	15	22	29	37
Water					
Wild and remote lakes and streams	3	6	8	9	10
Lakes and streams near roads	-3	-4	-6	-8	-10
Lake and stream sites adjoined by roads	8	15	22	29	37
Intensively developed water sites	12	23	34	47	61
Snow and Ice					
Wilderness and other roadless areas	-9	-15	-21	-26	-31
Undeveloped areas near roads	-12	-20	-28	-35	-41
Partially developed roaded areas	-19	-15	-21	-26	-31
Intensively developed winter sports sites	17	28	36	43	49

Source: U.S. Department of Agriculture, Forest Service, *Regional Demand and Supply Projections for Outdoor Recreation* (Washington, D.C.: U.S. Government Printing Office, August 1993), p. 14. *Primary source:* H. Ken Cordell et al (1990). *Note:* Assumes continuation of current trends.

★ 385 ★

Recreational Resources

Recreation Trips away from Home if Historical Decline of Resource Availability Continues, 1987-2040

"Driving for pleasure and sightseeing are expected to remain the top two activities through 2040, in terms of the nationwide volume of expected supply of annual trips. Neither activity ranks lower than fourth in any RPA region. Closely related activities that are often consumed together, sightseeing and driving for pleasure are both dependent on roads and motorized transportation.

"There is greater variety among the regions in the activities which are expected to show the greatest percentage increases in expected supply or trip consumption by 2040. Five activities are among the top 10 fastest growing activities in all regions. These include downhill skiing, sailing, rafting/tubing, running/jogging, and outdoor pool swimming. The RPA projections for downhill skiing, however, have met sharp criticism from more than one reviewer. Although an extension of recent past trends projects continued steady growth in the developed winter sports sites recreation environment, in reality, the number of downhill skiing resorts has declined in recent years. While larger resorts have been steadily increasing their skier capacity, the overall trend has been a reduction in skier capacity, and a gradual decline in the annual number of skier visits (United Ski Industries Association 1991).

"It also should be noted that the high projected growth rates of sailing and rafting/tubing are largely a function of their small number of base year trips, making moderate growth in trips appear deceptively large in terms of percent change. Moreover, the regression models for expected supply of sailing and rafting/tubing trips were among the least stable of all of the activity models. The sailing model explained 33% of the variation in sailing trips and the rafting/tubing model performed worst of all, with an adjusted R-square of 0.12."

[1987 base = millions of trips]

Resource category and activity (national region)	1987 base	Percent change from 1987 base				
		2000	2010	2020	2030	2040
Land						
Wildlife observation	69.5	107	113	120	120	130
Primitive camping	38.1	108	115	122	130	134
Backpacking	25.9	124	144	165	185	198
Nature study	70.7	99	101	103	107	108
Horseback riding	63.2	114	125	135	144	149
Day hiking	91.1	123	144	168	198	229
Photography	42.1	115	128	141	154	163
Visit prehistoric sites	16.7	127	148	173	203	236
Collecting berries	19.0	110	120	132	149	169
Collecting firewood	30.3	109	118	130	144	161
Walking for pleasure	266.4	116	132	148	168	183
Running and jogging	83.7	131	160	192	229	260
Bicycling	114.5	124	146	170	197	218
Offroad vehicle driving	80.2	104	108	112	118	121
Visiting museums	9.7	118	134	152	172	187
Attend special events	73.7	115	129	144	161	175
Visiting historic sites	73.0	117	133	152	178	204
Driving for pleasure	421.4	110	120	129	139	145
Family gatherings	74.4	121	139	160	182	202
Sightseeing	292.1	114	128	144	164	185
Picnicking	262.1	110	120	131	145	156
Developed camping	60.5	120	138	158	178	195
Water						
Canoeing/kayaking	39.7	113	126	138	153	163

[Continued]

★ 385 ★

Recreation Trips away from Home if Historical Decline of Resource Availability Continues, 1987-2040

[Continued]

Resource category and activity (national region)	1987 base	Percent change from 1987 base				
		2000	2010	2020	2030	2040
Stream/lake swimming	238.7	108	118	128	140	152
Rafting/tubing	9.0	123	151	182	229	267
Rowing/Paddling, etc.	61.8	110	120	130	142	150
Motorboating	219.4	107	114	122	131	138
Water-skiing	107.4	112	122	132	144	152
Outdoor pool swimming	221.0	135	166	200	237	267
Sailing	35.0	141	181	226	279	322
Snow and ice						
Cross-country skiing	9.7	125	136	142	141	126
Downhill skiing	64.3	160	207	256	305	338
Snowmobiling	17.7	120	131	137	141	137

Source: U.S. Department of Agriculture, Forest Service, *Regional Demand and Supply Projections for Outdoor Recreation* (Washington, D.C.: U.S. Government Printing Office, August 1993), pp. 23-4. *Primary source:* Outdoor Recreation and Wilderness Assessment Research, USDA Forest Service, Athens, GA. *Note:* Source also includes regional data.

★ 386 ★

Recreational Resources

Fastest Growing Recreation Activities away from Home if Historical Decline of Resource Availability Continues, 1987-2040

"Growth rates in trip consumption... vary by region, and reflect projected growth in regional population. All of the 10 fastest growing activities in the Pacific Coast region are expected to show increases of more than 200% by 2040."

[Rank]

Activity	Region			
	Pacific North	Rocky Coast	Mountains	South
Downhill skiing	1	6	1	4
Sailing	2	1	3	1
Outdoor pool swimming	3	4	5	5
Day hiking	4	-	9	8
Visiting prehistoric sites	5	-	7	9
Visiting historic sites	6	-	10	-
Running/jogging	7	3	4	3
Sightseeing	8	-	-	-
Backpacking	9	-	-	6
Rafting/tubing	10	2	2	2
Family gatherings	-	10	-	-
Collecting firewood	-	-	6	-

[Continued]

★ 386 ★

Fastest Growing Recreation Activities away from Home if Historical Decline of Resource Availability Continues, 1987-2040

[Continued]

Activity	Region			
	Pacific North	Rocky Coast	Mountains	South
Bicycling	-	5	8	7
Visiting museums	-	7	-	-
Developed camping	-	8	-	10
Walking for pleasure	-	9	-	-

Source: U.S. Department of Agriculture, Forest Service, *Regional Demand and Supply Projections for Outdoor Recreation* (Washington, D.C.: U.S. Government Printing Office, August 1993), p. 27. *Primary source:* Outdoor Recreation and Wilderness Assessment Research, USDA Forest Service, Athens, GA.

★ 387 ★

Recreational Resources

Recreation Trips away from Home with Resource Availability Unconstrained, 1987-2040

[1987=millions of trips]

Resource category and activity (national region)	1987 trips	Future number of trips as percentage of 1987 demand				
		2000	2010	2020	2030	2040
Land						
Wildlife observation	69.5	116	131	146	162	174
Primitive camping	38.1	114	127	140	154	164
Backpacking	25.9	134	164	196	230	255
Nature study	70.7	105	113	120	131	138
Horseback riding	63.2	123	141	160	177	190
Day hiking	91.1	131	161	198	244	293
Photography	42.1	123	143	165	188	205
Visit prehistoric sites	16.7	133	160	192	233	278
Collecting berries	19.0	133	126	143	166	192
Collecting firewood	30.3	113	127	143	161	183
Walking for pleasure	266.4	116	131	146	164	177
Running and jogging	83.7	133	163	197	234	262
Bicycling	114.5	125	148	173	202	222
Offroad vehicle driving	80.2	105	111	118	125	130
Visiting museums	9.7	118	136	153	174	188
Attend special events	73.7	114	127	141	157	168
Visiting historic sites	73.0	122	143	169	203	241
Driving for pleasure	421.4	115	128	142	157	167
Family gatherings	74.4	119	135	152	170	182
Sightseeing	292.1	118	136	156	183	212
Picnicking	262.1	108	117	126	136	144
Developed camping	60.5	120	137	155	173	186

[Continued]

★ 387 ★

Recreation Trips away from Home with Resource Availability Unconstrained, 1987-2040

[Continued]

Resource category and activity (national region)	1987 trips	Future number of trips as percentage of 1987 demand				
		2000	2010	2020	2030	2040
Water						
Canoeing/kayaking	39.7	113	126	140	157	169
Stream/lake swimming	238.7	105	110	117	124	129
Rafting/tubing	9.0	111	136	164	215	255
Rowing/paddling, etc.	61.8	112	124	136	150	159
Motorboating	219.4	106	111	117	123	127
Water-skiing	107.4	111	121	131	141	148
Outdoor pool swimming	221.0	137	169	205	242	269
Sailing	35.0	145	188	237	293	335
Snow and ice						
Cross-country skiing	9.7	147	177	199	212	195
Downhill skiing	64.3	153	197	247	298	333
Snowmobiling	17.7	119	128	134	137	130

Source: U.S. Department of Agriculture, Forest Service, *Regional Demand and Supply Projections for Outdoor Recreation* (Washington, D.C.: U.S. Government Printing Office, August 1993), pp. 29-32. *Primary source:* Outdoor Recreation and Wilderness Assessment Research, USDA Forest Service, Athens, GA. *Notes:* Demand is based on the number of trips households would take if future per trip costs were unchanged from the base year amount and resource availability were unconstrained. Source also contains regional data.

★ 388 ★

Recreational Resources

Fastest Growing Recreation Activities with Resource Availability Unconstrained, 1987-2040

[Rank]

Activity	Region Pacific North	Rocky Coast	Mountains	South
Downhill skiing	1	7	2	2
Sailing	4	1	3	1
Day hiking	2	-	4	5
Rafting/tubing	-	2	1	4
Pool swimming	7	-	5	3
Visiting prehistoric sites	3	-	8	8
Cross-country skiing	-	3	6	-
Visiting historic sites	6	-	10	10
Running/jogging	10	4	7	6
Sightseeing	5	-	-	-
Backpacking	9	5	9	7
Bicycling	-	6	-	9
Photography	-	8	-	-
Collecting berries	8	-	-	-

[Continued]

★ 388 ★

Fastest Growing Recreation Activities with Resource Availability Unconstrained, 1987-2040

[Continued]

Activity	Region Pacific North	Rocky Coast	Mountains	South
Visiting museums	-	9	-	-
Developed camping	-	10	-	-

Source: U.S. Department of Agriculture, Forest Service, *Regional Demand and Supply Projections for Outdoor Recreation* (Washington, D.C.: U.S. Government Printing Office, August 1993), p. 32. *Primary source:* Outdoor Recreation and Wilderness Assessment Research, USDA Forest Service, Athens, GA.

★ 389 ★

Recreational Resources

Gap Between Demand for Recreation Activities away from Home with Unconstrained Resource Availability and Expected Decline in Supply for Such Trips, 1987-2040

[1987=millions of trips; projections are a percent of 1987 trips]

Resource category and activity (national region)	1987 trips	2000 D/S/G[1]	2010 D/S/G	2020 D/S/G	2030 D/S/G	2040 D/S/G
Land						
Wildlife observation	69.5	116/107/9	131/113/17	146/120/26	162/120/42	174/130/44
Primitive camping	38.1	114/108/6	127/115/12	140/122/18	154/130/24	164/134/30
Backpacking	25.9	134/124/10	164/144/20	196/165/31	230/185/45	255/198/57
Nature study	70.7	105/99/6	113/101/12	120/103/17	131/107/24	138/108/30
Horseback riding	63.2	123/114/9	141/125/16	160/135/25	177/144/33	190/149/41
Day hiking	91.1	131/123/8	161/144/17	198/168/30	244/198/46	293/229/64
Photography	42.1	123/115/8	143/128/15	165/141/24	188/154/34	205/163/42
Visit prehistoric sites	16.7	133/127/6	160/148/12	192/173/19	233/203/30	278/236/42
Collecting berries	19.0	113/110/3	126/120/6	143/132/11	166/149/17	192/169/23
Collecting firewood	30.3	113/109/4	127/118/9	143/130/13	161/144/17	183/161/22
Walking for pleasure	266.4	116/116/0	131/132/0	146/148/0	164/168/0	177/183/0
Running and jogging	83.7	133/131/2	163/160/3	197/192/5	234/229/5	262/260/2
Bicycling	114.5	125/124/1	148/146/2	173/170/3	202/197/5	222/218/4
Offroad vehicle driving	80.2	105/104/1	111/108/3	118/112/6	125/118/7	130/121/9
Visiting museums	9.7	118/118/0	136/134/2	153/152/1	174/172/2	188/187/1
Attend special events	73.7	114/115/0	127/129/0	141/144/0	157/161/0	168/175/0
Visiting historic sites	73.0	122/117/5	143/133/10	169/152/17	203/178/25	241/204/37
Driving for pleasure	421.4	115/110/5	128/120/8	142/129/13	157/139/18	167/145/22
Family gatherings	74.4	119/121/0	135/139/0	152/160/0	170/182/0	182/202/0
Sightseeing	292.1	118/114/4	136/128/8	156/144/12	183/164/19	212/185/27
Picnicking	262.1	108/110/0	117/120/0	126/131/0	136/145/0	144/156/0
Developed camping	60.5	120/120/0	137/138/0	155/158/0	173/178/0	186/195/0
Water						
Canoeing/kayaking	39.7	113/113/0	126/126/0	140/138/2	157/153/4	169/163/6
Stream/lake swimming	238.7	105/108/0	110/118/0	117/128/0	124/140/0	129/152/0

[Continued]

★ 389 ★

Gap Between Demand for Recreation Activities away from Home with Unconstrained Resource Availability and Expected Decline in Supply for Such Trips, 1987-2040

[Continued]

Resource category and activity (national region)	1987 trips	2000 D/S/G[1]	2010 D/S/G	2020 D/S/G	2030 D/S/G	2040 D/S/G
Rafting/tubing	9.0	111/123/0	136/151/0	164/182/0	215/229/0	255/267/0
Rowing/paddling, etc.	61.8	112/110/2	124/120/4	136/130/6	150/142/8	159/150/9
Motorboating	219.4	106/107/0	111/114/0	117/122/0	123/131/0	127/138/0
Water-skiing	107.4	111/112/0	121/122/0	131/132/0	141/144/0	148/152/0
Outdoor pool swimming	221.0	137/135/2	169/166/3	205/200/5	242/237/5	269/267/2
Sailing	35.0	145/141/4	188/181/7	237/226/11	293/279/14	335/322/13
Snow and ice						
Cross-country skiing	9.7	147/125/22	177/136/41	199/142/57	212/141/71	195/126/69
Downhill skiing	64.3	153/160/0	197/207/0	247/256/0	298/305/0	333/338/0
Snowmobiling	17.7	119/120/0	128/131/0	134/137/0	137/141/0	130/137/0

Source: U.S. Department of Agriculture, Forest Service, *Regional Demand and Supply Projections for Outdoor Recreation* (Washington, D.C.: U.S. Government Printing Office, August 1993), pp. 33-6. *Primary source:* Outdoor Recreation and Wilderness Assessment Research, USDA Forest Service, Athens, GA. *Notes:* 1. D is the maximum preferred demand; S is the expected supply; and G is the percentage difference (gap) between demand and supply. D, S, and G are all expressed as percentages of the 1987 base number of trips. In the projection base year of 1987, demand is assumed to equal supply with zero gap, that is, demand and supply are in equilibrium. Source also contains regional data.

★ 390 ★

Recreational Resources

Outdoor Recreation Activities with the Largest Projected Gaps in Absolute Number of Trips by Region, 2040

"Regional differences are less apparent when examining projected gaps in terms of the absolute number of trips. Gaps in numbers of trips for sightseeing, driving for pleasure, and day hiking are among the top four activities with gaps in each of the four regions. Although no gap is projected for outdoor pool swimming for the North region, in each of the other regions that activity is projected to have relatively large gaps. In the two eastern regions, relatively large gaps in trips are predicted for wildlife observation, but not for horseback riding. The reverse is true for the two western regions.

"Almost every activity for which a small or zero gap was projected occurs primarily in an environment with developed recreation facilities. Recent trends in developed land and water resources indicate that the supply of such recreation opportunities will continue to increase fast enough to absorb additional trip demands. Growth in recreation resources and facilities implies reduced cost for trip production. Lower trip costs induce households to produce more trips. As a result, supply and consumption is greater, and gaps are less likely.

"Activities such as backpacking, day hiking, and wildlife observation that occur most often in less developed and more remote settings are projected, to a large extent, to experience growth in preferred demand that will outpace consumption and production of trips. The models predict that, as accessible recreation resources decline to fail to keep pace with growth in demand, households will not be able to produce the number of trips they would prefer to take in the future at the 1987 price. Here, preferred demand will exceed the expected supply of trips."

[Gap in percent (top five ranked gaps)]

Activity	Region			
	Pacific North	Rocky Coast	Mountains	South
Sightseeing	29.5	19.8	7.7	17.8
Driving for pleasure	17.8	42.0	8.1	27.1
Day hiking	18.2	15.8	10.1	12.6
Outdoor pool swimming	0	11.8	10.0	14.2
Visiting historic sites	10.8	5.4	3.0	5.8
Horseback riding	4.5	15.3	4.6	5.3
Wildlife observation	8.2	10.8	3.7	9.5

Source: U.S. Department of Agriculture, Forest Service, *Regional Demand and Supply Projections for Outdoor Recreation* (Washington, D.C.: U.S. Government Printing Office, August 1993), pp. 36-7. *Primary source:* Outdoor Recreation and Wilderness Assessment Research, USDA Forest Service, Athens, GA.

★ 391 ★

Recreational Resources

Outdoor Recreation Activities with the Largest Projected Percentage Gaps by Region, 2040

[Gap in percent (top five ranked gaps)]

Activity	Region			
	Pacific North	Rocky Coast	Mountains	South
Cross-country skiing	55	338	139	29
Rafting/tubing	--	--	318	--
Day hiking	43	115	130	46
Backpacking	16	266	143	28
Wildlife observation	26	121	69	40
Visiting prehistoric sites	40	48	54	27
Photography	24	166	57	36
Visiting historic sites	32	53	61	24
Horseback riding	18	133	76	26
Sailing	--	101	102	20

Source: U.S. Department of Agriculture, Forest Service, *Regional Demand and Supply Projections for Outdoor Recreation* (Washington, D.C.: U.S. Government Printing Office, August 1993), p. 36. *Primary source:* Outdoor Recreation and Wilderness Assessment Research, USDA Forest Service, Athens, GA.

Chapter 10
HEALTH, MEDICAL CARE, AND HUMAN SERVICES

Health Care: General Predictions

★ 392 ★

New Treatments in Brain Disorders, 2000

"Migraine headaches, substance abuse, strokes, depression, and memory loss are among the most common types of brain disorders for which scientists hope to find treatments by the year 2000.

"The newly formed Dana Foundation Alliance for Brain Initiatives, a consortium of neuroscientists and brain researchers, has identified several objectives for this field that could be realized within the next few years. The neuroscientists polled by the Alliance predicted that by the end of the decade brain research will:

—Identify genetic defects that lead to Huntington's disease (99%).

—Identify defective genes that cause Alzheimer's disease (89%).

—Develop better treatments for pain from migraine headaches (93%), arthritis (93%), and cancer (91%).

"Developing drugs to block addictive substances, identifying the cause behind hereditary deafness and blindness, and finding substances to reduce nerve-cell damage and speed recovery from strokes were among the longer-range goals of researchers."

Source: "Curing Brain Ailments," in *The Futurist*, September-October, 1993, p. 56. *Primary source:* The Dana Alliance for Brain Initiatives, 745 Fifth Avenue, Suite 700, New York, NY 10151.

★393★

Health Care: General Predictions

Number of Medically Uninsured Californians, 2000

"A new study by the Institute for the Future projects that the number of Californians who are medically uninsured will grow by more than 40% by the year 2000, increasing from 6 million to 8.5 million, of whom 2.4 million will be children.

"Almost 90% of California's uninsured are working people and families, and more than half live in households that earn well above the poverty line, says J. Ian Morrison, president of the Institute. Among the reasons: Small businesses are abandoning health coverage, and costs for individual insurance are escalating. 'In short, if nothing is done, a bad situation could get much worse,' says Morrison."

Source: "Health Crisis Foreseen in California," in *The Futurist*, January-February, 1993, p. 37. *Primary source:* Institute for the Future, "Working Families Under Stress: California Health Care Access in the 1990s," 2744 Sand Hill Road, Menlo Park, CA 94025-7020.

★394★

Health Care: General Predictions

Percentage of Children Immunized by Time of School Entry, 1970-2000

"[As of 1990], starting at age of 2 months, children in the United States receive[d] vaccinations against eight diseases: diphtheria, tetanus, pertussis, polio, hemophilus influenza type B, measles, mumps and rubella. In addition, hepatitis B vaccination was recommended for all infants in the United States in November 1991. All 50 States and the District of Columbia have immunization laws or immunization requirements for school entry. Some 95 percent of children are already fully immunized when they enroll in school."

[Percent vaccinated]

Year	
1970	90
1975	92
1980	93
1985	94
1990	95
1995	93
2000	95

Source: A report in response to the World Summit for Children, *A Culture of Caring: America's Commitment to Children and Families* (Washington, D.C.: U.S. Government Printing Office, September 1990), p. 18. *Primary source:* Center for Prevention Services (CDC). *Note:* Magnitudes estimated from published chart.

★ 395 ★

Health Care: General Predictions

Global Percentage of Pregnant Women Receiving First Trimester Prenatal Care: Blacks and Whites, 1970-2000

"U.S. objectives for the year 2000:

—Reduce the maternal mortality rate to no more than 3.3 percent per 100,000 live births (baseline: 6.6 per 100,000 in 1987).

—Increase to at least 90 percent the proportion of all pregnant women who receive prenatal care in the first trimester of pregnancy (baseline: 76 percent of live births in 1987)."

[Percent of live births]

Year	Whites	Blacks
1970	80	61
1975	80	60
1980	80	60
1985	80	60
1990	80	60
1995	80	60
2000	80	58

Source: A report in response to the World Summit for Children, *A Culture of Caring: America's Commitment to Children and Families* (Washington, D.C.: U.S. Government Printing Office, September 1990), p. 77. *Primary source:* National Vital Statistics System (CDC). *Note:* Magnitudes estimated from published chart.

★ 396 ★

Health Care: General Predictions

Physician Visits and Percent Change in Visits, 2000-2030

"The aging of the population will create a greater demand for physician care. According to projections based on 1989 physician contact rates and projections of the noninstitutionalized elderly population, the demand for physician contacts will increase by 22 percent (from 259 million to 296 million contacts) by the year 2000, and by 115 percent (to 556 million visits) by 2030.

"The disparity between the elderly and nonelderly populations in the use of physician services is not as great at the disparity for other forms of health care. In 1989, people 65+ represented 12 percent of the non-institutionalized population and accounted for 20 percent of physician contacts."

[Number of people and visits in thousands]

Year	Age		
	65+	65 to 74	75+
2000			
Noninstitutionalized population	34,882	18,243	16,639
Total physician contacts	295,613	147,480	148,133
% change in contacts, 1989-2000	14.2	1.0	31.1
2030			
Noninstitutionalized population	65,604	35,988	29,616
Total physician contacts	555,717	290,932	264,785
% change in contacts, 1989-2030	114.6	99.3	134.4

Source: U.S. Senate Special Committee on Aging, the American Association of Retired Persons, the Federal Council on the Aging, and the U.S. Administration on Aging, *Aging America: Trends and Projections* (Washington, D.C.: U.S. Government Printing Office, 1991), p. 129. *Primary source:* U.S. Administration on Aging. Unpublished projections based on physician visit rates from the 1989 National Health Interview Survey and population projections from the U.S. Bureau of the Census.

★ 397 ★

Health Care: General Predictions

Increase in Demand for Primary Care Physicians, 1970-2000

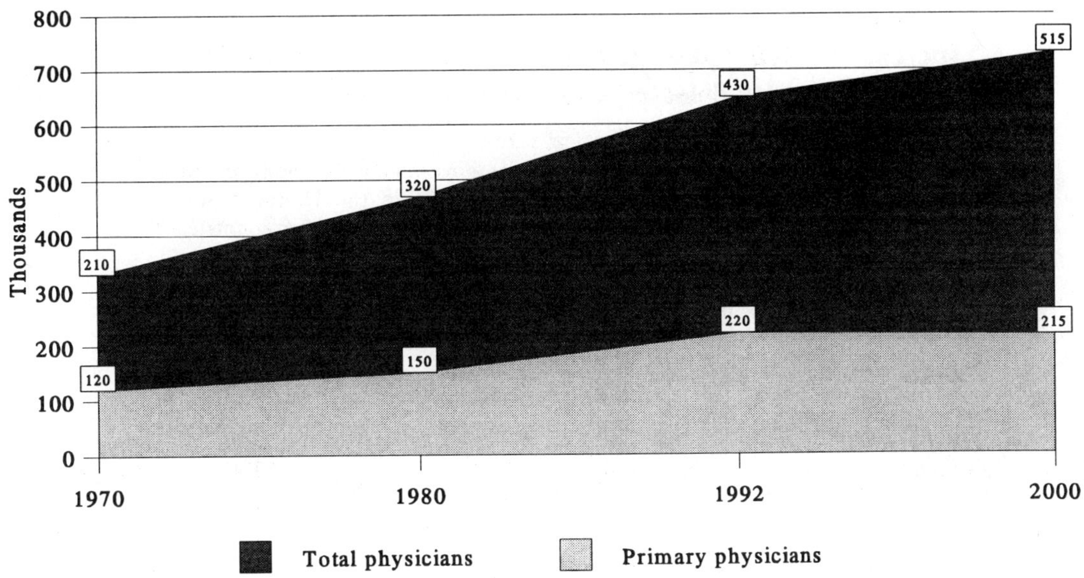

"As managed care replaces traditional fee for service... Americans will need more primary-care doctors but far fewer specialists. Today 41 million Americans are enrolled in HMOs [Health Maintenance Organizations], which employ doctors on salary or contract with physicians to treat patients for a fixed monthly fee. HMOs encourage their primary-care physicians to treat rashes, sprains, chest pain, and all other routine disorders themselves, sending patients to specialists only for surgery or complex diagnoses and treatment."

[Thousands]

Year	Total physicians	Primary physicians
1970	330	120
1980	470	150
1992	650	220
2000	720	215

Source: Shawn Tully, "Why We Need More Doctors," in *Fortune*, 23 August 1993, p. 74. *Primary source:* American Medical Association (AMA), Council for Opportunity in Graduate Management Education (COGME). *Note:* Magnitudes estimated from published chart.

Effects of Health Care Costs

★ 398 ★

Increase in Real Government Expenditures on Medical Care for Selected Countries, 1980-2025

"U.S. government expenditures on medical care will grow at a very rapid rate over the next several decades. For example, real government expenditures for medical care are projected to increase by 80 percent in the United States between 1980 and 2025. They will rise by 74 percent in Canada. Other countries are expected to have more modest increases."

[Percent; index: 1980=100]

Country	Year		
	1980	2000	2025
United States	100	130	180
France	100	117	130
West Germany	100	104	103
Italy	100	113	121
United Kingdom	100	105	115
Canada	100	128	174
Japan	100	130	147

Source: U.S. Senate Special Committee on Aging, the American Association of Retired Persons, the Federal Council on the Aging, and the U.S. Administration on Aging, *Aging America: Trends and Projections* (Washington, D.C.: U.S. Government Printing Office, 1991), p. 270. *Primary source:* Peter S. Heller, Richard Hemming, Peter W. Kohnert, and International Monetary Fund Staff, *Aging and Social Expenditure in the Major Industrial Countries, 1980-2025*, Occasional Paper 47, September 1986.

★ 399 ★

Effects of Health Care Costs

Increase in Health Care Costs, 2000-2001

"It may be the fate of every U.S. president to become bogged down in a dismal swamp. Lyndon Johnson had Vietnam. Richard Nixon had Watergate. George Bush wrestled with the double-dip recession. And Bill Clinton will have the U.S. health care system.

[Continued]

★ 399 ★

Increase in Health Care Costs, 2000-2001

[Continued]

"Consider the treacherous terrain that lies ahead for the president-elect. Exploding government health care programs are driving the federal budget deficit skyward. Left unchecked, they could add almost $1 trillion to the national debt by 2001. Spiraling health costs are breaking the backs of thousands of businesses and depressing workers' wages; at Ford, covering workers' health costs now runs to $800 per vehicle, roughly double the per-car cost of steel. At least 35 million Americans now lack health insurance —and Clinton says 100,000 more are losing their coverage each month...

"The incentives to act are enormous. National health spending is rising about 10 percent a year, or about 1.66 times the rate of nominal economic growth. If that trend continues, health care will absorb an ever growing share of the economy—from just under 14 percent now to 18 percent by the year 2000. But if the rise in health spending could be brought down in line with nominal economic growth—in other words, to about 7 percent a year—the savings would be extraordinary. Washington health economist Jack Meyer calculates that trimming overall health spending to that level could produce nearly $1 trillion in savings—and perhaps as much as $4 trillion—over the course of this decade."

Source: Susan Dentzer, "Clinton's Big Test," in *U.S. News & World Report*, 23 November 1992, pp. 26, 28.

★ 400 ★

Effects of Health Care Costs

Nationwide Health Care Expenditures by Type of Spending, 1992-2000

[Billions of dollars]

	1992	1995	2000
Hospital	100	420	675
Physician	150	200	320
Nursing Home	60	85	130
Drugs	60	75	110
Others	215	280	430

Source: Edward Felsenthal, "Health Care Business Practices Spark Debate Over Impact of Antitrust Rules," in *The Wall Street Journal*, 11 March 1993, p. A10. *Primary source:* Congressional Budget Office. *Notes:* Magnitudes estimated from published chart. Figures are excluded for years 1965-1991, 1993-1994, and 1996-1999.

★ 401 ★

Effects of Health Care Costs

Phased-in Cost of Universal Health Care Coverage, 1995-2000

"No matter how sharp his pencil, Clinton will face a sizable tax gap, with few attractive options for filling it. In years past, Franklin D. Roosevelt and Lyndon B. Johnson just ducked the question: Both Social Security and Medicare were launched without the funding needed for long-term soundness. In these deficit-ridden times that option isn't open to Clinton. With so little room to maneuver, the collision between his health promises and the nation's tax phobia could turn into a national train wreck."

[Billions of dollars]

Year	
1995	12
1996	25
1997	42
1998	60
1999	85
2000	92

Source: Mike McNamee and Susan B. Garland, with Paul Magnusson, "From Brainstorms to Headaches," in *Business Week*, 3 May 1993, pp. 26, 28. *Primary source:* Brookings Institution. *Note:* Magnitudes estimated from published chart.

★ 402 ★

Effects of Health Care Costs

Government Benefit Outlays with and without Health-care Reform, 1991- 1999

"The [Clinton] administration projects that the federal deficit, expected to be $234.8 billion this year, will drop to $165.1 billion next year if the president's health-care package passes as proposed or to $176.1 billion if it doesn't. Either way, Mr. Clinton boasted in his introduction to the budget, 'It will be the first time deficits have declined three years running since Harry Truman occupied the Oval office.' But unless federal health-care spending is restrained, the budget deficit will start widening again in fiscal 1997 and top $200 billion in 1999, the White House budget office said. The administration projects that if the president's health plan is adopted, health-care spending will be contained and the deficit will amount to $181 billion in 1999."

[Trillions of dollars]

Year	Benefits	Discretionary
1991	.60	0.55
1993	.65	0.55
1995[1]	.75	0.55
1997[1]	.90	0.55
1999[1]	1.05	0.55

Source: David Wessel and David Rogers, "Clinton Would Cut Money for Programs Democrats Cherish," in *The Wall Street Journal*, 8 February 1994, pp. A1, A13. *Primary source:* U.S. Office of Management and Budget. *Notes:* Magnitudes estimated from published chart . Source also includes data for 1979-1989. 1. Estimates assume health-care reform. Discretionary spending is annually appropriated spending on defense and domestic programs. Benefits include Social Security and Medicare, and exclude interest. Not adjusted for inflation.

★ 403 ★

Effects of Health Care Costs

Health Care Spending as a Percentage of GDP, 1965-2000

"Even if the current double-digit trend in medical spending growth slips a bit, the budget office said, the nation's health spending will still double by 2000, to $1.68 trillion—a staggering 18 percent of the projected gross domestic product—from $808 billion, or 13.6, in 1992.

"But if Federal spending for health could be held to the 1991 share of G.D.P., the budget office said the deficit could be pushed back to about 1 percent of potential G.D.P. in 2002, about where it was in the 1960's and 1970's, before soaring above 3 percent of G.D.P. in the 1980's."

[Percent of gross domestic product]

Year	
1965	6
1980	9.2
1985	10.4
1990	12
1992	13.7
1995	15.1
2000	18

Source: Milt Freudenheim, "Medical Costs: The Beat Goes On," in *The New York Times*, 22 December 1992, p. D2. *Primary source:* Congressional Budget Office. *Note:* Magnitudes estimated from published chart.

★ 404 ★

Effects of Health Care Costs

Major Areas of Difference in Estimates of the Health Security Act, 1995- 2000

"CBO's estimates of the Health Security Act tend to generate higher figures for expenditure items, and lower figures for revenue items than those of the Clinton Administration. Fewer consistent differences exist between the Lewin-VHI and the Clinton Administration estimates."

[Billions of dollars]

	Clinton Administration	Congressional Budget Office	Lewin-VHI
Employer subsidy	$93.1	$179 +92.3%	$142.9 +53.5%
Family subsidy	$193	$217 +12.4%	$195.5 +1.3%
Cushion for subsidy[A]	$41.2	N/A	N/A
Income and payroll taxes	$28.4	$24 -15.5%	$3.7 -113.0%

[Continued]

★ 404 ★

Major Areas of Difference in Estimates of the Health Security Act, 1995- 2000

[Continued]

	Clinton Administration	Congressional Budget Office	Lewin-VHI
Corporate assessment	$24.2	$8 -66.9%	$33 +36.4%
Recovered tax expenditures	$31.4	$10 -68.2%	$17 -45.9%

Source: U.S. Congress, Office of Technology Assessment, *Understanding Estimates of the Impact of Health Reform on the Federal Budget* (Washington, D.C.: U.S. Government Printing Office, July 1994), pp. 3-4. *Primary source:* Office of Technology Assessment. *Notes:* Health Security Act=HR 3600/S.1757. The percentage shown in the figures are the differences relative to the Clinton Administration's projections. A. Note that the Clinton Administration's estimates for subsidies do not include the potential behavioral responses to the subsidies. The Clinton Administration uses a separate "cushion" to cover the behavioral responses to subsidies. Neither CBO nor Lewin-VHI, Inc. (Fairfax, VA) adopted such methodology in their estimates of the subsidies.

★ 405 ★

Effects of Health Care Costs

Federal Budget Effects under the Health Security Act, 1995-2000

[Billions of dollars]

	Clinton Administration	Congressional Budget Office	Lewin-VHI
Family subsidy	$193	$217 +12.4%	$195.5 +1.3%
Employer subsidy	$93.1	$179 +92.3%	$142.9 +53.5%
Cushion for subsidy	$41.2	N/A	N/A
Medicare drug benefit expenditures	$69.1	$73 +5.6%	$59.3 -14.2%
Long-term care expenditures	$56.7	$61 +7.6%	$64.7 +14.1%
Medicare savings	$118.3	$112 -5.3%	$123.9 +4.7%
Medicaid savings	$60.8	$54 -11.2%	$66.7 +9.7%
Tobacco tax revenues	$67.4	$68.5 +1.6%	$65.8 -2.4%
Income and payroll taxes	$28.4	$24 -15.5%	$3.7 -113.0%
Corporate assessment	$24.2	$8 -66.9%	$33 +36.4%
Assessment for retiree subsidy	$11.4	$13 +14.0%	$12.1 +6.1%
Recovered tax expenditures	$31.4	$10 -68.2%	$17 -45.9%
New tax expenditures	$8.9	$8 -10.1%	$7.9 -11.2%

Source: U.S. Congress, Office of Technology Assessment, *Understanding Estimates of the Impact of Health Reform on the Federal Budget* (Washington, D.C.: U.S. Government Printing Office, July 1994), p. 11. *Primary source:* Office of Technology Assessment. *Notes:* N/A=not applicable. Health Security Act=HR 3600/S.1757. The percentages shown in the figure are the differences relative to the Clinton Administration's projections.

★ 406 ★

Effects of Health Care Costs

Federal Expenditures for Premium Subsidies, 1995-2000

"The general methodology used to estimate the premiums takes into account the baseline spending for the covered benefits, the inducement effects among the previously uninsured and underinsured individuals, and the number of persons with different family structures covered by regional alliances."

[Billions of dollars]

Premium subsidy estimates	Clinton Administration	Congressional Budget Office	Lewin-VHI	CBO vs. Clinton Administration $(%)	Lewin-VHI vs. Clinton Administration $(%)	Lewin-VHI vs. CBO $(%)
Family subsidy	$193.0	$217	$195.5	$24 (12.4%)	$2.5 (1.3%	-$21.5 (-9.9%)
Employer subsidy	93.1	179	142.9	85.9 (92.3)	49.8 (53.5)	-36.1 (-20.2)
"Cushion"	41.2	NA	NA	NA	NA	NA
Total gross subsidy	327.4	396	338.4	68.6 (21)	11 (3.4)	-57.6 (-14.5)

Source: U.S. Congress, Office of Technology Assessment, *Understanding Estimates of the Impact of Health Reform on the Federal Budget* (Washington, D.C.: U.S. Government Printing Office, July 1994), p. 13. *Primary source:* Office of Technology Assessment, based on data from Lewin-VHI, Inc., *The Financial Impact of the Health Security Act* (Fairfax, VA, 9 December 1993); U.S. Congress, Congressional Budget Office, *An Analysis of the Administration's Health Proposal*); U.S. Executive Office of the President, Office of Management and Budget, *Budget of the U.S. Government, FY 95* (Washington, D.C.: U.S. Government Printing Office, February 1994). *Note:* NA=not applicable.

★ 407 ★

Effects of Health Care Costs

Federal Expenditures for New Benefit Programs, 1995-2000

"Analysts' estimates of the Medicare Part-B prescription drug benefit represent less than one-fifth of the estimated new federal expenditures proposed under reform. In absolute monetary terms, the largest difference in analysts' estimates is less than $14 billion for the six years from 1995 through 2000...

"The estimates of federal outlays for the Medicare Part-B prescription drug benefit are determined by three factors.

—The baseline expenditures for prescription drugs by the potential beneficiaries.

—The assumption about the demand elasticity for prescription drugs (i.e., the inducement effect due to insurance coverage), and

—The number of eligible beneficiaries and the participation rate of the eligible population...

"As in the case of estimates for the Medicare drug benefit, analysts' estimates of the proposed community-based long-term care program represent less than one-fifth of the estimated additional federal expenditures under the Health Security Act. As shown in [the table below], in absolute terms, the largest difference among analysts' estimates is $8 billion for the period from 1995 through 2000.

"There is, however, one major difference between the Medicare prescription drug benefit and the new long-term care program for severely disabled individuals. The former is essentially part of an entitlement program, while the latter is designed as a federal grant program to states. The total amount of federal appropriation and the phase-in schedule for the long-term care program are specified in the Health Security Act. For the fiscal years from 1995 through 2000, the states would receive $4.5 billion, $7.8 billion, $11.0 billion, $14.7 billion, and $18.7 billion, for a six-year capped total of $56.7 billion. The Clinton Administration used these figures as its estimates of the federal outlays for the long-term care program."

[Billions of dollars]

Benefit provisions	Clinton Administration	Congressional Budget Office	Lewin-VHI	CBO vs. Clinton Administration $(%)	Lewin-VHI vs. Clinton Administration $(%)	Lewin-VHI vs. CBO $(%)
Medicare prescription drug benefit	$69.1	$73	$59.3	$3.9 (5.6%)	-$9.8 (-14.2%)	-$13.7 (-18.8%
Community-based long-term care benefit program	56.7	61	64.7	4.3 (7.6)	8.0 (14.1)	3.7 (6.1)
Total	125.8	134	124.0	8.2 (6.6)	-1.8 (-1.4)	-10 (-7.5)

Source: U.S. Congress, Office of Technology Assessment, *Understanding Estimates of the Impact of Health Reform on the Federal Budget* (Washington, D.C.: U.S. Government Printing Office, July 1994), pp. 17, 19. *Primary source:* Office of Technology Assessment, based on data from Lewin-VHI, Inc., *The Financial Impact of the Health Security Act* (Fairfax, VA, 9 December 1993); U.S. Congress, Congressional Budget Office, *An Analysis of the Administration's Health Proposal*); U.S. Executive Office of the President, Office of Management and Budget, *Budget of the U.S. Government, FY 95* (Washington, D.C.: U.S. Government Printing Office, February 1994).

★ 408 ★

Effects of Health Care Costs

Federal Savings from Medicare and Medicaid, 1995-2000

"Medicare and Medicaid savings represent a significant portion (about one-half) of the estimated source of funds under reform. As shown in [the table below], the Clinton Administration, CBO, and Lewin-VHI estimates of savings from both Medicare and Medicaid are reasonably close. CBO's and the Clinton Administration's estimates of Medicare savings differ by only approximately $6 billion, or 5 percent, while their estimates for Medicaid savings differ by approximately $7 billion, or 11 percent, for the period from 1995 through 2000.

"There are, however, some variations in the projected savings from specific sources. Lewin-VHI, for example, projected substantially higher Medicare savings from patient cost-sharing may have resulted from a much larger demand elasticity for laboratory or home health services than either the Clinton Administration or CBO. Lewin-VHI's higher estimates of Medicare savings from patient cost-sharing may have resulted from a much larger demand elasticity for laboratory and home health services than that assumed by the Clinton Administration and CBO. However, none of the three indicated what demand elasticity they used."

[Billions of dollars]

Medicare and Medicaid savings	Clinton Administration	Congressional Budget Office	Lewin-VHI	CBO vs. Clinton Administration $(%)	Lewin-VHI vs. Clinton Administration $(%)	Lewin-VHI vs. CBO $(%)
Reduced payments to providers (Medicare)	$88.4[A]	$81	$79.9	-$7.4 (-8.4%)	-$8.5 (-9.6%)	-$1.1 (-1.4%)
Additional Part-B premium/HI tax (Medicare)	17.6[A]	15	14.9	-2.6(-15)	-2.7(-15)	-0.1(-0.1)
Imposing patient cost-sharing (Medicare)	16.2	15	27.0	-1.2(-7.4)	10.8(66.7)	12(80)
Others (Medicare)	2.2[A]	3	2.1	0.8(36.4)	-0.1(-4.5)	-0.9(-30)
Total Medicare savings	118.3	112[B]	123.9	-6.3(-5.3)	5.6(4.7)	$11.9(10.6)
Total Medicaid savings	60.8	54	66.7	-6.8(-11.2)	5.9(9.7)	$12.7(23.5)

Source: U.S. Congress, Office of Technology Assessment, *Understanding Estimates of the Impact of Health Reform on the Federal Budget* (Washington, D.C.: U.S. Government Printing Office, July 1994), p. 21. *Primary sources:* Office of Technology Assessment, based on data from Lewin-VHI, Inc., *The Financial Impact of the Health Security Act* (Fairfax, VA, 9 December 1993); U.S. Congress, Congressional Budget Office, *An Analysis of the Administration's Health Proposal*); U.S. Executive Office of the President, Office of Management and Budget, *Budget of the U.S. Government, FY 95* (Washington, D.C.: U.S. Government Printing Office, February 1994). *Notes:* A. The Clinton Administration's February 1994 document did not provide information on these separate sources of savings. For illustrative purposes, the three figures shown here are drawn from the Administration's December 1993 estimates. Figures from the February 1994 estimates, if available, would be lower than what are shown here. B. Total savings shown are lower than the sum of individual savings sources due to rounding.

★ 409 ★

Effects of Health Care Costs

Sources of Funds for the Health Security Act, 1995-2000

[Billions of dollars]

	1995	1996	1997	1998	1999	2000	1995-2000
Medicare	2.1	9.0	14.3	22.1	31.6	39.2	118.3
Part A Savings	0.0	3.3	7.0	12.0	16.4	20.4	59.1
Part B Savings	1.9	2.4	2.7	5.3	8.7	11.5	32.4
Parts A and B Savings	0.2	1.5	2.2	2.6	4.2	5.0	15.8
HI Tax Extended to all State and Local Government Employees	0.0	1.6	1.6	1.5	1.5	1.5	7.6
Income Related SMI Premium with outlay and premium effects	0.0	0.2	0.9	0.7	0.8	1.0	3.6
Medicaid	0.0	0.8	3.5	9.2	20.1	27.1	60.8
Cash-Eligible Beneficiaries in Alliances	0.0	0.3	1.2	3.7	6.6	9.7	21.5
Reduced Disproportionate Share Hospital Payments	0.0	1.0	3.7	10.4	15.2	17.4	47.7
Less Supplemental Services for Children	0.0	-0.1	-0.4	-1.1	-1.6	-1.6	-4.8
Payment Lag, Administrative Savings, and Other Changes	0.0	-0.4	-1.0	-3.8	-0.1	1.6	-3.6
Other Federal Programs	0.0	0.4	1.2	6.9	9.8	10.9	29.2
Veterans Affairs: Third Party Receipts	0.0	0.6	1.7	4.4	5.8	6.1	18.5
Defense Department Health (a)	0.0	0.1	0.2	0.7	0.8	0.8	2.6
Federal Employees Health Benefits	0.0	-0.2	-0.7	1.8	3.2	4.0	8.2
Tobacco Tax/Corporate Assessment	12.0	15.0	16.2	16.2	16.1	16.1	91.6
Tobacco Tax	12.0	11.3	11.2	11.1	11.0	10.9	67.4
Corporate Assessment	0.0	3.8	5.0	5.1	5.1	5.2	24.2
Other Revenue Effects	0.1	0.8	8.4	20.0	28.8	34.5	92.6
Exclusion of Health Insurance from Cafeteria Plans	0.0	0.0	5.3	8.1	8.7	9.3	31.4
Effects of Mandate, Cost Containment, and Discounts	0.0	0.1	0.9	4.4	9.3	13.7	28.4
Dedicated Revenues for Academic Health Centers	0.0	0.5	1.6	4.3	5.5	5.8	17.7
Assessment on Employers for Retiree Discounts	0.0	0.0	0.0	2.4	4.3	4.7	11.4
Anti-Abuse Rule - Certain S Corp. Shareholders	0.0	0.2	0.5	0.5	0.5	0.5	2.2
Modify Tax Treatment of Certain Health Care Organizations	0.0	0.0	0.1	0.2	0.2	0.2	0.7
Reporting Penalties - Non-corp. Ind. Contractors	0.1	0.1	0.1	0.1	0.1	0.1	0.5
Modify Tax Treatment Retirement Funding Accounts	0.0	0.0	0.0	0.0	0.1	0.1	0.3
Recapture Retiree Discounts High-Income Recipients	0.0	0.0	0.0	0.0	0.1	0.1	0.2
Incentives for Health Providers in Shortage Areas	-0.0	-0.0	-0.0	-0.0	-0.0	-0.0	-0.1
Debt Service	0.3	0.6	0.5	0.2	0.6	2.0	4.2
TOTAL	14.5	26.7	44.0	74.7	107.0	129.8	396.8

Source: Executive Office of the President of the United States, Office of Management and Budget, *Budget of the United States Government* (Washington, D.C.: U.S. Government Printing Office, 1994), p. 189. *Notes:* A. Under the proposed legislation, the Secretary of Defense is to decide when the military system will be coordinated with national health reform. The table shows the estimated budgetary effects on the Department of Defense if the military system were to be fully coordinated with national health reform by 1998. These estimates were calculated using the economic assumptions in the 1995 budget. Estimates released in November 1993 were based on the economic assumptions in the 1993 Midsession Review. The numbers in this table for the years 1994-1999 are drawn from the budget database, except that they include the Vulnerable Population Adjustment and a Medicare adjustment based on more recent data than were available at the time the budget database was completed.

★ 410 ★

Effects of Health Care Costs

Use of Funds for the Health Security Act, 1995-2000

[Billions of dollars]

	1995	1996	1997	1998	1999	2000	1995-2000
Veterans, Public Health, New Administration, and Other	3.0	5.2	9.6	8.9	10.0	10.3	47.0
Veterans Health Care Investment Fund	1.0	0.6	1.7	0.0	0.0	0.0	3.3
New Public Health Initiatives	0.4	1.1	1.6	1.3	1.2	1.1	6.7
Net New Spending on Acad. Health Ctrs. and Grad. Med. Educ.	0.3	1.8	3.8	4.9	6.2	6.5	23.5
Advance Practice Nurses (Medicare)	0.0	0.2	0.4	0.5	0.6	0.6	2.2
New Federal Administrative and Start-Up Costs	1.3	0.9	1.2	0.9	0.6	0.6	5.4
Special Supplemental Food Program (WIC)	0.0	0.5	0.6	0.6	0.7	0.7	3.1
Vulnerable Population Adjustment	0.0	0.1	0.3	0.7	0.8	0.8	2.7
Long-Term Care	0.0	5.1	8.8	12.2	16.0	20.1	62.2
Home Based Care for the Disabled	0.0	6.0	10.2	13.9	18.2	22.8	71.1
Medicaid Offset	0.0	-1.5	-2.4	-2.9	-3.5	-4.1	-14.4
Liberalized Medicaid Eligibility and Personal Needs Allowance	0.0	0.4	0.5	0.5	0.5	0.5	2.4
Tax Incentives for Long-term Care	0.0	0.2	0.5	0.7	0.8	0.9	3.1
Medicare Drug Benefit	0.0	6.9	14.0	15.0	16.0	17.2	69.1
100% Tax Deduction for Self-Employed Health Insurance	0.5	0.6	0.9	1.7	2.5	2.8	8.9
Discounts	0.0	5.8	17.5	41.8	44.3	41.8	151.1
Discounts - Net of Cushion	0.0	4.5	13.6	31.4	31.7	28.8	109.9
Total Discounts	0.0	10.2	31.6	82.7	100.0	103.0	327.4
Employers (net of cushion)	0.0	3.0	9.2	23.7	28.4	28.7	93.1
Non-retired Households (net of cushion)	0.0	4.4	14.0	36.8	45.0	46.7	146.9
Retirees - low income discounts (net of cushion)	0.0	0.7	2.1	5.5	6.7	7.0	21.9
Retirees - added discounts (net of cushion)	0.0	0.4	1.4	3.7	4.5	4.8	14.8
Out-of-Pocket	0.0	0.3	1.0	2.6	2.7	2.8	9.4
Cushion	0.0	1.3	4.0	10.4	12.6	13.0	41.2
Offsets Made Possible by Health Reform	0.0	-4.4	-14.1	-40.9	-55.7	-61.2	-176.3
Medicaid	0.0	-3.4	-12.1	-34.9	-47.7	-53.2	-151.3
States' Required Maintenance of Effort	0.0	-2.0	-6.4	-18.1	-22.4	-23.4	-72.3
Discontinued Medicaid Coverage	0.0	-1.4	-5.7	-16.8	-25.3	-29.8	-79.0
Basic Benefits	0.0	-1.3	-5.2	-15.2	-22.9	-26.9	-71.5
Wrap-around Benefits	0.0	-0.1	-0.5	-1.6	-2.4	-2.9	-7.5
Medicare Offset for Employed Beneficiaries	0.0	-1.0	-2.0	-6.0	-8.0	-8.0	-25.0
Total Spending	3.5	23.5	50.9	79.4	88.8	92.1	338.3
Deficit Reduction	11.0	3.2	-6.9	-4.8	18.2	37.7	58.5
Total	14.5	26.7	44.0	74.7	107.0	129.8	396.8

Source: Executive Office of the President of the United States, Office of Management and Budget, *Budget of the United States Government* (Washington, D.C.: U.S. Government Printing Office, 1994), p. 190. *Notes:* These estimates were calculated using the economic assumptions in the 1995 budget. Estimates released in November 1993 were based on the economic assumptions in the 1993 Midsession Review. The numbers in this table for the years 1994-1999 are drawn from the budget database, except that they include the Vulnerable Population Adjustment and a Medicare adjustment based on more recent data than were available at the time the budget database was completed. WIC=Women, Infants, and Children.

★ 411 ★

Effects of Health Care Costs

Cost of Premium Discounts for the Health Security Act, 1995-2000

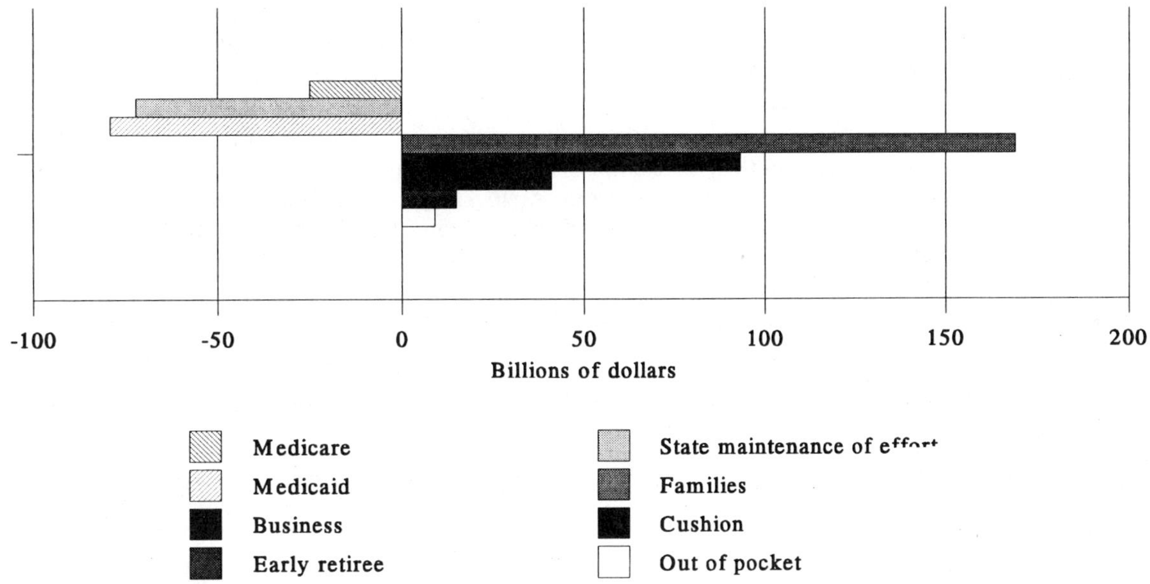

[Billions of dollars]

	Billions of dollars
Gross	327
Cushion	41
Out of pocket	9
Families	169
Early retiree	15
Business	93
Offsets	176
Medicare	25
State maintenance of effort	72
Medicaid	79
Net	151

Source: Executive Office of the President of the United States, Office of Management and Budget, *Budget of the United States Government* (Washington, D.C.: U.S. Government Printing Office, 1994), p. 191. *Notes:* These estimates were calculated using the economic assumptions in the 1995 budget. Estimates released in November 1993 were based on the economic assumptions in the 1993 Midsession Review.

★ 412 ★

Effects of Health Care Costs

Estimated Increased Revenue by Taxing Employer Contributions for Health Care Insurance, 1993-1997

"Last January, White House officials halted the printing of President Bush's federal budget after congressional Republicans protested that the 2,000-page document contained a proposal that amounted to political dynamite.

"The explosive suggestion? Taxing some of the health benefits of the nation's highest paid workers, a measure advocates contend would being more price sensitivity to the health-care market and also raise revenue to provide medical services for the poor. Frightened by its GOP colleagues' admonishments, the Bush administration dropped the idea and never mentioned it again.

"Now, as Bill Clinton prepares to take over the White House, taxing health benefits is back squarely on the table."

[Billions of dollars]

Year	
1993	10
1994	16
1995	19
1996	22
1997	26

Source: Hilary Stout, "Benefits-Taxation Idea Returns to White House under Clinton after Failing as a Bush Proposal," in *The Wall Street Journal*, 30 December 1992, p. 30. *Primary source: Congressional Budget Office.* Notes: *Includes only those individuals exceeding $335 a month per family or $135 a Month per Individual. Magnitudes estimated from published chart. GOP=Grand Old Party.*

★ 413 ★

Effects of Health Care Costs

Increase in Deficit Resulting from Clinton Health Plan, 1998-2004

"The White House estimates that health-insurance premiums employers pay for their workers will rise 9% annually in coming years if there is no health-care reform. Mr. Clinton proposes a law to cut that rate of increase in half. He describes this as a 'backstop' in case 'managed competition' fails to slow the growth in health costs. CBO figures the caps are about the only thing in the Clinton plan that will actually work to slow the growth of health-care spending. It accepts them because Mr. Clinton would write a law with teeth to enforce them. But laws last only as long as Congress and the public support them.

"'If the reliance is placed on premium caps...' says Sen. Danforth, 'it's the political problem of having the will to stick with those caps.' CBO predicts that the first problems will surface when Mr. Clinton's new National Health Board sets different premiums for different regions to reflect existing differences in health costs. Boston's premium could easily be twice the one set for El Paso, Texas. Americans tolerate wide regional disparities in private markets, but such disparities are hard to justify when determined by government. That's why Social Security benefits are the same across the country despite differing living costs. The pressure to spend more money will likely grow in the second year when the board sets growth rates for different regions, and the congressman from El Paso discovers that even though premiums there are lower than in Boston, they might be allowed to rise only by the same percentage. And if the regional caps survive that battle, there's still the substantial risk that the spending caps in and of themselves will provoke enough hospital closings, disgruntled doctors, long waiting times and horror stories to force Congress to raise them."

[Billions of dollars]

Year	Expected increase	Increase if premiums 10% higher
1998	32	52
2000	10	46
2004	0	48

Source: David Wessel, "Clinton's Health Plan Is a Fiscal Dice Roll," in *The Wall Street Journal*, 14 February 1994, p. A1. *Primary source:* Congressional Budget Office (CBO). *Note:* Magnitudes estimated from published chart.

Impacts of the AIDS Crisis

★ 414 ★

Adult HIV Infections Worldwide, 1980-2000

"Worldwide, more than 12 million people are infected with HIV. The great majority live in Africa, south of the Sahara. Asia is poised to become the plague's next epicenter."

[Millions of infections]

	1980	1985	1990	1995	2000
Africa	0	.55	.90	.80	.75
North America	0	.10	.05	.05	.025
Latin America	0	.05	.20	.20	.20
Europe	0	.01	.05	.025	.025
Asia	0.0	0.00	.30	.80	1.30

Source: "HIV Today and Tomorrow," in *Newsweek*, 22 March 1993, p. 49. *Primary source:* World Health Organization. *Note:* Magnitudes estimated from published chart.

★ 415 ★

Impacts of the AIDS Crisis

Effect of AIDS on Population Growth, 1960-2020

"The HIV/AIDS pandemic now seems likely to cause negative population growth rates even in the most severely affected countries, according to a U.S. Census Bureau study. The effects of AIDS may be offset by profound health and demographic transitions in developing nations—such as falling fertility rates, subsidence of infectious and parasitic diseases, and increased life-spans—that could make them resemble developed nations in the coming years, suggests Kevin Kinsella, the study's author. In China, for instance, life expectancy is projected to rise from 46 years for males and 48 years for females born in 1960 to 75 and 81, respectively, for those born in 2020."

Source: "No Population Decline Due to AIDS," in *The Futurist*, July-August 1993, p. 6. *Primary source:* U.S. Department of Commerce, Bureau of the Census, *Population and Health Transitions* (P95/92-2).

★ 416 ★

Impacts of the AIDS Crisis

Women and AIDS, 1992-2000

[Millions]

Year	Women with Aids	Women with HIV	Percent of victims who are women
1992	700,000	4,700,000	40
1995	1,500,000	15,000,000	45
2000	5,500,000	55,000,000	50

Source: Steven Findlay, "The Shock of the New," in *U.S. News & World Report*, 3 August 1992, p. 14. *Primary source:* World Health Organization, *AIDS in the World 1992* (Harvard University Press). *Notes:* Magnitudes estimated from published chart. 1995 and 2000 figures are projections.

★ 417 ★

Impacts of the AIDS Crisis

Cases of AIDS in San Francisco, 1985-1997

"The AIDS epidemic has passed its peak in San Francisco, the first city to be struck by the disease, the city's health department said yesterday. The number of new AIDS cases reached its highest level in 1992, 10 years after the peak year for newly reported infections with H.I.V., the virus that causes AIDS.

"[In 1993], the health department said, the number of new cases dropped by 50 percent, reflecting the effectiveness of prevention programs that were put into effect in the 1980s. Department researchers said they expected the number of new cases to continue to decline but more slowly over the next three years..."

[Thousands of cases]

Year	
1985	1,000
1992	3,326
1993	1,507
1994	1,400
1997	1,204

Source: Gina Kolata, "AIDS in San Francisco Hit Peak in '92, Officials Say," in *The Wall Street Journal*, 16 February 1994, p. A.10. *Primary source:* San Francisco Department of Public Health. *Notes:* Magnitudes estimated from published chart. Source also includes data for 1980-1984.

Nursing and Elderly Health Care

★ 418 ★

Federal Pension and Health Programs as a Percentage of GNP and the Budget, 1965-2040

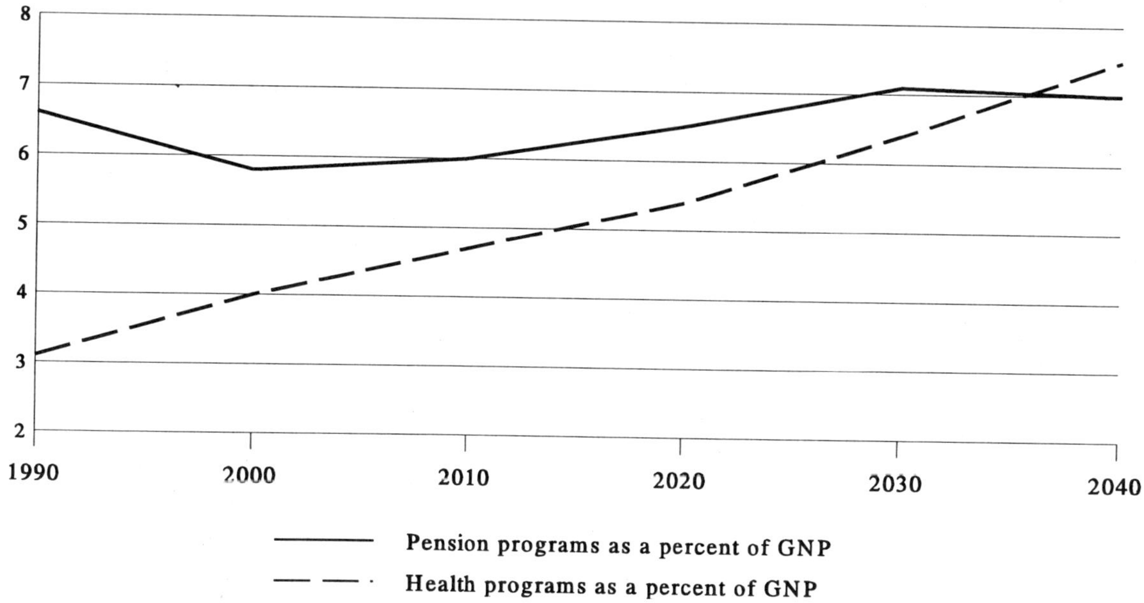

"Rising health care costs, rather than spending for retirement income, account for most of the current increase in public spending on the elderly. Social Security retirement and disability benefits, which grew from 2.5 percent of GNP in 1965 to 5.2 percent in 1983, are projected to decline to 4.2 percent by 2005, and then increase slightly to 5.7 percent by 2030. Other pension benefits paid from the federal budget are expected to decline from 2 percent of GNP currently to about 1.2 percent of GNP by 2030.

"On the other hand, health care costs will continue to grow steadily. In 1970, Medicare and other federal health programs accounted for only 1.4 percent of GNP; but by 1986, federal health spending had risen to 3.0 percent of GNP. With no change in current law, federal expenditures on health care are projected to increase to more than 6 percent of GNP by 2030... In short, if health care costs are not brought under control, federal spending on health care will equal, or even surpass, federal spending on retirement income within the next 50 years."

[Percent]

Year	Pension programs as a percent of GNP[1]	Health programs as a percent of GNP[1]	Total as a percent of GNP[1]	Total as a percent of budget[2]
1965	4.1	0.3	4.4	24.9
1970	4.7	1.4	6.1	30.0
1975	6.4	2.0	8.4	37.1
1980	6.5	2.3	8.8	38.2

[Continued]

★ 418 ★

Federal Pension and Health Programs as a Percentage of GNP and the Budget, 1965-2040

[Continued]

Year	Pension programs as a percent of GNP[1]	Health programs as a percent of GNP[1]	Total as a percent of GNP[1]	Total as a percent of budget[2]
1982	7.1	2.7	9.7	39.6
1984	7.0	2.8	9.8	39.7
1986	6.6	3.0	9.6	39.4
1988	6.4	3.2	9.6	39.4
1990	6.6[3]	3.1[3]	9.7	40.4
1995	6.2	3.7	9.9	41.3
2000	5.8	4.0	9.8	40.8
2005	5.6	4.4	10.0	41.7
2010	6.0	4.7	10.7	44.6
2015	6.0	5.0	11.0	45.8
2020	6.5	5.4	11.9	49.6
2025	7.0	5.9	12.9	53.9
2030	7.1	6.4	13.5	56.3
2035	7.1	7.0	14.1	58.8
2040	7.0	7.5	14.5	60.4

Source: U.S. Senate Special Committee on Aging, the American Association of Retired Persons, the Federal Council on the Aging, and the U.S. Administration on Aging, *Aging America: Trends and Projections* (Washington, D.C.: U.S. Government Printing Office, 1991), pp. 242-43. *Primary source:* John L. Palmer and Barbara B. Torrey, "Health Care Financing and Pension Programs." Paper prepared for the Urban Institute Conference on "Federal Budget Policy in the 1980s," 29-30 September 1983. *Notes:* 1. Estimates for 1984-1988 are based on Congressional Budget Office (CBO) baseline assumptions (August 1983); forecasts for 1990 and beyond are based on intermediate assumptions of the Social Security and Medicare actuaries. 2. Forecasts for 1990 and beyond are based on the assumption that the budget accounts for 24 percent of GNP. 3. The discontinuity in the estimates of pension and health benefits as a percent of GNP between 1986 and 1990 is due to the Social Security trustees assuming that Old Age, Survivors, and Disability Insurance (OASDI) will grow at a faster rate in the late 1980s than CBO assumes, and the Health Insurance trustees assuming that Medicare will grow at a slower rate than CBO assumes. CBO=Congressional Budget Office; GNP=Gross National Product.

★ 419 ★

Nursing and Elderly Health Care

The Failure of Nursing Home Insurance: Future Elderly, 2005

"Currently, Americans who need nursing home care face not only the loss of their ability to live independently, but a financial expense that is likely to be devastating. Today, nursing home costs average approximately $35,000 per year—and much more than that in many urban areas. Under our current health care system, individuals pay almost half of all nursing home costs out-of-pocket, making these expenses the largest out-of-pocket health cost for the elderly...

"The number of Americans who will need nursing home care and therefore face this devastating expenses is likely to double to 2030. Given this growing need, some policymakers and insurance industry representatives assert that private insurance will be the vehicle for making nursing home care affordable. To date only 2.4 million such policies have been sold, and many have already lapsed...

"[This] study finds that private nursing home insurance fails to make nursing home care affordable for the vast majority of Americans, middle-aged and older...

—Type I (copayment-weighted) nursing home insurance fails to make nursing home care affordable for over three-fourths (79%) of persons who will be 65-79 years old in the year 2005 and who first purchase insurance at that time.

—Type II (premium-weighted) nursing home insurance fails to make nursing home insurance affordable for 96 percent of persons who will be ages 65-79 in 2005 and who first purchase insurance at that time."

[Percent]

Age (in 2005)	Type I Policies (copayment-weighted)[A]	Type II Policies (premium-weighted)[A]
65-69	83	90
70-74	75	99
75-79[B]	78	99
Summary		
65-79	79	96

Source: Families USA Foundation, *Nursing Home Insurance: Who Can Afford it?*, February 1993, pp. 1, 3-4, 8. *Primary source:* Lewin/VHI, Inc. *Notes:* Private nursing home insurance fails to make nursing home care affordable if the annual premiums cost more than five percent of a person's annual income or copayments exceed the policyholder's income at age 80. A. For definitions of Type I and Type II policies see the Technical Appendix. B. Few insurance companies will sell nursing home insurance policies to consumers over age 79.

★ 420 ★

Nursing and Elderly Health Care

Real Pension Saving as a Share of Total Private Payroll, 1992-2063

"As the nation's largest 'tax expenditure' pensions remain an enticing plum to be picked for current expenditure. In fact, pecks have already been taken: In 1987, Congress chose to limit the ability of companies to 'overfund' their retirement plans, which tax considerations lead them to do.

"But taxing pensions misses the point in a big way. The U.S. desperately needs to encourage funding of retirement by any means possible. Pensions, where they are in force, are part of the answer. But because reductions in real wages and job-tenure have crimped prospective benefits in some cases, and because pension coverage hasn't kept pace with work force growth, existing plans aren't a match for the looming demand for old-age outlays.

"The magnitude of the generation shift ahead is apprehensible in the accompanying chart. It is from a paper by Stanford economist John Shoven and Sylvester Schieber, research director for benefits adviser Wyatt Co., who you might say have both made a life's work out of retirement. Their latest contribution was to organize the Washington conclave where this topic was aired.

"[The table below] effectively measures an expected depletion of private pensions assets as the baby-boom wrinkles. The authors caution that swings of this nature result from bulges in age cohorts and don't necessarily mean public policy has failed. (They do mean that asset prices are likely to suffer during the selling wave.) But the scope of this reversal in what is a $4 trillion source of savings in the American economy indicates stress in the system. The picture would look even more extreme if public pensions were included.

"At the same time, mind you, the Social Security surplus that was supposed to carry rock 'n' rollers through their golden years has shrunk dramatically from what was projected at the time of Mr. Greenspan's 1983 exercise. Instead of a 'trust fund' apex of more than $20 trillion in 2045, the peak is now seen to be about $5 trillion in 2025. That money will be exhausted by 2035, instead of 2063 as initially believed. Put all this together, and it's obvious the promised checks won't be in the mail for late boomers."

[Percent]

Year	
1992	.037
2000	.340
2010	.023
2020	.005
2030	-.010
2040	-.024
2050	-.034
2060	.035
2063	-0.040

Source: Tim W. Ferguson, "Pensions: The Shape of Things to Come," in *The Wall Street Journal*, 26 October 1993, p. A23. *Primary source:* Sylvester Schieber, John Shoven. *Note:* Magnitudes estimated from published chart.

★ 421 ★

Nursing and Elderly Health Care

Long-term Elderly Health Care, 1900-2050

"If current trends continue, Mr. [Donald M.] Charsky [president of Life Plans, a long-term care consulting company], estimates the nation will be paying $500 billion a year for long-term care in today's dollars by the year 2020, when the baby-boom generation becomes the elder boom.

"In 1990, only 4 percent of the population was over 65, according the Census Bureau. In 1990, that number grew to 12.5 percent of the population. By 2050, 20.6 percent of Americans will be forced to seek long term care."

Source: Peter Kerr, "Elderly Care: The Insurers' Role," in *The New York Times*, 16 March 1993, p. D1.

★ 422 ★

Nursing and Elderly Health Care

Nursing Home Expenditures for People Age 65+ by Source of Payment, 1990- 2020

"In 1988, Americans spent $43.1 billion on nursing home care. Nursing home residents and their families paid 48.4 percent of that amount, Medicaid paid 44.4 percent, and Medicare, 1.9 percent. Private insurance paid 1.1 percent of nursing home costs. In the future, older people will use more long-term care because more people will live long enough to need it. As a result, the number of older people in nursing homes will increase dramatically, as will total nursing home expenditures.

"In the last 10 years, out-of-pocket payments as a portion of total nursing home expenditures have increased. This trend is expected to continue."

[Billions of 1989 dollars]

Source of payment	1990	2005	2020
Nursing Home Care			
Medicare	$1.1	$1.8	$3.2
Medicaid	$15.7	$27.0	$45.0
Out-of-pocket	$20.8	$35.2	$63.4
Total	$37.6	$64.0	$112.6

Source: U.S. Senate Special Committee on Aging, the American Association of Retired Persons, the Federal Council on the Aging, and the U.S. Administration on Aging, *Aging America: Trends and Projections* (Washington, D.C.: U.S. Government Printing Office, 1991), p. 172. *Primary source:* Brookings/ICF *Long Term-Care Financing Model*, unpublished data, 1990.

★ 423 ★

Nursing and Elderly Health Care

Expected Role of Private Long-term Care Insurance, 1990-2020

"The cost of long-term care can place an unbearable financial strain on many Americans, particularly the elderly. Private long-term care insurance is now being marketed; however, only about 1.5 million policies have been sold. While the market is expected to grow, the cost of policies for the elderly is high, relative to their income.

"Recent estimates show that the proportion of long-term care expenditures covered by private long-term care insurance will slowly increase. For example, in 1990 about 2 percent of expenditures were covered by insurance. Assuming continued growth in the sales of long-term care insurance, by the year 2020, long-term care insurance will pay approximately 6.6 percent of total long-term care expenditures."

[Billions of 1989 dollars]

Year	Total LTC expenditures (in billions of 1989 dollars)	Percent of LTC expenditures covered by private insurance
1990	$46.0	2.0%
2005	$75.9	4.0%
2020	$132.6	6.6%

Source: U.S. Senate Special Committee on Aging, the American Association of Retired Persons, the Federal Council on the Aging, and the U.S. Administration on Aging, *Aging America: Trends and Projections* (Washington, D.C.: U.S. Government Printing Office, 1991), p. 175. *Primary source:* Brookings/ICF *Long Term-Care Financing Model*, unpublished data, 1990. *Note:* LTC=Long-term Care.

★ 424 ★

Nursing and Elderly Health Care

Decline in Retirement Income of Elderly Women Living Alone, 1970-2020

"Women continue to pour into the paid work force, but retirement income does not reflect their growing contributions. In 1970, women received 70% of the Social Security benefits men received. In 1989, that percentage had grown just to 73%. In 1974, women's average private pension income was 73% of men's; by 1987, that ratio had plummeted to 58%.

"By the year 2020, Social Security and pension systems will have practically ended poverty among older men and couples, but poverty will remain widespread among older women living alone—those who are divorced, widowed or never married."

Source: Older Women's League, "Heading for Hardship: Retirement Income for American Women in the Next Century," May 1990, p. 1. Copies available from OWL, 730 11th Street, N.W., Suite 300, Washington, D.C., 20001.

★ 425 ★

Nursing and Elderly Health Care

Elderly Women Living Alone in Poverty or Near-Poverty, 1987-2020

"In 40 years, when today's 25-year old retires, fewer women will be retiring married, and therefore fewer will have access to a husband's retirement income. Seven out of 10 baby-boom women will outlive their husband and can expect to be widows for at least 15 years. In the year 2030, only one of three women over age 65 will be married, compared to 40% today. In only 40 years, more than one out of every five older women will be divorced, a 400% increase over today."

[Percent]

Year	Female	Male
1987	45	37
2001-2005	45	15
2016-2020	38	5

Source: Older Women's League, "Heading for Hardship: Retirement Income for American Women in the Next Century," May 1990, p. 3. Copies available from OWL, 730 11th Street, N.W., Suite 300, Washington, D.C., 20001. *Primary source:* ICT estimates. *Note:* Magnitudes estimated from published chart.

★ 426 ★

Nursing and Elderly Health Care

Aging Veteran Population, 1980-2040

"As more of the country's veterans reach age 65, the health and long-term care system operated by the Department of Veterans Affairs (VA) will face increased demands for care. In 1986, 6.4 million veterans age 65+ were potential users of the system. By the year 2000, the number is projected to reach 8.5 million."

[Millions of veterans]

Year	Under 45	Age 45 to 64	65 and Older	Total
1980	12.0	13.0	4.0	29.0
1990	9.0	11.0	7.0	27.0
2000	5.0	11.5	8.5	25.0
2010	5.0	9.0	8.0	22.0
2020	5.0	5.5	7.5	18.0
2030	5.0	4.0	6.0	15.0
2040	5.0	3.0	5.0	13.0

Source: U.S. Senate Special Committee on Aging, the American Association of Retired Persons, the Federal Council on the Aging, and the U.S. Administration on Aging, *Aging America: Trends and Projections* (Washington, D.C.: U.S. Government Printing Office, 1991), p. 170. *Primary source:* Department of Veterans Affairs, 1990. *Note:* Magnitudes estimated from published chart.

★ 427 ★

Nursing and Elderly Health Care

Veteran Administration Nursing Home Census, 1988-2010

"An increase in the cost of care accompanies the increase in the number of veterans. From 1974 to 1983, the average daily census of veterans in all VA long-term care facilities grew from 31,900 to 38,000. During the same period, aggregate costs for long-term care of veterans rose from $183.1 million to $636.2 million. By 1986, VA costs had increased to $906.6 million. The VA provides or pays for a variety of long-term care services. Veterans Affairs nursing homes are located in the 172 VA medical centers; 27,200 veterans were served in such homes in 1988, where the number of daily residents average 11,300. In addition to care at its own facilities, the VA pays for some skilled and intermediate care in non-VA nursing homes. In 1988, approximately 42,000 veterans received care in 3,600 community facilities. The number of daily residents was approximately 12,400."

[Census in thousands]

Year	VA	Community	State Home	Total
1988	10	13	9	32
1989	10	10	9	29
1990	15	13	10	38
1995	18	19	11	48

[Continued]

★ 427 ★

Veteran Administration Nursing Home Census, 1988-2010
[Continued]

Year	VA	Community	State Home	Total
2000	25	22	11	58
2010	30	35	10	75

Source: U.S. Senate Special Committee on Aging, the American Association of Retired Persons, the Federal Council on the Aging, and the U.S. Administration on Aging, *Aging America: Trends and Projections* (Washington, D.C.: U.S. Government Printing Office, 1991), p. 171. *Primary source:* Department of Veterans Affairs. *Notes:* Magnitudes estimated from published chart. Average Daily Census. VA = Department of Veterans Affairs.

Human Services

★ 428 ★

Federal Spending on Entitlements, 1994-2004

"In 1994 [Senators Bob Kerry and John Danforth] called for raising the retirement age to 70 from the current 65, ending Medicare for wealthy senior citizens and raising costs for the rest, and creating a new mandatory private supplemental retirement account.

"They would also reduce annual cost of living increases for Social Security recipients and order a 10% reduction with further limits on growth for welfare and other entitlements."

[Billions of dollars]

Year	Social Security	Medicare	Medicaid
1994	325	170	85
1995	345	185	100
1996	360	205	110
1997	375	220	125
1998	395	245	135
1999	410	270	155
2000	325	300	175
2001	450	435	190
2002	475	450	210
2003	500	400	230
2004	523	435	250

Source: William M. Welch, "Benefit Cuts Proposal Under Fire," in *USA Today*, 12 December 1994, p. 6A. *Primary source:* Congressional Budget Office. *Note:* Magnitudes estimated from published chart.

★ 429 ★

Human Services

Growth in Entitlements, 1992-1998

"President Clinton has proposed cutting Medicare by about $50 billion over the next five years, and the Senate Finance Committee is prepared to cut an additional $31 billion, said the panel's chairman, Senator Daniel Patrick Moynihan of New York."

[Trillions of actual dollars]

	1992	1993	1994	1995	1996	1997	1998
Medicaid	.7	.8	.9	1.0	1.2	1.3	1.5
Medicare	1.3	1.5	1.6	1.8	2.0	2.3	2.6
Social Security	2.8	2.9	3.0	3.3	3.5	3.7	3.8
Other	2.2	2.4	2.4	2.4	2.3	2.6	2.7
TOTALS	7.0	7.6	7.9	8.5	9.0	9.9	10.6

Source: David E. Rosenbaum, "Answer: Cut Entitlements. Question: But How?," in *The New York Times*, 8 June 1993, p. A22. *Primary source:* Congressional Budget Office. *Note:* Magnitudes estimated from published chart.

★ 430 ★

Human Services

OASI and DI Tax Rates for Employees and Employers under Present Law and under Three Tax Reallocation Options, 1990-2045 and Later

[Percent of taxable earnings]

Calendar year	OASDI	OASI	DI
Present law:			
1990-99	6.20	5.60	0.60
2000 & later	6.20	5.49	0.71
Option 1:			
1990-92	6.20	5.60	0.60
1993-94	6.20	5.35	0.85
1995-99	6.20	5.34	0.86
2000 & later	6.20	5.33	0.87
Option 2:			
1990-92	6.20	5.60	0.60
1993 & later	6.20	5.40	0.80
Option 3:			
1990-92	6.20	5.60	0.60
1993 & later	6.20	5.49	0.71
Illustrative long-range financing schedule[1]			
1990-92	6.20	5.60	0.60

[Continued]

★ 430 ★

OASI and DI Tax Rates for Employees and Employers under Present Law and under Three Tax Reallocation Options, 1990-2045 and Later

[Continued]

Calendar year	OASDI	OASI	DI
1993-96	1	1	0.80
1997-2001	1	1	0.75
2002-2009	1	1	0.85
2010-2044	1	1	0.95
2045 & later	1	1	1.05

Source: Department of Health and Human Services, *The Social Security Disability Insurance Program: An Analysis* (Washington, D.C.: U.S. Government Printing Office, December 1992), Table 7. *Notes:* OASI=Federal Old-Age and Survivors Insurance. DI=Federal Disability Insurance. 1. Neither the OASI Trust Fund nor the DI Trust Fund is adequately financed in the long range (defined as the next 75 years). The illustrative financing schedule is included as an indication of the DI tax rates that would be required to fully cover projected DI costs over this period. As such, it is not intended as a reallocation option. It eventually will be necessary to adjust both the OASI and DI financing schedules and/or make appropriate changes to the benefit provisions in order to place each trust fund in actuarial balance over the long range. The financing schedules shown are based on the intermediate (alternative II) assumptions from the 1992 Trustees Report. Some adjustment will be required to reflect the latest actual experience and updated projections available at the time legislation is considered.

★ 431 ★

Human Services

Amounts of Change Required from Present Law to Prevent the DI Balance Ratio from Declining below the 20-percent Minimal Level, 1993-2001

"The following table shows the minimum amounts necessary to keep the DI balance ratio from falling below 20 percent. The amounts of (1) additional tax income, (2) benefit reductions, and (3) a combination of equal amounts of tax income and benefit reductions are shown for each year over the next 10 years. This period was chosen to coincide with the short-range projections period employed in the Trustees Report and because nominal dollar amounts become increasingly less meaningful with longer projection periods.

"The additional tax amounts required to meet the 20-percent goal differ somewhat from the reductions in benefit amounts. Tax rate changes affect assets (the numerator of the balance ratio) but not expenditures (the denominator); benefit changes affect both assets and expenditures simultaneously. Under the combined approach, one-half of the amount shown would be raised through additional tax income and one-half would be implemented through benefit reductions.

"The decrease in required amounts from 1999 to 2000 reflects the effect of the reallocation of tax rates between OASI and DI that is scheduled under present law for the year 2000. Under this schedule, the DI tax rate is set to increase from its current level of 0.60 percent (for employees and employers, each) to 0.71 percent."

[Billions of dollars]

Calendar year	Additional tax income only	Benefit reductions only	Total amounts of additional tax income and benefit reductions, under combined approach
1993	--	--	--
1994	--	--	--
1995	$1.4	$0.5	$0.9
1996	4.9	4.7	4.8
1997	6.5	6.3	6.4
1998	8.2	7.5	8.0
1999	10.1	11.8	10.9
2000	3.7	3.7	3.6
2001	4.8	4.0	4.4
Total, 1993-2001	39.6	38.5	39.0

Source: Department of Health and Human Services, *The Social Security Disability Insurance Program: An Analysis* (Washington, D.C.: U.S. Government Printing Office, December 1992), pp. 2-3. *Note:* Based on intermediate assumptions. DI = Federal Disability Insurance.

★ 432 ★

Human Services

Amounts of Change Required from Present Law for DI to Meet the Short-range Test of Financial Adequacy, 1993-2001

"Because the estimated DI balance for 1992 is 41 percent, the financial adequacy test requires that the fund achieve a 100-percent ratio by the beginning of 1997, and remain at or above 100 percent through 2001. For purposes of illustration, estimates were prepared of the changes that would be required to move steadily from the 41-percent balance ratio up to 100 percent at the beginning of 1997 and to remain at 100 percent through the year 2001.

"The following table shows the resulting estimated amounts of (1) additional tax income, (2) benefit reductions, (3) a combination of equal proportions of tax income and benefit reductions."

[Billions of dollars]

Calendar year	Additional tax income only	Benefit reductions only	Total amounts of additional tax income and benefit reductions, under combined approach
1993	$7.3	$4.2	$5.0
1994	8.8	6.1	8.1
1995	10.7	9.0	9.4
1996	12.8	10.1	11.7
1997	7.4	11.7	12.5
1998	9.2	8.2	3.6
1999	11.1	9.6	14.6
2000	4.7	11.8	8.3
2001	5.8	5.3	2.5
Total, 1993-2001	77.9	76.0	75.7

Source: Department of Health and Human Services, *The Social Security Disability Insurance Program: An Analysis* (Washington, D.C.: U.S. Government Printing Office, December 1992), p. 4. *Note:* Based on intermediate assumptions. DI = Federal Disability Insurance.

★ 433 ★

Human Services

OASI, DI, HI, and SMI Outgo as a Percent of Gross Domestic Product, 1994-2068

"The table below shows the estimated outgo from each trust fund as a percentage of estimated gross domestic product (GDP) in selected years and the percentage increase in outgo in relation to GDP from 1994 to 2068. OASI and DI increase at about the same rate over this period, while the increase in HI and particularly in SMI are much greater."

[Percent]

Trust Fund	1994	2020	2045	2068	% Increase
OASI	4.25	5.09	5.75	6.03	42
DI	.58	.85	.85	.83	43
HI	1.60	3.22	4.55	4.98	211
SMI	.93	3.27	4.10	4.37	370

Source: Social Security and Medicare Boards of Trustees, *Status of the Social Security and Medicare Programs: A Summary of the 1994 Annual Reports* (Washington, D.C.: U.S. Government Printing Office, April 1994), p. 9. *Notes:* OASI = Federal Old-Age and Survivors Insurance. DI = Federal Disability Insurance. HI = Federal Hospital Insurance. SMI = Federal Supplementary Medical Insurance.

★ 434 ★

Human Services

Financial Status of the OASI, DI, HI, and SMI Programs, 1994-2068

"The status of the Social Security and Medicare programs can be summarized by looking at the results of the tests used to evaluate the financial status of the trust funds and at the number of years before each trust fund is expected to be exhausted under the intermediate assumptions."

Trust Fund	Is the Test Met: Short-Range 10 Years (2004)	Is the Test Met: Long-Range 75 Years (2068)	Years Until Exhaustion
OASI	Yes	No	42
DI	No	No	1
OASDI (combined)	Yes	No	35
HI	No	No	7
The SMI trust Fund meets its test of actuarial soundness.			

Source: Social Security and Medicare Boards of Trustees, *Status of the Social Security and Medicare Programs: A Summary of the 1994 Annual Reports* (Washington, D.C.: U.S. Government Printing Office, April 1994), p. 9. *Notes:* OASI = Federal Old-Age and Survivors Insurance. DI = Federal Disability Insurance. HI = Federal Hospital Insurance. SMI = Federal Supplementary Medical Insurance.

★ 435 ★

Human Services

Social Security Benefits as a Percent of Social Security Taxes for Low, Average, and High Earners, 1985-2037

"Under current law, up to 50% of Social Security benefits are taxable for people with income and benefits over $25,000 for individuals and $32,000 for couples. Under Clinton's plan, up to 85% of Social Security benefits would be taxable."

[Percent of Social Security taxes]

Year	Low Earners	Average Earners	High Earners
1985	250	170	140
1993	160	115	90
2011	115	80	60
2027	115	80	55
2037	125	85	60

Source: Michael J. Mandel, "Social Security—Bad News for More and More People..." in *Business Week*, 5 April 1993, p. 69. *Primary source:* Social Security Administration. *Notes:* Measures lifetime ratio of old age, survivors, and disability benefits (OASDI) to employer and employee payroll taxes, adjusting for interest rates and inflation and not including income taxes paid on benefits. Magnitudes estimated from published chart.

National Health Goals

★ 436 ★

Increase in Persons Engaging in Physical Activity and Fitness, 1985-2000

"Regular physical activity can help to prevent and manage coronary heart disease, hypertension, noninsulin-dependent diabetes mellitus, osteoporosis, obesity, and mental health, problems such as depression and anxiety. Regular physical activity has also been associated with lower rates of colon cancer and stroke, and may be linked to reduced back injury. On average, physically active people outlive those who are inactive. Regular physical activity can also help to maintain the functional independence of older adults and enhance the quality of life for people of all ages."

[Percent]

	1985	1991	Year 2000 target
Persons 18-74 years	12	14	20
Low income persons 18-74 years	7	13	12

Source: U.S. Department of Health and Human Services, Public Health Service, Centers for Disease Control and Prevention, and National Center for Health Statistics, *Healthy People 2000 Review 1993* (Hyattsville, MD, June 1994), p. 7. *Primary source:* Centers for Disease Control and Prevention, National Center for Health Statistics, and the National Health Interview Survey. *Note:* Low income is defined as annual family income less than $20,000.

★ 437 ★

National Health Goals

Decline in Number of Overweight Adults 20-74 Years of Age, 1976-2000

"Dietary factors contribute substantially to preventable illness and premature death in the United States. For the majority of adults who do not smoke and do not drink excessively, what they eat is the most significant controllable risk factor affecting their long-term health. Five leading causes of death are associated with dietary factors: coronary heart disease, some types of cancer, stroke, noninsulin-dependent diabetes mellitus, and coronary artery disease. In general once-prevalent nutrient deficiencies have been replaced by excesses and imbalances of other food components in the diet. Malnutrition still occurs in some groups of people, however, including those who are isolated or economically deprived."

[Percent]

	1976-80	1988-91	Year 2000 target
All persons	26	34	20
Male	24	32	20
Female	27	35	20
Black women	44	49	30
Mexican American women	39	47	25

Source: U.S. Department of Health and Human Services, Public Health Service, Centers for Disease Control and Prevention, and National Center for Health Statistics, *Healthy People 2000 Review 1993* (Hyattsville, MD, June 1994), p. 14. *Primary source:* Centers for Disease Control and Prevention, National Center for Health Statistics, and National Health and Nutrition Examination Survey.

★ 438 ★

National Health Goals

Decline in Lung Cancer, 1987-2000

"Tobacco use is responsible for approximately one of every five deaths in the United States and is the single most important preventable cause of death and disease in our society. Cigarette smoking accounts for about 419,000 deaths yearly, including 21 percent of all coronary heart disease deaths, 87 percent of all lung cancer deaths, and 82 percent of all deaths from chronic obstructive pulmonary disease. Smoking is responsible for more than 5 million years of potential life lost each year."

[Rate per 100,000 population]

	1987	1988	1989	1990	1991	Year 2000 target
All persons	38.5	38.8	39.3	39.9	39.6	42

Source: U.S. Department of Health and Human Services, Public Health Service, Centers for Disease Control and Prevention, and National Center for Health Statistics, *Healthy People 2000 Review 1993* (Hyattsville, MD, June 1994), p. 23. *Primary source:* Centers for Disease Control and Prevention, National Center for Health Statistics, and National Vital Statistics System.

★ 439 ★

National Health Goals

Decline in Use of Alcohol and Other Drugs, 1988-2000

"Large numbers of Americans have used illicit drugs and misused alcohol; these behaviors can have serious health and social consequences. Alcohol is implicated in nearly half of all deaths caused by motor vehicle crashes and fatal intentional injuries such as suicides and homicides. Alcohol is the principal contributor to cirrhosis, the 11th leading cause of death in the United States in 1991. Intravenous drug users and their sexual partners are at high risk of infection with the human Immunodeficiency virus, the ninth leading cause of death in 1991."

[Percent]

	1988	1990	1991	1992	Year 2000 target
Alcohol:					
12-17 years	25.2%	24.5%	20.3%	15.7%	12.6%
18-20	57.9%	52.3%	57.0%	50.3%	29.0%
Marijuana:					
12-17 years	6.4%	5.2%	4.3%	4.0%	3.2%
18-25 years	15.5%	12.7%	13.0%	11.0%	7.8%

[Continued]

★ 439 ★

Decline in Use of Alcohol and Other Drugs, 1988-2000

[Continued]

	1988	1990	1991	1992	Year 2000 target
Cocaine:					
12-17 years	1.1%	0.6%	0.4%	0.3%	0.6%
18-25 years	4.5%	2.2%	2.0%	1.8%	2.3%

Source: U.S. Department of Health and Human Services, Public Health Service, Centers for Disease Control and Prevention, and National Center for Health Statistics, *Healthy People 2000 Review 1993* (Hyattsville, MD, June 1994), p. 30. *Primary source:* Office of Assistant Secretary, Substance Abuse Mental Health Services Administration, and National Household Survey of Drug Abuse.

★ 440 ★

National Health Goals

Adolescent Abstinence from Sexual Intercourse, 1988-2000

"More than three out of four young women and 85 percent of young men have had sexual intercourse by age 20. Each year, 1 out of 10 young women in this age group becomes pregnant. By age 20, approximately 40 percent of all women have been pregnant while 63 percent of black women have been pregnant. An estimated 84 percent of these teen pregnancies were unintended."

[Percent]

	1988	1990	1991	Year 2000 target
Ever sexually active girls 15-17 years	24	24	25	40
Ever sexually active boys 15-17 years	33	30	36	40

Source: U.S. Department of Health and Human Services, Public Health Service, Centers for Disease Control and Prevention, and National Center for Health Statistics, *Healthy People 2000 Review 1993* (Hyattsville, MD, June 1994), p. 36. *Primary source:* Centers for Disease Control and Prevention, National Center for Health Statistics, and National Survey of Family Growth.

★ 441 ★

National Health Goals

Decline in Death Rates for Suicide, 1987-2000

"In 1989, an estimated 3.3 million adults in the United States reported that they had a psychiatric disorder that interfered with one or more aspects of their daily life in the past year. Approximately 77 percent had sought help for their problem. Sixty-eight percent had used prescription medications and 23 percent had received government disability payments for their disorders.

"Suicide, one of the most serious potential outcomes of mental disorders, continues to be the target of many programmatic initiatives. Youth suicide prevention has been the focus of both school and community programs."

[Rate per 100,000 population]

	1987	1988	1989	1990	1991	1992	Year 2000 target
All persons	11.7	11.5	11.3	11.5	11.4	10.9	10.5
Youth 15-19 years	10.2	11.1	11.1	11.1	11.0	...	8.2
Men aged 20-24 years	25.2	25.2	24.9	25.1	25.4	...	21.4
White men 65 years and over	46.7	45.7	44.3	44.4	...	...	39.2
American Indian and Alaska Native	20.1	20.2	19.6	21.0	...	...	12.8

Source: U.S. Department of Health and Human Services, Public Health Service, Centers for Disease Control and Prevention, and National Center for Health Statistics, *Healthy People 2000 Review 1993* (Hyattsville, MD, June 1994), p. 42. *Primary source:* Centers for Disease Control and Prevention, National Center for Health Statistics, and National Vital Statistics System. *Note:* 1992 data are provisional.

★ 442 ★

National Health Goals

Decrease in Weapon-related Death Rates, 1987-2000

"Violent and abusive behaviors continue to be major causes of death, injury, and stress in the United States...

"Firearms play a major role in both interpersonal and self-directed violence, especially among younger victims. Handguns are the primary means for the majority of this violence, being used in 78 percent of all firearm crimes. While laws limiting access to firearms and mandatory sentences for felony firearms use appear to reduce and/or prevent violence injuries, a combined effort by law enforcement and public health services will be necessary to effectively address the problem of violence."

[Rate per 100,000 population]

	1987	1988	1989	1990	1991	Year 2000 target
All weapon-related	14.8	15.1	15.5	16.5	16.9	12.6
Firearms	13.0	13.4	13.7	14.6	15.2	...
Knives	1.8	1.8	1.8	1.8	1.8	...

Source: U.S. Department of Health and Human Services, Public Health Service, Centers for Disease Control and Prevention, and National Center for Health Statistics, *Healthy People 2000 Review 1993* (Hyattsville, MD, June 1994), p. 48. *Primary source:* Centers for Disease Control and Prevention, National Center for Health Statistics, and National Vital Statistics System.

★ 443 ★

National Health Goals

Decline in Death-rates for Unintentional Injuries, 1987-2000

"Unintentional injuries are the fifth leading cause of death in the United States, accounting for nearly 90,000 deaths annually...

"[Some decline in unintentional injuries has been seen] in areas related to motor vehicle fatalities, injuries, and use of vehicle occupant restraints. This improvement may be attributable to reduction in the amount of driving and alcohol consumption during the recent economic slowdown. The national rate of residential fire deaths and all special populations monitored as subobjectives show declining rates. These improvements may be associated with increased use of smoke detectors."

[Rate per 100,000 population]

	1987	1988	1989	1990	1991	1992	Year 2000 target
All persons	34.7	35.0	33.9	32.5	31.0	29.2	29.3
American Indian or Alaska Native	66.0	64.4	61.8	59.0	58.3	...	66.1
Black male	68.0	70.4	68.8	62.4	61.0	53.2	51.9
White male	49.8	50.0	47.8	46.4	43.9	41.7	42.9

Source: U.S. Department of Health and Human Services, Public Health Service, Centers for Disease Control and Prevention, and National Center for Health Statistics, *Healthy People 2000 Review 1993* (Hyattsville, MD, June 1994), p. 58. *Primary source:* Centers for Disease Control and Prevention, National Center for Health Statistics, and National Vital Statistics System.

★ 444 ★

National Health Goals

Decline in Non-fatal Work-related Injuries, 1987-2000

"Work-related injuries and deaths decrease the quality of life and produce stress among the workers and their families. A recent study by the RAND Corporation estimated that in 1989 the costs associated with work-related injuries exceeded $83 billion. While the human and financial costs of occupational injuries are extensive, efforts to reduce these injuries are successful and cost-effective. Although work-related deaths have declined slightly from a 1983-87 average of 6 per 100,000 workers to a rate of 5.0 in 1992, work-related injuries remain above the 1983-87 average of 7.7 per 100 (7.9 in 1991 and 8.3 in 1992). The leading cause of occupational deaths is motor vehicle accidents, reductions in this area are, in part, a consequence of increased legislation and enforcement of seat belt laws."

[Rate per 100 full-time workers]

	1987	1988	1989	1990	1991	1992	Year 2000 target
Full-time workers	7.7	8.3	8.2	8.3	7.9	8.3	6
Construction workers	14.9	14.4	14.2	14.1	12.8	12.9	10
Nursing and personal care workers	12.7	14.8	15.2	15.4	15.0	18.2	9
Farm workers	12.4	11.7	11.7	12.3	10.2	11.0	8

[Continued]

★ 444 ★

Decline in Non-fatal Work-related Injuries, 1987-2000

[Continued]

	1987	1988	1989	1990	1991	1992	Year 2000 target
Transportation workers	8.3	8.8	9.1	8.4	9.1	8.8	6
Mine workers	8.3	8.5	8.2	8.1	7.1	7.0	6

Source: U.S. Department of Health and Human Services, Public Health Service, Centers for Disease Control and Prevention, and National Center for Health Statistics, *Healthy People 2000 Review 1993* (Hyattsville, MD, June 1994), p. 65. *Primary source:* Department of Labor, Bureau of Labor Statistics, Annual Survey of Occupational Injuries and Illnesses, and Census of Fatal Occupational Injuries. *Note:* Includes only full-time workers.

★ 445 ★

National Health Goals

Increase in Proportion of People Who Live in Counties That Meet Air Pollution Standards, 1988-2000

"Environmental factors play a fundamental role in health and disease. One of the most famous public health interventions to control disease (cholera) succeeded through control of a contaminated public water supply. Despite this historic and other more recent successes, the etiology linking toxic exposure to disease is not well documented. The monitoring of public exposure to toxins and research into the relationship of toxic exposure to health and disease are important due to the increasing public and commercial use of hazardous substances.

"Research may clarify current ambiguity about exposure thresholds. Dioxin continues to be the focus of research, but lead has been shown to have toxic effects at even lower exposure levels than originally believed. Research will aid priority setting among environmental and public health interventions."

[Percent]

	1988	1989	1990	1991	1992	Year 2000 target
Any pollutant	49.7	65.3	69.4	65.3	78.4	85
Ozone	53.6	72.6	74.2	72.0	82.1	85
Carbon monoxide	87.8	86.2	91.1	92.0	94.3	85
Nitrogen dioxide	96.6	96.5	96.5	96.5	100.0	85
Sulfur dioxide	99.3	99.9	99.4	98.0	100.0	85
Particulates	89.4	88.8	92.3	91.4	89.6	85
Lead	99.3	99.4	97.8	94.1	98.1	85

Source: U.S. Department of Health and Human Services, Public Health Service, Centers for Disease Control and Prevention, and National Center for Health Statistics, *Healthy People 2000 Review 1993* (Hyattsville, MD, June 1994), p. 70. *Primary source:* Environmental Protection Agency, National Air Quality, and Emission Trends Report.

★ 446 ★

National Health Goals

Environmental Health Objective Status, 1988-2000

Objective	1988 baseline		1991	1992	Target 2000
	Original	Revised			
Asthma hospitalizations (per 100,000)	188[1]	...	196	183	160
a. Blacks and other nonwhites	334[1]	...	349	380	265
b. Children 14 years and under	284[1]	...	339	344	225
Mental retardation (per 1,000 school-aged children)	2.7[2]	...	---	---	2
Waterborne diseases (number of outbreaks)	31	16[3]	15	19	11
a. People served by community water systems	13	4[2]	2	5	6
Blood lead levels exceeding 15 & 25 ug/dL	3 million[4] & 234,000	...	---	---	500,000 & 0
a. Inner-city low-income black children 15 & 25 ug/dL	234,900[4] & 36,700	...	---	---	75,000 & 0
Proportion of people in counties that have not exceeded standards for air pollutants	49.7%	...	65.3%	78.4%	85%
Ozone	53.6%	...	72.0%	82.1%	85%
Carbon monoxide	87.8%	...	92.0%	94.3%	85%
Nitrogen dioxide	96.5%	...	96.5%	100%	85%
Sulfur dioxide	99.3%	...	98.0%	100%	85%
Particulates	89.4%	...	91.4%	89.6%	85%
Lead	99.3%	...	94.1%	98.1%	85%
Radon testing	Less than[5] 5%	...	7.4[6]	---	40%
a. Homes with smokers and former smokers	---	...	7.4[6]	---	50%
b. Homes with children	---	...	---	---	50%
Toxic agent releases					
DHHS list of carcinogens (billion pounds)	0.32	0.48[7]	0.23	---	0.24
ATSDR list of the most toxic chemicals (billion pounds)					
200 substances	2.62	3.50[7]	2.16	---	2.60
250 substances	3.70	4.48[7]	2.70	---	...
Solid waste (average pounds per person per day)	4.0	...	4.3[8]	---	3.6
People receiving safe drinking water	74%	73%[9]	72%	72%	85%
Number of Maximum Contaminant Level Standards in force	...	31	75	98	...
Impaired surface water	25%[10]	...	---	---	15%
Rivers	...	30%	---	38%	15%
Lakes	...	27%	---	44%	15%
Estuaries	...	29%	---	32%	15%
Homes tested for lead-based paint	...	Less[11,12] than 5%	---	---	50%
Number of States with construction standards to minimize radon concentrations	1[5]	...	---	3[13]	35
Disclosure of lead and radon concentrations (number of States)					
Disclosure of lead	2[5]	...	5	...[14]	30
Disclosure of radon	1[5]	...	5	13	30
Significant health risks from hazardous waste sites (indicators)					
Sites on list	1,082[8]	1,079[8,15]	---	1,199	...
Health assessments conducted	1,000[8]	1,379[8,15]	---	1,452	...

[Continued]

★ 446 ★

Environmental Health Objective Status, 1988-2000

[Continued]

Objective	1988 baseline		1991	1992	Target 2000
	Original	Revised			
Sites with public health concerns/hazards	...	250[8,15]	---	283	...
Sites where ATSDR recommendation followed	---	...	---	---	100%
Counties with programs for recyclable materials and household hazardous waste	850%[1] Programs in 41 States	...	---	---	75%
Permanent and temporary household hazardous waste recycling	...	300[1]	802	---	...
States with at least one program	...	28[1]	50	---	...
Number of States that track sentinel environmental diseases					
Plans established and monitored	...	0[8]	---	---	35
Federal law and funds	...	0[8]	8[13]	10[16]	---
State law and funds	...	29[8,17]	29[17]	31[17]	---

Source: U.S. Department of Health and Human Services, Public Health Service, Centers for Disease Control and Prevention, and National Center for Health Statistics, *Healthy People 2000 Review 1993* (Hyattsville, MD, June 1994), pp. 72-3. *Notes:* DHHS=Department of Health and Human Services; ATSDR=Agency for Toxic Substances and Disease Registry; ug=uniform gains; dl=decaliter. 1. 1987 data. 2. 1985-88 data. 3. Original baselines were averages of the years 1971-88; revised baselines are data from 1988 data. 4. 1984 data. 5. 1989 data. 6. Data represent the proportion of people who reported that they knew what radon was and had tested their homes for radon. 7. Baselines were revised to reflect updates from industry. 8. 1990 data. 9. Baselines was revised to correct for rounding error. 10. Baseline has been revised to reflect EPA reporting categories. 11. 1991 data. 12. Data represent the proportion of people with homes built before 1950 who report that their paint had been analyzed for lead content. 13. 1993 data. 14. By 1995, Federal regulation will require disclosure of lead-based paint in all pre-1978 housing during the sales or leasing. Because of this pending legislation, there are no current tracking activities. 15. Baselines were updated to reflect revised methodology. 16. 1994 funded. 17. Includes the District of Columbia.

★ 447 ★

National Health Goals

Increase in Proportion of Mothers Who Receive Prenatal Care in the First Trimester, 1987-2000

"Improving the health of mothers and infants is a national challenge. Of every 1,000 babies born in the United States each year, about 9 die before their first birthday. Although the infant mortality rate in the United States continues to decline and has reached an all-time low, in recent years the pace of progress has slowed. Important measures of increased risk of infant death, such as incidence of low birthweight and receipt of prenatal care, show little or no recent improvement. The mortality rate for black infants is twice the rate for white infants, and there is evidence that this difference is increasing."

[Percent of live births]

	1987	1988	1989	1990	1991	Year 2000 target
All races	76.0	75.9	75.5	75.8	76.2	90
Black	60.8	60.7	60.0	60.6	61.9	90
American Indian or Alaska Native	57.6	58.1	57.9	57.9	59.9	90
Hispanic	61.0	61.3	59.5	60.2	61.0	90

Source: U.S. Department of Health and Human Services, Public Health Service, Centers for Disease Control and Prevention, and National Center for Health Statistics, *Healthy People 2000 Review 1993* (Hyattsville, MD, June 1994), pp. 87-9. *Primary source:* Centers for Disease Control and Prevention, National Center for Health Statistics, and National Vital Statistics System. *Notes:* Data have been revised to reflect the change in tabulating births from the race of the child to the race of the mother.

★ 448 ★

National Health Goals

Decline in Age Adjusted Death Rates for Stroke, 1987-2000

"Over the past 20 years the death rate for cardiovascular disease has declined dramatically: 46 percent for all cardiovascular disease, 51 percent for coronary heart disease, and 60 percent for stroke. Even so, cardiovascular diseases—primarily coronary heart disease and stroke—kill nearly as many Americans as all other diseases combined. Cardiovascular disease is also among the leading causes of disability. The major modifiable risk sectors for cardiovascular disease are high blood pressure, high blood cholesterol, and cigarette smoking. Other important risk factors are obesity, physical inactivity, and diabetes mellitus."

[Rate per 100,000 population]

	1987	1988	1989	1990	1991	1992	Year 2000 target
All persons	30.4	29.9	28.3	27.7	26.8	26.1	20.0
Black	52.5	52.9	50.6	48.4	46.8	---	27.0

Source: U.S. Department of Health and Human Services, Public Health Service, Centers for Disease Control and Prevention, and National Center for Health Statistics, *Healthy People 2000 Review 1993* (Hyattsville, MD, June 1994), p. 93. *Primary source:* Centers for Disease Control and Prevention, National Center for Health Statistics, and National Vital Statistics System. *Note:* 1992 data are provisional.

★ 449 ★

National Health Goals

Decline in Age-Adjusted Death Rates for Female Breast Cancer, 1987-2000

"Cancer accounts for nearly one out of every four deaths in the United States. Cancer is not one disease, but a constellation of more than 1,000 different diseases, each characterized by the uncontrolled growth and spread of abnormal cells. Of the 250 million Americans now living, about 75 million will eventually have cancer. While the incidence of cancer has increased in the past two decades, death rates for those under 55 have fallen. More people are surviving cancer now than several decades ago. Research has demonstrated that many cancers can be prevented or, if detected and treated at early stages, cured."

[Deaths per 100,000 females]

	1987	1988	1989	1990	1991	Year 2000 target
Females	23.0	23.3	23.1	23.1	22.7	20.6

Source: U.S. Department of Health and Human Services, Public Health Service, Centers for Disease Control and Prevention, and National Center for Health Statistics, *Healthy People 2000 Review 1993* (Hyattsville, MD, June 1994), p. 101. *Primary source:* Centers for Disease Control and Prevention, National Center for Health Statistics, and National Vital Statistics System.

★ 450 ★

National Health Goals

Decline in Age-Adjusted Death Rates for Diabetes-related Causes, 1986- 2000

"As the population of the United States grows older, the problems posed by chronic and disabling conditions increasingly demand the Nation's attention. Chronic conditions such as heart disease, cancer, stroke, and lung and liver disease are joined in importance by other chronic and disabling conditions, such as diabetes, arthritis, deformities or orthopedic impairments, hearing the visual impairments, and mental retardation."

[Rate per 100,000 population]

	1986	1988	1989	1990	1991	Year 2000 target
All persons	38	38	38	38	38	34
Black	67	69	71	71	71	58
American Indian or Alaska Native	46	52	56	53	51	48

Source: U.S. Department of Health and Human Services, Public Health Service, Centers for Disease Control and Prevention, and National Center for Health Statistics, *Healthy People 2000 Review 1993* (Hyattsville, MD, June 1994), p. 108. *Primary source:* Centers for Disease Control and Prevention, National Center for Health Statistics, and National Vital Statistics System.

★ 451 ★

National Health Goals

Decreased Rate of Number of Diagnosed AIDS Cases per Year According to Selected Population Groups, 1989-2000

"An estimated 1 million people in the United States are infected with the human immunodeficiency virus (HIV). By the end of 1993, a total of 361,509 cases of AIDS had been reported. This count is based on the case definition used prior to the latest revision in January 1993. Although antimicrobial treatment extends survival, no treatment is yet available to prevent death among people with acquired immunodeficiency syndrome (AIDS). HIV and AIDS will continue to make major demands on health and social services systems for decades."

[Number of cases in thousands]

	1989	1990	1991	1992	Year 2000 target
All persons	49	55	68	87	98
Men who have sex with men	27	30	35	42	48
Black	15	17	22	31	37
Hispanic	8	10	12	15	18

Source: U.S. Department of Health and Human Services, Public Health Service, Centers for Disease Control and Prevention, and National Center for Health Statistics, *Healthy People 2000 Review 1993* (Hyattsville, MD, June 1994), p. 119. *Primary source:* Centers for Disease Control and Prevention, National Center for Infectious Diseases, and AIDS Surveillance System. *Notes:* Data have been revised. Original data were estimated based on preliminary analysis.

★ 452 ★

National Health Goals

Sexually Transmitted Diseases Objective Status, 1988-2000

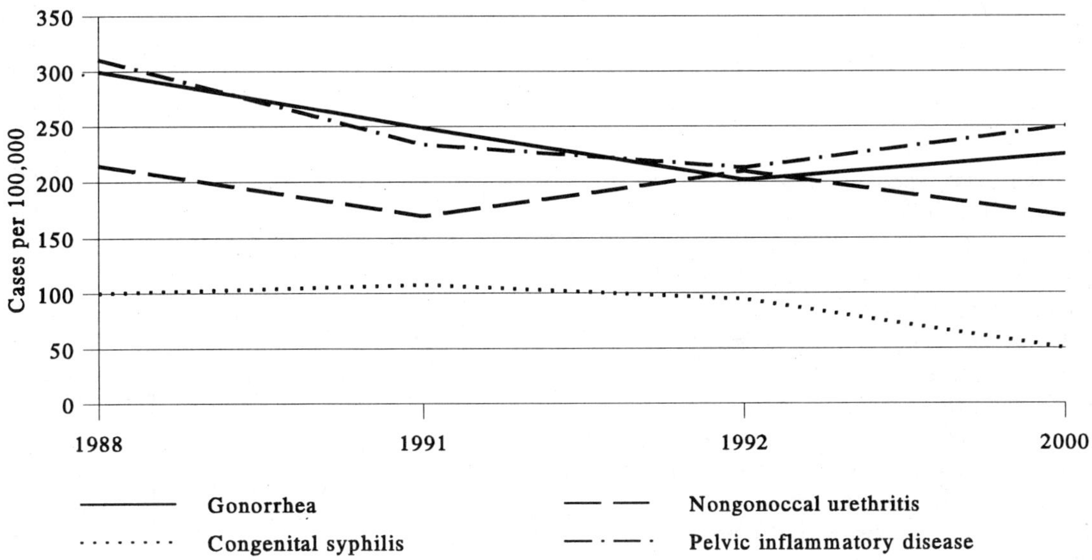

"In 1989, excluding infection with the human immunodeficiency virus (HIV), almost 12 million cases of sexually transmitted diseases were reported, 86 percent of them in people aged 15-29 years. By age 21, approximately one of every five young people has required treatment for a sexually transmitted disease. Women and children suffer a disproportionate amount of the sexually transmitted disease burden, with pelvic inflammatory disease, sterility, ectopic pregnancy, blindness, cancer associated with papilloma virus, fetal and infant deaths, birth defects and mental retardation among the most serious complications. Ethnic and racial minorities also shoulder a disproportionate share of the sexually transmitted disease burden, experiencing higher rates of disease and disability than the population as a whole."

Objective	1988 baseline		1991	1992	Target 2000
	Original	Revised			
Gonorrhea (per 100,000)	300[1]	...	249	202	225
a. Blacks	1,990[1]	...	1,720	1,434	1,300
b. Adolescents 15-19 years	1,123[1]	...	991	837	750
c. Females 15-44 years	501[1]	...	419	366	290
Nongonococcal urethritis (per 100,000)	215	...	170	210	170
Primary and secondary syphillis (per 100,000)	18.1[1]	...	17.3	13.7	10
a. Blacks	118[1]	...	124	92	65
Congenital syphilis (per 100,000 live births)	100.0[1,2]	44.7	107.5	94.7	50
Annual number of first-time consultations[3]					
Genital herpes	167,000	163,000[4]	285,000	139,000	142,000
Geniral warts	451,000	290,000[4]	282,000	218,000	385,000
Pelvic Inflammatory disease incidence (per 100,000)					
Females 15-44 years	311	...	234	213	250
Sexually transmitted hepatitis B (number of cases)	58,300[5]	47,593[2,5]	58,393	52,800	30,500
Repeat gonorrhea Infection	20%[5]	...	---	18%	15%
Adolescents who ever had sexual intercourse					
Adolescents 15 years					
Females	27%	...	36%[6]	---	15%
Males	33%	...	44%[6]	---	15%

[Continued]

★ 452 ★

Sexually Transmitted Diseases Objective Status, 1988-2000

[Continued]

Objective	1988 baseline		1991	1992	Target 2000
	Original	Revised			
Adolescents 17 years					
Females	50%	...	66%[6]	---	40%
Males	66%	...	68%[6]	---	40%
Condom use at last sexual intercourse					
Sexually active unmarried females 15-44 years	19%	...	---	---	50%
a. Sexually active females 15-19 years	26%	...	38%[7]	---	60%
b. Sexually active males 15-19 years	57%	...	54%[7]	---	75%
c. Intravenous drug abusers	34%	...	---	---	60%
Clinic services for HIV and other sexually transmitted diseases					
Family planning clinics	40%[1]	...	---	---	50%
Sexually transmitted disease education in schools	95%	...	---	---	100%
Correct management of sexually transmitted disease cases by primary care providers	70%	...	---	---	90%
Clinician counseling to prevent HIV and other sexually transmitted diseases	10%[5]	...	---	---	75%
Percent of clinicians routinely service to 81-100% of patients					
Counseling about HIV and STD prevention					
Family physicians	---	...	---	27%	...
Internists	---	...	---	30%	...
Obstetricians/Gynecologists	---	...	---	46%	...
Nurse practitioners	---	...	---	50%	...
Pediatricians	---	...	---	46%	...
Inquiry about sexual practices and STD's					
Family physicians	---	...	---	13%	...
Internists	--	...	---	18%	...
Obstetricians/Gynecologists	---	...	---	34%	...
Nurse practitioners	---	...	---	52%	...
Pediatricians	---	...	---	30%	...
a. Providers practicing in high incidence areas	---	...	---	---	90%
Partner notification of exposure to sexually transmitted diseases					
Patients with bacterial sexually transmitted diseases	20%	...	---	---	50%

Source: U.S. Department of Health and Human Services, Public Health Service, Centers for Disease Control and Prevention, and National Center for Health Statistics, *Healthy People 2000 Review 1993* (Hyattsville, MD, June 1994), pp. 126, 128. *Primary source:* Centers for Disease Control and Prevention, National Center for Prevention, National Center for Preventive Services, Sexually Transmitted Disease Surveillance System. *Notes:* 1. 1989 data. 2. Data have been revised. Original data were estimated based on preliminary analysis. 3. As measured by first-time visits to physician's offices. 4. Data have been revised to reflect updated methodology. 5. 1987 data. 6. Data were previously reported by high school grade; current data are by age. 7. 9th-12th grade students.

★ 453 ★

National Health Goals

Immunization and Infectious Diseases Objective Status, 1988-2000

Objective	1987 baseline		1991	1992	Target 2000
	Original	Revised			
Vaccine-preventable diseases (number of cases)					
Diphtheria among people 25 years and under	1[1]	...	2	3	0
Tetanus among people 25 years and under	3[1]	...	4	7	0
Polio (wild-type virus)	0[1]	...	0	0	0
Measles	3,058[1]	...	9,411	2,237	0
Rubella	225[1]	...	1,401	160	0
Congenital Rubella Syndrome	6[1]	...	47	11	0
Mumps	4,866[1]	...	4,263	2,572	500
Pertussis	3,450[1]	...	2,719	4,083	1,000
Epidemic-related pneumonia and influenza deaths among older adults (per 100,000)	9.1[2]	19.9[2,3]	14.6[4]	23.1[5]	7.3
Viral hepatitis cases (per 100,000)					
Hepatitis B (HBV)	63.5	...	42.6	37.7	40.0
Hepatitis A	31.0	33.0[6]	29.0	27.2	23.0
Hepatitis C	18.3	...	8.3	5.6	13.7
HBV cases (number of cases)					
a. Intravenous drug abusers	30,000	44,348[6]	12,666	10,576	22,500
b. Heterosexually active people	33,000	33,995[6]	43,795	46,152	22,000
c. Homosexual males	25,300	13,598[6]	14,598	6,730	8,500
d. Children of Asians/Pacific Islanders	8,900	10,817[6]	7,514	6,730	1,800
e. Occupationally exposed workers	6,200	3,090[6]	2,576	1,923	1,250
f. Infants (new carriers)	3,500	3,863[6]	2,235	2,464	550
g. Alaska Natives	15	...	15	15	1
Tuberculosis (per 100,000)	9.1[1]	...	10.4	10.5	3.5
a. Asians/Pacific Islanders	36.3[1]	...	41.8	46.6	15.0
b. Blacks	28.3[1]	...	31.9	31.7	10.0
c. Hispanics	18.3[1]	...	21.4	22.4	5.0
d. American Indians/Alaska Natives	18.1[1]	...	16.3	16.3	5.0
Surgical wound and nosocomial infections					
Device-associated nosocomial infection rates (per 1,000 device-days)					
Bloodstream infections					
Medical/Coronary ICUs	...	6.9[7]	---	---	6.2
Surgical/Medical-Surgical ICUs	...	5.3[7]	---	---	4.8
Pediatric ICUs	...	11.4[7]	---	---	10.3
Urinary tract infections					
Medical/Coronary ICUs	...	10.7[7]	---	---	9.6
Surgical/Medical-Surgical ICUs	...	7.6[7]	---	---	6.8
Pediatric ICUs	...	5.8[7]	---	---	5.2
Pneumonia					
Medical/Coronary ICUs	...	12.8[7]	---	---	11.5
Surgical/Medical-Surgical ICUs	...	17.6[7]	---	---	15.8
Pediatric ICUs	...	4.7[7]	---	---	4.2
Surgical wound infection rates (per 100 operations)					
Low-risk patients	...	1.1[7]	---	---	1.0
Medium-low-risk patients	...	3.2[7]	---	---	2.9
Medium-high-risk patients	...	6.3[7]	---	---	5.7

[Continued]

★ 453 ★

Immunization and Infectious Diseases Objective Status, 1988-2000

[Continued]

Objective	1987 baseline Original	1987 baseline Revised	1991	1992	Target 2000
High-risk patients	...	14.4[7]	---	---	13.0
Illness among international travelers (number of cases)					
Typhoid fever	280	...	351	---	140
Hepatitis A	1,280	4,475[6]	3,730	3,814	640
Malaria	2,000	932[6]	1,021	---	1,000
Bacterial meningitis (per 100,000)	6.3[8]	6.5[6,8]	---	---	4.7
a. Alaska Natives	33	...	17	---	8
Diarrhea among children in child care center					
Children 0-6 years	...	32[9]	---	---	24%
Children 0-3 years	...	38%[9]	---	---	28%
Ear Infections among children 4 years and under (restricted activity days per 100 children)	131	135.4[3]	155.7	155.2	105.0
Pneumonia-related illness (restricted activity days per 100 people)					
People 65 years and over	48.0	19.1[3]	78.5	63.5	38.0
Children 4 years and under	27.0	29.4[3]	24.1	19.4	24.0
Immunization (percent immunized)					
Basic immunization series among children					
Children 2 years and under	70-80%[10]	54-65%[3,11]	---	---	90%
Children 19-35 months					
Diptheria-tetanus-pertussis	---	...	60%[12,13]	83%[12,13]	...
Polio	---	...	53%[12,13]	72%[12,13]	...
Measles-containing	---	...	82%[13]	83%[13]	...
Haemophilus influenzae B	---	...	58%[13]	67%[13]	...
Children in licensed child care facilities	94%	94-95%[3,14]	94-96%[14]	---	95%
Children in kindergarten through post-secondary education institutions	97%	97-98%[5,14]	96-98%[14]	---	95%
Pneumococcal pneumonia and influenza immunizations					
Institutionalized chronically ill people or older people	---	...	---	---	80%
Noninstitutionalized high-risk population	10-20%[10]	14-30%[3,15]	16%[16]	---	60%
Hepatitis B immunizations					
Infants of antigen-positive mothers	...	40%[9]	---	---	90%
Occupationally exposed workers	...	37%[17]	---	50%	90%
IV-drug users in drug treatment programs	---	...	---	---	50%
Homosexual males	---	...	---	---	50%
Postexposure rabies treatments (number)	18,000	...	18,800	24,700	9,000
Immunization laws (number of States)	10[18,19]	10-40[3,17]	---	34-50	50
Provision of immunizations by clinicians	---	...	---	---	90%
Percent of clinicians routinely providing services to 81-100% of patients (children)					
DTP vaccination					
Pediatricians	...	86%[20]	---	---	...
Nurse practitioners	...	76%[20]	---	---	...
Family physicians	...	89%[20]	---	---	...
Oral polio vaccination					
Pediatricians	...	87%[20]	---	---	...

[Continued]

★ 453 ★

Immunization and Infectious Diseases Objective Status, 1988-2000

[Continued]

Objective	1987 baseline		1991	1992	Target 2000
	Original	Revised			
Nurse practitioners	...	76%[20]	---	---	...
Family physicians	...	89%[20]	---	---	...
Tetanus-diphtheria booster (under 18 years)					
Pediatricians	...	79%[20]	---	---	...
Nurse practitioners	...	71%[20]	---	---	...
Family physicians	...	70%[20]	---	---	...
Hib vaccination					
Pediatricians	...	85%[20]	---	---	...
Nurse practitioners	...	68%[20]	---	---	...
Family physicians	...	74%[20]	---	---	...
(adults)					
Tetanus-diphtheria booster (18 years and over)					
Nurse practitioners	...	38%[20]	---	---	...
Obstetricians/Gynecologists	...	4%[20]	---	---	...
Internists	...	29%[20]	---	---	...
Family physicians	...	28%[20]	---	---	...
Influenza vaccination (65 years and over)					
Nurse practitioners	...	42%[20]	---	---	...
Obstetricians/Gynecologists	...	6%[20]	---	---	...
Internists	...	49%[20]	---	---	...
Family physicians	...	31%[20]	---	---	...
Pneumococcal vaccination (65 years and over)					
Nurse practitioners	...	33%[20]	---	---	...
Obstetricians/Gynecologists	...	5%[20]	---	---	...
Internists	...	40%[20]	---	---	...
Family physicians	...	25%[20]	---	---	...
Financial barriers to immunization					
Employment-based insurance plans that provide coverage for immunizations					
Conventional insurance plans	45%[17]	...	---	53%	100%
Preferred Provider Organizational plans	62%[17]	...	---	65%	100%
Health Maintenance Organization plans	98%[17]	...	---	95%	100%
Public health department provision of immunizations	...	37-70%[18]	---	---	90%
Local health programs to identify tuberculosis	---	...	---	---	90%
Preventive therapy for tuberculosis					
(percent of infected persons completing therapy)	66.3%	...	64.9%	---	85%
Laboratory capability for influenza diagnosis					
Tertiary care hospitals	---	52%[21]	---	---	85%
Secondary care hospitals and HMOs	---	...	---	---	50%

[Continued]

★ 453 ★

Immunization and Infectious Diseases Objective Status, 1988-2000

[Continued]

Objective	1987 baseline		1991	1992	Target 2000
	Original	Revised			
Secondary care hospitals	---	45%[21]	---	---	...
HMOs	---	68%[21]	---	---	...

Source: U.S. Department of Health and Human Services, Public Health Service, Centers for Disease Control and Prevention, and National Center for Health Statistics, *Healthy People 2000 Review 1993* (Hyattsville, MD, June 1994), p. 133-5. *Primary source:* Centers for Disease Control and Prevention, National Center for Infectious Diseases, Sentinel Counties Hepatitis Investigation, and Viral Hepatitis Surveillance System. *Notes:* 1. 1988 data. 2. 1979-80 influenza season through 1986-87 influenza season. 3. Data have been revised to reflect updated methodology. 4. 1986-87 influenza season through 1988-89 influenza season. 5. 1987-88 influenza season through 1988-89 influenza season. 6. Data have been revised. Original data were estimated based on preliminary analysis. 7. 1986-90 data. 8. 1986 data. 9. 1991 data. 10. 1985 data. 11. 1985 data; range of antigen-specific immunization levels among 2-year-old children. 12. Three or more doses. 13. 1991 and 1992 data on immunization levels among children 19-35 months are not comparable. Changes between 1991 and 1992 are primarily the result of a redesign of the 1992 National Health Interview Survey vaccination section. 14. Range of antigen-specific immunization levels. 15. 1989 data; among people 65 years and over, 14 percent received pneumococcal vaccine and 30 percent received influenza vaccine. 16. Proportion of people 65 years and over who received both pneumococcal and influenza vaccines; 21 percent received pneumococcal vaccine and 42 percent received influenza vaccine. 17. 1989 data. 18. 1990 data. 19. Includes the District of Columbia. 20. 1992 data. 21. 1993 data.

★ 454 ★

National Health Goals

Clinical Preventive Services Objective Status, 1991-2000

"Clinical preventive services are those disease prevention and health promotion services—immunizations, screening for early detection of disease or risk factors, and patient counseling—that are delivered to individuals in a health care setting. The U.S. Clinical Preventive Services Task Force, a panel of prevention experts appointed by the U.S. Public Health Service, has reviewed the full range of scientific literature on clinical preventive services and developed scientifically sound recommendations for specific service based on age, gender, and other risk factors."

[Proportion of eligible people]

Objective	Baseline		1991	1992	Target 2000
	Original	Revised			
Years of healthy life	62.0[1]	64.0[2,3]	63.9	---	65
a. Blacks	56.0[1]	No change[2,3]	56.0	---	60
b. Hispanics	62.0[1]	64.8[2,3,4]	---	---	65
c. People 65 years and over[5]	12.0[1]	11.9[2,3]	11.8	---	14
Receipt of recommended service	...	13%[6,7]	---	---	50%
a. Infants up to 24 months	...	---	---	---	90%
b. Children 2-12 years	...	---	---	---	80%
c. Adolescents 13-18 years	...	---	---	---	50%
d. People 19-39 years	...	12%[6]	---	---	40%
e. People 40-64 years	...	18%[6]	---	---	40%
f. People 65 years and over	...	0%[6]	---	---	40%
g. Low-income people	...	8%[6,7]	---	---	50%
h. Blacks	...	13%[6,7]	---	---	50%
i. Hispanics	...	13%[6,7]	---	---	50%
j. Asians/Pacific Islanders	...	12%[6,7]	---	---	50%
k. American Indians/Alaska Natives	...	14%[6,7]	---	---	70%
l. People with disabilities	...	12%[6,7]	---	---	80%
Access to primary care (Percent with source of care)	82%[8]	...	80%	79%	95%
a. Hispanics	70%[8]	...	64%	65%	95%
b. Blacks	70%[8]	...	80%	77%	95%

[Continued]

★ 454 ★

Clinical Preventive Services Objective Status, 1991-2000

[Continued]

Objective	Baseline Original	Baseline Revised	1991	1992	Target 2000
c. Low-income people	80%[8]	...	72%	72%	95%
Financial barriers to receipt to clinical preventive services	---	...	72%	72%	95%
Proportion without health care coverage					
People under 65 years	...	16%[9]	17%[2]	---	...
Clinical preventive services from publicity funded programs (proportion of eligible people)	---	...	---	---	90%
Federal programs					
Screening	...	10-100%[10]	---	---	...
Counseling	...	40-100%[10]	---	---	...
Immunizations	...	10-96%[10]	---	---	...
Provisions of recommended services by primary care providers	---	...	---	---	50%
Percent of clinicians routinely providing service to 81-100% of patients (children)					
Hemoglobin/Hematocrit					
Pediatricians	...	78%[11]	---	---	...
Nurse practitioners	...	77%[11]	---	---	...
Family practitioners	...	52%[11]	---	---	...
Eye exam (for strabismus and amblyopia)					
Pediatricians	...	64%[11]	---	---	...
Nurse practitioners	...	67%[11]	---	---	...
Family practitioners	...	53%[11]	---	---	...
Blood pressure					
Pediatricians	...	78%[11]	---	---	...
Nurse practitioners	...	71%[11]	---	---	...
Family physicians	...	42%[11]	---	---	...
Height and weight					
Pediatricians	...	96%[11]	---	---	...
Nurse practitioners	...	88%[11]	---	---	...
Family physicians	...	89%[11]	---	---	...
DTP vaccination					
Pediatricians	...	86%[11]	---	---	...
Nurse practitioners	...	76%[11]	---	---	...
Family physicians	...	89%[11]	---	---	...
Oral polio vaccination					
Pediatricians	...	87%[11]	---	--	...
Nurse practitioners	...	76%[11]	---	---	...
Family physicians	...	89%[11]	---	---	...
Tetanus-diphtheria booster					
Pediatricians	...	79%[11]	---	---	...
Nurse practitioners	...	71%[11]	---	---	...
Family physicians	...	70%[11]	---	---	...
Hib vaccination					
Pediatricians	...	85%[11]	---	---	...
Nurse practitioners	...	68%[11]	---	---	...
Family physicians	...	74%[11]	---	---	...

[Continued]

★ 454 ★

Clinical Preventive Services Objective Status, 1991-2000

[Continued]

Objective	Baseline Original	Baseline Revised	1991	1992	Target 2000
(adults)					
Tetanus-diphtheria booster (18 years and over)					
Nurse practitioners	...	38%[11]	---	---	...
Obstetricians/Gynecologists	...	4%[11]	---	---	...
Internists	...	29%[11]	---	---	...
Family physicians	...	28%[11]	---	---	...
Influenza vaccination (65 years and over)					
Nurse practitioners	...	42%[11]	---	---	...
Obstetricians/Gynecologists	...	6%[11]	---	---	...
Internists	...	49%[11]	---	---	...
Family physicians	...	31%[11]	---	---	...
Pneumococcal vaccination (65 years and over)					
Nurse practitioners	...	33%[11]	---	---	...
Obstetricians/Gynecologists	...	5%[11]	---	---	...
Internists	...	40%[11]	---	---	...
Family physicians	...	25%[11]	---	---	...
Blood pressure					
Nurse practitioners	...	82%[11]	---	---	...
Obstetricians/Gynecologists	...	88%[11]	---	---	...
Internists	...	92%[11]	---	---	...
Family physicians	...	89%[11]	---	---	...
Cholesterol level					
Nurse practitioners	...	45%[11]	---	---	...
Obstetricians/Gynecologists	...	36%[11]	---	---	...
Internists	...	80%[11]	---	---	...
Family physicians	...	61%[11]	---	---	...
Breast exam (by clinician)					
Nurse practitioners	...	78%[11]	---	---	...
Obstetricians/Gynecologists	...	92%[11]	---	---	...
Internists	...	76%[11]	---	---	...
Family physicians	...	62%[11]	---	---	...
Pap smear					
Nurse practitioners	...	77%[11]	---	---	...
Obstetricians/Gynecologists	...	95%[11]	---	---	...
Internists	...	67%[11]	---	---	...
Family physicians	...	62%[11]	---	---	...
Mammogram					
Nurse practitioners	...	63%[11]	---	---	...
Obstetricians/Gynecologists	...	85%[11]	---	---	...
Internists	...	67%[11]	---	---	...
Family physicians	...	53%[11]	---	---	...
Local health department assurance of access to essential clinical preventive service					
Proportion of people served	---	...	---	---	90%
Proportion of local health departments providing:					
Health education	...	74%[12]	---	---	...

[Continued]

★ 454 ★

Clinical Preventive Services Objective Status, 1991-2000

[Continued]

Objective	Baseline		1991	1992	Target 2000
	Original	Revised			
Child health	...	84%[12]	---	---	...
Immunizations	...	92%[12]	---	---	...
Prenatal care	...	59%[12]	---	---	...
Primary care	...	22%[12]	---	---	...
Racial/ethnic minority representation in the health professions					
Degrees awarded to:					
Blacks	5.0%[13]	...	5.7%[14]	5.7%[15]	8.0%
Hispanics	3.0%[13]	...	4.3%[14]	4.8%[15]	6.4%
American Indians/Alaska Natives	0.3%[13]	...	0.4%[14]	0.5%[15]	0.6%

Source: U.S. Department of Health and Human Services, Public Health Service, Centers for Disease Control and Prevention, and National Center for Health Statistics, *Healthy People 2000 Review 1993* (Hyattsville, MD, June 1994), p. 139, 141-3. *Primary source:* Centers for Disease Control and Prevention, National Center for Statistics, and National Health Interview Survey. *Notes:* 1. 1980 data. 2. 1990 data. 3. Data have been revised to reflect updated methodology. 4. Estimate based on preliminary data. 5. Years of healthy life remaining at age 65. 6. 1991 data. 7. Among people 19 years and over. 8. 1986 data. 9. 1989 data. 10. 1991-92 data. 11. 1992 data. 12. 1990 data. 13. 1985-86 data. 14. Academic year 1990-91. 15. Academic year 1991-92.

Chapter 11
INCOME, TAXES, PRICES, AND SPENDING

Income

★ 455 ★

Personal Income by Type and Disposition, 1979-2005-I

[Billions of current dollars]

Category	1979	1989	1992	2005		
				Low	Moderate	High
Personal Income	$2,033.1	$4,380.3	$5,144.9	$12,174.4	$14,434.6	$15,730.6
Wages and salaries	1,255.5	2,586.4	2,973.1	7,646.4	8,722.0	9,570.7
Other labor income	124.3	251.9	322.7	762.8	855.9	931.8
Proprietors' income	181.8	347.3	414.3	882.6	1,045.2	1,214.3
Rental income	8.4	-13.5	-8.9	-35.1	90.9	210.2
Personal dividend income	50.4	126.5	140.4	278.9	306.6	377.6
Personal interest income	223.2	668.2	694.3	1,679.9	1,571.2	1,350.5
Net transfer income	264.8	609.3	609.1	1,520.1	1,842.8	2,075.5
Disposable personal income	1,753.0	3,787.0	4,500.2	10,512.1	12,558.1	13,764.3
Personal consumption	1,583.7	3,523.1	4,139.9	9,939.0	11,830.9	12,948.2
Interest and transfer payments	45.9	111.9	121.5	204.1	213.3	224.2
Personal savings	123.3	152.1	238.7	368.9	514.9	591.9
Disposable personal income (billions of 1987 dollars)	2,710.0	3,465.0	3,632.5	4,520.9	4,879.8	5,467.7
Per capita disposable personal income (1987 dollars)	12,023	13,922	14,219	16,032	17,304	18,598
Per capita disposable personal income (current dollars)	9,020	17,600	17,615	35,000	39,000	44,800
Personal savings rate (percent)	7.1	4.0	5.3	3.5	4.1	4.3

Source: U.S. Department of Labor, Bureau of Labor Statistics, *The American Work Force: 1992-2005* (Washington, D.C.: U.S. Government Printing Office, April 1994), p. 24. *Primary source:* Historical data, Bureau of Economic Analysis; projected data, Bureau of Labor Statistics.

★ 456 ★

Income

Personal Income by Type and Disposition, 1979-2005-II

[Billions of current dollars]

Category	Average annual rates of change					
	1979-89	1989-92	1979-92	1992-2005		
				Low	Moderate	High
Personal Income	8.0	5.5	7.4	6.9	8.3	9.0
Wages and salaries	7.5	4.8	6.9	7.5	8.6	9.4
Other labor income	7.3	8.6	7.6	6.9	7.8	8.5
Proprietors' income	6.7	6.1	6.5	6.0	7.4	8.6
Personal dividend income	9.6	3.5	8.2	5.4	6.2	7.9
Personal interest income	11.6	1.3	9.1	7.0	6.5	5.3
Net transfer income	8.7	.0	6.6	7.3	8.9	9.9
Disposable personal income	8.0	5.9	7.5	6.7	8.2	9.0
Personal consumption	8.3	5.5	7.7	7.0	8.4	9.2
Interest and transfer payments	9.3	32.8	7.8	4.1	4.4	4.8
Personal savings	2.1	16.2	5.2	3.4	6.1	7.2
Disposable personal income (billions of 1987 dollars)	2.5	1.6	2.3	1.7	2.3	3.2
Per capita disposable personal income (1987 dollars)	1.5	.7	1.3	.9	1.5	2.1
Per capita disposable personal income (current dollars)	6.9	.0	5.3	5.3	6.3	7.4

Source: U.S. Department of Labor, Bureau of Labor Statistics, *The American Work Force: 1992-2005* (Washington, D.C.: U.S. Government Printing Office, April 1994), p. 24. *Primary source:* Historical data, Bureau of Economic Analysis; projected data, Bureau of Labor Statistics.

★ 457 ★

Income

Disposable Income per Capita, 1979-2004

[Constant 1991-92 dollars]

Year ending	Middle alternative projections	Low alternative projections	High alternative projections
1994	17,385	$16,956	$17,851
1995	17,629	17,124	18,190
1996	17,863	17,328	18,459
1997	18,003	17,454	18,627
1998	18,123	17,563	18,767
1999	18,246	17,663	18,923
2000	18,395	17,806	19,090
2001	18,560	17,986	19,257
2002	18,717	18,160	19,416

[Continued]

★ 457 ★

Disposable Income per Capita, 1979-2004

[Continued]

Year ending	Middle alternative projections	Low alternative projections	High alternative projections
2003	18,850	18,290	19,578
2004	18,994	18,417	19,759

Source: U.S. Department of Education, Office of Educational Research and Improvement, National Center for Education Statistics, *Projections of Education Statistics to 2004* (Washington, D.C.: U.S. Government Printing Office, October 1993), p. 150. *Primary source:* DRI/McGraw-Hill "U.S. Quarterly Model." This table was prepared June 1993. *Notes:* Based on the Consumer Price Index for all urban consumers, Bureau of Labor Statistics, U.S. Department of Labor.

★ 458 ★

Income

Income of Working Women Compared to Men, 2000

"Working women still have plenty of ground to cover before catching up with men... [Women] who work full time year-round still earn only about 72 cents for every dollar men make. June O'Neill, a professor of economics at Baruch College in New York City and an authority on the wage gap, predicts women's pay will reach about 80 cents to the dollar by the end of the decade, as their average years of experience and education increase relative to men's, and employers discriminate less."

Source: Antony J. Michels, "Pay Gap Between the Sexes," in *Fortune*, 20 April 1992, p. 20. *Primary source:* Professor June O'Neill, Baruch College.

★ 459 ★

Income

Income of Working-wife Families by Age of Household Head, 1990-2000

"The number of households considered affluent will jump during the current decade, mainly because of working wives, a Conference Board study shows.

"Households earning $100,000 or more a year will double by the year 2000, to 4.3 million. There also will be an 'explosive' rise in households earning $50,000 or more a year, said Fabian Linden, Executive Director of the board's Consumer Research Center. Households earning at the $50,000 level and above, where both spouses are working, will increase about 50%, to almost 20 million by the year 2000 from 13.5 million in 1990, the study projects."

[Billions of 1990 dollars]

Age group	1990	2000
Under 25	$35	$34
25-35	366	366
35-45	525	744
45-55	416	727
55-65	211	296
Over 65	52	54

Source: Fred R. Bleakley, "Number of Affluent Households to Jump and Spending to Rise, Study Indicates," in *The Wall Street Journal*, 27 October 1993, p. A2. *Primary source:* The Conference Board.

★ 460 ★

Income

Economic Status of Elderly People Living Alone: 1990-2000

"The economic status of older men is expected to improve much more rapidly than that of women. For example, the poverty rate among older women who live alone is projected to decrease 54 percent by the year 2020 (from 26 percent in 1990 to 12 percent by 2020); among older men who live alone the poverty rate is projected to decline by 79 percent (from 19 percent in 1990 to 4 percent by 2020). Today, there are five times as many older women living alone below the poverty threshold as there are men. By the year 2020, poor women living alone will outnumber similarly situated men by a factor of ten."

[Percent]

Year	<100% Of Poverty	150-299% Of Poverty	100-149% Of Poverty	300% + Poverty
1990	19	30	27	24
2005	27	34	21	18
2020	37	37	16	11

Source: U.S. Senate Special Committee on Aging, American Association of Retired Persons, Federal Council on the Aging, U.S. Administration on Aging, *Aging America: Trends and Projections* (Washington, D.C.: U.S. Government Printing Office, 1991), p. 218. *Primary source:* Lewin/ICF estimates based on data from the *Current Population Survey* and the Brookings/ICF Long-Term Care Financing Model (1990). *Note:* May not add to 100 percent due to rounding.

★ 461 ★

Income

Number of Elderly People Living Alone below Poverty by Sex, 1990-2020

"Despite the overall anticipated improvement in the economic status of older people, by 2020 it is projected that more than 2 in 5 (41 percent) of elderly people living alone will continue to be economically vulnerable—that is, they will have incomes below 200 percent of the poverty threshold."

[Thousands]

Year	Men	Women
1990	370	1873
2005	232	1723
2020	145	1470

Source: U.S. Senate Special Committee on Aging, American Association of Retired Persons, Federal Council on the Aging, U.S. Administration on Aging, *Aging America: Trends and Projections* (Washington, D.C.: U.S. Government Printing Office, 1991), p. 219. *Primary source:* Lewin/ICF estimates based on data from the *Current Population Survey* and the Brookings/ICF Long-Term Care Financing Model (1990).

★ 462 ★

Income

Income Distribution of Impaired People Age 65+ as a Proportion of the Poverty Level, 1990-2020

[Thousands]

Income as proportion of poverty level	Year					
	1990		2005		2020	
	Number	Percent[1]	Number	Percent	Number	Percent
Total	5,913	100	7,540	100	9,914	100
<100%	1,593	27	1,341	18	1,153	12
100-149%	1,578	27	1,734	23	1,690	17
150-199%	745	13	1,067	14	1,343	14
200%+	1,997	34	3,398	45	5,728	58

Source: U.S. Senate Special Committee on Aging, American Association of Retired Persons, Federal Council on the Aging, U.S. Administration on Aging, *Aging America: Trends and Projections* (Washington, D.C.: U.S. Government Printing Office, 1991), p. 176. *Primary source:* Lewin/ICF estimates based on data from the *1984 Survey on Aging (SOA)* and the Brookings/ICF Long-Term Care Financing Model (1990). *Notes:* "Impaired people" includes people living in the community with ADL limitations and nursing home residents. ADL=Activities of Daily Living. 1. Totals may exceed 100 percent due to rounding. Projections assume constant age, sex, and marital status income are the result of expected growth in pension coverage, increases in real earnings, and higher rates for female labor force participation by women.

★ 463 ★

Income

Asset Distribution of Impaired People Age 65+, 1990-2020

"In 1990, about 3.5 million impaired older people had nonhousing financial assets below $25,000 (60 percent). By the year 2020, the number of impaired older people with modest assets is projected to rise to 5.2 million (52 percent)."

[Thousands]

Financial assets (Nonhousing, 1989 dollars)	Year					
	1990		2005		2020	
	Number	Percent	Number	Percent	Number	Percent
Total	5,913	100	7,540	100	9,914	100
<$25,000	3,548	60	4,222	56	5,155	52
$25,000+	2,365	40	3,318	44	4,759	48

Source: U.S. Senate Special Committee on Aging, American Association of Retired Persons, Federal Council on the Aging, U.S. Administration on Aging, *Aging America: Trends and Projections* (Washington, D.C.: U.S. Government Printing Office, 1991), pp. 177-78. *Primary source:* Lewin/ICF estimates based on data from the *1984 Survey on Aging (SOA)* and the Brookings/ICF Long-Term Care Financing Model (1990). *Notes:* Impaired people includes people living in the community with ADL limitations and nursing home residents. ADL=Activities of Daily Living. Totals may exceed 100 percent due to rounding. Projections assume constant age, sex, and marital status rates of disability for people in the community.

Taxes

★ 464 ★

Federal Government Receipts, 1994-1999

"1995 receipts are projected at $1,342.2 billion, an increase of $93.0 billion, or 7.4 percent, in the absence of the proposed health reform. All new receipts raised by OBRA-93 are deposited in the Deficit Reduction Fund created by an Executive Order of the President. The health reform proposal would add $11.6 billion in receipts, all to pay for health care.

"Receipts increases in 1995—as did those in 1994—reflect the President's deficit-reduction plan of last year, and the affected receipts sources grow the most rapidly as a result. The budget contains no tax increase proposals."

[Billions of dollars]

	1994	1995	1996	1997	1998	1999
Individual income taxes	550.0	597.2	630.6	663.9	698.6	739.4
Corporation income taxes	130.7	141.0	146.3	150.3	153.9	157.5
Social insurance taxes and contributions	461.9	492.1	518.5	546.1	576.0	604.7
Excise taxes	54.6	55.8	56.7	57.8	58.9	60.3
Other receipts	52.0	56.0	58.2	61.3	64.4	67.2
Total receipts	1,249.2	1,342.2	1,410.4	1,479.5	1,550.8	1,629.0
Total receipts without health care reform as a percent of GDP	18.8%	19.1%	19.0%	18.9%	18.7%	18.6%
Memorandum:						
Effect of health care reform proposal on receipts	-0.1	11.6	16.9	25.6	36.2	44.0
Total receipts with health care reform	1,249.1	1,358.1	1,427.3	1,505.1	1,586.1	1,672.9
Total receipts with health care reform as a percent of GDP	18.8%	19.3%	19.2%	19.2%	19.2%	19.1%

Source: Executive Office of the President of the United States, Office of Management and Budget, *Budget of the United States Government* (Washington, D.C.: U.S. Government Printing Office, 1994), p. 31.

★ 465 ★

Taxes

Federal Government Receipts by Source, 1993-1999

[Billions of dollars]

Source	1993 Actual	Estimate 1994	1995	1996	1997	1998	1999
Individual income taxes	509.7	549.9	595.0	627.7	664.1	701.6	745.1
Corporation income taxes	117.5	130.7	140.4	145.8	149.8	152.5	157.2
Social insurance taxes and contributions	428.3	461.9	490.4	518.3	548.5	580.0	610.2
(On-budget)	(116.4)	(125.7)	(135.2)	(143.6)	(151.0)	(158.6)	(165.0)
(Off-budget)	(311.9)	(336.2)	(355.2)	(347.7)	(397.5)	(421.4)	(445.1)
Excise taxes	48.1	54.6	71.9	71.7	72.7	73.6	74.9
Estate and gift taxes	12.6	12.7	13.9	15.0	16.1	17.3	18.5
Customs duties	18.8	19.2	20.9	21.3	22.2	23.1	24.0
Miscellaneous receipts	18.6	20.0	21.3	27.6	31.6	38.7	43.1
Total receipts	1,153.5	1,249.1	1,353.8	1,427.3	1,505.1	1,586.9	1,672.9
(On-budget)	(841.6)	(912.9)	(998.6)	(1,052.6)	(1,107.6)	(1,165.5)	(1,227.8)
(Off-budget)	(311.9)	(336.2)	(355.2)	(374.7)	(397.5)	(421.4)	(455.1)

Source: Executive Office of the President of the United States, Office of Management and Budget, *Budget of the United States Government* (Washington, D.C.: U.S. Government Printing Office, 1994), p. 236.

★ 466 ★

Taxes

State and Local Receipts, 1979-2005-I

[Billions of current dollars]

Category	1979	1989	1992	2005 Low	2005 Moderate	2005 High
Receipts	$330.6	$681.5	$837.8	$2,292.8	$2,565.8	$2,818.3
Personal taxes	50.5	131.5	154.0	461.0	526.2	591.1
Corporate profits taxes	13.6	24.2	26.0	75.5	130.5	187.6
Indirect business taxes	158.6	352.8	421.5	1,010.6	1,126.8	1,196.7
Social insurance contributions	27.4	54.8	64.9	150.8	162.1	188.6
Grants-in-aid from Federal Government	80.5	118.2	171.4	594.6	620.2	654.3
			Percent distribution			
Receipts	100.0	100.0	100.0	100.0	100.0	100.0
Personal taxes	15.3	19.3	18.4	20.1	20.5	21.0
Corporate profits taxes	4.1	3.6	3.1	3.3	5.1	6.7
Indirect business taxes	48.0	51.8	50.3	44.1	43.9	42.5
Social insurance contributions	8.3	8.0	7.7	6.6	6.3	6.7
Grants-in-aid from Federal Government	24.3	17.3	20.5	25.9	24.2	23.2

Source: U.S. Department of Labor, Bureau of Labor Statistics, *The American Work Force: 1992-2005* (Washington, D.C.: U.S. Government Printing Office, April 1994), pp. 21-2. *Primary source:* Historical data, Bureau of Economic Analysis; projected data, Bureau of Labor Statistics. Source also includes data on state and local expenditures (see entries 494-95).

★ 467 ★

Taxes

State and Local Receipts, 1979-2005-II

[Billions of current dollars]

Category	Average annual rates of change					
	1979-89	1989-92	1979-92	1992-2005		
				Low	Moderate	High
Receipts	7.5	7.1	7.4	8.1	9.0	9.8
Personal taxes	10.0	5.4	9.0	8.8	9.9	10.9
Corporate profits taxes	5.9	2.4	5.1	8.5	13.2	16.4
Indirect business taxes	8.3	6.1	7.8	7.0	7.9	8.4
Social insurance contributions	7.2	5.8	6.9	6.7	7.3	8.6
Grants-in-aid from Federal Government	3.9	13.2	6.0	10.0	10.4	10.9

Source: U.S. Department of Labor, Bureau of Labor Statistics, *The American Work Force: 1992-2005* (Washington, D.C.: U.S. Government Printing Office, April 1994), pp. 21-2. *Primary source:* Historical data, Bureau of Economic Analysis; projected data, Bureau of Labor Statistics. Source also includes data on state and local expenditures (see entries 494-95).

★ 468 ★

Taxes

Personal Tax and Nontax Payments to State and Local Governments, 1979- 2004

[Constant 1991-92 dollars per capita]

Year ending	Middle alternative projections	Low alternative projections	High alternative projections
1994	626	$609	$646
1995	659	631	691
1996	685	657	719
1997	704	675	741
1998	716	687	756
1999	725	697	768
2000	737	711	780
2001	750	727	793
2002	763	743	806
2003	775	757	820
2004	788	772	834

Source: U.S. Department of Education, Office of Educational Research and Improvement, National Center for Education Statistics, *Projections of Education Statistics to 2004* (Washington, D.C.: U.S. Government Printing Office, October 1993), p. 154. *Primary source:* DRI/McGraw-Hill, "U.S. Quarterly Model." This table was prepared June 1993. *Notes:* Based on the Consumer Price Index for all urban consumers, Bureau of Labor Statistics, U.S. Department of Labor.

★ 469 ★

Taxes

Property Taxes for State and Local Governments, 1994-2004

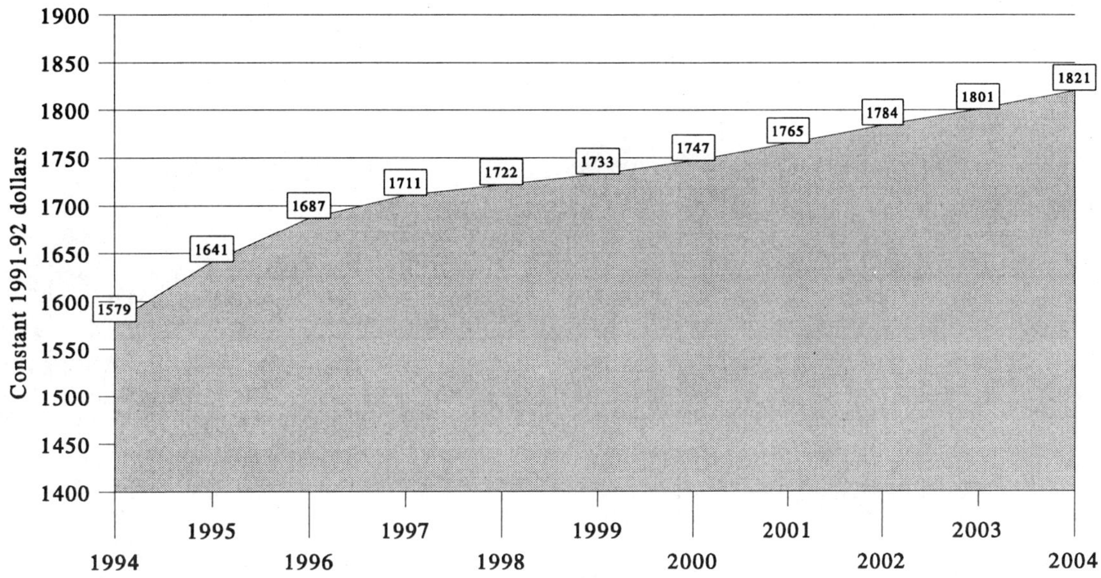

[Constant 1991-92 dollars per capita]

Year ending	Middle alternative projections	Low alternative projections	High alternative projections
1994	1,579	$1,538	$1,624
1995	1,641	1,586	1,706
1996	1,687	1,630	1,756
1997	1,711	1,652	1,785
1998	1,722	1,660	1,800
1999	1,733	1,668	1,814
2000	1,747	1,685	1,829
2001	1,765	1,706	1,847
2002	1,784	1,729	1,866
2003	1,801	1,747	1,885
2004	1,821	1,768	1,908

Source: U.S. Department of Education, Office of Educational Research and Improvement, National Center for Education Statistics, *Projections of Education Statistics to 2004* (Washington, D.C.: U.S. Government Printing Office, October 1993), p. 156. *Primary source:* DRI/McGraw-Hill, "U.S. Quarterly Model." This table was prepared June 1993. *Notes:* Based on the Consumer Price Index for all urban consumers, Bureau of Labor Statistics, U.S. Department of Labor.

★ 470 ★

Taxes

U.S. Information and Withholding Documents, 1991-1998

[Rounded to thousands]

	Projected							
	1991	1992	1993	1994	1995	1996	1997	1998
Grand Total	1,060,724	1,067,498	1,097,598	1,121,752	1,143,461	1,163,113	1,181,667	1,199,730
Total	200,142	194,130	201,307	205,667	209,278	211,403	212,468	212,968
W-2	198,471	192,261	199,225	203,359	206,730	208,602	209,400	209,619
W-2P	0	0	0	0	0	0	0	0
W-2G	1,671	1,869	2,082	2,308	2,548	2,801	3,068	3,349
Total	860,582	873,368	896,291	916,085	934,183	951,710	969,199	986,762
1099-DIV	96,352	96,128	96,993	97,491	98,401	99,614	100,663	101,856
1099-INT	337,928	342,258	351,470	358,442	362,885	367,498	372,819	379,181
1099-MISC	75,965	78,756	81,547	84,338	87,129	89,920	92,711	95,502
1099-OID	3,998	4,085	4,380	4,683	4,815	5,077	5,432	5,803
1099-PATR	2,172	2,357	2,610	2,930	3,317	3,773	4,300	4,902
1099-R	47,138	49,482	51,831	54,056	55,911	57,676	59,123	60,158
1099-B	57,493	57,573	58,889	59,307	60,218	60,899	61,698	61,706
1099-G	47,403	46,966	48,678	50,229	51,748	52,896	53,833	54,611
5498	59,946	59,523	58,978	58,513	58,206	57,781	57,219	56,949
1099-A	477	489	499	506	512	518	522	526
1098	57,125	58,231	60,733	63,410	66,401	69,129	71,756	74,165
1099-S	3,520	4,436	4,492	4,921	5,087	5,142	5,061	4,998
SSA/RRB-1099	43,360	44,174	45,003	45,847	46,707	47,583	48,476	49,385
K-1 (Form 1041)	5,334	5,474	5,624	5,776	5,931	6,090	6,253	6,420
K-1 (Form 1065)	17,688	18,287	18,949	19,640	20,326	21,032	21,758	22,515
K-1 (Form 1120S)	4,029	4,491	4,954	5,432	5,923	6,414	6,905	7,403
Foreign	654	658	661	664	666	668	670	672

Source: Department of Treasury, Internal Revenue Service, *Projections: Information and Withholding Documents Calendar Years 1991-98* (Washington, D.C.: U.S. Government Printing Office, April, 1991), p. 2. *Notes:* Beginning in 1991, Form W-2P will be combined with Form 1099-R. Source also includes actual data for 1990.

★ 471 ★

Taxes

Number of Returns to Be Filed, 1993-2001

[Counts in thousands]

Type of Return	Projected								
	1993	1994	1995	1996	1997	1998	1999	2000	2001
Grand Total	209,015	213,896	219,122	223,369	227,676	231,489	235,293	238,988	242,858
Primary Total	197,375	201,536	206,051	209,717	213,451	216,777	220,105	223,349	226,741
Individual, Total	115,408	117,961	120,525	122,543	124,654	126,419	128,183	129,855	131,675

[Continued]

★ 471 ★

Number of Returns to Be Filed, 1993-2001

[Continued]

Type of Return		Projected							
	1993	1994	1995	1996	1997	1998	1999	2000	2001
Forms 1040/A/EZ/PC	115,015	117,534	120,068	122,052	124,128	125,855	127,579	129,209	130,985
Form 1040	72,944	73,822	76,244	77,523	79,030	80,262	81,434	82,493	83,810
Form 1040A	20,245	19,058	18,990	18,654	18,617	18,624	18,701	18,794	19,056
Form 1040EZ	16,920	18,589	17,464	17,462	17,342	17,212	17,072	16,929	16,850
Form 1040PC	4,907	6,065	7,369	8,413	9,138	9,757	10,372	10,993	11,268
Forms 1040NR/PR/SS	392	427	457	491	527	564	604	645	690
Individual Estimated Tax	40,228	41,201	42,181	43,165	44,149	45,134	46,118	47,102	48,086
Fiduciary	2,931	2,980	3,033	3,087	3,146	3,204	3,262	3,320	3,380
Fiduciary Estimated Tax	697	715	728	741	755	769	783	797	811
Partnership	1,579	1,546	1,519	1,499	1,484	1,475	1,472	1,474	1,478
Corporation	4,584	4,736	4,899	5,059	5,215	5,367	5,522	5,682	5,845
Estate Tax	74	79	85	92	99	106	115	123	133
Gift Tax	202	219	236	253	267	281	293	305	315
Employment Tax	28,913	29,279	29,987	30,366	30,696	30,966	31,234	31,498	31,759
Form 1042	22	23	23	24	24	24	25	25	25
Exempt Organization	547	560	573	585	597	609	620	632	644
Employee Plans	1,267	1,327	1,374	1,418	1,460	1,500	1,537	1,573	1,608
Excise	833	814	793	801	817	833	850	866	883
Form 8752	72	73	75	78	80	83	86	89	92
Selected Supplemental	11,640	12,360	13,072	13,652	14,225	14,712	15,188	15,640	16,117
Form 1040X	1,866	1,952	2,054	2,133	2,207	2,268	2,325	2,378	2,433
Form 4868	5,775	6,176	6,556	6,846	7,136	7,373	7,603	7,818	8,048
Form 2688	1,870	2,047	2,211	2,349	2,487	2,608	2,727	2,842	2,963
Form 1120X	28	27	26	25	24	23	22	21	20
Form 7004	2,063	2,119	2,183	2,256	2,327	2,395	2,463	2,533	2,604
Form 1041A	38	40	41	42	44	45	47	48	50

Source: Internal Revenue Service, Research Division, *Fiscal Year Return Projections for the United States: 1993-2001* (Washington, D.C.: U.S. Government Printing Office, August 1993), p. 3. *Notes:* Detail may not add to subtotal/total due to rounding. Source also includes actual data for 1992.

★ 472 ★

Taxes

Federal Tax Incentive Proposals, 1993-1998

"The [Clinton economic] plan contains targeted tax provisions designed to provide an immediate boost to investment in the short term, and to encourage capital spending over the long run.

[Continued]

★ 472 ★

Federal Tax Incentive Proposals, 1993-1998

[Continued]

"**Permanent small business tax credit**. Small businesses will now be eligible for a permanent investment tax credit on their equipment. The credit will generally be 7 percent in 1993 and 1994 and 5 percent thereafter. Small businesses operate at the margin and need a permanent incentive to invest, grow and provide new employment opportunities. At the same time, the decrease in the rate from 7 percent to 5 percent after two years will provide an incentive to accelerate investment and add support for the current recovery.

"**Temporary marginal investment tax credit for all business**. Business will also be eligible for a tax credit on qualifying investments; the credit will be temporary and will apply only to 'marginal' investments acquired between December 3, 1992 and December 31, 1994. The credit will amount to 7 percent in 1993 and 1994, with somewhat lower rates applicable to shorter-lived property. To ensure that the credit is targeted to marginal investment by large companies, the credit each year is applied to investment over an historic base.

"**Simplifying and enhancing depreciation provisions for companies subject to the alternative minimum tax (AMT)**. Currently, property is depreciated for AMT purposes over a substantially longer period than for regular tax purposes. (For example, commercial aircraft are depreciated over 7 years for regular tax purposes and 12 years for AMT purposes). In addition, a corporation subject to the AMT must compute three depreciation schedules for federal tax purposes.

"The proposal substantially enhances the investment incentives for taxpayers subject to the AMT and simplifies the AMT by using the shorter regular tax depreciable lives for minimum tax as well as regular tax purposes. Thus, one depreciation period will be used for computation of both the minimum and regular tax, although the rate of depreciation will remain less rapid under the minimum tax than under the regular tax.

"Because they reduce the net cost of acquiring depreciable assets, the investment tax credit proposals will stimulate investment by both small and large businesses. The investment tax credit proposals, coupled with the liberalized depreciation under the minimum tax, will provide a strong and lasting stimulus to investment, encourage modernization of productive equipment, and help create good jobs."

Source: Executive Office of the President of the United States, Office of Management and Budget, *A Vision of Change for America* (Washington, D.C.: U.S. Government Printing Office, February 1993), pp. 38-9.

★ 473 ★

Taxes

Personal Income Tax Changes, 1993-1998

"The [Clinton economic] plan increases the top income tax rate from 31 percent to 36 percent for taxpayers with high incomes. The 36% tax rate will apply to taxable income in excess of $140,000 for couples and $115,000 for individuals, beginning [1993]. Average taxpayers with taxable income in excess of the $140,000/$115,000 thresholds will have adjusted gross income in excess of $180,000 on joint returns and $140,000 on individual returns. In addition, the package applies an additional 10 percent surtax for those people with taxable income over $250,000, resulting in a 39.6% tax rate for those income levels; and increases the Alternative Minimum Tax rate to 26 percent on AMT income less than $175,000 and 28 percent on AMT income over $175,000.

"These changes affect just over 1 percent of taxpayers and produce $26 billion of new revenues in 1997. Yet tax rates remain well below previous highs, preserving incentives to work and save.

"The plan also extends existing law rules on itemized deduction limitations and the personal exemption phaseout that are targeted to high income taxpayers. Those provisions are scheduled to expire in calendar years 1996 and 1997, respectively.

"The package also includes a number of other personal income tax changes that are designed to improve fairness. It reduces compensation that can be taken into account for purposes of benefits and contributions under qualified retirement plans to $150,000 (1993 cap is $235,840). This change will better target the benefit of tax deferral to middle income Americans and will raise almost $1 billion in 1997. It also disallows deductions for closing costs and meals incurred as a result of moving to a new residence. These expenses that are generally not deductible for other taxpayers should improve the equity of the tax system. The change in moving expense rules raises $0.5 billion in 1997."

Source: Executive Office of the President of the United States, Office of Management and Budget, *A Vision of Change for America* (Washington, D.C.: U.S. Government Printing Office, February 1993), p. 103.

★ 474 ★

Taxes

Business Tax Changes, 1993-1998

"The investment tax credits, the corporate alternative minimum tax changes and the favorable capital gains provisions in the stimulus and investment packages will spur investment and encourage the growth of all business, especially small business. At the same time however, large highly profitable companies will have to pay a greater portion of their net earnings in taxes. The package increases the corporate tax rate from 34 percent to 36 percent for taxable income above $10 million, raising $6 billion in 1997. Of the 2.2 million corporations, only about 2,700 large corporations will be affected by this proposal in any year.

"The [Clinton] package also contains a proposal to reduce the deductible portion of meals and entertainment from 80 percent to 50 percent. This will increase revenues by almost $4 billion in 1997. Meals and entertainment expenses involve a substantial component of personal consumption. A 50 percent split reasonably balances the mixed benefits of meals and entertainment expenses.

"The plan would deny certain other business deductions, including the deduction for compensation in excess of $1 million, unless linked to productivity. The goal is to encourage corporations to focus more carefully on their compensation policies and to shift business spending from excess pay to investment. This proposal would raise $.2 billion in 1997."

Source: Executive Office of the President of the United States, Office of Management and Budget, *A Vision of Change for America* (Washington, D.C.: U.S. Government Printing Office, February 1993), p. 104.

★ 475 ★

Taxes

Motor Fuel Taxes Added by Federal Region and Year, 1992-2010

"Retail prices for gasoline and diesel fuel include Federal and State taxes but do not include local and city taxes. The taxes added include a special 5-cent Federal tax implemented by the Budget Reconciliation Act of 1990 which is assumed to be renewed for the post-1995 time period. The amount of taxes are identical among scenarios and, with the exception of Region 9, remain constant throughout the forecast period. In Region 9, taxes are increased 1 cent per gallon for each year through 1995, reflecting scheduled increases in the October 1990 California tax bill."

[1991 dollars per million Btu]

Sector/Product	1	2	3	4	5	6	7	8	9	10
Current Taxes (1992)										
Diesel	2.99	3.07	2.94	2.48	3.91	2.80	2.53	2.69	3.00	2.80
Gasoline	3.05	2.78	2.80	2.42	2.86	2.68	2.47	2.71	2.86	2.87
1993 Additions to Current										
Diesel	0.00	0.00	0.00	0.00	0.00	0.00	0.00	0.00	0.19	0.00
Gasoline	0.00	0.00	0.00	0.00	0.00	0.00	0.00	0.00	0.22	0.00
1994 through 2010 Additions to Current										
Diesel	0.00	0.00	0.00	0.00	0.00	0.00	0.00	0.00	0.25	0.00
Gasoline	0.00	0.00	0.00	0.00	0.00	0.00	0.00	0.00	0.29	0.00

Source: U.S. Department of Energy, Energy Information Administration, *Assumptions for the Annual Energy Outlook 1993* (Washington, D.C.: U.S. Government Printing Office, 1993), pp. 57-8. *Primary source:* Aggregated from Energy Information Administration, *Petroleum Marketing Monthly*, August 1992, Table EN1; California Proposition Nos. 108 and 111. *Note:* Btu=British thermal units.

★ 476 ★

Taxes

National Environmental Markups for Gasoline and Distillate Fuel Oil by Sector and Fuel Type, 1992-2010

"[Retail prices in entry 475 above] include environmental markups which reflect cost increases resulting from several environmental regulations enacted since 1989. Incremental costs estimates are used only for regulations that specify dates and extent of coverage. As described below, the environmental markups include incremental costs resulting from portions of the Resource Conservation and Recovery Act (RCRA), the Superfund Amendments and Reauthorization Act of (SARA), the Oil Pollution Act, the Clean Air Act (CAA), and the Clean Air Act Amendments of 1990 (CAA90)."

[1991 dollars per million Btu]

Year	All Products	Diesel Fuel	Gasoline
1992	0.04	0.12	0.21
1993	0.04	0.45	0.22
1994	0.04	0.45	0.23
1995	0.01	0.42	0.36

[Continued]

★ 476 ★

National Environmental Markups for Gasoline and Distillate Fuel Oil by Sector and Fuel Type, 1992-2010

[Continued]

Year	All Products	Diesel Fuel	Gasoline
2000	0.00	0.41	0.50
2005	0.00	0.41	0.69
2010	0.00	0.41	0.81

Source: U.S. Department of Energy, Energy Information Administration, *Assumptions for the Annual Energy Outlook 1993* (Washington, D.C.: U.S. Government Printing Office, 1993), pp. 58-9. *Primary source:* Markups derived from U.S. Environmental Protection Agency (EPA), Office of Underground Storage Tanks, "Regulatory Impact Analysis of Technical Standards for Underground Storage Tanks," Exhibit ES-1 (Washington, D.C. August 24, 1988); EPA, final rule "Regulation of Fuels and Fuel Additives: Fuel Quality Regulations for Highway Diesel Fuel Sold in 1993 and Later Calendar Years" (Washington, D.C. 8 August 1990), pp. 7, 19; *Federal Register*, Vol. 55, no. 112, 11 June 1990, p. 23663; American Petroleum Institute, *Costs of Congressional Reformulated Gasoline*, Editorial and Special Issues Department, Public Affairs Group, 4 May 1990; 101st Congress, Second Session, *Congressional Record*, 26 October 1990, p. 12857; Congressional and Budget Office, *Clean Fuels for Conventional Vehicles: Implications and Proposed Standards*, September 1990, p. 1. *Note:* Btu=British thermal units.

★ 477 ★

Taxes

Reduction of U.S. Budget Deficit Resulting from Gas Tax, 1993-1997

[A] broad alliance of economists, business leaders and Clinton's own designated cabinet members is lining up behind the gas tax. Executives of the Big Three auto makers reiterated their support for such a tax during their meeting with Clinton last week, mainly because they prefer the tax to increasingly stringent fuel-efficiency regulations. Several economic studies now suggest that the levy's chief drawback—a brutal burden on the poor and middle class—may be less onerous than is widely thought.

"The gas tax has political staying power because it offers Clinton a vast new revenue pool. Increasing the federal tax, now 14.1 cents per gallon, by 50 cents over five years would produce $46 billion in new annual revenues by 1997, according to estimates by *U.S. News* and DRI/McGraw-Hill. That would cut the budget deficit by 15 percent—nearly one third of Clinton's stated goal—without trimming a single program or entitlement. Put another way, it's enough money to pay for almost all of the president-elect's ambitious programs in infrastructure, worker training, education reform and community development without raising another dime of taxes. By the fifth year, a 50-cent increase would cost the average American family $550 a year, assuming no change in driving habits. But because gas prices have dropped sharply since the early 1980s, that would still leave a gallon of gas cheaper than it was 10 years ago."

[Percent]

Year	
1993	0.9%
1994	5.0%
1995	8.8%
1996	12.5%
1997	15.1%

Source: David Hage and Sara Collins, "Driving Down the Deficit," in *U.S. News & World Report*, 18 January 1993, pp. 58-9. *Primary source: USN&WR*—basic data: DRI/McGraw-Hill and *USN&WR* estimates.

★ 478 ★

Taxes

Gas Tax Revenue Losses Due to Telecommuting, 1992-2002

[Millions of dollars]

	1992 Foregone Taxes	1997 5 year Foregone Taxes	2002 10 year Foregone Taxes
Upper Bound	$57.5	$199.2	$540.8
Lower Bound	$57.5	$153.2	$270.3

Source: U.S. Department of Transportation, *Transportation Implications of Telecommuting*, (Washington, D.C.: U.S. Government Printing Office, April, 1993), p. 75.

★ 479 ★

Taxes

New Tax Revenues from Income, Payroll, and Tobacco Products, 1995-2000

[Billions of dollars]

New tax revenues	Clinton Administration	Congressional Budget Office	Lewin-VHI	CBO vs. Clinton Administration $ (%)	Lewin-VHI vs. Clinton Administration $ (%)	Lewin-VHI vs. CBO $ (%)
Excise tax on tobacco products	$67.4	$68.5	$65.8	$1.1 (1.6%)	-$1.6 (2.4%)	-$2.7 (-3.9%)
Effects of universal coverage, cost containment, and premium subsidy	28.4	24	-3.7	-4.4 (-15.5)	-32.1 (-113.0)	-27.7 (-115.4)
Assessment for corporate alliances	24.2	8	33.0	-16.2 (66.9)	8.8 (36.4)	25.0 (312.5)
Assessment for retiree subsidy	11.4	13	12.1	1.6 (14)	0.7 (6.1)	-0.9 (-6.9)

Source: U.S. Congress, Office of Technology Assessment, *Understanding Estimates of the Impact of Health Reform on the Federal Budget* (Washington, D.C.: U.S. Government Printing Office, July 1994), p. 23. *Primary source:* Office of Technology Assessment, 1994, based on data from LewinnVHI, Inc., *The Financial Impact of the Health Security Act* (Fairfax, VA; 9 December 1993); U.S. Congress, Congressional Budget Office, *An Analysis of the Administration's Health Proposal* (Washington, DC; February 1994); U.S. Executive Office of the President, Office of Management and Budget, *Budget of the U.S. Government FY95* (Washington, DC: U.S. Government Printing Office, February 1994). *Note:* CBO = Congressional Budget Office.

★ 480 ★

Taxes

Decrease in Personal Tax Rates by Deferring Income, 1996-2011

"Even if taxes rise in the years ahead, deferring income today may still be a smart move. A study by Arthur Andersen shows that rates would have to increase dramatically for your future tax payment to exceed what you gain by deferring income and taxes now."

[Taxes in points]

If you defer income to...	You win unless tax rates rise by more than...
1996	6
2001	12
2007	18
2011	22

Source: Terence P. Pare, "Last-Minute Moves to Lower Your Taxes," in *Fortune*, 18 November 1991, p. 42. *Primary source:* Arthur Andersen.

★ 481 ★

Taxes

Annual Added Revenues from Taxing Capital Gains Held until Death, 1994- 1997

"Under current law, the amount a decreased person's property has appreciated isn't subject to capital gains taxes, and the person's heirs have to pay such taxes only on any appreciation that occurs after the date of death. In an interview with *The Wall Street Journal* [in December 1992], Mr. Clinton said he probably would look at eliminating this provision in an effort to attack the bulging budget deficit. Although he didn't offer any specifics, any Clinton proposal would surely include provisions to soften the impact on certain hard-hit groups."

[Billions of dollars]

	1994	1995	1996	1997
Include gains in last tax return of decreased	$3.2	$3.9	$4.6	$5.3
Enact supplemental 10% estate tax	0.5	0.5	0.6	0.6
Require that the "basis" of the decreased be carried over with the inherited asset	--[1]	1.4	1.7	2.0

Source: Rick Wartzman, "Clinton Suggestion of Possible Capital Gains Tax Upon Death Stirs Ire Among Powerful Interests," in *The Wall Street Journal*, 5 January 1993, p. A16. *Primary sources:* Congressional Budget Office; Joint Committee on Taxation. *Note:* 1. Less than $50 million.

★ 482 ★

Taxes

Government Revenues from Value-Added Tax (VAT), 1994-1998

"[The strongest selling point of the Value-added tax (VAT)] is its proven ability to produce gushers of revenue. A 5% tax applied over a broad base of goods and services could raise more than $100 billion a year by 1996. That's as much as the entire corporate income tax generates now. Exempt food, housing, and medical care, as many European countries do, and a 5% VAT would still produce nearly $60 billion annually after three years."

[Billions of dollars]

Year	5% Rate	5% Rate excluding, food, housing, and medical care
1994	0	0
1995	70	35
1996	105	55
1997	115	60
1998	125	65

Source: Rob Norton, "The Tax Idea That Won't Go Away," in *Fortune*, 17 May 1993, p. 77. *Primary source:* Joint Committee on Taxation.

★ 483 ★

Taxes

Government Revenues from Increased Taxation of Affluent Americans and Increasing Income Subject to the Medicare Payroll Tax, 1994-1998

"The president expects to collect $118 billion over the next four years by increasing marginal tax rates to 36% from 31% for couples with taxable incomes above $140,000 and to 39.6% for those with incomes above $250,000 and making them pay more in Medicare payroll taxes."

[Billions of dollars]

Year	
1994	30
1995	25
1996	29
1997	32
1998	34

Source: David Wessel, "It's the Argument Neither Party Wants to Hear: Increasing Tax Rates on the Rich Won't Work," in *The Wall Street Journal*, 27 April 1993, p. A22. *Primary source:* Treasury Department.

★ 484 ★

Taxes

Recovered Tax Expenditures from Repealing Cafeteria Plan for Health Benefits, 1995-2000

"In addition to new tax revenues from a higher excise tax on tobacco products, and potentially, from higher incomes and wages, the Health Security Act would attempt to raise additional funds from recovering certain health-related tax expenditures under current law. For example, the act would no longer allow the use of tax-exempt cafeteria plans for employer-sponsored health benefits. In addition, after 2004 the tax exclusion for health insurance premiums would be limited to the costs of the standard benefit package."

[Billions of dollars]

Clinton Administration	$31.4
Congressional Budget Office	$10
Lewin-VHI	$17.0
CBO vs. Clinton Administration $ (%)	-$21.4 (-68.2%)
Lewin-VHI vs. Clinton Administration $ (%)	-$14.4 (-45.9%)
Lewin-VHI vs. CBO $ (%)	$7.0 (70.0%)

Source: U.S. Congress, Office of Technology Assessment, *Understanding Estimates of the Impact of Health Reform on the Federal Budget* (Washington, D.C.: U.S. Government Printing Office, July 1994), p. 26. *Primary sources:* Office of Technology Assessment, 1994; based on data from Lewin-VHI, Inc., *The Financial Impact of the Health Security Act* (Fairfax, VA; 9 December 1993); U.S. Congress, Congressional Budget Office, *An Analysis of the Administration's Health Proposal* (Washington, DC; February 1994); U.S. Executive Office of the President, Office of Management and Budget, *Budget of the U.S. Government FY95* (Washington, DC: U.S. Government Printing Office, February 1994). *Note:* CBO = Congressional Budget Office.

★ 485 ★

Taxes

Increase in Future Generations' Net Payment of Taxes

"'Future generations...are estimated to make a 111% larger net payment [in taxes] to the government, on average, than those born in 1991,' the budget says.

"The average tax rate for all those generations-yet-to-come will be about 71% of income unless something changes, the budget office says. The analysis also illustrates the effects of two potential policies: a strict cap on the growth of spending on government benefits and stiff tax increase. Both would raise the tax rates on those now alive and lower the tax rates on those yet to come. But compared with a spending cap, the tax increase would fall much more heavily on today's children than on their parents, who would enjoy much the same retirement and health benefits as today's elderly."

Source: David Wessel, "Budget Office, Using Unlikely Script, Estimates Tax Bite for Yet-to-Be-Born," in *The Wall Street Journal*, 7 January 1993, p. A2.

Prices

★ 486 ★

Effect of Long-term Interest Rates on Consumer Prices, 1997

"[The] bond market remains a mystery to many Americans. But the impact of falling interest rates is as tangible as a cheap mortgage or a surge in auto sales. To gauge this impact, *U.S. News* asked The WEFA Group, a prominent forecasting firm, to stimulate the effects of lower interest rates using its econometric model of the American economy..."

[According to the WEFA group, prices will stabilize. With]:

—6% long-term interest rates, the inflation rate inches its way up to 4.1 percent by 1977.

—6.5% long-term interest rates, the inflation rate moves to 4 percent in 1997.

—7.5% long-term interest rates, the inflation rate hovers at 3.9 percent in 1997."

Source: David Hage, "Tonic for A Sick Economy," in *U.S. News & World Report*, 23 August 1993, pp. 44, 46.

★ 487 ★

Prices

Changes in Consumer Food Prices, 1991-2000

[Percent]

CPI category	Selected history		1995	1996	1997	1998	1999	2000
	1991	1992						
All food	2.9	1.3	2.8	3.1	2.9	3.2	3.1	3.2
Food away from home	3.4	2.1	3.2	3.3	3.5	3.5	3.4	3.4
Food at home	2.6	0.8	2.5	3.0	2.6	2.9	3.0	3.0
Meats	3.1	-1.4	1.7	3.3	3.0	3.4	4.1	3.6
Beef and veal	2.8	-0.1	0.8	1.4	2.1	3.9	5.0	4.4
Pork	3.3	-4.7	4.0	7.5	5.0	2.5	2.0	1.8
Other meats	3.7	0.2	0.8	1.4	2.2	3.9	4.9	4.4
Poultry	-0.8	0.4	2.5	-0.6	-0.4	1.0	1.9	1.7
Fish and seafood	1.1	2.5	2.6	2.7	2.9	2.9	2.9	2.8
Eggs	-2.3	-10.6	2.6	9.2	-4.8	8.1	-3.5	3.9
Dairy products	-1.1	2.7	2.7	3.7	3.2	2.8	3.0	2.6

[Continued]

★ 487 ★

Changes in Consumer Food Prices, 1991-2000

[Continued]

CPI category	Selected history		1995	1996	1997	1998	1999	2000
	1991	1992						
Fats and oils	4.3	-1.3	1.7	2.6	2.3	2.0	2.4	2.3
Fruits and vegetables	4.7	-0.3	2.6	2.6	2.8	2.8	3.0	3.2
Sugar and sweets	3.7	2.9	2.8	2.1	2.7	3.3	2.5	2.5
Cereals and bakery products	4.1	3.8	3.1	3.0	2.9	3.4	2.7	3.2
Nonalcoholic beverages	0.5	0.3	2.5	2.5	2.4	2.4	2.7	2.6
Other prepared foods	4.5	2.1	3.3	3.2	2.5	2.4	3.6	2.9

Source: U.S. Department of Agriculture, World Agricultural Outlook Board, Interagency Agricultural Projections Committee, *Long-term Agricultural Baseline Projections* (Washington, D.C.: U.S. Government Printing Office, October 1993), p. 46. *Note:* CPI = Consumer Price Index.

★ 488 ★

Prices

Consumer Food Price Indexes, 1991-2000

[Consumer Price Index, 1982-84 = 100; expenditures in billions of dollars]

CPI category	Selected history		1995	1996	1997	1998	1999	2000
	1991	1992						
Consumer price indexes:								
All food	136.2	138.0	148.1	152.7	157.2	162.2	167.3	172.6
Food away from home	137.9	140.8	153.4	158.4	164.0	169.7	175.5	181.4
Food at home	135.8	136.9	145.6	149.9	153.8	158.3	163.1	168.0
Meats	132.5	130.7	134.4	138.8	143.0	147.9	153.9	159.4
Beef and veal	132.4	132.3	133.1	135.0	137.9	143.3	150.4	157.0
Pork	134.1	127.8	139.3	149.7	157.2	161.1	164.3	167.2
Other meats	131.5	131.7	131.6	133.4	136.4	141.7	148.7	155.2
Poultry	131.5	132.0	137.4	136.6	136.0	137.4	140.0	142.4
Fish and seafood	148.3	152.0	164.1	168.5	173.4	178.5	183.6	188.8
Eggs	121.2	108.3	114.9	125.5	119.5	129.5	124.7	129.6
Dairy products	125.1	128.5	135.0	140.0	144.5	148.5	153.0	157.0
Fats and oils	131.7	130.0	136.5	140.0	143.2	146.0	149.5	153.0
Fruits and vegetables	155.9	155.5	164.5	168.8	173.6	178.5	183.8	189.7
Sugar and sweets	129.3	133.1	146.0	149.0	153.0	158.0	162.0	166.0
Cereals and bakery products	145.8	151.3	167.0	172.0	177.0	183.0	188.0	194.0
Nonalcoholic beverages	114.1	114.4	121.0	124.0	127.0	130.0	133.5	137.0
Other prepared foods	137.1	140.0	155.0	160.0	164.0	168.0	174.0	179.0
Food expenditures:								
Total food	570.4	592.4	675.0	706.4	739.7	775.2	811.7	849.9

[Continued]

★ 488 ★

Consumer Food Price Indexes, 1991-2000

[Continued]

CPI category	Selected history		1995	1996	1997	1998	1999	2000
	1991	1992						
At home	312.7	324.2	365.4	380.5	395.8	412.4	429.3	447.0
Away from home	257.7	268.2	309.6	325.9	343.9	362.8	382.4	402.9

Source: U.S. Department of Agriculture, World Agricultural Outlook Board, Interagency Agricultural Projections Committee, *Long-term Agricultural Baseline Projections* (Washington, D.C.: U.S. Government Printing Office, October 1993), p. 45. *Note:* CPI=Consumer Price Index.

★ 489 ★

Prices

Value of 1994 Cars, 1997

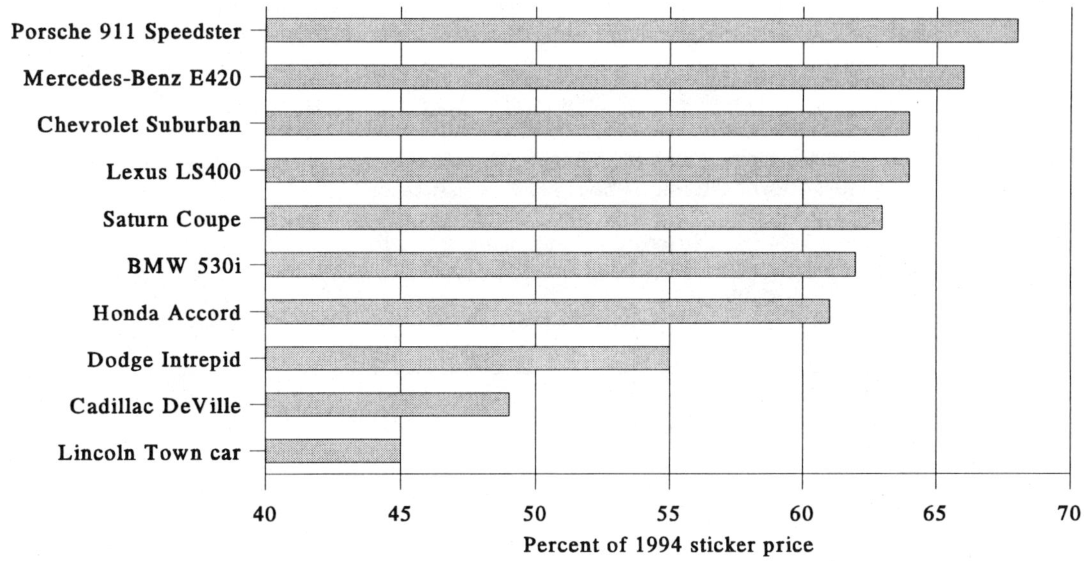

"Based on the percentage of the sticker price retained after three years of use, Mercedes Benz, Porsche, Lexus, and Honda stand up best. They are followed by Acura, Toyota, Nissan, and Mazda."

[Percent of 1994 sticker price]

	What '94 cars will be worth in '97 as a percent of today's sticker price
Lincoln Town car	45
Cadillac DeVille	49
Dodge Intrepid	55
Honda Accord	61
BMW 530i	62
Saturn Coupe	63
Lexus LS400	64
Chevrolet Suburban	64
Mercedes-Benz E420	66
Porsche 911 Speedster	68

Source: Alex Taylor III, "Have You Driven a (Used) Ford Lately?" in *Fortune*, 21 March 1994, p. 14. *Primary source:* Automotive Lease Guide.

★ 490 ★

Prices

Cost of Leasing versus Buying an Automobile, 1994-1997

"This year, nearly one out of every four customers will lease a new car rather than buy one—more than twice the number who leased three years ago, according to CNW Marketing/Research, a Bandon, Ore., firm that tracks the car market...

"Some one million short-term leases will expire [in 1994], another 1.5 million next year and 2.2 million in 1996, predicts CNW. Dealers anxious to unload this glut are already slashing finance rates for used-car buyers, extending warranties and/or offering 24-hour roadside assistance."

[Cost of a 1994 Honda Accord LX automatic sedan, list price $18,500, when leased for 2 1/2 years, versus cost when bought with an 8.4% loan over a three-year period]

	Lease	Buy
Term	30 months	36 months
Initial payment	$250 (deposit)	$3,700 (down payment)
Monthly payments	$239	$446
TOTAL COST	$7,170	$19,756

Source: Kerry Hannon, "Is Car Leasing a Good Deal for You?" in *Working Woman*, November 1994, p. 26. *Primary source:* Working Woman Research; Bank Rate Monitor.

★ 491 ★

Prices

Decrease in Personal Health Care Prices Despite Increase in Revenues per Physician, 1980-2000

"The best way to cure what ails health care is to unleash the free market. The market *does* work. Prices are already falling dramatically in large cities where an ample supply of doctors are competing hard for business."

[Revenues per physician in thousands of 1992 dollars]

Year	Revenues per physician
1980	$190
1992	$280
2000	$430

Source: Shawn Tully, "Why We Need More Doctors," in *Fortune*, 23 August 1993, p. 73. *Primary source:* American Medical Association; Health Care Financing Administration. *Note:* HMO = Health Maintenance Organization.

Spending

★ 492 ★

Federal Government Expenditures, 1979-2005-I

[Billions of current dollars]

Category	1979	1989	1992	2005 Low	2005 Moderate	2005 High
Expenditures	520.3	1,181.6	1,459.3	3,315.8	3,392.2	3,366.2
Purchases of goods and services	179.3	401.6	448.8	704.8	834.5	927.2
Transfer payments	209.7	471.5	624.5	1,395.7	1,487.8	1,544.2
Grants-in aid to State and local governments	80.5	118.2	171.4	594.9	620.2	654.3
Net interest paid	42.1	164.7	187.1	566.5	395.1	184.8
Subsidies less current surplus	8.6	25.5	27.5	53.9	54.6	55.7
Federal surplus	-15.7	-122.3	-276.3	-386.9	-1.2	402.0
			Percent distribution			
Expenditures	100.0	100.0	100.0	100.0	100.0	100.0
Purchases of goods and services	34.5	34.0	30.8	21.3	24.6	27.5
Transfer payments	40.3	39.9	42.8	42.1	43.9	45.9
Grants-in-aid to State and local governments	15.5	10.0	11.7	17.9	18.3	19.4
Net interest paid	8.1	13.9	12.8	17.1	11.6	5.5
Subsidies less current surplus	1.7	2.0	1.9	1.6	1.6	1.7

Source: U.S. Department of Labor, Bureau of Labor Statistics, *The American Work Force: 1992-2005* (Washington, D.C.: U.S. Government Printing Office, April 1994), p. 21. *Primary source:* Historical data, Bureau of Economic Analysis; projected data, Bureau of Labor Statistics.

★ 493 ★

Spending

Federal Government Expenditures, 1979-2005-II

[Billions of current dollars]

Category	Average annual rates of change 1979-89	1989-92	1979-92	1992-2005 Low	1992-2005 Moderate	1992-2005 High
Expenditures	8.5	7.3	8.3	6.5	6.7	6.6
Purchases of goods and services	8.4	3.8	7.3	3.5	4.9	5.7
Transfer payments	8.4	9.8	8.8	6.4	6.9	7.2
Grants-in aid to State and local governments	4.1	13.2	6.0	10.0	10.4	10.9
Net interest paid	14.6	4.3	12.2	8.9	5.9	-.1
Subsidies less current surplus	11.5	2.5	9.4	5.3	5.4	5.6

Source: U.S. Department of Labor, Bureau of Labor Statistics, *The American Work Force: 1992-2005* (Washington, D.C.: U.S. Government Printing Office, April 1994), p. 21. *Primary source:* Historical data, Bureau of Economic Analysis; projected data, Bureau of Labor Statistics.

★ 494 ★

Spending

State and Local Expenditures, 1979-2005-I

"Fiscal belt tightening will remain a fact of life for State and local governments throughout the next 13 years, especially with regard to social programs. This will be necessary to maintain balanced budgets in the face of increasing needs for public safety expenditures and incarceration facilities. The Bureau has further assumed that real grants-in-aid will grow at a rate of 2.8 percent over the next 13 years in response to infrastructure maintenance needs and expansion of the Medicaid program. As a result, State and local spending on goods and services are expected to maintain a constant share of GDP over the 13-year projection period—11.6 percent, in real terms."

[Billions of current dollars]

Category	1979	1989	1992	2005 Low	2005 Moderate	2005 High
Expenditures	305.5	636.7	830.6	2,234.6	2,449.6	2,684.9
Purchases of goods and services	269.2	573.6	683.0	1,573.9	1,828.6	1,999.8
Transfer payments	57.2	143.6	228.6	851.1	823.8	928.0
Net interest paid	-13.3	-52.3	-46.0	-100.1	-121.3	-152.7
Subsidies less current surplus	-5.7	-20.1	-24.8	-59.2	-58.7	-59.2
State and local surplus	25.1	44.8	7.2	61.5	116.2	133.4
Percent distribution						
Expenditures	100.0	100.0	100.0	100.0	100.0	100.0
Purchases of goods and services	88.1	90.1	82.2	70.4	74.6	74.5
Transfer payments	18.7	22.6	27.5	38.1	33.6	34.6
Nct interest paid	-4.4	-8.2	-5.5	-4.5	-5.0	-5.7
Subsidies less current surplus	-1.9	-3.2	-3.0	-2.6	-2.4	-2.2

Source: U.S. Department of Labor, Bureau of Labor Statistics, *The American Work Force: 1992-2005* (Washington, D.C.: U.S. Government Printing Office, April 1994), p. 22. *Primary source:* Historical data, Bureau of Economic Analysis; projected data, Bureau of Labor Statistics.

★ 495 ★

Spending

State and Local Expenditures, 1979-2005-II

"Fiscal belt tightening will remain a fact of life for State and local governments throughout the next 13 years, especially with regard to social programs. This will be necessary to maintain balanced budgets in the face of increasing needs for public safety expenditures and incarceration facilities. The Bureau has further assumed that real grants-in-aid will grow at a rate of 2.8 percent over the next 13 years in response to infrastructure maintenance needs and expansion of the Medicaid program. As a result, State and local spending on goods and services are expected to maintain a constant share of GDP over the 13-year projection period—11.6 percent, in real terms."

[Billions of current dollars]

Category	Average annual rates of change					
	1979-89	1989-92	1979-92	1992-2005 Low	1992-2005 Moderate	1992-2005 High
Expenditures	7.6	9.3	8.0	7.9	9.8	9.4
Purchases of goods and services	7.9	6.0	7.4	6.6	7.9	8.6
Transfer payments	9.6	16.8	11.2	10.6	10.4	11.4

Source: U.S. Department of Labor, Bureau of Labor Statistics, *The American Work Force: 1992-2005* (Washington, D.C.: U.S. Government Printing Office, April 1994), p. 22. *Primary source:* Historical data, Bureau of Economic Analysis; projected data, Bureau of Labor Statistics.

★ 496 ★

Spending

Estimates of New Tax Expenditures, 1995-2000

[Billions of dollars]

Clinton Administration	$8.9
Congressional Budget Office	$8
Lewin-VHI	$7.9
CBO vs. Clinton Administration $ (%)	-$0.9 (-10.1%)
Lewin-VHI vs. Clinton Administration $ (%)	-$1.0 (-11.2%)
Lewin-VHI vs. CBO $ (%)	-$0.1 (1.3%)

Source: U.S. Congress, Office of Technology Assessment, *Understanding Estimates of the Impact of Health Reform on the Federal Budget* (Washington, D.C.: U.S. Government Printing Office, July 1994), p. 28. *Primary source:* Office of Technology Assessment, 1994; based on data from Lewin-VHI, Inc., *The Financial Impact of the Health Security Act* (Fairfax, VA; 9 December 1993); U.S. Congress, Congressional Budget Office, *An Analysis of the Administration's Health Proposal* (Washington, D.C. February 1994); U.S. Executive Office of the President, Office of Management and Budget, *Budget of the U.S. Government FY95* (Washington, DC: U.S. Government Printing Office, February 1994). *Note:* CBO = Congressional Budget Office.

★ 497 ★

Spending

Annual Growth Rate in Real Government Pension Expenditures for Selected Countries, 1960-2025

"The historical and projected pension cost growth rates for the United States are a bit lower than average for the developed world. Between 1960 and 1980, real (i.e., inflation-adjusted) U.S. government pension costs grew by an average of 6.2 percent per year. Between 1980 and 2025, these costs are projected to grow at an average real rate of 2.5 percent. A similar slowdown in growth can be seen in other developed countries."

Country	1960-1980	1980-2025
United States	6.2	2.5
France	8.2	2.7
West Germany	4.9	2.5
Italy	8.5	3.6
United Kingdom	4.8	2.4
Canada	7.2	2.6
Japan	14.1	5.9

Source: U.S. Senate Special Committee on Aging, American Association of Retired Persons, Federal Council on the Aging, U.S. Administration on Aging, *Aging America: Trends and Projections* (Washington, D.C.: U.S. Government Printing Office, 1991), p. 268. *Primary source:* International Monetary Fund (IMF), *Aging and Social Expenditure in the Major Industrial Countries, 1980-2025*, by Peter S. Heller, Richard Hemming, Peter W. Kohnert, and IMF Staff. Occasional Paper 47 (September 1986).

★ 498 ★

Spending

World Spending on Promotional Advertising and Direct Mail, 1990-1996

"[Robert Coen of McCann-Erickson, an advertising agency], believes American advertising spending will rise by 7.2% this year, meaning that its share of (GDP) will increase once again. Worldwide, advertising spending (including direct mail and promotion) is set to grow by 5.2% this year and 6.7% in 1995, according to Zenith, a media-buying company owned by Britain's Saatchi & Saatchi. Although much of the growth will come from America and Britain, continental Europe's ad market is also showing signs of life. And in East Asia and Latin America, advertising spending is roaring ahead, though from small beginnings."

[Billions of dollars]

Year	Advertising	Direct mail, promotion expenditure
1990	210	70
1991	220	75
1992	225	80
1993	230	85
1994	240	90
1995	260	95
1996	275	100

Source: "Hubris and Humble Pie," in *The Economist*, 27 August 1994, p. 55. *Primary source:* Zenith Media Worldwide.

★ 499 ★

Spending

National Spending on Durable Goods, 1976-2000

[Money in billions of 1982 dollars; compound growth rate in percent]

Category	1976	1988	2000 (Projected)	1976-1988	1988-2000
Building Components	98.0	120.7	134.5	1.7	0.9
Durables Consumption[A,B]	324.6	574.5	753.1	4.8	2.3
Motor Vehicles and Parts	109.6	182.1	220.6	4.1	1.8
Other Durable Goods[B]	215.0	39.24	532.2	5.2	2.5
Producers' Durables[A]	186.2	364.8	530.1	5.6	3.2
Government Purchases	45.1	113.6	105.6	7.7	-0.6
Defense Durables	30.6	83.8	62.9	8.4	-2.4
Federal Nondefense	1.6	5.3	7.6	10.0	3.0
State & Local Governments	12.9	24.5	35.1	5.3	3.0
Balance of Trade	24.4	-46.2	0.0	N.A.	N.A.

[Continued]

★ 499 ★

National Spending on Durable Goods, 1976-2000

[Continued]

Category	1976	1988	2000 (Projected)	1976-1988	1988-2000
Durables Exports	112.9	236.1	500.0	6.1	6.3
Durables Imports	88.5	282.3	500.0	9.7	4.8

Source: U.S. Congress, Joint Economic Committee, Subcommittee on Technology and National Security, "Demographic Change and the Economy of the Nineties" (Washington, D.C.: U.S. Government Printing Office, December 1991), p. 76. *Primary source:* Norman C. Saunders, "The aggregate structure of the Economy," *Monthly Labor Review* (Bureau of Labor Statistics), November 1989, pp. 13-24. Also the U.S. National Income and Product Accounts and author's estimates. *Notes:* N.A. = Not Applicable. A. These projections for the year 2000 are obtained from BLS (see source above). Other projections are made by the author and elucidate in the text. B. Definitions of these categories are those used by Data Resources, Inc. (DRI) in its macroeconomic model and by BLS. These definitions differ somewhat within the personal consumption category from those of the National Income and Product Accounts.

★ 500 ★

Spending

Consumer Food Expenditures, 1991-2000

[Consumer Price Index, 1982-84 = 100; Food expenditures in billions of dollars]

CPI category	Selected history 1991	Selected history 1992	1995	1996	1997	1998	1999	2000
Consumer price indexes:								
All food	136.2	138.0	148.1	152.7	157.2	162.2	167.3	172.6
Food away from home	137.9	140.8	153.4	158.4	164.0	169.7	175.5	181.4
Food at home	135.8	136.9	145.6	149.9	153.8	158.3	163.1	168.0
Meats	132.5	130.7	134.4	138.8	143.0	147.9	153.9	159.4
Beef and veal	132.4	132.3	133.1	135.0	137.9	143.3	150.4	157.0
Pork	134.1	127.8	139.3	149.7	157.2	161.1	164.3	167.2
Other meats	131.5	131.7	131.6	133.4	136.4	141.7	148.7	155.2
Poultry	131.5	132.0	137.4	136.6	136.0	137.4	140.0	142.4
Fish and seafood	148.3	152.0	164.1	168.5	173.4	178.5	183.6	188.8
Eggs	121.2	108.3	114.9	125.5	119.5	129.2	124.7	129.6
Dairy products	125.1	128.5	135.0	140.0	144.5	148.5	153.0	157.0
Fats and oils	131.7	130.0	136.5	140.0	143.2	146.0	149.5	153.0
Fruits and vegetables	155.9	155.5	164.5	168.8	173.6	178.5	183.8	189.7
Sugar and sweets	129.3	133.1	146.0	149.0	153.0	158.0	162.0	166.0
Cereals and bakery products	145.8	151.3	167.0	172.0	177.0	183.0	188.0	194.0
Nonalcoholic beverages	114.1	114.4	121.0	124.0	127.0	130.0	133.5	137.0
Other prepared foods	137.1	140.0	155.0	160.0	164.0	168.0	174.0	179.0
Food expenditures:								
Total food	570.4	592.4	675.0	706.4	739.7	775.2	811.7	849.9

[Continued]

★ 500 ★

Consumer Food Expenditures, 1991-2000

[Continued]

CPI category	Selected history		1995	1996	1997	1998	1999	2000
	1991	1992						
At home	312.7	324.2	365.4	380.5	395.8	412.4	429.3	447.0
Away from home	257.7	268.2	309.6	325.9	343.9	362.8	382.4	402.9

Source: U.S. Department of Agriculture, World Agricultural Outlook Board, Interagency Agricultural Projections Committee, *Long-term Agricultural Baseline Projections* (Washington, D.C.: U.S. Government Printing Office, October 1993), p. 45.

★ 501 ★

Spending

Consumer Expenditures for Meats, 1991-2000

[Dollars]

	Selected history[1]		1995	1996	1997	1998	1999	2000
	1991	1992						
Beef, dollars per person	192.33	189.53	196.40	199.73	204.94	210.41	215.19	220.88
Percent of income	1.15	1.09	0.98	0.95	0.92	0.90	0.88	0.86
Percent of meat expenditures	51.52	51.35	49.90	49.69	49.76	49.62	49.28	49.07
Pork, dollars per person	106.76	104.07	113.61	116.20	119.17	122.60	126.42	130.29
Percent of income	0.64	0.60	0.57	0.55	0.54	0.53	0.51	0.50
Percent of meat expenditures	28.60	28.19	28.86	28.91	28.93	28.91	28.95	28.95
Broilers, dollars per person	56.27	58.05	64.69	66.53	68.82	71.79	75.34	78.87
Percent of income	0.34	0.33	0.32	0.32	0.31	0.31	0.31	0.31
Percent of meat expenditures	15.07	15.73	16.44	16.55	16.71	16.93	17.25	17.52
Turkeys, dollars per person	17.94	17.47	18.91	19.49	18.96	19.27	19.71	20.09
Percent of income	0.11	0.10	0.09	0.09	0.09	0.08	0.08	0.08
Percent of meat expenditures	4.81	4.73	4.80	4.85	4.60	4.54	4.51	4.46
Total meats, dollars per person	373.30	369.11	393.61	401.95	411.89	424.08	436.67	450.12
Percent of income	2.24	2.13	1.96	1.90	1.86	1.82	1.78	1.74

Source: U.S. Department of Agriculture, World Agricultural Outlook Board, Interagency Agricultural Projections Committee, *Long-term Agricultural Baseline Projections* (Washington, D.C.: U.S. Government Printing Office, October 1993), p. 35. *Notes:* 1. Historical data as of June 1993. Baseline projections shown in this report present one plausible scenario, representative of the long-term direction of the agricultural sector. The projections are a conditional, current law (as of June 1993) scenario with no shocks, based on a special set of assumptions regarding the macroeconomy, the weather, and international developments. The projections were prepared in June 1993, based on policy decisions and other information at the time. The short-term outlook would now differ from that used in these baseline projections, although it is expected that by 1995 the agricultural sector will have adjusted to the near-term disruptions in supply and use.

★ 502 ★

Spending

Consumer Expenditures for Personal Consumption by Method of Payment, 1980-2000

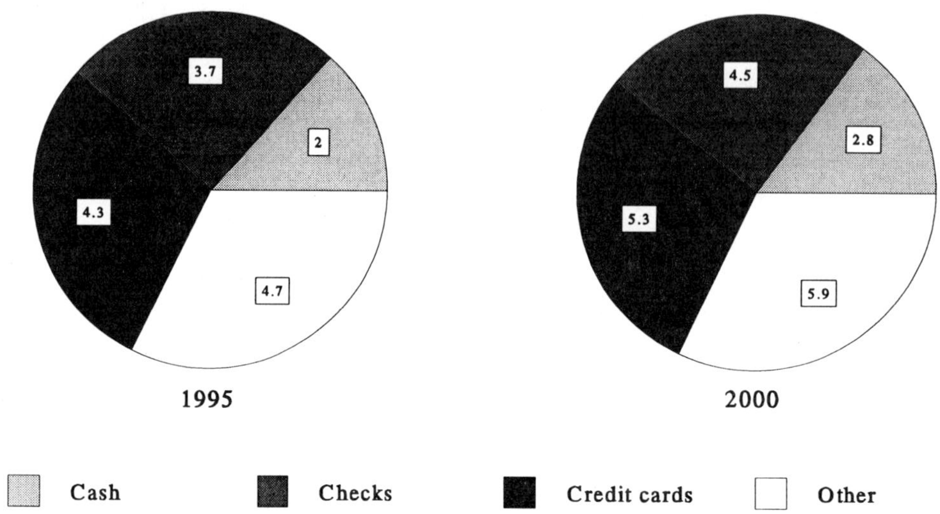

"[Banks] need an alternative source of earnings. After the credit-buying binge of the 1980s, in which consumers accumulated huge financing charges on credit-card purchases, banks are facing a new environment. Consumers are trying to take control of their financial lives by, among other things, eliminating the high finance charges associated with traditional cards."

[Trillions of dollars]

	1980	1985	1990	1995[2]	2000[2]
Cash	1.0	1.3	1.7	2.0	2.8
Checks	1.5	2.2	2.8	3.7	4.5
Credit cards	1.7	2.5	3.3	4.3	5.3
Other[1]	1.8	2.6	3.4	4.7	5.9
TOTAL	6.0	8.6	11.2	14.7	18.5

Source: Steven Lipin, "Banks' Push to Sell Debit Cards is Mostly Uphill," in *The Wall Street Journal*, 19 October 1993, p. B1. *Primary source:* The Nilson Report. *Notes:* 1. Includes debit cards, automatic payments, traveler's checks, ATM payments, home banking, money orders, prepaid cards and food stamps. 2. Estimate.

★ 503 ★

Spending

Number of Households Using Debit Cards for Purchases, 1990-1998

[Millions of households]

Year	
1990	6.5
1991	7.5
1992	8.5
1993	12.3
1994	17.2
1995	22
1996	26.3
1997	31.2
1998	35

Source: Andree Brooks, "These Cards Can Shop Without Using Credit," in *The New York Times*, 28 August 1993, p. 33. *Primary source:* Payment Systems Inc. *Note:* Figures for 1993-1998 are estimates.

★ 504 ★

Spending

Personal Consumption Expenditures by Type, 1979-2005-I

[Billions of 1987 dollars]

Category	1979	1989	1992	2005		
				Low	Moderate	High
Personal consumption	$2,448.3	$3,223.3	$3,341.8	$4,104.6	$4,426.5	$4,699.0
Durables	289.0	440.7	456.6	573.7	649.4	696.7
Motor vehicles and parts	130.5	196.4	182.3	223.3	257.6	265.9
Furniture	101.3	165.8	194.8	252.2	277.0	304.5
Other durables	57.2	78.5	79.5	98.2	114.8	126.3
Nondurables	862.8	1,051.6	1,062.9	1,163.7	1,283.6	1,358.6
Food and beverages	448.00	515.0	520.5	562.1	608.0	638.4
Clothing and shoes	124.1	187.8	193.7	225.5	253.7	266.0
Gasoline and oil	76.4	87.3	83.9	80.7	86.3	87.9
Fuel oil and coal	18.1	11.4	11.9	8.1	9.0	9.2
Other nondurables	196.3	250.2	252.9	287.3	326.6	357.1
Services	1,296.5	1,731.0	1,822.3	2,367.2	2,493.5	2,643.7
Housing	387.9	469.2	484.2	558.2	560.3	622.3
Household operation	162.9	202.6	211.7	252.3	276.5	295.8
Transportation	96.1	123.8	122.7	151.5	170.0	187.6
Medical care	290.9	408.6	449.2	629.2	677.6	705.3
Other services	358.7	526.9	554.4	775.6	809.1	823.7

[Continued]

★ 504 ★

Personal Consumption Expenditures by Type, 1979-2005-I

[Continued]

Category	1979	1989	1992	2005		
				Low	Moderate	High
			Percent distribution			
Personal consumption	100.0	100.0	100.0	100.0	100.0	100.0
Durables	11.8	13.7	13.7	14.0	14.7	14.9
Motor vehicles and parts	5.3	6.1	5.5	5.5	5.8	5.7
Furniture	4.1	5.1	5.8	6.2	6.3	6.5
Other durables	2.3	2.4	2.4	2.4	2.6	2.7
Nondurables	35.2	32.6	31.8	28.3	29.0	28.9
Food and beverages	18.3	16.0	15.6	13.7	13.7	13.6
Clothing and shoes	5.1	5.8	5.8	5.5	5.7	5.7
Gasoline and oil	3.1	2.7	2.5	2.0	1.9	1.9
Fuel and oil and coal	.7	.4	.4	.2	.2	.2
Other nondurables	8.0	7.8	7.6	7.0	7.4	7.6
Services	53.0	53.7	54.5	57.8	56.3	56.2
Housing	15.8	14.6	14.6	13.6	12.7	13.2
Household operation	6.7	6.3	6.3	6.1	6.2	6.3
Transportation	3.9	3.8	3.7	3.7	3.8	4.0
Medical care	11.9	12.7	13.4	15.3	15.3	15.0
Other services	14.7	16.3	16.6	18.9	18.3	17.7

Source: U.S. Department of Labor, Bureau of Labor Statistics, *The American Work Force: 1992-2005* (Washington, D.C.: U.S. Government Printing Office, April 1994), p. 15. *Primary source:* Historical data, Bureau of Economic Analysis; projected data, Bureau of Labor Statistics.

★ 505 ★

Spending

Personal Consumption Expenditures by Type, 1979-2005-II

[Billions of 1987 dollars]

Category	Average annual rates of change					
	1979-89	1989-92	1979-92	1992-2005		
				Low	Moderate	High
Personal consumption	2.8	1.2	2.4	1.6	2.2	2.7
Durables	4.3	1.2	3.6	1.8	2.7	3.3
Motor vehicles and parts	4.2	-2.5	2.6	1.6	2.7	2.9
Furniture	5.1	5.5	5.2	2.0	2.7	3.5
Other durables	3.2	.4	2.6	1.6	2.9	3.6
Nondurables	2.0	.4	1.6	.7	1.5	1.9
Food and beverages	1.4	.4	1.2	.6	1.2	1.6
Clothing and shoes	4.2	1.0	3.5	1.2	2.1	2.5
Gasoline and oil	1.3	-1.3	.7	-.3	.2	.4
Fuel oil and coal	-4.5	1.4	-3.2	-2.9	-2.1	-2.0

[Continued]

★ 505 ★

Personal Consumption Expenditures by Type, 1979-2005-II

[Continued]

Category	Average annual rates of change					
				1992-2005		
	1979-89	1989-92	1979-92	Low	Moderate	High
Other nondurables	2.5	.4	2.0	1.0	2.0	2.7
Services	2.9	1.7	2.7	2.0	2.4	2.9
Housing	1.9	1.1	1.7	1.1	1.1	1.9
Household operation	2.2	1.5	2.0	1.4	2.1	2.6
Transportation	2.6	-.3	1.8	1.6	2.5	3.3
Medical care	3.5	3.2	3.4	2.6	3.2	3.5
Other services	3.9	1.7	3.4	2.6	3.0	3.2

Source: U.S. Department of Labor, Bureau of Labor Statistics, *The American Work Force: 1992-2005* (Washington, D.C.: U.S. Government Printing Office, April 1994), p. 15. *Primary source:* Historical data, Bureau of Economic Analysis; projected data, Bureau of Labor Statistics.

Chapter 12
LABOR, EMPLOYMENT, OCCUPATIONS, AND EARNINGS

General Statistics on Labor

★ 506 ★

Trends in Labor, 1991-2000

"[Forecasters Cetron and Davies project the following trends for world and U.S. labor]:

—The world's labor force will grow by only 1.5% per year during the 1990s—much slower than in recent decades, but fast enough to provide most countries with the workers they need. In contrast, the United States faces shortages of labor in general, and especially of low-wage-rate workers.

—Multinational companies may find their operations handicapped by loss of employees and potential workers to the worldwide epidemic of AIDS, especially in Africa, since many firms rely on indigenous workers.

"The shrinking supply of young workers in many countries means that the overall labor force is aging rapidly.

—Persons aged 25 to 59 accounted for 65% of the world labor force in 1985; almost all growth of the labor force over the next decade will occur in this age group.

—Union membership is declining steadily in the United States. It reached 17.5% in 1986. According to the United Auto Workers, it will fall to 12% by 1995 and to less than 10% by 2000.

—Unionization in Latin America will be about the same as in the 1980s; unionization in the Pacific Rim will remain low; unionization in the developing world as a whole will remain extremely low.

—Increased use of robots, CAD/CAM, and flexible manufacturing complexes can cut a company's work force by up to one-third.

[Continued]

★ 506 ★

Trends in Labor, 1991-2000

[Continued]

—Growing use of artificial intelligence, which improves productivity, and quality, will make the companies adopting it more competitive, but will reduce the need for workers in the highly unionized manufacturing industries.

—People will change residences, jobs, and even occupations more frequently, especially in industrialized countries.

—High-speed MAGLEV trains will allow daily commutes of up to 500 miles.

—The number of people who retrain for new careers, one measure of occupational mobility, has been increasing steadily.

—The new information-based organizational management methods—nonhierarchical, organic systems that can respond quickly to environmental changes—foster greater occupational flexibility and autonomy.

"The wave of new entrepreneurs that appeared in the United States during the 1970s and 1980s is just the leading edge of a much broader trend.

—In 1986, the number of new businesses started in the United States hit a record 700,000. In 1950, there were fewer than 100,000 new business incorporations. A similar trend has appeared in Western Europe, where would-be entrepreneurs were until recently viewed with suspicion. And a new generation of entrepreneurs is growing throughout Eastern Europe and even in Japan.

—From 1970 to 1980, small businesses started by entrepreneurs accounted for most of the 20 million new jobs created in America. In 1987, small businesses accounted for 1 million new jobs, compared with 97,000 in large companies.

"More women will continue to enter the labor force.

—In both developed and developing regions, the percentage of working women has increased since 1950. Women represented 36.5% of the world's labor force in 1985. This growth is expected to continue at a moderate rate, with developed nations showing the fastest increases."

Source: Marvin J. Cetron and Owen Davies, "Trends Shaping the World," in *The Futurist*, September-October 1991, pp. 16-17. *Primary source:* Adapted from Owen and Davies, *Crystal Globe: The Haves and Have-nots of the New World Order* (St. Martin's Press, 1991).

★ 507 ★

General Statistics on Labor

Labor and Robotics

"When envisioning the world's future work force and the functions and tasks people will be expected to perform, contemporary literature has not accorded a large role to or reflected high expectations for the future applications of complex, robotic machines. In today's world, only a few repetitive functions have been allotted to robots. In fact, the leading application areas for robots ordered in the first quarter of 1992 were identified as welding, material handling, and assembly. According to figures published in the May 1992 edition of *Robotics News*, the current U.S. robot population is estimated to be 44,000 units at an average cost of $106,150 per unit, and the trends show increasing orders of greater complexity—with unit shipments increasing by 10 percent—since the first quarter of 1991, and the dollar value of net orders increasing by 13 percent for the same period. A growing recognition of the competitive value of robotics also prompted an increase in international sales, which accounted for 31 percent of new orders.

"Let me, then, make my bias clear. I think we need to imagine and prepare for a world in which robots will get cheaper and better and will come to replace human workers in dangerous, monotonous, and even very highly complex manufacturing as well as some service procedures. We should look forward to a day when humans will not perform most forms of manual labor nor depend on such categories of employment as a means of earning a livelihood. Consequently, we should begin to develop plans for occupational alternatives in order to guide the displaced work force in new directions. The solution to potential unemployment problems will focus on training people who have been replaced by robots to fill new jobs created by the evolution of industry. These solutions will have to be highly differentiated to take account of the categories of jobs robots will most likely assume and the humans they will subsequently relieve. The value of thinking about this now—and expecting that it will happen—is that we can possibly avoid the dislocations and trauma associated in the past transformations of the character of the work force, of the needs of the workplace, and of the venues for making such changes happen."

Source: Allan E. Goodman, *A Brief History of the Future: The United States in a Changing World Order*, Boulder, CO: Westview Press, 1993, p. 92.

★ 508 ★

General Statistics on Labor

Civilian Labor Force by Sex, Age, Race, and Hispanic Origin, 1979-2005

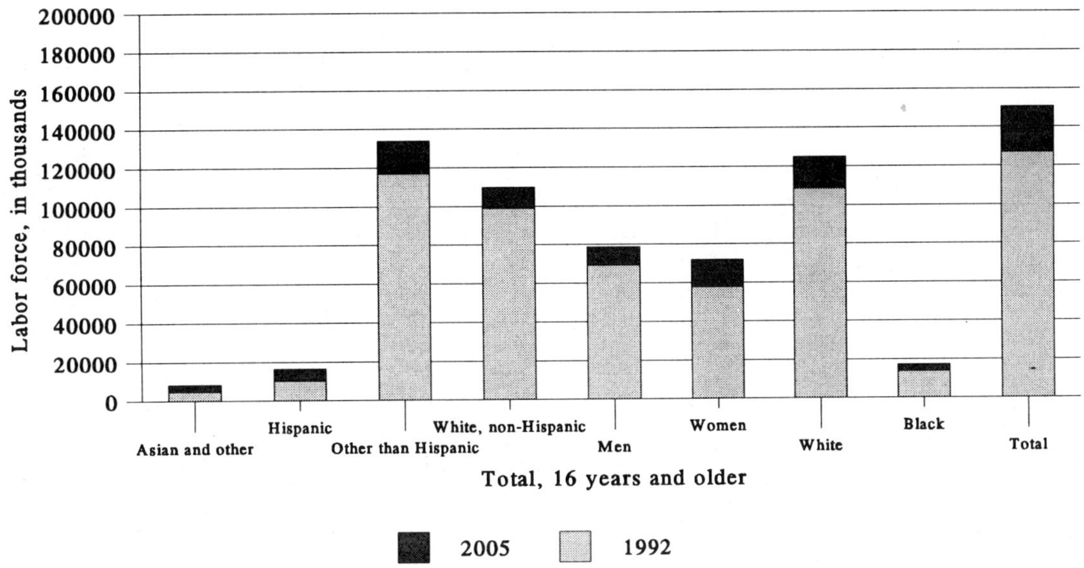

"By 2005, the labor force, those working or looking for work, is expected to number 151 million, an increase of 24 million from 1992, according to the latest projections made by the Bureau of Labor Statistics. This represents an increase of 19 percent, slightly less than the 21-percent increase over the previous 13-year period, 1979 to 1992, when the labor force grew by 22 million. For the first time in years, BLS projections show that the labor force increase in *numerical* terms will be larger in the projected period than in the corresponding historical period.

"The growth in women's labor force is expected to slow down, but will still increase at a faster rate than that of men. Women are projected to represent a slightly greater portion of the labor force in 2005 than in 1992. The number of men in the labor force is projected to grow at a rate similar to their growth in the immediate past. The projected labor force growth will be affected by the aging of the baby-boom generation, those born between 1946 and 1964: in the 1992-2005 period, the labor force of those aged 45 to 64 is expected to grow most rapidly. The different race or Hispanic origin groups have shown—and are projected to continue to show—widely varied growth rates as a consequence of divergent rates of population growth."

Group	Level (thousands)			Change (thousands)		Percent change		Percent distribution			Annual growth rate (percent)	
	1979	1992	2005	1979-92	1992-2005	1979-92	1992-2005	1979	1992	2005	1979-92	1992-2005
Total, 16 years and older	104,962	126,982	150,516	22,020	23,534	21.0	18.5	100.0	100.0	100.0	1.5	1.3
16 to 24	25,407	20,454	24,127	-4,953	3,673	-19.5	18.0	24.2	16.1	16.0	-1.7	1.3
25 to 54	64,520	91,097	105,054	26,577	13,957	41.2	15.3	61.5	71.7	69.8	2.7	1.1
55 and older	15,034	15,432	21,335	398	5,903	2.6	38.3	14.3	12.2	14.2	.2	2.5
Men, 16 years and older	60,726	69,184	78,718	8,458	9,534	13.9	13.8	57.9	54.5	52.3	1.0	1.0
Women, 16 years and older	44,235	57,798	71,798	13,563	14,000	30.7	24.2	42.1	45.5	47.7	2.1	1.7
White, 16 years and older	91,923	108,526	124,847	16,603	16,321	18.1	15.0	87.6	85.5	82.9	1.3	1.1
Black, 16 years and older	10,678	13,891	17,395	3,213	3,504	30.1	25.2	10.2	10.9	11.6	2.0	1.7
Asian and other, 16 years and older[1]	2,361	4,565	8,274	2,204	3,709	93.4	81.2	2.2	3.6	5.5	5.2	4.7
Hispanic, 16 years and older	[2]	10,131	16,581	[2]	6,450	[2]	63.7	[2]	8.0	11.0	4.3[3]	3.9

[Continued]

★ 508 ★

Civilian Labor Force by Sex, Age, Race, and Hispanic Origin, 1979-2005

[Continued]

Group	Level (thousands)			Change (thousands)		Percent change		Percent distribution			Annual growth rate (percent)	
	1979	1992	2005	1979-92	1992-2005	1979-92	1992-2005	1979	1992	2005	1979-92	1992-2005
Other than Hispanic, 16 years and older	[2]	116,851	133,935	[2]	17,084	[2]	14.6	[2]	92.0	89.0	1.1[3]	1.1
White, non-Hispanic	[2]	98,819	109,753	[2]	10,934	[2]	11.1	[2]	77.8	72.9	.9[3]	.8

Source: U.S. Department of Labor, Bureau of Labor Statistics, *The American Work Force: 1992-2005* (Washington, D.C.: U.S. Government Printing Office, April 1994), pp. 29-30. *Notes:* 1. The "Asian and other" group includes a) Asians and Pacific Islanders and b) American Indians and Alaska Natives. The historical data are derived by subtracting "black" from the "black and other" group; projections are made directly, not by subtraction. 2. Data for Hispanic origin is not available before 1980. 3. Data are for 1980-92.

★ 509 ★

General Statistics on Labor

Civilian Labor Force Participation Rates by Sex, Age, Race, and Hispanic Origin, 1979-2005

"The labor force participation rate for men dropped 2.2 percentage points in the 1979-92 period. For the period 1992-2005, participation is projected to drop 0.8 percentage point. Men's labor force participation dropped most rapidly over the 1979-85 period, 1.5 percentage points. But between 1986 and 1992 the decrease was only 0.7 percentage point. BLS projects that for the first part of the 1990's, participation of men will drop by only 0.1 percentage point, partly because the labor force rates of young men are expected to recover some of the decline in their participation. During the latter part of the projection period, labor force participation rates are expected to fall by 0.7 percentage point, as the oldest of the baby-boom generation approaches retirement. All men in the 25 and older age groups, except in the 55-64 age group, have lower labor participation rates in 2005 than in 1992."

Group	Participation rate (thousands)			Level (thousands)			Change (thousands)		Percent change		Annual growth rate (percent)	
	1979	1992	2005	1979	1992	1992-2005	1979-92	1992-2005	1979-92	1992-2005	1979-92	1992-2005
Total, 16 years and older	63.7	66.3	68.8	104,962	126,982	150,516	22,020	23,534	21.0	18.5	1.5	1.3
Men, 16 years and older	77.8	75.6	74.7	60,726	69,184	78,718	8,458	9,534	13.9	13.8	1.0	1.0
16 to 19	61.5	41.1	55.5	5,111	3,457	4,624	-1,564	1,077	-30.6	30.4	-2.8	2.1
20 to 24	86.4	83.3	84.4	8,535	7,242	8,111	-1,293	869	-15.1	12.0	-1.3	.9
25 to 34	95.3	93.8	93.5	16,387	19,355	16,509	2,968	-2,846	18.1	-14.7	1.3	-1.2
35 to 44	95.7	93.8	93.5	11,531	18,162	19,645	6,631	1,483	57.5	8.2	3.6	.6
45 to 54	91.4	90.8	90.2	10,008	12,101	18,065	2,093	5,964	20.9	49.3	1.5	3.1
55 to 64	72.8	67.0	69.7	7,212	6,701	9,560	-511	2,859	-7.1	42.7	-.6	2.8
65 and over	19.9	16.1	14.7	1,943	2,077	2,203	134	126	6.9	6.1	.5	.5
Women, 16 years and older	50.9	57.8	63.2	44,235	57,798	71,798	13,563	14,000	30.7	24.2	2.1	1.7
16 to 24	54.2	49.2	52.4	4,527	3,204	4,222	-1,323	1,018	-29.2	31.8	-2.6	2.1
20 to 24	69.0	71.2	73.6	7,234	6,461	7,169	-773	708	-10.7	11.0	-.9	.8
25 to 34	63.9	74.1	80.7	11,551	15,748	14,839	4,197	-909	36.3	-5.8	2.4	-.5
35 to 44	63.6	76.8	86.2	8,154	15,441	18,643	7,287	3,202	89.4	20.7	5.0	1.5
45 to 54	58.3	72.7	82.8	6,889	10,290	17,354	3,401	7,064	49.4	68.6	3.1	4.1
55 to 64	41.7	46.6	52.4	4,719	5,169	7,825	450	2,656	9.5	51.4	.7	3.2
65 and older	8.3	8.3	8.8	1,161	1,485	1,747	324	262	27.9	17.6	1.9	1.3
White, 16 years and older	63.9	66.7	70.2	91,923	108,526	124,847	16,603	16,321	18.1	15.0	1.3	1.1
Men	78.6	76.4	77.2	53,856	59,830	66,007	5,974	6,177	11.1	10.3	.8	.8
Women	50.5	57.8	62.6	38,067	48,696	58,840	10,629	10,144	27.9	20.8	1.9	1.5
Black, 16 years and older	61.4	63.3	66.2	10,678	13,891	17,395	3,213	3,504	30.1	25.2	2.0	1.7
Men	71.3	69.7	70.5	5,559	6,892	8,355	1,333	1,463	24.0	21.2	1.7	1.5
Women	53.1	58.0	62.6	5,119	6,999	9,040	1,880	2,041	36.7	29.2	2.4	2.0

[Continued]

★ 509 ★

Civilian Labor Force Participation Rates by Sex, Age, Race, and Hispanic Origin, 1979-2005

[Continued]

Group	Participation rate (thousands)			Level (thousands)			Change (thousands)		Percent change		Annual growth rate (percent)	
	1979	1992	2005	1979	1992	1992-2005	1979-92	1992-2005	1979-92	1992-2005	1979-92	1992-2005
Asian and other, 16 years and older[1]	66.1	65.6	66.6	2,361	4,565	8,274	2,204	3,709	93.4	81.2	5.2	4.7
Men	76.6	74.6	74.1	1,311	2,462	4,355	1,151	1,893	87.8	76.9	5.0	4.5
Women	56.4	57.5	59.9	1,049	2,103	3,918	1,054	1,815	100.5	86.3	5.5	4.9
Hispanic, 16 years and older	[2]	66.5	68.4	[2]	10,131	16,581	[2]	6,450	[2]	63.7	4.3[3]	3.9
Men	[2]	80.5	79.5	[2]	6,091	9,628	[2]	3,537	[2]	58.1	4.0[3]	3.6
Women	[2]	52.6	57.3	[2]	4,040	6,953	[2]	2,913	[2]	72.1	4.7[3]	4.3
Other than Hispanic, 16 years and older	[2]	66.3	68.8	[2]	116,851	133,935	[2]	17,084	[2]	14.6	1.2[3]	1.1
Men	[2]	75.1	74.1	[2]	63,093	69,090	[2]	5,997	[2]	9.5	.8[3]	.7
Women	[2]	58.2	64.0	[2]	53,758	64,846	[2]	11,088	[2]	20.6	1.8[3]	1.5
White non-Hispanic, 16 years and older	[2]	66.8	69.4	[2]	98,819	109,753	[2]	10,934	[2]	11.1	1.0[3]	.8
Men	[2]	75.9	74.7	[2]	53,997	57,218	[2]	3,221	[2]	6.0	.5[3]	.4
Women	[2]	58.3	64.4	[2]	44,822	52,535	[2]	7,713	[2]	17.2	1.6[3]	1.2

Source: U.S. Department of Labor, Bureau of Labor Statistics, *The American Work Force: 1992-2005* (Washington, D.C.: U.S. Government Printing Office, April 1994), p. 32. *Notes:* 1. The "Asian and other" group includes a) Asians and Pacific Islanders and b) American Indians and Alaska Natives. The historical data are derived by subtracting "black" from the "black and other" group; projections are made directly, not by subtraction. 2. Data for Hispanic origin is not available before 1980. 3. Data are for 1980-92.

★ 510 ★

General Statistics on Labor

Civilian Labor Force and Projected Entrants and Leavers, 1992-2005

"According to BLS projections, by 2005, 25.1 million men will have joined the 1992 labor force of 69.2 million, and 15.6 million men will have left the labor force, resulting in a labor force in 2005 of 78.7 million men. Similarly, 26.0 million women are expected to enter the labor force over the period 1992-2005, while 12.0 million women are projected to leave. The relatively fewer women leaving the labor force would raise the share of the labor force represented by women from 45.5 percent in 1992 to 47.7 percent in 2005.

"BLS is projecting that the number of entrants over the 1992-2005 period will be 14 percent greater than the 22.8 million who entered during the 1979-92 period. The number projected to leave the labor force would increase even more by 22 percent. Slightly more men than women entered the labor force, 51 percent, compared with 49 percent, in the 1979-92 period. This is reversed in the 1992-2005 period, as women are expected to account for 51 percent of the entrants."

Group	Labor force 1992	Entrants 1992-2005	Leavers 1992-2005	Labor force 2005
Numbers (In thousands)				
Total	126,982	51,215	27,681	150,516
Men	69,184	25,125	15,591	78,719
Women	57,798	26,090	12,090	71,798

[Continued]

★ 510 ★

Civilian Labor Force and Projected Entrants and Leavers, 1992-2005

[Continued]

Group	Labor force 1992	Entrants 1992-2005	Leavers 1992-2005	Labor force 2005
White, non-Hispanic	98,817	33,384	22,448	109,753
Men	53,995	16,107	12,884	57,218
Women	44,822	17,278	9,564	52,535
Black, non-Hispanic	13,694	6,096	3,160	16,630
Men	6,786	2,881	1,505	8,163
Women	6,908	3,215	1,656	8,467
Hispanic origin	10,131	7,801	1,352	16,581
Men	6,091	4,339	802	9,628
Women	4,040	3,462	550	6,953
Asian and other, non-Hispanic	4,340	3,958	746	7,552
Men	2,312	1,798	401	3,709
Women	2,028	2,135	320	4,843
Share (percent)				
Total	100.0	100.0	100.0	100.0
Men	54.5	49.1	56.3	52.3
Women	45.5	50.9	43.7	47.7
White, non-Hispanic	77.8	65.2	81.0	72.9
Men	42.5	31.4	46.5	38.0
Women	35.3	33.7	34.5	34.9
Black, non-Hispanic	10.8	11.9	11.4	11.0
Men	5.3	5.6	5.4	5.4
Women	5.4	6.3	6.0	5.6
Hispanic origin	8.0	15.2	4.9	11.0
Men	4.8	8.5	2.9	6.4
Women	3.2	6.8	2.0	4.6
Asian and other, non-Hispanic	3.4	7.7	2.7	5.0
Men	1.8	3.5	1.4	2.5
Women	1.6	4.6	1.2	2.6

Source: U.S. Department of Labor, Bureau of Labor Statistics, *The American Work Force: 1992-2005* (Washington, D.C.: U.S. Government Printing Office, April 1994), p. 34.

★ 511 ★

General Statistics on Labor

Three Projections of the Civilian Labor Force by Sex, Age, Race, and Hispanic Origin, 2005

"The range in the labor force between the low and high projections is 9 million. The range is greater for women than for men, 6 million versus 4 million, reflecting greater uncertainty about women's labor force participation. Labor force participation rates of the high-growth and low-growth scenarios differ from those in the moderate-growth scenario. In addition, the high-growth alternative assumes that population growth will follow the Census Bureau high net immigration growth path; the low growth uses the middle immigration path used for the moderate projections.

"In the high-growth alternative, the labor force would be 156 million by 2005, 6 million more than in the moderate scenario. In this alternative, 70 percent of the population 16 and older would be in the labor force, 90 percent of those aged 25 to 54 would be in the labor force, as would nearly 75 percent of youth. This higher growth of labor force reflects not only increased participation rates, but also higher net immigration, 1.2 million annually.

"Under the assumptions used to develop the low-growth projection, the labor force would include 147 million in 2005, 3 million fewer than in the moderate-growth projection. Two-thirds of the population would yield proportionately fewer people in the peak working years age group, which would depress the labor force participation rate."

	Participation rate (percent)			Level (thousands)		
	High	Moderate	Low	High	Moderate	Low
Total	70.1	68.8	67.3	156,454	150,516	147,252
Men	75.8	74.7	73.6	81,062	78,718	77,558
Women	65.0	63.2	61.4	75,391	71,798	69,694
Aged 16 to 24	69.1	67.5	65.6	25,315	24,127	23,436
Aged 23 to 54	88.9	87.8	86.4	108,726	105,054	103,348
Aged 55 years and over	34.9	33.6	32.3	22,413	21,335	20,469
White, 16 years and older	70.5	69.5	68.1	128,961	124,847	122,478
Black, 16 years and older	68.2	66.2	64.0	18,022	17,395	16,820
Asian and other, 16 years and older[1]	68.9	66.6	64.0	9,470	8,274	7,954
Hispanic, 16 years and older	70.9	68.4	66.0	18,286	16,581	16,006
Other than Hispanic, 16 years and older	70.0	68.8	61.5	138,168	133,935	119,632
White, non-Hispanic	70.5	69.4	68.3	112,357	109,753	107,906

Source: U.S. Department of Labor, Bureau of Labor Statistics, *The American Work Force: 1992-2005* (Washington, D.C.: U.S. Government Printing Office, April 1994), p. 35. *Notes:* 1. The "Asian and other" group includes a) Asians and Pacific Islanders and b) American Indians and Alaska Natives. The historical data are derived by subtracting "black" from the "black and other" group.

★ 512 ★

General Statistics on Labor

Effect of Industry and Occupation Employment Shifts on Weekly Compensation, 1970-2000

"According to [the data below], the effects of industrial and occupational change on the weekly compensation of rural production workers were *negative* throughout the 1970s and 1980s (- 2.8 and - 1.2 percent, respectively), negative effects that appear likely to continue into the future. For example, under the relatively optimistic equal growth scenario, weekly compensation for rural production workers is projected to go down at a ten-year rate of 0.8 percent, while under the more realistic '1980s growth' scenario, weekly compensation will fall even faster, at a 1.2 percent rate. Thus, not only are rural production workers likely to face weak demand for workers skills, they are also likely to face downward pressure on their pay levels from the effects of structural change."

[Ten-year rates of change][1]

Place and Occupation Level of Jobs	(1) 1970-79	(2) 1980-88	1988-2000 Based on BLS Projections (3) Equal Growth Scenario	(4) 1970s Growth Scenario	(5) 1980s Growth Scenario
National					
All Workers	2.2%	0.6%	-0.2%	-	-
Production	0.9	-1.0	-0.4	-	-
Supervisory	1.8	2.8	0.4	-	-
Metro					
All Workers	2.0%	1.3%	-0.1%	-0.1%	0.1%
Production	-0.4	-0.4	-0.3	-0.5	-0.2
Supervisory	2.7	0.5	0.3	0.8	0.4
Nonmetro					
All Workers	3.1%	-2.5%	-0.5%	0.2%	-1.3%
Production	-2.8	-1.2	-0.8	0.4	-1.2
Supervisory	0.7	0.9	0.6	-1.4	-0.3

Source: Economic Policy Institute, "The Myth of the Coming Labor Shortage in Rural Areas" by Ruy A. Teixeira and Lawrence Mishel, Briefing Paper #200, 1730 Rhode Island Avenue, NW, Washington, D.C., 20036, April 1992, pp. 13-14. *Primary source:* Authors' calculations. Industrial/occupational shift effects were estimated from a shift-share analysis of a twenty-three by twenty-three industry/occupation matrix for the years 1970-2000. For all industry/occupation categories, employment counts were based on wage and salary employment in that category (i.e., the self-employed (unincorporated) and unpaid family were excluded). For the historical analysis, employment counts for 1970 were obtained from the 1970 Census, 1979 counts from the March 1979 *Current Population Survey (CPS)*, 1980 counts from the 1980 Census and 1988 counts from the 1988 *CPS* Earning files. For projections, employment counts for 1988 and 2000 were obtained from the 1988-2000 Bureau of Labor Statistics (BLS) employment projections. Hourly and weekly wage data were derived from the 1988 *CPS* earnings file. *Notes:* 1. To facilitate comparisons of these time periods which are of different length the data have been converted to ten-year rates of change: the change if the annual rate of change in these time periods had continued for ten years.

★513★

General Statistics on Labor

Effects of NAFTA on the U.S. Labor Market, 1999

"Nafta will cause problems for low-skill Americans. Economists Gary Hufbauer and Jeffrey Schott of the Institute for International Economics, a nonpartisan Washington, D.C., research outfit, estimate that the U.S. will lose 150,000 low-skill jobs to Mexico by the end of the decade. But overall, free trade will be a strong net plus. The Commerce Department estimates that each additional $1 billion in exports creates 19,000 jobs. Mexico imported $33 billion of U.S. goods last year, two-thirds of them high-value-added capital goods like trucks, machinery, and computers. The bottom line: Hufbauer and Schott forecast that the U.S. will gain a net 325,000 well-paying jobs by 1999."

Source: Louis S. Richman, "Who Gains from a Free-trade Deal?" in *Fortune*, 7 September 1992, p. 8.

★514★

General Statistics on Labor

Women of Childbearing Age in the Labor Force, 1948-2005

"The history of the labor force participation of women over the past half century indicates that young women participate in the labor force more than older women. Because the childbearing years are defined as ages 15 to 44, a high proportion of the female labor force also is of childbearing age. However, this is changing slowly.

"When the Current Population Survey began in 1948 women of childbearing age were 71 percent of the female labor force. At its lowest point, the share was 60 percent in 1961 during the end of the baby-boom period. By 1987, women of childbearing age were 74 percent of the female labor force, the highest attained. The share has since dropped and is projected to continue to decline. Other measures indicate the importance of this group of the labor force as a whole. They were a fifth of the labor force as recently as 1961; currently, they are almost a third of the labor force. Women are a rising share of the labor force of 16-to-44 year-olds, and this is projected to continue. The labor force participation of this group of women is an additional uncertainty in projections: whatever happens, the general direction of these proportions are likely to prevail."

[Thousands]

	1948	1961	1987	1992	2000	2005
Population, women, 16 and older	17,335	23,806	53,658	57,798	66,555	71,798
Population, women, 16 to 44	12,286	14,371	39,466	40,854	44,059	44,872
As a percent Of women	70.9	60.4	73.6	70.7	66.2	62.5

[Continued]

★ 514 ★

Women of Childbearing Age in the Labor Force, 1948-2005

[Continued]

	1948	1961	1987	1992	2000	2005
Of the labor force	20.3	20.4	32.9	32.2	31.1	29.8
Of the 16 to 44 labor force	31.1	33.7	45.5	45.8	47.1	47.9

Source: U.S. Department of Labor, Bureau of Labor Statistics, *The American Work Force: 1992-2005* (Washington, D.C.: U.S. Government Printing Office, April 1994), p. 36.

Skill and Educational Requirements

★ 515 ★

Blue- and White-Collar Workers as a Percent of the Work Force, 1900-2000

[Percent of work forcc]

Year	Blue collar	White collar
1900	38	20
1910	40	22
1920	41	23
1930	42	25
1940	42	32
1950	42	38
1960	39	41
1970	36	48
1980	30	53
1991	28	59
2000	25	62

Source: John Huey, "Waking Up to the New Economy," in *Fortune*, 27 June 1994, p. 40. *Primary source:* Stephen R. Barley, Cornell University. *Note:* Magnitudes estimated from published chart.

★ 516 ★

Skill and Educational Requirements

Employment Gap Between Less- and More-Skilled Workers, 1950-2005

"During the industrial revolution, one of the gravest objections to industrial capitalism was that the division of labor, its key principle, also divided men and turned people into nothing but their hands. It stunted individuals, stifling their most human faculties of heart and brain and making them animated machines, shaking with the same repetitive movement for ten or 12 hours a day as if from palsy.

"The economic transformation now under way in the United States undeniably imposes disappointment and often hardship on many for whom high-paying, low-skill jobs will not be found. But it has a larger, deeply moving consequence for the American worker. Says Garry Berryman, who runs Honda's training center in Ohio: 'An organization, with all its greatest muscle—machinery, equipment, money, facilities—can't do anything unless it's got a brain. The brain is the people'."

[Millions of blue-collar jobs]

Year	More-skilled workers	Less-skilled workers
1950	7.7	15.8
1955	8.2	16.3
1960	8.4	15.7
1965	9.3	17.1
1970	10.0	17.7
1975	10.8	17.1
1980	12.3	18.2
1985	13.3	16.8
1990	14.0	17.2
2005	16.0	18.0

Source: "Today's U.S. Worker," in *Fortune*, 4 May 1992, pp. 60, 65. *Primary source:* U.S. Bureau of Labor Statistics. *Note:* Magnitudes estimated from published chart.

★ 517 ★

Skill and Educational Requirements

Effect of Industry and Occupation Employment Shifts on Skill and Education Requirements and Pay, 1970-2000

"A recent study analyzed the effects of both industry and occupation shifts on job-skill levels from 1960 to 1985 in 267 occupations and sixty-four industries (Howell and Wolff, ["Skill Changes in the U.S. Labor Force, 1960-1985," *Industrial and Labor Relations Review*, April] 1991). It found that, while structural upgrading of job skills took place in each decade, *the rate of upgrading declined substantially over time*. For example, the 'substantive complexity' of jobs went up 0.69 percent per year in the 1960s, 0.46 percent per year in the 1970s, and only 0.28 percent per year in 1980s. These results hardly suggest an impending explosion of skills upgrading from structural change."

[Ten-year rate of change][1]

Job Characteristic	1970-79	1980-88	BLS Projections 1988-2000
Pay Levels			
Hourly Wage	2.5%	1.5%	0.3%
Weekly Wage	2.8	1.5	0.2
Hourly Compensation	2.0	0.6	-0.0
Weekly Compensation	2.2	0.6	-0.2
Skill Indices			
General Education Development (GED)	2.3%	2.0%	0.8%
Numerical Aptitude	1.5	1.7	0.5
Verbal Aptitude	2.3	2.1	0.8
Intellectual Aptitude	2.3	2.0	0.8
Handling Data	4.0	4.3	1.4
Handling People	2.2	1.9	0.7
Handling Things	-1.4	-2.1	-0.4
Education			
Average Years of Schooling	1.4%	1.1%	0.5%
	(Percentage Point Change)		
Shares of Employment Requiring:			
Less Than High School	-1.4%	-0.9%	-0.4%
High School Graduate	-1.3	-1.9	-0.7

[Continued]

★517★

Effect of Industry and Occupation Employment Shifts on Skill and Education Requirements and Pay, 1970-2000

[Continued]

Job Characteristic	1970-79	1980-88	BLS Projections 1988-2000
Some College	0.6	0.6	0.3
College Graduate or More	2.2	2.0	0.8

Source: Economic Policy Institute, "The Myth of the Coming Labor Shortage in Rural Areas" by Ruy A. Teixeira and Lawrence Mishel, Briefing Paper #2000, 1730 Rhode Island Ave., NW. Washington, D.C., 20036, April 1992, p. 6. *Primary source:* Authors' calculations. Industrial/occupational shift effects were estimated from a shift-share analysis of a twenty-three by twenty-three industry/occupation matrix for the years 1970-2000. For all industrial occupation categories, employment counts were based on wage and salary employment in that category (i.e., the self-employed (unincorporated) and unpaid family were excluded). For the historical analysis, employment counts for 1970 were obtained from the 1970 Census, 1979 counts from the March 1979 *Current Population Survey (CPS)*, 1980 counts from the 1980 Census and 1988 counts from the 1988 *CPS* Earnings files. For projections, employment counts for 1988 and 2000 were obtained from the 1988-2000 Bureau of Labor Statistics (BLS) employment projections. Hourly and weekly wage data were derived from the 1988 *CPS* earnings file. All skill indices are taken from the *Dictionary of Occupational Titles (DOT)*, a compedium of occupational titles in common use in civilian U.S. labor markets. Skill ratings were based on scores from the 4th edition of *DOT*. Educational requirements are based on the educational levels of incumbents, drawn from the 1988 *CPS* earnings file. *Notes:* 1. To facilitate comparisons of these time periods which are of different length the data have been converted to ten-year rates of change: the change if the annual rate of change in these time periods had continued for ten years.

★518★

Skill and Educational Requirements

Metropolitan and Nonmetropolitan Growth in Job-Skill and Education Requirements and Pay, 1970-2000

"[As] the data in columns 3, 4, and 5 indicate, future changes in the job structure are likely to keep skill growth for rural production (and white collar) jobs at the same very low levels as previous decades—in fact, probably *lower*. Thus, rural production workers, in particular—the overwhelming majority of the rural workforce and the presumed chief target of an education-based, supply-push strategy—seem very unlikely to experience the demand-side conditions appropriate to such a strategy."

[Ten-year rates of change][1]

Job Characteristic	(1) 1970-1979		(2) 1980-1988		1988-2000 Based on BLS Projections					
					(3) Equal Growth Scenario		(4) 1970s Growth Scenario		(5) 1980s Growth Scenario	
	Metro	Nonmetro	Metro	Nonmetro	Metro	Nonmetro	Metro	Nonmetro	Metro	Nonmetro
Pay Levels										
Hourly Wage	2.3%	3.3%	2.0%	-1.4%	0.3%	0.1%	0.4%	0.8%	0.5%	-0.7%
Weekly Wage	2.7	3.5	2.2	-1.9	0.2	-0.1	0.3	0.6	0.4	-1.0
Hourly Compensation	1.8	3.0	1.2	-2.0	-0.0	-0.3	-0.0	0.4	0.1	1.0
Weekly Compensation	2.0	3.1	1.3	-2.5	-0.1	-0.5	-0.1	0.2	0.1	-1.3
Skill Indices										
General Educational Development (GED)	2.2%	2.9%	2.2%	1.1%	0.7%	0.9%	0.8%	1.3%	0.8%	0.5%
Numerical Aptitude	1.4	2.0	1.8	0.7	0.5	0.5	0.5	1.0	0.6	0.2
Verbal Aptitude	2.2	2.9	2.2	1.0	0.8	0.8	0.8	1.4	0.9	0.4
Intellectual Aptitude	2.2	2.9	2.2	0.9	0.7	0.8	0.7	1.3	0.8	0.4
Handling Data	4.0	4.7	4.7	1.9	1.3	1.4	1.3	2.2	1.5	0.6

[Continued]

★ 518 ★

Metropolitan and Nonmetropolitan Growth in Job-Skill and Education Requirements and Pay, 1970-2000

[Continued]

Job Characteristic	(1) 1970-1979		(2) 1980-1988		1988-2000 Based on BLS Projections					
					(3) Equal Growth Scenario		(4) 1970s Growth Scenario		(5) 1980s Growth Scenario	
	Metro	Nonmetro	Metro	Nonmetro	Metro	Nonmetro	Metro	Nonmetro	Metro	Nonmetro
Handling People	2.2	2.3	2.0	0.9	0.6	0.8	0.7	1.0	0.7	0.4
Handling Things	-1.7	-0.6	-2.3	-1.5	-0.4	-0.4	-0.5	-0.1	-0.4	-0.2
Education										
Average Years of School	1.3%	1.9%	1.2%	0.4%	0.5%	0.6%	0.5%	0.9%	0.5%	0.3%
	(Percentage Point Change)									
Shares of Employment Requiring										
Less than High School	-1.2%	-2.4%	-0.9%	-0.4%	-0.3%	-0.6%	-0.3%	-1.2%	-0.3%	-0.4%
High School Graduate	-1.6	-1.1	2.0	0.6	-.7	-.5	-.8	-.5	-.8	-0.1
Some College	0.6	1.1	0.6	0.8	0.3	0.4	0.2	0.8	0.3	0.3
College Graduate or more	2.2	2.	2.4	0.4	0.8	0.8	0.9	0.9	0.9	0.2

Source: Economic Policy Institute, "The Myth of the Coming Labor Shortage in Rural Areas" by Ruy A. Teixeira and Lawrence Mishel, Briefing Paper #200, 1730 Rhode Island Ave., NW, Washington, D.C., 20036, April 1992, pp. 9, 12. *Primary source:* Authors' calculations. Industrial/occupational shift effects were estimated from a shift-share analysis of a twenty-three by twenty-three industry/occupation matrix for the years 1970-2000. For all industry/occupation categories, employment counts were based on wage and salary employment in that category (i.e., the self-employed (unincorporated) and unpaid family were excluded). For the historical analysis, employment counts for 1970 were obtained from the 1970 Census, 1979 counts from March 1979 *Current Population Survey (CPS)*, 1980 counts from the 1980 Census and 1988 counts from the 1988 *CPS* Earnings files. For projections, employment counts for 1988 and 2000 were obtained from the 1988-2000 were obtained from the 1988-2000 Bureau of Labor Statistics (BLS) employment projections. Hourly and weekly wage data were derived from the 1988 *CPS* earnings file. All skill indices are taken from the *Dictionary of Occupational Titles (DOT)*, a compedium of occupational titles in common use in civilian U.S. labor markets. Skill ratings were based on scores from the 4th edition of *DOT*. Educational requirements are based on the educational levels of incumbents, drawn from the 1988 *CPS* earnings file. *Notes:* 1. To facilitate comparisons of these time periods which are of different length the data have been converted to ten-year rates of change: the change if the annual rate of change in these time periods had continued for ten years.

★ 519 ★

Skill and Educational Requirements

Effect of Industry and Occupation Employment Shifts on General Education Development (GED) Skill Requirements, 1970-2000

[Ten-year rates of change][1]

Place and Occupation Level of Jobs	(1) 1970-79	(2) 1980-88	1988-2000 Based on BLS Projections		
			(3) Equal Growth Scenario	(4) 1970s Growth Scenario	(5) 1980s Growth Scenario
National					
All Workers	2.3%	2.0%	0.8%	-	-
Production	2.1	1.8	0.9	-	-
Supervisory	1.0	1.7	0.5	-	-
Metro					
All Workers	2.2%	2.2%	0.7%	0.8%	0.8%
Production	1.7	1.2	0.8	0.8	0.9
Supervisory	1.6	0.7	0.5	0.5	0.5

[Continued]

★ 519 ★

Effect of Industry and Occupation Employment Shifts on General Education Development (GED) Skill Requirements, 1970-2000

[Continued]

Place and Occupation Level of Jobs	(1) 1970-79	(2) 1980-88	1988-2000 Based on BLS Projections		
			(3) Equal Growth Scenario	(4) 1970s Growth Scenario	(5) 1980s Growth Scenario
Nonmetro					
All Workers	2.9%	1.1%	0.9%	1.3%	0.5%
Production	0.9	1.4	0.9	1.4	0.6
Supervisory	1.2	0.8	0.6	0.5	0.3

Source: Economic Policy Institute, "The Myth of the Coming Labor Shortage in Rural Areas" by Ruy A. Teixeira and Lawrence Mishel, Briefing Paper #200, 1730 Rhode Island Ave., NW, Washington, D.C., 20036, April 1992, p. 12. *Primary source:* Authors' calculations. Industrial/occupational shift effects were estimated from a shift-share analysis of a twenty-three by twenty-three industry/occupation matrix for the years 1970-2000. For all industry/occupation categories, employment counts were based on wage and salary employment in that category (i.e., the self-employed (unincorporated) and unpaid family were excluded). For the historical analysis, employment counts for 1970 were obtained from the 1970 Census, 1979 counts from March 1979 *Current Population Survey (CPS)*, 1980 counts from the 1980 Census and 1988 counts from the 1988 *CPS* Earnings files. For projections, employment counts for 1988 and 2000 were obtained from the 1988-2000 Bureau of Labor Statistics (BLS) employment projections. Hourly and weekly wage data were derived from the 1988 *CPS* earnings file. Educational requirements are based on the educational levels of incumbents, drawn from the 1988 *CPS* earnings file. *Notes:* 1. To facilitate comparisons of these time periods which are of different length the data have been converted to ten-year rates of change: the change if the annual rate of change in these time periods had continued for ten years.

★ 520 ★

Skill and Educational Requirements

Effect of Industry and Occupation Employment Shifts on Years of Schooling Required, 1970-2000

"The results for average years of education [reveal] very slow growth in educational requirements for rural production workers in the 1970s and 1980s to be succeeded, according to projections estimates, by even slower growth in the future. Data for other skill and education measures (not shown here) fully accord with this picture: future growth in job-skill requirements for the bulk of the rural workforce will be sluggish at best, almost non-existent at worst."

[Ten-year rates of change][1]

Place and Occupation Level of Jobs	(1) 1970-79	(2) 1980-88	1988-2000 Based on BLS Projections		
			(3) Equal Growth Scenario	(4) 1970s Growth Scenario	(5) 1980s Growth Scenario
National					
All Workers	1.4%	1.1%	0.5%	-	-
Production	1.3	0.8	0.5	-	-
Supervisory	0.6	1.3	0.3	-	-
Metro					
All Workers	1.3%	1.2%	0.5%	0.5%	0.5%

[Continued]

★ 520 ★

Effect of Industry and Occupation Employment Shifts on Years of Schooling Required, 1970-2000

[Continued]

Place and Occupation Level of Jobs	(1) 1970-79	(2) 1980-88	1988-2000 Based on BLS Projections (3) Equal Growth Scenario	(4) 1970s Growth Scenario	(5) 1980s Growth Scenario
Production	0.8	0.7	0.5	0.5	0.5
Supervisory	1.2	0.5	0.3	0.4	0.3
Nonmetro					
All Workers	1.9%	0.4%	0.6%	0.9%	0.3%
Production	0.3	0.8	0.6	0.9	0.4
Supervisory	0.8	0.6	0.4	0.1	0.2

Source: Economic Policy Institute, "The Myth of the Coming Labor Shortage in Rural Areas" by Ruy A. Teixeira and Lawrence Mishel, Briefing Paper #200, 1730 Rhode Island Ave., NW, Washington, D.C., 20036, April 1992, pp. 12-13. *Primary source:* Authors' calculations. Industrial/occupational shift effects were estimated from a shift-share analysis of a twenty-three by twenty-three industry/occupation matrix for the years 1970-2000. For all industry/occupation categories, employment counts were based on wage and salary employment in that category (i.e., the self-employed (unincorporated) and unpaid family were excluded). For the historical analysis, employment counts for 1970 were obtained from the 1970 Census, 1979 counts from March 1979 *Current Population Survey (CPS)*, 1980 counts from the 1980 Census and 1988 counts from the 1988 *CPS* Earnings files. For projections, employment counts for 1988 and 2000 were obtained from the 1988-2000 Bureau of Labor Statistics (BLS) employment projections. Hourly and weekly wage data were derived from the 1988 *CPS* earnings file. Educational requirements are based on the educational levels of incumbents, drawn from the 1988 *CPS* earnings file. *Notes:* 1. To facilitate comparisons of these time periods which are of different length the data have been converted to ten-year rates of change: the change if the annual rate of change in these time periods had continued for ten years.

★ 521 ★

Skill and Educational Requirements

Average Annual Job Openings and Degree Awards for Natural Scientists and Engineers, 1984-1997

[Thousands]

Category	Engineers: Civil	Electrical and electronics	Mechanical	Chemical	Other	Total	Natural scientists: Life	Physical	Mathematical and computer	Total
1984-90										
Job openings	7.7	14.6	10.8	-0.1	30.9	63.9	6.3	8.8	38.6	117.6
Net separations	3.9	8.7	7.3	1.2	11.4	32.5	3.6	6.4	3.3	45.8
Growth	3.8	5.9	3.5	-1.3	19.4	31.3	2.7	2.4	35.4	71.8
Science and engineering graduates	8.9	24.5	18.9	6.3	14.1	72.7	55.9	20.1	50.7	199.4
Ratio of science and engineering graduates to job openings	1.15	1.68	1.74	[1]	.46	1.14	8.88	2.29	1.31	1.70

[Continued]

★ 521 ★

Average Annual Job Openings and Degree Awards for Natural Scientists and Engineers, 1984-1997

[Continued]

Category	Engineers						Natural scientists			Total
	Civil	Electrical and electronics	Mechanical	Chemical	Other	Total	Life	Physical	Mathematical and computer	
1991-97										
Job openings	8.3	18.7	12.4	1.5	20.6	61.6	5.7	9.0	30.0	106.2
Net separations	4.6	9.8	8.0	1.2	13.1	36.6	3.8	6.4	6.2	53.0
Growth	3.7	8.9	4.5	.4	7.5	24.9	1.9	2.6	23.7	53.2
Science and engineering graduates	6.8	19.6	15.2	3.9	8.6	54.1	43.1	14.4	47.4	159.0
Ratio of science and engineering graduates to job openings	.82	1.05	1.22	2.52	.42	.88	7.57	1.60	1.58	1.50

Source: Betty W. Su and Carl A. Chentrens, "Foreign Trade Alternatives for Employment and Occupations," in *Monthly Labor Review*, November 1994, p. 60. *Note:* 1. Not applicable. Midlevel alternative.

Employment by Occupation and Industry

★ 522 ★

Employment by Major Occupational Group, 1992-2005

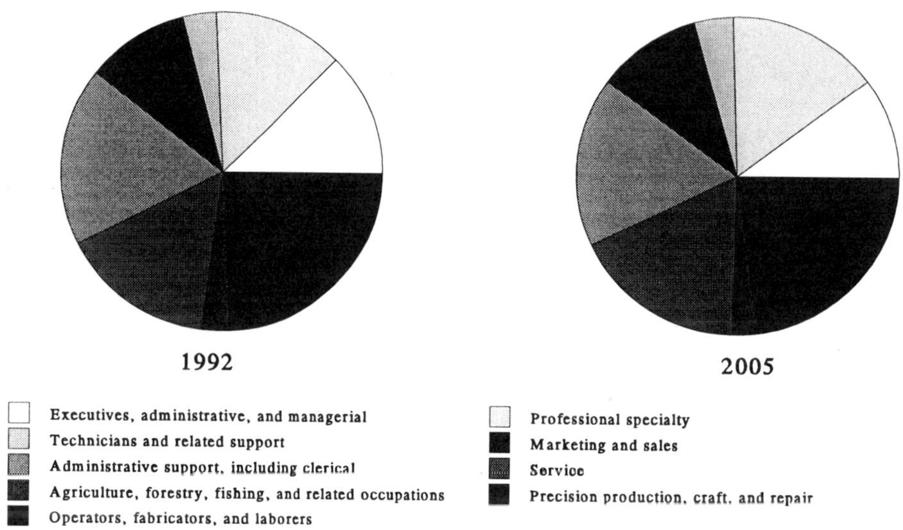

"Among the major occupational groups, employment in professional specialty occupations, technicians and related support occupations, and service occupations is projected to increase fastest. Executive, administrative, and managerial occupations also are projected to have faster-than-average employment growth, and the number of jobs for marketing and salesworkers is expected to grow about as fast as total employment. Employment in all other major occupational groups is expected to increase, but at a slower rate than total employment growth."

[Thousands and percent change]

Occupation	1992		2005		Percent change	
	Number	Percent	Number	Percent	1979-92	1992-2005
Total, all occupations	121,099	100.0	147,482	100.0	19.0	21.8
Executives, administrative, and managerial	12,066	10.0	15,195	10.3	50.4	25.9
Professional specialty	16,592	13.7	22,801	15.5	43.0	37.4
Technicians and related support	4,282	3.5	5,664	3.8	57.6	32.2
Marketing and sales	12,993	10.7	15,664	10.6	30.7	20.6
Administrative support, including clerical	22,349	18.5	25,406	17.2	15.0	13.7
Service	19,358	16.0	25,820	17.5	24.6	33.4
Agricultural, forestry, fishing, and related occupations	3,530	2.9	3,650	2.5	-5.2	3.4

[Continued]

★ 522 ★

Employment by Major Occupational Group, 1992-2005

[Continued]

Occupation	1992		2005		Percent change	
	Number	Percent	Number	Percent	1979-92	1992-2005
Precision production, craft, and repair	13,580	11.2	15,380	10.4	4.3	13.3
Operators, fabricators, and laborers	16,349	13.5	17,902	12.1	-10.3	9.5

Source: U.S. Department of Labor, Bureau of Labor Statistics, *The American Work Force: 1992-2005* (Washington, D.C.: U.S. Government Printing Office, April 1994), p. 57. *Notes:* The 1992 and 2005 employment data and the projected change 1992-2005 are derived from the industry-occupation employment matrices for each year. The data on 1979-92 percent change were derived from the Current Population Survey (CPS) because a comparable industry-occupation matrix for 1979 is not available. The CPS data represent estimates of employed persons and exclude the estimates of persons with more than one job that are included in the industry-occupation employment matrices. The CPS exclusions of dual jobholders affects the employment levels and trends of some occupational groups more than others. Therefore, the resulting comparisons of change between 1979-92 and 1992-2005 are only broadly indicative of trends.

★ 523 ★

Employment by Occupation and Industry

Fastest Growing Occupations, 1992-2005

"Most of the occupations with the fastest projected employment growth are concentrated in one or more of the rapidly growing industries. A large number of the 30 occupations with the fastest projected growth rate are concentrated in the health services sector which is expected to increase about twice as fast as the economy as a whole. Many human services workers, who are classified in the detailed occupation with the second fastest projected growth rate, are employed in health services, social services, and State and local governments. These employees hold professional and paraprofessional jobs in facilities and programs that serve the elderly, the mentally impaired, and the developmentally disabled. Employment in two other rapidly growing occupations—home health aides and personal and home care aides—is concentrated in the home health care services and individuals and miscellaneous social services industries. Home health aides are expected to be in great demand to provide personal and physical care for an increasing number of elderly people and for patients who are recovering from surgery and other serious health conditions. Personal and home care aides perform a variety of light housekeeping tasks for those in need of home care."

[Thousands]

Occupation	Employment		Numerical change	Percent change
	1992	2005		
Home health aides	347	827	479	138
Human services workers	189	445	256	136
Personal and home care aides	127	293	166	130
Computer engineers and scientists	211	447	236	112
Systems analysts	455	956	501	110
Physical and corrective therapy assistants and aides	61	118	57	93
Physical therapists	90	170	79	88
Paralegals	95	176	81	86
Teachers, special education	358	625	267	74
Medical assistants	181	308	128	71
Detectives, except public	59	100	41	70
Correction officers	282	479	197	70
Child care workers	684	1,135	450	66
Travel agents	115	191	76	66
Radiologic technologists and technicians	162	264	102	63

[Continued]

★ 523 ★

Fastest Growing Occupations, 1992-2005

[Continued]

Occupation	Employment 1992	Employment 2005	Numerical change	Percent change
Nursery workers	72	116	44	62
Medical records technicians	76	123	47	61
Operations research analysts	45	72	27	61
Occupational therapists	40	64	24	60
Legal secretaries	280	439	160	57
Teachers, preschool and kindergarten	434	669	236	54
Manicurists	35	55	19	54
Producers, directors, actors and entertainers	129	198	69	54
Speech-language pathologists and audiologists	73	110	37	51
Flight attendants	93	140	47	51
Guards	803	1,211	408	51
Insurance adjusters, examiners, and investigators	147	220	72	49
Respiratory therapists	74	109	36	48
Psychologists	143	212	69	48
Paving, surfacing, and tamping equipment operators	72	107	35	48

Source: U.S. Department of Labor, Bureau of Labor Statistics, *The American Work Force: 1992-2005* (Washington, D.C.: U.S. Government Printing Office, April 1994), pp. 72-3.

★ 524 ★

Employment by Occupation and Industry

Occupations with the Largest Job Growth, 1992-2005

"Several of the detailed occupations with the largest numerical job growth are concentrated in three industries that are expected to provide nearly half of the total growth in wage and salary jobs from 1992 to 2005—retail trade, health services, and educational services. The occupation that is expected to have the second largest increase overall is registered nurses (765,000 jobs). Other health-related occupations with large projected numerical increases are nursing aides, orderlies, and attendants (594,000 jobs); licensed practical nurses (261,000 jobs); and home health aides (479,000 jobs). The latter occupation is also among the fastest growing occupations."

[Thousands]

Occupation	Employment 1992	Employment 2005	Numerical change	Percent change
Salespersons, retail	3,660	4,446	786	21
Registered nurses	1,835	2,601	765	42
Cashiers	2,747	3,417	670	24
General office clerks	2,688	3,342	654	24
Truck drivers light and heavy	2,391	3,039	648	27
Waiters and waitresses	1,756	2,394	637	36
Nursing aides, orderlies, and attendants	1,308	1,903	594	45
Janitors and cleaners, including maids and housekeeping cleaners	2,862	3,410	548	19

[Continued]

★ 524 ★

Occupations with the Largest Job Growth, 1992-2005

[Continued]

Occupation	Employment 1992	Employment 2005	Numerical change	Percent change
Food preparation workers	1,223	1,748	524	43
Systems analysts	455	956	501	110
Home health aides	347	827	479	138
Teachers, secondary school	1,263	1,724	462	37
Child care workers	684	1,135	450	66
Guards	803	1,211	408	51
Marketing and sales worker supervisors	2,036	2,443	407	20
Teacher aides and educational assistants	885	1,266	381	43
General managers and top executives	2,871	3,251	380	13
Maintenance repairers, general utility	1,145	1,464	319	28
Gardeners and groundskeepers, except farm	884	1,195	311	35
Teachers, elementary	1,456	1,767	311	21
Food counter, fountain, and related workers	1,564	1,872	308	20
Receptionists and information clerks	904	1,210	305	34
Accountants and auditors	939	1,243	304	32
Clerical supervisors and managers	1,267	1,568	301	24
Cooks, restaurant	602	879	276	46
Teachers, special education	358	625	267	74
Licensed practical nurses	659	920	261	40
Cooks, short order and fast food	714	971	257	36
Human services workers	189	445	256	136
Computer engineers and scientists	211	447	236	112

Source: U.S. Department of Labor, Bureau of Labor Statistics, *The American Work Force: 1992-2005* (Washington, D.C.: U.S. Government Printing Office, April 1994), pp. 73-4, 76.

★ 525 ★

Employment by Occupation and Industry

Occupations with the Largest Job Decline, 1992-2005

"Industry employment change is the major cause of projected employment declines for farmers; textile draw-out and winding machine operators and tenders; electrical and electronic equipment assemblers, precision; electrical and electronic assemblers; and two occupations in the private household industry—cleaners and servants and child care workers. Declining occupations that are expected to be affected almost equally by industry employment changes and by occupational structure changes include farm workers; central office and PBX installers and repairers; central office operators; station installers and repairers; and directory assistance operators.

"Most of the other declining occupations are affected more by occupational structure changes than by industry employment changes. The large decline in employment for bartenders in the eating and drinking places industry is attributable to the projected decline in the consumption of alcoholic beverages outside of the home. Overall, the employment of bartenders is projected to decline by 32,000 jobs. The use of typists and word processors is expected to decrease significantly in most industries because of productivity improvements resulting from office automation and the increased use of word processing equipment by professional and managerial employees. Job losses for these workers are expected to be very substantial—125,000 jobs. The demand for computer operators, except peripheral equipment is expected to fall due to an expected decrease in the use of mainframe computers relative to personal computers. Employment for bank tellers is expected to decline because of increased use of automated teller machines, terminals, and other electronic equipment for customer fund transactions."

[Thousands]

Occupation	Employment		Numerical change	Percent change
	1992	2005		
Farmers	1,088	857	-231	-21
Sewing machine operators, garment	556	393	-162	-29
Cleaners and servants, private households	483	326	-157	-32
Farmworkers	849	716	-133	-16
Typists and word processors	789	664	-125	-16
Child care workers, private household	350	227	-123	-35
Computer operators, except peripheral equipment	266	161	-104	-39
Packaging and filling machine operators and tenders	319	248	-71	-22
Inspectors, testers, and graders, precision	625	559	-65	-10
Switchboard operators	239	188	-51	-21
Telephone and cable TV line installers and repairers	165	125	-40	-24
Textile draw-out and winding machine operators and tenders	192	157	-35	-18
Machine forming operators and tenders, metal and plastic	155	123	-32	-21
Bartenders	382	350	-32	-8
Butchers and meatcutters	222	191	-31	-14
Billing, posting, and calculating machine operators	93	66	-28	-29
Central office and PBX installers and repairers	70	45	-25	-36
Central office operators	48	24	-24	-50
Bank tellers	525	502	-24	-4
Electrical and electronic assemblers	210	187	-23	-11
Cutting and slicing machine setters, operators and tenders	94	73	-21	-23
Electrical and electronic equipment assemblers, precision	150	129	-21	-14
Station installers and repairers, telephone	40	20	-20	-50
Machine tool cutting operators and tenders, metal and plastic	114	95	-19	-17
Peripheral EDP equipment operators	30	12	-18	-60
Welding machine setters, operators, and tenders	97	80	-17	-17

[Continued]

★ 525 ★

Occupations with the Largest Job Decline, 1992-2005

[Continued]

Occupation	Employment 1992	Employment 2005	Numerical change	Percent change
Crushing and mixing machine operators and tenders	133	117	-16	-12
Industrial machinery mechanics	477	462	-15	-3
Directory assistance operators	27	13	-14	-51
Head sawyers and sawing machines operators and tenders, setters and set-up operators	59	46	-13	-22

Source: U.S. Department of Labor, Bureau of Labor Statistics, *The American Work Force: 1992-2005* (Washington, D.C.: U.S. Government Printing Office, April 1994), pp. 74, 77.

★ 526 ★

Employment by Occupation and Industry

Factors Affecting Demand Growth of Major Occupational Groups to 2005

"Between 1992 and 2005, total wage and salary employment is projected to increase by almost 23 percent in the moderate-growth projections developed by BLS [Bureau of Labor Statistics]. At the detailed occupational level of the projections, growth ranges from a high of 138.2 percent over the period for home health aides to a low of - 75.3 percent for central frame wirers. To assist the user of the projections in evaluating and understanding the sources of increase or decrease for individual occupations, a detailed analysis of the factors entering the projection process has been carried out. This is presented in [the table below] for major occupational groups. Such factor analyses have been carried out often in the past for industry output or industry employment, but this carries the analysis one step further, to the occupational level of detail."

[Percent Change from 1992]

Occupation	2005	Factor percent change: GDP level	Sector distribution	Commodity distribution	Production technology	Labor productivity	Staffing patterns	Interaction
Total, all occupations	22.6	35.9	3.3	-1.0	2.5	-12.4	0.0	-5.8
Executive, administrative, and managerial occupations	24.5	35.9	3.1	-0.9	3.5	-12.1	1.6	-6.7
Professional specialty occupations	39.4	35.9	10.2	-1.7	2.2	-12.2	8.1	-3.1
Technicians and related support occupations	32.3	35.9	8.6	-1.2	5.1	-12.9	2.0	-5.2
Marketing and sales occupations	23.1	35.9	1.7	-2.0	5.1	-14.1	1.9	-5.4
Administrative support occupations, including clerical	14.1	35.9	4.4	-1.0	4.0	-13.7	-7.6	-7.9
Service occupations	32.8	35.9	4.6	-1.1	0.2	-5.8	0.9	-2.0

[Continued]

★ 526 ★

Factors Affecting Demand Growth of Major Occupational Groups to 2005

[Continued]

Occupation	2005	Factor percent change						
		GDP level	Sector distribution	Commodity distribution	Production technology	Labor productivity	Staffing patterns	Interaction
Agriculture, forestry, fishing, and related occupations	15.9	35.9	2.2	-1.7	-1.1	-14.9	1.8	-6.4
Precision production, craft, and repair occupations	13.3	35.9	-2.5	-0.6	1.2	-12.3	-0.7	-7.6
Operators, fabricators, and laborers	9.8	35.9	-2.0	0.1	1.7	-17.0	-0.9	-7.9

Source: U.S. Department of Labor, Bureau of Labor Statistics, *The American Work Force: 1992-2005* (Washington, D.C.: U.S. Government Printing Office, April 1994), pp. 133, 135.

★ 527 ★

Employment by Occupation and Industry

Civilian Employment by Occupation under Low, Medium, and High Scenarios, 1992-2005-I

"Projected growth from 1992 to 2005 will vary widely among the individual occupations, ranging from an increase of 138 percent to a decline of 75 percent. In general, occupations that require a bachelor's degree or other post-secondary education or training are projected to have faster-than-average rates of employment growth. Also, many occupations requiring less formal education or training are projected to have above average growth. In addition to the growth rate, the size of the occupational stock of jobs is an important factor in determining the numerical growth in the occupation; therefore, it has a great effect on the structure of future employment. Many slower growing occupations, some requiring little education and training and others having significant educational requirements, are expected to add significant numbers of jobs primarily because of their large employment bases. As a result, the economy is projected to continue to generate jobs for workers at all levels of education and training.

"Most of the employment growth will occur in service-producing industries. As a consequence, occupations concentrated in those industries are more likely to experience rapid employment growth, compared with occupations in the goods-producing industries. Of the 26.4 million projected increase in total employment over the 1992-2005 period, more than 25 million jobs are projected in the service-producing industries and fewer than 1 million jobs are expected in the goods-producing industries."

[Thousands]

	Total employment				1992-2005 employment change					
	1992	Projected, 2005			Number			Percent		
		Low	Moderate	High	Low	Moderate	High	Low	Moderate	High
Total, all occupations	121,099	139,007	147,482	154,430	17,908	26,383	33,330	15	22	28
Executive, administrative, and managerial occupations	12,066	14,331	15,195	15,977	2,265	3,129	3,911	19	26	32
Managerial and administrative occupations	8,411	9,847	10,427	10,982	1,436	2,016	2,570	17	24	31
Administrative services managers	226	241	256	267	14	30	40	6	13	18
Communication, transportation, and utilities operations managers	144	146	158	166	2	14	22	1	10	15
Construction managers	180	254	265	309	73	85	128	41	47	71
Education administrators	351	412	432	448	62	81	97	18	23	28
Engineering, mathematical, and natural science managers	337	410	444	476	73	106	139	22	32	41
Financial managers	701	828	875	917	127	174	215	18	25	31
Food service and lodging managers	532	732	764	787	200	232	255	38	44	48
Funeral directors and morticians	27	31	32	32	4	5	5	16	18	20

[Continued]

★ 527 ★

Civilian Employment by Occupation under Low, Medium, and High Scenarios, 1992-2005-I

[Continued]

	Total employment				1992-2005 employment change					
	1992	Projected, 2005			Number			Percent		
		Low	Moderate	High	Low	Moderate	High	Low	Moderate	High
General managers and top executives	2,871	3,050	3,251	3,418	179	380	547	6	13	19
Government chief executives and legislators	73	71	76	79	-2	2	6	-3	3	8
Industrial production managers	203	189	208	224	-13	5	22	-7	2	11
Marketing, advertising, and public relations managers	432	548	588	616	116	156	184	27	36	43
Personnel, training, and labor relations managers	193	226	241	251	34	48	59	17	25	31
Property and real estate managers	243	317	328	347	74	85	104	30	35	43
Purchasing managers	221	234	252	266	13	31	45	6	14	20
All other managers and administrators	1,676	2,158	2,258	2,378	482	582	701	29	35	42
Management support occupations	3,654	4,484	4,767	4,995	829	1,113	1,340	23	30	37
Accountants and auditors	939	1,167	1,243	1,301	228	304	362	24	32	39
Budget analysts	67	75	81	85	8	13	17	12	20	26
Claims examiners, property and casualty insurance	33	39	42	42	6	9	9	18	26	26
Construction and building inspectors	66	80	86	92	15	20	26	22	30	40
Cost estimators	163	200	211	242	37	49	79	23	30	48
Credit analysts	33	33	35	35	[1]	1	2	-1	4	5
Employment interviewers, private or public employment service	79	90	96	99	11	17	20	14	22	26
Inspectors and compliance officers, except construction	155	186	196	205	31	42	50	20	27	32
Loan officers and counselors	171	230	239	241	60	68	70	35	40	41
Management analysts	208	283	297	313	75	89	105	36	40	50
Personnel, training, and labor relations specialists	281	360	383	398	79	102	117	28	36	42
Purchasing agents, except wholesale, retail, and farm products	222	200	216	232	-22	-6	10	-10	-3	4
Tax examiners, collectors, and revenue agents	64	71	75	78	6	10	14	10	16	21
Underwriters	100	116	124	125	16	24	24	16	24	24
Wholesale and retail buyers, except farm products	180	190	204	216	10	24	36	6	13	20
All other management support workers	892	1,163	1,240	1,292	271	348	400	30	39	45
Professional specialty occupations	16,592	21,640	22,801	23,681	5,048	6,209	7,089	30	37	43
Engineers	1,354	1,529	1,660	1,809	175	306	455	13	23	34
Aeronautical and astronautical engineers	66	69	75	80	4	9	15	6	14	22
Chemical engineers	52	57	62	66	5	10	15	10	19	28
Civil engineers, including traffic engineers	173	200	214	236	27	41	63	16	24	37
Electrical and electronics engineers	370	422	459	501	52	90	131	14	24	35
Industrial engineers, except safety engineers	119	126	138	151	8	20	32	6	17	27
Mechanical engineers	227	250	273	300	23	46	73	10	20	32
Metallurgists and metallurgical, ceramic, and materials engineers	19	22	24	26	3	5	7	18	28	38
Mining engineers, including mine safety engineers	4	3	4	4	[1]	0	0	-5	3	11
Nuclear engineers	17	16	17	18	-1	-	1	-5	0	6
Petroleum engineers	14	12	14	17	-2	[1]	3	-14	-2	19
All other engineers	295	350	380	409	56	85	115	19	29	39
Architects and surveyors	214	242	257	289	28	43	75	13	20	35
Architects, except landscape and marine	96	114	121	136	18	25	41	19	26	43
Landscape architects	19	23	24	26	4	5	7	21	26	37
Surveyors	99	105	112	127	6	13	27	6	13	28
Life scientists	182	210	222	231	28	40	49	16	22	27

[Continued]

★ 527 ★

Civilian Employment by Occupation under Low, Medium, and High Scenarios, 1992-2005-I

[Continued]

	Total employment				1992-2005 employment change					
	1992	Projected, 2005			Number			Percent		
		Low	Moderate	High	Low	Moderate	High	Low	Moderate	High
Agricultural and food scientists	29	31	33	35	3	4	6	9	14	20
Biological scientists	78	92	97	100	14	19	23	18	25	29
Foresters and conservation scientists	35	37	40	42	2	4	7	6	12	19
Medical scientists	39	48	51	52	9	12	14	24	31	35
All other life scientists	1	1	2	2	0	0	0	2	8	12
Computer, mathematical, and operations research occupations	758	1,418	1,530	1,616	660	772	858	87	102	113
Actuaries	15	18	19	19	3	4	5	21	29	32
Computer systems analysts, engineers, and scientists	666	1,300	1,403	1,485	634	737	819	95	111	123
Computer engineers and scientists	211	409	447	484	198	236	273	94	112	129
Systems analysts	455	891	956	1,001	436	501	546	96	110	120
Statisticians	16	17	18	18	0	2	2	3	9	13
Mathematicians and all other mathematical scientists	16	17	18	18	0	1	2	1	8	12
Operations research analysts	45	67	72	75	22	27	30	50	61	68
Physical scientists	197	227	243	257	29	45	60	15	23	30
Chemists	92	104	112	117	12	20	24	13	21	27
Geologists, geophysicists, and oceanographers	48	55	59	65	6	11	17	13	22	35
Meteorologists	6	7	8	8	1	1	2	17	24	30
Physicists and astronomers	21	19	20	21	-2	-1	0	-9	-3	1
All other physical scientists	30	42	45	46	11	14	16	37	46	54
Social scientists	258	337	353	369	80	95	111	31	37	43
Economists	51	61	64	67	10	13	15	19	25	30
Psychologists	143	204	212	222	60	69	78	42	48	55
Urban and regional planners	28	32	34	36	4	6	8	16	23	29
All other social scientists	35	40	42	44	5	7	9	14	20	25
Social, recreational, and religious workers	1,130	1,663	1,731	1,767	533	601	637	47	53	56
Clergy	189	238	245	250	49	56	61	26	30	32
Directors, religious activities and education	64	80	83	83	17	19	20	26	30	31
Human services workers	189	429	445	451	241	256	263	128	136	139
Recreation workers	204	270	282	290	66	78	86	32	38	42
Social workers	484	645	676	693	161	191	208	33	40	43
Lawyers and judicial workers	716	868	913	946	152	197	230	21	28	32
Judges, magistrates, and other judicial workers	90	87	92	96	-3	2	6	-3	2	7
Lawyers	626	781	821	850	155	195	224	25	31	36
Teachers, librarians, and counselors	5,984	7,642	8,010	8,284	1,658	2,026	2,300	28	34	38
Teachers, elementary	1,456	1,683	1,767	1,830	226	311	373	16	21	26
Teachers, preschool and kindergarten	434	646	669	682	212	236	248	49	54	57
Teachers, special education	358	594	625	648	236	267	290	66	74	81
Teachers, secondary school	1,263	1,640	1,724	1,789	377	462	526	30	37	42
College and university faculty	812	976	1,026	1,064	164	214	253	20	26	31
Other teachers and instructors	817	1,039	1,082	1,118	222	265	301	27	32	37
Farm and home management advisors	16	15	16	16	-1	1	0	-8	-3	1
Instructors and coaches, sports and physical training	260	343	355	363	82	94	102	32	36	39
Adult and vocational education teachers	540	681	712	739	141	172	199	26	32	37
Instructors, adult (nonvocational) education	235	285	296	309	50	60	73	21	26	31
Teachers and instructors, vocational education and training	305	396	416	430	91	111	125	30	36	41

[Continued]

★ 527 ★

Civilian Employment by Occupation under Low, Medium, and High Scenarios, 1992-2005-I

[Continued]

	Total employment				1992-2005 employment change					
	1992	Projected, 2005			Number			Percent		
		Low	Moderate	High	Low	Moderate	High	Low	Moderate	High
All other teachers and instructors	530	698	731	766	168	201	225	32	38	42
Librarians, archivists, curators, and related workers	160	172	181	188	11	21	28	7	13	17
Curators, archivists, museum technicians, and restorers	19	21	23	23	2	3	4	12	18	22
Librarians, professional	141	150	158	164	9	17	23	6	12	17
Counselors	154	195	204	211	40	50	56	26	32	37
Health diagnosing occupations	875	1,076	1,120	1,154	201	246	280	23	28	32
Chiropractors	46	60	62	65	14	16	19	31	36	42
Dentists	183	185	192	200	3	9	17	1	5	9
Optometrists	31	34	36	37	3	5	6	11	16	19
Physicians	556	720	751	769	164	195	213	29	35	38
Podiatrists	15	19	20	21	5	5	6	32	37	43
Veterinarians and veterinary inspectors	44	57	59	62	12	14	18	28	33	41
Health assessment and treating occupations	2,436	3,319	3,482	3,537	883	1,046	1,101	36	43	45
Dietitians and nutritionists	50	60	63	64	11	13	14	21	26	29
Pharmacists	163	198	211	217	35	47	53	21	29	33
Physician assistants	58	74	78	79	16	20	21	28	34	36
Registered nurses	1,835	2,479	2,601	2,637	644	765	802	35	42	44
Therapists	329	507	530	540	178	201	211	54	61	64
Occupational therapists	40	61	64	65	21	24	25	53	60	62
Physical therapists	90	163	170	173	72	79	82	80	88	91
Recreational therapists	30	41	42	43	10	12	13	34	40	42
Respiratory therapists	74	104	109	110	30	36	37	41	48	50
Speech-language pathologists and audiologists	73	105	110	113	32	37	40	45	51	56
All other therapists	23	34	36	37	11	13	14	49	56	59
Writers, artists, and entertainers	1,606	1,914	2,012	2,104	308	406	498	19	25	31
Artists and commercial artists	273	320	335	354	47	63	81	17	23	30
Athletes, coaches, umpires, and related workers	36	39	41	42	3	5	6	9	13	18
Dancers and choreographers	18	22	23	24	4	5	5	20	25	28
Designers	302	337	359	381	35	57	79	12	19	26
Designers, except interior designers	236	267	285	302	31	49	66	13	21	28
Interior designers	66	70	74	79	4	8	13	6	12	20
Musicians	236	285	294	304	49	59	69	21	25	29
Photographers and camera operators	118	141	147	153	23	29	35	20	25	30
Camera operators, television, motion picture, video	11	13	13	14	2	2	3	17	23	27
Photographers	107	129	134	140	21	27	32	20	25	30
Producers, directors, actors, and entertainers	129	190	198	205	61	69	76	47	54	59
Public relations specialists and publicity writers	98	117	123	127	19	26	30	20	26	30
Radio and TV announcers and newscasters	56	66	70	71	10	14	15	18	25	28
Reporters and correspondents	58	68	73	75	10	15	18	18	26	31
Writers and editors, including technical writers	283	328	348	367	45	66	84	16	23	30
All other professional workers	883	1,196	1,269	1,318	313	386	435	35	44	49
Technicians and related support occupations	4,282	5,324	5,664	5,895	1,042	1,383	1,613	24	32	38
Health technicians and technologists	2,028	2,710	2,848	2,897	682	821	870	34	40	43
Cardiology technologists	14	18	19	19	4	5	5	29	35	36
Clinical lab technologists and technicians	268	323	339	343	56	71	75	21	26	28
Dental hygienists	108	147	154	156	40	46	48	37	43	45
EEG technologists	6	9	10	10	3	3	4	47	54	55
EKG technicians	16	13	14	14	-3	-2	-2	-18	-14	-13
Emergency medical technicians	114	142	155	158	28	41	44	24	36	39

[Continued]

★ 527 ★

Civilian Employment by Occupation under Low, Medium, and High Scenarios, 1992-2005-I

[Continued]

	Total employment				1992-2005 employment change					
	1992	Projected, 2005			Number			Percent		
		Low	Moderate	High	Low	Moderate	High	Low	Moderate	High
Licensed practical nurse	659	879	920	933	220	261	274	33	40	42
Medical records technicians	76	118	123	125	42	47	49	54	61	64
Nuclear medicine technologists	12	17	18	18	5	6	6	43	50	52
Opticians, dispensing and measuring	63	81	86	88	18	22	25	28	36	39
Psychiatric technicians	72	86	90	91	15	19	19	20	26	27
Radiologic technologists and technicians	162	252	264	267	90	102	105	55	63	65
Surgical technologists	44	59	62	63	16	19	19	36	42	44
All other health professionals and paraprofessionals	413	564	595	612	151	181	199	36	44	48
Engineering and science technicians and technologists	1,253	1,372	1,482	1,609	118	229	356	9	18	28
Engineering technicians	695	761	827	899	66	132	204	10	19	29
Electrical and electronic technicians technologists	323	363	396	432	40	74	109	12	23	34
All other engineering technicians and technologists	372	399	431	466	27	59	94	7	16	25
Drafters	314	324	350	391	10	35	77	3	11	24
Science and mathematics technicians	244	286	305	319	42	61	75	17	25	31
Technicians, except health and engineering and science	1,000	1,243	1,334	1,389	242	333	388	24	33	39
Aircraft pilots and flight engineers	85	101	115	119	16	30	34	18	35	40
Air traffic controllers	23	24	25	26	1	2	3	3	10	14
Broadcast technicians	35	35	37	38	[1]	1	2	-1	4	6
Computer programmers	555	673	723	759	118	169	204	21	30	37
Legal assistants and technicians, except clerical	192	283	299	307	91	107	115	48	56	60
Paralegals	95	166	176	180	72	81	85	76	86	90
Title examiners and searchers	29	33	35	36	4	6	7	13	19	23
All other legal assistants, including law clerks	68	83	88	91	15	20	23	23	30	34
Programmers, numerical, tool, and process control	7	7	8	9	[1]	1	2	-3	8	21
Technical assistants, library	71	84	89	92	13	18	21	19	25	30
All other technicians	33	36	37	39	4	5	7	11	15	20
Marketing and sales occupations	12,993	14,659	15,664	16,336	1,665	2,671	3,342	13	21	26
Cashiers	2,747	3,201	3,417	3,520	453	670	773	17	24	28
Counter and rental clerks	242	314	331	341	72	88	99	30	36	41
Insurance sales workers	415	451	477	487	36	62	73	9	15	18
Marketing and sales workers supervisors	2,036	2,303	2,443	2,565	267	407	529	13	20	26
Real estate agents, brokers, and appraisers	397	446	461	490	48	63	93	12	16	23
Brokers, real estate	69	80	83	88	11	14	19	17	20	28
Real estate appraisers	45	60	63	66	15	17	20	33	38	45
Sales agents, real estate	283	305	315	337	22	32	53	8	11	19
Salespersons, retail	3,660	4,137	4,446	4,611	478	786	951	13	21	26
Securities and financial services salesworkers	200	250	265	270	50	65	71	25	33	35
Travel agents	115	167	191	196	52	76	81	45	66	70
All other sales and related workers	3,181	3,390	3,634	3,855	209	452	674	7	14	21
Administrative support occupations, including clerical	22,349	23,852	25,406	26,416	1,504	3,057	4,067	7	14	18
Adjusters, investigators, and collectors	1,152	1,412	1,510	1,545	260	358	393	23	31	34
Adjustment clerks	352	412	445	462	61	93	110	17	26	31
Bill and account collectors	235	309	328	339	75	94	104	32	40	45
Insurance claims and policy processing occupations	434	545	583	584	111	149	151	26	34	35

[Continued]

★ 527 ★

Civilian Employment by Occupation under Low, Medium, and High Scenarios, 1992-2005-I

[Continued]

	Total employment				1992-2005 employment change					
	1992	Projected, 2005			Number			Percent		
		Low	Moderate	High	Low	Moderate	High	Low	Moderate	High
Insurance adjusters, examiners, and investigators	147	205	220	220	58	72	73	39	49	49
Insurance claims clerks	116	149	158	159	33	43	44	29	37	38
Insurance policy processing clerks	171	191	205	205	20	34	34	12	20	20
Welfare eligibility workers and interviewers	93	103	109	114	10	16	21	10	17	22
All other adjusters and investigators	38	42	44	46	4	7	8	11	17	20
Communications equipment operators	327	219	234	241	-108	-93	-86	-33	-28	-26
Telephone operators	314	211	225	232	-103	-89	-82	-33	-28	-26
Central office operators	48	22	24	24	-26	-24	-24	-55	-50	-49
Directory assistance operators	27	12	13	14	-15	-14	-13	-55	-51	-49
Switchboard operators	239	117	188	194	-62	-51	-45	-26	-21	-19
All other communications equipment operators	13	8	9	9	-5	-4	-4	-38	-33	-32
Computer operators and peripheral equipment operators	296	162	173	181	-134	-122	-155	-45	-41	-39
Computer operators, except peripheral equipment	266	151	161	168	-115	-104	-97	-43	-39	-37
Peripheral EDP equipment operators	30	11	12	12	-19	-18	-18	-63	-60	-59
Information clerks	1,333	1,665	1,762	1,810	332	429	477	25	32	36
Hotel desks clerks	122	167	172	178	45	50	56	37	41	46
Interviewing clerks, except personnel and social welfare	71	90	95	96	20	24	26	28	34	36
New accounts clerks, banking	105	110	114	115	5	10	10	5	9	10
Receptionists and information clerks	904	1,149	1,210	1,245	245	305	341	27	34	38
Reservation and transportation ticket agents and travel clerks	131	149	171	176	18	39	45	14	30	34
Mail clerks and messengers	271	279	298	307	8	26	35	3	10	13
Mail clerks, except mail machine operators and postal service	132	146	155	160	14	24	28	11	18	22
Messengers	140	134	142	147	-6	2	7	-4	2	5
Postal clerks and mail carriers	361	325	362	390	-36	2	29	-10	0	8
Postal mail carriers	297	269	300	322	-28	3	25	-9	1	8
Postal service clerks	64	56	63	68	-7	-1	4	-12	-2	6

Source: U.S. Department of Labor, Bureau of Labor Statistics, *The American Work Force: 1992-2005* (Washington, D.C.: U.S. Government Printing Office, April 1994), pp. 56, 59-71. *Note:* 1. A decline of fewer than 1,000 workers.

★ 528 ★

Employment by Occupation and Industry

Civilian Employment by Occupation under Low, Medium, and High Scenarios, 1992-2005-II

"Projected growth from 1992 to 2005 will vary widely among the individual occupations, ranging from an increase of 138 percent to a decline of 75 percent. In general, occupations that require a bachelor's degree or other post-secondary education or training are projected to have faster-than-average rates of employment growth. Also, many occupations requiring less formal education or training are projected to have above average growth. In addition to the growth rate, the size of the occupational stock of jobs is an important factor in determining the numerical growth in the occupation; therefore, it has a great effect on the structure of future employment. Many slower growing occupations, some requiring little education and training and others having significant educational requirements, are expected to add significant numbers of jobs primarily because of their large employment bases. As a result, the economy is projected to continue to generate jobs for workers at all levels of education and training.

"Most of the employment growth will occur in service-producing industries. As a consequence, occupations concentrated in those industries are more likely to experience rapid employment growth, compared with occupations in the goods-producing industries. Of the 26.4 million projected increase in total employment over the 1992-2005 period, more than 25 million jobs are projected in the service-producing industries and fewer than 1 million jobs are expected in the goods-producing industries."

[Thousands]

	Total employment				1992-2005 employment change					
	1992	Projected, 2005			Number			Percent		
		Low	Moderate	High	Low	Moderate	High	Low	Moderate	High
Material recording, scheduling, dispatching, and distributing occupations	3,588	3,734	4,043	4,258	145	455	669	4	13	19
Dispatchers	222	249	268	282	28	46	60	13	21	27
Dispatchers, except police, fire, and ambulance	146	167	181	190	21	34	44	14	23	30
Dispatchers, police, fire, and ambulance	75	82	87	91	7	12	16	9	16	22
Meter readers, utilities	49	47	49	51	-3	0	2	-5	0	5
Order filers, wholesale and retail sales	187	200	216	232	13	29	45	7	16	24
Procurement clerks	61	50	54	57	-11	-7	-4	-17	-11	-6
Production, planning, and expediting clerks	239	248	272	292	8	31	52	3	13	22
Stock clerks	1,782	1,801	1,940	2,024	19	158	242	1	9	14
Traffic, shipping, and receiving clerks	824	889	971	1,034	65	147	209	8	18	25
Weighers, measurers, checkers, and samplers, recordkeeping	46	50	54	57	4	8	11	9	17	24
All other material recording, scheduling, and distribution workers	178	200	219	229	22	41	51	12	23	28
Records processing occupations	3,621	3,604	3,834	4,009	-17	213	388	[1]	6	11
Advertising clerks	17	22	23	24	5	6	7	28	37	43
Brokerage clerks	57	65	69	70	7	12	12	13	21	22
Correspondence clerks	31	31	33	34	0	2	3	0	7	10
File clerks	257	288	305	313	31	48	56	12	19	22
Financial records processing occupations	2,686	2,609	2,770	2,905	-77	84	219	-3	3	8
Billing, cost, and rate clerks	315	332	355	368	17	39	52	5	12	17
Billing, posting, and calculating machine operators	93	62	66	68	-31	-28	-25	-34	-29	-27
Bookkeeping, accounting, and auditing clerks	2,112	2,060	2,186	2,296	-52	73	184	-2	3	9
Payroll and timekeeping clerks	165	154	164	173	-11	-1	8	-7	[1]	5
Library assistants and bookmobile drivers	114	127	135	140	13	20	26	12	18	23
Order clerks, materials, merchandise, and service	300	289	313	331	-11	13	31	-4	4	10
Personnel clerks, except payroll and timekeeping	128	150	160	167	22	32	39	17	25	30
Statement clerks	31	24	25	25	-7	-6	-6	-23	-20	-19
Secretaries, stenographers, and typists	4,228	4,241	4,488	4,665	12	259	437	0	6	10
Secretaries	3,324	3,508	3,710	3,860	183	386	535	6	12	16
Legal secretaries	280	415	439	447	135	160	168	48	57	60
Medical secretaries	235	326	341	345	92	106	110	39	45	47
Secretaries, except legal and medical	2,810	2,766	2,930	3,067	-43	120	258	-2	4	9
Stenographers	115	107	113	117	-8	-2	3	-7	-1	2
Typists and word processors	789	626	664	688	-163	-125	-101	-21	-16	-13

[Continued]

★ 528 ★

Civilian Employment by Occupation under Low, Medium, and High Scenarios, 1992-2005-II

[Continued]

	Total employment				1992-2005 employment change					
	1992	Projected, 2005			Number			Percent		
		Low	Moderate	High	Low	Moderate	High	Low	Moderate	High
Other clerical and administrative support workers	7,172	8,211	8,702	9,011	1,039	1,530	1,839	14	21	26
Bank tellers	525	481	502	503	-444	-24	-22	-8	-4	-4
Clerical supervisors and managers	1,267	1,473	1,568	1,622	206	301	355	16	24	28
Court clerks	50	58	61	64	8	12	15	17	24	30
Credit authorizers, credit checkers, and loan and credit clerks	218	260	272	276	41	53	57	19	24	26
Credit authorizers	19	22	23	24	3	5	6	16	24	29
Credit checkers	41	45	48	50	4	7	9	10	17	22
Loan and credit clerks	142	172	179	180	31	37	38	22	26	27
Loan interviewers	17	21	22	22	4	4	5	22	26	27
Customer service representatives, utilities	127	141	151	156	13	24	29	11	19	23
Data entry keyers, except composing	432	482	515	534	50	83	101	12	19	23
Data entry keyers, composing	16	11	12	12	-5	-4	-4	-32	-26	-24
Duplicating, mail, and other office machine operators	162	172	183	189	10	21	27	6	13	17
General office clerks	2,688	3,143	3,342	3,489	455	654	801	17	24	30
Municipal clerks	22	25	26	27	2	4	5	10	17	22
Proofreaders and copy markers	27	26	28	29	1	2	3	-1	6	10
Real estate clerks	24	34	35	37	10	11	12	40	44	52
Statistical clerks	74	65	69	71	-8	-4	-2	-11	-6	-3
Teacher aides and educational assistants	885	1,209	1,266	1,308	324	381	423	37	43	48
All other clerical and administrative support workers	655	631	671	-23	16	39	-4	2	6	
Service occupations	19,358	24,609	25,820	26,438	5,241	6,461	7,080	27	33	37
Cleaning and building service occupations, except private household	3,284	3,726	3,913	4,039	442	629	755	13	19	23
Institutional cleaning supervisors	156	200	208	213	44	52	57	28	34	37
Janitors and cleaners, including maids and housekeeping cleaners	2,862	3,246	3,410	3,519	384	548	657	13	19	23
Pest controllers and assistants	49	48	51	53	-1	2	4	-2	5	8
All other cleaning and building service workers	217	232	244	254	15	27	37	7	12	17
Food preparation and service occupations	7,669	9,566	10,060	10,189	1,897	2,391	2,520	25	31	33
Chefs, cooks, and other kitchen workers	3,092	4,070	4,282	4,343	978	1,190	1,251	32	38	40
Cooks, except short order	1,155	1,488	1,564	1,590	33	409	435	29	35	38
Bakers, bread and pastry	146	202	216	222	55	69	75	38	47	51
Cooks, institution or cafeteria	406	449	470	479	43	64	73	11	16	18
Cooks, restaurant	602	837	879	889	235	276	286	39	46	48
Cooks, short order and fast food	714	921	971	978	207	257	264	29	36	37
Food preparation workers	1,223	1,661	1,748	1,775	438	524	552	36	43	45
Food and beverage service occupations	4,365	5,223	5,489	5,548	858	1,124	1,183	20	26	27
Bartenders	382	385	350	354	-47	-32	-28	-12	-8	-7
Dining room and cafeteria attendants and bar helpers	441	546	572	580	105	131	139	24	30	31
Food counter, fountain, and related workers	1,564	1,776	1,872	1,895	212	308	331	14	20	21
Hosts and hostesses, restaurant, lounge, or coffee shop	222	286	301	304	64	79	83	29	36	37
Waiters and waitresses	1,756	2,280	2,394	2,415	523	637	659	30	36	37
All other food preparation and service workers	212	273	289	298	61	77	86	29	36	40
Health service occupations	2,041	2,943	3,073	3,124	901	1,032	1,082	44	51	53
Ambulance drivers and attendants, except EMTs	15	16	18	18	1	3	3	6	17	19
Dental assistants	183	244	254	258	61	72	75	34	39	41
Medical assistants	181	296	308	313	115	128	132	63	71	73
Nursing aides and psychiatric aides	1,389	1,922	2,006	2,041	533	616	652	38	44	47
Nursing aides, orderlies, and attendants	1,308	1,824	1,903	1,937	515	594	628	39	45	48
Psychiatric aides	81	98	103	105	17	22	24	21	28	30
Occupational therapy assistant aides	12	20	21	21	8	9	9	71	78	80
Pharmacy assistants	54	72	76	77	19	22	24	35	42	44
Physical and corrective therapy assistants and aides	61	113	118	119	52	57	58	85	93	95
All other health service workers	147	260	273	276	113	125	129	77	85	88

[Continued]

★ 528 ★

Civilian Employment by Occupation under Low, Medium, and High Scenarios, 1992-2005-II

[Continued]

	Total employment				1992-2005 employment change					
	1992	Projected, 2005			Number			Percent		
		Low	Moderate	High	Low	Moderate	High	Low	Moderate	High
Personal service occupations	2,295	3,668	3,804	3,913	1,373	1,509	1,618	60	65	70
Amusement and recreation attendants	207	294	303	309	87	96	102	42	46	49
Baggage porters and bellhops	34	47	50	52	13	16	17	38	46	51
Barbers	71	67	69	73	-3	-1	3	-4	-2	4
Child care workers	684	1,100	1,135	1,183	415	450	499	61	66	73
Cosmetologists and related workers	676	893	915	947	217	240	271	32	35	40
Hairdressers, hairstylists, and cosmetologists	628	824	846	876	196	218	248	31	35	39
Manicurists	35	54	55	56	18	19	21	51	54	58
Shampooers	12	15	15	15	3	3	3	23	24	25
Flight attendants	93	121	140	144	28	47	51	30	51	55
Homemaker-home health aides	475	1,077	1,120	1,131	602	645	656	127	136	138
Home health aides	347	794	827	835	447	479	488	129	138	141
Personal and home care aides	127	283	293	296	156	166	168	122	130	132
Ushers, lobby attendants, and ticker takers	56	69	72	74	13	16	18	24	29	33
Private household workers	869	565	583	620	-304	-286	-249	-35	-33	-29
Child care workers, private household	350	220	227	242	-130	-123	-108	-37	-35	-31
Cleaners and servants, private household	483	316	326	347	-167	-157	-136	-35	-32	-28
Cooks, private household	9	7	7	8	-2	-2	-1	-21	-18	-13
Housekeepers and butlers	27	22	22	24	-5	-5	-3	-20	-18	-12
Protective service occupations	2,320	2,970	3,154	3,290	649	834	970	28	36	42
Firefighting occupations	305	334	354	372	29	50	67	10	16	22
Fire fighters	229	252	267	280	23	38	51	10	17	22
Fire fighting and prevention supervisors	62	68	72	75	6	10	13	9	16	22
Fire inspection occupations	14	15	15	16	1	2	3	7	13	20
Law enforcement occupations	982	1,198	1,271	1,333	216	289	351	22	29	36
Correction officers	282	452	479	503	169	197	221	60	70	78
Police and detectives	700	746	792	830	46	92	130	7	13	19
Police and detective supervisors	97	103	109	114	6	12	17	6	13	18
Police detectives and investigators	70	72	76	80	1	6	9	2	8	13
Police patrol officers	441	441	468	491	30	57	80	7	14	19
Sheriffs and deputy sheriffs	84	90	95	100	6	12	16	7	14	19
Other law enforcement occupations	38	41	43	46	3	5	8	8	14	20
Other protective service workers	1,034	1,438	1,529	1,586	405	495	552	39	48	53
Detectives, except public	59	94	100	104	35	41	45	60	70	77
Guards	803	1,138	1,211	1,255	335	408	452	42	51	56
Crossing guards	57	65	69	72	8	12	15	14	20	27
All other protective service workers	115	141	149	155	26	34	40	23	30	35
All other service workers	879	1,172	1,232	1,263	292	353	384	33	40	44
Agriculture, forestry, fishing, and related occupations	3,530	3,523	3,650	3,871	-7	120	341	[1]	3	10
Animal caretakers, except farm	103	138	143	151	36	41	48	35	40	47
Farm occupations	921	806	832	881	-115	-88	-40	-12	-10	-4
Farmworkers	849	696	716	758	-153	-133	-91	-18	-16	-11
Nursery workers	72	110	116	123	38	44	51	53	62	71
Farm operators and managers	1,218	984	1,014	1,081	-234	-204	-137	-19	-17	-11
Farmers	1,088	831	857	914	-257	-231	-174	-24	-21	-16
Farm managers	130	153	157	167	23	27	37	18	21	28
Fishers, hunters, and trappers	60	62	64	67	1	3	6	2	5	10
Captains and other officers, fishing vessels	8	8	9	9	0	1	1	4	7	12
Fishers, hunters, and trappers	52	53	55	58	1	2	5	2	5	10
Forestry and logging occupations	131	128	134	148	-3	3	17	-2	2	13
Forest and conservation workers	35	41	43	47	6	8	12	16	22	33
Timber cutting and logging occupations	96	87	91	101	-9	-5	5	-9	-5	6
Fallers and buckers	33	28	29	32	-5	-4	-1	-15	-11	-3
Logging tractor operators	26	26	27	30	[1]	1	4	-1	4	16
Log handling equipment operators	15	14	15	17	-1	-1	1	-9	-4	9
All other timber cutting and related logging workers	22	20	20	23	-2	-1	1	-10	-7	4

[Continued]

★ 528 ★

Civilian Employment by Occupation under Low, Medium, and High Scenarios, 1992-2005-II

[Continued]

	Total employment				1992-2005 employment change					
	1992	Projected, 2005			Number			Percent		
		Low	Moderate	High	Low	Moderate	High	Low	Moderate	High
Gardeners and groundskeepers, except farm	884	1,152	1,195	1,261	268	311	377	30	35	43
Supervisors, farming, forestry, and agricultural related occupations	71	80	83	89	9	12	17	13	17	24
All other agricultural, forestry, fishing, and related workers	142	173	184	194	31	42	52	22	29	36
Precision production, craft, and repair occupations	13,580	14,465	15,380	16,713	885	1,800	3,133	7	13	23
Blue-collar worker supervisors	1,757	1,844	1,974	2,131	87	217	374	5	12	21
Construction trades	3,510	4,116	4,295	4,826	606	786	1,317	17	22	38
Bricklayers and stone masons	139	167	174	200	29	36	62	21	26	44
Carpenters	978	1,131	1,176	1,317	153	198	338	16	20	35
Carpet installers	62	72	75	81	10	13	19	17	22	31
Ceiling tile installers and acoustical carpenters	12	11	12	14	-1	1	2	-5	-1	16
Concrete and terrazzo finishers	100	109	113	133	9	13	33	9	13	33
Drywall installers and finishers	121	159	165	190	38	44	70	32	37	58
Electricians	518	588	618	698	70	100	180	14	19	35
Glaziers	39	49	51	59	10	12	19	24	30	48
Hard tile setters	30	36	37	42	6	7	12	21	25	40
Highway maintenance workers	168	204	217	230	36	49	62	22	29	37
Insulation workers	57	76	79	92	19	22	36	34	40	63
Painters and paperhangers, construction and maintenance	440	547	569	624	107	128	184	24	29	42
Paving, surfacing, and tamping equipment operators	72	102	107	123	30	35	50	41	48	69
Pipelayers and pipelaying fitters	48	58	61	70	10	13	22	21	26	45
Plasterers	32	36	37	43	4	5	11	12	16	34
Plumbers, pipefitters, and steamfitters	351	362	378	428	11	27	76	3	8	22
Roofers	127	149	155	176	22	28	49	17	22	38
Structural and reinforcing metal workers	66	78	81	95	12	15	29	18	22	44
All other construction trades workers	150	181	190	214	31	40	64	20	26	43
Extractive and related workers, including blasters	231	211	226	263	-20	-6	32	-9	-2	14
Oil and gas extraction occupations	69	44	48	70	-25	-21	1	-36	-31	2
Roustabouts	33	20	22	32	-13	-11	-1	-38	-33	-2
All other oil and gas extraction occupations	36	24	26	38	-12	-10	2	-33	-29	5
Mining, quarrying, and tunneling occupations	21	17	19	20	-4	-3	-1	-18	-12	-6
All other extraction and related workers	141	149	159	173	9	18	32	6	13	23
Mechanics, installers, and repairers	4,819	5,240	5,581	5,929	421	762	1,110	9	16	23
Communications equipment mechanics, installers, and repairers	108	62	68	69	-46	-41	-39	-43	-38	-36
Central office and PBX installers and repairers	70	41	45	46	-29	-25	-24	-41	-36	-34
Frame wirers, central office	11	2	3	3	-8	-8	-8	-77	-75	-75
Radio mechanics	9	8	8	9	-2	-1	-1	-17	-11	-9
Signal or track switch maintainers	3	1	1	1	-2	-2	-2	-77	-75	-73
All other communications equipment mechanics, installers, and repairers	15	10	11	11	-5	-4	-4	-34	-30	-27
Electrical and electronic equipment mechanics, installers, and repairers	545	500	535	570	-45	-9	25	-8	-2	5
Data processing equipment repairers	83	112	120	128	29	38	45	35	45	55
Electrical powerline installers and repairers	108	110	117	126	3	9	18	2	9	17
Electronic home entertainment equipment repairers	39	35	37	38	-4	-2	1	-11	-5	-1
Electronics repairers, commercial and industrial equipment	68	68	73	78	0	5	9	0	7	14
Station installers and repairers, telephone	40	18	20	20	-22	-20	-19	-55	-50	-49
Telephone and cable TV line installers and repairers	165	117	125	134	-49	-40	-31	-29	-24	-19

[Continued]

★ 528 ★

Civilian Employment by Occupation under Low, Medium, and High Scenarios, 1992-2005-II

[Continued]

	Total employment				1992-2005 employment change					
	1992	Projected, 2005			Number			Percent		
		Low	Moderate	High	Low	Moderate	High	Low	Moderate	High
All other electrical and electronic equipment mechanics, installers, and repairers	42	40	43	46	-2	1	3	-5	3	8
Machinery and related mechanics, installers, and repairers	1,696	1,889	2,005	2,122	193	310	426	11	18	25
Industrial machinery mechanics	477	427	462	492	-50	-15	14	-11	-3	3
Maintenance repairers, general utility	1,145	1,388	1,464	1,542	243	319	397	21	28	35
Millwrights	73	74	79	88	1	6	15	1	9	20
Vehicle and mobile equipment mechanics and repairers	1,524	1,735	1,850	1,964	211	326	440	14	21	29
Aircraft mechanics and engine specialists	131	131	148	154	[1]	17	22	[1]	13	17
Aircraft engine specialists	26	26	28	30	-1	2	3	-2	8	13
Aircraft mechanics	105	106	120	124	0	15	19	0	14	18
Automotive body and related repairers	202	250	263	281	48	61	80	24	30	39
Automotive mechanics	739	857	907	960	117	168	220	16	23	30
Bus and truck mechanics and diesel engine specialists	263	305	327	348	42	64	85	16	24	32
Farm equipment mechanics	47	49	53	56	3	6	10	6	13	21
Mobile heavy equipment mechanics	96	94	100	109	-2	4	13	-3	4	13
Motorcycle, boat, and small engine mechanics	46	50	53	56	4	7	9	8	15	21
Motorcycle repairers	11	10	10	11	-1	[1]	0	-10	-4	1
Small engine specialists	35	40	43	45	5	7	9	14	21	27
Other mechanics, installers, and repairers	946	1,054	1,123	1,204	108	176	258	11	19	27
Bicycle repairers	14	18	20	20	5	6	7	36	45	51
Camera and photographic equipment repairers	8	8	9	9	1	1	2	10	16	23
Coin and vending machine servicers and repairers	20	19	20	20	-1	[1]	1	-6	[1]	3
Electric meter installers and repairers	13	12	13	13	-1	-1	[1]	-11	-6	-1
Electromedical and biomedical equipment repairers	10	12	13	13	3	3	4	30	37	39
Elevator installers and repairers	22	24	25	29	3	4	8	12	18	35
Heat, air conditioning, and refrigeration mechanics and installers	212	261	274	305	49	62	94	23	29	44
Home appliance and power tool repairers	74	69	74	77	-5	[1]	3	-6	[1]	4
Locksmiths and safe repairers	18	21	22	23	2	3	5	12	19	25
Musical instrument repairers and tuners	12	13	13	14	0	1	2	4	9	15
Office machine and cash register servicers	60	60	65	70	0	5	10	0	8	16
Precision instrument repairers	45	44	48	51	-1	3	6	-1	7	13
Riggers	12	11	12	13	-1	0	1	-6	1	10
Tire repairers and changers	80	89	95	99	8	15	19	10	18	24
Watchmakers	9	7	7	8	-2	-2	-2	-26	-23	-18
All other mechanics, installers, and repairers	338	386	413	439	48	75	100	14	22	30

Source: U.S. Department of Labor, Bureau of Labor Statistics, *The American Work Force: 1992-2005* (Washington, D.C.: U.S. Government Printing Office, April 1994), pp. 56, 59-71. *Note:* 1. A decline of fewer than 1,000 workers.

★ 529 ★

Employment by Occupation and Industry

Civilian Employment by Occupation under Low, Medium, and High Scenarios, 1992-2005-III

"Projected growth from 1992 to 2005 will vary widely among the individual occupations, ranging from an increase of 138 percent to a decline of 75 percent. In general, occupations that require a bachelor's degree or other post-secondary education or training are projected to have faster-than-average rates of employment growth. Also, many occupations requiring less formal education or training are projected to have above average growth. In addition to the growth rate, the size of the occupational stock of jobs is an important factor in determining the numerical growth in the occupation; therefore, it has a great effect on the structure of future employment. Many slower growing occupations, some requiring little education and training and others having significant educational requirements, are expected to add significant numbers of jobs primarily because of their large employment bases. As a result, the economy is projected to continue to generate jobs for workers at all levels of education and training.

"Most of the employment growth will occur in service-producing industries. As a consequence, occupations concentrated in those industries are more likely to experience rapid employment growth, compared with occupations in the goods-producing industries. Of the 26.4 million projected increase in total employment over the 1992-2005 period, more than 25 million jobs are projected in the service-producing industries and fewer than 1 million jobs are expected in the goods-producing industries."

[Thousands]

	Total employment				1992-2005 employment change					
	1992	Projected, 2005			Number			Percent		
		Low	Moderate	High	Low	Moderate	High	Low	Moderate	High
Production occupations, precision	2,956	2,737	2,965	3,205	-219	9	249	-7	0	8
Assemblers, precision	334	281	316	356	-54	-18	22	-16	-6	7
Aircraft assemblers, precision	26	25	27	29	-1	1	3	-4	4	12
Electrical and electronic equipment assemblers, precision	150	113	129	147	-37	-21	-2	-24	-14	-1
Electromechanical equipment assemblers, precision	48	37	42	47	-11	-6	-1	-24	-13	-2
Fitters, structural metal, precision	15	14	14	17	-1	[1]	2	-7	-1	14
Machine builders and other precision machine assemblers	57	52	59	66	-4	2	9	-8	4	17
All other precision assemblers	40	41	45	50	1	6	10	2	14	26
Food workers, precision	305	264	279	286	-41	-26	-19	-13	-8	-6
Bakers, manufacturing	43	44	45	46	1	2	3	2	6	7
Butchers and meatcutters	222	179	191	197	-42	-31	-25	-19	-14	-11
All other precision food and tobacco workers	40	41	43	43	1	2	3	2	6	7
Inspectors, testers, and graders, precision	625	511	559	598	-113	-65	-27	-18	-10	-4
Metal workers, precision	854	807	880	975	-46	26	121	-5	3	14
Boilermakers	26	24	25	28	-2	-1	2	-9	04	6
Jewelers and silversmiths	30	33	35	37	3	6	7	11	19	25
Machinists	352	315	348	382	-37	-4	30	-10	-1	8
Sheet metal workers and duct installers	208	229	244	279	21	36	71	10	17	34
Shipfitters	13	10	11	11	-3	-2	-2	-23	-18	-16
Tool and die makers	138	115	128	141	-22	-9	3	-16	-7	3
All other precision metal workers	88	81	89	97	-7	1	10	-8	1	11
Printing workers, precision	151	163	176	182	13	25	31	8	17	21
Bookbinders	8	8	9	9	0	1	1	6	14	18
Prepress printing workers, precision	130	133	143	147	3	13	18	2	10	13
Compositors and typesetters, precision	11	7	8	8	-3	-3	-3	-31	-27	-23
Job printers	15	9	10	10	-6	-5	-5	-39	-35	-33
Paste-up workers	22	17	18	19	-5	-4	-3	-25	-19	-16
Electronic pagination systems workers	18	29	32	33	12	14	15	65	78	84
Photoengravers	7	7	8	8	1	1	2	12	21	25
Camera operators	14	14	15	16	[1]	1	2	[1]	7	11
Strippers, printing	30	35	38	39	5	8	9	16	25	29
Platemakers	13	13	14	15	[1]	1	1	-1	7	10
All other printing workers, precision	13	23	24	25	9	11	12	72	85	91
Textile, apparel, and furnishing workers, precision	266	245	260	271	-21	-6	5	-8	-2	2
Custom tailors and sewers	113	103	109	114	-9	-4	1	-8	-4	1

[Continued]

★ 529 ★

Civilian Employment by Occupation under Low, Medium, and High Scenarios, 1992-2005-III

[Continued]

	Total employment				1992-2005 employment change					
	1992	Projected, 2005			Number			Percent		
		Low	Moderate	High	Low	Moderate	High	Low	Moderate	High
Patternmakers and layout workers, fabric and apparel	18	13	15	15	-5	-3	-3	-29	-18	-17
Shoe and leather workers and repairers, precision	22	16	17	18	-6	-4	-4	-26	-20	-17
Upholsterers	60	63	67	71	3	7	10	5	11	17
All other precision textile, apparel, and furnishings workers	54	50	52	53	-4	-1	[1]	-7	-2	-1
Woodworkers, precision	220	258	272	305	37	52	85	17	24	38
Cabinetmakers and bench carpenters	114	135	141	160	21	28	47	19	24	41
Furniture finishers	37	40	43	46	4	7	9	11	18	25
Wood machinists	46	56	60	67	10	13	21	22	29	45
All other precision woodworkers	24	26	28	32	2	4	8	10	18	33
Other precision workers	201	207	222	233	6	21	32	3	10	16
Dental lab technicians, precision	48	48	50	51	[1]	2	2	-1	3	5
Optical goods workers, precision	19	20	23	24	2	4	5	9	22	25
Photographic process workers, precision	14	17	18	18	3	4	4	21	26	31
All other precision workers	120	122	132	140	2	12	20	2	10	17
Plant and system occupations	308	317	340	359	9	32	51	3	10	17
Chemical plant and system operators	39	36	40	41	-3	0	2	-7	1	5
Electric power generating plant operators, distributors, and dispatchers	43	44	47	49	2	4	6	4	10	15
Power distributors and dispatchers	17	16	17	17	-1	0	1	-6	0	5
Power generating and reactor plant operators	26	29	30	32	3	4	5	10	16	21
Gas and petroleum plant and system occupations	31	27	30	33	-5	-2	2	-15	-5	7
Stationary engineers	31	31	33	34	[1]	2	3	-1	5	9
Water and liquid waste treatment plant and system operators	86	96	102	107	10	16	21	11	18	24
All other plant and system operators	78	83	89	95	6	12	17	7	15	22
Operators, fabricators, and laborers	16,349	16,603	17,902	19,103	254	1,553	,2754	2	10	17
Machine setters, set-up operators, operators, and tenders	4,676	3,958	4,326	4,579	-719	-350	-97	-15	-7	-2
Numerical control machine tool operators and tenders, metal and plastic	73	78	87	97	5	14	24	7	20	33
Combination machine tool setters, set-up operators, operators, and tenders	102	114	126	138	12	24	37	12	24	36
Machine tool cut and form setters, operators, and tenders, metal and plastic	674	530	586	643	-144	-89	-31	-21	-13	-5
Drilling and boring machine tool setters and set-up operators, metal and plastic	44	34	38	43	-9	-5	-1	-21	-12	-2
Grinding machine setters and set-up operators, metal and plastic	65	53	58	64	-13	-7	-1	-20	-11	-2
Lathe and turning machine tool setters and set-up operators, metal and plastic	69	52	58	64	-17	-11	-4	-24	-16	-6
Machine forming operators and tenders, metal and plastic	155	112	123	133	-43	-32	-22	-28	-21	-14
Machine tool cutting operators and tenders, metal and plastic	114	85	96	104	-29	-19	-9	-25	-17	-8
Punching machine setters and set-up operators, metal and plastic	45	34	38	41	-11	-7	-4	-25	-17	-8
All other machine tool cutting and forming, etc.	182	160	176	193	-23	-7	11	-12	-4	6
Metal fabricating machine setters, operators, and related workers	151	123	134	150	-29	-17	-1	-19	-11	-1
Metal fabricators, structural metal products	45	42	45	52	-3	0	7	-6	0	15

[Continued]

★ 529 ★

Civilian Employment by Occupation under Low, Medium, and High Scenarios, 1992-2005-III

[Continued]

	Total employment				1992-2005 employment change					
	1992	Projected, 2005			Number			Percent		
		Low	Moderate	High	Low	Moderate	High	Low	Moderate	High
Soldering and brazing machine operators and tenders	9	7	8	9	-2	-1	0	-21	-10	2
Welding machine setters, operators, and tenders	97	73	80	89	-24	-17	-8	-25	-17	-8
Metal and plastic processing machine setters, operators, and related workers	399	365	401	435	-34	3	36	-8	1	9
Electrolytic plating machine operators and tenders, setters and set-up operators, metal and plastic	42	37	41	46	-5	-1	4	-12	-2	10
Foundry mold assembly and shakeout workers	9	8	9	10	-1	0	1	-6	3	14
Furnace operators and tenders	20	17	19	20	-3	-1	1	-16	-6	3
Heaters, metal and plastic	3	3	3	4	[1]	[1]	0	-13	-4	4
Heating equipment setters and set-up operators, metal and plastic	6	5	5	6	-1	-1	[1]	-22	-13	-5
Heat treating machine operators and tenders, metal and plastic	19	15	16	18	-4	-3	-1	-22	-14	-5
Metal molding machine operators and tenders, setters and set-up operators	38	31	34	37	-8	-4	-1	-20	-11	-2
Nonelectrolytic plating machine operators and tenders, setters and set-up operators, metal and plastic	7	6	7	7	-1	-1	0	-18	-9	1
Plastic molding machine operators and tenders, setters and set-up operators	150	148	161	171	-3	11	21	-2	7	14
All other metal and plastic machine setters, operators, and related workers	104	96	106	115	-7	2	11	-7	2	11
Printing, binding, and related workers	375	411	444	459	36	69	85	10	18	23
Bindery machine operators and set-up operators	68	73	79	81	5	11	13	8	16	20
Prepress printing workers, production	24	21	22	23	-4	-2	-1	-15	-9	-5
Photoengraving and lithographic machine operators and tenders	5	5	5	5	0	0	1	3	11	14
Typesetting and composing machine operators and tenders	20	16	17	18	-4	-3	-3	-19	-13	-10
Printing press operators	217	237	255	264	20	38	47	9	18	22
Letterpress operators	13	10	11	12	-3	-2	-2	-21	-15	-12
Offset lithographic press operators	79	101	108	112	22	29	33	28	37	42
Printing press machine setters, operators and tenders	110	109	118	122	-1	8	12	[1]	7	11
All other printing press setters and set-up operators	14	16	17	18	2	3	4	12	19	24
Screen printing machine setters and set-up operators	25	31	34	35	6	9	10	23	37	42
All other printing, binding, and related workers	41	49	54	56	8	12	15	20	30	36
Textile and related setters, operators, and related workers	1,041	733	829	843	-308	-212	-198	-30	-20	-19
Extruding and forming machine operators and tenders, synthetic or glass fibers	23	19	21	22	-4	-2	-1	-17	-10	-5
Pressing machine operators and tenders, textile, garment, and related materials	78	80	86	86	2	8	8	3	10	11
Sewing machine operators, garment	556	338	393	396	-217	-162	-159	-39	-29	-29
Sewing machine operators, non-garment	124	103	114	118	-21	-10	-6	-17	-9	-5

[Continued]

★ 529 ★

Civilian Employment by Occupation under Low, Medium, and High Scenarios, 1992-2005-III

[Continued]

	Total employment				1992-2005 employment change					
	1992	Projected, 2005			Number			Percent		
		Low	Moderate	High	Low	Moderate	High	Low	Moderate	High
Textile bleaching and dyeing machine operators and tenders	29	23	26	27	-6	-3	-3	-21	-11	-9
Textile draw-out and winding machine operators and tenders	192	140	157	161	-52	-35	-32	-27	-18	-16
Textile machine setters and set-up operators	39	29	32	33	-10	-7	-6	-26	-17	-15
Woodworking machine setters, operators, and other related workers	121	92	96	110	-28	-24	-10	-24	-20	-9
Head sawyers and sawing machine operators and tenders, setters and set-up operators	59	44	46	53	-15	-13	-6	-26	-22	-10
Woodworking machine operators and tenders, setters and set-up operators	62	48	51	57	-13	-11	-4	-22	-18	-7
Other machine setters, set-up operators, and tenders	1,741	1,512	1,622	1,702	-229	-119	-39	-13	-7	-2
Boiler operators and tenders, low pressure	18	15	16	17	-2	-1	-1	-14	-8	-3
Cement and gluing machine operators and tenders	35	26	28	30	-9	-7	-4	-26	-20	-13
Chemical equipment controllers, operators and tenders	77	70	76	80	-7	-1	2	-10	-2	3
Cooking and roasting machine operators and tenders, food and tobacco	28	31	32	33	3	4	4	10	13	15
Crushing and mixing machine operators and tenders	133	109	117	124	-24	-16	-9	-18	-12	-7
Cutting and slicing machine setters operators and tenders	94	68	73	76	-26	-21	-18	-28	-23	-19
Dairy processing equipment operators, including setters	15	16	17	17	1	1	2	4	9	10
Electronic semiconductor processors	32	28	33	39	-4	1	7	-12	4	22
Extruding and forming machine setters, operators and tenders	99	93	101	106	-6	2	7	-6	2	7
Furnace, kiln, or kettle operators, and tenders	27	24	25	28	-3	-2	1	-13	-6	3
Laundry and drycleaning machine operators and tenders, except pressing	162	228	237	241	66	75	79	41	46	49
Motion picture projectionists	9	7	7	7	-3	-2	-2	-29	-26	-24
Packaging and filling machine operators and tenders	319	232	248	257	-86	-71	-62	-27	-22	-19
Painting and coating machine operators	151	140	152	166	-10	2	15	-7	1	10
Coating, painting, and spraying machine operators, tenders, setters, and set-up operators	107	98	107	117	-9	0	11	-8	0	10
Painters, transportation equipment	44	43	45	48	-1	1	4	-3	3	10
Paper goods machine setters and set-up operators	50	59	64	66	8	13	16	17	26	31
Photographic processing machine operators and tenders	49	55	59	60	6	9	11	12	19	23
Separating and still machine operators and tenders	21	13	14	15	-8	-7	-6	-37	-33	-30
Shoe sewing machine operators and tenders	16	9	10	10	-7	-6	-6	-46	-38	-36
Tire building machine operators	14	10	11	12	-4	-3	-3	-29	-22	-19
All other machine operators, tenders, setters, and set-up operators	390	279	302	319	-111	-88	-71	-28	-23	-18

[Continued]

★ 529 ★

Civilian Employment by Occupation under Low, Medium, and High Scenarios, 1992-2005-III

[Continued]

	Total employment				1992-2005 employment change					
	1992	Projected, 2005			Number			Percent		
		Low	Moderate	High	Low	Moderate	High	Low	Moderate	High
Hand workers, including assemblers and fabricators	2,528	2,422	2,630	2,833	-106	102	305	-4	4	12
Cannery workers	73	80	82	83	7	10	10	10	13	14
Coil winders, tapers, and finishers	20	12	14	16	-8	-7	-4	-41	-32	-22
Cutters and trimmers, hand	49	40	44	46	-10	-5	-3	-19	-10	-7
Electrical and electronic assemblers	210	164	187	213	-47	-23	3	-22	-11	1
Grinders and polishers, hand	71	66	72	80	-5	1	8	-8	2	12
Machine assemblers	49	44	49	54	-5	[1]	5	-11	-1	10
Meat, poultry, and fish cutters and trimmers, hand	127	163	169	171	35	42	43	28	33	34
Metal pourers and casters, basic shapes	10	8	9	10	-2	-1	0	-16	-7	2
Painting, coating, and decorating workers, hand	29	35	37	40	6	8	11	19	28	37
Portable machine cutters	11	5	6	6	-5	-4	-4	-48	-40	-39
Pressers, hand	16	13	15	15	-3	-1	-1	-17	-7	-6
Sewers, hand	23	20	22	22	-3	-1	[1]	-14	-5	-1
Solderers and brazers	21	20	23	25	-1	2	4	-3	8	18
Welders and cutters	306	326	352	388	21	46	82	7	15	27
All other assemblers and fabricators	1,113	921	1,007	1,096	-192	-107	-18	-17	-10	-2
All other hand workers	400	505	542	568	105	142	169	26	36	42
Transportation and material moving machine and vehicle operators	4,694	5,336	5,719	6,087	642	1,025	1,393	14	22	30
Motor vehicle operators	3,429	4,001	4,285	4,524	572	856	1,095	17	25	32
Bus drivers	562	633	681	701	71	119	139	13	21	25
Bus drivers	167	163	177	182	-5	10	15	-3	6	9
Bus drivers, school	395	471	504	519	76	109	124	19	28	31
Taxi drivers and chauffeurs	120	133	142	148	13	22	28	11	18	23
Truck drivers	2,720	3,202	3,428	3,639	482	708	919	18	26	34
Driver/salesworkers	329	366	389	404	37	60	74	11	18	22
Truck drivers light and heavy	2,391	2,836	3,039	3,235	446	648	845	19	27	35
All other motor vehicle operators	27	33	34	36	5	7	9	20	27	33
Rail transportation workers	116	131	141	150	14	25	34	12	21	29
Locomotive engineers	19	19	21	22	[1]	2	3	[1]	8	16
Railroad brake, signal, and switch operators	35	35	38	40	[1]	3	5	-1	8	15
Railroad conductors and yardmasters	29	34	37	40	5	8	11	18	28	37
Rail yard engineers, dinkey operators, and hostlers	9	9	9	10	[1]	1	1	-2	6	14
Subway and streetcar operators	22	33	35	37	11	13	15	48	57	65
All other rail vehicle operators	2	1	1	1	-1	-1	-1	-55	-52	-48
Water transportation and related workers	134	130	144	155	-4	10	21	-3	8	16
Able seamen, ordinary seamen, and marine oilers	22	18	21	23	-4	-1	1	-18	-5	5
Captains and pilots, ship	16	14	16	18	-2	[1]	2	-13	[1]	10
Mates, ship, boat, and bridge	7	6	7	7	-1	[1]	0	-20	-7	3
Ship engineers	9	7	8	9	-2	-1	[1]	-20	-9	[1]
All other transportation and related workers	79	85	92	98	5	13	18	7	16	23
Material moving equipment operators	983	1,039	1,111	1,218	56	129	235	6	13	24
Crane and tower operators	46	49	53	59	3	7	13	7	16	29
Excavation and loading machine operators	72	83	86	100	11	14	28	15	20	38
Grader, dozer, and scraper operators	102	118	123	142	15	21	39	15	20	38

[Continued]

★ 529 ★

Civilian Employment by Occupation under Low, Medium, and High Scenarios, 1992-2005-III

[Continued]

	Total employment				1992-2005 employment change					
	1992	Projected, 2005			Number			Percent		
		Low	Moderate	High	Low	Moderate	High	Low	Moderate	High
Hoist and winch operators	12	12	13	14	[1]	1	2	-1	6	20
Industrial truck and tractor operators	413	410	442	471	-3	29	58	-1	7	14
Operating engineers	136	152	159	179	16	23	43	12	17	32
All other material moving equipment operators	201	216	234	254	14	33	52	7	16	26
All other transportation and material moving equipment operators	32	35	38	41	3	5	8	9	16	25
Helpers, laborers, and material movers, hand	4,451	4,887	5,227	5,604	436	776	1,153	10	17	26
Freight, stock, and material movers, hand	845	885	955	1,011	41	111	166	5	13	20
Hand packers and packages	685	715	770	804	30	85	119	4	12	17
Helpers, construction trades	452	509	530	624	57	79	172	13	17	38
Machine feeders and offbearers	255	239	256	274	-16	2	19	-6	1	7
Parking lot attendants	63	81	85	90	19	22	277	30	35	44
Refuse collectors	121	126	134	141	4	13	19	4	11	16
Service station attendants	190	168	180	189	-22	-10	-1	-12	-5	-1
Vehicle washers and equipment cleaners	219	255	271	288	36	52	69	16	24	31
All other helpers, laborers, and material movers, hand	1,621	1,908	2,044	2,183	287	423	562	18	26	35

Source: U.S. Department of Labor, Bureau of Labor Statistics, *The American Work Force: 1992-2005* (Washington, D.C.: U.S. Government Printing Office, April 1994), pp. 56, 59-71. *Note:* 1. A decline of fewer than 1,000 workers.

★ 530 ★

Employment by Occupation and Industry

Total Employment by Industry, 1979-2005

"Employment in the U.S. economy is projected to increase by 26.4 million over the 1992-2005 period, rising from 121.1 million to 147.5 million. The projected annual average growth rate of 1.5 percent is slightly faster than the 1.4-percent rate recorded for the preceding 13-year period, 1979 through 1992. Nonfarm wage and salary jobs are projected to rise from 107.9 million to almost 133 million, and to account for 25.1 million of the 26.4 million increase in total employment. The number of nonfarm self-employed and unpaid family workers is projected to increase from 8.8 million to 10.4 million. For the agricultural sector, the combined number of self-employed workers and wage and salary workers is projected to remain unchanged at 3.3 million workers. The number of private household workers is expected to continue to decline, falling from the 1992 level of 1.1 million to 0.8 million.

"There are several macroeconomic factors that are expected to affect industry output and employment growth: demographic changes (aging of the population, slowing rate of growth of the labor supply), a projected decline in defense spending, expected continued growth of business investment in equipment, a strong increase in personal consumption expenditures, and a gradual decline in the exchange rate of the dollar concomitant with a gradually improving net export of level. All of these factors have general effects of industry output and employment, and some will have special effects on specific industries."

Industry description	Standard Industrial Classification	Employment (in thousands)					Annual growth rate[1]	
		1979	1992	2005			Employment, 1992-2005 (moderate scenario)	Output, 1992-2005
				Low	Moderate	High		
Nonfarm wage and salary[2]		89,491	107,888	124,931	132,960	138,944	1.6	[3]
Mining	10-14	958	631	510	562	690	-.9	0.4
Metal mining	10	101	53	57	64	67	1.4	2.3
Coal mining	12	259	126	85	90	96	-2.5	3.1
Crude petroleum, natural gas, and gas liquids	131, 132	198	187	138	164	197	-1.0	-1.3

[Continued]

★ 530 ★

Total Employment by Industry, 1979-2005

[Continued]

Industry description	Standard Industrial Classification	Employment (in thousands) 1979	1992	2005 Low	2005 Moderate	2005 High	Annual growth rate[1] Employment, 1992-2005 (moderate scenario)	Output, 1992-2005
Oil and gas field services	138	276	164	130	136	214	-1.4	-.7
Nonmetallic minerals, except fuels	14	124	102	101	107	118	.4	2.2
Construction	15, 16, 17	4,463	4,471	5,407	5,632	6,643	1.8	1.8
Manufacturing	20-39	21,040	18,040	15,981	17,523	18,866	-.2	2.4
Durable manufacturing	24, 25, 32-39	12,730	10,237	8,738	9,673	10,788	-.4	2.7
Lumber and wood products	24	782	674	699	690	832	.2	1.9
Logging	241	89	78	65	68	78	-1.0	1.5
Sawmills and planing mills	242	237	179	160	167	196	-.5	1.6
Millwork and structural wood members, n.e.c.	24, 31, 4, 9	157	190	249	250	317	2.2	3.1
Veneer and plywood	2435,6	77	49	38	39	48	-1.7	1.7
Wood containers and miscellaneous wood products	244,9	140	123	107	115	127	-.5	2.1
Mobile homes	2451	58	40	32	33	44	-1.6	-1.1
Prefabricated wood buildings	2452	26	16	18	18	24	1.0	1.7
Furniture and fixtures	25	498	476	479	523	561	.7	1.9
Household furniture	251	329	270	265	283	294	.4	2.0
Partitions and fixtures	254	65	75	82	90	103	1.4	2.4
Office and miscellaneous furniture and fixtures	252, 3, 9	104	132	133	150	165	1.0	1.7
Stone, clay, and glass products	32	674	512	409	437	492	-1.2	1.1
Glass and glass products	321, 2, 3	199	152	114	124	129	-1.6	.9
Cement, concrete, gypsum, and plaster products	324, 327	249	204	166	174	207	-1.2	1.3
Stone, clay, and miscellaneous mineral products[4]	325, 6, 8, 9	226	156	129	140	156	-.8	1.1
Primary metal industries	33	1,254	693	556	618	680	-.9	1.2
Blast furnaces and basic steel products	331	571	250	201	224	247	-.9	1.4
Iron and steel foundries	332	241	120	88	97	108	-1.6	.1
Primary nonferrous metals	333	73	43	36	40	43	-.6	1.4
Miscellaneous primary and secondary metals	334, 9	51	41	38	42	46	.2	3.2
Nonferrous rolling and drawing	335	220	162	120	133	148	-1.5	.5
Nonferrous foundries	336	100	77	74	81	89	.4	2.1
Fabricated metal products	34	1,713	1,322	1,101	1,196	1,327	-.8	1.2
Metal cans and shipping containers	341	80	45	30	31	32	-2.8	1.0
Cutlery, handtools, and hardware	342	184	123	98	106	116	-1.1	1.6
Plumbing and nonelectric heating equipment	343	77	56	49	50	59	-.9	.9
Fabricated structural metal products	344	516	390	311	331	383	-1.2	.7
Screw machine products, bolts, rivets, etc.	345	116	90	76	85	92	-.4	1.9
Forgings	3462,3	63	36	32	35	37	-.2	1.1
Automotive stampings	3465	118	98	103	113	120	1.1	1.7
Stampings, except automotive	3466,9	121	83	53	59	64	-2.6	.1
Metal services, n.e.c.	347	107	115	127	142	159	1.7	4.1
Small arms and small arms ammunition	3482, 3484	29	20	14	15	15	-2.1	.1
Ammunition and ordinance, except small arms	3483, 3489	35	46	26	27	27	-4.0	-1.0
Miscellaneous fabricated metal products	349	269	222	183	203	222	-.7	.7

[Continued]

★ 530 ★

Total Employment by Industry, 1979-2005

[Continued]

Industry description	Standard Industrial Classification	Employment (in thousands) 1979	1992	2005 Low	2005 Moderate	2005 High	Annual growth rate[1] Employment, 1992-2005 (moderate scenario)	Output, 1992-2005
Industrial machinery and equipment	35	2,508	1,922	1,638	1,868	2,160	-.2	4.6
Engines and turbines	351	145	87	61	69	76	-1.8	.7
Farm and garden machinery	352	182	93	81	91	103	-.2	2.5
Construction machinery	3531	161	73	63	71	81	-.2	3.2
Mining and oil field machinery	3532, 3	120	55	52	59	62	.5	.6
Materials handling machinery and equipment[4]	3534, 5, 6, 7	101	75	75	84	97	.9	2.3
Metalworking machinery	354	395	302	290	332	377	.7	1.8
Special industry machinery	355	193	148	109	126	147	-1.2	2.0
General industrial machinery	356	304	236	208	238	273	.1	2.0
Computer equipment[4]	3571, 2, 5, 7	318	353	195	237	312	-3.0	8.1
Office and accounting machines[4]	3578, 9	68	38	21	27	36	-2.7	1.6
Refrigeration and service industry machinery	358	189	173	169	184	205	.5	3.0
Industrial machinery, n.e.c.	359	332	290	315	351	391	1.5	2.8
Electronic and other electric equipment	36	1,793	1,526	1,185	1,354	1,537	-.9	3.3
Electric distributing equipment	361	120	83	60	68	81	-1.5	.9
Electrical industrial apparatus	362	242	158	104	119	137	-2.1	1.3
Household appliances	363	177	116	89	94	97	-1.6	2.2
Electric lighting and wiring equipment	364	227	174	138	155	176	-.9	1.0
Household audio and video equipment	365	115	82	60	63	65	-2.1	3.2
Telephone and telegraph apparatus[4]	3661	171	108	68	81	93	-2.3	1.4
Broadcasting and communications equipment[4,5]	3663, 9	128	128	104	116	130	-.8	4.4
Semiconductors and related devices	3674	201	218	188	224	264	.2	5.6
Miscellaneous electronic components[4]	3671, 1, 5-9	309	307	255	300	348	-.2	3.5
Storage batteries and engine electrical parts	3691, 4	118	89	77	85	90	-.3	2.5
Electrical equipment and supplies, n.e.c.[4,5]	3692, 5, 9	77	62	43	49	56	-1.8	3.3
Transportation equipment	37	2,059	1,822	1,610	1,765	1,891	-.2	2.3
Motor vehicles and equipment	371	990	809	686	759	817	-.5	2.6
Motor vehicles and car bodies	3711	463	314	213	241	256	-2.0	2.6
Motor vehicle parts and accessories	3714	441	417	379	413	447	-.1	2.4
Truck and bus bodies, trailers, and motor homes	3713, 5, 6	86	77	94	105	114	2.4	4.8
Aircraft	3721	333	332	274	302	330	-.7	1.2
Aircraft and missile engines	3724, 3764	163	149	133	146	156	-.2	3.0
Aircraft and missile parts and equipment, n.e.c.	3728, 3769	120	170	236	255	275	3.2	4.2
Guided missiles and space vehicles	3761	81	105	69	73	74	-2.8	-.3
Ship building and repairing	3731	173	124	74	77	78	-.36	-2.3
Boat building and repairing	3732	53	45	53	59	61	2.0	5.9
Railroad equipment	374	74	28	34	38	43	2.5	3.4
Miscellaneous transportation equipment	375, 9	74	60	51	56	57	-.5	1.3
Instruments and related products	38	1,006	925	796	887	969	-.3	3.4
Search and navigation equipment[4]	381	227	228	161	177	198	-1.9	2.1
Measuring and controlling devices, watches[4]	382, 387	431	300	226	255	282	-1.2	3.7
Ophthalmic goods	385	45	38	34	40	41	.4	3.3
Medical instruments and supplies	3841-3	144	216	269	295	317	2.4	6.1
X-ray and other electromedical	3844-5							

[Continued]

★ 530 ★

Total Employment by Industry, 1979-2005

[Continued]

Industry description	Standard Industrial Classification	Employment (in thousands) 1979	1992	2005 Low	2005 Moderate	2005 High	Annual growth rate[1] Employment, 1992-2005 (moderate scenario)	Output, 1992-2005
apparatus[4,5]		26	48	51	58	66	1.5	3.7
Photographic equipment and supplies	386	134	95	55	62	65	-3.2	1.3
Miscellaneous manufacturing Industries	39	445	363	294	334	340	-.6	1.9
Jewelry, silverware, and plated ware	391	61	50	41	47	49	-.4	1.0
Toys and sporting goods	394	121	107	81	95	95	-.9	2.2
Manufactured products, n.e.c.[4]	393, 5, 6, 9	263	207	172	192	195	-.6	1.9
Nondurable manufacturing	20-23, 26-31	8,310	7,804	7,243	7,851	8,079	.0	1.9
Food and kindred products	20	1,733	1,655	1,589	1,648	1,660	.0	1.5
Meat products	201	358	434	475	496	500	1.0	1.3
Dairy products	202	180	152	127	134	135	-1.0	1.0
Preserved fruits and vegetables	203	250	246	252	261	263	.4	1.9
Grain mill products, fats and oils	204, 7	189	156	133	139	141	-.9	2.6
Bakery products	205	237	207	183	192	193	-.6	1.0
Sugar and confectionery products	206	113	104	89	91	92	-1.0	.7
Alcoholic beverages	2082, 3, 4, 5	86	66	52	53	54	-1.7	.7
Soft drinks and flavorings	2086, 7	153	109	81	84	84	-2.0	1.3
Miscellaneous foods and kindred products	209	165	180	197	198	199	.7	1.3
Tobacco manufacturers	21	70	49	35	37	39	-2.1	.7
Textile mill products	22	885	671	510	571	585	-1.2	1.2
Weaving, finishing, yarn, and thread mills	221, 2, 3, 4, 6, 8	528	360	255	287	291	-1.7	.7
Knitting mills	225	231	202	152	173	173	-1.2	.4
Carpets and rugs	227	61	59	65	68	75	1.1	3.3
Miscellaneous textile goods	229	66	51	39	43	45	-1.4	2.2
Apparel and other textile products	23	1,304	1,005	651	760	765	-2.1	.7
Apparel	231-8	1,115	807	467	556	556	-2.8	.0
Miscellaneous fabricated textile products	239	189	198	184	205	210	.2	2.6
Paper and allied products	26	697	687	672	729	752	.4	2.5
Pulp, paper, and paperboard mills	261, 2, 3	262	239	204	224	227	-.5	2.5
Paperboard containers and boxes	265	214	211	215	231	241	.7	2.2
Converted paper products, except containers	267	221	238	253	274	285	1.1	2.8
Printing and publishing	27	1,235	1,504	1,621	1,751	1,810	1.2	2.9
Newspapers	271	420	451	477	513	532	1.0	1.9
Periodicals	272	82	123	135	146	152	1.3	3.2
Books	273	102	118	130	146	151	1.7	3.2
Miscellaneous publishing	274	46	80	108	117	121	3.0	3.9
Commercial printing and business forms	275, 6	451	577	612	656	676	1.0	3.0
Greeting card publishing	277	24	26	27	30	31	1.0	3.3
Blankbooks and bookbinding	278	63	69	71	78	79	1.0	3.2
Printing trade services	279	47	59	61	65	68	.8	3.2
Chemicals and allied products	28	1,109	1,083	1,006	1,090	1,132	.1	2.3
Industrial chemicals	281, 6	333	290	234	255	265	-1.0	1.7
Plastics materials and synthetics	282	212	173	144	158	167	-.7	2.5
Drugs	283	193	256	277	297	300	1.1	2.9
Soap, cleaners, and toilet goods	284	140	154	153	167	173	.7	2.3
Paints and allied products	285	69	58	52	56	62	-.4	2.4
Agricultural chemicals	287	70	58	42	45	45	-2.0	1.3
Miscellaneous chemicals products	289	93	93	105	113	120	1.5	3.9
Petroleum and coal products	29	210	159	118	128	137	-1.6	.8

[Continued]

★ 530 ★

Total Employment by Industry, 1979-2005

[Continued]

Industry description	Standard Industrial Classification	Employment (in thousands) 1979	1992	2005 Low	2005 Moderate	2005 High	Annual growth rate[1] Employment, 1992-2005 (moderate scenario)	Output, 1992-2005
Petroleum refining	291	165	120	84	92	98	-2.0	.6
Miscellaneous petroleum and coal products	295, 9	45	39	34	36	40	-.5	2.8
Rubber and miscellaneous plastics products	30	821	872	979	1,066	1,125	1.6	3.5
Tires and inner tubes	301	127	82	59	64	67	-1.8	.2
Rubber products, plastic hose and footwear	302, 5, 6	208	171	142	158	160	-.6	2.3
Miscellaneous plastics products, n.e.c.	308	486	619	778	843	898	2.4	4.2
Leather and leather products	31	246	119	63	71	73	-3.9	-2.2
Footwear except rubber and plastic	313, 4	161	69	33	39	41	-4.4	-2.5
Luggage, handbags, and leather products, n.e.c.	311, 5, 6, 7, 9	85	51	30	33	33	-3.4	-2.1
Transportation, communications, utilities	40-42, 44-49	5,136	5,709	5,909	6,497	6,763	1.0	2.3
Transportation	40-42, 44-47	3,019	3,486	3,866	4,310	4,507	1.6	2.8
Railroad transportation	40	556	254	233	252	270	-1.	2.4
Local and interurban passenger transit	41	263	359	332	383	386	.5	1.7
Trucking and warehousing	42	1,339	1,606	1,866	2,109	2,130	1.8	2.3
Water transportation	44	214	173	132	154	171	-.9	1.9
Air transportation	45	438	729	835	967	996	2.2	4.0
Pipelines, except natural gas	46	20	19	17	18	19	-.2	1.2
Transportation services	47	189	346	452	516	535	3.1	3.5
Passenger transportation arrangement[4]	472	92	183	260	300	307	3.9	2.5
Miscellaneous transportation services[4]	473, 4, 8	96	163	192	216	229	2.2	4.2
Communications	48	1,309	1,268	1,030	1,116	1,142	-1.0	2.7
Communications, except broadcasting[4]	481, 2, 9	1,095	912	660	724	742	-1.8	3.1
Radio and television broadcasting, cable TV[4]	483, 4	214	355	370	392	400	.8	1.4
Electric, gas, and sanitary services	49	807	955	1,013	1,072	1,115	.9	1.1
Electric utilities including combined services	491, pt. 493	493	553	554	582	606	.4	1.5
Gas utilities including combined services	492, pt. 493	220	205	184	190	205	-.6	-.9
Water and sanitation including combined	494, 5, 6, 7, pt. 493	94	197	274	299	304	3.3	3.7
Wholesale trade	50, 5	5,221	6,045	6,641	7,191	7,761	1.3	2.9
Retail trade	52-59	14,972	19,346	22,254	23,777	24,336	1.6	2.2
Retail trade, excluding eating and drinking places	52-57, 59	10,459	12,744	13,926	14,999	15,511	1.3	2.4
Eating and drinking places		4,513	6,602	8,329	8,778	8,825	2.2	1.4
Finance, insurance, and real estate	60-67	4,975	6,571	7,585	7,969	8,078	1.5	2.2
Depository institutions[4]	60	1,890	2,103	2,107	2,195	2,201	.3	2.9
Nondepository; holding and investment offices[4]		276	615	921	949	957	3.4	4.5
Security and commodity brokers	62	204	439	528	570	575	2.0	4.0
Insurance carriers	63	1,200	1,480	1,549	1,660	1,661	.9	1.7
Insurance agents, brokers, and service	64	443	652	906	971	972	3.1	3.3
Real estate	65	963	1,282	1,574	1,624	1,712	1.8	2.6
Services[2]	70-87, 89	16,779	28,422	39,808	41,788	42,766	3.0	3.5
Hotels and other lodging places	70	1,060	1,572	2,136	2,209	2,281	2.6	4.1
Personal services	72	821	1,111	1,352	1,382	1,388	1.7	2.0
Laundry, cleaning, and shore repair[4]	721, 5	367	418	458	475	476	1.0	1.7
Personal services, n.e.c.[4]	722, 9	98	216	286	292	294	2.3	2.1
Beauty and barber shops	723, 4	318	392	510	516	518	2.1	2.5

[Continued]

★ 530 ★

Total Employment by Industry, 1979-2005

[Continued]

Industry description	Standard Industrial Classification	Employment (in thousands) 1979	1992	2005 Low	2005 Moderate	2005 High	Annual growth rate[1] Employment, 1992-2005 (moderate scenario)	Output, 1992-2005
Funeral service and crematories	726	69	85	98	99	100	1.2	1.0
Business services	73	2,410	5,313	7,799	8,370	8,664	3.6	4.7
Advertising	731	146	226	268	288	299	1.9	2.4
Services to buildings	734	487	805	937	1,000	1,029	1.7	3.9
Miscellaneous equipment rental and leasing[4]	735	-	205	298	325	343	3.6	3.9
Personnel supply services	736	508	1,649	2,408	2,581	2,656	3.5	2.8
Computer and data processing services	737	271	831	1,507	1,626	1,697	5.3	5.9
Detective, guard, and security services[4]	7381, 2	-	505	658	716	742	2.7	2.4
Photocopying, commercial art, photofinishing[4]	7334, 5, 6; 7384	-	190	274	291	302	3.4	4.3
Business services, n.e.c.[4]	732; 7331, 8; 7383, 9	-	903	1,450	1,543	1,597	4.2	5.5
Auto repair, services, and garages	75	575	878	1,229	1,293	1,401	3.0	2.3
Automotive rentals, without drivers[4]	751	118	159	206	222	236	2.6	4.1
Automobile parking, repair, and services	752, 3, 4	457	719	1,023	1,071	1,165	3.1	1.9
Miscellaneous repair shops	76	22	345	421	449	467	2.0	2.4
Electrical repair shops	762	84	108	131	140	143	2.0	2.4
Watch, clock, jewelry, and furniture repair	763, 4	29	27	27	29	30	.7	.2
Miscellaneous repair shops and related services	769	169	210	262	280	295	2.2	2.6
Motion pictures	78	228	404	476	499	511	1.6	2.3
Motion pictures	781-3	228	279	374	392	401	2.6	2.8
Video tape rental	784	-	125	103	110	107	-1.2	-1.3
Amusement and recreation services	79	751	1,169	1,595	1,626	1,646	2.6	3.2
Producers, orchestras, and entertainers	792	84	143	194	201	208	2.6	2.0
Bowling centers	793	102	88	84	85	86	-.2	-.2
Commercial sports	794	70	113	133	135	138	1.4	.9
Amusement and recreation services, n.e.c.	791, 9	494	826	1,184	1,205	1,215	3.0	4.1
Health services	80	4,993	8,523	11,998	12,539	12,632	3.0	3.3
Offices of health practitioners	801, 2, 3, 4	1,200	2,387	3,468	3,617	3,667	3.2	2.9
Nursing and personal care facilities	805	951	1,543	2,215	2,306	2,330	3.1	3.4
Hospitals, private	806	2,608	3,760	4,801	5,039	5,048	2.3	3.4
Health services, n.e.c.	807, 8, 9	234	833	1,514	1,577	1,587	5.0	3.9
Legal services	81	460	915	1,280	1,355	1,380	3.1	3.4
Educational services	82	1,090	1,700	2,047	2,162	2,174	1.9	2.8
Elementary and secondary schools	821	259	467	616	616	618	2.2	3.0
Colleges and universities	822	717	1,025	1,124	1,236	1,245	1.5	2.7
Libraries, vocational, and other schools	823-9	114	208	307	310	312	3.1	2.9
Social services	83	1,081	1,958	3,584	3,691	3,715	5.0	5.1
Individual and miscellaneous social services	832,9	390	703	1,129	1,162	1,167	3.9	5.1
Job training and related services	833	187	271	401	418	421	3.4	3.7
Child day care services	835	303	449	757	777	780	4.3	2.8
Residential care	836	201	535	1,297	1,355	1,348	7.3	7.8
Museums, zoos, and membership organizations	84, 86, 8733	1,652	2,164	2,601	2,674	2,703	1.6	4.1
Museums and noncommercial organizations, n.e.c.	84; 765, 9; 8733	201	298	383	393	399	3.3	5.9
Business and professional associations	861, 2	117	156	190	200	203	1.9	1.9
Labor, civic, and social organizations	863, 4	453	559	648	661	669	1.3	1.4
Religious organizations[5]	866	882	1,151	1,380	1,420	1,432	1.6	4.8
Engineering, management,	87 (less							

[Continued]

★ 530 ★

Total Employment by Industry, 1979-2005

[Continued]

Industry description	Standard Industrial Classification	Employment (in thousands)					Annual growth rate[1]	
		1979	1992	2005			Employment, 1992-2005 (moderate scenario)	Output, 1992-2005
				Low	Moderate	High		
and services, n.e.c.	8733), 89	1,341	2,370	3,290	3,538	3,804	3.1	3.4
Engineering and architectural services	871	515	746	928	1,001	1,173	2.3	2.4
Research and testing services	8731, 2, 4	235	417	522	553	564	2.2	3.3
Management and public relations	874	273	655	1,026	1,110	1,153	4.1	5.5
Accounting, auditing, and services, n.e.c.	872, 89	318	553	816	876	914	3.6	2.2
Government		15,947	18,653	20,836	22,021	23,041	1.3	1.5
Federal Government		2,773	2,969	2,628	2,815	2,950	-.4	.6
Federal enterprises		876	985	826	915	984	-.6	2.7
U.S. Postal Service		661	792	674	751	807	-.4	3.2
Federal electric utilities		52	28	18	19	21	-2.7	.4
Federal Government enterprises, n.e.c.		163	165	135	144	156	-1.0	1.8
Federal general government		1,897	1,984	1,802	1,901	1,966	-.3	-.2
State and local government		13,174	15,683	18,208	19,206	20,091	1.6	2.0
State and local enterprises		733	938	1,007	1,137	1,223	1.5	1.9
Local government passenger transit		130	204	214	254	271	1.7	1.1
State and local electric utilities		63	81	81	88	96	.6	1.0
State and local government enterprises, n.e.c.		540	653	712	795	856	1.5	2.2
State and local general government		12,441	14,745	17,201	18,069	18,868	1.6	2.0
State government education		1,378	1,797	2,191	2,301	2,403	1.9	2.4
Local government education		5,107	6,222	7,627	8,012	8,366	2.0	2.7
State and local general government, n.e.c.		4,847	5,637	6,193	6,506	6,793	1.1	1.3
Agriculture[6]	01, 02, 07, 08, 09	3,398	3,295	3,221	3,325	3,535	.1	1.6
Livestock and livestock products	pt. 01, pt. 02	1,268	1,117	959	993	1,049	-.9	1.1
Other agricultural products	pt. 01, pt. 02	1,506	1,088	827	846	897	-1.9	1.8
Agricultural services	7	547	984	1,304	1,351	1,442	2.5	3.1
Forestry	8	21	38	49	52	61	2.4	2.5
Fishing	9	57	69	81	83	86	1.4	.1
Private households	88	1,264	1,116	777	802	853	-2.5	-1.0
Nonagricultural self-employed and unpaid family[7]		7,210	8,794	10,078	10,397	11,098	1.3	[3]
Total[8]		101,363	121,093	139,007	147,483	154,430	1.5	2.4

Source: U.S. Department of Labor, Bureau of Labor Statistics, *The American Work Force: 1992-2005* (Washington, D.C.: U.S. Government Printing Office, April 1994), pp. 39, 50-54. *Primary source:* Historical output data are from the Bureau of Economic Analysis, U.S. Department of Commerce. *Notes:*—=Data not available. n.e.c.=Not otherwise classified. 1. Rates are based on moderate scenario. 2. Excludes SIC 074,5,8 (agricultural services) and 99 (nonclassifiable establishments). The data therefore are not exactly comparable with data published in *Employment and Earnings*. 3. Comparable estimate of output growth is not available. 4. Current Employment Statistics (CES) figures are not available for 1979 for this industry (or for at least one component in a group of industries). Estimates were produced by the Bureau's Office of Employment Projections for the purpose of those projections. 5. Does not meet usual publication criteria of Current Employment Statistics program. 6. Excludes government wage and salary workers, and includes private SIC 08, 09 (forestry and fisheries). 7. Excludes SIC 08, 09 (forestry and fisheries). 8. Wage and salary data are from the Current Employment Statistics (payroll) survey, which counts jobs, whereas self-employed, unpaid family worker, agricultural, and private household data are from the Current Population Survey (household survey), which counts workers. These totals for 1979 and 1992, therefore, differ from the official employment estimates of the Bureau of Labor Statistics.

★ 531 ★

Employment by Occupation and Industry

Employment by Major Industry Division, 1979-2005-I

[Thousands]

Industry	Employment level					Change			
	1979	1992	2005			1979-92	1992-2005		
			Low	Moderate	High		Low	Moderate	High
Nonfarm wage and salary[1]	89,491	107,888	124,931	132,960	138,944	18,398	17,043	25,072	31,055
Goods producing	26,461	23,142	21,898	23,717	26,200	-3,319	-1,244	575	3,058
Mining	958	631	510	562	690	-327	-121	-69	59
Construction	4,463	4,471	5,407	5,632	6,643	8	936	1,161	2,172
Manufacturing	21,040	18,040	15,981	17,523	18,866	-3,000	-2,059	-517	826
Durable	12,730	10,237	8,738	9,673	10,788	-2,493	-1,499	-564	551
Nondurable	8,310	7,804	7,243	7,850	8,079	-506	-561	46	275
Service producing	63,030	84,746	103,034	109,243	112,744	21,717	18,287	24,497	27,512
Transportation, communications, utilities	5,136	5,709	5,909	6,497	6,753	573	200	788	1,054
Wholesale trade	5,221	6,045	6,641	7,191	7,761	824	596	1,146	1,716
Retail trade	14,972	19,346	22,254	23,777	24,336	4,374	2,908	4,431	4,990
Finance, insurance, and real estate	4,975	6,571	7,585	7,969	8,078	1,596	1,014	1,398	1,507
Services[1]	16,779	28,422	39,808	41,788	42,766	11,644	11,386	13,365	14,344
Government	15,947	18,653	20,836	22,021	23,041	2,706	2,183	3,368	4,388
Agriculture[2]	3,398	3,295	3,221	3,325	3,535	-103	-74	30	240
Private households	1,264	1,116	777	802	853	-148	-339	-314	-263
Nonagricultural self-employed and unpaid family workers[3]	7,210	8,794	10,078	10,396	11,098	1,584	1,284	1,602	2,304
Total[4]	101,363	121,093	139,007	147,483	154,430	19,731	17,924	26,390	33,336

Source: U.S. Department of Labor, Bureau of Labor Statistics, *The American Work Force: 1992-2005* (Washington, D.C.: U.S. Government Printing Office, April 1994), p. 45. *Primary source:* Historical output data are from the Bureau of Economic Analysis, U.S. Department of Commerce. *Notes:* 1. Excludes SIC 074, 5, 8 (agricultural services) and 99 (nonclassifiable establishments). The data therefore are not exactly comparable with data published in *Employment and Earnings*. 2. Excludes government wage and salary workers, and includes private SIC 08, 09 (forestry and fisheries). 3. Excludes SIC 08, 09 (forestry and fisheries). 4. Wage and salary data are from the Current Employment Statistics (payroll) survey, which counts jobs, whereas self-employed, unpaid family worker, agricultural, and private household data are from the Current Population Survey (household survey), which counts workers.

★ 532 ★

Employment by Occupation and Industry

Employment by Major Industry Division, 1979-2005-II

[Thousands]

Industry	Percent distribution of wage and salary employment					Annual rate of change			
	1979	1992	2005			1979-92	1992-2005		
			Low	Moderate	High		Low	Moderate	High
Nonfarm wage and salary[1]	100.0	100.0	100.0	100.0	100.0	1.4	1.1	1.6	2.0
Goods producing	29.6	21.4	17.5	17.8	18.9	-1.0	-.4	.2	1.0
Mining	1.1	.6	.4	.4	.5	-3.2	-1.6	-.9	.7
Construction	5.0	4.1	4.3	4.2	.5	0	1.5	1.8	3.1

[Continued]

★ 532 ★

Employment by Major Industry Division, 1979-2005-II

[Continued]

Industry	Percent distribution of wage and salary employment					Annual rate of change			
	1979	1992	2005			1979-92	1992-2005		
			Low	Moderate	High		Low	Moderate	High
Manufacturing	23.5	16.7	12.8	13.2	13.6	-1.2	-.9	-0.2	.3
Durable	14.2	9.5	7.0	7.3	7.8	-1.7	-1.2	-0.4	.4
Nondurable	9.3	7.2	5.8	5.9	5.8	-0.5	-.6	0	.3
Service producing	70.4	78.6	82.5	82.2	81.1	2.3	1.5	2.0	2.2
Transportation, communications, utilities	5.7	5.3	4.7	4.9	4.9	.8	.3	1.0	1.3
Wholesale trade	5.8	5.6	5.3	5.4	5.6	1.1	.7	1.3	1.9
Retail trade	16.7	17.9	17.8	17.5	17.6	2.0	1.1	1.6	1.8
Finance, insurance, and real estate	5.6	6.1	6.1	6.0	5.8	2.2	1.1	1.5	1.6
Services[1]	18.7	26.3	31.9	31.4	30.8	4.1	2.6	3.0	3.2
Government	17.8	17.3	16.7	16.6	16.6	1.2	.9	1.3	1.6
Agriculture[2]	-	-	-	-	-	-.2	-.2	.1	.5
Private households	-	-	-	-	-	-1.0	-2.7	-2.5	-2.0
Nonagricultural self-employed and unpaid family workers[3]	-	-	-	-	-	1.5	1.1	1.3	1.8
Total[4]	-	-	-	-	-	1.4	1.1	1.5	1.9

Source: U.S. Department of Labor, Bureau of Labor Statistics, *The American Work Force: 1992-2005* (Washington, D.C.: U.S. Government Printing Office, April 1994), p. 45. *Primary source:* Historical output data are from the Bureau of Economic Analysis, U.S. Department of Commerce. *Notes:* - = Data not available. 1. Excludes SIC 074, 5, 8 (agricultural services) and 99 (nonclassifiable establishments). The data therefore are not exactly comparable with data published in *Employment and Earnings*. 2. Excludes government wage and salary workers, and includes private SIC 08, 09 (forestry and fisheries). 3. Excludes SIC 08, 09 (forestry and fisheries). 4. Wage and salary data are from the Current Employment Statistics (payroll) survey, which counts jobs, whereas self-employed, unpaid family worker, agricultural, and private household data are from the Current Population Survey (household survey), which counts workers.

★ 533 ★

Employment by Occupation and Industry

Output by Major Industry Division, 1979-2005-I

[Billions of 1987 dollars]

Industry	Gross duplicated output					Percent distribution				
	1997	1992	2005			1979	1992	2005		
			Low	Moderate	High			Low	Moderate	High
Total	6,915.0	8,660.8	10,688.2	11,809.1	13,133.1	100.0	100.0	100.0	100.0	100.0
Goods producing	2,913.2	3,284.8	3,855.8	4,356.2	5,060.1	42.1	37.9	36.1	36.9	38.5
Mining	168.8	147.5	134.2	155.6	190.1	2.4	1.7	1.3	1.3	1.4
Construction	522.1	559.9	657.0	708.0	879.3	7.6	6.5	6.1	6.0	6.7
Manufacturing	2,222.4	2,577.3	3,064.8	3,492.7	3,990.7	32.1	29.8	28.7	29.6	30.4
Durable	1,193.3	1,338.6	1,639.2	1,903.3	2,263.3	17.3	15.5	15.3	16.1	17.2
Nondurable	1,029.0	1,238.8	1,425.5	1,589.3	1,727.4	14.9	14.3	13.3	13.5	13.2
Service producing	3,816.6	5,162.7	6,593.0	7,195.0	7,798.1	55.2	59.6	61.7	60.9	59.4
Transportation, communications, utilities	613.3	712.5	846.3	956.6	1,050.0	8.9	8.2	7.9	8.1	8.0
Wholesale trade	337.5	428.5	554.6	621.3	706.1	4.9	4.9	5.2	5.3	5.4
Retail trade	531.8	782.2	931.1	1,031.9	1,115.7	7.7	9.0	8.7	8.7	8.5

[Continued]

★ 533 ★

Output by Major Industry Division, 1979-2005-I

[Continued]

Industry	Gross duplicated output					Percent distribution				
	1997	1992	2005			1979	1992	2005		
			Low	Moderate	High			Low	Moderate	High
Finance, insurance, and real estate	903.1	1,162.9	1,453.1	1,544.1	1,680.3	13.1	13.4	13.6	13.1	12.8
Services	923.3	1,446.8	2,085.3	2,272.0	2,438.4	13.4	16.7	19.5	19.2	18.6
Government	507.7	629.7	722.5	768.9	807.6	7.3	7.3	6.8	6.5	6.1
Agriculture	177.3	203.2	231.6	248.9	265.6	2.6	2.3	2.2	2.1	2.0
Private households	7.9	10.2	7.8	8.9	9.3	.1	.1	.1	.1	.1

Source: U.S. Department of Labor, Bureau of Labor Statistics, *The American Work Force: 1992-2005* (Washington, D.C.: U.S. Government Printing Office, April 1994), p. 46. *Primary source:* Historical output data are from the Bureau of Economic Analysis, U.S. Department of Commerce.

★ 534 ★

Employment by Occupation and Industry

Output by Major Industry Division, 1979-2005-II

[Percent]

Industry	Annual rate of change			
	1979-92	1992-2005		
		Low	Moderate	High
Total	1.7	1.6	2.4	3.3
Goods producing	.9	1.2	2.2	3.4
Mining	-1.0	-.7	.4	2.0
Construction	.5	1.2	1.8	3.5
Manufacturing	1.1	1.3	2.4	3.4
Durable	.9	1.6	2.7	4.1
Nondurable	1.4	1.1	1.9	2.6
Service producing	2.4	1.9	2.6	3.2
Transportation, communications, utilities	1.2	1.3	2.3	3.0
Wholesale trade	1.9	2.0	2.9	3.9
Retail trade	3.0	1.3	2.2	2.8
Finance, insurance, and real estate	2.0	1.7	2.2	2.9
Services	3.5	2.9	3.5	4.1
Government	1.7	1.1	1.5	1.9
Agriculture	1.1	1.0	1.6	2.1
Private households	2.0	-2.1	-1.0	-.7

Source: U.S. Department of Labor, Bureau of Labor Statistics, *The American Work Force: 1992-2005* (Washington, D.C.: U.S. Government Printing Office, April 1994), p. 46. *Primary source:* Historical output data are from the Bureau of Economic Analysis, U.S. Department of Commerce.

★ 535 ★

Employment by Occupation and Industry

Defense-related Employment by Major Sector and Occupational Group, 1977- 1997

"It is illuminating to note that the runup in the defense spending between 1977 and 1987 was $111 billion in real terms, and was accompanied by an increase of 2.1 million defense-related jobs in the private sector. The 1987-97 defense cutbacks... amount to a decline of $97 billion, accompanied by declines of 1.8 million jobs in the private sector of the economy. In short, the impact of the cutbacks on the private economy is less than the impact of the decade-earlier surge in defense spending.

"Excluding impacts to the Federal Government itself, major areas of the economy that would likely absorb the greatest declines in defense-related jobs are manufacturing (594,000 fewer jobs), retail and wholesale trade (139,000 fewer), and transportation (62,000 fewer)."

[Thousands]

Sector or occupational group	1977	1987	1992	1997	Level change			
					1977-87	1987-92	1992-97	1987-97
Sector								
Total defense-related employment	4,861.0	7,204.8	6,308.1	4,451.3	2,343.8	-896.7	-1,856.8	-2,753.5
Agriculture, forestry, fisheries	16.1	27.5	20.2	11.8	11.4	-7.3	-8.4	-15.7
Mining	26.1	31.2	27.4	18.2	5.1	-3.8	-9.2	-13.0
Construction	104.8	185.1	152.7	99.8	80.3	-32.4	-52.9	-85.3
Manufacturing	1,087.8	1,857.0	1,406.8	812.4	769.2	-450.2	-594.4	-1,044.6
Transportation	116.6	200.9	168.9	107.2	84.3	-32.0	-61.7	-93.7
Communications	24.3	38.0	28.5	15.5	13.7	-9.5	-13.0	-22.5
Public utilities	18.9	34.6	28.4	17.2	15.7	-6.2	-11.2	-17.4
Trade	203.8	496.8	428.2	289.6	293.0	-68.6	-138.6	-207.2
Finance, insurance, and real estate	41.5	87.1	72.9	47.2	45.6	-14.2	-25.7	-39.9
Services	178.5	920.6	947.0	660.8	742.1	264.	-286.2	-259.8
Government (including military)	3,042.6	3,326.0	3,027.1	2,371.6	283.4	-298.9	-655.5	-954.4
Occupational group								
Total, all civilian occupations	...	5,038.8	4,330.1	3,010.6	...	-708.7	-1,319.5	-2,028.2
Executive, administrative, and managerial	...	631.9	549.0	406.0	...	-82.9	-143.0	-225.9
Professional specialty occupations	...	724.6	629.8	495.5	...	-94.8	-134.3	-229.1
Technicians and related support occupations	...	288.6	253.5	194.5	...	-35.1	-59.0	-94.1
Marketing and sales occupations	...	275.5	248.5	174.4	...	-27.0	-74.1	-101.1
Administrative support occupations	...	927.7	828.2	564.4	...	-99.5	-263.8	-363.3
Service occupations	...	408.6	362.8	253.2	...	-45.8	-109.6	-155.4
Agriculture, forestry, and fishing occupations	...	71.9	63.2	42.5	...	-8.7	-20.7	-29.4
Precision production, craft, and repair	...	819.7	672.3	442.7	...	-147.4	-229.6	-377.0
Operators, fabricators, and laborers	...	890.3	722.8	437.4	...	-167.5	-285.4	-452.9

Source: Norman C. Saunders, "Employment Effects of the Rise and Fall in Defense Spending," in *Monthly Labor Review*, April 1993, pp. 4-5.

★ 536 ★

Employment by Occupation and Industry

Employment of Wage and Salary Workers in Construction by Occupation, 1990-2005

"Employment in the construction industry is expected to grow 18 percent through the year 2005, about as fast as the average for all industries. Employment growth is projected to add more than 900,000 new jobs in construction over the 1990-2005 period, and many job openings will also result each year from the need to replace experienced workers who leave jobs in the industry.

"Employment in this industry depends primarily on the level of construction and remodeling activity. New construction is usually cut back during periods when the economy is not expanding, and the number of job openings in construction fluctuates greatly from year to year. Employment growth in various segments of the construction industry varies greatly depending on what the industry is hired to construct."

[Thousands]

Industry	1990 Employment	1990-2005 Percent change
Total construction	5,136	17.9
General building contractors	1,308	7.8
Residential building construction	651	10.3
Operative builders	39	-45.6
Nonresidential building construction	618	8.5
Heavy construction contractors	763	25.7
Highway and street construction	241	30.9
Heavy construction, except highways	522	23.3
Special trade contractors	3,065	20.4
Plumbing, heating, and air-conditioning	656	15.5
Painting and paperhanging	178	14.9
Electrical work	554	27.0
Masonry, stonework, and plastering	487	20.1
Carpentering and floor work	198	19.6
Roofing, siding, and sheet metal work	212	29.2
Concrete work	232	11.7
Water well drilling	20	4.6
Miscellaneous special trade	530	22.8

Source: U.S. Department of Labor, Bureau of Labor Statistics, *A Career Guide to Industries* (Washington, D.C.: U.S. Government Printing Office, September 1992), pp. 12, 16. *Primary source:* Bureau of Labor Statistics.

★ 537 ★

Employment by Occupation and Industry

Employment of Wage and Salary Workers in Mining and Quarrying by Occupation, 1990-2005

"Employment in mining and quarrying is expected to decline about 9 percent by the year 2005, continuing the long-term decline in mining employment due to technological changes and expected low growth in demand for metals and other minerals. Slow employment growth in metal mining and the production of nonmetallic minerals is expected to be offset by employment declines in the larger coal mining segment of the industry."

[Thousands]

Occupation	1990 Employment		1990-2005 Percent change
	Number	Percent	
All occupations	318	100.0	-8.2
Operators, fabricators, and laborers	131	41.3	-5.8
Helpers, laborers, and material movers	26	8.3	-16.3
Truck drivers	21	6.6	3.9
All other material moving equipment operators	19	5.9	7.3
Grader, dozer, and scraper operators	12	4.0	-11.9
Excavating and loading machine operators	12	3.8	2.6
Crushing machine operators	10	3.3	9.0
Welders and cutters	7	2.1	-11.0
Industrial truck and tractor operators	5	1.6	-0.4
Operating engineers	4	1.3	3.5
Separating and still machine operators	3	1.3	-21.5
Precision production, craft, and repair	117	36.7	-11.0
Mining, quarrying, and tunneling occupations	23	7.2	-20.1
Blue collar worker supervisors	22	6.8	-13.7
Industrial machinery mechanics	16	5.0	-7.2
All other extraction and related workers	16	4.9	-11.9
Maintenance repairers, general utility	9	2.8	-10.2
Mobile heavy equipment mechanics	8	2.6	-0.9
Electricians	6	2.0	-5.0
Administrative support	24	7.6	-16.6
Secretaries	5	1.5	-18.4
Bookkeeping, accounting, and auditing clerks	4	1.3	-28.9
General office clerks	4	1.2	-6.0
Weighers, measurers, checkers, and samplers, recordkeeping	3	0.9	1.7

[Continued]

★ 537 ★

Employment of Wage and Salary Workers in Mining and Quarrying by Occupation, 1990-2005

[Continued]

Occupation	1990 Employment		1990-2005 Percent change
	Number	Percent	
Stock clerks, stockroom, warehouse, or yard	2	0.7	-1.7
Executive, administrative, and managerial	25	6.0	-6.9
General managers and top executives	7	2.1	9.1
Professional specialty occupations	10	3.1	2.7
Mining engineers	3	0.8	-5.2
Geologists, geophysicists, and oceanographers	2	0.7	15.2
Surveyors	2	0.8	-5.2
Technician and related	5	1.5	2.4
Engineering and science technicians	4	1.2	6.3
Other occupations	7	2.1	-6.7

Source: U.S. Department of Labor, Bureau of Labor Statistics, *A Career Guide to Industries* (Washington, D.C.: U.S. Government Printing Office, September 1992), pp. 21-2. *Primary source:* Bureau of Labor Statistics.

★ 538 ★

Employment by Occupation and Industry

Employment in Oil and Gas Extraction for Selected Groups, 1973-2005

"Most occupational groups will experience stability or small declines in employment according to Bureau of Labor Statistics (BLS) projections. The number of managers and administrators (38,000 in 1990) is expected to decline 5.4 percent between 1990 and 2005. The moderate growth projection is for just under 36,000 of these workers in 2005. Management support occupations are projected to decline from 21,475 in 1990 to 21,150 in 2005, a fall of 1.5 percent. However, within the management support category, the number of personnel, training, and labor relations specialists is expected to increase 4.6 percent, from about 1,620 in 1990 to close to 1,700 in 2005. Activities involving these occupations are expected to grow in importance."

[Thousands]

Year	All workers	Production workers	Women workers
1973	280	185	25
1976	350	240	35
1979	480	315	60
1982	700	485	100

[Continued]

★ 538 ★

Employment in Oil and Gas Extraction for Selected Groups, 1973-2005

[Continued]

Year	All workers	Production workers	Women workers
1985	590	370	95
1988	400	355	70
1992	355	240	60
1996	385[1]	--	--
2000	385[1]	--	--
2005	385[1]	--	--

Source: U.S. Department of Labor, Bureau of Labor Statistics, *Technology and Labor in Oil and Gas Extraction and Commercial Banking* (Washington, D.C.: U.S. Government Printing Office, October 1993), pp. 14-15. *Primary source:* Bureau of Labor Statistics. *Notes:* Magnitudes estimated from published chart. 1. Based upon moderate scenario; source also includes high and low projections.

★ 539 ★

Employment by Occupation and Industry

Employment of Wage and Salary Workers in Oil and Gas Extraction by Occupation, 1990-2005

"Little change in employment in the oil and gas extraction industry is expected through the year 2005. Employment in the industry as a whole is projected to decline 4.3 percent, as the decline in employment in crude petroleum, natural gas, and natural gas liquids segment of the industry—expected to drop by 12 percent—more than offsets the expected small increase—only 3.4 percent—for oil and gas field service employment.

"These divergent rates of employment change reflect how the two parts of this industry are responding to declining domestic production of crude petroleum. As domestic oil reservoirs have become depleted and the risks increase for deeper well drilling, lower oil prices and worldwide surpluses have reduced the incentive to launch new domestic oil exploration. Low oil prices also have discouraged the adoption of horizontal drilling and other new technologies. Increased environmental constraints are hampering development of both onshore and offshore sites. Thus, the outlook is for a continued decline in domestic production and increased reliance on imported oil."

[Thousands]

Occupation	1990 Employment		1990-2005 Percent Change
	Number	Percent	
All occupations	394	100.0	-4.3
Precision production, craft, and repair	141	35.9	-3.2
All other oil and gas extraction occupations	40	10.2	-0.6
Roustabouts	38	9.6	-3.6
Blue-collar worker supervisors	23	5.9	-6.9

[Continued]

★ 539 ★

Employment of Wage and Salary Workers in Oil and Gas Extraction by Occupation, 1990-2005

[Continued]

Occupation	1990 Employment Number	1990 Employment Percent	1990-2005 Percent Change
All other extraction and related workers	8	2.0	-4.5
Industrial machinery mechanics	6	1.6	3.5
Operators, fabricators, and laborers	60	15.3	0.9
All other material moving equipment operators	23	5.8	-2.8
Truck drivers	13	3.2	9.6
Administrative support including clerical	59	15.1	-18.8
Secretaries, except legal and medical	18	4.5	-19.2
Bookkeeping, accounting, and auditing clerks	12	3.0	-31.3
General office clerks	11	2.7	-6.1
Executive, managerial, and administrative	59	15.1	-4.0
General managers and top executives	15	3.7	-6.0
All other managers and administrators	12	3.0	-8.8
Accountants and auditors	10	2.6	0.7
Professional specialty	45	11.4	1.1
Geologists, geophysicists, and oceanographers	15	3.9	0.0
Petroleum engineers	14	3.5	-1.4
Other occupations	10	2.6	6.4

Source: U.S. Department of Labor, Bureau of Labor Statistics, *A Career Guide to Industries* (Washington, D.C.: U.S. Government Printing Office, September 1992), pp. 26, 28. *Primary source:* Bureau of Labor Statistics.

★ 540 ★

Employment by Occupation and Industry

Employment of Wage and Salary Workers in Aerospace Manufacturing by Occupation, 1990-2005

"Employment in the aerospace industry is expected to remain nearly unchanged. Over the 1990-2005 period, employment is projected to decline slightly from 892,000 to 879,000, a decline of 1.5 percent. Employment in the large aircraft and parts sector of the industry is projected to increase 1.3 percent, offsetting a decline of 11.7 percent in employment in the smaller guided-missiles and space-vehicles sector. Factors affecting the employment outlook in the aerospace industry include Federal defense expenditures, commercial aircraft sales, and exports."

[Thousands]

Occupation	1990 Employment		1990-2005 Percent Change
	Number	Percent	
All occupations	892	100.0	-1.4
Precision production, craft and repair	240	26.9	-2.7
Mechanics, installers, and repairers	55	6.1	3.5
Assemblers, precision	53	5.9	-10.4
Inspectors, testers, and graders, precision	39	4.3	-6.3
Blue-collar worker supervisors	26	2.9	-6.0
Machinists	21	1.2	4.7
Tool and die makers	11	1.2	1.5
Sheet metal workers	9	1.0	-3.8
Professional specialty	208	23.3	11.6
Engineers	155	17.4	10.5
Systems and analysts and computer scientists	17	1.9	34.6
Operators, fabricators, and laborers	147	16.4	-15.6
Machine setters, setup operators, and tenders	74	8.4	-11.7
Hand workers, including assemblers and fabricators	47	5.2	-26.7
Executive, administrative, and managerial	112	12.6	3.9
Engineering, mathematical, and natural science managers	14	1.5	8.7
Purchasing agents	11	1.3	7.9
Industrial production managers	10	1.1	1.3
Administrative support	109	12.2	13.7
Secretaries, stenographers, and typists	22	2.5	-22.7

[Continued]

★ 540 ★

Employment of Wage and Salary Workers in Aerospace Manufacturing by Occupation, 1990-2005

[Continued]

Occupation	1990 Employment Number	1990 Employment Percent	1990-2005 Percent Change
Production planning and expediting clerks	20	2.3	-7.3
Stock clerks, stockroom warehouse or yard	12	1.3	-14.7
Technicians and related	56	6.3	5.7
Engineering technicians	36	4.0	5.5
Computer programmers	10	1.1	22.9
Other occupations	21	2.3	-2.1

Source: U.S. Department of Labor, Bureau of Labor Statistics, *A Career Guide to Industries* (Washington, D.C.: U.S. Government Printing Office, September 1992), pp. 31, 33. *Primary source:* Bureau of Labor Statistics.

★ 541 ★

Employment by Occupation and Industry

Employment of Wage and Salary Workers in Apparel and Other Textile Products by Occupation, 1990-2005

"Employment in the apparel industry is expected to decline through the year 2005. This decline will affect mainly the production occupations. Although employment in the industry is declining, a large number of job openings will occur as experienced workers transfer to other industries, retire, or leave the workforce."

[Thousands]

Occupation	1990 Employment Number	1990 Employment Percent	1990-2005 Percent Change
All occupations	1,043	100.0	-18.7
Operators, fabricators, and laborers	758	72.6	-21.6
Sewing machine operators, garment	486	46.6	-26.7
Sewing machine operators, nongarment	58	5.6	-10.2
Pressing machine operators and tenders, textile, garment, and related	25	2.4	-1.4
Cutters and trimmers, hand	18	1.7	-19.9

[Continued]

★ 541 ★

Employment of Wage and Salary Workers in Apparel and Other Textile Products by Occupation, 1990-2005

[Continued]

Occupation	1990 Employment		1990-2005 Percent Change
	Number	Percent	
Freight, stock, and material movers, hand	19	1.8	-13.1
Hand packers and packagers	23	2.2	-11.0
Portable machine cutters	11	1.1	-4.0
All other assemblers and fabricators	18	1.7	-23.9
All other laborers and material movers	19	1.8	-13.1
Precision production, craft and repair	110	10.5	-10.7
Blue-collar worker supervisors	32	3.1	-13.5
Inspectors, testers, and graders	31	3.0	-15.3
Mechanics, installers, and repairers	19	1.8	-4.4
Patternmakers and layout workers, fabric and apparel	12	1.5	-4.5
Custom tailors and sewers	7	0.7	-7.4
Administrative support, including clerical	93	8.9	-19.0
Material recording, scheduling, and distributing occupations	36	3.5	-15.4
Financial records processing occupations	18	1.7	-30.8
Executive, administrative, and managerial	40	3.9	-6.1
General managers and top executives	17	1.7	-14.7
Other occupations	42	4.1	-0.4

Source: U.S. Department of Labor, Bureau of Labor Statistics, *A Career Guide to Industries* (Washington, D.C.: U.S. Government Printing Office, September 1992), pp. 36-7. *Primary source:* Bureau of Labor Statistics.

★ 542 ★

Employment by Occupation and Industry

Employment of Wage and Salary Workers in Chemical and Allied Products by Occupation, 1990-2005

"Employment in the chemical and allied products industry, excluding drugs, is projected to decline by 6 percent over the 1990 to 2005 period. The growth in the industry that characterized the 1970's and 1980's is not expected to continue. The decline can be attributed to factors that affect the entire U.S. economy but will have stronger impact on the chemical industry. More efficient production processes, increased plant automation, growth of environmental awareness, health and safety concerns, increased foreign competition, and an emphasis on specialty chemicals will influence chemical industry employment significantly."

[Thousands]

Occupation	1990 Employment		1990-2005 Percent Change
	Number	Percent	
All occupations	855	100.0	-6.0
Operators, fabricators, and laborers	262	30.1	-10.8
Chemical equipment controllers	53	6.2	-20.7
Helpers, laborers, and material movers, hand	53	6.1	-5.3
Transportation and material moving machine and vehicle operators	30	3.6	-5.1
Packaging and filling operators	29	3.4	-12.1
Crushing and mixing operators	24	2.9	4.0
Precision production, craft, and repair	180	21.0	-9.5
Blue-collar worker supervisors	43	5.0	-10.5
Chemical plant and system operators	30	3.5	-16.9
Maintenance repairers	21	2.5	15.5
Industrial machinery mechanics	19	2.2	0.6
Inspectors, testers, and graders	15	1.7	-7.5
Administrative support, including clerical	119	13.9	-14.9
Secretaries	28	3.3	-17.0
Bookkeeping, accounting, and auditing clerks	11	1.2	-28.9
Executive, managerial, and administrative	103	12.1	13.2
General managers and top executives	17	2.0	-10.5
Industrial production managers	11	1.3	12.5
Accounts and auditors	8	1.0	4.4

[Continued]

★ 542 ★

Employment of Wage and Salary Workers in Chemical and Allied Products by Occupation, 1990-2005

[Continued]

Occupation	1990 Employment		1990-2005 Percent Change
	Number	Percent	
Professional specialty	88	10.3	3.7
Science and math technicians	36	4.3	-0.8
Chemists	26	3.0	1.7
Chemical engineers	17	1.9	-3.0
Technicians and related	52	6.1	0.6
Engineering and science technicians	47	5.5	-1.5
Other occupations	52	6.0	11.1

Source: U.S. Department of Labor, Bureau of Labor Statistics, *A Career Guide to Industries* (Washington, D.C.: U.S. Government Printing Office, September 1992), pp. 41-2. *Primary source:* Bureau of Labor Statistics.

★ 543 ★

Employment by Occupation and Industry

Employment of Wage and Salary Workers in Drug Manufacturing by Occupation, 1990-2005

"Wage and salary jobs in drug manufacturing are expected to reach 293,000 in the year 2005, an increase of more than 23 percent, about the average rate for all industries. Demand will be stimulated primarily by population growth—particularly the growing number of older people who require more health care services—and by the growth of public and private health care insurance programs, which generally cover the cost of drugs and medicine. Other factors expected to increase the demand for drugs include greater personal income, the rising health consciousness of the general public, and the discovery of new drugs. Biotechnology offers great opportunities for the development of revolutionary new drugs and products. Although the drug industry is now the predominant user of biotechnology, many other industries including the agricultural sector are also using biotechnology. Employment in the biotechnology segment of the industry is therefore expected to grow faster than the industry average."

[Thousands]

Occupation	1990 Employment		1990-2005 Percent Change
	Number	Percent	
All occupations	238	100.0	23.3
Operators, fabricators, and laborers	55	23.0	8.4
Packaging and filling machine operators	18	7.4	3.8
Chemical equipment controllers and operators	6	2.7	3.7
Hand packers and packagers	5	2.3	16.7
Crushing and mixing machine operators	4	1.5	29.7
Administrative support, including clerical	42	17.5	7.1
Secretaries	14	5.7	3.8
General office clerks	4	1.9	20.7
Traffic, shipping, and receiving clerks	3	1.2	16.1
Bookkeeping and accounting clerks	3	1.1	-11.2
Professional specialty	39	16.4	39.7
Engineers	5	2.1	36.3
Biological scientists	10	4.2	39.9
Medical scientists	4	1.6	55.6
Systems analysts and computer scientists	5	2.1	61.3
Chemists	9	3.8	29.7

[Continued]

★ 543 ★

Employment of Wage and Salary Workers in Drug Manufacturing by Occupation, 1990-2005

[Continued]

Occupation	1990 Employment		1990-2005 Percent Change
	Number	Percent	
Executive, administrative, and managerial	37	15.5	29.9
General managers and top executives	5	2.0	11.5
Engineering, mathematical, and natural science managers	5	2.0	38.1
Marketing, advertising, and public relations managers	4	1.8	42.7
Industrial production managers	3	1.3	41.1
Precision production, craft, and repair	29	12.4	20.4
Blue-collar supervisors	8	3.5	16.7
Mechanics, installers, and repairers	8	3.4	21.2
Inspectors, testers, and graders	7	3.0	16.7
Technicians and related support	18	7.6	53.2
Science and mathematics technicians	14	5.7	57.4
Marketing and sales	10	4.1	45.2
Other occupations	9	3.6	16.7

Source: U.S. Department of Labor, Bureau of Labor Statistics, *A Career Guide to Industries* (Washington, D.C.: U.S. Government Printing Office, September 1992), pp. 45, 48. *Primary source:* Bureau of Labor Statistics.

★ 544 ★

Employment by Occupation and Industry

Employment of Wage and Salary Workers in Electronics Manufacturing by Occupation, 1990-2005

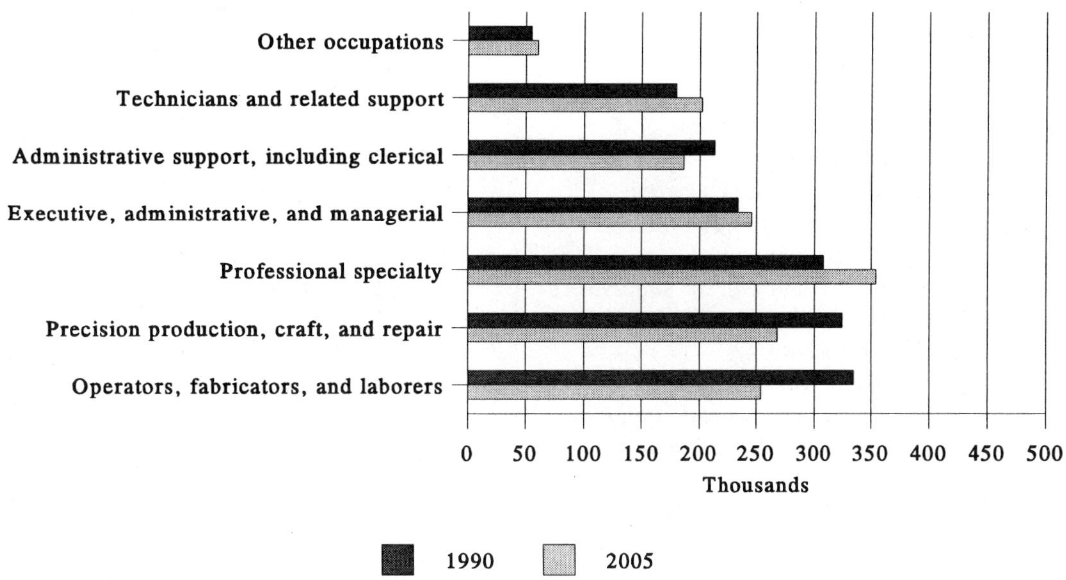

"Despite the electronics industry's reputation for dynamic growth, overall employment is expected to decline between 1990 and 2005. The industry is expected to continue its rapid productivity growth, meaning that fewer production worker should be needed, even though the output of products is expected to continue to increase. Furthermore, it is becoming increasingly common for products to have labor-intensive operations performed in low-wage countries in the Far East or Mexico. The industry will also very likely continue to encounter competition from imports of electronic goods and components, especially from Japan, but also from other countries in Asia and Europe.

"Expected employment of engineers, technicians, and managers should grow slowly, but employment of production workers, especially assemblers, is expected to decrease significantly. Employment in clerical occupations is also expected to decline."

[Thousands]

Occupation	1990 Employment		1990-2005 Percent Change
	Number	Percent	
All occupations	1,650	100.0	-4.8
Operators, fabricators, and laborers	335	20.3	-24.2
Electrical and electronic assemblers	105	64.	-44.5
All other assemblers and fabricators	62	3.7	-22.3

[Continued]

★ 544 ★

Employment of Wage and Salary Workers in Electronics Manufacturing by Occupation, 1990-2005

[Continued]

Occupation	1990 Employment		1990-2005 Percent Change
	Number	Percent	
Precision production, craft, and repair	325	19.7	-17.6
Electrical and electronic equipment assemblers, precision	105	6.4	-47.9
Blue-collar worker supervisors	44	2.7	-1.5
Mechanics, installers, and repairers	39	2.4	4.9
Metal workers, precision	23	1.4	7.0
Electromechanical equipment assemblers, precision	19	1.1	-36.6
Professional specialty	308	18.7	15.0
Engineers	241	14.6	13.0
Electrical engineers	119	7.2	14.4
Industrial engineers	21	1.3	13.9
Mechanical engineers	20	1.2	11.9
Computer systems analysts	24	1.5	44.3
Executive, administrative, and managerial	234	14.2	5.1
Engineering, math, and natural science managers	43	2.6	10.4
General managers, and top executives	26	1.6	-8.9
Industrial production managers	24	1.5	15.2
Administrative support, including clerical	213	12.9	-12.5
Secretaries	44	2.6	-17.1
Technicians and related support	180	10.9	12.2
Electrical and electronic technicians and technologists	89	5.4	16.0
All other engineering technicians and technologists	31	1.9	8.5
Other occupations	55	3.3	9.9

Source: U.S. Department of Labor, Bureau of Labor Statistics, *A Career Guide to Industries* (Washington, D.C.: U.S. Government Printing Office, September 1992), p. 51. *Primary source:* Bureau of Labor Statistics.

★ 545 ★

Employment by Occupation and Industry

Employment in Food Processing by Occupation, 1990-2005

"Employment in food processing is expected to decline 6 percent by the year 2005. Like other manufacturing industries, food processing is becoming less labor intensive. Technological innovations should result in continuing increases in productivity among production workers. Although professional specialty occupations and technicians comprise a very small proportion of industry employment, employment in some of these occupations—such as engineers and computer science—is expected to grow, reflecting the industry's continuing emphasis on scientific research to improve food products and production processes.

"The need to replace workers who transfer to jobs in other industries to stop working should result in many job openings. Replacement needs may be particularly significant in this industry because of the high rate of turnover among many low-skilled production workers."

[Thousands]

Occupation	1990 Employment		1990-2005 Percent Change
	Number	Percent	
All occupations	1,668	100.0	-6.4
Operators, fabricators, and laborers	887	53.2	-7.7
Meat, poultry, and fish cutters and trimmers, hand	121	7.2	12.4
Packaging and filling machine operators and tenders	118	7.1	-18.3
Truckdrivers	102	6.1	-9.0
Hand packers and packagers	96	5.7	-3.5
Cannery workers	78	4.7	-7.2
Industrial truck and tractor operators	38	2.3	-8.2
Freight, stock, and material movers, hand	37	2.2	-8.9
Cooking and roasting machine operators and tenders	29	1.8	-14.9
Crushing and mixing machine operators and tenders	27	1.7	2.7
Dairy processing equipment operators	18	1.1	-12.9
Machine feeders and offbearers	18	1.1	-10.7
Precision production, craft, and repair	324	19.4	-5.9
Blue-collar worker supervisors	62	3.7	-7.2
Butchers and meatcutters	62	3.7	-16.3
Industrial machinery mechanics	44	2.6	4.3
Bakers, manufacturing	30	1.8	-4.4
Maintenance repairers, general utility	28	1.7	-9.8
Inspectors, testers, and graders, precision	27	1.6	-2.6

[Continued]

★ 545 ★

Employment in Food Processing by Occupation, 1990-2005

[Continued]

Occupation	1990 Employment		1990-2005 Percent Change
	Number	Percent	
Administrative support, including clerical	152	9.1	-15.7
Secretaries	22	1.3	-19.6
Traffic, shipping, and receiving clerks	21	1.3	-8.2
Bookkeeping, accounting, and auditing clerks	19	1.1	-30.3
General office clerks	19	1.1	-6.7
Executive, administrative, and managerial	117	7.0	0.3
General managers and top executives	27	1.6	-11.7
Industrial production managers	19	1.1	10.7
Marketing and sales	69	4.1	3.9
Service	57	3.4	3.9
Janitors and cleaners	33	2.0	-12.1
Other occupations	62	3.7	7.9

Source: U.S. Department of Labor, Bureau of Labor Statistics, *A Career Guide to Industries* (Washington, D.C.: U.S. Government Printing Office, September 1992), pp. 55-7. *Primary source:* Bureau of Labor Statistics.

★ 546 ★

Employment by Occupation and Industry

Employment of Wage and Salary Workers in Furniture and Fixtures by Occupation, 1990-2005

"Employment in the furniture and fixtures industry is expected to grow about as fast as the average for all jobs through 2005, increasing 21 percent during the 1990-2005 period. Factors influencing demand in this industry include economic cycles, construction starts, disposable incomes, not demographic trends. As the Nation's population, personal income, and business expenditures grow, the demand for furniture and fixtures will increase.

"The rate of growth will vary among the various sectors. Stimulated by the rising demand from stores and offices, the partitions and fixtures industry will grow much faster than the average, with a 36 percent increase in employment expected. Office and miscellaneous furniture and fixtures will also experience strong employment gains, growing faster than average through 2005. Despite the recent slowdown, commercial real estate construction will continue generating job opportunities for workers in this industry."

[Thousands]

Occupation	1990 Employment		1990-2005 Percent Change
	Number	Percent	
All occupations	510	100.0	21.2
Operators, fabricators, and laborers	256	50.3	14.8
Hand workers, including assemblers and fabricators	100	19.7	0.1
Helpers, laborers, and material movers, hand	40	7.9	19.8
Woodworking machine setters, operators, and other related workers	33	6.4	29.9
Sewing machine operators, nongarment	20	3.9	31.9
Machine tool cut and form setters, operators, and tenders, metal and plastic	16	3.2	4.4
Coating, painting, and spraying machine operators, tenders, setters, and setup operators	10	1.9	19.7
Truck drivers	8	1.6	4.4
Precision production, craft, and repair	143	28.1	25.6
Precision woodworkers	62	12.3	24.5
Cabinetmakers and bench carpenters	28	5.5	24.6
Wood machinists	16	3.2	19.3
Furniture finishers	13	2.6	27.2
All other precision woodworkers	5	1.0	34.3
Upholsterers	26	5.1	20.6

[Continued]

★ 546 ★

Employment of Wage and Salary Workers in Furniture and Fixtures by Occupation, 1990-2005

[Continued]

Occupation	1990 Employment		1990-2005 Percent Change
	Number	Percent	
Blue-collar worker supervisors	21	4.0	25.0
Machinery and related mechanics, installers, and repairers	8	1.5	28.8
Inspectors, testers, and graders, precision	8	1.5	23.1
Administrative support, including clerical	51	9.9	17.6
Traffic, shipping, and receiving clerks	9	1.7	24.6
Financial records processing occupations	8	1.5	0.0
Secretaries	6	1.2	12.9
General office clerks	6	1.2	31.0
Executive, administrative, and managerial	33	6.4	37.7
General managers and top executives	11	2.1	20.9
Other occupations	22	4.3	79.4

Source: U.S. Department of Labor, Bureau of Labor Statistics, *A Career Guide to Industries* (Washington, D.C.: U.S. Government Printing Office, September 1992), pp. 60-1. *Primary source:* Bureau of Labor Statistics.

★ 547 ★

Employment by Occupation and Industry

Employment in Motor Vehicle and Equipment Manufacturing by Occupation, 1990-2005

"Employment in the motor vehicle and equipment manufacturing industry is expected to decline 8 percent, or 65,000 jobs, over the 1990-2005 period. Nevertheless, the need to replace workers who transfer to jobs in other industries or stop working will result in many job openings.

"Employment in the industry is projected to decline from 809,000 to 744,000 for several reasons. The growing intensity of international and domestic competition has compelled domestic motor vehicle manufacturers to seek productivity and quality improvements through the application of high technology production techniques, including robots, computers, and programmable equipment. Increasing productivity should more than offset increasing demand for motor vehicles, and this should be the primary cause of declining industry employment."

[Thousands]

Occupation	1990 Employment		1990-2005 Percent Change
	Number	Percent	
All occupations	809	100.0	-8.1
Operators, fabricators, and laborers	434	53.7	-17.6
Hand workers, including assemblers and fabricators	229	28.2	-22.6
Machine setters, operators, and tenders	150	18.6	-15.4
Helpers, laborers, and material movers, hand	31	3.9	-6.3
Transportation and material moving machine and vehicle operators	24	3.0	.5
Precision production, craft, and repair	166	20.5	1.3
Mechanics, installers, and repairers	48	5.9	4.9
Blue-collar worker supervisors	28	3.5	-2.6
Inspectors, testers, and graders	28	3.4	-2.6
Tool and die makers	13	1.6	3.9
Electricians	12	1.5	8.9
Sheet metal workers	10	1.2	8.3
Executive, administrative, and managerial	59	7.3	6.8
General managers and top executives	7	.8	-7.0
Industrial production managers	6	.8	17.8

[Continued]

★ 547 ★

Employment in Motor Vehicle and Equipment Manufacturing by Occupation, 1990-2005

[Continued]

Occupation	1990 Employment		1990-2005 Percent Change
	Number	Percent	
Administrative support, including clerical	55	6.8	-9.9
Material recording, scheduling, dispatching, and distributing occupations	21	2.6	-5.4
Secretaries, stenographers, and typists	10	1.2	-17.2
Professional specialty	48	6.0	17.3
Engineers	36	4.5	17.3
Technicians and related support	23	2.8	5.4
Engineering technicians	14	1.8	8.9
Drafters	5	.7	-13.5
Service	14	1.7	-7.4
Janitors and cleaners	9	1.1	-9.9
Other occupations	10	1.3	21.0

Source: U.S. Department of Labor, Bureau of Labor Statistics, *A Career Guide to Industries* (Washington, D.C.: U.S. Government Printing Office, September 1992), pp. 65-6. *Primary source:* Bureau of Labor Statistics.

★ 548 ★

Employment by Occupation and Industry

Supply of Natural Scientists and Engineers by Selected Variables, 1970- 1997

"[The] market conditions experienced by natural science and engineering graduates in the late 1980's and early 1990's are likely to depress further the proportion of young people earning degrees in these fields. That is, the decline in the number of degrees awarded in natural science and engineering probably will be greater than the decline that would be projected by a simple demographic model. Moreover, for the 1991-97 period, the projected decline in the number of degrees awarded in natural science and engineering is greater than the projected decline in the number of job openings in those fields.

"In 1991, based on a review of literature, L. L. Leslie and R. L. Oaxaca concluded that both economic and demographic factors affect choices of college major and, therefore, the types and numbers of future degree awards. In 1990, the National Science Foundation had reported that it could not establish any such empirical relationship, concluding that 'statistical correlations between annual production of [natural science and engineering] bachelors with starting salary data from the College Placement Council...show that in the past there has been virtually no relationship between changes in the relative starting salaries ([that is,] relative to other fields such as business, the social sciences and health sciences) and degree production in the combined fields herein defined as [natural science and engineering].' However, in 1991, Eileen L. Collins reported that lagged median starting salaries were significant in explaining degree output. Our analysis of 1967-85 data from the College Placement Council indicates a strong and persistent relationship between relative starting salaries of natural scientists and engineers and the rate of degrees awarded in these fields, albeit a relationship lagged in nature, with the number of natural science and engineering degrees increasing (decreasing) approximately 4 to 5 years after increases (decreases) in relative salaries in the fields."

[Thousands]

Year	Number of 22-year-olds (millions)	Number of high school graduates (millions)	Graduates with bachelor's degree		Graduates with bachelor's degree including engineering technology degree		Lagged salary premium
			Number (thousands)	Degree awards rate[1]	Number (thousands)	Degree awards rate[1]	
Actual:							
1970	3.5	2.8	144	4.1	...	...	...
1971	3.5	2.7	146	4.2	147	4.2	...
1972	3.5	2.7	148	4.2	150	4.3	.16
1973	3.7	2.8	155	4.2	156	4.3	.16
1974	3.8	2.9	160	4.2	162	4.3	.14
1975	3.9	2.9	157	4.1	160	4.1	.12
1976	4.0	3.0	160	4.0	163	4.1	.13
1977	4.1	3.0	163	4.0	168	4.1	.13
1978	4.1	3.1	168	4.1	173	4.2	.13
1979	4.3	3.1	173	4.0	178	4.2	.16
1980	4.3	3.2	177	4.0	184	4.3	.22
1981	4.3	3.2	183	4.2	190	4.4	.25
1982	4.3	3.1	189	4.4	199	4.6	.29
1983	4.4	3.1	197	4.5	211	4.8	.33
1984	4.3	3.0	206	4.8	222	5.2	.34
1985	4.2	3.0	214	5.1	230	5.5	.37
1986	4.2	3.0	214	5.2	231	5.6	.39
1987	4.0	2.9	208	5.2	222	5.6	.39
1988	3.8	2.8	194	5.1	208	5.5	.38
1989	3.7	2.7	184	5.0	198	5.4	.37
1990	3.6	2.6	177	5.0[2]	191	5.2	.34

[Continued]

★ 548 ★

Supply of Natural Scientists and Engineers by Selected Variables, 1970- 1997

[Continued]

Year	Number of 22-year-olds (millions)	Number of high school graduates (millions)	Graduates with bachelor's degree		Graduates with bachelor's degree including engineering technology degree		Lagged salary premium
			Number (thousands)	Degree awards rate[1]	Number (thousands)	Degree awards rate[1]	
Estimated:							
1991	3.7	2.7	...	...	...	...	.34
1992	3.8	2.8	...	...	...	...	.30
1993	3.9	2.8	...	...	...	...	.25
1994	3.6	2.7	...	...	...	...	.24
1995	3.4	2.5	...	...	...	...	.26
1996	3.3	2.4	...	...	...	...	.31
1997	3.4	2.5	...	...	...	...	.31

Source: Michael G. Finn and Joe G. Baker, "Future Jobs in Natural Science and Engineering: Shortage or Surplus?" in *Monthly Labor Review*, February 1993, pp. 54-5, 57. *Primary source:* Column 1 data, Dougals J. Braddock, "Scientific and Technical Employment, 1990-2005," *Monthly Labor Review*, February 1992, table 4, p. 39. Column 2, National Center for Education Statistics, *Projections of Education Statistics to 2002*, table 26. Columns 3 and 5, National Science Foundation (with Oak Ridge Institute for Science and Education), *Science and Engineering Degrees, 1966-1989*. Column 4, column 3, divided by column 1. Column 6, column 5 divided by column 1. Column 7, calculated by the authors from annual College Placement Council reports. *Notes:* 1. The degree awards rate is the number of degree awards in natural science and engineering as a percent of the 22-year-old population. 2. Braddock assumed a 5-percent 1990 participation rate; based on data from the National Center for Education Statistics, the authors estimate that the 1990 participation rate was 4.8 percent.

★ 549 ★

Employment by Occupation and Industry

Employment of Wage and Salary Workers in Printing and Publishing by Occupation, 1990-2005

"Spurred by increased demand for printed materials, employment in the printing and publishing industry is expected to grow about as fast as the average for all industries through the year 2005. Wage and salary employment in the printing industry is expected to increase by 21 percent during the 1990-2005 period. Factors stimulating demand include rising levels of personal income, increasing school enrollments, and higher levels of educational attainment. The rate of growth will differ among various sectors of the industry.

"Predictions that computers would turn us into a paperless society have not come true. The printing industry will continue to supply products for education, business, and leisure for a long time to come. Although the industry is expected to continue growing through 2005, it will grow at a slower rate than during the 1980's, largely due to slower economic growth, competition from nonprint media, and increasing use of nontraditional printing technologies."

[Thousands]

Occupation	1990 Employment		1990-2005 Percent change
	Number	Percent	
All occupations	1,574	100.0	20.7
Executive, managerial, and administrative	147	9.3	28.1
General managers and top executives	53	3.4	16.3
Marketing, advertising, and public relations managers	22	1.4	46.3
Professional specialty	163	10.3	27.6
Writers, artists, and entertainers	144	9.4	24.8
Marketing and sales	170	10.8	43.9
Administrative support	343	21.8	7.8
Precision production, craft, and repair	218	13.9	21.7
Prepress workers, precision	172	11.4	23.3
Compositors and typesetters	8	0.5	-5.2
Job printers	13	0.8	22.7
Paste-up workers	30	1.9	13.3
Electronic pagination workers	12	0.7	33.3
Photoengravers	8	0.5	13.2
Camera operators	16	1.0	21.2
Strippers, printing	32	2.0	34.3

[Continued]

★ 549 ★

Employment of Wage and Salary Workers in Printing and Publishing by Occupation, 1990-2005

[Continued]

Occupation	1990 Employment		1990-2005 Percent change
	Number	Percent	
Platemakers	14	0.9	23.5
All other precision	11	0.7	25.6
Prepress workers, product	28	1.7	21.5
Photoengraving and lithographic machine operators	2	0.1	5.7
Typesetting and composing machine operators and tenders	26	1.2	22.9
Operators, fabricators, and laborers	504	32.0	16.0
Printing, binding, and related workers	281	17.8	19.6
Printing press operators	162	10.3	21.1
Letterpress operators	16	1.0	-10.1
Offset lithographic operators	80	5.1	32.8
Printing press machine setters, operators, and tenders	59	3.8	13.4
Screen print machine setters and operators	9	0.6	36.9
All other printing press setters	8	0.5	22.9
Binding or finishing workers	69	4.3	10.3
Bookbinders	6	0.4	15.7
Bindery machine operators	63	4.0	9.7
All other printing, binding, and related workers	18	1.2	28.6
Other occupations	28	1.7	28.5

Source: U.S. Department of Labor, Bureau of Labor Statistics, *A Career Guide to Industries* (Washington, D.C.: U.S. Government Printing Office, September 1992), pp. 70-1. *Primary source:* Bureau of Labor Statistics.

★ 550 ★

Employment by Occupation and Industry

Employment Trends in the Pulp, Paper, and Paperboard Industries, 1973- 2005

"Employment in pulp, paper, and paperboard mills fell in more than half of the years during the 1973-93 period, and the average annual rate of decline over this period was 0.6 percent. Over the years 1973-79, total employment decreased at an annual rate of 0.2 percent, although production workers experienced a sharper decline (0.7 percent)."

[Thousands]

Year	All employees	Production workers
1973	265	208
1977	260	202
1981	246	198
1985	244	187
1989	239	188
1993	234	181
1992	228	--
1997	233[1]	--
2001	228[1]	--
2005	223[1]	--
	Average annual percent change	
1973-1979	-.2	-.7
1979-1993	-.8	-.8
1992-2005[1]	-.5	-.5

Source: U.S. Department of Labor, Bureau of Labor Statistics, *Technology and Labor in Pulp, Paperboard and Selected Converting Industries* (Washington, D.C.: U.S. Government Printing Office, June 1994), p. 10. *Primary source:* Bureau of Labor Statistics. *Notes:* Annual rate of change taken from table 2, p. 10. Some magnitudes estimated from published chart. 1. Projections based on moderate scenario; source also includes high and low projections.

★ 551 ★

Employment by Occupation and Industry

Job Expectations of Workers Employed in the Publishing Industry, 1999

"The respondents [in the survey reported below] were almost exactly divided between males and females, and the average age was 44; 40% had college degrees and a further 20% graduate degrees. They had been in their current jobs an average of 6.5 years, in the publishing industry as a whole an average of 14.8 years—somewhat belying the idea of publishing as a constant game of musical chairs. Over 36% had come into publishing from another career, whereas over 62% had never worked anywhere else."

[Percent]

Where respondents expected to be in 1999[1]	
In my current job	26.0
In a higher position in this company	21.2
Self-employed	15.1
In a similar job in a different company	13.3
Retired	9.2
In a different industry	5.5
In a different area of the publishing industry	5.2
In a higher position with another company	2.8

Source: John F. Baker, "Your Personal Bottom Line," in *Publishers Weekly*, 25 April 1994, pp. 37-8. *Primary source: PW* survey. *Notes:* Total exceeds 100% due to multiple answers. Base=543 respondents. 1. Not a question. This response a write-in.

★ 552 ★

Employment by Occupation and Industry

Information Workers as a Percent of the Labor Force, 1992-2002

"Telecommuting represents a fundamental change in the way companies and employees view work. This kind of innovation would inherently require a substantial number of years for widespread adoption even for jobs and individuals perfectly suited to remote work, with supportive managers and sophisticated technologies. The uncertainties about costs and benefits and the need for individuals and firms to work out appropriate telecommuting programs are matters which will take time to resolve. In some areas particularly afflicted with congestion and air quality problems, these impediments will be confronted by public sector requirements to reduce travel, and those situations can be expected to be among the first to experience relatively widespread telecommuting; the Los Angeles area is the leading example."

Year	U.S. Population[1] (millions)	Labor Force[2] (millions)	Information Workers	
			Number (millions)	Pct. of Labor Force
1992	253.3	127.6	72.1	56.5%
1993	255.2	129.1	73.3	56.8%
1994	256.9	130.7	75.6	57.1%
1995	258.7	132.3	75.7	57.2%
1996	260.5	133.9	76.8	57.4%
1997	262.3	135.5	78.2	57.7%
1998	264.1	137.1	79.6	58.1%
1999	266.0	138.7	81.0	58.4%
2000	267.8	140.4	82.5	58.8%
2001	269.7	142.1	84.0	59.1%
2002	271.6	143.8	85.5	59.5%

Source: Department of Transportation, *Transportation Implications of Telecommuting* (Washington, D.C.: U.S. Government Printing Office, April 1993), p. 55. *Notes:* 1. 0.7% increase annually. 2. 1.2% increase annually.

★ 553 ★

Employment by Occupation and Industry

Employment of Wage and Salary Workers in Blast Furnaces and Basic Steel Products by Occupation, 1990-2005

"Employment in the steel industry is expected to decline over the 1990-2005 period. The decline can be attributed, in part, to increased use of laborsaving technologies and machinery. Other factors affecting employment in the industry include overall economic conditions, development in minimills, foreign trade, and environmental regulations. Despite the continuing decline in employment, qualified workers will be needed to replace workers as they retire or leave the industry.

"The condition of the overall economy and of the industries that use steel strongly affect the steel industry. In good economic times, consumers buy more goods and therefore use more steel. Conversely, the importation of goods and equipment made with foreign-produced steel decrease demand for domestically produced steel. For example, if the automotive industry, a major user of steel is doing well, it will purchase more steel to manufacture more cars; however, foreign-made cars reduce the demand for domestic cars and steel. Industries that are significant users of steel include structural metal products, motor vehicles and related parts and equipment, fabricated structure metal products, miscellaneous fabricated metal products, household appliances, and metal cans and containers."

[Thousands]

Occupation	1990 Employment		1990-2005 Percent change
	Number	Percent	
All occupations	275	100.0	-19.6
Operators, fabricators, and laborers	130	47.3	-23.6
Helpers, laborers, and material movers, hand	34	12.5	-24.4
Machine tool cut and form setters, operators, and tenders, metal and plastic	28	10.0	-34.5
Crane and tower operators	11	4.2	-11.8
Furnace operators and tenders	6	2.1	-11.4
Industrial truck and tractors operator	6	2.1	-20.7
Welder and cutters	5	1.9	-20.2
Truckdrivers	3	1.1	-11.6
Precision production, craft, and repair	85	30.9	-16.3
Blue-collar worker supervisors	19	6.9	-20.2
Industrial machinery mechanics	13	4.6	-11.4
Metal workers, precision	8	2.9	-13.3

[Continued]

★ 553 ★

Employment of Wage and Salary Workers in Blast Furnaces and Basic Steel Products by Occupation, 1990-2005

[Continued]

Occupation	1990 Employment		1990-2005 Percent change
	Number	Percent	
Maintenance repairers, general utility	7	2.7	-23.2
Inspectors, testers, and graders, precision	7	2.5	-20.3
Millwrights	7	2.4	-11.4
Electricians	6	2.4	-16.4
Administrative support including clerical	22	8.1	-25.9
Material recording, scheduling, dispatching, and distributing occupations	9	3.3	-22.1
Professional specialty	9	3.2	-1.9
Engineers	6	2.2	-5.0
Other occupations	24	8.7	-11.5

Source: U.S. Department of Labor, Bureau of Labor Statistics, *A Career Guide to Industries* (Washington, D.C.: U.S. Government Printing Office, September 1992), pp. 74-5. *Primary source:* Bureau of Labor Statistics.

★ 554 ★

Employment by Occupation and Industry

Employment in the Steel Industry, 1973-2005

"According to projections by the Bureau of Labor Statistics, U.S. employment in the steel industry is expected to decline at an average annual rate of 1.4 percent from 1990 to 2005 (moderate projection).

"No employment increases are projected for any major occupational groups in the industry. And, with only a few exceptions, employment is projected to decline for all occupations, although the amount of decline varies from one occupation to another."

[Thousands]

Year	All workers	Production workers
1973	605	485
1976	540	425
1979	555	440

[Continued]

★ 554 ★

Employment in the Steel Industry, 1973-2005

[Continued]

Year	All workers	Production workers
1982	505	375
1985	340	255
1988	365	255
1992	250	185
1996	245[1]	--
2000	235[1]	--
2005	225[1]	--
	Average annual percent change	
1973-1993	-4.5	-4.8
1973-1979	-1.0	-1.2
1979-1993	-6.1	-6.5
1992-2005[1]	-1.4	--

Source: U.S. Department of Labor, Bureau of Labor Statistics, *Technology and Its Effect on Labor in the Steel Industry* (Washington, D.C.: U.S. Government Printing Office, May 1994), pp. 3-4. *Primary source:* Bureau of Labor Statistics. *Notes:* Annual rate of change taken from table 1, p. 3. Some magnitudes estimated from published chart. 1. Projections based on moderate scenario; source also includes high and low projections.

★ 555 ★

Employment by Occupation and Industry

Employment of Wage and Salary Workers in Radio and Television Broadcasting by Occupation, 1990-2005

"Employment in the broadcasting industry is expected to increase about 15 percent, nearly as fast as the average for all industries from 1990 through the year 2005. Beside job openings due to growth, many openings will result from the need to replace experienced workers who retire, die, or leave the industry for other reasons. Competition will be keen, however, for entry level positions because the industry traditionally attracts large number of jobseekers. Most entry level positions are likely to be in small stations; the stations in major metropolitan areas such as New York or Los Angeles usually seek highly experienced personnel. Work experience in the industry is important, and students with experience gained through internships or part-time work should have the best job prospects."

[Thousands]

Occupation	1990 Employment		1990-2005 Percent change
	Number	Percent	
All occupations	364	100.0	15.2
Professional specialty	108	29.6	26.2
Radio and TV announcers and newscasters	53	14.5	21.3
Producers, directors, actors, and entertainers	13	3.6	29.6
Photographers and camera operators	11	3.0	36.8
Reporters and correspondents	11	3.0	30.7
Writers and editors, including technical writers	6	1.6	16.2
Administrative support, including clerical	78	21.6	5.6
Secretaries, stenographers, and typists	15	4.0	-1.0
Other clerical and administrative support workers	30	8.2	11.3
Marketing and sales	47	12.8	5.6
Precision production, craft, and repair	46	12.5	-10.8
Telephone and cable TV line installers and repairers	32	8.8	-18.7
Executive, administrative, and managerial	44	12.0	23.8
General managers and top executives	14	4.0	12.7

[Continued]

★555★

Employment of Wage and Salary Workers in Radio and Television Broadcasting by Occupation, 1990-2005

[Continued]

Occupation	1990 Employment		1990-2005 Percent change
	Number	Percent	
Marketing, advertising, and public relations workers	9	24	39.4
Technicians and related	36	10.0	10.0
Broadcast technicians	28	7.8	4.5
Other occupations	5	1.3	15.1

Source: U.S. Department of Labor, Bureau of Labor Statistics, *A Career Guide to Industries* (Washington, D.C.: U.S. Government Printing Office, September 1992), pp. 89-90. *Primary source:* Bureau of Labor Statistics.

★ 556 ★

Employment by Occupation and Industry

Employment of Wage and Salary Workers in Telephone Communications by Occupation, 1990-2005

"Wage and salary jobs in the telephone industry are expected to decline more than 23 percent from 1990 through the year 2005. Technological innovations such as fiber-optic cable networks, electronic switching systems, digital data transmission, and office automation will continue to reduce personnel requirements, making for poor employment prospects in many occupations, particularly in craft occupations and for operators. These productivity improvements should more than offset the potential employment gains from strong growth in residential and business demand for telephone services, the development of new markets such as cellular phone services and electronic fund transfer systems, and the transmission of data to home televisions or computers via the phone system.

"The job outlook in specific telephone occupations may not follow the trend of the overall industry. Employment prospects for directory assistance and central office operators are expected to be poor as automation continues to increase these workers' productivity and reduce their employment to less than half of present levels. Computer voice recognition technology—if perfected—could totally eliminate directory assistance operators. This technology would enable customers to request numbers from a computer rather than a human. This technology could also eliminate many central office operator jobs."

[Thousands]

Occupation	1990 Employment		1990-2005 Percent change
	Number	Percent	
All occupations	947	100.0	-23.6
Administrative support, including clerical	400	42.2	-26.2
Telephone operators	87	9.2	-58.7
Customer service representative utilities	60	6.0	-.4
General office clerks	49	5.2	-6.3
Clerical supervisor and managers	40	4.2	-9.6
Material recording scheduling, dispatching, and distributing occupations	26	2.8	-47.0
Adjusters, investigators, and collectors	22	2.3	-4.4
Records processing occupations, financial	21	2.2	-20.2
Financial records processing occupations	20	2.1	-30.4
Secretaries, stenographers, and typists	19	2.0	-29.0

[Continued]

★ 556 ★

Employment of Wage and Salary Workers in Telephone Communications by Occupation, 1990-2005

[Continued]

Occupation	1990 Employment		1990-2005 Percent change
	Number	Percent	
Precision production, craft, and repair	303	32.0	-41.6
Central office and PBX installers and repairers	79	8.3	-43.3
Telephone and cable TV line installers and repairers	64	6.7	-47.6
Station installers, and repairers, telephone	43	4.6	-59.4
Blue-collar worker supervisors	37	3.9	-40.4
Electrical powerline installers and repairers	15	1.6	-19.0
Frame wirers, central office	11	1.2	-60.1
Executive, administrative, and managerial	90	9.5	-1.5
Communication, transportation and utilities operations managers	17	1.8	3.9
General managers and top executives	15	1.6	-12.1
Professional specialty	58	6.1	16.0
Engineers	29	3.1	6.4
Systems analysts and computer scientists	12	1.3	59.7
Marketing and sales	49	5.2	-.2
Technicians and related	36	3.8	2.3
Electrical and electronic technicians/technologists	13	1.4	3.3
Other occupations	11	1.2	-11.3

Source: U.S. Department of Labor, Bureau of Labor Statistics, *A Career Guide to Industries* (Washington, D.C.: U.S. Government Printing Office, September 1992), pp. 93, 95. *Primary source:* Bureau of Labor Statistics.

★ 557 ★

Employment by Occupation and Industry

Employment of Wage and Salary Workers in Trucking and Warehousing by Occupation, 1990-2005

"The number of wage and salary jobs in the trucking and warehousing industry is expected to grow by 25 percent, faster than the average from 1990 through 2005. Opportunities in this industry should be good for truckdrivers and mechanics.

"One of the main factors influencing the welfare of the trucking and warehousing industry is the state of national economy. Growth in the industry parallels economic upswings and downturns. As the national economy grows, more goods are produced and sold; and thus more transportation services are needed to move them from the producer to the consumer. In a recession, the industry is one of the first to slow down as orders for goods and shipments decline.

"Competition in the trucking and warehousing industry is intense, both among trucking companies and, in some long-haul truckload segments, with the railroad industry. Trucking companies compete by slashing rates or offering more customized service. Motor carriers must balance quoting rates high enough to cover costs but low enough to remain competitive. It is hard to become and remain a successful owner-operator."

[Thousands]

Occupation	1990 Employment		1990-2005 Percent change
	Number	Percent	
All occupations	1,638	100.0	25.0
Operators, fabricators, and laborers	1,052	64.3	27.0
Transportation and material moving machine and vehicle operators	853	52.1	30.2
Truckdrivers	777	47.4	30.6
Industrial truck and tractor operators	48	2.9	30.0
Helpers, laborers, and material movers, hand	195	11.9	13.3
Hand packers and packagers	25	1.5	22.8
Refuse collectors	32	1.9	13.5
All other helpers, laborers, and material movers, hand	130	7.9	11.0
Administrative support, including clerical	273	16.7	14.4
Billing, cost, and rate clerks	26	1.6	-4.6
Bookkeeping, accounting, and auditing clerks	27	1.7	-8.8
Stock clerks, stockroom, warehouse or yard	16	1.0	1.6

[Continued]

★ 557 ★

Employment of Wage and Salary Workers in Trucking and Warehousing by Occupation, 1990-2005

[Continued]

Occupation	1990 Employment		1990-2005 Percent change
	Number	Percent	
General office clerks	50	3.1	24.5
Clerical supervisors and managers	21	1.3	21.3
Dispatchers	36	2.2	36.9
Traffic, shipping and receiving clerks	17	1.1	25.8
Secretaries, stenographers, and typists	28	1.7	4.9
Precision and production, craft, and repair	136	8.3	23.9
Blue-collar workers supervisors	46	2.8	20.4
Bus and truck mechanics and diesel engine specialists	54	3.3	26.5
Machinery and related mechanics, installers, and repairers	17	1.1	19.9
Executive, administrative, and managerial	114	6.9	28.9
Communication, transportation, and utilities operators manager	34	2.1	39.8
General managers and top executives	52	3.2	19.7
Other occupations	62	3.8	34.5

Source: U.S. Department of Labor, Bureau of Labor Statistics, *A Career Guide to Industries* (Washington, D.C.: U.S. Government Printing Office, September 1992), pp. 98, 100. *Primary source:* Bureau of Labor Statistics.

★ 558 ★

Employment by Occupation and Industry

Employment of Wage and Salary Workers in Department, Clothing, and Accessory Stores by Occupation, 1990-2005

"Wage and salary jobs in department, apparel, and accessories stores are projected to increase nearly 23 percent over the 1990-2005 period, about as fast as the average for all industries. Large numbers of job openings will result from the high job turnover in this large industry.

"Young workers have traditionally supplied a large proportion of this industry's workers. The pool of workers under the age of 25 is expected to continue to shrink through the mid-1990's; after the year 1996 their numbers will begin to grow. This industry will continue to offer plentiful opportunities—not only for young workers, but also for first-time job seekers, persons with limited job skills, senior citizens, people with young children seeking part-time work, displaced workers, and handicapped persons."

[Thousands]

Occupation	1990 Employment		1990-2005 Percent change
	Number	Percent	
All occupations	3,305	100.0	22.9
Marketing and sales	2,216	67.0	26.3
Salespersons, retail	1,418	42.9	25.4
All other sales and related workers	292	8.8	43.2
Stock clerks, sales floor	268	8.1	15.1
Cashiers	223	6.7	23.3
Administrative support	490	14.8	9.1
General office clerks	78	2.4	17.8
Stock clerks, storeroom, warehouse or yard	64	1.9	3.8
Adjustment clerks	59	1.8	19.6
Bookkeeping, accounting, and auditing clerks	40	1.2	-8.0
Traffic, shipping, and receiving clerks	38	1.1	16.2
Executive, administrative, and managerial	219	6.6	24.3
General managers and top executives	96	2.9	21.4
All other managers and administrators	16	.5	16.8
Wholesale and retail buyers, except farm products	31	.9	25.3

[Continued]

★ 558 ★

Employment of Wage and Salary Workers in Department, Clothing, and Accessory Stores by Occupation, 1990-2005

[Continued]

Occupation	1990 Employment		1990-2005 Percent change
	Number	Percent	
Service occupations	135	4.1	15.5
Janitors and cleaners, including maids and housekeeping cleaners	31	.9	6.6
Other occupations	245	7.4	21.0

Source: U.S. Department of Labor, Bureau of Labor Statistics, *A Career Guide to Industries* (Washington, D.C.: U.S. Government Printing Office, September 1992), pp. 104-05. *Primary source:* Bureau of Labor Statistics.

★ 559 ★

Employment by Occupation and Industry

Employment of Wage and Salary Workers in Eating and Drinking Places by Occupation, 1990-1995

"Job opportunities in eating and drinking places should be plentiful through the year 2005. Wage and salary jobs in eating and drinking places are expected to increase by 33 percent over the 1990-2005 period, much faster than the average rate of growth for all industries. In addition to the openings that will arise from employment growth, thousands of additional openings will occur each year due to the need to replace experienced workers who find other jobs or stop working. Job turnover is high in this industry, particularly among part-time workers, many of whom are students. Thus, plenty of industry jobs will be available, including many for persons with limited job skills, first-time job seekers, senior citizens, women with young children seeking part-time work, displaced workers, and handicapped persons.

"Many factors will contribute to growth in eating and drinking places. Among these are population growth, rising personal incomes, and changing life styles—including both more leisure time and more two income families. Some of this increased demand will be met by wider adoption of laborsaving innovations, such as salad bar and untended meal stations, automated beverage stations, and central kitchens servicing a number of establishments in the same restaurant chain. However, most of the increased demand for services will increase the need for additional workers."

[Thousands]

Occupation	1990 Employment		1990-2005 Percent change
	Number	Percent	
All occupations	6,565	100.0	32.7
Executive, managerial, and administrative	388	5.9	41.1
Food service and lodging managers	233	3.5	52.7
General managers and top executives	133	2.0	21.3
Accountants and auditors	16	.3	40.0
Marketing and sales	414	6.3	33.9
Cashiers	363	5.5	33.7
Sales persons, retail	36	.6	30.0
Administrative support, including clerical	128	2.0	21.0
Bookkeeping and accounting clerks	52	.8	18.5
Service occupations	5,461	83.2	32.3
Janitors and cleaners	80	1.2	15.5
Food preparation and service occupations	5,131	78.2	32.3
Waiters and waitresses	1,388	21.2	24.9

[Continued]

★ 559 ★

Employment of Wage and Salary Workers in Eating and Drinking Places by Occupation, 1990-1995

[Continued]

Occupation	1990 Employment Number	1990 Employment Percent	1990-2005 Percent change
Food counter, fountain, and related workers	1,214	18.5	36.4
Cooks, short order, and fast food	690	10.5	32.7
Food preparation workers	566	8.6	36.3
Cooks, restaurant	463	7.1	47.2
Dining room, and cafeteria attendants and bartenders' helpers	304	4.6	37.9
Bartenders	259	4.0	7.2
Hosts and hostesses	153	2.3	24.9
Cooks, institutional or cafeteria	36	.6	66.5
Bakers, bread and pastry	33	.5	38.8
All other food preparation and service workers	23	.4	38.8
Precision production, craft and repair	28	.4	64.8
Operators, fabricators, and laborers	135	2.1	30.1
Driver-sales workers	72	1.1	24.6
Truckdrivers	58	.9	38.1
Other occupations	13	.2	7.4

Source: U.S. Department of Labor, Bureau of Labor Statistics, *A Career Guide to Industries* (Washington, D.C.: U.S. Government Printing Office, September 1992), pp. 108-10. *Primary source:* Bureau of Labor Statistics.

★ 560 ★

Employment by Occupation and Industry

Employment of Wage and Salary Workers in Wholesale Trade by Occupation, 1990-2005

"Wage and salary jobs in wholesale trade are projected to grow over 16 percent through the year 2005, nearly as fast as the average for the entire economy. Wholesale trade is an intermediary in the market process, and its employment growth is inseparably tied to the growth of the economy. Industry trends, however, will change the composition and nature of much wholesale trade employment. Consolidation of the industry into fewer firms and the spread of new technology should slow growth in some occupations, but many new jobs will be created in others as firms provide a growing array of support services. In addition, these trends will change the roles of many other workers."

[Thousands]

Occupation	1990 Employment		1990-2005 Percent change
	Number	Percent	
All occupations	6,204	100.0	16.2
Administrative support, including clerical	1,650	26.6	9.6
Material recording, scheduling, dispatching, and distributing occupations	491	7.9	12.4
General office clerks	223	3.6	22.9
Secretaries	213	3.4	6.1
Bookkeeping, accounting, and auditing clerks	198	3.2	-9.1
Clerical supervisors and managers	102	1.7	19.6
Marketing and sales	1,633	26.3	11.2
All other sales and related workers	1,352	21.8	8.7
Salespersons, retail	135	2.2	24.4
Stock clerks, sales floor	86	1.4	18.6
Operators, fabricators, and laborers	1,206	19.4	17.9
Truckdrivers	389	6.3	31.4
Freight, stock, and material movers, hand	192	3.1	18.8
Hand workers, including assemblers and fabricators	130	2.1	-.8
Drivers/sales workers	110	1.8	19.1
Hand packers and packagers	100	1.6	19.0
Machine setters, setup operators, operators, and tenders	76	1.2	5.3
Industrial truck and tractor operators	59	1.0	3.4
Executive, administrative, and managerial	748	12.0	21.8
General managers and top executives	386	6.2	16.1
Purchasing managers	70	1.1	15.7

[Continued]

★ 560 ★

Employment of Wage and Salary Workers in Wholesale Trade by Occupation, 1990-2005

[Continued]

Occupation	1990 Employment		1990-2005 Percent change
	Number	Percent	
Wholesale buyers, except farm products	66	1.1	24.2
Precision production, craft, and repair	592	9.2	23.5
Vehicle and mobile equipment mechanics and repairers	139	2.2	20.1
Other mechanics, installers and repairers	117	1.9	21.4
Machinery and related mechanics, installers, and repairers	88	1.4	29.5
Blue-collar worker supervisors	87	1.4	19.5
Other occupations	374	6.0	39.0

Source: U.S. Department of Labor, Bureau of Labor Statistics, *A Career Guide to Industries* (Washington, D.C.: U.S. Government Printing Office, September 1992), pp. 124-25. *Primary source:* Bureau of Labor Statistics.

★ 561 ★

Employment by Occupation and Industry

Employment of Wage and Salary Workers in Banking by Occupation, 1990- 2005

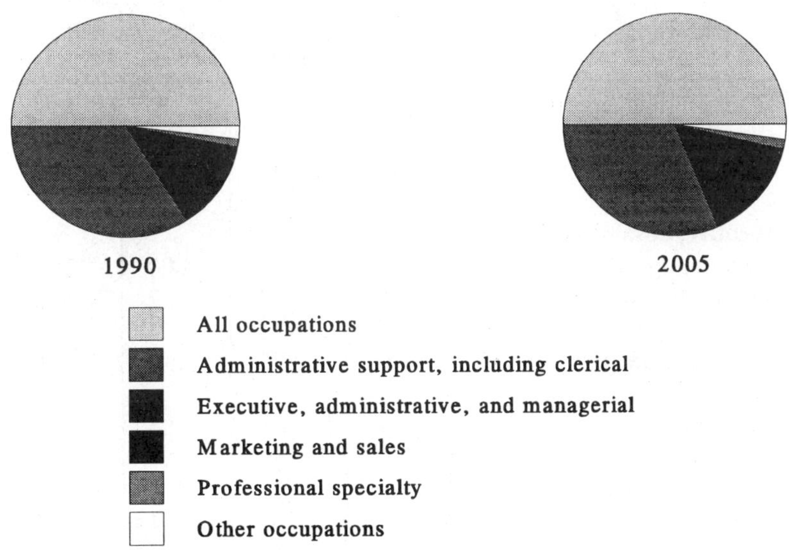

"Employment in the banking industry is expected to increase about 10 percent by the year 2005, more slowly than the average for all industries. Employment growth in this industry will be hindered by bank closings, consolidations, and mergers, as well as by technological developments such as electronic fund transfers which increase productivity, especially that of clerical workers.

"During the 1980's, many banks, especially savings and loans, made unwise loans, many of which may never be repaid. Consequently, more than 1,000 banks—mainly savings and loans—have failed in the past 10 years, and hundreds more are expected to do so in the next few years. Many banks in trouble have or will be merged or consolidated. On the other hand, employment is expected to grow in credit unions due to an expected increase in the number of credit union customers and credit unions' diversification into other banking services."

[Thousands]

Occupation	1990 Employment		1990-2005 Percent change
	Number	Percent	
All occupations	2,278	100.0	10.2
Administrative support, including clerical	1,549	68.0	2.2
Bank tellers	512	22.5	-5.1
Clerical supervisors and managers	138	6.1	12.3
General office clerks	115	5.0	16.6
Secretaries, except legal and medical	106	4.7	6.0
New accounts clerks, banking	104	4.6	13.0

[Continued]

★ 561 ★

Employment of Wage and Salary Workers in Banking by Occupation, 1990- 2005

[Continued]

Occupation	1990 Employment		1990-2005 Percent change
	Number	Percent	
Bookkeeping, accounting, and auditing clerks	97	4.3	-14.9
Loan and credit clerks	94	4.1	12.7
Executive, administrative, and managerial	547	24.0	24.4
Financial managers	129	5.7	36.3
Loan offices and counselors	123	5.4	19.6
General managers and top executives	72	3.2	12.9
All other management support workers	64	2.8	24.6
Accountants and auditors	39	1.7	29.0
Marketing and sales	54	2.4	42.6
Professional specialty	48	2.1	47.4
Other occupations	80	3.5	23.1

Source: U.S. Department of Labor, Bureau of Labor Statistics, *A Career Guide to Industries* (Washington, D.C.: U.S. Government Printing Office, September 1992), pp. 129-31. *Primary source:* Bureau of Labor Statistics.

★ 562 ★

Employment by Occupation and Industry

Employment of Wage and Salary Workers in Insurance by Occupation, 1990- 2005

"Wage and salary jobs in the insurance industry are expected to increase nearly 22 percent from 1990 to 2005, about as fast as the average for all industries. Employment in the insurance agents, brokers, and service segment of the industry should grow at a faster rate than anticipated with insurance carriers. In addition to new jobs that will become available, thousands of openings will occur as employees retire or leave their jobs for other reasons.

"Future demand for workers in this industry depends on the volume of insurance sales. Growing demand for long-term health care and pension benefits for the increasing number of retirees should spur insurance sales. Life insurance sales also should grow as more families seek policies designed to provide retirement income and educational funds for their children. Working women's growing need for life insurance and disability protection should increase demand also. Rising incomes and a concern for financial security also may stimulate sales of insurance, fixed and variable annuities, and other financial products and services."

[Thousands]

Occupation	1990 Employment		1990-2005 Percent change
	Number	Percent	
All occupations	2,118	100.0	21.8
Administrative support, including clerical	1,151	54.4	14.5
Insurance policy processing clerks	170	8.0	18.6
General office clerks	146	6.9	24.4
Insurance adjusters, examiners, and investigators	132	6.2	30.5
Secretaries	100	4.7	10.7
Clerical supervisors and managers	95	4.5	21.5
Insurance claims clerks	80	3.8	20.2
Typists and word processors	68	3.2	-18.0
Bookkeeping, accounting, and auditing clerks	68	3.2	-5.0
File clerks	46	2.2	-3.9
Data entry keyers, except composing	33	1.5	3.0
Executive, administrative, and managerial	429	20.3	28.2
General managers and top executives	98	4.7	26.4
Underwriters	98	4.6	23.5
Accountants and auditors	31	1.5	38.3
Claims examiners, property and casualty insurance	30	1.4	30.6
Marketing and sales	347	16.4	27.4
Insurance sales workers	291	13.7	25.6
Professional specialty	94	4.4	46.3
Systems analysts and computer scientists	29	1.4	66.4

[Continued]

★ 562 ★

Employment of Wage and Salary Workers in Insurance by Occupation, 1990- 2005

[Continued]

Occupation	1990 Employment		1990-2005 Percent change
	Number	Percent	
Technicians and related support	66	3.1	44.6
Computer programmers	38	1.8	56.7
Other occupations	32	1.5	16.5

Source: U.S. Department of Labor, Bureau of Labor Statistics, *A Career Guide to Industries* (Washington, D.C.: U.S. Government Printing Office, September 1992), pp. 134-35. *Primary source:* Bureau of Labor Statistics.

★ 563 ★

Employment by Occupation and Industry

Employment of Wage and Salary Workers in Securities and Commodities by Occupation, 1990-2005

"Employment in the security and commodity brokers and dealers industry is projected to increase 26 percent between 1990 and the year 2005, faster than the average for all industries. Most job openings, however, are expected to arise when workers transfer to other industries or leave the labor force.

"Most of the factors that contributed to the rapid growth in output and employment over the last decade should moderate in the future, resulting in a lower rate of growth in output and employment through the year 2005. Several factors should begin to moderate those trends: The volume of stock market transactions should level off and firms will not need to hire as many new employees in the future; the influx of foreign investment money will probably be less in the future as the dollar stabilizes; and insider trading scandals may discourage the participation of individual investors in the market. Furthermore, the rapid growth in mergers, acquisitions, and leveraged buyouts is probably over. High risk bonds or 'junk bonds,' will probably be used less to finance corporate mergers in the future."

[Thousands]

Occupation	1990 Employment		1990-2005 Percent change
	Number	Percent	
All occupations	427	100.0	26.7
Administrative support, including clerical	186	43.5	9.6
Brokerage clerks	48	1.1	5.6
Secretaries	39	9.1	8.1
General office clerks	17	4.0	28.8
Clerical supervisors and managers	15	3.6	22.7
Bookkeeping, accounting, and auditing clerks	12	2.9	-6.6

[Continued]

★ 563 ★

Employment of Wage and Salary Workers in Securities and Commodities by Occupation, 1990-2005

[Continued]

Occupation	1990 Employment		1990-2005 Percent change
	Number	Percent	
Data entry keyers, except composing	7	1.6	6.4
Communications equipment operators	5	1.2	-8.5
Computer operators, except peripheral equipment	5	1.1	15.3
Receptionists and information clerks	5	1.1	36.7
Marketing and sales	129	30.3	44.4
Securities and financial services sales workers	110	25.8	45.8
Executive, administrative, and managerical	81	19.0	30.2
General managers and top executives	21	5.0	21.9
Financial managers	12	2.9	26.0
Accountants and auditors	7	1.6	38.5
Professional specialty	16	3.7	47.9
Computer, mathematical, and operations research analysts	6	1.5	72.7
Technicians and related support	9	2.2	59.6
Computer programmers	8	1.8	62.7
Other occupations	6	1.3	23.2

Source: U.S. Department of Labor, Bureau of Labor Statistics, *A Career Guide to Industries* (Washington, D.C.: U.S. Government Printing Office, September 1992), pp. 138-39. *Primary source:* Bureau of Labor Statistics.

★ 564 ★

Employment by Occupation and Industry

Employment of Wage and Salary Workers in Advertising by Occupation, 1990-2005

"Employment in the advertising industry is projected to grow nearly 45 percent over the 1990-2005 period, much faster than the average for all industries. Despite this expected growth, competition for jobs will be keen because the industry traditionally attracts large numbers of job seekers.

"Several factors will create increased demand for advertising services. Among these are the production of more products and services that will be met by labor-saving innovations such as graphics software used with personal computers, but most of the increased demand will be met by hiring additional workers."

[Thousands]

Occupation	1990 Employment		1990-2005 Percent change
	Number	Percent	
All occupations	238	100.0	44.9
Administrative support	73	30.8	30.4
Secretaries	17	7.3	24.2
General office clerks	12	5.1	44.5
Bookkeeping, accounting, and auditing clerks	9	3.9	6.3
Clerical supervisors and managers	7	3.0	40.1
Receptionists and information clerks	6	2.3	55.2
Executive, managerial, and administrative	53	22.5	55.0
Marketing, advertising, and public relations managers	18	7.7	70.8
General managers and top executives	17	7.0	43.0
Purchasing agents, except wholesale, retail, and farm products	6	2.5	62.1
Professional specialty	51	21.3	46.1
Artists and commercial artists	16	6.9	39.7
Designers, except interior designers	14	5.8	55.2
Writers and editors, including technical writers	10	4.2	38.5
Marketing and sales	42	17.5	58.0
All other sales and related workers	41	17.3	58.0
Other occupations	13	7.7	40.4

Source: U.S. Department of Labor, Bureau of Labor Statistics, *A Career Guide to Industries* (Washington, D.C.: U.S. Government Printing Office, September 1992), pp. 65-6. *Primary source:* Bureau of Labor Statistics.

★ 565 ★

Employment by Occupation and Industry

Employment of Wage and Salary Workers in Amusement and Recreation Services by Occupation, 1990-2005

"Wage and salary jobs in amusement and recreation services are projected to increase more than 31 percent over the 1990-2005 period, faster than the average for all industries. Higher incomes, growth of leisure time, and increasing awareness of the health benefits of physical fitness will all affect employment growth.

"Personal income and the amount of leisure time are expected to increase, leaving workers with more disposable income and the time to use it. This will provide a larger market for establishments providing amusement and recreational facilities and services."

[Thousands]

Occupation	1990 Employment		1990-2005 Percent change
	Number	Percent	
All occupations	1,088	100.0	31.2
Service	428	39.3	27.1
Amusement and recreation attendants	93	8.5	20.5
Waiters and waitresses	65	6.0	25.6
Cleaning and building service occupations	44	4.1	14.3
Food counter, fountain, and related workers	37	3.4	37.4
Bartenders	31	2.9	.5
Protective service occupations	26	2.4	26.3
Ushers, lobby attendants, and ticket takers	20	1.8	41.2
Professional specialty	225	20.7	33.5
Instructors and coaches, sports and physical training	67	6.1	27.4
Musicians	54	5.0	24.2
Producers, directors, actors, and entertainers	26	2.4	51.6
Social, recreational, and religious workers	17	1.5	38.1
Adult and vocational education teachers	16	1.5	32.6
Athletes, coaches, umpires, and referees	15	1.4	37.8
Marketing and sales	108	9.9	34.9
Cashiers	57	5.3	32.3
Counter and rental clerks	20	1.9	28.1
Administrative support, including clerical	85	7.8	20.9
Information clerks	22	2.0	2.2
Secretaries, stenographers, and typists	17	1.6	12.7
Financial records processing occupations	19	1.8	-1.8

[Continued]

★ 565 ★

Employment of Wage and Salary Workers in Amusement and Recreation Services by Occupation, 1990-2005

[Continued]

Occupation	1990 Employment		1990-2005 Percent change
	Number	Percent	
Executive, administrative, and managerial	82	7.5	34.5
General managers and top executives	38	3.5	24.5
Financial managers	10	1.0	31.0
Agriculture, forestry, fishing and related	76	7.0	45.1
Gardeners and groundskeepers, except farm	65	6.0	47.1
Other occupations	85	7.8	35.3

Source: U.S. Department of Labor, Bureau of Labor Statistics, *A Career Guide to Industries* (Washington, D.C.: U.S. Government Printing Office, September 1992), pp. 143-44. *Primary source:* Bureau of Labor Statistics.

★ 566 ★

Employment by Occupation and Industry

Employment of Wage and Salary Workers in Child Care Facilities by Occupation, 1990-2005

"Wage and salary jobs in the child care services industry are projected to grow 42 percent over the 1990-2005 period, much faster than the average for all industries. In addition to openings created by employment growth, an unusually large number of job openings will result each year from the need to replace experienced workers who leave the industry. Turnover is very high, reflecting the low wages and relatively meager benefits. Rapid growth coupled with high turnover, however, should create excellent employment opportunities, especially for direct care providers.

"The child care services industry will continue to experience rapid growth, but it will be considerably slower than over the previous 15 years. This projected slowdown stems from an expected easing of demographic pressures as the increase in the population of women in their childbearing years continues to slow. An actual decline is projected in the number of working women between the ages of 20 and 34, when women are most likely to have preschool children."

[Thousands]

Occupation	1990 Employment		1990-2005 Percent change
	Number	Percent	
All occupations	457	100.0	42.7
Professional specialty	191	41.9	52.0
Teachers, preschool and kindergarten	174	38.0	55.1
Social workers	4	.9	16.5

[Continued]

★ 566 ★

Employment of Wage and Salary Workers in Child Care Facilities by Occupation, 1990-2005

[Continued]

Occupation	1990 Employment		1990-2005 Percent change
	Number	Percent	
Administrative support, including clerical	101	22.1	34.8
Teacher aides and education assistants	84	18.5	41.6
Bookkeeping, accounting and auditing clerks	6	1.3	-11.8
Secretaries	6	1.3	3.1
Service occupations	115	25.2	42.1
Child-care workers	78	17.2	51.3
Cooks, institutional or cafeteria	17	3.6	28.8
Janitors and cleaners, including maids and housekeeping cleaners	11	2.3	7.2
Executive, managerial, and administrative	41	9.0	23.9
Education administrators	15	3.3	32.5
General managers, and top executives	15	3.2	15.5
Operators, fabricators, and laborers	7	1.5	28.1
Busdrivers	6	1.4	28.5
Other occupations	2	.4	7.4

Source: U.S. Department of Labor, Bureau of Labor Statistics, *A Career Guide to Industries* (Washington, D.C.: U.S. Government Printing Office, September 1992), pp. 153-54. *Primary source:* Bureau of Labor Statistics.

★ 567 ★

Employment by Occupation and Industry

Employment of Wage and Salary Workers in Computer and Data Processing Services by Occupation, 1990-2005

"The computer and data processing services industry has grown extremely rapidly over the last 10 years mainly due to the development of the personal computer. This industry is projected to continue to grow rapidly, with employment expected to nearly double by 2005. The price of computers and related hardware continues to fall. With an ever increasing amount of computing power available, computer and data processing services firms are often engaged by individuals and organizations to maximize the return on their investments in equipment. Clients specialize in types of business other than computers, so when situations arise that challenge them beyond their limited knowledge of computers, they will continue turn to specialists."

[Thousands]

Occupation	1990 Employment		1990-2005 Percent change
	Number	Percent	
All occupations	784	100.0	90.6
Administrative support	252	32.1	55.8
Data entry keyers	52	6.6	26.5
Secretaries	33	4.2	66.2
Computer and peripheral, equipment operators	32	4.0	21.8
General office clerks	21	2.7	93.5
Bookkeeping, accounting, and auditing clerks	16	2.0	42.3
Clerical supervisors and managers	17	2.2	87.4
Professional specialty	158	20.1	137.3
Systems analysts and computer scientists	73	9.3	170.0
Electrical and electronics engineers	42	5.3	98.1
Technicians and related support	150	19.2	72.9
Computer programmers	131	16.8	66.2
Engineering technicians	16	2.1	124.6
Executive, managerial and administrative	127	16.2	104.4
General managers and top executives	37	4.7	86.2
Engineering, mathematical, and natural science managers	21	2.7	121.3
Marketing and sales	55	7.0	111.0
Precision production, craft, and repair	27	3.5	135.1

[Continued]

★ 567 ★

Employment of Wage and Salary Workers in Computer and Data Processing Services by Occupation, 1990-2005

[Continued]

Occupation	1990 Employment		1990-2005 Percent change
	Number	Percent	
Data processing equipment repairs	20	2.6	149.3
Other occupations	15	1.9	88.9

Source: U.S. Department of Labor, Bureau of Labor Statistics, *A Career Guide to Industries* (Washington, D.C.: U.S. Government Printing Office, September 1992), pp. 156, 159. *Primary source:* Bureau of Labor Statistics.

★ 568 ★

Employment by Occupation and Industry

Employment of Wage and Salary Workers in Educational Services by Occupation, 1990-2005

"Employment in the educational services industry is expected to grow by 25 percent, faster than the average for all industries, by the year 2005. In addition to employment growth, the need to replace experienced workers who find jobs in other industries or stop working will create many job openings. Given the large size of this industry, the number of jobs arising from replacement needs is particularly significant.

"Projected employment growth varies by occupation. Those expected to grow the fastest include counselors; school busdrivers; special education, adult education, and secondary school teachers; and teacher aides. Moderate growth is projected for college and university faculty, kindergarten and elementary school teachers, and education administrators. Relatively slow growth is expected for library workers—librarians, library technicians, and library assistants. Projected growth should result from demographers and enrollment increases, declines in class size in elementary and secondary schools, government legislation affecting education, expanded responsibilities of workers, and efforts to improve the quality of education."

[Thousands]

Occupation	1990 Employment		1990-2005 Percent change
	Number	Percent	
All occupations	9,440	100.0	24.5
Professional specialty	5,145	54.5	27.6
Teachers, elementary school	1,317	14.0	23.2
Teachers, secondary school	1,279	13.6	34.2
College and university faculty	711	7.5	18.9
Teachers, special education	332	3.5	40.5
Adult and vocational education teachers	260	2.8	30.5
Teachers, preschool and kindergarten	159	1.7	23.2
Instructors and coaches, sports and physical training	117	1.2	18.9
Registered nurses, therapists, and dietitians	102	1.1	28.8

[Continued]

★ 568 ★

Employment of Wage and Salary Workers in Educational Services by Occupation, 1990-2005

[Continued]

Occupation	1990 Employment		1990-2005 Percent change
	Number	Percent	
Counselors	99	1.1	34.9
Librarians	89	1.0	7.8
Farm and home management advisors	12	0.1	6.0
All other teachers and instructors	380	4.0	21.6
Administrative support, including clerical	1,793	19.0	17.7
Teacher aides	660	7.0	32.9
Secretaries, stenographers, and typists	481	5.1	1.7
Library assistants and bookmobile drivers	58	0.6	12.1
Service occupations	1,165	12.3	16.4
Janitors and cleaners	478	5.1	11.0
Chefs, cooks, and other kitchen workers	337	3.6	11.9
Food and beverage service workers	85	0.9	21.9
Executive, administrative, and managerial	538	5.7	24.4
Education administrators	282	3.0	24.4
Operators, fabricators, and laborers	362	3.8	30.5
Busdrivers, school	295	3.1	34.6
Other occupations	436	4.6	33.1

Source: U.S. Department of Labor, Bureau of Labor Statistics, *A Career Guide to Industries* (Washington, D.C.: U.S. Government Printing Office, September 1992), pp. 162, 164. *Primary source:* Bureau of Labor Statistics.

★ 569 ★

Employment by Occupation and Industry

Employment in the Federal Government by Occupation, 1990-2005

"Little or no change is expected in the overall level of Federal Government employment through the year 2005. The distribution of employment will change, however. Employment reductions are expected in the Department of Defense and overall increases are anticipated among the remaining executive agencies.

"Department of Defense employment is expected to gradually decline because of a reduced threat of world peace due to the dissolution of the Soviet Union as well as increasing concern over Federal budget deficits. Employing half of all Federal workers, the Department of Defense should gradually reduce its workforce through attrition over the next decade. Blue-collar workers, 3 out of 4 of whom work for Defense, may be particularly hard-hit. On the other hand, employment in other executive agencies is expected to increase slightly or at least remain stable due to population increases and growing needs for Federal programs."

[Thousands]

Occupation	1990 Employment		1990-2005 Percent change
	Number	Percent	
All occupations	2,266	100.0	-1.4
Professional specialty	605	26.7	8.8
Engineers	113	5.0	10.2
Systems analysts and computer scientists	50	2.2	34.2
Registered nurses	47	2.1	3.2
Life scientists	38	1.7	6.4
Physicians	35	1.6	3.2
Administrative support, including clerical	526	23.2	-17.7
Secretaries	107	4.7	-17.4
Typists and word processors	57	2.5	-38.1
Bookkeeping, accounting, and auditing clerks	45	2.0	-29.3
Executive, administrative, and managerial	370	16.3	4.5
Accountants and auditors	74	3.3	5.1
Inspectors and compliance officers, except construction	46	2.0	13.5
Purchasing agents, except wholesale, retail, and farm products	39	1.7	3.2
Tax examiners, collectors, and revenue agents	32	1.3	0.6

[Continued]

★ 569 ★

Employment in the Federal Government by Occupation, 1990-2005

[Continued]

Occupation	1990 Employment		1990-2005 Percent change
	Number	Percent	
Precision production, craft, and repair	262	11.6	-3.5
Mechanics, installers, and repairers	131	5.8	-4.0
Construction trades	41	1.8	-0.4
Blue-collar worker supervisors	40	1.7	-7.1
Technicians and related	206	9.1	6.7
Engineering technicians	65	2.9	6.4
Service	140	6.2	-0.5
Operators, fabricators, and laborers	116	5.1	-8.9
Other occupations	42	1.9	-2.9

Source: U.S. Department of Labor, Bureau of Labor Statistics, *A Career Guide to Industries* (Washington, D.C.: U.S. Government Printing Office, September 1992), pp. 169, 171-72. *Primary source:* Bureau of Labor Statistics.

★ 570 ★

Employment by Occupation and Industry

Employment of Wage and Salary Workers in Health Services by Occupation, 1990-2005

"Employment in the health services industry is projected to grow 44 percent during the period from 1990 through the year 2005, much faster than the 20-percent average for all industries. Employment growth is expected to add nearly 3.9 million new jobs—17 percent of all wage and salary jobs added to the U.S. economy by 2005—which will be more than in any other industry. Projected rates of employment growth for the various segments of this industry range from 27 percent in hospitals, the largest industry range from 27 percent in hospitals, the largest industry segment, to 107 percent in the much smaller home health care services."

[Thousands]

Occupation	1990 Employment		1990-2005 Percent change
	Number	Percent	
All occupations	8,927	100.0	43.6
Professional specialty	2,531	28.4	47.8
Registered nurses	1,416	15.9	48.6
Physicians	392	4.4	43.8
Therapists	196	2.2	64.5
Social workers	110	1.2	53.3
Service occupations	2,517	28.2	43.4
Nursing aides and psychiatric aides	1,001	11.2	47.2
Food preparation and service occupations	384	4.3	23.7
Janitors and cleaners	329	3.7	21.3
Dental assistants	172	1.9	34.5
Homemaker-home health aides	159	1.8	97.5
Medical assistants	157	1.8	77.0
Administrative support	1,723	19.3	38.1
Secretaries	376	4.2	50.2
Receptionists and information clerks	279	3.1	65.4
General office clerks	238	2.7	40.9
Bookkeeping, accounting, and auditing clerks	112	1.3	12.4
Typists and word processors	104	1.2	-7.0
Technicians and related support	1,396	15.6	45.1
Licensed practical nurses	527	5.9	42.2
Clinical laboratory technologists and technicians	238	2.7	26.1
Radiologic technologists	144	1.6	71.8
Dental hygienists	96	1.1	41.5
Executive, administrative, and managerial	439	4.9	44.4
Health services managers	257	2.9	42.0

[Continued]

★ 570 ★

Employment of Wage and Salary Workers in Health Services by Occupation, 1990-2005

[Continued]

Occupation	1990 Employment		1990-2005 Percent change
	Number	Percent	
General managers and top executives	87	1.0	52.4
Other health services managers and administrators	170	1.9	36.6
Precision production, craft and repair	169	1.9	26.8
Operators, fabricators, and laborers	100	1.1	31.8
Marketing and sales	36	0.4	56.6
Other occupations	15	0.2	51.6

Source: U.S. Department of Labor, Bureau of Labor Statistics, *A Career Guide to Industries* (Washington, D.C.: U.S. Government Printing Office, September 1992), pp. 176-77. *Primary source:* Bureau of Labor Statistics.

★ 571 ★

Employment by Occupation and Industry

Employment in Hospitals, 1963-2005

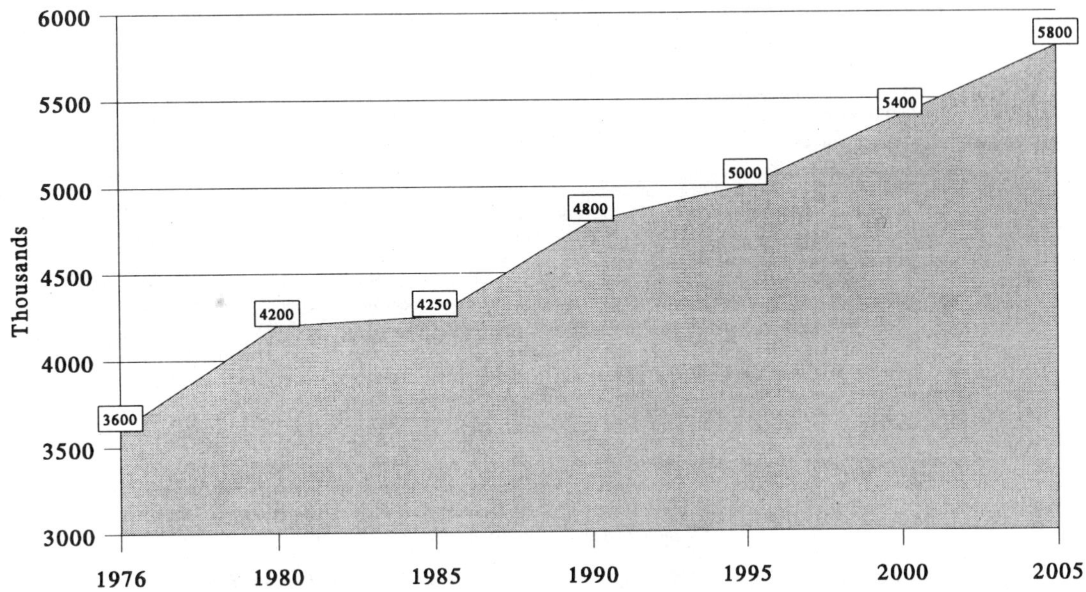

"Employment in hospitals has grown steadily in recent years. The number of employees is expected to continue to grow through the year 2005. Furthermore, employment and the structure of occupations will undergo further modification as technological and other changes are implemented more widely.

"The rate of employment growth has varied over the past two decades. Total combined employment for public and private hospitals grew from 3.6 million in 1976 to 4.9 million in 1990, a growth rate of 1.8 percent annually. Total employment grew an average of 3.2 percent a year from 1976 to 1979 and 1.5 percent annually from 1979 to 1990."

[Thousands]

Year	All hospital employees[3]	Private hospital employees	Government hospital employees
1976	3,600	2,350	550
1980	4,200	2,800	1,000
1985	4,250	3,000	750
1990	4,800	3,400	750
1995	5,000[1]	--	--
2000	5,400[1]	--	--
2005	5,800[1]	--	--
	Average annual percent change[2]		
1976-1990	1.8	3.0	0.1
1976-1979	3.2	4.1	2.9

[Continued]

★ 571 ★

Employment in Hospitals, 1963-2005

[Continued]

Year	All hospital employees[3]	Private hospital employees	Government hospital employees
1979-1990	1.5	2.3	-0.5
1990-2005[4]	1.6	--	--

Source: U.S. Department of Labor, Bureau of Labor Statistics, *Outlook for Technology and Labor in Hospitals* (Washington, D.C.: U.S. Government Printing Office, May 1992), pp. 16-17. *Primary source:* Bureau of Labor Statistics. *Notes:* Annual rate of change taken from table 2, p. 16. 1. Based on moderate scenario; source also includes high and low projections. 2. Least squares trend method used for percent changes in historical data; compound interest method for projected data. 3. BLS data on all government employees only available since 1976. 4. BLS makes employment projections based upon low, moderate, and high levels of economic growth. The projected data include State and local hospital employment but exclude Federal hospital employment. Some magnitudes estimated from published chart.

★ 572 ★

Employment by Occupation and Industry

Employment of Wage and Salary Workers in Hotels and Other Lodging Places by Occupation, 1990-2005

"Job opportunities in the hotel, motel, and other lodging places will be plentiful from 1990 through the year 2005. Wage and salary employment is projected to increase 32 percent, faster than the average rate of growth for all industries over the period. This rate of growth, however, will be slower than the industry's record growth in the past 10 years. The main reasons for slowdown in growth are slower population growth, overbuilding of hotels in the 1980's, and the elimination of tax incentives by the Tax Reform Act of 1986 associated with building of new hotels.

"Workers under the age of 25 have traditionally filled a significant proportion of the lodging industry's jobs. The pool of these young workers in the labor force—which declined rapidly in size between 1985 and 1990—will continue to shrink through the mid-1990's, and then start increasing again as the children of the baby-boomers begin entering the labor force. To attract and retain workers, the industry will place more emphasis on hiring, training, and retaining employees and more actively recruit part-time, older workers, disabled workers, and new immigrants. The hotel and lodging industry will also increasingly automate."

[Thousands]

Occupation	1990 Employment		1990-2005 Percent change
	Number	Percent	
All occupations	1,649	100.0	31.84
Service	1,063	64.5	29.5
Housekeepers, institutional	50	3.1	23.0
Janitors, cleaners, and maids	356	21.6	23.6
Cooks, restaurant	68	4.1	33.5
Food preparation workers	78	4.8	34.1
Bartenders	47	2.9	14.9

[Continued]

★ 572 ★

Employment of Wage and Salary Workers in Hotels and Other Lodging Places by Occupation, 1990-2005

[Continued]

Occupation	1990 Employment		1990-2005 Percent change
	Number	Percent	
Dining room and cafeteria attendants and bar helpers	53	3.2	32.7
Food counter, fountain, and related workers	40	2.4	31.6
Hosts and hostesses	19	1.1	22.0
Waiters and waitresses	193	11.7	33.7
Amusement and recreation attendants	37	2.2	38.7
Baggage porters and bellhops	25	1.5	37.2
Administrative support	230	13.9	25.2
Bookkeeping and accounting clerks	26	1.6	1.7
Hotel desk clerks	117	7.1	34.6
Secretaries	21	1.3	18.8
Executive, managerial, administrative	119	7.2	45.4
Food service and lodging managers	39	2.4	51.2
General managers and top executives	30	1.9	33.1
Marketing, advertising, and public relations managers	8	0.5	63.4
Accountants and auditors	11	0.6	51.2
Marketing and sales	78	4.8	45.3
Cashiers	48	2.9	43.1
Sales persons, retail	6	0.4	39.4
All other sales persons	25	1.5	51.2
Precision production, craft and repair	69	4.2	42.2
Maintenance repairers, general utility	50	3.0	43.1
Operators, fabricators, and laborers	49	3.0	30.2
Laundry and drycleaning machine operators	30	1.8	26.7
Agriculture, forestry, fishing and related	20	1.2	48.2
Gardeners and groundskeepers	19	1.2	48.2

Source: U.S. Department of Labor, Bureau of Labor Statistics, *A Career Guide to Industries* (Washington, D.C.: U.S. Government Printing Office, September 1992), pp. 182-85. *Primary source:* Bureau of Labor Statistics.

★ 573 ★

Employment by Occupation and Industry

Employment of Wage and Salary Workers in Management and Public Relations Services by Occupation, 1990-2005

"Wage and salary jobs in the management and public relations service industry are expected to grow about 76 percent by the year 2005, three times faster than average for all industries, but much slower than the industry has grown in recent years. The reasons for the projected slowdown in employment growth are twofold: The growth rate of the U.S. economy is slowing in general, which will necessarily slow industry growth, and as the industry matures, it will be more difficult for established firms to expand or new firms to enter the market.

"The increasing complexity of business will most contribute to industry growth. Among other things, today's managers must worry about rapid technological innovations, changes in government regulation, growing environmental concerns, and the continuing reduction of trade barriers and the globalization of markets. Because it has become difficult to keep abreast of these changes, corporations, institutions, and governments will increasingly need the aid of well trained, well informed management and public relations services professionals."

[Thousands]

Occupation	1990 Employment		1990-2005 Percent change
	Number	Percent	
All occupations	622	100.0	76.4
Executive, administrative, and managerial	185	29.7	85.2
General managers and top executives	46	7.4	70.1
Management analysts	21	3.3	104.0
Financial managers	18	2.9	74.8
Marketing, advertising, and public relations managers	11	1.8	108.7
Administrative services managers	11	1.7	74.7
Accountants and auditors	10	1.6	93.2
Administrative support, including clerical	177	28.5	53.8
Secretaries	54	8.7	51.8
General office clerks	18	2.8	76.7
Bookkeeping, accounting, and auditing clerks	16	2.6	29.9
Clerical supervisors and managers	16	2.5	71.2
Professional specialty	105	16.9	89.5
Public relations specialists and publicity writers	17	2.7	56.0
Designers	10	1.6	89.0
Systems analysts and computer scientists	9	1.5	146.7
Electrical and electronics engineers	9	1.4	105.7
Service workers	48	7.6	77.3
Guards	10	1.6	61.3
Food preparation and service occupations	10	1.6	89.8

[Continued]

★573★

Employment of Wage and Salary Workers in Management and Public Relations Services by Occupation, 1990-2005

[Continued]

Occupation	1990 Employment		1990-2005 Percent change
	Number	Percent	
Technicians and related support	39	6.3	101.1
Computer programmers	15	2.4	127.7
Engineering technicians	10	1.6	94.5
Marketing and sales	24	3.8	93.1
Precision production, craft, and repair	24	3.8	75.2
Other occupations	21	3.3	58.9

Source: U.S. Department of Labor, Bureau of Labor Statistics, *A Career Guide to Industries* (Washington, D.C.: U.S. Government Printing Office, September 1992), pp. 189, 192. *Primary source:* Bureau of Labor Statistics.

★574★

Employment by Occupation and Industry

Employment of Wage and Salary Workers in Motion Picture Production and Distribution by Occupation, 1990-1995

"Job opportunities in the motion picture production and distribution industry should be plentiful through the year 2005. Wage and salary jobs are projected to increase 38 percent over the 1990-2005 period, much faster than the average rate of growth for all industries. Rapid employment growth in motion picture production and distribution will be due to a growing demand for film and tape production for domestic and foreign television, cable television, feature film markets, home video, and for informational, educational, and industrial films. Job opportunities should be especially good in film reproduction, distribution, and rental, as more large studios turn to this part of business. In addition to new jobs, many more jobs will arise as workers leave this high-turnover industry.

"Growth is expected to be faster than the average for executives and managers; producers, directors, actors, and entertainers; artists; writers and editors; engineering technicians; camera operators; distribution personnel; and craft workers. However, many people seek these jobs so competition for them is expected to continue to be keen. Only the most talented will find regular employment."

[Thousands]

Occupation	1990 Employment		1990-2005 Percent change
	Number	Percent	
All occupations	164	100.0	38.1
Professional specialty	58	35.4	48.0
Producers, directors, actors, and entertainers	29	17.4	47.1
Artists and commercial artists	5	3.1	32.4
Photographers and camera operators	5	3.1	47.1
Writers and editors	3	1.7	31.2
Administrative support, including clerical	40	24.6	21.4
Secretaries, stenographers, and typists	12	7.6	14.8
Material recording, scheduling, dispatching, and distributing occupations	6	3.4	29.4
Financial records processing occupations	5	3.3	2.8
Executive, managerial, and administrative	27	16.6	39.0
General managers and top executives	11	6.7	31.9
Financial managers	4	2.2	35.5
Marketing, advertising, and public relations managers	4	2.4	61.8
Marketing and sales	15	9.2	48.7
Precision production, craft, and repair occupations	7	4.2	27.1
Production occupations, precision	4	2.7	21.5

[Continued]

★ 574 ★

Employment of Wage and Salary Workers in Motion Picture Production and Distribution by Occupation, 1990-1995

[Continued]

Occupation	1990 Employment		1990-2005 Percent change
	Number	Percent	
Technicians and related support	7	4.5	53.0
Engineering and science technicians	6	3.7	48.2
Operators, fabricators, and laborers	7	4.2	18.7

Source: U.S. Department of Labor, Bureau of Labor Statistics, *A Career Guide to Industries* (Washington, D.C.: U.S. Government Printing Office, September 1992), pp. 197, 199. *Primary source:* Bureau of Labor Statistics.

★ 575 ★

Employment by Occupation and Industry

Employment of Nongovernment Wage and Salary Workers in Social Services by Occupation, 1990-2005

"Job opportunities in social services should be numerous through the year 2005 because the number of nongovernment wage and salary jobs is expected to increase much faster than average. Employment is projected to grow 64 percent—more than three times the rate of the economy as a whole. Expected growth rates for the various segments of the industry range from 29 percent in job training and related services to 94 percent in residential care over the 1990-2005 period. Employment growth is not the only source of job openings, however. Workers who retire or transfer to other occupations will also need to be replaced. In large occupations with easy entry, relatively low pay, and high turnover, many job openings will occur.

"The expected rapid growth is due to expanding services for the elderly, disabled, mentally ill, mentally retarded, and families in crisis. Older people, who are a rapidly expanding part of the population, are more likely to need services. American families are losing extended family support systems, forcing individuals to look elsewhere for help in times of trouble. In addition, businesses are implementing more employee counseling programs. Programs are also increasing for special groups, such as those for adults who were abused as children or child protective services. Interest in fitness and health is increasing as well."

[Thousands]

Occupation	1990 Employment		1990-2005 Percent change
	Number	Percent	
All occupations	1,354	100.0	64.1
Service occupations	451	33.3	83.0
Homemaker-home health aides	159	11.8	99.1
Food preparation and service occupations	74	5.5	75.7
Nursing aides and psychiatric aides	71	5.3	85.0
Child care workers	48	3.5	85.4
Janitors and cleaners	43	3.2	50.2

[Continued]

★ 575 ★

Employment of Nongovernment Wage and Salary Workers in Social Services by Occupation, 1990-2005

[Continued]

Occupation	1990 Employment		1990-2005 Percent change
	Number	Percent	
Professional specialty	364	26.9	64.9
Social workers	115	8.5	53.1
Human services workers	73	5.4	89.8
Adult education teachers	34	2.5	57.1
Recreation workers	24	1.7	60.5
Registration nurses	24	1.8	84.3
Teachers, preschool and kindergarten	21	1.6	52.1
Counselors	15	1.1	44.5
Administrative support	198	14.6	37.2
Secretaries	52	3.9	34.0
Bookkeeping, accounting, and auditing clerks	25	1.8	15.3
Teacher aides and educational assistants	22	1.5	62.5
Executive, administrative, and managerial	158	11.7	58.8
General managers, and top executives	58	4.3	53.1
Operators, fabricators, and laborers	87	6.4	30.4
Hand workers	31	2.3	2.2
Motor vehicle operators	28	2.0	59.5
Precision production, craft, and repair	39	2.8	50.6
Technician and related support	34	2.5	89.0
Licensed practical nurses	18	1.3	97.0
Marketing and sales	17	1.3	54.2
Other occupations	7	0.5	75.0

Source: U.S. Department of Labor, Bureau of Labor Statistics, *A Career Guide to Industries* (Washington, D.C.: U.S. Government Printing Office, September 1992), pp. 207-08. *Primary source:* Bureau of Labor Statistics.

★ 576 ★

Employment by Occupation and Industry

Employment of Wage and Salary Workers in State and Local Government by Occupation, 1990-2005

"State and local government employment is projected to increase over 19 percent during the period 1990-2005, about as fast as the average for all industries. Employment growth will be fueled by the rising demand for services at the State and local levels. Since the early 1980's, government has decentralized and States have had to take on more responsibility for providing necessary services for their residents. Federal grants to State and local governments have declined from 15 percent of all Federal outlays in 1980 to 11 percent 1990. As a result, many policy decisions have been shifted to the State level, and States are dealing with transportation problems, health care issues, energy policies, and poverty. For example, in the past, the Federal Government provided 90 percent of funding for interstate highways, but now under a new plan Federal aid will be cut 75 percent, giving States more responsibility in this area.

"Future employment growth may be dampened by budgetary constraints despite the increased rule of State and local governments. These governments are having increasing difficulty meeting the growing demand for services because tax revenues and Federal aid are declining. Many States have cut their workforces recently in an effort to reduce spending and keep budgets balanced."

[Thousands]

Occupation	1990 Employment		1990-2005 Percent change
	Number	Percent	
All occupations	6,366	100.0	19.5
Service occupations	1,658	26.0	28.7
Law enforcement occupations	848	13.3	35.4
Firefighting occupations	267	4.2	25.5
Other protective services	115	1.8	13.2
Cleaning and building service occupations, except private household	111	1.7	15.0
Nursing aides and psychiatric aides	104	1.6	25.4
Administrative support, including clerical	1,416	22.4	3.8
Typists and word processors	181	2.9	-24.5
Secretaries	176	2.8	1.0
Welfare eligibility workers and interviewers	88	1.4	17.4
Bookkeeping, accounting, and auditing clerks	87	1.4	-13.5
Professional specialty	925	14.6	23.4
Social, recreational, and religious workers	301	4.7	18.1
Lawyers and judicial workers	104	1.6	26.0
Teachers, librarians, and counselors	100	1.6	16.7
Health assessment occupations	92	1.5	24.2
Engineers	87	1.4	28.1
Executive, administrative, and managerial	790	12.4	20.2
General managers	93	1.5	5.9

[Continued]

★ 576 ★

Employment of Wage and Salary Workers in State and Local Government by Occupation, 1990-2005

[Continued]

Occupation	1990 Employment		1990-2005 Percent change
	Number	Percent	
Inspectors and compliance officers, except construction	80	1.3	37.1
Government chief executives and legislators	70	1.1	4.4
Accounts and auditors	66	1.0	27.4
Precision production, craft, and repair	672	10.6	23.0
Construction trades	239	3.4	24.7
Mechanics, installers, and repairers	203	3.2	25.9
Highway maintenance workers	151	2.4	24.5
Blue-collar worker supervisors	96	1.5	14.4
Operators, fabricators, and laborers	465	7.3	13.4
Transportation and material moving machine operators	230	3.6	25.6
Helpers, laborers, and material movers	223	3.5	2.1
Technicians and related support	277	4.4	27.4
Health technicians	95	1.5	24.0
Technicians, except health and engineering	94	1.5	35.3
Engineering and science technicians and technologies	88	1.4	22.8
Other occupations	163	2.6	24.9

Source: U.S. Department of Labor, Bureau of Labor Statistics, *A Career Guide to Industries* (Washington, D.C.: U.S. Government Printing Office, September 1992), pp. 211, 213. *Primary source:* Bureau of Labor Statistics.

Chapter 13
POPULATION AND VITAL STATISTICS

U.S. Population by Selected Variables

★577★

Population by Regions and Divisions, 1970-2010

[Thousands]

Year	1970	1980	1990	2000	2010
Total	203,302	226,546	248,710	267,747	282,055
			REGIONS		
Northeast	49,061	49,135	50,809	51,810	52,496
Midwest	56,590	58,866	59,669	59,596	59,018
South	62,813	75,372	85,446	96,919	104,919
West	34,838	43,172	52,786	59,422	65,622
			DIVISIONS WITHIN REGIONS		
NORTHEAST					
New England	11,847	12,348	13,207	13,775	14,243
Middle Atlantic	37,213	36,787	37,602	38,035	38,253
MIDWEST					
East North Central	40,263	41,682	42,009	41,746	41,111
West North Central	16,328	17,183	17,660	17,850	17,907
SOUTH					
South Atlantic	30,679	36,959	43,567	50,002	55,110
East South Central	12,808	14,666	15,176	16,285	16,847
West South Central	19,326	23,747	26,703	30,632	32,961

[Continued]

★ 577 ★

Population by Regions and Divisions, 1970-2010

[Continued]

Year	1970	1980	1990	2000	2010
WEST					
Mountain	8,290	11,373	13,659	16,022	17,679
Pacific	26,548	31,800	39,127	43,400	47,943

Source: Congressional Research Service, Library of Congress, *Demographic Change and the Economy of the Nineties* (Washington, D.C.: U.S. Government Printing Office, December 1991), p. 43. *Primary source:* U.S. Bureau of the Census, *Projections of the Population of States by Age, Sex, and Race: 1988 to 2010; Current Population Reports*, Series P-25, No. 1017, Washington, Govt. Print. Off., 1988. p. 20-21; *State Population and Household Estimates to 1985, with Age and Components of Change; Current Population Reports*, Series P-25, No. 998, Washington, Govt. Print. Off., 1986, p. 39. The 1990 decennial census population figures are from: U.S. Bureau of the Census, *Commerce News. U.S. Population Up Nearly Two-Thirds in 40 Years; Nevada, California Lead 40-Year Period Growth*. CB91-07. Washington, Jan. 7, 1991, p. 6.

★ 578 ★

U.S. Population by Selected Variables

Total Population Growth by Decade, 1900-2050

[Millions]

Year	
1990	16.5
1910	14.0
1920	17.0
1930	9.0
1940	20.1
1950	27.6
1960	23.7
1970	23.3
1980	22.2
1990	27.0
2000	24.2
2010	25.5
2020	24.2
2030	21.5
2040	20.5

Source: Jennifer Cheeseman Day, U.S. Department of Commerce, Economics and Statistics Administration, Bureau of the Census, *Population Projections of the United States, by Age, Sex, Race and Hispanic Origin: 1993 to 2050* (Washington, D.C.: U.S. Government Printing Office, November 1993), Series P25-1104, p. xiv. *Notes:* 1900 through 1940 excludes Alaska and Hawaii. Magnitudes estimated from published chart.

★ 579 ★

U.S. Population by Selected Variables

U.S. Population Growth: 1989 vs. 1992 Projections, 1990-2050

"New long-term projections released in December by the Census Bureau indicate that the nation is expected to become more diverse, older, and substantially more populous than previously thought. *Population Projections of the United States by Age, Sex, Race, and Hispanic Origin: 1992 to 2050* presents the first set of bureau projections since January 1989. Originally scheduled to appear in late 1991, the new projections were delayed by the crush of other analyses flowing from the 1990 Census. The Census Bureau now plans to revise its U.S. population projections every odd-numbered year, with the first update expected late this year.

"This report contains some innovations. It is the first to present separate projections for Asian Americans and Native Americans—as well as for whites and blacks. It is also the first to incorporate the impact of AIDS in the middle series. And—a boon to data-users everywhere—it is the first to separate all racial groups into their Hispanic and non-Hispanic components, so that racial/ethnic breakdowns add to 100 percent.

"*Warning label*. It is sometimes said that statistics should come with a warning label. This volume does just that, with a headnote that reads: 'Many of the trends described here are substantially different from those shown in the previous projections, (*Current Population Reports*, Nos. 995 and 1018). These differences are primarily due to the changeover to the 1990 Census base and three significant changes in our assumptions: 1) Future fertility is assumed to remain near current levels; 2) Future immigration is assumed to remain near current levels; and 3) Fertility and mortality differentials by race/ethnic group are assumed to continue their current trends. The future course of population change could be substantially different—depending on the actual trends in births, deaths, and net migration.

"One big difference: the old projections assumed that the total fertility rate (TFR, or average lifetime births per woman) would converge at 1.8 for all racial/ethnic groups by 2050. The no-convergence scenario in the new projections shows fertility slowly increasing as the proportion of higher fertility groups in the population rises. In the middle series of projections, the TFR—which was 2.095 in 1990—is projected to reach 2.12 in 2050."

[Millions]

Year	Projections as of 1992	Projections as of 1989
1990	255	255
2010	300	283
2030	342	300
2050	385	295

Source: Kelvin Pollard, "Faster Growth, More Diversity in U.S. Projections," in *Population Today*, February 1993, p. 3. *Primary source:* U.S. Bureau of the Census, *Population Projections of the United States by Age, Sex, Race and Hispanic Origin: 1992 to 2050.*

★ 580 ★

U.S. Population by Selected Variables

U.S. vs. Third-world Population Growth, 2050

"With the fastest-growing population in the industrialized world, the United States is increasingly mimicking the growth rates of Third World countries, say Carl Haub and Machiko Yanagishita, demographers at the Population Reference Bureau. The United States adds nearly 3 million people per year to its total population, a large number of whom (800,000 in 1992) are immigrants. The United States now absorbs, through immigration, 1% of the people added to world population each year. The trend suggests that the United States will reach a total population of 383 million by 2050 and will continue to grow well beyond that time. Previously, the U.S. population was expected to plateau at 302 million in 2038 and decline slowly thereafter, according to Haub and Yanagishita."

Source: "U.S. Growth Rivals Third World," in *The Futurist*, September-October 1993, p. 5. *Primary source:* Population Reference Bureau, Inc., 1875 Connecticut N.W., Ste. 520, Washington, D.C., 20009.

Population Projections by Race and Sex

★ 581 ★

U.S. Population by Race: The End of Zero-population Growth, 1992-2050

"Experts for years talked about an America with 'ZPG,' or zero population growth. That term all but died last week when the Census Bureau, after reviewing immigration and fertility trends, overhauled its 21st-century projections. Steady growth is now expected in each of the next six censuses, with population in 2050 reaching 383 million, up 50 percent from now. The Census Bureau, which once assumed that all racial groups would eventually have similar fertility rates, now expects that black and Hispanic women will keep bearing children at higher rates than white women. If the projections prove true, a nation that is now three-fourths non-Hispanic white will be 53 percent non-Hispanic white in 2050."

	1992		2050	
	Millions	Percent	Millions	Percent
White	191	75	202	53
Black	32	12	62	16
Hispanic[1]	24	9	81	21
Asian	9	3	41	11
Indian	2.2	0.8	4.6	1.2

Source: "Forget Zero Population Growth," in *U.S. News and World Report*, 14 December 1992, p. 18.
Note: 1. Hispanics may be of any race.

★ 582 ★

Population Projections by Race and Sex

Population by Race and Hispanic Origin, 1990-2050

"The race and Hispanic-origin distribution of the U.S. population is projected to change. A combination of three factors contribute to this shift: differential fertility, net immigration, and age distribution among the race and Hispanic-origin groups.

"Although three-quarters of the population was non-Hispanic White in 1990, this group would contribute only 35 percent of the total population growth during this decade. After 2030, the non-Hispanic White population would contribute nothing to the nation's population growth because it would be declining in size.

"The non-Hispanic White share of the U.S. population would steadily fall from 76 percent in 1990 to 72 percent in 2000, 60 percent in 2030, and 53 percent in 2050.

"By the middle of next century, the Black population would double its 1990 size to 62 million. After 2012, more Blacks than non-Hispanic Whites would be added to the population each year.

"The fastest-growing race/ethnic group (with the highest rate of increase) would be the Asian and Pacific Islander population with annual growth rates that may exceed 4 percent during the 1990's.

"The race/ethnic group adding the largest number of people to the population would be the Hispanic-origin population. In fact, after 1996 the Hispanic population is projected to add more people to the United States every year than would any other race or origin group. By 2010, the Hispanic-origin population may become the second-largest race/ethnic group."

[Resident population in thousands]

Year	Total	Race				Hispanic origin[3]	Not of Hispanic origin, by race			
		White	Black	American Indian[1]	Asian[2]		White	Black	American Indiana[1]	Asian[2]
ESTIMATE										
1990	249,415	209,150	30,620	2,075	7,570	22,554	188,559	29,400	1,806	7,096
PROJECTIONS										
Lowest Series										
2050	285,502	214,054	42,026	3,323	26,099	57,643	161,382	38,933	2,807	24,738
Middle Series										
1995	263,434	218,334	33,117	2,226	9,756	26,798	193,900	31,648	1,927	9,161
2000	276,241	226,267	35,469	2,380	12,125	31,166	197,872	33,741	2,055	11,407
2005	288,286	233,343	37,793	2,543	14,608	35,702	200,842	35,793	2,190	13,759
2010	300,431	240,297	40,224	2,719	17,191	40,525	203,441	37,930	2,336	16,199
2020	325,942	254,791	45,409	3,090	22,653	51,217	208,280	42,459	2,641	21,345
2030	349,993	267,457	50,596	3,473	28,467	62,810	210,480	46,934	2,960	26,810
2040	371,505	277,232	55,917	3,894	34,461	75,130	209,148	51,489	3,314	32,424
2050	392,031	285,591	61,586	4,346	40,508	88,071	205,849	56,346	3,701	38,064
Highest Series										
2050	522,098	378,408	79,722	5,039	58,930	128,255	262,855	71,675	4,221	55,093

Source: Jennifer Cheeseman Day, U.S. Department of Commerce, Economics and Statistics Administration, Bureau of the Census, *Population Projections of the United States, by Age, Sex, Race and Hispanic Origin: 1993 to 2050* (Washington, D.C.: U.S. Government Printing Office, November 1993), Series P25-1104, pp. vii, xxii. *Primary source:* Current Population Reports, Series P25-1095. *Notes:* As of July 1. 1. American Indian represents American Indian, Eskimo, and Aleut. 2. Asian represents Asian and Pacific Islander. 3. Persons of Hispanic origin may be of any race.

★ 583 ★

Population Projections by Race and Sex

Percent of Total Population Growth by Race and Hispanic Origin, 1990- 2050

Resident population

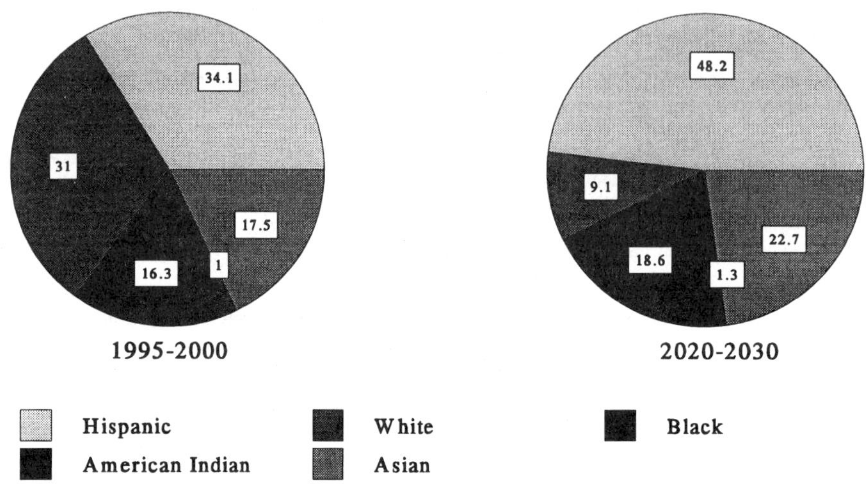

"Growth of the Hispanic-origin population will probably be a major element of the total population growth. The Hispanic population would contribute 32 percent of the nation's population growth from 1990 to 2000, 39 percent from 2000 to 2010, 45 percent from 2010 to 2030, and 60 percent from 2030 to 2050. This growth of the Hispanic population over the next six decades may be influenced more by natural increase than immigration."

[Resident population]

Year	Total	Race				Hispanic origin[3]	Not of Hispanic origin, by race			
		White	Black	American Indian[1]	Asian[2]		White	Black	American Indian[1]	Asian[2]
Projections										
1990 to 1995	100.0	65.5	17.8	1.1	15.6	30.3	38.1	16.0	0.9	14.7
1995 to 2000	100.0	61.9	18.4	1.2	18.5	34.1	31.0	16.3	1.0	17.5
2000 to 2005	100.0	58.7	19.3	1.4	20.6	37.7	24.7	17.0	1.1	19.5
2005 to 2010	100.0	57.3	20.0	1.4	21.3	39.7	21.4	17.6	1.2	20.1
2010 to 2020	100.0	56.8	20.3	1.5	21.4	41.9	19.0	17.8	1.2	20.2
2020 to 2030	100.0	52.7	21.6	1.6	24.2	48.2	9.1	18.6	1.3	22.7
2030 to 2040	100.0	45.4	24.7	2.0	27.9	57.3[4]	--	21.2[4]	1.6[4]	26.1[4]
2040 to 2050	100.0	40.7	27.6	2.2	29.5	63.0[4]	--	23.7[4]	1.9[4]	27.5[4]

Source: Jennifer Cheeseman Day, U.S. Department of Commerce, Economics and Statistics Administration, Bureau of the Census, *Population Projections of the United States, by Age, Sex, Race and Hispanic Origin: 1993 to 2050* (Washington, D.C.: U.S. Government Printing Office, November 1993), Series P25-1104, pp. xxiii-xxiv. *Primary source:* Current Population Reports, Series P25-1095. *Notes:* As of July 1. 1. American Indian represents American Indian, Eskimo, and Aleut. 2. Asian represents Asian and Pacific Islander. 3. Persons of Hispanic origin may be of any race. 4. These percentages do not add to 100 percent due to the declining size of White, not Hispanic population.

★ 584 ★

Population Projections by Race and Sex

Rising Minority Populations for All Age Groups, 1992-2025

"The popular image of minorities as uniformly powerless and poor is clearly not an accurate picture. Minorities are overrepresented among America's low-income population, but minority status is no longer synonymous with poverty. A growing segment of minorities are achieving affluence within mainstream society. The number of minorities in the highest income categories nearly doubled during the 1980s. Also, more minority politicians are being elected to public office...

"The trend toward greater diversity is challenging traditional views about minorities that underlie public policies and government programs. One traditional belief has been that over time minorities will almost automatically blend into America's cultural melting pot, as did the European immigrants of the 19th and early 20th centuries...

"An emerging model may be pluralism, in which minorities participate fully in all aspects of society while maintaining their racial and ethnic identities—forming a cultural mosaic or kaleidoscope. As we move into the 21st century, government at all levels will be grappling with the new realities of America's minority population."

[Percent of age group who are minority]

	1992	2025
Minority children (under age 18)	32	47
Working-age minorities (ages 18-64)	25	39
Older minorities (ages 65+)	14	25

Source: William P. O'Hare, "Diversity Trend: More Minorities Looking Less Alike," in *Population Today*, April 1993, p. 2. *Primary source:* "America's Minorities—The Demographics of Diversity," Population Reference Bureau, *Population Bulletin* 47, No. 4.

★ 585 ★

Population Projections by Race and Sex

Asian-American Population Growth Rate, 1991-2000

"The number of Asians and Pacific Islanders living in the United States grew by 80% between 1980 and 1989, increasing from 3.8 million to 6.9 million. Their rate of growth was twice that of Hispanics, six times that of blacks, and 20 times that of non-Hispanic whites, according to the report's authors, William P. O'Hare of the University of Louisville's Urban Research Institute and Judy C. Felt of PRB...

"O'Hare and Felt conclude that, 'as their numbers grow, the various Asian-American groups will gain a larger voice in the nation's economic, educational, and political systems. In the 1990s, Asian Americans are likely to become a much more visible and active minority group'."

Source: "Asian Americans Increase Rapidly," in *The Futurist*, September-October 1991, pp. 51-2. *Primary source:* "Asian Americans: America's Fastest Growing Minority Group," by William P. O'Hare and Judy C. Felt. Published by the Population Reference Bureau, Inc., February 1991. 16 pages $5. Available from the Circulation Department, Population Reference Bureau, Inc., P.O. Box 96152, Washington, D.C. 20090-6152.

★ 586 ★

Population Projections by Race and Sex

Black Population Growth by Age and Sex, 2010

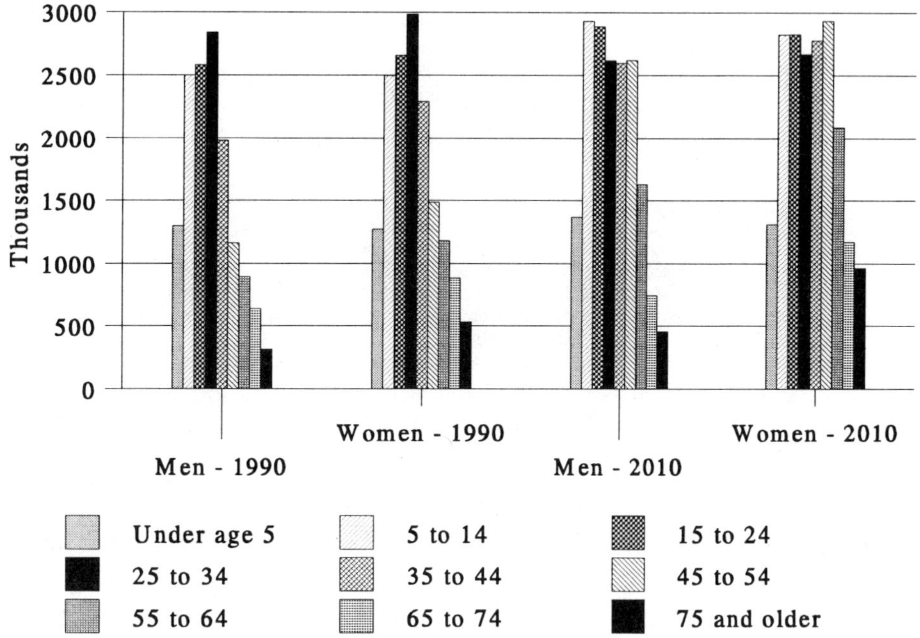

"Black America had its own baby boom in the 1950s and 1960s—in fact, the increase in births among black women was even higher than the increase for whites in those years. The black boom was followed by a black baby bust in the late 1960s and 1970s that mirrored the white baby bust. The result is a smaller generation of blacks, now in their teens and 20s, that will age through the population over the next 60 years. Between 1990 and 2010, the number of black Americans aged 25 to 34 will actually decline. But the number of blacks in their 40s and 50s should increase faster than the national average for those ages, as the large black baby boom reaches middle age."

[Thousands]

	1990		2010		Percent change 1990-2010	
	Men	Women	Men	Women	Men	Women
ALL AGES	14,204	15,782	17,841	19,558	26%	24%
Under age 5	1,297	1,272	1,366	1,312	5%	3%
5 to 14	2,499	2,497	2,931	2,822	17	13
15 to 24	2,581	2,658	2,888	2,826	12	6
25 to 34	2,840	2,984	2,617	2,666	-8	-11
35 to 44	1,978	2,290	2,595	2,778	31	21
45 to 54	1,162	1,484	2,620	2,933	125	98
55 to 64	895	1,181	1,628	2,084	82	76
65 to 74	636	884	741	1,171	17	33
75 and older	316	532	454	964	44	81

Source: Thomas G. Exter, "Blacks to 2010," in *American Demographics*, December 1992, p. 63. *Primary source:* The Urban Institute. *Notes:* Assumes current levels of fertility, mortality, and international migration will continue. For more information see "The Future Immigrant Population of the United States" from the Urban Institute, telephone (202) 857-8709.

★ 587 ★

Population Projections by Race and Sex

Growth in Number of Black and Hispanic Elderly People Living Alone, 1990-2020

[Thousands]

Year	Hispanic	Black
1990	221	925
2005	482	1365
2020	930	2381

Source: U.S. Senate Special Committee on Aging, The American Association of Retired Persons, the Federal Council on the Aging, and the U.S. Administration on Aging, *Aging America: Trends and Projections* (Washington, D.C.: U.S. Government Printing Office, 1991), p. 216. *Primary source:* Lewin/ICF estimates based on data from the *Current Population Survey* and the Brookings/ICF Long-Term Care Financing Model (1990).

★ 588 ★

Population Projections by Race and Sex

Population Growth Rates and Racial Distributions: Alaska, 1990-2010

"Between 1959 and 1990, the population of Alaska grew by 329,600, an increase of almost 150%. Growth rates historically have varied greatly from a high of 9.8% growth in the oil pipeline boom year 1974-75 and 7.1% during the peak in capital expenditures in 1982-83 to a low of - 1.8% during the oil market collapse in 1987. The key characteristic of Alaska's growth is its rapid fluctuation from year to year. The average annual growth rate over the 1959-90 period however has been 2.73%. The annual average growth rate of the 1980's was 2.75%. The Native population of Alaska grew from 64,103 in 1980 to 86,300 in 1990 at an average rate of 2.97% per year during the decade."

Race	1990 Population	2000 Population	2010 Population	% Annual Growth Rate 1990-2000	% Annual Growth Rate 2000-2010	% Racial Distribution 2000	% Racial Distribution 2010
Low Series	553,600	679,900	787,400	2.05	1.47	100.0	100.0
White	417,850	513,500	589,700	2.05	1.38	75.50	74.89
Native	86,300	102,800	121,000	1.75	1.63	15.10	15.37
Other	49,450	63,600	76,700	2.50	1.87	9.40	9.74
Middle Series	553,600	716,500	868,300	2.57	1.92	100.00	100.00
White	417,850	540,900	648,900	2.57	1.82	75.50	74.73
Native	86,300	108,700	135,200	2.30	2.17	15.10	15.57
Other	49,450	66,900	82,400	3.00	2.29	9.40	9.70
High Series	553,600	755,800	961,500	3.09	2.40	100.00	100.00
White	417,850	571,500	720,500	3.11	2.31	75.60	74.93
Native	86,300	112,800	144,400	2.66	2.46	14.90	15.02
Other	49,450	71,500	96,600	3.65	2.99	9.50	10.05

Source: State of Alaska, Alaska Department of Labor, Administrative Services Unit, *Alaska Population Projections 1990-2010* (Alaska: ASSETS, November 1991) p. 15. *Primary source:* Alaska Department of Labor, Research and Analysis, Demographics Unit.

★ 589 ★

Population Projections by Race and Sex

Race/Ethnicity and Migration Scenario: Texas, 1990-2030

"Three projection scenarios which produce three alternative sets of population values for the State and each county are presented in these projections. These scenarios assume the same set of mortality and fertility assumptions in each scenario but differ in their assumptions relative to net migration. The net migration assumptions made are derived from 1980-90 patterns which have been altered relative to expected future population trends. This is done by systematically and uniformly altering the adjusted 1980-90 net migration rates by age, sex and race/ ethnicity. The scenarios so produced are referred to as the zero migration (0.0) scenario, the 1980-90 (1.0) scenario, and the middle-range (0.5) scenario."

YEAR	TOTAL	ANGLO	BLACK	HISPANIC	OTHER
SCENARIO 0.0					
1990	16,986,510	10,308,444	1,980,693	4,339,900	357,473
1995	17,904,322	10,574,268	2,112,704	4,831,056	386,294
2000	18,643,966	10,723,280	2,218,141	5,291,822	410,723
2005	19,289,201	10,815,860	2,310,862	5,730,403	432,076
2010	19,840,642	10,852,953	2,388,927	6,149,989	448,773
2015	20,365,919	10,867,782	2,460,405	6,574,889	462,833
2020	20,836,758	10,844,578	2,520,463	6,997,441	474,276
2025	21,207,459	10,754,716	2,566,382	7,403,877	482,484
2030	21,480,275	10,611,299	2,598,668	7,783,769	486,539
SCENARIO 0.5					
1990	16,986,510	10,308,444	1,980,693	4,339,900	357,473
1995	18,277,904	10,686,309	2,132,926	5,030,606	428,063
2000	19,513,687	10,975,395	2,273,806	5,759,330	505,156
2005	20,729,189	11,203,675	2,408,270	6,527,032	590,212
2010	21,956,819	11,395,645	2,540,455	7,336,409	684,310
2015	23,232,974	11,565,845	2,672,991	8,206,504	787,634
2020	24,537,475	11,704,903	2,799,157	9,134,311	899,104
2025	25,803,746	11,772,397	2,913,585	10,101,252	1,016,512
2030	27,002,353	11,761,420	3,013,915	11,090,706	1,136,312
SCENARIO 1.0					
1990	16,986,510	10,308,444	1,980,693	4,339,900	357,473
1995	18,683,704	10,805,635	2,158,492	5,244,548	475,029
2000	20,448,727	11,225,939	2,329,783	6,268,351	624,654
2005	22,326,401	11,593,532	2,499,086	7,419,493	814,290
2010	24,359,245	11,930,252	2,669,512	8,705,544	1,053,937
2015	26,600,706	12,253,625	2,843,732	10,150,263	1,353,086
2020	29,050,389	12,545,300	3,015,472	11,768,637	1,720,980
2025	31,679,129	12,773,838	3,179,442	13,559,602	2,166,247
2030	34,469,595	12,927,904	3,332,837	15,514,378	2,694,476

Source: Department of Rural Sociology, Texas Agricultural Experiment Station, Texas A & M University System, *Projections of the Population of Texas and Counties in Texas by Age, Sex, and Race/Ethnicity* (Population Estimates and Projections Program, Texas State Data Center, Texas Department of Commerce, February 1993), pp. 10-13.

Population by Age

★ 590 ★

U.S. Resident Population by Age, 1990-2050

"The oldest age groups are projected to increase during the next six decades, both in number and as a proportion of the population. In 1990, there were 31 million people aged 65 and over, about 12.5 percent of the population. By 2000, this group would grow to almost 35 million and 12.8 percent of the population, and by 2050, over 80 million and represent 20.4 percent of the population."

[Thousands]

Year	Total	Under 5 years	5 to 13 years	14 to 17 years	18 to 24 years	25 to 34 years	35 to 44 years	45 to 64 years	65 years and over	85 years and over	100 years and over
ESTIMATE											
1990	249,415	18,874	32,000	13,312	26,829	43,136	37,765	46,277	31,224	3,050	37
PROJECTIONS											
Lowest Series											
1995	262,951	19,892	34,140	14,519	25,281	41,435	42,023	51,308	33,452	3,547	50
2000	270,259	18,034	35,869	15,564	25,306	37,286	44,565	59,183	34,450	4,101	66
2005	276,316	16,951	34,668	16,542	27,309	35,121	41,898	68,678	35,148	4,564	92
2010	281,180	16,653	32,100	16,425	29,005	35,934	37,703	76,255	37,104	5,055	112
2020	289,553	17,336	31,272	14,404	26,764	40,218	36,362	76,118	47,079	5,127	146
2030	292,902	16,519	31,773	14,792	25,260	36,593	40,553	68,577	58,836	5,808	177
2040	290,351	16,202	30,299	14,537	26,092	35,429	36,957	71,429	59,405	8,229	192
2050	285,502	16,250	30,174	13,986	24,920	36,106	35,791	71,628	56,647	9,894	285
Middle Series											
1995	263,434	20,181	34,262	14,591	25,465	41,670	42,150	51,465	33,649	3,598	52
2000	276,241	19,431	36,547	15,811	25,911	38,237	45,123	59,860	35,322	4,333	75
2005	288,286	19,333	36,843	16,947	28,238	36,792	43,075	70,089	36,970	5,082	120
2010	300,431	20,017	36,213	17,388	30,220	38,179	39,659	78,651	40,104	5,969	170
2020	325,942	21,957	38,701	17,119	30,456	43,553	39,662	81,147	53,348	6,959	299
2030	349,993	22,689	41,528	18,820	31,802	43,572	45,040	76,365	70,175	8,843	477
2040	371,505	23,978	43,069	19,747	34,510	46,127	45,134	81,925	77,014	13,840	659
2050	392,031	25,382	45,742	20,630	35,710	49,462	47,739	87,257	80,109	18,893	1,208
Highest Series											
1995	264,715	20,470	34,380	14,659	25,643	41,907	42,294	51,590	33,773	3,626	52
2000	281,957	20,938	37,206	16,045	26,498	39,198	45,797	60,411	35,864	4,483	80
2005	299,941	22,076	39,099	17,333	29,131	38,444	44,443	71,290	38,122	5,445	136
2010	319,536	24,108	40,756	18,331	31,383	40,358	41,772	80,792	42,035	6,644	208
2020	363,213	27,960	47,760	20,174	34,302	46,735	43,000	85,836	57,447	8,405	439
2030	410,991	31,472	54,296	23,745	39,423	50,832	49,467	83,713	78,042	11,410	827
2040	463,579	36,246	61,516	26,653	44,998	58,392	53,705	91,733	90,335	18,736	1,315
2050	522,098	41,404	70,680	30,400	50,494	65,872	61,394	102,413	99,441	27,318	2,676

Source: Jennifer Cheeseman Day, U.S. Department of Commerce, Economics and Statistics Administration, Bureau of the Census, *Population Projections of the United States, by Age, Sex, Race and Hispanic Origin: 1993 to 2050* (Washington, D.C.: U.S. Government Printing Office, November 1993), Series P25-1104, p. xvi. *Primary source:* Current Population Reports, Series P25-1095.

★ 591 ★

Population by Age

Growth in Population by Age Group, 1980-2050

"The growth of the 85+ population is one of the major achievements of improved disease prevention and health care in this century. However, it also has far-reaching implications for public policy because of the high probability of health problems in this age group and a corresponding need for health and social services.

"Life expectancy at age 85 rose by 33 percent between 1960 and 1987 and is projected to increase further over the next several decades. Between 1989 and 2050, the population age 85+ is expected to jump from about 1 to 5 percent of the total population and from 10 to 22 percent of the 65+ population.

"More people are also surviving into their 10th and 11th decades. As noted earlier, the Census Bureau estimates that there were about 61,000 people age 100+ in 1989 and that there will be over 100,000 by 2000. Because of the increase in the very old population, it is increasingly likely that older people will themselves have at least one surviving parent."

[Percent increase]

	1980-2000	1980-2030	1980-2050
Under 55	16	11	8
55 to 64	11	61	70
65 to 74	17	130	102
75 to 84	54	176	178
85+	104	258	574

Source: U.S. Senate Special Committee on Aging, the American Association of Retired Persons, the Federal Council on the Aging, and the U.S. Administration on Aging, *Aging America: Trends and Projections* (Washington, D.C.: U.S. Government Printing Office, 1991), p. 11. *Primary source:* U.S. Bureau of the Census, "Projections of the Population of the United States by Age, Sex, and Race: 1988 to 2080," by Gregory Spencer, *Current Population Reports* Series P-25, No. 1018 (January 1989).

★ 592 ★

Population by Age

Population by Age Categories and Regions, 1980-2010

[Population in thousands]

Year and Region	Age Category						
	0-17	18-24	25-34	35-44	45-64	65+	Total
1970							
Northeast	16,041	5,348	5,852	5,729	10,915	5,176	49,061
Midwest	19,855	6,452	6,787	6,290	11,502	5,704	56,590
South	21,852	7,643	7,725	7,065	12,511	6,017	62,813
West	11,958	4,288	4,565	4,023	6,922	3,082	34,838
Total	69,707	23,728	24,930	23,107	41,850	19,980	203,302

[Continued]

★ 592 ★

Population by Age Categories and Regions, 1980-2010

[Continued]

Year and Region	Age Category						
	0-17	18-24	25-34	35-44	45-64	65+	Total
1980							
Northeast	13,083	6,163	7,707	5,580	10,531	6,072	49,135
Midwest	16,918	7,872	9,427	6,474	11,483	6,692	58,866
South	21,638	10,065	12,215	8,526	14,440	8,488	75,372
West	12,116	5,922	7,732	5,055	8,049	4,298	43,172
Total	63,755	30,022	37,082	25,635	44,503	25,549	226,546
1990							
Northeast	11,900	5,123	8,719	7,581	10,167	7,089	50,577
Midwest	15,607	6,112	10,374	8,829	11,121	7,735	59,777
South	22,622	9,248	15,101	13,031	16,329	10,946	87,276
West	13,908	5,415	9,535	8,386	9,228	5,789	52,261
Total	64,037	25,897	43,728	37,827	46,843	31,560	249,891
2000							
Northeast	12,007	4,421	7,184	8,670	12,179	7,348	51,810
Midwest	14,988	5,535	7,955	9,671	13,535	7,914	59,596
South	23,668	9,226	13,252	15,698	22,266	12,809	96,919
West	15,049	5,806	8,562	9,801	13,394	6,812	59,422
Total	65,713	24,987	36,952	43,841	61,473	34,882	267,747
2010							
Northeast	11,001	4,777	6,818	7,216	15,012	7,674	52,496
Midwest	13,504	5,669	7,649	7,534	16,401	8,262	59,018
South	23,043	10,013	13,622	13,658	29,432	15,150	104,919
West	15,098	6,452	9,287	8,724	17,786	8,277	65,622
Total	62,646	26,911	37,375	37,131	78,630	39,362	282,055

Source: Congressional Research Service, Library of Congress, *Demographic Change and the Economy of the Nineties* (Washington, D.C.: U.S. Government Printing Office, December 1991), 102nd Congress, 1st Session, p. 43. *Primary sources:* U.S. Bureau of the Census, *Projections of the Population of States by Age, Sex, and Race: 1988 to 2010; Current Population Reports,* Series P-25, No. 1017, Washington, Govt. Print. Off., 1988, pp. 29-42; *State Population and Household Estimates to 1985, with Age and Components of Change; Current Population Reports,* Series P-25, No. 998, Washington, Govt. Print. Off., 1986, p. 39; U.S. Bureau of the Census, *State Population and Household Estimates, with Age, Sex, and Components of Change: 1981-1988, Current Population Reports,* Series P-25, no. 1044, Washington, Govt. Print. Off., 1989, pp. 20-29. The 1990 figures are from population projections, not from the 1990 decennial census, because the census data are not yet available by age category. Columns and rows may not sum to totals because of independent rounding by the Census Bureau. *Notes:* Source also includes data for 1970. Columns and rows may not sum to totals due to independent rounding by the Census Bureau.

★ 593 ★

Population by Age

Percent of Children and Elderly in the Population, 1900-2030

[Percent]

Year	Age	
	0 to 17	65+
1900	40	4
1980	28	11
2030	21	22

Source: U.S. Senate Special Committee on Aging, the American Association of Retired Persons, the Federal Council on Aging, and the U.S. Administration on Aging, *Aging America: Trends and Projections* (Washington, D.C.: U.S. Government Printing Office, 1991), p. 9. *Primary source:* 1900 figures, which exclude Alaska, Hawaii, and Armed Forces overseas: U.S. Bureau of the Census, "Estimates of the Population of the United States, by Single Years of Age, Color, and Sex: 1900 to 1959," *Current Population Reports* Series P-25, No. 311 (July 1965). 1980 and 2030 figures: U.S. Bureau of the Census, "Projections of the Population of the United States by Age, Sex, and Race: 1988 to 2080," by Gregory Spencer, *Current Population Reports* Series P-25, No. 1018 (January 1989).

★ 594 ★

Population by Age

Population Age 0-17 by Race, 1990-2010

"Looking out to the year 2000 and beyond, we can see some interesting shifts. The total U.S. population continues to increase, but at a slower rate, up to 267.7 million in 2000 (7.1 percent), and up to 282.2 million in 2010, (only 5.3 percent). However, America's youth population (age 0-17) goes up from 64.4 million in 1990 to 67.4 million in 2000, then DECLINES to 64.9 million in 2010, according to Census Bureau projections. This decline is already foreseeable in the decline in the number of females moving into the child-bearing years. Fewer women producing fewer children seems a safe hypothesis. The decline will be in the number of white youth particularly...

"A key rule of demographics is, if you weren't born, you don't count. It's silly to mourn the loss of 3.8 million white youth. As pragmatists, we must ensure that the additional 4.4 million nonwhite young people get the best education and access to good jobs as we possibly can, for the nation's health, and also because they will be funding our Social Security payments."

[Millions]

Youth	1990	2010	Change
Total youth[1]	64.4	64.9	+0.5
White, non-Hispanic	45.2	41.4	-3.8
Hispanic (of any race)	7.2	9.8	+2.6
Black[2]	10.2	11.4	+1.2
Other Races[2]	2.2	2.8	+0.6

[Continued]

★ 594 ★

Population Age 0-17 by Race, 1990-2010

[Continued]

Youth	1990	2010	Change
Increase in total non-white youth	-	-	+4.4
Decrease in total white youth	-	-	-3.8

Source: Harold L. Hodgkinson, Center for Demographic Policy, Institute for Education Leadership, *A Demographic Look at Tomorrow* (Washington, D.C.: Institute for Education Leadership, June 1992), pp. 5-6. *Primary source:* U.S. Census Bureau as cited in National Center for Education Statistics, *Youth Indicators 1991*. *Notes:* 1. May not add exactly because of rounding. 2. Includes small number of Hispanics; "other races" are primarily Asian and Native American.

★ 595 ★

Population by Age

Percent Nonwhite Youth in Selected States, 2010

"By 2010, 12 states plus the District of Columbia will have significant minority youth populations. About half of the nation's 64.4 million young people will reside in these 12 states. The question that arises from this situation is *what should we call 'minorities' when they are more than half of the population?* In 26 cities in California in 1990, no single racial or ethnic group made up a majority of the population. As a result, no elections could be won by any single racial or ethnic group including whites. Coalition politics was the only winning pattern.

"We normally think of 'high minority' states as being in the deep south. That was true in 1940, as blacks were, for all practical purposes, the only statistically significant minority group. Since about 1970, the process has been one of making America more ethnically diverse. Looking at the list of states [below], one sees many of our largest and most politically powerful states as well as some states in the deep south. In New York, California, Texas and Florida, each racial and ethnic group is expanding, beginning with the youngest portion of each group. By 2010, these FOUR states will contain 21 million of the nation's total 64.4 million youth, one-third of all youth (age 0 to 17) in the U.S. (New York is a special case. Although youth in New York will decline from 4.2 million in 1990 to 3.8 million in 2010, the decline is virtually among the white group. New York still remains a very large and powerful state.) As the nonwhite youth majority moves through the age range in these four key states, we will see first a majority of entry level workers, new households, new parents, promotions, voters, volunteers, semi-retirees and finally minority Social Security recipients, in that order."

State	Percent Nonwhite	State	Percent Nonwhite
D.C.	93.2%	Louisiana	50.3%
Hawaii	79.5%	Mississippi	49.9%
Texas	56.9%	New Jersey	45.7%
California	56.9%	Maryland	42.7%
Florida	53.4%	Illinois	41.7%

[Continued]

★ 595 ★

Percent Nonwhite Youth in Selected States, 2010

[Continued]

State	Percent Nonwhite	State	Percent Nonwhite
New York	52.8%	South Carolina	40.1%
U.S.	38.2%		

Source: Harold L. Hodgkinson, Center for Demographic Policy, Institute for Education Leadership, *A Demographic Look at Tomorrow* (Washington, D.C.: Institute for Education Leadership, June 1992), pp. 6-7. *Primary source:* U.S. Census Bureau as cited in *American Demographics*, May 1989. *Note:* Includes persons aged 0-17 years.

★ 596 ★

Population by Age

Change in the Number of High-School Graduates, 1989-1990 to 1999-2000

"If the U.S. population is increasing all through the next two decades but the youth populations decline after 2000, it means that the nation's average age will go up like a rocket after 2000. The eldest baby boomers, now 46, will begin to retire in droves after 2000. The baby boomlet is now working its way through junior high, but half of this increase in youth is in California, Texas, and Florida. There is no boomlet in most heartland and mid-Atlantic states as [the figures below make] clear."

State	% Change	State	% Change
Alabama	-11	Minnesota	+14
Alaska	+70	Mississippi	-1
Arizona	+32	Missouri	+4
Arkansas	-3	Montana	+3
California	+41	Nebraska	+1
North Carolina	-5	Nevada	+62
South Carolina	+2	New Hampshire	+10
Colorado	+22	New Jersey	-3
Connecticut	+1	New Mexico	+24
North Dakota	+9	New York	0
South Dakota	+11	Ohio	-5
Delaware	-2	Oklahoma	+27
Florida	+26	Oregon	+8
Georgia	+19	Pennsylvania	-1
Hawaii	+4	Rhode Island	+3
Idaho	-4	Tennessee	-2
Illinois	-6	Texas	+14
Indiana	-9	Utah	+45
Iowa	-5	Virginia	+21
Kansas	+15	West Virginia	-16
Kentucky	-3	Vermont	+13
Louisiana	+13	Washington	+25

[Continued]

★ 596 ★

Change in the Number of High-School Graduates, 1989-1990 to 1999-2000

[Continued]

State	% Change	State	% Change
Maine	-3	Washington, DC	-7
Maryland	+3	Wisconsin	+6
Massachusetts	-5	Wyoming	0
Michigan	-4		

Source: Harold L. Hodgkinson, Center for Demographic Policy, Institute for Education Leadership, *A Demographic Look at Tomorrow* (Washington, D.C.: Institute for Education Leadership, June 1992), p. 6. *Primary source:* Western Interstate Commission for Higher Education.

★ 597 ★

Population by Age

Median Age of the Population, 1950-2050

"The projected growth in the older population is expected to raise the median age of the U.S. population to 36 by the year 2000, to 42 by the year 2030, and to 43 in 2040. Between 1989 and 2030 the 65+ population is expected to more than double. In fact, if current fertility and immigration levels remain stable, the older population will be the only age group to experience significant growth in the next century.

"During the next 20 years, the elderly population is expected to grow more slowly than it has in many decades: from 1989 to 2010, for example, it will increase by about 1.1 percent a year, in contrast to an average annual growth of 2.4 percent during the 1950 to 1989 period. After 2010, however, the number and proportion of elderly will grow very rapidly. Between 2010 and 2030, the elderly population is projected to grow by 2.6 percent annually, while the under-65 population will decline by an average of 0.2 percent annually. By 2020, assuming no significant changes in mortality, the elderly population will reach 52 million, and by 2030, the graying of the baby boom will result in 65.6 million elderly. During this period the proportion of elderly will rise from 13 percent in 2000 to 21.8 percent in 2030, after which it will rise slowly to 22.9 percent by 2050."

[Median age]

Year	
1950	30
1960	29
1970	28
1980	30
1990	33
2000	36
2010	39
2020	40
2030	42

[Continued]

★ 597 ★

Median Age of the Population, 1950-2050

[Continued]

Year	
2040	43
2050	43

Source: U.S. Senate Special Committee on Aging, the American Association of Retired Persons, the Federal Council on the Aging, and the U.S. Administration on Aging, *Aging America: Trends and Projections* (Washington, D.C.: U.S. Government Printing Office, 1991), p. 6. *Primary source:* U.S. Bureau of the Census, *Statistical Abstract of the United States: 1985*, December 1984; Gregory Spencer, U.S. Bureau of the Census, "Projections of the Population of the United States, by Age, Sex, and Race: 1988 to 2008," *Current Population Reports*, Series P-25, No. 1018, January 1989.

★ 598 ★

Population by Age

Growth of the Older Population, 1900-2050

[Thousands]

Year	Total population all ages	55 to 64		65 to 74		75 to 84 years		85+		65+	
		Number	Percent	Number	Percent	Number	Percent	Number	Percent	Number	Percent
1900	76,303	4,009	5.3	2,189	2.9	772	1.0	123	0.2	3,084	4.0
1910	91,972	5,054	5.5	2,793	3.0	989	1.1	167	0.2	3,950	4.3
1920	105,711	6,532	6.2	3,464	3.3	1,259	1.2	210	0.2	4,933	4.7
1930	122,775	8,397	6.8	4,721	3.8	1,641	1.3	272	0.2	6,634	5.4
1940	131,669	10,572	8.0	6,375	4.7	2,278	1.7	365	0.3	9,019	6.8
1950	150,967	13,295	8.8	8,415	5.6	3,278	2.2	577	0.4	12,270	8.1
1960	179,323	15,572	8.7	10,997	6.1	4,633	2.6	929	0.5	16,560	9.2
1970	203,302	18,608	9.2	12,447	6.1	6,124	3.0	1,409	0.7	19,980	9.8
1980	226,546	21,703	9.6	15,580	6.9	7,729	3.4	2,240	1.0	25,549	11.3
1990	250,410	21,364	8.5	18,373	7.3	9,933	4.0	3,254	1.3	31,559	12.6
2000	268,266	24,158	9.0	18,243	6.8	12,017	4.5	4,622	1.7	34,882	13.0
2010	282,575	35,430	12.5	12,039	7.4	12,208	4.3	6,115	2.2	39,362	13.9
2020	294,364	41,087	14.0	30,973	10.5	14,443	4.9	6,651	2.3	52,067	17.7
2030	300,629	34,947	11.6	35,988	12.0	21,487	7.1	8,129	2.7	65,604	21.8
2040	301,807	35,537	11.8	30,808	10.2	25,050	8.3	12,251	4.1	68,109	22.6
2050	299,849	37,004	12.3	31,590	10.5	21,655	7.2	15,287	5.1	68,532	22.9

Source: U.S. Senate Special Committee on Aging, the American Association of Retired Persons, the Federal Council on the Aging, and the U.S. Administration on Aging, *Aging America: Trends and Projections* (Washington, D.C.: U.S. Government Printing Office, 1991), p. 7. *Primary source:* 1900 to 1980 data are tabulated from the Decennial Censuses of the Population and exclude Armed Forces overseas. Projections, which are middle series projections and include Armed Forces overseas, are from the U.S. Bureau of the Census, "Projections of the Population of the United States, by Age, Sex, and Race: 1988 to 2080," by Gregory Spencer, *Current Population Reports* Series P-25, No. 1018, January 1989.

★ 599 ★

Population by Age

Growth of the Minority Elderly Population, 1900-2050

"Today, the nonwhite and Hispanic populations have a smaller proportion of elderly people than the white population. In 1989, 13 percent of whites were age 65+, compared with only 8 percent of blacks, 7 percent of people of other races (Native Americans and Asian/Pacific Islanders), and 5 percent of Hispanics.

"These proportions are expected to remain relatively stable through the end of the century. However, beginning in the early part of the next century, the older minority population is expected to increase more rapidly than the older white population. This growth will be the result of higher fertility for the nonwhite and Hispanic populations than the white population. Between 1990 and 2030, the older white population will grow by 92 percent, compared with 247 percent of the older black population and people of other races and 395 percent of older Hispanics. Nevertheless, the percentage of elderly among white non-Hispanics in 2030 (24 percent) will still be higher than the percentage for blacks and other races (17 percent) or Hispanics (13 percent)."

[Minority age 65+ as a percent of the total 65+ population]

Year	
1990	14
2000	16
2010	20
2020	22
2030	25
2040	28
2050	32

Source: U.S. Senate Special Committee on Aging, the American Association of Retired Persons, the Federal Council on Aging, and the U.S. Administration on Aging, *Aging America: Trends and Projections* (Washington, D.C.: U.S. Government Printing Office, 1991), pp. 14, 16. *Primary source:* Figures computed by Donald G. Fowles, U.S. Administration on Aging, from data in U.S. Bureau of the Census, "Projections of the Hispanic Population: 1983-2080," by Gregory Spencer. *Current Population Reports* Series 25, No. 995 (November 1986) and in U.S. Bureau of the Census. "Projections of the Population of the United States by Age, Sex, and Race: 1988 to 2080," by Gregory Spencer. *Current Population Reports* Series P-25, No. 1018 (January 1989).

★ 600 ★

Population by Age

Population Age 55+ by Age Group, 1910-2050

"By 1980, the proportion of people age 65+ had increased to 11 percent and the proportion of young people had decreased to 28 percent. Census Bureau projections indicate that by the year 2030 there will be proportionately more elderly than young people in the population: 22 percent of the population will be 65+ and 21 percent will be under the age of 18."

[Millions]

Year	55 to 64	65 to 74	75 to 84	85+	Total
1910	5.0	1.5	0.5	NA	7.0
1930	9.0	5.0	1.0	NA	15.0
1950	14.0	10.0	2.0	0.5	26.5
1970	19.0	13.0	6.0	1.0	39.0
1990	21.0	16.0	11.0	6.0	54.0
2010	36.0	20.0	12.0	9.0	77.0
2030	36.0	37.0	19.0	11.0	103.0
2050	38.0	32.0	13.0	25.0	108.0

Source: U.S. Senate Special Committee on Aging, the American Association of Retired Persons, the Federal Council on Aging, and the U.S. Administration on Aging, *Aging America: Trends and Projections* (Washington, D.C.: U.S. Government Printing Office, 1991), p. 8. *Primary source:* 1900 to 1980 data are tabulated from the Decennial Censuses of the Population and exclude Armed Forces overseas. Projections, which are middle series projections and include Armed Forces overseas, are from the U.S. Bureau of the Census, "Projections of the Population of the United States by Age, Sex, and Race: 1988 to 2080," by Gregory Spencer, *Current Population Reports* Series P-25, No. 1018, January 1989. *Notes:* Source also includes data for 1900, 1920, 1940, 1960, 1980, 2000, 2020, and 2040. Magnitudes estimated from published chart.

★ 601 ★

Population by Age

The 65+ Population by State, 2010

"[There] are nearly 500 nonmetropolitan 'retirement counties' where the population age 60+ grew by at least 15 percent from in-migration during 1970-1980. These counties are scattered throughout the United States with concentrations in Maine, the Appalachian and Piedmont regions, Florida, the upper Peninsula of Michigan, the Ozark mountains, the Texas Hill Country, the Pacific Northwest coast, and selected counties in Arizona, New Mexico, Nevada, and California. Although many of these counties have high percentages of older people, some of them are also receiving large numbers of young im-migrants as well."

State	Number of 65+		Percent of total Population	Percent change, 1989-2010
	Rank	Value (000's)		
U.S., total	(x)	39,362	14.0	27.0
Alabama	21	645	14.4	23.4
Alaska	50	40	6.0	84.0

[Continued]

★ 601 ★

The 65+ Population by State, 2010

[Continued]

State	Number of 65+		Percent of total Population	Percent change, 1989-2010
	Rank	Value (000's)		
Arizona	14	841	15.2	81.1
Arkansas	29	422	16.5	18.6
California	1	4,680	12.3	52.4
Colorado	28	433	12.8	33.5
Connecticut	26	513	14.6	16.4
Delaware	44	120	12.8	51.0
District of Columbia	47	87	13.9	15.1
Florida	2	3,917	19.9	72.1
Georgia	11	1,055	11.2	61.6
Hawaii	37	225	14.1	88.7
Idaho	43	131	13.3	8.2
Illinois	6	1,532	13.2	6.6
Indiana	17	765	13.5	10.3
Iowa	32	391	17.4	-8.7
Kansas	33	381	15.3	11.1
Kentucky	25	526	14.8	11.6
Louisiana	24	536	13.8	10.1
Maine	38	192	13.4	17.3
Maryland	18	757	11.7	48.7
Massachusetts	13	895	13.9	10.0
Michigan	10	1,184	12.7	7.7
Minnesota	22	644	13.9	17.3
Mississippi	31	395	13.8	21.1
Missouri	15	838	14.8	16.6
Montana	45	103	14.9	-2.9
Nebraska	35	232	16.1	3.4
Nevada	39	192	11.9	58.3
New Hampshire	40	190	11.5	50.7
New Jersey	8	1,258	14.2	23.2
New Mexico	36	228	11.9	42.0
New York	3	2,583	14.2	10.3
North Carolina	9	1,209	13.8	51.4
North Dakota	48	82	15.4	-10.6
Ohio	7	1,512	14.0	8.1
Oklahoma	27	448	16.8	4.6
Oregon	30	413	14.1	5.3
Pennsylvania	5	1,845	15.3	1.4

[Continued]

★ 601 ★

The 65+ Population by State, 2010

[Continued]

State	Number of 65+		Percent of total Population	Percent change, 1989-2010
	Rank	Value (000's)		
Rhode Island	42	155	14.1	4.9
South Carolina	23	563	13.1	44.2
South Dakota	46	103	14.7	0.2
Tennessee	16	828	14.5	32.5
Texas	4	2,351	13.1	37.2
Utah	41	181	9.6	23.6
Vermont	49	80	12.2	18.5
Virginia	12	983	12.0	49.7
Washington	19	711	13.2	25.3
West Virginia	34	240	16.2	-11.7
Wisconsin	20	690	14.8	5.9
Wyoming	51	39	10.7	-16.0

Source: U.S. Senate Special Committee on Aging, the American Association of Retired Persons, the Federal Council on Aging, and the U.S. Administration on Aging, *Aging America: Trends and Projections* (Washington, D.C.: U.S. Government Printing Office, 1991), pp. 32-3. *Primary source:* U.S. Bureau of the Census, "Projections of the Population of the States by Age, Sex, and Race: 1989 to 2010," by Signe I. Wetrogan, *Current Population Reports* Series P-25, No. 1053 (January 1990), and unpublished data. *Note:* (x) Not applicable.

★ 602 ★

Population by Age

Increase in Number of People 65+ Living Alone, 1990-2020

"While the percentage of elderly people who live alone is projected to remain stable, their numbers will grow dramatically. Projections for the year 2020 indicate that the number of people age 65+ who live alone will grow to 15.2 million.

"Women accounted for almost four-fifths (78 percent) of all elderly people living alone in 1989. Whereas older men are almost five times more likely to live with a spouse than live alone, nearly equal numbers of women age 65+ live alone and with spouses. With increasing age, older men continue to be more likely to live with a spouse than to live alone. Older women, however, become more likely beyond the age of 74 to live alone."

[Millions]

Year	People age 65+
1990	9.2
2005	10.9
2020	15.2

Source: U.S. Senate Special Committee on Aging, the American Association of Retired Persons, the Federal Council on Aging, and the U.S. Administration on Aging, *Aging America: Trends and Projections* (Washington, D.C.: U.S. Government Printing Office, 1991), p. 210. *Primary source:* Lewin/ICF estimates based on data from the *Current Population Survey* and the Brookings/ICF Long-Term Care Financing Model (1990).

★ 603 ★

Population by Age

Population Age 65+ and Age 80+ in Selected Countries, 1990-2025

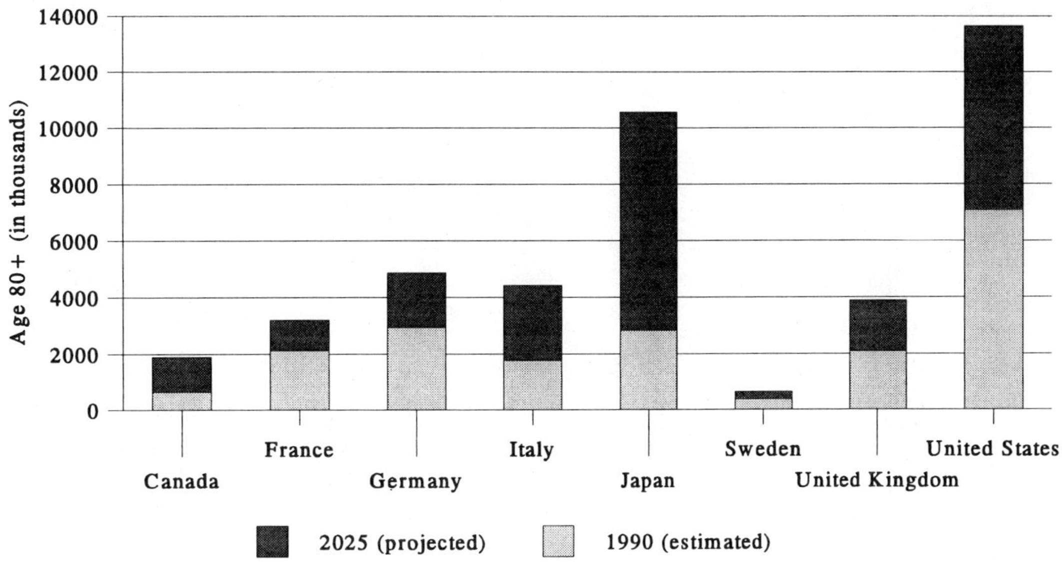

"Despite its very large elderly population, the United States is one of the 'younger' developed nations, at least as measured by the proportion of the population age 65+. In 1990, 12.6 percent of the U.S. population could be classified as elderly, using age 65+ as the defining age for 'elderly.' This was in sharp contrast to the much smaller Sweden, whose 1.5 million elderly comprised 17.9 percent of the population. That same year, France, Germany, Italy, and the United Kingdom also had greater proportions of elderly in their populations than did the United States."

Country	65+						80+					
	Number (in thousands)			Percent of total			Number (in thousands)			Percent of total		
	1990 (estimated)	2025 (projected)	Percent change 1990 to 2025	1990 (estimated)	2025 (projected)	Percent change 1990 to 2050	1990 (estimated)	2025 (projected)	Percent change 1990 to 2025	1990 (estimated)	2025 (projected)	Percent change 1990 to 2025
Canada	3,053	7,350	140.7	11.5	21.8	89.6	634	1,894	198.7	2.4	5.6	133.3
France	7,928	13,102	65.3	14.1	21.8	54.6	2,119	3,208	51.4	3.8	5.3	39.5
Germany	11,779	18,182	54.4	15.0	24.4	62.7	2,938	4,875	65.9	3.7	6.5	75.7
Italy	8,472	13,771	62.5	14.7	25.1	70.7	1,770	4,428	150.1	3.1	8.1	161.3
Japan	14,655	31,897	117.7	11.8	26.3	123.0	2,824	10,559	273.9	2.3	8.7	278.3
Sweden	1,527	2,032	33.1	17.9	23.7	32.4	375	640	70.8	4.4	7.5	70.4
United Kingdom	8,977	13,016	45.0	15.6	21.9	40.4	2,078	3,880	86.7	3.6	6.5	80.6
United States	31,560	59,713	89.2	12.6	20.0	58.7	7,082	13,658	92.8	2.8	4.6	64.3

Source: U.S. Senate Special Committee on Aging, the American Association of Retired Persons, the Federal Council on Aging, and the U.S. Administration on Aging, *Aging America: Trends and Projections* (Washington, D.C.: U.S. Government Printing Office, 1991), p. 250. *Primary source:* U.S. Bureau of the Census. International Data Base.

★ 604 ★

Population by Age

Increase in the 85+ Population, 1900-2050

"With increases in the number of people surviving into the upper age ranges, the elderly population is growing older. In 1990, the younger elderly (age 65 to 74) outnumbered the older elderly (age 75+) by more than 4 to 3. By the turn of the century, half (52 percent) of the elderly population is expected to be between the ages of 65 and 74 and half (48 percent) will be age 75+."

[Millions]

Year	
1900	0.10
1910	0.15
1920	0.20
1930	0.30
1940	0.40
1950	0.60
1960	0.80
1970	1.20
1980	2.10
1990	3.40
2000	4.30
2010	6.20
2020	6.30
2030	8.00
2040	12.40
2050	15.0

Source: U.S. Senate Special Committee on Aging, the American Association of Retired Persons, the Federal Council on Aging, and the U.S. Administration on Aging, *Aging America: Trends and Projections* (Washington, D.C.: U.S. Government Printing Office, 1991), p. 12. *Primary source:* U.S. Bureau of the Census, "America in Transition: An Aging Society," by Cynthia M. Taeuber, *Current Population Reports* Series P-23, No. 128 (September 1983); U.S. Bureau of the Census, "Projections of the Population of the United States by Age, Sex, and Race: 1988 to 2080," by Gregory Spencer, *Current Population Reports* Series P-25, No. 1018 (January 1989). *Note:* Magnitudes estimated from published chart.

Vital Statistics: Birth, Fertility, Mortality, and Life Expectancy Rates

★ 605 ★

Comparison of Principal Fertility, Mortality, and Net Immigration Assumptions between Old and New Census Bureau Projections, 1992-2050

"Specific component starting points and assumed ending points for this set of projections compared with the earlier projections are highlighted in [the table below]. Most assumptions used in this report are very similar to assumptions used in the last report. For complete information refer to the Detailed Methodology section. The fertility assumption in the middle series remains the same as the prior report with one exception. The fertility rates for Asian and Pacific Islander and also for Hispanic-origin women are projected to slowly decrease after 1995 instead of after 2000. The starting fertility rates were updated since the last report using the most current fertility data from the National Center for Health Statistic.

"The mortality assumptions for the middle series have changed minimally from the previous report. The average annual rate of change from 1980 to 1990 was projected from 1992 to 2050 for each age, sex, race, and ethnicity group. To maintain reasonableness in the survival rates by 2050, however, some general conditions were imposed. The starting mortality rates also were updated since the last report using the most current data.

"The previous immigration assumptions in the middle series are unchanged. Legislative policy has not changed since 1990, and currently there is no evidence of different patterns of future immigration. The distribution of net immigration by age, sex, race, and Hispanic origin used for this report is based on the 1992 estimates of net immigration."

[Millions series]

Subject	P25-1092		New	
	1992	2050	1993	2050
Total Fertility Rate[1]				
Total	2,052	2,119	2,074	2,150
White	1,951	2,009	1,973	2,054
Black	2,459	2,444	2,470	2,452
American Indian[2]	2,865	2,840	2,778	2,718
Asian[3]	2,327	2,078	2,514	2,134
Hispanic origin[4]	2,650	2,358	2,900	2,473
White, not Hispanic	1,850	1,850	1,840	1,840
Black, not Hispanic	2,450	2,450	2,450	2,450
American Indian, not Hispanic[2]	2,900	2,900	2,760	2,760
Asian, not Hispanic[3]	2,300	2,057	2,480	2,100
Life Expectancy at Birth[5]				
Total	75.8	82.1	76.0	82.6
White	76.4	83.0	76.8	83.8
Black	71.0	76.6	70.4	75.5
American Indian[2]	78.0	84.1	76.9	82.9

[Continued]

★ 605 ★

Comparison of Principal Fertility, Mortality, and Net Immigration Assumptions between Old and New Census Bureau Projections, 1992-2050

[Continued]

Subject	P25-1092		New	
	1992	2050	1993	2050
Asian[3]	83.2	88.0	82.9	88.0
Hispanic origin[4]	78.2	83.1	79.0	84.2
White, not Hispanic	76.4	83.1	76.6	83.8
Black, not Hispanic	70.8	76.0	70.2	74.8
American Indian, not Hispanic[2]	78.0	84.3	76.3	82.6
Asian, not Hispanic[3]	83.4	88.3	82.9	88.3
Yearly Net Immigration (thousands)				
Total	880	880	880	880
White	463	463	482	482
Black	80	80	81	81
American Indian[2]	0	0	0	0
Asian[3]	337	337	317	317
Hispanic origin[4]	324	324	322	322
White, not Hispanic	174	174	193	193
Black, not Hispanic	60	60	61	61
American Indian, not Hispanic[2]	0	0	0	0
Asian, not Hispanic[3]	323	323	304	304

Source: Jennifer Cheeseman Day, U.S. Department of Commerce, Economics and Statistics Administration, Bureau of the Census, *Population Projections of the United States, by Age, Sex, Race and Hispanic Origin: 1993 to 2050* (Washington, D.C.: U.S. Government Printing Office, November 1993), Series P25-1104, pp. viii-ix. *Notes:* 1. Adjusted for under-registration of births and undercount in the 1990 census as measured by Demographic Analysis. 2. American Indian represents American Indian, Eskimo, and Aleut. 3. Asian represents Asian and Pacific Islander. 4. Persons of Hispanic origin may be of any race. 5. Adjusted for net census coverage error in the 1990 census as measured by Demographic Analysis.

★ 606 ★

Vital Statistics: Birth, Fertility, Mortality, and Life Expectancy Rates

Principal Fertility, Life Expectancy, and Net Immigration Assumptions, 1993-2050

"Estimates indicate fertility rates increased in the last few years averaging about 2.1 births per woman in the early 1990's. Birth expectations have remained about the same since 1976 for all women at about two lifetime births. It is uncertain whether this level will continue, increase, or decrease. Based on this current lack of direction, the fertility assumption holds constant age-specific fertility rates at 1990 levels in the middle series for non-Hispanic White; non-Hispanic Black; and the non-Hispanic American Indian, Eskimo, and Aleut. A fifteen percent decrease in fertility rates between 1995 and 2050, however, is assumed for the Hispanic origin and the non-Hispanic Asian and Pacific Islander populations because the share of their fertility contributed by the foreign-born population is expected to decrease (foreign-born women tend to have higher fertility rates than native born). No covergence of birth rates by race and Hispanic origin is assumed...

"Life expectancy is assumed to increase in the middle series from 75.9 years in 1993 to 82.6 years in 2050. As in the previous projections report, this series replicates the mortality improvement experienced in the decade of the 1980's for the next 60 years, but also includes some negating effects of AIDS. The impact of AIDS is assumed to slowly diminish after the turn of the century, returning to current levels. No race-origin/sex convergence is assumed...

"[The table below] also shows that net immigration is assumed in the middle assumption to remain constant throughout the projection period at 880,000 per year (about 1,040,000 immigrants and 160,000 emigrants). This reflects the 1990 immigration law changes and current knowledge of emigration, undocumented migration, and movement to and from Puerto Rico. The high assumption of 1,370,000 includes higher numbers of these components (with a decrease of emigration), consistent with Immigration and Naturalization Service suggestions that the cap on legal immigration may be pierced by family-sponsored immigration, and that refugee immigration could potentially increase. The low assumption of 350,000 projects that immigration would decrease and emigration would increase, with legal and refugee immigration similar to the level in the mid-1980's (about 500,000), net undocumented immigration [decreasing] to 100,000, and emigration [increasing] to 260,000. Both the high and the low levels would be first reached in 1995."

Item	1993	2050 level		
		Low assumption	Middle assumption	High assumption
Fertility	2,074	1,892	2,150	2,622
Life expectancy	76.0	75.3	82.6	87.5
Yearly net immigration (thousands)	880	350	880	1,370

Source: Jennifer Cheeseman Day, U.S. Department of Commerce, Economics and Statistics Administration, Bureau of the Census, *Population Projections of the United States, by Age, Sex, Race and Hispanic Origin: 1993 to 2050* (Washington, D.C.: U.S. Government Printing Office, November 1993), Series P25-1104, pp. xi-xii.

★ 607 ★

Vital Statistics: Birth, Fertility, Mortality, and Life Expectancy Rates

Women in Childbearing Ages, 1990-2050

"By 2005, the crude birth rate may drop to a record low of 13.8 births per thousand population. Soon after the turn of the century, the crude birth rate is projected to rise, and the number of births would reach over 4 million again by 2006, instigated by an increasing number of women in their childbearing years. Many of these births will be the grandchildren of the baby boomers. The number of births may continue to increase throughout the end of the projected period. In fact, the 2012 the annual number of births would exceed the highest annual number of births ever achieved in the United States during the 20th century. At the same time, the crude birth rate would slowly decrease again from 14.1 to 13.4 by 2029 and remain constant. The annual number of births would continue to rise, setting new records each year. By 2018, births may exceed 4.5 million and top 5 million by 2041."

[Thousands Middle series]

Year	Number of women						Percent of total population
	15 to 44 years	15 to 19 years	20 to 24 years	25 to 29 years	30 to 34 years	35 to 44 years	
Estimate							
1990	58,700	8,645	9,387	10,575	11,006	19,087	23.5
Projections							
1995	59,820	8,659	9,088	9,623	11,212	21,238	22.7
2000	60,365	9,651	8,838	9,191	9,987	22,697	21.9
2005	60,164	10,162	9,808	8,938	9,553	21,702	20.9
2010	60,444	10,895	10,323	9,891	9,297	20,038	20.1
2020	63,090	10,502	10,678	11,087	10,762	20,060	19.4
2030	67,054	11,446	11,010	10,725	11,126	22,746	19.2
2040	70,050	12,124	12,025	11,657	11,472	22,773	18.9
2050	73,893	12,604	12,445	12,311	12,476	24,057	18.8

Source: Jennifer Cheeseman Day, U.S. Department of Commerce, Economics and Statistics Administration, Bureau of the Census, *Population Projections of the United States, by Age, Sex, Race and Hispanic Origin: 1993 to 2050* (Washington, D.C.: U.S. Government Printing Office, November 1993), Series P25-1104, p. xxix. *Primary source:* Current Population Reports, Series P25-1095.

★ 608 ★

Vital Statistics: Birth, Fertility, Mortality, and Life Expectancy Rates

American Indian, Eskimo, and Aleut, not Hispanic Females: Total Fertility Rates and Fertil Rates by Age, 2000-2050

[Live births per 1,000 women]

Projections for year ending June 30th	Total fertility rate	Birth rates for year ending June 30th								Mean age of childbearing	Median age of childbearing
		10 to 14 years	15 to 19 years	20 to 24 years	25 to 29 years	30 to 34 years	35 to 39 years	40 to 44 years	45 to 49 years		
LOW FERTILITY ASSUMPTION											
2000	2,483.2	1.9	92.4	170.9	126.5	67.6	29.0	6.2	0.3	25.30	24.43
2001	2,454.2	1.8	92.0	169.1	124.8	67.1	28.6	6.1	0.3	25.30	24.43
2002	2,425.5	1.8	91.2	167.3	123.4	66.7	28.2	6.0	0.3	25.30	24.43
2003	2,379.2	1.8	90.5	165.3	122.1	66.0	27.8	5.9	0.3	25.30	24.44
2004	2,369.2	1.8	89.3	163.3	120.9	65.0	27.5	5.8	0.3	25.30	24.43

[Continued]

★ 608 ★

American Indian, Eskimo, and Aleut, not Hispanic Females: Total Fertility Rates and Fertil Rates by Age, 2000-2050

[Continued]

Projections for year ending June 30th	Total fertility rate	Birth rates for year ending June 30th 10 to 14 years	15 to 19 years	20 to 24 years	25 to 29 years	30 to 34 years	35 to 39 years	40 to 44 years	45 to 49 years	Mean age of childbearing	Median age of childbearing
2005	2,341.5	1.9	87.7	161.2	119.7	64.0	27.3	5.7	0.3	25.30	24.43
2006	2,314.2	1.9	86.1	159.2	118.6	63.1	27.2	5.6	0.3	25.30	24.43
2007	2,287.2	1.9	84.9	157.3	117.3	62.4	27.1	5.5	0.3	25.30	24.43
2008	2,260.5	1.8	84.7	155.4	115.9	61.8	26.9	5.5	0.3	25.30	24.43
2009	2,234.1	1.8	85.3	153.6	114.5	61.3	26.4	5.4	0.3	25.30	24.43
2010 and beyond	1,208.0	1.7	85.5	151.9	112.9	60.8	25.9	5.4	0.3	25.30	24.43
MIDDLE FERTILITY ASSUMPTION											
1993 and beyond	2,760.0	2.0	104.7	190.0	140.1	75.5	32.7	6.9	0.3	25.30	24.42
HIGH FERTILITY ASSUMPTION											
2000	2,887.5	2.2	107.4	198.8	147.1	78.6	33.8	7.2	0.4	24.30	24.42
2001	2,902.0	2.2	108.7	200.0	147.6	79.4	33.8	7.2	0.4	25.30	24.41
2002	2,916.6	2.2	109.7	201.1	148.3	80.2	33.9	7.2	0.4	25.30	24.41
2003	2,931.3	2.2	110.6	202.1	149.3	80.7	34.0	7.3	0.4	25.30	24.41
2004	2,946.0	2.3	111.1	203.0	150.3	80.8	34.2	7.3	0.4	25.30	24.41
2005	2,960.8	2.4	111.0	203.8	151.4	80.9	34.5	7.2	0.4	25.30	24.42
2006	2,975.7	2.4	110.8	204.7	152.5	81.1	34.9	7.2	0.4	25.30	24.42
2007	2,990.7	2.4	111.0	205.6	153.4	81.6	35.4	7.2	0.4	25.30	24.42
2008	3,005.7	2.3	112.6	206.6	154.2	82.2	35.7	7.3	0.4	25.30	24.42
2009	3,020.8	2.3	114.8	207.6	154.8	82.9	35.7	7.3	0.4	25.30	24.42
2010 and beyond	3,036.0	2.3	116.4	208.8	155.3	83.6	35.6	7.4	0.4	25.30	24.41

Source: Jennifer Cheeseman Day, U.S. Department of Commerce, Economics and Statistics Administration, Bureau of the Census, *Population Projections of the United States, by Age, Sex, Race and Hispanic Origin: 1993 to 2050* (Washington, D.C.: U.S. Government Printing Office, November 1993), Series P25-1104, p. A-9. *Notes:* Includes low, middle, and high assumptions. Births are adjusted for underregistration and the female population is adjusted by Demographic Analysis for net census undercount. Source also includes data for 1993-1999 under the low and high fertility assumptions.

★ 609 ★

Vital Statistics: Birth, Fertility, Mortality, and Life Expectancy Rates

Asian and Pacific Islander, not Hispanic Females: Total Fertility Rates and Fertility Rate Age, 2000-2050

[Live births per 1,000 women]

Projections for year ending June 30th	Total fertility rate	Birth rates for year ending June 30th 10 to 14 years	15 to 19 years	20 to 24 years	25 to 29 years	30 to 34 years	35 to 39 years	40 to 44 years	45 to 49 years	Mean age of childbearing	Median age of childbearing
LOW FERTILITY ASSUMPTION											
2000	2,231.3	0.7	24.7	84.6	145.5	123.0	55.7	11.5	1.2	29.04	29.03
2001	2,205.2	0.6	24.7	83.2	143.8	121.9	55.0	11.4	1.2	29.04	29.04
2002	2,179.5	0.6	24.5	81.8	142.1	120.7	54.3	11.2	1.2	29.04	29.02
2003	2,154.0	0.6	24.3	80.7	140.3	119.2	53.6	11.1	1.1	29.04	29.03
2004	2,128.9	0.6	24.0	79.8	138.6	117.5	52.9	10.9	1.1	29.04	29.02
2005	2,104.0	0.6	23.6	79.1	136.8	115.7	52.5	10.8	1.1	29.04	29.03
2006	2,079.4	0.6	23.2	78.5	135.0	114.1	52.2	10.6	1.1	29.04	29.02
2007	2,055.2	0.6	22.8	77.7	133.3	112.8	51.7	10.5	1.1	29.04	29.04
2008	2,031.2	0.6	22.5	76.9	131.7	111.7	51.0	10.3	1.1	29.04	29.03
2009	2,007.4	0.6	22.1	76.0	130.2	110.5	50.1	10.2	1.0	29.04	29.03
2010 and beyond	1,984.0	0.6	22.0	75.0	128.8	109.5	49.2	10.2	1.0	29.04	29.04
MIDDLE FERTILITY ASSUMPTION											
2000	2,443.5	0.7	27.2	92.8	159.3	134.9	61.1	12.6	1.3	29.04	29.03
2001	2,436.2	0.7	27.3	92.1	158.9	134.8	60.9	12.6	1.3	29.04	29.03
2002	2,429.0	0.7	27.4	91.5	158.4	134.6	60.7	12.6	1.3	29.04	29.03
2003	2,421.8	0.7	27.4	91.1	157.8	134.1	60.5	12.5	1.3	29.04	29.02
2004	2,414.6	0.7	27.3	90.9	157.2	133.3	60.3	12.4	1.3	29.04	29.03

[Continued]

★ 609 ★

Asian and Pacific Islander, not Hispanic Females: Total Fertility Rates and Fertility Rate Age, 2000-2050

[Continued]

Projections for year ending June 30th	Total fertility rate	Birth rates for year ending June 30th: 10 to 14 years	15 to 19 years	20 to 24 years	25 to 29 years	30 to 34 years	35 to 39 years	40 to 44 years	45 to 49 years	Mean age of childbearing	Median age of childbearing
2005	2,407.4	0.7	27.2	90.9	156.6	132.5	60.3	12.4	1.3	29.04	29.01
2010	3,372.0	0.7	26.2	89.9	154.1	130.8	59.0	12.2	1.2	29.04	29.02
2015	2,337.0	0.7	26.2	87.8	151.9	129.2	58.4	11.9	1.2	29.04	29.02
2020	2,302.5	0.7	25.9	87.0	149.4	127.0	57.7	11.8	1.2	29.04	29.03
2025	2,268.6	0.7	25.5	85.8	147.4	125.6	56.7	11.7	1.2	29.04	29.01
2030	2,235.2	0.7	25.1	84.5	145.2	123.5	56.2	11.5	1.2	29.04	29.03
2035	2,202.2	0.6	24.7	83.2	143.1	121.6	55.1	11.4	1.2	29.04	29.03
2040	2,169.8	0.6	24.3	81.9	140.9	119.8	54.2	11.1	1.1	29.04	29.03
2045	2,137.8	0.6	24.0	80.7	138.8	118.1	53.4	11.0	1.1	29.04	29.03
2050	2,106.3	0.6	23.7	79.5	136.8	116.4	52.7	10.8	1.1	29.04	29.04
HIGH FERTILITY ASSUMPTION											
2000	2,594.6	0.8	29.0	98.7	169.1	143.3	65.1	13.4	1.4	29.04	29.02
2001	2,607.6	0.8	29.4	98.8	170.0	143.3	65.1	13.5	1.4	29.04	29.02
2002	2,620.7	0.8	29.7	99.0	170.8	145.2	65.7	13.6	1.4	29.04	29.02
2003	2,633.9	0.7	29.9	99.4	171.6	145.8	66.0	13.6	1.4	29.04	29.03
2004	2,647.1	0.7	30.0	99.9	172.4	146.2	66.3	13.7	1.4	29.04	29.03
2005	2,660.4	0.7	30.1	100.6	173.1	146.5	66.9	13.8	1.4	29.04	29.02
2006	2,673.8	0.7	30.1	101.4	173.9	147.1	67.4	13.8	1.4	29.04	29.03
2007	2,687.3	0.7	30.2	102.1	174.6	147.8	67.8	13.9	1.4	29.04	29.03
2008	2,700.8	0.8	30.2	102.7	175.5	148.6	67.8	13.9	1.4	29.04	29.03
2009	2,714.4	0.8	30.2	103.2	176.4	149.5	68.0	14.0	1.4	29.04	29.03
2010 and beyond	2,728.0	0.8	30.2	103.6	177.3	150.4	68.0	14.1	1.4	29.04	29.02

Source: Jennifer Cheeseman Day, U.S. Department of Commerce, Economics and Statistics Administration, Bureau of the Census, *Population Projections of the United States, by Age, Sex, Race and Hispanic Origin: 1993 to 2050* (Washington, D.C.: U.S. Government Printing Office, November 1993), Series P25-1104, p. A-10. *Notes:* Includes low, middle, and high assumptions. Births are adjusted for underregistration and the female population is adjusted by Demographic Analysis for net census undercount. Source also includes data for 1993-1999.

★ 610 ★

Vital Statistics: Birth, Fertility, Mortality, and Life Expectancy Rates

Total Females, Total Fertility Rates, and Fertility Rates by Age, 2000-2050

[Live births per 1,000 women]

Projections for year ending June 30th	Total fertility rate	Birth rates for year ending June 30th: 10 to 14 years	15 to 19 years	20 to 24 years	25 to 29 years	30 to 34 years	35 to 39 years	40 to 44 years	45 to 49 years	Mean age of childbearing	Median age of childbearing
LOW FERTILITY ASSUMPTION											
2000	1,951.7	1.3	55.7	110.8	111.5	75.0	29.4	5.1	0.2	26.53	26.21
2001	1,937.9	1.3	55.4	109.9	110.7	74.9	29.1	5.1	0.2	26.53	26.23
2002	1,924.2	1.3	54.9	109.0	110.1	74.7	28.8	5.0	0.2	26.54	26.23
2003	1,910.6	1.3	54.4	108.2	109.4	74.1	28.5	5.0	0.2	26.54	26.24
2004	1,897.2	1.3	54.0	107.3	108.7	73.3	28.3	4.9	0.2	26.54	26.26
2005	1,884.2	1.4	53.7	106.5	108.0	72.4	28.3	4.9	0.2	26.54	26.25
2010	1,822.7	1.3	53.3	103.0	104.0	70.8	27.3	4.7	0.2	26.53	26.25
2015	1,832.3	1.4	53.7	104.1	104.4	70.8	28.2	4.7	0.2	26.52	26.21
2020	1,839.9	1.4	54.0	104.6	104.5	71.0	28.2	5.0	0.2	26.51	26.19
2025	1,848.8	1.3	54.0	105.1	104.9	70.8	28.4	5.0	0.2	26.51	26.19
2030	1,858.1	1.4	54.1	105.6	105.2	71.1	28.2	5.1	0.2	26.51	26.17
2035	1,866.4	1.4	54.7	106.1	105.5	71.4	28.5	5.0	0.3	26.51	26.18
2040	1,873.9	1.4	55.3	106.6	105.8	71.8	28.8	5.1	0.3	26.51	26.16
2045	1,882.1	1.4	55.7	107.1	106.1	72.0	29.0	5.2	0.3	26.50	26.16
2050	1,892.1	1.5	56.1	107.7	106.4	72.2	29.2	5.3	0.3	26.49	26.14
MIDDLE FERTILITY ASSUMPTION											
2000	2,097.1	1.5	60.2	119.3	119.6	80.3	31.5	5.5	0.3	26.51	26.21
2001	2,098.9	1.5	60.4	119.3	119.7	80.8	31.4	5.5	0.3	26.51	26.20

[Continued]

★ 610 ★

Total Females, Total Fertility Rates, and Fertility Rates by Age, 2000-2050

[Continued]

Projections for year ending June 30th	Total fertility rate	Birth rates for year ending June 30th								Mean age of childbearing	Median age of childbearing
		10 to 14 years	15 to 19 years	20 to 24 years	25 to 29 years	30 to 34 years	35 to 39 years	40 to 44 years	45 to 49 years		
2002	2,100.6	1.5	60.4	119.3	119.9	81.2	31.4	5.5	0.3	26.52	26.21
2003	2,102.3	1.5	60.4	119.2	120.1	81.3	31.3	5.5	0.3	26.52	26.21
2004	2,104.2	1.5	60.4	119.2	120.3	81.0	31.4	5.5	0.3	26.52	26.21
2005	2,106.2	1.6	60.5	119.2	120.3	80.6	31.6	5.5	0.3	26.52	26.23
2010	2,119.0	1.6	62.4	120.0	120.2	82.0	31.8	5.5	0.3	26.51	26.19
2015	2,128.8	1.6	63.1	121.0	120.3	81.7	32.9	5.6	0.3	26.49	26.16
2020	2,136.1	1.7	63.5	121.6	120.3	81.7	32.7	5.9	0.3	26.47	26.12
2025	2,143.5	1.7	63.7	122.2	120.5	81.4	32.8	5.8	0.3	26.46	26.11
2030	2,149.3	1.7	64.1	122.6	120.6	81.5	32.6	5.9	0.3	26.45	26.09
2035	2,151.6	1.7	64.5	122.8	120.4	81.6	32.8	5.9	0.3	26.45	26.09
2040	2,151.4	1.8	64.9	122.8	120.1	81.5	33.0	5.9	0.3	26.44	26.07
2045	2,150.9	1.8	65.3	122.9	119.7	81.2	33.1	6.0	0.3	26.43	26.04
2050	2,150.4	1.8	65.7	123.1	119.3	80.8	33.0	6.1	0.3	26.41	26.03
HIGH FERTILITY ASSUMPTION											
2000	2,263.0	1.5	64.6	128.5	129.3	87.0	34.1	6.0	0.3	26.53	26.21
2001	2,284.8	1.6	65.4	129.6	130.5	88.3	34.4	6.0	0.3	26.53	26.22
2002	2,306.6	1.6	65.8	130.7	131.9	89.6	34.6	6.0	0.3	26.54	26.21
2003	2,328.4	1.6	66.3	131.7	133.4	90.4	34.9	6.1	0.3	26.55	26.22
2004	2,350.5	1.6	66.9	132.8	134.7	90.9	35.3	6.2	0.3	26.55	26.23
2005	2,372.9	1.7	67.5	140.4	134.7	91.4	35.9	6.2	0.3	26.55	26.23
2010	2,489.1	1.8	72.0	140.4	141.6	97.0	37.8	6.6	0.3	26.55	26.24
2015	2,507.7	1.8	72.5	141.8	142.3	97.1	39.2	6.7	0.3	26.55	26.20
2020	2,523.5	1.8	73.1	142.9	142.7	97.5	39.2	7.1	0.4	26.54	26.19
2025	2,540.9	1.9	73.5	144.1	143.7	97.5	39.5	7.1	0.4	26.53	26.18
2030	2,558.8	1.9	74.5	145.0	144.5	98.3	39.6	7.2	0.4	26.52	26.17
2035	2,575.7	1.9	75.4	146.0	145.0	99.0	40.1	7.2	0.4	26.52	26.16
2040	2,591.3	2.0	76.2	147.0	145.4	99.4	40.6	7.4	0.4	26.52	26.14
2045	2,606.8	2.0	77.0	148.1	145.9	99.5	40.9	7.5	0.4	26.50	26.12
2050	2,622.5	2.0	77.7	149.3	146.5	99.8	41.0	7.6	0.4	26.49	26.09

Source: Jennifer Cheeseman Day, U.S. Department of Commerce, Economics and Statistics Administration, Bureau of the Census, *Population Projections of the United States, by Age, Sex, Race and Hispanic Origin: 1993 to 2050* (Washington, D.C.: U.S. Government Printing Office, November 1993), Series P25-1104, p. A-1. *Notes:* Includes low, middle, and high assumptions. Births are adjusted for underregistration and the female population is adjusted by Demographic Analysis for net census undercount. Source also includes data for 1993-1999.

★ 611 ★

Vital Statistics: Birth, Fertility, Mortality, and Life Expectancy Rates

U.S. Infant Mortality Rate, 1970-2000

"In 1988, the United States had the 23rd lowest infant mortality rate among nations of the world. Although most babies in America are born strong and healthy, in 1989, for example, over 39,000 infants died in the United States before their first birthday. Black infants died at twice the rate of white infants, and the rates for some Native American groups and for Puerto Rico were also higher than that for whites. Thus, the United States recognizes there is much more progress to be made."

[Deaths per 1,000 live births]

Year	
1970	20
1975	17
1980	15
1985	14

[Continued]

★611★

U.S. Infant Mortality Rate, 1970-2000

[Continued]

Year	
1990	12
1995	11
2000	9

Source: "Office of the President of the United States, *A Culture of Caring: America's Commitment to Children and Families* (Washington, D.C., U.S. Government Printing Office). *Primary source:* National Vital Statistics System, CDC.

★612★

Vital Statistics: Birth, Fertility, Mortality, and Life Expectancy Rates

Alternative Projections of Life Expectancy and Population Age 65+, 2040

"A recent analysis by researchers at the National Institute on Aging and the University of Southern California (NIA/USC) projects that in 2040 there could be 87 million people age 65+. This figure, which represents almost 19 million more elderly people than the Census Bureau's middle series projection, was based on a 2-1 percent annual mortality decline, an assumption that is more optimistic than those used by the Census Bureau but which is consistent with mortality declines experienced by the U.S. population in recent years. According to the NIA/USC projection, the population age 85+ could number 24 million in 2040, almost twice as many as the middle series Census projection and nearly eight times the current level."

Subject	Bureau of the Census			NIA/ USC
	Middle series (series 14)	High mortality (series 23)	Low mortality (series 5)	
Life expectancy at birth (years)				
Men	75.9	73.0	80.8	85.9
Women	82.8	80.3	87.1	91.5
Population (in thousands)				
65+, total	68,109	60,936	80,110	86,805
65 to 74	30,808	29,111	33,205	32,075
75 to 84	25,050	22,516	29,224	31,212
85+	12,251	9,309	17,681	23,519
Percent change, 1989-2040				
65+, total	120	97	159	180
65 to 74	69	60	83	76

[Continued]

★ 612 ★

Alternative Projections of Life Expectancy and Population Age 65+, 2040

[Continued]

Subject	Bureau of the Census			NIA/ USC
	Middle series (series 14)	High mortality (series 23)	Low mortality (series 5)	
75 to 84	157	131	199	220
85+	303	206	481	673

Source: U.S. Senate Special Committee on Aging, the American Association of Retired Persons, the Federal Council on Aging, and the U.S. Administration on Aging, *Aging America: Trends and Projections*, Washington, D.C.: U.S. Bureau of the Census, "Projections of the Population of the United States by Age, Sex, and Race: 1988 to 2080," by Gregory Spencer, *Current Population Reports* Series P-25, No. 1018 (January 1989); U.S. Bureau of the Census, "U.S. Population Estimates, by Age, Sex, Race, and Hispanic Origin: 1989," by Frederick W. Homman, *Current Population Reports* Series P-25, No. 1057 (March 1990); Jack M. Guralnik, Machiko Yangishita and Edward L. Schneider, "Projecting the Older Population of the United States: Lessons From the Past and Prospects for the Future," *The Millbank Quarterly* Vol. 66, No. 2 (1988). *Notes:* NIA/USC = National Institute on Aging and the University of Southern California.

★ 613 ★

Vital Statistics: Birth, Fertility, Mortality, and Life Expectancy Rates

Life Expectancy at Birth by Race, Hispanic Origin, and Sex, 2000-2050-I

[Years]

Projections for calendar year	Life expectancy at birth									
	Total		Race							
			White		Black		American Indian, Eskimo, and Aleut		Asian and Pacific Islander	
	Male	Female	Male	Female	Male	Female	Male	Female	Male	Female
LOW ASSUMPTION										
2000	71.9	79.2	72.9	79.8	64.9	74.2	71.6	81.5	79.5	85.7
2001	71.9	79.2	72.8	79.8	64.9	74.2	71.6	81.5	79.5	85.7
2002	71.8	79.2	72.8	79.8	64.6	74.1	71.5	81.5	79.5	85.7
2003	71.7	79.2	72.7	79.8	64.5	74.1	71.5	81.5	79.5	85.7
2004	71.7	79.2	72.7	79.8	64.3	74.0	71.5	81.5	79.5	85.7
2005 and beyond	71.6	79.2	72.6	79.8	64.2	74.0	71.5	81.5	79.5	85.7
MIDDLE ASSUMPTION										
2000	73.2	80.2	74.3	80.9	65.3	75.1	73.6	83.1	81.1	86.9
2001	73.3	80.3	74.4	81.0	65.4	75.2	73.7	83.2	81.2	87.0
2002	73.4	80.4	74.6	81.1	65.5	75.3	73.8	83.3	81.3	87.0
2003	73.6	80.5	74.7	81.2	65.6	75.4	73.9	83.4	81.3	87.1
2004	73.7	80.6	74.8	81.3	65.8	75.5	74.0	83.5	81.4	87.2
2005	73.8	80.7	74.9	81.4	65.9	75.5	74.0	83.5	81.5	87.3
2010	74.5	81.3	75.6	82.0	66.5	76.0	74.5	84.0	81.9	87.6
2015	75.1	81.8	76.2	82.5	67.0	76.4	74.9	84.5	82.3	88.0
2020	75.7	82.3	76.9	83.1	67.6	76.9	75.4	84.9	82.8	88.4
2025	76.4	82.9	77.6	83.7	68.2	77.3	75.8	85.4	83.2	88.8
2030	77.0	83.4	78.3	84.2	68.8	77.8	76.3	85.8	83.6	89.2

[Continued]

★ 613 ★

Life Expectancy at Birth by Race, Hispanic Origin, and Sex, 2000-2050-I

[Continued]

Projections for calendar year	Life expectancy at birth									
	Total		Race							
			White		Black		American Indian, Eskimo, and Aleut		Asian and Pacific Islander	
	Male	Female	Male	Female	Male	Female	Male	Female	Male	Female
2035	77.7	83.9	78.9	84.8	69.4	78.2	76.7	86.3	84.0	89.5
2040	78.4	84.5	79.6	85.3	70.1	78.7	77.2	86.8	84.4	89.9
2045	79.0	85.0	80.3	85.9	70.7	79.1	77.6	87.2	84.9	90.3
2050	79.7	85.6	81.0	86.5	71.3	79.6	78.1	87.7	85.3	90.7
HIGH ASSUMPTION										
2000	74.0	80.9	74.8	81.5	68.0	76.5	73.2	82.9	80.7	86.9
2001	74.2	81.1	75.0	81.7	68.2	76.7	73.3	83.1	80.9	87.1
2002	74.4	81.3	75.1	81.9	68.4	76.9	73.5	83.3	81.0	87.2
2003	74.6	81.5	75.3	82.0	68.6	77.1	73.7	83.5	81.1	87.3
2004	74.8	81.7	75.5	82.2	68.8	77.4	73.8	83.6	81.3	87.5
2005	75.0	81.9	75.7	82.4	69.0	77.6	74.0	83.8	81.4	87.6
2010	75.9	82.9	76.6	83.4	70.1	78.7	74.9	84.7	82.1	88.4
2015	76.8	83.8	77.5	84.3	71.2	79.9	75.8	85.7	82.8	89.1
2020	77.8	84.8	78.4	85.3	72.3	81.0	76.7	86.6	83.4	89.8
2025	78.8	85.9	79.4	86.3	73.5	82.2	77.6	87.5	84.1	90.6
2030	79.8	86.9	80.3	87.3	74.6	83.4	78.5	88.5	84.8	91.3
2035	80.7	87.9	81.3	88.3	75.8	84.6	79.4	89.4	85.5	92.1
2040	81.8	89.0	82.2	89.3	77.0	85.9	80.4	90.4	86.3	92.9
2045	82.8	90.0	83.2	90.4	78.2	87.1	81.3	91.4	87.0	93.6
2050	83.8	91.1	84.2	91.4	79.4	88.4	82.3	92.4	87.7	94.4

Source: Jennifer Cheeseman Day, U.S. Department of Commerce, Economics and Statistics Administration, Bureau of the Census, *Population Projections of the United States, by Age, Sex, Race and Hispanic Origin: 1993 to 2050* (Washington, D.C.: U.S. Government Printing Office, November 1993), Series P25-1104, p. B-1. *Notes:* Source also includes data for 1993-1999. The 1993 to 2050 values are consistent with population totals adjusted for undercount by Demographic Analysis.

★ 614 ★

Vital Statistics: Birth, Fertility, Mortality, and Life Expectancy Rates

Life Expectancy at Birth by Race, Hispanic Origin, and Sex, 2000-2050-II

[Years]

Projections for calendar year	Life expectancy at birth									
	Hispanic origin[1]		Race							
			White		Black		American Indian, Eskimo, and Aleut		Asian and Pacific Islander	
	Male	Female	Male	Female	Male	Female	Male	Female	Male	Female
LOW ASSUMPTION										
2000	73.8	82.3	73.0	79.8	64.6	74.0	71.2	81.3	79.9	86.0
2001	73.6	82.2	72.9	79.8	64.4	73.9	71.2	81.3	79.9	86.0
2002	73.5	82.2	72.9	79.8	64.3	73.9	71.2	81.3	79.9	86.0
2003	73.3	82.2	72.9	79.8	64.1	73.8	71.2	81.3	79.9	86.0
2004	73.2	82.1	72.8	79.8	64.0	73.8	71.2	81.3	79.9	86.0
2005 and beyond	73.0	82.1	72.8	79.8	63.8	73.7	71.2	81.3	79.9	86.0
MIDDLE ASSUMPTION										
2000	75.3	83.5	74.4	80.8	64.9	74.8	73.3	82.9	81.4	87.1

[Continued]

★ 614 ★

Life Expectancy at Birth by Race, Hispanic Origin, and Sex, 2000-2050-II

[Continued]

Projections for calendar year	Life expectancy at birth									
	Hispanic origin[1]		Race							
			White		Black		American Indian, Eskimo, and Aleut		Asian and Pacific Islander	
	Male	Female	Male	Female	Male	Female	Male	Female	Male	Female
2001	75.4	83.6	74.5	80.9	65.0	74.9	73.4	83.0	81.5	87.2
2002	75.5	83.7	74.7	81.0	65.1	75.0	73.5	83.1	81.6	87.2
2003	75.6	83.7	74.8	81.1	65.2	75.0	73.6	83.2	81.6	87.3
2004	75.7	83.8	74.9	81.2	65.3	75.1	73.6	83.3	81.7	87.4
2005	75.9	83.9	75.1	81.3	65.4	75.2	73.7	83.4	81.8	87.5
2010	76.4	84.3	75.7	81.9	66.0	75.6	74.1	83.8	82.2	87.8
2015	77.0	84.7	76.4	82.4	66.6	76.0	74.6	84.3	82.6	88.2
2020	77.5	85.0	77.0	83.0	67.1	76.5	75.0	84.7	83.1	88.6
2025	78.1	85.4	77.7	83.5	67.7	76.9	75.4	85.2	83.5	89.0
2030	76.7	85.6	78.4	84.1	68.3	77.3	75.9	85.7	83.9	89.4
2035	79.2	86.2	79.1	84.6	68.8	77.7	76.3	86.2	84.3	89.7
2040	79.6	86.6	79.8	85.2	69.4	78.1	76.7	86.6	84.7	90.1
2045	80.4	87.0	80.5	85.7	70.0	78.6	77.2	87.1	85.2	90.5
2050	81.0	87.4	81.2	86.3	70.6	79.0	77.6	87.6	85.6	90.9
HIGH ASSUMPTION										
2000	76.3	83.8	74.9	81.4	67.7	76.2	72.7	82.9	81.0	87.1
2001	76.5	83.9	75.0	81.6	67.9	76.4	72.9	83.1	81.1	87.3
2002	76.6	84.1	75.2	81.8	68.1	76.7	73.0	83.3	81.3	87.4
2003	76.8	84.2	75.4	82.0	68.3	76.9	73.2	83.5	81.4	87.5
2004	76.9	84.3	75.6	82.2	68.5	77.1	73.4	83.7	81.5	87.7
2005	77.0	84.5	75.8	82.4	68.7	77.3	73.6	83.9	81.7	87.8
2010	77.8	85.2	76.7	83.4	69.8	78.4	74.5	84.8	82.3	88.5
2015	78.5	85.9	77.7	84.4	70.9	79.6	75.4	85.8	83.0	89.1
2020	79.3	86.6	78.8	85.4	72.0	80.7	76.3	86.8	83.7	89.8
2025	80.0	87.4	79.6	86.4	73.1	81.9	77.3	87.8	84.4	90.5
2030	80.8	88.1	80.6	87.4	74.3	83.0	78.2	88.8	85.1	91.2
2035	81.5	88.8	81.6	88.5	75.4	84.2	79.2	89.8	85.8	91.9
2040	82.3	89.6	82.6	89.5	76.6	85.4	80.1	90.9	86.5	92.6
2045	83.1	90.3	83.7	90.6	77.8	86.7	81.1	91.9	87.2	93.3
2050	83.9	91.1	84.7	91.7	79.0	87.9	82.1	93.0	87.9	94.0

Source: Jennifer Cheeseman Day, U.S. Department of Commerce, Economics and Statistics Administration, Bureau of the Census, *Population Projections of the United States, by Age, Sex, Race and Hispanic Origin: 1993 to 2050* (Washington, D.C.: U.S. Government Printing Office, November 1993), Series P25-1104, p. B-1. *Notes:* Source also includes data for 1993-1999. The 1993 to 2050 values are consistent with population totals adjusted for undercount by Demographic Analysis. 1. Persons of Hispanic origin may be of any race.

★ 615 ★

Vital Statistics: Birth, Fertility, Mortality, and Life Expectancy Rates

Life Expectancy at Age 65 by Race, Hispanic Origin, and Sex, 2000-2050-I

[Years]

Projections for calendar year	Life expectancy at 65									
	Total		Race							
			White		Black		American Indian, Eskimo, and Aleut		Asian and Pacific Islander	
	Male	Female	Male	Female	Male	Female	Male	Female	Male	Female
LOW ASSUMPTION										
2000	15.5	19.4	15.6	19.5	14.0	18.1	18.9	23.8	20.0	24.4
2001	15.5	19.5	15.6	19.5	14.0	18.1	18.9	23.8	20.0	24.5
2002	15.5	19.5	15.6	19.5	14.0	18.1	18.9	23.9	20.0	24.5
2003	15.6	19.5	15.6	19.5	14.0	18.1	18.9	23.9	20.0	24.5

[Continued]

★ 615 ★

Life Expectancy at Age 65 by Race, Hispanic Origin, and Sex, 2000-2050-I

[Continued]

Projections for calendar year	Life expectancy at 65									
	Total		Race							
			White		Black		American Indian, Eskimo, and Aleut		Asian and Pacific Islander	
	Male	Female	Male	Female	Male	Female	Male	Female	Male	Female
2004	15.6	19.5	15.6	19.5	14.0	18.1	18.9	24.0	20.0	24.5
2005 and beyond	15.6	19.5	15.6	19.5	14.0	18.1	18.9	24.0	20.0	24.5
MIDDLE ASSUMPTION										
2000	16.4	20.0	16.5	20.1	14.4	18.5	20.1	24.9	21.1	25.2
2001	16.5	20.1	16.6	20.1	14.5	18.5	20.2	25.0	21.1	25.3
2002	16.6	20.2	16.7	20.2	14.5	18.6	20.2	25.0	21.2	25.4
2003	16.7	20.2	16.8	20.3	14.6	18.6	20.3	25.1	21.2	25.4
2004	16.7	20.3	16.9	20.4	14.6	18.7	20.3	25.2	21.3	25.5
2005	16.8	20.4	16.9	20.5	14.6	18.7	20.4	25.2	21.4	25.5
2010	17.2	20.8	17.4	20.8	14.9	18.9	20.7	25.5	21.7	25.8
2015	17.6	21.1	17.8	21.2	15.1	19.1	21.0	25.8	22.0	26.1
2020	18.0	21.5	18.2	21.6	15.3	19.3	21.4	26.1	22.3	26.4
2025	18.5	21.9	18.7	22.0	15.5	19.5	21.7	26.4	22.6	26.7
2030	18.9	22.3	19.1	22.5	15.7	19.8	22.0	26.8	23.0	27.0
2035	19.4	22.7	19.6	22.9	16.0	20.0	22.4	27.1	23.3	27.3
2040	19.8	23.2	20.1	23.3	16.2	20.2	22.7	27.4	24.0	27.7
2045	20.3	23.6	20.6	23.8	16.4	20.4	23.1	27.7	24.0	28.0
2050	20.8	24.0	21.1	24.2	16.7	20.7	23.4	28.1	24.3	28.3
HIGH ASSUMPTION										
2000	16.4	20.5	16.5	20.6	14.6	19.0	19.7	24.5	20.8	25.3
2001	16.5	20.6	16.6	20.7	14.7	19.2	19.8	24.6	20.9	25.5
2002	16.6	20.8	16.7	20.9	14.8	19.3	19.9	24.7	20.9	25.6
2003	16.7	20.9	16.8	21.0	14.9	19.4	20.0	24.9	21.0	25.7
2004	16.8	21.1	16.9	21.2	15.0	19.5	20.1	25.0	21.1	25.8
2005	16.9	21.2	17.0	21.3	15.1	19.6	20.2	25.1	21.2	25.9
2010	17.5	21.9	17.6	22.0	15.5	20.3	20.7	25.8	21.7	26.5
2015	18.1	22.7	18.2	22.8	15.9	20.9	21.2	26.5	22.2	27.1
2020	18.7	23.4	18.8	23.6	16.4	21.6	21.7	27.2	22.7	27.7
2025	19.3	24.2	19.4	24.4	16.8	22.3	22.3	28.0	23.2	28.3
2030	19.9	25.0	20.1	25.2	17.3	23.0	22.8	28.7	23.7	28.9
2035	20.6	25.9	20.8	26.0	17.8	23.7	23.4	29.5	24.2	29.6
2040	21.3	26.7	21.5	26.9	18.3	24.5	24.0	30.3	24.7	30.2
2045	22.0	27.6	22.2	27.8	18.8	25.2	24.6	31.1	25.3	30.9
2050	22.7	28.6	22.9	28.8	19.4	26.0	25.2	32.0	25.8	31.6

Source: Jennifer Cheeseman Day, U.S. Department of Commerce, Economics and Statistics Administration, Bureau of the Census, *Population Projections of the United States, by Age, Sex, Race and Hispanic Origin: 1993 to 2050* (Washington, D.C.: U.S. Government Printing Office, November 1993), Series P25-1104, p. B-2. *Notes:* Includes low, middle, and high assumptions. The 1993 to 2050 values are consistent with population totals adjusted for undercount by Demographic Analysis. Source also includes data for 1993-1999.

★ 616 ★

Vital Statistics: Birth, Fertility, Mortality, and Life Expectancy Rates

Life Expectancy at Age 65 by Race, Hispanic Origin, and Sex, 2000-2050-II

[Years]

Projections for calendar year	Life expectancy at 65									
	Hispanic origin[1]		Race							
			White		Black		American Indian, Eskimo, and Aleut		Asian and Pacific Islander	
	Male	Female	Male	Female	Male	Female	Male	Female	Male	Female
LOW ASSUMPTION										
2000	18.3	22.0	15.5	19.4	13.8	18.0	18.9	24.3	20.1	24.6
2001	18.3	22.0	15.5	19.4	13.8	18.0	18.9	24.3	20.1	24.6
2002	18.3	22.0	15.5	19.4	13.8	18.0	18.9	24.3	20.1	24.6
2003	18.3	22.0	15.5	19.4	13.8	18.0	18.9	24.3	20.1	24.6
2004	18.3	22.0	15.5	19.4	13.8	18.0	18.9	24.3	20.1	24.6
2005 and beyond	18.3	22.0	15.5	19.4	13.8	18.0	18.9	24.3	20.1	24.6
MIDDLE ASSUMPTION										
2000	19.3	22.7	16.4	20.0	14.3	18.4	20.1	25.1	21.1	25.4
2001	19.4	22.7	16.5	20.0	14.3	18.4	20.2	25.1	21.2	25.4
2002	19.4	22.8	16.6	20.1	14.4	18.5	20.3	25.2	21.3	25.5
2003	19.5	22.8	16.6	20.2	14.4	18.5	20.3	25.3	21.3	25.5
2004	19.6	22.9	16.7	20.2	14.4	18.5	20.4	25.3	21.4	25.6
2005	19.6	22.9	16.8	20.3	14.5	18.6	20.5	25.4	21.4	25.7
2010	19.9	23.2	17.2	20.7	14.7	18.7	20.8	25.7	21.8	26.0
2015	20.2	23.4	17.6	21.1	14.9	18.9	21.1	26.0	22.1	26.3
2020	20.5	23.7	18.0	21.5	15.0	19.1	21.5	26.4	22.4	26.6
2025	20.8	24.0	18.5	21.9	15.2	19.3	21.8	26.7	22.7	26.9
2030	21.1	24.2	18.9	22.3	15.4	19.5	22.1	27.0	23.0	27.2
2035	21.5	24.5	19.4	22.7	15.6	19.7	22.5	27.4	23.4	27.5
2040	21.8	24.8	19.8	23.1	15.8	19.9	22.8	27.7	23.7	27.8
2045	22.1	25.1	20.3	23.5	16.0	20.1	23.2	28.0	24.1	28.1
2050	22.5	25.3	20.8	24.0	16.2	20.3	23.6	28.4	24.4	28.4
HIGH ASSUMPTION										
2000	19.2	22.9	16.4	20.6	14.5	18.9	19.8	25.4	20.9	25.5
2001	19.2	23.0	16.5	20.7	14.6	19.0	19.9	25.6	20.9	25.7
2002	19.3	23.1	16.6	20.8	14.7	19.1	20.0	25.7	21.0	25.8
2003	19.4	23.2	16.7	21.0	14.8	19.3	20.1	25.8	21.1	25.9
2004	19.5	23.3	16.8	21.1	14.8	19.4	20.2	26.0	21.2	26.0
2005	19.6	23.4	16.9	21.3	14.9	19.5	20.3	26.1	21.3	26.1
2010	20.0	23.9	17.5	22.0	15.3	20.1	20.8	26.8	21.8	26.7
2015	20.5	24.5	18.1	22.8	15.7	20.7	21.3	27.5	22.3	27.3
2020	20.9	25.0	18.7	23.6	16.2	21.3	21.9	28.2	22.8	27.9
2025	21.4	25.6	19.3	24.4	16.6	22.0	22.5	29.0	23.3	28.5
2030	21.9	26.2	20.0	25.3	17.0	22.6	23.0	29.7	23.8	29.1
2035	22.4	26.8	20.7	26.1	17.5	23.3	23.6	30.5	24.3	29.7
2040	22.9	27.4	21.3	27.0	18.0	24.0	24.2	31.3	24.8	30.4

[Continued]

★ 616 ★

Life Expectancy at Age 65 by Race, Hispanic Origin, and Sex, 2000-2050-II

[Continued]

Projections for calendar year	Life expectancy at 65									
	Hispanic origin[1]		Race							
			White		Black		American Indian, Eskimo, and Aleut		Asian and Pacific Islander	
	Male	Female	Male	Female	Male	Female	Male	Female	Male	Female
2045	23.4	28.0	22.1	28.0	18.4	24.8	24.9	32.2	25.4	31.1
2050	23.9	28.7	22.8	29.0	18.9	25.5	25.5	33.0	25.9	31.7

Source: Jennifer Cheeseman Day, U.S. Department of Commerce, Economics and Statistics Administration, Bureau of the Census, *Population Projections of the United States, by Age, Sex, Race and Hispanic Origin: 1993 to 2050* (Washington, D.C.: U.S. Government Printing Office, November 1993), Series P25-1104, p. B-2. *Notes:* Includes low, middle, and high assumptions. The 1993 to 2050 values are consistent with population totals adjusted for undercount by Demographic Analysis. Source also includes data for 1993-1999. 1. Persons of Hispanic origin may be of any race.

★ 617 ★

Vital Statistics: Birth, Fertility, Mortality, and Life Expectancy Rates

Gap in Life Expectancy for Men and Women (Female Life Expectancy Minus Male Life Expectancy), 1950-2050

[Size of gap in years]

Year	At birth	At age 65
1950	5.50	2.25
1960	6.70	3.00
1970	7.40	3.75
1980	7.30	4.00
1990	6.80	4.50
2000	6.80	4.75
2010	6.80	4.90
2020	6.80	4.90
2030	6.80	4.90

[Continued]

★ 617 ★

Gap in Life Expectancy for Men and Women (Female Life Expectancy Minus Male Life Expectancy), 1950-2050

[Continued]

Year	At birth	At age 65
2040	6.80	5.00
2050	6.80	5.00

Source: U.S. Senate Special Committee on Aging, the American Association of Retired Persons, the Federal Council on the Aging, and the U.S. Administration on Aging, *Aging America: Trends and Projections* (Washington, D.C.: U.S. Government Printing Office, 1991), pp. 14-16. *Primary source:* U.S. Bureau of the Census, "Projections of the Population of the United States by Age, Sex, and Race: 1988 to 2080," by Gregory Spencer, *Current Population Reports* Series P-25, No. 1018 (January 1989); National Center for Health Statistics, *Health, United States, 1988* DHHS Pub. No. (PHS) 89-122, Washington: Department of Health and Human Services, March 1989; National Center for Health Statistics, "Life Tables," *Vital Statistics of the United States, 1987* Vol. II, Section 6 (February 1990). *Notes:* Life expectancy estimates (1950-1987) are taken from National Center for Health Statistics data, while life expectancy projections (1990-2050) are drawn from Census Bureau data. The use of two different data bases accounts for the slight jump in the life expectancy differential between men and women at age 65 from 1987-1990. Magnitudes estimated from published chart.

Effects of Immigration and Migration on the U.S. Population

★ 618 ★

Percent Distribution of Births, Deaths, and Net Immigration by Race and Hispanic Origin, 1 2050

"[The table below illustrates] the shifting proportional race/ethnic shares of births over the projection period. As the non-Hispanic White population decreases its share of total births, the other groups would gain. In 1995, about 63 percent of all births would be non-Hispanic White. About 1 in 6 births would be Black, and 1 in 6 would be of Hispanic origin....

"Between 1993 and 2050 the total number of annual deaths is projected to increase by 85 percent, from 2.2 million in 1993 to 4.1 million in 2050. Although life expectancy at birth would increase from 72.5 years for males to 79.7 in 2050 and from 79.3 for females to 85.6 in 2050, the increased volume of deaths is caused by the increased number of people in older ages where mortality is high.

"The crude death rate would increase steadily until the latter half of the 2040's when the rate would peak at 10.4. The crude death rate in the United States has not been this high since before 1930.

"Most of the deaths would occur to the non-Hispanic White population. Although their proportion of all deaths is projected to decrease from 82 percent to 66 percent by 2050, the non-Hispanic White population is more at risk of dying because they are the most numerous race/ethnic group and comprise a relatively high percentage of the elderly population. For similar reasons, the percentage of deaths occurring to the other groups are expected to rise as well, as these groups both age and increase their share of the population. By the middle of the next century, the increase in share of deaths from current levels increases slightly for Blacks and American Indians, increases five-fold for Asians, and triples for the Hispanic-origin population.

"Net immigration is projected to be a predominant factor in future population growth. The middle series projects 880,000 net immigrants a year composed of 322,000 Hispanics; 304,000 non-Hispanic Asians; 193,000 non-Hispanic Whites; and 61,000 non-Hispanic Blacks. In both the low and high assumptions, the Hispanic population is assumed to have the highest number of annual immigrants.

"In the middle series, 2 of every 3 people added to the population through net immigration would be Hispanic or Asian, 1 in 5 would be non-Hispanic White, and 1 in 10 would be Black.

"As natural increase declines, the compounding impact of immigration on the U.S. population growth would increase each year. In 1993, almost one-third of the population growth would be caused by net immigration. By the turn of the century, net immigration would account for over 37 percent of the post-1992 population increase. Eventually, about 86 percent of the population growth during the year 2050 may be due to post-1992 net immigration."

[Percent distribution]

Year	Total	Race				Hispanic origin[3]	Not of Hispanic origin, by race			
		White	Black	American Indian[1]	Asian[2]		White	Black	American Indian[1]	Asian[2]
BIRTHS										
Middle Series										
1995	100.0	77.7	17.0	1.0	4.2	15.9	63.2	16.1	0.8	3.9
2000	100.0	76.1	17.7	1.1	5.2	17.5	60.1	16.6	0.9	4.8
2005	100.0	74.8	18.1	1.2	6.0	19.0	57.5	17.0	1.0	5.5
2010	100.0	73.8	18.5	1.2	6.5	20.3	55.4	17.3	1.0	6.0
2020	100.0	72.3	18.9	1.2	7.6	22.9	51.6	17.5	1.0	7.0
2030	100.0	70.0	19.9	1.3	8.9	25.5	46.8	18.3	1.1	8.2
2040	100.0	68.5	20.5	1.4	9.6	27.6	43.5	18.8	1.2	8.8
2050	100.0	67.1	21.2	1.4	10.3	29.4	40.5	19.4	1.3	9.4
Lowest Series										
2050	100.0	71.5	17.7	1.3	9.4	27.7	46.2	16.2	1.1	8.8

[Continued]

★ 618 ★

Percent Distribution of Births, Deaths, and Net Immigration by Race and Hispanic Origin, 1995-2050

[Continued]

Year	Total	Race				Hispanic origin[3]	Not of Hispanic origin, by race			
		White	Black	American Indian[1]	Asian[2]		White	Black	American Indian[1]	Asian[2]
Highest Series										
2050	100.0	69.1	18.0	1.2	11.8	33.6	38.8	15.9	1.0	10.8
DEATHS										
Middle Series										
1995	100.0	85.6	12.8	0.5	1.2	4.5	81.4	12.6	0.4	1.1
2000	100.0	84.7	13.3	0.5	1.5	5.3	79.8	13.0	0.4	1.4
2005	100.0	84.1	13.5	0.5	1.9	6.0	78.6	13.2	0.4	1.8
2010	100.0	83.4	13.7	0.5	2.4	6.7	77.2	13.3	0.5	2.2
2020	100.0	81.6	14.4	0.6	3.3	8.3	74.0	14.0	0.6	3.2
2030	100.0	80.3	14.8	0.7	4.2	9.8	71.4	14.2	0.6	4.0
2040	100.0	79.5	14.7	0.7	5.1	11.4	69.1	14.1	0.6	4.8
2050	100.0	78.3	14.9	0.7	6.1	13.5	66.0	14.1	0.6	5.8
Lowest Series										
2050	100.0	79.2	14.8	0.8	5.2	13.3	67.0	14.0	0.7	5.0
Highest Series										
2050	100.0	78.8	13.6	0.7	6.9	14.3	65.8	12.8	0.6	6.5
NET IMMIGRATION										
Middle Series										
1993-2005	100.0	54.8	9.2	0.0	36.0	36.6	21.9	6.9	0.0	34.5
Lowest Series										
1995-2050	100.0	40.1	7.7	0.0	52.1	40.3	2.9	6.0	0.0	50.9
Highest Series										
1995-2050	100.0	57.9	9.5	0.0	32.7	36.2	25.6	7.1	0.0	31.2

Source: Jennifer Cheeseman Day, U.S. Department of Commerce, Economics and Statistics Administration, Bureau of the Census, *Population Projections of the United States, by Age, Sex, Race and Hispanic Origin: 1993 to 2050* (Washington, D.C.: U.S. Government Printing Office, November 1993), Series P25-1104, pp. xxx-xxxi. *Notes:* 1. American Indian represents American Indian, Eskimo, and Aleut. 2. Asian represents Asian and Pacific Islander. 3. Persons of Hispanic origin may be of any race.

★ 619 ★

Effects of Immigration and Migration on the U.S. Population

Post-1970 Immigrant Growth, 1970-2050

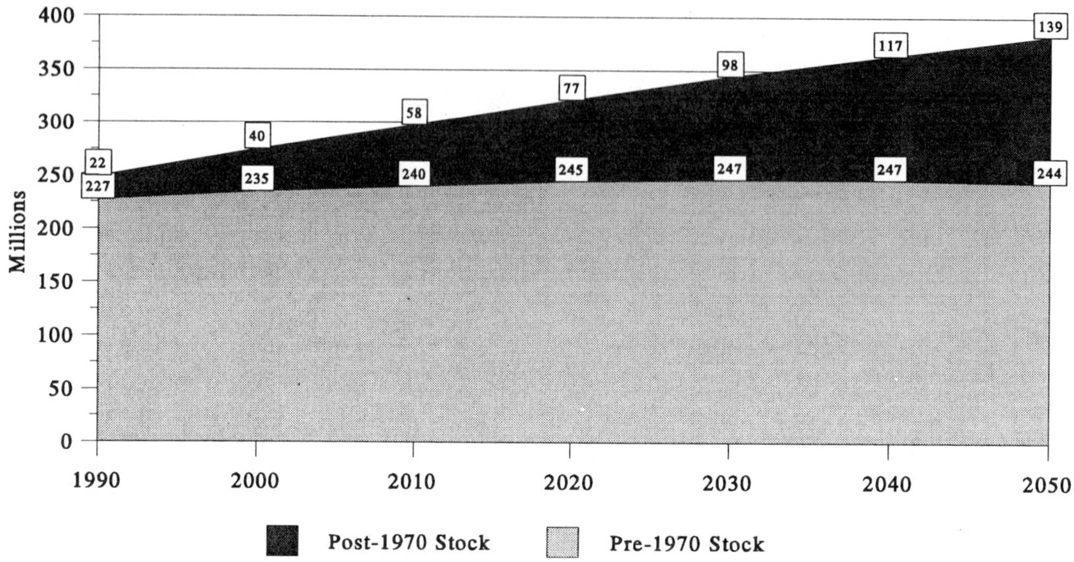

"Dr. Bouvier [former vice-president of the Population Reference Bureau] projects that post-1970 immigrants and *all* their descendants contributed 25 million people to the population between 1970 and 1990, and will make up about two-thirds of U.S. population growth during the 1990s. Thereafter, they will supply virtually all of the population growth, since pre-1970 Americans and their descendants will have achieved relative population stability.

"By 2050, the Census Bureau estimates the U.S. population will reach 383 million. By Dr. Bouvier's count, at the point more than a third (36 per cent) of the population will be post-1970 immigrants and their descendants—a staggering 139 million people."

[In millions]

Year	Total Population	Pre-1970 Stock	Post-1970 Stock
1970	203	203	-
1980	227	214	13
1990	249	227	22
2000	275	235	40
2010	298	240	58
2020	322	245	77
2030	345	247	98
2040	364	247	117
2050	383	244	139

Source: Peter Brimelow and Joseph E. Fallon, "Controlling Our Demographic Destiny," in *National Review*, 21 February 1994, p. 42. *Primary source:* Leon Bouvier, Urban Institute.

★ 620 ★

Effects of Immigration and Migration on the U.S. Population

Net Immigration as a Percentage of U.S. Population Growth, 1901-2040

"After 2050, Americans of European descent, who were 89 per cent of the U.S. population in 1960, will be a minority of less than 50 per cent, according to the estimates of Leon Bouvier, former vice president of the Population Reference Bureau and a leading authority on immigration. But there is nothing natural or inevitable about this' demographic revolution. It is essentially a result of U.S. Government policies after 1965 that had the effect of decreasing immigration from Europe and increasing immigration from the Third World."

[Percent]

Year	Net immigration as % of Population Growth
1901-1920	28%
1911-1920	15%
1921-1930	17%
1931-1940	net emigration
1941-1950	10%
1951-1960	9%
1961-1970	11%
1971-1980	33%
1981-1990	37%
1991-2000	35%
2001-2010	41%
2011-2020	45%
2021-2030	53%
2031-2040	63%

Source: Peter Brimelow and Joseph E. Fallon, "Controlling Our Demographic Destiny," in *National Review*, 21 February 1994, p. 42. *Primary source:* Leon Bouvier, Urban Institute.

★ 621 ★

Effects of Immigration and Migration on the U.S. Population

Elderly Inmigrants, Outmigrants, and Net Migrants 65+: Alabama Projection Study, 1985-2025

"Increasing numbers of elderly people are choosing to relocate. Indeed, the attraction of elderly migrants has been called the 'growth industry' of the 1990s. These migrants often bring with them substantial monetary assets and thus they may provide a boon to the local economy. Elderly migrants are viewed as a stimulus to local services, they enhance the tax base and provide a pool of volunteers with a wide range of expertise. Yet, some planners and policy makers fear the retiree migrants drive up housing prices and demands for a wide range of community services. As they become more frail, they may also place increased demands on local health care resources and social services. Reaction to social changes resulting from elderly immigrants may also fuel what has been termed a 'gray peril' mentality."

[People aged 65 and older]

Projection Year	Total	Study Area		Morgan	Contiguous
		Madison	Marshall		
Immigrants 65+					
1985	4037	1818	1023	1196	2665
1990	4528	2039	1147	1342	3047
1995	4958	2233	1256	1469	3393
2000	5186	2335	1314	1537	3608
2005	5236	2357	1327	1551	3578
2010	4241	2365	1331	1556	3739
2015	5597	2520	1418	1658	4023
2020	6211	2797	1574	1840	4474
2025	6856	3087	1737	2031	4944
Outmigrants 65+					
1985	1534	742	347	446	2434
1990	2064	998	466	600	2786
1995	2555	1236	577	742	3129
2000	2996	1449	677	870	3292
2005	3306	1599	747	960	3428
2010	3536	1710	799	1027	3473
2015	3907	1889	883	1135	3963
2020	4278	2069	966	1243	4067
2025	4724	2285	1067	1372	4507
Net Migrants 65+					
1985	2503	1076	676	751	231
1990	2464	1041	681	742	261
1995	2403	997	679	727	264
2000	2190	886	637	666	316
2005	1929	759	580	591	250
2010	1715	655	532	529	266
2015	1690	631	536	523	330

[Continued]

★ 621 ★

Elderly Inmigrants, Outmigrants, and Net Migrants 65+: Alabama Projection Study, 1985-2025

[Continued]

Projection Year	Total	Study Area		Morgan	Contiguous
		Madison	Marshall		
2020	1933	728	607	598	407
2025	2132	803	670	659	437

Source: Graham D. Rowles, et al, *Impact of Migration of the Elderly*, Final report to the Appalachian Regional Commission (March 1992), pp. i, 131.

★ 622 ★

Effects of Immigration and Migration on the U.S. Population

Migrant Population and Annual Elderly Growth Rate: Pennsylvania Case Study, 1980-2005

	Nation	Study	Contiguous
1980			
Total	226,545,800	87,680	1,410,233
65+	25,549,430	11,946	190,520
75+	9,968,822	4,173	68,716
M. Age	34.0183	35.592	35.9982
1985			
Total	234,693,900	101,598	1,452,878
65+	28,365,100	14,443	210,368
75+	11,706,850	5,230	79,391
M. Age	34.7981	37.1292	36.5306
R 65+ (%)	2.0909	3.7963	1.9820
R 75+ (%)	3.2142	4.5155	2.8881
1990			
Total	241,564,500	113,878	1,493,624
65+	30,841,770	17,422	223,316
75+	13,209,420	6,483	92,147
M. Age	35.4842	37.8085	36.9528
R 65+ (%)	1.6742	3.7505	1.1946
R 75+ (%)	2.4151	4.2954	2.9800
1995			
Total	246,588,700	124,261	1,525,635
65+	32,173,520	19,380	227,347
75+	14,298,940	7,506	100,067
M. Age	36.2478	38.5905	37.4005
R 65+ (%)	0.8455	2.1302	0.3578
R 75+ (%)	1.5851	2.9304	1.6491

[Continued]

★ 622 ★

Migrant Population and Annual Elderly Growth Rate: Pennsylvania Case Study, 1980-2005

[Continued]

	Nation	Study	Contiguous
2000			
Total	249,855,200	132,971	1,546,647
65+	32,165,310	20,131	217,703
75+	15,349,050	8,8114	103,646
M. Age	37.0915	39.536	37.9631
R 65+ (%)	-0.0051	-0.7604	-0.8669
R 75+ (%)	1.4174	3.2128	0.7028
2005			
Total	251,975,000	140,259	1,559,472
65+	32,057,140	20,912	209,143
75+	15,601,210	9,408	101,967
M. Age	37.914	40.556	38.5849
R 65+ (%)	-0.0674	-0.7612	-0.8023
R 75+ (%)	0.3259	1.3044	-0.3266

Source: Graham D. Rowles, et al, *Impact of Migration of the Elderly*, Final report to the Appalachian Regional Commission (March 1992), p. 145.

Population Projections for Selected States

★ 623 ★

Population and Other Selected Variables: Delaware, 1990-2020

"All of the projections have been rounded to the nearest 50. This should in no way be interpreted as a measure of statistical accuracy. Further, this rounding may produce differences between the sum of a table and the printed totals. The total is the rounded sum of the column; not the sum of the rounded entries of the column."

	1990	1995	2000	2005	2010	2015	2020
Population	666,168	701,750	731,050	757,800	782,700	808,150	832,850
Labor Force		380,200	396,850	414,100	429,000	438,300	441,550
Employed Persons		359,300	375,050	391,350	405,400	414,200	417,300
Jobs		380,850	397,550	414,800	429,750	439,050	442,300
Self-employed		28,000	29,200	30,200	31,000	32,000	33,000
Agricult. emp.		6,800	6,600	6,400	6,200	6,000	5,800
Resident Jobs		346,050	361,750	378,200	392,550	401,050	403,500
Births		52,500	49,200	48,300	48,300	50,700	52,950
Deaths		31,900	35,000	36,750	38,550	40,400	42,750
Net Migrants		15,000	15,100	15,200	15,150	15,100	14,550
Households		270,200	284,450	298,800	314,700	331,950	347,650
Net New Units		17,300	14,250	14,350	15,900	17,250	15,700

[Continued]

★ 623 ★

Population and Other Selected Variables: Delaware, 1990-2020

[Continued]

	1990	1995	2000	2005	2010	2015	2020
Proj. Employment		364,500	381,200	398,200	413,000	422,000	425,000
Net Commuting		18,500	19,500	20,000	20,500	21,000	21,500
Resident Emp.		346,000	361,700	378,200	392,500	401,000	403,500

Source: Delaware Population Consortium: Population Projections (Dover, Delaware: University of Delaware, January 1993), Version 1992.0, pp. 7-8.

★ 624 ★

Population Projections for Selected States

Numbers and Percentages of Persons by Age Group: Ohio, 1990-2015

"The age groups from 25-29 years up through 60-64 years all show similar patterns for the future. Each group will first increase as the baby boom generation swells its size, then decline sharply with the subsequent replacement of this group by the smaller cohorts born in the 1970's. None subsequently will return to the size reached when it contained the birth cohorts of 1955 to 1964.

"One way to examine the aging of the population is to focus on those age 65 and older. The 65 and over group has grown by 20.3 percent in the last 10 years—1,169,500 in 1980 and 1,407,000 in 1990. These cohorts made up 10.8 percent of the total population in 1980, and 13.0 percent in 1990. The percentage of the entire population that is 65 years and older will be 13.7 by 2015. These numbers will increase by 203,500 from 1990 to 2015.

"The population age 85 and over is projected to grow also, one result of the very old benefiting from health maintenance care improvements. The percentage of this group in the total population was 1.27 in 1990 and is projected to rise to 1.60 in 2015. The actual number was 138,000 in 1990 and is projected to be 188,100 in 2015.

"Even as the overall population becomes older, so will the elderly population itself become older. At present, 9.81 percent of those in the 65 and over age group are 85 and over. This percentage will grow steadily to 11.7 in 2015."

Year	Age 0-14	Age 15-64	Age 65 and over	Age 85 and over	Age 5-14	Age 0-14	Age 15-64	Age 65 and over	Age 85 and over	Age 85+ /65+
1990	2,347,000	7,093,100	1,406,900	138,000	1,561,900	21.64%	65.39%	12.97%	1.27%	9.8%
1995	2,383,400	7,196,300	1,465,300	147,500	1,567,800	21.58%	65.15%	13.27%	1.34%	10.1%
2000	2,390,600	7,351,600	1,446,200	165,100	1,595,700	21.37%	65.71%	12.93%	1.48%	11.4%
2005	2,392,000	7,526,900	1,426,400	172,800	1,603,300	20.08%	66.34%	12.57%	1.52%	12.1%
2010	2,398,000	7,666,800	1,457,000	188,500	1,586,700	20.81%	66.54%	12.65%	1.64%	12.9%
2015	2,443,900	7,699,200	1,620,400	188,100	1,603,500	20.79%	65.51%	13.70%	1.60%	11.7%

Source: Ohio Data Users Center, Ohio Department of Development, *Population Projections: Ohio and Counties by Age and Sex: 1990 to 2015* (Columbus, Ohio: January 1993), pp. 5-6. *Primary source:* Ohio Data Users Center, The Ohio Department of Development, Columbus, Ohio, 1993.

★ 625 ★

Population Projections for Selected States

Total Population by Age and County: Maine, 1988-1998

Age	1988 Estimated Population	1991	1992	1993	1994	1995	1996	1997	1998
All ages	1,205,620	1,252,413	1,259,036	1,269,443	1,283,956	1,291,144	1,299,596	1,306,608	1,321,392
Under 5 years	86,230	89,752	89,366	89,791	90,125	89,911	88,543	88,450	88,090
5-9 Years	86,392	91,460	91,319	91,724	92,513	92,518	92,871	93,028	93,455
10-14 Years	81,548	88,487	88,932	89,491	89,596	89,771	89,635	89,241	89,569
15-17 Years	55,164	49,080	50,065	50,743	52,202	52,322	52,836	52,869	53,155
18-19 Years	41,943	38,794	37,214	36,321	36,130	36,312	36,959	37,602	38,957
20-24 Years	107,795	103,403	101,907	100,468	98,710	95,364	92,379	90,654	90,924
25-34 Years	180,780	192,345	192,348	192,025	192,159	191,011	189,558	186,107	183,034
35-44 Years	169,332	186,308	187,310	189,361	193,367	196,587	200,977	205,177	210,896
45-64 Years	227,463	236,143	241,644	248,370	256,145	262,538	269,098	275,320	284,165
65-74 Years	95,057	98,560	99,564	100,520	101,271	101,983	102,759	103,249	103,495
75-84 Years	55,725	58,309	59,090	59,836	60,471	61,087	61,747	62,240	62,583
85 & Over Years	18,191	19,772	20,277	20,793	21,267	21,740	22,234	22,671	23,068

Source: Maine Department of Human Services, Office of Data, Research, and Vital Statistics, *Maine Population Projections: 1989-1998, by Minor Civil Divisions, Sex, Age Group and County* (Augusta, Maine: April 1991), p. 39. *Note:* Source also includes data for 1989 and 1990.

★ 626 ★

Population Projections for Selected States

Life Expectancies: North Carolina, 1950-2020

"Between April 1990 and April 2000, North Carolina's population is expected to grow by roughly 3/4 of a million people (11.2 percent), increasing from 6,628,637 to 7,373,000 by the end of the decade. Almost half of this growth, some 348,000 people, will be the result of net migration into the state. The rest will be due to natural increase...

"Life expectancy at birth will continue to increase for all race-sex groups. For white males, life expectancy will increase by about 1.5 years, increasing from 71.8 in 1990 to 73.3 in the year 2000. White females show a somewhat smaller increase, 1.2 years, with life expectancy going from 79.7 in 1990 to 80.9 in the year 2000. Life expectancy for nonwhite males will increase by roughly twice as much, 2.8 years, during this decade, going from 65.7 in 1990 to 68.5 in the year 2000. Life expectancy for nonwhite females will increase by 2.1 years, going from 74.7 in 1990 to 76.8 in the year 2000."

[Years]

Year	White Male	White Female	Other Male	Other Female
1950	66.527	72.891	58.460	62.832
1960	66.936	74.744	59.095	65.330
1970	66.756	75.706	58.820	67.805
1980	70.015	78.533	63.663	73.582

[Continued]

★ 626 ★

Life Expectancies: North Carolina, 1950-2020

[Continued]

Year	White Male	White Female	Other Male	Other Female
1990	71.810	79.687	65.727	74.707
2000	73.327	80.936	68.491	76.842
2010	74.259	81.758	70.311	78.347
2020	74.756	82.172	71.512	79.348

Source: North Carolina Office of State Planning, *North Carolina Population Projections, 1991-2020* (Raleigh, North Carolina: Office of State Planning, July 1992), pp. 1, 4.

★ 627 ★

Population Projections for Selected States

Population of Metropolitan Areas: Oklahoma, 1990-2020

[Years]

	1990	1995	2000	2005	2010	2015	2020
State Total	3,145,585	3,299,150	3,426,000	3,532,150	3,619,850	2,681,900	3,717,500
Metro Areas:	1,869,842	1,975,100	2,061,850	2,135,950	2,195,650	2,236,400	2,259,450
Enid MA	56,735	58,900	60,750	62,450	63,850	64,800	65,150
Ft. Smith, MA (Oklahoma portion)	33,828	35,450	36,850	38,050	38,950	39,500	39,750
Lawton, MA	111,486	119,850	127,100	134,100	140,650	146,300	150,500
Oklahoma City, MA	958,839	1,010,600	1,052,700	1,087,350	1,113,900	1,130,100	1,139,700
Tulsa, MA	708,954	750,350	784,500	814,000	838,300	855,700	864,350
Non-Metro Areas:	1,275,743	1,324,050	1,364,150	1,396,200	1,424,200	1,445,500	1,458,050

Source: Oklahoma Department of Commerce, *Population Projections for Oklahoma: 1990-2020* (Oklahoma City, Oklahoma: Oklahoma Department of Commerce, April 1993), p. 6. *Notes:* MA=Metropolitan Area. Enid=Garfield County; Ft. Smith=Sequoyah County; Lawton=Comanche County; Oklahoma City=Canadian, Cleveland, Logan, McClain, Oklahoma, and Pottawatomie Counties; Tulsa=Creek Osage, Rogers, Tulsa, and Wagoner Counties.

★ 628 ★

Population Projections for Selected States

Population by Five Year Age Group: Utah, 1980-2020

Age	1980	1990	1995	2000	2005	2010	2015	2020
0-4	189,962	169,633	180,057	194,027	214,011	230,430	237,404	243,132
5-9	146,187	183,674	169,283	177,220	195,399	219,018	232,728	238,428
10-14	125,681	183,846	175,231	164,555	176,317	197,733	218,907	231,507
15-19	138,903	152,455	182,521	169,473	163,330	177,338	194,709	213,104
20-24	155,676	137,822	155,320	182,070	176,245	174,839	183,142	197,753

[Continued]

★ 628 ★

Population by Five Year Age Group: Utah, 1980-2020

[Continued]

Age	1980	1990	1995	2000	2005	2010	2015	2020
25-29	135,087	137,321	147,771	152,533	188,883	189,718	182,945	190,243
30-34	105,688	137,577	130,770	140,480	151,540	194,256	190,668	182,016
35-39	79,178	124,209	136,781	127,522	141,594	156,620	195,903	191,137
40-44	63,628	100,463	128,384	135,089	129,860	146,931	158,512	195,695
45-49	57,021	77,148	106,460	126,429	136,119	133,950	148,094	158,562
50-54	55,845	61,333	81,595	104,552	126,110	138,216	134,102	147,199
55-59	52,701	54,930	62,783	79,203	102,989	125,997	136,419	131,829
60-64	46,260	52,481	53,443	59,994	76,716	101,151	122,179	131,763
65-69	38,183	48,676	49,872	50,566	57,377	74,026	96,324	115,695
70-74	29,637	39,511	45,177	45,413	46,541	53,281	67,789	87,546
75-79	20,242	29,266	34,778	38,198	38,781	40,188	45,515	57,529
80-84	12,306	18,894	22,856	25,988	28,775	29,517	30,280	34,158
85+	8,852	13,611	16,219	18,736	21,661	24,634	25,899	26,723
Total	1,461,037	1,722,850	1,879,301	1,992,048	2,172,248	2,407,843	2,601,519	2,774,019
Median	23	25	26	27	28	29	30	31

Source: Demographic and Economic Analysis, Utah Office of Planning and Budget, *State of Utah: Economic and Demographic Projections 1992* (Salt Lake City, Utah: May 1992), p. 27. *Notes:* 1980 and 1990 populations are April 1 census populations; all others are July 1 populations.

★ 629 ★

Population Projections for Selected States

Metropolitan Area Populations: Virginia, 1980-2010

[Years]

	1980	1990	1995	2000	2010
VIRGINIA TOTAL	5,346,818	6,189,314	6,551,559	6,896,557	7,451,158
Charlottesville MSA	113,568	131,373	139,635	147,504	162,786
Danville MSA	111,789	108,728	108,348	107,986	107,313
Virginia Portion of Johnson City-Kingsport-Bristol (TN-VA) MSA	90,597	87,517	86,569	85,668	84,240
Lynchburg MSA	182,207	193,928	199,866	205,524	215,322
Virginia Portion of Norfolk-Virginia Beach-Newport News (VA-NC) MSA	1,189,909	1,431,095	1,525,546	1,615,499	1,782,925
Richmond-Petersburg MSA	761,311	865,640	916,590	965,115	1,057,901
Roanoke MSA	220,393	224,589	225,701	226,759	228,290

[Continued]

★ 629 ★

Metropolitan Area Populations: Virginia, 1980-2010

[Continued]

	1980	1990	1995	2000	2010
Virginia Portion of Washington (DC-MD-VA-WV) PMSA	1,296,158	1,732,436	1,912,731	2,084,442	2,315,396
Total MAs	3,965,932	4,775,306	5,114,986	5,438,497	5,954,173
Percent of State	74.2	77.2	78.1	78.9	79.9
Remainder of State	1,380,886	1,414,008	1,436,573	1,458,060	1,496,985
Percent of State	25.8	22.8	21.9	21.1	20.1

Source: Virginia Employment Commission, Economic Information Services Division, *Virginia: Population Projections, 2010* (Virginia). *Note:* MSA = Metropolitan Statistical Area.

★ 630 ★

Population Projections for Selected States

Population in Three Broad Age Groups: Wisconsin, 1990-2020

"Strong population growth is projected for Wisconsin in the 1990s. An increase of nearly five percent is forecast for the first half of the decade.

"Wisconsin's population in 2020 is projected at 5.7 million, 800,000 more than the 1990 census count of 4.9 million.

"Wisconsin's working-age population (age 18 to 64) will peak in 2015 at 3.5 million, an increase of 522,000 from 1990.

"Population growth in the state is expected to slow in the 2010-2020 period. The state will add only 165,000 persons in that decade.

"The number of births in Wisconsin will remain relatively stable over the 30-year projection period, but the volume of deaths will increase substantially due to the aging population. As a result, natural increase, the excess of births over deaths, will fall steadily from about 134,000 in the first half of the 1990s to 64,000 in the 2015-2020 period."

[Millions]

Year	0 to 17	18 to 64	65+	Total
1990	1.30	2.95	.75	4.95
1995	1.40	3.00	.70	5.10
2000	1.40	3.15	.75	5.30
2005	1.35	3.35	.70	5.40
2010	1.30	3.50	.75	5.55
2015	1.30	3.45	.90	5.65
2020	1.35	3.35	1.00	5.70

Source: Demographic Services Center, Wisconsin Department of Administration, *Official Population Projections: 1990-2020* (Madison, Wisconsin: June 1993), p. 7.

World Population Statistics

★ 631 ★

Trends in World Population Growth, 1991-2020

Forecasters Cetron and Davies project the following trends in world and U.S. population:

"In the industrialized countries, the 'birth dearth' has cut growth almost to nothing, while in the developing world, the population bomb is still exploding.

—The rich get richer, the poor have children: Throughout the industrialized world, workers can look forward to national retirement programs or social security. In the developing lands, those too old for labor rely on their children to support them—so they have as many as they can.

—Thanks to better health care, children have a greater chance to survive into adulthood and produce children of their own. This will tend to accelerate population growth, but contraceptive use is increasing, with an opposite effect on growth.

—In the developed world, the vast Baby Boom generation is approaching middle age, threatening to overwhelm both medical and social security programs. These costs will consume an increasing portion of national budgets until about 2020.

"The AIDS epidemic will slaughter millions of people worldwide, especially in Africa.

—According to the World Health Organization, the AIDS-causing human immunodeficiency virus will have infected up to 40 million people by 2000.

—By 1990, some 5 million people in sub-Saharan Africa already carried the disease—twice as many as just three years earlier. In some cities, as much as 40% of the population may be infected.

"A host of new medical technologies will make life longer and more comfortable in the industrialized world. It will be many years before these advances spread to the developing countries.

"As the West grows ever more concerned with physical culture and personal health, developing countries are adopting the unhealthy practices that wealthier nations are trying to cast off: smoking, high-fat diets, and sedentary lifestyles. To those emerging from poverty, these deadly luxuries are symbols of success.

—In the United States, smokers are kicking the habit. Only 35% of American men smoke, down from 52% twenty years ago; 29% of women smoke, down from a peak of 34%.

[Continued]

★ 631 ★

Trends in World Population Growth, 1991-2020

[Continued]

—However, the developing world continues to smoke more each year. Even Europe shows little sign of solving this problem.

"Better nutrition and the 'wellness' movement will raise life expectancies.

—In developed countries, children born in the 1980s will live to an average age of 70 for males, 77 for females. In developing countries, the average life expectancies will remain stalled at 59 years for males and 61 for females."

Source: Marvin J. Cetron and Owen Davies, "50 Trends Shaping the World," in *The Futurist*, September-October 1991, pp. 12-13. *Primary source:* Cetron and Davies, *Crystal Globe: The Haves and Have-nots of the New World Order* (St. Martin's Press, 1991).

★ 632 ★

World Population Statistics

World Population Growth Rate, 1993-2010

"The 1993 edition of PRB's *World Population Data Sheet* now shows a world population growth rate of 1.63 percent, down from 1.68 on last year's edition. This marks the lowest world growth rate recorded since PRB's first edition of the annual wallchart in 1962. Total world population is still growing rapidly, however, as evidenced by another benchmark: 1993's world population total is 5.5 billion people—rapidly approaching the 6 billion mark expected by about 1997 or 1998. PRB now estimates that the world population is growing by 90 million annually."

[Thousands]

Country/region (world rank)	Population 1993	Projected pop. change 1993-2010	Annual births	Annual deaths	Annual natural increase
World	5,505,914,000	1,535,472	141,226	51,192	90,034
More developed	1,230,101,000	86,795	16,898	11,632	5,267
Less developed	4,275,813,000	1,448,677	124,327	39,560	84,767
Less developed (excluding China)	3,097,287,000	1,229,390	102,831	31,782	71,049
Africa	676,684,000	404,508	28,952	9,219	19,733
Sub-Saharan Africa	549,522,000	352,384	24,923	8,280	16,643
Northern Africa	154,569,000	67,762	5,257	1,309	3,948
Western Africa	187,534,000	127,471	8,680	2,914	5,765
Nigeria (10)	95,060,000	66,909	4,259	1,340	2,918
Eastern Africa	213,949,000	142,001	9,946	3,454	6,492
Middle Africa	75,984,000	47,151	3,515	1,173	2,341
Southern Africa	44,648,000	20,123	1,555	368	1,186
Asia	3,257,181,000	918,132	84,394	27,986	56,408
Asia (excl. China)	2,078,655,000	698,845	62,897	20,208	42,690
Western Asia	144,339,000	79,250	5,230	1,180	4,050
Southern Asia	1,253,157,000	463,474	42,046	13,768	28,278
India (2)	897,443,000	268,750	27,641	9,244	18,398
Pakistan (8)	122,398,000	68,322	5,349	1,616	3,733

[Continued]

★ 632 ★

World Population Growth Rate, 1993-2010

[Continued]

Country/region (world rank)	Population 1993	Projected pop. change 1993-2010	Annual births	Annual deaths	Annual natural increase
Bangladesh (9)	113,882,000	50,904	4,157	1,469	2,688
Southeast Asia	459,770,000	132,904	12,660	3,881	8,779
Indonesia (4)	187,638,000	51,192	4,804	1,689	3,115
East Asia	1,399,915,000	242,504	24,458	9,158	15,300
China (1)	1,178,526,000	219,287	21,496	7,778	13,718
Japan (7)	124,767,000	5,630	1,235	836	399
North America	286,591,000	44,853	4,563	2,399	2,164
United States (3)	258,328,000	40,281	4,133	2,196	1,937
Latin America	460,225,000	128,978	12,003	3,128	8,874
Central America	120,851,000	43,772	3,693	726	2,967
Caribbean	34,714,000	8,078	874	282	592
South America	304,660,000	77,128	7,436	2,120	5,316
Brazil (5)	151,989,000	33,624	3,455	1,125	2,310
Europe	512,717,000	10,124	6,169	5,239	929
Northern Europe	93,404,000	3,556	1,287	1,033	254
Western Europe	179,407,000	669	2,096	1,813	283
Eastern Europe	96,591,000	4,728	1,223	1,084	139
Southern Europe	143,315,000	1,171	1,564	1,309	254
Russia (6)	149,001,000	4,033	1,803	1,699	104
Oceania	27,691,000	6,307	537	217	320

Source: Carl Haub, "China's Fertility Drop Lowers World Growth Rate," in *Population Today*, June 1993, pp. 1, 10. *Primary source:* PRB's 1993 World Population Data Sheet. *Note:* PRB = Population Reference Bureau.

★ 633 ★

World Population Statistics

World Population Growth, 7000 B.C.-2025 A.D.

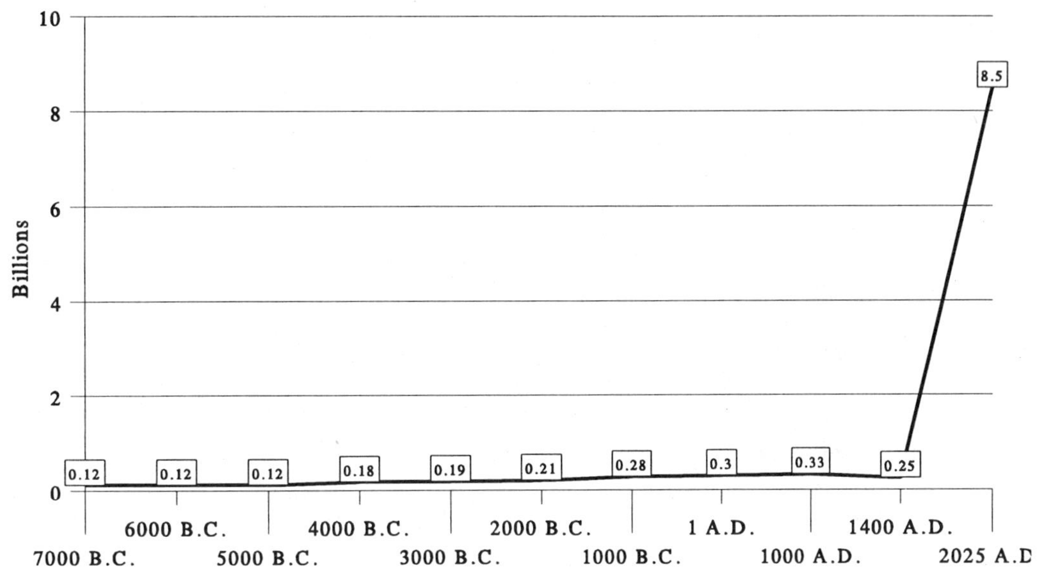

"Thomas Merrick, president of [Population Reference Bureau (PRB)], in his 1989 monograph, "World Population in Transition," identifies two periods of major population growth: 1750 to 1950 and 1950 to the present. Until 1750, the birth rate was high everywhere, but so was the death rate, due to generally poor health and nutrition, famines, epidemics, and wars—perhaps roughly in line with [Thomas] Malthus's theory. Even so, the world population reached about 760 million in 1750.

"After 1750, most relatively developed countries sooner or later began to experience a so-called *demographic transition*, at which time the death rate dropped sharply as a result of improved medical, social, and economic conditions. Meanwhile, the birth rate declined less rapidly as living standards improved. So during that period the population increased substantially. By the end of this transition, the population in most developed countries had leveled off or was growing only very slowly, as the declining birth rate caught up with the declining death rate. In the meantime the world population grew to 2.5 billion by 1950, due in part to the growth in the developed nations. Between 1950 and the mid-1980s the world population doubled to five billion, largely as a result of the surge in the growth rates in the less developed and underdeveloped countries of Asia, Africa, and Latin America."

[Billions]

New Stone Age	
7000 B.C.	.12
6000 B.C.	.12
5000 B.C.	.12
4000 B.C.	.18

[Continued]

★ 633 ★

World Population Growth, 7000 B.C.-2025 A.D.

[Continued]

Bronze Age	
3000 B.C.	.19
2000 B.C.	.21
Iron Age	
1000 B.C.	.28
1 A.D.	.30
Middle Ages	
1000 A.D.	.33
1400 A.D. (The Black Death)	.25
Modern Age	
2025 A.D.	8.50

Source: Walter J. Karplus, *The Heavens Are Falling: The Scientific Predictions of Catastrophes in Our Time* (New York: Plenum Press), 1992, pp. 216-217. *Primary source:* Population Reference Bureau, Inc.

★ 634 ★

World Population Statistics

World Population and Average Annual Rates of Growth by Region and Development Category, 1950-2020

"Estimated at 1.65 billion in 1990, the world population is now expected to be about 6.3 billion at the next turn of the century. With an estimated 5.4 billion at midyear 1991, it has more than doubled since 1950. Another 95 million persons, more than the current population of Mexico, are added each year. By the period 2015 to 2020, about 100 million will be added annually, bringing the 2020 population of the world to about 8.2 billion.

"Ten countries now have over 100 million inhabitants, led by China with nearly 1.2 billion or more than one-fifth of the world's people. The United States ranks fourth in size, with a quarter of a billion people.

"Sub-Saharan Africa is the only region whose population is growing faster than 3 percent annually. Its growth is equivalent to adding another Ghana each year. Growth rates in other regions have stabilized or have begun to decline. By the period 2010 to 2020, according to the latest projections, the population growth rate will have declined to about 2.6 percent in Sub-Saharan Africa; and that of Near East and North Africa, which is currently about 2.7 percent, will have declined to 2.1 percent annually. By that same period, the growth rate in both Asia (excluding Japan) and Latin America and the Caribbean is projected to reach about 1.2 percent per year. Due to its low level of fertility and aging population, Japan's growth rate is likely to become negative (that is, the population itself will begin to get smaller) during the period 2010 to 2020."

[Midyear population in millions]

Region	1950	1960	1970	1980	1990	1991	2000	2010	2020
World	2,564	3,050	3,722	4,478	5,329	5,423	6,285	7,240	8,233
Developing	1,732	2,105	2,672	3,341	4,117	4,203	5,008	5,913	6,874
Developed	832	945	1,049	1,137	1,213	1,219	1,276	1,327	1,360
Sub-Saharan Africa	193	238	305	402	541	558	736	984	1,279
Near East and North America	87	112	144	190	252	259	327	412	506
Asia	1,368	1,628	2,038	2,497	2,992	3,046	3,528	4,015	4,500
Developing	1,284	1,533	1,933	2,380	2,868	2,922	3,400	3,885	4,373
Developed	84	94	104	117	124	124	128	130	128
Latin America and the Caribbean	166	218	286	364	449	458	537	624	705
North America	166	199	226	252	277	279	298	314	328
Europe	392	425	460	484	501	502	516	523	522
Soviet Union	180	214	243	266	291	293	312	334	355
Oceania	12	16	19	23	27	27	31	35	38
Developing	2	3	4	5	6	6	8	9	11
Developed	10	13	15	18	20	21	23	25	27
Excluding China									
World	2,002	2,399	2,901	3,495	4,196	4,271	4,981	5,820	6,692
Developing	1,169	1,454	1,852	2,358	2,983	3,052	3,705	4,493	5,332

[Continued]

★ 634 ★

World Population and Average Annual Rates of Growth by Region and Development Category, 1950-2020

[Continued]

Region	1950	1960	1970	1980	1990	1991	2000	2010	2020
Asia	805	977	1,217	1,514	1,858	1,894	2,225	2,595	2,959
Developing	721	883	1,113	1,397	1,735	1,770	2,097	2,464	2,831

Source: U.S. Department of Commerce, Bureau of the Census, *World Population Profile: 1991* (Washington, D.C.: U.S. Government Printing Office, December 1991), pp. 1, A-I. *Note:* Figures may not add to totals because of rounding.

★ 635 ★

World Population Statistics

Population of World Metropolitan Areas, 1992-2000

[Millions]

	1992	2000
Tokyo	25.8	28.0
Sao Paulo, Brazil	19.2	22.6
New York City	16.2	16.6
Mexico City	15.3	16.2
Shanghai	14.1	17.4
Bombay	13.3	18.1
Los Angeles	11.9	13.2
Buenos Aires	11.8	12.8
Seoul	11.6	13.0
Beijing	11.4	14.4
Rio de Janeiro	11.3	12.2
Calcutta	11.1	12.7
Jakarta, Indonesia	10.0	13.4
Tianjin, China	9.8	12.5
Metro Manilla	9.6	12.6
Cairo	9.0	10.8
New Delhi	8.8	11.7
Lagos, Nigeria	8.7	13.5
Karachi, Pakistan	8.6	11.9
Bangkok	7.6	9.9
Dacca, Bangladesh	7.4	11.5

Source: Eugene Linden, "Megacities," in *Time*, 11 January 1993, p. 36. *Primary source:* Population Division U.N. Secretariat. *Notes:* Urban area estimates vary widely, depending on area definitions and recency of census.

★ 636 ★

World Population Statistics

World Population under Different Fertility Assumptions, 1990-2130

"Recognizing the thinness of the ice on which they are skating, most demographers carefully refrain from making 'predictions' that imply quantitative forecasts, and prefer to talk instead of 'projections'—another word for 'scenarios'. [The table below] shows five different projections made by the United Nations. The fertility assumption, the year when the replacement level of 2.1 will be reached, is different for each projection, yet all five 'predict' zero population growth at some point in the future. The *when* depends on the many assumptions that affect future birth and death rates. At best we can look forward to a world population of about 8.75 billion, at worst close to 14 billion.

"(PRB) demographer Leon Bouvier went out on a limb in 1984 and ventured a prediction of the world population in 2034 and how the population would then be distributed over the globe. He had to assume many things—no nuclear wars, continued exponential growth in science and technology, sufficient food and energy resources, worldwide use of contraceptive devices, and a well-regulated world economy. Many would strongly argue with these assumptions, but they led Bouvier to opt for one of the more optimistic of the United Nations projections. His prediction for the world population on July 1, 2034 is a shade over 8 billion. This is twice the population in 1976 and represents an average growth rate over the period of 1.2% per year (compared with around 1.8% at present). He foresees some difficulties in adjusting to this population growth, but no out-and-out catastrophes. About 15% of the world's population will live in the 'least developed countries,' including some in Africa and the Middle East as well as in Bangladesh, and these people will truly have rough lives." All others will be able to keep their nose above the water to a greater or lesser extent.

[Billions]

Year	Replacement fertility reached:				
	By 2000	By 2020	By 2040	By 2060	By 2080
1990	5.2	5.2	5.2	5.2	5.2
2010	6.2	6.6	6.9	7.2	7.6
2030	7.4	8.3	8.9	9.4	10.2
2050	8.2	9.3	10.0	11.0	12.2
2070	8.5	9.6	10.5	11.8	13.2
2090	8.7	9.7	10.7	12.2	13.8
2110	8.8	9.8	10.8	12.4	14.0
2130	8.8	9.8	10.8	12.4	14.0

Source: Walter J. Karplus, *The Heavens Are Falling: The Scientific Prediction of Catastrophes in Our Time* (New York: Plenum Press), 1992, pp. 224-25. *Primary source:* Population Bureau, Inc.

★ 637 ★

World Population Statistics

World Migration, 1950-2025

"In a report replete with surprises, the United Nations Population Fund last week found people around the world migrating on a scale never known before. At least 100 million people live outside the countries in which they were born, including perhaps 30 million who have moved to America or Western Europe since 1980. But despite perceptions, most migrants do not move to industrial countries. Instead, they remain in the Third World. Each year, 20 million to 30 million leave the countryside for urban areas. By the end of this decade, the Third World is expected to include 17 of the world's 20 biggest 'megacities,' led by Mexico City (25.6 million) and Sao Paulo, Brazil (22.1 million). New York, No. 1 in 1950, is projected to be fifth in 2000. London and Paris, No. 2 and No. 4 in 1950, won't even make the top 20."

[Scale: 100 million inhabitants = percentage]

Year	Industrialized nations	Developing nations
1950	33	67
1990	23	77
2025	16	84

Source: "Migration: 'The Human Crisis of Our Age,' " in *U.S. News & World Report*, 19 July 1993, p. 16. *Primary source:* Basic data: United Nations Population Division.

★ 638 ★

World Population Statistics

Sex Ratio of the Population by Age in Selected Countries, 1990-2025

"The result of longer life expectancy for a woman is a dearth of men in the upper ages, especially in the oldest population, a situation that has enormous consequences for the status and living arrangements of women. Reference is made frequently to the sex ratio, or number of men per 100 women. In many developed nations, there are roughly 67 men for every 100 women in the total elderly population, but in Germany—which is experiencing the effect of exceptionally high war deaths—the ratio is only 51... Sweden had the most favorable sex ratio at age 65: as of 1990, there were 74 older men for every 100 women 65+.

"Developed countries are expected to experience an improvement in the sex ratio of the elderly by the year 2025, although few countries will duplicate Germany's increase of 26 older men per 100 older women. In other developed countries, the increase will range from about 6 to 11 per 100 women.

"As unfavorable as the sex ratio is at age 65, it is even more extreme at age 80. Again, the ratio is lowest in Germany, where there are only 39 men age 80+ for every 100 women. The picture is similar in the United Kingdom and France, with ratios of 42 and 44, respectively; both of these countries suffered extreme casualties during World War I that are reflected in current sex ratios."

[Number of men per 100 women in age group]

Country	1990			2025		
	All ages	65+	85+	All ages	65+	85+
Canada	97.2	71.9	52.4	95.7	77.4	59.4
France	95.1	64.4	44.3	95.6	74.0	55.0
Germany	92.7	50.5	39.0	96.5	76.0	52.9
Italy	94.4	67.1	49.5	95.4	75.3	56.1
Japan	96.7	67.6	55.1	96.1	78.5	61.6
Sweden	97.3	74.1	53.7	97.3	79.6	61.2
United Kingdom	95.3	66.3	42.4	97.1	77.7	57.8
United States	95.4	68.7	47.1	95.5	77.1	53.3

Source: U.S. Senate Special Committee on Aging, the American Association of Retired Persons, the Federal Council on the Aging, and the U.S. Administration on Aging, *Aging America: Trends and Projections* (Washington, D.C.: U.S. Government Printing Office, 1991), p. 259. *Primary source:* U.S. Bureau of the Census. International Data Base.

★ 639 ★

World Population Statistics

World Population Dependency Ratios, 1950-2050

"[The table below] shows the proportion of the world's population that is dependent on others. This is estimated by the number of people aged 14 and under or over 65 (assumed to be too young or too old to support themselves) for every 100 people between those ages. The average ratio for the world is declining. It fell from 65 in 1950 to 62 in 1990. By 2050 it is expected to be 55 or below."

[Per 100 people of working age]

	1950	1990	2050
Africa	84	91	48
Latin America	76	68	58
Asia	67	60	55
Oceania	57	54	60
North America	80	50	64
Europe	50	48	68
World	62	59	52

Source: "Emerging-Market Indicators," in *The Economist*, 24 September 1994, p. 114. *Primary source:* United Nations. *Note:* Magnitudes estimated from published chart.

★ 640 ★

World Population Statistics

Average Annual Growth Rates of the Elderly Population by Age for Selected Countries, 1990-2025

"Over the next 35 years, the elderly population will increase numerically and as a percentage of total population in developed countries throughout the world.

"Numerical increases will be especially pronounced in Canada and Japan, where the number of elderly will more than double. The United States also will experience a relatively sharp increase of almost 90 percent in the number of people age 65+...

"Segments of populations will age at varying rates in different countries over the next several decades. Largely as a result of low birth rates of the 1930s, the 65 to 79 age group in the United States will increase at the relatively low annual rate of 0.3 percent between 1990 and 2005. In many other countries, however, this age group will grow more rapidly during this period. For example, Japan's annual rate of growth for the population age 65 to 79 (3.0 percent) will be the most rapid in the developed world—10 times that of the United States. In contrast, negative growth rates are projected for Sweden and the United Kingdom."

[Percent]

Country	1990-2005		2005-2025	
	65 to 69	80+	65 to 79	80+
Japan	3.00	4.30	0.70	3.40
Canada	1.60	3.80	2.90	2.60
France	1.30	1.30	1.70	1.10
Germany	1.90	0.80	0.60	1.90
Italy	1.50	3.10	0.60	2.20
Sweden	-0.60	2.00	1.40	1.20
United Kingdom	-0.1	2.10	1.40	1.60
United States	0.30	2.70	2.90	1.30

Source: U.S. Senate Special Committee on Aging, the American Association of Retired Persons, the Federal Council on Aging, and the U.S. Administration on Aging, *Aging America: Trends and Projections* (Washington, D.C.: U.S. Government Printing Office, 1991), p. 252. *Primary source:* U.S. Bureau of the Census. International Data Base.

★ 641 ★

World Population Statistics

Percent of Population Age 80+ in Selected Countries, 1990 and 2025

"No consistent growth pattern will characterize the following 20 years, although in most countries, the annual growth rate of the oldest will be slower than that projected for 1990 to 2005. Germany will be an exception to this trend. In some countries, such as Canada, France, Sweden, and the United States, the oldest old will also grow at a slower rate than the younger elderly between 2005 and 2025, but in Germany, Italy, Japan, and the United Kingdom, the opposite will happen. Nonetheless, both numerically and as a proportion of the population, the oldest old in many nations will increase more sharply than the total aged population over the next several decades. The increase will be greatest in Japan, where the number of people age 80+ will increase by 274 percent, and the proportion of age 80+ by 278 percent. By 2025, between 5 percent and 9 percent of the populations of the developed nations will be at least 80 years of age."

[Percent]

Country	1990	2025
Sweden	4.3	7.3
France	3.9	5.3
Germany	3.8	6.2
United Kingdom	3.7	6.2
Italy	3.2	8.0
United States	2.7	4.5
Canada	2.4	5.7
Japan	2.3	8.7

Source: U.S. Senate Special Committee on Aging, the American Association of Retired Persons, the Federal Council on Aging, and the U.S. Administration on Aging, *Aging America: Trends and Projections* (Washington, D.C.: U.S. Government Printing Office, 1991), pp. 254-255. *Primary source:* U.S. Bureau of the Census. International Data Base. *Note:* Magnitudes estimated from published chart.

Chapter 14
SCIENCE AND TECHNOLOGY

General Scientific and Technological Predictions

★ 642 ★

Science and Technology, 1960-2050

"[Forecasters Marvin Cetron and Owen Davies predict the following trends in science]:

"High technological turnover rates are accelerating.

—All the technological knowledge we work with today will represent only 1% of the knowledge that will be available in 2050.

"Technology has come to dominate the economy and society in the developed world. Its central role can only grow.

—For some economists, the numbers of cars, computers, telephones, facsimile machines, and copiers in a nation define how 'developed' the country is.

—Personal robots will appear in homes in the developed world by 2000. Robots will perform mundane commercial and service jobs and environmentally dangerous jobs, such as repairing space-station components in orbit.

"The technology gap between developed and developing countries will continue to widen.

—Developed countries have 10 times as many scientists and engineers per capita as the developing world. The gap between their spending on research and development grew threefold from 1970 to 1980.

—Technologically underdeveloped countries face antiquated or nonexistent production facilities, a dearth of useful knowledge, ineffective organization and management, and a lack of technical abilities and skills. Under these conditions, underdevelopment is often self-perpetuating, which weakens the country's ability to compete in international markets.

[Continued]

★ 642 ★

Science and Technology, 1960-2050

[Continued]

—The widening technology gap will aggravate the disparity in North-South trade, with the developed nations of the Northern Hemisphere supplying more and more high-tech goods. The less-developed countries of the South will be restricted to exporting natural resources and relatively unprofitable low-tech manufactured products.

"Nations will exchange scientific information more freely, but will continue to hold back technological data.

—Basic research is done principally in universities, which have a tradition of communicating their findings.

—Fifty-three percent of Ph.D. candidates in U.S. science and engineering programs are from other countries. Anything they learn will return to their homelands when they do.

—The space-faring nations—soon to include Japan—will share their findings more freely.

—Technological discoveries, in contrast, often spring from corporate laboratories, whose sponsors have a keen interest in keeping them proprietary. More than half of the technology transferred between countries will move between giant corporations and their overseas branches or as part of joint ventures by multinationals and foreign partners.

"Research and development (R&D) will play an ever-greater role in the world economy.

—R&D outlays in the United States have varied narrowly (between 2.1% and 2.8% of the GNP) since 1960 and have been rising generally since 1978.

—R&D spending is growing most rapidly in the electronics, aerospace, pharmaceuticals, and chemical industries."

Source: Marvin Cetron and Owen Davies, "50 Trends Shaping the World," in *The Futurist*, September-October 1991, p. 15. *Primary source:* Marvin J. Cetron and Owen Davies, *Crystal Globe: The Haves and Have-Nots of the New World Order* (St. Martin's Press), 1991.

★ 643 ★

General Scientific and Technological Predictions

Research and Development Goals: A Japanese View, 1993-2011

"Polling some 2,800 of the nation's leading specialists in public and private research institutes and universities, Japan's Science and Technology Agency has identified key R&D goals for the next 30 years...

[Continued]

★ 643 ★

Research and Development Goals: A Japanese View, 1993-2011

[Continued]

"The five most-important goals and the year they are expected to be achieved are:

1. Commercialization of technologies to eliminate air pollutants such as the oxides of nitrogen (2003).
2. Invention of a computer to operate faster than 10 teraflops (10 trillion calculations per second) (2004).
3. Discovery of the major development mechanism of cancer (2010).
4. Commercialization of effective methods to prevent the spread of cancer (2007).
5. Diffusion of global-scale environmental preservation technologies (2011)."

Source: "Technology Goals: A Japanese View," in *The Futurist*, September-October 1993, p. 8. *Primary source:* Hajime Nagahama, "Technopolicy," in *Look Japan*, May 1993.

Federal Research and Development

★ 644 ★

Federal Budget for Technology Research and Development, 1993-1997

"Candidate Bill Clinton promised a technology policy that would make U.S. industry more competitive. What has the President delivered so far?

"Congress will probably increase the Commerce Department's civilian technology budget by about $36 million, to a total of $162 million, at Clinton's request. One result: The seven federal manufacturing extension centers around the U.S. will be able to take on more 'students'; these are primarily small and medium-size manufacturing companies that want to learn such techniques as designing parts with CAD/CAM equipment. Commerce hopes to increase the number of centers to 100 by 1997.

[Continued]

★ 644 ★

Federal Budget for Technology Research and Development, 1993-1997

[Continued]

"In recent years about 60% of all that Washington spends on research and development—a total of $69 billion for 1993—has gone to the military. Clinton would like R&D money split equally between defense and civilian projects. Presumably part of the civilian share would be spent on undertakings like one he has praised, Senmatech, designed to vault U.S. companies ahead of their Japanese rivals in the art of making the machines that in turn make seminconductors.

"But Washington changes direction as fast as a supertanker turns around. R&D spending for fiscal 1994 will be biased about sixty-four toward the Pentagon, as usual. It is not likely to approach fifty-fifty before 1997."

Source: Suneel Ratan, "Clinton Gets Technical—Slowly," in *Fortune*, 20 September 1993, p. 16.

★ 645 ★

Federal Research and Development

Federal Proposals for Technology and Business Reinvestment and Defense Conversion, 1994-1998

[Millions of dollars]

	1994	1995	1996	1997	1998	1994-1997 Total
NASA civil aviation	36	121	171	222	267	550
NASA short-haul aircraft research	3	10	17	20	20	50
Dual-use technology for defense reinvestment and transition (DOD)	133	322	420	456	480	1,331
Federal Coordinating Council for Science, Engineering and Technology (research initiatives)	100	266	383	457	514	1,206
Crosscutting high performance computing (NSF, NIH, NASA, and NIST)	53	158	253	320	362	784
National Inst. of Standards and Technology growth	56	219	403	628	805	1,306
National labs (non-defense)	14	35	47	50	50	146
Information highways (Commerce)	6	42	98	129	150	275
National Science Foundation	134	451	758	954	1,100	2,297
Government automation and efficiency	204	652	850	943	735	2,649
Extend R&E tax credit (tax incentive)	1,207	1,503	1,750	1,977	2,200	6,437
Subtotal, Technology and Business Reinvestment and Defense Conversion	1,946	3,779	5,150	6,156	6,683	17,031

Source: Executive Office of the President of the United States, Office of Management and Budget, *A Vision of Change for America* (Washington, D.C.: U.S. Government Printing Office, 17 February 1993), p. 136. *Notes:* Source also includes data for 1994. DOD=Department of Defense; NASA=National Aeronautics and Space Administration; NIH=National Institute of Health; NIST=National Institute of Standards and Technology; NSF=National Science Foundation.

★ 646 ★

Federal Research and Development

Federal Technology Proposal Highlights, 1993-1997

"To move ahead of our competitors in technological research and development, this initiative will provide incentives to explore new technologies. It will create high-wage jobs and help push America toward the cutting edge of goundbreaking technologies. It will create markets that encourage the use of universities in an effort to ensure that innovative products have the label 'Made in America.'

"**NSF/Enhancing university-based competitive science and engineering research in the U.S.** Studies show that investments in research and development (R&D) tend to be the strongest and most consistent positive influence on productivity growth. Most of NSF's investments are in university-based R&D programs which are competitively selected on their merit by members of the science and engineering community. These activities contribute to the Nation's productivity by generating new scientific and engineering knowledge and contribute to the training of the next generation of scientists and engineers. In 1992, NSF had $1 billion of unfunded proposals that were rated excellent through peer review. Thus, it appears that NSF has the capacity to invest more funds in a broad range of important research areas, including strategically targeted research in improving our understanding of the climate system and improved engineering approaches to mitigate environmental problems; advanced computers and digital networks; biotechnology; materials processing; advanced manufacturing; math and science and education; and smart highways, bridges, and other civil infrastructure. This proposal—which adds $2.3 billion over four years, and $954 million in 1997—also includes funds to support the Nation's university-based research facilities and instrumentation.

"**Commerce/Increase civilian R&D at the National Institute of Standards and Technology (NIST).** America's competitiveness rests ultimately with the private sector. Yet, the Federal Government has an important role to play in promoting economic growth, in part by supporting research and development. This proposal provides aggressive growth for the National Institute of Standards and Technology (NIST). NIST is the only Federal lab with the principal mission of supporting U.S. industry and has provided a steady stream of technology support to U.S. firms for over 90 years. This proposal provides for: 1) an increase of $138 million in 1994, rising to $680 million, by 1997, for the Advanced Technology Program to provide matching grants for industry-led R&D projects, including funding for consortia like SEMATECH; 2) over 100 manufacturing extension centers nationwide by 1997 to assist manufacturers to modernize their production capability; and 3) doubling the amount of R&D performed in the NIST labs by 1998. This proposal would increase total NIST funding from $381 million in 1993 to $1.2 billion in 1997 (budget authority).

[Continued]

★ 646 ★

Federal Technology Proposal Highlights, 1993-1997

[Continued]

"**Commerce 'Information Highways' Demonstrations.** The development of a broadband, interactive telecommunications network linking the Nation's businesses, schools, libraries, hospitals, governments, and others could pay enormous dividends to the U.S. economy. Engineers working on the same problem, teachers and students, and patients and doctors would all be able to communicate instantly no matter how much distance separated them. This proposal builds on the 1993 stimulus initiative by providing new seed money to 'jumpstart' the development of these networks. In 1994, $54 million will be made available to the Department of Commerce for grants to States, local governments, universities, school systems, and non-profits to link public facilities in such a network. Between 1995 and 1998, $150 million annually would be made available...

"**Crosscutting high performance computing (NSF/NIH/NASA/NIST).** This investment builds directly on a stimulus program to develop applications which use advanced computers and communication networks to solve problems in health care, education, manufacturing, and more. For example, under a pilot test in Boston, a physician could transit images (X-rays, CAT scans, photos) quickly to a specialist across town for immediate consultation. This program would be part of the multi-agency High Performance Computing and Communications program and would be coordinated by the Office of Science and Technology Policy's Federal Coordinating Council for Science, Engineering, and Technology (FCCSET). 1997—$320 million; four year total—$784 million.

"**NASA/Civil aviation**. The quality of the air transportation system has a direct impact on the quality of life of every U.S. citizen. This investment option would expand NASA aeronautics research in its support of the aviation industry and its enhancement of the safety and capacity of the national airspace system. One area of investment, advanced subsonics research, would focus on developing technology that would increase the competitiveness of U.S. commercial transport aircraft and enhance the safety and productivity of the national aviation system. The other area of investment, high-speed research, would focus on resolving critical environmental issues and establishing the technology base for an economical, supersonic aircraft. These investments will help counter aggressive government-supported foreign competition. In addition, it will provide technologies that improve the environmental compatibility of existing and future aircraft by reducing noise and engine emissions. Funding will reach an additional $222 billion in 1997, for a four year total increase of $550 million.

"**NASA/Short-haul aircraft research.** This initiative will expand NASA aeronautics research to develop technologies for short-haul aviation. Short-haul aircraft includes commuter aircraft, rotorcraft, and general aviation airplanes. There are roughly 220,000 short-haul aircraft in the United States, making up 98 percent of the total civil aviation fleet. To help bolster the competitive position of the U.S. short-haul industry, NASA would develop technologies for both rotary and fixed wing aircraft to enable a new mode of high utility, safe, fast, and direct transportation linking thousands of smaller communities. The program would take advantage of ongoing and new Federal Aviation Administration (FAA) and industry cooperation to accelerate application of these advanced technologies to U.S. aircraft and engine manufacturers. Estimated outlay increase: in 1997, $20 million; over four years, $50 million.

[Continued]

★ 646 ★

Federal Technology Proposal Highlights, 1993-1997

[Continued]

"Greatly increase non-defense Cooperative Research and Development Agreements (CRADAs) at the national labs. Cooperative Research and Development Agreements (CRADAs) are one of the mechanisms by which the national laboratories can work with industry to transfer lab-developed technology and know-how to the private sector. The funds go to the labs to pay for the share of the jointly agreed-upon R&D in the CRADA. The laboratory work under each CRADA is proprietary to the private-sector partner, who also hold the patent rights to inventions made under the CRADA. The current funding for CRADAs to transfer technology developed by DOE non-defense programs is $9 million, but there is more demand from industry for assistance through CRADAs than can be funded with that amount of money. This investment initiative provides an additional $30 million in 1994 and $50 million per year over the baseline in 1995-97.

"Modernizing Social Security Administration computer systems. The Social Security Administration (SSA) relies heavily on its information systems to provide services and pay benefits. To meet current and future demands, SSA and State Disability Determination (DDSs) must abandon their labor-intensive, paper-driven tradition and automate. The proposal would invest in the pilot tested Intelligent workstations and local area networks and (IWS/LAN), creating a standard, state-of-the-art, computing network for all SSA and DDSs. The investment funding includes modular workstations, and design/site preparation/installation. Estimated cost: over four years—$880 million; 1997—$245 million.

"Modernize Internal Revenue Service. IRS currently processes tax returns using technology from the 1960s. These out-of-date systems result in long delays for taxpayers and extra costs for the Federal government. Tax Systems Modernization (TSM) represents IRS's effort to move to an up-to-date, automated approach to processing taxes. With TSM, tax returns will be processed and stored using modern technology. Tax returns will be available in electronic files instead of remote warehouses. As a result, IRS employees will be able to provide immediate responses to most taxpayer questions over the phone. TSM will enable IRS to reduce the risks and costs associated with operating their current systems while also improving their ability to serve the public in the administration of the nation's tax system into the 21st century. Estimated cost: over four years—$1.8 billion; 1997—$0.7 billion."

Source: Executive Office of the President of the United States, Office of Management and Budget, *A Vision of Change for America* (Washington, D.C.: U.S. Government Printing Office, 17 February 1993), pp. 52-5. *Notes:* NASA=National Aeronautics and Space Administration; NIH=National Institute of Health; NSF=National Science Foundation; R&D=Research and Development.

Technological Developments for Specific Industries

★ 647 ★

High-definition Television Technology, 1987-1996

"A scant three years ago, experts said it couldn't be done. Broadcasting high-definition television in digital form within the narrow confines of American TV channels was believed to be for beyond the state of the technician's art. The best that anyone expected when the Federal Communications Commission belatedly launched a competition in 1987 to select an advanced American television standard was a somewhat poorer version of the analog HDTV system now being transmitted from satellites in Japan.

"But an announcement last week in Washington shows how dramatically the TV picture has improved. Prodded by the FCC's advisory committee, proponents of the four rival HDTV systems remaining in the FCC's competition formed a 'grand alliance' to merge the best of the best of their technical schemes into a single industry proposal. Although extensive tests had produced no clear winner, every one, significantly, demonstrated better pictures than the present Japanese system...

"The alliance's new proposal will be tested next year, and then the FCC must decide if it is satisfactory. If there are no serious glitches, the first purchasers of HDTV sets could watch the 1996 Summer Olympics in spectacular, wide-screen color."

Source: William J. Cook, "A Clear Picture for TV," in *U.S. News & World Report*, 7 June 1994, p. 60. *Note:* FCC = Federal Communications Commission; HDTV = High-definition Television.

★ 648 ★

Technological Developments for Specific Industries

Global Technological Projects, 1995-2015

"Global development projects are revolutionizing people's lives. They are the driving force behind continuing advances in the quality of life...

"There are more than 1,000 worldwide development ventures involving investments of at least $1 billion and/or achieving scientific or technological breakthroughs of global significance. In addition to energy, water, urban development, space, and scientific research 'super projects,' there is great interest in forging new global links through communications and transportation projects such as airports, railways, tunnels, highways, and bridges, as well as fiber-optic and satellite communications joint ventures...

[Continued]

★ 648 ★

Global Technological Projects, 1995-2015

[Continued]

"In the United States, Boeing would like to borrow $10 billion in the year 2000 and privately develop its own supersonic transport (SST). Boeing officials project a need for 400 to 500 SSTs by the next century.

"The successes of high-speed trains in France and the 'bullet train' in Japan have spurred a number of such projects around the world. The Community of European Railroads has planned an 18,630-mile (30,000-km) network linking all major cities. Each nation would build its own high-speed links according to a three-stage plan, with competition dates in 1995, 2005, and 2015...

"Under consideration [in the United States] are high-speed lines proposed for Texas, California, Ohio, Florida, the northern midwest region (Chicago, Milwaukee, and Minnesota), and the southwest (Los Angeles to Los Vegas).

"Other super-project transportation links in the works include conventional rail lines, highways, and superships."

Source: McKinley Conway, "Super Projects: New Wonders of the World;" in *The Futurist*, March-April 1993, pp. 25-8. *Primary source:* McKinley Conway, *Site World*, Conway Data, Inc., 1991, with supplemental material from Conway Data, Inc., *Site World: The 1992 Yearbook of Global Super Projects*, 1992, and World Development Council, *Super Projects Newsletter*, October 1992. *Note:* SST = Supersonic Transport.

★ 649 ★

Technological Developments for Specific Industries

Major Technological Changes in Hospitals

"Technological innovations in health care are increasing. As hospitals' share of gross national product has grown, the resources devoted to medical science and equipment have expanded. Some medical care advances increase costs and labor requirements. Other changes—such as synthetic antibiotics, surgical advances, and robotics for the handicapped—lower costs while increasing the efficiency of care."

Technology	Description	Labor implications	Diffusion
Advances in diagnostic imaging and monitoring	Improved diagnostic imaging, diagnostic catherizations, and better monitoring procedures have made earlier detection of many diseases possible and reduced the need for exploratory surgery. Patients often carry diagnostic monitoring equipment on or in their bodies for long-term diagnostic purposes relating to biochemical balances, brain and sleep disorders, heart and vascular disease, and metabolic problems. More accurate, easy-to-use equipment has been introduced.	Although less exploratory surgery is needed, early detection of cancer probably increases the number of tumor surgeries and the efficacy of these excisions. At present, the number of vascular surgeries is increasing, but the long-run result of diagnostic advances may be less thoracic and vascular surgery, and more preventive and dietary treatment. These procedures increase the demand for a variety of technologists, technicians, dietitians, and therapists. The need for surgical personnel may eventually decline.	Some advances require very expensive equipment, which has tended to concentrate some diagnostic activity in large teaching hospitals or in specialized facilities. The capital outlays involved in CT technology, magnetic reasonance, and nuclear medicine are impractical for many community hospitals and rural facilities.
Laboratory testing	New rapid testing techniques, improved equipment, and continual expansion of conditions that can be detected through specimen tests have tended to expand the role of laboratory testing in routine hospital patient care. The growth in the variety of tests has caused an increase in the use of outside laboratories by hospitals, but rapid techniques are most effectively used in-house, so on site laboratories remain necessary. New tests for AIDS, hepatitis, cancer, and genetic diseases have been developed.	More work is being concentrated on the day shift, because technical activity to culture and observe specimens over a long period of time is less needed than in the past. Although new equipment has improved productivity in the laboratory, specimens must still be obtained manually. The expansion of available test boosts demand for laboratory services. The net result is a growth in demand for laboratory technicians and technologists. Rapid techniques and more outpatient testing may reduce hospitalization and the demand for some	Generally, the easy access to offsite laboratory facilities and simple use test kits speed diffusion. Some newer tests diffuse slowly due to expense, limited availability, complexity, safety, controversy, or because another available procedure has been shown to be effective. Chorionic villus sampling is an example of slow diffusion due to limited availability and safety questions.

[Continued]

★ 649 ★

Major Technological Changes in Hospitals

[Continued]

Technology	Description	Labor implications	Diffusion
		inpatient support staff.	
Prepackaged materials	Prepackaged, single use, disposable materials and kits have replaced many reusable materials. These include tubing and catheters, syringes, needles, toilet kits, razors, draping materials, sutures, and even bedding and patient gowns.	Because of disposable supplies, central service workers in hospitals must contend with larger, changing inventories, but they package few supplies themselves. With the development of improved inventory management systems, productivity increases may reduce the number of central service workers over the coming decade, but hospitals face a growing need to find envionmentally safe methods to dispose of used materials.	Most small equipment and materials are packaged outside hospitals today. The rate of diffusion is rapid, unless the expense involved is very high. Disposable patient and surgical clothing is available, but reusable clothing is still more common.
Drugs, chemotherapy, and recombinant DNA technologies	Constant progress has been made in developing new drugs. With the growth of knowledge in biological processes and the effects of certain drugs, it has become possible to tailor chemicals to produce specific effects. Manipulation of genetic material to produce new biochemicals is providing enzymes, hormones, antibodies, and new medicines. Other pharmaceutical advances are providing new antibiotic, anti-hypertensives, immunosuppresives, cancer treatments, psychoactive agents, and other drugs.	Demand for hospital pharmacy workers is increasing because medical treatments that make use of pharmaceuticals is growing. Although some medicines and chemicals may prolong the hospitalization of terminal patients, most drugs eliminate or shorten hospital stays, and drugs that cut the need for surgery tend to reduce labor requirements of hospital staff outside of the pharmacy.	New drug treatments are often used first in teaching hospitals and other research-oriented hospitals. Once the FDA approves a new drug, chemotherapy, or other biological agent, diffusion occurs throughout the country, sometimes in a matter of months. Production constraints may in some cases slow diffusion, but delays rarely last more than a year. Physicians and hospitals face liability risk if they do not use the best available, approved treatments.
Computer-based information, record, and accounting systems	Use of computers for data processing, record keeping, cross-referencing, billing, accounting, diagnostic support, inpatient monitoring, and equipment monitoring.	The employment of clerical workers in accounting, billing, and medical records is projected to remain flat or to decline. The employment of accounts, auditors, systems analysts, and computer programmers and operators is expected to grow substantially. Medical professionals learn computer skills and use computers or computer output at a steadily increasing rate.	The costs of computing equipment and software have fallen enough to allow most hospitals to have in-house computer facilities for automated patient records and accounting data bases. Smaller hospitals are joining together to share computer facilities. Some hospitals are contracting out for these services or receiving them through management contracts. Even very small, rural hospitals have access to this technology. A growing number of hospitals are using computers as aids in diagnosis, inpatient monitoring, and equipment and inventory control.
Shock-wave treatments	Involve a high-intensity, soundwave generating device that can pulverize many kidney stones. It allows thousands of patients to avoid surgery. The first "lithotripser" required anesthesia and immersion in a tank. A newer version eliminates both the tank and general anesthesia, and permits a greater number of shock waves per treatment.	Lithotripsy eliminates or sharply cuts inpatient lengths-of-stay for those patients who can use this alternative to surgery. Lithotripsy reduces the demand for hospital beds and surgical services. It lowers the demand for hospital employment, except in radiology, urology, and specific lithotripsy services.	Because the cost of a lithotripsy units is in the $2 million range, this technology is mainly found in larger hospitals. Many metropolitan areas only require a single unit to meet all local demand for this service. For medical centers that have the tank system in place, the newer version is often too expensive to add. A similar treatment for gallstones is being developed, and it may eventually become the prevailing treatment for gallstones.
Surgical advances	Increasing technical skill, improved diagnostic imaging, better equipment, and laparoscopic techniques have made less invasive surgery possible. Incisions are smaller than in the past and recovery from surgery is often more rapid. Lasers, computers, senography, magnetic resonance imaging, stereo optiscopes, miniature precision tools, fiber optics, imaging chemicals and isotopes, and better x-ray equipment are factors in these advances.	Outpatient surgery and reduced lengths-of-stay for hospitalized surgery patients reduces the demand for hospital ward personnel. The expansion of possible surgical procedures increases the demand for surgical and recovery room personnel. The need for diagnostic and laboratory support is expanded.	The appearance of outpatient surgical facilities that operate independently of hospitals has stimulated many urban hospitals to create their own outpatient surgical facilities. Since many outpatient procedures are elective and the potential patients now have access to such facilities. The other advances relating to less invasive surgery and more sophisticated equipment are tending to concentrate some surgical procedures in large or specialized hospitals.
Incision closing	Surgical staples are an alternative to suturing. Although several times more expensive than sutures, they require less skill to insert and speed surgical procedures. They also promote more rapid healing and recovery. New systems use super adhesives and plastic coverings	These are labor-saving technologists. They reduce the demand for surgical and hospital ward personnel, and there is no counter-balancing increase in employment.	The spread of these technologies is accelerating, as acceptance by surgeons has grown.

[Continued]

★ 649 ★

Major Technological Changes in Hospitals

[Continued]

Technology	Description	Labor implications	Diffusion
	instead of either sutures of staples.		
Implantable infusion systems	Miniature pumps that administer medicines hormones, insulin, and chemotherapy agents.	These pumps increase the demand for some surgery, since they must be implanted and removed. They reduce hospitalization and may eventually reduce the surgical need for cancer excision, and cardiovascular surgeries related to long-term diabetes, such as detached retinas and venous atrophy. This could reduce the demand for hospital labor.	Such pumps are still in the developmental stages and are confined to research and teaching facilities. Diffusion to community hospitals is unlikely to occur until the late 1990's.
Nuclear medicine	Nuclear medicine is used in the treatment of cancers and benign tumors. Treatment can involve the use of x rays at various energy levels and the use of radioisotopes. Because different isotopes have distinct properties and are absorbed differently in the tissues of the body, nuclear medicine also plays important roles in testing and diagnosis.	Refinements in these technologies expand the role of nuclear medicine in the hospital. Advances have created more specialties and more technical positions. However, improvements in treatment and diagnosis can reduce hospitalization and lengths-of-stay in hospitals. Patients suffer fewer side effects from treatments and procedures. This tends to reduce the demands for surgery and in-hospital nursing care.	Diffusion of advances in nuclear diagnosis and imaging tends to take place among most large and medium-sized hospitals. The use of nuclear medicine for treatment is restricted in general to less than half of of the large hospitals in the United States. Even by the end of the 1990's, the percent of large hospitals with nuclear treatment programs is not expected to be much more than 50 percent. Among the major medical centers with large nuclear medicine departments, advances diffuse rapidly. These centers are found in all the regions of the United States.
Transplantation and immunology	Transplantation of organs and other body parts has grown very rapidly. Improvements in immune system suppression makes it possible for the human body to tolerate foreign tissue, instead of rejecting it. The most common implantation is of plastic lenses into the eyes of cataract patients. Over 1 million are done each year. Thousands of synthetic blood vessels, joints, bones, middle ears, and teeth are also implanted. Transplantation of living tissues includes hearts, livers, lungs, kidneys, pancreases, corneas, and skin or bone from one part of a patient to another part.	Transplants, implants, and immune treatment activity greatly increase the demand for labor in hospitals. Virtually all of these procedures are very labor intensive. They require highly skilled medical and clinical workers. These procedures account for a large and growing portion of surgeries. They also require great amounts of administrative and clerical support.	The incentives to adopt new transplantion and related technology is very strong. This area of medicine involves substantial revenues and prestige. Diffusion is being slowed by the massive costs and skill acquisition required to adopt these technologies and by a shortage of organs available for transplantation. Third party payers are attempting to limit the spread of these procedures to no more than a few facilities per region. This is because there are economies of scale and skill level benefits involved with restricting the number of approved centers. Diffusion is also being limited by payers who refuse to pay for experimental or dubious procedures and by the inability of most private payers to meet the high costs of new procedures.
Dialysis	Dialysis is available to all patients requiring it in the United States. This Government funded system provides treatment to 55,000 people. The large size of this program has created the proper environment for the improvement and refinement of methods and equipment. Important advances include more and better venous shunts (now usually internal); better, more compact machinery; more rapid treatment; and more complete cleansing of the patient's blood. Procedural simplification makes it easier for patients to be treated at home.	Most dialysis is done on an outpatient basis. Many clinics are freestanding, and many patients are treated at home. Hospitals have been playing a declining role in the provision of dialysis, and this trend is expected to continue. Hospitals play an important role in the provision of mental health services and education of dialysis patients. They also are important in monitoring the patient's physical status. These programs require several thousand hospital-based professionals.	Because of the universal nature of this Government program, improvements in dialysis treatments diffuse very rapidly.
Diabetic treatment	Diabetes affects over 12 million Americans. It poses one of the most serious health problems. Diabetics tend to suffer from many ailments that require hospitalization and intensive treatment. These include pregnancy complications, blindness, circulatory diseases, organ failure, and diabetic coma.	Improvements in the health status of diabetics resulting from new treatment technologies could have a substantial impact on hospitalization rates. The treatments mainly rely on patient activities. There may be some increase in the demand for diabetic specialists among nurses, technologists, and physicians, but other labor demand could fall.	Diffusion of new treatment technology has been slower than expected. Old treatment methods are entrenched, and too few patients understand the gravity of their illness. To speed the improvements of treatment systems, a large increase in physician and patient education will be required. Improved education is being actively promoted.
Generic research	Researchers are experimenting with the direct insertion of genetic material to cure or repair tissues. This can potentially be used for genetic diseases and cancer treatment.	If this research results in a healthier population, there will be less hospitalization. This would lower hospital employment in general. However, there will be a growth in the demand for geneticists, microbiologists, and related occupations.	This research and clinical testing is confined to a few major research and medical centers. Any effective treatments will diffuse quite rapidly across the country because the initial research is focused on very serious or fatal illness.

[Continued]

★ 649 ★

Major Technological Changes in Hospitals

[Continued]

Technology	Description	Labor implications	Diffusion
Intensive care and shock-trauma units	Specialized treatment systems for serious medical conditions including cardiac emergencies, strokes, burns, wounds, severe bone fractures, hemorrhaging, life-threatening infections, intense seizure sequences, concussions, and complex post-operative care. Rather then using conventional emergency room and wards, hospitals develop and employ specialized units and support areas of serious injuries and diseases.	These forms of treatment delivery require highly skilled labor in surgical, nursing, physical therapy, cosmetic prostheses, construction, hematology, and numerous other medical and nonmedical areas. This category of health care delivery tends to be extremely labor intensive.	Intensive care units have spread to most medium-size and large hospitals. In teaching hospitals these units are further subdivided into surgical, medical, respiratory, and other specialized units. Metropolitan areas try to designate a single large hospital to specialize in burn or severe shock-trauma. Most rural areas lack these forms of medical care due to the capital expenses and skilled labor required. Few for-profit hospitals are heavily involved in these forms of health care delivery because the high costs are difficult to recover.
Nonmedical service	Hospitals are increasing the productivity of laundry, food, housekeeping, plant and equipment maintenance, and other services through the use of computerized inventory control, automated laundry equipment, specialized contract services, and pooled, computer-coordinated, interhospital services to achieve economies of scale.	In these services, hospitals are striving to use technology to reduce labor requirements. The outlook is for strong productivity growth in nonmedical services and for some reductions in total employment in these areas.	All hospitals are looking for ways to cut nonmedical employment. Small hospitals will experience trouble adopting expensive solutions. Larger hospitals throughout the country are investing to boost nonmedical productivity.

Source: U.S. Department of Labor, Bureau of Labor Statistics, *Outlook for Technology and Labor in Hospitals* (Washington, D.C.: U.S. Government Printing Office, May, 1992), pp. 2-6.

★ 650 ★

Technological Developments for Specific Industries

Major Technological Changes in Oil and Gas Extraction

"Refinements in measuring instruments and the rapid advance of computer technology are causing significant changes in exploration and field development. The level of discovery risk has fallen. The number of dry holes drilled per discovery has declined for companies using computer-aided exploration. This tends to lower the cost of exploration by reducing the amount of time, equipment, and labor needed to bring a productive well on line. However, the uncertainly of future oil prices has curtailed exploration and development of new fields.

"Other significant technology advances in oil and gas extraction include total process integration, better metals, equipment refinements, improved maintenance, horizontal drilling, and the enhancement and expansion of computer applications. Quality and process improvement efforts have frequently been successful and have been crucial in preventing more rapid erosion in domestic oil production."

Technology	Description	Labor implications	Diffusion
Advances in the identification and imaging of potential oil and gas fields	The combination of accumulated exploration experience, advances in computer hardware, and software improvements has made it possible to more accurately identify potential sites for oil and gas drilling and to predict with a significant probability the size of deposits that may lie beneath the land or sea sites. The use of computer-aided oil exploration (CAEX) means that the number of "dry holes" drilled per successful discovery is declining. Explosives have given way to sonar analysis. Laser-based measurements and satellite and aerial photography data are also important inputs. Air guns in large arrays and multiple sensor arrays combine to yield data bases that can produce three-dimensional, color images of rock structures thousands of feet beneath the sea or land.	Although less exploratory drilling is conducted than in the past, the sites are often more difficult to develop. The lowered need for drilling causes the employment of oil field workers to decline. However, the greater difficulties in exploration that result from remote locations, offshore locations, and the increased average depth of potential oil fields tends to increase the need for labor. Moreover, to the extent that technology provides a higher success rate in drilling, the cost of producing oil and gas is lowered. This downward pressure on costs means that drilling can take place at lower anticipated market price levels than would otherwise be the case. This tends to improve the employment prospect of oil field workers when oil prices are relatively low.	The more challenging the potential exploration sites in terms of remoteness, field depth, and offshore location, the more likely computerized imaging techniques and computer analyses will be used. At present, smaller oil companies are less likely to use the most recent techniques, since many are working in areas adjacent to established fields, and at relatively accessible depths. Yet, as costs drop and precision improves, virtually all exploration will use computerized imaging and analysis. Over 60 percent of seabed oil and gas exploration involved CAEX in 1991 and over 20 percent of land-based oil and gas exploration used CAEX.
Horizontal drilling	Horizontal drilling is responsible for most of the new drilling taking place in	Horizontal drilling is a boon to oil field workers. Largely because of this technical	In some reservoirs, horizontal drilling has slashed the drilling cost per barrel of oil

[Continued]

★ 650 ★

Major Technological Changes in Oil and Gas Extraction

[Continued]

Technology	Description	Labor implications	Diffusion
	the United States. This technique starts conventionally by drilling downward, but the drill then follows a curved path and approaches potential oil bearing rock horizontally. This system has proven so effective that it allows for drilling in geological formations where drilling was considered uneconomical in the recent past. Slant drilling is a simpler variation on horizontal drilling that can be used in shallow fields with good results under the right conditions.	advance, oil and gas field employment actually increased in 1990 after several years of decline. For these workers, there is no downside to this technology. Without horizontal drilling and slant drilling, employment would face an even more difficult future.	produced from $12 a barrel to $4. An advance this dramatic will diffuse as rapidly as new equipment can be produced and marketed, and new skills given to the drilling teams. The technique has spread throughout Texas in less than 3 years. It should be used nationwide within 5 years. During the coming 20 years, much of the additional oil that will be produced in the United States will come from enhanced recovery techniques and from drilling techniques that both improve the extraction of oil and lower the cost of bringing the oil out of the ground. Increasing the level of total oil recovery from each field allows mature fields to stay in production longer, and it raises the feasibility of developing new, smaller fields.
Refinements in established methods and equipment	Work methods and organization are undergoing steady improvements. Much of this is because oil and gas prices have been relatively low. This increases the pressure to organize work efficiently and to lower costs. Improvements in drilling hardware contributed to the development of horizontal drilling. Newer equipment--such as more powerful top drives--is easier to use, more durable, safer, and more economical over the life span of the part or material. Valves and safety cut-offs are more reliable and effective. Growing modularity in equipment design, easier methods of assembling and tearing down drilling sites, and better equipment accessibility for maintenance also have tended to lower operating costs. Safety measures, such as spill containment systems sensors and extinguishing systems are improving the work environment. Waste management and recycling are being upgraded.	Although these changes lower the demand for labor, the associated lower costs also mean that drilling and production become feasible at lower market prices, which can increase employment opportunities. The changes in equipment also have tended to raise safety levels. However, the changes in work methods often expose temporary workers to greater danger. This is because temporary workers who come on-site only when needed tend to have less safety training than permanent workers. Their lower skill levels also increase their chances of having accidents.	Changes in the work methods diffused rapidly in the mid and late 1980's. However, the diffusion of new equipment is available at low prices, and many drilling and production organizations try to use their existing equipment stock for as long as feasible. It will be many years before this older equipment is discarded.
Enhanced oil recovery materials and techniques	Oil producers have steadily improved their proportion of extraction of the oil and gas located at each production site. At first they used water, other drive fluids, steam, gas, and air to boost production from older wells. In recent years they have used chemical additives and inexpensive, free-flowing, but bulky, polymergels to boost production in fractured rock that tends to be bypassed by drive fluids. High energy gas injection also is being used to fracture rock and increase flow rates. Efforts to improve fracture stimulation technology have had significant success, which will help maintain production levels in the coming decade. Explosives have been used for decades to fracture rock and increase the flow of oil and gas. However, the past decade has witnessed improvements in explosive formulations and controls that have made this approach more precise and productive. Although not considered to be part of EOR, these advances affect how and where EOR techniques are used.	Oil recovery enhancement raises the demand for oil field workers. Higher skill levels and additional engineering work are usually needed to enhance recovery. These methods keep fields in production longer. In most cases, these fields produce oil for additional years or decades. In general, enhancement techniques do not expose workers to dangerous substances or other work hazards when conducted properly, nor do they lower quality of the work environment. Fracture stimulation technology requires new skills in geoscience, explosives, and compressed gases.	The United States has aging oil fields in widely dispersed areas. Although these fields vary in geological settings, the enhanced recovery techniques spread quickly to any appropriate field. The extent to which enhanced recovery methods are used depends on oil prices. Some of the best systems can only be used at high price levels. At present, the National Petroleum Council estimates that at least a million barrels a day are added to U.S. production due to enhanced recovery. There are some very small, stripper fields located on family farms and private plots that are not benefiting from the newer methods and materials, but they account for less than 1 percent of the national oil and gas output.

[Continued]

★ 650 ★

Major Technological Changes in Oil and Gas Extraction

[Continued]

Technology	Description	Labor implications	Diffusion
Computer-based and related systems	This technology involves the use of computers for management information systems, office procedures, word processing, voice mail, facsimile transmission, accounting, data processing, record keeping, cross-referencing, billing, inventory control, and equipment and work-site monitoring. Computers also are used to manage and plan production levels, and programmable logic controllers manage many aspects of oil production.	The employment of clerical workers in accounting, billing, and records keeping is projected to remain flat or to decline. The employment of accountants, auditors, systems analysts, and computer programmers and operators is expected to grow substantially, but automation in accounting and auditing, as well as sharper than anticipated declines in domestic oil and gas activity, may alter this projection. Oil and gas industry professionals are learning computer skills and are using computers or computer output at a steadily increasing rate. At production sites, computer based systems and programmable logic controllers are raising productivity, lowering training requirements, and reducing the need for some kinds of production workers.	The costs of computing equipment and software have fallen enough to allow most of this industry to have in-house computer facilities for automated records and accounting data bases. Smaller companies may contract out for some of these services. Programmable logic controllers were adapted from automobile production to some offshore oil production functions and are now spreading to every aspect of offshore and onshore production.
Offshore drilling and production	Although improvements in steering and site location technologies have made free floating drilling feasible, it is still uncertain if the cost of drilling in deep ocean sites justifies any significant production from free-floating rigs in the near future. Eventually, free-floating rigs may play a major role in offshore oil and gas production. The established oil platform technology will continue to be important on continental shelves. Platforms are being designed to better withstand severe storms and to prevent or extinguish platform fires. Platform assembly and transporting techniques have undergone some important improvements. Computer aided design and engineering are reducing the cost of designing and planning oil platforms. Piping and loading systems also have been improved.	Some refinements in assembly techniques and some changes in platform configuration may lower slightly the demand for labor. New equipment used on the platforms and improved drilling equipment may also reduce the demand for labor slightly. These changes improve safety and the work environment to which workers are subjected.	Oil platform production is limited and the capital requirements are quite large. Any significant improvements diffuse throughout the industry in under 5 years.

Source: U.S. Department of Labor, Bureau of Labor Statistics, *Technology and Labor in Oil and Gas Extraction and Commercial Banking* (Washington, D.C.: U.S. Government Printing Office, October 1993), pp. 2, 6-8.

★ 651 ★

Technological Developments for Specific Industries

Major Technological Changes in Commercial Banking, 1993-2000

"Computerization has had profound effects on banking operations. Telecommunications have tended to centralize administration and some decision making, but the improvement in communication has also empowered some workers at the branch bank level and off-site workers, and increased their ability to make decisions. Interbank operations have benefited from electronic fund transfers, better sorting and processing systems, and improved computer links. A variety of optical and imaging technologies have improved data entry systems and altered document verification systems, although the potential future uses for optical imaging and optical character recognition remain largely untapped. Refinements in accounting and evaluation methods are causing major changes in financial institutions. The recent success in developing more precise evaluation procedures have begun to alter the cost structure of banking, and these techniques reduce the amount of equipment and labor needed to bring a customer account on line. Equipment and computer software continue to improve. Because of problems in the 1980's, risk assessment systems are becoming more computerized and complex. Risk management pertains to many areas. For example, increased automation entails risks that a general system crash could compromise or abort thousands of transactions. High level of concern over the volatility of future interest rates has made designing loan risk management systems more difficult, but future risk-management developments will depend on the business environment. A long-term period of economic growth with low inflation and steady, low interest rates could reshape the priorities of risk management."

Technology	Description	Labor implications	Diffusion
Computerization	Banks are among the most computerized businesses. Recent technology changes include improvements and innovations in on-line operations, open systems, fault-tolerant minicomputers, multitalented workstations, multiuser systems, and mainframe computer partitioning. Future developments may include intelligent networks that better use personal computers and linked workstations. Computer systems are becoming easier to use and more resistant to accepting date entry errors. Computerization has made it practical for banks to create new mortgage products, such as reverse equity mortgages, shared equity mortgages, and a variety of adjustable rate mortgages. New consumer loan products and equity loan products have also entered banking markets, and new commercial loan products are expected to grow in importance.	Some of these developments increase the demand for systems experts and some programmers. Due to shared peripheral equipment in multiuser systems and open system architecture, the total amount of computer hardware needed for banking tasks may be reduced, which means less demand for computer hardware maintenance and repair personnel. The simplification of procedures and higher speeds of processing reduce labor requirements for bank tellers, secretaries, and clerical workers. Increasing the variety of banking products tends to increase the demand for customer service representatives and related loan officers. Bank tellers have become more involved in direct marketing of bank products to consumers. Some management opportunities are created to oversee the development and marketing of new types of loans and new debit card operations. Computer controlled voice response units have reduced the demand for low-level customer service representatives and operators.	Some modern technology is useful only in very large banking and bank service operations with established mainframe computer centers. However, many recent computer technology innovations and improvements are applicable to all levels of banking, and some of the initial costs can be recouped within a short period. Less expensive technologies of this sort diffuse nationwide within 2 or 3 years. For the expensive, new systems, the rate of diffusion is hard to predict. Banks have become more cautious than in the past about investing in new, complex systems. The unknown potential and costs of competing minicomputer systems and workstation networks also makes it difficult to predict the future need for mainframe systems and computer partitioning. Many new products made feasible by computerizaton are designed to lower the banks' risks in making loans. Such products tend to diffuse rapidly. Products needed to maintain or expand market share also spread rapidly.
Telecommunications	The integration of advanced telecommunication systems with the computer networks in banking operations has allowed some activities to be centralized, yet it has allowed other activities to be offered at new sites, such as supermarkets. There have been major advances in Automatic teller machines and telephone-based banking services.	Telecommunications have eliminated entire branch operations and some jobs in bank branches are disappearing. These systems have made automatic teller machines even more useful than they were in the past because the telephone line network linkage systems operate more rapidly and reliably.	Diffusion of telecommunication systems is slowed by cost and by the need to maintain a human presence in some market areas. Banks can lose business when there are no longer convenient branches where customers can talk face-to-face with bank service representatives. The leveling off and modest decline in ATM sales at the end of the 1980's stimulated the development of more versatile ATM equipment. Sales have strengthened, and rate of diffusion of these new machines should increase. The telephone companies' delay in switching to all-digital systems and line problems in less populated areas adversely affects the growth of banking telecommunications. Competition among telephone companies and the potential for proprietary telecommunication systems to become cheaper and more user-friendly should increase the rate and economy of banking telecommunication advances and diffusion by the late 1990's. Because they affect the customer cost basis of telecommunications through rate setting, State telephone regulatory agencies may play a role in this transition.

[Continued]

★ 651 ★

Major Technological Changes in Commercial Banking, 1993-2000

[Continued]

Technology	Description	Labor implications	Diffusion
Interbank operations	Improvements in computers and software have made the Federal Reserve clearing centers, and the intra-branch and inter-bank transaction clearing operations more efficient and automated.	Automation and simplification/verification of data entry processes has outpaced the growth in bank transactions. The result is a reduced need for clerical workers in clearing operations, but managers and more skilled professionals continue to experience modest job growth.	The Federal Reserve system has adopted new technology and methods. The rapidity of diffusion to other clearing operations depends on the scope and size of these operations, because the costs of conversion can be steep. Some smaller clearing houses have been merged into larger scale operations to take advantage of new technology.
Optical data entry, data storage, and related systems	The improvement and price declines in optical scanners and related technology are allowing banks to eliminate some of their manual data entry systems. Optical disk data storage allows banks to store both new and old data quickly and economically.	Optical entry and storage systems reduce paperwork and the need for clerks and computer keying. These system have no effect on the demand for management, customer service representative, professional staff, and other highly skilled staff.	The rate of diffusion has been slowed by the problems associated with older scanners and by the cost of optical scanning and data storage. Diffusion is proceeding at a rapid rate among large banks, and optical data entry and storage may be common in smaller banks by the late 1990's.
	Biometric scanning is used to verify signatures, fingerprints, and other traits that can uniquely identify an individual. Related, optical systems for currency verification are being developed.	If biometric scanning becomes common, demand for tellers and some related clerical staff will decline. Less staff training related to these forms of identity verification may be required by banks. Automated currency verification would have similar implications.	If the cost of biometric scanning continues to decline and reliability proves to be good, these devices will in general use by the end of the century. Newer copying and computerized printing technology has increased the threat of counterfeiting. Reliable currency verification systems may diffuse rapidly.
Accounting technologies and integrated information systems	Accounting for transactions and evaluating bank performance is now incorporated in relational databases that have evolved from the process technology of distributive data processing. Advanced telecommunications tie branch and remote office data into the central systems as the transactions are recorded. Auditing through the computer became routine during the 1980's. The availability of interactive, modular software, management information systems, relational databases, expert systems, and related software technology has made information about all aspects of bank operations, balance sheets, and accounts easily available to bank management and financial professionals.	Accounting is more centralized than in the past. Automation means fewer accounting clerks, but the demand for CPA's and high-level accountants and auditors continues to grow in spite of automation, centralization, and bank mergers. The major reason for this is the growth in the number of bank products. Integrated information systems tend to centralize management. Demand for branch staff professionals and managers declines. Some layers of management can be eliminated because so much information and measuring criteria have become available without intermediaries. However, the growth in the volume of data and information to be processed also can create work for programmers, systems analysts, technical librarians, and other information specialists. Rule-based expert systems and artificial intelligence systems will continue to improve work accuracy and reduce fraud loss.	The diffusion of new techniques and software is very rapid. The major constraint is the time necessary to evaluate the cost-benefits of new methods, equipment, and software, and recruiting or training of staff. Diffusion of integrated information systems has been very rapid among larger banks. Most intermediate sized banks will probably move into advanced, integrated information systems during the coming 10 years. Many small banks do not need the full capabilities of these systems.

[Continued]

★ 651 ★

Major Technological Changes in Commercial Banking, 1993-2000

[Continued]

Technology	Description	Labor implications	Diffusion
Other office automation	Banks are benefiting from the same new office systems found in other important businesses. These automated, computerized systems handle filing, ordering goods and services, inventory control, tracking and overseeing maintenance and repair functions, monitoring and controlling office and building environmental control systems, word processing, mail systems, and payroll/personnel management.	Office automation has been slow to produce labor savings, but there is a growing trend in that direction. The 1990's are expected to experience more rapid productivity because adjustments in work patterns that were needed to benefit from the changes in office technology are now well underway. Branch office personnel demands at all levels may decline, and there may be some reduction in central and secretarial staffs.	Because of stricter oversight of procurement costs, the rate of office automation growth in the 1990's may slow from the rate experienced in the 1980's. Banks will not abandon useful older equipment without a very clear idea of significant benefits from buying or leasing newer systems.
Credit card and debit card operations	The knowledge and technology gained from credit card operations have been extended into debit card operations. A debit card can credit and debit accounts on a near-instantaneous basis through the use of automatic teller machines and point-of-sale terminals linked directly to the banking system or a linked intermediary. Magnetic strips on the cards are "read" by these machines. The central data bases authorize and record transactions. "Smart cards" that use integrated circuitry in place of, or in addition to, magnetic strips may replace the present cards before the end of the century.	Processing credit card slips remains relatively labor intensive, although some credit card fund transfers are largely electronic in nature. In contrast, debit card operations are among the most automated in the banking industry. These cards are becoming more useful and widely applied as electronic fund transfer technology advances. As this technology grows, fewer clerical workers and bank tellers may be needed. Because "smart cards" are more versatile than the present cards, labor requirements will decline even more if these cards come into general use.	Credit cards will continue to be widely used. The more widespread use of debit cards may be one of the most important changes in the economic patterns in the 1990's. By the end of the decade, debit cards may be used in many situations presently involving checks or cash. Bankers hope to eventually replace most checks transactions with debit card transactions. The cost-benefits of "smart cards" appear very favorable. These cards are capable of multiple functions and a single card could serve as a health card, calling card, credit card, driver's license, and virtually any other use a card could serve. However, the reluctance to merge all these functions and the capital invested in magnetic stripe equipment should slow the acceptance of "smart cards."

Source: U.S. Department of Labor, Bureau of Labor Statistics, *Technology and Labor in Oil and Gas Extraction and Commercial Banking* (Washington, D.C.: U.S. Government Printing Office, October 1993), pp. 21, 26-8.

Impacts of Information Technology

★ 652 ★

The Information Superhighway, 2000

"Bill Clinton's idea of progress is decidedly old-fashioned. He believes that making things makes money, and he proposes renovating the once fabulous American thing-making, wealth-generating machine through new technologies.

[Continued]

★ 652 ★

The Information Superhighway, 2000

[Continued]

"Clinton's leading technology proposal is to move the nation's infrastructure into the 21st century with advanced electronic communications highways—an idea that Japan has already poured billions into. The goal is to enhance productivity by moving vast quantities of digital data seamlessly over high-capacity networks as sound, graphics and video between universities, corporations, industrial research centers, health-care facilities—and ultimately everyone's home. With such a capability, corporations could send computer-generated drawings across the nation in an instant to cooperate in the design and manufacture of new products. Remote communities could send x-rays over the wire for expert diagnosis at regional health-care centers. Telecommuters could work at home by tapping into a corporation's computer systems."

Source: William J. Cook, "Sparking the Future: Clinton Sees Technology as the Linchpin of Industrial Revitalization," in *U.S. News & World Report*, 16 November 1992, pp. 90, 92.

★ 653 ★

Impacts of Information Technology

Effects of Information Technology on Personal Freedom, 1980-2040

"Despite the fact that the planet seems threatened now by the technologies produced during the two hundred years of the industrial revolution, by the twenty-first century science may offer a strong opportunity to reduce these threats substantially as well as to improve the conditions of human life. If present trends continue, these developments are likely to create benefits for human life and relationships that far exceed the technological advances of the past five hundred years. In the past, the engine of change has been war. During periods of conflict, technology has been developed to improve the righting capacity of one monarch, country, or ethnic group. The driving force behind the technology of the future, it seems to me, is much more likely to be peace. Innovations will grow out of the need to make peace between warring ethnic or regional groups and to avoid further conflict over the planet's scarce and clearly hard-pressed basic resources.

"No one knows, of course, whether the earth was designed to contain 5 or 6 billion inhabitants. But the more we discover about our collective impact on the planet, the more capable we become of protecting and conserving it. We have also not yet scientifically determined whether the future climate of the earth will be warmer or cooler. The topic of global warming is a significant issue on the agenda of international affairs these days, and virtually everyone has a sense that the earth's climate has gotten hotter and drier since the late 1980s. The causes of the phenomenon are unclear, but the consequences of global warming for food production, coastlines, desertification and deforestation, and population growth and movements are not hard to imagine. Should these forecasts increasingly appear likely, technology will be called on to ameliorate the consequences. This in turn will increase the sense that people possess the potential to master the environment and, in the longer run, to improve their methods of managing the earth.

[Continued]

★ 653 ★

Effects of Information Technology on Personal Freedom, 1980-2040

[Continued]

"We should also be prepared for the alternate prospect of global cooling, which I think is much more likely by the years 2030 to 2040. The earth has already exceeded the longest of about twenty-four periods of global warming, as measured by the earth's core and ocean floor sediment samples. Each has lasted about ten thousand years, except for the present Holocene, which is in its eleventh millennium. Conceivably, the use of fossil fuels has prolonged this warm period just as the population has exploded, requiring longer growing seasons and larger harvests. Should the Holocene end and world temperatures drop 5 to 10 degrees Fahrenheit, technology and international cooperation will be no less important to finding a way to cope with this development.

"Nevertheless, in the case of either prospect, the relationship between people and governments will change. As communities and ethnic groups are affected by global temperatures changes, they will expect more from government. They may also demand a larger share of the assets and resources—especially food, warmth, and space—controlled by other groups and communities that might be less adversely affected. Governments at all levels will be obliged to assume the role of mediator and to balance conflicting and competing demands. They will have to offer protection to both the displaced populations and original inhabitants as populations shift to more desirable locations and settlements. Moreover, because the shifts were made necessary by nature, the problems of governance will often transcend national boundaries and require regional cooperation and integration on continent-wide scales.

"Consequently, one major feature that will be unique about the future will be its proportions. For the past thousand years, the scope of human interaction and problems has been narrowing as more and more states have been created and greater differentiation has occurred. Religions, ethnic groups, and money have allowed people to remain isolated and to develop and improve their lives at vastly different rates. Just fifty years ago, the wealthy everywhere could be confident that by the conservation of their capital, the judicious application of the interest compounded on it, and the other forms of leverage it generated, they could guarantee the quality of their life styles more or less indefinitely and insulate themselves from the pressures and conflicts of the poor in their home countries and around the globe. Few people, rich, or poor, think that way today.

[Continued]

★ 653 ★

Effects of Information Technology on Personal Freedom, 1980-2040

[Continued]

"The technology of tomorrow seems far more inclined toward and capable of scattering its power and benefits on a global scale than that which characterized the industrial revolution. Contact with the technology of the latter was limited to a few, usually those who worked in factories and on the manufacturing process. Far more than the consumers of their products or the managers who profited from their labor, the workers were normally the only people aware of the practical power of machines to produce materials better, faster, and cheaper. When workers eventually discovered that their skills in operating these technologies could translate into political power, they organized and were alternately powerful and repressed. In retrospect, labor unions and movements in nearly every country undergoing industrialization didn't achieve a degree of influence for very long. This was attributed in part of the fact that workers did not own or control the technology, no matter how they understood its operation. When the whistle blew and the workers left the shop floor, they left behind the benefits of the new technology. Only later as wages rose and the prices of manufactured goods began to decline in proportion to the workers' purchasing power did laborers actually see a relationship between what machines did for them at work and what they did for their families at home.

"Today, farmers or workers can live in a world where the large-scale functions of machines at work can be downsized and replicated in their personal lives. Most technologies available to the chairman of IBM are available to the company's least-paid employee—as well as to the mechanic who services cars employees drive to work or the clerk in the grocery store who bags the food they consume. Although large amounts of capital will still be necessary to invent the applications of tomorrow, the machines and processes that are created will likely be reproduced to the point where the unit cost will be affordable to average people everywhere. And this distribution is bound to change people's expectations about their own lives and about the future they can provide for their children. As this occurs, the role and the nature of government are also likely to change. People may find they need less assistance from government because they have access to more of the ideas and processes that will improve their lives. But above all, they will expect governments to facilitate equal access to the devices and procedures that improve the way we live as individuals and with each other. Governments have never before been held to this standard. But never have so many people been aware of the potential for technology to increase their productivity and security. Clearly, the technology of the future will be indispensable as well as accessible to everyone interested in freedom.

"There is no telling what genius and creativity lie ahead as people are liberated by technology in the service of the idea of freedom. But consider the consequences. Currently, probably a quarter of the world's population cannot even read; half do not attend school for more than a few years. Yet these people's brain size and capacity for absorbing and applying knowledge are roughly the same as those of the reader of this book. Who can make a case that our future will be anything but brighter as these minds come on stream?"

Source: Allan E. Goodman, *A Brief History of the Future: The United States in a Changing World Order* (Boulder, CO: Westview Press), 1993, pp. 58-60.

★ 654 ★

Impacts of Information Technology

Implications of Computer Monitoring, 1993-2013

"Picture this as the workplace of the future: A computer tells you if you are making too many typos and suggests that you take a break from typing. Or it tells your boss if you are talking to a customer. Or taking too long a break. Or what you are saying on the phone. Through a computer, your boss can see what you are doing every minute and every second while you are at work.

"Does this description sound like a portrayal of the far-off future? It isn't. It's today. Currently, as many as 26 million workers in the United States are monitored in their jobs, and this number will increase as computers are used more and more within companies and as the cost of these monitoring systems goes down. By the end of the decade, as many as 30 million people may be constantly monitored in their jobs. But exactly how will these monitoring systems change in the next 20 years, and how will they affect workers?

"Alan Westin, a professor at Columbia University, believes that monitoring can be done in a humane fashion if employees are guaranteed several rights, including access to all information gathered through monitoring. Furthermore, it can be motivational to give employees personal access to this information. As Michael J. Smith, a professor at the University of Wisconsin—Madison, asserts, 'Information given to the supervisor often turns out to be a club, but when it goes directly to the worker, it can become a positive motivator.'"

Source: Kristen Bell DeTienne, "Big Brother or Friendly Coach?: Computer Monitoring in the 21st Century," in *The Futurist*, September-October 1993, pp. 33-4.

★ 655 ★

Impacts of Information Technology

Impact of Information Technologies on Consumerism, 1990-2010

"During the 1990s and the first decade of the twenty-first century, new information technologies promise to help consumers make more-informed shopping decisions. These technologies—including optical fiber, personal communication services, and multimedia computers—will qualitatively change shopping, transforming what might be called Industrial Age shopping into Information Age shopping.

"Here's a preview of some of the things we can expect from the empowered consumers of the Information Age.

[Continued]

★ 655 ★

Impact of Information Technologies on Consumerism, 1990-2010

[Continued]

"First of all, advertising-financed media will disappear. Mass media consist of two components: editorial or entertainment content and advertising. Traditionally, the editorial component has almost always been used to attract the consumer to the advertising component. The principle is that you can force consumers to take in something they don't want (the advertising) by offering something they do want (the editorial matter).

"But this system can thrive only in an era of passive media such as we have today. Once media become interactive and consumers can separate the advertising from the editorial components of media, this system of advertising-financed media will collapse...

"If consumers no longer have to see ads, how will they learn about new products they may want to buy? One answer may be information agents...

"When the Industrial Age separated production and consumption, it created buyers and sellers—the basis for the modern market economy. The Information Age should bring a second and equally profound division of labor, this time involving the separation of those who supply products from those who provide information about them.

"The result will be improved information to consumers. The product information we get today is biased because it is provided by the same people who want to sell the products; i.e., it is 'promotional' information. All other things being equal, consumers would always prefer to get their information from impartial rather than promotional sources. Until now, all other things have not been equal: Promoters have been more efficient at collecting and distributing information than independent information sources.

"Now, however, the development of new and more efficient information infrastructures could change this equation. These infrastructures will change the economics of gathering and using information in a way that favors impartial information sources."

Source: James H. Snider, "Shopping in the Information Age," in *The Futurist*, November-December 1992, pp. 14-15.

Environmental Technologies

★ 656 ★

Sulfur Dioxide Reductions Resulting from Clean Coal Technology, 1980-2030

"The Clean Air Act and its 1977 amendments created, in effect, two major categories of coal-burning power plants in the U.S.: (1) those built before 1978 which typically have little, if any, pollution control equipment (except, in some cases, devices that capture small particles of ash called *particulates*) and (2) those built after 1978 which are equipped with *flue gas scrubbers* (until recently the scrubber was the only commercial technology capable of achieving the 70% to 90% SO_2 reduction standard).

"The nation's clean air laws were tightened substantially in 1990 when Congress again amended the 1970 Clean Air Act. The amendments constituted the most sweeping changes in environmental legislation since the original Act, with provisions to reduce releases of virtually every airborne pollutant from smog-causing automobile emissions to toxic pollutants from factories and chemical plants. The acid rain provisions of the new legislation were among the most stringent. They affect almost every existing power generator in the U.S. and will influence the choice of fuel and technology for every new power plant to be built in this country in the foreseeable future.

"Under the new legislation, signed by President Bush on November 15, 1990, utilities will have to cut their sulfur dioxide emissions by 10 million tons from 1980 levels by the year 2000 (with a 4-year time extension if certain clean coal technologies are used). After that time, a nationwide utility SO_2 emission cap of 8.9 million tons per year will go into effect. All new power generators that burn fossil fuels after 2000 will have to stay within the SO_2 cap, either offsetting sulfur releases from new plants by cutting emissions at existing plants or by purchasing emission 'credits' from utilities that have made greater-than-required SO_2 reductions.

[Millions of tons]

Year	
1980	17.0
1990	15.5
2000	8.9
2010	8.9

[Continued]

★ 656 ★

Sulfur Dioxide Reductions Resulting from Clean Coal Technology, 1980-2030

[Continued]

Year	
2020	8.9
2030	8.9

Source: U.S. Department of Energy, *Clean Coal Technology* (Washington, D.C.: U.S. Government PrMarch 1992), pp. 9-11. *Note:* Magnitudes estimated from published chart.

★ 657 ★

Environmental Technologies

Earth 21: Technological Developments to Limit Air Pollutant Emissions, 1993-2050

"Reducing carbon dioxide is a hard task, even in a long-range view. Nevertheless, we should make long-term efforts to mitigate global warming as much as possible. Among the many new technologies, these will play key roles in the future, though they may not be sufficient solutions:

"*Short-term future (present to 2010)*: Energy-conservation technologies and high-efficiency energy-conversion technologies (such as thermo-electric and chemical-electric energy conversion).

"*Intermediate future (2010 to 2050)*: Nuclear technologies (such as inherently safe systems and fast breeder reactors), small-scale photovoltaics, and carbon-dioxide-removal technology.

"*Long-term future (2050 and beyond)*: Large-scale photovoltaics, and energy-system photovoltaics and energy-system restructuring (such as redesign of residential areas)."

Source: Yasuhiko Ishida, "Regreening the Earth: Japan's 100-year Plan," in *The Futurist*, July-August 1993, p. 24. *Note:* CFC = Chloroflurocarbons.

Industrial and Energy Technologies

★658★

Development of Chlorofluorocarbon-free Refrigerator Technology, 1992-1997

"In an innovative effort to overcome market barriers that have slowed the commmercialization of more energy-efficient consumer appliances, 25 U.S. utilities joined to offer a 'Golden Carrot' in the form of a $30-million award to the winner of a design competition for an advanced, energy-saving refrigerator that is free of ozone-depleting chloroflurocarbons (CFCs). The consortium, the Super-Efficient Refrigerator Program, Inc. (SERP), was formed in collaboration with the U.S. EPA Global Change Division's green programs, EPRI, and others. Its member utilities provide electric service to more than one quarter of the Nation's households. The award will provide the winning manufacturer with a subsidy of over $100 per refrigerator. In return, the new super-efficient refrigerator will be delivered in participating utilities' service areas before it is available to other distributors...

"The competition challenged manufacturers to commit to producing a CFC-free refrigerator at least 25 percent more efficient than the 1993 Federal energy efficient standards require and to deliver them to participating utilities' service areas in 1994-97. The manufacturer must agree to assemble the refrigerators in North America. Additional points in the competition could be awarded for achieving greater efficiency levels.

"Bids were due in October 1992 and all but 1 of the 15 major U.S. manufacturers entered the competition. Submittals were reviewed based on a number of key factors including proposed design, efficiency levels, incentive requested, marketing plans, and technological experience. In December 1992, Whirlpool Corp. and Frigidaire Co. were selected as finalists to design the new refrigerator.

"The winner announced in June 1993 was Whirlpool Corp., which will deliver about 250,000 SERP refrigerators in various models between 1994 and 1997. SERP refrigerators will be priced the same as other models with similar features.

"EPA estimates that a super-efficient refrigerator has the potential to save 300 to 400 kWh/year over its lifetime and save its owners a total of about $500 on utility bills. It also is expected to eliminate 9,000 pounds of carbon dioxide emissions compared with current models."

Source: U.S. Congress, Office of Technology Assessment, *Energy Efficiency* (Washington, D.C.: U.S. Government Printing Office, September 1993), pp. 75-6. *Primary source:* U.S. Environmental Protection Agency, Office of Atmospheric Programs, *1992 Accomplishments and Prospects for 1993*, vol. 1: Global Change Division, EPA 430-K 92-031, November 1992, pp. 11-12; Gary Fernstrom, "Building a Better Refrigerator," *Environment*, September/October 1992, p. 27; Utilities sponsoring "Super-Fridge Contest to Get an Edge in Marketing," *Electric Utility Week*, 5 July 1993, p. 4. *Notes:* CFC= Chlorofluorocarbons; EPRI=Environmental Protection Research Institute; SERP=Super-Efficient Refrigerator Program.

★ 659 ★

Industrial and Energy Technologies

Predictive Technology Equipment Maintenance, 1992-1997

"Many industries such as aerospace are beginning to recognize the benefits of 'predictive'—rather than crisis—maintenance of equipment, according to Frost & Sullivan, an international market-research publisher.

"Leading the way, the aerospace industry spent more than $38 million on so-called condition-monitoring equipment in 1992. Other industrial sectors are now increasing their spending on vibration sensing, oil-debris analysis, and thermographic and other condition-monitoring equipment, pushing total sales to an expected $246 million a year by 1997, up from $195 million in 1992.

"'Commercial pressures to increase life expectancy and maximize service and maintenance intervals have been a major driving force behind the widespread adoption of condition monitoring practice,' says Frost & Sullivan."

Source: "Predicting Equipment Breakdowns," in *The Futurist*, March-April 1993, p. 8. *Primary source:* Frost & Sullivan International.

★ 660 ★

Industrial and Energy Technologies

Energy Use for Major Industrial Processes under Alternate Technology Scenarios, 1980-2010

"At any given time, the mix of technologies used by industry ranges from outdated to state-of-the-art. Energy efficiency improves as older facilities are replaced with state-of-the-art ones. In the petroleum refining, chemical, pulp and paper, steel, aluminum, cement, and glass industries, most state-of-the-art technologies use 12 to 38 percent less energy than the mix of processes currently used. This comparison does not imply that these industries would find it economical to bring all their existing plants to state-of-the-art levels at once, but instead shows the energy savings that can be expected as plants are modernized. Energy efficiency also improves as advanced technologies are developed to become the state-of-the-art of tomorrow. Advanced technologies, not yet commercialized, could possibly reduce energy use in the various processes by an additional 9 to 35 percent."

Process	Current[A]	(Year)	State-of-the-art (2010)	Advanced (2010)	
Petroleum refining	602	(1989)	405	363	thousand Btu/barrel of crude oil
Miscellaneous chemicals					
Sulfuric acid[B]	-1,860	(1988)	-2,120	-3,230	thousand Btu/ton of sulfuric acid
Nitrogen and oxygen[C]	3,730	(1985)	3,150	2,820	thousand Btu/ton of oxygen and nitrogen
Ethylene	58.2	(1988)	57.4	52.4	million Btu/ton of ethylene
Pulp and paper[D]					
Chemical process (kraft)	39.4	(1985)	26.7	20.0	million Btu/ton of paper
Mechanical (stone groundwood)	35.1		29.0	-	
Semichemical	36.6		26.5	20.5	
Thermomechanical	40.9		31.9	28.2	
Chemimechanical (nonsulfur)	-		-	13.9	

[Continued]

★ 660 ★

Energy Use for Major Industrial Processes under Alternate Technology Scenarios, 1980-2010

[Continued]

Process	Current[A]	(Year)	State-of-the-art (2010)	Advanced (2010)	
Biological	-		-	23.2	
Repulping recycled paper	23.8		18.5	14.8	
Steel[E]					
Basic oxygen process	26.0	(1983)	16.1	-	million Btu/ton of finished steel
Electric process (scrap-based)	15.4		10.2	8.8	
Direct steelmaking	-		-	14.0	
Aluminum					
Alumina and aluminum production	196	(1980)	162	137	million Btu/ton of aluminum
Aluminum smelting only	160		135	110	
Cement[F]	5,070	(1988)	3,780	3,110	thousand Btu/ton of cement
Glass					
Flat glass	15.0	(1985)	10.3	6.9	million Btu/ton of glass
Container glass	15.6		12.1	8.9	
Pressed and blown glass	27.4		22.8	15.2	
Fibrous glass	24.5		21.6	14.0	

Source: U.S. Congress, Office of Technology Assessment, *Industrial Energy Efficiency* (Washington, D.C.: U.S. Government Printing Office, August 1993), p. 67-8. *Notes:* The energy values in this table are unlike most others in this report in that they account for purchased electricity at 10,500 Btu/kWh. This inconsistency arises because of how the figures were reported in the original sources; that is, generation and transmission losses are included. A. Average of currently implemented technologies. B. Figures for sulfuric acid are negative because the production process is exothermic—it produces more energy than it consumes. C. Assumes production of 58 percent nitrogen and 42 percent oxygen. D. Mix of paper products is 8 percent newsprint, 30 percent printing and writing paper, 4 percent industrial paper, 7 percent tissue paper, 49 percent paperboard, and 2 percent construction paper. E. Steel figures embody: 65 percent continuous casting and 35 percent ingot casting in the current case; 95 percent continuous casting and 5 percent ingot casting in the state of the art case; and 68 percent strip casting, 27 percent continuous casting, and 5 percent ingot casting in the advanced case. Mix of steel products is 21 percent hot rolled sheet and strip, 38 percent cold rolled sheet and strip, 9 percent heavy plate, 7 percent shapes and rails, and 25 percent bars and wire rods. F. Cement produced from domestic clinker.

★ 661 ★

Industrial and Energy Technologies

Energy Use by Selected Chemical Production Technologies under Alternate Scenarios, 1993-2010

"In the 1980s, the chemical industry restructured itself by closing inefficient and obsolete plants, streamlining production processes, reorganizing corporate activities, and placing more emphasis on specialty chemicals with high profit margins. As a result, the chemical industry currently uses relatively state-of-the-art technologies. There remain, however, large opportunities for new cogeneration capacity."

[Thousand Btu/ton of end product]

Process	Energy use		
	Current[A] (1993)	State-of-the-art (2010)	Advanced (2010)
Sulfuric acid (1988)[B]			
Energy consumption	232	-	-
Export steam	-2,093	-	-
Total (net energy production)	-1,861	-2,117	-3,226
Nitrogen and oxygen production (1985)[C]			
Separation	540	351	244
Compression (80 percent of production)	409	409	409
Liquefaction (20 percent of production)	1,720	1,720	1,720
Electricity losses	2,517	2,124	1,902
Total	3,728	3,146	2,818
Ethylene (1988)			
Feedstock energy	53,600	53,600	49,000
Process energy	4,600	3,800	3,400
Total	58,200	57,400	52,400

Source: U.S. Congress, Office of Technology Assessment, *Industrial Energy Efficiency* (Washington, D.C.: U.S. Government Printing Office, August 1993), pp. 88, 90. *Primary source:* Energetic Inc., *Industry Profiles: Chemicals*, prepared for the U.S. Department of Energy, Office of Industrial Technologies, December 1990. Some data modified by the Office of Technology Assessment. *Notes:* A. Average of currently implemented technologies. B. Figures for sulfuric acid are negative because the production process is exothermic—it produces more energy than it consumes. C. Assumes production of 58 percent nitrogen and 42 percent oxygen.

★ 662 ★

Industrial and Energy Technologies

Energy Use by Pulp and Paper Production Technologies under Alternate Scenarios, 1988-2010

"Paper mills process cellulose fibers, primarily from wood, into writing paper, newsprint, magazine stock, paperboard, card boards, sanitary tissues, and various other decorative and structural papers. The wood is first ground and pulped to separate the fibers from each other and suspend them in water. Later, the pulp is filtered onto wire screens, dried, and formed into paper. Along the way, the fibers may be beaten for strength, bleached for whiteness, or sized to improve their writing characteristics. There are five principle process steps in paper production: 1) wood preparation, 2) pulping, 3) bleaching, 4) chemical recovery, and 5) papermaking...

"On average, about 35 million Btu are used to produce a ton of paper (based on 1988 data). The most energy-intensive steps are the papermaking, pulping, and chemical recovery steps. Widespread adoption of state-of-the-art technologies can reduce energy consumption by an estimated 29 percent from current average practices. The potential reductions are greatest for the papermaking stage. Advanced technologies, not yet commercialized, could possibly reduce energy use an additional 27 percent."

[Million Btu/ton of product]

Process	Process mix			Measure	Energy use			Product
	Current (1988)	State-of-the-art (2010)	Advanced (2010)		Current[A] (1988)	State-of-the-art (2010)	Advanced (2010)	
Wood preparation	0.71	0.71	0.71	tons of wood per ton of pulp	0.5	0.4	0.4	Wood
Pulping								
Chemical: kraft	55.3	55.2	42.5	% pulp produced	8.3	4.9	4.4	Pulp
Chemical: sulfite	1.8	2.1	1.4	% pulp produced	8.6	6.3	5.7	Pulp
Chemical: other[B]	1.6	1.5	1.4	% pulp produced	16.0	8.8	7.9	Pulp
Semichemical: neutral sulfite	5.0	5.0	2.1	% pulp produced	9.8	7.2	6.5	Pulp
Mechanical: stone groundwood	2.0	2.1	-	% pulp produced	14.5	13.2	-	Pulp
Mechanical: refiner mechanical[C]	2.0	-	-	% pulp produced	18.6	-	-	Pulp
Thermomechanical	2.8	5.0	5.0	% pulp produced	19.7	15.8	15.8	Pulp
Chemimechanical	-	-	-	% pulp produced	-	14.5	-	Pulp
OPCO process	-	-	-	% pulp produced	-	-	12.6	Pulp
Non-sulfur process	-	-	10.6	% pulp produced	-	-	3.2	Pulp
Biological	-	-	5.7	% pulp produced	-	-	11.4	Pulp
Alcohol	-	-	2.1	% pulp produced	-	-	2.2	Pulp
Waste paper	19.6	20.4	20.4	% pulp produced	4.3	4.0	4.0	Pulp
Market pulp drying	9.9	8.7	8.7	% pulp produced	4.2	4.0	1.3	Pulp
Subtotal	1.11	1.13	1.13	tons of pulp per ton of paper	7.9	5.5	4.9	Pulp
Bleaching	0.3	0.3	0.3	fraction of pulp bleached	7.5	5.6	4.5	Pulp
Chemical recovery								
Kraft	55.3	55.2	42.5	% pulp produced	10.1	6.4	4.2	Pulp
Sulfite	1.8	2.1	1.4	% pulp produced	7.5	4.8	3.1	Pulp
Semichemical	5.0	5.0	2.1	% pulp produced	6.0	3.8	2.5	Pulp
Subtotal	0.62	0.62	0.46	fraction of pulp with a chemical recovery stage	9.7	6.1	4.1	Pulp
Papermaking								
Newsprint	7.6	8.0	8.0	% paper produced	8.2	5.5	3.7	Paper
Printing and writing paper	27.8	30.1	30.1	% paper produced	13.8	9.3	5.6	Paper
Industrial paper	6.4	4.0	4.0	% paper produced	14.1	9.5	5.7	Paper
Tissue paper	7.0	7.3	7.3	% paper produced	11.2	8.3	8.3	Paper
Paperboard	37.5	37.6	37.6	% paper produced	13.6	9.2	5.5	Paper
Recycled paperboard	11.2	11.3	11.3	% paper produced	13.6	9.2	5.5	Paper

[Continued]

★ 662 ★

Energy Use by Pulp and Paper Production Technologies under Alternate Scenarios, 1988-2010

[Continued]

Process	Process mix			Measure	Energy use			Product
	Current (1988)	State-of-the-art (2010)	Advanced (2010)		Current[A] (1988)	State-of-the-art (2010)	Advanced (2010)	
Construction paper	2.4	1.7	1.7	% paper produced	12.7	8.6	5.1	Paper
Subtotal	1.00	1.00	1.00	ton of paper	13.1	8.9	5.6	Paper
Auxiliary equipment								
Lighting, space heating, and power plant	1.00	1.00	1.00	ton of paper	2.9	2.7	2.7	Paper
Total	1.00	1.00	1.00	ton of paper	34.5	24.6	18.0	Paper

Source: U.S. Congress, Office of Technology Assessment, *Industrial Energy Efficiency* (Washington, D.C.: U.S. Government Printing Office, August 1993), pp. 90-1, 93. *Primary source:* A. Elaahi and Howard E. Lowitt, Energetics Inc., *The U.S. Pulp and Paper Industry: An Energy Perspective*, prepared for the U.S. Department of Energy, Office of Industrial Programs (Springfield, VA: National Technical Information Service, April 1988). Energetics Inc., *Industry Profiles: Paper*, prepared for the U.S. DOE, Office of Industrial Technologies, December 1990. *Notes:* Purchased electricity is counted at 10,500 Btu/kWh; generation transmissions and losses are included. Estimated losses in 1988 were approximately 4.3 million Btu per ton of paper. A. Average of currently implemented technologies. B. Chemical processes for dissolving pulps and alpha pulps. C. For state-of-the-art, refiner mechanical pulping is assumed to be replaced by thermomechanical pulping with heat recovery.

★ 663 ★

Industrial and Energy Technologies

Energy Use by Steel Production Technologies under Alternate Scenarios, 1989-2010

"Steel products are produced from iron ore and iron scrap using a variety of pyrometallurgical, eletrolytic, and mechanical processes. Integrated mills rely mostly on ore-based processes, the most common of which involves reducing pelletized iron ore into pig iron using coke (in a blast furnace); refining the iron into steel (in a basic oxygen furnace); and casting, forming, and treating the steel into sheet, bars, beams, and other products. The major steps are: ore preparation, cokemaking, ironmaking, steelmaking, primary casting, secondary finishing, and heat treating...

"The most energy-intensive steps are ironmaking and electric steelmaking. Reductions in energy intensity can result from shifts in the mix of processes, improvements in the efficiency of the processes, and improvements in yields. Currently, about 22 million Btu are used on average to produce a ton of finished steel (based on 1990 and 1991 and data)...

"Widespread adoption of state-of-the-art technologies can reduce energy consumption by about 34 to 38 percent from current average practices. Advanced technologies, not yet commercialized, could possibly reduce energy use an additional 13 percent."

[Million Btu/ton of product]

Process	Process mix			Tons input per ton output or percent	Energy use			Product
	Current (1988)	State-of-the-art (2010)	Advanced (2010)		Current[A] (1988)	State-of-the-art (2010)	Advanced (2010)	
Agglomeration								
Pelletizing	1.11	1.11	1.11	Pellets/pig iron	0.4	0.2	0.2	Pellets
Sintering	0.38	0.38	0.38	Sinter/pig iron	1.5	1.2	1.2	Sinter
Cokemaking	0.54	0.54	0.54	Coke/pig iron	6.0	3.0	3.0	Coke
Ironmaking	0.85	0.85	0.85	Pig iron/BOF steel	13.9	10.2	10.2	Iron
	0.66	-	-	Pig iron/OH steel	13.9	-	-	Iron
Steelmaking								
Basic oxygen furnace (BOF)	59.6	62.0	31.0	percent	0.5	-0.1	-0.1	BOF steel
Open hearth (OH)	4.5	-	-	percent	3.3	-	-	OH steel
Electric arc furnace (EAF)	35.9	38.0	38.0	percent	6.3	5.0	5.0	EAF steel

[Continued]

★ 663 ★

Energy Use by Steel Production Technologies under Alternate Scenarios, 1989-2010

[Continued]

Process	Process mix			Tons input per ton output or percent	Energy use			Product
	Current (1988)	State-of-the-art (2010)	Advanced (2010)		Current[A] (1988)	State-of-the-art (2010)	Advanced (2010)	
Direct steelmaking	-	-	31.0	percent	-	-	9.9	Direct steel
Raw steel production, subtotal								
Ore/coke/iron/BOF route	-	-	-	-	15.9	10.5	10.5	BOF steel
Ore/coke/iron/OH route	-	-	-	-	15.2	-	-	OH steel
Scrap/electric furnace route	-	-	-	-	6.3	5.0	5.0	EAF steel
Direct steelmaking route	-	-	-	-	-	-	9.9	Direct steel
Average	1.00	1.00	1.00	Ton of raw steel	12.4	8.4	8.2	Raw steel
Primary casting								
Ingot casting	35.1	5.0	5.0	percent	2.7	0.7	0.7	Cast steel
Continuous casting	64.8	95.0	27.0	percent	1.0	0.2	0.2	Cast steel
Strip casting	-	-	68.0	percent	-	-	[B]	Cast steel
Average	0.91	0.94	0.94	Cast steel/raw steel	1.6	0.3	0.1	Cast steel
Forming, finishing, heat treating, and annealing								
Sheet/strip: hot rolled	21.1	21.1	-	percent	2.5	1.5	-	Finished steel
Sheet/strip: cold rolled	37.9	37.9	-	percent	6.2	3.8	-	Finished steel
Heavy plate	9.0	9.0	-	percent	3.2	2.4	-	Finished steel
Sheet/strip: hot rolled (strip cast).	-	-	21.1	percent	-	-	0.7	Finished steel
Sheet/strip: cold rolled (strip cast).	-	-	37.9	percent	-	-	1.6	Finished steel
Heavy plate (strip cast)	-	-	9.0	percent	-	-	1.0	Finished steel
Shapes and rails	6.7	6.7	6.7	percent	4.4	1.9	1.9	Finished steel
Bars/wire rods	25.3	25.3	25.3	percent	5.0	2.7	2.7	Finished steel
Average	0.91	0.94	0.94	Finished steel/raw steel	4.7	2.8	1.7	Finished steel
Unallocated energy[C]	-	-	-	-	1.9	1.8	1.6	Raw steel
Total	-	-	-	-	20.1	13.1	11.5	Raw steel
					22.2	13.9	12.2	Finished steel

Source: U.S. Congress, Office of Technology Assessment, *Industrial Energy Efficiency* (Washington, D.C.: U.S. Government Printing Office, August 1993), pp. 97-99. *Primary sources:* Sayed A. Azami and Howard E. Lowitt, Energetics, Inc., *The U.S. Steel Industry: An Energy Perspective*, prepared for the U.S. Department of Energy, Office of Industrial Programs (Springfield, VA: National Technical Information Service, January 1988). Energetics Inc., *Industry Profiles: Steel*, prepared for the U.S. Department of Energy, Office of Industrial Programs (Springfield, VA: National Technical Information Service, January 1988). Energetics Inc., *Industry Profiles: Steel*, prepared for the U.S. DOE, Office of Industrial Technologies, December 1990. F. T. Sparrow, Argonne National Laboratory, *Energy and Materials Flows in the Iron and Steel Industry* (Springfield, VA: National Technical Information Service, August 1979). Some data modified by the Office of Technology Assessment. *Notes:* Purchased electricity is counted at 10,500 Btu/kWh; generation transmissions and losses are included. Estimated losses in 1989 were approximately 3.0 million Btu per ton of raw steel. BOF=basic oxygen furnace; OH=open hearth furnace; EAF=electric arc furnace. A. Average of currently implemented technologies. B. All energy use for direct strip casting is charged to appropriate forming and finishing processes; hot and cold rolled sheet/strip and heavy plate. C. Includes galvanizing, electrolyte tinning, fuel-fired boiler operations, power generation services, and other miscellaneous services.

★ 664 ★

Industrial and Energy Technologies

Energy Use by Aluminum Production Technologies under Alternate Scenarios, 1980-2010

"Electric power accounts for about 26 percent of the aluminum industry's production costs, other energy sources account for an additional 1 percent (based on 1990 data). As a consequence, aluminum production capacity is located in areas of abundant, inexpensive electricity. In the United States, smelter capacity is located roughly one-third in the Pacific Northwest, one-third in the Ohio Valley, and the rest in the Carolinas, New York, and Texas. Because of rising electricity prices, very little aluminum smelting capacity has been built in the United States in the recent past and none is expected to be built in the future. Most new capacity, is being located in Australia, Canada, Brazil, and Venezuela.

"The Bayer refining process produces pure alumina from bauxite. The bauxite is crushed and ground, then digested in hot (280 to 450F) caustic soda (NaOH) solution. The alumina minerals in the ore react with the caustic soda and dissolve as sodium-aluminate. Most of the impurities in the ore precipitate out as 'red mud,' which is removed by countercurrent decantation and filtration. The solution is then seeded with starter crystals and agitated to crystallize out alumina hydrate. This material is then calcined in kilns (to remove the water) and the result is pure alumina.

"Alumina refining accounts on average for about 27 percent of the energy used in aluminum production (based on 1980 data). State-of-the-art technologies can reduce energy use in alumina production by 24 percent. However, these savings do not apply to all aluminum production, because about half of U.S. alumina supplies are imported instead of refined domestically."

[Million Btu/ton of aluminum]

Process	Energy use		
	Current (1980)	State-of-the-art (2010)	Advanced (2010)
Alumina refining: Bayer process	35.5	27.0	27.0
Alumina smelting: Hall-Heroult process			
Electrolysis (kWh per lb of aluminum)	49.5 (7.3)	42.3 (6.2)	
Fume recycling and other electricity	3.4 (0.5)	2.7 (0.4)	
Anode production: heat and energy	5.4	3.3	
Anode production: raw materials	14.6	12.5	
Fluoride production	2.0	0.4	
Subtotal	74.9	61.2	49.0[B]
Holding, casting, melting, alloying, and scrap remelting.	9.5	9.5	9.5
Total end use energy			
Based on domestic alumina refining	119.8	97.7	85.4
Based on imported alumina	84.3	70.7	58.4

[Continued]

★ 664 ★

Energy Use by Aluminum Production Technologies under Alternate Scenarios, 1980-2010

[Continued]

Process	Energy use		
	Current (1980)	State-of-the-art (2010)	Advanced (2010)
Electricity losses[C]	75.6	64.2	51.7
Total[D]	177.7	148.4	123.6

Source: U.S. Congress, Office of Technology Assessment, *Industrial Energy Efficiency* (Washington, D.C.: U.S. Government Printing Office, August 1993), pp. 105-6. *Primary sources:* S.Y. Shen, Argonne National Laboratory, *Energy and Materials Flows in the Production of Primary Aluminum* (Springfield, VA: National Technical Information Service, October 1981). R.M. Arons and A.M. Wolsky, Argonne National Laboratory, *Energy and Materials Flows in the Fabrication of Aluminum Products* (Springfield, VA: National Technical Information Service, August 1988). Energetics, Inc., *Industry Profiles: Aluminum*, prepared for the U.S. Department of Energy, Office of Industrial Programs December 1990. *Notes:* Purchased electricity is counted at 10,500 Btu/kWh; generation transmissions and losses are included. A. Average of currently implemented technologies. B. Based on estimated 20 percent improvement in smelting energy efficiency. C. Assumes that 65 percent of electricity is produced from thermal sources (68 percent losses) and 35 percent produced from hydro sources (10 percent losses). D. Assumes that half of the alumina is refined domestically and half is imported.

★ 665 ★

Industrial and Energy Technologies

Energy Use by Cement Production Technologies under Alternate Scenarios, 1988-2010

"There are two principal categories of cement production, the wet process and the dry process. In the wet process, water is added to the process stream at the grinding stage and later the materials are fed into the kiln as a slurry. In the dry process, the raw materials are ground without water, then preheated or precalcined, and finally fed into the kiln as a dry meal that contains less than 7 percent moisture. The preheat and precalcined stage uses waste heat from the kiln. In some plants, this intermediate stage is skipped and the dry ground materials are fed directly into the kiln...

"[Raw materials production], which includes the crushing, proportioning, drying, grinding, and blending of the various minerals, accounts for about 8 percent of the energy used in cement manufacturing. The grinding stage, which consumes the most energy, is done either wet or dry. The wet process requires less energy at the grinding stage, but much more energy in clinker production. Grinding is particularly inefficient, with an estimated 2 to 5 percent of the input energy going to breaking materials apart, and the remainder going into heat and vibration. Full use of state-of-the-art technologies such as the dry process, with additional drying in the mills and improved classification schemes, are estimated to reduce energy use in raw materials preparation by about 19 percent from current average practices. Technologies, not yet commercialized, such as advanced sensors and instrumentation, modeling and controls for grinding circuits, and differential grinding, may be able to reduce the energy use an additional 23 percent.

"Sintering and fusing the ground materials into clinker is the most energy-intensive stage of the process. It accounts for approximately 80 percent of the energy used in cement production. The dry process with precalcining or preheating uses the least energy, the wet process uses the most. Advances in the preheater and precalciner processes have led to significant improvements in the overall energy efficiency of cement production in recent years."

[Thousand Btu/ton of clinker]

Process	Process mix (fraction of clinker processed, except where noted)			Energy use		
	Current (1988)	State-of-the-art (2010)	Advanced (2010)	Current[A] (1988)	State-of-the-art (2010)	Advanced (2010)
Raw materials preparation						
Primary crushing	1.00	1.00	1.00	26	24	42
Secondary crushing	1.00	1.00	-	32	28	B
Proportioning	1.00	1.00	1.00	21	19	19
Drying	0.16	-	-	270	-	-
Raw grinding (wet)	0.34	-	-	275	-	-
Raw grinding (dry)	0.66	1.00	1.00	312	270	203
Blending	1.00	1.00	1.00	2	2	2
Subtotal				425	343	266
Clinker production						
Long kiln (wet)	0.34	-	-	4,932	-	-
Long kiln (dry), no preheat/precalcine	0.16	-	-	4,294	-	-
Short kiln (dry), with preheat	0.20	0.20	-	3,469	3,000	-
Short kiln (dry), with precalcine	0.30	0.80	0.80	3,322	3,000	2,500
Stationary clinkering, with precalcine	-	-	0.20	-	-	2,360
Clinker cooling	1.00	1.00	1.00	63	57	57
Subtotal				4,121	3,057	2,529
Finish grinding						
Ball milling	0.95	-	-	525	-	-
Ball milling, with pregrinding	0.05	0.99	0.70	473	378	321

[Continued]

★ 665 ★

Energy Use by Cement Production Technologies under Alternate Scenarios, 1988-2010

[Continued]

Process	Process mix (fraction of clinker processed, except where noted)			Energy use		
	Current (1988)	State-of-the-art (2010)	Advanced (2010)	Current[A] (1988)	State-of-the-art (2010)	Advanced (2010)
Roller milling	-	0.01	0.20	-	420	315
Nonmechanical grinding	-	-	0.10	-	-	300
Subtotal				522	378	318
Total						
From domestic clinker	97%	93%	74%	5,067	3,778	3,112
From imported clinker	3%	7%	6%	522	378	318
From secondary materials	-	-	20%	-	-	-
Weighted average				4,925	3,528	2,325

Source: U.S. Congress, Office of Technology Assessment, *Industrial Energy Efficiency* (Washington, D.C.: U.S. Government Printing Office, August 1993), pp. 108-110. *Primary source:* S. R. Venkateswaren and Howard E. Lowitt, Energetics Inc., *The U.S. Cement Industry: An Energy Perspective*, prepared for the DOE, Office of Industrial Programs (Springfield, VA: National Technical Information Service, May 1988). Energetics, Inc., *Industry Profiles: Cement*, prepared for the U.S. Department of Energy, Office of Industrial Programs, December 1990. *Notes:* Purchased electricity is counted at 10,500 Btu/kWh; generation transmissions and losses are included. A. Average of currently implemented technologies. B. Included in primary crushing.

★ 666 ★

Industrial and Energy Technologies

Energy Use by Glass Production Technologies under Alternate Scenarios, 1985-2010

"Glass is produced by melting silica, limestone, and soda ash, in a furnace and allowing them to cool to an amorphous (noncrystalline) state. Other elements may be added to alter the color or other properties. While still molten, the glass is formed into a variety of products including: windows, mirrors, bottles, jars, light bulbs, tableware, and fiberglass. The principal processing steps are batch preparation, melting and refining, forming, and postforming. "The energy used to manufacture glass varies significantly among the major categories of glass products: flat, containers, pressed and blown, and fibrous. Currently, between 15 and 27 million Btu are used on average to produce a ton of glass, depending on the product (based on 1985 data). For the industry as a whole, widespread adoption of state-of-the-art technologies can reduce energy consumption by an estimated 21 percent from current average practices. The estimated reductions are greatest for flat glass and smallest for fibrous glass. Advanced technologies, not yet commercialized, could possibly reduce energy use an additional 30 percent."

Process	Process mix (tons of product/ton of finished glass)			Energy use (million Btu/ton product)			Product
	Current (1985)	State-of-the-art (2010)	Advanced (2010)	Current[A] (1985)	State-of-the-art (2010)	Advanced (2010)	
Flat glass							
Batch preparation	1.32	1.32	1.26	0.27	0.24	0.24	Batch processed glass
Melting and refining							
Large fossil fuel melter	1.26	1.26	-	8.10	5.10	-	Melted glass
Advanced melter with batch preheat	-	-	1.20	-	-	3.00	Melted glass
Subtotal	1.26	1.26	1.20	8.10	5.10	3.00	Melted glass
Forming	1.26	1.26	1.20	1.45	1.30	1.17	Formed glass

[Continued]

★ 666 ★

Energy Use by Glass Production Technologies under Alternate Scenarios, 1985-2010

[Continued]

Process	Process mix (tons of product/ton of finished glass)			Energy use (million Btu/ton product)			Product
	Current (1985)	State-of-the-art (2010)	Advanced (2010)	Current[A] (1985)	State-of-the-art (2010)	Advanced (2010)	
Post-forming							
Annealing	1.20	1.20	-	0.42	0.27	-	Postformed glass
Tempering	0.60	0.60	-	3.03	2.14	-	Postformed glass
Laminating/autoclaving	0.40	0.40	-	0.82	0.75	-	Postformed glass
Advanced	-	-	1.20	-	-	1.36	Postformed glass
Subtotal	1.20	1.20	1.20	2.20	1.59	1.36	Postformed glass
Total	1.00	1.00	1.00	15.03	10.28	6.93	Finished glass
Container glass							
Batch preparation	1.32	1.32	1.24	0.53	0.48	0.48	Batch processed glass
Melting and refining							
Large fossil fuel melter	1.01	1.01	-	5.50	3.90	-	Melted glass
Small fossil fuel melter	0.19	0.19	-	9.42	8.35	-	Melted glass
Small electric melter	0.06	0.06	-	10.50	8.90	-	Melted glass
Advanced melter with batch preheat	-	-	1.19	-	-	3.00	Melted glass
Subtotal	1.26	1.26	1.19	6.34	4.82	3.00	Melted glass
Forming	1.20	1.20	1.13	4.01	3.20	2.88	Formed glass
Post-forming							
Annealing	1.13	1.13	-	1.84	1.40	-	Postformed glass
Advanced	-	-	1.13	-	-	1.33	Postformed glass
Subtotal	1.13	1.13	1.13	1.84	1.40	1.33	
Total	1.00	1.00	1.00	15.59	12.14	8.91	Finished glass
Pressed and blown glass							
Batch preparation	1.51	1.51	1.51	0.76	0.68	0.68	Batch processed glass
Melting and refining							
Small fossil fueled melter	1.30	1.30	-	10.10	8.00	-	Melted glass
Small electric melter	0.14	0.14	-	9.90	8.90	-	Melted glass
Advanced melter with batch preheat	-	-	1.30	-	-	3.00	Melted glass
Moly-lined electric melter	-	-	0.14	-	-	6.70	Melted glass
Subtotal	1.44	1.44	1.44	10.08	8.09	3.37	Melted glass
Forming	1.37	1.37	1.37	5.31	4.50	4.05	Formed glass
Post-forming							
Fire polishing	1.37	1.37	-	1.20	1.10	-	Postformed glass
Annealing	1.37	1.37	-	2.04	1.79	-	Postformed glass
Advanced	-	-	1.37	-	-	2.74	Postformed glass
Subtotal	1.37	1.37	1.37	3.24	2.89	2.74	Postformed glass
Total	1.00	1.00	1.00	27.37	22.80	15.18	Finished glass
Fibrous glass							
Batch preparation	1.30	1.30	1.30	1.15	1.04	1.04	Batch processed glass
Melting and refining							
Small fossil-fueled melter	1.11	1.11	-	9.89	9.08	-	Melted glass
Small electric melter	0.12	0.12	-	9.90	8.90	-	Melted glass
Advanced melter with batch preheat	-	-	1.11	-	-	3.00	Melted glass
Moly-lined electric melter	-	-	0.12	-	-	6.70	Melted glass

[Continued]

★ 666 ★

Energy Use by Glass Production Technologies under Alternate Scenarios, 1985-2010

[Continued]

Process	Process mix (tons of product/ton of finished glass)			Energy use (million Btu/ton product)			Product
	Current (1985)	State-of-the-art (2010)	Advanced (2010)	Current[A] (1985)	State-of-the-art (2010)	Advanced (2010)	
Subtotal	1.24	1.24	1.24	9.89	9.06	3.37	Melted glass
Forming	1.11	1.11	1.11	7.24	6.00	5.40	Formed glass
Post-forming							
Curing	1.00	1.00	-	1.10	0.94	-	Postformed glass
Drying	1.00	1.00	-	1.64	1.40	-	Postformed glass
Advanced	-	-	1.11	-	-	2.22	Postformed glass
Subtotal	1.00	1.00	1.11	2.74	2.34	2.22	Postformed glass
Total	1.00	1.00	1.00	24.51	21.56	13.98	Finished glass

Source: U.S. Congress, Office of Technology Assessment, *Industrial Energy Efficiency* (Washington, D.C.: U.S. Government Printing Office, August 1993), pp. 112-14. *Primary sources:* E. Babcock, E. Elaahi and Howard E. Lowitt, Energetics Inc., *The U.S. Glass Industry: An Energy Perspective*, prepared for the DOE, Office of the Industrial Programs (Springfield, VA: National Technical Information Service, September 1988). Energetics, Inc., *Industry Profiles: Glass*, prepared for the U.S. Department of Energy, Office of Industrial Programs, December 1990. *Notes:* Purchased electricity is counted at 10,500 Btu/kWh; generation transmissions and losses are included. Estimated losses in 1985 were approximately 2.6 million Btu/ton of flat glass; 4.4 million Btu/ton of container glass; 9.2 million Btu/ton of pressed and blown glass; and 7.6 million Btu/ton of fibrous glass. A. Average of currently implemented technologies.

★ 667 ★

Industrial and Energy Technologies

Residential Energy Efficiency Technologies, 1993-2010

"There are a variety of technologies available to cut residential energy use without diminishing the services provided. The basic strategies for cutting electricity use in the residential sector are:

—Improving residential building shell efficiency through better insulation by cutting conductive heat losses and gains through ceilings, walls, and floors; installing storm doors and windows; and cutting air infiltration by caulking gaps and weather-stripping around doors, windows, joints and other spaces.

—Choosing more efficient appliances for new installations and accelerating the retirement of older less efficient appliances.

—Improving the management of residential energy use through better maintenance, energy management controls, load shifting, and changes in occupant behavior.

"Improving the energy efficiency of existing buildings is one of the most promising and vital areas of energy savings. Space heating and cooling account for 30 percent of residential electricity use. Improved thermal integrity in new and existing residential buildings can reduce heating and cooling loads and save electricity.

[Continued]

★ 667 ★

Residential Energy Efficiency Technologies, 1993-2010

[Continued]

"Replacement of existing buildings by energy-efficient new buildings is slow and expensive; most of the existing housing stock will continue in use for the next 30 to 40 years or more. There are over 90 million residential units in the United States, and we are adding between 1 and 2 million units per year. Although by the year 2000 there will be 10 to 15 million new units, about 90 percent of the units existing in 2000 have already been built, and by the year 2010 it is estimated that about 70 percent of homes will consist of housing stock built before 1985.

"The most cost-effective time to incorporate energy-saving measures into buildings is when they are built, remodeled or rehabilitated. In fact, failure to make accommodation for energy-saving technology in material and design choices at this stage causes lost energy saving opportunities—for example, using the standard 2-by-4 dimension lumber in exterior walls instead of 2-by-6 construction that allows for more insulation, or not selecting the most energy efficient windows...

"Together, refrigerators and freezers make up about 24 percent of residential electricity demand. Both technologies have seen substantial increases in efficiency over the past 20 years, but opportunities for significant improvements in performance remain.

"The typical refrigerator on the market today uses just 45 percent of the electricity needed to run the average 1972 model. A combination of technological gains has produced these savings, including: more efficient fans, motors, and compressors; better or more compact insulation; improved door seals and gaskets; and dual compressors. DOE researchers believe that it is technically feasible to cut electricity needed to run today's average new model almost 50 percent further. EPRI's analysis estimates that more efficient refrigerators could cut energy use about 22 to 48 percent in 2000 over the 1987 stock. Even more efficient refrigerators are available today than those assumed in the EPRI report, so that the maximum potential savings probably understate the potential...

"About 15 percent of household electricity load is lighting. As in other sectors, use of more energy-efficient lighting products can save electricity for residential customers. OTA's recent report *Building Energy Efficiency* estimated that efficient lighting could cut residential lighting electricity use by one-third if one-half of all residential incandescent lights were replaced by compact fluorescents. Assuming the light is used 6 hours per day, OTA calculated a payback period of 1.7 years for a $20 compact fluorescent bulb. Compact fluorescents also last 10 to 13 times longer than standard incandescent bulbs. EPRI estimated maximum potential lighting related savings at from 20 to 40 percent in 2000...

[Continued]

★ 667 ★

Residential Energy Efficiency Technologies, 1993-2010

[Continued]

"Electric ranges and ovens account for 4 percent of household electricity demand. Newer models, particularly self-cleaning ovens, are more efficient than current stock owing to a number of changes: more insulation, better seals, improved heating elements and reflective pans, reduced thermal mass, reduced contact resistance, and better controls. The penetration of microwave ovens, convection ovens, and induction cooktops also offer energy savings. It is uncertain whether microwave ovens, which cook food with one-third the electricity required for standard electric ranges and ovens, will actually result in reduced cooking loads as consumers may tend to use them more as an adjunct to conventional appliances. EPRI estimates that replacement of the 1987 stock of ranges and ovens with more efficient models could produce savings of 10 to 20 percent in electricity demand for cooking in 2000.

"Dishwashers account for about 2 percent of household electricity use and are found in 43 percent of households. Energy-saving features such as better insulation, water temperature boosters, water saver cycles, and air drying cycles can cut electricity consumption. Total savings are dependent on the customers use of energy-saving cycles. EPRI estimates that improved dishwashers could cut dishwasher electricity demand in 2000 by 10 to 30 percent over 1987 stock.

"The remaining household electric appliances, such as clothes washers and dryers, televisions, stereos and other electronic equipment, vacuums, small household appliances, power tools, and home computers account for about 13 percent of present residential electricity use. This portion of household electricity demand is expected to grow with greater saturation of clothes washers and electronic equipment. Newer models will be more energy efficient, and EPRI estimate, that this trend is expected to result in electricity consumption that is 10 to 20 percent less than equivalent 1987 models by 2000."

Source: U.S. Congress, Office of Technology Assessment, *Energy Efficiency* (Washington, D.C.: U.S. Government Printing Office, September 1993), pp. 69, 74, 76-6. *Notes:* DOE=Department of Energy; EPRI=Environmental Protection Research Institute; OTA=Office of Technology Assessment.

★ 668 ★

Industrial and Energy Technologies

Increase in Number of Microprocessor Controller Chips Used in a Typical Car, Office and Home, 1970-2000

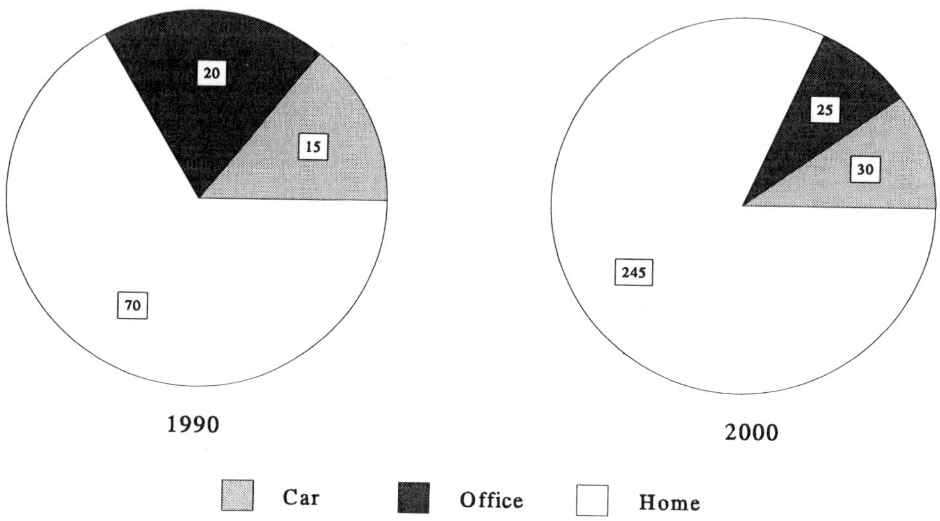

"Motorola reckons the number of 'controller chips' in use in every home, office and car will soar during the 1990s. So far about 1,000 manufacturers are using or experimenting with [Palo Alto, Ca., chip designer] Echelon's technology, among them AT&T, Hewlett-Packard, Schlumberger, ABB and Phillips. Working with Oracle, Echelon has developed systems that could control a houseful of gadgets. And IntelliNet, based in Naples, Florida, has developed a LonWorks-based network that allows homeowners to control everything from video systems to the swimming-pool temperature via a series of keypads located throughout their home."

[Number of chips]

Year	Car	Office	Home	Total
1970	0	0	0	0
1980	0	0	10	10
1990	15	20	70	105
2000	30	25	245	300

Source: "A Smaller, Friendlier Future," in *The Economist*, 17 September 1994, p. 20. *Primary source:* Motorola. *Note:* Magnitudes estimated from published chart.

Chapter 15
TRANSPORTATION

Transportation: General Statistics

★ 669 ★

Transportation Activity by Mode, 1970-2010

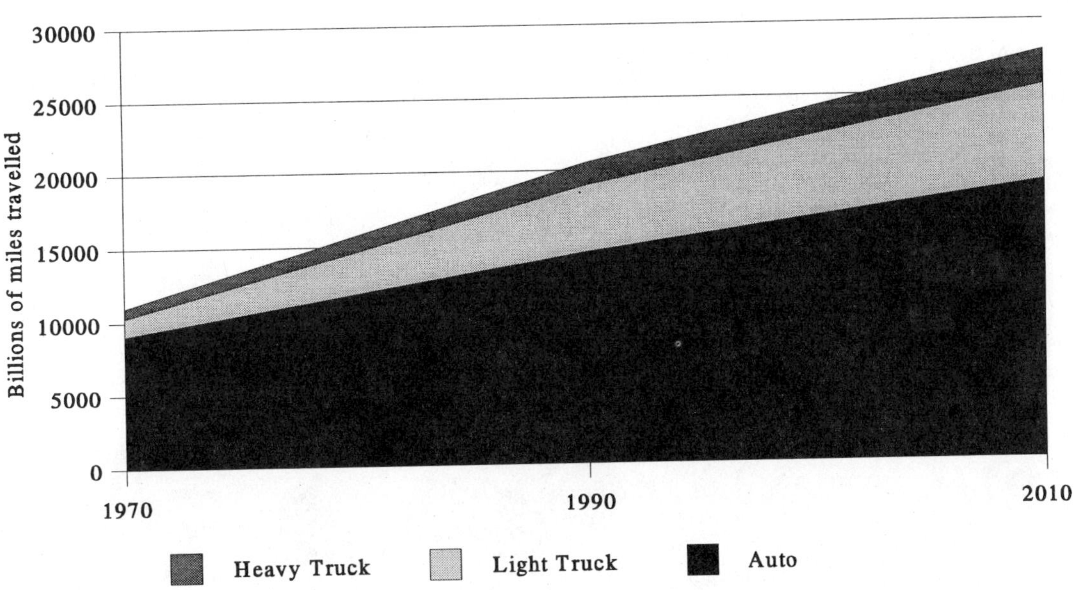

"[The table below] summarizes historical and projected trends in transportation activity—vehicle-miles of travel for highway modes and ton-miles or passenger-miles of travel for nonhighway modes. Stripped of efficiency assumptions, the forecast shows slow and steady moderation in travel growth, particularly for passenger modes. Relatively slow population growth, the aging of the 'baby boom' and other population segments, and only modest increases in personal income depress growth in personal travel demand. With increasing traffic congestion, telecommunications substitutes for a growing share of local trips. Long-distance trips continue to be by the same modes, but absent the 'extraordinary events' responsible for much of their recent performance, growth slows to more moderate levels. 'Extraordinary' events include airline, rail, and motor carrier deregulation; the near total shift to diesel engines in class 8 trucks; the development of Alaskan oil fields, which rapidly boosted coastal tanker traffic; and tighter regulations on the fuel economy, emissions, and safety of cars than of light trucks, which in turn increased price, performance, and capacity disparities (and altered consumer preferences). The sole 'extraordinary' event included in the baseline scenario is the growth in coal use forecast by the National Energy Policy Plan. Because we assume that all incremental coal production comes from sources west of the Mississippi, relatively longer lengths of haul result in a disproportionate increase in rail ton-miles traveled, even if much of the increased coal traffic is transhipped to waterborne modes."

★ 669 ★

Transportation Activity by Mode, 1970-2010

[Continued]

Year	Highway Modes				Nonhighway Modes		
	Auto (10^9VMT)	Light Truck (10^9VMT)	Heavy Truck (10^9VMT)	Total (10^9VMT)	Air[A] (10^9RPM)	Rail (10^9TMT)	Marine[A] (10^9TMT)
1970	907	123	67	1,110	109	771	596
1975	1,023	201	87	1,328	137	759	566
1980	1,105	291	115	1,527	204	932	922
1985	1,260	373	131	1,774	278	898	893
1990	1,447	453	153	2,094	344	1,075	911
1995	1,546	517	167	2,270	410	1,252	899
2000	1,657	570	186	2,444	487	1,490	912
2010	1,895	659	237	2,795	669	2,069	999
Average annual percentage change							
1970-1985	2.22	7.68	4.57	3.18	6.44	1.02	2.77
1990-2010	1.36	1.89	2.21	1.45	3.38	3.33	0.46

Source: M. M. Mintz and A. D. Vyas, U.S. Department of Energy, Energy Systems Division, Argonne National Laboratory, *Forecast of Transportation Energy Demand through the Year 2010* (Washington, D.C.: U.S. Government Printing Office, November 1990, revised April 1991), pp. 57-8, 61. *Notes:* VMT = Vehicle miles traveled; RPM = Revolutions Per Minute; TMT = Ton-Miles Traveled. A. Domestic operations of U.S. flag carriers.

★ 670 ★

Transportation: General Statistics

Transportation Energy Use by Mode, 1970-2010

[Energy use in 10^{15} Btu]

Year	Highway Modes			Nonhighway Modes				
	Auto	Light Truck	Heavy Truck[1]	Air[2]	Rail[3]	Marine[4]	Other[5]	Total
1970	8.526	1.540	1.611	1.307	0.575	0.753	0.993	15.305
1975	9.611	2.240	1.908	1.274	0.596	0.851	0.849	17.329
1980	9.037	2.951	2.564	1.528	0.645	1.677	0.915	19.317
1985	8.673	3.630	3.085	1.881	0.501	1.311	0.781	19.862
1990	9.066	3.988	3.654	2.298	0.529	0.956	0.690	21.182
1995	9.356	4.337	3.927	2.544	0.604	1.020	0.737	22.533
2000	9.713	4.630	4.166	2.765	0.704	1.101	0.748	23.828
2010	9.586	4.871	5.103	2.988	0.950	1.304	0.712	25.513
Average annual percentage change								
1970-1985	0.11	5.88	4.43	2.46	-0.91	3.77	-1.59	1.68
1990-2010	0.28	1.01	1.68	1.32	2.97	1.56	0.16	0.93

Source: M. M. Mintz and A. D. Vyas, U.S. Department of Energy, Energy Systems Division, Argonne National Laboratory, *Forecast of Transportation Energy Demand through the Year 2010* (Washington, D.C.: U.S. Government Printing Office, November 1990, revised April 1991), p. 56. *Notes:* 1. Includes buses. 2. Passenger, freight, and general aviation. 3. Freight only. 4. Domestic freight and U.S. fuel purchases for international shipping. 5. Pipeline, transit, and rail passengers.

★ 671 ★

Transportation: General Statistics

Transportation Research Funding, 1992-1997

[Millions of dollars]

	Authorization Levels by Fiscal Year						
	1992	1993	1994	1995	1996	1997	Total
BTS	5	10	15	15	20	25	90
Bus Testing	4	0	0	0	0	0	4
University Centers	5	6	6	6	6	6	35
Research Institutes	11	9	9	6	6	6	47
IVHS	94	113	113	113	113	113	659
Total	119	138	143	140	145	150	836

Source: Edward Weiner, U.S. Department of Transportation, *Urban Transportation Planning in the United States: An Historical Overview*, rev. ed. (Washington, D.C.: U.S. Government Printing Office, November 1992), p. 242. *Note:* BTS=Boeing Test Support; IVHS=Intelligent Vehicle-Highway Systems.

Aircraft and Air Passenger Traffic

★ 672 ★

Active Pilots by Type of Certificate, 1988-2005

[Thousands]

AS OF JANUARY 1	RECREATIONAL[2]				AIRLINE		GLIDER	TOTAL	INSTRUMENT
	STUDENTS	LIGHTER-THAN-AIR[3]	PRIVATE	COMMERCIAL	TRANSPORT	HELICOPTER			RATED[1]
Historical[4]									
1988	146.0	1.2	300.9	143.6	91.3	8.7	7.9	699.7	266.1
1989	136.9	1.1	299.8	143.0	97.0	8.6	7.6	694.0	273.8
1990	142.5	1.1	293.2	144.5	102.1	8.9	7.7	700.0	282.8
1991	128.7	0.1	299.1	149.7	107.7	9.6	7.8	702.7	297.1
1992	120.2	0.2	293.3	148.4	112.2	9.9	8.0	692.1	303.2
1993E	114.6	0.2	288.1	146.4	115.9	9.7	8.2	683.0	306.2
Forecast									
1994	115.0	0.3	288.9	148.6	118.2	9.7	8.2	688.9	309.8
1995	116.8	0.4	289.8	150.1	120.5	9.8	8.3	695.7	313.6
1996	118.5	0.5	290.7	151.6	122.9	10.0	8.4	702.6	317.3
1997	120.3	0.7	291.6	153.2	127.5	10.1	8.5	711.9	321.4
1998	121.5	0.8	292.4	154.6	132.1	10.3	8.6	720.3	325.3
1999	122.7	0.9	293.3	156.2	137.0	10.4	8.7	729.2	329.9
2000	123.4	1.0	294.1	157.7	140.7	10.5	8.7	736.1	334.8
2001	124.0	1.1	295.0	159.3	144.5	10.6	8.8	743.3	339.5
2002	124.6	1.2	296.0	160.9	148.4	10.7	8.8	750.6	344.2
2003	125.2	1.3	296.8	162.5	151.4	10.8	8.8	756.8	348.4

[Continued]

★ 672 ★

Active Pilots by Type of Certificate, 1988-2005

[Continued]

AS OF JANUARY 1	RECREATIONAL[2] STUDENTS	LIGHTER-THAN-AIR[3]	PRIVATE	COMMERCIAL	AIRLINE TRANSPORT	AIRLINE HELICOPTER	GLIDER	TOTAL	INSTRUMENT RATED[1]
2004	125.8	1.3	297.7	164.1	154.4	10.9	8.9	763.1	352.6
2005	126.5	1.4	298.6	165.8	157.5	11.0	9.0	769.8	356.1

Source: U.S. Department of Transportation, Federal Aviation Administration, *FAA Aviation Forecasts: Fiscal Years 1994-2005* (Washington, D.C.: Government Printing Office, 1994), p. IX-26. *Notes:* Detail may not add to total due to independent rounding. E=Estimate. 1. Instrument rated pilots should not be added to other categories in deriving total. 2. Recreation rating not available until 1991. 3. Lighter-than-air type rating is no longer issued after 1990. 4. Source: *FAA Statistical Handbook of Aviation.*

★ 673 ★

Aircraft and Air Passenger Traffic

World Commercial Aircraft Fleet Changes, 1993-2015

"The success of a next generation of large aircraft—if there is to be one—will be driven by their costs. The previous generation of wide-body aircraft, especially the Boeing 747, revolutionized air travel in terms of the large number of passengers that could be flown long distances.

"But a successor, whether it has 600, 800 or more seats, will compete in a very different environment. Air travel today has become more of a commodity than when Pan American bought the first 25 747s. Passengers demand lower fares, more nonstop flights and greater frequency of service. Airport and airway congestion both point toward the use of larger aircraft to maximize landing and takeoff slot utilization, but in most markets operating short and medium-haul wide-body twins rather than bigger jumbos may satisfy that requirement."

[Number of Aircraft]

Seat Category	2015
81-150	7,975
151-210	3,450
211-300	3,238
301-400	2,301
401-600	443
More than 600	360
TOTAL	17,767[1]

Source: Michael Mecham, "Cost, Not Size, to Drive Success of Superjumbo," in *Aviation Week & Space Technology*, 21 November 1994, p. 45. *Primary source:* ICAO. *Note:* 1. Compared to 7,934 in 1993.

★ 674 ★

Aircraft and Air Passenger Traffic

Civil Aircraft Sales, 1960-2000

"Having lost $15 billion over the past four years, the world's big airlines are expected to edge into profit this year. But the days when the market for commercial aircraft grew at a rate of 7% a year are gone for good. Even in the buoyant Asia-Pacific market, air travel is becoming a mature industry. And rather than buy new aircraft, cash-strapped airlines are going first to rejuvenate their older aircraft (some 150 surplus jets are currently parked in the dry Arizona desert) with quieter and more efficient engines and modern electronics. Aircraft makers such as Boeing, Airbus and McDonnell Douglas will be lucky if they see annual sales grow as high as 4% for the rest of the decade. Meanwhile, defence budgets for aircraft and helicopters are declining by 4% a year."

[1993 prices in billions of dollars]

Year	
Historical trend:	
5-7% rise per year	
1960	5
1965	7
1970	14
1975	11
1980	18
1985	20
1990	28
New trend:	
2-4% rise per year	
1995	32
2000	33

Source: "The New Arithmetic," in *The Economist*, 3 September 1994, p. 7. *Primary source:* Booz Allen & Hamilton. *Notes:* Magnitudes estimated from published chart. Figures through 1993 actual; 1994-2000 based on an average rate of increase.

★ 675 ★

Aircraft and Air Passenger Traffic

World Scheduled Air Passenger Traffic, 1991-2011

"Worldwide passenger traffic is expected to increase at an average of 6.7% annually between 1991 and 2011. This is somewhat less than the 7.3% average rate experienced between 1971 and 1991. The first 10 years of the forecast produces a slower rate of growth than the latter 10-year period, 6.4% for 1991-2001 vs. 7.1% for 2001-2011. This is primarily due to the two economic slowdowns projected through 2001 compared to only one during the latter period.

"Much of the long term growth is attributed to burgeoning international travel markets where industrial globalization is a key factor. As corporations become increasingly multinational in scope with production sites worldwide, demand for both business and pleasure transportation will expand as economic growth is stimulated. These are primarily Asian-related markets, driven by projected strong economic development. Over the forecast period, passenger traffic on international routes is expected to develop at 7% annually, while domestic markets (excluding the former U.S.S.R.) will grow far slower at just 5.5%.

Route	1991-2011 Average Growth (%)	Share of World RPKs (%)	
		1991	2011
U.S. Domestic	4.6	32.5	20.8
North Atlantic	4.8	11.6	7.7
Europe-Far East	8.2	7.6	9.5
North and Mid Pacific	10.9	7.4	15.1
Intra-Far East and Pacific	11.1	7.2	15.3
Intra-Europe	5.7	4.8	3.8
Japan Domestic	6.1	3.1	2.6
Europe-Africa	6.8	2.8	2.7
Other Far East Domestic	10.6	2.7	5.2
North America-Central America	6.8	2.3	2.2
Total Major Routes	7.2	82.0	84.9
Total World[1]	7.0	100.0	100.0

Source: McDonnell Douglas Corp., Douglas Aircraft Company, Market Assessment, Mail Code 7-82, *1992-2011 Outlook for Commercial Aircraft* (Long Beach, CA, 90846-0001), pp. 15-16. *Notes:* RPK=Revenue-Passenger Kilometers. 1. Excludes former USSR. The data in this document are forecasts only. No representation or warranty by McDonnell Douglas Corporation is either intended or implied.

★ 676 ★

Aircraft and Air Passenger Traffic

Air Passenger Traffic by Domiciled Region, 1991-2011

"Airlines located in Asia/Pacific will expand the fastest, averaging 9.7% growth per year. By 2011, these carriers will fly 2,300 RPKs, or about 35% of the world total."

[Billions of Revenue Passenger Kilometers (RPKs)]

Year	1991	2001	2011
North America	800	1,250	2,375
Europe[1]	475	800	1,250
Asia/Pacific	400	995	2,300
Middle East/Africa	100	150	225
Latin America	95	150	310

Source: McDonnell Douglas Corp., Douglas Aircraft Company, Market Assessment, Mail Code 7-82, *1992-2011 Outlook for Commercial Aircraft* (Long Beach, CA, 90846-0001), pp. 17-18. *Notes:* Magnitudes estimated from published chart. 1. Excludes former USSR. The data in this document are forecasts only. No representation or warranty by McDonnell Douglas Corporation is either intended or implied.

★ 677 ★

Aircraft and Air Passenger Traffic

Air Passenger Traffic Growth by Domiciled Region, 1991-2011

"By 2011, traffic carried by airlines domiciled in North America will barely exceed that of Asia/Pacific operators. With RPKs forecast to grow at 5.7% annually, the North American domiciled carrier share of world traffic will drop to 35% from the current 43%.

"Spurred by substantial economic growth. Latin American airlines are forecast to produce the second highest traffic growth, averaging 6.8% from 1991 to 2001 and 7.3% for 2001 to 2011.

"Airlines based in Europe and Middle East/Africa, along with North American carriers, will develop at similar rates through 2011, ranging between 5% and 6%. These are all below the world average."

[Annual percent change in Revenue Passenger Kilometers (RPKs)]

	1981-1991	1991-2001	2001-2011
North America	5.6	5.0	6.0
Europe[1]	5.6	4.9	5.4
Asia/Pacific	7.3	9.8	9.6
Middle East/Africa	3.8	5.3	5.5

[Continued]

★ 677 ★

Air Passenger Traffic Growth by Domiciled Region, 1991-2011

[Continued]

	1981-1991	1991-2001	2001-2011
Latin America	4.1	6.3	7.1
World[1]	5.3	6.3	6.9

Source: McDonnell Douglas Corp., Douglas Aircraft Company, Market Assessment, Mail Code 7-82, *1992-2011 Outlook for Commercial Aircraft* (Long Beach, CA, 90846-0001), p. 17. *Notes:* The data in this document are forecasts only. No representation or warranty by McDonnell Douglas Corporation is either intended or implied. 1. Excludes former U.S.S.R. Magnitudes estimated from published chart.

★ 678 ★

Aircraft and Air Passenger Traffic

U.S. Commercial Air Carriers and Regionals/Commuters: Total Scheduled Passenger Traffic, 1988-2005

FISCAL YEAR	REVENUE PASSENGER ENPLANEMENTS (Millions)			REVENUE PASSENGER MILES (Billions)		
	DOMESTIC	INTERNATIONAL	TOTAL	DOMESTIC	INTERNATIONAL	TOTAL
Historical[1]						
1988	441.2	34.3	475.5	329.9	90.5	420.4
1989	443.6	36.8	480.4	333.2	100.6	433.8
1990	456.6	41.3	497.9	344.9	115.1	460.0
1991	447.3	39.7	487.0	339.3	113.5	452.8
1992	462.0	42.6	504.6	352.8	128.3	481.1
1993E	463.7	45.0	508.7	353.8	134.4	488.2
Forecast						
1994	480.5	47.7	528.2	366.4	141.2	507.6
1995	500.8	51.3	552.3	382.5	151.6	435.1
1996	520.3	55.9	576.2	398.1	163.1	561.2
1997	541.8	60.4	602.2	415.4	175.4	590.8
1998	563.3	64.7	628.0	432.4	187.5	619.9
1999	586.5	69.1	655.8	449.7	200.2	649.9
2000	606.2	73.3	679.5	466.6	212.6	679.2
2001	628.2	77.8	705.8	483.9	224.8	708.7
2002	650.0	82.0	732.0	501.2	237.5	738.7
2003	671.9	86.6	758.5	518.7	250.9	769.6
2004	695.0	91.3	786.3	536.3	264.8	801.1

[Continued]

★ 678 ★

U.S. Commercial Air Carriers and Regionals/Commuters: Total Scheduled Passenger Traffic, 1988-2005

[Continued]

FISCAL YEAR	REVENUE PASSENGER ENPLANEMENTS (Millions)			REVENUE PASSENGER MILES (Billions)		
	DOMESTIC	INTERNATIONAL	TOTAL	DOMESTIC	INTERNATIONAL	TOTAL
2005	715.7	96.3	812.0	553.8	279.6	833.4

Source: U.S. Department of Transportation, Federal Aviation Administration, *FAA Aviation Forecasts: Fiscal Years 1994-2005* (Washington, D.C.: Government Printing Office, 1994), p. IX-12. *Notes:* E=Estimate. 1. Research and Special Programs Administration (RSPA), Forms 41 and 298-C.

★ 679 ★

Aircraft and Air Passenger Traffic

U.S. Commercial Air Carriers: Scheduled Passenger Traffic, 1988-2005

FISCAL YEAR	REVENUE PASSENGER ENPLANEMENTS (Millions)			REVENUE PASSENGER MILES (Billions)		
	DOMESTIC	INTERNATIONAL	TOTAL	DOMESTIC	INTERNATIONAL	TOTAL
Historical[1]						
1988	414.2	34.3	448.5	325.5	90.5	416.0
1989	415.6	36.8	452.4	328.4	100.6	429.0
1990	424.1	41.3	465.4	339.2	115.1	454.3
1991	413.3	39.7	453.0	333.6	113.5	447.1
1992	429.2	42.6	471.8	346.5	128.5	475.0
1993E	428.8	45.0	473.9	346.8	134.4	418.2
Forecast						
1994	442.7	47.7	490.4	358.6	141.2	499.8
1995	460.6	51.5	512.1	374.0	151.6	525.6
1996	477.9	55.9	533.8	389.0	163.1	552.1
1997	497.2	60.4	557.6	405.7	175.4	581.1
1998	515.9	64.7	580.6	422.0	187.5	609.5
1999	534.6	69.1	603.7	438.4	200.2	638.6
2000	553.0	73.3	626.3	454.6	212.6	667.2
2001	571.6	77.6	649.2	471.0	224.8	695.8
2002	590.2	82.0	672.2	487.5	237.5	725.0
2003	608.8	86.6	695.4	504.1	250.9	755.0
2004	627.3	91.3	718.6	520.7	264.8	785.5
2005	645.9	96.3	742.2	537.4	279.6	817.0

Source: U.S. Department of Transportation, Federal Aviation Administration, *FAA Aviation Forecasts: Fiscal Years 1994-2005* (Washington, D.C.: Government Printing Office, 1994), p. IX-13. *Notes:* E=Estimate. 1. Research and Special Programs Administration (RSPA), Forms 41 and 298-C.

★ 680 ★

Aircraft and Air Passenger Traffic

U.S. Commercial Air Carriers: Scheduled International Passenger Traffic, 1988-2005

FISCAL YEAR	REVENUE PASSENGER ENPLANEMENTS (MIL)				REVENUE PASSENGER MILES (BIL)			
	ATLANTIC	LATIN AMERICA	PACIFIC	TOTAL	ATLANTIC	LATIN AMERICA	PACIFIC	TOTAL
Historical[1]								
1988	14.6	11.5	8.2	34.3	46.1	14.2	30.2	90.5
1989	15.0	11.8	10.0	36.8	49.1	14.7	36.8	100.6
1990	16.1	13.0	12.2	41.3	53.7	16.0	45.4	115.1
1991	12.2	14.7	12.8	39.7	47.1	18.3	48.1	113.5
1992	14.8	13.6	14.2	42.6	57.7	17.1	53.6	128.5
1993E	15.6	15.8	13.6	45.0	61.1	20.8	52.5	134.4
Forecast								
1994	16.3	17.3	14.1	47.7	64.2	22.9	54.1	141.2
1995	17.4	19.2	14.9	51.5	68.4	25.6	57.6	151.6
1996	18.6	21.3	16.0	55.9	73.1	28.4	61.6	163.1
1997	19.9	23.5	17.0	60.4	78.3	31.5	65.6	175.4
1998	21.1	25.5	18.1	64.7	83.3	34.3	69.9	187.5
1999	22.5	27.4	19.2	69.1	88.8	37.0	74.4	200.2
2000	23.8	29.2	20.3	73.3	94.1	39.6	78.9	212.6
2001	24.9	31.2	21.5	77.6	98.8	42.4	83.6	224.8
2002	26.1	33.1	22.8	82.0	103.7	45.2	88.6	237.5
2003	27.4	35.1	24.1	86.6	108.9	48.1	93.9	250.9
2004	28.7	37.1	25.5	91.3	114.3	51.0	99.5	264.8
2005	30.1	39.2	27.0	96.3	120.0	54.1	105.5	279.6

Source: U.S. Department of Transportation, Federal Aviation Administration, *FAA Aviation Forecasts: Fiscal Years 1994-2005* (Washington, D.C.: Government Printing Office, 1994), p. IX-14. *Notes:* E=Estimate. 1. Research and Special Programs Administration (RSPA), Forms 41 and 298-C.

★ 681 ★

Aircraft and Air Passenger Traffic

U.S. Regionals/Commuters: Scheduled Passenger Traffic, 1988-2005

[Millions]

FISCAL YEAR	REVENUE PASSENGER ENPLANEMENTS			REVENUE PASSENGER MILES		
	48 STATES	HAWAII/ PUERTO RICO/ VIRGIN ISLANDS	TOTAL	48 STATES	HAWAII/ PUERTO RICO/ VIRGIN ISLANDS	TOTAL
Historical[1]						
1988	28.4	1.7	30.1	4,875.3	152.6	5,027.9
1989	30.7	1.4	32.1	5,504.8	125.3	5,630.1
1990	35.5	1.7	37.2	6,513.1	140.7	6,653.8
1991	37.0	1.7	38.7	6,870.1	139.4	7,009.5
1992	41.1	1.7	42.8	8,091.7	137.2	8,228.9

[Continued]

★ 681 ★

U.S. Regionals/Commuters: Scheduled Passenger Traffic, 1988-2005

[Continued]

FISCAL YEAR	REVENUE PASSENGER ENPLANEMENTS			REVENUE PASSENGER MILES		
	48 STATES	HAWAII/ PUERTO RICO/ VIRGIN ISLANDS	TOTAL	48 STATES	HAWAII/ PUERTO RICO/ VIRGIN ISLANDS	TOTAL
1993E	45.6	1.6	47.2	9,402.6	142.9	9,545.5
Forecast						
1994	50.2	1.8	52.0	10,540.3	163.8	10,704.1
1995	54.5	2.0	56.5	11,720.8	182.0	11,902.8
1996	58.7	2.1	60.8	12,904.6	191.1	13,095.7
1997	63.1	2.2	65.3	14,130.6	200.2	14,330.8
1998	67.6	2.3	69.9	15,416.5	209.3	15,625.8
1999	72.1	2.4	76.5	16,665.2	218.4	16,883.6
2000	76.9	2.5	79.4	17,998.4	227.5	18,225.9
2001	81.8	2.6	84.4	19,384.3	236.6	19,620.9
2002	86.8	2.7	89.5	20,741.2	245.7	20,986.9
2003	91.9	2.8	94.7	22,151.6	254.8	22,406.4
2004	97.2	2.9	101.1	23,613.6	263.9	23,877.5
2005	102.3	3.0	105.3	25,054.0	273.0	25,327.0

Source: U.S. Department of Transportation, Federal Aviation Administration, *FAA Aviation Forecasts: Fiscal Years 1994-2005* (Washington, D.C.: Government Printing Office, 1994), p. IX-21. *Notes:* E=Estimate. 1. Research and Special Programs Administration (RSPA), Forms 41 and 298-C.

★ 682 ★

Aircraft and Air Passenger Traffic

Average Seats Per Aircraft by Domiciled Region (Active Fleet), 1991-2011

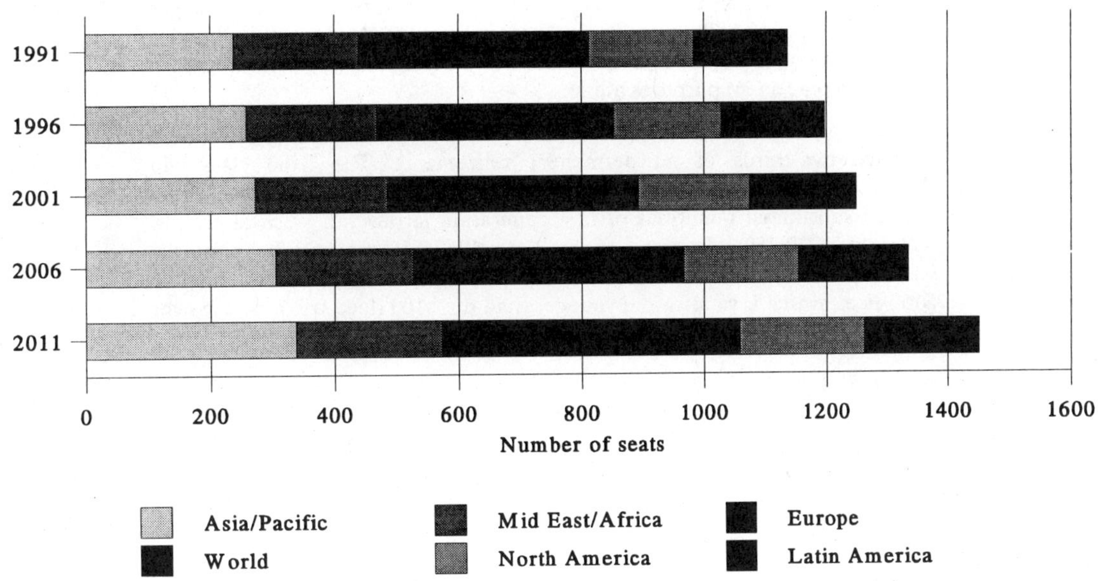

"With the relative emphasis on larger aircraft, average seats per aircraft worldwide will rise to 247 by 2011 from the 187-seat average in 1991. Average aircraft seating will, therefore, expand by 3 seats each year. Asia/Pacific airlines, currently leading all regions with 238 seats per aircraft, will produce the highest seating growth of any region. With its expanding traffic volumes, average aircraft seats will rise by 1.8% annually for Asia/Pacific carriers, advancing to 338 seats per aircraft by 2011."

[Number of seats]

Region	1991	1996	2001	2006	2011
Asia/Pacific	238	258	272	305	338
Mid East/Africa	201	210	213	222	235
Europe	188	193	203	220	238
World	187	192	203	220	247
North America	170	176	183	188	205
Latin America	155	169	175	180	188

Source: McDonnell Douglas Corp., Douglas Aircraft Company, Market Assessment, Mail Code 7-82, *1992-2011 Outlook for Commercial Aircraft* (Long Beach, CA 90846-001), p. 27. *Notes:* The data in this document are forecasts only. No representation or warranty by McDonnell Douglas Corporation is either intended or implied. Magnitudes estimated from published chart.

★ 683 ★

Aircraft and Air Passenger Traffic

World Passenger Aircraft Permanent Retirements by Generic Class and Domiciled Region, 1992-2011

"The results from the McDonnell Douglas Aircraft Retirement Model indicate that 4,886 aircraft will be permanently retired from active passenger service over the next 20 years. This equates to about 62% of the today's active passenger fleet. Thus, an average of 244 new aircraft must be produced each year for replacement purposes alone.

"Short-range aircraft, with 5,300 units in active passenger service, will produce two-thirds of all permanent retirements. The S100 class will dominate short-range aircraft retirements with over 2,000 planes. These include substantial quantities of first generation jet aircraft, such as DC-9s. 737s, and 727-100s delivered in the late 1960s. These will be primarily withdrawn from active service during the 1990s to meet noise regulations. The S150 fleet, which is smaller and younger than the S100 fleet, will produce over 1,200 permanent retirements composed mainly of the 727-200 model."

[Number of units]

Type/region of	Number retired
Type of Aircraft	
S100	2,054
S150	1,240
M200	323
L200	60
L300	328
M400	104
L400	215
M600	21
Other	631
Region	
North America	2,207
Europe	897
Asia/Pacific	643
Latin America	725
Middle East/Africa	414
TOTAL	4,886

Source: McDonnell Douglas Corp., Douglas Aircraft Company, Market Assessment, Mail Code 7-82, *1992-2011 Outlook for Commercial Aircraft* (Long Beach, CA 90846-001), pp. 31-2. *Notes:* The data in this document are forecasts only. No representation or warranty by McDonnell Douglas Corporation is either intended or implied. Magnitudes estimated from published chart.

★ 684 ★

Aircraft and Air Passenger Traffic

Passenger Aircraft Deliveries by Domiciled Region and Seat Class, 1992- 2011

"Between 1992 and 2011, the forecast indicates that 14,072 new passenger aircraft deliveries will be required to satisfy projected traffic levels. Expressed in constant 1992 U.S. dollars, these planes will cost $1,034 billion. Nearly 4,900 of these deliveries (35%) will be for replacement purposes, while 9,200 units (65%) will be required for traffic growth.

"Short-range aircraft will account for 41% of total deliveries, a relatively low proportion considering today's fleet composition of 67%. This reflects decreased airline reliance on the S100 class, with little growth of its fleet expected over time.

"The M200 class will produce the second highest delivery requirement, and quadruple in fleet count. It benefits substantially from S150 capacity upgrades in order to meet departure guidelines.

"The 300-seat and 400-seat widebody classes will require nearly the same number of deliveries to satisfy growing international markets. The proportion of long-range requirements, however, is considerably larger with the 400-seat class."

[Thousands of units]

Class	Latin America	Middle East/ Africa	Asia/ Pacific	Europe/ North America	Total
S100	.20	.05	.25	1.80	2.30
S150	.25	.15	.60	2.37	3.37
M200	.25	.15	.50	1.80	2.70
L200	.05	.05	.10	.50	.70
M300	.12	.12	.41	.55	1.10
L300	.12	.10	.58	.30	1.10
M400	--	.10	.40	.40	.90
L400	.10	.20	.60	.42	1.32
M600	--	--	.25	.10	.35
L600	--	--	.30	.10	.40

Source: McDonnell Douglas Corp., Douglas Aircraft Company, Market Assessment, Mail Code 7-82, *1992-2011 Outlook for Commercial Aircraft* (Long Beach, CA 90846-001), pp. 35-6. *Notes:* The data in this document are forecasts only. No representation or warranty by McDonnell Douglas Corporation is either intended or implied.

★ 685 ★

Aircraft and Air Passenger Traffic

World Passenger Aircraft Deliveries by Generic Class, 1992-2011

"Passenger aircraft deliveries will vary considerably over the forecast time frame. Faced with current overcapacity problems and two economic slowdowns assumed during the first half of the forecast, new delivery requirements through 2001 will be somewhat moderate compared to that projected for the 2002-2011 period. The airframe industry will need to manufacture an average of 566 aircraft annually for the first half of the forecast, escalating its production to an average of 841 jetliners during the latter half of the forecast. There is a gradual shift from low-capacity narrow-body and low-capacity widebody classes to higher capacity aircraft classes that allow increased operating efficiencies."

[Number of units]

Generic Class	1992-1996	1997-2001	2002-2006	2007-2011	Total
S100	639	653	438	605	2,335
S150	728	868	1,019	788	3,403
M200	411	547	782	965	2,705
L200	130	94	71	66	361
M300	182	153	371	490	1,196
L300	264	183	371	326	1,144
M400	60	168	261	410	899
L400	250	295	412	471	1,428
M600	9	11	55	144	219
L600	0	14	108	260	382
Total	2,673	2,986	3,888	4,525	14,072
Average Per Year	535	597	778	905	704

Source: McDonnell Douglas Corp., Douglas Aircraft Company, Market Assessment, Mail Code 7-82, *1992-2011 Outlook for Commercial Aircraft* (Long Beach, CA 90846-0001), p. 39. *Notes:* The data in this document are forecasts only. No representation or warranty by McDonnell Douglas Corporation is either intended or implied.

★ 686 ★

Aircraft and Air Passenger Traffic

Decline in Operating Costs and Revenue Yields of World Passenger Airlines, 1960-2010

"The world's international airlines think that they are at a turning point. With economic recovery in the industrial world, aircraft are beginning to fill up again with passengers and freight...

"So recovery is in the air. Or is it? Look at the new orders again and ask yourself whether this can be the same industry that has 1,000 redundant aircraft still parked in America's Mojave desert. Or the industry in which America's four big carriers—American Airlines, United, USAir and Delta—are struggling to stay aloft. Or where European airlines such as Air France are pleading for cash from their state-owned parents. Incredibly, it is. This, after all, is aviation, an industry built on a belief in defying gravity.

"Last time the airlines got their sums wrong, it was because they added far more capacity than they did passengers. This time around, IATA reckons that revenues are about to rise faster than capacity for the second year running. That is already filling up planes: passenger load-factors rose by three percentage points in the first four months of this year. NatWest Securities, a London broker, reckons that airlines will fly 67% full this year—just above that 66.5% break-even point. Once they have crossed the break-even point, profits can increase dramatically. By 1997, NatWest predicts, load-factors will top 70% and profits will have risen to $13.2 billion.

"However, some of these figures need to be taken with care. To begin with, IATA's forecast for last year—that losses would halve—turned out to be incorrect. More important, while revenues overall may be recovering, yields—or the amount of revenue that an airline gets from filling a seat—have been falling, forcing airlines to cut costs frantically."

Year	Yields/cents per passenger mile	Operating costs per mile[1]
1960	32.0	100
1965	28.0	72
1970	24.0	52
1975	23.0	50
1980	22.0	53
1985	17.0	40
1990	17.0	40
1995	15.5	40
2000	11.5	37
2005	10.2	34
2010	10.0	32

Source: "Those Foolhardy Firms in Their Flying Machines," in *The Economist*, 25 June 1994, p. 63. *Primary source:* Boeing. *Notes:* Magnitudes estimated from published chart. IATA = International Air Transport Association. 1. 1960 = 100.

★ 687 ★

Aircraft and Air Passenger Traffic

World Passenger Open Aircraft Market, 1992-2011

"With current airline overcapacity relative to demand, a modest open market is projected through 1996, particularly in short-range classes. Retirements attributed to noise regulations will turn demand around for smaller aircraft in the latter 1990s. Since only 314 aircraft orders are scheduled for delivery during the 1997-2001 time frame, the open market for passenger aircraft will rise to nearly 2,700 units.

"Open market demand will continue to expand during the latter half of the forecast as incremental annual traffic gains become greater. This will create increased demand for larger capacity widebody aircraft, keeping departure growth at acceptable levels. The open market will climb to nearly 3,900 aircraft during the 2002-2006 period, further rising to over 4,500 units during the last 5 years with nearly 10% of this demand satisfied by the 600-seat aircraft class. Since no current orders are scheduled for delivery past 2001, the open market for commercial aircraft equates to airline delivery requirements."

[Number of units]

Generic Class	1992-1996	1997-2001	2002-2006	2007-2011	Total
S100	58	593	438	605	1,694
S150	101	810	1,019	788	2,718
M200	58	488	782	965	2,293
L200	16	94	71	66	247
M300	11	128	371	490	1,000
L300	56	155	371	326	908
M400	3	138	261	410	812
L400	48	241	412	471	1,172
M600	2	11	55	144	212
L600	0	14	108	260	382
Total	353	2,672	3,888	4,525	11,438

Source: McDonnell Douglas Corp., Douglas Aircraft Company, Market Assessment, Mail Code 7-82, *1992-2011 Outlook for Commercial Aircraft* (Long Beach, CA, 90846-0001), p. 45. *Notes:* The data in this document are forecasts only. No representation or warranty by McDonnell Douglas Corporation is either intended or implied.

★ 688 ★

Aircraft and Air Passenger Traffic

Helicopter Technology Improvement

"Helicopters could play an increasingly large role in intercity air transportation in the near future.

[Continued]

★ 688 ★

Helicopter Technology Improvement

[Continued]

"Improvement in the helicopter technology 'promises the long-sought and unattained trick of economically combining high speed and vertical flight in the same vehicle, teasing us with thoughts of intercity travel between downtown heliports at 300 miles an hour,' says David S. Lawrence, director of market planning at United Technologies' Sikorsky Aircraft division. For example, advanced technology such as "tiltrotors" (rotor blades that can be angled to increase a helicopter's speed) will make helicopters more competitive with airplanes in terms of speed.

"But technology advances should not be overemphasized, Lawrence adds. Even without improving the technology, helicopters are capable of playing a more important part in city-to-city transportation, he argues. 'It's important not to lose sight of the technology of *today*—that of the conventional, garden-variety helicopter; and how close it now is to being a suitable, useful, even essential component of our national transportation system—no longer an underutilized novelty, or a success-by-default, but a fully acceptable vehicle of choice,' he notes."

Source: "More Helicopters in Our Future?" in *The Futurist*, September-October 1991, p. 48. *Primary source:* "Helicopters and Today's Air Transportation System," *Transportation Quarterly*, April 1991. Published by the Eno Foundation for Transportation, Box 2055, Westport, CN 06880-2055.

★ 689 ★

Aircraft and Air Passenger Traffic

Active Rotorcraft Fleet and Hours Flown, 1988-2005

AS OF JANUARY 1	ACTIVE FLEET (Thousands)			HOURS FLOWN[1] (Millions)		
	PISTON	TURBINE	TOTAL	PISTON	TURBINE	TOTAL
Historical[2]						
1988	2.6	3.3	5.9	0.6	1.9	2.5
1989	2.4	3.6	6.0	0.7	1.9	2.6
1990	3.0	3.9	6.9	0.7	1.6	2.3
1991	3.2	3.7	6.9	0.6	2.0	2.6
1992	2.5	3.8	6.3	0.5	1.9	2.4
1993E	2.2	3.6	5.8	0.4	1.8	2.2
Forecast						
1994	2.1	3.6	5.7	0.4	1.9	2.3
1995	2.1	3.8	5.9	0.4	2.1	2.5
1996	2.0	4.0	6.0	0.4	2.2	2.6
1997	2.0	4.2	6.2	0.4	2.3	2.7
1998	2.0	4.4	6.4	0.4	2.5	2.9
1999	2.0	4.6	6.6	0.4	2.6	3.0
2000	1.9	4.8	6.7	0.4	2.8	3.2

[Continued]

★ 689 ★

Active Rotorcraft Fleet and Hours Flown, 1988-2005

[Continued]

AS OF JANUARY 1	ACTIVE FLEET (Thousands)			HOURS FLOWN[1] (Millions)		
	PISTON	TURBINE	TOTAL	PISTON	TURBINE	TOTAL
2001	1.9	5.0	6.9	0.4	2.9	3.3
2002	1.9	5.2	7.1	0.4	3.1	3.5
2003	1.8	5.4	7.2	0.4	3.2	3.6
2004	1.8	5.6	7.4	0.4	3.4	3.8
2005	1.8	5.8	7.6	0.4	3.5	3.9

Source: U.S. Department of Transportation, Federal Aviation Administration, *FAA Aviation Forecasts: Fiscal Years 1994-2005* (Washington, D.C.: Government Printing Office, 1994), p. IX-14. *FAA Statistical Handbook of Aviation. Notes:* E=Estimate. 1. Helicopter hours flown are on a fiscal year basis. 2. Source: *FAA Statistical Handbook of Aviation.*

Motor Vehicles

★ 690 ★

Worldwide Increase in Number of Automobiles and Motorcycles, 2000-2015

"Royal Dutch/Shell believes that the number of cars worldwide could double to 1 billion by 2000. A planner at one large company believes that there could be 70 million motorcycles, 30 million lorries and 100 million cars in China by 2015. Huge scope for further growth would remain. After all, the American market is still growing, even though it has more cars than drivers."

Source: "Onward and Upward," in *The Economist*, 18 June 1994, p. 2. *Primary source:* Royal Dutch Shell.

★ 691 ★

Motor Vehicles

Personal Vehicles by Type and Size Class, 1985-2010

Type and Size	Year			Change, 1985-2010 (%/yr)
	1985	2000	2010	
Automobiles (10^6)	122.3	161.5	184.7	1.66
Subcompact	32.8	44.6	59.2	2.39
Compact	24.3	32.7	37.8	1.78
Midsize	34.5	45.2	49.3	1.44

[Continued]

★ 691 ★

Personal Vehicles by Type and Size Class, 1985-2010

[Continued]

Type and Size	Year			Change, 1985-2010 (%/yr)
	1985	2000	2010	
Large	30.7	39.1	38.4	0.90
Light trucks (10^6)	23.5	39.6	44.6	2.60
Compact	3.5	6.8	9.3	3.99
Standard	12.6	19.5	20.4	1.95
Minivan/sm. utility	1.7	5.1	4.4	3.88
Standard van/utility	5.7	8.2	7.8	1.26
Total LDV[A] (10^6)	145.8	201.2	229.4	1.83
Autos per capita	0.511	0.602	0.654	0.99
Light trucks per capita	0.098	0.148	0.158	1.93
LDV per capita	0.609	0.750	0.812	1.16
Auto share of LDVs	0.839	0.803	0.805	-0.17

Source: M. M. Mintz and A. D. Vyas, U.S. Department of Energy, Energy Systems Division, Argonnne National Laboratory, *Forecast of Transportation Energy Demand through the Year 2010* (Washington, D.C.: U.S. Government Printing Office, November 1990, revised April 1991), p. 22. *Note:* A. Light-duty vehicles.

★ 692 ★

Motor Vehicles

Vehicle-Miles Traveled by Type and Size of Personal Vehicle, 1985-2010

Type and Size	Travel (VMT), by Year			Change, 1985-2010 (%/yr)
	1985	2000	2010	
Automobiles (10^6)	1,057.8	1,386.6	1,570.3	1.59
Subcompact	292.9	392.6	514.7	2.28
Compact	210.9	282.5	322.5	1.71
Midsize	297.0	387.5	418.8	1.38
Large	257.0	323.9	314.4	0.81
Light trucks (10^9)	209.3	345.4	384.9	2.47
Compact	31.1	59.8	81.1	3.91
Standard	110.3	167.6	173.6	1.83
Minivan/sm. utility	16.2	46.5	59.1	5.31
Standard van/utility	51.7	71.6	71.1	1.28
Total LDV[A] (10^9)	1,267.0	1,732.0	1,955.1	1.75
LDV VMT per capita	5,295	6,455	6,918	1.08

[Continued]

★ 692 ★

Vehicle-Miles Traveled by Type and Size of Personal Vehicle, 1985-2010

[Continued]

Type and Size	Travel (VMT), by Year			Change, 1985-2010
	1985	2000	2010	(%/yr)
LDV VMT/vehicle	8,690	8,608	8,523	-0.08
LDV VMT/household	14,579	16,355	16,942	0.60

Source: M. M. Mintz and A. D. Vyas, U.S. Department of Energy, Energy Systems Division, Argonnne National Laboratory, *Forecast of Transportation Energy Demand through the Year 2010* (Washington, D.C.: U.S. Government Printing Office, November 1990, revised April 1991), p. 23. *Notes:* VMT = Vehicle Miles Traveled. A. Light-duty vehicles.

★ 693 ★

Motor Vehicles

Travel and Fuel Use by Personal Motor Vehicles, 1985-2010

Item	Value, by Year					Change, 1985-2010
	1985	1990	1995	2000	2010	(%/yr)
Vehicle-Miles Traveled (10^9)						
Autos	1057.8	1235.8	1307.7	1386.6	1570.3	1.59
Trucks	209.3	266.0	312.9	345.4	384.9	2.47
Total	1267.0	1501.8	1620.5	1732.0	1955.1	1.75
Energy (10^{15} Btu)						
Autos	7.396	7.825	8.045	8.265	8.085	0.36
Trucks	1.921	2.223	2.544	2.743	2.718	1.40
Total	9.317	10.047	10.589	11.009	10.803	0.59
Energy by Fuel Type (10^{15} Btu)						
Gasoline	9.206	9.956	10.507	10.901	10.665	0.59
Diesel	0.110	0.091	0.081	0.107	0.138	0.90
Fuel Economy (mpg)						
Autos	17.9	19.1	20.3	21.0	24.3	1.23
Trucks	13.6	14.5	15.4	15.7	17.7	1.05
Total	17.0	18.0	19.1	19.7	22.7	1.15
Vehicles (10^6)						
Autos	122.3	140.4	150.6	161.5	184.7	1.66
Trucks	23.5	29.6	35.4	39.6	44.6	2.59
Total	145.8	170.0	186.0	201.2	229.4	1.83

Source: M. M. Mintz and A. D. Vyas, U.S. Department of Energy, Energy Systems Division, Argonne National Laboratory, *Forecast of Transportation Energy Demand through the Year 2010* (Washington, D.C.: U.S. Government Printing Office, November 1990, revised April 1991), p. 2. *Notes:* Includes household-based vehicles only. Fleets are excluded. Btu = British thermal unit.

★ 694 ★

Motor Vehicles

Highway Vehicles, Fuel Economy, and Miles Traveled, 1985-2010

Item	Value, by Year					Change, 1985-2010 (%/yr)
	1985	1990	1995	2000	2010	
Vehicles (10^6)						
Autos						
Personal	122.3	140.4	150.6	161.5	184.7	1.66
Fleet	8.9	9.2	9.9	10.8	13.0	1.52
Total	131.2	149.6	160.6	172.3	197.7	1.66
Light Trucks						
Personal	23.5	29.6	35.4	39.6	44.6	2.59
Commercial	12.0	13.6	14.7	16.2	19.6	1.96
Total	35.6	43.2	50.2	55.8	64.2	2.39
Heavy Trucks	5.3	6.1	6.6	7.3	9.2	2.21
Fuel Economy (mpg)						
Autos	18.2	20.0	20.7	21.3	24.7	1.24
Light Trucks	13.0	14.2	14.9	15.4	17.0	1.08
Personal	13.6	15.0	15.4	15.8	17.7	1.05
Commercial	12.2	13.3	14.3	15.0	16.0	1.09
Heavy Trucks	5.8	5.9	6.1	6.4	6.6	0.52
Medium	8.0	8.1	8.2	8.3	8.4	0.21
Lt.-Heavy	6.9	7.0	7.2	7.3	7.4	0.31
Heavy-heavy	5.4	5.6	5.7	6.1	6.3	0.60
All Trucks	10.6	11.6	12.2	12.7	13.6	1.00
Vehicle-Miles Traveled (10^9)						
Autos	1262.5	1446.5	1546.4	1656.9	1894.7	1.64
Light Trucks						
Personal	209.3	266.0	312.9	345.4	384.9	2.47
Comml. Gasoline	157.9	180.3	196.4	215.4	258.9	2.00
Comml. Diesel	4.7	6.5	7.7	9.3	14.9	4.73
Total	371.8	452.8	517.0	570.1	658.6	2.31
Heavy Duty Vehicles						
Gas Trucks	39.3	37.2	36.7	35.9	37.2	-0.22
Diesel Trucks	91.9	115.6	130.5	150.3	199.7	3.15
Buses	6.3	6.7	7.0	7.4	7.7	0.81
Total	137.5	159.4	174.1	1932.6	244.6	2.33
Total, All Vehicles	1771.8	2058.7	2237.5	4159.6	2797.9	1.84

Source: M. M. Mintz and A. D. Vyas, U.S. Department of Energy, Energy Systems Division, Argonne National Laboratory, *Forecast of Transportation Energy Demand through the Year 2010* (Washington, D.C.: U.S. Government Printing Office, November 1990, revised April 1991), p. 6.

★ 695 ★

Motor Vehicles

Characteristics of the Personal Vehicle Fleet, 1985-2010

Vehicle Type and Size (Seats)	1985			2000			2010		
	Curb Weight (lb)	Engine Power (hp)	Fuel Economy (mpg)	Curb Weight (lb)	Engine Power (hp)	Fuel Economy (mpg)	Curb Weight (lb)	Engine Power (hp)	Fuel Economy (mpg)
Automobile									
Small (2-4)	2,205	75	22.7	1,906	63	25.8	1,645	54	29.3
Compact (4)	2,674	90	19.2	2,312	77	22.6	1,988	66	25.7
Midsize (5)	3,178	108	16.8	2,747	93	19.8	2,363	80	22.6
Large (6)	3,874	135	14.6	3,349	116	17.2	2,880	100	19.6
Light truck									
Compact	3,496	90	17.2	3,121	84	19.5	2,778	77	21.5
Std. truck	4,158	130	13.1	3,712	119	14.8	3,304	107	16.4
Minivan/sm. utility (7-8)	4,126	101	16.7	3,604	101	19.0	3,208	92	21.1
Std. van/utility (11-15)	4,926	140	12.4	4,398	127	14.0	3,914	115	15.5

Source: M. M. Mintz and A. D. Vyas, U.S. Department of Energy, Energy Systems Division, Argonne National Laboratory, *Forecast of Transportation Energy Demand through the Year 2010* (Washington, D.C.: U.S. Government Printing Office, November 1990, revised April 1991), p. 20. *Notes:* Average values applicable to all vehicles on the road. Lb=pound; hp=horsepower; mpg=miles per gallon.

★ 696 ★

Motor Vehicles

Fuel Economy of Personal Vehicles, 1985-2010

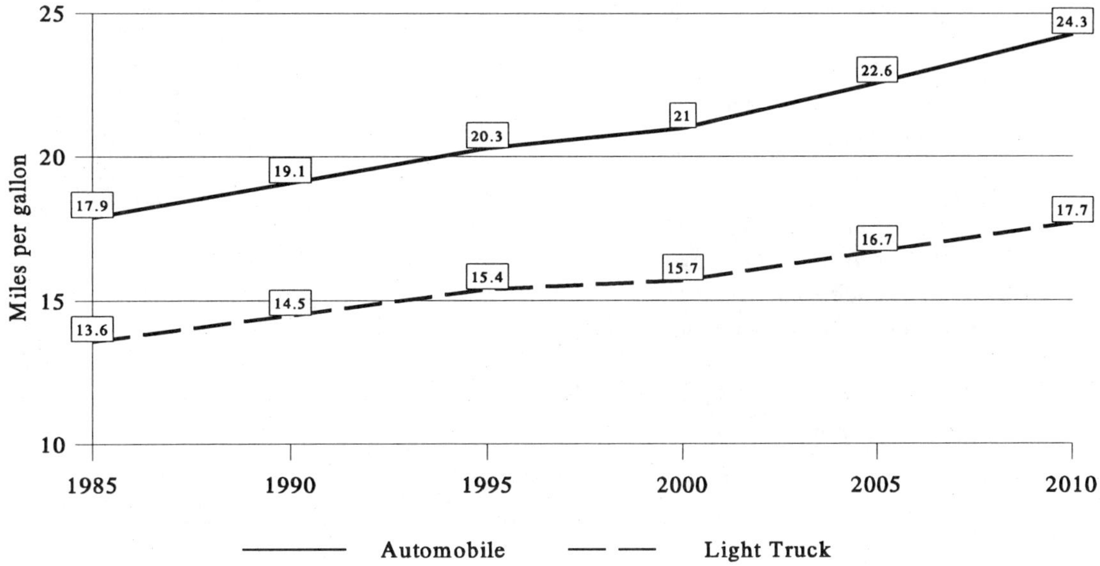

[Miles per gallon]

Year	Fuel Economy		
	Automobile	Light Truck	Total
1985	17.9	13.6	17.0
1990	19.1	14.5	18.0
1995	20.3	15.4	19.1
2000	21.0	15.7	19.7
2005	22.6	16.7	21.1
2010	24.3	17.7	22.6

Source: M. M. Mintz and A. D. Vyas, U.S. Department of Energy, Energy Systems Division, Argonne National Laboratory, *Forecast of Transportation Energy Demand through the Year 2010* (Washington, D.C.: U.S. Government Printing Office, November 1990, revised April 1991), p. 24.

★ 697 ★

Motor Vehicles

Truck Technology and Operating Improvements, 1990-2010

"[The table below] summarizes the market penetration and fuel efficiency benefit of specific truck technologies and other operating improvements assumed under the baseline scenario."

Technology or Operating Improvements[A]	Efficiency Gain (%)[B]	Penetration of Heavy-Heavy Trucks (%)		
		1990	2000	2010
Advanced drag reduction	25	1	19	45
Improved tires & lubricants	5	1	50	80
Electronic transmission controls	4	5	30	75
Electronic engine controls	4	5	30	70
Turbocompound diesel engine	5	0	1	10
Increased load factors (TMT/VMT)	10-14[C]	D	D	D

Source: M. M. Mintz and A. D. Vyas, U.S. Department of Energy, Energy Systems Division, Argonne National Laboratory, *Forecast of Transportation Energy Demand through the Year 2010* (Washington, D.C.: U.S. Government Printing Office, November 1990, revised April 1991), p. 44. *Notes:* VMT=Vehicle miles traveled. A. Low-heat rejection diesels and turbine engines are not included in the baseline scenario. All improvement listed could be made to a single base vehicle. B. On-road improvement in miles per gallon (MPG). C. Improvements in British thermal unit (Btu) Ton-Mile-Traveled (TMT).

★ 698 ★

Motor Vehicles

Commercial Truck Vehicle Miles Traveled (VMT) and Energy Use by Size Class, 1970-2010

"Recent trends in heavy-truck energy consumption and VMT are shown in [the table below]. The heavy-truck share of total transportation energy increased from 9.8% in 1970 to 14.9% in 1985. Energy consumption increased by 94.7% between 1970 and 1985. In contrast, automobile energy consumption increased from 1970 to 1978 and then declined, resulting in an overall increase of only 1.7% between 1970 and 1985. Combined auto and light-truck energy consumption increased 22.2% during the same period. The rate of growth in heavy-truck VMT was 104.8% between 1970 and 1985, compared with a 57.1% increase in combined automobile and light-truck VMT."

Feature	Forecast, by Year					Change, 1985-2010 (%/yr)
	1985	1990	1995	2000	2010	
Energy (10^{15}Btu)						
Light	1.6699	1.7652	1.7930	1.8871	2.1533	1.02
Medium	0.1169	0.1374	0.1481	0.1618	0.2001	2.17
Lt. heavy	0.4643	0.5365	0.5776	0.6326	0.7926	2.16
Hvy. heavy	2.4852	2.8112	3.0248	3.1877	3.9199	1.84

[Continued]

★ 698 ★

Commercial Truck Vehicle Miles Traveled (VMT) and Energy Use by Size Class, 1970-2010

[Continued]

Feature	Forecast, by Year					Change, 1985-2010 (%/yr)
	1985	1990	1995	2000	2010	
Total	4.7363	5.2502	5.5436	5.8691	7.0659	1.61
VMT (10^9)						
Light	162.6	186.8	204.1	224.7	273.8	2.11
Medium	7.4	8.8	9.6	10.6	13.2	2.33
Lt. heavy	25.2	29.4	32.2	35.6	42.9	2.16
Hvy. heavy	98.6	114.5	125.4	140.0	178.8	2.41
Total	293.8	339.6	371.2	387.3	473.3	1.93
Fuel economy (mpg)						
Light	12.2	13.3	14.3	15.0	16.0	1.09
Medium	8.0	8.1	8.2	8.3	8.4	0.20
Lt. heavy	6.9	7.0	7.2	7.3	7.4	0.28
Hvy. heavy	5.4	5.6	5.7	6.1	6.3	0.62
Total	8.8	9.4	9.9	10.3	10.8	0.82

Source: M. M. Mintz and A. D. Vyas, U.S. Department of Energy, Energy Systems Division, Argonne National Laboratory, *Forecast of Transportation Energy Demand through the Year 2010* (Washington, D.C.: U.S. Government Printing Office, November 1990, revised April 1991), pp. 44, 46. *Notes:* Btu=British thermal units; VMT=Vehicle Miles Traveled; MPG=Miles per gallon.

★ 699 ★

Motor Vehicles

Motor Carrier Safety Funding, 1992-1997

[Millions of dollars]

	Authorization Levels by Fiscal Year						Total
	1992	1993	1994	1995	1996	1997	
Safety Grants	65	76	80	83	85	90	479
Safety Functions	49	0	0	0	0	0	49
Other	7	1	1	0	0	0	9
Total	121	77	81	83	85	90	537

Source: Edward Weiner, U.S. Department of Transportation, *Urban Transportation Planning in the United States: An Historical Overview*, rev. ed. (Washington, D.C.: U.S. Government Printing Office, November 1992), p. 242.

Other Transportation Modes

★ 700 ★

Travel and Fuel Use by Nonpersonal Motor Vehicles, 1985-2010

Item	Value, by Year					Change, 1985-2010 (%/yr)
	1985	1990	1995	2000	2010	
Passenger Travel						
Fleet Autos						
VMT (10^9)[A]	204.7	210.7	238.7	270.4	324.5	1.86
Energy (10^5Btu)	1.286	1.242	1.320	1.448	1.501	0.62
Buses[B]						
VMT (10^9)[A]	6.3	6.7	7.0	7.4	7.7	0.81
Energy (10^{15}Btu)	0.161	0.169	0.176	0.184	0.190	0.67
Passenger Aircraft						
RPM (10^9)[D]	277.8	344.3	410.2	487.0	668.5	3.57
Energy (10^{15}Btu)[D]	1.697	2.103	2.331	2.532	2.723	1.91
General Aviation[B]						
Operations (10^6)	37.5	38.4	42.8	47.7	54.3	1.49
Energy (10^{15} Btu)	0.144	0.148	0.163	0.180	0.201	1.33
Domestic Freight						
Ton-Miles Traveled (TMT, 10^9)						
Trucks	1653.3	1965.3	2201.9	2491.7	3202.7	2.68
Rail	898.0	1075.4	1252.1	1490.2	2068.8	3.39
Marine	893.3	911.1	898.5	912.0	998.7	0.45
Air[E]	1.8	2.5	3.0	3.8	5.5	4.48
Pipeline	763.9	763.1	749.6	729.6	675.7	-0.49
Total	4210.3	4717.3	5105.2	5627.3	6951.4	2.03
Energy (10^{15}Btu)						
Trucks	4.737	5.250	5.544	5.869	7.066	1.61
Rail	0.446	0.529	0.604	0.704	0.950	3.07
Marine	0.329	0.337	0.334	0.340	0.376	0.54
Air[E]	0.040	0.047	0.049	0.053	0.064	1.91
Pipeline	0.657	0.676	0.722	0.733	0.696	0.23
Total	6.209	6.839	7.253	7.699	9.152	1.56
Energy Intensity (10^3 Btu/TMT)						
Trucks	2.865	2.671	2.518	2.355	2.206	-1.04
Rail	0.497	0.492	0.482	0.472	0.459	-0.31
Marine	0.368	0.370	0.372	0.373	0.376	0.09
Air[E]	21.670	18.809	16.255	14,037	11.618	-2.46

[Continued]

★ 700 ★

Travel and Fuel Use by Nonpersonal Motor Vehicles, 1985-2010

[Continued]

Item	Value, by Year					Change, 1985-2010 (%/yr)
	1985	1990	1995	2000	2010	
Pipeline	0.860	0.886	0.963	1.005	1.030	0.72
Other Subsectors[B]						
Energy (10^{15} Btu)						
Foreign vessels	0.686	0.619	0.686	0.761	0.928	1.22
Military aviation	0.657	0.681	0.681	0.681	0.681	0.15
Rail transit	0.014	0.014	0.015	0.015	0.016	0.50

Source: M. M. Mintz and A. D. Vyas, U.S. Department of Energy, Energy Systems Division, Argonne National Laboratory, *Forecast of Transportation Energy Demand through the Year 2010* (Washington, D.C.: U.S. Government Printing Office, November 1990, revised April 1991), pp. 3-4. *Notes:* Btu=British thermal units; RPM=Revolutions Per Minute. A. Vehicle-miles traveled. B. Not included in ANL-90 forecast. Values shown are extrapolations. C. Revenue-passenger miles. D. Includes U.S. fuel purchases by foreign flag carriers. E. All-cargo aircraft only.

★ 701 ★

Other Transportation Modes

Mass Transit Funding, 1992-1997

[Millions of dollars]

	Authorization Levels by Fiscal Year						
	1992	1993	1994	1995	1996	1997	Total
Discretionary	1,342	2,030	2,050	2,050	2,050	2,900	12,422
Formula	1,823	2,604	2,643	2,643	2,643	3,741	16,096
Rural	106	152	154	154	154	218	937
I Substitutions	160	165	0	0	0	0	325
Elderly & Disabled	55	70	69	69	69	97	428
Plan & Research	120	164	161	161	161	224	987
Administration	37	50	49	49	49	49	304
Total	3,643	5,235	5,125	5,125	5,125	7,250	31,499

Source: Edward Weiner, U.S. Department of Transportation, *Urban Transportation Planning in the United States: An Historical Overview*, rev. ed. (Washington, D.C.: U.S. Government Printing Office, November 1992), p. 242.

★ 702 ★

Other Transportation Modes

Rail Freight Ton-Miles, Fuel Consumption, and Fuel Efficiency, 1985-2010

"In 1985, railroads accounted for 2.5% of the energy consumed in transportation. [The table below] shows trends in rail energy consumption and intensity, in terms of Btu per ton-mile-traveled (Btu/TMT). Rail energy intensity was relatively stable before 1975. Since then, a series of events—including the energy price shocks of 1973-1974 and 1979, increased intermodal competition spurred by deregulation, labor renegotiations (permitting, among other things, smaller crews and the elimination of carbooses on intermodal runs), locomotive replacement, and a spate of mergers and acquisitions—have improved rail productivity and energy intensity. The energy intensity of Class 1 railroads improved by 28.6% between 1975 and 1985. Because ton-miles rose only 10% over this period, rail energy use declined by 16%."

	Value, by Year						Growth, 1985-2010 (%/yr)
	1985	1990	1995	2000	2005	2010	
TMT (10^9)							
ANL	898	1,075	1,252	1,490	1,756	2,069	3.39
EIA	868[A]	917	993	1,044	1,107	1,187	1.43
Fuel (10^{15} Btu)							
ANL	0.446	0.529	0.604	0.704	0.818	0.950	3.07
EIA	0.441[A]	0.465	0.504	0.503	0.562	0.603	1.43
Efficiency (Btu/TMT)							
ANL	497	492	482	472	466	459	-0.32
EIA	508[A]	507	508	508	508	508	0

Source: M. M. Mintz and A. D. Vyas, U.S. Department of Energy, Energy Systems Division, Argonne National Laboratory, *Forecast of Transportation Energy Demand through the Year 2010* (Washington, D.C.: U.S. Government Printing Office, November 1990, revised April 1991), pp. 45, 49. *Notes:* TMT=Ton-Mile Traveled; ANL=Argonne National Laboratory; EIA=Energy Information Administration; Btu=British thermal unit. A. 1988.

★ 703 ★

Other Transportation Modes

Domestic Waterborne Freight Ton-Miles, Energy Use, and Energy Intensity, 1970-2010

"Recent trends in marine ton-miles, energy use, and energy intensity are summarized in [the table below]. Between 1975 and 1980 the composition of domestic shipping changed dramatically. As large volumes of Alaskan Oil began moving to the lower-48 states, coastal traffic rose sharply and came to account for a far larger share of domestic shipping demand. However, since coastal tankers have relatively more energy-efficient engines and duty cycles than push/tow boats operating in inland waters, this compositional change had virtually no impact on energy consumption. Because the baseline scenario assumes steady declines in Alaskan oil output, the Alaskan oil effect is modeled as a one-time upward shift in demand by the crude oil sector that is slowly eroded over time."

Year	TMT (10^9)	Energy Use (10^{15}Btu)	Energy Intensity (Btu/TMT)
1970	596	0.325	545
1975	566	0.311	549
1980	922	0.330	358
1985	893.3	0.329	368
1990	911.1	0.337	370
1995	898.5	0.334	372
2000	912.0	0.340	373
2010	998.7	0.376	377
	Average annual percentage change		
1970-1985	2.73	0.08	-2.58
1985-2010	0.45	0.54	0.10

Source: M. M. Mintz and A. D. Vyas, U.S. Department of Energy, Energy Systems Division, Argonne National Laboratory, *Forecast of Transportation Energy Demand through the Year 2010* (Washington, D.C.: U.S. Government Printing Office, November 1990, revised April 1991), pp. 49-50. *Note:* TMT=Ton-Mile Traveled; Btu=British thermal unit.

★ 704 ★

Other Transportation Modes

Domestic Air Freight Ton-Miles, Energy Use, and Energy Intensity, 1970-2010

Year	TMT[A] (10^9)	Energy Use (10^{15}Btu)		Energy Intensity (Btu/TMT)	
		Total	All-Cargo	Total[B]	All-Cargo Cargo
1970	3.01	NA[C]	NA	NA	26,821
1975	3.47	NA	NA	NA	21,530
1980	4.53	NA	NA	NA	23,750[D]
1985	6.16	0.061	0.040	9903	21,670
1990	7.75	0.074	0.047	9548	18,809
1995	8.93	0.082	0.049	9183	16,255
2000	10.42	0.092	0.053	8829	14,037
2010	14.54	0.119	0.064	8184	11,618
		Average annual percentage change			
1970-1985	4.89	NA	NA	NA	-1.41
1985-2010	3.50	2.71	1.9	-0.76	-2.46

Source: M. M. Mintz and A. D. Vyas, U.S. Department of Energy, Energy Systems Division, Argonne National Laboratory, *Forecast of Transportation Energy Demand through the Year 2010* (Washington, D.C.: U.S. Government Printing Office, November 1990, revised April 1991), p. 53. *Notes:* TMT=Ton-Miles Traveled; Btu=British thermal units. A. Total includes belly freight. B. Weighted average of all-cargo and belly freight. Belly freight assigned a value of zero since fuel is already included in passenger totals. C. NA= Data not available. D. 1979.

★ 705 ★

Other Transportation Modes

Gap between Automobile and Bicycle Production, 1950-2000

"Clearly, bikes are cheaper to own than cars. As [Lester Brown and Ed Ayres of the Worldwatch Institute] note, 'The bottom line on the economics of automobile and bicycle ownership is that, over the last two decades, the number of people who have reached the automobile level of affluence has been quite small, while the number reaching the bicycle level of affluence has been quite large. Less than 10% of the world's people can afford cars, whereas an estimated 80% can buy bikes.

"The number of bicycles produced in the world climbed to 105 million in 1988, compared with 36 million automobiles. There are now 2.6 bikes built for every car, according to the Worldwatch Institute."

[Millions]

Year	Bicycle	Automobile
1960	20	60
1970	35	22
1980	59	30
1990	100	35
2000	152	45

Source: "Bikes vs. Cars," in *The Futurist*, March-April 1993, p. 53. *Primary source:* Worldwatch Institute. *Notes:* Magnitudes estimated from published chart. Source also includes data for 1950.

The Transportation Infrastructure: Highways

★ 706 ★

Increase in Road Traffic Congestion, 1992-2012

"Enormous 'hidden' subsidies, paid for by society at large, make driving in the United States seem much cheaper than it actually is. The result is ever-worsening traffic congestion, according to a recent World Resources Institute report...

"Over the next 20 years, freeway use is projected to increase fourfold and travel on the roads to double. If current trends continue, the average speed on Los Angeles freeways, now about 30 miles per hour, would drop to 11 miles per hour by the year 2010."

Source: "The Real Costs of Driving," in *The Futurist*, November-December 1992, pp. 59-60. *Primary source:* James J. MacKenzie, Roger C. Dower, and Donald D. T. Chen, "The Going Rate: What It Really Costs to Drive," World Resources Institute, June 1992, 32 pp. $9.95 plus $3 shipping and handling: WRI Publications, P.O. Box 4852, Hampden Station, Baltimore, MD, 21211.

★ 707 ★

The Transportation Infrastructure: Highways

Federal Highway Development, 1993-2013

"The Federal Highway Administration is spending $150 million a year on innovative systems, including one that would allow cars separated by only a few feet to travel at high speeds and even change lanes without accident, a boon for places like California, which are running out of room and money for new highways. Malcolm Currie, retired CEO of Hughes Aircraft Co., now heads Project California, an attempt to reverse the state's job losses. 'Over the next 20 years,' he says, 'smart highways could employ up to 20,000 people manufacturing sensors and designing command and control systems.' The trick—one whose solution is still some years away—is to figure out how to make an inexpensive car brain as smart as that of a $1 million cruise missile..."

Source: Lee Smith, "Can Defense Pain Be Turned to Gain?" in *Fortune*, 8 February 1993, p. 96.

★ 708 ★

The Transportation Infrastructure: Highways

Surface Transportation Funding, 1992-1997

[Millions of dollars]

	Authorization Levels by Fiscal Year						
	1992	1993	1994	1995	1996	1997	Total
NHS	3,003	3,599	3,599	3,599	3,600	3,600	21,000
I Construction	1,800	1,800	1,800	1,800	0	0	7,200
I Maintenance	2,431	2,913	2,914	2,914	2,914	2,914	17,000
I Substitutions	240	240	240	240	0	0	960
STP	3,418	4,096	4,096	4,096	4,097	4,097	23,900
Bridge Repair & Rehaul	2,288	2,762	2,762	2,762	2,763	2,763	16,100
Demo Projects	543	1,225	1,159	1,101	1,101	1,101	6,230
Congress & Air Quality	858	1,028	1,028	1,028	1,029	1,029	6,000
Other Programs	1,875	761	816	801	828	828	5,910
Equity Adjust	2,236	2,055	2,055	2,055	4,055	4,055	16,512
Total	18,692	20,479	20,469	20,396	20,387	20,389	120,812

Source: Edward Weiner, U.S. Department of Transportation, *Urban Transportation Planning in the United States: An Historical Overview*, rev. ed. (Washington, D.C.: U.S. Government Printing Office, November 1992), p. 241. *Note:* STP = Surface Transportation Program.

★ 709 ★

The Transportation Infrastructure: Highways

Highway Safety Funding, 1992-1997

[Millions of dollars]

	Authorization Levels by Fiscal Year						
	1992	1993	1994	1995	1996	1997	Total
State/Community	126	171	171	171	171	171	981
Safety R&D	44	44	44	44	44	44	264
Traffic & Vehicle Safety	69	71	74	77	0	0	291
Other Programs	39	11	11	11	4	4	80
Total	278	297	300	303	219	219	1,616

Source: Edward Weiner, U.S. Department of Transportation, *Urban Transportation Planning in the United States: An Historical Overview*, rev. ed. (Washington, D.C.: U.S. Government Printing Office, November 1992), p. 241. *Note:* R&D = Research and Development.

Airports and Aircraft Operations

★ 710 ★

Air Terminal Redevelopment, 2005

"In their preliminary designs, Boeing's New Large Airplane and Airbus' A3XX anticipate wingspans in the 75-80 meter range. The proposed McDonnell Douglas DC-12 is slightly smaller at about 70 meters.

"**JEAN-JACQUES HUBER**, an Airbus Industrie A3XX manager, says there is an industry consensus that the length and wingspan of new jumbos cannot exceed an 80 X 80-meter footprint.

"Wilkins said that studying the implications of larger aircraft on the costs of terminals will be the next ACI task. They will be more complex than figuring out added runway costs.

" 'If you're talking about a 10-year time scale [between planning for a new terminal and its completion], between now and 2005, a lot of airports will have to have major redevelopment of terminals or build new ones anyway. The question is, how much more will those facilities cost if they're going to be built for an 80-meter wingspan than if they're going to be built for a 65-meter wingspan like the 747-400' he said."

Source: Michael Mecham, "Airport Officials: Superjumbos Mean New Headaches," in *Aviation Week & Space Technology*, 21 November 1994, p. 76. *Note:* ACI = Airports Council International.

★ 711 ★

Airports and Aircraft Operations

Super Airport Development, 2000

"The concept of 'The Airport City,' which I supported in the 1970s, now appears to be in full bloom. The large new super airports and the wayports of the future must, of necessity, be planned as new towns having unique features.

"Closely related to the airport development situation is the progress being made on a new generation of aircraft. These range from TAVs (Trans Atmospheric Vehicles), capable of operating at high supersonic speeds in space, to tilt-rotor machines capable of vertical takeoff and landing at small fields.

"In the United States, Boeing would like to borrow $10 billion in the year 2000 and privately develop its own supersonic transport (SST). Boeing officials project a need for 400 to 500 SSTs by the next century."

Source: McKinley Conway, "Super Projects: New Wonders of the World," in *The Futurist*, March-April 1993, p. 25.

★ 712 ★

Airports and Aircraft Operations

Total Aircraft Operations at Airports with FAA Traffic Control Service, 1985-2001

"To measure increases in system use, the FAA forecasts tower activity or total operations at airports with FAA traffic control service. In 1989, aircraft operations reported by the 399 airports with FAA-run towers reached 61.4 million, representing steady growth through the 1980s largely because of increased demand for commercial air service. Growth of FAA tower activity, as represented [below], is expected to increase at an average annual rate of 2.1 percent, reaching 79.2 million operations by 2001.

"Although a 2.1-percent annual increase in tower activity may not seem like a dramatic jump in demand, it must be remembered that in addition to being nearly three times the projected rate of national population growth, capacity constraints already limit growth in aviation at many of the more heavily used airports; without increasing capacity, some of the future demand for air services may go unmet. In fact, some argue that without immediate changes in public policy leading to construction of new airports and expansion of existing congested facilities, meeting future demand for air travel much above current levels may not be possible."

[Millions of operations]

Year	
1985	58
1986	59
1987	61
1988	61.5
1989	62
1990	63
1991	64
1992	66.5
1993	67.5
1994	69.5
1995	70.5
1996	72.5
1997	74
1998	74.8
1999	76.5
2000	78
2001	79.2

Source: 102nd Congress 1st Session, *Demographic Change and the Economy of the Nineties*, Report prepared for the Subcommittee on Technology and National Security of the Joint Economic Committee, Congress of the United States (Washington, D.C.: U.S. Government Printing Office, December 1991), p. 186. *Primary source:* Federal Aviation Administration, *Aviation Forecasts*, March 1990, p. 201. *Note:* Magnitudes estimated from published chart.

★ 713 ★

Airports and Aircraft Operations

Aviation Operations for Major Airports: Air Route Traffic Control Centers, 1991-2005

"Aircraft operations at the centers [below] are expected to grow at an average rate of 2.3 percent a year between 1991 and 2005. In absolute numbers, center operations are forecast to increase from 36.4 million aircraft handled in 1991 to 48.2 million in 2005... In 1991, 50.3 percent of the traffic handled at centers were air carrier flights. This proportion is expected to increase only slightly to about 51.3 percent in 2005."

[Thousands of operations]

Air Route Traffic Control Centers	1991	2005
Albuquerque	1,420	1,850
Atlanta	2,200	3,000
Boston	1,510	1,970
Chicago	2,590	3,350
Cleveland	2,300	2,930
Ft. Worth	2,500	2,500
Denver	1,420	2,010
Houston	1,670	2,010
Indianapolis	1,850	2,420
Jacksonville	1,620	2,350
Kansas City	1,660	2,300
Los Angeles	1,810	2,260
Memphis	1,800	2,430
Miami	1,770	2,430
Minneapolis	1,610	2,360
New York	1,915	2,480
Oakland	1,660	2,785
Salt Lake City	1,230	1,505
Seattle	1,275	1,770
Washington	2,185	2,680

Source: U.S. Department of Transportation, Federal Aviation Administration, Office of System Capacity and Requirements, *1993 Aviation System Capacity Plan* (Washington, D.C.: U.S. Government Printing Office, 1993), p. I-8, I-II. *Primary source:* Office of Aviation Policy and Plans (APO) forecast of Instrument Flight Rules (IFR) Aircraft handled by Air Route Traffic Control Center (ARTCC), Fiscal Years 1992-2005, June 1992. *Note:* Magnitudes estimated from published chart.

★ 714 ★

Airports and Aircraft Operations

Annual Air Carrier Delay in Excess of 20,000 Hours for Major Airports, 1991-2002

1991	
Chicago O'Hare	ORD
Atlanta Hartsfield	ATL
Dallas-Ft. Worth	DFW
Los Angeles	LAX
Newark	EWR
San Francisco	SFO
Boston	BOS
New York John F. Kennedy	JFK
St. Louis	STL
Phoenix	PHX
Miami	MIA
Philadelphia	PHL
Washington National	DCA
Pittsburgh	PIT
Detroit	DTW
Orlando	MCO
Minneapolis	MSP
Charlotte	CLT
Denver Stapleton[1]	DEN
Honolulu	HNL
Houston	IAH
Seattle-Tacoma	SEA
New York La Guardia	LGA
2002	
Chicago O'Hare	ORD
Dallas-Ft. Worth	DFW
Atlanta Hartsfield	ATL
San Francisco	SFO
Washington Dulles	IAD
Newark	EWR
St. Louis	STL
Los Angeles	LAX
Phoenix	PHX
New York John F. Kennedy	JFK
Miami	MIA
Philadelphia	PHL
Boston	BOS
Detroit	DTW
Pittsburgh	PIT
New York La Guardia	LGA
Orlando	MCO
Minneapolis	MSP
Washington National	DCA
San Diego	SAN

[Continued]

★ 714 ★

Annual Air Carrier Delay in Excess of 20,000 Hours for Major Airports, 1991-2002

[Continued]

Charlotte-Douglas	CLT
Cincinnati	CVG
Honolulu	HNL
Houston	IAH
Las Vegas	LAS
Windsor Locks	BDL
Memphis	MEM
Baltimore Washington	BWI
Ontario	ONT
Nashville	BNA
Raleigh-Durham	RDU
Seattle-Tacoma	SEA
Salt Lake City	SLC

Source: U.S. Department of Transportation, Federal Aviation Administration, Office of System Capacity and Requirements, *1993 Aviation System Capacity Plan* (Washington, D.C.: U.S. Government Printing Office, 1993), p. I-21. *Notes:* 1. No projection for Denver can be made under this assumption since the increased level of activity projected for Denver in 2002 cannot be handled at the existing Denver Stapleton Airport.

★ 715 ★

Airports and Aircraft Operations

Airport Enplanements by Major Airport, 1990-2005

[Thousands of enplanements]

City-Airport	Airport ID	Rank	Enplanements FY90	Enplanements FY2005	%Growth
Chicago O'Hare Int'l	ORD	1	27,949	42,250	51.2
Dallas-Fort Worth Int'l	DFW	2	24,270	40,860	68.4
Atlanta Hartsfield Int'l	ATL	3	24,134	35,678	47.8
Los Angeles Int'l	LAX	4	22,277	34,277	53.9
San Francisco Int'l	SFO	5	14,694	28,570	94.4
New York Kennedy Int'l	JFK	6	14,451	22,283	54.2
Denver Stapleton Int'l[1]	DEN	7	12,767	26,555	108.0
Miami Int'l	MIA	8	12,192	21,672	77.8
New York LaGuardia	LGA	9	11,410	16,371	43.5
Boston Logan Int'l	BOS	10	11,085	18,888	70.4
Newark Int'l	EWR	11	11,012	23,048	109.3
Phoenix Sky Harbor Int'l	PHX	12	10,877	24,281	123.2
Detroit Metro Wayne County	DTW	13	10,555	19,304	82.9
Honolulu Int'l	HNL	14	10,417	15,546	49.2
St. Louis Lambert Int'l	STL	15	10,057	18,838	87.3
Minneapolis-St. Paul	MSP	16	9,715	17,005	75.0
Las Vegas McCarran	LAS	17	9,301	19,832	113.2
Orlando Int'l	MCO	18	8,684	16,733	92.7
Pittsburgh Int'l	PIT	19	8,531	16,907	98.2

[Continued]

★ 715 ★

Airport Enplanements by Major Airport, 1990-2005

[Continued]

City-Airport	Airport ID	Rank	Enplanements		%Growth
			FY90	FY2005	
Houston Intercontinental	IAH	20	8,127	15,164	86.6
Philadelphia Int'l	PHL	21	8,001	13,683	71.0
Seattle-Tacoma	SEA	22	7,863	14,720	87.2
Washington National	DCA	23	7,809	9,452	21.0
Charlotte Douglas Int'l	CLT	24	7,784	13,298	70.8
Salt Lake City Int'l	SLC	25	5,580	9,605	72.1
San Diego Lindbergh	SAN	26	5,488	11,725	113.6
Tampa Int'l	TPA	27	5,307	12,059	127.2
Washington Dulles Int'l	IDA	28	5,112	13,256	159.3
Baltimore-Washington Int'l	BWI	29	5,028	8,469	68.4
Raleigh-Durham Int'l	RDU	30	4,601	10,815	135.1
Cincinnati Int'l	CVG	31	4,538	11,866	161.5
Fort Lauderdale Int'l	FLL	32	4,427	8,833	99.5
Memphis Int'l	MEM	33	4,231	8,589	103.0
Cleveland Hopkins Int'l	CLE	34	4,188	6,477	54.7
Houston Hobby	HOU	35	3,990	7,953	99.3

Source: U.S. Department of Transportation, Federal Aviation Administration, Office of System Capacity and Requirements, *1993 Aviation System Capacity Plan* (Washington, D.C.: U.S. Government Printing Office, 1993), p. A-5. *Notes:* Includes only the top 100 airports, ranked by 1990 enplanements. 1. Assumes development of a new airport at Denver and increased hubbing activity in 1993-1995.

★ 716 ★

Airports and Aircraft Operations

Total Airport Operations, 1990-2005

[Thousands of operations]

City-Airport	Airport ID	Rank	Operations		%Growth
			FY90	FY2005	
Chicago O'Hare Int'l	ORD	1	811	848	4.6
Atlanta Hartsfield Int'l	ATL	2	779	950	22.0
Dallas-Fort Worth Int'l	DFW	3	725	1,198	65.2
Los Angeles Int'l	LAX	4	669	856	27.9
Santa Ana John Wayne	SNA	5	523	730	39.6
Phoenix Sky Harbor Int'l	PHX	6	497	646	30.0
Long Beach	LGB	7	483	551	14.1
Denver Stapleton Int'l	DEN	8	475	655	37.9
Miami Int'l	MIA	9	463	644	39.1
Charlotte Douglas Int'l	CLT	10	452	644	39.1
Boston Logan Int'l	BOS	11	448	552	23.2
St. Louis Lambert Int'l	STL	12	443	550	24.2
San Francisco Int'l	SFO	13	437	722	65.2
Honolulu Int'l	HNL	14	407	509	25.1
Philadelphia Int'l	PHL	15	405	540	33.3
Las Vegas McCarran	LAS	16	395	509	28.9
Detroit Metro Wayne County	DTW	17	391	543	38.9

[Continued]

★ 716 ★

Total Airport Operations, 1990-2005

[Continued]

City-Airport	Airport ID	Rank	Operations FY90	Operations FY2005	%Growth
Oakland Metro Int'l	OAK	18	389	609	56.6
Pittsburgh Int'l	PIT	19	385	556	44.4
Newark Int'l	EWR	20	384	449	16.9
Minneapolis-St. Paul	MSP	21	382	579	51.6
New York La Guardia	LGA	22	365	381	4.4
Seattle-Tacoma	SEA	23	354	430	21.5
New York Kennedy Int'l	JFK	24	342	397	16.1
Memphis Int'l	MEM	25	330	503	52.4
Chicago Midway	MDW	26	322	408	26.7
San Jose Int'l	SJC	27	320	550	71.9
Washington National	DCA	28	320	356	11.3
Houston Intercontinental	IAH	29	310	458	47.7
Baltimore-Washington Int'l	BWI	30	304	416	36.8
Salt Lake City Int'l	SLC	31	302	406	34.4
Cincinnati Int'l	CVG	32	285	548	92.3
Raleigh-Durham Int'l	RDU	33	283	454	60.4
Orlando Int'l	MCO	34	278	588	111.5
Cleveland Hopkins Int'l	CLE	35	273	303	11.0
Portland (OR) Int'l	PDX	36	272	367	34.9
Houston Hobby	HOU	37	267	382	43.1
Nashville Metro	BNA	38	259	375	44.8
Washington Dulles Int'l	IAD	39	240	395	64.6
West Palm Beach Int'l	PBI	40	239	255	6.7
Burbank	BUR	41	235	301	28.1
Tucson Int'l	TUS	42	229	491	114.4
Tampa Int'l	TPA	43	227	367	61.7
Albuquerque Int'l	ABQ	44	226	467	106.6
Indianapolis Int'l	IND	45	225	730	224.4
Fort Lauderdale Int'l	FLL	46	224	383	71.0
Port Columbus Int'l	CMH	47	224	286	27.7
Anchorage	ANC	48	219	280	27.9
San Antonio Int'l	SAT	49	219	380	73.5
Dallas Love	DAL	50	214	410	91.6
San Diego Lindbergh	SAN	51	212	345	62.7
Milwaukee Mitchell Int'l	MKE	52	209	268	28.2
Islip Long Island MacArthur	ISP	53	209	336	60.8
San Juan Luis Munoz Marin Int'l	SJU	54	205	287	40.0
Birmingham Municipal	BHM	55	199	278	39.7
Dayton Int'l	DAY	56	197	321	62.9
Tulsa Int'l	TUL	57	195	285	46.2
Austin Robert Mueller	AUS	58	193	378	95.8
Albany	ALB	59	184	234	27.2
Rochester Monroe County	ROC	60	184	295	60.3
Syracuse Hancock Int'l	SYR	61	193	279	52.5
Windsor Locks Bradley Int'l	BDL	62	182	337	85.2
Providence Green State	PVD	63	180	189	5.0

[Continued]

★ 716 ★

Total Airport Operations, 1990-2005

[Continued]

City-Airport	Airport ID	Rank	Operations FY90	Operations FY2005	%Growth
El Paso Int'l	ELP	64	179	335	87.2
Kahului	OGG	65	179	271	51.4
Colorado Springs Municipal	COS	66	177	234	32.2
Wichita Mid-Continent	ICT	67	175	320	82.9
Grand Rapids Kent County Int'l	GRR	68	169	265	56.8
Boise	BOI	69	168	324	92.9
Sarasota-Bradenton	SRQ	70	168	222	32.1
Knoxville McGhee-Tyson	TYS	71	167	200	19.8
Reno Cannon Int'l	RNO	72	164	244	48.8
Sacramento Metro	SMF	73	162	313	93.2
Kansas City Int'l	MCI	74	162	355	119.1
Norfolk Int'l	ORF	75	161	241	49.7
Louisville Standiford	SDF	76	160	221	38.1
Richmond Int'l	RIC	77	160	213	33.1
Omaha Eppley	OMA	78	153	201	31.4
New Orleans Int'l	MSY	79	152	236	55.3
Greensboro Regional	GSO	80	151	220	45.7
Ontario Int'l	ONT	81	151	454	200.7
Little Rock Adams	LIT	82	149	257	72.5
Jacksonville Int'l	JAX	83	148	196	32.4
Des Moines	DSM	84	146	280	91.8
Oklahoma City Will Rogers Wld	OKC	85	145	215	48.3
Buffalo Int'l	BUF	86	140	184	31.4
Harrisburg	MDT	87	140	190	35.7
Lubbock Int'l	LBB	88	133	208	56.4
Charleston (SC) AFB Int'l	CHS	89	132	187	41.7
Spokane Int'l	GEG	90	121	228	88.4
Lihue	LIH	91	114	150	31.6
Columbia (SC) Metro	CAE	92	113	217	92.0
Portland Int'l Jetport (ME)	PWM	93	112	156	39.3
Savannah Int'l	SAV	94	109	172	57.8
Charlotte Amalie St. Thomas (VI)	STT	95	105	128	21.9
Hilo General Lyman	ITO	96	100	115	15.0
Midland Int'l	MAF	97	97	182	87.6
Amarillo	AMA	98	86	129	50.0
Fort Myers SW Florida Regional	RSW	99	69	158	129.0
Greer Greenville-Spartanburg	GSP	100	69	104	50.7
Total			25,968	37,986	

Source: U.S. Department of Transportation, Federal Aviation Administration, Office of System Capacity and Requirements, *1993 Aviation System Capacity Plan* (Washington, D.C.: U.S. Government Printing Office, 1993), p. A-8. *Primary source:* Federal Aviation Administration, *Terminal Area Forecasts Fiscal Year 1992-2005*, July 1992. *Note:* Includes only the top 100 airports, ranked by 1990 operations.

Transportation Impacts of Telecommuting

★ 717 ★

Projected Telecommuters, 1992-2002

"Information occupations play a large role in today's economy, accounting for over 50 percent of the labor force. As fewer workers are involved in physical production, more information related jobs are evolving.

"The information sector is the one of primary interest. 'Information work' should not be seen as involving only information technology, advanced computer systems, etc. Information workers are simply individuals whose primary economic activity involves the creation, processing, manipulation or distribution of information. It is generally agreed that most information workers, because of the nature of their job functions, could potentially telecommute at least on a part-time basis. However, the counting of information workers, and thus of potential telecommuters, is not straightforward. This is due to the gross nature of census occupational data and the fact that there are many job functions, not typically categorized in the information sector, which deal with information to such an extent that telecommuting is possible at least part time. The ultimate fraction of the total labor force that will be involved with information work is not clear.

"The analysis in this report is based on the assumption that information workers currently constitute about 56 percent of the U.S. workforce, and will gradually increase to around 59 percent in 2002..."

Year	Projected Telecommuters					
	Upper Bound			Lower Bound		
	Number (millions)	Pct. of Labor Force	Pct. of Information Workers	Number (millions)	Pct. of Labor Force	Pct. of Information Workers
1992	2.0	1.6%	2.8%	2.0	1.6%	2.8%
1993	2.5	2.0%	3.5%	2.5	2.0%	3.5%
1994	3.2	2.5%	4.3%	3.1	2.4%	4.2%
1995	4.0	3.0%	5.3%	3.7	2.8%	4.8%
1996	5.0	3.7%	6.5%	4.2	3.1%	5.5%
1997	6.2	4.6%	7.9%	4.8	3.5%	6.1%
1998	7.6	5.5%	9.5%	5.3	3.9%	6.7%
1999	9.2	6.7%	11.4%	5.8	4.2%	7.2%
2000	10.9	7.8%	13.3%	6.4	4.6%	7.8%
2001	12.9	9.1%	15.4%	6.9	4.9%	8.3%
2002	15.0	10.4%	17.5%	7.5	5.2%	8.8%

Source: Department of Transportation, *Transportation Implications of Telecommuting* (Washington, D.C.: U.S. Government Printing Office, April 1993), pp. 54, 59.

★ 718 ★

Transportation Impacts of Telecommuting

Transportation Fuel Savings Resulting from Telecommuting, 1992-2002

"Using [a] projected VMT [Vehicle Miles Traveled] reduction [assumption], it is estimated that a national total potential savings of 4.2 million barrels [of fuel] per year could be obtained in 1992 and 40 million barrels by 2002 through telecommuting. The total amount of fuel consumed by passenger cars in 1990 was 72.4 billion gallons (U.S. DOT, FHWA, Highway Statistics). The estimated 1992 savings of 178 million gallons represents 0.25 percent of this total, rising to 2.1 percent by 2002. A typical telecommuter who works at home an average of 2 days per week would realize a net fuel savings of about 96.6 gallons, or 2.3 barrels, per year. This is 19 percent of the average yearly per-vehicle fuel consumption."

		1992		1997 - 5 year		2002 - 10 year	
		Saved	% of Total	Saved	% of Total	Saved	% of Total
Upper Bound	Gallons of Gasoline (millions)	178	0.25%	619	0.8%	1,679	2.1%
	Barrels of Gasoline (millions)	4.2		14.7		40	
Lower Bound	Gallons of Gasoline (millions)	178	0.25%	475.9	0.6%	840	1.1%
	Barrels of Gasoline (millions)	4.2		11.3		20	

Source: Department of Transportation, *Transportation Implications of Telecommuting* (Washington, D.C.: U.S. Government Printing Office, April 1993), p. 74. *Note:* DOT=Department of Transportation; FHWA=Federal Highway Administration.

★ 719 ★

Transportation Impacts of Telecommuting

Transportation Impacts of Telecommuting, 1992-2002

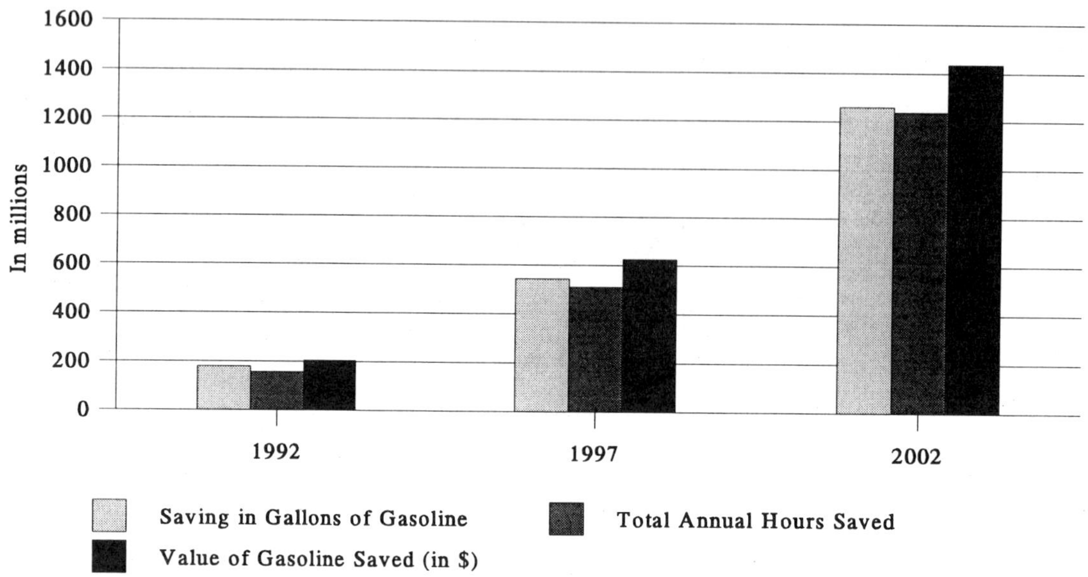

"Telecommuting is at such an early stage that prediction of its rate of growth and transportation impacts is difficult. Many factors contribute to a high level of uncertainty in the estimates presented [below]. The actual degree to which jobs, individuals, and employers will be suited to telecommuting is not clear. Most demonstration or pilot programs have been limited in scale and have involved carefully selected workers and managers. Directly relevant data concerning travel behavior, emissions, and fuel use are not available and would vary from region to region."

TRANSPORTATION IMPACTS	1992	1997	2002
Saving in Vehicle Miles Traveled (VMT) (billions)	3.7	10.0-12.9	17.6-35.1
Percentage Saving in Total Passenger VMT	0.23%	0.49%-0.63%	0.7%-1.4%
Percentage Saving in Commuting VMT	0.70%	1.6%-2.0%	2.3%-4.5%
Saving in Gallons of Gasoline (millions)	178	475.9-619	840-1,679
Percentage Saving in Gasoline	0.25%	0.6%-0.8%	1.1%-2.1%
Value of Gasoline Saved (millions)	$203	$543-$706	$958-$1,914
Percentage Saving in Emissions			
NO_x	0.23%	0.6%-0.8%	1.1%-2.2%
HC	0.31%	0.8%-1.1%	1.4%-2.7%
CO	0.36%	1.0%-1.3%	1.7%-3.4%
Annual Hours Saved for Average Telecommuter	77	93	110.3
Total Annual Hours Saved (millions)	156	444-577	826-1,652

Source: Department of Transportation, *Transportation Implications of Telecommuting* (Washington, D.C.: U.S. Government Printing Office, April 1993), p. ix.

★ 720 ★

Transportation Impacts of Telecommuting

Safety Implications of Telecommuting, 1992-2002

		1992		1997 - 5 year		2002 - 10 year	
		Number	% of Total	Number	% of Total	Number	% of Total
Upper Bound	Lives Saved	87	0.19%	300	0.69%	815	1.97%
	Accidents Avoided	28,520	0.23%	65,770	0.63%	117,700	1.43%
Lower Bound	Lives Saved	87	0.19%	231	0.54%	408	0.99%
	Accidents Avoided	27,520	0.23%	50,355	0.49%	58,850	0.72%

Source: Department of Transportation, *Transportation Implications of Telecommuting* (Washington, D.C.: U.S. Government Printing Office, April 1993), p. 82.

Transportation and Tourism

★ 721 ★

World and U.S. International Visitor Arrivals and Receipts, 1960-2000

"Globally, spending on travel and tourism represents nearly 10 percent of the world Gross National Product, generating a conservative estimate of $527 billion, or an optimistic projection of $720 billion, in worldwide revenues (excluding passenger fares). Expenditures on travel abroad represent about seven percent of world trade, placing tourism among the three largest items in international trade.

"With respect to employment, tourism creates nearly 100 million jobs, and is likely to employ even more people in the future based on its continued growth. Tourism is significant as a major contributor to balance of payments for many countries and is often used as a tool for economic development. Some of the social benefits of tourism, such as cultural interactions and exposure to different traditions, cannot be measured as precisely but are equally as important because of their contribution to international understanding."

Year	World Arrivals (Millions)	USA Arrivals (Millions)	USA Share (Percent)	World Receipts (Billions $)	USA Receipts (Billions $)	USA Share (Percent)
1960	69.3	5.6	8.1	$6.9	$1.0	14.8
1965	112.9	7.8	6.9	$11.6	$1.5	13.3
1970	165.8	12.4	7.5	$17.9	$2.3	13.0
1975	222.3	15.7	7.1	$40.7	$4.7	11.5
1980	287.8	22.3	7.7	$102.4	$10.6	10.3
1985	329.6	25.4	7.7	$115.4	$17.9	15.5
1986	340.8	26.0	7.6	$139.8	$20.5	14.7
1987	366.8	29.4	8.0	$171.6	$23.7	13.8
1988	393.9	34.1	8.7	$197.7	$27.9	15.0
1989	427.9	36.6	8.5	$210.8	$36.6	17.3
1990	455.6	39.5	8.7	$255.1	$43.4	17.0
1991	455.1	42.9	9.4	$261.1	$48.8	18.7
1992 (P)	475.6	45.4	9.5	$278.7	$55.2	19.8
1993 (P)	503.6	47.9	9.5	$334.0	$60.1	18.0
1994 (P)	533.4	50.9	9.5	$389.0	$67.3	17.3
1995 (P)	564.8	54.2	9.6	$445.0	$75.3	16.9
2000 (P)	752.0	77.4	10.3	$720.0	$132.1	18.3

Source: U.S. Department of Commerce, U.S. Travel and Tourism Administration, *World Tourism at the Millennium: An Agenda for Industry, Government and Education*, (Washington, D.C.: U.S. Government Printing Office, April 1993), p. 67. *Primary source:* Compiled by Ron Erdmann, Market Research Analyst, U.S. Travel and Tourism Administration from World Tourism Organization and U.S. Travel and Tourism Administration data on world and U.S. international tourism arrivals and receipts, March 1993. *Note:* P=Projected (Receipts are in 1992 dollars).

★ 722 ★

Transportation and Tourism

Tourist Arrivals to the U.S.: Germany and the United Kingdom, 1985-2000

[Millions of arrivals]

Year	German Increase in Arrivals 1985-2000 1130%	UK Increase in Arrivals 1985-2000 598%
1985	861	509
1990	2,244	1,203
1995	3,680	2,650
2000	6,260	6,010

Source: U.S. Travel and Tourism Administration, *Pow Wow Europe: European Travel to the United States, 1987-1992,* (Washington, D.C.: U.S. Government Printing Office, September 1993). *Primary source:* U.S. Travel and Tourism Administration.

★ 723 ★

Transportation and Tourism

Tourist Arrivals to the U.S.: France, Italy, and the Netherlands, 1985-2000

[Thousands of arrivals]

Year	France Increase in Arrivals 1985-2000 242%	Italy Increase in Arrivals 1985-2000 273%	Netherlands Increase in Arrivals 1985-2000 377%
1985	336	220	131
1990	716	396	284
1995	895	645	420
2000	1,150	820	625

Source: U.S. Travel and Tourism Administration, *Pow Wow Europe: European Travel to the United States, 1987-1992,* (Washington, D.C.: U.S. Government Printing Office, September 1993). *Primary source:* U.S. Travel and Tourism Administration.

INDEX OF FORECASTS BY YEAR

The Index of Forecasts by Year contains complete references to all dates in the tables and entries above. Each reference is followed by an entry number that appears between two stars. Entry numbers are also followed by inclusive page numbers for each entry. To search *SFUS* by topic or subject, consult the subject index on page 793.

SUBJECT INDEX

The Subject Index contains nearly 3,000 terms referring to topics and issues examined in *Statistical Forecasts of the United States*. As in the Year Index (p. 777), each term is followed by one or more entry numbers (bordered by stars) and the page number or numbers where the entries may be found. For access to *SFUS* by year of forecast, refer to the Year index.